SECOND EDITION

Managing the Global Corporation

Case Studies in Strategy and Management

José de la Torre
The Anderson School at UCLA

Yves Doz
INSEAD

Timothy Devinney
Australian Graduate School of Management

Boston Burr Ridge, IL Dubuque, IA Madison, WI New York San Francisco St. Louis
Bangkok Bogotá Caracas Lisbon London Madrid
Mexico City Milan New Delhi Seoul Singapore Sydney Taipei Toronto

McGraw-Hill Higher Education

A Division of The ***McGraw-Hill*** *Companies*

MANAGING THE GLOBAL CORPORATION
CASE STUDIES IN STRATEGY AND MANAGEMENT

Published by Irwin/McGraw-Hill, an imprint of The McGraw-Hill Companies, Inc., 1221 Avenue of the Americas, New York, NY 10020.

This book is printed on acid-free paper.

1 2 3 4 5 6 7 8 9 0 QPD/QPD 0 9 8 7 6 5 4 3 2 1 0

ISBN 0–07–234798-8

Vice president/Editor-in-chief: *Rob Zwettler*
Senior sponsoring editor: *Jennifer Roche*
Editorial assistant: *Tracy Jensen*
Marketing manager: *Brad Shultz*
Project manager: *Kelly L. Delso*
Production supervisor: *Lori Koetters*
Coordinator freelance design: *Craig Jordan*
Supplement coordinator: *Mark Sienicki*
Cover designer: *Crispin Prebys*
Interior design: *Photonica, Metal Globe, by Stephen Webster*
Compositor: *Carlisle Communications, Ltd.*
Typeface: *10/12 Times Roman*
Printer: *Quebecor Printing Book Group/Dubuque*

Library of Congress Cataloging-in-Publication Data

Torre, José de la, 1950-
Managing the global corporation : case studies in strategy and management / José de la Torre, Yves Doz, Timothy Devinney.-- 2nd ed.
p. cm. -- (McGraw-Hill advanced topics in global management)
Rev. ed. of: Managing the global corporation / William Harley Davidson, José de la Torre. 1989
Includes index.
ISBN 0–07–234798–8 (softcover : alk. paper)
1. International business enterprises--Management. I. Doz, Yves L. II. Devinney, Timothy Michael, 1956- III. Davidson, William Harley, 1951- Managing the global corporation. IV. Title. V. Series.

HD62.4 .T67 2000
658′.049--dc21 00–027781

www.mhhe.com

About the Authors

José de la Torre is professor of international business strategy and director of UCLA's Center for International Business Education and Research. He received his doctorate from the Harvard Business School following degrees in engineering and management from Penn State. Previously, he has taught at INSEAD, Georgia State University, and has held a number of visiting positions in Europe and Latin America. He is currently President of the Academy of International Business and on the editorial board of several academic journals in the field. A member of the Board of Advisors of the *Los Angeles Times* until 1996, he has consulted with many global corporations and currently serves on the board of two such companies. Author of more than 10 books, 30 journal articles and 50 case studies, his recent papers dealing with multinational corporate reaction to regional market liberalization, political risk management and international collaborative agreements have appeared in *Management Science,* the *International Journal of Forecasting,* the *Journal of International Business Studies* and *Organization Science.*

Yves Doz is the Associate Dean for Executive Education and the Timken Professor of Global Technology and Innovation at INSEAD. He received his doctorate from Harvard University and is a graduate of HEC in Jouy-en-Josas, France. He has also taught at Harvard Business School, Stanford, and Aoyama Gakuin (Japan). Doz's research on the strategy and management processes of multinational corporations has led to four books including *Strategic Management in Multinational Companies* (1986), *The Multinational Mission: Balancing Local Demands and Global Vision* (1987, with C.K. Prahalad) and *Alliance Advantage* (1998, with Gary Hamel). He is currently finishing a project with two INSEAD colleagues that deals with competition in the knowledge economy with the title of *From Global to Metanational.* He has consulted with many major multinational companies in projects ranging from the restructuring of the top management of a leading European firm to designing and implementing competitive revitalization programs.

Timothy Devinney is a Professor at the Australian Graduate School of Management (AGSM), University of New South Wales, Sydney, and Director of the school's Centre for Corporate Change. Before joining the AGSM he held positions on the faculties of the University of Chicago, Vanderbilt University, and the University of California, Los Angeles (UCLA). He holds Ph.D., MBA, and MA degrees from the University of Chicago and a BSc from Carnegie Mellon University, and has been a visiting faculty member at numerous universities in Europe and Asia. He has published four books and more than 30 articles in leading journals such as *Management Science,* the *Journal of Business, The Academy of Management Review, Organization Science,* and *the Strategic Management Journal.*

Contents

List of Contributors

FACULTY:

Christopher A. Bartlett	Professor, The Harvard Business School, Boston, Massachusetts, USA
Francis Bidault	Professor, Theseus Institute, Sophia Antipolis, France
J. Stuart Black	Professor, Thunderbird, The American Graduate School of International Management, Phoenix, Arizona, USA
Behrouz Chahid-Nourai	Professor, CEDEP, Fontainebleau, France
Sriram Dasu	Associate Professor, Marshall School of Business, University of Southern California, Los Angeles, California, USA
William H. Davidson	Chairman, Mesa Research, Palos Verdes, California, USA
Timothy Devinney	Professor, The Australian Graduate School of Management, University of New South Wales, Sydney, Australia
Yves Doz	Professor, INSEAD, Fontainebleau, France
Kasra Ferdows	Professor, Georgetown University, Washington, D.C., USA
Charles Galunic	Associate Professor, INSEAD, Fontainebleau, France
Sumantra Ghoshal	Professor, London Business School, London, England
Philippe Haspeslagh	Professor, INSEAD, Fontainebleau, France
Dominique Héau	Professor, INSEAD, Fontainebleau, France
Andrew C. Inkpen	Professor, Thunderbird, The American Graduate School of International Management, Phoenix, Arizona, USA
Uday S. Karmarkar	Professor, The Anderson School at UCLA, Los Angeles, California, USA
Karel Kool	Professor, INSEAD Fontainebleau, France
Mitchell Koza	Professor, Cranfield School of Management, Cranfield, Bedfordshire, United Kingdom
Stefanie Lenway	Professor, The Carlson School of Management, University of Minnesota, Minneapolis, Minnesota, USA
David Lewin	Professor, The Anderson School at UCLA, Los Angeles, California, USA
Jon Martínez	Professor, Escuela de Negocios, Universidad Adolfo Ibáñez, Viña del Mar, Chile
Bruce McKern	Professor and Dean, Mt. Eliza Business School, Melbourne, Australia
Arnoud de Meyer	Professor, INSEAD, Fontainebleau, France
Allan J. Morrison	Professor, The Ivey School, University of Western Ontario, London, Ontario, Canada
Thomas Murtha	Professor, The Carlson School of Management, University of Minnesota, Minneapolis, Minnesota, USA

John Naman Assistant Professor, Katz School of Business, University of Pittsburgh, Pittsburgh, Pennsylvania, USA
Arvind Phatak Professor, Temple University, Philadelphia, Pennsylvania, USA
Peter Smith Ring Professor, Loyola Marymount University, Los Angeles, California, USA
Ravi Sarathy Professor Northeastern University, Boston, Massachusetts, USA
Gordon Shillinglaw Professor Emeritus, Columbia University, New York, New York, USA
Helmut Schütte Affiliate Professor, Euro-Asia Center, INSEAD, Fontainebleau, France
Jonathan Story Professor, INSEAD, Fontainebleau, France
José de la Torre Professor, The Anderson School at UCLA, Los Angeles, California, USA
Wesley B. Truitt Visiting Professor The Anderson School at UCLA, Los Angeles, California, USA
Paul Verdin Professor, The Catholic University, Leuven, Belgium
John Weeks Assistant Professor, INSEAD, Fontainebleau, France
Peter J. Williamson Professor, INSEAD, Fontainebleau, France
George S. Yip Professor, The Judge Institute, Cambridge University, Cambridge, England

RESEARCH ASSOCIATES, FELLOWS AND ASSISTANTS:

Mary Ackenhusen
Dag Anderson
Jean-Louis Barsoux
T.C.A. Bashyam
Sibel Berzeg
Alessandro Brenna
Deborah Clyde-Smith
Mark-Antoine Cousin
Deborah Dralle
Marie-Aude Dalsace
Beniamino Finzi
Jacopo Franzan
Elizabeth Fulcher
Marco Gabbiani
Francesca Gee
David Harkleroad
James Howe
Katherine Johnston
Andy Khodjamirian
Alice de Koning
L.N. Krishna
Barbara Lewis
Michael Maier
Tammy Masden
Jukka Nihtila
Juan Carlos Páez
Adam Pearson
Irina Petrova
Marie-Claude Reney
Nasser Sagheb
Nicola de Sanctis
A. Schmidt
Mary Schweinsberg
Esteban S. Skoknic
Marcelle Speller
Tanya Spyridakis
Anna Lisa Tazartes
Charles W. Thomson
Martine van den Poel
Jan Visser
Kris Vogelsong
Peter Wei Gang Lu

INSTITUTIONS

The Anderson Graduate School of Management
UCLA
Los Angeles, California, USA

The Australian Graduate School of Management
University of New South Wales
Sydney, Australia

Escuela de Negocios de Valparaíso
Universidad Adolfo Ibáñez
Viña del Mar, Chile

INSEAD, The European Institute of Business Administration
Fontainebleau, France

IMD, The Institute for Management Development
Lausanne, Switzerland

The McDonough School of Business
Georgetown University
Washington, D.C., USA

The College of Business
Northeastern University
Boston, Massachusetts, USA

Theseus Institute
Sophia Antipolis, France

Thunderbird, The American Graduate School of International Management
Phoenix, Arizona, USA

Preface

Our Global Environment

There is little doubt that our perception of the size of the world is shrinking by the day. As new technologies and government policies bridge distances and reduce obstacles to international transactions, both producers and consumers expand their horizons from local to global markets and sources. Regardless of the type of endeavor in which businesses engage, the playing field is now the globe.

Modern advances in communication technologies and transport have brought distant lands and events into nearly everyone's field of vision and within the scope of personal experience. National cultural achievements—whether gastronomic, artistic, or literary—are rapidly shared by a world eager to savor humanity's inventiveness and to complement traditional domestic choices. Scientific discoveries spread widely at astonishing speed; they are often replicated across the globe within weeks of their first announcement. The advent of e-commerce makes many products, music, or ideas available in nearly all nations instantaneously, whether or not the owners or producers planned it that way. Even in the arena of sporting events, teams and stars are no longer the domain of any one city or nation. Players like Michael Jordan and Ronaldo—and their teams, the Chicago Bulls and Inter Milan—are recognized and followed worldwide. Yet, it is in the field of business that the transformation from a national to a global economy has been most dramatic.

In the immediate postwar period, the ratio of world trade to world output was considerably less than 10 percent. By the late 1980s this ratio had doubled, and at the end of the century is hovering around 25 percent. World trade in manufactured goods now represents more than 35 percent of total output, with more than 50 percent of this being intracompany transfers, i.e., trade between divisions of the same company located in different national jurisdictions. Overall, trade volume expanded at a pace above 7 percent per annum during the last half-century, far outpacing and significantly contributing to the unprecedented economic growth the world has experienced during this period.

Trade in so-called invisibles—tourism, the myriad of services from engineering to telecommunications that are critical to any modern society, dividend and financial flows, and other international transfers—grew at an even faster rate and have consistently outpaced merchandise trade export growth. Led by the globalization of financial services and markets and propelled by the Internet revolution, this component of world trade promises to remain the fastest growing segment. In 1998, services export trade was on the order of $1.5 trillion and merchandise export trade around $5.5 trillion. In fact, the liberalization of trade in services, particularly in financial and telecommunication services, as well as the international protection of intellectual property rights, are two of the top priorities of the World Trade Organization (WTO) for the next decade.

International capital flows, both portfolio investments as well as foreign direct investment (FDI), have also grown dramatically in the last half-century. With annual flows of more than $600 billion in 1998 (versus less than $40 billion in the early 1980s), FDI has become the major weapon of choice in international competition. In fact, according to the annual UNCTAD survey of multinational investment, sales by foreign affiliates of major multinational companies exceeded $12 trillion in 1998, nearly twice the volume of world trade. In recent years, this growth has been accompanied by considerable diversification in the sources and destinations of investment. For example, the United States, once the principal source of international investment capital, has now become also its major recipient. The U.S. share of the total stock of FDI has dropped from nearly 60 percent in the early 1970s, to less than 40 percent by the late 1990s. Even in the shadow of the Asian economic crisis, Asia now accounts for about one-third of all outward FDI, and this includes firms from Korea, Taiwan, Hong Kong, and Singapore, and not just Japanese multinationals. The same is happening in Latin America, where Mexican, Brazilian, Chilean, and Argentinean firms are increasingly venturing outside their home markets.

The share of FDI going into emerging markets has also grown dramatically during the 1990s. China has led the list with incoming FDI flows that exceeded $40 billion annually in recent years, followed by Brazil and Mexico. The large number of privatizations of state-owned companies and the adoption of liberal economic regimes throughout Asia, Latin America, and Eastern Europe has contributed to this shift.

International investment activity in stocks, bonds, real estate, and other assets now plays a central role in securities markets, as greater integration of the world's major capital markets is driven by deregulation and technological change. By the turn of the century annual foreign exchange transactions approached $600 trillion per annum, nearly 100 times the volume of world trade! The collapse of several Asian currencies and economies in 1997 was blamed by many on the perfidious nature of international capital flows, which later targeted Russia and Brazil. Whether this is fact or fiction is not really relevant; the reality is that governments have lost much of the control they had in manipulating their economic policy to gain strategic advantage. For example, international securities transactions represented over 600 percent of Britain's GDP in 1998 (and nearly 200 percent of the GDPs of Germany and the United States, respectively). The creation of the Euro in 1999 will accelerate this trend.

Yet, concurrent with this expansion in direct foreign investment we find a growing diversification in the prevailing organizational forms and structures adopted by international companies. Joint ventures, licensing arrangements, as well as a multitude of nonequity collaborative agreements appear to be gaining ground relative to traditional investment patterns in wholly owned subsidiaries, as new companies and new countries enter the international arena. Partnerships and alliances represent one of the most dynamic dimensions of the global business environment at the turn of the century. This is particularly evident in the global expansion of "dot.com" companies as they seek local content and acceptability together with financial contributions from those markets into which they wish to grow. In fact, their rapid and instantaneous access to global markets of these "born global" companies may call into question our traditional understanding of the internationalization process.

Finally, the speed of technological diffusion has risen markedly since the early 1950s. Then, less than 20 percent of U.S. innovations would be transferred abroad within the first three years following their introduction to the domestic market. The figure by the mid 1980s was closer to 65 percent. Today, no high-tech company can afford to delay the international expansion of its new products without substantial risks to its global position. For products amenable to e-commerce distribution—computer software, music, images, and books—instant worldwide availability has become ubiquitous. Furthermore, although it used to be safe to predict an international life cycle that started in the United States and moved first to Europe, then to Japan, and eventually to the rest of the world (with a gap of maybe 5 to 10 years between each major stage), major innovations today have an equal probability of emanating from any of the Triad countries and are almost instantaneously adopted by the others. The rapid growth of Japanese and European firms among the top earners of U.S. patents corroborates this trend. And yet, the growing interdependence of world markets means that the source of innovation and the location of production are increasingly divorced both from each other as well as from demand.

One ignores these trends only at their own peril. Business executives need to understand the factors driving industries and firms to compete on a global basis and to develop management strategies and policies to deal with this reality. Although the speed and degree of globalization will vary by industry according to a variety of technical and environmental factors, all modern executives, in any field of specialization, must incorporate a global perspective in the execution of their tasks.

Organization of the Book

We have written and designed this book to enrich the advanced student's understanding of business issues and problems encountered in managing global businesses. The field of international management encompasses a broad range of skills and disciplines. Case studies represent ideal vehicles for integrating the various perspectives needed to master typical international business situations. The cases printed in this volume reflect the authors' belief that international business is a cross-disciplinary field that can only be mastered through the integration of various skills, functions, and disciplines. The book is organized into 5 sections and 14 units with primary focus on individual areas of management concern.

Section I: Introduction

The first two cases in the book serve as an excellent introduction to the set of issues that will preoccupy us throughout the entire collection. The first case (Case 1–1) describes the process by which Cemex consolidated its position in its home market in the 1970s and 80s, and then faced the decision as to whether it should expand abroad or not. This is an industry with established world producers and one in which exports are difficult beyond a regional basis due to high transportation costs. The case addresses the logic of Cemex's acquisition of two cement companies in Spain from a strategic and financial perspective: is this the best utilization of the company's resources, what are Cemex's unique capabilities that can be transferred abroad, and what are the risks associated with such an internationalization strategy? As such, Cemex's dilemma resembles that faced by many firms in the early stages of their internationalization. The (B) case (Case 1–2) describes the Spanish venture in more detail and permits the class to deepen their discussion of the fit of this opportunity with the company's skills and resources. A third case, available for in-class distribution, updates the company's international expansion through the late 1990s and describes the issues it has encountered and the responses taken as Cemex has grown to become the third largest cement company in the world.

Section II: Global Competitive Strategies in Transition

Considerable debate and confusion surround the questions of what constitutes a global industry and what may be termed global, multinational, international, or transnational companies. For our purposes, *global industries* are characterized by fairly homogenous market demand worldwide and exhibit minimum-scale requirements (in innovation, production, or service) that exceed the size of any single national market. Global corporate structures are derived from an overwhelming economic imperative to amortize R&D costs, exploit economies of scale, or take advantage of other firm-specific resources on a global basis. These industries (e.g., commercial aircraft or mainframe computers) are typically but not exclusively populated by *global companies,* that is, firms that optimize their activities as if the world were a single market, a definition rooted in their organizational and operating logic and not on industry association or international scope. They are typically governed and managed with considerable degree of centralization in all strategic and many operational decisions.

In contrast, we define *multinational companies* as those consisting of a loosely coupled network of national subsidiaries, enjoying varying degrees of self-sufficiency and acting in a governance structure more akin to a *federal* model. These firms can successfully inhabit both global industries, where they pursue strategies of raising domestic barriers to entry for global competitors, or *fragmented industries* (e.g., processed foods or retail banking), where they position themselves to compete against purely domestic firms by emphasizing certain advantages derived from their multicountry operations. Finally, *international companies* is a term we reserve to those mainly domestic companies that nonetheless participate opportunistically in the international economy through exports and a few nonintegrated subsidiaries, licensees, and agents.

The cases in this section illustrate the different strategic and organizational challenges that face firms competing in a wide variety of industries with distinct technological and political dimensions in their respective global business environments. They also provide insights into the process and dynamics of industry globalization and the unique competitive interrelationships found in industries subject to international competition under models that range from strong globalization to national fragmentation. The ascendancy of global economic and technological conditions have characterized the last quarter of a century for many industries. How firms adapt or fail to accommodate to the requirements of such changing conditions is the thrust of this first set of cases. We also focus on the particular problems peculiar to service industries and entrepreneurial firms, both of which are populating the ranks of multinational companies to an increasing degree in the last decade.

In Unit 2—From International to Global Competition—the Michelin tire industry series (Cases 2–1, 2–2, and 2–3) takes us a step back in time in order to allow for a longitudinal analysis of the process of industry globalization. These cases permit extensive analysis of individual competitors in an industry experiencing rapid technological change and global market integration. The cases also address some public policy issues that often play a central role in determining the conditions for success in international business. The three cases in the book describe the situation that prevailed in North America in the early 1970s when Michelin made its first foray into this market. Two additional cases available for in-class distribution take the evolution of the industry and Michelin's strategy through the early 1980s and 1990s, respectively. Altogether, these five cases represent a unique opportunity to witness a process that is characteristic of many other industries as the nature of competition shifts from individual markets to the global arena.

The cases in Unit 3—Global Competition in Fragmented Sectors—deal with competitive strategies in fragmented sectors, where globalizing forces are weak and national requirements are dominant. The Heineken case (3–1) presents the evolution of the company's European strategy in the face of domestically oriented competitors. The economics of brewing do not call for extensive globalization. Yet, the company has been active in world markets for over a century. Heineken now faces a reassessment of its international strategy with a view to increase the commitment of resources to fully owned subsidiaries in major European markets. The second case (3–2) deals with the definition of responsibilities between the geographic area coordinators and the worldwide functional managers at Heineken headquarters, and how these may need to change given the new strategy. Two additional cases (Athenian Brewery S.A. and J. J. Murphy's Brewery) are available for in-class distribution. These serve to test the validity of Heineken's proposed new European strategy in two very different contexts. Finally, a case updating the company's development through the late 1990s and posing a new set of strategic challenges is also available for use in class. This set of five cases richly illustrates the complexities of managing a loose federation of companies where the forces of global integration must be kept in check.

The final case in Unit 3 discusses the extraordinary success associated with Häagen Daz's globalization strategy (Case 3–3). Its European entry, however, pits the company against an established and powerful producer, Unilever, in the latter's home market. The case serves to exemplify competitive interaction in multinational markets of this type.

Unit 4—Global Expansion in Service Industries—presents three examples of one of the most pervasive phenomena in the last 20 years, the globalization of services. Egon Zehnder International (Case 4–1) tells the story of the world's number one, top-end executive search firm and its struggle to determine which, if any, of the Asian economies are amenable to its style of executive search. A major concern facing the firm's management is that Asian businesses seem not to respond positively to Egon Zehnder's relational style. A follow-up case is available for in-class distribution that describes subsequent events in one Asian market: India. Kenny Rogers Roasters in China (A) (Case 4–2) ostensibly deals with issues of goal formulation, strategy content and joint venture partner selection. However, more important perhaps is the question of the degree of control over operations and quality that is required in such a global franchise business. Here again, two additional cases are available for in-class distribution to cover subsequent events. The final case in this unit, ENDESA-Chile (Case 4–3), brings in the issues of the political and economic risk facing service companies as they expand away from familiar domestic markets, and the transferability of their competitive skills. ENDESA is attempting to ride the wave of privatization moving through South America's electric supply industry. The company's board must evaluate the risk/return trade-off of further international expansion into the Argentine market relative to domestic diversification or expansion elsewhere.

Unit 5—Global Strategy in Entrepreneurial Firms—explores issues of international expansion in smaller, entrepreneurial firms and the travails they face in being "born global." The Australian Motorcycle Company case (5–1) presents the story of a company that has developed a state-of-the-art motorcycle, but is stymied by the choice of distribution and marketing strategy available in foreign markets. International Service System (Case 5–2) is an example of a company that has entered a low-status, price-conscious business with a service concept that upgrades its image and allows it to charge a premium price for its services. ISS has embraced an organizational model of distributed multinational entrepreneurship, and developed the key management processes and roles required to make it effective. Finally, the Acer Group case (5–3) describes a company that has been focused on internationalization since its outset in a tough global industry. Acer has grown with a strategy of encouraging local investment by joint venture partners in a borderless networked company.

Section III: Managing the Globalization Process

Corporations can participate in individual markets in a variety of ways. They may choose to enter a market by engaging the services of an agent or distributor, through a licensee, by undertaking a variety of joint ventures at different stages of the value-added chain, through acquisition, or by the formation of a wholly owned subsidiary. The issues and frameworks relevant to these decisions are the central points of this section.

Assessing and managing the political environment is an integral element of such a decision and part of the job of any senior international manager. Political constraints often make the best economic strategy unfeasible. Compromises that call for suboptimal economic performance may yield unexpected benefits in the form of political patronage, privileged access to markets, or procurement opportunities. But these advantages may be short-lived, requiring difficult trade-offs on the part of management. And when hostile environments cannot be avoided, the task of managing the possible negative fallout is critically important.

Traditionally, foreign investors undertook joint ventures and other forms of collaboration only when they had been coerced by host country regulations or in response to political risks. For the past decade or two, however, we have witnessed exponential growth in intercorporate alliances and collaborations between partners of equal standing and involving operations in industrial countries. Similarly, market entry by acquisition is an increasingly favorite choice for firms to cope with the structural rationalization accompanying the process of globalization in many industries.

The cases in Unit 6—Market Entry Strategies and Managing Political Risks—focus on the special concerns that arise in multinational companies' relationships with governments, either as customers, suppliers, partners or regulators, and in assessing and incorporating political risks into market entry decisions. The first case (6–1) is the story of Enron Corporation's somewhat acrimonious entry into the Indian energy market. Enron had to decide what to do when a newly elected government in the Indian state of Maharashtra canceled its $2.8 billion power project after considerable front-end investments. In Deng's Legacy: China On-Line (Case 6–2), the case describes the changing telecommunications environment in China. Lacking an indigenous capability to deal with the need for rapid improvement in this vital infrastructure area, the Chinese government must appeal to a number of multinational operators. A set of cases on potential foreign partners that include Alcatel, AT&T, Motorola, Nortel, Siemens, LM Ericsson, and three others (available for in-class distribution by the instructor) describe the situation from the perspective of each of these companies, allowing for a negotiation simulation exercise on the terms of entry.

The third case on PaintCo Brasileira (Case 6–3) addresses the issue of how a company should incorporate political risk in its assessment of various entry alternatives—licensing, joint venture, acquisition or start-up—in terms of both its strategic and financial objectives. A detailed spreadsheet allows for simulation of most scenarios on financial returns and permits the students to quantify these risks. Finally, an additional case on the insurance industry (Colonial Insurance vs. National Mutual Insurance: The Battle for a China License) is available for the instructor to use to explore similar issues in the context of a service industry and the issuance of operating licenses to partners or agents in risky markets.

Unit 7—Alliances, Partnerships and Acquisitions—allows for a closer examination of the strategic and managerial issues associated with different modes of market entry. The first two cases focus principally on partner choice and venture design, whereas the last two focus more on the managerial aspects of alliances and acquisitions. Northrop Grumman and Advanced Technology Transport Bus Program (Case 7–1) discusses the need for the company to seek a partner in order to exploit a radically new design for an urban transit bus. Born out of the U.S. government defense technology conversion program, the project presents the company with a dilemma since it does not possess the necessary skills to succeed in this market. The questions posed include how to select a partner and on what basis. In the case on FIAT and Peugeot's Sevelnord Venture (A) (Case 7–2) we are presented with a situation where the companies have been operating a successful joint venture for some years and want to expand their relationship further. However, the conditions in the proposed new product/market area are different than those prevailing in the original venture. Two additional cases available for in-class distribution provide the relative perspectives of each of the two companies. These and a detailed spreadsheet allow the students to role play a joint venture design negotiation and discuss the issues that may affect its successful development under uncertain conditions.

General Electric-SNECMA (A) (Case 7–3) tells the history of a successful joint venture in the aircraft engine business that is undergoing a challenge from a changing competitive environment. The partners need to determine how to modify their arrangement in order to cope with these changes. Two additional cases are available for in-class distribution that follow the development of the relationship over a 10-year period. The last case in this section, Electrolux: The Acquisition and Integration of Zanussi (Case 7–4) focuses on the importance of post-merger integration in terms of the strategic, operational and organizational priorities of the acquirer. For Electrolux the issue is how to make Zanussi part of Electrolux while preserving its distinct identity and reviving the fighting spirit that had been the hallmark of the proud Italian company.

This last unit in this section, Unit 8—Network Organizations and E-business—presents issues that have risen to the fore in the management of firms seeking to operate flexibly in the new global economy. Nexia International (Case 8–1) is a loose affiliation of accounting firms that includes members in 68 countries and correspondents in 5 others, operating 292 offices with 881 partners and 7,769 staff. For Nexia the key question is how to keep the strategic loyalty of its members in the face of centrifugal forces and asymmetric conditions. Issues of quality consistency and the value and costs of central network services are critical to this question. PixTech (Case 8–2) is a small firm in an industry dominated by big players. The company is facing a number of strategic issues regarding its network of technology partners, such as the need to assimilate low-cost, high-quality, and high-volume manufacturing capabilities from its Taiwanese associate. Much of the company's concerns are due to the fast moving nature of the industry, the design and manufacturing of field emission displays, an alternative technology in the flat panel display industry, and the problems of integrating disparate contributions from the partners.

Aspect Development, Inc. (A) (Case 8–3) describes the early history of a leading provider of component databases and parts information management software to original equipment manufacturers in the electronics industry. Having grown rapidly since their founding in 1991, the company is evaluating how to position itself for the next big growth spurt in intermediation of global value-added chains in the late 1990s. This would include the online provision of their services and expansion to global markets. A follow-up case is available for in-class distribution to trace the company's decision and development over this later period.

Section IV: Managing Global Operations

This section addresses key strategic, operational, structural, and managerial issues associated with the management of different global functions—marketing, finance, manufacturing, R&D and knowledge, and people. In each case the optimal balance of global integration and local responsiveness is bound to respond to different political conditions and technical requirements, as well as having to respond to markedly varying internal pressures. The purpose of the cases in the following units is to develop expertise in diagnosing the right set of forces that apply in each instance, and in designing organizational solutions and managerial approaches that are suitable to the moment, yet remain flexible to accommodate change over time.

The first set of cases in this section, Unit 9—Managing the Global Marketing Function—deal with these issues in the context of marketing decisions. Among the most critical issues facing any manager with global marketing responsibilities are the selection of markets which the firm will enter and the extent to which product positioning and marketing strategies need to be adapted to local circumstances. In fact, the debate on the relative advantages of standardization versus adaptation has been at the core of the international marketing literature for over 20 years. Related to these issues, and often defining the choices, is how the international marketing function is structured to balance the twin objectives of uniformity across markets and responsiveness to the idiosyncrasies of domestic consumers.

The case on Procter & Gamble: Ariel Ultra's Eurobrand Strategy (Case 9–1) describes P&G's efforts to develop a compact laundry detergent for the European market. Competitive developments in the French market, however, argue for a quick and different response from that planned for the European launch, still two months away. This calls into question the entire regional strategy and requires a reassessment of its premises. Hewlett-Packard: Global Account Management (A) (Case 9–2) describes HP's move from a local to a global marketing strategy for their global customers. The shift from a product or market-focused sales/account program to a customer-focused approach requires the company to know which types of customers should be identified as global accounts, how to establish a balance between its global accounts and its geographic strategies, and how to manage both simultaneously.

Unit 10—Managing the Global Finance Function and Risks—examines the management of corporate finance in global markets and its associated risks. The two cases in this unit encapsulate a number of complex issues. In China Southern Airlines (Case 10–1) the immediate question of what is the appropriate price for an initial public offering (IPO) for a Chinese state-owned company brings up the problem of cash flow and risk assessment in environments subject to little due diligence and managerial control. The analysis is relevant not just to those contemplating IPOs but to anyone doing valuation analysis of companies in less developed countries. SouthGold (Case 10–2) is a company going through radical change induced by globalization. The South African mining industry, newly open to international scrutiny, is rapidly focusing its operations around primary metals. In the gold sector this has led to the creation of a number of gold-only companies, one of which is SouthGold. The question facing SouthGold is how to handle Southern Africa's production cost disadvantage with the use of derivatives? It is also an excellent opportunity to discuss how companies utilize outside investors to mitigate the influence of local politicians.

The next set of cases in Unit 11—Managing Global Manufacturing and Logistics—deal with the management of operations in a global setting. The key theme throughout is the balance and coordination of international manufacturing facilities. BOK Fibers International (Case 11–1) describes the Latin American fiber operations of a large diversified chemical firm. Traditionally organized in a series of bilateral relationships with significant local equity partners in each country, the company has to adjust to the advent of a more integrated and liberal market environment. This calls for much higher degree of integration among the subsidiaries. What are the relative costs and benefits of such integration and how to achieve it are the main subjects of the case. In BMW: Globalizing Manufacturing Operations (Case 11–2) the reader finds the story of BMW's new plant at Spartanburg, South Carolina. In a record-breaking 24 months, BMW had put together a state-of-the-art facility and BMW management was considering expanding the plant's capacity ahead of schedule in order to accommodate a faster ramp-up of production for the Z3—a brand new roadster produced only at Spartanburg. Al Kinzer, President of BMW Manufacturing Corp., was under pressure to formulate a strategy for dealing with this unexpected demand that relates to BMW's global manufacturing strategy.

The cases in Unit 12—Managing Research, Knowledge, and New Product Development—tackle the issues of technology and knowledge transfer in multinational companies as well as providing insights into the product development process from an R&D and technology management perspective. Salomon: Strategic Entry into the World Snowboard Market (Case 12–1) examines the know-how requirements facing Salomon as it expands from skis, boots and bindings to snowboards. The problem facing the firm is that while the products are technically similar, they are radically different from a marketing perspective. Nestlé S.A. (Case 12–2) operates a distributed R&D function that puts heavy emphasis on centralization of basic scientific endeavors (in Switzerland) and the geographic dispersion of product development and specialized research to a number of labs throughout the world. The case allows us to examine these competing pressures testing this system and the organizational mechanisms necessary to make it work. Case 12–3, Managing Knowledge at Booz-Allen & Hamilton, represents one of the hot topics of the last decade, knowledge management. Booz-Allen is faced with classic knowledge management problems—how to ensure that people have an incentive to codify what they know; how to develop systems that allow people to access what others know; and how to do so without commoditizing the firm's proposition to consumers—all of this in a broad international context.

The last unit in this section, Unit 13—Managing People in a Global Company—addresses the issues associated with the management of human resources and corporate culture in a global context. Federal Express (A) and (B) (Cases 13–1 and 13–2) describe the acquisition by Federal Express of the Flying Tiger organization in the late 1980s and the subsequent problems it encountered as it attempted to impose its HR practices and values outside the U.S. context. The cases raise the question as to whether these problems could have been predicted and avoided, and how. A third case available for distribution in class continues the company's handling of these issues into the 1990s. Case 13–3, Nizhlak: The Top Management Team, tackles the complex issue of the competence and composition of the top management team in a Russian-German joint venture. The case provides an opportunity to address the sensitive issues of coalition formation and communication breakdowns when two different cultures get together for a single purpose.

The last case in this series, Ciba-Geigy Management Development (Case 13–4) focuses on the human resources management function in a sophisticated global corporation. The triggering decision is the need to appoint a new pharmaceutical marketing manager for the French operating company. Top management of Ciba-Geigy France have one view, whereas the management development staff and division management at headquarters have another. Detailed information on the company's strategy, organization, and management development system allow for a thorough discussion of the merits of each position and of the role of the human resource management function as "glue" in a diversified global company.

Section Five: Synthesis and Integration

The purpose of the cases in this last section is to integrate all the material covered in the book. In A.B. Thorsten (1) (Case 14–1) a dispute arises between the management of the Swedish subsidiary of a diversified Canadian chemical company and its headquarters' staff regarding an investment in Sweden. The situation escalates and comes to the attention of top management, who must deal with a proposal of small financial importance but of great significance for the future structure and management culture of the entire organization. This case serves as an excellent bridge to the organizational problems typical of the transition from international to multinational and global structures. Henkel Asia-Pacific (Case 14–2) discusses an interesting situation where Henkel's business units were initially leery of Asia expansion. An Asian unit is thus created to promoted business development, which leads to the various divisions to change their minds and begin entering Asia willy-nilly. The case highlights the difficulties of decision making, co-ordination and integration across business divisions in a diversified multinational, and presents a case for and against regional structures.

Case 14–3 outlines the problems faced by Alfa-Laval Agri, the world's leading supplier of milking equipment and farm supplies to dairy farmers. The company's problems began with its reaction to the opening of Eastern Europe after 1989. Having formed a matrix structure to share responsibility between business units and local market companies, the company found that the business units were accused of thinking too "Scandinavian" and not listening to customer demands. The market companies, on the other hand, were reluctant to stop customizing at great costs, or to report to "not knowledgeable" people at the center who were constantly asking for market information. Rank Xerox (A) (Case 14–4) brings us back to an analysis of the global strategy of the company, where the book began. Rank Xerox is in the throes of a major reorganization and must completely reorient itself into a customer driven global player. How to break the country-focused strategy of the past, and what is the best transition path to their new structure, are the main issues on the strategic agenda. A follow-up case describing some of their actions is available for in-class distribution and discussion.

The Teaching and Practice of International Business

Our intention in writing this casebook was to make more accessible for teachers and students of international business complex and current materials that reflect the reality of operating in a global competitive environment. Each case study reproduced here represents a set of problems or issues that are commonly encountered by managers who may be operating at various levels of responsibility in the global business arena. The cases were selected and arrayed to permit an effective application of current theory and knowledge in the area of international business management to problems ranging from the definition of competitive strategy to policy issues in all major functional areas.

The appropriate mix of case problems, and the theoretical readings and lectures which must accompany them, can best be determined by individual instructors based on their preferences and on the specific circumstances of their students' curriculum. These are, however, complex and advanced problems more suitable to students having considerable exposure to the full range of business courses required in a core business studies program as well as familiarity with the international economic issues that frame the environment in which trade and investment take place. The number and sequence of cases presented in this casebook reflect a relatively comprehensive catalog of the issues we believe are most critical to the international manager. Obviously, it would be difficult, if not impossible, to use all these cases in any single course. The selection provided here is meant to offer a sufficient variety and a set of options from which each instructor can design his or her most effective course structure.

Although the cases were selected partly because of their focus on broad interdisciplinary issues, they also permit a rather narrow analysis of specific functional areas and issues, while encouraging a more integrated perspective on international management problems. We believe that analysis of the situations presented in these studies will yield significant insights into the general principles that underlie the successful practice of management in a global business environment.

Acknowledgments

First and foremost we wish to express our appreciation to all who contributed materials for this casebook. These individuals and institutions made significant commitments of time, effort and financial resources to an activity that is not often rewarded in academic circles. For their dedication to pedagogical objectives and their willingness to allow us to use their material we are most grateful. Second, we wish to acknowledge a great intellectual debt to Professor William H. Davidson, who coauthored the earlier edition of this casebook. Time constraints and his very busy schedule as a researcher and consultant did not allow Bill to contribute to this new edition, and he generously ceded his place to others with the time to do so. We are appreciative of your earlier efforts, Bill, and most grateful for your support in this endeavor.

Third, we would like to acknowledge the valuable collaboration of a large number of case writers and research assistants who have worked diligently with us over the years and across four continents in the preparation of these and other international management cases. In particularly José de la Torre wishes to thank Michel Bacchetta, Dana Dyas, Martin Flash, Burkhardt Fuchs, David Harkleroad, Hansoo Kang, Andy Khodjamirian, Nasser Sagheb, Marcelle Speller, and Martine van den Poel. Yves Doz is thankful for the assistance of Jean-Louis Barsoux, Marie-Aude Dalsace, Francesca Gee, L. N. Krishna, and Martine van den Poel. Finally, Timothy Devinney wishes to express his gratitude to Marco Gabbiani, Marc-Antoine Cousin, Elizabeth Fulcher, Irina Petrova, A. Schmidt, Kris Vogelsong, and Peter Wei Gang Lu.

The willingness of many leading international companies to allow these cases to be written also merits our sincere gratitude. Large and small, some more global than others, these firms have had the courage to have their strategies, policies and decisions aired publicly. Whatever the circumstances or results, the frankness and honesty with which these firms have allowed others to learn from their experiences is indeed commendable. We thank them all collectively for their deep concern about the quality of management education and their contribution to the cases in this book. We would like to single out some of the executives and companies that were particularly helpful to the three of us. José de la Torre is most appreciative of the extensive cooperation of executives at Heineken, especially its former chairman G. van Schaik and board members Hans Drost and Robert van den Vijver, Hans Hüther at Akzo-Nobel, and Bob Nelson at Northrop Grumman Corporation. Yves Doz wishes to acknowledge the collaboration of many executives at Ciba-Geigy, GE-SNECMA, Alfa Laval and Rank Xerox that made those cases possible. Timothy Devinney is grateful to the contributions of executives at Egon Zehnder worldwide, especially Ashley Stephenson, Damien O'Brien and Bill Henderson, to Ruby Lu and Ching Tao of Goldman Sachs (Hong Kong), Li Yong Zhen of China Southern Airways, Alan Beanland and Matthew Percival of Colonial Insurance, and Geoff Webb of National Mutual.

The support of a number of institutions should also be acknowledged. The majority of the cases in this book were written while the authors and many of the contributors were at INSEAD. Professor de la Torre was supported there over a 13-year period through the late 1980s, as were Professors Ferdows, Ghoshal, and Koza, all now elsewhere. Others, including Professors Doz, Galunic, Haspeslagh, Héau, Kool, de Meyer, Schütte, Story, Weeks, and Williamson are still on the INSEAD faculty. The Institute generously allowed us to use their cases in this volume, for which we are most grateful. We are also appreciative of the authorization given by other institutions, particularly IMD in Lausanne, the Theseus Institute in Sophia Antipolis, France, and Thunderbird in Phoenix, for their continued support of case writing. Finally, we would like to express our thanks to our current employers for allowing us the time to complete this project. The Anderson School at UCLA has been most generous in its support of Professor de la Torre's international activities. Professor Devinney also wishes to thank the staff of the Frank Lowy Library at the Australian Graduate School of Management, especially Mary McDonnell, and his students in the MBA and executive program classes at the Australian Graduate School of Management, CEIBS and City University (Hong Kong).

Any project of this nature requires the assistance of several indefatigable people, who will look after a myriad of details and keep us in line. Our secretaries, Noëlle Triaureau and Jenna Radomile (at UCLA), Marie-Françoise Piquerez (at INSEAD) and Leone Kennedy (at the AGSM) were all extraordinary in keeping us focused and reasonably on time. Our editors at McGraw-Hill, Jennifer Roche, Tracy Jensen, and Kelly Delso were superb in their support and encouragement. We wish to thank also our students at all three institutions who have let us try new material on them, sometimes with less than perfect results, and our colleagues Dominique Héau (INSEAD) and George Yip (now at Cambridge University) for their constant insights and contributions to our own ideas.

In closing, we dedicate this book to a giant of our field whose death this past year left a great vacuum in the teaching and understanding of international business. Ray Vernon was an uncommon academic whose devotion to the study of multinational corporations and to his students is worthy of emulation by future generations of students and researchers. We will remember him fondly and try to follow in his relentless pursuit of knowledge and relevance.

José de la Torre
Yves Doz
Timothy Devinney

SECTION

I Introduction

UNIT 1 The Globalization Process

Case 1-1

Cemex (A)

Cemex was the largest cement company in North America, and the fourth largest in the world, with about 24 million tons of capacity at the end of 1991, and a 63 percent share of the Mexican market. From its original base of operations in the northeast of Mexico (in 1972 the company had only 2.2 million tons of installed capacity and controlled less than 15 percent of the Mexican market), it expanded across Mexico first and then internationally. By 1991, sales amounted to 5.3 trillion pesos (about $1.7 billion), of which exports accounted for about 15 percent. Exhibits 1–3 provide detailed income statement, balance sheet and cash flow information for Cemex for the period 1986–91.

The Market for Cement in Mexico

Total Mexican cement consumption was 21.2 and 23.3 million tons in 1990 and 1991, respectively, making it the 13th largest market in the world. Mexican consumers preferred cement over other building materials, partly because wood was scarce and bricks were more expensive. Rising incomes in recent years had also allowed people to move up from cheaper materials such as corrugated metal and adobe to more durable cement.

Cement was a cyclical business. Sales were dependent on population changes, economic growth, and construction expenditures. In developing countries, cement expenditures grew at about 1.5 to 2 times the rate of growth in GDP (see Exhibit 4 for Mexican data). In 1990, Mexico's population was estimated at 81 million, growing at more than 2 percent per year it would surpass 100 million by the year 2000. Demand for a first residence principally arises from people in the 20 to 25 years of age bracket, a segment that represented approximately 16 million households in Mexico. Of these, about 35 to 40 percent did not currently own their own home but would like to do so, suggesting an estimated housing shortage of about 6 million units. The housing sector could thus be expected to generate significant demand for cement in the coming years.

Mexico had both adhered to the GATT agreements and joined the OECD[1] in the late 1980s, resulting in a significant unilateral decrease in import tariffs. More open trade with the United States and others, and privatization

[1]The Organization for Economic Cooperation and Development was an association of 24 industrialized countries encompassing most of Europe, the United States and Canada, Japan, Australia, and New Zealand.

This case was prepared by Professor Ravi Sarathy at Northeastern University for purposes of class discussion. Revised by Professor José de la Torre at the Anderson School of UCLA, February 1999.

EXHIBIT 1 **Cemex S.A. and Consolidated Subsidiaries—Income Statements, 1987–91**
($ millions, except earnings per share)

	Years Ended December 31				
	1987	1988	1989	1990	1991
Net Sales	$ 524	$ 616	$ 1,075	$ 1,305	$ 1,706
Cost of Sales	352	430	841	928	1,064
Gross Profit	172	186	234	377	642
Selling Expenses	(*)	(*)	37	52	79
Administrative Expenses	(*)	(*)	94	126	142
Total Selling and Administrative Expenses	48	61	131	178	221
Operating Income	124	124	103	199	420
Financial Expenses	(73)	(77)	(368)	(393)	(330)
Financial Income	106	86	361	150	286
Foreign Exchange Gain/Loss, Net	(45)	5	(35)	(84)	(44)
Monetary Position Gain/Loss, net	14	(12)	99	322	212
Net Comprehensive Financing Income/Cost	2	2	57	(5)	124
Other Income/Expenses, Net	41	70	5	(42)	(47)
Income Before Taxes and Profit Sharing	167	196	165	152	497
Income Tax Benefit/Expense and Business` Asset Tax, Net	14	(4)	(7)	33	5
Employees' Statutory Profit Sharing	0	(7)	(5)	(10)	(11)
Equity in Income of Affiliates	1	9	5	3	11
Minority Interest in Net Income	23	26	27	30	60
Majority Interest in Net Income	159	168	131	148	442
Earnings Per Share ($)	0.53	0.51	0.4	0.45	1.34

Notes: All figures are rounded to the nearest $1 million.
(*) Amounts were not reported separately in the audited consolidated financial statements.
Source: Cemex Prospectus, March 13, 1992.

of the extensive state-owned industrial holdings, were expected to lead the Mexican economy to grow at a rate between 4 and 6 percent a year. As a result, government and private expenditures on infrastructure could be expected to increase dramatically. The road system in Mexico was inadequate for the country's needs, for example, and there were plans to build 5,000 additional kilometers of four-lane toll highways and seven international toll bridges by 1994. This compared to the 4,000 km of four-lane highways currently in use. Most roads were constructed of asphalt, which was cheaper initially but required higher maintenance. With the private sector being given more leeway to build toll roads, bridges, and airports, a shift toward greater use of cement would follow.

About 60 percent of cement expenditures in Mexico were for residential construction, 20 percent for public works, and 20 percent for nonresidential private construction. The construction sector accounted for about 4 percent of Mexican GDP, which compared to 4.9 percent in the United States and a European average of 12 percent.

Cement was costly to transport over land, being relatively heavy and with a low value-to-weight ratio. As a result, it was considered uncompetitive to move cement over land more than 100 to 200 miles from a production site. Because of Mexico's north-south mountain ranges and the location of its large cities inland (see map in Exhibit 5), logistics were a major problem. Mexico's three largest markets were all far from seaports: Guadalajara at

EXHIBIT 2 Cemex S.A. and Consolidated Subsidiaries—Balance Sheets, 1987–91
($ millions)

	Years Ended on December 31				
	1987	1988	1989	1990	1991
Cash and Temporary Investments	$ 187	$ 190	$ 186	$ 145	$ 202
Trade Receivables, Net	23	46	83	91	109
Other Receivables	36	59	59	111	139
Inventories	78	112	182	175	211
Total Current Assets	324	407	510	522	661
Investments in Affiliated Companies	57	183	110	122	113
Property, Plant and Equipment	1,511	2,042	3,536	3,982	4,729
Accumulated Depreciation	-744	-1,002	-1,769	-1,966	-2,243
Construction in Progress	15	81	270	341	128
Net Property, Plant and Equipment	782	1,121	2,037	2,357	2,614
Excess Over Book Value in Acquisitions	(*)	(*)	275	381	396
Other Deferred Charges	(*)	(*)	26	91	131
Accumulated Amortization	(*)	(*)	-18	-36	-67
Net Deferred Charges	11	5	283	436	460
Total Assets	1,174	1,716	2,940	3,437	3,848
Bank Loans and Notes Payable	19	54	320	213	68
Current Portion of Long-Term Debt	42	15	40	48	76
Short-Term Debt	61	69	360	261	144
Trade Accounts Payable	15	17	40	30	34
Other Accrued Expenses	73	111	122	197	126
Total Current Liabilities	149	197	522	488	304
Bank Loans	(*)	(*)	484	609	232
Debentures	(*)	(*)	293	325	157
Notes Payable	(*)	(*)	(*)	157	954
Others	(*)	(*)	55	(*)	(*)
Current Portion of Long-Term Debt	(*)	(*)	-40	-48	-76
Long-Term Debt	135	143	792	1,043	1,267
Other Non-Current Liabilities	3	17	40	34	36
Minority Interest	134	182	306	474	408
Stockholders' Equity	753	1,177	1,280	1,398	1,833
Total Liabilities and Stockholders' Equity	1,174	1,716	2,940	3,437	3,848

Notes: Figures are rounded to the nearest $1 million.
(*) Amounts were not reported separately in the audited financial statements.
Source: Cemex Prospectus, March 13, 1992.

220 km, and Monterrey and Mexico City at over 300 km each. This meant a choice between many small inefficient plants or expensive inland transportation across mountains in a country with relatively few new highways. However, cement could be shipped economically over long distances by sea, allowing cement produced in large-scale plants near marine transportation facilities to compete with domestic production in port cities in countries with large cement markets. Mexico, despite 16,000 km of coastline, had few well developed harbors. In fact, Houston was the most important single port of entry for goods destined for the Mexican market.

EXHIBIT 3 Cemex S.A. and Subsidiaries—Changes in Financial Position, 1987–91
($ millions)

	Years Ended December 31				
	1987	1988	1989	1990	1991
Operations:					
Majority Interest Net Income	$ 159	$ 168	$ 131	$ 148	$ 442
Items Not Affecting Cash Flows	116	88	136	169	230
Resources Provided by Operations	275	256	267	317	672
Trade Accounts Receivables, Net	(7)	(12)	(38)	6	(5)
Other Receivables and Other Current Assets	(27)	(7)	9	(42)	(15)
Inventories	(14)	(12)	(110)	(15)	(29)
Trade Accounts Payable	12	(5)	22	(17)	0
Other Accounts Payable and Accrued Expenses	61	(31)	58	55	(99)
Other Assets and Liabilities, Net	—	—	—	—	(3)
Net Investment in Working Capital	25	(67)	(59)	(13)	(151)
Net Resources from Operations	300	189	208	304	521
Financing Activities:					
Proceeds from Short-Term Bank Loans	15	27	167	(192)	(38)
Proceeds from Long-Term Bank Loans	118	(48)	326	43	(459)
Debentures	(*)	(*)	293	(17)	(212)
Notes Payable	(*)	(*)	102	125	640
Investment by Subsidiaries	—	—	—	—	(113)
Dividends	(11)	(16)	(17)	(16)	(18)
Other Financing (repayments)	(21)	13	8	(12)	1
Resources Provided by Financing Activities	101	(24)	879	(69)	(199)
Investing Activities:					
Property, Plant & Equipment, & Deferred Charges	(290)	(89)	(1,121)	(392)	(121)
Minority Interest	51	—	45	117	(172)
Other	(110)	(161)	69	(32)	8
Resources Used in Investing Activities	(349)	(250)	(1,096)	(307)	(285)
Increase (decrease) in Cash and Investments	52	(85)	(9)	(72)	37
Cash and Investments at Beginning of the Year	124	187	190	186	145
Effect of Inflation on Cash and Investments	11	88	5	31	20
Cash and Investments at End of Year	187	190	186	145	202

Notes: Figures are rounded to the nearest $1 million.
(*) Amounts were not reported separately in the audited consolidated financial statements.
Source: Cemex Prospectus, March 13, 1992.

Most cement was usually sold as a commodity. The Mexican market was different, however, in that most cement was purchased in branded bags. This was partly because small contractors and individuals were responsible for much of the home construction business, often timing their projects and buying materials as their income allowed. While most cement in developed countries was purchased by large industrial and commercial buyers, Cemex estimated that about 78 percent of demand for cement in Mexico was from the retail sector.

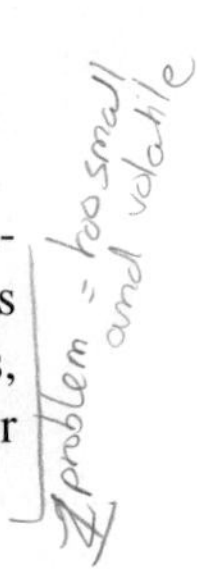

EXHIBIT 4 Mexican GDP and Cement Consumption

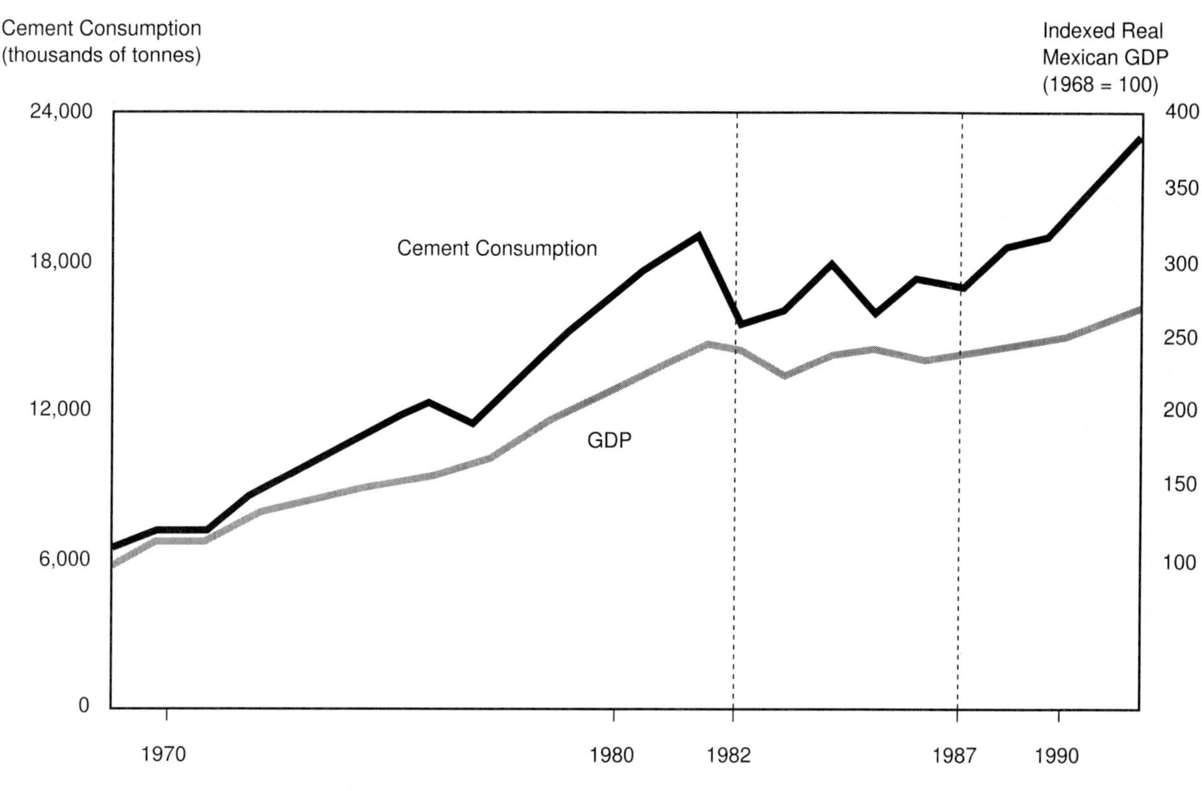

Source: Canacem; Banco de Mexico.

Cemex in the Mexican Market

In 1991, Cemex branded, bagged cement was sold through 4,500 exclusive retail distributors. These distributors were largely family businesses, and Cemex enjoyed considerable brand loyalty both at the distributor and retail customer level. Cemex provided technical and marketing assistance to the dealers and, on average, dealers had been associated with Cemex for nearly 10 years. Cemex employed a number of different regional brands such as Cemento Monterrey, Cemento Tolteca, and Cemento Anahuac, which derived from the original companies that had been acquired by Cemex over the previous decade. These brands were advertised in newspapers, billboards, radio, and, sometimes, television. Cemex's global competitors, on the other hand, sold principally bulk cement in a commodity market. Exhibit 6 presents data on Cemex sales by distribution channel.

By the end of 1991, Cemex had 42 sales offices and 29 distribution sites throughout Mexico, with a storage capacity of 330,000 tons, including 4 marine terminals used for exports. Partly through acquisitions, Cemex controlled a significant portion of cement-handling facilities at Mexican ports. The map in Exhibit 7 shows most Cemex plants and ready-mix sites across Mexico. Exhibit 8 summarizes the group's sales volume over the period 1984 to 1992.

As in other developed markets, the ready-mix line of cement products was gaining importance rapidly. Cement was often mixed by the end-user at the construction site with aggregates and water in order to form concrete. An alternative was ready-mix concrete, which was prepared by the cement producer and delivered in ready-mix trucks to the site, where it was poured as needed. Ready-mix concrete sales were dependent on trucking facilities, and involved greater investment in transportation, loading,

EXHIBIT 5 Mexican Topographic Map

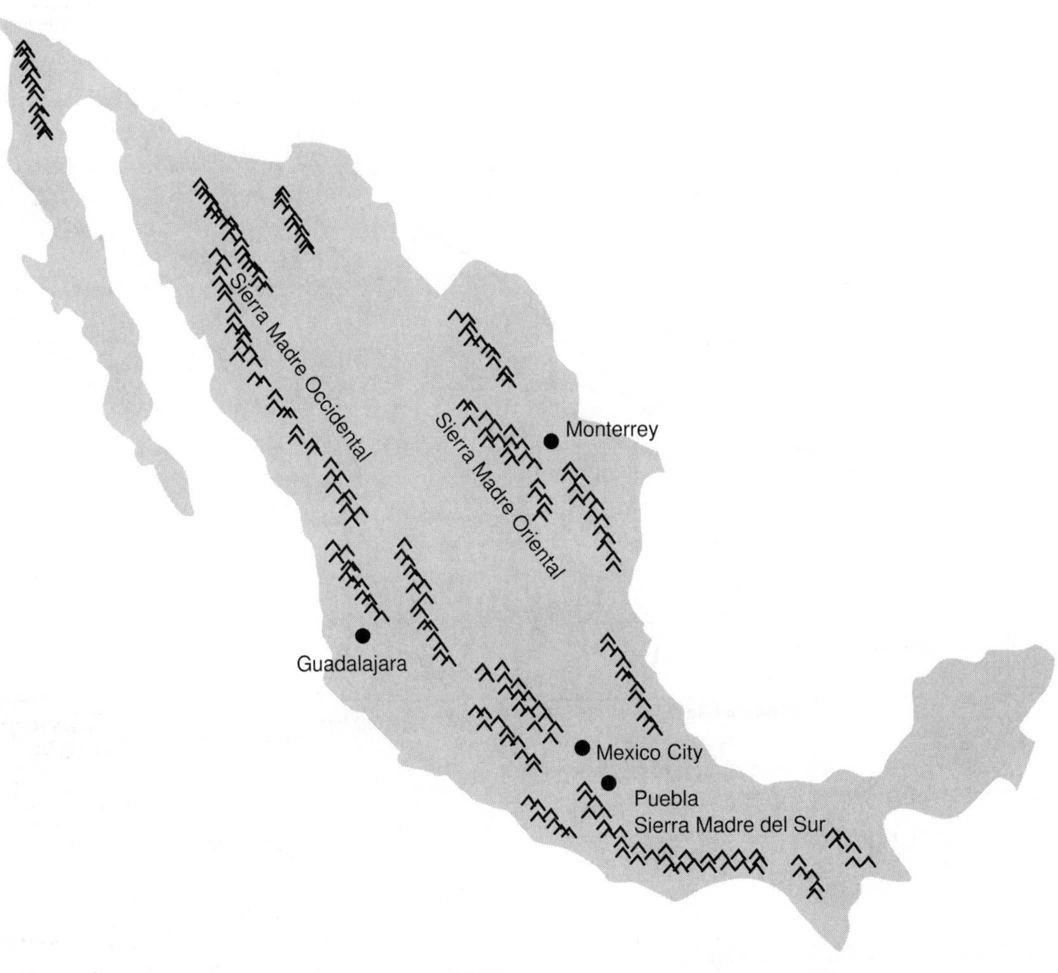

Source: Morgan Stanley Emerging Markets Investment Research, June 1992.

EXHIBIT 6 Cemex Sales of Cement in Mexico by Channel of Distribution, 1987–91

	1987	1988	1989	1990	1991
Retail Distributors (bags)	78.5%	79.7%	76.2%	76.6%	74.6%
Ready-Mix (mainly in trucks)	3.2	3.3	7.2	8.2	8.9
Industry, Government, Etc.	18.3	17.0	16.6	15.2	16.5

Source: Company Records.

EXHIBIT 7 Cemex: Location of Cement Plants and Ready-Mix Sites in Mexico

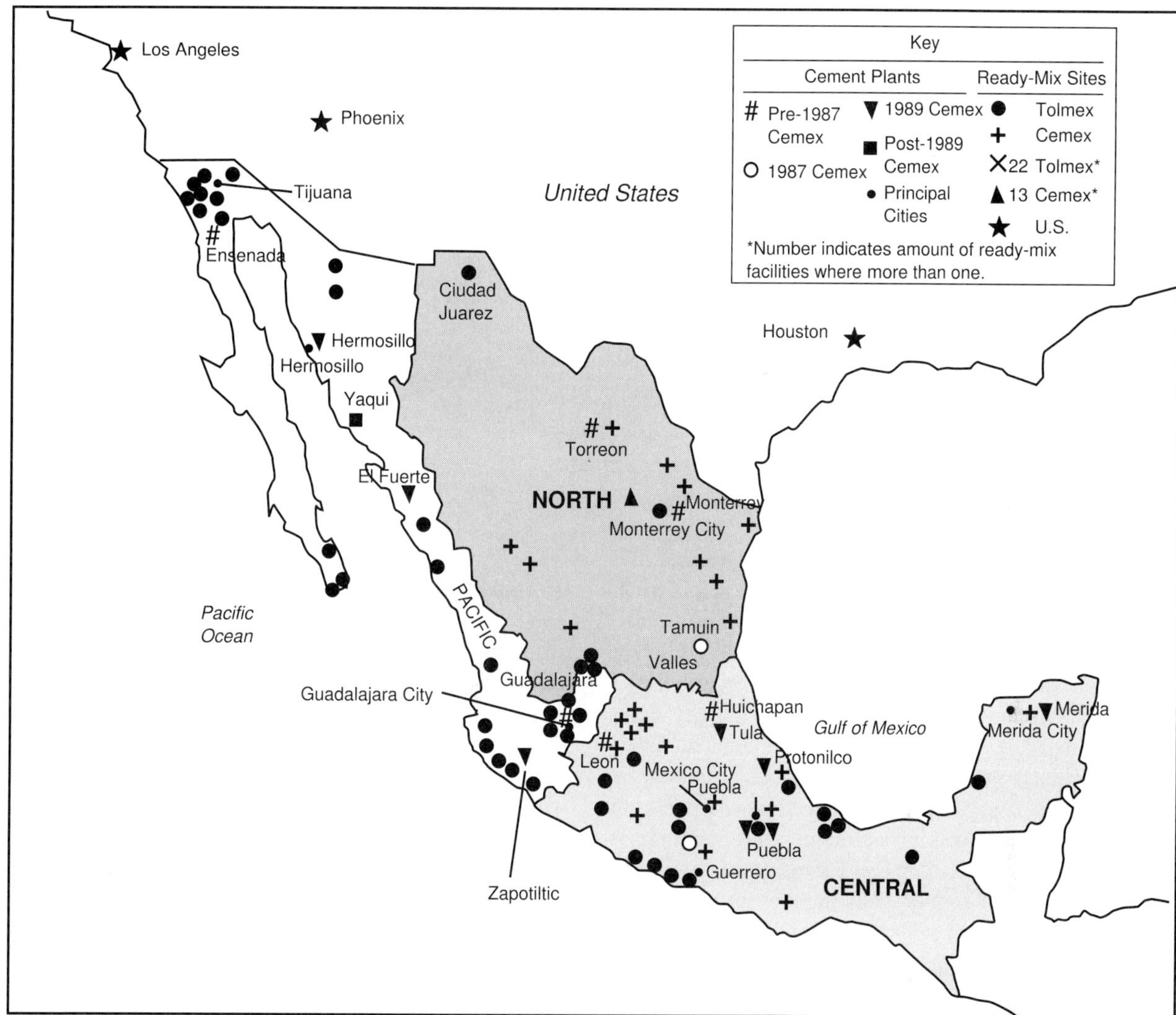

Source: Cemex Prospectus, March 13, 1992, p. 25.

and mixing equipment. Larger scale projects made relatively more use of ready-mix concrete, in order to ensure greater quality control and because of time and labor saved by using ready-mix products. For example, use of ready-mix concrete in Korea had increased from 17 to 54 percent of total cement sales in the period from 1983 to 1989. In industrialized countries, ready-mix accounted for as much as 80 percent of total cement sales.

Ready-mix concrete had traditionally been less important in Mexico because of the relatively small size of construction projects as well as the low cost of labor. About 3 cubic meters of ready-mix could be made from one ton of cement, while one cubic meter of ready-mix sold for about the same price as one ton of cement. The incremental cost of producing 3 cubic meters of ready-mix (costs of sand, water, gravel, pumping and mixing) was about equal to the cost of producing one ton of cement. Thus, ready-mix offered superior margins.

About 11 percent of Cemex sales were in ready-mix concrete, in which it had a 72 percent market share

EXHIBIT 8 Cemex Group Cement Volumes and Mexican GDP Growth

	1984	1985	1986	1987	1988	1989	1990	1991	1992
Domestic Cement									
Thousands of Tons	5,453	6,121	5,618	8,950	8,528	12,651	13,834	15,200	16,950
Increase (percent)	—	12.3	(8.2)	59.3	(4.7)	48.3	9.4	9.9	11.5
Export Cement									
Thousands of Tons	535	574	897	2,826	3,046	3,424	2,266	1,400	1,500
Total	5,988	6,695	6,515	11,776	11,574	16,075	16,100	16,600	18,450
Ready-Mix									
Thousands of Cubic Meters	—	2,800	2,100	2,600	2,600	2,700	3,400	3,900	4,800
Increase (percent)	—	—	(25.0)	23.8	0	3.8	25.9	14.7	23.0
Real GDP Growth (percent)	3.6	2.6	(3.8)	1.8	1.4	3.1	3.9	4.3	4.6
Real Construction Growth (%)	3.9	3.6	(9.9)	1.9	(1.3)	3.2	7.6	2.6	7.5

Source: Morgan Stanley Emerging Markets Investment Research, June 26, 1992.

nationally, principally because of the Tolteca acquisition. Cemex operated about 122 ready-mix plants in 40 cities in Mexico, and about 850 ready-mix trucks. Ready-mix concrete sales doubled in Mexico City in 1990 from previous year levels, while increasing by 13 percent in Monterrey and by 34 percent in areas along the U.S. border. Wages were higher there, and labor shortages had developed because of demand for labor by maquiladoras. As Mexico increased expenditures on large housing projects, infrastructure, and commercial and industrial projects, demand for ready-mix could increase along with tighter construction schedules and higher quality control with exact specifications for cement strength and uniformity.

Cemex's Cost Structure and Price Liberalization

Cement is made by quarrying and grinding limestone, feeding it through a kiln, grinding again, then mixing with gypsum. Plants were typically located near limestone sites. This resulted in a high fixed cost business. While raw materials such as limestone, gypsum, and aggregates (rock and sand) were variable costs, other inputs including labor, depreciation, energy and fuel were mostly fixed costs.

Cemex's cost structure was determined by the modernity of its plants (state of the art technology and productivity) and by the costs of electricity, fuel oil, and labor. Cemex had placed considerable stress on energy efficiency, with fuel consumption (measured by Kcal per kg of clinker produced) declining by 15 percent between 1982 and 1990. Similarly, electricity consumption per unit declined by 9 percent over the same period. Sixteen of 17 Cemex plants use the "dry process" whereby, instead of adding water to form slurry and then drying it, dry materials were heated to high temperatures to reduce them to powder. Most Cemex kilns recovered waste heat to preheat raw materials, and Cemex plants had been modernized to enable them to switch easily from fuel oil to natural gas as prices dictated.

Because of the prevalence of bagged cement, cement operations in Mexico were somewhat more labor intensive. Cemex averaged 1.17 man-hours per ton in 1991. Its newest Yaqui plant, however, with automated bagging equipment registered significant productivity gains and reached a level of 0.47 man-hours per ton.

Forecasts suggested that electricity prices were likely to rise at the rate of inflation, while real wage costs were likely to increase at between 3 and 4 percent a year over the inflation rate. Fuel oil was pegged to U.S. fuel prices, but in January 1992, the Mexican government announced a reduction of the price of fuel by 25 percent. Fuel represented about 17 percent of Cemex's costs. In general, input costs could therefore be expected to be volatile and increase slightly. Transportation costs averaged about 9 percent of cost of goods sold over the period 1984 to 1991, but should decline because of geographic diversification and improved logistics following the Tolteca acquisition.

As part of economic reforms being implemented in the last months of the de la Madrid administration, Mexico adopted a system of price controls in December 1987. This had a serious impact on Cemex's profitability in 1988 and 1989. The PECE program *(Pacto de Estabilidad y Crecimiento Económico)* established by President Salinas in 1989, placed greater emphasis on voluntary control of prices, which allowed Cemex to increase prices from $52.6 per ton in August 1988 to $77 per ton by December 1991. This was, nonetheless, substantially below international prices at the time, which ranged between $85 and $90 per ton, on average. Cement prices were completely deregulated in April 1992. In consequence, Mexican cement prices increased to $83 per ton in May 1992, with effective prices being around $79–80 a ton, after discounting.

Cemex's Investment Programs

Cemex's expansion beyond northeast Mexico had been achieved through acquisitions and investment. Since 1982 alone, Cemex had invested over $2 billion on acquisitions and plant expansion and on modernization. With a network of 17 cement plants and 134 ready-mix concrete facilities across the country, the company had become a national producer (see Exhibit 9). Its total capacity was broadly distributed with 31 percent in the Central region, 37 percent in the Pacific region and 32 percent in the Northern region. The next largest competitors in 1991 were Cementos Apasco (with 17 percent of the Mexican market) and Cruz Azul (13 percent). Apasco was 60 percent-owned by Holderbank of Switzerland, the world's largest cement producer. All other independent producers represented less than 7 percent of the market.

Exhibit 10 summarizes Cemex's recent acquisitions and their impact on capacity and market share. Cemex spent $880 million on these acquisitions, including two significant purchases of major competitors. *Cementos Anahuac,* acquired in 1987, was then Mexico's third largest cement producer. Its purchase increased Cemex's capacity to 15.2 million tons and its domestic market share to 43 percent, and it gave Cemex a significant share of the critical Mexico City market as well as access to the Gulf Coast export markets. *Empresas Tolteca,* was Mexico's second largest producer and Cemex's chief competitor. Controlled by the British firm, Blue Circle Cement, the acquisition in 1989 increased Cemex's capacity to 21.7 million tons and gave it a 63 percent domestic market share. More importantly, it allowed Cemex to dominate the domestic ready-mix market by increasing its

EXHIBIT 9 Cemex Production by Plant and Subsidiary, 1991

(in thousands of tons)

	Production of Gray Cement[1]	Domestic Market Region
CEMENTOS MONTERREY		
Cementos Mexicanos:		
Monterrey[2]	1,618	North
Torreon	1,408	North
Huichapan	1,280	Central
Valles	887	North
CEGUSA		
Cementos Guadalajara		
Guadalajara	1,178	Pacific
Ensenada	602	Pacific
Cementos del Yaqui		
Yaqui[3]	752	Pacific
TOLTECA		
Cementos Tolteca		
Atotonilco	2,050	Central
Zapotiltic	1,494	Pacific
Tula[2]	—	Central
Cemento Portland Nacional		
Hermosillo	1,318	Pacific
Cementos Atoyac		
Puebla	164	Central
Cementos Sinaloa		
El Fuerte	375	Pacific
GRUPO EMPRESARIAL MAYA		
Cementos Maya		
Leon	554	Central
Merida	589	Central
Grupo Anahuac:		
Barrientos	1,829	Central
Tamuin[4]	335	North
TOTAL	16,432	

Notes: (1) Represents thousands of tons produced during the calendar year and may differ from sales figures.
(2) These production figures do not include white cement production. Monterrey produced 158,000 tons, and Tula 94,000 tons of white cement in 1991.
(3) In 1991, the Yaqui plant was on start-up phase and did not produce to full capacity.
(4) Plant was closed for part of the year for modernization and labor restructuring.
Source: Cemex Prospectus, March 13, 1992, p. 31.

EXHIBIT 10 Cemex Group Investments and Acquisitions

Year	Company/Plant	Installed Capacity (thousand tons)	Accumulated Capacity (thousand tons)	Purchase Price (in 1990 $ per ton)	Domestic Market Share (percent)
1960	Cementos Maya/Merida	40	2,540	$ 88	—
1973	Cementos Portland del Bajo	450	2,600	82	18%
1976	Cementos Guadalajara	740	3,200	90	25
1983	New Kilns and Plant (1976–83)	—	9,600	—	31
1985	Huichapan Plant (1984–85)	—	10,700	—	33
1987	Cementos Anahuac	4,500	15,200	43	43
1988	49% interest in Cementos de Chihuaha[1]	—	—	—	—
1989	Tolteca	6,800	21,700	82	63
1990	New Plant and Expansion	2,200	23,900	—	63

Note: (1) Capacity not reflected since Cemex Group did not acquire control.
Source: Company data, Morgan Stanley Emerging Markets Investment Research, June 26, 1992, Table 7.

share from 33 to 72 percent in one stroke. Tolteca's modern plants and distribution terminals complemented Cemex's existing network, gave it additional facilities in the Pacific and Central markets, and strengthened its abilities to export to Pacific Rim countries. Through Tolteca, Cemex also obtained control of U.S. ready-mix operations, aggregates, terminals, and distribution facilities.

Such geographic diversification, in addition to putting plants closer to major markets, also allowed for production rationalization. Cemex could begin to shift output to those plants in areas with the highest demand and prices, or to those with the lowest costs. Regional diversification also allowed Cemex to develop and maintain a portfolio of regional brands. These acquisitions were made at a time when the Mexican economy was relatively weak following the 1982 debt crisis and the devaluation of 1987. Thus, Cemex was able to acquire capacity relatively cheaply. In the case of Tolteca, its cost per ton of capacity acquired was about $90. This compares with the cost of greenfield investment to generate new capacity in excess of $200 per ton.

During this period, Cemex also spent $950 million on new plant and environmental control equipment that yielded an additional 4.8 million tons of capacity, principally in the Pacific and Central regions. Newer plants were more energy efficient, and the newer equipment helped raise labor productivity. Another $330 million was spent to develop international operations, including U.S. distribution facilities in Arizona, Texas, and California, as well as on two beach-front hotels in Mexico. Between 1989 and 1991, Cemex spent about $250 million on environmental control equipment.

Future Plans

Looking to the future, Cemex had announced plans to invest $1 billion over the period 1992–1994. Of this, $815 million was earmarked for two new cement plants and the modernization and expansion of four existing plants. These expenditures would increase Cemex capacity by 37 percent, or 8.8 million tons by 1994. About $100 million more would be spent on environmental control equipment, and the remainder on the expansion of existing and new ready-mix plants. Ready-mix capacity would double as a result. Exhibit 11 provides details on Cemex's planned investments.

Cemex's capital investment programs allowed the company to reduce labor and transportation costs, which, along with low energy costs in Mexico, made the company a low international cost producer. Compared to an average cost of production in the United States of about $36 per ton of cement, for example, Cemex's average cost was $27 a ton. Furthermore, its cost structure in the newest plants was even lower, at about $22 to $23 a ton,

EXHIBIT 11 Projected Investments, 1992–94

Company Plant	Projected Capacity Expansion in Tons	Projected Start-up Year
TOLMEX		
Guadalajara	400,000	1993
Atotonilco		
Phase I	500,000	1992
Phase II	500,000	1993
Puebla	2,400,000	1993
Bajío/Colima	2,400,000	1994
GRUPO EMPRESARIAL MAYA		
Merida[1]		
Phase II	100,000	1991
Phase III	500,000	1994
CEMENTOS MEXICANOS		
Huichapan	2,000,000	1993
TOTAL	8,800,000	

Note: (1) The first expansion phase of the Merida plant was completed in 1991.
Source: Cemex Prospectus, March 13, 1992, p. 30.

at par with Korea (Exhibit 12). As part of its focus on the use of technology to reduce costs, Cemex had acquired a 51 percent participation in a joint venture with F.L. Schmidt, a leading design and manufacturing firm of cement-making equipment.

A major uncertainty remained, however, over interest and exchange rates. High real rates of interest could hurt the housing market, making mortgage and construction loans less affordable. Devaluation of the peso had lagged the interest rate differentials between the U.S. and Mexican economies resulting in a somewhat overvalued peso and making export prices higher in international markets. Over the period 1987–1991, Mexican inflation, interest rates and peso exchange rates are summarized in Exhibit 13.

Cemex's International Activities

Cemex's international sales reached $234 million in 1991, about 14 percent of total sales. Exports from Mexico totaled $58.3 million, with 65 percent going to the United States, 32 percent to the Far East, and the rest to the Caribbean. Sales from U.S. distribution facilities in Southern California, Arizona, and Texas amounted to

EXHIBIT 12 Average Cost in $ per Metric Ton, 1991

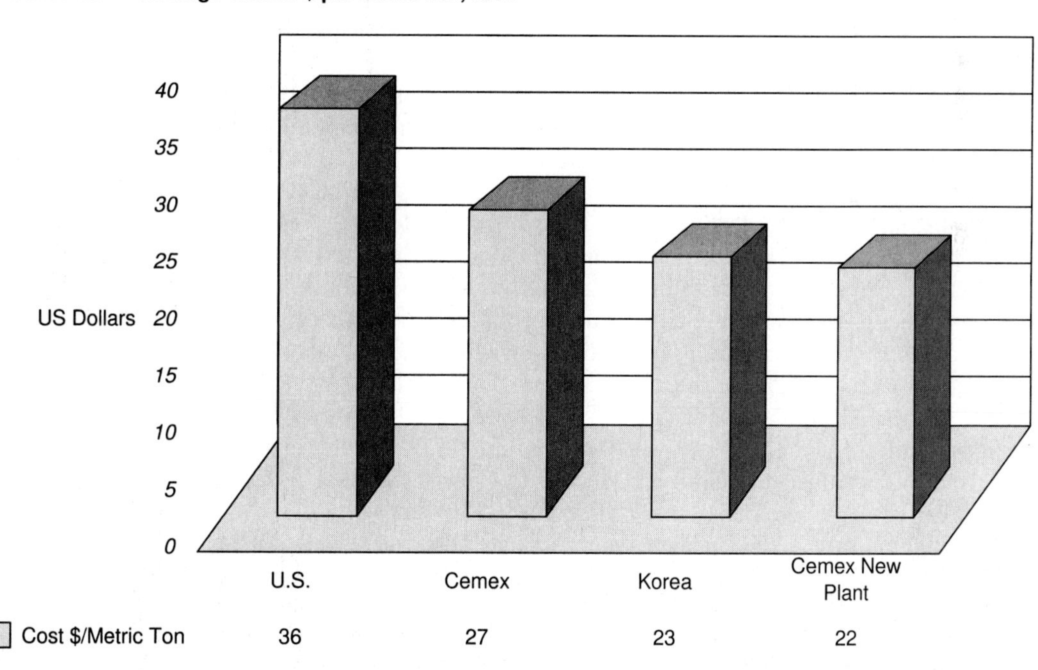

EXHIBIT 13 Inflation, Interest Rates, and Exchange Rates for Mexico, 1987–91

	1987	1988	1989	1990	1991
Inflation (CPI)	159.2%	51.7%	19.7%	29.9%	18.8%
Average 90-Day Treasury Bill Rate	104.8%	36.2%	31.9%	29.3%	18.0%
Exchange Rate, Year End (Pesos/$)	2,204	2,273	2,647	2,949	3,086
Exchange Rate Average (Peso/$)	1,419	2,268	2,462	2,813	3,018

EXHIBIT 14 Cemex—Key Operating Companies in the United States

Acquisition	Date	Location	Operations
Pacific Coast Cement	1990	Southern California	Terminal and Distribution
BCW	1989	Arizona and So. California California	Ready-Mix and Aggregates Terminal and Distribution
Sunbelt Cement[1]	1987	Arizona and So. California	Terminals and Distribution
Sunstar Cement[2]	1989	Texas	Ready-Mix, Aggregates, Grinding and Distribution
Sunbelt White[3]	1988	Texas	Pennsylvania White cement; Production and Distribution
Sunbelt Management[4]	1988	Texas	Terminals and Distribution

Notes: (1) Originally joint venture with Southdown Inc.; Cemex Group acquired 100% in 1989.
(2) Holds 100% of Houston Shell & Concrete, Gulf Coast Portland Cement, and Houston Concrete Products.
(3) Holds 29% interest in Lehigh White Cement.
(4) Holds 50% interest in Texas Sunbelt.
Source: Company data, Morgan Stanley Emerging Markets Investment Research, June 26, 1992, p. 15.

$175.6 million. Cemex had spent $156 million to acquire an integrated ready-mix and aggregates business in Southern California, as well as two maritime terminals in Spain. Cemex's U.S. properties, managed collectively as the Sunbelt Group, include 18 distribution terminals, 48 ready-mix plants, 7 aggregates facilities, and about 360 ready-mix trucks. Exports were shipped from Veracruz, Manzanillo, and other ports and also by rail or truck to the United States. Cemex has emphasized Texas and California as the U.S. markets with greater potential (see Exhibit 14 for a list of U.S. operating companies).

The company suffered a major setback in October 1990, when the U.S. Department of Commerce issued an antidumping order against Cemex, imposing additional duties of 58 percent on its U.S. shipments. As a consequence, exports to the United States fell from 21 percent of Cemex production in 1989, to 14 percent in 1990, and 5 percent in 1991. Overall, exports declined from 3.6 million tons in 1989, to 1.4 million tons in 1991. However, Cemex was able to sell more of its production in the expanding domestic market and increased its exports to Asia and the Caribbean. Thus, capacity utilization rates did not suffer much.

In July 1992, Cemex announced that it would acquire Spain's two largest cement companies. Cemex made a tender offer for the outstanding shares of Compañía Valenciana de Cementos after reaching agreement to acquire the shares of three major shareholders: the Serratosa family of Spain and two foreign cement companies, Norway's Aker group and Sweden's Industri AB Euroc. Cemex would pay about $1.25 billion for Valenciana, Europe's second largest cement company, with 1991 sales of $637 million and profits of $102 million. Shortly thereafter, Cemex agreed to buy Sansón, Spain's second-largest cement producer for $600 million. Sansón's 1991 sales were $461 million, with profits of $93 million. The two companies together controlled 28 percent of the Spanish market.

Case 1-2

Cemex (B)

Cemex, through its dominance of the Mexican cement market (see the A case), had been generating considerable free cash flow in the late 1980s and early 1990s. The company had several alternatives for use of this surplus cash: (1) reduce its debt significantly; (2) increase dividend payments; (3) diversify outside the cement industry within Mexico or elsewhere; or (4) expand its position within the cement industry on a global scale. Cemex already had some U.S. cement operations which might constitute a good base for further expansion into that market. Brazil was the only other Latin American country with a large domestic market, but none of the Brazilian cement companies seemed available. Asia had its own large and efficient producers, and Cemex had considered acquisition opportunities in Malaysia and Thailand, before dismissing them as being geographically too remote to be managed efficiently. Europe, and Spain specifically, loomed large in the company's perspective.

The Move into Spain

In July 1992, Cemex announced that it would acquire Spain's two largest cement companies. First, it made a tender offer for the outstanding shares of Compañía Valenciana de Cementos after reaching agreement to acquire the shares of three major shareholders: the Serratosa family of Spain and two foreign cement companies, Norway's Aker group and Sweden's Industri AB Euroc. Cemex would be paying about $1.25 billion for Valenciana, Europe's second largest cement company with 1991 sales of $637 million and profits of $102 million. Shortly thereafter, Cemex agreed to buy Sansón, Spain's second-largest cement producer for $600 million. The two companies together controlled 28 percent of the Spanish market. Sansón's 1991 sales were $461 million and had profits of $93 million.

Valenciana's operations were located mainly in southeastern Spain, while Sansón's plants were in the central region. Sansón had the most modern facilities within the Spanish industry and the lowest production costs. The two companies together had 11.4 million tons of installed capacity, and complemented Cemex's previous purchase of deep-water marine terminals in southern Spain (see Exhibit 1). The Spanish market was similar to Mexico's in that bagged cement was one of the most important product segments.

This case was prepared by Professor Ravi Sarathy at Northeastern University for use in classroom discussion.

EXHIBIT 1 Cement Plants and Capacity of Valenciana and Sansón, 1992

Valenciana		Sansón	
Cement Plants	Capacity (million tons)	Cement Plants	Capacity (million tons)
Valenciana	3.2	La Auxiliar	1.0
Cementos del Mar	1.5	Portland Iberia	1.5
Cementos del Atlántico	1.6	Cementos Portland M. de Jalón	1.0
Portland de Mallorca	0.45	Cementos de las Islas	0.2
Total	6.75	Total	3.7
8 Cement Kilns		4 Cement Kilns	
110 Ready-Mix Plants		40 Ready-Mix Plants	
Capacity: 4.5 Million Cubic Meters		Capacity: 1.8 Million Cubic Meters	
18 Percent of Industry Capacity		10 Percent of Industry Capacity	
1991 Sales: 5.3 Million Tons		1991 Sales: 4.2 Million Tons (includes outside purchases)	
Capacity Utilization: 79 Percent		Capacity Utilization: 95 Percent	

Cemex management indicated various reasons for its Spanish acquisitions. They preferred to remain within the cement industry, and they saw this as an opportunity to buy a large market share in an important market all at once. Spain was culturally akin to Mexico, and it was the third largest producer and market for cement in Europe, about 15 percent of total European demand.

Cemex also thought that it would be possible to integrate the two neighboring companies and use its own management and logistics expertise to reduce costs. By creating an integrated network of 12 cement plants in Spain, transportation costs could be reduced. Furthermore, only about 30 percent of Spanish demand was for ready-mix cement, while the European average was around 50 percent, indicating strong growth potential for this product.

The Spanish recession in 1990–92 had resulted in the price of cement falling to between \$85 and \$95 per ton, from a peak of \$100 a ton. Imported cement from Turkey, which had a 12 percent share of the market, contributed to the lower prices. As a result, Cemex was once again acquiring assets at discounted values. Cemex paid about \$180 per metric ton of capacity for the two Spanish companies, whereas previous cement acquisitions in Europe had gone for more than \$300 per ton. In comparison, Ciments Français had offered to buy out the remaining minority interests of Cementos Rezola in Spain for about \$154 per ton a few months earlier.

Cement Consumption in Spain

Construction activity in Spain had slowed down after the building boom for the Olympic Games and Expo '92. While the current recession reduced demand for cement in Spain through 1993, the longer-term outlook was more attractive. Spain's economic growth during the 1980s had been faster than the average for the entire European Economic Community. Starting from a lower income and industrial base when compared to the wealthy nations in the E.C., Spain had benefited enormously from membership in the E.C. This rate of growth required massive infrastructure investments in the construction of highways, railroads, and housing, in which cement was extensively used. During the period 1986–90, cement demand grew at between 2 and 3 times the rate of growth of Spanish GDP (see Exhibit 2).

As the Spanish government dampened its economy to cut inflation, a necessary consequence of being in the European Exchange Rate Mechanism (ERM)[1], the construction and cement industries suffered. A forecast from the Construction Institute of Catalunya suggested that construction output would grow at 2 percent in 1993. Furthermore, public sector spending accounted for about one-third of total construction expenditures in Spain, and budget deficits were forcing the government to cut back on infrastructure spending for the time being. The Spanish government had followed a policy of holding public infrastructure investment to an average of about 5 percent of GNP, with long-term plans to triple the highway system and to build up the country's high-speed railroads. The prevailing economic situation meant that these plans would have to be put on hold. Budget constraints also led the government to delay payments to contractors. As the industry volume dried up, more competition emerged for the fewer public tenders put out to auction, leading to lower bids and decreased profits. Exhibit 3 summarizes recent demand for cement in Spain.

[1]Under this agreement, all member nations undertook to prevent their currencies from fluctuating more than 2.25 percent on either side of the average of a basket of other E.C. member country currencies.

EXHIBIT 2 Spanish GDP and Cement Sales Growth, 1984–1991

	1984	1985	1986	1987	1988	1989	1990	1991
Growth of GDP (%)	2.93	2.31	3.28	5.57	5.17	4.76	3.61	2.46
Cement Sales (million tons)	16.2	16.5	18.2	20.2	22.7	26.0	28.5	28.0
Sales Growth (%)	-(9.5)	1.9	10.2	10.7	12.4	14.5	9.6	1.0
Public Sector Tenders (billion Ptas)	na	na	593	725	990	1464	2079	1501
GDP/Cement Multiplier.	neg.	0.8	3.1	1.9	2.4	3.0	2.6	0.4

EXHIBIT 3 Cement Demand in Spain, 1990–91
(in millions of tons)

	1990	1991
Domestic Cement	25.7	25.5
Imports	2.8	3.3
Total Consumption	28.5	28.8

EXHIBIT 4 Regional Market Shares for Valenciana and Sansón

Region	Valenciana	Sansón
Catalunya (Barcelona)	10%	11%
Aragon (Zaragoza)	-	87%
Levante (Valencia)	36%	-
Centro (Madrid)	-	22%
Andalucia (Seville)	15%	-

Import competition from plants in Turkey, Romania, and Tunisia was having an impact primarily along the Mediterranean coastal regions—Barcelona, Valencia, and Seville—where much of the construction boom had focused. In Valencia, because of import competition, prices had dropped to $77 per ton in 1992, compared to $85–90 a ton in Madrid and Aragon.

EXHIBIT 5 Funding Sources for Acquisition of Valenciana and Sansón

	Valenciana	Sansón
Total Acquisition Cost ($ millions)	1,250	600
Less:		
Disposition of Non-Cement Assets	200	100
Cemex Cash Payments	250	250
Private Placement:	0	90
Balance: To be Financed with Debt	800	160

Market Position: Valenciana and Sansón

The Spanish cement industry had installed capacity of about 35–38 million tons. Sansón and Valenciana together accounted for 28–30 percent of this capacity, or about 11 million tons. Their joint market share was about 30 percent, but their share of the ready-mix segment was about 15 percent. They were market leader in the most highly fragmented segment of the industry. Major competitors and their overall market shares included LaFarge Coppée (13 percent), Holderbank (9 percent), a joint venture of Italcementi and Ciments Français (8 percent), with the remaining 40–42 percent held by smaller firms. Overall, the cement industry was becoming increasingly concentrated on a global basis. Major global players include Holderbank (Switzerland), LaFarge Coppée (France), Blue Circle (U.K.) and Italcementi (Italy), of which only Holderbank had a significant position in the Mexican market. Furthermore, all of the major cement companies in Europe had entered Spain since 1986, taking significant market positions.

However, given high transportation costs for cement, regional market shares were perhaps more pertinent measures of strategic position than national market (or international) shares. Exhibit 4 indicates the regional distribution of Valenciana and Sansón's market positions. The only market overlap occurred in Catalunya, and the integration of the two companies under Cemex direction could take place without much duplication of regional distribution facilities or customer bases. Valenciana derived about 80 percent of its sales, both in cement and ready-mix, from Andalucia and Valencia. Sansón was concentrated in the Central and Aragon areas. Neither of the two companies had much market exposure in the northwest of Spain.

Valenciana's productive capacity, adjusted for ready-mix, was 7.8 million tons, whereas its 1991 sales volume reached 6.2 million tons. Valenciana's capacity also included nearly one-half million tons of white cement, of which it was the largest producer in Spain. Sansón, on the other hand, had a deficit in capacity and had been forced in recent years to purchase nearly one million tons from other producers in order to satisfy its regional market demand in Aragon.

Financial Aspects of the Acquisition

Exhibit 5 summarizes the financial impact of the acquisition. Borrowing the $960 million the plan called for, would raise Cemex's debt to total capital ratio from 15 percent to nearly 40 percent. In addition, Cemex would be assuming existing obligations by the two Spanish companies totaling about $500 million. Since the two acquired companies had upgraded their plants within the last few years, no extensive capital expenditures would be required, permitting Cemex to pay off the increased acquisition-related debt from future cash flows. Cemex was also contemplating selling a minority stake in Cemex España (as the new holding company would be known) on the local stock market as a means of reducing debt. Disposition of the non-cement assets of Valenciana, including real estate, transportation and farming interests, as well as a valuable art collection, would further help reduce debt related to the acquisition. Exhibit 6 summarizes financial results for 1991 for both Spanish companies and for Cemex.

Future Outlook for Cemex

Actions taken by the Mexican government in 1992 in order to reduce inflation had led to higher interest rates and a slowdown of the Mexican economy. Econometric forecasts had the economy's growth rate falling to around 4 percent in 1993 before resuming to a level of 5 percent or better after 1994. These projections, however, were based on the positive conclusion of the negotiations for a North American Free Trade Area. Exhibit 7 summarizes the forecasts available at the time. Based on the macroeconomic situation for Mexico, as well as expected Spanish growth, pro-forma forecasts of overall sales volume at Cemex were prepared, and they are shown in Exhibit 8.

Cemex management had stunned the company's shareholders when it announced the magnitude of its Spanish acquisitions. Most investors, unhappy with Cemex's strategy of using its cash flow from the high growth Mexican market to invest in the more competitive and slower growth Spanish market, dumped their shares. In consequence, Cemex share prices fell by nearly 50 percent in the weeks following the announcement. Cemex management, nonetheless, was serenely confident that the Spanish acquisitions were a necessary step in making Cemex one of the key players in a global cement industry. In discussing the move, Mr. Lorenzo Zambrano, Cemex's CEO commented, "Had we not gone into Spain [at this time], we would be left out of Europe forever."

EXHIBIT 6 Financial Summary for Cemex, Valenciana and Sansón, 1991
(in millions of U.S. dollars and percent)

	Cemex		Valenciana		Sansón	
	$ millions	Percent	$ millions	Percent	$ millions	Percent
Sales	1,706	100	630	100	461	100
EBITD[1]	567	33.2	167	26.5	126	27.4
EBIT[2]	420	24.6	126	20.0	103	22.3
Net Income	442	25.9	102	16.2	93	20.2
Total Assets	3,848	100	754	100	961	100
Total Debt	1,411	36.7	329	43.6	194	20.2

(1) Earnings before interest, taxes and depreciation.
(2) Earnings before interest and taxes.

EXHIBIT 7 Mexico: Macroeconomic Forecast, 1993–96

	1993	1994	1995	1996
GDP Growth	4.2%	5.7%	5.5%	6.8%
Construction Growth	7.2%	9.1%	7.3%	9.7%
Inflation (CPI)	110.2%	11.5%	10.4%	10.4%
CETES (interest rate)	12.4%	13.3%	12.8%	12.2%

EXHIBIT 8 Cemex Group: Forecast of Cement Sales Volumes, 1993–96
(in thousands of tons or cubic meters)

	1993	1994	1995	1996
Mexico: Cement Sales	18,180	21,730	23,050	26,490
Annual Growth Rate (%)	11.1	14.0	11.2	14.9
Cement Exports	1,630	1,780	1,980	2,220
Total	19,810	22,510	25,030	28,710
Ready-Mix Sales (m^3)	5,500	7,040	8,610	11,180
Annual Growth Rate (%)	22.2	28.0	22.3	29.8
Spain: Cement Sales	8,250	8,400	8,580	8,850
Annual Growth Rate (%)	—	1.8	2.1	3.1

Sources for all exhibits: Cemex News Releases, various dates; Mickey Schleien, "Cemex: The Price of Diversification," *Morgan Stanley Research Report,* July 22, 1992; and Mark Stockdale, "Cemex Recommendation," *S.G. Warburg Securities,* August 12, 1992.

SECTION

II Global Competitive Strategies in Transition

UNIT 2 From International to Global Competition

INSEAD

Case 2-1

Pneumatiques Michelin I–A

In July 1969, the Michelin Tire Company announced it would establish production facilities in Nova Scotia, Canada. Approximately 85 percent of its production of steel-belted truck tires was reported to be for export to the United States, with the balance for Canada, the Caribbean, and South America. Local government officials and politicians were overjoyed at the news of the planned investment of nearly $100 million and the creation of 1,300 jobs. Their happiness was renewed in late 1971, when the plant began operating and the company announced an intended expansion of $40 million which would add a facility for making passenger car tires and which could create another 1,300 jobs.

This case was prepared by David Harkleroad, Research Assistant, under the supervision of Professors Dominique Héau and José de la Torre at the European Institute of Business Administration (INSEAD), Fontainebleau, France. It incorporates material from a case series entitled "Michelin Tires Manufacturing Co. of Canada (A) through (D), prepared by David E. Osborn under the supervision of Professor Donald H. Thain at the University of Western Ontario, Canada.
INSEAD revision, 1982. This version, 1999.

The Michelin investment in Canada was induced by major grants and other financial assistance by both federal and provincial governments. In a discussion of the details before the Public Accounts Committee of the Nova Scotia Legislature on March 28, 1972, Finance Minister Peter Nicholson said there was "nothing new or strange in this day and age for international companies such as Michelin to be given incentives of various types. Countries all over the world were offering incentives, and few eyebrows were raised."

Nicholson's comments were made in response to the reaction of the powerful American tire and rubber lobby. On February 8, 1972, this organization had initiated a complaint with the U.S. Treasury Department of unfair export competition. The Treasury Department began an investigation to determine whether the Canadian government assistance to Michelin constituted a "bounty or grant" in violation of U.S. laws deserving of tariff retaliation. The outcome of the investigation threatened a new round in an international trade war, a chilling prospect to those concerned about Canada's chance for success in such a war.

Michelin

Michelin was Europe's largest tire manufacturer and the third largest worldwide. Its history was inseparably linked with that of the pneumatic tire. The Michelin organization began in 1889 when the brothers Edouard and

André Michelin made tires for horse-drawn carriages in Clermont-Ferrand, France, where the company headquarters were still located in 1972. In 1891, Michelin took out its first patent on the pneumatic tire and, since that time, the company had constantly introduced innovations in the field. The most notable of these was the radial tire, which Michelin first introduced in France in 1948.

In 1959, François Michelin took command of the organization. His two main objectives were to reinforce Michelin's specialization in tire manufacture and to test the radial tire on European markets. From 1960 to 1965, the company increased the number of manufacturing plants from eight to ten in France and added five others in the rest of Europe. In 1963, it built a test center with 32 kilometers of roads, second only in size to Goodyear's Nevada test track in the United States. In the same year, he created the Michelin Investment Holdings Co. in Bermuda to serve as a focal point for the group's future activities in the Western Hemisphere.

A high priority was given at Michelin to technical research and development, and the resulting product improvements played a major role in the growing "radialization" of the European tire market. In addition, quality control and marketing planning were known to be stressed. The Michelin radial tire enjoyed a reputation as one of the world's premier automobile tires and accounted for 80 percent of Michelin's production in 1971. The company's early commitment to the radial market put it at a great advantage relative to its European competitors, who did not begin radial tire production until the mid-1960s. By the end of the decade Michelin controlled over one-third of the total European tire market through its dominant position in the radial segments. This represented a total volume of about 200,000 tires per day.[1]

One characteristic of the Michelin organization was its penchant for secrecy, which led to many rumors and anecdotes about its real nature. Complex security arrangements limited company personnel to their own departments or work areas and all management personnel were required to take an oath of secrecy. Journalists, bankers, and academics received little information from the company even when it had a good story to tell. It was said that only two or three people outside the Michelin family knew all of the company's organization.

The secrecy surrounding Michelin had not obscured its financial success. Although its reported figures were inadequate for complete analysis, Michelin's operating margins appeared to be 13 percent of sales. It had a record of steadily rising profits, unlike the four U.S. giants—Goodyear, Firestone, Uniroyal, and Goodrich—and unlike its chief European rival, Dunlop-Pirelli. In Europe, where it ranked first in tire sales, it employed over 70,000 people, its 1971 sales were over $1,500 million, and its cash flow that year was estimated at just under $200 million. These figures did not include Michelin holdings in Citroën automobiles or in Kléber-Colombes (the number two French tire manufacturer), independently managed companies registered on the Paris Stock Exchange.

The Canadian Tire Industry

The Canadian tire industry in 1972 was almost totally comprised of subsidiaries of foreign (mainly U.S.) tire manufacturers. Six companies, with a total of ten plants, were engaged in the manufacture of tires. Seven of these plants were located in Ontario, two were in Quebec, and one was in Alberta. Goodyear Canada was the largest with four plants. Its U.S. parent was the world's largest rubber producer with total 1971 sales of $3,200 million, 60 percent of which were tires. Other subsidiaries were: Firestone, Uniroyal, B.F. Goodrich, Dunlop, and Mansfield-Denman General Ltd. Canadian subsidiaries, except Goodyear, did not publish financial information before 1972, when the government required federally incorporated companies to file certain financial information. Exhibit 1 summarizes available information.

Passenger car tires dominated the tire market (Exhibit 2), and subsidiaries of major U.S. auto manufacturers were the main consumers of the original equipment (OEM) tire production. Original equipment sales had been cyclical following the auto industry, despite the boost which the 1965 Auto Pact (see Appendix) gave to the Canadian segment of that industry. Replacement tires accounted for approximately two-thirds of Canadian tire production by volume and for a higher portion by sales value and profits. Industry growth had been slow in recent years due to several factors: low auto production years in 1969 and 1970, the growth of foreign car imports, longer-lasting tires, and the increasing popularity of European radial tires which were considered by many consumers to be technically superior to American tires.

Although domestic production was roughly equivalent to domestic sales, the volume and value of imported tires had increased markedly in recent years (Exhibit 3). At the same time, the Canadian industry had found it increasingly

[1] In 1965, Sears and Roebuck, the world's largest retailer, had begun distributing Michelin's radials in the United States under its own private label. This line represented an annual volume of one million units by 1971.

EXHIBIT 1 Selected Financial Information—Canadian Subsidiaries of U.S. Tire Manufacturers

Goodyear

Year	Gross Revenue (C$ million)	Operating Profit Margin Before Taxes (%)	Net Income (C$ thousand)
1966	136.6	9.2	4,533
1967	149.8	8.6	4,128
1968	154.2	3.0	171
1969	175.8	4.8	1,232
1970	175.6	9.7	3,291
1971	185.4	13.3	7,753

	B.F. Goodrich (C$ million)		**Firestone** (C$ million)	
	1970	1971	1970	1971
Sales	84.8	98.5	136.5	147.8
Operating Profit	5.2	6.9	13.4	15.1
Net Income	2.0	1.8	4.2	5.6
Dividend	0.3	0.3	2.7	0.8
Operating Profit Margin Before Taxes	6.1%	7.0%	9.8%	10.2%
Current Assets	37.7	41.7	81.4	80.4
Fixed Assets	20.6	19.7	61.0	60.0
Other Assets	0.6	0.6	1.6	1.3
Total Assets	58.9	62.0	144.0	141.7
Equity	27.9	30.4	54.6	59.4
Long-Term Debt	8.4	7.6	27.5	26.0

Source: Financial Post Corporation and company reports.

difficult to maintain its exports to foreign markets, where local productive capacity was greatly enlarged during the 1960s. In the opinion of industry spokesmen, the import threat was likely to increase. Canada was bound, as a signatory to the General Agreement on Tariffs and Trade (GATT), to gradually lower tariffs on a wide range of products, including tires and rubber products. This would create obvious difficulties for the Canadian industry, which had developed behind a high tariff wall of 17.5 percent.

Federal–Provincial Relationships in Canada

In the early 1970s, Prime Minister Pierre Trudeau was at the height of his popularity because of his charisma and because of a booming economy. He had been elected Prime Minister in 1969, and the ruling Liberal Party had been in power for a decade. Trudeau had a slim majority in the national legislature, but Canadian politicians almost always voted with the party, and even a majority of one would virtually ensure the passage of important legislation. The opposition was divided between the Conservatives and the New Democrats, a socialist party that had its roots in Western Canada. Four of the provincial governments (Nova Scotia, New Foundland, Prince Edward Island, and Quebec) were controlled by Liberal governments, three by the Conservatives and three by the New Democrats. The Atlantic Provinces had traditionally been a Liberal stronghold. Ironically, Robert Stanfield, the Conservative Party leader, was born in Nova Scotia, not far from the location of the Michelin plants.

EXHIBIT 2 Canadian Tire Production, 1962–1971

Year	Passenger Car Tires	Truck, Bus and Grader Tires	Industrial Tires	Tractors and Implement Tires	Airplane Tires	Motorcycle Tires
1962	9,180,939	1,077,875	70,149	415,028	15,577	1,141
1963	10,545,390	1,207,215	75,944	515,205	13,340	1,154
1964	11,431,427	1,356,874	85,201	476,428	10,279	1,503
1965	12,052,428	1,491,641	133,924	458,261	11,907	1,320
1966	13,527,315	1,784,264	181,848	509,888	13,013	2,229
1967	13,998,051	1,849,185	176,740	488,769	18,268	1,579
1968	14,577,416	1,777,826	170,203	382,235	9,014	720
1969	16,614,725	2,006,635	239,744	332,522	9,775	1,650
1970	17,720,048	2,086,849	176,405	300,269	1,914	591
1971	16,891,603	2,213,828	206,093	327,050	n.a.	1,391

n.a. = not available.
Source: Rubber Association of Canada.

EXHIBIT 3 Canadian Tire Production and Trade, 1967–1971

	Volume (thousands of units)			Value ($ million)				
				Imports			Exports	
Year	Production	Imports	Exports	Total	United States	France	Total	United States
1967	16,535	2,767	825	17.4	10.5	n.a.*	15.5	11.1
1968	16,917	4,901	801	40.6	30.7	3.4	11.9	8.6
1969	19,206	6,237	529	51.6	38.9	3.7	n.a.†	n.a.†
1970	20,285	5,752	987	46.0	27.2	5.0	n.a.†	n.a.†
1971	19,640	3,623	634	69.4	41.9	7.7	18.7	14.7

n.a. = not available.
*Statistics for Europe not broken down by country.
†Statistics for exports given only for rubber industry, not broken down for tires.
Sources: "Trade by Commodities," *OECD Abstracts;* D.B.S.

Trudeau had increased the role of the federal government in economic affairs, and the federal assistance offered Michelin was a direct result of his actions to channel money from the industrial provinces into the more traditionally agricultural provinces. Previously, the national government had not played as large a role in internal matters as in the United States. The provincial governments had power over taxes, health, education, welfare, and natural resources.

Nova Scotia and the Atlantic Provinces

Nova Scotia is one of Canada's easternmost provinces, almost an island, connected to the mainland by a narrow land-bridge. Before the American Revolution, Halifax, the provincial capital, was one of the continent's main ports of call. As the years passed, however, the westward expansion moved industries inland toward the Great Lakes area. The province's major activities include coal

EXHIBIT 4 Trends in Income, Labor Markets, Investments and Production Each Region Compared to Canada, 1950–1971
(Averages for Periods Shown, Canada = 100)

Regions	Years	Earned Income Per Head*	Unemployment Rate	Labor Force Participation Rate	In Manufacturing Per Head: Total Investment	In Manufacturing Per Head: Value Added†
Atlantic	1950–1959	63	176	88	44	35
	1960–1969	66	167	87	66	35
	1970–1971	69	132	86	131	35
Quebec	1950–1959	86	131	100	39	105
	1960–1969	89	134	98	88	102
	1970–1971	88	131	98	67	99
Ontario	1950–1959	120	74	105	142	153
	1960–1969	119	71	105	143	151
	1970–1971	120	77	104	137	150
Prairie	1950–1959	99	61	99	51	38
	1960–1969	95	63	102	42	40
	1970–1971	92	73	102	46	41
British Columbia	1950–1959	118	116	96	138	95
	1960–1969	110	117	99	129	92
	1970–1971	108	119	102	120	87
Canada (actual levels)	1950–1959	C$1,169	4.2%	53.5%	C$ 98	C$537
	1960–1969	C$1,177	5.1%	54.6%	C$146	C$691
	1970–1971	C$2,653	6.2%	55.9%	C$288	C$920

*Earned income = Personal income *minus* government transfer payments (excluding interest) *minus* interest, dividends and miscellaneous investment income of persons.

†The last two figures for each region and Canada apply to 1960–1967 and 1968–1969 respectively.

Source: Statistics Canada.

mining, fishing, shipbuilding, and farming. There were few industries and a lack of a skilled industrial labor force. The coal industry was a major employer until the 1960s, when a major mine disaster and the general trend away from coal as a primary fuel significantly reduced the importance of this industry for the region.

The Atlantic provinces, which included Nova Scotia, New Foundland, Prince Edward Island and New Brunswick, traditionally had been areas of low industrial development and high unemployment, as can be seen in Exhibit 4.

Business–Government Relations in the Canadian Tire Industry

During World War II, industry members had been encouraged to cooperate to obtain maximum efficiency and effectiveness for the war effort. This cooperation continued until 1952, when all Canadian tire manufacturers, a distribution company and the Rubber Association of Canada (RAC) were convicted of price-fixing and prohibited from further cooperative activities with respect to the manufacture and sales of tires and tubes. Henceforth, competition was keen and cooperation only occurred in areas of obvious common interest such as briefs to the government on such matters as legislation and freight rates.

In the early 1960s, discussions were held between industry executives and officials of the Federal Department of Industry on the question of including tires in the U.S.–Canada Auto Pact, an agreement intended to liberalize trade between the two nations in automobiles and automotive components. Eventually, due in part to the apprehension among industry leaders about the wisdom of such a move, tires were excluded from the 1965 agreement. In 1966, a survey on the amount of value added in production by Canadian manufacturers was conducted with the implied intention of adding tires to the Auto Pact, but nothing concrete developed.

These events lingered in the minds of industry leaders, and as one later stated, they were "sick of playing 20 questions with the government." However, by the late 1960s, many executives were concerned about the low profitability and the ever-widening gap in productivity between U.S. and Canadian producers, particularly with respect to production of industrial products. A productivity gap was suspected in tire production as well, but there were no meaningful comparative figures due to the lack of cooperation within the industry. Some thought that the problems of the tire industry were those of distribution: tires, due to their bulkiness, had high distribution and handling costs. Others thought that savings could be effected by rationalization with their American parents, but one study by Goodyear indicated that the possible savings were not as much as expected. Nevertheless, the financial and manpower resources of the tire companies in Canada were being stretched very thin. The number of tires (i.e., types of tires) had proliferated tremendously in the 1960s, and, in addition to their own brand names, the companies were producing private brands for a multitude of outlets. The resulting short runs, rising costs and rising interest rates caused financial problems, which were exacerbated in some companies by expensive union strikes.

In 1969, talk about rationalization resumed among industry executives, initiated by W. V. Turner, the president of the RAC. However, fear of antitrust caused them to go to the newly formed Department of Industry, Trade and Commerce (DITC), which appointed a study team. Despite a long- standing antagonism toward the government, industry executives agreed to provide cost figures on which a complete analysis of industrial rubber products could be based, even though they would not divulge such information to each other.

This third attempt at industry–government cooperation was to fare no better than the first two. At a meeting of the RAC Board of Directors in late 1969, the members reopened the question of some study on the tire industry to determine whether a program of rationalization should be analyzed in detail. Government officials scheduled a series of meetings with the presidents of each company, but these were later postponed. No explanation for the postponement was given until January 1970, when Turner was asked to come to Ottawa. At that meeting, he was informed that the federal government would allow Michelin to import radials not produced in its Nova Scotia plant duty-free for a period of three years, in addition to other financial assistance. Turner listened in stunned silence, asked some questions to ensure that he understood completely, and reported back.

The industry was shocked by the news. It maintained that it had no opposition to the incentives offered to Michelin, especially since these grants were available to all. The contentious point was the remission of duty agreement. To the industry, the government, in addition to "bankrolling" Michelin with loans and grants, had by virtue of the duty-free provision created an effective rationalization program, which they had been seeking but which would not benefit them.

The Origins of the Michelin Deal

The story of Michelin's introduction to Canada was one of intrigue and political maneuvering on a complex, international scale. One of the central figures was Robert Manuge, the executive vice president of Industrial Estates Ltd (IEL), a Crown Corporation which was the industrial development agency of Nova Scotia. On a flight from New York to Montreal in November 1967, Mr. Manuge shared a newspaper with a lady beside him. He discovered that she was the wife of the Canadian head of Citroën, and he met her husband upon landing at Montreal airport. An appointment was arranged for Manuge with Maurice Sodoyer, the Michelin representative in Montreal, who suggested that Manuge contact Michelin headquarters in Clermont-Ferrand.

IEL had been organized in 1957 to introduce secondary manufacturing to Nova Scotia. It was empowered to lend as much as 100 percent of the cost of land and buildings, and at least 60 percent on machinery, all at current interest rates. Up to 1971, IEL's clients numbered 70 companies, 20 of which were already in business before they received any IEL grants. Of these, 17 either sold out to other companies or ceased operations entirely, but 80 percent of the new IEL-sponsored companies survived. The biggest blots on the IEL record were two bad investments in Clairtone Sound Corporation and Deuterium of Canada Ltd. IEL management participated in the initial project started by Clairtone costing roughly $4.5 million for a stereo hi-fi plant, and in the first phase of the Deuterium heavy-water plant which represented a $30 million investment. Expansion of these projects ultimately resulted in total investments of $20 million for Clairtone and $120 million for Deuterium. One newspaper report said: "it was no secret that the Michelin deal might go some way to getting IEL management off the hook." The same could undoubtedly have been said of many Nova Scotia politicians and businessmen who took part in these earlier decisions.

In December 1967, Manuge wrote a letter to Michelin setting out the advantages of a Nova Scotia location to serve both the U.S. and Canadian markets. He received a reply which stated that the company was interested, but that negotiations must be carried out in secret. In February 1968, Manuge began a series of negotiations, involving over 40 trans-Atlantic flights, under the name Project Y. Almost all of his colleagues were unaware of the real nature of Project Y, and all visits of Michelin officials to Halifax were carefully disguised. At the same time, a New York lawyer was carrying on an investigation with IEL officials on behalf of an undisclosed client about the possibilities of locating in Nova Scotia. Manuge discovered much later that the lawyer had been retained by Michelin to establish independently IEL's veracity and competence.

On July 28, 1969, Frank H. Sobey, President of IEL, announced that the negotiations with Michelin had been successfully concluded. The company was to establish two plants in Nova Scotia: (1) a steel cord plant in the town of Bridgewater, to employ 500 persons, at an estimated cost of $10.1 million; and (2) a tire factory in the town of Granton, which would use the output of the steel cord plant to produce steel-belted radial truck tires. Total output was estimated by industry sources to be between 5,000 and 8,000 truck tires a day. The tire factory would cost $41 million and would employ 800 persons. Cost overruns eventually brought plant costs to $22.5 and $62.2 million for Bridgewater and Granton respectively.

Disappointment about the IEL announcement was particularly evident in Quebec. A Quebec government source said that François Michelin was so bitterly opposed to Charles de Gaulle and his love affair with Quebec that it was almost impossible for Michelin even to discuss the possibility of locating a plant in Quebec.

The Agreement and Incentives

The package announced in January 1970, included provincial, local, and federal incentives:

1. IEL agreed to provide a $50 million, 6 percent loan to Michelin (Canada) to finance the construction of the two plants in two parts, a 10-year loan of $34 million and an 18-year loan of $16 million, both secured by a mortgage on the land, buildings, and machinery owned by Michelin in Nova Scotia.
2. IEL would grant a total of $7.6 million for capital costs ($5 million) and training of employees ($2.6 million).
3. The municipalities of Granton and Bridgewater would reduce taxes payable by Michelin to 1 percent of the real and personal property tax assessment for a period of 10 years. In the absence of such agreements, the tax would have been 3.7 percent in Bridgewater and 2.1 percent in Granton.
4. The 40-acre plant site valued at $10,000 was donated to Michelin by the town of Bridgewater.
5. Federal assistance included a cash grant of $8.07 million under the Area Development Incentives Act.[2] The grant was based on the amount of investment and number of jobs created, and it would be advanced once commercial production levels were achieved.
6. Also provided under the A.D.I.A., was an accelerated depreciation of capital costs. The company could write off building costs at 20 percent per year, and machinery at 50 percent per year, profits permitting.
7. Michelin was allowed to import much of its manufacturing machinery duty free.
8. The federal government would grant Michelin Canada the right to import tires into Canada free of duty for a period of three years. The imported tires had to be of a type and size not produced by Michelin in Canada, and the offer was conditional upon the duty-free privilege not disrupting the operations of existing tire producers in Canada. The confidential letters of offer, written by then Finance Minister Edgar Benson, with the approval of his cabinet colleagues, were imprecise as to the date of commencement for the duty-free privilege, but suggested that it would occur no later than commencement of production in Canada.

The first three forms of federal assistance (items 5–7 above) were available to all qualifying companies. The tariff remission was a form of assistance which the Government of Canada had granted in the past in special circumstances. The tariff remission meant that Michelin would not have to pay the duty of 17.5 percent otherwise imposed on tires imported into Canada. Tires imported into Canada and subsequently exported to the United States would still be subject to the U.S. duty on tires of 4 percent, as if they were imported directly from France. It was argued that if Canada had not agreed to compensate

[2]The A.D.I.A. was an outgrowth of a program begun in 1963 to attract industry to areas where there was an exceptionally high degree of unemployment. New industries locating in such areas were eligible for a three-year tax holiday and accelerated capital cost allowances. These income tax benefits did not prove as great an incentive as had been expected, as the applicant companies often had little net income in their first few years of operation. To correct this deficiency, Parliament passed the A.D.I.A. in 1965, which provided cash grants to companies locating in areas designated by degree of unemployment, non-farm family income and distribution of income.

Michelin for the amount of duty payable on imports of such tires, the company might have planned a different and less efficient product mix, or it would probably have produced a lower volume of tires of a greater variety of types and sizes, which might have reduced the employment opportunities offered by the project.

Michelin officials made it quite clear that they were not seeking any special treatment or benefit, that they would have no objection to the same arrangement being made with other Canadian manufacturers, and that they had no objection to the tariff on tires being reduced or removed altogether. This latter course was not acceptable to the government as there was not sufficient time to assess its impact on the total industry. However, the chance for increasing employment in a region where unemployment was unusually high was of considerable interest, and the government was also attracted by the fact that it was an industrial development project rationalized to meet the standards of world competition. Michelin would manufacture a limited line of truck tires in Canada, and import the balance of other types and sizes of truck, passenger and light commercial vehicle tires from its European plants. Michelin's Canadian market was, of course, not large enough to warrant manufacture in Canada solely for the domestic market, but the import provisions would allow long production runs, which would ensure that the Nova Scotia plant remained competitive on an international basis.

Canadian Industry Reaction

Some Canadian government officials had formed the opinion that the tire industry was poorly managed and fraught with bickering and lack of direction. The existing companies had different strengths and weaknesses and different commitments to the future. It was thus impossible to agree on any common action, since any suggestion invariably favored one company over another. Unanimity was reached only on the demand that the government rescind the tariff agreement with Michelin. One proposal that received some support was that, as was the case under the Auto Pact, manufacturers could import tires duty-free provided they maintained certain production levels in Canada and increased such production proportionately to the Canadian tire market. The agreement lasted two days, as one company immediately opposed it. Discussions continued through 1970 and into 1971, but nothing was accomplished. When Michelin's plant produced its first tires in October 1971, the issue arose again.

In late 1971, the Executive Committee of the Rubber Association of Canada met with government officials for further general discussion. The industry representatives discovered that one of their members, Uniroyal, had made a proposal to the government before their arrival, asking the Minister of Finance for duty-free entry of radial steel tires and equipment when imported by that company into Canada. This proposal was meant to equate Uniroyal with the arrangement made for Michelin. In addition, it was implied by Uniroyal that they would use whatever influence they had in the United States to get the Rubber Manufacturers' Association to back off its stand on countervailing duties. The proposal therefore had considerable appeal at that time to government officials. The break in ranks left the RAC floundering again.

The government persisted, especially since duty-free imports would permit increasing efficiency through specialization. The original proposal was later expanded into four:

1. Duty-free entry of radial steel tires and equipment, when imported by manufacturers of radial steel tires in Canada.
2. Duty-free entry of radial steel tires and equipment, when imported by manufacturers of tires generally.
3. Duty-free entry of radial steel tires and equipment by any company doing business in Canada.
4. A reduction of the tariff from 17.5 to 4 percent on all tires on a most-favored nation-basis.

The manufacturers rejected the third proposal, which would permit their customers to import directly from the United States. The fourth proposal upset the companies greatly, since it would radically change the nature of Canadian production. Dunlop, which did not plan to produce radials in Canada, favored the second proposal. However, Firestone had recently decided to invest in Canadian steel-cord production and would oppose any scheme that would eliminate what it thought was a competitive advantage. Goodyear wanted nothing less than the Michelin deal, though it preferred that the deal be dropped. The disagreement left most executives believing that their problems would have to be solved by themselves.

Growing U.S. opposition to Michelin was beginning to concern Canadian government officials. One company president felt that if any proposal were accepted, it would mean the companies would agree to dissuade their American parents from opposing Michelin. However, the Michelin threat was different in each country in both nature and degree, and the Canadian government could not be sure how much influence the subsidiaries could have on their parents.

U.S. Industry Reaction to the Michelin Grants

In bringing their complaint before the U.S. Customs Court, the U.S. industry requested that the government apply duties ranging from $41.60 a tire in 1972, to $1.06 a tire from 1982 to 1989. Though directed at Michelin, such action would bring the whole Canadian policy of regional development into question. This was happening at a time when the United States had suffered its worst balance of trade deficit in history (and the first since World War II), which had led to the "Nixon shock" of August 1971 and the subsequent devaluation of the dollar by 10 percent in December of that year. Facing growing subsidies and grants for industrial development in Canada, Europe, and the developing world, U.S. officials wondered where to draw the line. Section 303 of the Tariff Act provided that:

> Whenever any country . . . or other political subdivision of government . . . shall pay or bestow, directly or indirectly, any bounty or grant upon the manufacture or production or export of any article . . . manufactured or produced . . . in such country . . ., and such article is dutiable under . . . this Act, then, upon the importation of any such article . . . into the United States . . . whether . . . imported directly from the country of production or otherwise, there shall be levied and paid, . . . in addition to the duties otherwise imposed by this Act, an additional duty equal to the net amount of such bounty or grant. . .

There was obviously plenty of room for interpretation. The fact that 1972 was an election year in both Canada and the United States would probably influence the weight accorded to different factors in the final decision. Yet, countervailing duty was a strong weapon. It had first been used in the United States in the 1890s to protect the domestic sugarbeet industry from German producers who received direct export subsidies. The legislation had later been amended to provide relief from all bounties on exports to the United States, but had been used sparingly and not at all from 1959 to 1967. Its application against Michelin would provide a further strain on the already sensitive U.S.–Canadian trade relations (see Exhibit 5).

For the Canadian government, the issue was also crucial. Over 50 percent of Canada's manufacturing sector was in foreign hands, and mostly U.S. hands. If U.S. laws were interpreted in such a way that Canada's regional aid programs were declared subject to countervailing duty, the future effectiveness of such programs could be substantially reduced. The political fallout would be great if a negative decision were handed down.

APPENDIX: THE AUTOMOTIVE PRODUCTS TRADE AGREEMENT OF 1965[3]

In 1962, Canada established a rebate on duties paid on the import of certain automobile products. In 1963, this was replaced by a new order allowing for duty-free imports on car parts that would then be re-exported. The response of the auto parts manufacturers in the United States was strong and unambiguous. They asserted that the Canadian rebate was a grant to stimulate Canadian exports. In such an instance, the Tariff Act requires the U.S. Secretary of the Treasury to apply countervailing duties.

In 1964, automotive products trade between the two countries was about $700 million, about 9 percent of the $8 billion in total annual trade between Canada and the United States. The two industries were very similar since consumers in both countries generally preferred the same types of cars and over 90 percent of Canadian auto products were made by subsidiaries of U.S. manufacturers. There was little scope for trade, particularly since Canada imposed a 17.5 percent duty on cars and up to a 25 percent duty on parts. U.S. duties amounted to 6.5 percent on cars and 8.5 percent on parts.

Canada's protective tariffs had stimulated industry growth, but not efficiently. Canadian manufacturers were encouraged to include at least 60 percent Canadian value in their output. Most subsidiaries duplicated U.S. facilities and, because of the limited Canadian market, were unable to achieve similar economies of scale. As a result, Canadian autos cost about 10 percent more than those made in the U.S.

The Johnson Administration chose to negotiate the conflict with Canada rather than risk the possibility of retaliation in case countervailing duties were imposed. Also, security considerations required the installation of an early warning radar system along the Arctic Circle which needed Canadian consent. Eventually, an agreement was reached that provided for:

- duty-free imports of automotive products into Canada only when imported by automotive manufacturers;
- Canadian manufacturers to maintain existing production rates and to sign letters of intent to increase production to follow the growth of the Canadian market; and
- remission of duties on all imports into the U.S. from Canada.

Exhibit 6 shows the impact of the pact on the Canadian balance of automotive trade with the United States for 1965–1971.

---

[3]Source: Taken in part from Lawrence A. Fouraker, "The Automotive Products Trade Act of 1965", in Raymond Vernon, *Manager in the International Economy*, Prentice Hall, 1968, p. 242.

EXHIBIT 5 U.S.–Canadian Trade, 1968–1971
(US$ million)

	1968	1969	1970	1971
U.S. Exports to Canada				
Agriculture	462	527	556	544
Minerals and Fuels	810	916	1,296	1,135
Manufactures	6,634	7,500	6,935	8,397
Total	7,906	8,943	8,787	10,076
As Percent of Total U.S. Exports	23	24	21	23
As Percent of Total Canadian Imports	73	73	71	70
Canadian Exports to United States				
Agriculture	504	568	669	659
Minerals and Fuels	2,326	2,476	2,758	3,142
Manufactures	5,698	6,754	7,399	8,278
Total	8,527	9,798	10,826	12,079
As Percent of Total Canadian Exports	68	71	65	68
As Percent of Total U.S. Imports	27	29	28	28
Net Balance to United States	(621)	(855)	(2,039)	(2,003)

Source: OECD Trade Statistics.

EXHIBIT 6 Automotive Trade Balance for Canada, 1965–1971
(Net Trade in C$ millions)

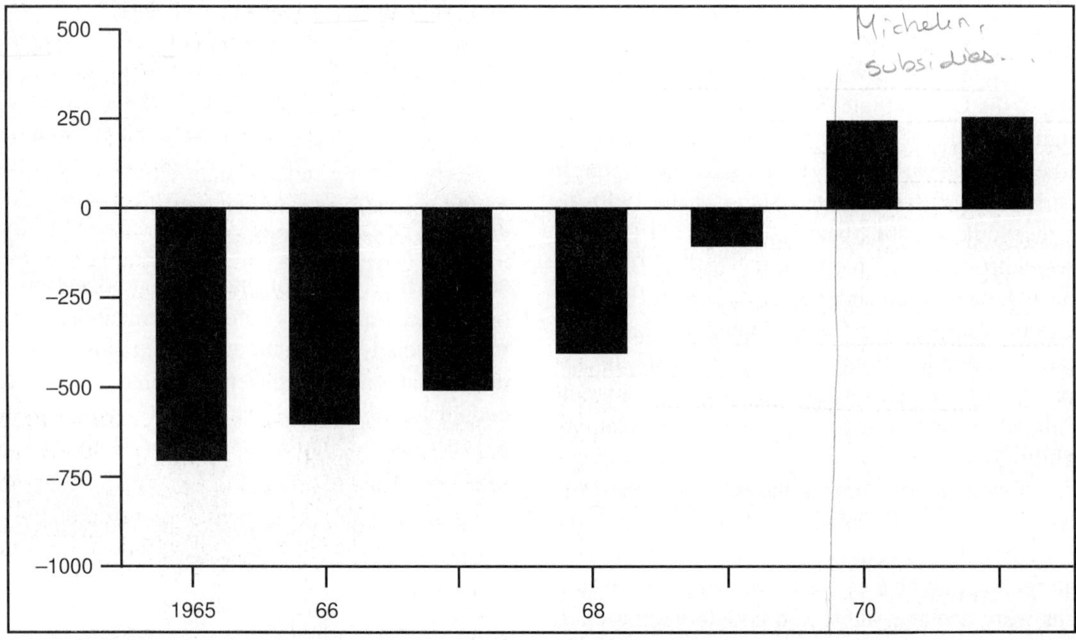

Case 2-2

INSEAD

Pneumatiques Michelin I–B

The world's tire industry was at a crossroads in the early 1970s. Long dominated by five large U.S. manufacturers, new competitors and new technologies were rising to challenge their leadership position. Bridgestone and other Japanese tire manufacturers were making rapid inroads in many markets, targeting the Eastern Bloc and Third World Nations as well as the lower end of the U.S. market with inexpensive, conventional tires. In the U.S. market alone, total Japanese share had grown from less than 1 percent in 1968 to over 4 percent in 1972. These imports appeared solely in the low price (under $20) segment. Michelin of France threatened on the opposite end of the spectrum with its high-quality radial tires, boasting longer tread life, improved safety and handling, and increased gas mileage.

The U.S. Tire Industry[1]

By the early 1970s, over 200 million tires a year were being sold in the United States, at a value of over $5 billion. Roughly 80 percent of the units and 65 percent of the value was for car tires; 15 percent of the units and 25 percent of the value was for truck and bus tires; the remainder was for farm-implement, specialty, and motorcycle tires. In the automobile market, roughly one-third of the tires were sold to automobile manufacturers, and the remaining two-thirds were sold as replacement tires.

The U.S. tire industry began in the late 19th century when several firms began producing bicycle tires. Soon it became closely linked with automobile production, and, by 1920, there were over 175 different tire manufacturers making over 30 million tires a year. In the 1930s, falling demand and the resulting overcapacity, heightened by severe price competition between Goodyear and Firestone, forced many of the smaller manufacturers out of business. The cyclical nature of the industry had led many manufacturers to diversify to ensure more steady profit growth, and only those companies with superior financial strength survived the decade. By 1945, there were only 23 tire manufacturers left, a number that was further reduced to 14 by 1965.

Significant quality improvements had been made in the first half of the century. The average tire life in 1910 was estimated at nine months of normal use; by 1937, average tire life was nearly three years. The war years brought government subsidies to seek rubber substitutes and resulted in the discovery and introduction of synthetic rubber (butadiene) as a major raw material. Most of the subsequent improvements were the result of new materials and of better tread and rim design.

Beginning in the 1960s, manufacturers experimented with new tire types. Traditionally, tires consisted of four cord plies laid at 45-degree angles to the tread (the Appendix describes the various types of tires). Early in the 1960s, in an attempt to reduce labor input,[2] manufacturers reduced the number of plies from four to two while keeping the overall thickness constant. However, customers rejected this change, partly due to quality problems, resulting in one of the industry's major marketing disasters. Undaunted, Armstrong Rubber Co., a relatively small firm in the industry, introduced the bias-belted tire in 1966, which consisted of the traditional four-ply construction while adding a belt between the plies and the tread. This higher-quality tire, which improved safety and durability, was heavily supported by advertising when all major competitors entered the market in 1967. Bias-belted tire sales grew spectacularly as shown in Exhibit 1.

By 1971, almost all U.S. manufacturers were producing at least one line of radial tires, but they were reluctant to abandon their concentration on bias-belted tires. By 1972, bias-belted tires were expected to account for about 82 percent of the original equipment market and for 35 percent of the replacement market.

Industry Structure

Manufacture of traditional tires was characterized by low technological barriers to entry. The production process, which consisted of rubber mixing, stock preparation, tire building, and tire curing, was not considered difficult to master (see Appendix). Though significant advances in

[1]Some of the information in this case comes from *Economic Report on the Manufacture and Distribution of Automotive Tires,* U.S. Government Printing Office, March 1966. Industry observers thought the report's conclusions were still valid in the early 1970s.

This case was prepared by David Harkleroad, Research Assistant, under the supervision of Professors Dominique Héau and José de la Torre at the European Institute of Business Administration (INSEAD), Fontainebleau, France.

[2]The wrapping of layers of fiber cord around the tire mold was done entirely by hand and required significant expertise.

EXHIBIT 1 U.S. OEM Passenger Tire Market Share by Type of Construction

	Radial	Bias-Belted	Conventional (4-ply)
1968	2%	6%	92%
1969	2	33	65
1970	3	65	32
1971	4	70	26
1972(e)	5	82	13

Source: Jules Pogrow, *The International Tire and Rubber Industry,* Cambridge, Mass., Harvard Business School, 1971.

EXHIBIT 2 After-Tax ROI in Various U.S. Industries

	1947–1964	1959–1964
Motor Vehicles	18.0%	16.4%
Office Equipment	17.1	16.0
Soaps and Detergents	13.6	14.0
Cigarettes	12.8	14.1
Tires	12.0	9.4
Metal Containers	9.7	8.5

Source: Federal Trade Commission.

automation had been made, a substantial amount of labor input was still necessary in the tire building stage, particularly because of the large number of types and sizes of tires produced. U.S. Census data indicated the breakdown of production costs in 1967 to be 51 percent materials, 20 percent labor, and 29 percent overheads. The industry in North America was also highly unionized. According to the United Rubber Workers (URW) Union, a member of the AFL-CIO Federation, total membership covered nearly 190,000 workers in all rubber-related industries, and included about 90 percent of U.S. and Canadian tire production.

The industry was characterized by limited economies of scale in production. A plant size of 5,000 to 8,000 tires a day, representing less than 1 percent of the U.S. market, was considered cost competitive, although this depended on the mix of models in production. Investment costs for such a plant were estimated at about \$10 million, plus \$2 million for each thousand units of daily capacity. Larger plants, over 10,000 units per day, with more automated production systems, would cost about \$50 million, plus \$1 million per thousand units after the first 10,000. Lead times for construction and start-up of a new plant normally exceeded two years.

Given the high cost of molds and the long set-up times involved, the average length of production run per model had a larger impact on unit costs than total plant size. Truck tires, which had to support heavier loads, required more plies and thus a greater labor input. They also required more expensive molds which were used to produce fewer tires. The additional steps necessary to produce belted tires also tended to reduce productivity by approximately 15 percent relative to conventional or bias-belted tires. Optimal plant size was also influenced by the need to be located close to volume buyers since land transport costs for the bulky tires were high. In highly competitive markets, where no tariffs were involved, the maximum radius for shipping tires overland was about 300 miles.

Low technological and production barriers to entry would seem to imply a low industry concentration level. Yet, according to the U.S. Federal Trade Commission, "the tire industry was one of the most concentrated in our economy." In 1971, the four largest manufacturers accounted for 71 percent of shipments and the eight largest for 90 percent.

In recent years, the industry was characterized by low profit margins. Large volume distributors often slashed retail prices in attempts to gain market share, forcing tire manufacturers to do the same, or forcing them to provide lower-quality tires at competitive prices. Government antitrust action also had a role in keeping prices depressed. In 1959, the Federal Trade Commission charged the industry with price fixing, but the manufacturers cut prices by up to 19 percent two months later and the case was settled out of court in 1962. Profitability in the tire industry was lower than that in most other industries with similar concentration ratios, as shown in Exhibit 2. As a percent of sales, tire industry profits before tax averaged about 7.8 percent during the 1960s, which compared with 8.4 percent for all manufacturing industries.

The key to the industry's profitability was the automotive market; over 50 kilograms of rubber products other than tires went into every automobile manufactured in the United States. Thus, when automotive demand slowed down in the late 1960s, the industry suffered accordingly: it experienced an operating cash deficit of \$1.1 billion for the 1965–1969 period; debt-to-equity ra-

EXHIBIT 3 Manufacturer's Share of the U.S. OEM Market, 1966/1972
(percentages)

	General Motors	Ford	Chrysler	American Motors	Total OEM
Goodyear	8/20	30/18	77/68	70/70	30/n.a.
Firestone	25/20	43/43	4/10	0/25	25/n.a.
Goodrich	20/10	16/10	19/9	30/5	16/n.a.
Uniroyal	42/37	4/13	0/0	0/0	25/n.a.
General Tire	5/13	7/10	0/13	0/0	4/n.a.
Michelin	0/0	0/6	0/0	0/0	0/n.a.

n.a. = not available.
Source: *Rubber World*, January 1966; *Modern Tire Dealer*, January 1973.

tios rose on the average from 0.3 in 1961 to nearly 0.75 in 1970; and corporate liquidity (the quick ratio) declined by two-thirds. It was estimated that to support the 1971 level of capital expenditures (7.5 percent of net sales), the industry must realize a return on assets of 10.6 percent, nearly double what was actually achieved. Recovery was closely related to the success of the higher price, higher profit bias-belted tires.

Tire manufacturers also attempted to defend their profitability through both vertical and horizontal integration, coupled with modest research and development programs. Backward vertical integration included rubber plantations, chemical plants, and textile mills; forward vertical integration was limited to wholesale and retail sales. Manufacturers also integrate horizontally into associated products, such as mechanical rubber goods, foam products, and wheels.

Markets

The *original equipment market* (OEM) generally accounted for about one-third of total industry shipments of passenger car, truck, bus, and other tires. Automobile manufacturers set specifications on tire characteristics and durability and bought solely on the basis of price within these specifications. They would change suppliers if a tire manufacturer could offer a substantial price reduction, but since the market was highly competitive (OEM tires might be sold for as little as variable cost), only the large firms could compete. The advantage of supplying OEM tires lay in the need to run plants at capacity and the fact that OEM suppliers could attract replacement sales. Only the top five tire companies sold tires in the OEM market, and their shares of this market in 1966 and 1972 are shown in Exhibit 3.

While OEM market shares remained fairly stable over time, automakers used the semiannual price and supply reviews mainly as a penalty/reward system to keep price and service characteristics of the five suppliers in line with their needs. In addition, this was a highly cyclical industry. While new car production had grown at 4.5 percent annually between 1961 and 1971, annual fluctuations were large. Estimated new car sales for 1972 were nearly 11 million, a 7 percent increase over 1971.

The *replacement market* typically accounted for two-thirds of the unit volume and a higher than proportionate share of sales and profits. In the replacement market, since one tire appeared much the same as another, consumers often could not determine quality differences and bought either the least expensive or the brand with which their cars had been originally equipped. A 1965 survey determined that price was the most important factor to consumers, followed by wearability and general quality. Brand was a factor only to 7 percent of respondents.

In addition to the three basic technology offerings, manufacturers were forced to provide an array of sizes and styles to meet the buying public's demand. The general assortment of combinations offered by most major manufacturers included a range of features: (1) physical characteristics such as height, width, wheel diameter, and tubeless; (2) tread patterns such as all season, snow, or off-highway; and (3) cosmetics factors such as white walls, raised letters, and specialty stripes. For a major tire producer such as Goodyear or Firestone, offering a full line of tires meant maintaining a product line with over 8,000 distinct products. Prices for tires within the three

EXHIBIT 4 Price Segments in the U.S. Replacement Tire Market, 1972
(percent of total demand by type)

Price Bracket	Conventional	Bias-Belted	Radial
Over $50	4.5	4.2	68.6
$42.50 to $50	6.8	10.5	21.3
$37.50 to $42.49	10.5	20.4	—
$32.50 to $37.49	16.5	30.2	10.1
$27.50 to $32.49	26.3	20.1	—
$22.50 to $27.49	22.1	8.5	—
Under $22.50	13.3	6.1	—
	100.0	100.0	100.0
Median price	$28.05	$34.45	$55.20

Source: National Rubber Tire Dealer's Association.

basic categories reflected this wide range of products as shown in Exhibit 4.

Passenger-car tires accounted for about 85 percent of total replacement tire production. Demand fluctuated on the basis of the number of two-year old cars on the road, average annual mileage per vehicle, and prevalent tire life. Although the average annual miles driven per car remained relatively constant, the larger pool of cars in the road translated into a 4.4 percent annual increase in total vehicle miles driven. Despite improved tire construction, a faster rate of replacement occurred during the 1960s because of higher driving speeds, heavier cars, greater popularity of power systems, the imposition of federal and state tire-safety laws, including tread depth minima, and a generally more safety-conscious public. Annual increases in replacement shipments during the sixties averaged about 7 percent. The main uncertainty concerning future growth in the market centered on the tire-life of the new bias-belted tires.[3]

Producers were expecting both the OEM and replacement markets to converge on the bias-belted tire. Consumers had increased their spending on tires since 1964 (average unit price had gone up from $21.50 to nearly $30 in 1969), which had motivated producers to broaden their lines with many new styles and performance models.

Distribution

Since the early 1900s, replacement tires had been distributed through independent dealers. Some dealers sold a variety of brands, but many specialized in the tires of a single manufacturer. In 1926, 80 percent of replacement tires were sold through this channel. Retail margins on major brands averaged 25–30 percent, but independent dealers realized most of their profits on automotive service work.

In the 1930s, the large oil companies, in an effort to gain competitive advantages against each other, began offering automotive supplies, including tires, at their service stations. They were followed by large retail chain and mail order stores which, by buying in large volume, could offer attractive prices, usually under their own private brand names. By 1940, three chains accounted for about a quarter of the replacement market. Almost 90 percent of the major oil company tires came from one of the four major tire producers in 1962, and these were distributed through over 200,000 outlets nationwide. Sears, the largest of the retail and mail order chain stores, sold its tires through over 800 stores and, by the early 1970s, sold more tires than anyone but Goodyear and Firestone. By 1970, private label tires accounted for 40 percent of all tires sold in the domestic replacement market. The breakdown of automobile replacement tire sales by type of outlet is shown in Exhibit 5.

The oil companies' share of distribution had significantly eroded over the past few years, with the advent of self-service gas stations and increasing competition from integrated automotive service centers. These behaved much like OEMs in their buying, in that they spread their business over several major manufacturers who would emboss the same name on the tire. For example, Atlas

EXHIBIT 5 Replacement Sales by Outlet Type
(percent)

	1965	1972(e)
Independent Dealers	36.5	52.4
Chain, Mail-Order Stores	20.5	17.2
Service Stations	25.6	13.7
Tire Company Stores	9.9	10.1
Department, Discount Stores	5.6	4.2
Cooperatives	1.5	2.1
Direct	0.4	0.4
	100.0%	100.0%

[3]One industry estimate was that, while conventional tires had an average life of 17,500 miles, bias-belted tires might average about 20,500. In contrast, radial tires would typically exceed 30,000 miles.

tires (Exxon) were made by Firestone, General, Goodrich, and Goodyear.

Chain and mail order distribution had also eroded over the past 10 years. In this channel, chains such as Sears or Montgomery Ward contracted the manufacture of private brands for their exclusive use (e.g., Allstate, Riverside). They also exercised a certain amount of market power in their buying behavior. Discount chains were often included in the same category as mail order distributors for planning purposes. Firestone and Armstrong accounted for 70 percent of sales to chain and mail order distributors.

Company-owned stores became popular as more manufacturers integrated forward to try to capture retail margins and associated service contributions. Manufacturers only offered their company brand and house brands in company stores, but usually had better inventory selection due to close communication with warehouses. Companies felt direct retail exposure gave them added information on customer buying habits and helped to build brand loyalty via service. However, ownership of retail outlets did involve increases in fixed costs and overhead in a generally fragmented service market with varying degrees of overcapacity. Firestone and Goodyear had the largest number of company-owned stores with 1,950 and 1,750 respectively.

Truck tires were sold mainly through wholesalers who provided customer service such as balancing or alignment. Though there was some transfer of brand image from automobile tires, durability was the key selling point. Truckers often bought a specified number of miles or a specified number of retreads, rather than buying just a tire. Fleet buyers were even more demanding and had better information on relative performance.

International Competition

The U.S. tire industry had faced economic problems which were usually attributed to low productivity, high labor costs, and outmoded production facilities. However, the 1960s and early 1970s brought a new source of woe to them: severe competition from foreign-made goods. Between 1963 and 1970, imported tires went from 1.8 to 10.6 percent of the U.S. domestic market, and would have been even higher in 1971 if the Nixon Administration had not imposed a 10 percent import surcharge.[4] The growth of imports as a percentage of the large replacement tire market was occurring at an even faster rate. Over the same period, U.S. tire exports exhibited a declining growth rate and the net effect was a constant year-to-year deterioration in the U.S. balance of trade in tires. By 1971, the Rubber Manufacturers' Association estimated the unfavorable balance of trade in the U.S. rubber industry at $163 million. Exhibit 6 presents recent financial information on all major U.S. producers. Exhibits 7–10 summarize data on production, value added and trade for the U.S. tire industry.

The tire import threat was three-pronged. First, imported cars, with imported tires, had been taking around 16 percent of the U.S. auto market. Second, Japanese and other low-wage foreign producers had been shipping in millions of replacement tires, competing for sales mainly on a price basis in small sizes (less than 13 inches). In 1970, these imports took 5.7 percent of the replacement market, up from less than 1 percent in 1963. In the first five months of 1971, imports from Japan soared by 195 percent over 1970 figures. The third part of the import threat was premium-priced, high-margin radial tires.

The major shares of the import market for replacement tires in the early 1970s were estimated to be as follows: France (24 percent); Italy (20); Germany (12); Japan (8); Canada (7); and the U.K. (5). Imports from Canada were mainly brought in by U.S. parent companies to buffer domestic inventories in periods of cyclical shortages. Michelin had become the major source of imported automobile tires in recent years, primarily due to its contract to supply private label radials to the Sears distribution network, and it was also a major factor in truck tire imports.

The RMA attributed the apparent loss of U.S. competitiveness to three factors: (1) lower wage costs abroad (hourly compensation for production workers in the industry were estimated in 1970 to be $6 in the U.S., $5 in Canada, $2.35 in France, and $1.75 in Japan); (2) significantly higher tariffs in other markets (12.5 percent in Japan and 9 percent in the EEC); and (3) unfair incentives granted exporters in other countries. Yet, the higher growth rate prevalent in overseas tire markets (113 percent versus 74 percent in the U.S. during the 1960s) was thought to limit foreign suppliers' capacity to expand sales to the U.S. market.

Nonetheless, the major U.S. companies were strongly represented in world markets through direct foreign investments. Based on their dominant position in the home country and their ties to affiliates of U.S. car makers overseas, they had established a strong presence in foreign tire markets since the 1920s, as

[4]This measure lasted only six months and was eliminated after the dollar was devalued by 10 percent in December 1971.

EXHIBIT 6 Financial Information on Major U.S. Tire Companies, 1966–1971

	Total Sales ($ millions)	Operating Profit (% margin before taxes)	Net Income ($ millions)	Cash Flow (% of sales)
		Goodyear Tire and Rubber Co. Ltd.		
1966	2,476	9.5	118.5	8.2
1967	2,638	9.2	127.1	8.4
1968	2,926	10.7	148.3	8.6
1969	3,215	10.5	158.2	8.4
1970	3,195	9.0	129.2	7.9
1971	3,602	10.4	170.2	8.4
		Firestone Tire and Rubber Co. Ltd.		
1966	1,815	10.6	101.8	9.0
1967	1,875	10.8	102.3	9.0
1968	2,131	12.1	127.0	9.4
1969	2,279	10.6	116.7	8.6
1970	2,335	8.1	92.8	7.8
1971	2,484	9.3	113.5	8.9
		Uniroyal, Inc.		
1966	1,324	7.1	45.3	6.2
1967	1,265	5.4	33.0	5.4
1968	1,429	8.5	57.0	7.0
1969	1,554	6.6	45.6	6.6
1970	1,556	4.1	24.1	4.8
1971	1,678	5.6	43.1	5.7
		B.F. Goodrich Co. Ltd.		
1966	1,039	8.6	48.6	8.7
1967	1,066	5.8	29.5	7.3
1968	1,140	8.3	44.9	7.9
1969	1,229	7.6	39.9	7.2
1970	1,205	5.2	12.3	5.6
1971	1,300	6.9	29.8	6.8

Source: Michelin Tires Manufacturing Co. of Canada (A), University of Western Ontario, 1973.

EXHIBIT 7 **U.S. Tire Production and Trade, 1963–1971**
(market in million units; value in US$)

	Total Market*			Replacement Market			Value ($ million)		
Year	Market	Imports	Imports as Percent of Market	Market	Imports†	Imports as Percent of Market	Imports	Exports	Net Balance
1963	139.0	2.6	1.8	90.1	0.6	0.6	28.3	66.5	38.2
1964	152.0	4.0	2.6	101.2	1.4	1.4	40.4	74.2	34.0
1965	170.0	4.7	2.8	108.5	1.5	1.4	45.1	85.6	40.5
1966	176.0	6.9	3.9	116.9	2.3	2.0	61.1	79.7	18.6
1967	178.0	9.4	5.3	124.3	3.3	2.7	88.3	66.6	−21.7
1968	206.0	13.4	6.5	139.2	5.2	3.7	125.7	88.2	−37.5
1969	215.0	16.3	7.8	149.6	6.5	4.3	147.1	87.2	−59.9
1970	n.a.	n.a.	10.6	n.a.	n.a.	5.7	215.0	75.0	−140.0
1977	n.a.	n.a.	n.a.	n.a.	n.a.	n.a.	250.0‡	87.0‡	−163.0‡

*Automotive and truck tires only; includes tires on imported vehicles.
†Over 85 percent of these were passenger car tires.
‡Estimates.
n.a. = not available
Source: "Trade by Commodities," *OECD Abstracts;* Rubber Manufacturers Association.

EXHIBIT 8 **U.S. Tire Shipments, 1966–1971**
(in thousand units)

	Original Equipment	Replacement	Export	Total Shipments	Total Production
		Passengers Car Tires			
1966	47,362	101,812	1,783	150,957	154,516
1967	40,827	108,499	1,653	150,979	141,896
1968	49,873	121,088	2,667	173,628	177,408
1969	46,172	129,112	1,850	177,134	180,480
1970	37,535	129,608	1,497	168,640	164,571
1971	48,610	135,009	1,558	185,177	187,725
		Truck and Bus Tires			
1966	7,401	14,613	650	22,664	22,872
1967	6,873	14,418	465	21,756	21,165
1968	8,488	16,257	532	25,277	25,533
1969	9,430	17,439	569	27,438	27,211
1970	8,560	16,713	402	25,675	25,680
1971	10,251	18,386	391	29,028	28,428

Note: Years cited are calendar years.

EXHIBIT 9 U.S. Tire Industry Statistics

	Value of Shipments ($ million)	Wages ($ million)	Value Added ($ million)	Capital Expenditures ($ million)	Total Employees (thousands)	Production Workers (thousands)	Value Added Per Production Worker-Hour ($)
1966	$3,716	$537	$1,768	$153	85.3*	66.3*	10.03*
1967	3,734	574	1,823	199	92.7	68.7	13.35
1968	4,269	687	2,102	243	98.5	76.0	13.35
1969	4,717	754	2,304	342	103.0	80.0	13.51
1970	4,616	713	2,389	272	102.0	78.0	13.58
1971	5,322	797	2,767	220	n.a.	n.a.	n.a.
				Percent Change			
1971/1970	15.3	11.8	15.8	(19.1)			
1971/1966	7.4	8.2	9.4	7.5			
1963/1970					2.6	2.3	5.5

*Refers to 1963.

Note: The number of establishments was 182. The four (eight) largest manufacturers accounted for 71% (90%) of domestic production.

n.a. = not available.

shown in Exhibit 11. Exhibit 12 provides some estimates of the major market positions held by the largest five U.S. companies plus Michelin and Bridgestone in selected world markets. Exhibit 13 shows relative market shares in the U.S. replacement tire market for the same group of firms.

Potential for Radials in the United States

The future of the radial tire in the United States was, at best, uncertain in 1971. The radial tire offered some significant advantages such as longer life (Michelin offered a 40,000 mile guarantee in the late 1960s when other manufacturers were offering a 20,000 to 25,000 mile guarantee for conventional tires), 5 to 10 percent better gas mileage, and improved safety because of reduced distortion, friction, and tire heat and hence fewer blowouts. Ralph Nader, the American consumer advocate, had recently come out in favor of radial tires. However, radials were from 30 to 40 percent more expensive than other tires, and they were designed for European driving habits where the average car owner kept his car longer than the average U.S. car owner, where fuel was often double U.S. prices, where much of the driving occurred on winding mountainous roads not at all similar to the large U.S. superhighways, and where cars were designed with stiffer suspensions. In Europe, by 1971, 65 percent of the market had converted to radial tires and some observers had been predicting since the late 1960s that as many as 70 million radials a year would be sold in the United States by the mid-1970s. However, Goodyear's Chairman, Ralph de Young, predicted in 1971 that the radial would "remain a third choice for American motorists for many years to come."

De Young's statement about radials, though applicable to U.S. consumers' needs, undoubtedly also reflected resistance on the part of U.S. manufacturers to convert to radial production. The conversion from four-ply to bias-belted tires had been made, generally speaking, by expanding plant capacity to take account of lower productivity. Radial production, on the other hand, would require expensive new molds and machines and a retraining of the labor force in the more exacting and more labor-intensive production process. Estimates of conversion costs ran as high as $2.5 million per every 3,000 daily units of capacity. Though all the major American manufacturers were producing limited quantities of radi-

EXHIBIT 10 **U.S. Tire Industry Variables**

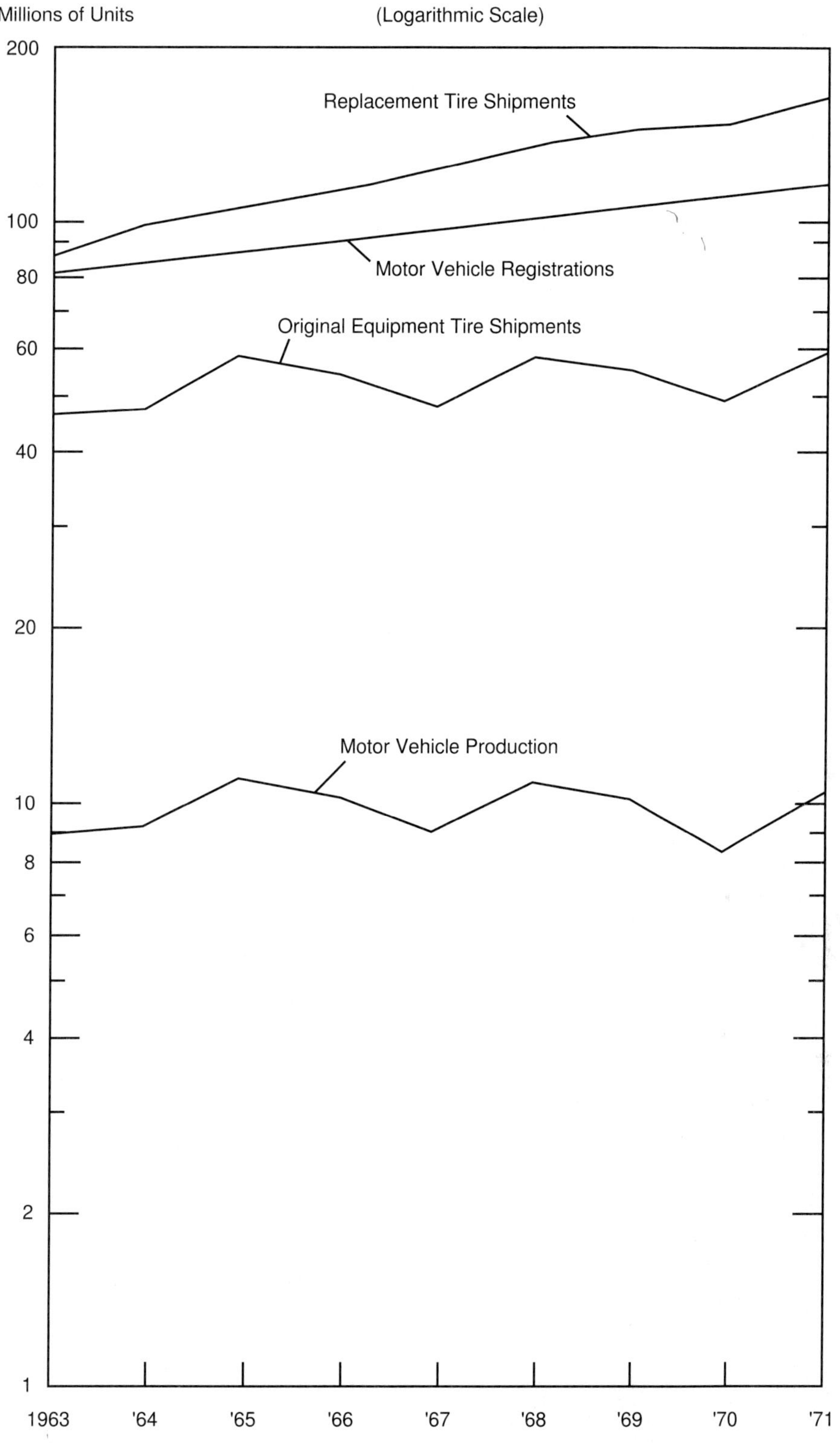

Source: Automobile Facts and Figures and BDC.

EXHIBIT 11 Investment Overseas by Company and Year

Country	Goodyear	Firestone	Goodrich
Canada	1917	1919	1918
United Kingdom	1927	1928	1934
Argentina	1930	1930	—
Brazil	1938	1939	1953
Sweden	1938	1945	1939
Philippines	1956	1957	1975
Japan	1956	1962	1963
France	1959	1960	1967
Portugal	1960	1958	—
West Germany	1961	1960	1964
Italy	1963	1966	1972
Taiwan	1971	—	1973(e)

Source: Company reports.

als, they had not yet perfected this production process. In fact, two U.S. manufacturers had recently introduced bias-belted tires into European markets to challenge the radials in their home ground.

APPENDIX: TYPES OF TIRES AND PRODUCTION METHODS

Tires in 1971 consisted of three basic types: conventional, bias-belted, and radial tires.

Conventional tires or bias-ply tires were made of four cord plies laid out at right angles to each other in a crisscross fashion and at a 45 degree angle to the tread. In the early 1960s, manufacturers reduced the number of plies to two, while doubling ply thickness to reduce the amount of labor content in tire making, but the two-ply was less durable and consumers rejected the change.

Bias-belted tires were of essentially the same ply construction as conventional tires, but were strengthened by the addition of a belt of rayon, polyester, or fiberglass between the plies and the tread.

Radial tires consisted of plies perpendicular to the tread, following the radius of the tire, and had a belt of steel cord between the plies and the tread. Radial tires were more expensive to produce because of increased labor input needed to align exactly the plies and the steel belts and because of the higher cost of steel compared to textiles and fiberglass.

Tire production consisted of four production steps: preparation of materials, components subassembly, assembly and curing.[5] Tires were made of five different components: plies of rubber-coated fabric or steel; an airtight safety liner for tubeless tires; an outer tread; sidewalls, which gave the tire strength and flexibility; and strands of steel wire called beads, which formed the inner circumference of tires and allowed them to be tightly joined into a slat on the rim of the wheel.

Preparation of Materials: natural and synthetic rubber and other chemicals were blended in various combinations depending on the types of tire and the particular component involved. The rubber was then formed into a continuous sheet and laid on skids and stocked.

Component Subassembly: fabric (rayon, nylon or polyester), or steel in the case of radials, was dipped into a special solution and then dried. It was then passed between rolls which pressed the warm and pliable sheets of rubber on to the sides and between the threads or strands. The resulting plies were then cut into standard widths and angles depending on the type of tire to be made. For tubeless tires, an airtight liner was then bonded on to what would then be the inner ply. Other machines cut tread and sidewall stock to the proper width. Some machines allowed the forming of tread and sidewall stock as single units. Beads were made of high tensile strength wire strands, which were bound together by a special insulating compound.

Tire Building: tire components were assembled on a semiautomatic precision machine with a collapsible drum. The workman wrapped the plies on the drum, layer by layer. If the tire were belted, a layer of rayon, fiberglass or cord belt was wrapped over the plies. The machine automatically set the beads in place, turned the plies around the beads and then stitched them together. The tread and sidewall units were then added and stitched to the rest. The workman then collapsed the drum, removed the tire and checked it for appearance.

Curing: the tire was then placed in a mold, where it was vulcanized, or treated with sulphur and heat, to bond the components into an integral unit and to form the pattern on the tread. This process was entirely automated and tightly controlled as to time, temperature and pressure.

[5]This description is adapted from Pogrow, Jules, *The International Tire and Rubber Industry,* Harvard Business School, 1971.

EXHIBIT 12 World Market Position of Major Tire Producers, 1971

	Major Producers' Market Share (percentage)								Market
	Goodyear	Firestone	Uniroyal	Goodrich	General	Michelin	Bridgestone	Market Size (millions of units)	Growth Rate* (% of units)
Argentina	29	26	—	—	8†	—	4	5.64	6.1
Benelux	34	9†	7†	6†	—	35	—	8.98	8.5
Brazil	32	28	—	8†	—	—	5	10.99	9.3
Canada	33	26	3†	17	3†	14	—	26.68	6.4
Costa Rica	45	39	—	—	—	—	4	0.88	(8.6)
France	6	6	7	—	—	62	—	37.99	7.7
India	13	14	—	10†	—	—	12	3.41	6.5
Italy	7	8	6	—	—	35	—	20.30	(1.4)
Japan	—	—	—	—	—	—	45	67.42	1.6
Kenya	—	80	—	—	—	3	8	0.31	(4.1)
Mexico	31	11	5	31	14	—	3	7.81	14.5
New Zealand	13	33	—	—	—	—	18	1.94	5.3
Portugal	8	26	—	14	39	15	—	1.91	3.0
South Africa	24	12†	8	—	9†	—	—	5.86	(1.5)
Sweden	13	22	—	9†	—	18	—	5.26	(1.5)
Thailand	22	26	—	—	—	—	29	1.70	13.5
United Kingdom	20	8	7†	6†	—	20	—	29.39	1.4
Venezuela	31	20	15	11†	16	—	6	2.98	10.5
W. Germany	9	7†	6†	5†	—	33	—	43.20	4.3

*3-year average of annual compounded growth rate.
†Casewriter's estimate.

EXHIBIT 13 Major Tire Producer's Share of U.S. Replacement Market, 1966–1972
(percent)

Year	Goodyear	Firestone	Goodrich	Uniroyal	General	Aggregate Imports	Michelin	Bridgestone
1966	27.5	25.3	9.2	11.0	2.6	1.0	n.a.	n.a.
1967	28.1	24.1	8.6	10.0	2.8	1.4	n.a.	n.a.
1968	28.1	24.5	8.8	10.0	2.7	2.0	n.a.	n.a.
1969	28.5	22.9	7.8	10.1	3.1	2.6	n.a.	n.a.
1970	28.6	21.6	7.6	9.9	3.6	3.6	n.a.	n.a.
1971	27.1	21.5	8.6	9.4	4.3	4.5	n.a.	n.a.
1972	27.2	22.2	9.0	9.7	3.8	5.6	1.6	0.46

n.a. = not available.

Case 2-3

INSEAD

Pneumatiques Michelin II

At the time of its investment in a Canadian truck tire plant in 1969 (see the case I–A in this series), Michelin was estimated to have about a third of the European automobile tire market and more than half of the European truck tire market. The company, however, given its penchant for secrecy, stated that "present statistical methods [did] not permit the evaluation of [our] share of . . . the market with sufficient precision." Through its success in Europe, Michelin had grown from being the seventh largest tire manufacturer in the world in 1959, to the third largest in 1971. Its future performance, however, appeared to be linked to its ability to penetrate the large North American market where the company's market share was less than 1 percent in 1971.

The Keys to Michelin's Success

In 1959, François Michelin took command of the company with the goal of expanding the sales of radial tires, which Michelin had introduced in Europe in 1948. Like other tire companies, which had seen sales and profits fluctuate wildly during the first half of the century, Michelin had bought into unrelated companies, such as Citroën (automobiles) and Machines Bull (computers), to ensure steady profit growth. After taking control of the company, Mr. Michelin either sold off its nontire assets, as in the case of Machines Bull, or gave complete autonomy to the director, as in the case of Citroën, so that Michelin could concentrate exclusively on its tire business.

Michelin began by trying to dominate the French market with an emphasis on quality at a high price. In addition, the company spared no expense in its research and development effort, with the result that Michelin had often led the competition in introducing new and superior products. Some of the company's innovations since its founding included:

- 1891—patent on a removable bicycle tire
- 1894—the first automobile tire
- 1899—the first tire able to withstand speeds of 100 km/h (60 mph)
- 1924—the removable steel wheel
- 1934—a nonskid tire
- 1937—the "metallic" tire, opening the use of steel cord in tire manufacturing
- 1948—the first steel-belted radial tire (the "X" tire)
- 1965—the asymmetric tire, adapted to high performance automobiles.

Most of Michelin's research was geared to radial tire technology, and there was little doubt in anybody's mind that in 1972 Michelin still had a clear technological lead in that area. Most of the specialized production machinery was developed in-house and when the patent on the famous "X" tire ran out in 1967, such production know-

---

This case was prepared from published sources by David Harkleroad, Research Assistant, under the supervision of Professors Dominique Héau and José de la Torre at the European Institute of Business Administration (INSEAD), Fontainebleau, France.

how became a key protection against potential competitors. Voya Peters, head of Michelin's U.S. operations, explained: "Anybody can make a steel-belted radial tire; but to make 100 of them of uniform quality is our secret."[1] Michelin ensured that it would remain at the forefront of tire technology by devoting a large effort to R&D. In 1972, it employed about 4,000 R&D people, representing roughly 4–5 percent of its total workforce worldwide, and R&D expenses were estimated at around 3–4 percent of sales.

Until the 1960s, only French motorists seemed convinced of the value of Michelin's radials, which lasted longer and performed better than conventional tires. In the early 1960s, Michelin took a 27.8 percent interest in Kléber-Colombes, the number two manufacturer in France, a move interpreted by industry observers as an attempt by Michelin to prevent other tire manufacturers from buying into its home market. Michelin also obtained a one-fifth share in Semperit, the major Austrian tire producer, apparently intended to secure a position outside the EEC market.

Having established his market position in France, François Michelin was then free to devote his efforts to the rest of the European market, where the company had built a few plants before the war, and to the building of a strong dealer network. The number of Michelin tire factories increased from eight to ten in France and from eight to thirteen in the rest of Europe between 1960 and 1965. Michelin exported to countries where it had no plants and, by 1971, about 75 percent of total group sales were outside of France, including about 40 percent of the output of the French manufacturing facilities (see Exhibit 1).

Michelin's investment in Canada was the first time the company had gone outside of Europe with large-scale production facilities. Until then, sales of high-priced, high quality radial tires to non-European markets had been secured largely through exports. In this respect, because of the high cost of shipping tires, Michelin was at a considerable disadvantage vis-à-vis other international manufacturers. Production capacity of U.S. manufacturers outside the United States (including minority participations in Japan) was three times that of Michelin's total capacity; and their combined capacity in Europe alone was greater than that of Michelin, the largest European manufacturer (see Exhibit 2).

EXHIBIT 1 Michelin Group Sales, 1969–1971
(millions of French francs)

	1969	1970	1971
Domestic Sales	1,472	1,748	1,992
French Exports	750	991	1,409
Total France	2,222	2,740	3,402
Group Total	**5,500**	**6,700**	**7,900**

Source: *Michelin Prospectus,* February 24, 1976.

Another key to the company's success was its management style. François Michelin's prime concern was loyalty to the company, and job applicants were investigated to the extent that one publication called "draconian." Once hired, apprentices were taught "*la sincérité vis-à-vis des hommes et vis-à-vis des faits, l'observation, l'esprit de progrès et par dessus tout, l'amour de l'ouvrage bien fait.*" Even managers with extensive prior experience underwent an 18-month training program, during which they learned the company's philosophy and policies, their job requirements and how to make tires by spending several weeks on the production line. The company had introduced Taylorized production lines before World War II, and increased salaries or gave bonuses to *"ces 'bons ourvriers' qui [savaient] 'faire mieux et moins cher.'* "[2]

Industry observers said that Michelin's workers were better paid than those in comparable jobs in other companies. This went hand in hand with François Michelin's strict antiunion stance, which came from his belief that unions had been formed only in reaction to bad management. Only about 8 percent of Michelin's employees belonged to unions, as opposed to a French national average of 20 percent.

Monsieur François, as he was known to his employees, *"éternellement vêtu d'un costume gris et d'un imperméable sans âge,"* was aware that in the battle for world supremacy, he faced adversaries with strong financing and whose potential was underemployed. Cutting costs was essential, except for research and production; rumor had it that "while factories are regularly modernized, the offices have not been refurbished since the turn of the century."

[1] *Forbes,* April 15, 1973.

[2] Most of these quotes come from *Entreprise,* September 21, 1973.

EXHIBIT 2 Estimated Tire Production Capacity, 1969

	U.S. Companies						Other				Grand
	Firestone	Goodyear	Uniroyal	Goodrich	Other	Total	Dunlop	Michelin	Pirelli	Other	Total
United States*	206	246	123	91	308	973	23†	—	—	—	997
Canada	21	31	16	8	5	81	8	—	—	—	89
Western Europe	73	82	36	20	8	218	100	201‡	72	123	714
Asia‡	13	115	11	51	1	190	29	—	—	29	247
Latin America	17	25	3	7	9	61	—	—	11	1	73
Rest of the World	8	16	3	6	2	35	20	1	6	2	63
Total	**338**	**515**	**191**	**182**	**332**	**1,558**	**179**	**202**	**89**	**154**	**2,183**

(thousands of daily units)

*1968 figures.

† 1970 estimates.

‡ Includes production of minority-owned affiliates, e.g., Bridgestone (20% owned by Goodyear) and Yokohama (34% owned by Goodrich), Kléber-Colombes (28% owned by Michelin); and other smaller participations by Firestone (Japan and Germany), Uniroyal (Sweden and Japan), Goodrich (Sweden and New Zealand), and Dunlop (Japan and Australia).

Source: Jules Pogrow, *The International Tire and Rubber Industry,* Cambridge, Mass., Harvard, 1971.

EXHIBIT 3 Michelin's Organization

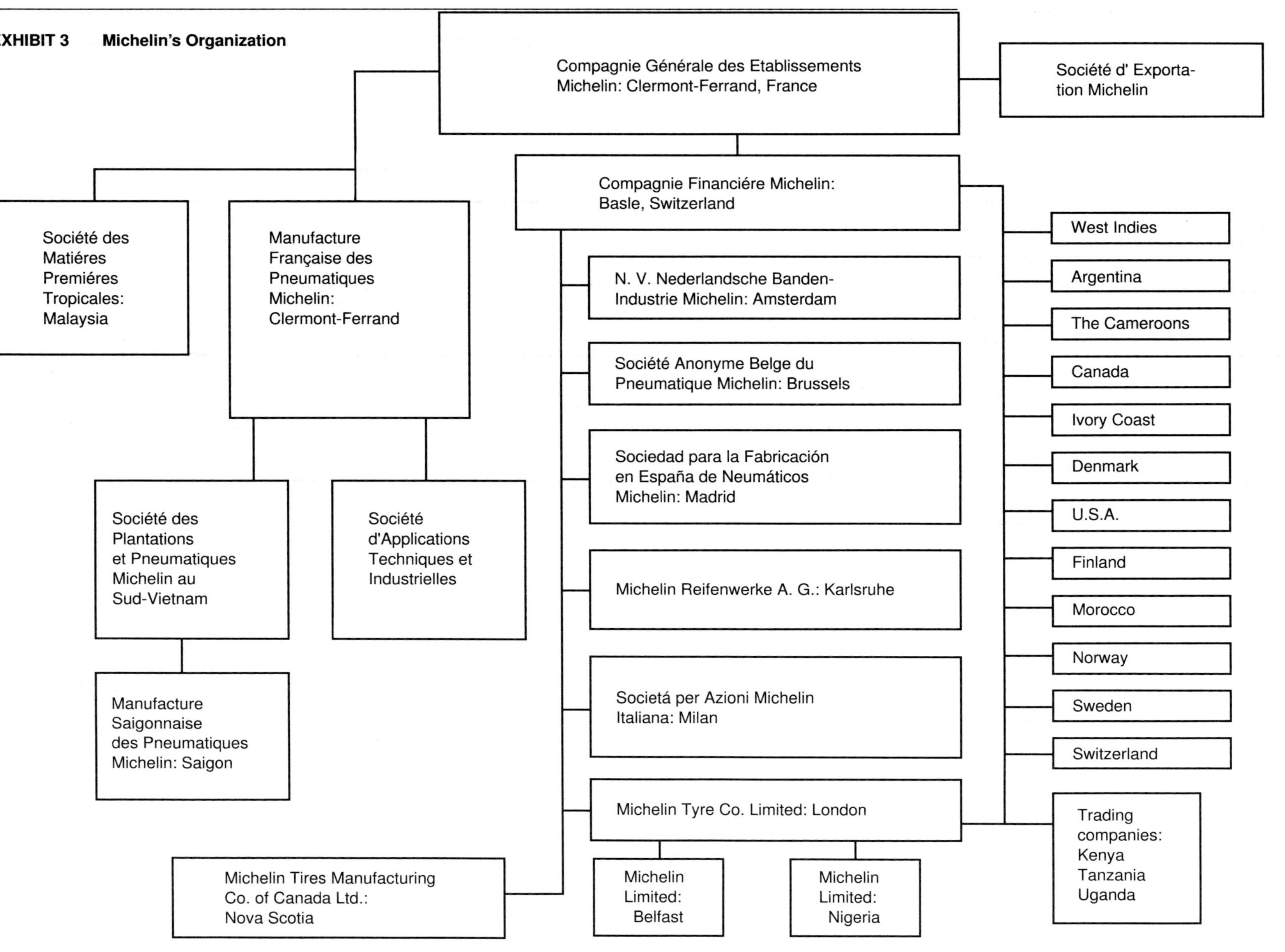

Source: Michelin Tire Co. of Canada, University of Western Ontario.

Michelin knew that he would be permitted no errors and the danger of industrial espionage led him to restrict employees to their own work areas, which they could enter only with special badges. Outsiders were prohibited from entry:

> Michelin has an iron-clad rule that permits no visitors. As François Michelin puts it: "You need ten years to develop a machine and five minutes to understand it, and thus to copy it." Some years ago, when General de Gaulle visited Clermont-Ferrand (French company headquarters) a Michelin employee recalls: "We politely showed him the sales room, then we politely showed him the display room, then we politely showed him the executive offices, and then we politely escorted him to his limousine in the parking lot. No one but Michelin people ever goes into a Michelin plant."[3]

The secrecy extended to all but the most senior managers and even the organizational structure was unknown. One attempt at its description is shown in Exhibit 3. Managers' responsibilities were a function of the person rather than the position. "The theory is that without an organizational chart, executive responsibility can be shifted without hurting feelings."

The success of the strategy can be gauged from its market performance. Michelin had solidified its hold on the French car tire market (see Exhibit 4). In addition, Michelin was estimated to have 20 percent of the U.K. market, behind Dunlop, and 25 percent of the Italian market, behind Pirelli. It was among the market leaders in Germany, with 15–20 percent of that market, and was the leader in all other European countries. In terms of sales growth, Michelin had far outstripped its American competitors in the years 1968 to 1970, achieving an average annual growth rate of 23 percent versus 7 percent for Goodyear, 5 percent for Firestone, and 3 percent for Goodrich.

This sales growth required large investments in plant, equipment, and inventories. The sales to total assets ratio for the industry was between 1.1 and 1.2, and inventories represented about 30 percent of total assets. In 1970, when Michelin operated 30 plants throughout the world (13 in France), it raised 110 million French francs (at the time 5FF = $1) in new capital, in addition to its internal cash flow, which was estimated to be 10 to 12 percent of sales. In 1971, it added one new plant in France and seven elsewhere in Europe for a total investment in fixed assets of over 1.7 billion FF. The total uses of funds for the year were 2.2 billion FF (1.8 billion in fixed assets and 400 million in inventory), of which 988 million FF came from internally generated cash. That year, the company issued its first bonds since 1963, providing another 664 million FF. It also reduced its cash balances by 321 million FF and raised another 251 million FF from other sources. On top of this, Michelin was planning on issuing 170 million FF of share capital in France in 1972. Exhibits 5–8 present available financial information about Michelin.

EXHIBIT 4 Market Shares in the French Automotive Tire Market, 1972

	OEM	Replacement
Michelin	45–50%	40–56%
Kléber-Colombes	25–28	18–20
Dunlop	15–20	12–14
Uniroyal	3–4	8–9
Firestone	4	8
Goodyear	3–4	7–8

Source: *Enterprise*, September 21, 1973.

The Michelin family held about 50 percent of the shares of *Compagnie Générale des Etablissements Michelin,* a nonlimited liability holding company, which owned virtually all of the shares of *Manufacture Française des Pneumatiques Michelin,* the French production arm, and all of the shares of *Compagnie Financière Michelin,* located in Switzerland, which was responsible for "coordinating and developing the industrial activities of the Michelin Group outside of France and [was] responsible for managing and coordinating such subsidiaries and for raising the funds required to meet their short, medium and long-term financial needs."[4] François Michelin was estimated to own about 3 percent of the holding company, but the family holdings gave him complete control.

In addition, Michelin held 51 percent of the shares in Citroën, the third largest French car manufacturer. The remaining 49 percent had been acquired by Italy's Fiat when Michelin tried to sell off its interests to concentrate on the tire business. The French government, however, appeared determined to keep Citroën in French hands and the arrangement between Fiat and Michelin was un-

[3]As quoted in *Business Week,* July 26, 1976.

[4]Michelin *Prospectus,* February 24, 1976.

EXHIBIT 5 Michelin Financial Flows, 1968–1971
(in millions of French francs)

Group (consolidated)	1968	1969	1970	1971
Sales	4,380	5,500	6,700	7,900*
Sales of French Subsidiary†	1,900	2,200	2,750	3,402*
Cash Flow	525	670	724*	988*
Net Profit	254	338	290	400
Investment in Plant	420	600	1,200	1,700*
Cash Flow/Sales	11.9%	12.2%	10.8%	12.5%

*Various Michelin publications
† Before VAT
Source: *Enterprise*, September 21, 1973.

EXHIBIT 6 Consolidated Balance Sheets, 1971
(in millions of French francs)

Assets	
Plant and Equipment (net)	3,652
Interests in Unaffiliated Companies and Goodwill	661
Inventory	1,839
Net Cash, Negotiable Assets, and Current Liabilities	(191)
	5,961
Liabilities	
Shareholders' Capital	450
Retained Earnings	1,590
Capital and Other Reserves	1,985
Minority Interests	67
Medium- and Long-Term Debt	1,869
	5,961

Note: Although the figures given are thought to be representative by the source, they were pieced together from available information and should not be considered exact.
Source: Goy, Huvette et Cie.

EXHIBIT 7 Group Cash Flow, 1971
(in millions of French francs)

Sources	
Internally Generated Funds	361
Depreciation	627
Operating Cash Flow	988
Increase in Medium- and Long-Term Debt	664
Increase in Other Liabilities	169
Exceptional Items	82
Decrease in Cash Balances	321
	2,224
Uses	
Investment in Plant	1,967
Investment in Other Fixed Assets	142
Increase in Inventory	385
	2,224

Note: Figures pieced together from available information and should not be considered exact.
Source: Goy, Huvette et Cie.

satisfactory to both. Michelin was considering reacquiring Fiat's shares, but Citroën was having financial difficulties (see Exhibit 9), and a large amount of time and money would be needed to restructure its finances and modernize its plants.

Michelin had integrated backwards in the 1930s into rubber plantations and steel-wire plants. Though the plantations were becoming less important as the use of synthetic rubber increased, the investment in steel wire plants had been an astute move. Thus, the company could not only control fully the quality of the wire used in its radials, but by its proprietary position make it difficult for other companies to obtain sufficient quantities of similar wire. Finally, the famous Michelin guides and maps, excellent publicity tools, represented about 1 percent of sales.

EXHIBIT 8 Michelin Group Cash Flows and Investments, 1970 and 1971
(In millions of French francs)

	Cash Flows			Investments	
	1970	1971		1970	1971
Generale des Etablissements	36	62		—	—
Manufacture Francaise	193	278	France	443	534
Great Britain (consolidated)	72	99	Great Britain (consolidated)	146	237
Italy	123	149	Italy	223	329
Spain	128	164	Spain	188	213
Germany	29	69	Germany	165	375
Belgium	(1)	13	Belgium	1	5
Low Countries	0	9	Low Countries	0	3
Switzerland (year ending in June)	131	160			
Synthetic Rubber Plant*	0	0	Synthetic Rubber Plant*	—	13
Other	13	(15)			
Total	724	998		1,166	1,709

*50% owned by Goodyear.
Note: Figures pieced together from available information and should not be considered exact.
Source: Goy, Huvette et Cie.

EXHIBIT 9 Citroën, Financial Results, 1966–1971
(in millions of French francs)

	Sales	Profits After Tax	Fixed Assets
1966*	3,777	22	1,048
1967*	3,847	12	1,354
1968	3,326	(119)	1,823
1969	3,655	(63)	1,661
1970	4,390	(373)	1,808
1971	5,738	25	1,709

*S.A. Andre Citroën; *Automobiles Citroën* for the following years.
Source: Annual reports.

Competition

In 1971, radial tires accounted for about 60 percent of the European tire market, up from 30 percent in 1965. European competitors had shifted production to radial tires to supply this growing demand, but none had been as successful as Michelin. Over 80 percent of Michelin's production was in radials and the company planned to phase out nonradial tires completely. Other companies, notably Pirelli, had introduced radial tires with fiber belts, rather than with steel belts, but Michelin's management considered the quality to be inferior to that of its own products. By 1968, all the European subsidiaries of U.S. tire companies had at least one production line of radials, typically using fiberglass or polyester belts. Although not as strong nor as long-lasting as steel-belted radials, they were cheaper to produce.

The European tire market was very fragmented in the late 1960s, and increasing competition had led to numerous attempts at rationalization. The American companies had expanded aggressively during the 1960s, and by 1969 they were operating 29 subsidiary plants in Europe. General Tire and Goodrich stressed minority participation with local producers, but the others had invested directly in major expansion programs. Their European plants were among the largest and most highly automated in the world. In addition to introducing their bias-belted tires, described as a cross between conventional and radial tires, they attacked the market aggressively, offering dealers large discounts and trying to secure broad distribution networks. They also sought agreements with the

U.S. automotive companies operating in Europe to supply them with OEM tires.

As profitability among European manufacturers declined, a number of companies sought to create groups that would permit them to rationalize their operation. One such attempt was the so-called "German solution," where Bayer, a large diversified German chemical firm, acquired 30 percent of Continental Gummiwerke, the fourth largest European tire manufacturer, 62 percent of Phoenix, the eighth largest, and 35 percent of Metzeler, the tenth largest. All of these manufacturers were located in Germany.

A second major group consisted of Dunlop, the major British tire manufacturer and the second largest in Europe, and Pirelli, the major Italian manufacturer and the third largest in Europe, who agreed to unite in 1970. Some 65 percent of Dunlop's sales and 35 percent of Pirelli's were in tires, and their union made them the second largest tire group in Europe, just behind Michelin. Dunlop was weak in radial tires, holding third place in the European radial market behind Michelin and Pirelli, but it had a wider geographic spread, covering Europe, the Commonwealth, Asia, and North America. Pirelli was strong in Southern Europe and South America. In only two areas, the United Kingdom and Germany, did production facilities overlap, but this did not seem to pose major problems. Together they controlled 45 percent of the British market, 35 percent of the Italian market, 18 percent of the German market, and 13 percent of the French market. Dunlop had decided to end its expensive racing support of Formula 1 cars in 1970, leaving the field to Goodyear, Firestone, and Michelin, who began discreetly equipping Formula 1 cars that same year. Financially, the two companies were not particularly complementary, since both had high debt ratios. Because the merger had caused a decline in profitability, it was not clear that it would survive.

Exhibit 10 shows tire production capacity by company and country for Europe in 1964 and 1969. Exhibit 11 presents summary 1969 financial data for all major tire manufacturers.

All major competitors in Europe had strong R&D capabilities. Pirelli had just developed a triangular-section tire, and Dunlop had introduced its Donova, which was highly regarded by the market. Many manufacturers were working on puncture-resistant or run-flat tires, and, since Michelin had not modified its tire concept since 1948, these developments could be expected to give the steel-belted radial strong competition.

Market Trends

During the 1960s, growth in the U.S. tire market was 74 percent, which compared to 113 percent elsewhere. The higher growth outside the United States was attributed to the increase in automobile usage and the expansion of highway systems in these countries. From 1957 to 1968, U.S. automobile production increased at a 4.5 percent annual rate while production elsewhere increased at a 17.2 percent annual rate. Industry sources predicted that more than 60 percent of the tires sold in the world in the 1970s would be sold outside the United States and Canada. Exhibit 12 shows these predictions for OEM and replacement passenger tires for 1968–1978.

The North American market was relatively mature, with sales growth at a 10 percent annual rate from 1957 to 1971, and expected to slow down considerably afterwards (see the case I–B in this series). Japan was the second largest tire-producing country in the world after the United States, and growth had averaged over 12 percent a year from 1967 to 1971. Demand was predominantly for traditional tires, and approximately half the market was controlled by Bridgestone, in which Goodyear had a minority position, and another quarter was held by Yokohama, in which Goodrich held 34 percent. Japan's strict foreign investment laws had prevented foreign tire companies from investing there, except in the case of minority ownerships or licensing agreements. Imports, representing about 2 percent of the market, were also strictly controlled. Dunlop was the only radial tire producer in Japan (in a joint venture), making tires for Toyotas destined for the European market. However, the investment laws had recently been liberalized, and several companies, including Michelin, were talking with Japanese companies about the possibility of creating additional joint ventures. These investments would not take place before the mid-1970s, even if satisfactory agreements were reached.

The European tire market had been growing at a fairly steady rate of 9 percent a year in the 1960s and the trend was expected to continue. The growth in radial tires was expected to be higher, approaching 13 percent. Already, 80 percent of the French and 60 percent of the European market was estimated to be radialized. U.S. producers had introduced their bias-belted tires, but were shifting to radial production to meet demand. For the rest of the world, most sales in the less developed countries were for traditional tires, and radials for passenger cars were not expected to show much growth and would most likely be supplied through imports.

EXHIBIT 10 Estimated Tire Production Capacity, Western Europe, 1964 and 1969
(thousands of daily units)

U.S. Companies

	Firestone		Goodyear		Uniroyal		Goodrich		Others		Subtotal	
	1964	1969	1964	1969	1964	1969	1964	1969	1964	1969	1964	1969
United Kingdom	11.5	18.3	17.8	29.0	3.8	4.0	—	—	—	—	32.1	51.3
France	4.0	6.5	3.5	9.0	6.0	9.0	16.0*	—	—	—	29.5	24.5
Germany	9.3*	14.3*	9.3	16.0	4.5	10.0	—	—	—	—	23.1	40.3
Italy	—	5.3	1.9	5.0	—	—	—	—	17.5*	—	19.4	10.3
Sweden	2.3	5.7	6.3	9.1	2.3*	4.0*	4.7*	6.0*	—	—	15.6	24.7
Other	11.8	23.3	7.5	13.8	4.7	8.5	6.0	13.5	7.8	7.6	37.8	66.7
Total	38.9	73.4	46.3	81.9	20.3	35.5	26.7	19.5	25.3	7.6	157.5	217.8

European Companies

	Dunlop		Pirelli		Michelin		Others		Subtotal		Grand Total	
	1964	1969	1964	1969	1964	1969	1964	1969	1964	1969	1964	1969
United Kingdom	53.4	56.5	2.9	5.7	10.0	30.0	4.5	7.5	70.8	99.7	102.9	151.0
France	19.0	18.5	—	—	48.0	104.0†	2.0	3.5	69.0	126.0	98.5	150.5
Germany	15.0	25.0	7.5	9.0	1.5	13.0	30.0	60.0	54.0	107.0	77.1	147.3
Italy	—	—	30.5	50.0	15.0	35.0	—	36.0	45.5	121.0	64.9	131.3
Sweden	—	—	—	—	—	—	—	0.1	—	0.1	15.6	24.8
Other	—	—	3.7	7.5	7.8	19.0‡	12.7	16.0	24.2	42.5	62.0	109.2
Total	87.4	100.0	43.7	72.2	81.3	201.0	49.2	123.1	263.5	496.3	421.0	714.1

* Minority interests.
† Including Kléber-Colombes.
‡ Mostly Spain.
Source: Jules Pogrow, *The International Tire and Rubber Industry,* Cambridge, Mass., Harvard, 1971.

Michelin's Outlook

Europe. Over the next four years, in order to maintain its share of the French truck tire market at about 80 percent and its share of the French car tire market at about 50 percent, Michelin planned to build three or four new plants, expand another three, and modernize the rest at a cost of 1.5 billion FF. To increase its penetration of other European markets, it would build another 12 plants in Italy, Spain, Great Britain and Germany. Capital expenditures were expected to reach 600–700 million FF per country. Other investments and increases in working capital, for all of Europe, were expected to require an additional 1.5 to 2.0 billion FF. An alternative to building its own new plants would be to reach a coproduction agreement with Bayer and the German group. Michelin was rumored to be considering such a possibility.

North America. The North American market, representing over 40 percent of the world's total, was not unknown to Michelin. It had already built a factory in the United States in 1907, but was forced to close it during the depression. Its westward drive began anew in 1948, when it began exporting radials to the United States through a sales office. In 1963, it created a financial subsidiary in Bermuda to direct future North American activities, and in 1965 it agreed to supply Sears, Roebuck

EXHIBIT 11 **Selected Financial Data on Major Tire Companies, 1969**
(U.S.$ millions)

	European Companies							U. S. Companies					
	Dunlop (U.K)	Pirelli (Italy)	Continental (Germany)	Kléber-Colombes (France)	Trelleborg & Tretorn (Sweden)	Semperit (Austria)	Phoenix Germany)	Goodyear	Goodrich	Firestone	Uniroyal	General	Brdigestone (Japan)
Turnover (net)	1,188	345	339	136	125	123	120	3,215	1,229	2,279	1,554	1,088	478
Cost of Goods Sold	n.a.	n.a.	n.a.	n.a.	n.a.	n.a.	n.a.	2,266	871	1,562	1,128	886	348
Depreciation	41	24.2	15.6	9	5.6	7.2	4.7	111	49	82	46	36	22
Selling, General & Administrative	n.a.	n.a.	n.a.	n.a.	n.a.	n.a.	n.a.	502	215	395	277	94	84
Earnings Before Interest and Taxes	79.1	(4.7)	24.2	9.5	n.a.	6.7	11.1	357	100	263	108	88	n.a.
Interest	n.a.	n.a.	n.a.	n.a.	n.a.	n.a.	n.a.	54	30	31	22	16	n.a.
Income Taxes	n.a.	n.a.	n.a.	n.a.	n.a.	n.a.	n.a.	144	28	114	35	33	n.a.
Other Charges	n.a.	n.a.	n.a.	n.a.	n.a.	n.a.	n.a.	2	—	4	4	4	n.a.
After Tax Profits	34.4	(3.7)	10.8	2.4	1.7	1.7	4.9	158	—	117	47	35	21
Cash Flow	75.4	20.5	26.4	11.4	7.3	8.9	9.6	278	100	205	94	71	43
(as % of turnover)	6.3	5.9	7.8	8.4	5.8	7.2	8	8.6	8.1	9.0	6.0	6.4	9.0
Current Assets	598.3	324.6	121	65.4	66.7	57.5	53.2	1,664	615	1,141	741	434	159
Fixed Assets	379.2	283.4	123.8	65.4	32.2	43.5	23.4	1,034	593	765	470	270	240
Other	—	—	—	—	—	—	—	67	49	113	47	120	—
Total Assets	977.5	608	244.8	130.8	98.9	101	76.6	2,764	1,257	2,019	1,258	824	399
Current Liabilities	331	157.2	74.7	47.2	29.5	28.6	18.7	821	362	473	321	206	122
Long-Term Debt	251.3	240.8	55.2	34.5	20.9	43.5	16.4	577	256	417	232	198	108
Other	—	—	—	—	—	—	—	98	44	65	90	30	—
Equity Capital	395.2	210	114.9	49.1	48.5	28.9	32.5	1,267	594	1,064	524	390	169
Capital Investment	82.1	42.6	21.1	16.1	8.4	7.4	8.7	293	138	165	29	55	n.a.
Employment (thousands)	108	25.3	27.5	9	9.1	10.8	8.2	134	53	100	67	34	11
Dividend Payments	n.a.	n.a.	n.a.	n.a.	n.a.	n.a.	n.a.	59	25	47	23	18	6

n.a. = not available
Source: Annual reports and estimates.

EXHIBIT 12 Ten-Year Tire Potential Outside the United States and Canada
(thousands of units)

	Original Equipment Tires			Replacement Passenger Tires		
	1968	1978	Growth (%)	1968	1979	Growth (%)
Western Europe	59,300	105,100	77	62,300	112,500	81
Latin America	7,800	14,000	80	8,600	15,400	79
Africa & Middle East	5,000	9,500	89	5,000	9,300	86
Far East & Oceania	18,300	39,500	116	13,000	28,400	118
Total Outside the U.S. and Canada	90,400	168,100	86	88,900	165,600	86

Source: Jules Pogrow, *The International Tire and Rubber Industry,* Cambridge, Mass., Harvard, 1971.

and Co., the world's largest retailer, with radial tires. These would be sold under Sears' Allstate brand name:

> Sears wanted a top-of-the-line tire. "We had to convince Michelin to develop an American-sized tire; they were reluctant," [said] a Sears official. "But we saw the market developing, and we wanted the best. . ." For Michelin, Sears represented a guaranteed demand base on which it could [later] build a U.S. tire business under its own name.[5]

By the 1970s, Sears was selling about a million premium-priced Michelin radials a year, representing about 0.5 percent of the market. In addition, Ford Motor Co. had begun equipping its luxury Lincoln Continental with imported Michelin radials which, Ford believed, helped increase the sales appeal of the car. There were rumors that Ford executives were considering offering radials as options on other cars. However, other automotive companies refused to consider Michelin's radials since the company had no production facilities in the United States.

Michelin had been approached by several smaller competitors about the possibility of a joint venture, merger, or other similar agreement. Contacts had been made with General Tire and with Armstrong. Although an acquisition or merger would give Michelin a ready-made distribution network and access to capital markets, the cost of converting traditional tire plants to radial tire manufacturing was estimated to be more expensive than building a completely new plant, and Michelin's penchant for secrecy led many to believe it would never submit to the scrutiny of a partner or to SEC financial disclosure requirements. Finally, Ralph Nader had been attacking the safety of U.S.-produced tires, and had endorsed Michelin's radials. The publicity resulting from this was a tempting attraction to the French firm.

Other countries. Michelin planned to continue to supply demand for radial car tires in developing countries from France, but two countries showed promise for the construction of truck tire plants: Brazil and Egypt. Michelin estimated that it would need to invest $60 million in Egypt and $150 million in Brazil to supply the Middle East and South American markets for truck tires. In Japan, Michelin seemed to have no immediate interest, but was talking to a large trading group about a longer-term investment. Entry into Eastern Europe would require investing there, but Michelin was reluctant to consider this given Fiat's experience with its car plant in the Soviet Union. Shortly thereafter, Russian-made Fiats began appearing in European markets. Kléber-Colombes and Semperit, which did not share Michelin's secret radial technology, had filled the void by building plants in Bulgaria, East Germany, Yugoslavia, and Hungary.

Motorcycle tires. In 1971, some three million motorcycles were sold in the world and the market for motorcycle tires, though small, was attractive. Michelin completed an in-depth survey of the motorcycle tire market in 1971, but since most motorcycles were produced in Japan, it would have to produce there in order to tap the OEM market. Dunlop already supplied tires for all Japanese motorcycles exported to Europe.

[5]*Forbes,* April 15, 1973.

Materials. Rayon, the traditional material used in belting tires, was about half as expensive as polyester and fiberglass, though belts made of the latter lasted much longer. However, rayon's price was increasing while the price of the other two was declining, and all major U.S. manufacturers had introduced at least one line of fiberglass and polyester belted tires in the early 1970s. Steel wire for radials, because of the technical difficulties of drawing it to the proper thickness, was found by U.S. manufacturers to be uneconomical. Yet, there was some speculation that a newly developed wire spinning process would allow U.S. producers to compete in the steel-belted radial market. Perhaps the most striking new material was Kevlar, a synthetic fiber developed by Dupont Chemicals for the Apollo space program, which had the same strength as steel while being much less dense. If tests were conclusive, Goodyear and Firestone seemed more likely to be able to obtain the fiber than Michelin since supply would be limited for at least several years due to Dupont's limited capacity. However, Kevlar was much more expensive than steel, and any company planning to use it would need several years to test its application for tires before putting the product on the market.

Organization and Social Considerations

As stated earlier, Michelin's centralized organization structure, reinforced by extensive training programs, created an *esprit de maison* unmatched elsewhere in the industry. However, it was not clear that François Michelin could maintain his highly centralized, secretive, and paternalistic organization as the number of employees worldwide approached 100,000, and as the company competed in more diverse markets. Significant investments outside of Continental Europe would certainly require more delegation of authority to managers in order for them to be able to respond quickly to different and changing operating conditions in each market.

Michelin's antiunion stance had led to the development of a company town in Clermont-Ferrand. The company had constructed housing for its employees and had provided hospitals, nurseries, and schools where, until recently, religious instruction was mandatory. It had been in advance of French government legislation by many years in providing social and welfare benefits such as free medical service, family allowance, paid vacations, and pensions. In addition, Michelin employees were reputedly better paid than their colleagues in similar positions in other companies. In fact, it was said that one of the reasons Michelin chose to invest in Nova Scotia was that unemployment was high and unionization was low in that area.

However, should the company decide to expand its investments abroad, it would have to deal with a workforce whose culture and values were drastically different. For example, in the United States, Michelin would face the strong United Rubber Workers Union, where periodical wage negotiations invariably resulted in high wage settlements or strikes. Michelin's workers had never gone on strike.

UNIT 3 Global Competition in Fragmented Sectors

INSEAD

Case 3–1

Heineken N.V.

During the early 1980s, the Executive Board of Heineken N.V., the famous Dutch beer and beverage company, had met a number of challenges to the basic strategy they had defined for the organization. Since the acquisition of the Amstel Brewery in 1968, Heineken had accelerated a process of diversification aimed at reducing its dependency on exports of Dutch beer. This had led to renewed efforts to be present in all European beer markets and to expand its activity in other continents, in addition to a growing commitment to nonbeer beverages. Presently, Heineken's management felt the need to evaluate the performance of the company in this respect and to make use of past experience and forecasted market conditions to define a clear set of objectives that would guide the group's future geographical spread and product diversity.

Historical Background

Heineken N.V. was founded by Mr. G. A. Heineken in 1864, when he purchased for *f* 48,000[1] one of the largest breweries of the time, *de Hooiberg* (the Haystack), which had been operating in the center of Amsterdam since 1592. In 1868, a new brewery was built in the meadows outside Amsterdam (now in the center of the city) and, as business was prosperous, a second Heineken brewery was inaugurated in Rotterdam in 1874. For a number of years, all Heineken beer was produced in these two breweries.

Modest export activities started as early as the 1860s, principally to India and the East and West Indies' markets, and developed rapidly to other countries. In 1927 Heineken made its first foreign investment when it acquired 100 percent of the shares of Brasserie Leopold, a family-owned brewery in Brussels. Shortly thereafter, the end of prohibition in the United States opened what was to become Heineken's largest single export market. Singapore, Indonesia, and Egypt were also important markets during this period.

In the postwar years, Heineken bought a second brewery in Singapore, which had been confiscated from the Germans, and expanded to Malaysia and Australian New Guinea. Through a Belgian associate, Heineken obtained access to breweries in Zaire, Burundi, Rwanda, and Congo-Brazzaville, and in West Africa, Heineken started operations with United Africa Company (a Unilever affiliate) on a 50/50 basis in Nigeria, followed later by Ghana, Sierra Leone, and Chad. In the Caribbean, the company acquired interests in Trinidad, St. Lucia, Martinique, and Jamaica.

Perhaps the most important event in the company's postwar expansion was the purchase of Amstel Brewery in 1968, the second largest Dutch brand with a market share of 15 percent. The merger gave Heineken a combined 50 percent of the domestic market, a broader product range with which it could stop further competitive threats, and a number of important affiliates in the Middle East, Africa, and the Caribbean.

In recent years Heineken continued its expansion into new and existing markets. A licensing agreement with Britain's Whitbread in 1968 was followed by the 1972 acquisition of a financial participation in a French group of breweries, which later led to a fully-owned subsidiary in this large market. Two years later, Heineken entered into a joint venture in Italy with Whitbread. Further expansion in South America and the Caribbean opened new geographical areas to Heineken. Since 1975, Norway, Sweden, and Ireland were added to the European countries where the Heineken or Amstel brands were produced under license. See Exhibits 1 and 2 for a summary of these developments.

This case was written by Mr. André Khodjamirian and Professor José de la Torre as a basis for class discussion. The generous contribution of many Heineken executives is gratefully acknowledged, but the authors retain all responsibility for any errors or misinterpretation of facts.

[1]Dutch guilders (or "florins" at the time). Current exchange rates are shown in Exhibit 4.

EXHIBIT 1 Heineken's International Activities, 1863–1982

Year	Activity
1864–85	Limited exports to various countries such as France, Belgium, England, East and West Indies, Turkey, Egypt, and Spain
1878	Brasserie Bavaro rented in **Belgium,** with an option to purchase; withdrew in 1879
1894	Exports begin to the **United States**
1927	**Belgium:** Acquisition of Brasserie Leopold; sold in 1964
1930	**Singapore:** Joint venture and technical contract in Malayan Breweries (42 percent)
1933	Exports resume to the **United States** after prohibition
1936	**Indonesia:** Minority participation taken in Surbaja Brewery; Heineken brand produced locally until 1963; holding later increased to 77 percent
1937	Participation (via indirect holding) in some African countries such as **Egypt** (nationalized under the Nasser regime) and the **Belgian Congo** (Zaire), and in **Indo-China** (sold in the 1950s)
1940	Exports stopped due to World War II
1949	**Nigeria:** Joint venture with United Africa Company (UAC) in Nigerian Breweries (first 50 percent, now 13 percent)
1950	**Venezuela:** Majority participation and Heineken license; divested in 1963
1952	**French Congo** (Brazzaville): Indirect participation and technical contract in Brasserie de Brazzaville
1955	**Surinam:** Amstel minority participation (now 38 percent) and technical contract **Belgium:** Participation in Moutery Albert (malting plant), later fully owned
1956	**Burundi:** Indirect participation (now 59 percent) and technical contract in Burundi
1958	**Jordan:** Minority participation and licensed production of Amstel
1959	**Rwanda:** Indirect participation and technical contract in Bralirwa (now 70 percent)
1960	**Netherlands Antilles:** Amstel license and minority participation (now 52 percent) in Antillian Brewery **Lebanon:** Amstel license and minority participation **Italy:** Minority participation and technical contract in Dreher Beer, later fully owned
1961	**Ghana:** Joint venture with UAC and technical contract in Kumasi Brewery Ltd. **Angola:** Participation and technical contract in Nova Empressa de Angola (27 percent)
1962	**Martinique:** Minority participation in Brasserie Lorraine; later increased to 58 percent
1963	**Chad:** Minority participation and technical contract in Brasserie du Logone **Sierra Leone:** Joint venture with UAC and technical contract in Sierra Leone Brewery (now 22 percent) **Greece:** Amstel minority participation, license and technical contract in Athenian Brewery S.A.; later increased to 98 percent
1964	**Papua New Guinea:** Indirect participation via Malayan Brewery and technical contract
1965	**South Africa:** Amstel license and technical contract **Spain:** Joint venture with UAC; sold in 1969
1969	**United Kingdom:** Heineken license and technical contract with Whitbread
1972	**Sierra Leone:** Heineken license **France:** Majority participation in Alsacienne des Brasseries (Albra) **Trinidad:** Participation (38 percent), technical contract and Heineken license with National Brewing Co. **Jamaica:** Heineken license and technical contract
1975	**Norway:** Heineken license **Portugal:** Technical contract **New Caledonia:** Technical contract and later on participation (86 percent) via Albra **Sweden:** Heineken license to Falken; terminated in 1978
1976	**Haiti:** Technical contract and Heineken license in 1977 **St. Lucia:** Participation (65 percent), Heineken and Amstel license and technical contract in Windward & Leeward Brewery **Tahiti:** Technical contract, Heineken and Green Sands licenses **Italy:** Heineken license
1978	**Ireland:** Heineken license and technical contract with J.J. Murphy's
1979	**France:** Amstel license for low-calorie beer; terminated in 1982
1980	**Finland:** Technical contract **Morocco:** Heineken license **Nigeria:** Green Sands license **Trinidad:** Green Sands license
1981	**France:** Heineken license **Italy:** Amstel license to Peroni **South Korea:** Heineken license and technical contract **Canada:** Acquisition (100 percent) of existing brewery renamed Amstel Brewery, Canada
1982	**Sweden:** Amstel license **Central Africa:** Doubling of participation in Zaire (60 percent) **Rwanda** (70 percent), **Burundi** (59 percent), the **People's Republic of Congo** (100 percent) and **Angola** (27 percent) by acquiring shares from Banque Lambert

Source: Company records.

EXHIBIT 2a Licensing Operations Worldwide, 1983 (Third Parties)

Note: **H** = Heineken; **A** = Amstel. Figures in parentheses represent number of breweries.
Source: Company records.

EXHIBIT 2b Heineken Participations Worldwide, 1983

Note: **H** = Heineken; **A** = Amstel. Figures in parentheses represent number of breweries.
Source: Company records.

Financial Performance

Heineken could be qualified by any standards as a successful company. Besides being one of the largest beer exporters in Europe, and probably the world, the company enjoyed a solid image and followed a quality-conscious approach to producing beer that had won its product worldwide fame. Sales proceeds increased four-fold, from *f* 1.1 billion in 1972, to over *f* 4.2 billion in 1982. The company had increased trading profits 2.2 times during the same period, but overall profitability had declined in the last three years (see Exhibits 3 through 5 for details). Income from technical fees related to agreements with foreign operations contributed a small but important (in profit terms) fraction of total revenue. The rest originated from sales of beer, spirits, wine, and soft drinks.

Beer accounted for around 80 percent of Heineken's total income (see Exhibit 6). In fact, beer had increased its share of the company's business throughout the 1970s in spite of heavy investments in product diversification. Domestic sales in hectoliters rose from around 0.3 million in 1951, to over 7 million in 30 years (see Exhibit 7). Beer sales outside the Netherlands represented about 70 percent of total volume, and turnover in the Western Hemisphere, which included Heineken's major foreign market, the United States, grew from 5 percent of sales in 1973, to 15 percent in 1983 (see Exhibits 8 and 9).

Investments in plants and other installations increased by about four times in the 1972–82 period. Asset turnover rate remained fairly constant, around 0.9, and the company had an average financial leverage (calculated on the basis of total debt to equity) of about 0.9.

Organization and Planning

After the Amstel merger in 1968, the company operated through three major divisions: Commercial, responsible for all Dutch sales; Technical, handling all production and technical assistance worldwide; and International, with line authority over exports, licenses, and financial participations. Each member of the Executive Board acquired direct operational responsibility for one division, and four regional groupings—Europe, Asia/Australia, Africa, and Western Hemisphere—were created at this time.[2]

During the 1970s, the corporate marketing, exports, and technical areas were given worldwide responsibility, but regional subgroups were established within each function. Simultaneously, four regional "coordinators" were given strategic and coordinating responsibility for their respective regions of the world and were placed under the direct supervision of one of the members of the board. The objective of this matrix structure was to balance the need for geographic focus and coordination with the requirement for close control of critical corporate functions. Exhibit 10 presents a simplified version of the company's organizational structure in 1983.

Following the regionalization of foreign activities and their increased autonomy, the need for systematic planning was strongly felt. Beginning in 1980, a "planning letter" was sent by the Executive Board to all major affiliates early in the year. The letter would outline major objectives for the corporation and for the respective affiliate for the near future. This would then form the basis for a detailed subsidiary five-year plan that would be discussed with the board, the regional coordinator, and other key corporate executives. Such meetings were held at least once yearly, but could be scheduled more frequently for certain critical activities.

Financial policy was highly centralized in Heineken. Retaining family control and avoiding falling "in the claws of the banks" were two important objectives. Headquarters would decide on how best to balance an affiliate's capital structure based on a number of criteria, the most critical of which was not to exceed an overall debt to equity ratio of 0.8–0.9 to 1. For this reason, affiliates were measured on a return on assets (ROA) basis, and cash flows were controlled centrally subject to legal and financial requirements. In this context, Dutch law was extremely generous in that profits earned abroad were not taxable in Holland when remitted as dividends; on the other hand, foreign losses were not deductible against Dutch income.

Human resource policy was also centrally determined. All major appointments at the affiliates were submitted to the board for approval by the director of Social Affairs with the concurrence of the appropriate regional coordinator and the local general manager. The technical function had traditionally been the most international at Heineken, since wherever the company was involved, and whether it participated in the equity or not, a Heineken brewmaster would be present. This had generated a cadre of expatriate technical personnel with significant international experience. Nontechnical functions tended to be staffed by nationals of each country, but Heineken's rapid international expansion in recent years

[2]For a more detailed discussion of the company's organization, see the case Heineken N.V.—Organizational Issues in this series.

EXHIBIT 3 Balance sheets, 1974–1982
(*f* million)

	1982	1981	1980	1979	1978	1977	1976	1975	1974
Assets									
Fixed assets									
Plants and Installations	2,174.0	2,113.5	2,088.1	1,776.9	1,571.8	1,397.0	1,154.3	1,071.3	901.9
Other Real Estate	73.5	61.5	61.8	58.8	57.7	57.4	51.2	55.7	48.6
Participations	67.6	69.0	60.3	60.1	56.6	59.8	56.9	59.6	57.3
Miscellaneous	89.1	78.6	76.2	69.6	77.0	74.9	61.7	73.0	69.3
	2,404.2	2,322.6	2,286.4	1,965.4	1,763.1	1,589.1	1,324.1	1,259.6	1,077.1
Current Assets									
Stocks	605.0	504.8	480.3	403.1	375.1	358.3	278.5	278.7	231.4
Accounts Receivable	343.7	325.9	286.2	277.0	261.8	227.6	179.6	167.7	177.3
Cash & Securities	372.0	199.0	97.1	90.6	74.1	95.4	83.0	38.8	39.1
	1,320.7	1,029.7	863.6	770.7	711.0	681.3	541.1	485.2	447.8
Total	**3,724.9**	**3,352.3**	**3,150.0**	**2,736.1**	**2,474.1**	**2,270.4**	**1,865.2**	**1,744.8**	**1,524.9**
Liabilities									
Group Funds									
Share Capital	361.2	361.2	361.3	289.0	289.0	231.2	231.2	177.8	177.8
General Reserve	673.7	572.4	497.8	557.7	465.1	459.2	382.7	392.1	350.4
Revaluation Reserve	691.4	650.6	544.8	429.3	361.9	222.8	192.6	152.5	124.2
Shareholders' Equity	1,726.3	1,584.2	1,403.9	1,276.0	1,116.0	913.2	806.5	722.4	652.4
Minority Interests	74.8	51.1	33.9	23.6	39.6	37.6	27.5	47.6	44.5
	1,801.1	1,635.3	1,437.8	1,299.6	1,155.6	950.8	834.0	770.0	696.9
Investment Equalization Account	101.9	98.4	90.8	48.8	27.1	14.5	8.4	5.5	4.6
Provision for Tax and Other	485.8	428.8	427.3	307.1	272.3	360.8	251.2	177.9	164.8
	587.7	527.2	518.1	355.9	299.4	375.3	259.6	183.4	169.4
Debt									
Long-Term Debt	341.8	326.3	330.9	227.5	239.1	214.5	202.9	201.6	205.7
Current Liabilities	994.3	863.5	863.2	853.1	779.9	729.8	568.7	589.8	452.9
	1,336.1	1,189.8	1,194.1	1,080.6	1,019.0	944.3	771.6	791.4	658.6
Total	**3,724.9**	**3,352.3**	**3,150.0**	**2,736.1**	**2,474.0**	**2,270.4**	**1,865.2**	**1,744.8**	**1,524.9**

Note: Figures from 1971 to 1978 are as of 30 September, and from 1979 onward are as of 31 December.
Source: Annual reports.

EXHIBIT 4 Income Statements, 1974–1982
(*ƒ* million)

	1982	1981	1980	1979	1978	1977	1976	1975	1974
Sales Proceeds	4,150.1	3,552.2	3,178.3	3,427.9	2,623.1	2,428.2	2,095.6	1,811.3	1,549.2
Income from Technical Fees	47.6	44.8	37.6	43.5	34.8	26.7	26.6	16.8	23.0
Miscellaneous Income	17.1	16.2	14.0	17.8	13.8	15.3	14.7	14.0	12.0
Turnover	**4,214.8**	**3,613.2**	**3,229.9**	**3,489.2**	**2,671.7**	**2,470.2**	**2,136.9**	**1,842.1**	**1,584.2**
Raw Materials	430.5	368.9	301.1	337.6	280.7	250.0	228.9	202.5	175.4
Packing Materials	533.1	487.6	423.0	430.5	316.9	298.2	228.2	195.8	138.3
Merchandise	163.2	153.0	160.7	171.0	118.9	104.0	92.1	106.2	92.0
Selling Expenses	332.9	301.2	269.8	265.4	232.0	212.0	190.6	361.0	283.3
Other Expenses	516.3	470.5	433.2	419.0	284.1	273.4	248.8		
Excise Duties	909.6	627.7	594.5	662.1	505.2	477.6	444.1	381.0	352.1
Salaries and Social Security	766.8	676.7	623.3	687.6	513.5	451.4	378.4	344.0	285.5
Depreciation	268.4	267.7	227.3	228.3	164.3	155.6	128.1	105.0	94.6
	3,920.8	3,353.3	3,032.9	3,201.5	2,415.6	2,222.2	1,939.2	1,695.5	1,421.2
Trading Profit	**294.0**	**259.9**	**197.0**	**287.7**	**256.1**	**248.0**	**197.7**	**146.6**	**163.0**
Interest Paid	60.3	69.5	71.9	52.4	39.1	39.6	33.6	37.4	24.3
Miscellaneous Revenues & Charges	26.8	12.7	8.5	8.4	5.6	4.6	2.2	4.1	2.4
Profit Before Tax	260.5	203.1	133.6	243.7	222.6	213.0	166.3	113.3	141.1
Taxation on Profit	108.9	82.2	53.9	104.0	105.0	106.9	84.9	55.3	65.9
Profit After Tax	**151.6**	**120.9**	**79.7**	**139.7**	**117.6**	**106.1**	**81.4**	**58.0**	**75.2**
Dividend from Participations	10.4	3.6	7.2	4.8	4.4	5.6	7.3	8.7	7.3
Group Profit	162.0	124.5	86.9	144.5	122.0	111.7	88.7	66.7	82.5
Minority Interests	8.8	4.1	-3.8	-0.8	-3.3	-2.2	3.4	3.9	-1.5
Net Profit	**153.2**	**120.4**	**83.1**	**143.7**	**118.7**	**109.5**	**92.1**	**70.6**	**81.0**
Memoranda									
Dividends Declared	50.6	50.6	50.6	50.9	40.5	32.4	32.4	24.9	24.9
Trading Profit as Percent of Turnover	7.0	7.2	6.1	8.6	9.6	10.0	9.3	8.0	10.3
Profit as Percent of Capital Employed	7.8	7.8	6.3	9.0	10.4	10.9	10.6	8.4	10.7
Net Profit as Percent of Equity	8.9	7.6	5.9	9.9	10.6	11.8	11.3	9.7	12.3
Dividend as Percent of Net Profit	33.0	42.0	60.9	35.4	34.1	29.5	35.1	35.3	30.7
Average Exchange Rate (*ƒ*/$)	2.67	2.50	1.99	2.01	2.16	2.45	2.87	2.73	2.70

Source: Annual reports.

EXHIBIT 5 Average Breakdown of Costs for Recent Years
(in percent of sales)

	Labor	Materials	Capital	Other	Total
Production	9.2	28.1	4.5	15.5	57.3
Marketing and Distribution	6.9	—	0.4	7.4	14.7
General and Administrative	2.8	—	—	0.6	3.4
Total Operations	18.9	28.1	4.9	23.5	75.4
Excise Duties					17.4
Interest Expense					0.7
Income Taxes					2.4
Net Profits					4.1
Total					100.0

Source: Corporate records.

had placed significant strain on the company's ability to provide sufficient human resources to meet its foreign operational requirements.

The Move into Beverages

Heineken was first involved in nonbeer beverages as early as 1939, with the acquisition of a 20 percent share participation in Hoppe, an established Dutch manufacturer of *jenever* (a grain-based spirit similar to gin but flavored with juniper berries). Nearly 30 years later, in 1967, a British company, Allied Breweries, entered the Dutch market by acquiring two local medium-sized breweries. Allied's move was viewed as a significant threat by the management of Heineken, as it had been active in the local food and drink trade for years and had established a foothold in the Dutch distribution network.

Heineken's immediate response was the acquisition of Amstel Brewery, an important milestone in the company's strategy. The threat of losing market dominance to Allied and the subsequent merger with Amstel removed any feelings of complacency that may have developed over the years as market leader. Between 1967 and 1970, Heineken resolved to make up for lost time in non-beer activities and proceeded to consolidate its operations on all fronts.[3]

[3]For a more detailed description of Heineken's nonbeer strategy and activities, see the case Distilled Trading International, Ltd., INSEAD, 1985.

Growth by Acquisition

In a rush of acquisitions dating to the early 1960s, Heineken obtained equity positions in a series of companies manufacturing and/or distributing soft drinks, wine and distilled products. Some of the rationale for these moves derived from a study made by McKinsey and Co. in 1969, which suggested that "spirits and wines represent a significant portion of the 'drink' market not yet fully exploited by Heineken," and that important opportunities for "synergism" existed between these sectors, particularly in export markets. By the end of 1973, Heineken's nonbeer product portfolio included a number of established brands in soft drinks (including 7Up and Pepsi Cola), *jenevers,* wine, and liqueurs for the Dutch market.

In 1972, an in-house team from the newly established corporate finance group carried out a detailed study of the spirits and wine market in the Netherlands. They concluded that branded products would gain in importance as home consumption increased over time (although some supermarket chains demanded "popular" staple products, particularly in the wine business), and that the Dutch market for distillates was comparatively small. Therefore, if Heineken wanted to continue a strategy of diversification into spirits, they would have to acquire some major brands and gain access to foreign markets, simultaneously.

The board's internal debate on how best to proceed in the distillates business—either a Dutch base with some sales

EXHIBIT 6 Turnover by Product Group, 1973–1982
(*ƒ* million and percent)

	1982	1981	1980	1978–1979	1977–1978	1976–1977	1975–1976	1974–1975	1973–1974
In *ƒ* Million									
Beer Sales	3,422.5	2,841.7	2,481.5	2,114.3	2,019.1	1,883.9	1,564.0	1,351.9	1,156.6
Soft Drinks	326.6	288.1	279.7	241.0	203.3	183.7	179.0	167.2	134.5
Spirits and Wine	300.1	317.6	308.6	336.0	282.0	264.2	154.3	205.9	179.9
Other Trading Income	100.8	104.7	108.6	134.6	118.7	96.4	88.9	86.3	78.2
Total	4,150.0	3,552.1	3,178.4	2,825.9	2,623.1	2,428.2	2,095.6	1,811.3	1,549.2
In Percent									
Beer Sales	82.5	80.0	78.0	74.8	77.0	77.6	74.6	74.6	74.7
Soft Drinks	7.9	8.1	8.8	8.5	7.7	7.6	8.5	9.2	8.7
Spirits and Wine	7.2	8.9	9.8	11.9	10.8	10.9	12.6	11.4	11.6
Other Trading Income	2.4	3.0	3.4	4.8	4.5	3.9	4.3	4.8	5.0
Total	100.0	100.0	100.0	100.0	100.0	100.0	100.0	100.0	100.0

Note: Financial years 1973/1974 to 1977/1978 are from 1 October to 30 September.
Financial year 1978/1979 was for 15 months, but figures have been adjusted on a calendar-year basis.
Financial years from 1980 correspond to calendar years.
Source: Annual reports.

EXHIBIT 7 Beer Sales of the Netherlands Breweries

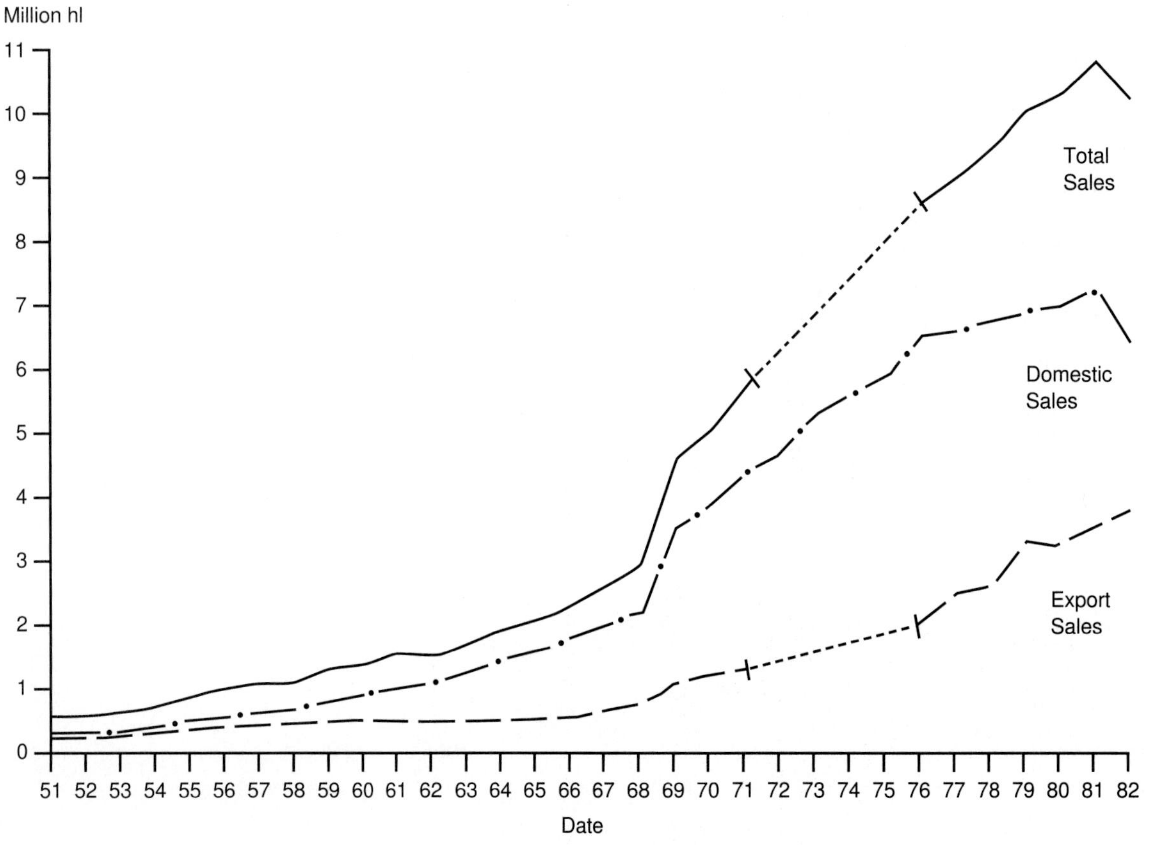

Note: 1 hl = 100 liters = 26.42 gallons = 0.611 barrels
Source: Annual reports.

abroad, or a major international position in spirits—remained unresolved after the company acquired a 30 percent interest in the English distiller Duncan, Gilbey and Matheson (DGM), early in 1975. DGM's relatively insignificant share in the distilled trade and few known brands led one Heineken Board member to describe the decision as follows: "The board decided we would be a beer company with beverages in a supporting role, specially as a protection against further incursions into our home market. As far as international spirits were concerned, we would continue to do it the 'creepy-crawly' way. DGM was an example of this; it was just fun to do!" By March 1979, however, under the terms of the original agreement, Heineken was forced to take over the outstanding shares of DGM and gained full control of the company. The stakes in the game had increased significantly.

The Bols Affair

N.V. Koninklijke Distilleerderijen Erven Lucas Bols produced a range of internationally known drinks, namely *jenevers* and liqueurs, had a dominant 20 percent share in the domestic spirits market and had established distribution outlets in many countries. Bols was also the Dutch import agent for several prestigious French wines, Courvoisier cognac and a few whisky brands. Furthermore, Bols was the only distillery in the Netherlands that was backward integrated and distilled its own grain alcohol.

Heineken management believed that a merger of the two companies would have a number of very obvious advantages, namely the combination of Bols' product range and brand image with Heineken's access to worldwide distribution, plus improved capacity utilization in distillates and lower capital requirements per unit of

EXHIBIT 8 Worldwide Beer Sales, 1973–1982

	1982	1981	1980	1978–1979	1977–1978	1976–1977	1975–1976	1974–1975	1973–1974
Total Sales (million hl)									
The Netherlands	6.4	7.3	7.0	6.9	6.7	6.6	6.6	5.9	5.6
Rest of Europe	7.8	7.2	7.1	7.1	6.6	6.1	6.2	5.5	5.5
Western Hemisphere	4.0	3.8	3.6	3.1	2.4	1.9	1.5	1.1	0.9
Africa	6.3	6.0	5.8	5.3	5.7	5.7	5.6	6.0	5.8
Australasia/Asia	2.4	2.5	2.4	2.2	2.0	1.8	1.6	1.7	1.6
	26.9	26.8	25.9	24.6	23.4	22.1	21.5	20.2	19.4
Percentage of Sales									
The Netherlands	24	27	27	28	29	30	31	29	29
Rest of Europe	29	27	27	29	28	28	29	27	28
Western Hemisphere	15	14	14	13	10	8	7	6	5
Africa	23	23	23	21	24	26	26	30	30
Australasia/Asia	9	9	9	9	9	8	7	8	8
	100	100	100	100	100	100	100	100	100

Note: Figures are total sales of beer brewed under Heineken supervision.
Source: Annual reports.

EXHIBIT 9 Heineken and Amstel Sales by Source

	1982		1975–1976		1970–1971	
	Total Sales (hl)	Percent exported from Holland	Total Sales (hl)	Percent Exported from Holland	Total Sales (hl)	Percent Exported from Holland
Europe Except the Netherlands	4,544,000	6.1	3,343,000	11.8	1,036,000	34.0
Western Hemisphere	3,220,000	90.2	1,312,000	88.7	641,000	86.1
Africa	499,000	37.1	414,000	71.3	393,000	42.0
Australasia/Asia	486,000	57.0	136,000	62.5	258,000	88.0
Total	8,749,000*	41.7	5,205,000	37.2	2,328,000	55.7

*Excluding duty-free.

Source: Annual reports and company records.

EXHIBIT 10 Organizational Structure, 1983

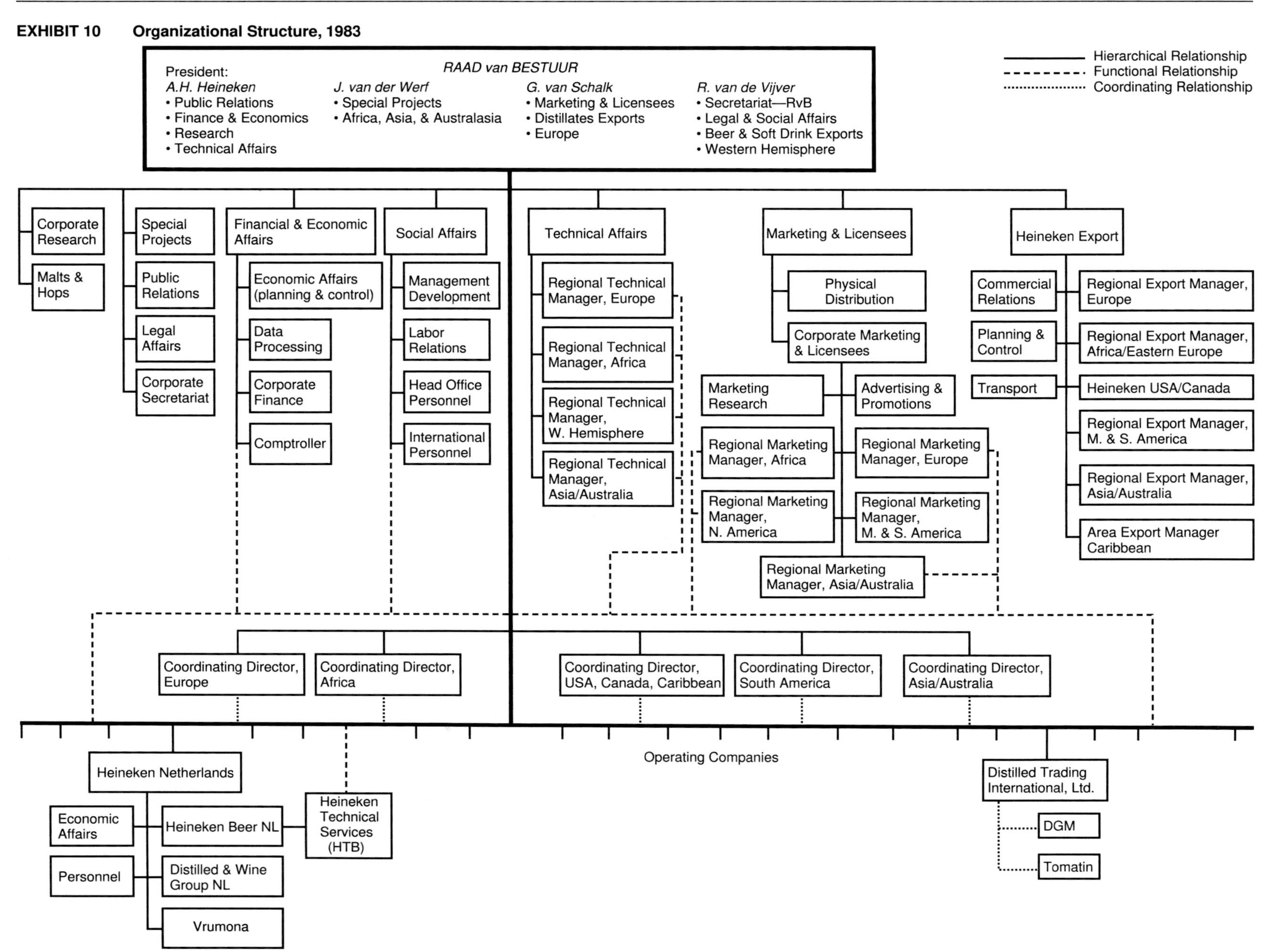

sales. In March 1976, the top executives of both companies discussed the possibility of a merger, but Bols' management did not appear enthusiastic. A month later, Heineken launched a hostile takeover bid for Bols, but failed as the target company undertook a protective share issue.

Several other companies were then examined for acquisition. Even the possibility of starting up a distillery and yeast factory outside the Netherlands was considered. Faced with repeated failures in finding an external solution, the Heineken Board turned to the construction of its own distillery in Zoetermeer. Construction began in 1977, and the integrated plant became fully operational by mid-1979 at a cost of *f* 60 million.

The 1979 St. Moritz Review

Early in 1979, following the DGM takeover, an overview was made regarding Heineken's position in distillates, mindful of capital limitations. At a meeting in the Swiss resort town of St. Moritz in the winter of 1979, Heineken's board adopted a company policy with regard to distillates. Some excerpts of that document are as follows:

> Heineken will not be interested in large takeovers of distilled companies because of financial restrictions. This policy, however, would not apply to companies producing whisky and cognac. The importance and authenticity of these spirits is such that it would provide Heineken with the independence and presence it seeks in the spirits trade.
>
> The U.K. being the center of the spirits trade, Heineken's distilled products operation should ultimately relocate to that country . . . An active development program should be started to create an "own" brand franchise with high margins . . . Distillates companies within the Heineken group should be autonomous in canvassing markets but should be assisted by "signals" from the beer people. Distillates companies within the group should . . . seek out small local markets where Heineken is present and export there.
>
> An Executive Board member should be appointed to supervise the distillates operations.

Several months later, two possibilities for entering the whisky business came up: Bell's and Tomatin. Bell's, one of the top-selling brands in the business, was judged to be too expensive (over *f* 100 million for a minority share). Instead, Heineken acquired 20 percent of Tomatin, a blender and exporter of bulk whisky without any major international brands for £1.55 million (about *f* 8 million). By the end of 1982, after two bad years of significant downturns in the spirit markets, the company was still reassessing its position in distillates.

The Major European Beer Markets

As evident from the company's historical chronology, Heineken's foreign involvement through the late 1960s was based essentially on the Far East, Africa, and the United States, with limited commitment to European markets other than through exports. Elsewhere the company held small shares and/or technical assistance agreements, with or without licensing, in a number of independent companies. Thus, the volume of beer brewed under Heineken supervision amounted to nearly as much as that brewed in Heineken-owned facilities. This prompted an executive to comment that "Heineken has never been an empire; it is more like a commonwealth."

The integration of Amstel into the Heineken group brought about a reassessment of this "low profile" approach to foreign markets. Since Amstel had been more actively involved in foreign activities under its own name, many of the key executives in the newly integrated company thus developed a more aggressive attitude toward foreign markets and were willing to argue forcefully for taking bigger risks with the promise of larger rewards. Also the Dutch beer market had stabilized since the relatively rapid growth in the immediate postwar period. With a market share of over 50 percent of its home market and little prospects for domestic sales growth, the joint Heineken-Amstel organization had the motivation and the resources to consider significant expansion of its European activities.

The next few years saw the company responding to market or investment opportunities that came into Heineken's field of vision from a multitude of sources. This is perhaps best illustrated by the history of some of the various countries where Heineken took positions during this period.

Belgium. After operating a local small brewery since 1927, urban renewal threatened to force Brasserie Leopold to move its facilities elsewhere. Heineken, facing extensive relocation costs and the fact that Leopold had sales of only 200,000 hl (5 percent of the Belgian market), sold the brewery to its major Belgian competitor, Stella Artois.

United Kingdom. Traditionally, the U.K. beer market was a difficult one to enter. The close relationship between the brewers and the pubs, where nearly 90 percent of beer consumption took place, prevented outside brewers from making inroads into this market. Only the shop (take-home) trade was accessible without a connection with a local brewer. Heineken had been exporting beer to independent bottlers in the U.K. since the 1920s, but the volume had rarely exceeded 30,000 hl per year.

In the late 1950s, the lager market in Britain was showing signs of increasing growth at the expense of traditional British ale. Whitbread, one of the "big six" British brewers, approached Heineken to discuss the possibility of setting up a joint venture that would first import Heineken into the country and eventually build a lager brewing facility for the local market. An agreement was reached by which tankers of specially brewed Heineken (see below) were imported into Britain for distribution by Whitbread and other allied bottlers. By 1969 the other bottlers were no longer involved and a technical contract and licensing agreement was concluded with Whitbread to produce Heineken locally. In 10 years, Heineken beer became a major product in Whitbread's portfolio (over 2 million hl per annum) and profits.

Heineken's market position in the U.K. was in many ways an anomaly. The Heineken formula was highly prized by the company, which had consistently resisted attempts to alter the beer in order to suit a particular market. The tax system and customer palate in the U.K., however, demanded a change of policy. For the first time Heineken beer was brewed with a lower alcohol content than elsewhere in the world. Furthermore, the brand was positioned in the middle of the lager range, a marked contrast to other markets where it traditionally sold as a premium beer. Throughout Heineken, it was said, "the British exception confirms the rule."

France. Other than exporting limited amounts of beer to France since 1875, Heineken's involvement in that market had been relatively minor. Imported by Moët-Hennessy and priced and sold as premium beer, Heineken's volume never exceeded 100,000 hl per year. In 1972, Heineken's involvement in the French market entered a new phase. Four small regional French breweries had consolidated their operations by forming Alsacienne de Brasserie (Albra), which controlled about 6 percent of the French market. A proposal to acquire Albra revived Heineken's interest in the French market.

Two other options were examined. Kronenbourg, the largest brewery in France, was discarded as a potential partner on the basis that cooperation could be overshadowed by competition. Union de Brasseries, the second largest, had rather fragmented operations and did not appear to suit Heineken's objectives. Heineken's Finance Department was not overly enthusiastic about the Albra proposal on the grounds that the operation seemed to be too small. Nonetheless, in the summer of 1972, Heineken's board made a public offer for a controlling interest in Albra. By November, 76 percent of Albra's shares were in Heineken's hands. Over the next few years, the remaining minority shares were taken over and, in March 1981, Heineken France, a 100 percent-owned subsidiary was created.

Since the Albra acquisition, Heineken's marketing staff had been concerned about their relatively low market share in France. Losses had been accumulating and the general view in Amsterdam was that this could not be allowed to continue. The option to produce Heineken locally came under study in 1977, and it presented an opportunity to possibly reposition the brand as in the British case and increase volume considerably from 130,000 hl at the time. A forecast of 3–4 million hl was made provided Heineken was sold as a "de luxe" (i.e., standard) brand with a wider popular appeal. This option was rejected after much discussion, and a policy decision was made that the Heineken brand should not be used to compete with lower priced brands to gain volume.

Also in 1978, as part of its general review of the French market, Heineken reconsidered Union de Brasseries (UdB) as a vehicle for expansion. UdB's product range, a market share of nearly 30 percent and its distribution network were all attractive. But the French brewer's condition was not all that sound, with losses running at about FF 30–50 million per year. Most of its five breweries were old, to the point that two would have to be closed down (a difficult proposition for a Dutch company in France), and preliminary estimates showed a need for an investment of around *f* 550 million over five years to pull the company out of the red. After lengthy deliberations, Heineken decided not to bid for UdB (a separate proposal was made to use their distribution system), and to concentrate on improving its position with Albra's facilities. By 1982, Heineken France was operating profitably for the first time.

Italy. Heineken first entered the Italian market in 1960, when the second largest brewer in the country approached the company for assistance. Heineken, which had no significant presence in the Italian market, offered Dreher a technical assistance contract that included a Heineken brewmaster to work in Italy, and acquired a 7 percent share and a seat on Dreher's board.

In August 1974, Dreher's owners wanted out of the business altogether. The Dreher group was worth around *f* 40 million and with 7 breweries controlled nearly 20 percent of the Italian market. The offer interested Heineken, but the investment and risk were considered too large. They contacted Whitbread, Heineken's British licensee, and eventually both companies acquired the Dreher operation on a 50/50 basis. Whitbread agreed to assume all financial and administrative functions in Dreher, since Heineken was short of staff at the time. By May 1976, Heineken bottled beer was being produced locally and marketed together with the Dreher brand.

Management problems and market difficulties, however, resulted in growing losses for the Italian company. Local management was hired, the organization was trimmed, marketing revamped and discounts cut, all of which helped to reduce losses partially, even though in the process Dreher lost around 8 percent in market share. In 1979, the French BSN group acquired 30 percent of Wührer, the third largest brewery in Italy with a market share of about 10 percent, bringing increased competition to the market. The next year, Whitbread, alarmed by the situation, withdrew completely from Dreher, selling its share to Heineken, which assumed total control of the company. Heineken overhauled the Italian company's financial strategy and banking arrangements and closed two unprofitable breweries. By 1982, Dreher's domestic market share was back up to 17 percent and the operation was again profitable.[4]

Norway. Heineken started brewing locally under license in 1975, following a period of limited imports. The beer was brewed by Arendals Bryggeri A/S, which was also the local Coca Cola bottler. Sales had grown satisfactorily and production reached 80,000 hl per year by 1980. However, sales had declined perceptibly since then causing headquarters marketing staff to reassess the wisdom of their position in the Norwegian market.

Sweden. Exports to Sweden had been limited until the mid 1970s when Heineken licensed a local brewer, Falken Bryggeri AB. Sales of locally produced Heineken reached 100,000 hl per year, but stiff competition prevented the brand from increasing market share. In 1979, another major Swedish brewer, which produced Carlsberg under license, bought the Falken Brewery and assumed full control. Heineken was faced with the decision of whether to remain in the market in cooperation with a brewer that also carried a major competing international brand or pull out. The European marketing regional manager felt that a termination of the licensing agreement would sacrifice their hard-earned market position. The executive board overruled him and terminated the agreement with Falken, thus resuming the importation of beer into Sweden.

The Swedish market was considered by many to be the most complicated in Europe. The government, in a drive to curb alcohol consumption, had decreed a complex system of beer categories by alcohol content and a fragmented distribution and import policy. In 1982, Heineken granted an Amstel license to another Swedish brewer, Wärby Bryggeri in Stockholm. Wärby was also to take over the distribution of the Heineken brand, but being a cooperative brewer, it has access only to cooperative outlets. This factor limited Heineken's market coverage and necessitated the setting up of a parallel distribution system. The different classes of beer, the fragmentation of outlets and multiple packaging needs resulted in high production costs in Holland and the loss of one-way bottles. Although Amstel sales surpassed Heineken's in 1982, volumes were insignificant. One senior marketing executive in Amsterdam stated: "The only possibility to survive is to go local. We need a partner in Sweden."

Greece. In 1963, Amstel Brewery began negotiations to participate in a new brewery in Greece, Athenian Brewery, with a 25 percent share in partnership with local interests. Production started in 1965 in Athens with a capacity of 50,000 hl, and Athenian joined the Heineken family after the 1968 merger. A second brewery was built in Thessalonika in 1974, after which market share rose rapidly to approximately 45 percent of the Greek market. Following the death of Athenian's founder in 1976, Heineken proceeded to expand its ownership position through various capital increases and complex negotiations, until it acquired complete control in 1979.

The rapid growth of the Greek beer market attracted significant competition in the late 1970s. Two local companies, Fix and Henninger (a German joint venture), were joined by Carlsberg (a United Breweries licensee) and Löwenbräu. Heineken responded by licensing its affiliate to produce Heineken locally in 1981, and by major increases in its advertising and promotion budgets. Both policies were aimed to maintain its dominant position in this growing market. After incurring severe losses during the first 18 months of operations, Carlsberg approached Heineken in late 1982 with an offer to sell its local brewery to Athenian.

[4]In 1981, to the consternation of its Italian management, Heineken licensed the Amstel brand to their main competitor in Italy, the Peroni group, the largest brewery in the country with about 25 percent of the market.

Ireland. Introduced to the Irish market by Whitbread, Heineken licensed Ireland's third largest brewery, J.J. Murphy's and Co. Ltd, in 1978. Murphy's had been looking for a lager brand to enter a market dominated by stout, where Guinness held a formidable 90 percent share. Lager sales were expanding rapidly and the Heineken brand did well during its first three years, reaching 9 percent of the lager segment, or 51,000 hl by 1981. Murphy's, however, was encountering severe financial difficulties and made repeated pleas to Heineken for financial help. In July 1982, Murphy's went into receivership, and Heineken's board was faced with the difficult decision of whether to acquire the failing company's assets or abandon the Irish market.

Germany. The German beer market was characterized by its "purity law," establishing production standards that aimed to protect German barley growers. The market was also very fragmented (the four largest brands held less than 15 percent of the total market) and many locally entrenched brewers "produced and sold beer around the church steeple." German beer was of high quality, and Heineken had for years debated how it could enter this large but difficult market where there were no national brands.

Spain. Heineken had made an ill-fated attempt to enter the Spanish market in the 1960s by setting up a joint venture with United Africa Co. in Burgos. After that venture failed, Heineken continued to export small quantities (8–10,000 hl per year) to Spain, but faced problems due to the high seasonality of sales (over 70 percent in the summer months), low stock rotation, and high luxury taxes on imported beer. The changing Spanish environment after 1975 and lower import duties permitted Heineken to drop its price premium to 67 percent above local competition by 1982. Volume rose to 25,000 hl, and a second distributorship was established to sell keg beer with estimated 1983 volume of an additional 25,000 hl. Corporate marketing staff advocated a fresh look at the Spanish market with the objective of establishing a major position through local production in the near future.

An Emerging Beer Strategy for Europe

As these situations illustrate, the company's objective to establish Heineken as a premium brand in all major European markets, suffered from a lack of clear guidelines as to which markets should be given priority and what levels of commitment and risk were necessary or tolerable. The rather opportunistic approach taken frequently caused differences of opinion between the company's top management and its marketing, finance, or production executives. A good example of this problem was the 1978 proposal to acquire Union de Brasseries in France.

The UdB acquisition would have given Heineken a major share of the French market, but at significant cost and risks. UdB was by no means an easy situation to handle, but lack of specific corporate guidelines prevented Heineken from making a broad evaluation of the situation, and the acquisition was seen only in light of its own value. As one senior staff member put it, "Heineken always tries to get a front row seat for 10 cents. The UdB acquisition would have required investments in excess of *f* 500 million over five years. We settled instead for the third balcony." The internal debate on UdB and on the correct positioning for Heineken in the French market served as a catalyst, however, and prompted the executive board to propose a set of criteria in regards to marketing of Heineken beer with worldwide implications.

The 1979 Review

Based on a study prepared at the request of the board by the corporate marketing department in September 1979, corporate strategy was discussed extensively, particularly in the European context. It was decided that a number of countries—the Netherlands, France, Italy, Greece, and the United States (because of its impact on European operations)—would be designated as "primary markets" where the company would have "greater aspirations."[5] Since Europe in general was of primary interest, a number of "secondary priority" markets—Belgium, Britain, Ireland, Germany, and Spain—were also identified. Smaller markets in Scandinavia, Switzerland, Portugal, and Eastern Europe were considered less critical.

The objectives of the company in primary markets were stated as follows:

- To obtain in each country a substantial long-term profitable position in the beer market;
- To assure an optimal exploitation of the Heineken brand, always in conjunction with its worldwide policy as a premium product; and
- To aim for a positive contribution to corporate results by local brands and Amstel.

[5]Although this document did not deal with them, Indonesia, Singapore, and Malaysia were also considered by the company to be primary markets.

In addition, objectives for each country were also defined. For example, Athenian Brewery was to maintain its current market position in Greece while improving financial results, and investigate the possibility of filling gaps in the "high class" beer niche with other beers such as a special (export), a "light," and Heineken. For Ireland, the objective was to reach 18 percent of the lager market without getting financially involved for the time being. For Spain, the short-term objective was to continue to expand turnover by way of exports and to explore the start of local production in the long term.

The staff argued that in order to meet increasing market segmentation and product differentiation in world markets, Heineken was compelled to formulate logical and consistent product and brand policies. New markets could be entered by exporting or by setting up local production, either through licensing or by acquisition. Whenever local production was done through a licensee, the staff recommended that Heineken also assume a small financial participation. The criteria for selecting which entry strategy to use would depend on the following factors:

- Is the country designated a primary market?;
- Brands and type of beer consumed;
- Import restrictions;
- Availability of suitable prospective partner;
- Local market circumstances;
- Investment required;
- Legal restrictions on ownership;
- Price measures and controls;
- Restrictions on royalties;
- Transfer problems for dividends/cash flows; and
- Risk of nationalization.

The document also outlined a series of policy guidelines. Fully-owned operating companies should be set up only in primary markets due to the limitation of available funds. Outside these areas, an entry by investment would have to be justified by expected or actual ROA, protecting existing volume, or the need to retain a licensing agreement. Furthermore, partnerships with "like-minded," ambitious international breweries should be avoided; cooperation with weak partners nearly always produced bad results. Local production in any given market should go hand-in-hand with technical assistance agreements, which must extend to all the brands produced by the local partner. Local beers should be positioned so as to not affect corporate brands, and outlets where Heineken or Amstel beer was sold must have a certain image to appeal to the international consumer. Finally, it was suggested that all subsequent policies at lower levels of management should derive from the global policy of the corporation, that operating policies in the commercial and R&D area should be made more specific, and that executives should be encouraged to "stick their necks out and say, for example, by 1985 we want to be there."

Licensing Policy

Throughout the years, Heineken had gained extensive experience in licensing agreements, but rarely had an in-depth evaluation of the relative merits of licensing as an entry vehicle into new markets been done. One member of the board described the tenor of their reflection as follows: "When we license, is it because licensing is good, or is it because we lack the necessary funds to participate financially? In other words, does the company look at these two operations separately or in conjunction with one another?"

The board saw a number of advantages in licensing, such as a smaller financial commitment, lower costs for higher volume, speed in getting on stream, and flexibility as its involvement could be increased as the market became better understood. Equally, a potential licensee stood to gain from having a "prestige brand to piggyback" on its existing production and distribution systems, getting access to the technological knowhow of Heineken, and tapping an additional profit source.

But there were also risks in licensing. Overflow of technical knowhow could lead to local brands gaining quality parity with the Heineken brand, although this risk could partly be diminished by putting a Heineken brewmaster on the spot. Issues of "brand positioning" between Heineken and local brands could also be a possible source of conflict with the licensee. And there was a certain vulnerability vis-à-vis local government regulations in terms of royalties, prices, packaging quality, and re-exports to neighboring markets. As a result, the board agreed that the Heineken brand, being the flagship of the company, would be licensed with greater care, and that market penetration strategies would be confined to Amstel. In this respect, the board wanted to further differentiate the image of the two corporate brands.

The New European Beer Strategy

In November 1981, a study prepared by a multidisciplinary team of corporate executives laid the foundation for what became known as the European Beer Strategy. This study made a critical analysis of the position of the Heineken and Amstel brands on the European scene and proceeded to make a series of recommendations. While brand pricing, positioning, and other details would be looked upon on a country by country basis, they should not deviate from basic Heineken principles of price differentiation, quality, and image. The major conclusions of the study were:

1. A viable long-term presence in the European beer market would require bulk production of beer due to factors such as economies of scale and price pressures. Also, in order to maintain its position with the trade and to absorb overheads, the company should carry small but profitable market segments.
2. The expansion capacity of the company must be quantified. This would depend on the financial norms for the group, the possibility of disposing of unprofitable and strategically unimportant investments, and the ownership position required in existing subsidiaries.
3. Priorities must be set, taking into account these factors, to seek optimal return on operations in primary markets. Since a large proportion of the European market must be approached through licensing arrangements, with or without participation, a policy should be established on potential partners in different markets.
4. Export activities should also be stepped up as an efficient means of gaining initial presence in a market.
5. The Heineken brand should be consistently priced 10–20 percent above local standard beer. The experience of downgrading Heineken in some markets shows a contribution loss not compensated by an increase of turnover.
6. Heineken subsidiaries should increase their efforts, where applicable, to develop standard local brands.

The study also identified a number of key environmental trends that would influence future strategic choices:

- Wine demand was increasing in beer markets, and, conversely, premium beer was becoming more popular in predominantly wine areas such as southern Europe.
- The bulk beer segment was stagnating due mainly to overcapacity, brand proliferation, price competition, and lower profits.
- Market concentration was on the rise, especially among European companies and brands, following the American experience.
- An increasing trend toward price and product differentiation created contradictory demands for economies of scale and segment differentiation.
- "Everyone was entering everyone else's markets," and their aim seemed to be overall European brand leadership.
- Distribution was the key to growth and profits.

To "capture and control" distribution became of paramount importance. Local brewers, sensing this, were protecting themselves by forward integration, buying wholesalers. High volume outlets provided a brewer with an important competitive advantage, namely for the sales of bulk or draft beer. Furthermore, the trend toward an increasing number of large hypermarkets would affect a brewery's marketing and promotion approaches as well as the price structures of premium beers.

In view of these factors, the goals of the European Beer Strategy was to obtain in each major market "at least 3rd place in market share, not less than 25 percent of the leader's share, and a minimum of 10 percent of the market. This would serve as the ground rule in evaluating the company's presence in each market, whether through exports, licensing, or direct participation." Exhibits 11 and 12 present an analysis of Heineken's current position in selected markets and a list of its major competitors in Europe. Exhibit 13 shows 1981 production for the world's largest beer companies.

Options and Implications

Heineken's success in exporting beer to the United States and becoming the highest selling imported beer in that country, and to other markets in Africa and the Americas, was not considered to be a valid model for Europe. The U.S. market was such that local production was believed to ruin a foreign brand's image, as was demonstrated by Löwenbräu and Tuborg. Elsewhere, conditions differed greatly from country to country, but the share of local production to total sales of Heineken and Amstel brands was generally on the rise (see Exhibit 9). Therefore, the European Beer Strategy was, as its name implied, almost exclusively related to European markets.

Increasing brand proliferation among breweries had diminished market differentiation between imports and local production. In some countries, this factor put imported premium beer (which was more costly) at a disadvantage, thus implying that continued profitability from exports was in doubt. Other factors mitigating against an export based strategy were environmental restrictions, such as the mandatory use of returnable bottles, import tariffs and custom duties protecting local brewers, and the fact that

EXHIBIT 11 **Consumption and Market Share in Selected Markets, 1982**

	Beer Consumption (thousand hl)	Population (million)	Per capita Consumption (liters)	Number of Breweries	Heineken company*: Heineken (thousand hl)	Heineken company*: Other Brands (thousand hl)	Heineken company*: Total Share (%)
Europe							
Germany	91,586	61.6	148.6	1,292	—	—	—
United Kingdom	61,780	56.1	110.3	138	2,084	—	3.4
France	24,302	54.2	44.8	63	402	1,332	7.1
Spain	21,519	37.9	56.7	39	22	4	0.1
Belgium/Luxemb.	13,213	10.2	129.3	134	38	1	0.3
Netherlands	11,728	14.3	82.0	22	4,935	1,469	54.6
Italy	11,624	56.6	20.5	30	352	1,744	18
Switzerland	4,605	6.5	71.2	40	11	6	0.4
Sweden	4,158	8.3	49.9	17	35	90	3
Ireland	3,761	3.5	108.0	5	49	114	4.3
Portugal	3,737	10.0	37.4	4	—	—	—
Greece	2,870	9.8	29.3	8	56	1,200	43.8
Norway	1,926	4.1	46.8	17	72	—	3.7
Americas							
United States	234,176	232.1	100.9	82	2,495	42	1.1
Brazil	29,500†	126.8	23.3	32	—	—	—
Mexico	27,583†	74.0	37.2	7	—	—	—
Canada	23,667†	24.6	96.2	42	65	60	0.5
Venezuela	12,000†	14.7	81.6	5	0.7	—	—
Argentina	2,237†	28.4	7.9	9	0.8	—	—
Asia							
Japan	47,335†	118.4	40.0	27	28	—	—
Australia	19,682†	15.2	127.7	16	7	—	—
Philippines	7,700†	48.4	15.9	4	0.3	—	—
S. Korea	5,988†	38.1	15.7	2	45	—	0.8
Taiwan	2,825†	17.6	16.1	1	—	—	—
Singapore/Malaysia	1,950†	15.8	12.3	4	0.5	700	35.9
Indonesia	800†	146.9	0.5	5	6	447	56.6
Africa							
S. Africa	12,000†	30.1	39.9	5	0.2	299	2.5
Nigeria	10.380†	77.1	13.5	25	—	2,322	22.4
Egypt	425	42.2	1.0	2	—	—	—

*Includes under "other brands" beer brewed under the supervision of Heineken.

† Production only.

Source: Company records.

EXHIBIT 12 Major European Competitors

1. Norway–Sweden–Finland
In each of these markets, one or two groups controlled over 60 percent of local consumption. None, however, were of European scale or potential.

2. Denmark
United Breweries Ltd. had a strong home market. They appeared to prefer licensing agreements except when defending existing subsidiaries. Otherwise, they did not seem inclined to take many risks or important participations, and their financial capacity was limited.

3. Ireland
Guinness was strong but its product had limited appeal and was not a potential European competitor.

4. United Kingdom
Five groups controlled over 70 percent of the market. Some were looking to Europe for expansion but their activities to date were limited.

5. Germany
Highly fragmented market with three largest groups amounting to less than 20 percent of the local market. No German brewer had shown any intentions of launching a European strategy.

6. France
BSN (Kronenbourg) and UdB dominated the market with over 70 percent. BSN had a clear international ambition that paralleled Heineken's. Given their late start, they were following a three-stage strategy: succeed in Europe, follow with a "conquest of the New World" in the United States, and later expand overseas to "the four corners of the world." They had started by licensing third parties (e.g., in the U.K.) and by direct participations in Belgium, Spain, and Italy. BSN was strong financially and had an active acquisition program under way in food products.

BSN was probably Heineken's most dangerous competitor on a European scale. How serious a threat they were in the near future would depend on what opportunities they got to buy market share, the relative investment priorities between food and beverages, and their experience in the United States.

7. Belgium
Stella and Pied Boeuf shared nearly 60 percent of their home market. Their growth was limited to about 300 km from Leuven/Liege, and they presented no major threat in Europe. Stella had a few licensing arrangements in Africa and South America.

8. Portugal
Two state-owned groups controlled the market but should not be a factor elsewhere.

9. Spain
Largest five companies shared about 65 percent of the local market. None were potential European competitors.

10. Switzerland
Two groups dominated the market but were limited by their internal cartel rules.

Not competitive outside their home market.

11. Austria
Difficult to enter because of strict cartel rules, but not a factor outside Austria.

12. Italy
The five largest groups had 65–70 percent market share. Only Peroni was large enough to compete at the European level but it had not shown any indication to do so.

13. Greece
Both major groups with 75 percent of the market were related to foreign companies.

14. United States
Anheuser Busch had begun to enter Europe by licensing third parties. Their choice has always been made on the basis of market leadership: BSN in France, Prypp in Sweden, Oëtker in Germany. Only if they were to shift to a strategy of direct participation would they become a credible threat. Philip Morris, in the meantime, was building up its relationship with Löwenbräu. They had good in-house European marketing know-how through their cigarette business.

Source: Casewriter estimates.

access to distribution channels was becoming increasingly dependent on having a high-volume "carrier" brand, usually one belonging to a major local producer.

Licensing made a carrier brand available and provided access to local distribution outlets. It allowed Heineken to concentrate on its corporate brands, as opposed to its own subsidiaries where the carrier brand was "owned" and required time and investment. Furthermore, licensing was less costly in terms of the consequences of a wrong choice of third party carrier, as a "pull out" option always existed. The study recommended that licensees should get more profit from the Heineken brand than from their own. To compensate for its additional promotion and manufacturing costs, it was therefore necessary for Heineken to be priced at least 10–15 percent above the standard local beer.

In order to implement the European Beer Strategy exclusively with fully owned subsidiaries, on the basis of an investment of D*f* 175 per hectoliter, D*f* 3,500

EXHIBIT 13 World's Largest Beer Companies

Company	1981 Production (million hl)	Percent
Anheuser Busch (U.S.)	64	24.4
Miller (U.S.)	47	17.9
Kirin (Japan)	29	11.1
Heineken (Netherlands)	27	10.3
B.S.N. (France)	18	6.9
United Breweries (Denmark)	18*	6.9
Pabst (U.S.)	16	6.1
Allied Breweries (U.K.)	14	5.3
Bass Ltd. (U.K.)	14	5.3
Artois (Belgium)	8	3.1
Dub Schultheiss (Germany)	7	2.7
Total, 11 largest breweries	262	100

*Estimated
Source: Drexel Burnham Lambert, Inc.

million would be required, a sum not within Heineken's present financial capabilities. Whatever cash flows might be made available for capital expenditures of this sort could be increased further by lowering current financial ratios, disposing of activities no longer fitting the overall strategy, or reducing some Heineken 100-percent participations to a lower percentage (but not below 60 percent).

The 1983 Planning Letter

The executive board in its 1983 Planning Letter set out a series of objectives that should guide future strategic choices. The board once more asserted that Heineken should be "an international beverage company with a strong accent on beer." Emphasis should be placed on improving investments already made in Europe and on the United States, although this should not exclude looking at other opportunities that might arise. ROA should be improved with an overall corporate objective of 10 percent. Guidelines were established whereby ROA should be 25 percent on new investments, 15 percent on expansion of existing operations, and 10 percent on replacement. The board also placed greater emphasis on the need to be a good corporate citizen everywhere, to safeguard the quality and reliability of the company's products, and to let all employees know what their contribution should be to the achievement of these objectives.

INSEAD

Case 3–2

Heineken N.V.—Organizational Issues

Concomitant with the rapid expansion of Heineken's international activities, a number of organizational issues arose in the early 1980s that centered on what should be the proper division of responsibilities between headquarters staff, functional directors, and the management of the operating companies. The increasing complexity and diversity of national subsidiaries and licensees, together with the different stakes held by Heineken in each local company, made any universal approach to managing these relationships difficult if not unworkable.

It was increasingly obvious that operating companies should be as autonomous and self-reliant as possible in order to exploit to the best of their ability all domestic market opportunities. Since market conditions, competition, and political factors varied enormously among the more than 40 countries where Heineken operated, it was widely accepted that no central organization could deal effectively with this diversity. Nonetheless, Heineken's top management felt that there were a number of issues that must be either directed or closely controlled from Amsterdam. For example, it was argued that major deviations from corporate functional policies across countries could entail considerable difficulties for the company's desire to achieve a uniform worldwide corporate image, as well as for its effectiveness. Thus, the essence of the argument was how best to reconcile these two divergent requirements and foster a willing acceptance by managers, both in the operating companies and at head office, that none could be wholly independent of the other.

Organizational Evolution

During the past 20 years, Heineken had lived through a series of structural reorganizations typical of any large company which was both growing rapidly and diversifying its activities on several fronts. In the early 1960s, the company was managed by a three-man executive board

This case was written by Professor José de la Torre as a basis for class discussion. The generous contribution of many Heineken executives is gratefully acknowledged, but the author retains all responsibility for any errors or misinterpretation of facts.

(*Raad van Bestuur*) which reported to a larger Supervisory Council composed mainly of external directors. Below the board, in addition to some limited corporate functions, the company was organized into two major groups: Heineken Netherlands was responsible for exports, finance, production and technology, personnel, and commercial affairs; whereas Heineken International handled foreign participations, licensing agreements, and international finance. The three managing directors, while having direct supervisory responsibility for different aspects of the business, were jointly accountable for the whole.

After the Amstel merger in 1968, the company was reorganized into three major divisions: Commercial, responsible for all Dutch sales; Technical, handling all production and technical assistance worldwide; and International, with line authority over exports, licenses, and participations. Given that each member of the board had direct operational responsibility for one division, many minor decisions were constantly pushed up to them for resolution. Faced with this problem, the company gradually returned to a collegial board management and to a geographic structure whereby all domestic operations—production and sales of beer, soft drinks and distilled products—were grouped in one division, and the International Division retained control over foreign licensing and participations as well as exports from Holland. Four regional groups—Europe, Asia/Australia, Africa, and Western Hemisphere—were created at this time.

Throughout the 1970s, the company rebalanced its structure in a number of small but meaningful ways. A critical step was to bring the control of exports and foreign participations back to a central corporatewide level. The corporate marketing, exports, and technical areas were given worldwide responsibility, and regional subgroups were established within each function. Simultaneously, four overall "regional coordinators" were given strategic and coordinating responsibility for their respective regions of the world (later expanded to five) and were placed under the direct supervision of one of the members of the board. In this fashion, whenever a decision had to be taken which concerned a specific country or region, the regional coordinators could call on their counterparts within the corporate functional staff. The objective of this matrix structure was to balance the need for geographic focus and coordination with the requirement for close control of critical corporate functions. Finally, beginning in 1976, greater autonomy was given to the operating units both in the Netherlands and abroad. Exhibit 1 presents a simplified version of the company's organizational structure in 1983.

Heineken as a Shareholder

Heineken expected to exercise a primary influence on any strategic decisions by its subsidiaries and be entitled to an adequate return on its invested capital. Hence, it was to have the right to full information regarding the local company's financial matters and business conduct. The executive board of Heineken N.V., assisted by corporate staff from its Amsterdam head office, would handle subjects such as investment proposals, plans for the disposition of retained earnings, appraisals of operating company's performance, and key executive appointments. A list of specific points for which agreement from headquarters must be sought or which would be dealt with by the parent company included:

- Major changes in organizational structure;
- Approval of operational plans and major investments;
- Acquisition, granting, renewal, or relinquishment of licenses;
- Joint operations and/or participation agreements with third parties;
- International supply contracts;
- Use of corporate brands, trademarks, and patents;
- Setting standards for and monitoring the quality of corporate products;
- Changes in product quality outside general specifications;
- Activities that could affect other companies in which Heineken had an interest;
- Deviations from corporate functional policies;
- Development of employees for and actual appointment to key positions;
- Terms of service of expatriates;
- Remuneration, bonuses and terms of service for, and the development and career planning of, managers in the higher echelons; and
- Appraising operating company results and assessing their future broad plans and prospects.

Heineken as a Service Company

A second major role of Heineken N.V. was to provide assistance and services which operating companies might require in order to carry out their activities within their specific territories. In addition to monitoring and control functions implied in the various categories listed above, some of which included certain service components (e.g., maintenance of quality standards), Heineken viewed its service role to include the following areas:

- The management of each operating company was responsible for achieving both short- and long-term

EXHIBIT 1 Organizational Structure, 1983

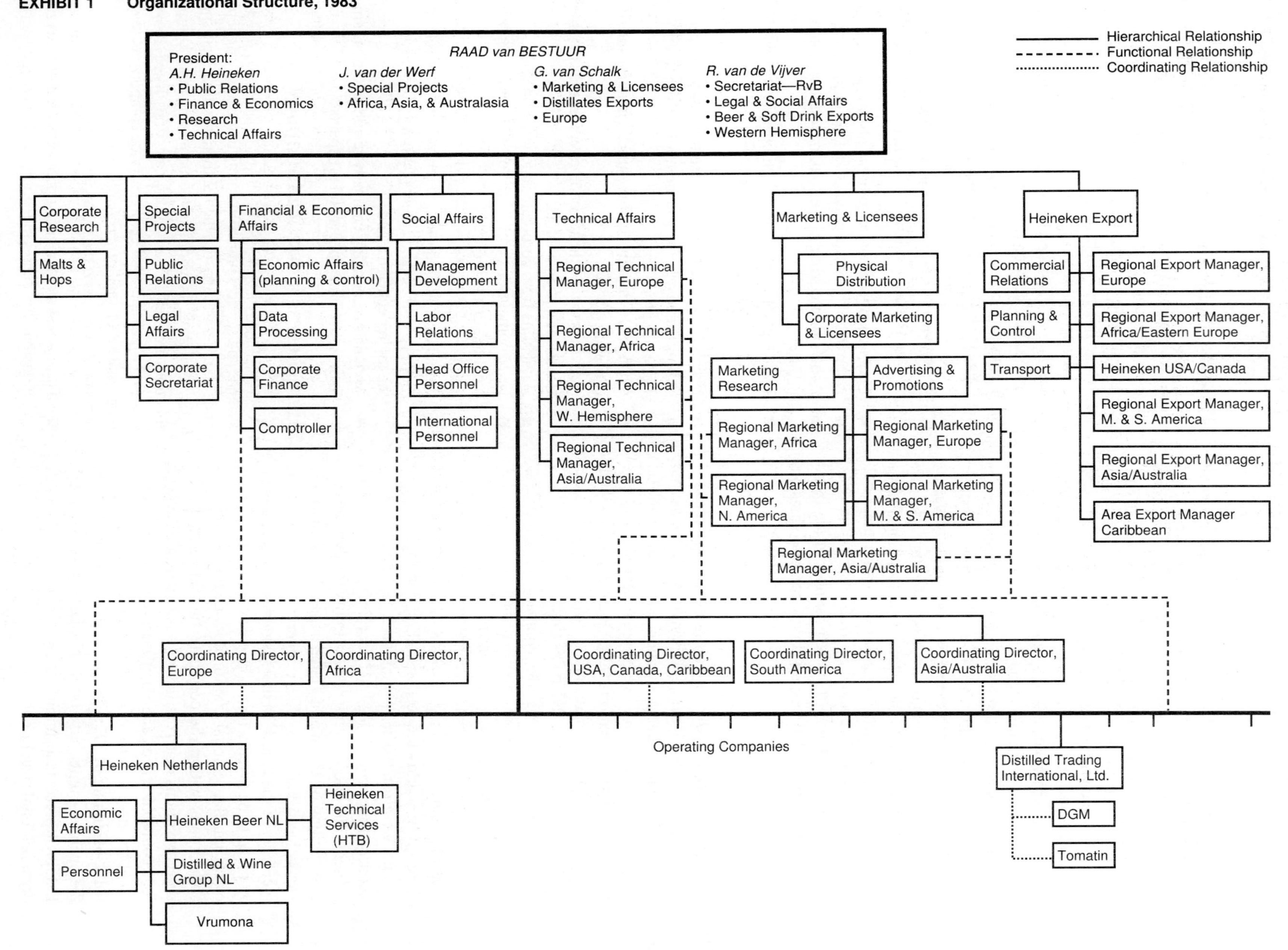

objectives. For those policies, however, which it could not establish or evaluate autonomously, local management would decide and request any assistance required from Heineken N.V. staff.

- To the extent that the management of an operating company developed experience and expertise in certain areas which might be of value to other affiliates elsewhere, Heineken N.V. would act as a focal point for the collection and dissemination of such knowledge for the benefit of all Heineken companies.
- Whenever the management of an operating company might wish to establish a policy which they were unable to evaluate fully, either because this required knowledge pertaining to affairs outside their jurisdiction or because it might prejudice the affairs of other Heineken companies, advice must be obtained from Heineken N.V.

The Annual Planning Letter and Strategy Review

The major vehicle through which the executive board exercised control over the activities of operating companies was the annual operational and strategic review of each subsidiary and affiliated company. Beginning in 1980, a planning letter was prepared by the executive board every year and sent to each operating company. The general (corporatewide) and specific (pertaining to that affiliate) objectives laid out in the letter would constitute the basis for the preparation of a detailed five-year plan and a one-year operational plan by the affiliate. This plan was first discussed with the appropriate regional coordinator and then brought to the board and other key corporate executives for discussion and approval. This process took place normally once a year, but could occur more often if special circumstances required it.

Regional Coordinating Directors

The executive board had delegated to the regional coordinating directors (RCD) some of the aspects of the shareholding relationship with the operating companies. The degree of delegation and supervision varied considerably from region to region and, within regions, from company to company. A number of factors contributed to this variation:

- The personality, management style, and availability of the executive board member responsible for that region, the RCD and the local general manager.
- The knowledge and length of service of the RCD as well as his familiarity with the issues prevalent in his region.
- The size and complexity of the operating company.
- Heineken's stake in the ownership of the operating company.
- The history of relations between the operating company and headquarters.

As of January 1983, the Heineken world was organized along five regions: Europe, Africa, North America and the Caribbean, Central and South America, and Asia/Australia. Each was headed by a regional coordinator responsible to the executive board or to one of its members for:

1. Promoting harmony between the operating companies with their local viewpoint, and functional coordinators and other departments in the head office with their global viewpoints.
2. Appraising the operating company from the point of view of a shareholder in terms of the employment of capital already invested and the conduct of the company's operations.
3. Reviewing, in cooperation with the relevant functional directors, investment projects and agreeing with the operating company on its targets and objectives.
4. Advising, in cooperation with the relevant functional directors, on management appointments.
5. Keeping fellow coordinating directors and functional directors informed on political and economic affairs within the region for the purpose of their duties.
6. Seeing to it that Heineken N.V.'s viewpoint on broad policy issues, investment prospects, corporate objectives and targets, and staff development and appointments was provided to all affiliates within their region.
7. Aiding upon request: (a) corporate functional directors to resolve their own or their staff's differences with operating companies, and (b) general managers to resolve differences between their organization and corporate functional directors or their staff.

Functional Directors

In principle, functional directors had no authority outside Heineken's corporate office other than for the promulgation of functional policies and for monitoring the adherence thereto. They were expected not to adopt an authoritative role toward an individual operating company or group of companies. Functional directors "should structure their respective organizations in such a manner that they can adequately support the regional coordinators in providing, as economically and efficiently as possible, the help and advice that operating companies require." As a result, most functional directors had chosen to structure their staff along geographic lines. Should differences of opinion arise from the interpretation by operating companies of functional policies, it would be the functional director's responsibility to bring these to the attention of the corresponding RCD and/or to the Heineken executive board.

As of January 1983, the principal functional areas at Heineken included: (1) financial and economic affairs, including planning and control and all data processing activities; (2) social affairs, including management development and industrial relations; (3) marketing and licenses, including physical distribution, marketing research, and advertising and promotions; (4) Heineken export, which handled imports into all countries where Heineken operated; (5) corporate research; and (6) technical affairs. Heineken Technical Services was housed within the Heineken Netherlands operating company, but its services to international subsidiaries were channeled through the corporate office of technical affairs and its regional technical managers. The offices of special projects (e.g., the on-going negotiations for entry into China), public relations, legal affairs, and the corporate secretariat were also located at headquarters and reported directly to the executive board. Specifically, functional directors were responsible to the board for:

1. Providing the executive board with functional advice.
2. Initiating functional worldwide targets, objectives, and policies.
3. Initiating new ideas and methods of improving performance for use in specific operating companies or throughout Heineken as a whole.
4. Providing staff suitable for international service.
5. Providing advice and service to: (a) regional coordinating directors to assist them in the functional aspects of their work, (b) other units in Heineken's corporate office, and (c) operating companies so as to assist them in achieving agreed targets and objectives.
6. Monitoring the adherence to established functional policies.
7. Providing operating companies with enough information on the outcome of the appraisal of their business conduct to enable the general manager to remedy weaknesses in his company or to contest the validity of the appraisal.

Since the various corporate functional directors were expected to provide all necessary support to the regions, including day-to-day assistance to operating companies as required, the regional coordinating directors would not normally need any staff. Some of the larger and more complex areas, however, whether as a result of the importance of their business or their geographical disparity, might require that the RCD be assisted by one or two qualified professionals. It was not expected, however, that regional coordinating directors would develop their own capability to monitor functional (as opposed to strategic or financial) performance among the various affiliates within their region. They should rely, instead, on the regional functional staff for these purposes.

As an example, Exhibit 2 illustrates the multitude of relationships involved in the technical function and the respective roles of the corporate office of technical affairs, the technical staff in the Netherlands, the operating company's management, and the regional coordinating director.

The Future

In commenting on the balance of responsibility between headquarters and the operating subsidiaries, a member of the executive board stated:

> In principle we want to decentralize as much as possible; people in the field should be responsible for their contribution. But we are mainly a one-brand, one-product company, which limits their freedom in terms of image and price. If you take away brand and advertising policy, financial policy, and the technology for main products, this leaves local managers with responsibility only for day-to-day and local people management issues. Is that enough?
>
> We are struggling with this problem; operating freedom means different things to various people. It is important that we balance centralized controls with the need to maintain local identity and initiative. We have made some progress in enlarging the scope for local managers, but perhaps we need to do more.

EXHIBIT 2 The Technical Management Function at Heineken, 1983

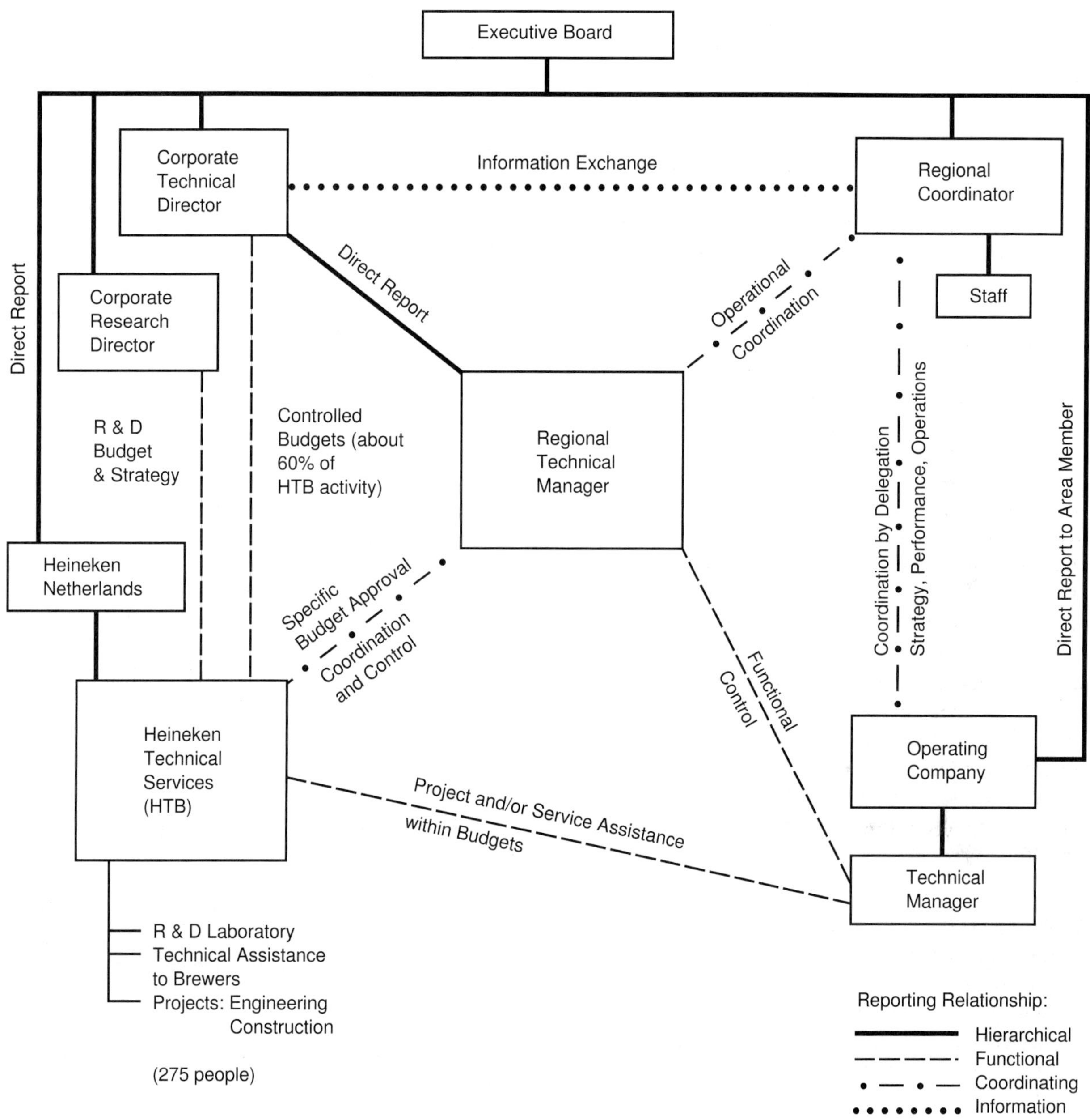

INSEAD

Case 3–3

Häagen Dazs and the European Ice-Cream Industry in 1994

In 1990, Häagen Dazs jumped on the European scene and took all ice-cream makers by surprise with its luscious superpremium ice-cream. It immediately took a dominant share of this very fast growing and high margin segment. By 1993, it held 80 percent of French superpremium ice-cream sales through retailers. By 1994, Häagen Dazs had achieved its very bold bet: to establish a strong brand identity and share position in the two countries it had targeted: France and the UK. Observed Lars Olofsson, Chairman of Gervais, "Häagen Dazs has been extremely successful exactly where we failed ten years ago."[1]

Despite Häagen Dazs's startling success, there were questions about the future. Stated the *Financial Times* in its review of GrandMet, the parent company of Häagen Dazs: "The boldest international foray has been by Häagen Dazs. . . . Expansion in Europe and Japan has helped double annual sales to about $500 million in five years, and is the most striking advertisement of GrandMet's claims to expertise in taking food brands across frontiers. But Häagen Dazs has yet to show a profit."[2]

In addition, competitors' actions were expected: "Some observers, even inside GrandMet, fear it may become vulnerable to more powerful competitors such as Unilever and Nestlé, which both plan rival 'superpremium' ice-cream brands." As Sir Michael Perry, Unilever's Co-Chairman, put it: "to Unilever ice-cream is so important that . . . we all get down on our knees and pray for a good summer."[3]

This case was prepared by Karel Cool, Professor at INSEAD, with the help of Alessandro Brenna, MBA 1994, and Anna Lisa Tazartes, MBA 1994. It is intended to be used as a basis for class discussion rather than to illustrate either effective or ineffective handling of an administrative situation.

Financial support from the INSEAD Alumni Fund European Case Programme is gratefully acknowledged.

[1]In 1984, Gervais launched an "American ice-cream" in small bulks (750 ml) very similar to the ones of Haägen Dazs, but with no success.

[2]*Financial Times,* "Burgers, Booze and Bull," 24 November 1993.

[3]*Business Week,* "The ice-cream wars turn red-hot," 4 July 1994. Ice-cream, beverages and snacks accounted for 12 percent of Unilever's revenues and 16 percent of operating profits; they were on average 40 percent more profitable than the remaining businesses.

The European Market for Ice-Cream

The 1993 market for industrial ice-cream in the four major countries (UK, France, Germany, and Italy) was estimated at 1.5b liters. In the period 1988–1992, the market had grown at about 5 percent per year. However, bad weather conditions and the recession in 1993 had produced flat sales in 1993. See Exhibit 1 for several characteristics of the European ice-cream industry.

The difference in size of the various markets was partly explained by the very different consumption per person in each country. Industrial ice-cream consumption per capita in 1992 was 5.8 liters in France, 5.5 liters in Germany, 6.7 liters in Italy, and 7.4 liters in the UK. This compared to the 15 liters per person in Sweden and the other North European countries and the 23 liters in the United States. The market also was very seasonal and affected by weather conditions.

The market could be divided into three main categories: *impulse, desserts,* and *catering*. Impulse or hand-held ice-cream such as cornets, lollies, and choc ices were usually consumed within minutes of purchase outside the home. The dessert market consisted of tubs, family specialities, desserts, and gateaux for household consumption and were sold at supermarkets and other retail outlets. Finally, the segment of catering to restaurants, bars, etc., remained throughout Europe a more or less unexploited sector.

Exhibit 1 gives the 1993 estimated breakdown (in volume) of the various segments. Since the price per liter of impulse ice-cream was up to four times the price of take-home ice-cream sold in retail outlets, the figures were significantly different when expressed in value.

Weather sensitivity was particularly felt in the impulse segment. In its review of the ice-cream business, the *Monopolies and Mergers Commission*[4] of the UK mentioned that sales of impulse ice-cream could be double or half the level of sales in any week depending on the weather. For example, Unilever's UK subsidiary, Wall's, was reported to have shipped 9 percent of its annual sales in a four-day working week at the end of May 1992. The sales fluctuations in impulse ice-cream sales for one national manufacturer in the UK are shown in Exhibit 2. In the 90s, sales in the impulse segment had been relatively stagnant.

[4]Monopolies and Mergers Commission, *Ice-cream. A report on the supply in the UK of ice-cream for immediate consumption,* London: HMSO, March 1994.

EXHIBIT 1 Characteristics of the European Ice-Cream Markets, 1993

Sales (m liters)	1988	1989	1990	1991	1992	1993
France	258	284	311	314	331	338
Germany	298	321	347	391	410	373
Italy	330	337	340	345	353	367
UK	377	400	403	410	420	433
TOTAL	1,263	1,342	1,401	1,460	1,514	1,511

	Seasonality		**Distribution**
	Peak season	Percent of Sales	Multiple's Share
France	May-September	60%	70%
Germany	May-August	60	75
Holland	April-September	60	65
Italy	April-September	85	50
Portugal	April-September	80	60
Spain	April-September	85	65
UK	May-August	60	64
Belgium	April-September	60	60

	Products			**Suppliers**	
	Dessert	Impulse	Catering	Industrial	Artisanal
France	75%	6%	19%	85%	15%
Germany	66	16	18	79	21
Holland	62	18	20	90	10
Italy	51	41	8	50	50
Portugal	34	51	15	90	10
Spain	40	40	20	80	20
UK	81	11	8	90	10
Belgium	75	5	20	85	15

Home consumption for desserts represented the largest segment in most European countries. This market had been growing at an annual rate of about 6 percent since the early 90s. The increasing ownership of freezers throughout Europe had had a very positive effect on ice-cream consumption. In France, Spain, and Germany, over 70 percent of households had some capacity to store frozen food. Italy, on the other hand, still had a lower penetration rate for freezers. The growth in this segment was explained also by manufacturers' product innovation, growth in multipacks, quality improvements, etc. In addition, consumers generally had less time to prepare meals at home and preferred ready-to-eat desserts such as ice-cream. The dessert market also was much less seasonal than the impulse market, though sales of ice-cream bar multipacks were weather dependent. The price per single item sold in multipacks by the large retailers was about 20–30 percent lower than when sold at a cornershop.

In addition to the industrial (i.e., wrapped) ice-cream sales, there also was a substantial artisanal segment in each country as shown in Exhibit 1. This segment included

EXHIBIT 2 Monthly Fluctuations in Impulse Ice-Cream Sales for One UK Manufacturer in 1992

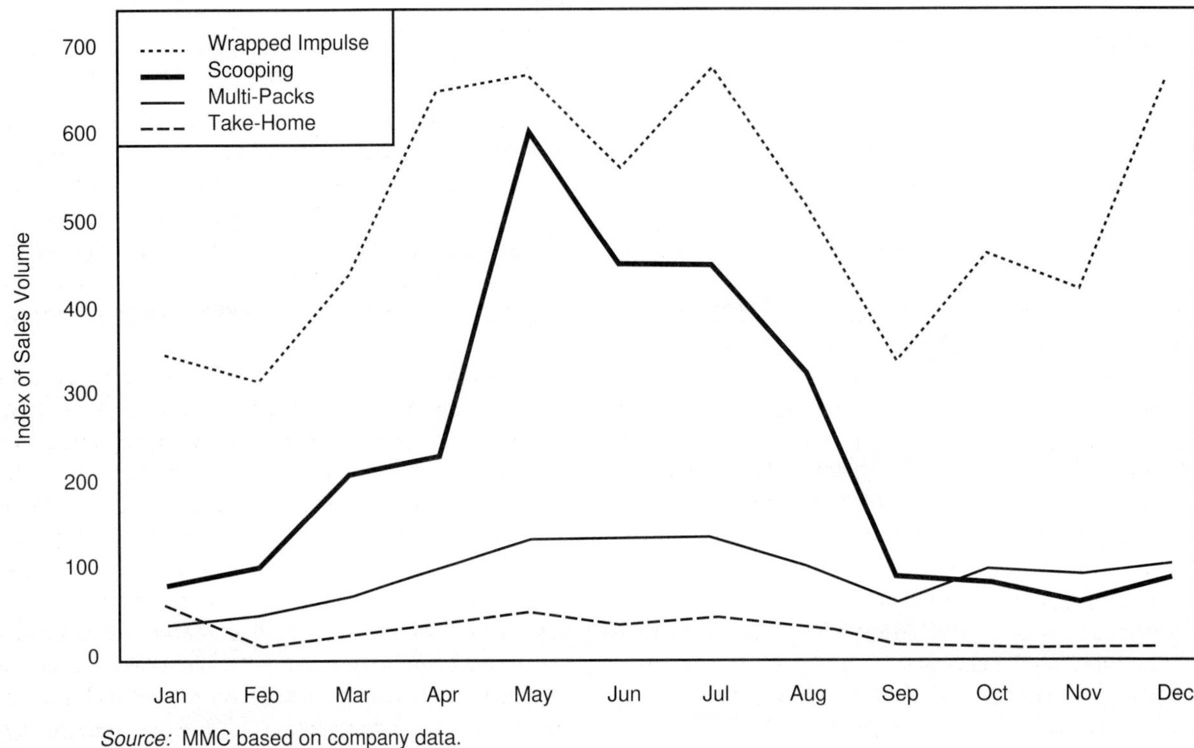

Source: MMC based on company data.

home-made ice-cream, sales of ice-cream in bars, cafés, etc., produced by the tenant, ice-cream sold on the street by local vendors, etc. Artisanal ice-cream was virtually absent from the take-home market. There were only rough guesses as to the size of this segment.[5]

The market could also be segmented into standard, premium, and superpremium ice-cream. This distinction depended on the ingredients used (especially fat content), the quality of the products, and the price level. The superpremium ice-cream, which Häagen Dazs had pioneered was available at the retail level and for impulse purchase. These products were targeted toward adults, and in particular, toward young professionals. An additional segment, frozen yoghurt, has been created in Europe in recent years.

In general, the adult ice-cream market in Europe had grown in importance. Ice-cream traditionally had been a product marketed to and consumed by children. In Italy, for instance, children under 10 years were thought to consume around 20 percent of all ice-cream; those aged between 11 and 20 years consumed a further 38 percent of total sales, leaving just 42 percent for those over 20 years of age. However, during the 80s the number of children between 5 and 14 years had steadily fallen. The adult market therefore had received more attention from the producers. Several prod-

[5]In value, artisanal ice-cream represented a much higher percentage, e.g., 30 percent in France, 35 percent in Belgium. The European Commission estimated that the share of artisanal ice-cream of the impulse market in France was 52 percent in volume and 51 percent in value. The corresponding figures for Belgium were 33 percent and 54 percent. The share of artisanal ice-cream of the catering market in France was 23 percent in volume and 32 percent in value. The corresponding figures for Belgium were 30 percent and 41 percent. European Commission N° IV/M.422 Unilever France/Ortiz Miko (II).

ucts had been launched that were bigger, richer, and more sophisticated with added emphasis on packaging.

The Ice-Cream Value Chain

Production. The production of ice-cream had always been very standardized since the 16th century when ice-cream had first been concocted by a Sicilian chef and sold in France. Today, ice-cream could still be produced quite easily. However, manufacturers had recently invested in new, sophisticated plants and machines to increase their flexibility in production and the quality of the final product. By 1994, the cost of a new, efficient manufacturing facility ranged between £15 and £40 million, depending on the size. Both recently installed plants of Mars and Häagen Dazs in Europe were estimated to have cost about $60 million. The industrial production of ice-cream was spread equally throughout the year so that the consumption peaks in the summer were met by winter production and long-term storage. This kind of production required additional investments in large storage areas.

Ice-cream production roughly followed the following stages. First, raw materials were put together and solid components (such as sugar, proteins, butter, flavoring materials) were added to the liquid. The mixture was then slightly heated to help the melting process. The blend was then passed under high pressure in a small tube to achieve a homogeneous mixture (homogenization). To guarantee the hygienic quality of the product, the mixture was also pasteurized. Then it went through a plate cooler and was stored at a temperature of 5°C for a time anywhere between 8 to 24 hours. From the mixing containers, the blend was moved to freezing machines and quickly frozen down to minus 8–10°C. It was at this stage that the injection of air took place to give the product the desired consistency. Leaving the freezer, the mixture passed a fruit feeder which "threw" fruit chips, chocolate and/or other ingredients at a fixed dosage into the mixture. Finally, the product was packaged and stored at a temperature of about −30°C. According to the kinds of product, the ingredients used in the process and the air content, the temperature at which the mixture had to be kept could vary substantially. For instance, the process was slightly different for the production of sorbets in which no milk was used.

The cost of raw materials, production, and packaging represented roughly 30 percent of manufacturer's sales. Milk (or water), fat and sugar, which accounted for 99 percent of the volume accounted only for 80 percent of the value. The flavors (eggs, powder and fruits) represented 20 percent of the value but only 1 percent in volume.[6]

Legislation regarding ingredients differed substantially across countries: fat content was highly regulated (e.g., French legislation forbids the use of vegetable fats); some countries did not allow the use of artificial sweeteners (e.g., Italy, France, and UK) and the regulation of artificial additives and flavors also differed by country. A more unified EC legislation was expected. In the meantime, these different requirements did not create an obstacle to centralized manufacturing, because flexible production equipment allowed rapid change-overs.

Product innovation. In the recent past, manufacturers had followed a policy of continuous innovation in terms of ingredients, flavor mix, shape, packaging, and color. In the impulse market, many products were tied to a specific event, movie (Dinosaurs from Jurassic Park, Flintstones), and lasted only one season. For major companies like Unilever, the sales from new products in the impulse market typically represented 20–30 percent in any given year. While there were staple products like Cornetto, which had been launched in 1959, there was a need for continuous innovation. The dessert market had also become more innovation intensive. For example, in advanced markets such as France, Carte D'Or of Unilever offered about 25 flavors. Every year, four to five new flavors were launched (or old ones were reintroduced). Häagen Dazs estimated an average life of one year for every version of its Extrãas product line. This high degree of product innovation led to a large number of stock keeping units (SKUs) within the industry. For example, Unilever had within Europe roughly 3,000 SKUs and an average of 180 per country.

Logistics. In moving ice-cream from the factory to the customer, a company could use its own chain or third party distribution. A well developed logistics network was particularly important in the impulse market where sales were very seasonal. Independent distributors were often used for the final delivery to the cornershop. It was

[6]British ice-cream historically had differered from that in most countries: it was mainly made up of nondairy products containing vegetable fat. This had its origins in the Second World War when UK ice-cream companies were prohibited from using milk and dairy fats in ice-cream production. By 1994, most UK ice-cream was still made up of nondairy products.

estimated that a distributor could make about 35 to 45 calls a day when the ice-cream had not been pre-ordered and about 40 to 60 visits with pre-ordered deliveries. In the high season, they had to visit each cornershop roughly once a week, some even once a day. Outside the hot season, this was only once every other week. Given the large number of shops where ice-cream was sold (e.g., more than 100,000 in Italy, 50,000 in the UK excluding summer kiosks, 220,000 in Germany) and the small sales volume per shop (see Exhibit 3), logistics took on a special importance in the impulse market. Furthermore, the need to transport and store ice-cream at lower temperatures than required for frozen food demanded dedicated transportation and storage facilities.[7]

EXHIBIT 3 Distribution of Annual Sales of Impulse Ice-Cream (Excl VAT)

Annual Sales per Shop	Percent of Total
less than £800	34–38
£800—£1,000	8–10
£1,000—£3,000	38–42
£3,000—£4,000	6–8
over £4,000	8–10

Source: Various industry estimates, MNC report.

The UK *Monopolies and Mergers Commission* estimated that the cost of distribution through (nonexclusive) wholesalers was about 25 percent of manufacturer's sales. For a major manufacturer with a dedicated distribution, this was roughly 20 percent. About 85 percent of distribution costs was accounted for by local distribution, from the regional center or depot to the retail outlet.

Distribution. Channels differed according to the segments. In the impulse segment, there had been a dominance of cornershops (confectionery, tobacconists, newsagent outlets—CTN). Their role was slightly declining but at different speeds depending on the country. In the UK, mobile units and kiosks accounted for about 37 percent of the volume of this segment and were eroding the role of the confectioners. The role of grocery stores in this segment was still not very important, although some producers had started to put their own refrigerators in supermarkets to capture impulse consumption.

In the take-home segment (desserts), grocery outlets were the dominant distribution channel. The trend was for a continued increase of the share of multiple retailers at a rate of 1–2 percent per year, mainly at the expense of independent grocers and other outlets. Exhibit 1 shows the share of grocery chains and other multiples of take-home ice-cream purchases by 1993.

The importance of multiples in the take-home segment was expected to grow also because of the importance of "distributor own brands." In the UK, for example, own labels accounted for 47 percent of take-home ice-cream sales and 32 percent of take-home premium ice-cream products, as multiples had introduced their premium own-label products. In contrast, in Italy and Spain, own-label accounted for only a small amount (6–7 percent), mainly because of a generally underdeveloped own-label strategy. Throughout Europe, own-label products had a share of about 16 percent of 1993 dessert sales. In impulse multipacks, the own-label share was about the same while the own-label share in single impulse sales was about 2 percent.

Freezer centers were an increasingly important distribution channel and had grown fast, especially in the UK and France. These outlets usually only sold take-home and multipack ice-creams, often own-labelled, and at a discount.

In the take-home segment, the proliferation of products had made retailers less keen to provide additional shelf space in freezers to newcomers. In the distribution through cornershops, it had been uncommon to find many different brands in the same outlet. While any manufacturer could propose to retailers to put in their shop one of their freezers, many small shops preferred to have only one freezer, primarily for a lack of space. As a consequence, there was intense competition across Europe to get freezer exclusivity. This resulted in large numbers of changes in freezer accounts. For example, in the year ending September 1992, Unilever in the UK had won 8,549 new accounts and lost 2,985. For 1993, the corresponding figures were 8,366 and 2,246. In the same year, Nestlé had gained 4,000 accounts and lost over 2,000.

However, as illustrated by the fall of Lyons Maid in the UK, freezer exclusivity was not a guarantee for success. In the early 1980s, the Allied Lyons subsidiary had about 40 percent of the impulse market. Despite its large

[7]Ice-cream quality was irrecoverably compromised when its temperature was higher than −15°C (it melted and then produced ice crystals on its surface when refrozen). Therefore, it had to be maintained in freezers at very low temperatures (−26°C to −40°C), which were often lower than that required for the storage of other frozen foods.

base of exclusive cabinets, its share slipped to 18 percent by 1991. This was largely due to a lack of significant product development, insufficient advertising, and only modest investment in manufacturing plant. Then, in February 1992, Mr. Henry Clarke bought Lyons Maid and added it to the three existing plants he had acquired the year before. In one year, he became the second largest UK ice-cream manufacturer. However, by October 1992, he was forced into receivership. Problems in commissioning new plants prevented the new Clarke Foods from achieving more than one-quarter of its planned output. Retailers began to turn elsewhere for supplies. A major advertising campaign and an exceptionally wet August meant that, like the rest of the industry, Clarke Foods experienced poor sales. In the face of acute liquidity problems, Mr. Clarke was forced to sell out to Nestlé. By 1992, the share of Lyons Maid was down to 10 percent.

Marketing. The importance of branding was demonstrated by the traditional strategy followed by the large multinationals entering different geographical markets: acquisition of existing companies. Substantial investments were necessary to create brand awareness and loyalty. To launch "I Cestelli" in the UK, Unilever had budgeted a £3m campaign, and to launch "Yolka," a new ice-cream with frozen yoghurt, the company was said to have budgeted more than FF15m for its communication campaign in France (in May 1994, 100 "30-second" spots appeared on TV). When Mars entered the UK market with their Mars bar, they reportedly spent £5m per year during the first three years and £2–3m per year thereafter. Advertising spending for major launches could easily equal the amount of sales during the first year.

Packaging had a strong impact on customer perception. It had to display the products in order to entice the consumer and reflect both product quality and brand positioning. Consequently, the weight of packaging costs tended to increase for premium and super-premium ice-creams.

Advertising and promotion expenses had been steadily growing in all the countries and on average accounted for about 4.5–7 percent of ice-cream sales. In all countries the leading advertiser was Unilever with about 15–17 percent of sales spent on advertising and promotion. The other manufacturers had followed Unilever, however. For example, Unilever's (Wall's) UK share of total industry advertising for ice-cream had fallen from over 80 percent in 1989 to 45 percent in 1992. Advertising was heavily concentrated on TV, representing around 80 percent of the total expenditure. Sampling was the second largest promotional expenditure. Häagen Dazs had pioneered another approach with its "dipping" shops, where customers could try the ice-cream in a dedicated setting.

Finally, there were some other important costs including depreciation of the large capital investments in machinery, trucks and storage facilities. For major players, the fixed assets-to-sales ratio could be as high as 0.50. Administration was another cost which represented about 5 percent of sales. Gross margins on average were 50 percent. However, the margins in impulse ice-cream sales tended to be between 55 and 60 percent while those in desserts were closer to 35–40 percent.

Competition

Until the major push of the multinational food companies in ice-cream in the mid-80s, bulk ice-cream production had been dominated by dairy firms and farmers' cooperatives. They saw ice-cream as a by-product of their milk business. It gave them, in addition, slightly higher margins than the milk business. However, unfamiliar with the practice and skill of branding products, bulk ice-cream remained a commodity product.

By 1994, four types of players could be identified. First, there were Unilever and Nestlé, which were present in every country in Europe and in all segments. They had grown through acquisitions of local companies and, so far, had avoided price battles. Second, there were multinational manufacturers which had entered the ice-cream market with a niche strategy: Mars and Häagen Dazs. Third, there were national manufacturers without a significant international presence, which had been able to gain a strong position in their domestic market. Recently, these companies had been acquisition targets. For example, Italgel, the second Italian manufacturer, had been acquired by Nestlé in 1993, and Ortiz-Miko, the second French manufacturer, was bought by Unilever in 1994. Only Schöller, the second German player with a 31 percent market share was still independent. Fourth, there remained a host of small national manufacturers with minor market shares acting as marginal local players. In the UK, for example, there were over 1,000 registered ice-cream makers.

In all European countries, the share of total sales held by the three largest competitors was over 60 percent and growing (see Exhibit 4). Exhibit 5 gives the estimated sales and market shares of the largest manufacturers in

EXHIBIT 4 Concentration and Shares of Ice-Cream Sales in Europe

Country	Top Three Competitors	Share of Top Three
France	Unilever, Nestlé Ortiz-Miko*	72%
Germany	Unilever, Schöller Eisman	72%
UK	Unilever, Nestlé Mars	52%
Belgium	Unilever, Ijsboerke, Ysco	60%
Italy	Unilever, Italgel** Sammontana	69%
Holland	Unilever Campina-Melkunie Hertog	65%
Spain	Unilever, Nestlé Avidesa	71%
Portugal	Unilever	85%

* Acquired by Unilever in 1994.
** Acquired by Nestlé in 1993.

EXHIBIT 5 European Sales of Top Companies, 1993

Company	Sales (£ million)	Market Share
Unilever	1,500	38.5%
Nestlé *	700	18%
Schöller	400	10%
Häagen Dazs	50	1.2%
Mars	150	3.6%

* With Italgel.

Europe. See also Exhibits 6 and 7 for the position of the players in Europe and worldwide.

Unilever. In the early 80s, Unilever commissioned a study from McKinsey to evaluate the future of their ice-cream business. The recommendation of the consulting firm was to sell. However, Unilever management decided that the business had substantial potential if a major position could be obtained. In the years following this decision, Unilever dramatically changed its ice-cream business and, by the same token, the ice-cream business in the world.

EXHIBIT 6 The Major Players in Ice-Cream Worldwide in 1994 ($b)

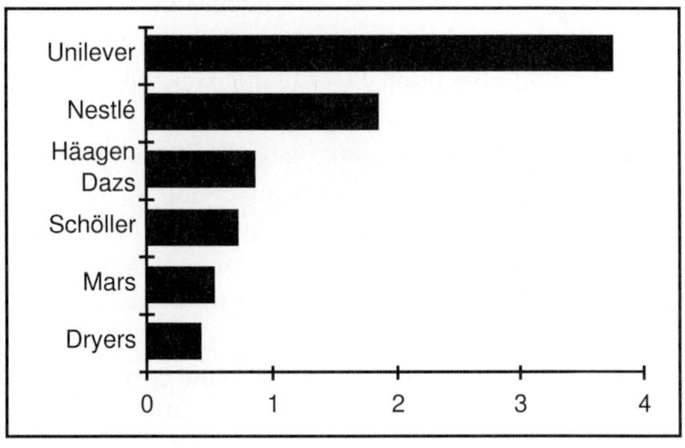

They first attacked the dessert market with their star brands, Viennetta and Carte D'Or, and set out to build a strong European position. They were to focus on ice-cream products with a high degree of sophistication. In the impulse market, Unilever sought to substantially upgrade the products in all dimensions (availability, taste, packaging, etc.). They used their 10 years of "cone" research to develop a much better cone, etc. The "Cornetto" brand was chosen as a focal brand and was rolled out internationally. The expansion was supported by acquisitions in many countries to snap up locally known brand names.

Toward the mid-80s, the company made a concerted effort to achieve rationalization across Europe: information about suppliers was shared, production was rationalized, etc. At the same time, a major expansion program outside Europe was planned. In 1994, Unilever's chairman, Mr. Tabaksblat, highlighted the achievements since 1989. Unilever had invested more than £2 billion in ice-cream capital expenditures and acquisitions. Of the acquisitions, 15 had been in the previous two years and seven of these had been in the developing world. Unilever was now present in 29 countries. Of their 49 factories, six had just been opened including one in Beijing. There were four more under construction. Sales had grown at a compounded 12 percent since 1989. Their 1993 market share position in Europe is shown in Exhibit 8, as well as their estimated ice-cream sales worldwide.

EXHIBIT 7a **Market Shares in Impulse Singles in W. Europe, 1994**

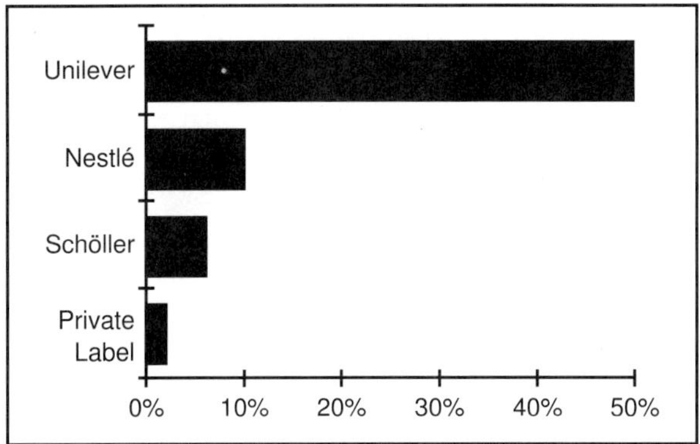

EXHIBIT 7b **Market Shares in Impulse Multipacks in W. Europe, 1994**

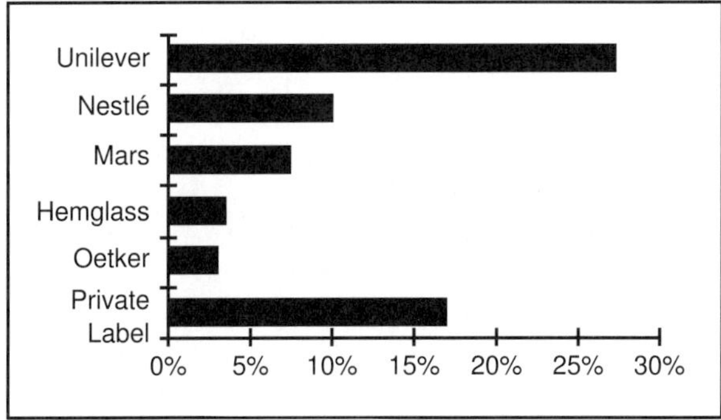

EXHIBIT 7c **Market Shares in Dessert Ice-Cream in W. Europe, 1994**

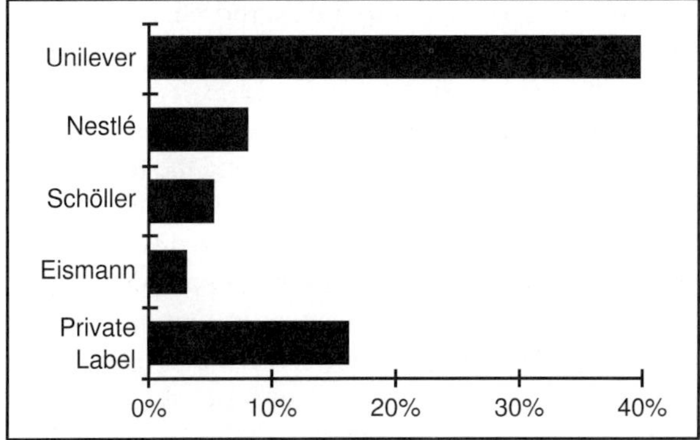

Unilever's expansion had been very dramatic in the United States. They had expanded Lipton's $150 million foothold with the "Good Humor" ice-cream into a $750 million market leadership through the $100 million Gold Bond deal, the $155 million acquisition of Klondike in 1992, and the 1993 acquisition for $275 million of Breyer's/Sealtest from Kraft. They moved very rapidly to rationalize the three businesses and achieved national distribution by 1994. New products were being added including dessert brands developed in Europe. See Exhibit 9 for an overview of the U.S. market.

A hallmark of Unilever's expansion strategy in the impulse market in Europe had been their practice of "Free-on-Loan (FOL)" freezers for the cornershops. They lent retailers cabinets of various sizes (0.5m–2m) on the condition that the freezer was exclusively stocked with Unilever ice-cream. To provide retailers an incentive to sell, they gave year-end bonuses calculated as a percentage of their purchases. Retailers who had bought their own "Non-Exclusive (NE)" freezers also received a bonus depending on their sales volume. To compensate for the investment cost, Unilever paid a higher bonus to owners of NE freezers. This practice was also followed by many other ice-cream manufacturers. Exhibit 10a gives an overview of the 1992 bonus structure for CTNs in the UK for Unilever. Exhibit 10b provides a breakdown of the sales range by cabinet size. For sales to large chains, different rates were negotiated. By 1994, Unilever was estimated to have FOL freezers in about 40–50 percent of European cornershops.

The *Monopolies and Mergers Commission* estimated that the cost of cabinets to Unilever in the UK was roughly 7 percent of sales. Their 1992 capital cost per freezer was estimated at £288. Unilever's annual cost of maintaining the cabinets was shown to be about £48 per cabinet. The cost to Mars was estimated at £44 per cabinet. The price of popular sized freezers was roughly £250–300 with discounts for large purchases. Unilever estimated their useful life at 12 years. While contract terms differed across Europe, it was typical to find an initial contract period of 12 months. Thereafter, either the retailer or the manufacturer could terminate the agreement with one month's notice.

Unilever was thought to have a very efficient logistics and distribution system. Their distribution costs as a percentage of sales were estimated at 16–18.5 percent. In the early 1980s, Unilever experimented with a fully owned distribution system which tried to exploit synergies across their range of frozen products. However, they quickly found that the cornershops' requirements for relatively

EXHIBIT 8 Unilever's European Market Position (1993) and Worldwide Sales

Country	Industrial ice-cream (£ million)	Unilever market share	Percentage of European sales
Germany	1,200	36%	25%
Italy	1,000	40%	19%
UK	700	40%	13%
Scandinavia	600	35%	11%
Spain	350	30%	7%
France	800	17%*	5%
Benelux	300	35%	7%
Other	550	50%	11%
Total	5,500	38.5%	100%

* Before the acquisition of Ortiz-Miko; 48 percent with Ortiz included.

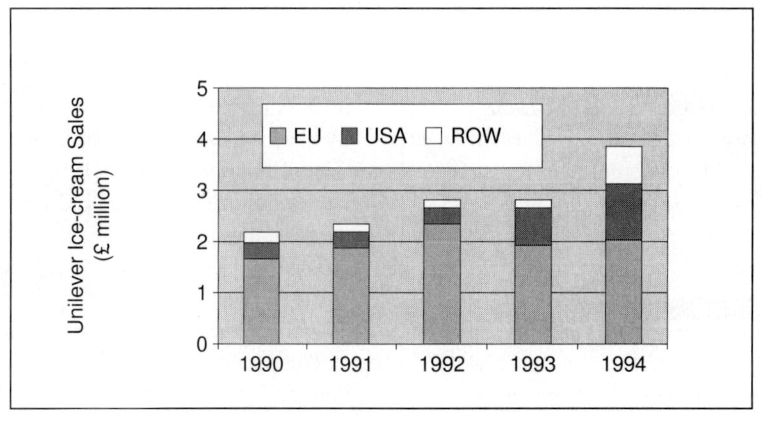

small drop, frequent delivery and small lead times for impulse ice-cream were not compatible with the requirements for its other frozen foods. By the mid-80s, they moved to a hybrid system where independent concessionaires would, within 24 hours of receiving an order, deliver the ice-cream. They also provided sales incentives to expand the customer base. Its UK concessionaires had a turnover which varied between £1–4 million.

Recently, Unilever had scored a big hit with the introduction of its "Magnum" ice-cream bar. It had been prompted by the aggressive entry of Mars with its ice-cream bar. By 1993, "Magnum was sold in 32 countries, and grew by 36 percent in 1993 to an estimated $400 million."[8] Unilever had also been surprised, like the other ice-cream makers, by the success of Häagen Dazs in France and the UK. In 1994, it launched "I Cestelli" as a product in the superpremium segment. The launch in Italy had reportedly been very successful and the results from its introduction in Germany were also very encouraging. However, neither in Germany nor Italy had Häagen Dazs recently attempted to establish a major position.

Because of their strong position in Europe, Unilever frequently had to justify themselves in court. Unilever's

[8]*Business Week,* "Unilever's global fight," 4 July 1994, pp. 40–45.

EXHIBIT 9 The U.S. Supermarket Ice-Cream Trade in 1993 (Total = $1.5 billion)

Firm	Major Brands	Share(%)
Unilever	Good Humor, Klondike, Vienetta, Sealtest, Popsicle	17.0
Nestlé	Drumstick, Crunch, Flintstones, Disney, Bon Bons, Dole, Health	14.4
Mars	Dove, Mars, Snickers, Rondos	7.8
Eskimo	Eskimo Pie	4.8
Heinz	Weight Watchers	4.6
GrandMet	Häagen Dazs	4.0
Private Label		14.4
Others		33.0

EXHIBIT 10a Unilever Bonus Rates in the UK, 1992

Retailer Purchases (excl VAT)	FOL Cabinet (%)	Non-Exclusive cabinet (%)
£0 - £799	0	0
£800 - £1,069	0	6
£1,070 - £1,579	2.5	6
£1,580 - £1,959	3	7
£1,960 - £2,389	3.5	7
£2,390 - £2,919	4	8
£2,920 - £3,469	5	8
£3,470 - £4,059	6	9
£4,060 - £4,609	7	9
£4,610 and more	8	10

Source: Birds Eye Wall's–Unilever in: MMC Report, *Ice-Cream,* March 1994, p. 9.

EXHIBIT 10b Estimated Range of Annual Purchases by Retailers by Size of Cabinet

Cabinet size	Minimum	Maximum
0.5m	£600	£1,200
1.0m	£750	£1,500
1.5m	£1,250	£2,500
2.0m	£3,250	£6,500

Source: Birds Eye Wall's–Unilever in: MMC Report, *Ice-Cream,* March 1994, p. 10.

most arduous challenger was Mars, with which they were involved in a number of court cases concerning freezer and shop exclusivity. When they acquired Ortiz-Miko in 1994, the European Commission had consented only after Unilever had agreed not to take over the Spanish and Portuguese operations of Ortiz; to sell the German Ortiz unit, Warncke; to honour all distribution agreements Ortiz had with other ice-cream makers for two more seasons; and to sell the frozen foods unit to the French food multinational, BSN.

Nestlé. A worldwide giant in food products, it was not until the late 80s that Nestlé started to aggressively build its ice-cream business. Since then, it has sought to build a position by acquisitions. Among the major acquisitions were the second largest UK ice-cream manufacturer, Clarke Foods, and the second largest Italian ice-cream manufacturer, Italgel. Nestlé's growth strategy in ice-cream was quite similar to Unilever's acquisition of national companies. However, Nestlé's products had remained quite national, using different brands in different markets. The only exception was the successful ice-cream bar "Nuts and Crunch" with which the company had the second position after Mars in almost all European countries. Neither was the Nestlé name extensively used as a European "umbrella" brand.

Though Nestlé attempted to keep pace with Unilever, it was still a distant second in Europe and worldwide. It had not yet been very successful with its UK acquisition. Since it acquired Lyons Maid, Lyons' share of the UK market had only inched up from 10 percent in 1992 to 11 percent in 1993. This followed the rise of Mars in the UK from 1 percent in 1989 to 14 percent in 1993.

Mars. The worldwide leader for confectionery products ("Mars," "Bounty," "Twix," "Snickers") surprised the ice-cream industry by creating the ice-cream bar segment in Europe. It already had a presence in the ice-cream industry in the United States through its Dove International division. In Europe, Mars first entered the UK market in 1989 and invested £40 million to build a plant of 50 million tons capacity near Strasbourg to serve the entire European market. By 1994, it was by far the leader in the ice-cream bar segment in every European market (e.g., 64 percent share of retail sales in France versus 17 percent for the second player, Nestlé).

Mars' entry had effectively created a new segment in the market: impulse ice-cream bars for adults. Arguing that its products were of higher quality (real chocolate, dairy ice-cream, etc.), they priced their bars at roughly double the average price of children's ice-creams. When competitors launched similar products (e.g., Unilever with "Sky," Nestlé with "Crunch"), they promptly followed the price increases.

A Gallop poll Mars had commissioned had indicated that if consumers were not able to get their preferred brand in an outlet, 65 percent would buy another brand, 8 percent would buy a different type of product, 14 percent would look elsewhere, and 13 percent would buy nothing. Therefore, Mars set out to build a strong distribution presence. Mars immediately made alliances with local ice-cream manufacturers to distribute their products. There were some questions about these distribution agreements now that the distributors for the major European markets (Italy, UK, and France) had been acquired by the big players.

To get access at the retail level, Mars provided nonexclusive freezers on the condition that their entire product range was stocked. They also rapidly expanded their freezer base with another deal to retailers: Mars would sell the retailer a cabinet. In return, the retailer would receive a free supply of Mars ice-cream equal to the cost of the cabinet. In the UK, Mars also had a distribution agreement with Nestlé. In 1990, they had reached an agreement with Lyons Maid whereby a limited range of Mars products was distributed into outlets with Lyons Maid freezers. This agreement was renewed in April 1993 and the earliest termination period was 31 March 1995.

Mars had not been afraid to use legal proceedings to obtain access to distribution. In 1991, Mars had started proceedings with the European Commission against Langnese-Iglo, Unilever's German ice-cream unit, and Schöller. Both competitors provided in Germany FOL freezers to retailers on the condition that they accepted "shop exclusivity" (i.e., no other ice-cream manufacturer could place a freezer in those shops). Mars argued that those contracts were anticompetitive and infringed both Articles 85 and 86 of the EC Treaty. In 1992, the Commission agreed with Mars and forced both Unilever and Schöller to abandon the requirement of shop exclusivity. The Commission did not make any ruling on the practice of freezer exclusivity. However, the Commission mentioned "the insulating effect [of this practice] on the relevant market as a whole."

Mars had attacked Unilever also in the Republic of Ireland and the UK. In Ireland, Unilever held a share of the impulse ice-cream market of over 70 percent. They had vigorously defended the practice of freezer exclusivity and in May 1992 had obtained an injunction against Mars when Mars had persuaded retailers to put their products in Unilever cabinets. Disagreeing with this judgement, Mars had made an appeal to the Irish Supreme Court. By the end of 1994, there was still no decision. Mars had also initiated, in 1991, proceedings with the European Commission against Unilever's Irish subsidiary. A decision was expected in 1995.

In the UK, Mars's actions had led to an investigation by the *Monopolies and Mergers Commission.* The purpose of the investigation was to establish whether there was a monopoly situation in the supply of ice-cream. The specific focus was on the competitive effects of freezer exclusivity. However, in March 1994, the Commission concluded that freezer exclusivity did not operate against the public interest.

Mars was also known for their very special culture. The most secretive of companies, the Mars brothers, Forest and John, had the reputation of "the worst, most feared enemy: totally unpredictable, capable of anything."[9] The $13 billion company had remained privately held and reportedly was run in a very autocratic way. Paying top salaries (which were publicly known in the company), they expected total dedication from their employees. The brothers also were obsessed with product quality and maximum plant utilisation, which counted toward monthly salaries.

They had never been afraid of making investments with only long-term payoffs and were obsessed with their strategy of global expansion. Mars had been losing share in the confectionery business in the United States to Hershey, and to Philip Morris and Cadbury Schweppes in Europe. However, they had invested aggressively in Eastern Europe and Russia, and competitors were unsure whether Mars was losing share because they were losing touch with the market or because they were expanding globally. A former Mars executive warned against premature conclusions: "Mars's real strength, to their credit, is excellent on-the-ground operations. You can go back three years after it opens, and their brands have distribution on a wide scale."[10] What move Mars would make in its confectionery business was unknown. Neither was it clear what the implications were, if any, for its ice-cream business.

Schöller. The company was the second most important ice-cream producer in Germany with a share of 25–30 percent. It was also present in other European countries, such as Austria, Belgium, France, Netherlands, Luxembourg, and the UK. Its most international brand was Mövenpick, which was particularly popular in central Europe. In some of these markets, Schöller was present through its own

---

[9] *Fortune,* November 28, 1994.
[10] *Ibid,* p. 56.

sales subsidiaries, in others through cooperation with local wholesalers. In Germany, Schöller was the leader in both the premium ice-cream segment with an estimated share of 45 percent, and in the large, household pack segment.

The majority of the shares in Schöller were privately held. So far, Schöller had remained an independent company. While the industry was rife with speculation as to who could buy Schöller, there had been no report of acquisition talks. In 1991, Schöller had concluded a cooperation agreement with Jacobs Suchard, a subsidiary of Philip Morris, for the development, production and distribution of ice-cream and ice-cream bars.

Along with Langnese-Iglo, Schöller had been obliged by the European Commission to change their FOL contracts which insisted on shop exclusivity. For Schöller, this was an unexpected outcome. In 1985, they had notified the Commission of the contracts they used with the trade. The same year, the Commission had communicated that, based on the facts they had, the contract was not in violation of Community laws. Yet, in 1991, the Commission started proceedings, leading to the requirement to change the contracts.

Häagen Dazs

Häagen Dazs ice-cream was introduced in the United States in 1960. It was the product of a family business created by Reuben and Rose Mattus in New York. Reuben Mattus, the son of a soldier who was killed in World War I, was brought to the United States from Poland in 1921 by his widowed mother. They settled in the Bronx and Mrs. Mattus set up a small business, Senator, selling lemon ice. The business prospered until the 1950s when the major manufacturers were muscling out small, local brands. It was then that Reuben Mattus said: "I cannot slug it out with the sluggers. I figured I had to find another niche." That niche was Häagen Dazs.

Observed Mattus, "The realization came to me that the aerated ice-cream being sold in the supermarket tasted different from the hand-packed kind you used to get at the drugstore. I looked around me and saw young people who had never tasted real ice-cream. . . . The quality of ice-cream had deteriorated to the point that it was just sweet and cold!" So Mattus created an ice-cream rich in egg yolks and fresh cream and gave it a made-up name, wanting it to sound cold, clear, luxurious, and Danish, because a family friend told him about the successful, rich ice-creams sold there.[11]

Häagen Dazs quickly gained a reputation as a dense, richly textured, luxury ice-cream, and many serious eaters were willing to pay more for what they perceived as the best, which had the added cachet of an unpronounceable name.[12] From the outset, key characteristics were present. The product was made with the finest, all natural ingredients which were purchased from only the best sources in the world: vanilla from Madagascar, chocolate from Belgium, strawberries from the second picking in Oregon, and Macademia nuts from Hawaii. To obtain a product much more dense and therefore creamy, the content of air was much lower than in traditional ice-cream (15–20 percent versus 50–60 percent).

Häagen Dazs was aimed at adults (25 to 35 years old) and sold only in pint or 3 1/2 ounce sizes, unlike the industry standard of half a gallon (1.8 liter) containers. This was much more convenient for the 55 percent of the population that had a one or two person household. Observed *Fortune* in 1981, "it is apparently a perfect product for the demographics of the Eighties: designer ice-cream. . . . It is a frozen snack for adults, arriving just in time for the maturing post-war baby boom . . . according to one study, these adults are eating three times as much ice-cream as children, and men are consuming the most." As the Häagen Dazs line went, "not everyone can afford a Rolls Royce or a Louis Vuitton handbag, but all can afford the best at $1.65 a pint." And Häagen Dazs production grew at 25 percent between 1976 and 1980 compared with an industry average of only 4 percent.

In 1980, Häagen Dazs had profits of $1.5 million on revenues of $30 million. It was selling at a 75 percent price premium over its rivals and growing at 25 percent per annum. It promoted the brand through franchised "dipping stores" that allowed customers to sample the product. By 1980 Häagen Dazs had sold franchises for 70 dipping stores where 18 flavors were dispensed in scoops and cups. Häagen Dazs' advantage in the fight for space in deep freezers was its premium price. The high profits per volume made it immediately attractive to retailers.

The commitment to in-house, highly concentrated production sites and a willingness to accept high transportation costs as the necessary price for preserving quality standards, had all come to characterize Häagen Dazs. Due to the nature of the ingredients, the product was more sensitive to thawing and refreezing than any traditional industrial ice-cream. Therefore it required more control during the whole distribution process.

---

[11] *Fortune*, "Ice-Cream Chic Häagen Dazs," 9 March 1981, pp. 117–120.

[12] *The New York Times*, "Reuben Mattus, 81, The Founder of Häagen Dazs," 29 January 1994.

By 1981 the business was still owned and run by the Mattus family, headed by Reuben as President. Despite the fact that Mr. Mattus did not believe in advertising and did not use any market research, Häagen Dazs was sold in supermarkets, restaurants, and franchise stores all over the United States, except in three states. It became one of the very few ice-cream brands sold nationally.

In the early 80s, Mr. Mattus was considering selling Häagen Dazs, and was thus readying the business to maximize the price. In an effort to increase the attractiveness, he decided to take the brand international and went to Canada in 1982. A licensing agreement was set up with control of the foreign organization from the Canadian partner (Ault). Due to the regulations regarding limited movement of dairy products across borders, the product was made by a subcontractor in Canada with little incentive toward preserving the distinctive features and high quality of the product. In 1983, with over 369 franchised stores and sales of over $100 million, Mattus sold Häagen Dazs to Pillsbury for $75 million and a consulting contract for himself.

Pillsbury already owned very strong brands and was intent on developing Häagen Dazs as a global brand. In April 1985, Pillsbury opened the second Häagen Dazs plant in California, adding to the one located in New Jersey. Three years later, the company undertook three more projects: implementation of strict new quality control standards to preserve the Häagen Dazs image and avoid the product recalls plaguing other US ice-cream manufacturers; significant expansion of the company-owned distribution system critical to preserve quality; revitalization of the more than 300 franchise-owned ice-cream shops which accounted for only 10 percent of the volume, but provided a critical marketing tool. The plan was designed to provide more flexibility and financial options by offering to convert franchise operations to licensees in selected areas. Pillsbury left the business arrangement in Canada relatively untouched. As a consequence, the brand never really took off in this market during the 1980s.

Pillsbury's global strategy for Häagen Dazs started with the launch of the product in Japan and Hong Kong in 1984 through joint ventures with Suntory and Pinedale, respectively. This introduction was a huge success, doubling its sales in the second year of operation and increasing the number of shops to 20. The success of these ventures could be attributed to three factors: the choice of truly capable partners, the structure of the venture, and the marketing strategy.

The joint venture partners had excellent executive and operational experience, as well as an understanding of and contacts in local markets. In addition, they were committed to making the business a success. The structure was such that Häagen Dazs retained control, with a 50 percent stake in the venture. The main partner held a 40 percent stake with responsibilities including locating and developing sites and developing relationships with the retailers. A minority stockholder, Tagamashi, held a 10 percent stake, with responsibility for manufacturing the product. All products were made in Japan given the regulatory and logistical (cost) constraints around importing dairy products from the United States.

The strategy was to introduce the brand via exclusive shops in high traffic locations. This meant securing stores in the center of large cities, such as train stations and shopping areas. While identifying the key sites was not difficult, securing these sites was a major challenge. However, the markets were ripe for the Häagen Dazs strategy of high quality, high priced products. By 1988, the number of shops in Japan alone had increased to 65, and the business was growing in Hong Kong and Singapore (also a joint venture with Pinedale).

In contrast to the Asian experience, efforts to enter the European market were much less successful. According to a former GrandMet/Häagen Dazs executive, Pillsbury made several launch errors. The product was launched in the wrong markets, namely Cologne and Frankfurt, in Germany, which are not known for trend setting or being "cosmopolitan." Erasco, Pillsbury's German subsidiary, simply transplanted the American execution of the brand image, which at that time was a more mature, widely available brand name, and thus was slightly less upscale. The introduction in Europe was not helped by Pillsbury's general lack of international launch expertise.

Then, in 1988, GrandMet made a successful bid for Pillsbury. One former company executive, who was part of the Pillsbury acquisition team and later joined the Häagen Dazs Europe team, stated that GrandMet was not even sure what brands they were buying when they successfully bid for Pillsbury. After the take-over, again like other GrandMet take-overs, "everything was up for sale." GrandMet's Ian Martin, then chief executive for foods, thought Häagen Dazs "might be a prime candidate for disposal."[13] It was only after GrandMet executives saw the high level of interest in this brand from several outside buyers that they took a closer look and decided the brand had global potential. The brand was split off from Pillsbury and began operating as a separate company within the GrandMet empire.[14]

---

[13]*Marketing*, "Häagen Dazs pushes cold front across world," 4 October 1990.

[14]See also the Appendix for a brief description of Grand Met.

Also following the GrandMet take-over, Reuben Mattus lost his consulting contract. Then, at the age of 80, he and his family began testing and eventually marketing a low fat ice-cream, which was first shipped in November 1992. He expected to sell half a million gallons in 1993.[15] However, in January 1994, Reuben Mattus at the age of 81 suffered a fatal heart attack while holidaying in Florida.

Once having made the decision to globalize the brand, GrandMet wasted no time in executing it. The company set up an office in Paris in charge of Häagen Dazs International (Canada, Asia, and Europe) and went out to hire a capable team with experience in international brands. They first hired Mr. Ovay Sorenson, a Dane from PepsiCo, to head the operation. Mr. Sorenson brought four other senior executives with him from Pepsi, whose mission was to develop and implement the plan to "take Häagen Dazs international!" Häagen Dazs' objective was very simple: to become the world's biggest ice-cream brand and get into as many mouths as possible.[16]

The GrandMet team completely restructured the deal in Canada, regaining control of operations and product quality. This business was then turned over to Häagen Dazs USA, in order to allow the international team to focus on their primary growth markets, Asia and Europe.

As the Asian joint venture operations were hugely successful (a former executive referred to them as "licences to print money"), GrandMet continued the expansion there, extending the existing joint ventures. A new management team was appointed in the area: its major decision was to increase the marketing effort in Japan. They chose a very provocative advertising campaign with the tag line "Shall we Häagen Dazs?" that got people talking about Häagen Dazs and generated lots of public relations. Finally, GrandMet was able to increase the profitability in 1991 due to a change in Japanese tariff regulations. At this time import tariffs on dairy products were reduced, such that it was actually less expensive to make the product in the California plant and ship it, frozen, all the way to Asia. Due to the very high costs in Japan, this resulted in a 40 percent savings in the cost of goods sold.

The number of retail shops in Asia increased to 81, and negotiations were completed to begin marketing Häagen Dazs in Korea through another joint venture. The following year, sales in the Far East increased a further 58 percent. Finally, in 1993, Häagen Dazs entered Taiwan, bringing the number of countries in the Far East with operations up to five.

[15]*Forbes*, "Life Begins at 80," 29 March 1993, p. 112.
[16]*Marketing*, 4 October 1990, p. 21.

Due to the relative strength of the business in Asia versus Europe, the team decided to concentrate its efforts on building the business in Europe. At the time of the take-over, Häagen Dazs Europe consisted of "three lousy shops in Germany." The European relaunch strategy was based on a slightly different positioning for the product than in the United States. In Europe it was to be clearly established as a luxury product. The only occupants of the super premium segment were local artisan producers who were more prevalent in some European countries (e.g., Italy) than in others.

The team devised a plan to become very big very fast, which required a huge capital investment on the part of GrandMet. They wanted to open 75 branded shops, basically at the same time, in order to close out the competition and control the superpremium market. The team felt that although it was a high risk strategy, if it worked they would "win big." The stated goal was to reach $300 million in sales in Europe in 4 1/2 years. A key milestone would be attaining $100 million in sales, at which point GrandMet would invest the capital required to build a plant in Europe. GrandMet approved the plan, which in the words of a former executive was "a huge roll of the dice."

The plan consisted of three elements: opening of branded exclusive shops in high traffic locations (unlike in the United States, these original shops were company-owned and run, and not franchised); broad scale sampling, including free testing, to further build brand recognition; and securing distribution through retailers. Executing this plan presented several challenges. First, getting space in the right locations was incredibly difficult. Trying to execute this simultaneously in 7 countries added to the difficulties. The team was stretched, building an organization in each country, from top management to shop employees. Each shop employed 50–60 people requiring significant training to ensure the right ambiance. Product procurement presented another challenge given tariff barriers and the sensitive nature of the product. However, the decision was made not to subcontract but to import all products from the United States.

The second element was to spread the brand name as fast as possible. They wanted the brand name to appear overnight and everywhere. Critical to this was to get exposure at high image events and among the opinion leaders. To further build brand awareness in year two, advertising was developed, but given the costs of the shop opening, there was not much budgeted for it. Thus, the team decided to go for a very inexpensive but provocative print campaign which was run only once. The objective was to visualise the Häagen Dazs experience in a way never before done with ice-cream—a very sensual, fashion-orientated, "art world" execution.

The final challenge was to get the product into retail shops where the bulk of the volume would be generated long term. The major retailers in Europe were very powerful, requiring huge listing fees for new brands. Despite these common practices and the desire of Häagen Dazs to enter retailers, the budget did not include money for listing fees nor promotional allowances. Further, the initial selling price was set at four times the United States price, already viewed as quite expensive there. The decision was made not to approach retailers but rather to wait for them to come to Häagen Dazs, thus establishing the power in the relationship. Sales offices were set up generally on the first floor of Häagen Dazs' shops, so that when the retailers did come, they were hit with the whole experience: branding, atmosphere and of course product sampling. Again, this was a risky strategy but with potentially high rewards.

The decision was made to start in the UK where the launch of Mars ice-cream had broken new ground in the premium market. Establishing the affordable luxury aura meant getting the product into the right mouths first. The initial distribution through London's upscale Harrods was followed by distribution via a number of high-class delicatessens and extensions into quality hotels and restaurants, where the printing of the brand name on menus helped build brand recognition. The launch was accompanied by salacious advertising that tantalized the taste buds of the consumer. The campaign worked better than expected. Due to the novel, somewhat controversial ads, the $1 million investment was estimated to have generated about $10-15 million in public relations.

The next step was Häagen Dazs ice-cream parlours where the product could be sampled in the right attractive environment. The first shop in London was opened in 1990 in Leicester Square and Häagen Dazs carts, catering, samples, etc. appeared at Ascot, Wimbledon, Henley, Hyde Park concerts, and all other major events. Following this was the extension to the leading supermarket chains, concentrating on shops in the vicinity of their ice-cream parlors. Finally, the expansion included an extension to other supermarket chains with a large number of in-store tastings and the opening of more franchised parlor operations.

Having met their first milestone of $100 million in sales, Häagen Dazs opened a $60 million ice-cream and frozen yoghurt plant at the end of 1992 in Arras, France—the "virtual center" of Europe's 350 million consumers. The new plant manufactured all products sold in Europe, and thus provided a hub for supply and distribution as it was located within a 24 hours' drive of all key markets and distribution points in Europe. The company also claimed that the location decision was based in part on the proximity to high quality local suppliers of dairy products. Local farmers supplied about 60 percent of the ingredients needed for the product. The plant had a capacity of 43 million liters annually; start-up capacity utilisation was 21million liters.

Häagen Dazs in 1994

Häagen Dazs had become the leading superpremium ice-cream brand in the United States and Japan with a growing presence in Europe and the Far East. In 1993, Häagen Dazs had a 4 percent market share of the U.S. ice-cream market and a decisive market leadership position with 58 percent of the U.S. superpremium segment. In Europe, volumes grew by 62 percent in 1993 and sales exceeded £75 million. Entry into European countries continued at a pace of about three to four each year, increasing distribution to 14 countries. In the Far East, Häagen Dazs was now in five countries, holding the number one spot in Japan in the superpremium category with sales of £140 million and volume growth of 20 percent. Future expansion plans included Saudi Arabia, Lebanon and Israel. Exhibit 11 gives the geographic split of sales in 1990 and the targeted breakdown for 1995, as well as market share positions in several markets and products.

In 1993, Häagen Dazs was selling 32 flavours in their basic pint containers, the Extrăas line of ice-cream with lots of "mix-ins," frozen yoghurts, a line of sorbets, and stick bars. The novelties were positioned toward the health-conscious consumer, but remained consistent with the Häagen Dazs brand equity of luxury and pleasure.

Products were developed by a small R&D team (10 people) located in New Jersey, USA. Along with developing innovative flavor combinations, this team worked with the marketing department to come up with exciting names, such as Caramel Cone Explosion and Cappuccino Commotion, two new flavors in the recently introduced Extrăas line. In addition, Häagen Dazs developed an information system in the United States called CSR (Corporate Sales Reporting) that allowed its marketing managers at headquarters to know in real time and with the highest level of detail which items sold (flavors, packaging) and where (nations, regions, single retailers; parlors, retailers, other channels). This quick, detailed information showed exactly "how many cases of Extrăas our distributors were buying, where each was selling best and what type of outlets were doing the most business when we first distributed the product in New England."[17] The

[17]Doug Hambry, Marketing Manager for Eastern US; SCOOP!, February 1993, p. 26.

EXHIBIT 11 Häagen Dazs Sales and Market Position in Selected Countries and Products

Sales Breakdown	1990	1995 (e)
United States	78.8%	50%
Europe	3.0%	30%
Pacific Rim	18.2%	20%
Total ($ million)	330	1,000

Market Shares*	1992	1993
France	3.2%	4.6%
UK	0.5%	3.9%
Belgium	na	4.4%
Germany	na	0.4%
Sweden	0.5%	1.6%
Japan	5.0%	5.7%

U.S. Market Shares**	1991	1992	1993
Singles	60%	60%	60%
Multi-packs	61%	61%	58%
Ice-cream Tubs	22%	22%	25%
Yoghurt Tubs	25%	27%	26%

* In value, of the total ice-cream market
** In value, of the superpremium ice-cream market.

advantages of CSR were not only evident in new product introductions, but also in analyzing trends in the market place and for setting production levels and mix. Extension to Europe was already foreseen in the near future.

The long-term company objective was to sell about 30 percent of their products through shops and 70 percent through retail outlets. They also had firmly established themselves in the emerging freezer centers such as Picard in France. In addition, they were experimenting with a range of innovative and unique outlets which fitted with the brand image of leisure and pleasure. Examples included movie theatres, Virgin Megastores and Blockbuster video rental stores in the United States.

In 1992, when Häagen Dazs had only 60 shops open in Europe, they served an average of 350,000 customers per week, more than 18 million a year. By August 1994 the company had 141 shops in Europe. With annual growth of 40–50 percent per year, it expected to have 300 shops open in two years. Observed John Riccitiello, General Manager of Häagen Dazs International: "We want our shops to be an event, a place where consumers and staff celebrate the experience of something that tastes great and gives you—even if just for a moment—a sense that it's worth being alive. It became our mission to provide that feeling."[18] There were two categories of shops: company-owned and franchised. The company-owned shops (about 45 of the total 141) were operated on a break-even basis, while the franchise shops were significant profit contributors.

One of the keys to Häagen Dazs' retail strategy was the provision of branded freezers for exclusive use of their products. These freezers allowed relatively easy sell-in, as they did not require the retailer to give up other products to provide space for Häagen Dazs. Along with the in-store advertising and brand awareness provided by the freezers,

[18] *Harvard Business Review*, "The Reinvention Roller Coaster: Risking the Present for a Powerful Future," Nov–Dec 1993.

the product quality was maintained as the temperature was closely monitored. In addition, the very high margins gave them relatively easy access to the stores. They currently had about 14,000 freezers in European retail outlets (at an average investment of FF 8,000) and aimed to double this penetration over the coming three to four years.

Much of Häagen Dazs' marketing efforts went toward distribution and sampling of the product either through their exclusive boutiques or via other innovative outlets (e.g., Virgin Megastores). In addition, they advertised through print and movie theatres, focusing on the pleasure and sensuality of the Häagen Dazs experience. In 1993 the company started using television in the UK and in 1994 did the same in France. The general thrust of advertising expenditures worldwide was to seek to unify the brand across all distribution channels, capitalizing on the range of outlets that Häagen Dazs' competitors so far had not matched. In the United States, Häagen Dazs' strategy was to raise their profile at the local community level through a strong program of local marketing and special event advertising.

The marketing efforts had particular success in de-seasonalizing demand. According to company sources, its sales volume on average was two times higher in the summer months than during the rest of the year which was quite low in comparison with other brands which, depending on the geography, reached ratios of 4:1 to 7:1.

Despite the high costs to enter the ice-cream market, there were several well-established major ice-cream manufacturers which were attempting to imitate Häagen Dazs. Unilever had been successful with its "Magnum" brand ice-cream stick bar. With "I Cestelli," Unilever was trying to establish a high-quality bulk product to be widely sold in retail outlets. In addition, both Unilever and Nestlé were reinforcing their market share position through the acquisition of the largest national players. In France, the acquisition of Ortiz-Miko enabled Unilever to double its overall market share, gain control over the catering segment (Ortiz-Miko was the leader in supplying restaurants), force Mars to change its French distributor, and exploit its Spring '93 launch of their upscale ice-cream brand (called "Maison Ortiz") sold in 500ml containers, priced 10–20 percent less than its direct competitor Häagen Dazs. This was happening while retailers were reducing the number of brands offered: in France they usually kept in addition to premium-price and own-labels, only two brands for each product segment and one of them had to be the leader.

The threat to Häagen Dazs was not limited to the major players. Also niche players had shown resolve to enter Häagen Dazs' segment. The most apparent threat in this arena was Ben & Jerry's. This company was the key U.S. competitor of Häagen Dazs, with a very similar product and marketing approach. In April 1994, Ben & Jerry's was launched in Europe, starting in the UK and using a strategy closely mirroring that which Häagen Dazs had used five years before. Ben & Jerry's started at Harrods and then moved into independents and supermarkets, first in London and the southeast of England. Ben & Jerry's ranked second only to Häagen Dazs in the U.S. premium sector. The growth of the Vermont-based company was 36 percent in volume in 1993, much higher than Häagen Dazs' 10 percent, with sales in the United States reaching $150 million. Its entry possibly posed a significant threat to Häagen Dazs if it replicated its U.S. success by ignoring traditional advertising techniques, relying instead on public relations generated from its campaigning on social and environmental issues (they donated 7.5 percent of pretax profits to charity). As with Häagen Dazs, Ben & Jerry's intended to import during the first two to three years, after which a UK manufacturing site was planned.

Although the company stated that, as of 1993, Häagen Dazs' European business had become profitable, some industry experts doubted their potential to generate profit in Europe. "In the year to September 30, 1991 [Häagen Dazs] had a turnover of just over £5 million in the UK, on which it made a pretax loss of £3.2 million."[19] Some competitors thought that in the French market Häagen Dazs had cumulated 1993 losses of FF 80 million out of revenues of around FF 250 million.

One of the major issues was the need to ensure a high level of utilization of the new plant in Arras. According to the expansion plans for Europe, Häagen Dazs had to reach $300 million in sales by 1995. This meant a 63 percent average annual increase for the years 1994 and 1995, over the $112 million revenues of 1993. Moreover the plan budgeted to complete the volume expansion of the Arras plant in only one year, doubling the volumes produced during 1994, in addition to the 1993 volume increase of 62 percent. This all took place in an atmosphere of increasing tension in the Paris European headquarters: "Once victory was achieved, bureaucracy took over. Paris headquarters began to quarrel with country management teams. Marketing began to flex its muscles at the expense of sales and operations. Headquarters in the United States were too worried about Ben & Jerry's encroachments to notice. The young hotshots in Europe began to wonder how to protect their position and, more important, what they could do for an encore."[20]

---

[19]*The Economist Intelligence Unit Limited*—EIU Retail Business N°424, June 1993.

[20]*Harvard Business Review,* "The Reinvention Roller Coaster: risking the present for a powerful future," November–December 1993, p. 97–108.

Under pressure of competition and profitability, Häagen Dazs had undertaken a set of moves to increase its sales volumes. It had introduced TV advertising, extended its penetration in restaurants and had gone into yoghurt-ice-cream. However, some retailers had refused to keep Häagen Dazs's freezers long after the launch phase as profitability had not been high enough to justify the space. In addition, Unilever's and Danone's (BSN) FF 100 million joint venture into yoghurt-ice-cream, as well as the introduction of a new product in this segment by Chambourcy (Nestlé), posed a formidable challenge to Häagen Dazs.

APPENDIX: GRAND METROPOLITAN, 1980–1993

GrandMet was started in 1962 as a small hotel and restaurant business in the UK. In its 32-year history, "GrandMet's executives have demonstrated little interest in corporate strategy, preferring the thrill of buying and selling assets at a dizzying pace."[21] Thus, GrandMet grew into a very large, highly diversified firm, primarily through acquisitions (and divestitures). Along with hotels and restaurants, holdings over the years have included betting shops, pub estates, milk and cheese products, optical stores, childcare centers and many other businesses. The company has been described as an "unpredictable maverick" with a "torrent of deals bewildering some observers."[22] Exhibit 12 describes the major acquisitions and disposals since 1980.

This reputation for being a conglomerate with little or no strategic focus had had a negative effect on the company's share price, and thus in the past decade company executives have been struggling to convince investors that this was no longer the case. Sir Allen Sheppard, Chairman and Group Chief Executive from 1986 to 1993, started to establish the company's strategic focus as an *international food, drinks and retailing group*. In fact, a major aim of the frenetic dealing which led up to and included the Pillsbury acquisition in 1988 for $5.8 billion was "to erase GrandMet's image as a conglomerate."[23]

This choice of focus was likely a result of the company's most successful business, branded alcoholic beverages. In 1972 GrandMet acquired International Distillers & Vintners; numerous other acquisitions since then in the branded drinks business made GrandMet into the largest player in the world in alcoholic beverages. GrandMet's portfolio of brands included J&B Scotch, Smirnoff Vodka, Gilbey's Gin, and Bailey's Irish Cream. This division has been the star of the group, with its success attributed to "brand building, securing distribution, innovative product development and marketing, and most of all, an awareness of consumer trends."[24]

[21]*Business Week,* "A Grand Design for Grand Met," 20 December 1993.

[22]*Financial Times,* "Burgers, Booze and Bull," 24 November 1993.

[23]*Fortune,* "GrandMet's Recipe for Pillsbury," 13 March 1989, p. 39.

[24]Harvard Business School Case Study #9-590-056, *Grand Metropolitan Adding Value to Foods,* December 13, 1989.

EXHIBIT 12 Acquisitions and Disposals by GrandMet since 1980

Year	Acquisitions	Disposals
1980	The Paddington Corporation	
	Carillon Importers	
	ALPO Pet Foods	
	Atlantic Soft Drink Company	
	Pepsi Cola San Joaquin Bottling Company	
	Liggett Group Inc.	
	L&M do Brasil	
	The Pinkerton Tobacco Company	
	Diversified Products Corporation	
1981	Inter-Continental Hotels Corporation	

Year	Acquisitions	Disposals
1982	Rumple Minza (liquer)	
1983	Children's World (education services)	
1984		CC Soft Drinks
1985	Quality Care (home healthcare) Cinzano (25% interest) Ritz & Casanova Hotels (minority interest) Pearle Optical (eye care) Sambuca Romana (liquer) G. Ruddle& Company (brewing) Hamard Catering Strathleven Bonded Warehouse	L&M do Brasil The Pinkerton Tobacco Company Express (northern milk activity) Mecca Leisure
1986		Liggett Group Inc. Stern Brauerei Brouwerij Maes Watney Mann and Truman Maltings Drybrough & Co. Ltd.
1987	Heublein Inc. (wines & spirits) Almaden Vineyards Inc. S. Reece Dairy Produce Packers Ltd. Saccone & Speed and Roberts & Cooper (wines & spirits and off licenses) Martell Cognac (10% interest) MacCormac Products, Connacht Foods (specialty milk powder manufacturing) Jim Dandy Company (pet foods) Fleur de Lys (frozen cakes & pastries) The Hervin Company (pet food)	Diversified Products Corporation Children's World (education services) Quality Care (home health care) Strathleven Bonded Warehouse Express Foods USA North Sea Oil interests Compass Services, Compass Vending, GIS, GM Health Care McGuinness Distillers
1988	Vision Express Healthworks (snacks) Eye + Tech J. Thayer & Sons (ice-cream) Kaysens (frozen cakes) Peter's Savory Products (meat & pastry) The William Hill Organization (retail betting) Wienerwald & Spaghetti Factory Restaurants	Atlantic Soft Drink Company Pepsi Cola San Joaquin Bottling Company Inter-Continental Hotels Corporation Meurice Hotel (Paris)
1989	The Pillsbury Company (includes Burger King) Wimpy Restaurants Sileno (wine & spirit distribution) Christian Brothers Metaxa (wine & spirit distribution) UB Restaurants	Wienerwald & Spaghetti Factory Restaurants The William Hill / Mecca Bookmakers Steak & Ale, Bennigan's Restaurants (acquired with Pillsbury) Pillsbury South American operations Pillsbury Grain Merchandising Pillsbury Seafood Operations Bumble Bee
1990	Remy Cointreau (20% interest)	Pubs into Inntrepreneur joint ventures with Courage
1991		Pizzaland and Pastificio Restaurants Express Dairy Foods
1992	Mcglynn Bakery Cinzano (full control)	
1993	Roush Products Company (foodservice & wholesale bakery suppliers) Buton (spirits) Gonzàles Byass (30% interest) North British Distillery (JV with Robertson & Baxter) Glen Ellen & M G Vallejo (California wines) Laurent-Perrier Champagne (21% interest)	Chef & Brewer Restaurants / Pubs Oakland Fast Food

Sources: Company Reports, Harvard Business School Case #9-590-056, *Financial Times.*

UNIT 4 Global Expansion in Service Industries

Case 4–1

Egon Zehnder International: Asian Expansion

Several issues were concerning Egon Zehnder International in 1994. The firm had been successful in a highly competitive market and had managed to grow without losing its distinctive character: an egalitarian group of highly professional and experienced consultants offering assistance to companies looking for top executives.

However, the partnership felt that in order to continue its expansion, the firm had to increase its presence in the Asia-Pacific region. The economic potential of such an action was appealing, but the past experience of the firm in the region was not entirely without its problems. The approach to executive search employed by Egon Zehnder International was alien to Asian markets and not all the offices of the firm were doing well in the region. Also, the recent expansion in the United States had put considerable strain on the firm's resources. Egon Zehnder International's Asia Pacific offices were in Sydney, Melbourne, Tokyo, Hong Kong, and Singapore.

Egon Zehnder International

History of the Firm

Egon Zehnder International was founded in Zurich, Switzerland, in 1964 by Dr. Egon P.S. Zehnder, a Swiss national and a graduate of Harvard Business School. In the early 1960s, he was attempting to establish Spencer Stuart, one of the leading American executive search firms, in Europe. Executive search was virtually unknown in Europe at that time, and the American ostentatious and brokerage-driven way of conducting search was perceived very negatively by the European corporate environment.

Egon Zehnder International (EZI) was created in response to the specific values and needs expressed by the European business community. Service was discreet and based on fixed fees, one profit centre, and long-term client relationships. The firm was to be managed conservatively and finance its development without relying on debt.

In keeping with this orientation, the firm relied on its own partners for its geographical expansion. The specificity of its culture and philosophy made Egon Zehnder International wary of expanding through the acquisition of local firms. The only exceptions to the rule were an unsuccessful joint venture with William Clark & Associates in the USA and the successful acquisition of the Canadian firm J. Robert Swidler Inc. in 1989.

Since 1964, the firm has progressively expanded in Europe, America, and the Asia-Pacific—by 1974 it had 10 offices and 37 consultants, by 1984 it had 20 offices and 100 consultants and by 1994, 39 offices and 159 consultants. The firm has shown steady growth in the worldwide executive search "league table"—in 1985, it was ranked 6th worldwide, in 1990 3rd, and since 1992, second. It is the number one executive search firm in Western Europe with \$70 million in billings (10 percent market share) and 25 offices. In the United States, the firm is ranked 9th, with \$10.1 million in billings (an estimated 1 percent of the executive search market) and 5 offices. In the Asia-Pacific region, the firm has 5 offices and \$11.5 million in billings. The 10 leading firms in the Asia-Pacific region record total revenues of \$100 million.

The industry structure is very different in Europe and in the USA: in Europe the 10 largest firms serve 47 percent of the market, while in the United States the 10 largest firms serve 28 percent of the market only.

Over one-third of Egon Zehnder International's assignments are searches for presidents and CEOs, with another 50 percent of searches being for executives who

This case was written by Professor Timothy Devinney and Marc-Antoine Cousin, MBA, as a basis for class discussion and not for the purpose of illustrating either the good or bad handling of a specific management situation.

report directly to senior management. Between 30 percent and 40 percent of their assignments are cross-border searches.

Philosophy and Structure

The Egon Zehnder International philosophy and culture is unique for the executive search business. The three cornerstones of its approach to executive search are as follows.

The one-firm concept

Egon Zehnder International is a completely integrated organisation acting as one single profit centre. All offices are fully owned by the partnership. Its compensation structure is unique to the industry, with the distribution of profits to the partners depending on the results of the firm worldwide and seniority only. No record is kept on individual performance, and all partners own an equal share of the equity of the company. In 1994, approximately $30 million in profits were shared among the firm's 80 partners, with shares ranging from 0.8 percent for a junior partner to 1.65 percent for a partner with 15 years or more experience with the company. At the nonpartner level, consultants receive fixed compensation with a bonus loosely tied to their performance.

The firm has an extremely low consultant turnover rate. In an industry where, on average, 30 percent of consultants change jobs in a year, Egon Zehnder International has a turnover rate of less than 2 percent a year. Each consultant is expected to conduct approximately 12 searches per year, with the average billings per search ranging from $60,000 to $90,000.

The firm has an extremely lean organisation structure. The CEO (Dan Meiland, since 1992) has almost no central staff and has the various office managers reporting directly to him. There are 39 office managers, 120 partners and consultants, and approximately 40 researchers—typically young university graduates. The central administrative staff consists of a controller, a secretary, and one accountant. The smaller offices tend to have at least two consultants, one researcher, and one or two support staff.

Consulting services

Egon Zehnder International prides itself on being more than a mere provider of executive search services. Although ultimately an executive search firm, it views itself as an "executive recruitment consultancy"—offering intelligence on the market and guidance in framing the roles and needs of the position in relationship to the strategy of company. A typical search process is detailed in Exhibit 1.

Richard Bahner, former Vice President of Human Resources at Citibank in Hong Kong, details an aspect of the consulting service he perceives as being offered by Egon Zehnder International:

> I'm looking for a full service provider. [. . .] I am looking for somebody who is going to be a partner. [. . .] I want someone who can put me in contact with what's going on. I want someone who can supply me with critical information, [. . .] give a view point of how we are perceived as an employer, [. . .] educate me on what is going on within the industry and what's going on in different market places. [. . .] I am looking for a consultant and intelligence first, and search is important but it is in some ways secondary [. . .]

To achieve this level of service and professionalism, Egon Zehnder International hires executives or management consultants with strong credentials—typically two university degrees, extensive international experience, and a strong record of achievements—and creates the conditions for a co-operative and financially attractive environment. The firm never hires anyone having worked for a competitor. Exhibit 2 details the composition of the consulting staff.

All consultants receive formal training at the beginning of their employment and ongoing development training every year. Partners meet twice a year. A general conference for all consultants and their spouses is held every second or third year. Regional conferences are held every one or two years.

All consultants, partners or nonpartners, do basically the same work. From the time of first contact, they personally interact with the client and potential or actual candidates. As a novice consultant's experience increases, they progressively create and maintain their own portfolio of clients.

Consistent with the consulting orientation of it service, the firm applies *a fixed-fee* structure. This is in stark contrast to the common practice in the industry of charging a fee proportional to the compensation package of the placed candidate—typically between 20 percent and 35 percent of the executive's compensation package. EZI's fee depends on the complexity of the assignment, its geographical scope, the level of responsibility, and the expected amount of time needed to complete the placement successfully.

A focus on long-term relationships

Egon Zehnder International focuses on the long-term client relationship instead of the pursuit of short-term profitability based on contingency fees. This aspect of their approach to search finds its expression in each stage

EXHIBIT 1 The Executive Search Process*

A typical search lasts for about three to five months and involves the following steps:

A. Understand the client's situation

Through research and meetings with and observations of the client organisation, the search consultant sought to understand as much about the client organisation and its specific needs as possible. This helped the consultant place in perspective the executive position to be filled. According to Mark Schappell, a consultant in Egon Zehnder International's New York office, *redefinition of the clients' needs right at the outset is the most important part of our work. You must understand the specific goals the client organisation has in mind for the candidate who will fill the position. You must understand the exact role to be filled, its tasks and responsibilities, and the skills and personal attributes necessary.*

B. Confirm proposal and specification

The consultant wrote a thorough proposal describing how he or she would approach the search. A detailed description of the position to be filled along with the past experience and personal characteristics of the ideal candidate were included.

C. Conduct systematic search

Consultants, along with researchers, conducted in-depth searches first for target companies, then for potential candidates through a variety of sources. These included industry research, internal and external databases, consultant's mental Rolodex, and the firm's contacts. A list of names was derived based on screening of the *hard facts:* industry-specific and functional skills, relevant achievements such as having successfully executed a turnaround of a distressed company and other requirements such as language ability. Consultants personally contacted potential candidates and references to obtain as much input as possible on each of them. In some instances, usually for general management positions, there were as many as 100 potential candidates and in others, such as narrowly defined financial services posts in derivatives or specific foreign markets, as few as 10 suitable candidates would be contacted.

D. Interview potential candidates

The consultants then appraised potential candidates on the *soft facts:* personality, charisma, drive, and other human qualities— through face-to-face interviews. The consultant's goal was to separate those candidates who would likely have a good fit with the client's organisation from those who were merely qualified. Comprehensive written reports of 8 to 15 pages per candidate were prepared and presented to the client for review. Such reports were not the industry norm but as one consultant said, Egon Zehnder International wanted its clients to feel that *we understand the problem better than anyone else does.*

E. Present candidates and check references

Egon Zehnder International not only arranged meetings between potential candidates and clients, but they were also the only major search firm whose policy was to attend each initial meeting between client and candidate. Fortunat F. Mueller-Maerki, a New York-based partner who, as a Swiss national, had been with Egon Zehnder International for 19 years, commented: *How can you call yourself a consultant if you aren't actually there for the meetings between your client and the candidates? If you spend a day with your client locked in a room away from telephone calls and responsibilities, and meet with each candidate, and see how they interact with the client, then and only then are you prepared to offer your recommendation, should you be asked to do so.* In addition, consultants solicited numerous references on each candidate, which further influenced the final decision.

F. Assist in negotiations and follow-up

The consultant assisted the client in negotiations with the finalist. The firm also helped clients to structure their offer and acted as an intermediary between the two parties.

*Source: Harvard Business Case 9–395–076, *Egon Zehnder International.*

of the service: consulting and search, due diligence on the background of the candidates and needs of the client, and follow-up with the candidate and client to assure the search was successful for both parties. The importance of consulting *and* search is summarised by Mike Thibouville, Regional Director of Human Resources at DHL in Hong Kong, as follows:

> We keep EZI briefed on an ongoing basis of the developments within DHL, even when we do not have a current search for them to undertake. By doing this, they are kept up to date with the developments and therefore understand the changes in the organisation. We then prepare a detailed brief on each particular position and are largely able to leave them to their own devices because they understand the culture and politics of the organisation.
>
> The other key issue for me is that they treat the candidates in the way that I would treat them directly—explaining how the process is proceeding and briefing unsuccessful candidates on why they were not successful. They realise that we feel that these candidates are also customers and therefore must be treated with the same respect that successful candidates are treated with. It is this attention to detail that makes EZI one of the best.

In the search process, it is a common practice in the executive search industry to put a client company and the placed candidate *off-limits* for an agreed period after the search has been completed. The executive search firm will not recruit the placed executive again and will not search for candidates in the client company during this period. Theoretically, all international firms offer this guarantee, but varying levels of interpretation of the concept are found in practice. At one end of the spectrum are firms that claim they put the client and the candidate off-limits for two years but do not adhere to their commitment. On the other end of the spectrum, Egon Zehnder International puts the candidate off-limits as long as s/he stays with the client organisation, and the company itself off-limits for three years.

In the process of selecting suitable candidates, Egon Zehnder is perceived as a unique firm. David Tang, Commercial Manager of Cubertias in Hong Kong, explains how he was recruited for his current position by EZI:

> With EZI, I actually spent over an hour with them the first time. Then two guys from EZI actually sat down to speak to me, and they went through a lot of things which I did not ex-

EXHIBIT 2 Composition of Consulting Staff

Citizenship[1]	Consultants
United States	24
United Kingdom	16
Germany	17
Switzerland	11
The Netherlands	9
France	10
Italy	9
Australia	5
Canada	7
Japan	6
Spain	8
Belgium	4
Denmark	5
Sweden	5
Argentina	3
Brazil	3
Austria	4
Finland	2
Greece	2
Hungary	2
Malaysia	1
Mexico	3
Portugal	1
Singapore	2
Turkey	1
Norway	1
China	1
Hong Kong	1

Degrees[2]	Consultants
MBA (or equivalent)	96
Miscellaneous Doctorates	20
Law Degree (JD or equivalent)	20
Masters Degree (MA, MSc)	52

Gender	
Female	12
Male	147

(1) May not add up because of dual citizenship.
(2) Includes foreign equivalent degrees.
Source: Egon Zehnder International.

pect them to go through, more personal kind of things. They were interested in my childhood, they were interested in my personal hobbies and other things that I do. [. . .] So apart from your qualifications and experience they are also interested in your personal profile, what kind of person you are. Are you this type of guy who will be a follower, or are you a natural leader, are you likely to be honest, your track record, those kind of things. And the locals [search firms], they never do anything like that.

Finally, the consultant who has placed the candidate remains in contact with him/her. Rex Au Yeung, Managing Director of Principal Insurance in Hong Kong, describes the relationship he has maintained with the consultant in the following terms:

> After I joined the company, the consultant at EZI has been maintaining contact with me. Ensuring that: 'how are you doing?' Mind you he was polite enough not to really poke his nose in and ask: 'tell me what you are doing?' He did it very discreetly, which is very good. [. . .] I think he views it as part of his role to ensure that the match is there and that he is putting the right person with the right company. I value that because I think it makes me feel that I am not a commodity. It makes me feel like a human being. They are recommending me to this company and, at the same time, making sure that I am enjoying it. A lot of companies, [. . .] once they have assigned someone and walked away with the consulting fee, they consider that the file is closed.

Egon Zehnder International in Asia

Egon Zehnder International opened its first Asian office in Tokyo in 1973, followed by a Singapore office in 1981 and a Hong Kong office in 1986. Exhibits 3 to 5 summarise the position of the firm in each of the Asia-Pacific markets.

Japan

Egon Zehnder International was the first executive search firm to establish a practice in Japan. The initial 10 years were difficult as the firm had to educate the market to the whole concept of executive search. Most of their clients were foreign multinationals in search of Japanese executives for their local operations. There was no shortage of qualified potential candidates, but the Japanese culture of lifetime employment and the associated disapproval of job switching made it very difficult to convince executives to change employers. This was worsened by the fact that foreign companies were less valued by employees than Japanese and working for them often was an irreversible decision: no return into the Japanese corporate world was possible.

By the early 1990s, executive search had progressively gained acceptance, as a decline in lifetime employment and an increasing acceptance of foreign companies by Japanese executives had made search easier. Increasingly, European and US multinationals were looking for Japanese executives in Japan instead of expatriates. Finally, a very small but increasing market of Japanese companies targeting their Japanese competitors for talent is slowly arising. Still, in spite of these trends, more than 90 percent of Egon Zehnder International's Japanese market clients are foreign companies. On the other hand, 90 percent of the placed executives are Japanese. Only 5 percent of clients and candidates are of non-Japanese Asian origin.

EXHIBIT 3 Characteristics, Revenue, and Position of EZI Offices in Asia-Pacific (1992)

	Egon Zehnder International					Executive Search Market Statistics		
Office/ Country	Revenue ($ millions)	Number of Consultants	Revenue Per Consultant ($ 000)	Number of Assignments	Cross-Border Searches as a Percent of All Searches	Revenue Leader $m	Revenue Top 10 $m	Market Size (est.) $m
Japan	3.9	6	650	90	25	5.2	25.1	120(1)
Singapore	2.4	4	600	64	98	2.4	11.5	n/a
Hong Kong	2.4	4	600	41	89	6.5	28.5	40(2)

(1) Estimate.
(2) Revenue of top 25.
Source: EIU, March 1994.

EXHIBIT 4 Breakdown of the Origins of EZI Clients and Candidates in the Asia-Pacific Region 1992

Office/ Country	Client Break-Down (percent)				Candidate Breakdown (percent)			
	Local	Other Asia-Pacific	American	European	Local	Other Asia-Pacific	American	European
Japan	10	5	45	40	90	5	2	3
Singapore	24	16	31	29	36	55	5	4
Hong Kong	18	11	33	38	52	34	11	3

Source: EIU, March 1994.

EXHIBIT 5 Origins of Clients for EZI Asian Offices

Offices → Origin of Clients	Japan	Singapore	Hong Kong
China			
Hong Kong		Y	Y
India			
Indonesia		Y	Y
Japan	Y	Y	Y
Malaysia		Y	Y
New Zealand	Y		
Singapore		Y	Y
South Korea	Y		
Thailand		Y	Y

Source: EIU, March 1994.

Singapore

In 1981, Egon Zehnder International was the fourth of the international executive search firms to open an office in Singapore. At that time, most large American firms were opening offices in Hong Kong. Egon Zehnder International preferred to wait for more information about the possible evolution of Hong Kong's political and economic situation.

Norman Wright, a partner from the Australian practice, managed the Singapore office. The first few years were difficult because of the small size of the Singapore market, the fact that many local companies of relevant size were government owned, and a local lack of understanding of executive search as it was being offered by Egon Zehnder International.

Charles Tseng, the managing partner of the Singapore office, explains this last point:

> Egon Zehnder has a consulting approach to executive search which is something a lot of Asians do not understand. Asians are very practical people, find someone and you get a commission, just like you find a house and you get a commission. We had a very challenging time in explaining and in pioneering our approach. [. . .] The immediacy of results was very important. So, frankly, many people could not see the difference between putting an ad in the paper and executive search.

Eventually the practice, carried on with determination and supported by the firm's global partnership, prevailed. It established a strong team of talented Chinese consultants and built a small but loyal domestic base in each of the Asian countries served by the office. It also benefited from the increasing investment by American and European multinationals in the region. Singapore saw heavy Foreign Direct Investment in the late 1980s with Malaysia coming into its own in the early 1990s.

In 1994, the Singapore office is among the best performing practices in the firm worldwide.

Hong Kong

In 1986, Norman Wright, while still developing the Singapore operation, established an office in Hong Kong. However, a lack of active support from the European headquarters and the fragmentation of Wright's efforts between the Singapore and Hong Kong offices resulted in less than average performance. One of the main reasons for these difficulties was to be found in the insufficient education of the local team to the unique culture of the firm. As Damien O'Brien, now the managing partner of the Hong Kong office, explains:

> They didn't have the leadership they needed, they were basically people from business—obviously not from search—so they came from industry into an environment with no partner and no leadership to help them build a new presence

in the local business community.

The office was unable to develop a strong local client base. Moreover, the referrals from other offices decreased as trust in the quality of the Hong Kong consultants' work deteriorated.

Perspective on the Asian Market of Executive Search

Development of Foreign Direct Investment in Asia

The stock of Foreign Direct Investment (FDI) in the whole of developing East Asia (China, the Asian NIEs,[1] Indonesia, Malaysia, the Philippines, and Thailand) is estimated to have increased by as much as $130 billion between 1980 and 1992. In the ASEAN countries (excluding Brunei), the growth rate of FDI reached an average of 14 percent p.a. during this period. In China it reached 15 percent p.a. and 25 percent p.a. in 1988–92. Between 1992 and 1994, FDI into China increased by 74 percent annually, suggesting a significant diversion of investments to China from other destinations, particularly the ASEAN countries.

Japan was the main source of FDI to developing East Asia. During the period 1985–1992 cumulative outward flows of Japanese FDI amounted to about $220 billion. Most of it was directed to nonmanufacturing activities in the USA. In contrast, the bulk of Japanese FDI in East Asia continued to be directed at manufacturing activities.

The United States and Europe continued to be important sources of FDI in East Asia. However the Asian NIEs have contributed increasingly to the FDI stock, mostly to ASEAN and China, and reached a cumulative value of close to $40 billion in 1980–92. A recent phenomenon is the increase in FDI from developing East Asia in the USA, which has reached a cumulative stock of about $10 billion. Exhibits 6–8 detail the evolution of inward FDI, venture capital and GDP in various Asian countries. Exhibit 9 gives an estimation of the geographic breakdown of subsidiaries of multinationals. Exhibit 10 shows the evolution of the number of listed companies in selected emerging economies.

Hadi Soesastro[2] explains that FDI in East Asia has been influenced by both push and pull factors. Four waves can be identified. The first took place in the 1960s and early 1970s and was motivated by protected local markets and the first major yen revaluation. Investment was concentrated mainly in joint ventures in textiles and household electrical appliances. In the 1970s, the region's bright prospects and the availability of low cost capital stimulated the second wave. This period was exemplified by import substitution projects in basic industries and the creation of American export platforms in consumer electronics and semiconductors. The third wave involved the relocation of labour-intensive industry from Japan and the Asian NIEs to ASEAN. It resulted principally from the appreciation of the yen and several NIE currencies in the 1980s. This shift was strongly encouraged by an improved investment climate in ASEAN countries.

The current, fourth, wave is characterised by the massive increase in FDI in China. Several reasons have been invoked to explain this boom. There is the obvious attraction of China's huge domestic market. This might signify a shift in interest to the disadvantage of ASEAN. Another reason is the dramatic increase in multinational investment activities from overseas Chinese networks, mainly from Hong Kong and Taiwan. These flows concern not only China but ASEAN countries also. Japan, with its massive outward production investment, also contributes significantly to this fourth wave. As China and ASEAN upgrade their technological capability, they are increasingly able to participate in global high-technological production networks originated in Japan and Asian NIEs.

Exhibit 11 provides a few indicators of the performance of various countries in terms of economic development.

Corporate Organisations in Asia

Traditionally, the family of the founder controls Asian conglomerates. Typically, the founder is an enormously energetic entrepreneur with remarkable business judgement. These companies are well integrated into a powerful network of connections in their home market. They also usually expand nationally and across borders along the lines of this network. This network provides preferential access to resources and markets.

However, in order to expand further afield and to credibly face international competition these family-based

---

[1]New Industrialised Economies: Hong Kong, Taiwan, South Korea, Singapore.

[2]In Edward K.Y. Chen & Peter Drysdale (eds), *Corporate Links and Foreign Direct Investment in Asia and the Pacific*, New York: Harper Educational, 1995, 1–8.

EXHIBIT 6A FDI Inflows 1971–1992 (& million)

	China	Hong Kong	Taiwan	Indonesia	Malaysia	Philippines	Korea	Singapore	Thailand	India
1971–80	300	1,757	775	2,052	4,101	1,339	1,084	4,158	945	n/a
1981–90	18,683	12,888	6,700	4,176	11,046	3,299	4,048	23,456	7,329	337(1)
1991–92	15,522	4,169	4,806	3,256	8,191	772	1,666	10,030	4,130	n/a
1993–94	56,259	n/a	n/a	4,051	8,581	2,300	1,489	11,200	2,018	n/a

EXHIBIT 6B Compounded Average Growth Rate FDI Inflows

	China	Hong Kong	Taiwan	Indonesia	Malaysia	Philippines	Korea	Singapore	Thailand	India
1971–80	n/a	31%	23%	3%	28%	8%	−9%	30%	19%	n/a
1980–90	33%	17%	29%	20%	10%	17%	46%	16%	29%	n/a
1990–92	79%	8%	8%	27%	33%	−34%	−12%	3%	−7%	n/a
1992–94	74%	n/a	n/a	9%	3%	153%	21%	0%	−45%	n/a

EXHIBIT 6C Compounded Average Growth Rate of GDP at Constant Prices

	China	Hong Kong	Taiwan	Indonesia	Malaysia	Philippines	Korea	Singapore	Thailand	India
1971–80	n/a	n/a	n/a	8%	8%	6%	8%	9%	7%	3%
1980–90	9%	n/a	n/a	5%	5%	2%	9%	7%	8%	6%
1990–92	11%	n/a	n/a	7%	12%	0%	7%	7%	8%	3%
1992–94	13%	n/a	n/a	7%	12%	3%	7%	10%	8%	5%

(1) Estimation based on U.N. Centre on Transnational Corporations, *World Investment Directory,* 1992.
Source: IMF

companies must overcome inherent inefficiencies—a lack of information systems resources, managerial competencies, and human resource management. Moreover, as T.C. Chu and Trevor MacMurray point out: "the real challenge, [. . .] lies in the management ranks. Middle management is often thin, senior management overloaded, and decision making too centralised in the hands of a few. Growth puts an enormous burden on this kind of management structure."[3]

These conglomerates are carrying on deep changes in their organisational structure and operating modes. An example is provided by Bangkok Bank,[4] a traditional Chinese business. In the past, the bank used to lend to clients on the basis of their connection to the bank's founder, Chin Sophonpanich. Trust or reciprocation of favours drove lending. The bank supplied financing to ethnic Chinese across South-East Asia. By the 1980s, the bank had become very westernised. Sophonpanich was no longer accessible to his old contacts. His son, Chatri, born outside

[3]The road ahead for Asia's leading conglomerates, *McKinsey Quarterly,* March 1993, p. 125.

[4]Example given by the East Asia Analytical Unit of the Australian Department of Foreign Affairs and Trade in the journal, *World Executive Digest,* May 1997, p. 25.

EXHIBIT 7 Distribution of Inward Foreign Investment Stocks by Source, 1980–92

Destination →	China			NIEs			ASEAN			All East Asia		
Source Country	1980	1988	1986–92	1980	1988	1986–92	1980	1988	1986–92	1980	1988	1986–92
United States	16.9%	15.8%	8.0%	35.6%	31.9%	n/a	12.0%	13.2%	13.5%	20.0%	20.7%	n/a
Europe	14.6%	9.5%	4.4%	22.4%	20.4%	n/a	20.5%	26.0%	15.6%	19.8%	20.5%	n/a
Japan	5.8%	7.2%	10.2%	24.1%	32.0%	n/a	32.9%	28.8%	25.8%	24.4%	25.5%	n/a
NIEs	55.8%	63.1%	70.9%	6.7%	6.2%	n/a	24.3%	22.3%	29.5%	26.0%	24.7%	n/a
ASEAN	0.5%	0.8%	0.8%	2.1%	1.1%	n/a	0.7%	1.0%	2.5%	1.1%	1.0%	n/a
Other	6.5%	3.6%	5.6%	9.0%	8.4%	n/a	9.5%	8.7%	13.1%	8.7%	7.6%	n/a
	100.0%	100.0%	100.0%	100.0%	100.0%	n/a	100.0%	100.0%	100.0%	100.0%	100.0%	n/a

Source: UNCTC, 1992, in Peter A. Petri, *The interdependence of trade and investment in the Pacific—Corporate links and FDI in Asia and the Pacific* New York: Harper Educational, 1995.

EXHIBIT 8 Venture Capital Pool in Asia (1993)

Country	Total ($ million)	Sources of Venture Capital			Stage of Development		
		Local	Other Asian	Non Asian	Start-up	Expansion	Mezzanine
Hong Kong/China	3,095	13%	24%	63%	11%	57%	14%
India	149	73%	2%	25%	59%	21%	13%
Indonesia	99	62%	32%	6%	1%	46%	53%
Japan	17,750	86%	4%	10%	3%	41%	53%
Korea	1,687	88%	3%	10%	36%	40%	20%
Malaysia	160	66%	14%	20%	27%	38%	35%
Philippines	58	35%	47%	19%	32%	68%	0%
Singapore	1,013	33%	26%	42%	14%	52%	31%
Taiwan	508	86%	8%	5%	23%	41%	30%
Thailand	98	17%	42%	41%	14%	61%	21%
Vietnam	0.01	0%	6%	94%	7%	81%	0%

Note on development stages: Start-up (establishing the business), Expansion (expanding production or marketing capabilities), Mezzanine (raising capital and finding strategic shareholders before public offering).
Source: The Guide to Venture Capital in Asia, *Asian Venture Capital Journal,* AVCJ Holdings Ltd, 1994/95.

EXHIBIT 9 Distribution of Subsidiaries of a Sample of 98 Western and Japanese Multinationals Across Countries

Country	Number of Subsidiaries
China	5
Hong Kong	27
India	21
Indonesia	14
Japan	42
Malaysia	22
Philippines	13
South Korea	10
Singapore	25
Taiwan	14
Thailand	16
Total in Asia-Pacific	253
Total Number of Subsidiaries Worldwide	1129

Sample taken from a population of 452 companies.
Source: John M. Stopford, *Directory of Multinationals,* New York: MacMillan, 1992.

China and Western-educated, became CEO. His links with Chinese networks are much weaker. The bank is now growing more slowly but more carefully than in the past. It has a public affairs/corporate affairs division, formally trained staff and is now a public company. An older ethnic businessman in Yangon summarised the impact of the transformation of Bangkok Bank: *I received my start in business with a loan from Chin Sophonpanich, whom I knew, to set up several factories. If I were starting out today, Bangkok Bank would demand to see well-kept business records and a detailed business plan before it would lend me even a modest amount.*

The typical pattern of evolution of these family owned firms is as follows:

From a Traditional Asian Firm . . .

A Expertise from outside the immediate family but within the clan is brought to the firm.

B Senior management control weakens as the firm expands and one or two middle managers are brought in.

C Capital is raised from sources outside the clan network, perhaps from a bank.

D The firm begins to seek closer relations with the political elite.

E Outside, professional managers are brought in.

F The firm is restructured and streamlined.

EXHIBIT 10 Evolution of the Number of Companies Listed in the Stock Market of Selected Emerging Economies

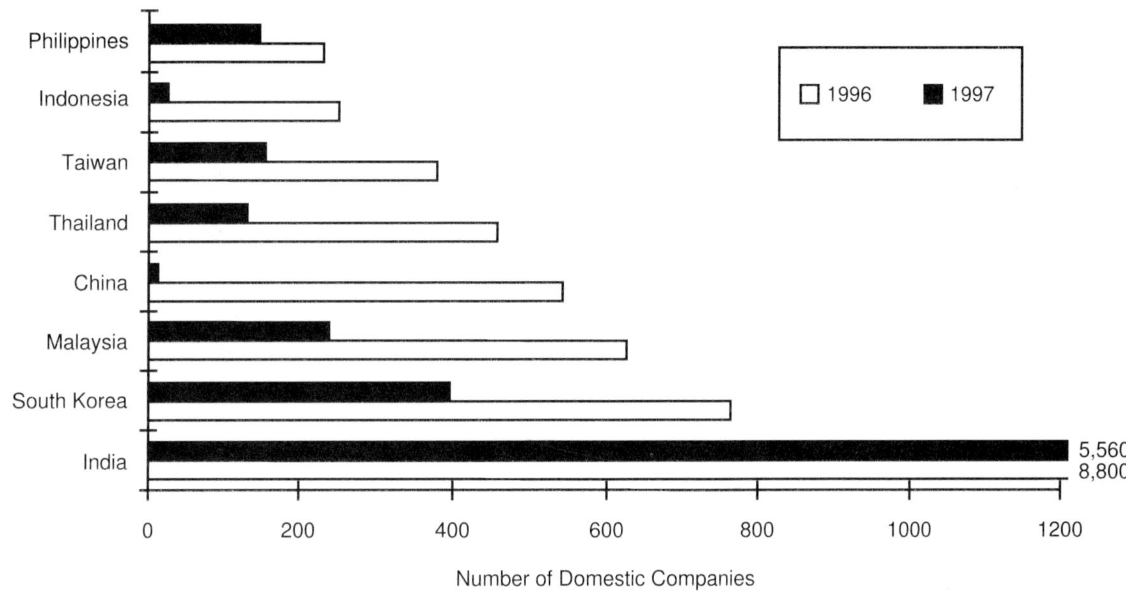

Source: International Finance Corporation as reported in *The Economist,* 26 July 1997, p. 100.

G The firm may list on the local stock exchange; capital may be raised on international bond markets.

H The family sells down its stock to a bare majority holding.

. . . to a Western-style Firm

Source: *World Executive Digest,* May 1997.

Family-owned conglomerates tend to find ways to protect the interests of the family, no matter how large the company becomes. Usually these companies are formed into a squat pyramid format, with a private holding company at the apex, a second tier holding the most prized assets—usually privately held—and a third tier comprising the group's publicly listed companies. The idea is the following: what is profitable is 100 percent mine, what is not—or is risky—is mostly not mine.

Even in its later stages of development, and typically when the CEO is not a member of the clan, these companies are characterised by a strong involvement of the owner in the strategic aspects of management. Dennis Ku, EZI consultant in the Hong Kong office and previously General Manager in a publicly listed Hong Kong toy company, describes the situation in the following terms:

> . . . you may be given a General Manager title, but you have got to be proactive—find out what they (the owner and Managing Director) do; find out where they demonstrate their weaknesses. [. . .] A good dynamic manager for a family company is 'tell me the areas you are interested in doing and I will do the rest for you'. Number two is 'I will make observations by the way, in areas that you do want to work on, and I will find out some of your problems'. [. . .] My job as a General Manager is to make it work. I don't have to be too protective about whom (in the lower ranks of managers) they cannot talk to; whom they can talk to.

Western multinationals, which function with a much more depersonalised culture, require more formal and structured means of cascading responsibility and centralised reporting. Senior managers are accountable for the results and enjoy autonomy vis-à-vis the means. They usually participate in the definition of the goals of the company.

Contemporaneous with the third wave of FDI in Southeast Asia in 1980s, many companies adopted the transnational model.[5] This structure holds that customer needs are growing more homogeneous throughout the world, so companies should no longer duplicate their

[5]John A. Quelch and Helen Bloom, The return of the country manager, *McKinsey Quarterly,* February 1996, 31–45.

EXHIBIT 11 Performance Figures of Selected Economies

	Unit	China	Hong Kong	India	Indonesia	Japan	Malaysia	Philippines	Singapore	South Korea	Taiwan	Thailand	Total Selected
Area	*000 km^2*	9600	1.1	3288	1948	377.7	329.8	300	0.6	99.2	36	543	24206
Population	*m*	1158.2	5.5	875.2	185	124.2	18.6	60.7	2.8	43.6	20.6	57.6	2570
Urban Population as Percent of Total Population	–	26%	n/a	28%	31%	77%	60%	48%	100%	74%	80%	27%	32%
University Students	*000*	2060	50	2050	1760	2290	70	1700	60	800	610	880	12860
University Students as Percent of Total Population	–	0.2%	0.9%	0.2%	1.0%	1.8%	0.4%	2.8%	2.1%	1.8%	3.0%	1.5%	0.5%
Workforce	*m*	583.6	2.8	314	80.5	65.8	7.06	26	1.55	19.3	8.58	32.7	1150
Workforce as Percent of Total Population	–	50%	51%	36%	44%	53%	38%	43%	55%	44%	42%	57%	45%
Literacy Rate	–	n/a	n/a	52.1%	77.0%	99.8%	80.0%	93.5%	90.0%	n/a	93.6%	90.0%	n/a
GDP Per Capita (1991)	*$*	390	14,341	361	638	27,233	2,448	743	11,845	6,498	8,083	1,604	2,061
Avg. GDP Growth (1987–91)	–	6.2%	4.6%	5.9%	6.8%	4.9%	8.3%	3.8%	6.7%	9.5%	7.9%	10.4%	5.4%
Merchandise Exports (1991)	*$ m*	71,910	98,560	17,664	29,142	314,786	34,349	8,767	59,025	71,870	81,047	28,428	855,907
Merchandise Imports (1991)	*$ m*	63,791	100,255	20,418	25,869	236,999	36,648	13,041	66,293	81,525	58,328	37,591	778,239
Trade Balance (1991)	*$ m*	8,119	(1,695)	(2,754)	3,273	77,787	(2,299)	(4,274)	(7,268)	(9,655)	22,719	(9,163)	77,668
GNP 1994 (1)	*$m*	509,566	116,018	296,749	168,888	4,629,459	67,163	65,764	68,666	378,086	n/a	141,519	
GNP Per Capita	*$/capita*	440	21,094	339	913	37,274	3,611	1,083	24,524	8,672	n/a	2,457	
GNP Growth 1993–94	–	–7%	14%	15%	11%	9%	12%	19%	19%	14%	n/a	15%	
FDI Abroad 1994	*$m*	2000	n/a	0	0	18100	0	404	2177	2524	n/a	493	
FDI Abroad growth 1993–94	–	–55%	n/a	0	0	31%	0	54%	22%	85%	n/a	123%	

Data is from 1992 unless noted otherwise.

(1) Data for Hong Kong extrapolated from data of 1992 from World Bank, *World Tables 1994*.

Source: IMF financial data, *Far Eastern Economic Review, Asia Yearbook*.

manufacturing and product development in each national market, but should leverage their capabilities across borders to achieve global economies, respond to local markets and transfer best practices. Senior managers were expected to think, operate, and communicate along three dimensions: product, geography, and function.

Today, however, the role of country manager is again on the rise, powered by opportunities for growth in emerging markets. The transnational model and the related weak definition of a country manager proved inappropriate for several reasons: (1) gaining entry into emerging markets, making contacts, and winning government contacts are becoming priorities; (2) globalisation notwithstanding, most multinationals still make the bulk of their profits on local sales and have to service local customers responsively. Their competition includes not only other multinationals but also fast moving and highly responsive local companies; and (3) most multinationals are responding to global competition and local political requirements by expanding their operations through local acquisitions or joint ventures.

These changes require senior resident country managers with good people skills, cultural sensitivity, the power to make decisions, and the ability to function well in the complex and often matrix-like organisational structure of the company.

Neville Kiang, Human Resources Manager with Rabobank in Singapore, explains the characteristics of successful managers in his organisation:

> Luckily, they also have the ability to develop relationships. First, communication style is different in Asia compared to different parts of the world. And even within this part of Asia, you have Chinese-based, Malay-based types of clients. The approach, the handling, has got to be different. But most of our managers are Asians in the first place, and they would have been used to handling different kinds of Asians. They are also Western educated. So dealing with people from America or from Europe is not a very difficult thing. Language ability is a very useful skill to have. Most of us can speak Mandarin and we learn a bit of Malay. [. . .] I would say our competent manager is a product specialist, a strong relationship builder and has total ability with our language.

European MNEs tend to source the local executive functions using local competencies. US MNEs tend to send executives from within the organisation to fulfil the function of local CEO.

Business Culture in Asia

Ethnic Chinese make up only 10 percent of the population of Southeast Asia, excluding China, but they control more than 70 percent of the region's corporate wealth. They are, therefore, unavoidable business partners or competitors in the region. Exhibit 12 gives an estimate of the ethnic breakdown of the population of several countries of East Asia.

The Chinese people, wherever they live, attach great importance to cultivating, maintaining and developing *guanxi* (connection or relationship). Guanxi can be translated as friendship between two persons, with implications of a continual exchange of favours in spite of official policies or rules. Guanxi is more a utilitarian relationship than an emotional bond.

The ethical obligation to return favours comes from the necessity to maintain face. Guanxi usually favours the weaker party, as the latter expects more help from the relationship than his *friend*. This reflects the Confucian principle of family cohesion. The reward for the strongest friend lies in the increase in *face* he receives. Face has two dimensions: *lian* and *mianzi*. Lian is the reputation and prestige attached to one's ethical and socially responsible behaviour. Mianzi is a measure of one's success. It is a measure of the size and usefulness of one's active *guanxi wang* (connection network). Though guanxi does not necessarily imply an emotional bond, expressing graceful attentions, giving gifts and compliments showing one's respect and feelings on appropriate occasions (*renqing:* humanised obligation) are civilised and powerful means of creating and strengthening relationships.

The Chinese network is formed from a collection of one-to-one relationships. Confucianism proposes five cardinal relationships that form the basis of the *da jia* (big family). These relationships are: sincerity between father and son, righteousness between ruler and subjects, distinction or separate functions between husband and wife, order between older brothers and younger brothers, and faithfulness among friends. They can be understood in literal terms or metaphorically. For example, the relationship between a teacher and a student is a form of father-son link, while the relationship between two colleagues of different experience connects to the idea of an older-younger brother link. By excelling in the immaculate art of one-to-one relationship building, a person can manipulate the notion of family and include very heterogeneous people linked to other members through one-to-one links (*zi jia ren:* one's own family people).

The social culture clearly affects the way business is conducted but also the way a manager is expected to behave in a company with Chinese employees. Bill Henderson, EZI consultant in Hong Kong, stresses this latter point, when asked to describe a competent manager:

EXHIBIT 12 Ethnic Breakdown of Selected Asian Countries' Population (1995 estimates)

	Population (*million*)	Chinese (*percent*)	Malay (*percent*)	Indian (*percent*)	Thai (*percent*)	Kinh (*percent*)	Korean (*percent*)	European (*percent*)	Others (*percent*)
Hong Kong	5.5	98.0%							2%
Taiwan	21.5	93.0%							7%
Singapore	2.9	76.4%	14.9%	6.4%					2%
Malaysia	19.7	32.0%	56.0%	9.0%					
Thailand	60.3	14.0%			75.0%				11%
Indonesia	203.6	2.5%	93.5%						4%
Philippines	73.3	1.0%	99.0%						
Vietnam	74.4	3.0%				90.0%			7%
India	936.5			97.0%					3%
China	1,203.0	92.0%							8%
Korea	45.6	0.1%					99.9%		
Australia	18.3	2.0%						94.4%	3.6%
Total with China and India									
Millions	2,664.6	1,157.6	274.4	910.4	45.2	67.0	45.6	17.3	146.7
Percent	100%	43%	10%	34%	2%	3%	2%	1%	6%
Total excluding China and India									
Millions	525.1	50.8	274.4	2.0	45.2	67.0	45.6	17.3	22.3
Percent	100%	10%	52%	0%	9%	13%	9%	3%	4%

Source: *The SBS WORLD GUIDE, 5th Edition,* Melbourne: Reed Reference Australia, 1996.

> These are the same qualities which make for success in managers in most environments, except that in Hong Kong and China there is a strong Confucian component. [. . .] A degree of paternalism, by showing the manager cares for his staff, [. . .] is important in terms of building a stable and successful organisation and retaining people.

This system can be usefully compared to the Japanese social system, as described by Chie Nakane:[6]

> The Japanese family system differs from that of the Chinese system, where family ethics are always based on relationship between particular individuals such as father and son, brother and sisters, parent and child, husband and wife, while in Japan they are always based on the collective group, i.e., members of a household, not on the relationship between individuals.

The Japanese system results in strong organisational loyalty because the sanction for deception is severe and irreversible: being ostracised by your old *family* and not being able to be accepted into new *family* relationships.

The Chinese system results in strong loyalty to the network. If the organisation and the network do not coincide, then a fairly low level of loyalty may be expected.

In this regard the Koreans are more similar to the Chinese. The *inhwa* (harmony) relationship binds two or more individuals, usually of unequal rank, without reference to organisational or other group membership. There is little organisational loyalty.[7]

Chinese and Malays share the same type of culture in terms of focusing on harmony instead of control, on relationship more than on task, being very aware and respectful of traditions, and seeking long-term results. But Malays tend to push these characteristics further than Chinese do. Furthermore, they are keener on being a decent person than achieving some earthly goal. Chinese are more balanced in this respect. Both cultures are very formal, context sensitive, have a strong respect for hierarchy, and low praise for individualism.

[6] *Japanese Society,* New York: Penguin, 1970, quoted in Min Chen, *Asian Management Systems: Chinese, Japanese and Korean Styles of Business,* London: Routledge, 1995, 59–60.

[7] Jon P. Alston, Wa., Guanxi and Inhwa: Managerial principles in Japan, China, Korea, *Business Horizons,* March/April 1989, 26–31.

Availability of Competent Managers

In Southeast Asia, managers having the professional competencies required to operate in the increasingly global economy are a scarce resource. As Eugene Y.K. Tan, Executive Director, Monsanto Singapore, explains:

> In Asia you have to identify the skill resources available from the location that you are going to. [. . .] Singapore and Malaysia provide a good pool of managerial human resources for Vietnam and Indonesia. Malaysia, in general, has limited or poor resources for managing in China. For China, besides Singapore and Hong Kong, one may find suitable candidates from Taiwan or maybe even from Japan. There are also fundamental custom, historical and cultural differences. Thus, for example, if you have facilities in Korea, you don't get Japanese to run the operations there.

On the other hand, the Indian subcontinent seems to offer a satisfactory pool of managerial competency.

> I can quite comfortably say, in all the support areas, in all the functional areas that I see, we Indians probably have the benefit of having some of the best talent in Asia. I see quality people here being, generally speaking, much better than in other Asian countries for almost every functional area you can think of. (Pradeep Mathur, Managing Director, Tupperware India)

One major issue in terms of the managerial pool in Asia, relates to the evolution of competencies. As the local economies progress toward maturity, will they continue to depend on the external world for providing managerial competency? Bill Henderson is fairly sceptical regarding this evolution:

> I don't see any major changes in the foreseeable future, [. . .] unless there is a huge economic downturn in which the demands of foreign multinationals to expand are put on hold, [. . .] you're still, certainly over the course of the next five to ten years, going to see immature labour markets here. [. . .] Because of the very high element of personalism in terms of allegiance to management, you will still [. . .] see senior managers moving, either being promoted out of the region, or alternatively moving as a result of executive search activity and then the management layer below them drifting away, either following them where they are going or alternatively accepting other positions.

Neville Kiang, HR Manager with Rabobank, gives a different view on this same issue:

> Singapore is now the feeding tank of talent for the economies that are around here. As these economies start funding their own infrastructure, the requirement for [. . .] experienced managers will increase. The strain on Singapore's resources will increase as well and that's why the sourcing will have to expand further, because Singapore is not big enough. Eventually what will happen is that the trend will go in reverse in the way that Singapore will receive experienced managers from the now emerging economies around. But this is probably not before ten years.

Exhibits 13 and 14 give information about compensation levels of executive in various cities.

Competition

Executive search was virtually unknown in Asia before 1965, when Boyden first opened an office in Hong Kong. The profession has expanded considerably since then and reached varying levels of maturity across countries. Exhibits 15 and 16 present the relative positions of the leading firms in the region in terms of revenue, assignments and consultants.

In Hong Kong, Korn/Ferry and GKR opened their offices in the late 1960s, but it took 10 years for the market to develop. In the late 1970s, Spencer Stuart began operations, soon followed by Amrop International and Russell Reynolds. In the mid 1980s, TASA, Egon Zehnder, and Norman Broadbent opened offices. By the late 1980s local firms began appearing: Anthony Au & Associates (now included in Ward Howell International), LTA, and Executive Access, founded by Ranjan Marwah, which is now the major volume player in Hong Kong. In 1992, the total billings of the 13 leading firms amounted to $28.8 million.

In Singapore, the search market was developed initially by Korn/Ferry in 1976. As in Hong Kong, the major international firms have all opened offices in Singapore. In the early 1990s several local firms established themselves: Lena Lim & Associates and Executive Talent, with $0.4 and $0.9 million revenue in 1992 respectively.

In Taiwan, Boyden opened an office in 1982, but the market only began to develop by the end of the decade. In South Korea, the executive search market began to develop in the late 1980s with Boyden, Ward Howell, and T.A.O. being the three major players.

Korn/Ferry opened an office in Kuala Lumpur in 1976 and was still the only international firm with operations in Malaysia in 1992. In Indonesia, Boyden is the only international player in the market, having established an office in 1992.

Thailand and India are still very undeveloped markets, and once again Boyden proved to be the pioneer in both markets. In Thailand, Korn/Ferry and T.A.O. also have established offices while Executive Access, utilising the connections of its Indian founder, does a considerable

EXHIBIT 13 Compensation Levels, Cost of Living and Office Rental Levels in Various Cities

	Gross Salaries ($/year)[1]			Purchasing Power ($/year)[2]			Cost of Living Base: HK = 100		CBD Office Rents ($/m²)[4]
	Senior Mgr	Middle Mgr	Junior Mgr	Senior Mgr	Middle Mgr	Junior Mgr	1996	1994	
Zurich	166,785	n/a	70,287	115,091	80,786	55,227	105	109	n/a
Frankfurt	158,689	98,860	61,363	108,495	74,622	48,644	86	92	n/a
Hong Kong	141,624	73,723	40,104	120,380	65,893	39,005	100	100	1,363
Tokyo	141,345	87,766	54,495	89,373	59,555	38,636	133	171	1,011
Paris	123,065	76,008	46,945	89,972	59,472	39,202	90	95	n/a
Singapore	119,137	61,382	31,626	96,055	48,294	25,283	94	94	895
Milan	116,135	68,716	40,659	74,632	46,942	30,326	84	82	n/a
Seoul	115,903	64,585	35,989	97,262	58,617	34,739	98	99	788
Taipei	111,741	62,664	35,140	95,109	57,645	33,616	91	100	559
London	95,741	57,067	34,015	75,018	48,547	30,628	81	85	n/a
Sydney	92,870	60,154	38,964	64,671	45,370	32,840	80	79	444
Kuala Lumpur	80,541	36,148	16,296	67,518	33,851	16,520	76	79	252
Bangkok	73,202	31,834	13,844	70,196	34,173	15,882	76	80	272
Jakarta	72,141	26,342	11,135	60,395	26,640	11,256	83	83	209
Manila	47,581	22,343	10,961	40,833	20,769	10,827	72	73	464
Shanghai[3]	32,340	12,154	6,798	26,484	10,431	6,095	101	n/a	801[5]
Ho Chi Minh	22,740	12,519	6,870	n/a	n/a	n/a	83	77	n/a

(1) Median at each level. Survey does not include expatriate pay.

(2) Median of net income after tax of a married person with two children, with cost of living factored in, using Hong Kong as a base. Expatriates are excluded.

(3) Manufacturing only.

(4) Collier Jardine Asia Pacific Property Trends (1997).

(5) Estimation from other sources.

Source for (1)–(3): Change is in the Air, *World Executive Digest,* April 1997.

EXHIBIT 14 Breakdown of Salaries by Function (dollars/year)

	Finance & Administration		Sales & Marketing		Manufacturing & Engineering		HR / Personnel		EDP / Computers	
	Senior Mgr	Entry-level Mgr	Senior Mgr	Entry-level Mgr	Senior Mgr	Entry-level Mgr	Senior Mgr	Entry-level Mgr	Senior Mgr	Entry-level Mgr
Bangkok	74,383	12,683	62,343	12,612	60,516	11,577	69,750	10,917	67,977	14,917
Hong Kong	149,381	38,181	137,172	40,804	141,752	36,967	131,594	41,295	135,664	38,800
Jakarta	80,874	11,875	73,537	12,336	68,311	9,023	86,761	11,639	71,863	12,109
Kuala Lumpur	84,705	15,844	79,347	16,192	87,565	14,755	82,288	13,223	101,205	15,036
Manila	41,237	8,810	57,623	9,586	46,618	9,449	52,136	8,860	42,869	8,960
Seoul	103,417	31,247	113,815	34,548	100,278	33,187	113,449	36,337	102,376	34,434
Singapore	120,829	33,020	126,580	32,852	109,351	30,702	114,816	29,712	122,320	32,124
Taipei	113,878	29,248	100,290	30,146	93,517	32,160	125,004	29,618	120,554	31,377

Survey does not include expatriate pay.
Senior Mgr: Head of division or head of a critical function. 11–50 subordinates. 6–10 years experience.
Entry-level Mgr: Supervisor or technical specialist. Minimal experience.
Source: Change is in the Air, *World Executive Digest,* April 1997.

EXHIBIT 15 Leading Executive Search Firms' Office's Revenue by Country Where Offices Are Open, 1992 ($ millions)

Firm	China	Hong Kong	India	Indonesia	Japan	Malaysia	Philippines	Singapore	South Korea	Taiwan	Thailand	Total Selected	Total World	Asia-Pacific as Percent of Total
Russell Reynolds		4.6			4.1			2.0				10.7	85.0	12.6%
Egon Zehnder International		2.4			3.9			2.4				8.7	95.2	9.1
Korn/Ferry		2.2			5.2	0.8		1.2			0.3	9.7	118.0	8.2
Spencer Stuart		3.0			3.0							6.0	6.4	0.9
Ward Howell		2.2			2.1				0.5	0.7		6.5	44.8	13.4
Executive Access		6.5										6.5	6.5	100.0
Boyden		2.1	0.8		0.7			0.7	0.4	0.5	0.6	5.8	24.5	23.7
Amrop		0.6						0.9		0.6		2.1	70.5	3.0
International Search Partnership		2.5						1.0		0.6		4.1	33.8	12.1
TASA		1.5						0.7				2.2	31.5	7.0
GKR Neumann		1.0			2.3							3.3	53.0	6.2
LTA		1.2						1.2				2.4	2.4	100.0
Paul Ray/Berndtson					0.8							0.8	52.0	1.5
Total	0	28.8	0.8	n/a	22.1	0.8	n/a	10.1	0.9	2.0	0.9	68.8	788.6	8.7

Source: EIU, 1994.

EXHIBIT 16 Leading Executive Search Firms' Office's Assignments and Consultants by Country Where Offices Are Open (1992)

	Hong Kong		India		Japan		Malaysia		Singapore		South Korea		Taiwan		Thailand	
Firm	Assig..	Cons.	Assig.	Cons.	Assig.	Cons.	Assig.	Cons.	Assig.	Cons.	Assig.	Cons.	Assig.	Cons.	Assig.	Cons.
Russell Reynolds	100	6			85	7			48	4						
Egon Zehnder International	41	4			80	6			64	4						
Korn/Ferry	72	5			120	9	30	3	74	5					18	1
Spencer Stuart	110	6			62	6										
Ward Howell	58	3									45	5	n/a	2		
Executive Access	105	10														
Boyden	100	7	77	4	30	0			41	2	28	2	51	3	60	8
Amrop	32	2							42	3			30	2		
International Search Partnership/Norman	95	4														
Broadbent																
TASA	1.5	n/a							40	0.7						
GKR Neumann	28	1			50	2.3										
LTA	1.2	n/a							1.2	n/a						
Paul Ray/Berndtson					0.8	17										
Total	847.2	48	77	4	427.8	47.3	30	3	310.2	18.7	73	7	81	7	78	9

Assig. = Assignments.
Cons. = Consultants.
Source: EIU-1994.

amount of work in India from its Hong Kong base. However, corruption, strong family ties, unofficial networks, and low average compensation levels contribute to make India a difficult market to crack.

In China, there are significant constraints on how executive search firms can operate. This state of affairs forces firms wanting to conduct China searches to do so from their Hong Kong offices. Potential candidates are contacted initially from Hong Kong with the consultant travelling into China to informally meet them at a later stage. However, in spite of the difficulties, some firms, such as Korn/Ferry, were considering opening offices in Shanghai.

The executive search industry encompasses a very diverse group of firms: from one-man shops operated by a local ex-executive using his personal address book to highly professional international firms practising extensive systematic research. In between are local firms that do a volume business by recycling resumes with minimal prescreening. It appears that differentiation between firms is difficult to establish, and the whole sector suffers from unprofessional individual behaviour. Bill Henderson stresses this point:

> I think that there is, in various segments of the market place, a degree of disillusionment with professional search which is reflected in comments of: 'they're all the same' [or] 'they're all unprofessional' [. . .] To that extent, the whole search environment is degraded by comparison with the situation that prevails in other mature markets.

Firms also try to differentiate themselves by their recruiting *philosophy.* Egon Zehnder International, with extensive off-limit rules and its consulting style of search, is at one end of the spectrum, while firms like Executive Access, the number-one firm in Hong Kong, dominate the volume business. The latter has an approach very different from that pursued by EZI—they extensively broker executives to organisations and receive a commission related to the compensation package of the selected candidate. Executive Access directs its efforts toward those executives who have the strongest bargaining position in the market.

Among executive search firms, there are generalists and sectoral or functional specialists. Firms also tend to specialise on specific levels of management. Exhibit 17 details organisational information and functional specialisation for the leading firms. Egon Zehnder, Korn/Ferry, Russell Reynolds and Spencer Stuart all compete for searches for top general or divisional managers and are often perceived by clients as being very comparable firms.

Among international firms, differences also exist in terms of the type of consultants they employ. Russell Reynolds, Korn/Ferry and Spencer Stuart will employ local *grey-haired* Chinese with the requisite political connections. Egon Zehnder International prefers to grow their own local consultants and inculcate them in the unique EZI culture.

Overall, the executive search market is divided in several niches, and as Bill Henderson points out, firms do not find themselves often in a direct competitive situation:

> We are occasionally involved in, as we call them, 'shoot out' situations with one or two of our quality competitors, but I would say that probably 50, 60, maybe even 70 percent of the work that we get is obtained as a result of either direct business development initiatives or alternatively, it comes [. . .], direct from clients without the competition being involved.

Asian Expansion?

As the partners prepared for the 1994 annual partner's meeting, there was a clear sense that a decision needed to be made in regard to Egon Zehnder International's Asia strategy. Should the firm *wait and see* as some partners were proposing. As one consultant said: *After all we have been successful in operating from Tokyo, Singapore, and Hong Kong. Why not build on that success?* Interestingly, the partners from the Asia Pacific region were proposing expansion but could not achieve consensus on where to expand.

Case 4–2

Kenny Rogers Roasters in China (A)

It was mid-October 1995 and Tony Wang, President of Franchise Investment Corporation of Asia (FICA), had just returned to Hong Kong from a one week visit to Beijing. FICA had earlier in the year been granted the franchise

This case was prepared by Professor Allen J. Morrison in collaboration with Professor J. Stewart Black and Tanya Spyridakis. Additional assistance was provided by Jan Visser. The case study is not intended to illustrate either effective or ineffective handling of a managerial situation.

EXHIBIT 17 Ownership Structure, Functional Breakdown of Searches, Fee Structures and Incentive System of the Leading Executive

		Assignments by Function				Fee and Compensation	
Firm	Ownership Basis	Corporate Executive, Chairman	Divisional Executives	Functional Executives	R&D Technical, Production	Fee Structure (1)	Consultant Bonus Based on: (2)
Russell Reynolds	Global	10%	20%	60%	10%	Fixed	Individual/Subsidiary
Egon Zehnder International	Global	36%	4%	45%	15%	Fixed	World-wide
Korn/Ferry	Global	23%	26%	34%	17%	Fixed/percentage	Individual/Subsidiary
Spencer Stuart	Global	52%	0%	38%	10%	Percentage	Individual/Subsidiary
Ward Howell	Local	17%	20%	50%	13%	Fixed/percentage	Individual
Executive Access	Local	25%	10%	55%	10%	Percentage	Individual
Boyden	Local	20%	16%	50%	14%	Percentage	Subsidiary
Amrop	Local	27%	21%	47%	5%	Fixed/percentage	Subsidiary
Norman Broadbent	Global	8%	23%	58%	11%	Percentage	Individual
TASA	Global	16%	0%	69%	15%	Fixed/percentage	Individual/Subsidiary
GKR Neumann	Global	46%	0%	39%	15%	Fixed	Individual/World-Wide
LTA	Local	19%	0%	65%	16%	Percentage	Individual/World-Wide
Paul Ray/Berndtson	Local	20%	25%	40%	15%	Percentage	Individual

(1) **Fixed** describes a fee structure in which the level of fee does not depend on the salary of the successful candidate. **Percentage** describes the opposite situation.

(2) The incentive structures of firms vary from a system in which consultants are rewarded on their **individual** performance only to a system where compensation bonuses depend exclusively on the global performance of the firm **worldwide.** An intermediate situation involves bonuses based on the performance of the local **subsidiary.**

Source: EIU, 1994.

rights for Kenny Rogers Roasters (KRR), a rotisserie chicken restaurant concept, for both Beijing and Shanghai. While Wang was eager to move forward, serious concerns had emerged over the challenges of doing business in China. Just as most foreign companies had looked to local partners to help ameliorate some of these concerns, Wang had begun joint venture discussions with three companies. Although each potential partner appeared eager to work with FICA, Wang was wondering whether the time was right to proceed and if so, with which company.

KRR Overview

The driving force behind KRR was John Y. Brown, an entrepreneur with a long history in the food service industry. In 1964, Brown, who at the time was a 29 year old Kentucky lawyer, and his partner, 60 year old Jack Massey, purchased Kentucky Fried Chicken from 74 year old Harland Sanders for $ 2 million. Over the next 5 years the partners added 1,000 new stores and grew sales by an average of 96 percent per year. Observers attributed this growth to two main factors: (1) the company's reliance on less costly franchise expansion over company-owned stores, and (2) Brown's ability to select hard charging and entrepreneurial franchisees. KFC was sold to Heublen Inc. in 1971 for $275 million making both partners wealthy men.

During the 1970s Brown went on to become Governor of the State of Kentucky and owner of three professional basketball teams including the Boston Celtics. In 1979 he married 1971 Miss America, Phyllis George. During the early 1980s Brown helped launch Miami Subs and Roadhouse Grill franchises and bankrolled his wife's Chicken by George line of prepared chicken sold in grocery stores.

By the late 1980s, Brown was becoming increasingly convinced of the enormous market potential for roasted chicken. The health craze that swept the United States in the 1980s significantly increased the demand for lighter, nonfried food options. This affected many segments of the food industry, and the poultry industry was no exception. Many restaurant owners began investing in rotisserie ovens and introducing more healthy menus.

In looking for a new way to grab the customer's attention, Brown thought it a natural to team with long-time friend Kenny Rogers. Kenny Rogers, once described as "the most popular singer in America," had a career that spanned more than three decades, half of which as a solo artist. Rogers's popularity manifested itself in the many awards and honors that he had received over the years: three Grammies, 11 People's Choice Awards, 18 American Music Awards, five Country Music Association Awards, eight Academy of Country Music Awards, four platinum albums, five multiplatinum, one platinum single, and numerous gold albums and singles. Rogers also dabbled in several businesses including a partnership in Silver Dollar City, considered country music's capital, in Branson, Missouri. When Brown came up with the concept of a rotisserie chicken restaurant chain, Rogers was very enthusiastic.

> When I saw this concept, I thought it was so outstanding I was willing to put my reputation on the line, not just as an endorser, but as an owner and partner . . . I believe nonfried chicken is the wave of the 90s, and working with folks who made fried chicken a billion dollar business gives me the confidence we are doing it right.

Kenny Rogers Roasters (KRR) began operations on January 17, 1991, in Louisville, Kentucky and opened its first restaurant in August of that year in Coral Gables, Florida. The menu: citrus and herb-marinated wood roasted chicken and about a dozen side dishes such as mashed potatoes and gravy, corn-on-the-cob, baked beans, and pasta salad. Growth was rapid. From an original group of five people, the company grew to include a corporate staff of more than 100. By late 1995, the company had moved headquarters to Ft. Lauderdale, Florida, and had over 310 stores. KRR operated in approximately 35 U.S. states, had more than a dozen stores in Canada and had at least one store in Greece, Cyprus, Israel, Malaysia, Korea, the Philippines, Japan, Jordan, and Singapore. Company plans called for the addition of almost 1,200 new stores in the United States and 240 stores internationally by 2002.

The Rotisserie Chicken Business

The market's switch to rotisserie chicken did not escape the competition. In 1993, KFC spent $100 million to roll out its Colonel's Rotisserie Gold in all 5,100 of its stores in the United States. Rotisserie chicken constituted about 25 percent of *KFC* sales in company-owned stores by the end of 1995. In all, KFC enjoyed a 58 percent share of the retail chicken industry, and gross sales of over $3.5 billion. Other fast-food restaurants, noting the trend, also attempted to expand into the nonfried market. For example, Popeye's Famous Chicken entered the nonfried market despite its lack of capital; it featured a roasted chicken that could be cooked in the same ovens as its biscuits. Boston Market (formerly known as Boston Chicken) was another up-and-coming competitor in the rotisserie chicken segment. Opening its first store in 1985, by 1993 the company had 166 stores in approximately 25 states, and sales of

$154 million (more than triple its 1992 sales). By the end of 1995, Boston Market had become a public company with over 825 stores operating (none outside the United States) and was opening a new store each business day.

While sales of rotisserie chicken were still considerably smaller ($700 million versus $6 billion for fried chicken in 1993), advocates of nonfried chicken firmly believed that the gap would close within 10 years. Statistics confirmed the growing popularity of nonfried chicken in the United States: sales of fried chicken consumed outside the home grew an average of 3.5 percent from 1989 to 1995, while sales of nonfried chicken grew an average of 10.75 percent in the same period. Annual growth in per capita chicken consumption between 1984 and 1994 was 38.5 percent.

Despite its rapid growth, rotisserie chicken had several drawbacks. Uncooked rotisserie chicken had a shorter shelf life than fried chicken. Rotisserie chicken took 75 to 90 minutes to cook compared to 30 minutes for fried chicken. Additionally, a cooked rotisserie chicken needed moisture and would spoil if kept under a heat lamp for too long; this, however, posed no problem for fried chicken. Finally, customer demand would often be greater than supply in peak hours, which was difficult for rotisserie chicken vendors due to the longer cooking times.

Kenny Rogers Roasters

By 1995 KRR was still a privately held company, with no immediate plans to go public. The equity breakdown was approximately John Y. Brown, Jr. 28 percent; Kenny Rogers 14.5 percent; and a group of Malaysian investors 35 percent; various friends of Brown and Rogers held the remaining 22.5 percent. Brown served as the company's CEO and Chairman of the Board. Rogers sat on the board of directors and, though he was not directly involved in running the company, attended many meetings and assisted in promoting the company. In building his management team, Brown recruited several people with whom he had worked in his days at KFC. Other management talent was recruited from fast-food chains such as Wendy's, Burger King, Pizza Hut, Arby's, and McDonald's.

In the United States, KRR's restaurants averaged 2,800 square feet in size, with seating capacity for 80 to 100 people. The stores had a country-western motif and were decorated with memorabilia from Rogers's career. Television monitors were also located throughout the restaurant showing customized music videos featuring performances by Rogers and other country and western entertainers. Advertising and promotional messages were interspersed with the music videos. A signature wood-fire rotisserie with surrounding wood piles were placed in full view of the customer. The serving counter was buffet-like in style, with a wide range of side dishes kept warm in a glass display case. Servers on the other side of the counter put together plates for customers based on their choice of entree and side dishes.

All menu items at KRR restaurants were prepared onsite. The chicken was marinated overnight and roasted the next day over a hard-wood fire to an internal temperature of about 180°. Most side dishes were made from scratch, though a few items were prepared from mixes developed at the company's training and development center near the corporate headquarters. The labor-intense nature of KRR was not without its downside; labor costs averaged between 26 and 27 percent of sales, food costs ran just under 30 percent.

A free-standing Kenny Rogers restaurant with a drive-through window generally went through 1,800 chickens a week and generated approximately $1 million in annual sales. By 1995, take-out orders comprised about 45 to 50 percent of sales; the company's goal was to increase this to around 60. Total KRR revenues in 1995 were estimated at $321 million, up from $68.7 million in 1993 and $150 million in 1994.

KRR Franchises

From the very beginning, franchising played a big part of the company's expansion. By 1995, franchise stores accounted for about 85 percent of KRR's 310 stores. All of KRR's international stores were owned by franchisees. Though the company had solicited a few of its franchisees, most franchisees had approached KRR. The company carefully screened all franchisees for previous restaurant experience, especially multiunit operations experience, references, credit rating, and net worth. KRR wanted franchisees who knew and liked the restaurant business, who were or had been in it, and who appreciated the difference the company was trying to make with customer service and product quality.

KRR set up *franchise* and *development* contracts. Both typically had a duration of 20 years. A franchise agreement was for a single store; a development agreement was for a specified number of restaurants, within a set time frame, in a designated area. When signing development agreements, KRR typically awarded territories in small clusters of five to 50 restaurants. The boundaries of the territory varied depending on the size and experience of the group or individual involved, as well as availability within the region requested.[1]

The costs involved in a franchise agreement included the initial franchise payment of $29,500; a royalty fee of 4.5 percent of gross sales; and contributions to the company advertising production fund, the national advertising fund, as well as a local or regional advertising fund of 0.75 percent, 2 percent, and (a minimum of) 3 percent of gross sales, respectively. The initial franchise fee was due upon signing the franchise agreement; all other fees were due monthly once the store was in operation. Fees related to a development agreement were similar to those of a franchise agreement. In addition to normal franchise fees, a developer was typically required to pay a development fee of $10,000 for each restaurant covered under the agreement. This fee was nonrefundable and was due (along with the full $29,500 for the first store to be built) upon signing the development agreement. The development fee was to be applied in equal portions as a credit against the initial franchise fee for each restaurant to be developed under the development agreement. The balance of each additional store's (within a development area) franchise fee was due as each store went into construction, according to the development schedule.

Company research showed that the average costs to build a new restaurant in the United States ranged from $560,000 to $672,000; the costs to convert an existing site ranged from $405,000 to $545,000. These costs included such expenses as property rental or payments, architectural and engineering fees, insurance, business licenses, equipment, furniture, signs, office supplies, opening inventory, and so forth.

Training and Development

KRR put great emphasis on training and provided franchisees and operators with three training courses. These courses took place at the company's training and development center located near corporate headquarters in Ft. Lauderdale, Florida. All expenses (travel, living, etc.) incurred in the training process were the responsibility of the franchisee. The first course was an optional three-day executive orientation program for all first-time franchisees and partners. The remaining two courses were not optional. All franchisees were required to certify and maintain a minimum of two managers for each store. The company's level one course for all managers was an intense four-week program held four to six weeks prior to the store's opening. Dubbed as KRR's version of boot camp, management-trainees essentially lived with their trainer, learning all aspects of daily operations. Once a developer had opened a substantial number of stores within the designated territory, it was possible to apply for accreditation, that is, to set up its own level-one management training program. The second level of management training was required for any manager before being promoted to a general store manager. Held either before or after a store opening, this six-day program focused not so much on operational procedures, but rather on how to deal with the more sensitive issues of management, i.e., how to deal with staff members and customers, especially when there were problems.

In addition, for each new store opening, franchisees were provided an opening team to assist in the initial training of hourly employees. The size of the team and the duration of its stay depended on the number of stores the franchisee already had in operation. The opening team would be sent once KRR had received a "Certificate of Occupancy" and a completed "Pre-Opening Checklist" from the franchisee. The franchisee was responsible for making sure that the store was ready for preopening training, though the opening date of the store could be pushed back if the store was not ready.

In the United States, typically 60 to 65 hourly employees were hired for each new store. Of those initially hired, approximately 60 percent would quit within the first few months. KRR's training and development center designed a 12 part video training program which demonstrated proper operating procedures for equipment and preparation of food items. These videos were used to train new employees in all stores, both domestic and international.

Control Issues

Menu adjustments were a particular concern for international stores. Some side dishes did not go over well in various parts of the world. For example, baked beans with bacon was not served in Jordan and other Muslim countries. Franchisees were encouraged to offer alternative side dishes that would be better received in their country or region of the world, while still meeting the company's quality standards. Sometimes recipes of ex-

[1]The franchising scheme of KKR's principal rival, Boston Market, differed considerably. Boston Market sold whole regions and provided up to 75 percent of its franchisees' financing. Boston Market did have an unusual caveat that accompanied the financing plan: After two years, Boston Market had the right to convert the unpaid debt into an ownership share in the franchise.

isting dishes had to be altered for regional tastes. Most notably sugar content had to be reduced for dishes served in the Asia-Pacific region where people had less of a "sweet tooth" than Americans. All new menu items or variations in recipes had to preapproved by corporate headquarters.

In addition to approving menus, KRR developed standards and specifications for most of its food products and equipment. To ensure consistency, KRR approved suppliers of chickens, breads, spices, mixes, marinades, plastic products, packaging, and so forth, in each territory or country where the company operated. Generally, finding approved local suppliers for chickens and other major food products was not a problem. However, many overseas franchisees ordered such specialized products as marinades and packaging materials from KRR's contracted United States distributor.

In order to maintain constant communication between KRR's corporate office and any given store, franchisees were required to install computer systems in each store. This system allowed KRR to instantly receive information concerning sales of each restaurant, and, in turn, to provide franchisees with information necessary to prepare financial statements and better manage the restaurant. Also, the company had standard forms for use in such areas as inventory control, profit-and-loss control, and monitoring daily and weekly sales.

Tony Wang and KRR in China

KRR's efforts in China were spearheaded by Ta-Tung (Tony) Wang, a former KFC executive with considerable experience in the Far East. Wang was born in Sichuan province in the People's Republic of China in 1944 and raised in Taiwan. In the late 1960s he moved to the United States to complete graduate work. Upon graduation he took a management position with KFC in Louisville, Kentucky. A series of promotions culminated with Wang's appointment as KFC Vice President for Southeast Asia in 1986. The position, based in Singapore, charged Wang with aggressively expanding KFC throughout the Asia Pacific region. Wang focused his efforts primarily on China, a country of 1.2 billion people with an undeveloped food service industry. In 1987, he gained considerable international notoriety by opening the first Western style fast food restaurant in China. The store was KFC's largest in the world and was located just opposite Mao's mausoleum off Tiananmen Square.

Wang credited the careful selection of joint venture partners as key in securing the store's prime location and in expediting the opening of the store. Three Chinese partners were selected and each played a different role in the start-up and on-going operation of the store: Beijing Animal Production Bureau (which owned 10 percent of the joint venture) accessed locally grown chickens; Beijing Tourist Bureau (which had a 14 percent ownership position) helped with site selection, permits, lease issues, and hiring; and the Bank of China (which had a 25 percent ownership position) assisted in converting soft currency renminbi profits to hard currency. Despite high chicken prices (KFC approved chicken in China cost over $1 per pound, well over twice U.S. levels), the operation was a major success. In reflecting back on that time Wang noted: "We were the first Western quick service restaurant in any communist country. It was very exciting. There were crowds lining up outside the store in the morning even before we opened. It was not unusual for us to have to call the police to control the crowds."

After opening additional restaurants in China, in September, 1989, Tony Wang left KFC to become president of CP Food Services Co., a subsidiary of the Charoen Pokphand Group, the largest agri-business company in Asia. In September 1991, Wang moved back to the United States to become president of Grace Food Services, a subsidiary of W.R. Grace & Co. A year later Tony Wang left Grace to become president of Foodmaker International, the $1.2 billion parent company of Jack-in-the-Box and Chi-Chi's restaurants. Wang had a mandate to open 800 new restaurants over an eight-year period, primarily in the Pacific Rim. In January 1993, catastrophe struck when contaminated hamburgers were served at a Seattle Jack-in-the Box restaurant. Although the tainted hamburger was traced to a California-based supplier, Foodmaker was hit with a series of costly lawsuits and devastating publicity. Sales nose-dived and, in order to conserve finances, the company's international expansion plan was shelved.

Wang sensed an important win-win opportunity for all and offered to continue the company's expansion using his own money. An agreement was struck whereby Wang's own company, QSR (*Quick Service Restaurant*), became a Jack-in-the-Box Master Licensee with franchise and development rights for 20 countries in the Middle East and Asia (including China but not Japan). The agreement with Foodmaker, which came into effect on January 1, 1994, and lasted 10 years, gave QSR complete control over the selection and development of all franchises within these 20 countries. QSR had the right to select stand alone franchisees, establish joint ventures with franchisees, or set itself up as a franchisee within any or all of the designated countries. Under the Master License agreement, Foodmaker and QSR split all franchise fees for Jack-in-the-Box restaurants. In assessing Foodmaker's rationale in setting up the Master License agreement, Wang commented: "this is a mutually beneficial concept for both parties. If they have the know-how but not the money, what have they got? They have a great concept but are not able to implement it internationally."

FICA (Franchise Investment Corporation of Asia)

Once Wang left Foodmaker, he began to explore other franchise investment opportunities in Asia. For assistance, Wang turned to American International Group, Inc. (AIG), one of the largest U.S.-based insurance companies.[2] Wang had been discussing franchise investment concepts with several senior AIG (Asia) managers since the late 1980s. In 1990, AIG (Asia) formed FICA as a subsidiary company designed to pursue multiple franchise options and invited Wang to serve as its first president. Wang declined, saying that he thought it was premature at the time. Consequently, FICA was put on hold.

In early 1994, Wang reopened discussions with AIG and in January 1995 joined FICA as its president and co-owner. FICA's ownership was split between AIG (60 percent) and QSR (40 percent). Wang served as president and primary decision maker in an office which was established by FICA in Hong Kong. Wang commented on the ownership structure: "as president of FICA, I am also an employee of FICA. I am president because of my skills and contacts. But my 40 percent ownership is based on financial contribution."

FICA had a three-fold mandate: (1) to develop and invest in franchise concepts in Asia, (2) to act as a consultant to franchisees in the region, and (3) to establish food processing and other franchise support/commissary functions. Primary emphasis focused on investing in established franchise concepts. The philosophy was explained by Wang:

> Every franchiser has a very strict noncompete clause for products in the same category. Our strategic plan was for FICA to become a multiconcept regional franchise investment and development company. We began to look at categories of products that did not compete.

After considerable effort, FICA signed far-reaching franchise agreements with Circle-K for both the Philippines and Thailand and with Carvel Ice Cream for China. By the fall of 1995, the company was continuing negotiations with these companies for additional franchise territories within Asia Pacific. In 1994, FICA also began investigating KRR in the context of a broader China strategy. (Economic and social trends for China are shown in Exhibit 1.) Wang explained why KRR seemed natural for China:

> We identified various franchise categories and one of those was chicken. I knew a lot of people at KRR who used to work for KFC. I knew John Brown and Loy Weston [former General Manager of KFC in Japan and for 18 months President of KRR Pacific]. Some of the best people who worked for KFC now work for KRR. I also knew Lenny Abelman, [KRR's newly appointed vice president in charge of International Development] who I had used as a consultant while I was at Foodmaker. But beyond having a lot of contacts, KRR made good business sense for China. It represents American lifestyle. It is not fast food like KFC or McDonald's. It is an entirely new category. Also, young people in China really like Kenny Rogers as a singer.

Wang's negotiations focused on gaining the franchise rights for KRR for both Shanghai and Beijing.

> I didn't need the rights to the whole country. Beijing and Shanghai are on the leading edge of China. I am sure that KRR will not partner with anyone else until they see what happens in Beijing and Shanghai. If they can get someone else to do it better, fine. But if I do a good job, why would John Brown want someone else to do it? In any case, Beijing and Shanghai are both huge.

In the spring of 1995, FICA was granted the KRR rights for both Beijing and Shanghai. While FICA did not pay a fee for the KRR rights to these two cities, it did agree to pay an up-front franchise fee for each store based on opening 15 stores in total. According to Wang, the up-front franchise fees "were consistent with U.S. per store fees discounted by an allowance for new market development." FICA's 1995 structure is presented in Exhibit 2.

Beyond franchise fees, Wang recognized that considerable money would be required to build the first KRR store. Costs were not directly comparable with U.S. levels. The location of the store, terms and conditions of the lease, and size of the store all affected costs. To Wang, "I didn't even ask what a U.S. store cost. I knew it would be irrelevant. U.S. stores are 90 percent free standing. They

[2] In 1994, AIG had net profits in excess of $4 billion on revenues in excess of $24 billion and assets of approximately $130 billion.

EXHIBIT 1 Economic and Social Trends in China

Economic Indicators	1989	1990	1991	1992	1993	1994	1995*	1996*	1997*	1998*	1999*
GNP at Current Market Prices ($ bn)	424.8	369.9	380.1	435.9	544.6	477.2	525.9	569.6	616.7	670.4	730.2
Real GNP Growth (%)	4.4	4.1	8.2	13.0	13.4	11.8	9.8	8.6	8.3	8.4	8.5
GNP, Per Capita ($)	380.0	324.0	330.0	374.0	462.0	399.0	434.0	463.0	494.0	530.0	569.0
Consumer Price Inflation (%)	17.5	1.6	3.0	5.4	13.0	25.0	18.0	12.0	11.5	11.5	11.0
Exchange Rate (av.) Rmb: $ (official Rate)	3.8	4.8	5.3	5.5	5.8	8.6	8.6	9.5	10.0	10.5	11.0
Av. Growth Rate in Wages; Urban Workers (%)[a]	10.8	10.5	9.4	15.8	19.6	18.0	15.0	13.0	12.5	13.0	12.5

Demographics	1989	1990	1991	1992	1993	1994[b]
Urban Population (billion)	295.4	301.9	305.4	323.7	333.5	
Rural Population (billion)	831.6	841.4	852.8	848.0	851.7	
Total Population (billion)	1,127.0	1,143.3	1,158.2	1,171.7	1,185.2	

A: State enterprises only.
B: Data not yet available.

Demographic and Social Trends	1991	1996*	2001*	Annual Average % Change 1991–2001*
Total Population (billion)	1.15	1.13	1.31	1.3
Population Growth Rate (% per year)				1.3
Age Profile (% of population)				
0-14	27.5	26.9	26.4	0.9
15-64	66.5	66.9	67.2	1.4
65+	6.2	6.4	6.4	2.0
Life Expectancy (years)				
Male	66	67	68	N/A
Female	69			N/A
Literacy Rate (% of population) 10 Years and Over	80	82	84	N/A
Labor Force (million)	584	645	712	2.0

*EIU estimates.
Source: These tables were compiled from China: *Country Report* and *Country Forecast. Economist Intelligence Unit,* 1995.

also involve a lot of real estate. None in China are or will be free standing. Also you can't buy real estate in China."

In deciding on a Beijing or Shanghai location for the first store, Wang commented:

> I didn't make the decision of predetermining where the first store would be located. I looked at the opportunities and at supporting functions. The first concern was where we could get good employees and managers. We settled on Beijing.

Finding a Partner

Once the decision had been made to focus on Beijing, Wang began the process of finding an appropriate local partner. Despite years of open door economic policies, Chinese investment regulations remained complex and cumbersome. There were also legal issues to be considered. Wang explained:

> The law in China is both clear and uncertain in the area of ownership. The regulations state that you cannot have 100 percent foreign ownership in food services. Beyond that it is not clear. So we had to think about a partner or several partners . . . I wanted to find a partner who could bring me some skills and organizational strength. The organizational strength might be an understanding of retailing in Beijing or an understanding of real estate or something else valuable.

Wang initially thought of contacting his old KFC partners. However, this was ruled out because of strict noncompete agreements that Wang had forced upon each partner when the original KFC joint venture was established in 1987. Wang then turned to East City Food Services and Distribution Co., a firm with which he had some familiarity. East City was a city government owned enterprise with 30 different Chinese style sit-down restaurants and over 100 retail food outlets in the greater Beijing area. Preliminary discussions with East City's management indicated

EXHIBIT 2 FICA (Franchise Investment Corporation of Asia), 1995

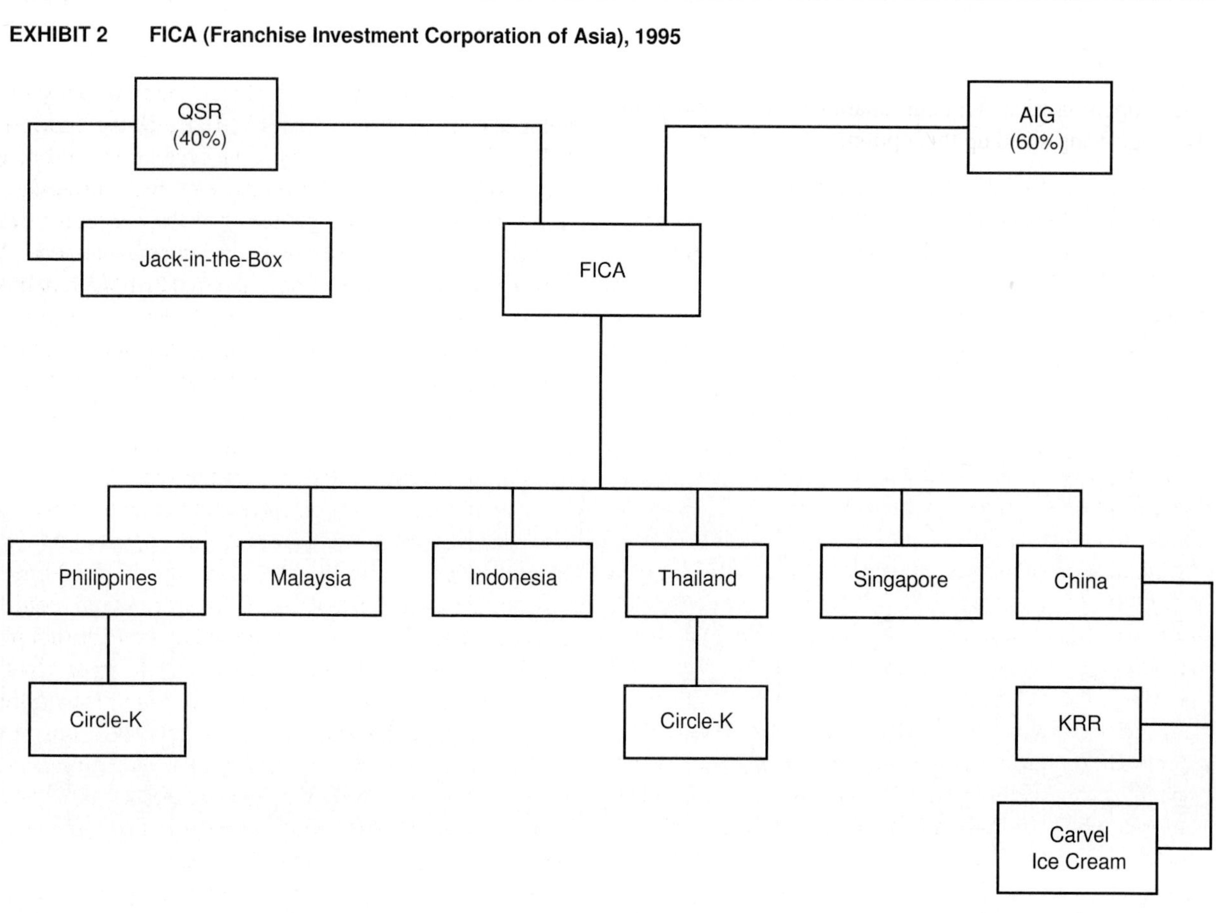

considerable excitement at partnering with KRR. East City promised access to its extensive labor pool that could either be transferred to KRR or hired through the company's normal channels. East City also had extensive local market knowledge and could be useful in marketing efforts and pricing issues. Finally, through their up-stream contacts, the company promised to assist in accessing chickens and various food ingredients that would be essential in the smooth running of KRR restaurants. In assessing their potential contributions, Wang commented:

> We would save some starting legwork by partnering with them. They could represent a smart option given my other FICA commitments. I think they are seriously worth considering. One drawback, however, is that they couldn't provide much in the way of finances.

A second option Wang was considering was the Beijing Branch of the China Great Wall Trading Co., a major investor-owned international trading company. China Great Wall had extensive international contacts and was very familiar with Western business practices. They were also very entrepreneurial and were seeking new investment opportunities with multinational corporations in Beijing. Wang sized up this option:

> China Great Wall has a lot of appeal because it can provide a bridge between the Chinese and American ways of doing business. Mr. Lu Hong Jun, the General Manager, was someone I have known for some time. He seems quite easy to work with. I admire his entrepreneurial spirit. China Great Wall also seems to have plenty of money, including access to hard currency.

As a third option, Wang considered D&D Realty Co. D&D was a Hong Kong based real estate development and leasing company with revenues in excess of $1.8 billion. In 1993 it began a major push in to China and in 1994 opened its first office in Beijing. In early 1995 it signed a contract as leasing agent for a new 14 story office complex being built by Hong Kong investors in a commercial area in central Beijing. It was interested in filling ground floor space with a signature store and in September 1995 approached FICA with an offer to form a partnership with KRR. D&D communicated its plans for aggressive expansion in Beijing and promised Wang that as a partner it could provide relatively easy access to prime retail space within the city. Wang was clearly intrigued by the potential. "It is a very interesting concept. My worry is that they are still new and don't have mature contacts. Still, they deserve careful consideration."

Future Direction

Wang was clearly committed to moving KRR forward in Beijing in as expeditious a manner as possible. While he clearly had other responsibilities as President of FICA, Wang realized KRR's approach to the Beijing market would set a clear precedent for the expansion of other FICA retailing concepts in China. He was also aware that the competition was not standing still. By the fall of 1995, McDonald's had 17 restaurants running in Beijing; KFC was operating 10. Other restaurant companies including Hard Rock Cafe, Pizza Hut, and TGI Friday's, had either established operations or had broken ground for new stores in the Beijing area.

Despite the obvious popularity of Western food and the enormous potential of the Chinese market, the Chinese food service industry remained poorly developed and at risk. McDonald's and KFC were both involved in difficult lease negotiations. In February 1995, McDonald's managers were informed that its flagship restaurant in Beijing (and McDonald's largest in the world) would be razed to accommodate the construction of an enormous shopping, office, and residential complex being developed by Hong Kong billionaire Li Ka-Shing. McDonald's refused to vacate its building arguing that it had a valid long-term lease. Demolition of the surrounding area continued and by October 1995 the restaurant was still operating, but in what appeared to be a war zone. A spokesperson for the developer asserted that McDonald's never had a clean lease on the property. Rumors that McDonald's had cut a special deal with Li Ka-Shing's group were circulating among Western business people in Beijing. One other rumor circulating was that KFC would not renew its 10 year lease on its flagship Tiananmen Square store because of soaring rent costs.

The problems of doing business in China did not stop with leasing issues. Wang learned that import duties for equipment and materials would average 50 to 100 percent. It was estimated that each KRR store would require a minimum of $150,000 in imported equipment (not including lease-hold improvements). While import permits were relatively straight forward, Wang lacked the staff to manage the development of 15 new stores in a short period of time. Another concern was hiring and training the new workers. With 15 restaurants, over 1,000 new employees would be required over the next few years. Who would interview them, hire them and train them? No one in KRR's training group spoke Mandarin nor were Chinese language training materials available.

Wang also learned that wage rates had climbed substantially over the past decade. Multinational companies were paying from a low 1,500 RMB per month for office clerks who spoke some English to as high as 10,000 RMB per month for senior managers who spoke fluent English.[3] Over 95 percent of employees in Beijing worked for state-owned enterprises where salaries averaged between 500 to 700 RMB per month. In Beijing, anyone—including those who worked for multinational companies—making less than 2,000 RMB per month was entitled to subsidized housing. Government subsidies reduced rent costs to less than 80 RMB per month. The cheapest unsubsidized apartments started at over 1,000 RMB per month and increased sharply according to location, size, and quality.

Wang was also acutely aware that by October 1995 none of the local food suppliers had been either identified or approved by KRR's head office. Related to this was a real concern over the menu. KRR's menu had never been tested in Beijing. While chicken was commonly eaten in China, would the Chinese be attracted to a premium product that was promoted in the United States as a healthy alternative to fried chicken? Furthermore, should KRR develop new menu items for China and if so, who would actually develop the concepts? Even if tasty new concepts could be developed, how long would they take to get corporate approval and could they be produced economically without costly new equipment?

These were all questions that were weighing heavily on Wang's mind. One thing that was clear was that whoever was selected as FICA's local partner would have a major impact on the success or failure of KRR in China. With so many unresolved issues, Wang was wondering whether the time was right to formalize a partnership.

Case 4–3

ENDESA-Chile

Buenos Aires, May 15, 1992. José Yuraszeck, president of the board of ENDESA, and Jaime Bauzá, chief executive officer, embraced each other euphorically in the board room of SEGBA, one of Argentina's major electrical utilities participating in the privatization process. They had just learned that their consortium, led by ENDESA, had won the bidding for a 60 percent share in Central Costanera, S.A. Located in Buenos Aires, this thermal generation plant with 1,260 megawatts of installed capacity was the largest such plant in South America.

This was the first foreign investment by ENDESA (the *Empresa Nacional de Electricidad. S.A.*), the leading firm in electrical generation and distribution in Chile. With total assets of more than $3 billion and income of roughly $300 million, ENDESA was also the largest private firm in Chile (see Exhibit 1).

Buenos Aires, August 3, 1992. An Argentine newspaper headline read, "Chileans Take Lead in Buenos Aires Electrical Business," referring to the winning bid by the Distrelec Consortium for 51 percent of Edesur, a firm responsible for the distribution of electrical energy to more than half of the Buenos Aires metropolitan district. ENDESA had an 11 percent share in Distrelec.

Santiago, November 18, 1992. The board of ENDESA met to decide what position to take regarding the coming privatization auctions in the Argentine electrical sector. Chief among these properties were the hydroelectric facilities of Hidronor, scheduled to be sold in February 1993.

In less than one year from its first decision to expand outside Chile, ENDESA had already invested more than $96 million in Argentina. An investment in Hidronor could easily double this figure. Various members of the board wondered if it was appropriate to *continue* investing in Argentina, or if they should wait for opportunities that would undoubtedly present themselves in other Latin American countries.

Although the privatization of the Argentine electrical sector, a process which was barely a year old, was going forward as planned, macroeconomic developments in the country were less favorable. The apparent overvaluation of the peso, the lack of competitiveness of the labor force, and signs of diminished confidence by the international financial community were all troublesome. These issues brought to the fore questions about the economic

[3]In October 1995, the Chinese renminbi (RMB) had an exchange rate of $1= 8.11 RMB.

This case was prepared by Esteban S. Skoknic, executive of ENDESA and a graduate of the Executive MBA program at the Escuela de Negocios de Valparaíso, Universidad Adolfo Ibáñez, in Santiago, Chile, and Professor Jon Martínez, of the same university. The case is intended to serve as the basis for class discussion and not as an illustration of either proper or improper management of a given situation. This translation is based on a earlier one by Professor Donald Lessard at the MIT Sloan School of Management.

EXHIBIT 1 ENDESA—Financial Statements
(In millions of U.S. dollars, unless otherwise stated)

	1992*	1991	1990	1989	1988	1987
Consolidated Balance Sheets						
Cash and Deposits	103	88	84	125	103	56
Liquid Investments	12	13	37	50	36	39
Receivables	101	103	79	96	116	112
Other	32	43	33	29	10	11
Total Current Assets	**248**	**247**	**233**	**300**	**265**	**218**
Plant and Equipment	4,231	3,872	2,864	2,532	2,737	2,545
Accumulated Depreciation	−1,502	−1,328	−1,181	−982	−1,006	−895
Net Fixed Assets	2,729	2,544	1,683	1,550	1,731	1,650
Construction in Progress	155	109	430	460	149	125
Total Fixed Assets	**2,884**	**2,653**	**2,113**	**2,010**	**1,880**	**1,775**
Affiliated Companies	84	38	164	2	57	46
Long-Term Receivables	52	70	115	128	29	56
Other	49	42	47	40	15	5
TOTAL ASSETS	**3,317**	**3,050**	**2,672**	**2,480**	**2,246**	**2,100**
Short-Term Debt	101	109	99	73	65	55
Accounts Payable	7	8	24	34	18	14
Other	77	52	26	9	12	17
Total Current Liabilities	**185**	**169**	**149**	**116**	**95**	**86**
Long-Term Debt	1,064	1,006	791	818	660	717
Other Obligations	54	40	34	38	28	26
Minority Interests	18	16	0	50	17	2
Capital and Reserves	1,888	1,722	1,619	1,381	1,299	1,207
Current Profits	158	179	104	105	179	62
Declared Dividends	−50	−82	−25	−28	−32	n.a.
Total Equity	**1,996**	**1,819**	**1,698**	**1,458**	**1,446**	**1,269**
TOTAL LIABILITIES	**3,317**	**3,050**	**2,672**	**2,480**	**2,246**	**2,100**
Profit and Loss Statement						
Income from Operations	**217**	**437**	**432**	**349**	**389**	**300**
Operating Costs	−82	−216	−296	−222	−222	−174
Administrative and Sales Costs	−11	−17	−14	−12	−13	−15
Operating Profits	**124**	**204**	**122**	**115**	**154**	**111**
Financial Income	3	9	15	14	9	20
Financial Expenses	−39	−77	−63	−60	−67	−68
Monetary Corrections	70	41	21	18	58	−16
Other Non-Operational Results	4	7	9	19	24	15
Income Before Taxes	**162**	**184**	**104**	**106**	**178**	**62**
Income Taxes	−2	−3	0	0	0	0
Minority Interests	−2	−2	0	0	0	0
Net Profits	**158**	**179**	**104**	**106**	**179**	**62**
Memorandum						
Exchange Rate (Pesos/$)	358.7	374.5	337.1	297.4	247.2	238.1
No. of Shareholders	60,436	56,882	51,883	63,629	37,901	5,129
No. of Shares Outstanding (millions)	8,002	8,001	7,976	7,945	7,935	7,919
Share Price (Pesos)**	156.50	118.50	32.00	21.00	13.90	15.20
Market Capitalization** (million $)	3,491	2,532	757	561	446	506

*All figures are for years ending on December 31, except for 1992, which are for the half-year to June 30.

**Data are for prices on December 31, except for 1992, which correspond to October 30.

Source: ENDESA.

and political stability of Argentina that ENDESA's board had posed since they first considered foreign investment.

Company Background

ENDESA was established in 1943 with the mission of carrying out the national electrification plan developed by CORFO (the Chilean state development corporation), in response to a serious electricity shortage that had existed in the country since the mid 1930s. ENDESA was set up as an independent, limited liability company (a *Sociedad Anónima*) controlled by CORFO, in order to give it substantial autonomy of operation.

Its early activity was the design and construction of major works, primarily hydroelectric plants and transmission systems. In fulfilling its mission, ENDESA was responsible for the construction and operation of more than 70 percent of all electric generation capacity installed in Chile in the last 50 years (85 percent if only public services are included), and developed the transmission systems that formed the basis for the Central and Northern interconnected grids. These investments, together with the development of distribution systems in various other zones of the country, extended the supply of energy to more than 90 percent of Chile's inhabitants by 1992, from less than 25 percent in 1940. During this same period, annual per capita consumption rose from 125 to 1,060 kWh.

Two aspects marked ENDESA's activities since its creation: the development of a national engineering capability and technological excellence. The former consisted in the development of a group of technicians and professionals that could solve problems in areas where previously there was no experience in Chile. Thus, ENDESA was able to carry out large scale civil works with its own engineering staff and manage its operations efficiently. They gained a level of prestige in Latin America to the point that its consultancy services were in considerable demand in other countries. The emphasis on technical excellence had also led to high service quality, even relative to international standards. This emphasis on efficient management was also reflected in the stability of the management of the firm. During the 45 years that ENDESA was controlled by the state, it had only eight general managers.

Privatization

ENDESA was responsible for carrying out the National Electrification Plan until 1978, the year in which the National Energy Commission was created. This entity became responsible for sectoral policy, limiting ENDESA to a productive role. One of the principal activities of the Commission was to define a new strategy for the sector, one that would be coherent with the general political economy of the government. This strategy emphasized economic efficiency, with the state assuming a secondary role, and led to a policy of decentralization and deconcentration of electric generation, transmission, and distribution activities, mainly through the creation of several enterprises that would share these tasks.

Beginning in 1980, ENDESA launched its own transformation process by forming regional distribution companies, shifting certain key hydroelectric plants (Pullinque and Pilmaiquén) to subsidiaries, spinning off other large generating plants (Colbún-Machicura and Pehuenche) as independent CORFO subsidiaries, and transferring back to CORFO electrical enterprises that were outside the region covered by the Central Interconnected Grid. Between 1981 and 1986, the distribution subsidiaries and the Pullinque and Pilmaiquén plants were transferred to the private sector. In the second half of 1987, CORFO began privatizing ENDESA, through a preferential share offering to its workers and public employees, as well as through a direct sale of shares to the public. As a result of these efforts, ENDESA's shares were held by more than 60,000 shareholders. Exhibit 2 shows the evolution of ownership of ENDESA since 1986.

In April 1990, the first board of directors of ENDESA without government representation was elected. The board named Jaime Bauzá as the company's chief executive officer. Bauzá was a 47 year-old civil engineer, with long experience in the national electrical sector, having been a director of Chilectra, general manager and a director of Chilgener, and at the time of his appointment, the general manager of Pehuenche.

Modernization

Management's first concern was to modernize ENDESA and convert it into a highly efficient organization that could grow and optimize its use of resources. In order to encourage decentralization of decision making and more effective management control, ENDESA was split into separate enterprises as shown in Exhibit 3, each reporting directly to the board and relating to each other through "arms-length" market mechanisms. The generation and transmission of electrical energy, ENDESA's principal activities, remained divisions of the firm for tax reasons.

Engineering and project management staffs were organized as a subsidiary firm, Ingendesa, that provided services

EXHIBIT 2 Ownership Distribution of ENDESA
(percentages)

	1992 (June)	1991	1990	1989	1988	1987	1986
CORFO	0	0	1	7	46	90	99
Pension Fund Managers	29	29	26	22	21	4	0
Enersis	12	12	12	11	0	0	0
Other Institutions	25	23	19	7	3	2	1
Individual Investors	34	36	42	53	30	4	0
Total	100	100	100	100	100	100	10

to the group but could also contract with outside national and international firms. It was expected that by 1992, 35 percent of its billings would be to third parties. Pangue S.A. was established as a separate firm to carry out the construction of a hydroelectric facility of the same name on the Bío-Bío river, and later to operate that plant. Employee health services were shifted to Ispén, a closed HMO, and Enigesa was created to manage the nonproductive properties of ENDESA. At the same time, certain corporate activities were centralized including financial management, human resource management, and capital budgeting.

Equally important to these structural changes were changes in administrative policies. In the finance area, these included the recruitment of new executives from the private sector and an aggressive shift toward capital market based financing. In human resource management, seniority-based promotion criteria and pay scales were changed to systems tied to market comparisons and linked to productivity. As a result of this reorganization, ENDESA concluded that it could reduce its staff by nearly 20 percent by the end of 1992. In June, the company and its affiliates employed 2,369 people.

ENDESA's shares had become one of the most heavily traded on the Chilean stock exchange, accounting for 15–20 percent of the total daily volume and also showing a substantial increase in price since privatization. Exhibit 1 shows closing share prices in the Santiago stock exchange, as well as the total market capitalization in each year since privatization.

ENDESA in 1992

One can distinguish three stages in the delivery of electricity to customers: generation or production, transmission, and distribution. The Chilean regulatory regime provided incentives for regulated competition in generation. It recognized the existence of natural monopolies in distribution, and thereby granted regional concessions. And it regulated the transmission stage through a system of payment of tolls, providing access to all generators to transmission networks whenever these had been established by public fiat or had benefited from the imposition of right-of-way provisions to private parties.

By mid-1992, ENDESA was engaged in the production and transport of electrical energy within the Central Interconnected Grid (CIG), which accounted for 95 percent of all public service energy consumption in Chile (see the Appendix for more details). ENDESA's generation division managed 1,928 MW of installed capacity (83 percent of which was hydroelectric) in 15 generating plants, and through its subsidiary, Pehuenche, a 500 MW hydroelectric facility. Several other firms operated in this market, including Chilgener, a private enterprise with 756 MW of capacity, and Colbún (490 MW), a state-owned enterprise, as well as several minor producers with a total capacity of 156 MW. ENDESA's share of total electricity generation for the CIG oscillated between 40 and 60 percent of the total, depending upon hydrological conditions as can be seen in Exhibit 4.

Decisions regarding construction of power plants that would go into service through 1997 had already been taken and, in some cases, construction had already started. A simulation of future operations indicated that ENDESA and its subsidiaries would retain around a 60 percent share of total energy generation in the CIG through the 1990s. In terms of sales, ENDESA typically had around a 65 percent market share, with the difference purchased from other generators. Production and sales were expected to balance in the coming years.

ENDESA's transmission division owned over 9,000 kilometers of transmission lines, about 75 percent of the high tension grid of the CIG. Its dominant role would be maintained in the future, given that no significant expansion

EXHIBIT 3 Corporate Structure and Shareholdings

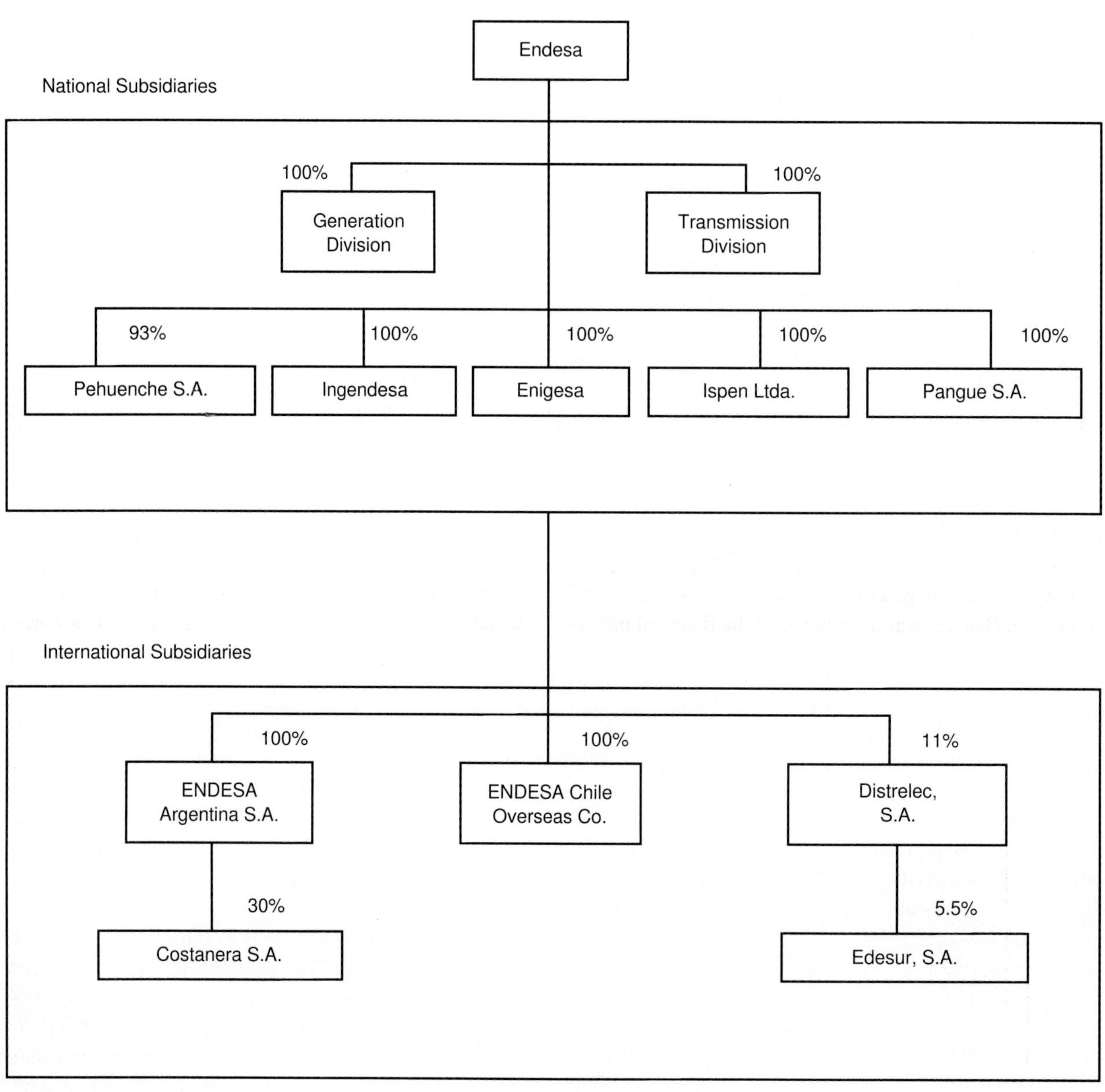

Note: Percentages represent direct and indirect participation as of October 1992.

EXHIBIT 4 Endesa's Share of Electricity Generation in the Chilean Central Integrated Grid
(percentages)

	1992 (June)	1991	1990	1989	1988	1987
Endesa	42	44	49	50	58	60
Pehuenche	19	14	0	0	0	0
Chilgener	12	17	31	29	17	8
Colbún	21	19	14	15	19	24
Other	6	6	6	6	6	8
Total	100	100	100	100	100	100

of the grid was planned. Eighty-six percent of the income of the transmission division in 1992 came from toll payments made by the generation division and the Pehuenche plant.

The Internationalization of ENDESA

In line with its reorganization, ENDESA began to outline a long-term development strategy. "Our starting point," noted Mr. Bauzá, "was an analysis of the financial projections for the firm. In order to meet our principal objective, which is to supply energy to the CIG, we needed to make investments ranging from $1.2 to $1.4 billion in the next 10 years. We realized that our expected funds flow would allow us to meet this investment program and, without violating our agreements to the banks or our rating, make additional investments in the order of $500 million."

Mr. Yuraszeck added that, "Given its capabilities, the firm can do much more than what it is required to do in its sector, but to diversify away from energy within Chile would not be easy. If ENDESA sought to diversify into other sectors such as telecommunications, forestry, or mining, it would convert itself into a 'little monster' that our country would probably not be willing to accept. I don't believe that very large firms have a place in Chile."

Given its capabilities, ENDESA chose to explore options in sectors that were intensive in energy use and hydraulic resources, and in activities related to projects with high engineering content such as civil works and hydraulic works. The latter included projects abroad, taking advantage of opportunities that were opening in neighboring countries in the electrical and energy sectors. As a result, the board approved the possibility of investing in foreign electrical projects up to a limit of 10 percent of ENDESA's total assets.

The electrical sector in almost all Latin American countries was in crisis: low rates, inefficient management, and poor investment decisions had resulted in serious financial problems and, in some cases, significant shortages of supply (see Appendix for more details). A favored solution to these problems was to bring in private capital to the sector, almost totally absent at the time, which would contribute funding as well as project management and operational capabilities. Most countries in the region included the electrical sector as one of those which would be subject to deep transformation as part of a process of structural reforms. In many cases this process began with a discussion of the privatization of existing installations.

The Argentine Opportunity

Argentina decided in 1991 to privatize all electrical generation, transmission, and distribution then in the hands of the federal government through three enterprises: SEGBA, Hidronor, and Agua y Energía. The process would begin with the sale of two large thermoelectric plants located in Buenos Aires (Puerto with 1,009 MW and Costanera with 1,260 MW), and would continue with some of the smaller thermoelectric plants, the transmission grid, and the hydroelectric plants. At the same time, distribution of electric power in Buenos Aires would be divided into two firms and auctioned off. Such a process was consistent with the policy of the new government of President Menem to restructure the country into a liberal market economy.

The proposed sale of the Argentine generating plants coincided with ENDESA's search for new investments. This was an opportunity to acquire functioning plants of a large size, within an electrical system that was three times the size of the Chilean CIG. The possibility of establishing a physical connection of the two grids via a 200-megawatt line between the cities of Santiago and

Mendoza had been considered for many years. However, the decision to invest in Argentina was independent of the eventual realization of this interconnection.

José Yuraszeck, who in addition to being president (the equivalent of chairman of the board) of ENDESA was also the general manager of Enersis (the major transmission company in Chile and owner of 12 percent of ENDESA), affirmed that, "opportunities such as this come only once in a lifetime" and added, "in a world as interrelated as ours, the international expansion of a growing firm is a natural part of its development."

Along with the decision to participate in Argentina's privatization process, ENDESA had to decide how to do it. Should it invest only in the largest plants that would justify the effort required, or should it start by investing in smaller plants and learn along the way? Should it wait for the auctioning of the large hydroelectric plants that were much closer to their own experience and presented fewer technical problems?

Regardless of the outcome, ENDESA's executives decided that it was critical to begin an analysis of the Argentine electrical sector, including its structure, regulatory framework, labor and tax laws, etc. The Chilean firms were the only private electrical firms in Latin America that operated under a set of rules similar to those that were under study for Argentina and other countries. Said José Yuraszeck: "It is significant that Chilean firms in general, and ENDESA in particular, have already lived through an experience similar to that facing other countries."

In the case of the large thermal plants, Argentina was looking to sell a 60 percent share in each firm. The remaining 30 percent would be sold later in an IPO (initial public offering) in the local stock market, with the last 10 percent offered to the workers. The Puerto and Costanera plants were to be sold with a contract for the sale of energy to the distribution companies for 8 years, at a price expressed in dollars and indexed to the price of fuel. In accordance with current regulations, these plants should operate in a coordinated fashion with the other plants in the National Interconnected Grid (NIG) that constituted the market for the sale and purchase of surpluses and deficits with respect to the various generation and distribution contracts. These conditions had been selected to provide an incentive for the efficient utilization of resources, as well as to reduce the risks associated with changes in the Argentine economy and decisions by third parties regarding additions to the country's generation capacity.

Regarding the mode of entering Argentina, José Yuraszeck stated that, "I think that it would be crazy for a Chilean firm to go to Argentina without local partners. Argentina is a much larger country than Chile. It takes knocking on several doors and many meetings to reach the highest levels of local companies."

In order to participate in the first auctions, ENDESA put together a consortium in which it controlled 50.1 percent. Other investors included the Chilean distribution and transmission firm Distribuidora Chilectra Metropolitana and the holding Enersis (owner of 70 percent of Chilectra) with a total of 20 percent, various enterprises of the powerful Argentine group Pérez Companc with 25 percent, and a U.S. firm, Public Services of Indiana, with 5 percent. ENDESA would be responsible for operating the plants. The investment would take place through a new subsidiary, Endesa-Argentina, created for this purpose.

Later that year, ENDESA took a 10 percent stake in Inversora Distrelec, a consortium that paid $511 million for 51 percent of the energy distribution firm for the south of Buenos Aires, Edesur. Other firms in this group were Enersis and Chilectra (with 39.5 percent), the Pérez Companc group (40.5 percent), and Public Services of Indiana (10 percent). Chilectra Metropolitana would be the operator in this case.

Experience in Costanera

Gunther Prett, a Chilean engineer with 40 years of experience at ENDESA and former head of its transmission division, commented that time had never passed so quickly as it had during his recent months as general manager of Costanera. He was putting in 12 hours a day at the plant, and that did not seem to be enough to deal with the many problems that arose daily, of which the technical ones were the least difficult. Nevertheless, Mr. Prett felt very good about the results obtained thus far. On the day ENDESA took over as operator, the plant was operating at 435 MW. By October, it had surpassed 900 MW and showed positive earnings of $2.2 million.

As operator, ENDESA was responsible for the technical management, especially assuring a high yield from the machinery, and for the efficient administration of the enterprise. Costanera's machinery was in relatively bad condition and it had never operated as a business unit. The consortium planned to invest $200 million in refurbishing Costanera's machinery. The first payments for the fabrication of new equipment and working capital had been lent to Endesa-Argentina by the consortium partners. It was expected that in the near future Endesa-Argentina would be able to borrow on its own to meet additional requirements.

Of the 14 executives at the level of general manager or assistant general manager in Costanera (see Exhibit 5), 10 were named by ENDESA and 4 were proposed by the

EXHIBIT 5 Organizational Structure for Central Costanera

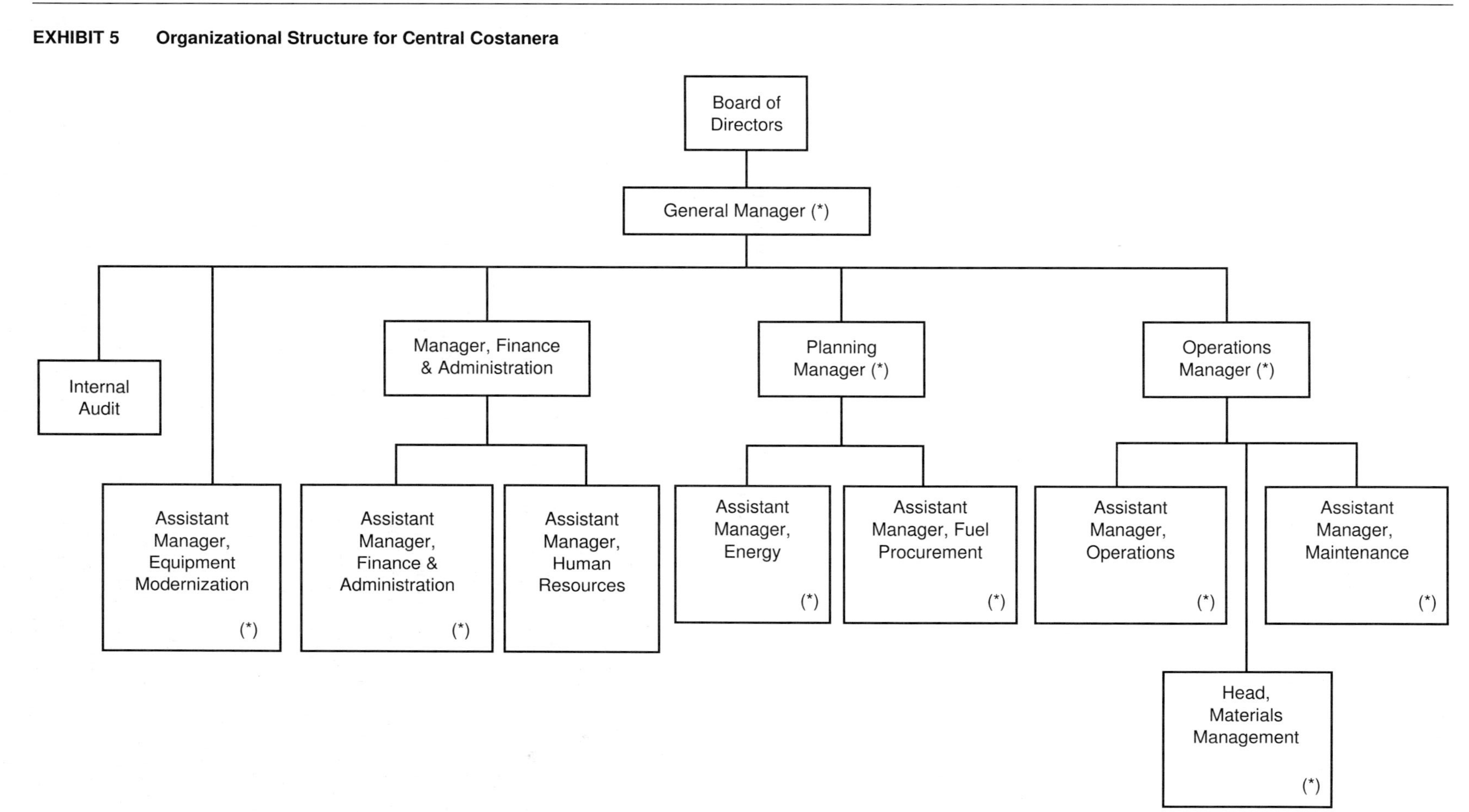

Note: (*) Denotes Chilean national.

EXHIBIT 6 Characteristics of ENDESA's Top Management Resources

	Corporate Staffs	Generation Division	Transmission Division
Age			
Less than 40	8	2	2
40 to 50	17	6	4
50 to 60	15	6	9
Over 60	2	6	1
Average	48	54	52
Length of Service with ENDESA			
Less than 10 years	21	2	1
10 to 20	3	1	3
20 to 30	12	5	6
Over 30	6	9	6
Average	16	27	27
Occupation			
Engineers	22	16	15
Business/Economics Training	5	2	1
Lawyers	9	0	0
Other	6	2	0
Post-Graduate Degree in:			
Business Administration	2	1	0
Finance or Project Evaluation	3	2	1
Experience with Other Companies	21	3	1

Argentine partners. There were a total of 18 Chileans in the plant, supplemented by other technical and management people who traveled to Costanera when needed. It was not always easy to fill these positions (see Exhibit 6 for summary statistics on ENDESA's senior professional staff). In the opinion of Rodrigo Manubens, vice president of ENDESA, "This is a problem that we hadn't predicted. Our people are very concerned about their children, leaving their parents, etc., even considering how close Argentina is, the ease of travel and communications, and how attractive is Buenos Aires. This is a phenomenon that will take some time to solve, something that all Chilean firms that are internationalizing share."

José Yuraszeck added: "Nobody entered ENDESA to have an international career. At the most they expected to study abroad for one or two years and then return. As ENDESA took the decision to invest outside Chile only one year ago, there hasn't been sufficient time to prepare." This, he noted, was especially critical since, "ENDESA's business is to export middle management and technology."

One management area that was expected to be difficult was labor relations. ENDESA felt that Costanera was drastically overstaffed when they took it over, and that many work habits, some established by rule and others just accepted as norms, were incompatible with efficient operations. The first step taken was to offer a voluntary retirement plan for which it was necessary to add to the funds normally provided for this purpose by the government. Retirement arrangements were also made for all those employees that met the legal requirements. As a result of these measures, total staff was reduced by 320 workers, bringing the number down to 730 by the end of the year. Nevertheless, management felt that this number was still too high.

Another critical issue was the establishment of a new collective bargaining contract that would be more flexible and would include incentives for improving efficiency up to international standards. Toward the end of September, conversations had begun with the unions that were still on-going. Although there had been no specific problems to date, it was known that other firms that had attempted to make similar changes had experienced difficulties, including acts of sabotage against their productive capacity.

Gunther Prett was of the opinion that, "to any group of engineers, the ability to do things that could not be done before due to the lack of resources, is a source of professional satisfaction. But the rest of the staff, with whom I have held many conversations, are just waiting to hear the results of the collective bargaining negotiations. Their concerns are in areas such as changes in the work schedule, restrictions on overtime, grievance procedures, and so on."

Business practices were also different from those at ENDESA. Mr. Prett noticed, for example, that when they put service or purchase contracts up for bid, there was no real competition among suppliers. They acted as if they were not convinced that the rules of the game were objective or that they would be applied in the interest of the company.

Management control for ENDESA's affiliates was exercised through their boards, but the situation at Costanera required special handling. In fact, Jaime Bauzá, who was President of Costanera's board, was spending a great deal of his time on this affiliate.

Issues for the Future

Jaime Bauzá thought that ENDESA's initial results were extremely successful, particularly when compared with their expectations. Regarding his concerns for the future, he noted,

> "The first point that worries me is the current organization of ENDESA, which I would define as being in a growth crisis. All of us, in whatever area of the firm, find ourselves in a very hectic situation (*'una especie de zafarancho'*). This can only last for a short time. I must urgently restructure the organization so that it can operate in this new stage that we're living. . . . [I need to] decentralize to the extent possible, but establish a certain scheme of control that allows me to know exactly what's going on so that I can make the right decisions at the right moment.
>
> The second point that concerns me is to continue to have sufficient information to identify the best alternatives by which we can realize our plan to invest $500 million outside of the existing businesses.
>
> The third point is that all of this expansion will be financed ultimately by additional borrowing, and we have to make sure we have adequate sources of financing to get the best results."

The active Argentine privatization process, with the pending sale of the hydroelectric plants of Hidronor and the distribution grid, forced ENDESA to review its investment strategy. Argentina's economic situation, which had taken off with the "convertibility plan" of Finance Minister Domingo Cavallo, was showing signs of deterioration with its associated political risks. The trade balance for 1992, for example, showed a deficit of more than one billion dollars, the first negative balance in more than 10 years. Cumulative inflation had reached 41.4 percent since the exchange rate was fixed in 1989. To boot, wages in Argentine's industrial sector had not been competitive with those in either Chile or Brazil prior to the start of the plan. The last steps announced by the government, including export tax rebates and an increase in import tariffs, represented a disguised devaluation. Industrial production had been stagnant since March, and a slight decline was expected for 1993. The government also expected a reduction of capital inflows in 1993 as well. In spite of considerable improvement in its external image, Argentina was still viewed as risky, ranking 54 (up from 78 three years earlier) out of 169 countries included in *Euromoney's* 1992 Risk Rating (see Exhibit 7).

This discouraging panorama undercut confidence and was reflected in a 50 percent drop in the Buenos Aires stock market since the end of May. To top it all, the labor unions, traditionally the main source of support for the Peronistas, had called their first general strike against the Menem government for November 9, 1992. (See Exhibits 8 and 9 for information on the macroeconomic situation in Argentina.) Given these developments, ENDESA's management was considering the possibility of putting further investments in Argentina on hold, perhaps in favor of other Latin American countries that presented favorable opportunities as they restructured their economies.

Other Opportunities

The country that was most advanced in the privatization process was **Peru.** It was expected that their regulatory legislative proposal, very similar to that in effect in Chile, would be approved shortly. The sale of existing properties could begin as early as the first quarter of 1993. The government had already begun to reorganize the electric utilities as independent business units with the main generating plants placed in two companies, Electroperú and Electrolima, to be sold separately. Given the high perceived political risk associated with Peru, the sales price of key assets could be very attractive.

In **Colombia,** a supply crisis in the last few months had resulted in blackouts or brownouts covering up to 25 percent of consumers. This had precipitated the drafting of a congressional bill to restructure the sector, which allowed participation by private investors. Nevertheless, it

EXHIBIT 7 Country Risk Ratings, Selected Countries

Rank 1992	Rank 1991	Country	Total Score (Max = 100)	Political Risk (Max = 20)
1	1	Japan	99.6	20.0
4	4	Germany	98.2	19.7
6	7	United States	98.1	19.6
9	14	United Kingdom	96.9	19.5
14	19	Singapore	92.8	18.0
17	17	Spain	91.6	17.1
20	21	Taiwan	90.1	17.3
25	28	Hong Kong	85.6	16.2
29	25	S. Korea	75.5	16.6
35	**47**	**Chile**	**69.6**	**14.3**
40	32	Indonesia	63.5	12.6
45	**34**	**Mexico**	**59.4**	**13.7**
47	36	S. Africa	53.9	11.9
48	**61**	**Colombia**	**53.8**	**11.5**
51	**45**	**Venezuela**	**51.1**	**10.2**
54	**78**	**Argentina**	**45.0**	**10.6**
57	51	India	44.1	6.4
70	**65**	**Brazil**	**37.2**	**7.8**
85	**99**	**Bolivia**	**31.6**	**7.8**
94	**85**	**Ecuador**	**28.8**	**7.6**
95	**115**	**El Salvador**	**28.7**	**4.8**

Source: *Euromoney*, September 1992.

was expected that the outright sale of assets would be delayed due to the diversity of players and regional interests that participated in the sector.

The privatization of the electrical sector in **Venezuela** had been on the table for a long time. An attempted *coup de état* by a group of military officers in 1992, however, had cast doubt on the stability of the government of Carlos Andrés Pérez, and set back the timetable for the sale of electricity generation assets. It was hoped that the new regulatory law would be approved in early 1993 and that the privatization process would resume afterwards.

The government of **Uruguay** was scheduled to seek approval of a new "Public Enterprise Law" through a national plebiscite. Only then would they be allowed to proceed with the privatization of activities currently under control of the state. The new government in **Brazil** had announced that it would not undo the privatization program currently underway, but slow progress was expected given its declaration that any privatization in areas of strategic importance (and electricity generation would certainly be considered one) would require approval by the Congress. In any event, Brazilian electrical enterprises were so large that it would be difficult for ENDESA to bid for them.

Legislation approved 1991 in **Costa Rica** allowed only very limited private participation in the generation of electrical energy. In **Mexico,** where the government had put in place a very broad program for the sale of public enterprises, the electrical sector was reserved to the State by the constitution, and no changes were seen in the near term. A new government in **Ecuador** was beginning a process of reorganization of the sector and would be studying a new regulatory framework. Any action here, however, would be months or years away. Finally, in **El Salvador,** regulatory reform for the electricity sector was under way, and it was expected that their hydroelectric plants might be put up for sale by early 1993.

Against this backdrop, Argentina remained the only Latin American country in which the process of privati-

EXHIBIT 8 Argentina: Selected Economic Indicators

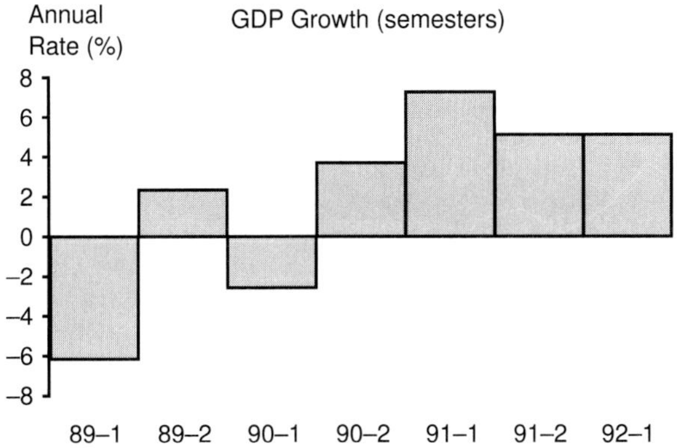

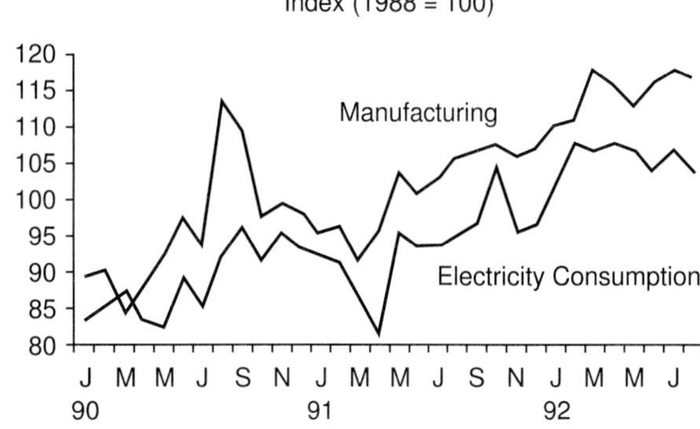

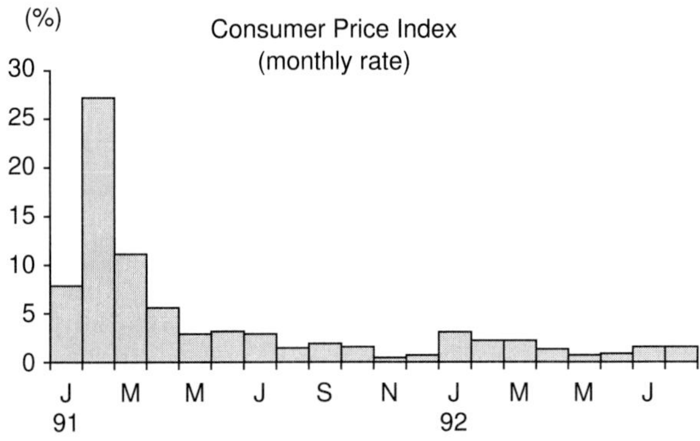

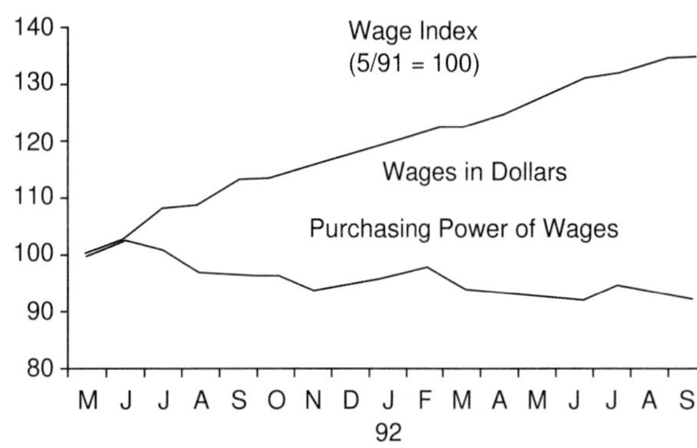

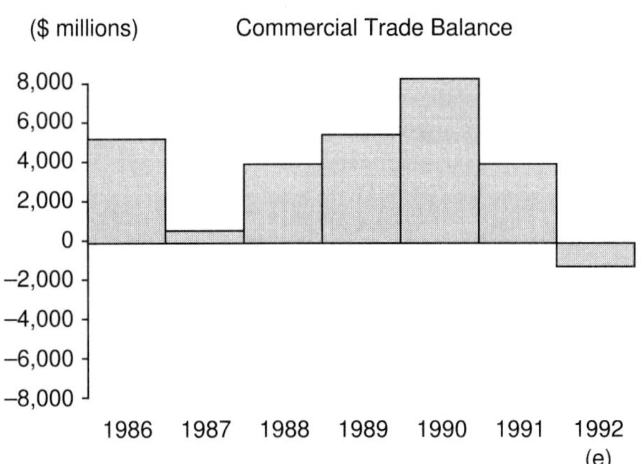

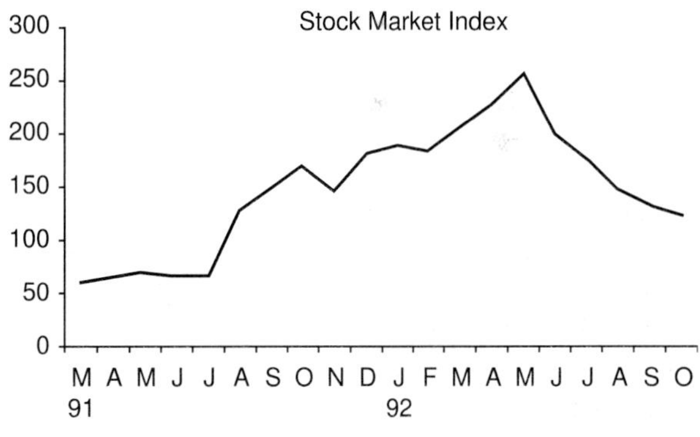

Sources: CEPAL, Central Bank, Stock Market.

EXHIBIT 9 Exchange Rate "Dutch" Disease in Latin America

Though Latin America's reforming vanguard—Chile, Mexico, and Argentina—can expect historically moderate 13–30 percent inflation this year, their inflation containment has wrought major changes in relative prices, both domestic and vis-à-vis the outside world.

Relative price changes signal investors concerning the prospective profitability of investment in different sectors. The term "Dutch disease" recalls the 1970s Netherlands' experience of profit compression in manufacturing under the relative price changes bred by natural gas development. The disease propagates readily when overall inflation control is disproportionately enforced by real exchange rate appreciation—conspicuous now in Argentina (since 1989 and sustained by the peso's fixed dollar rate), prominent in Mexico (since late 1990), and noticeable in Chile (in the past year).

Strong currencies have been favored in the region to fight inflation expectations. And they come to look sustainable while capital floods in from abroad amid financial investor euphoria. Latin America's own previous history, however, shows that the economic consequences may be less benign in the medium term (and the currency strength ultimately untenable). Particularly troubling in this connection are the steep rises apparent in Argentina and Mexico in the terms of trade of domestic services sectors relative to manufacturing. The positive interpretation is that these illustrate the constructive power of competition through trade liberalization; the negative is the effective twist of investment incentive toward service activities sheltered from international competition, to the progressive enfeeblement of tradables output that will lead to eventual external payments problems.

Real Effective Exchange Rates
(1987 = 100)

160
140
120
100
80
60
Argentina
Mexico
Chile
1990
1991
1992

Domestic Terms of Trade
(Ratio of consumer to wholesale prices of manufacturers, 1987 = 100)

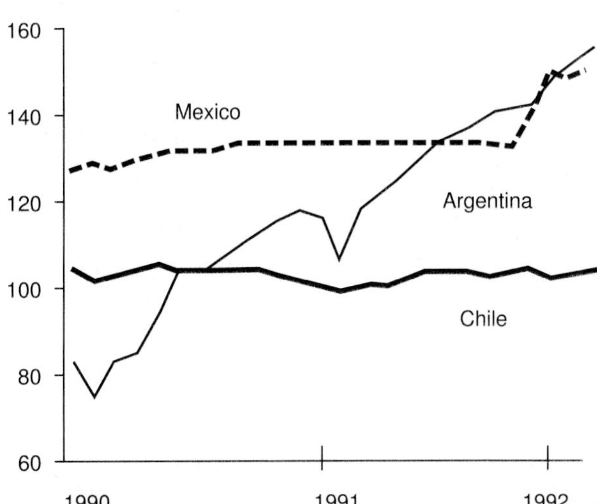

Source: Morgan Guaranty, *World Financial Markets,* May/June 1992.

zation had a fixed time table and clear rules of the game. All other countries were still working out the basic issues, and they were not yet at the stage in which they could assure the conditions nor the timetable under which privatization would take place.

The Hidronor Project

Given that hydroelectric plants were ENDESA's strength, its participation in the auction for Hidronor plants seemed logical. Further, these were large-scale plants, which would permit subsequent expansion and growth with a concentrated effort. As shown in Exhibit 10, the public auction would include plants of 450, 1,000, 1,320, and 1,650 MW, to be sold in a very short period of time. Therefore, the ENDESA consortium would have to establish priorities. If it were to win the bid for one of the larger plants, it would practically double the amount of power that it operated in Argentina and extend its investment there proportionally.

These hydroelectric installations were relatively new and would be turned over under concession contracts

EXHIBIT 10 Size and Characteristics of the Hidronor Power Generation Stations

The various hydroelectric plants associated with the Hidronor complex were built (or under construction) on the rivers Neuquén and Limay in the northern Patagonia, approximately 1,200 km. southwest of Buenos Aires. They were organized into four separate companies:

Companies/Plants	Date of Construction	Installed Capacity (MW)	Average Energy Production (Gwh)	Expected Bid Price Range ($ millions)
Planicie Banderita	1978	450	1,510	50–100
Alicurá	1984	1,000	2,360	100–200
Chocón y Arroyito	1973, 1983	1,320	4,070	150–250
Piedra del Águila & Pichi Picún Leufú	1993–1996	1,650	6,613	300–400

Each of these operations had received a 60-year concession for the exploitation of all related works and the hydrological resources associated with them. Given the impact of the dams on the economic operation of the hydro-electrical system, their management was placed in the hands of the plant operators. However, these various dams (with the exception of Alicurá) had multiple objectives—flood control, irrigation, and electricity generation—of which electric generation had the lowest priority. In order to guarantee the observance of these objectives and preserve the integrity of the hydroelectric operation, the concession agreements included restrictions to the operation of the dams under specified circumstances. As long as these operating rules were observed, the plant operators would be exempt from any responsibility for damages downstream in the event of flood or drought.

For the plants currently under construction (Piedra del Águila and Pichi Picún Leufú), the state would transfer all related contracts to the new operators. The state would also assume any costs associated with possible deficiencies in the dams associated with these plants. An inspection visit by ENDESA engineers to the various facilities concluded that the electro-mechanical equipment was, in general, in very good state of maintenance. Some problems with filtration in the dams of El Chocón and Piedra del Águila were being corrected.

These plants were all relatively far from any population centers, so that work camps and housing were provided by the plants. The energy produced in these plants was transmitted to Buenos Aires through three high voltage lines belonging to the transmission company.

Source: Company records.

running 60 years. The equipment was in very good condition, and no major investments were anticipated in the short term. There were some issues, however, regarding the dams of El Chocón and Piedra de Águila, that had to be resolved. The existence of a provincial authority controlling the hydrological resources made matters more complex. The management of the dams, however, given their impact on the reliability and cost of electricity production, would be handled by the operators of the plants.

Yet, in contrast to Costanera, which was covered against the risk of changes in electricity and fuel spot prices by its long-term sales contract, the hydroelectric plants would remain exposed to spot prices whether or not they had long-term contracts. They would likely have excess capacity in wet conditions, and be forced to buy in the spot market during dry conditions. Given that the overall demand for energy was a function of economic growth, its income and the prices in the spot market would be correlated with economic variables independent of climatic conditions. Thus, a critical aspect of the operation would depend on the company's ability to design sales contracts that incorporated prevalent energy costs during periods of drought.

ENDESA had decided to seek different partners for the hydroelectric business. It formed a new consortium in which it held a 40 percent share, with another 40 percent from ENDESA-Spain (no relation) and 20 percent from an Argentine enterprise. ENDESA-Spain was a state-owned firm with an important presence in the Spanish electrical sector, including 11,550 MW of installed capacity of which 2,770 MW were from hydroelectric plants. The joint venture agreement called for ENDESA-Chile to be the operator of the plant in consultation with ENDESA-Spain. The latter was already involved in Argentina, participating in a consortium with Electricité de France and the Argentine firm Astra, which had purchased Edenor, the second major distribution company serving the north of Buenos Aires.

Chilean firms were investing in a large number of sectors in Argentina, including food, supermarkets and shopping centers, disposable diapers and paper products, steel, copper manufacturing, etc. Even though Minister Cavallo stated that he was, "very pleased with Chilean investments in the process of privatization," few doubted that it was a sensitive subject for public opinion. ENDESA executives believed that a foreign presence in the electrical sector would create problems only if there were failures with the supply of power. Yet, the government had needed to pass a special decree to allow Chilean companies to bid on Hidronor, given the location of these plants near their common border, a legacy of previous conflicts between the two countries. And if ENDESA were to win its bid for one of Hidronor's large plants, over 25 percent of all capacity in the national grid would be in Chilean hands.

Finally, there was always the option to slow down the process of internationalization. There were several domestic sectors in which ENDESA could have a competitive advantage, such as infrastructure projects and other energy intensive sectors. But these sectors would not fully occupy ENDESA's financial capacity, making it necessary to seek projects in other large-scale sectors in which the country had a comparative advantage such as wood, paper, cellulose or mining.

APPENDIX: THE ELECTRIC INDUSTRY IN CHILE AND LATIN AMERICA

Electric power was one of the most versatile forms of energy. It could be easily transformed into any of the basic energy needs of modern society (light, heat, movement, communications, etc.), and it could be produced from any form of primary energy (coal, oil, nuclear, or hydraulic). This accounted for the systematic increase of electric power's share in overall energy consumption throughout the world. In developing countries, the elasticity between electric power consumption and economic activity was greater than one.

Certain characteristics conditioned the way in which electric power was produced and organized. And these had traditionally resulted in the creation of large public utility electric power systems to satisfy national needs. Among the main characteristics were:

- It was not economical to store great quantities of electric power, thus, power must be produced as it was consumed.
- There was need for transmission and distribution networks to connect producers and consumers.
- Consumption had important variations by hours and seasons, typical of the daily cycle of economic activity and of people's habits.
- There were large economies of scale in generation (through unit size), transmission (higher tension), and distribution (charge density).
- The most economic sites for the location of power plants were often distant from the major consumption centers.
- Different production technologies presented complementary economic and operational characteristics, so it was typical that lower costs could be obtained by a combination of different types of power plants (hydraulic, steam and gas turbines, and so on).
- The sector was highly capital intensive.

The aggregate installations that constitute an electric power system could be classified in three types of activities. Production or generation of electric power was made up of power plants where thermal or hydraulic power was transformed into electricity. Electric power transmission consisted of the lines transporting energy from the power plants to consumption areas, including the substations that served as distribution and voltage transforming nodes in the system. Finally, distribution were the networks which fed individual consumers and businesses users directly from the transmission system substations.

The ability to establish physical connections between different production and consumption centers, and the high cost to users of a failure in supply had led to a system of coordinated operation of generation and transmission facilities in interconnected grids. This need, together with the long construction cycles associated with new facilities, had placed a premium on careful planning for the gradual expansion of national power systems.

Production Technologies

In interconnected grids, power generation tended to be performed typically in large plants. Although electric power could be produced from virtually all primary energy sources, only some transformation processes had competitive costs that permitted mass production, mainly hydraulic and thermal generation from coal, oil derivatives, and uranium. Other primary sources of power such as solar, wind, geothermal or biomass, were competitive only under certain conditions. Although their market penetration was growing, it was not expected that they would generate a significant percentage of electric power in the coming decade.

The traditional forms of production had achieved relatively high levels of efficiency and, thus, technological advances had been rather slow in the last years, as compared with other productive sectors. Consequently, the useful life of facilities was high. The most promising technologies for the near future were those that enhanced fuel efficiency in power generation.

Economies of scale in design, manufacturing and sale had led to the globalization of competition in equipment manufacturing for the power generation and transmission industries. As a result, technology diffused rapidly through these sectors and the latest advances in materials, design or control systems were promptly integrated into new facilities throughout virtually the whole world. Meanwhile, technology for low voltage transmission and in distribution was quite standardized, resulting in local production of equipment in many countries.

Organization of the Electric Sector

The sector's technical characteristics had led to a general acceptance of the concept of a natural monopoly. A legal and regulatory framework evolved to regulate the sector (whether in private or public hands), accompanied in many cases with restrictions on market entry. In practice, this resulted in the creation of vertically integrated monopolies, controlling the generation, transmission, and distribution of electric power in a certain geographic area, or in the existence of an oligopoly for generation-transmission activities coupled with geographic monopolies for distribution.

In the early years, most countries' suppliers were private companies. In some countries, mainly developed ones (United States, Belgium, Spain, among others), this structure of regulated private companies was maintained. Others, such as France, Italy, or Scandinavia, were characterized by publicly owned utilities. In the case of most developing countries, pressures to eliminate foreign investors, lack of capital, and a desire to extend coverage by subsidizing the consumer, led to the formation of state-owned corporations. This was done either through the nationalization of existing companies, or through the creation of state companies that undertook the sector's development. There was general agreement that a sector so critical to economic and social development should be in the hands of the state.

In the 1980s, some countries began to question the efficiency of the traditional mode of organization of the electric sector. Debate began on the possibility of establishing a regulatory framework that would create competitive conditions in certain stages of the process, allowing the existence of regulated private monopolies with incentives to strive for efficiency. With such a framework, introduced in 1982, Chile pioneered in changing its electric industry regulations. It also led in the privatization of state-owned companies, which began in 1981 and was completed by 1989.

International Collaboration

The establishment of interconnected electric systems has been a constant in all countries. The benefits they entail (greater safety, reserve reduction, larger size units, and fuel economy) offset the costs of developing the associated transmission systems. These arguments were valid not only within national frontiers but also at the international level. Thus, connecting lines had been built among countries in Western Europe and in Eastern Europe, between Canada and the United States, between the United States and the north of Mexico, between several Central American countries, and so on. Many of these interconnections had been justified by increases in service reliability, by marginal economic exchanges and a few by long-term supply contracts. However, the amounts of energy involved in international exchange were, generally, small as compared with national production.

Other possibilities for international collaboration existed, although they were less frequent. One example was the joint development of hydroelectric projects on international rivers that led to an interconnection between the electric systems of the countries concerned. This was the case for the Salto Grande power plant (Argentina-Uruguay) or the Itaipú dam (Brazil-Paraguay). Other possibilities included sharing in the investment in interconnected power plants, or supplying border zones.

The Electric Sector in Latin America[1]

In 1950, most electric companies in Latin America were privately owned and served only the most important population centers. Over the next two decades, widespread nationalizations led to the creation of large public electric utilities in all countries. Significant progress in geographic coverage and in generation capacity took place since then. However, a series of problems arose that led to a deep crisis in the electric sector, one also associated with the general economic crisis the region faced in the mid-1980s. Poor allocation of resources, inefficient management of the sector's public companies, subsidized prices, and high debt levels all became evident, and resulted in lack of maintenance of existing facilities and delays in bringing into service new projects. Thus, service levels deteriorated markedly.

Argentina. The National Interconnected Grid (NIG) covered 93 percent of electric power consumption and spread over virtually all of Argentina, excepting the southern Patagonian zones and the northern province of Misiones. Additionally, the NIG was interconnected with Uruguay through de Salto Grande power plant, on the Uruguay River, established as a binational entity.

The installed power in the NIG, at the end of 1990, was of 13,210 MW, of which 6,370 were of thermal origin, 5,820 hydraulic, and 1,020 nuclear. Hydraulic power accounted for 38 percent of all power produced. The consumption of public service power had grown at annual rates of 7.9, 7.8, and 2.8 percent in the decades of the 1960s, 1970s, and 1980s, respectively. Forty percent of this consumption was concentrated in Buenos Aires. Consumption growth was estimated at 5 to 6 percent for the near term. This increment would be supplied mainly by the start of hydroelectric power plants (Piedra del Águila, Yaciretá, and Pichi Picún Leufú) and the nuclear power plant Atucha II, all of which were under construction. Any additional power to be installed would probably be based on natural gas.

Up to 1991, almost all the installed capacity and distribution were in the hands of federal or provincial companies, the main ones being Agua y Energía (3,940 MW), SEGBA (2,680 MW), Hidronor (2,720 MW), Salto Grande (1,260 MW), and the National Commission for Atomic Power (1,020 MW). In 1991, the government undertook the privatization of the existing facilities—with the exception of the binational entities, Salto Grande and Yaciretá, and the nuclear power plants—and established the legal basis for the development of the sector.

The regulatory framework established that power generation activities were incompatible with transmission or distribution and required coordinated operations by all power plants interconnected to the NIG. A spot market was made available to all generators, distributors and large clients, where transactions could take place at the system's marginal cost of production on a minute to minute basis. Finally, the framework opened the possibility for generators and distributors to enter freely into fixed-price contracts, established free competition in generation, and a regulated monopoly in transmission and distribution.

Bolivia. Supply was based mainly on hydroelectric power, however, thermal generation had grown recently in response to the availability of natural gas in the country. Consumption growth rates of 9.3 percent per annum were expected for the next few years. The Empresa Nacional de Electricidad (ENDE), was state owned and responsible for the generation and transmission of electric power, while regional companies were in charge of distribution.

Notwithstanding the increase in electric service coverage in the last two decades, Bolivia had one of the lowest levels in the region. During the 1980s, the electric sector achieved a satisfactory financial performance and required few government contributions.

Brazil. Most power generation was hydroelectric and will continue to be so in spite of new additions of coal and natural gas thermal generation. An annual growth rate of consumption of 5.5 percent had been projected for the 1990s. The Brazilian electric sector was among the largest in the world. ELETROBRAS, federally owned, acted both as a holding company and as a development bank for the sector. Its four subsidiaries (Furnas, Chef, Eletrosul, and Eletronorte) were responsible for the generation and transmission of high voltage electricity. It also managed the Brazilian 50 percent share of the binational power plant at Itaipú. Generally, the provincial governments owned the distribution companies in their respective states.

A low price policy, aimed at controlling inflation, had hindered the financial stability and economic efficiency of the sector and made necessary large contributions by the government. The resources needed to fund planned investments (nearly $9 billion per year)

[1]This section is based on data taken from "The Evolution, Situation and Prospects of the Electric Power Sector in the Latin American and Caribbean Countries," World Bank-OLADE, 1991. See Exhibit 11 for summary statistics on some of the region's main electric power markets.

EXHIBIT 11 Summary Statistics for the Latin American Electrical Sector

	Total Population 1990 (millions)*	Per Capita GDP 1990 (US $)*	Annual Growth in GDP 1980-90 (%)*	Service Coverage 1989 (%)*	Installed Capacity 1991 (MW)**	Annual Production 1991 (GWh)**	Hydroelectric Generation 1989 (%)***	Annual Growth in Generation 1980-90 (%)**
Argentina	32.3	2,370	−0.4	95	17,197	64,808	30	2.8
Bolivia	7.2	630	−0.1	25	683	2,293	66	2.3
Brazil	150.4	2,680	2.7	70	54,136	256,681	93	5.7
Columbia	32.3	1,260	3.7	64	8,925	38,226	77	6.0
Costa Rica	2.8	1,900	3.0	90	915	3,408	98	4.8
Chile	13.2	1,940	3.2	91	5,100	19,566	54	4.7
Ecuador	10.3	980	2.0	65	2,322	7,175	86	6.2
El Salvador	5.2	1,110	0.9	46	703	2,099	69	3.5
Guatemala	9.2	900	0.8	31	696	2,319	90	4.1
Honduras	5.1	590	2.3	34	290	1,095	80	1.9
Mexico	86.2	2,490	1.0	66	27,338	119,600	19	6.7
Nicaragua	3.9	n.a.	−2.2	38	395	1,073	25	0.1
Panama	2.4	1,830	0.2	58	898	2,800	78	4.1
Paraguay	4.3	1,110	2.5	46	6,528	2,893	100	15.3
Peru	21.7	1,160	−0.3	38	4,187	14,471	27	3.8
Dominican Republic	7.1	830	2.1	38	1,065	3,843	18	5.4
Uruguay	3.1	2,560	0.3	87	1,795	5,191	68	6.2
Venezuela	19.7	2,560	1.0	85	18,822	65,294	57	5.9

Sources:
*World Bank.
**International Commission on Electric Energy (CIER); United Nations, Economic Commission for Latin America (CEPAL).
***CEPAL.

could not be financed internally, and important contributions of outside capital would be needed.

Colombia. Electric power generation was mainly hydroelectric, and would remain so over the next few years. An annual growth rate of consumption of 6.7 percent was expected over the decade. Almost all the energy was generated, transmitted, and distributed by seven companies: three municipal companies (in Bogotá, Medellín, and Cali), three regional companies owned by the government (CVC, CORELCA, and ICEL), and a fourth one that was a subsidiary of the latter three (ISA). The sector was in poor financial condition due to high debt levels, insufficient fund generation, and currency depreciation, among others.

Ecuador. Hydroelectric generation was the norm, resorting to thermal generation in emergency cases. Annual consumption growth of 6.7 percent was expected for the next few years. INECEL, a government-owned company, was responsible for all generation and transmission, supplying electric power to 18 regional distribution companies. Due to low electricity rates and high foreign debt, the electric sector would have difficulties to fund the expansion projects needed for an adequate future supply of energy.

El Salvador. Most generation was hydroelectric or geothermal, a condition that was expected to continue throughout the 1990s, with a projected consumption growth of 4.2 percent per annum. Virtually all power generation was in the hands of a government corporation, Comisión Ejecutiva del Río Lempa (CEL), which sold electric power to privately owned regional distribution companies. The electric sector was seriously affected by the economic situation in the country and exhibited a level of accrued debt and a scarcity of resources that hindered both maintenance of existing facilities and the investments needed for expansion.

Mexico. Oil-fired thermal generation was dominant, with a small hydroelectric complement. The share of thermal generation was increasing, with most of the expansion based on coal plants. Annual consumption growth rate was estimated at 6.7 percent. The Comisión Federal de Electricidad (CFE) and its distribution affiliate, Compañía de Luz y Fuerza del Centro, supplied all the electric power consumed domestically. The electricity sector had added significantly to the government's fiscal deficit, due mainly to the existence of subsidized electrical rates.

Peru. Although most generation was hydroelectric, an important increase in thermic generation was expected in the future. Annual consumption growth rate had been estimated at 6.6 percent. A national corporation, Electroperú, and 10 regional companies supplied all electric power. The most important among them, Electrolima, served one-half of the country's consumers around the nation's capital. Over the 1980s, inefficient operations and low rates were characteristic of the Peruvian electric sector, resulting in a significant accumulation of foreign debt. This and the difficult economic and political conditions prevalent in Peru throughout the decade, had seriously affected the sector's expansion.

Uruguay. Consumption was mainly supplied by hydroelectric generation from Uruguay's own power plants and from the binational plant of Salto Grande. Thermal generation was to increase slightly in the future. Generation, transmission, and distribution were under the control of the Administración Nacional de Usinas y Transmisiones Eléctricas (UTE). The sector had progressed adequately, but the heavy debt burden brought about by the hydroelectric project investments forced a reduction of the planned expansion of distribution facilities and a corresponding drop in service.

Venezuela. Supply was mainly hydroelectric, complemented by oil thermal generation, a situation likely to continue into the near future. Consumption growth was forecast for the next few years at 8.1 percent per annum. The electric sector was made up of four state-owned companies (CADAFE, EDELCA, ENELVEN, and ENELBAR) and seven privately owned firms. The most important among the latter was Electricidad de Caracas, which supplied the city of Caracas and its suburbs. The sector had achieved an important development in the last years, to which end it had used up a significant share of the country's resources. At present, it faced serious problems caused by an inadequate price policy and a weak financial situation.

The Chilean Electric Sector

The Chilean electric sector consisted of public service companies, and a few industrial and mining companies that produced electric power to supply their own needs (auto-producers) and sold any excess to the national grid.

Total installed capacity in the country was 5,100 MW. For 1992, electric generation was expected to reach approximately 21,500 GWh. Three different zones could be identified in Chile with distinctive characteristics.

Norte Grande Zone. The northern zone comprised the regions of Tarapacá and Antofagasta. The Norte Grande Interconnected Grid (NGIG) was developed to link the cities between Arica and Antofagasta and the mining centers at Chuquicamata and La Escondida. This is a desert area, with almost no hydroelectric resources. Generation, based mainly on coal-fired plants, accounted for 18 percent of Chilean electric power production.

The principal generator in Norte Grande was CODELCO (the national copper mining company), which owned the thermal generating plant at Tocopilla with 563 MW capacity. In addition to supplying power to the mine at Chuquicamata, this plant sold power to Edelnor, a 96 MW plant and the only public utility generator in the NGIG.

Central Zone. This zone comprised the regions between Taltal in the north and Chiloé Island in the South (some 2000 km in length) and was supplied by the Central Interconnected Grid (CIG). The central zone consumed 81 percent of the country's electric power. Power generation was mainly hydroelectric (accounting for between 60 and 95 percent of generated power depending on hydrological conditions), complemented by coal-fired thermal generation.

Total installed capacity by public utilities represented 3,830 MW, of which 78 percent was hydroelectric. The main generators were ENDESA (1,928 MW), Chilgener (756 MW), Pehuenche (500 MW) and Colbún-Machicura (490 MW). All auto-producers had a total installed capacity of 300 MW. The main distribution companies were Chilectra Metropolitana, Chilectra Quinta Región, Compañía General de Electricidad Industrial, Saesa, Frontel, EMEL, EMELAT y EMEC.

Austral Zone. This zone included the regions of Chiloé Continental (mainland), Aysén, and Magallanes, in the extreme south. This zone is characterized by few small population centers, located in far-off places and very distant from one another. Electric power production, which accounts for about 1 percent of the country's total, was basically hydroelectric at Aysén and from a gas-fired thermal plant in Magallanes. Generation and distribution were in the hands of two companies, EDELAYSEN and EDELMAG.

Annual growth rates of power consumption in Chile for the 1960s, 1970s, and 1980s were 5.1, 4.5 and 4.5 percent, respectively. The figures for the CIG zone were 6.8, 5.7 and 4.8 percent over the same periods, and was expected to grow at a cumulative 5 to 6 percent per annum for the decade of 1990s. Exhibit 12 summarizes figures for power consumption for each of the three main regions for 1991.

Evolution of the Chilean Electric Sector

From the first public lighting installations, at the end of the 19th century, to the beginning of the 1940s, electric power in Chile was supplied exclusively by private companies. A supply crisis in the 1930s, partly related to the world financial crisis and increasing government regulations, brought about the active participation of the state through the creation of ENDESA, an affiliate of the Corporación de Fomento a la Producción, the Chilean state development corporation. When Chilectra was nationalized in 1970, virtually all public service power generation and transmission, and around 90 percent of distribution were in the hands of the state.

In 1978, a new approach toward the sector began to be implemented with the creation of the Comisión Nacional de Energía (CNE), whereby the state's regulating role was explicitly separated from its business role. Later, in 1982, a new regulatory framework was introduced, and the change process was completed with the privatization of the generation, transport, and distribution companies owned by the state.

The activities of the electric power industry in Chile were regulated by the Decree-Law No.1 of 1982, issued by the Ministry of Mining. This decree established different

EXHIBIT 12 Chilean Consumption of Electric Energy—1991

(GWh)

	Public Utilities	Auto-Producers	Total
Norte Grande	824	2,674	3,498
Central Integrated Grid	14,733	1,323	16,056
Austral Zone	138	115	253
Total	15,695	4,112	19,807

rules for the generation, transport, and distribution of electric power, according to characteristics particular to each of these stages. It was accepted, for example, that there were no extraordinary economies of scale at the generation level and that the purpose of the regulations should be to create the best conditions for regulated competition. As a result:

- There would be no need of a special authorization for the construction of a power plant, except for those aspects related to water rights and safety.
- There would be price freedom for the supply to large clients (more than 2 MW of power).
- Regulated prices were established on the basis of short-term marginal costs for the system.
- All generators would coordinate activities and would transfer energy among them at a spot price based on the marginal cost of the system at that instant.
- All generators would have free and equal access to the transmission systems.

In contrast, significant economies of scale existed at the transmission level. Generators must pay for the use of third-party transmission systems on the basis of their annual mean costs of investment and operation. However, these costs were not to be fixed by the authority, but determined by mutual accord or through arbitration.

The existence of a natural monopoly in distribution was accepted for each geographic area. Distribution concessions were thus granted to companies that were compelled to provide service to their assigned territory. The regulatory authority would determine prices to small consumers (less than 2 MW) on the basis of the average cost of power obtained from the generators, plus a mean distribution cost. The latter was calculated for a typical distribution company under the assumptions of adequate management of investment decisions and operational efficiency. These costs were revised every four years by independent consultants hired jointly by the authority and the companies.

In 1989, the last year in which the calculations had been made, the CNE had determined that the contribution of each stage of the production process to the total cost of electric power in Chile were as follows (in U.S. cents per kWh): generation, 3.2¢; transmission, 0.7¢; and distribution, 2.4¢.

UNIT 5 Global Strategy in Entrepreneurial Firms

Case 5-1

The Australian Motorcycle Company: Born Global or Stillborn?

The volume of enthusiastic press coverage his company was receiving pleased Rod Hunwick, the general manager of the newly formed Australian Motorcycle Company (AMC). The Hunwick Hallam motorcycle had "*won rave reviews from the international motorcycle press and strong expressions of interest from potential distributors and customers*"[1]. Alan Cathcart, a world renowned, independent journalist visited Australia twice to test ride both the cruiser and the race prototypes and gave strong endorsements of both machines. Detailed articles about the new bikes appeared in over 20 motorcycle magazines around the world and Motorcycle Online, the premier motorcycle "e-zine" (see Exhibit 1 for some article extracts).

However, Hunwick had some pressing concerns. The location for the factory had yet to be decided, although some attractive proposals had been received from both the New South Wales and Victorian State governments. The first of 30 Hunwick Hallam Boss PowerCruisers was due to roll off the line in November 1998. No decision to go ahead could be made until suitable financing had been secured. Attempts to secure a local provider of venture capital for the start up phase had been fruitless. Of equally great importance to the success of the firm was the choice of which markets to target for export and the question of how to distribute its product in foreign markets.

[1]*Business Review Weekly*, 7 July 1997, p. 34.

This case was written by Marco Gabbiani, MBA, under the supervision of Professor Timothy Devinney as a basis for class discussion and not for the purpose of illustrating either the good or bad handling of a specific management situation.

The Australian Motorcycle Company

The Founders

The Australian Motorcycle Company was formed in 1994 to develop, manufacture, and sell a prestige Australian built motorcycle. Rod Hunwick joined forces with Paul Hallam to design a unique engine and motorcycle to be branded "Hunwick Hallam" (HH). To date, Hunwick has spent over A$3 million of his own funds on product development.

Hunwick has four motorcycle dealerships and two car outlets in his Action Motor Group (AMG). Action retails Honda, Suzuki, Moto Guzzi, and Bimota motorcycles and Suzuki four wheeled vehicles. Hunwick has proven his expertise in selling motorcycles: The branch in Parramatta, a suburb west of Sydney, is the most successful Honda outlet in Australia, selling over 1,000 bikes a year. Hallam, an engineer, has designed engines and motorcycles for a variety of purposes and has won international renown for his work in developing superbike[2] racing engines. A team of eight people was involved in prototype development. After three years of development effort, prototypes for three different models have been developed (see Exhibit 2 for HH product types and pictures).

Strategy

AMC's aim is to capture a previously ignored market niche: high-end customers prepared to pay a large premium for a high quality, individually customized, handmade motorcycle. These riders desire unique and stylish machines that deliver high levels of reliability, resale value, and performance. Most of the potential customers are offshore and, with simple modifications, the bike's design can be tailored to any market. Limited production runs and a range of factory customizing options are aimed at delivering a unique product to each customer. Gross margins of over 50 percent are expected from direct

[2]Superbike racing is based on production motorcycles and has many local series as well as an international series that is in the FIM stable.

EXHIBIT 1a Australian Motorcycle Company High Performance Engineering in Every Sense by Ken Edwards

With a mixture of high-tech lilt and super speedway "bark," Australia's first locally designed and built high performance motorcycle has thundered into life. The effort of a small team headed by leading Australian motorcycle and automotive retailer Rod Hunwick and world recognized race engineer Paul Hallam, the fuel-injected DOHC 90-degree V-twin has been under development for almost three years. Designed by Hallam, the powerplant will initially be constructed in three distinct versions. These in turn will power a three-bike model range built in Australia and marketed under the Hunwick Hallam banner.

It is planned that the first motorcycle to wear their distinctive HH logo will be the 1350cc BOSS V-PowerCruiser. A 1000cc X1R Sportbike that will feature Formula One-style pneumatic valve actuation and be eligible for the World Superbike Championship will follow this. The final model in the line-up will be an unfaired 1100cc Rage streetrod. Both PowerCruiser and Superbike versions of the engine have undergone extensive dyno testing and are registering competitive levels of horsepower in their intended roles.

Many people have likened the Hunwick Hallam to New Zealand's Britten, however the two Australians responsible for this machine had higher aims than to build just one, or even a handful of bikes. "We have kept the development and design of the engines secret," said project pioneer Rod Hunwick, "However, the whole Hunwick Hallam project has reached the stage that we can make public some of our efforts."

These guys are intent on taking on the world. World Superbikes actually. To do this, a volume build is required. The enterprising pair have formed a manufacturing arm—the Australian Motorcycle Company—with the intent of building 500 Hunwick Hallam motorcycles per year to be exported around the world. With large-capacity and prestige motorcycle sales experiencing a resurgence worldwide, the export potential of the new Hunwick Hallam venture is considerable. "We are currently negotiating regarding the future of our enterprise, including the location and scope of the manufacturing facilities," said Hunwick.

"What Paul (Hallam) has designed and we have produced is a world class powerplant—in its various versions it is the first step to producing a range of motorcycles that we believe will take on the world's best," added Hunwick. Details of the innovative eight-valve 1350cc PowerCruiser powerplant include a 102.5 x 82mm bore and stroke, sequential electronic fuel-injection and an ultra-compact cylinder-head design featuring Hallam's own Axial Targeted Combustion process.

"We set out to design the world's best four-stroke motorcycle powerplant," designer and engineer Hallam said. "Taking the best from all facets of combustion engineering, the engines are both innovative and practical. The elemental design has the potential to provide quite astonishing figures—both versions are already producing more horsepower than their potential competitors," Hallam revealed.

Production documentation and tooling is also well advanced. Already the BOSS V-PowerCruiser is a running concern in prototype form, with final testing and compliance with Australian Design Rules a priority. The 1350cc 90-degree V-twin BOSS cruiser is set to offer significant performance increases for the powercruiser market. Handling and styling won't disappoint either.

However, the bike everybody wanted to see was the X1R Superbike. Former Australian Superbike Champion Mal Campbell has assumed the role of race/test rider for Hunwick Hallam, and completed the first laps ever ridden on the bike recently between races at Phillip Island during the 1997 World Superbike event there. The World Superbike Championship-eligible powerplant that is (literally) the backbone of this motorcycle, will offer features previously found only in Formula One car racing.

"While the Australian market is important, we believe that most of our production will be for export," stated Hunwick. "The demand for high quality, innovative and exciting motorcycles is increasing worldwide. This is a very important project in a number of ways. Hunwick Hallam will showcase both the design talent of Paul and our team, and Australia's manufacturing industry as a whole." At this stage no firm rollout date has been set for the first of the Hunwick Hallam models, however Hunwick said design and construction is well advanced. "Our Sydney based team is well down the road to completing our initial prototype program," Hunwick revealed. "We're in the business of producing motorcycles, not design exercises. No embargo."

EXHIBIT 1b Hunwick Hallam X1R Superbike: The First Ride by Ken Edwards

Hunwick Hallam's X1R Superbike rolled out into the public gaze for its first time during round one of the 1997 World Superbike Championship at Phillip Island. A brave move on the part of the Australian Motorcycle Company, as the bike had not been tested previously. Apart from running the engine up on a dyno, the X1R had never turned a wheel before. The bike was rolled out of the truck much to the awe of international Superbike teams and the Australian public. A jet-black carbon fiber-covered beauty that looked like no other. This wasn't any concept bike drawn up by under-worked Japanese motorcycle designers. This was the real thing. Sex on wheels.

Bike designer Paul Hallam had the honors of rolling the bike up to pit lane. Clearly it was the moment he had waited for. After three years working in secret, at last the world would see his creation. Would the bike start? Would the bike run? What if. . . .? A million questions going through the heads of all that watched. Paul Hallam was quietly confident. The bike is bump started into action. The sound is a beautiful thump that only a V-twin can offer.

Hallam handed the bike over to the highly experienced racer and development rider Malcolm Campbell, the only man ever to win a race on Honda's notorious NR750. Taking off from pit lane, Superbike teams were all outside their garages watching history take place. Campbell and the X1R disappear over the hill on the main straight to the delight of the patriotic crowd.

Paul Hallam was asked what he felt the highest pinnacle was so far in the development of the new racing machine. "Here and now," was the reply. As the bike came down the main straight it seemed that all the garages were empty. Hallam's creation was on its first flying lap of any racetrack in the world. On completion of the second lap Campbell pulled into the pits as instructed. An eager Hallam awaited the news. "Power is great, needs some adjustment on the rear suspension," comments the rider.

The Hunwick Hallam X1R entered its first competitive meeting soon after this debut at round three of the Australian Superbike Series at Winton, Victoria. However, Campbell crashed out of the race in a first corner incident with another rider. The X1R had qualified ninth in wet conditions.

For the remainder of this year, the X1R will be competing in a special "prototype" class for no prize money or points in the Australian Superbike Series. The bike must comply with all Superbike Rules as per Motorcycling Australia's General Competition Rules (GCR's), except for volume sales. GCR's are identical to FIM rules for World Superbike, where the Hunwick Hallam team hopes to compete by next season.

Hunwick Hallam Debuts Its BOSS PowerCruiser

Australian Superbike manufacturer Hunwick Hallam has announced details of its stunning BOSS PowerCruiser prototype. The pioneering Australian marquee's debut machine is set to take street cruisers to a new plane—in terms of styling and design as well as performance.

The first of three debut models to wear the Hunwick Hallam badge, the BOSS PowerCruiser is propelled by a 1350cc version of Hunwick Hallam's own V-Power, fuel injected, eight valve, DOHC, 90-degree V-twin. In its PowerCruiser guise, the ultra-modern, short-stroke, Axial Targeted Combustion, air/liquid-cooled powerplant is claimed to produce in excess of 100 horsepower—despite a very mild state of tune.

Already, racing versions of the same power plant are producing over 160 hp per liter. Designed to take the street cruiser concept into the next century, the Hunwick Hallam BOSS PowerCruiser has been designed from HH's first principles concept. That is, while some motorcycles are designed in isolation as a powerplant and chassis, HH has treated the motorcycle as one component. As such, the HH design sees its engine act as the major chassis component, eliminating the need for a conventional frame. The BOSS PowerCruiser's cast-alloy steering head, rear sub-assembly and rear swingarm bolt directly to the central engine-transmission unit. So too does its rear suspension componentry—Hunwick Hallam's own rising rate asymmetric RamRoc monoshock system.

Hunwick Hallam's engine/chassis design offers weight reduction and packaging benefits as well as facilitating production savings and easing routine maintenance. Visually however, the benefit of this approach is clear. The visual aspect of the Hunwick Hallam design is that the PowerCruiser is almost elemental in its appearance. Wheels, engine and controls—nothing ancillary.

In this respect, the BOSS PowerCruiser is a hint of things to come. It certainly breaks the 'in vogue' cruiser mold. Like the prototype, the production BOSS PowerCruiser will use top level componentry: Fully adjustable Dutch-made WP suspension units, and braking via Brembo componentry. Road and track testing of the PowerCruiser have already indicated good handling characteristics.

Indeed, could the HH PowerCruiser deliver handling characteristics more akin to a conventional sportbike? This ability, while not detracting from the traditional attraction of cruisers, has the added bonus of appealing to riders who have been frustrated by the poor dynamic performance of the current crop of cruisers. Hunwick Hallam claims the BOSS PowerCruiser promises 50 percent more power than its opposition, while boasting a 50 percent weight advantage in the cruiser arena.

At this stage it is anticipated that the BOSS PowerCruiser will commence production in 1998. Currently, the company is negotiating with venture capital partners and is in discussions with State Government bodies regarding the establishment of its manufacturing facility. Since the venture was made public with release of details of the new powerplant in January, interest at both business and end-user levels has been promising.

Source: Motorcycle Online at http://www.motorcycle.com/. Article at .../mo/mcken/hunwick.html.

EXHIBIT 2a Hunwick Hallam 1998/99 Product Range

Model	Style	Engine Capacity	Share of Sales (est.)
Boss PowerCruiser	Cruiser	1350 cc	70%
Rage	Cruiser	1100 cc	20%
X1R	Supersport	1000 cc	10%

EXHIBIT 2b Boss PowerCruiser

EXHIBIT 2c Hunwick Hallam Rage

EXHIBIT 2d Hunwick Hallam X1R

customer sales. Sales to distributors will run at margins of over 40 percent. The after-tax profit margin is expected to be around 5 percent.

Hunwick's understanding of the market is based on his extensive experience in selling expensive motorcycles in Australia. He believes that HH customers around the world share similar needs. AMC's strategic emphasis is on the product's design and performance rather than after-sales service and promotion. The main promotion vehicle for the product is a high profile racing program.

The racing program will serve two important purposes. First, racing raises the profile of the company and is a useful promotional tool. Second, race development is an effective way to evolve a reliable and robust design, as racing conditions are more demanding than those prevailing on the road. AMC expects its race development orientation to substitute effectively for a large advertising budget.

> We don't think we will have to run huge international marketing campaigns, because our experience is that people already know the bike for its unique qualities [. . .] We believe that it can generate its own demand.[3]

AMC is keen to emphasize its differentiated product positioning. Bikes will be individually handmade to customer specifications. Rapid order turnaround of approximately one month is aimed at maintaining high levels of customer service. Customers will be invited to visit the factory to get a better idea of how they may wish to customize their machine. AMC plans to export directly to customers in markets where there is no distribution structure.

Recent Progress

Five prototypes have been built and the road bike is ready for production. The X1R race bike has entered a number of local races and won on a few occasions. Power output figures are very promising for competition at the international level. AMC is seeking a partner with a 30 percent share of equity and requires approximately A$7 million dollars in external funds to start production. Negotiations for equity investment are progressing with an Asian venture capital fund.

Apart from the domestic market, AMC expects to concentrate its export efforts on Europe and Japan. Consultants who evaluated AMC's prospects were unwilling to sign off on the size of the market that HH motorcycles could capture. This problem arose because Hunwick's target segment has never been targeted before. Apart from racing motorcycles and a few limited edition special models (like Honda's NR750 which sold for over A$80,000), no other manufacturer sells motorcycles in volume[4] at the A$35,000–A$40,000 price level (see Exhibit 3 for examples of Australian motorcycle prices).[5] However, many purchasers of expensive motorcycles buy accessories to customize their motorcycles, resulting in gross purchase values of well over $30,000.

The World Motorcycle Market

The Heavyweight Segment

The bulk of world production is in small commuter motorcycles. The market that AMC is targeting is the so-called "heavyweight" market for motorcycles with engine capacities in excess of 750cc.[6] Exhibit 4 gives production figures for the major motorcycle producing countries. China, India, and South East Asian countries only manufacture bikes up to 150cc. These machines are predominantly used for transport purposes.

The heavyweight market is concentrated in Europe, Japan, North America, and Australia/ New Zealand. The Japanese "Big Four"—Honda, Kawasaki, Suzuki, and Yamaha—dominate this part of the motorcycle industry. Since the late 1960's, they have accounted for more than half of the world's heavyweight motorcycle production. The non-Japanese, or 'Western', producers focus on the larger bike market (represented by engine capacities of 125cc or more). Harley Davidson is the single largest manufacturer in the US. The European industry has been reduced to a few major players: BMW in Germany, Triumph in the UK, Cagiva/Ducati, and Aprilia in Italy.

Customer Preferences

In most developed countries motorcycles sales have been in decline since the 1970s.[7] The role of the motorcycle has changed from a means of cheap transportation to that of a lifestyle accessory, and changing fashions have led to the rising and declining popularity of motorcycles. During the 1970s motorcycles suffered from negative social images and a very poor safety record. The 1990s have revealed a small recovery in the motorcycle industry, and it is becoming fashionable to be on two wheels again. Many celebrities and high profile business people now openly advertise their affection for motorcycles. These customers place a premium on the exclusivity of their mount with little concern for price.

---

[3]Rod Hunwick, *Business Review Weekly,* 7 July 1997, p. 34.

[4]Specialist builders like Harris, Over, and Egli rarely produce more than 50 of each model.

[5]Harley Davidson's most expensive model retails for just under A$30,000 in Australia.

[6]Some observers include 750cc bikes in the heavyweight segment.

[7]See Exhibit 5 for data on the history of motorcycle sales in Australia and the UK. This pattern is representative of that seen in other Western markets as well.

EXHIBIT 3 Australian Price Guide—Selected Motorcycles (1997)

Manufacturer/Model	Type	Actual CCs	Weight (Kgs-dry)	Price (A$)
Bimota				
SB6	Supersport	1074	190	$35,700
DB3 Mantra	Supersport	904	172	$25,990
BMW				
K1100LTSE	Sport/tourer	1092	290	$24,900
R1100TR	Sport/tourer	1085	282	$23,500
R1100GS	Sport/tourer	1085	243	$18,500
Ducati				
916SPS	Supersport	995	195	$35,995
M900 Monster	Standard	904	184	$16,995
Harley Davidson				
FLHTCUI Electra Glide Ultra Classic	Tourer	1340	347	$29,250
FLSTF Fat Boy Two Tone	Cruiser	1340	284	$24,250
XL1200 Sportster Sport	Cruiser	1200	226	$14,995
Honda				
GL1500SEV Gold Wing	Tourer	1520	370	$29,990
GL1500C2V Valkyrie Cruiser	Cruiser	1520	309	$19,990
CBR1100XV Blackbird	Sport/tourer	1137	227	$16,500
VT1100C2V Ace	Cruiser	1099	260	$14,490
CBR900RRV	Supersport	918	183	$15,900
Kawasaki				
Vulcan 1500 Classic	Cruiser	1470	292	$16,390
ZZR–1100	Sport/tourer	1052	233	$16,490
ZX9–R	Supersport	899	215	$15,490
Suzuki				
VS1400GLPV	Cruiser	1360	243	$12,599
GSX–R750V	Supersport	749	179	$14,999
Triumph				
Trophy 1200	Sport/tourer	1200	235	$18,950
T595 Daytona	Supersport	955	198	$18,990
Thunderbird	Cruiser	900	220	$16,250
Yamaha				
XVZ1300ATJ Royal Star Tour Classic	Cruiser	~1270	~310	$19,990
XV1100SH Virago	Cruiser	1063	221	$11,999
YZF1000RK	Supersport	993	198	$15,999

Note: The highest priced motorcycle and the largest cc bikes are listed when possible.
Source: *Australian Motorcycle Trader,* 12 September 1997.

EXHIBIT 4a World Motorcycle Production—Selected Countries

Year	1995	1993	1992	1991	1990	1989	1988	1987	1986	1985	1984	1983
Japan	1,213,000	3,023,154	3,196,535	3,028,616	2,806,895	2,794,362	2,945,618	2,630,608	3,396,643	4,536,347	4,026,307	4,807,379
France	*325,904*	*327,731*	329,558	324,143	333,212	330,958	311,462	279,978	291,218	448,369	449,317	518,487
Italy	*477,550*	*527,850*	578,150	628,450	909,899	882,492	899,513	700,046	839,828	808,250	716,675	861,050
Germany	*89,333*	*81,059*	72,785	85,171	56,237	49,446	50,030	60,830	65,779	85,840	120,023	139,592
UK	*5,950*	*4,675*	3,400	2,678	850	900	640	800	350	2,000	2,300	2,300
Netherlands	*21,250*	*22,557*	23,863	25,678	26,476	21,700	18,500	28,900	12,600	7,400	6,200	8,000
Spain	*285,842*	*299,181*	312,519	321,390	384,565	335,922	328,056	255,431	182,621	173,473	177,156	179,174
Austria		*3,872*	7,248	14,456	20,904	16,352	23,049	55,737	98,691	160,799	145,949	134,119
Yugoslavia						66,480	68,563	87,092	78,978	76,818	86,346	74,472
USA	*91,630*	*84,291*	76,951	66,210	62,272	120,000	110,000	125,000	105,000	130,000	155,000	100,000
India	*1,257,896*	*1,367,379*	1,476,861	1,601,333	1,875,522	1,750,406	1,547,966	1,401,819	1,359,668	1,125,606	851,354	759,183
Total	***3,768,851***	***5,741,747***	**6,077,870**	**6,098,125**	**6,476,832**	**6,303,018**	**6,369,397**	**5,626,241**	**6,431,376**	**7,554,902**	**6,736,627**	**7,583,747**

Note: Italicized numbers for 1993 and 1995 are estimates.
Source: Automobile associations in each country and *Guide to the Motor Industry of Japan,* Japan Motor Industry Federation, INC (JMIF).

EXHIBIT 4b World Motorcycle Production Estimates for 1996

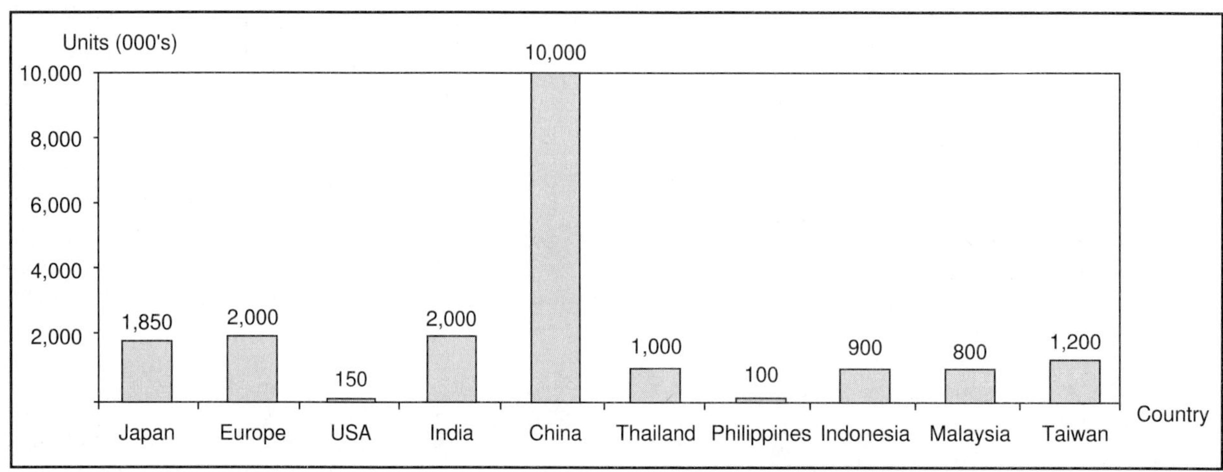

Source: International Motorcycle Manufacturers Association, Geneva (IMMA). Phone interview 15 August 1997.

EXHIBIT 5 History of UK and Australian Motorcycle Sales, 1970–97

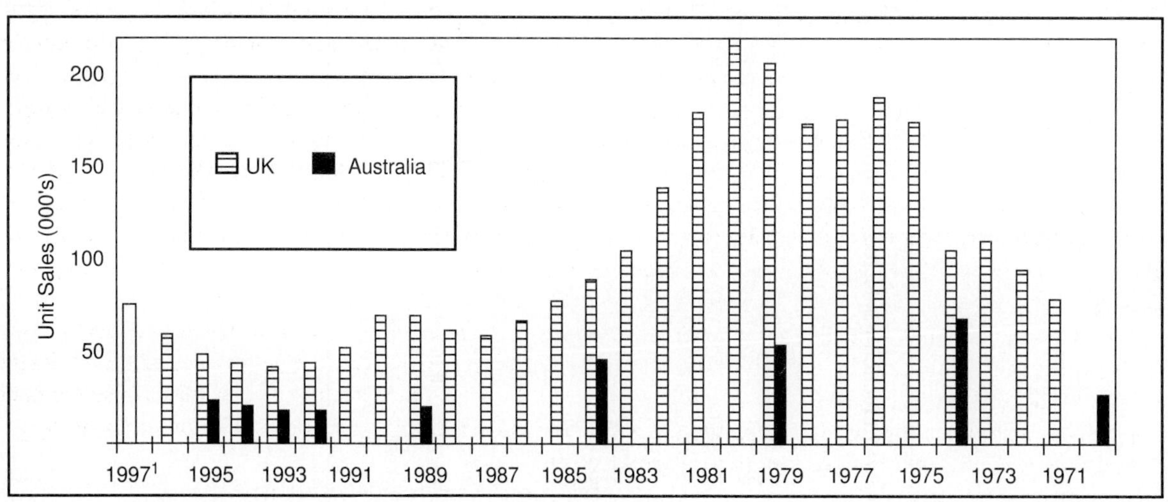

Note: (1)1997 figure annualized from January–July sales figures.
Source: UK Motorcycle Industry Association (MCIA) and ABS, *Motor Vehicles in Australia,* Publication 9311.0, 1997.

Australia and New Zealand

AMC's home market is small by world standards in terms of total volume. However, the high proportion of large motorcycles purchased makes Australia an attractive top-end market. The total market has been growing since 1993, and the fastest growth has been in the over 750cc segment. This can be seen in the dramatic increase in the average price paid for an imported motorcycle in Exhibit 6.

Harley Davidson has the highest share of the over 750cc market (see Exhibit 6), and this share has consistently increased since they entered the market. Harley Davidson's success reflects the increasing popularity of cruisers as well as a validation of their own efforts. In light of the lessons learned from Harley Davidson's success in Australia, AMC plans to sell its product directly from a showroom/factory facility. Along with capitalizing on Hunwick's experience selling motorcycles, direct selling facilitates the customer's selection of custom options.

Europe

Europe is the largest heavyweight market in the world if one includes the 750 class machines that are popular in Europe (those that have capacities just under 750 cc). The four largest markets are Germany, France, Britain, and Italy. Britain has the highest concentration of large motorcycles but a relatively low concentration of cruisers compared to its European peers. Although, the cruiser segment is growing in all European countries, it is still small compared to the US cruiser segment. This is attributable, at least in part, to European buyers' preference for performance—acceleration, braking, and cornering—over ostentatious styling. All of this is reflected in Harley Davidson's weaker competitive position in Europe. Exhibit 7 presents selected data on the European market.

The integration of the European Union (EU) market has pluses and minuses for the industry. Certification requirements are common across the EU and there is also no duty payable when transferring goods between member countries. However, noise and emissions controls for motorcycles are becoming stricter, and some politicians have been active in attempting to reduce the power output of high performance motorcycles. According to IMMA, *"it is only a matter of time before the 100 hp limit is imposed on Europe by the European Parliament"*.[8]

Japan

For a country with a large population of motorcycles, the over 750cc motorcycle segment is relatively small in Japan. Japan has a registered motorcycle population 83 percent of the size of the US motorcycle population, but a heavyweight market that is only 20 percent of the size of the US segment.[9] A combination of numerous capacity classes for registration purposes and higher fees on large motorbikes have resulted in a heavyweight segment that is proportionally smaller than other major markets. However, cruisers are very popular, as can be seen from Harley Davidson's share of the heavyweight segment (see Exhibit 8).

North America

The home of Harley Davidson is the largest heavyweight market and the largest cruiser market in the world. American motorcycle buyers are very loyal to their brands and their country. Anti-Japanese motorcycle attitudes are apparent in many parts of the US motorcycle fraternity. Harley Davidson has a very dominant position in the heavy cruiser market with a 60 percent share of a still growing segment and has had the largest market share since 1987 (see Exhibit 9). Lower speed limits and poorly enforced helmet regulations have led to the popularity of "wind in the hair" motorcycling. Motorcycle performance is perceived to be less important than styling, individuality and brand by a majority of buyers.

The highly litigious nature of the American market increases the risk of selling recently developed products. Audi's travails were a case in point. Audi led the field when it introduced drive-by-wire technology to the US but damaging litigation regarding this technology was very costly. Litigation is a particular concern for AMC since their technology is so new. The ability to alter motorcycle geometry and engine characteristics radically with little effort creates the danger that customers may customize their bikes in a potentially unsafe manner.

Export Distribution Channels

Motorcycle distribution follows a pattern similar to that seen in the car industry. Dealerships are usually independent of the manufacturers but are frequently franchised or part of a chain store system. Most dealers sell

---

[8] International Motorcycle Manufacturers Association, Geneva, phone interview.

[9] Source US Census bureau, *Japan Statistical Yearbook 1997*, and *Harley Davidson 1996 Annual Report*.

EXHIBIT 6a **Australian Motorcycle Registrations by Manufacturer**

Company	1995	1994	1993	1989	1984	1979	1974	1969
BMW	867	861	663	546	1,503	415	607	65
Cagiva	93	49	25	2				
Ducati	641	445	299	300	456	464	953	242
Harley Davidson	3,258	3,095	2,587	1,755	847	500	519	53
Honda	6,530	6,436	5,611	5,609	15,896	19,010	26,025	11,252
Husqvarna	210	200	159	87	144	86	68	1
Kawasaki	2,916	2,669	2,562	3,187	6,382	6,336	6,102	1,705
KTM	427	333	143	130	214	27	14	
Moto Guzzi	162	102	104	173	256	114	80	16
Suzuki	2,331	1,816	1,940	3,409	9,063	11,515	11,280	5,658
Triumph	481	466	265	3	4	371	321	971
Vespa	59	2	5	61	50	100	230	227
Yamaha	4,284	3,973	3,018	4,964	10,673	14,067	17,999	4,584
Other	86	58	44	227	391	942	3,365	2,496
Total	**22,345**	**20,505**	**17,425**	**20,453**	**45,879**	**53,947**	**67,563**	**27,270**

EXHIBIT 6b **The Average Value of Motorcycle Imports Per Registered Motorcycle**
(estimates $A)

Company	1995	1994	1993	1989	1984	1979	1974	1969
BMW	16,344	14,124	16,525	10,533	4,397	3,101	2,092	1,277
Japan	10,410	9,304	9,717	5,844	1,823	602	529	252
Harley Davidson	25,938	23,715	23,394	18,289	7,503	4,466	844	472
Average	**18,098**	**16,626**	**17,277**	**11,207**	**2,071**	**683**	**577**	**279**

Note: Average value defined as the value of imports divided by the total number of registered vehicles.

EXHIBIT 6c **Value of Motorcycle Imports by Source**
(A$ millions)

Country	1995	1994	1993	1992	1991	1990	1989	1984	1979	1974	1969
Germany	14.17	12.16	10.96	8.92	3.93	4.87	5.75	6.61	1.29	1.27	0.08
Japan	167.19	138.57	127.59	115.35	87.85	88.38	100.34	76.58	30.68	32.46	5.86
USA	84.51	73.40	30.52	54.39	39.10	29.34	32.10	6.35	2.23	0.44	0.02
Other	138.52	116.78	101.99	83.90	79.48	84.46	91.03	5.48	2.64	4.80	1.65
Total	**404.39**	**340.91**	**301.05**	**262.56**	**210.37**	**207.05**	**229.22**	**95.02**	**36.84**	**38.97**	**7.61**

Source: Australian Bureau of Statistics (ABS), *Motor Vehicles in Australia,* publication 9311.0, 1997.

EXHIBIT 7a European Motorcycle Market Data

(units sold)

Country	1996	1995	1994
UK	58,802	*46,695	44,729
France	115,814	84,461	84,870
Germany	271,467	217,495	212,848
Italy	87,927	80,320	73,914
Spain	30,570	34,251	34,811
Austria	20,781	18,160	16,212
Europe (Total)	**676,417**	**567,290**	**541,851**

*The UK MCIA quotes a figure of 47,429.

EXHIBIT 7b Number of Greater than 750cc Models by Sales Ranking in the European Market

	Top 50			Top 10		
Country	1996	1995	1994	1996	1995	1994
UK	20	19	21	4	3	3
France	13	18	16	3	2	2
Germany	17	21	16	0	0	1
Italy	11	8	12	1	0	0
Spain	5	8	6	0	0	0
Austria	22	22	20	4	3	3
Europe (Total)	**16**	**16**	**18**	**1**	**1**	**1**

EXHIBIT 7c Sales Volume of Top-Ranked Model and the 50th-Ranked Model in the European Market

(high ranking scooters and mopeds and Honda C90 excluded)

	Top-Ranked model			50th-Ranked model		
Country	1996	1995	1994	1996	1995	1994
UK	2,460	1,830	1,783	292	243	254
France	4,250	2,174	1,989	643	531	594
Germany	5,880	7,047	7,846	1,662	1,463	1,365
Italy	2,678	2,819	2,975	444	402	415
Spain	1,185	1,456	1,501	157	169	185
Austria	726	746	695	113	96	94
Europe (Total)	**13,643**	**11,896**	**12,944**	**3,539**	**3,038**	**2,940**

EXHIBIT 7d Sales Volume of Top-Ranked Model in the Greater than 750cc Class in Europe

Country	1996	1995	1994
UK	2,460	1,649	1,783
France	2,947	1,666	1,860
Germany	3,924	3,794	3,859
Italy	1,803	1,110	941
Spain	305	409	331
Austria	726	472	464
Europe (Total)	**8,518**	**7,032**	**9,059**

EXHIBIT 7e Market Share of the Top 50 Models in the European Market

Country	1996	1995	1994
UK	65%	61%	62%
France	66%	62%	59%
Germany	66%	64%	66%
Italy	73%	67%	65%
Spain	72%	74%	73%
Austria	72%	76%	78%
Europe (Total)	**49%**	**47%**	**48%**

more than one brand of motorcycle, and it is not uncommon to see larger dealers selling two or more of the Big Four brands and a handful of European models. Harley Davidson is an exception to this rule with 75 percent of its North American and 50 percent of its European dealers being exclusive Harley Davidson operations. Harley Davidson is beginning to vertically integrate by taking over some Harley Davidson franchises, and it already owns the importers in many of its larger export markets. In most countries there is a single importer of each brand and independent and subsidiary importers appear to be equally common.[10]

Dealer margins do not appear to vary to a great degree given the consistency of motorcycle pricing around the world after freight and taxes are taken into account. In the UK, the typical dealer margin of 15 percent[11] is often negotiated to a figure well below this level. The revenue gained from accessory sales, financing, and after-sales service can help to offset this margin erosion. The margins on high-end motorcycles tend to be somewhat higher than the average to compensate for lower sales volumes and higher inventory costs. AMC estimates that its retail margin is similar to that obtained by brands like Harley Davidson and Bimota. The importer or distributor in each

[10]Volume exports of motorcycles are shipped by sea. Shipping costs per motorcycle are approximately A$250.

[11]Source: phone interview with Motorcycle Industry Association, Coventry UK.

EXHIBIT 7f Sales Volume and Brand of the Top-Ranked Cruiser (over 750cc) Model in Europe

	Sales Volume (units)			Top-Ranked Brand		
Country	1996	1995	1994	1996	1995	1994
UK	361	428	369	Yamaha	Yamaha	Yamaha
France	1,261	802	708	Kawasaki	Honda	Harley Davidson
Germany	2,705	3,058	3,051	Kawasaki	Suzuki	Suzuki
Italy	535	586	767	Harley Davidson	Harley Davidson	Suzuki
Spain	305	227	210	Harley Davidson	Harley Davidson	Kawasaki
Austria	726	456	416	Kawasaki	Yamaha	Yamaha
Europe (total)	**7,192**	**5,277**	**5,423**	**Kawasaki**	**Yamaha**	**Yamaha**

Note: Shaded cells denote a large capacity bike (greater than 1100cc). Unshaded cells denote a small capacity bike (greater than 750cc but less than 900cc).

Source: Australian Motorcycle Company provided all the data for exhibits 7a–7f.

EXHIBIT 8a Sales in the Major Markets of Greater-than-750cc Motorcycles
(thousand units)

	1995	1994	1993	1992	1991	1990	1989	1988	1987	1986
North America	140.3	124.0	100.5	92.3	80.7	84.2	70.1	92.5	97.3	107.2
Europe	139.9	128.7	129.8	128.0	104.0	96.1				
Japan/Australia	35.5	34.0	31.8	28.2	24.6	26.1	20.9	19.8	16.5	12.6

Source: Harley Davidson, *Annual Report,* 1995; R.L. Polk & Co., Giral S.A., JAMA, ABS.

EXHIBIT 8b Sales in the Major Markets of Greater than 650cc Motorcycles and Harley Davidson's Share
(thousand units)

	1996		1995		1994	
	Units	Harley Davidson (segment share)	Units	Harley Davidson (segment share)	Units	Harley Davidson (segment share)
North America	178.5	47.6%	163.1	47.2%	150.4	46.2%
Europe	224.7	6.9%	207.2	7.4%	201.9	7.1%
Japan/Australia	37.4	21.9%	39.8	19.8%	38.8	19.6%

Source: Harley Davidson, *Annual Report,* 1996; R.L. Polk & Co; Giral S.A.; JAMA; ABS.

EXHIBIT 8c Manufacturers' Share of the Greater than 750cc Motorcycle Markets, 1995
(percent)

	North America	Europe	Japan	Australia	World[1]
Harley Davidson	54.9	10.9	17.0	40.9	31.7
Honda	17.8	14.2	9.5	13.0	15.4
Kawasaki	8.7	11.6	25.9	9.8	11.5
Suzuki	7.9	14.6	10.0	4.9	11.0
Yamaha	4.2	16.5	23.3	7.8	11.4
Japan	38.6	56.9	68.7	35.5	49.3
BMW	3.0	19.7	5.4	9.9	10.8
Cagiva/Ducati		5.0	4.3	4.8	2.7
Triumph		5.2		7.2	2.5
Moto Guzzi				1.5	0.0
Other	3.5	2.3	4.5	0.2	3.0
Market size (units)	**140,300**	**139,900**	**27,534**	**7,966**	**315,700**

Note: (1) Estimate. All Harley Davidson models have capacities of 883cc or more. Therefore the number of HD's units sold in greater than 650cc and greater than 750cc markets is the same. Because the greater than 650cc market includes more models, HD's share of this segment is smaller than in the greater than 750cc segment. The heavyweight segment is sometimes defined as greater than 650cc or 750cc.

Source: Harley Davidson, *Annual Report,* 1995; R.L. Polk & Co, Giral S.A.; JAMA; ABS.

EXHIBIT 9 U.S. Market Analysis for Greater than 650cc Motorcycles, 1992–96

	1996	1995	1994	1993	1992
Units sold	*165.7*	*151.2*	*140.8*	*123.8*	*104.2*
Share (percent)					
Harley Davidson	48.2	47.7	46.3	47.9	50.1
Honda	18.8	20.2	22.5	20.1	17.9
Kawasaki	12.2	10.6	9.8	9.7	9.1
Suzuki	8.7	9.6	10.6	12.1	13.1
Yamaha	5.9	5.8	5.6	5.8	5.3
Other	6.2	6.1	5.2	4.4	4.5
Tourers and cruisers	80.0	78.0	76.0		
HD Share of Tourers and Cruisers	**60.3**	**61.2**	**60.9**		

Source: Harley Davidson, *Annual Report,* 1996; R.L. Polk & Company. The registered motorcycle population in 1994 as 3,679,701 units. Source: US. Census Bureau.

country usually controls after-sales service training, marketing planning, and advertising.

Motorcycle Product Segmentation

Market segmentation in the motorcycle market is done by engine capacity and/or by the type of motorcycle. Different types of motorcycles are designed for different road or off-road conditions. The most important types of larger and expensive (i.e., greater than 125cc) machines are the tourers, sportbikes, and cruisers. Road bikes are matched by racing machines in their variety of configurations and styles.

The large motorcycle market is completely dominated by four-stroke engine machinery. The benefits of the four-stroke engine are better fuel consumption, less noise and smoke, and better reliability and ease of use. A small fraction of performance sportbikes and a large proportion of scooters and mopeds still use two-stroke engines. Two-stroke engines give the best power-to-weight delivery (and often power-to-price ratio) at the cost of poor fuel consumption, high exhaust emissions, smoke and noise, and a narrower spread of power. The majority of cruisers use a V-twin engine layout. V-twin engines are blessed with more low speed torque, a distinctive exhaust note (that is a favorite of many bikers) and narrower-across-the-frame dimensions than other engine layouts. The result is a power delivery that is more predictable and relaxed. Previously the sole preserve of Harley Davidson and Ducati, an increasing number of new models are adopting the twin V format.

Supersport

Sportbikes, being derived from racing machines, emphasize handling and speed. However, there is considerable blurring between the definition of a sportbike and a tourer. In some markets Honda's VFR750 is called a tourer, in others it is called a sportbike. The most narrowly focused sportbikes cannot be ridden over long distances comfortably. This results from the need to have low handlebars (to concentrate the rider's weight over the front wheel) and high foot-pegs (to provide high levels of cornering clearance for spectacular lean angles of 30 degrees or less). High-end sportbikes use the most expensive brakes, wheels, and suspension components, and a great deal of effort and expense goes into making the bikes small and light and the engines powerful. High performance motorcycle engines demonstrate higher specific output than any road going car engines. The best-known sportbike producers are the Big Four and Ducati. Sportbike sales are linked to the performance of the manufacturer in racing competition. Ducati and Honda's success on racetracks has led to impressive sales figures for their sportbikes.

Tourers

Harley Davidson pioneered this category with the Electra Glide model. Large windscreens, comfortable seats, luggage panniers and other amenities for long distance travel are the hallmark of a tourer. The engine is designed for "roll-on" response rather than top end power to reduce reliance on gear down-changes for brisk acceleration. Although some other manufacturers, such as Honda and Moto Guzzi, have followed Harley Davidson into this segment, most manufacturers produce only sport tourers. The lack of emphasis on performance and focus on comfort results in a large and heavy machine carrying lightly stressed, large capacity engines.

Sport Tourers

Sport tourers are high-speed versions of tourers and attempt to satisfy a dual role. BMW is regarded as the leading brand in this segment. Sport tourers are designed for traveling with luggage and a passenger on board. They are large and heavy with very powerful motors for high-speed cruising. Cornering and braking performance tends to be adequate, and the bodywork is designed for high-speed aerodynamic performance and rider protection. Some sports tourers are the fastest of all production bikes. Honda's Blackbird and Kawasaki's ZZR–1100 are both capable of speeds over 280 km/h in standard trim. Features like ABS,[12] heated hand grips, center stands luggage racks, and panniers are common on high-end machines. Rider and pillion comfort mandates the use of plush suspension systems, higher unsprung mass and larger distances from seat to handlebars to foot-pegs. This results in a large and heavy design.

Cruiser

The cruiser is the most curious and fastest growing motorcycle segment. *"In 1989, the cruiser market accounted for 19 percent of worldwide sales. This figure is now 33 percent and is predicted to grow even further."*[13]

Profit margins on cruisers are high.[14] Harley Davidson defined the cruiser with its retro styled laid back designs. In order to cash in on this lucrative, large, and growing segment, manufacturers around the world are releasing an increasing variety of models. The trend is akin to that of four-wheel drive vehicles where purchases are driven by image rather than function.

The Japanese manufacturers began making Harley look-alikes in the mid-1980s. The Europeans have begun to make cruisers in the last few years. Triumph released its Thunderbird in 1995 (its first model for the US market), and BMW released its R1200 in 1997. The typical cruiser is not purchased for performance reasons. Unseasoned cruiser riders complain of poor performance, weak braking and poor cornering clearance while suffering from high levels of vibration, noisy exhausts, and buffeting from the wind. Individualized retro styling, a distinctive exhaust note, a "laid back" riding position, and strong acceleration off the mark are the major attractions for aficionados of such bikes. Harley's association with "biker" gangs and movies like *Easy Rider* have given the cruiser a bad boy image despite its laid back performance and riding style. This has increased its appeal to retired rebels who still like to flaunt their individuality.

> Most cruiser buyers haven't owned or ridden a motorcycle for many years. They are 35–45 years old, white collar, they've got money, they've got a license. Their skills are a bit rusty but they want a bike.[15]

The emphasis of cruiser design is on styling and individual customization. It took the Japanese manufactures a considerable amount of time to realize that their cruisers needed to vibrate more and be noisier in order to sell. Harley Davidson is now attempting to patent the "potato-potato" exhaust note in response to the increasingly accurate copies of its own designs.

Image is a crucial factor in the cruiser market. Price, performance, and quality often take second place to the power of the brand.

> The Japanese and Germans build great bikes, but if it doesn't have a Harley badge it doesn't matter [. . .] their [Harley Davidson] biggest asset is their heritage—that's something the other companies can't buy. Resistance to non-Harley's is weakening—but it is still there to some extent.[16]

The US cruiser market is still very parochial. The latest Japanese models are designed and manufactured in the USA and clearly badged to advertise this fact.

Accessory purchases are a lucrative source of revenue. Almost 20 percent of Harley Davidson's revenue comes from parts and accessories and general merchandise (see Exhibit 11). In order to increase the individuality of their motorcycles, owners purchase accessories to distinguish their machine even further. Frequently the aim is to have a bike that looks like no other.

---

[12]Anti-lock brakes.

[13]Dr Michael Ganal, General Manager, BMW Motorcycle division, quoted in *AMCN*, 13 June 1997, p. 32.

[14]This can be seen in Exhibit 11 by comparing Harley Davidson's high profit relative to sales when compared to BMW and Yamaha.

[15]Guy Allen, former *AMCN* editor, quoted in the *Sunday Herald*, 27 July 1997, p. 52.

[16]Guy Allen, ibid.

A cruiser is a lifestyle thing, so you have to dress up your bike and get the right gear for the rider. Most cruiser buyers spend another $3,000 to $4,000 on accessories.[17]

Standard

Substantial proportions of motorcycles are of a conventional design that has remained unchanged for many years. These bikes use simpler and cheaper components and are aimed at more utilitarian roles and basic transport needs. Naked bikes are modern copies of older styles that had no fairings or windscreens and emphasize visibility of the engine.

On/Off Road

Another popular design style is based on off-road motorcycles. These road bikes generally use single or twin cylinder engines and long travel suspensions. They mirror their off-road cousins but add lights, instruments, and road tires. This style has become very popular in France: customized "*super motards*" are produced by a number of specialists.

Other Categories

Racing motorcycles are designed for a wide variety of conditions and road surfaces. AMC's X1R is aimed at the superbike racing class that is based on production road machines. Homologation rules require an annual build volume of 500 units. Ducati and the Big Four sell customized versions of their superbikes for from A$90,000 to three times this figure.

Scooters and mopeds constitute a large volume segment. In general, their design is utilitarian, although recently these models have become fashionable again. Engine capacities never exceed 250cc, with the most common models having 80cc to 150cc engines.

Off-road motorcycles are predominantly used for racing competitions like enduro and moto cross. Small numbers are designed for military and agricultural use.

Custom builders make small numbers of special models and also make bikes to order. Some builders have their own brand of motorcycle that are usually based on existing designs. However, most builders simply modify existing bikes. Cruiser owners are big spenders on nonfactory custom modifications.

[17]Guy Allen, ibid.

Competitors

Exhibit 10 lists the major manufacturers and Exhibit 11 provides selected financial information on some of the major players. AMC's product goal is a highly individualized and premium quality product. Through its combination of product attributes, it aims to avoid direct competition with any existing product. The companies described below compete in the high-price segment and are thought to pose the biggest threat to AMC's success.

Harley Davidson and Buell

Arguably one of the most spectacular marketing success stories of the 1990s, Harley Davidson continues to increase its already large market share. Harley Davidson's success has forced other manufacturers to build the types of bikes that Harley invented. HD's typical customer is male, aged in their mid-forties, has an income of US$68,000, purchases the motorcycle for recreational purposes, and is an experienced motorcycle rider.[18] The brand has intense customer loyalty. For example, there is little evidence of any other brand name (of any product) being tattooed onto the bodies of customers with such regularity. The Harley Owners Group (HOG) has a membership of over 300,000.

Company research has consistently shown a repurchase intent of 92 percent since 1988.[19]

Harley's strategy has been to maintain supply at levels below demand. Long waiting lists and high resale prices have been enduring facts of life for customers. This may change now that Harley is expanding capacity rapidly and cruiser buyers are starting to switch to Harley copies. HD is planning to add capacity to reach production levels of 145,000 units in 1998, ramping up to 200,000 units by 2003. Models are cosmetically updated every year to maintain high levels of unique identity.

Harley has introduced advanced operations management techniques to keep costs down and improve quality. It sells 23 different models with three engine sizes. US prices range from $5,200 to $18,500 and are typically 50 percent higher than those for comparable competitors' models. Sales are shifting to the higher priced and more profitable models. Accessories are an important part of the business that further feed customer desires to customize their machines. HD is a highly focused company. Its sole line of business is motorcycles, accessories, and HD merchandise clothing and personal effects.

[18]*Harley Davidson 1996 Annual Report,* p. 4.
[19]Ibid., p. 4.

EXHIBIT 10a Established Manufacturers' Product Range

Company	Sport	Sport/Touring	Touring	Cruiser	Standard	On/Off Road	Off Road	Racing
Honda	✓	✓	✓	✓	✓	✓	✓	✓
Yamaha	✓	✓	✓	✓	✓	✓	✓	✓
Suzuki	✓	✓		✓	✓	✓	✓	✓
Kawasaki	✓	✓		✓	✓	✓	✓	✓
Harley Davidson			✓	✓				✓
Buell[1]	✓							
BMW		✓		✓	✓	✓		
Aprilia	✓				✓	✓		✓
Cagiva		✓			✓	✓		
Ducati	✓	✓						✓
Bimota	✓							
Triumph	✓	✓			✓	✓		
Moto	✓		✓	✓	✓	✓		
Laverda	✓							
KTM						✓	✓	✓
Husqvarna[2]							✓	✓

Notes: (1) 49% owned by Harley Davidson; (2) 100% owned by Cagiva.

EXHIBIT 10b Emerging Manufacturers

Company	Sport	Sport/Touring	Touring	Cruiser	Standard	On/Off Road	Off Road	Racing
MZ					✓			
Polaris				✓				
Hunwick	✓			✓				✓
Hallam								

EXHIBIT 10c Custom Builders

Company	Country
Egli	Switzerland
Spondon	UK
Harris	UK
Over	Japan
Britten	New Zealand
Vee Two	Australia
Drysdale	Australia
Segale	France
Voxsan	France

EXHIBIT 11 Selected Financial Results, 1996

	Harley Davidson (US$ m)	BMW (DM m)	Yamaha (US$ m)
Sales Revenue	1,531	935	3,984
Operating Expenses	1,311		3,770*
Operating Income	221		
Profit	**143**	**19**	**214**
Assets	790		3,179
Capital Expenditure	179		232
Motorcycle Sales Revenue	1,199		
Parts and Accessory Revenue	210		
General Merchandise Revenue	91		
Cost of Goods Sold	1,041		
Selling, Admin & Engineering	262		
Units Sold	118,771	50,340	
Employees	5,200	1,754	
World Market Share (> 750cc)	31.7%	10.8%	11.4%
Revenue Per Bike (US $)	10,097		
Accessory Revenue Per Bike (US $)	1,770		
Bikes Produced/Employee	22.8	28.7	

*Includes taxes

Source: Company annual reports, 1996.

The Harley trademark is its air-cooled 45-degree V-twin engine. Like the rest of the bike, the engine is robust, reliable, and heavy. There is little use of advanced technology except for the recent introduction of fuel injection to meet forthcoming emissions regulations. Harley now owns 49 percent of Buell. Buell makes HD-engined sportbikes. 1996 sales were over 2,000 units. Prices are equivalent to mid-range Harley's.

BMW

BMW has a conservative image. Its motorcycles are oriented to a touring role and emphasize practicality, comfort, and reliability over outright performance. BMW also has a long heritage and is famous for its flat-twin engine. BMW is renowned for its high quality and has a good track record for introducing innovative technology. Recent model introductions have signaled a shift in BMW's image. The new K1200RS is the first motorcycle to exceed BMW's self-imposed 100 hp limit and does so by a substantial 30 hp margin. BMW's styling has also become more adventurous. The recently released R1200C is BMW's first cruiser and is seen as a risky and bold step for the company. The BMW motorcycle division is a small part of the BMW group better known for its automobile products. BMW pricing is slightly below that of HD but more than the Japanese equivalents. Resale values are above average for the market.

Ducati

Ducati has built its reputation on sports and racing machines. Top of the range Ducati's, like the 916SPS, command prices above those for HD. Customers often purchase performance enhancing accessories after the purchase of an already expensive high performance machine. Ducati's image is based on desmodromic valve actuation, 90-degree V-twin engines, and steel tube space frame chassis. Ducati has just been bought by a Texas investment bank and is slated for a listing on the NYSE. Prices are generally well in excess of equivalent Japanese machines and resale values are high.

Bimota

Bimota is a very small and relatively young producer that specializes in sportbikes. Bimota is one of the most innovative stylers and designers of bikes. All but one of its models use existing Japanese or Italian engines. Resale values are not very high compared to their high retail prices. Sales volumes increased dramatically when prices were reduced. The best selling model, the Suzuki based SB-6, has sold several thousand units at a price of around A$35,000 whereas previous models sold only a few hundred units at prices A$10,000 higher.

Polaris

Polaris is the first American-based challenger to HD to emerge with a finished product. A few other start-ups that revived old American brand names like Indian and Excelsior-Henderson have floundered. Polaris released a large capacity V-twin cruiser that closely mimics HD's design approach. Pricing is expected to be below that of HD. The parent company began with snowmobile production and has diversified into personal watercraft (better known as Jet skis).

Triumph

Triumph is a very old brand with a strong heritage that fell on hard times in the last several decades. However, the British brand has been revived and is now beginning to flex its muscles with the release of its second generation of motorcycles. Most of Triumph's product range is sports or touring oriented. The Thunderbird, released in 1995 is a retro styled "naked" bike designed to appeal to the American market. It is not a cruiser in the strict sense but shares some cruiser characteristics like retro styling, a lazier power delivery, a more relaxed seating position and a famous model name from the 1960s. Triumph's prices have generally been higher than the Japanese equivalents and residual values have been competitive.

The Japanese Big Four

The undisputed market leadership of the Japanese is eroding. Harley Davidson has made the greatest inroads into the Japanese share of large motorcycles. The Japanese produce the broadest product ranges and price at the bottom of the range in most product categories. The products are recognized as offering the best value for money and models are updated frequently. Their styling is faddish and, although the Japanese brands are criticized for lacking character and individuality, their performance and handling is the best in the industry. Their reliability and quality is quite variable but is generally considered to be the best in its class. The resale values of big-four bikes are the lowest in the industry except for a few models.

Japanese responses to Harley Davidson's strategy have not been very successful until recently. The latest designs are almost indistinguishable from the real thing except for the brand name. All the Big Four are diversified producers. Only Yamaha generates the bulk of its revenue from motorcycles.

Specialist Builders

High prices are paid for small volume specialist bikes. The limited resources of the smaller firms limit development that often results in flawed designs that may perform well but do not have the same all round quality of larger manufacturers' products. These products are attractive because of their highly unique nature; however, their resale value tends to be very low.

Hunwick Hallam Motorcycle Product Range

The Motorcycles

The company initially aims to produce three different motorcycles: a large and medium-size cruiser and a supersports machine that will be homologated for racing in the World Superbike series. The flagship Boss PowerCruiser is expected to provide the bulk of sales and will be the first model ready for sale. All models are aimed at the high end of the motorcycle market. Hand assembly, parts of the highest quality, advanced design, and individual customizing of each bike at the factory prior to delivery are aimed at delivering value to customers who are paying the premium price these machines command.

Product Features

All HH motorcycles will share the same basic power plant. The V-twin engine can be built in capacities ranging from 1000cc to 2000cc. Because the engine is the main structural member there is no frame. The front and rear end are literally bolted on to the engine. This is a key design feature that allows the geometry of each model to be customized very easily by simply changing the (relatively inexpensive) parts that connect the engine to the suspension, handlebars, and seat units. Thus designs as dissimilar as sportbikes and cruisers can be based on the same engine and have different capacities. A further benefit of using a high-performance engine is that the HH cruisers will have class-leading power and torque. Hunwick believes that many potential cruiser owners are not satisfied by the poor performance of cruisers on the market. The HH engine and innovative "chassis" will deliver more power with less weight by a substantial margin over current cruiser designs. High quality suspension, brakes, and tires will improve handling quality to levels well in excess of cruisers sold today.

The engine bristles with advanced technology and high quality features: Electronic fuel injection, torsional vibration dampers, rolling element bearings (instead of cheaper plain bearings), an advanced combustion design, and Formula 1-derived pneumatic valve actuation: a first on any motorcycle. The electronic fuel system allows engines to be tailored to different export markets requirements and individual customer tastes. Modifications to the engines' characteristics will be able to be executed by internet-based links to AMC. Engine tuning and fault finding can then be performed from any location. This remote tuning technology has already been proven by Lamborghini and is also to be used by Bimota.

AMC has been painstaking in its attention to details. The HH design is aimed at ease of assembly and maintenance. As a consequence, AMC anticipates a work-force requirement of only 48 staff once production ramps up to 1,200 units. Forethought has also been given to addressing servicing and assembly errors. For example, if the timing belt is incorrectly fitted, no engine damage will occur. Most high performance engines will be seriously damaged if such an error occurs. According to Motorcycle Online "*The Hunwick Hallam design is, in a word—Bulletproof.*"

The other key element of the HH family is that the appearance of the bikes can be easily altered. From the outset, the designers made sure that fairing panels, fuel tanks, headlights, and fenders of differing shapes could be bolted onto the same attachment points. This is essential to realizing individual customization at a lower cost.

Parts Sourcing

Unlike most motorcycle start ups AMC has decided to develop and manufacture most of the parts that make up its motorcycles. In-house development of components, in particular the engine, is very expensive. According to Hallam "[we] *set out to build the world's best four-stroke motorcycle powerplant.*"

The engine, chassis, and electronic fuel injection control system are all to be made in house. The wheels, bodywork, exhaust system, and ancillary parts like handlebars, foot pegs, and gear linkages are to be made in Australia to Hallam's design specifications. The gearbox, brakes, tires, instrumentation, and suspension are top of the range components sourced from the world's best suppliers (like Suzuki, Brembo, and WP). AMC is aiming to build bikes with a sufficiently high local content to win export credits which can be used to offset import duties on certain components.

The Way Forward?

AMC's difficulties in raising finance are largely based on the lack of certainty about the sales potential of HH motorcycles and a lack of understanding of the motorcycle industry. The industry is small and documentation is scarce. Hunwick is determined to press ahead with production, as he believes strongly in his product. The choices of export markets and distribution methods are crucial to the success of the venture. These decisions are required to add certainty to the marketing plan. The domestic market is a certain target but too small to sustain the venture alone. The choice of which foreign markets to enter first is a trade off: Take on Harley loyalists in the litigious and parochial but massive US cruiser market or tackle the diversified, more performance-oriented but smaller European cruiser market. The choice of distribution method, particularly in Europe is also difficult. The options include direct sales to existing dealers, selling to different importers, selling to a centralized importer, setting up a European subsidiary to supply all of Europe or enter joint ventures with a handful of large dealers in major cities.

INSEAD

Case 5-2

ISS—International Service System A/S

With a turnover of 11.4 billion DKK (Danish kroner), equivalent to nearly 2 billion dollars, and employing over 115,000 people in 17 countries spread around 3 continents, ISS is an anomaly in the world of megacorporations. The company counts advanced technology, high levels of professional skills, and a global brand image among its key sources of competitive advantage. It is not in the business of computers or pharmaceuticals, however, nor in packaged foods or luxury cosmetics. ISS, as

This case was written by Mary Ackenhusen, Research Associate, under the supervision of Sumantra Ghoshal, Professor at INSEAD. We are grateful to Sandeep Sander for helping to make this case possible. It is intended to be used as a basis for class discussion rather than to illustrate either effective or ineffective handling of an administrative situation.

described by Poul Andreassen, the company's President since 1962, "is the world's largest and best cleaning service company." In a highly fragmented industry in which the three key success factors are believed to be "cost, cost, and cost", ISS is rarely the low cost vendor. Yet, in 1992, over 80 percent of its worldwide revenues and over 92 percent of its profits came from the "mom and pop" business of daily office cleaning.

Poul Andreassen believes that opportunities for further development are practically unlimited for ISS:

> The business is ours to lose. Where ISS will be in the future all depends on ourselves because the market is out there. There is not a serious threat unless we are not doing what we're saying, what we believe in.

Sven Ipsen, the head of the Scandinavian division, which contributes half of ISS' worldwide profits, concurs with this assessment:

> I see no major threats for ISS Scandinavia for the next five years apart from a severe recession. We operate with very small margins and we understand the market well enough to know which levers to pull if we begin to lose market share. We know where to go if we have to tighten our belt. I think we have a very flexible organization.

ISS' ambition is to continue improving its service levels so that, "Someday, ISS and the word service will be synonymous just like Xerox and photocopying once were." To achieve this vision, however, Andreassen believes that two key hurdles have to be first overcome.

In the second half of the 1980s, ISS achieved spectacular growth in both sales and profits: 17 percent and 25 percent, respectively, per annum (see Exhibits 1–3 for financial information). Yet, its relative profitability at 3 percent of sales remained several percentage points lower than that of either ServiceMaster or BET, its two key competitors. Improving profitability is, therefore, the first priority.

EXHIBIT 1 ISS Income Statement 1990–1992
(amounts in DKK million)

	1992	1991	1990
Consolidated turnover	**11,356.0**	**11,805.7**	**9,610.1**
Staff Cost	8,326.5	8,572.3	6,931.4
Cost of Goods Sold	783.6	929.8	1,139.5
Other Operating Costs	1,379.0	1,398.9	1,139.5
Depreciation	329.9	322.8	289.7
Operating Profit	**537.0**	**581.9**	**413.6**
Amortisation of Goodwill	60.7	62.2	17.8
Income from Participating Interests	3.4	8.9	10.1
Interest Receivable and Similar Income	74.1	73.7	42.8
Interest Payable and Similar Charges	180.0	270.6	182.7
Interest Receivable (payable), Net	(105.9)	(196.9)	(139.9)
Profit on Ordinary Operations	**373.8**	**331.7**	**266.0**
Other Income	35.1	10.6	103.8
Other Expenses	31.9	13.8	101.7
Other Income (expenses), Net	3.2	(3.2)	2.1
Profit Before Tax	**377.0**	**331.7**	**268.1**
Tax on Profit for the Year	105.9	82.0	62.5
Consolidated Profit	**271.1**	**246.5**	**205.6**
Minority Interests	(5.2)	(2.8)	(1.0)
ISS Consolidated Net Profit	**265.9**	**243.7**	**204.6**

Source: ISS Annual Report, 1992.

EXHIBIT 2 ISS Consolidated Balance Sheet December 31, 1992
(amounts in DDK million)

Assets		Liabilities	
Fixed Assets		**Equity**	
Intangible Assets		Share Capital	432.9
Goodwill	990.0	Reserves	564.6
Development Costs	7.8		
Leasehold Improvements	47.0	**ISS Shareholders' Equity**	**997.5**
	1,044.8		
		Minority Interests	**129.8**
Tangible Assets			
Land and Buildings	392.2	**Total Consolidated Equity**	**1,127.3**
Production Plant	70.5		
Service Equipment, Vehicles and Fixtures	751.9	**Provisions for Liabilities and Charges**	
Assets Under Construction	53.3		
	1,267.9	Deferred Tax	101.4
		Other Provisions	226.2
Financial Assets			
Investments in Associated Companies	4.4	**Total Provisions**	**327.6**
Other Securities	18.3		
Other Receivables	75.6	**Long-Term Creditors**	
	98.3	Bond Loan	477.3
		Mortgage Debt	35.0
		Bank Loans and Other Debt	679.3
Total Fixed Assets	**2,411.0**	**Total Long-Term Creditors**	**1,191.6**
Current Assets		**Short-Term Creditors**	
Stocks	254.9	Bond Loan	0
		Mortgage Debt	1.4
Debtors		Bank Loans and Other Debt	117.9
Trade Debtors	1,123.9	Trade Creditors and Other Debt	1,197.1
Other Debtors	249.9	Prepayments from Customers	66.9
	1,373.8	Corporation Tax	50.2
		Tax Withholdings, VAT, Etc	545.7
Securities	**89.4**	Dividend	43.3
Cash at Bank and In Hand	**539.9**		
Total Current Assets	**2,258.0**	**Total Short-Term Creditors**	**2,022.5**
		Total Provisions and Creditors	**3,541.7**
Total Asset	**4,669.0**	**Total Liabilities**	**4,669.0**

Source: ISS Annual Report, 1992.

EXHIBIT 3 ISS B-Shares (1983 = 100)

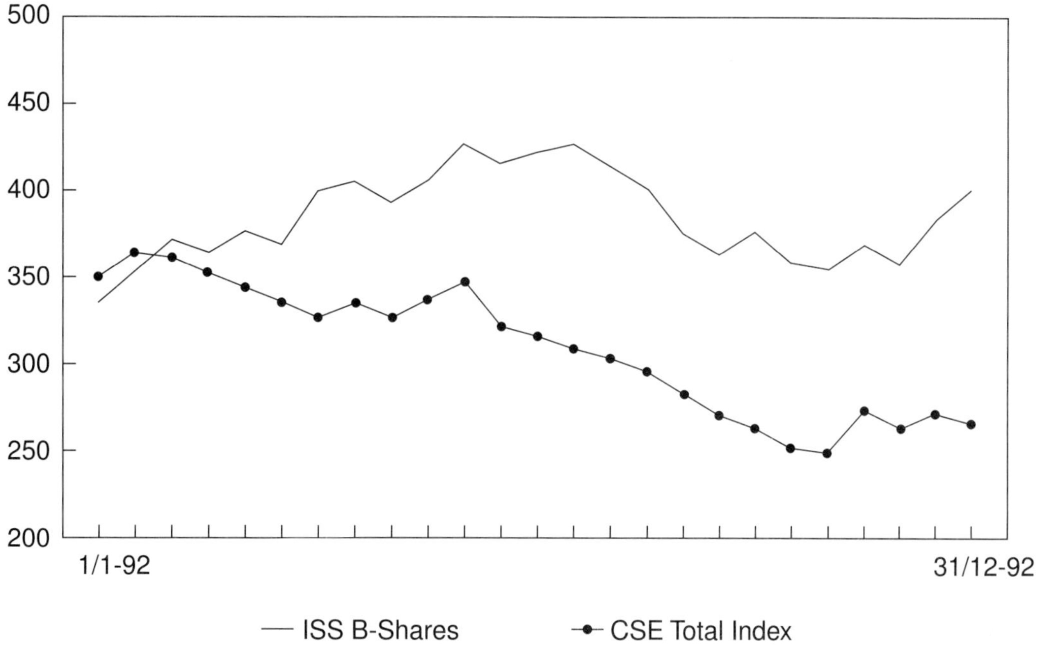

CSE = Copenhagen Stock Exchange Total Index.

> I have seen too many 'wheeler-dealer' companies grow rapidly only to go under for not taking quality seriously. They did not try to compile resources for product development, to build personnel development systems, or invest to create a modern way of managing their enterprises. To improve service quality, we must continue to make these investments. But for that, we must achieve 5 percent profit before tax, at the least.

Second, ISS' admirable pace of growth has thus far come primarily from acquisitions. This strategy of acquisitive growth has reached its limit, and the company's target of 15 percent annual growth through the 1990s must now come from in-house developments. Given the size of the company, continued growth through acquisitions would require either too many small acquisitions or acquisitions of very large companies, both of which would entail unacceptable levels of risk. Importantly, there is a large amount of goodwill on the corporate balance sheet, thus, the new strategy of organic growth must achieve a consistent improvement in earnings per share in order to protect and enhance the value of ISS' stock.

While ample opportunities for organic growth remain available, the company needs to reassess its organizational approach and replenish its management skills to reorient itself to this new growth process. Many managers feel that the company is too conservative, financially, and does not provide the funding necessary to build new businesses from scratch. However, this is where Andreassen sees growth and profitability improvement as two inseparably intertwined objectives:

> We've invested a lot of money over the years in management training and now is the time to show for it. We have got to come up and make the 5 percent before tax. Then we will have a very important cash flow and can make available those funds the businesses need to grow.

ISS Spreads its Wings

ISS was created in 1901 by a Danish lawyer to provide security services for office buildings in Copenhagen. The company grew in the security business, and in 1934, it expanded its activities to include commercial cleaning. By the time Andreassen took over the management of the company in 1962, it had grown to 2,000 employees and 50 million DKK in sales.

At this time, office cleaning was considered to be neither an attractive nor a sophisticated business. The margins were very low and the companies which served the market were almost entirely small businesses. Andreassen likes to emphasize how negatively people viewed their positions as cleaners by recalling experiences of employees who left their houses at 5 A.M. in full tennis garb, drove to their building sites and then changed into their cleaning clothes. They did not ever want the neighbors to know what they really did between 5 and 8 in the morning. Andreassen spent the next 30 years of his life working to mold ISS into a professionally managed service company which would combat the low-class image of the industry.

The 60s: Professional Management

The market for commercial cleaning and security services was changing at the time Andreassen took over the management of ISS in the early 60s. Companies were beginning to focus on their main lines of business and contracting out secondary activities such as cleaning, security, and food service. This "structural rationalization" trend supported Andreassen's personal philosophy that cleaning was a professional business and must be managed as such.

Prior to ISS, Andreassen had earned a degree in industrial engineering and then worked in positions ranging from time-study engineer to plant manager in several multinational companies including Remington Rand and SAS. In his new job, he immediately began applying some of the basic management techniques he had learned in a manufacturing environment to the cleaning business.

In his first days as President, Andreassen was somewhat surprised to find that the only information collected to measure the work of the cleaners was how much material (cleaning products) had been used. Since this comprised only 3 percent of the cost of a contract and wages accounted for 65–70 percent, Andreassen began his task of professionalizing ISS' operations by developing a system to better plan the work. The new planning system assured the job would be performed efficiently and to a given standard by specifying the work methods, the frequency of each task, and how the various jobs were to be distributed among the workers. With this innovation, a cleaner now had a personalized job sheet of the tasks to be performed by him or her each day. The planning system also allowed ISS to accurately bid for new business.

The system remains a key tool at ISS in 1992, though it is now more sophisticated and computerized. When a tender offer is being prepared for a new site, a group of planners estimate the labor, equipment, and material content by entering the building parameters, including the size of the area to be cleaned, types of floors, number of toilets, frequency of cleaning tasks, etc., into a special computer program developed by ISS. The program then calculates the estimated cost of the job using the pre-established standards for cleaning.

To address the efficiency of his workers, Andreassen implemented a combination of improvements to substantially increase the cleaning rate, which stood at 40 square meters per hour. Often the rate could be increased by improved tools such as better cleaning products, specially designed mops and dust rags, and new or additional machinery. Likewise, the growing popularity of carpets in office buildings helped boost the productivity of the cleaning operators. By 1992, average cleaning rates had been improved to 250–350 square meters per hour.

At the same time, Andreassen hired a chemical engineer to take responsibility for the technical function of developing and producing new cleaning products. Referring to the bad-image of the cleaning business, Andreassen remembers that in 1962 when he placed an advertisement for this position in a Copenhagen paper, he had no responses because "Who wants to be in the cleaning business?" In the end, he pressured a friend into taking the position. The result of this drive for state-of-the-art cleaning tools was the establishment in 1963 of a separate company, Darenas, under the ISS banner.

His next action was to break the company up into profit centers, units with full operational and financial responsibility. This change supported his philosophy that the most motivated managers were those who thought of the business as their own. To monitor these relatively autonomous business units, he adopted a financial reporting system, the Management Reporting System (MRS), which provided a detailed profit and loss statement, called the after-calculation, for each business unit (see Exhibit 4 for a sample report). This information was compiled monthly, and the report was distributed to all senior managers of the company including Andreassen.

The basis of the report was a cost accounting system starting at the contract level which deducted all direct costs such as material, equipment, and wage costs for every cleaning contract against the contract's turnover, to figure the "contract contribution". Enabling management to understand their overhead costs, the expenses of each successive layer of management (i.e., branch, district, and country) were subtracted to calculate CBI (contribution I), CBII, and CBIII. CBIII was the operating profit earned by the business unit after all costs were deducted.

EXHIBIT 4 Profit and Loss Statement

ISS Servisystem Marischka
Company N°: 412 Beträge in A.S.

September 1992

SA: 10 R: 1 D: 3
Distriktmanager; Steinreiber Erich

	Month				Year to Date				Total Year			
	Budget		Actual		Budget		Actual		Budget		Estimated	
	%	Amount	%	Amount	%	Amount	%	Amount	%	Amount	%	Amount
Sales External	100.0	7,894	100.0	8,063	100.0	67,075	100.0	70,388	100.0	90,227	100.0	92,000
Sales to Sub-Group Co.S	0.0	0	0.0	0	0.0	0	0.0	0	0.0	0	0.0	0
Sales to Other ISS Co.S	0.0	0	0.0	0	0.0	0	0.0	0	0.0	0	0.0	0
Sales to Other Groups Co.S	0.0	0	0.0	0	0.0	0	0.0	0	0.0	0	0.0	0
TOTAL SALES	100.0	7,894	100.0	8,063	100.0	67,075	100.0	70,388	100.0	90,227	100.0	92,000
Net Wages	36.0	2,839	37.6	3,029	36.1	24,196	36.7	25,839	36.2	32,619	36.9	33,919
Additional Wages & Social Chg	26.3	2,077	27.7	2,233	26.4	17,724	27.1	19,063	26.5	23,883	27.2	25,024
Total Wages	62.3	4,916	65.3	5,262	62.5	41,920	63.8	44,902	62.6	56,502	64.1	58,943
Subcontractors	0.0	0	0.0	0	0.0	0	0.0	0	0.0	0	0.0	0
Total Wages + Subcontractors	62.3	4,916	65.3	5,262	62.5	41,920	63.8	44,902	62.6	56,502	64.1	58,943
Transportation	2.2	173	201	173	2.2	1,502	2.3	1,592	2.2	2,027	2.3	2,151
Material Consumption	2.6	209	2.6	207	2.6	1,776	2.3	1,649	2.7	2,393	2.4	2,230
Machinery & Equipment	1.3	1.6	1.2	95	1.5	1,007	1.2	848	1.5	1,356	1.4	1,248
Supervision	5.1	400	3.6	292	5.1	3,388	3.9	2,777	5.1	4,599	4.2	3,850
Other Production Costs	1.1	88	0.9	70	1.2	790	1.0	683	1.2	1,049	1.1	970
Total Direct Production Costs	74.6	5,892	75.6	6,099	75.1	50,383	74.5	52,451	75.3	67,926	75.4	69,392
CONTRACT CONTRIBUTION	25.4	2,002	24.4	1,964	24.9	16,692	25.5	17,937	24.7	22,301	24.6	22,608
Branch Management	3.1	245	2.0	165	3.3	2,218	2.3	1,642	3.3	2,971	2.5	2,312
CONTRIBUTION I	22.3	1,757	22.3	1,799	21.6	14,474	23.2	16,295	21.4	19,330	22.1	20,296
District Planing Costs	0.0	0	0.0	0	0.0	0	0.0	0	0.0	0	0.0	0
District Stock Costs	0.0	0	0.0	0	0.0	0	0.0	0	0.0	0	0.0	0
District Sales Costs	0.0	0	0.0	0	0.0	0	0.0	0	0.0	0	0.0	0
District Office Costs	0.0	0	0.0	0	0.0	0	0.0	0	0.0	0	0.0	0
District Management	0.0	0	0.0	0	0.0	0	0.0	0	0.0	0	0.0	0
District Joint Costs	0.0	0	0.0	0	0.0	0	0.0	0	0.0	0	0.0	0
Reg. Management + Joint Costs	0.0	0	0.0	0	0.0	0	0.0	0	0.0	0	0.0	0
Tot. District + Region Costs	0.0	0	0.0	0	0.0	0	0.0	0	0.0	0	0.0	0
CONTRIBUTION II	22.3	1,757	22.3	1,799	21.6	14,474	23.2	16,295	21.4	19,330	22.1	20,296

Source: ISS Marischka.

Monthly, the budgeted direct costs were compared with the actual results using the after-calculation report, giving the unit manager immediate insight into the profitability of each job under his or her control.

The MRS had two major benefits. Firstly, it focused at the smallest and most basic unit of performance, the cleaning contract and team, and provided the transparency necessary for corrective actions at that level. Secondly, this financial system became the basis for measuring a manager's success and identifying areas which needed improvement. Andreassen explains the value of the system:

> One of the most important ingredients of management is that all levels of management know exactly on which criteria to measure whether or not a manager is successful. This takes care of half of the management process as . . . one does not have to kick everybody around. [With MRS] people were well aware when they were successful, and they knew how to take corrective actions if they had bad results.

When ISS acquired a company, the implementation of this system was the priority management action in order to immediately improve profitability.

With the realization that people were his largest cost on a contract, Andreassen was convinced that he must focus his attention on the individuals doing the cleaning, the cleaners. Beyond his drive to improve the efficiency and standards of cleaning, Andreassen wanted to improve his employees' satisfaction with their work. Andreassen's mother had been a shop steward in a tobacco company, and this gave him an appreciation for the feelings of workers who performed manual labor and a desire to improve their status.

Andreassen began improving his workforce's self-image by giving ISS employees an identity of which they could be proud. All ISS employees were given attractive uniforms with the ISS logo. All supervisors were given company cars to drive with the ISS blue letters emblazoned on the side. Andreassen explained:

> We all need a certain degree of recognition. We want to identify with something . . . I want a cleaner to be able to point out to her children, the smart white car in the street with its blue stripes driving past, and say to them, 'This is my company'.

Likewise, Andreassen extended the existing training programs for the cleaners and added new training programs for his management to help them carry out the work in a professional manner. He recalls:

> At the time, there was a growing understanding of the importance of this type of work, that it had to be carried out in a professional manner and that the persons doing the work were entitled to wages on a level with the industrial workers. The work had to be done professionally in order for us to be able to develop the systems and methods . . . and this called for resources for both training and professional management.

This era was one of expansion within Scandinavia and the rest of Europe. ISS is believed to be the first cleaning company to have worked outside of its home country when it entered Sweden in the 40s and Norway in the 50s. In the 60s, ISS increased its international presence by entering Germany, Switzerland, Holland, and the UK through local acquisitions.

The 70s: Service Management

By the early 1970s, ISS had a strong system of procedures and standards which assured high quality, efficient cleaning, but management realized that the market was beginning to demand more. As Sven Ipsen remembers:

> Earlier we thought that if we gave the customer the quality he wanted, shiny floors, clean lavatories, then he should be satisfied because that was what he paid for. Then we realized that we needed to not only focus on what we delivered as service, but how we delivered it.

ISS' new service philosophy was based on "The Magic Formula" (see Exhibit 5). The thrust of the formula was that every market segment had unique characteristics, i.e., hospitals, schools, or office buildings. Thus, the service package, including methods and product offerings, should reflect the needs of each segment. A unique delivery system for each segment was the most effective way of handling the different needs of the segment, yet the company could still be tied together by one identity, such as a common logo. Additionally, the company should carry the same culture for a high level of service throughout all aspects of the operation.

Thus, instead of the same workers cleaning hospitals, schools, and other buildings using the same methods and equipment, there was a recognition of the difference in customer needs. This drove ISS to set up separate organizations to serve each of its markets. While before, the only separate groups were security, food service, and cleaning, now cleaning was broken into groups to meet the special, different needs of offices, schools, hospitals, and food (mainly slaughterhouses known as abattoirs). The cleaners and managers received special training on the specific needs of these areas and remained dedicated to a market segment in order to build the experience and expertise needed to effectively serve customers in these segments.

Focused attention on specific market segments allowed ISS to leverage its knowledge of a customer's

EXHIBIT 5 The ISS Magic Formula

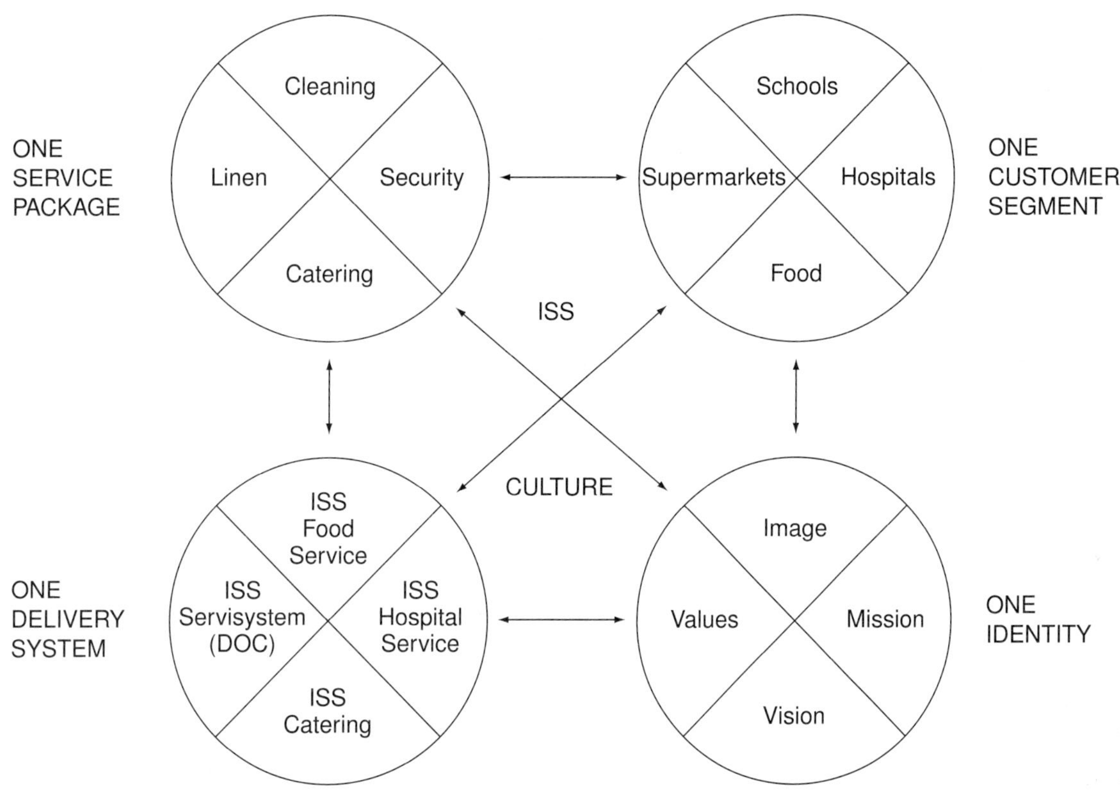

business with its on-site presence to offer special cleaning and other services. For example, in a supermarket, ISS would gain entrance to the customer through a contract to do traditional cleaning of the shop area and offices. Over time, after ISS had proven its professionalism in cleaning, it expanded its service offering to include special cleaning of the meat section, freezers, shopping carts, or even air filters as well as noncleaning tasks such as labeling, coffee making, uniform cleaning, lighting, and repair of shopping carts.

A key element of the "Magic Formula" is to nurture the "front line" which is the primary contact with the customer: the supervisors and workers. Close attention is paid to the hiring, training, and retention of these employees. For example, in Denmark, all managers including the Managing Director, spend up to two days per month interviewing candidates for the cleaning operator position. Then, a video presentation of what a cleaner can expect from his or her job is shown to each candidate, and a formal job bank is used to try to match cleaners to jobs, primarily based on location of the job relative to the cleaner's home.

The high turnover which is usually found in low paying jobs such as cleaning (cleaners earn close to the bottom of the wage scale) has always been a concern to ISS. The actual turnover rate of ISS varies greatly between countries from 50 percent to 100 percent annually, depending somewhat on the tightness of the labor market in that country. As Andreassen explains:

> Many, perhaps 60 percent of them will stay many years, a lot for 25 years . . . but the last 40 percent is turning around 2 or 3 times. Some of that you can not avoid because they are coming in to earn money for a wedding or other special event so they only stay a couple of months. Also we hire quite a few students.

ISS believes a good supervisor can reduce the turnover. Though the supervisors are responsible for training, quality control, and scheduling of their work team, the most important part of their job is letting the cleaners know that they care. As described by one of the supervisors:

> The ISS advantage is that the supervisor is there for the people . . . that they can come to us for time, for a coffee. It's not always possible to help them, but they need someone to listen. If they know this, they'll work for a supervisor on Saturdays and Sundays.

The supervisor also serves as the primary customer contact, interacting with the customer daily to assure that he or she is satisfied with the service as well as to suggest added services which might be performed either regularly, such as more frequent waxing of the floors, or on a one-time basis, such as cleaning the telephones.

The company uses a whole array of formal reports and surveys to measure customer satisfaction, in addition to regular customer contact by the branch and district management, yet it is the supervisors who help most in differentiating ISS from the other cleaning companies. As one of the supervisors explained:

> Other cleaning companies are cheaper but they have less supervision. We supervisors are a very good internal control system. Also, we are there for the customer, an on-site answer for all the customer's problems.

Service management layered on top of the professional methods and quality standards proved to be a successful formula which helped ISS to grow to be a 3 billion DKK business by the end of the 1970s. Contributing to this geographic and market growth, were the additional acquisitions of cleaning services in Europe, the purchase of Clorius, an energy control company, and its first expansion into North America through the purchase of a majority share in Prudential Building Maintenance Corporation of New York.

The 80s: Strategic Planning

By the beginning of the 1980s, ISS was operating in 3 continents and had ventured into a dozen specialized cleaning and related businesses. With the good fortune to have too many growth opportunities, both geographically and market-wise, Andreassen decided it was time to formally guide the further development of ISS through the adoption of a strategic planning system.

The ISS "team planning process" is a top-down, bottom-up participative system to develop detailed and integrated plans to support defined corporate objectives. The key elements of the plan answer the questions "Where are we?", "Where do we want to go?", "How do we get there?" and "Who does what and how?", that is: status, goals, strategies, and action plans. The process involves many team members at each level, necessitating that it begin in April each year in order to finish by the end of October.

The team planning process begins with training for all participants new to the process to assure that everyone "speaks the same language". Starting from the top at the corporate level, a planning team is formed which will develop both qualitative and quantitative goals and objectives to be passed down to the next level, the divisions, as input to their plans. The divisions will also each have a team which will develop its mission, goals, and objectives. This continues in the same manner down each of the levels of management and stops at the level of branch management within each country. Then the plans with the detailed proposals on how the various units expect to meet the corporate guidelines flow upward by management level with the lower level management plan becoming input for the next higher level. Therefore, each planning team at each level has two major planning sessions per year as the plans flow downward and then climb back up. To assure smooth communication of plans between levels, planning teams include members from the management level directly above and below.

The process is designed to complement the autonomy granted to the local operating managers with each level of management giving the level below it a framework of strategic guidelines. Andreassen and his management team place a high value on the process:

> The process holds our organization together and is the basis for our development and success. . . It is the national leaders of ISS, with their teams, who contribute to the corporate strategy, the strategy for the development of each national unit, adapted not only to each country's particular personnel, social and legal conditions, but also the cultural and behavioral conditions. This complex task can not be dealt with from behind a desk in Copenhagen.

The tool is credited for helping to build and maintain the ISS culture through extensive communication of mission, guidelines, rules, and expectations.

Guided by this formal strategic planning process, ISS continued its growth throughout the 1980s by expanding the U.S. cleaning business nationwide through acquisition, acquiring additional cleaning companies in Denmark, Sweden, and Germany, sponsoring further acquisitions of energy companies under the Clorius umbrella and by acquiring a hospital service company, Mediclean, in the UK.

The 90s: Total Quality Management

Poul Andreassen does not worry about other service companies copying the ISS formula because he drives ISS to continuously develop new initiatives. He likes to say, "Walking in the footsteps of somebody else will not put you in front." To this end, ISS initiated a program in 1991 to implement Total Quality Management as the next step for achieving service excellence. The TQM mission, as stated by the company, is to:

> Target the Group's functions and resources throughout the entire supply chain towards the creation of a perceived service quality which, as a minimum, fulfils the customers' demands and expectations, with the specific objectives of increasing customer satisfaction, reducing the loss of contracts, increasing sales to existing customers and reducing the staff turnover.

The primary two tools of TQM are extensive measurement systems in important areas, such as employee and customer satisfaction, and work analysis. The objective of the work analysis is to improve the operational processes used in ISS by identifying every step of the current process backwards from the customer to the beginning of the ISS supply chain and then looking for ways to rationalize the process (process mapping). This extensive analysis will eventually be done for every activity within the company.

The TQM program is envisioned to extend through 1995 for the training phase alone. To support this massive effort, a special subsidiary, ISS Quality Institute A/S, was established in 1992 near Copenhagen with its own Managing Director. One reason for the separate operating company was because a program which was perceived to be a "corporate program" would not be easily accepted.

Still, various divisional and country managers had difficulties accepting the importance, as well as the 20 million DKK price tag, of TQM when Andreassen first introduced the idea. Even its supporters admit that when comparing this focus to the Service Management thrust of the 70s, "It looks like old wine in new bottles, to some extent." One of the country managers comments that he has been providing quality all along, and remarks, "You can not turn a switch and say 'Now we start TQM'. What's TQM? It all comes through the people."

As the concept grew to address other ISS needs beyond its stated objectives, its internal acceptance increased. TQM is now envisioned to be a marketing tool to other multinational corporations who are also embracing the concept in their own businesses; it is a means of enabling cleaners to more easily involve themselves in initiating and implementing new ideas; and it is an integration tool to help transfer best practices between business units.

Flemming Schandorff, the Managing Director for the cleaning business in Denmark, is enthusiastic about TQM and feels it could make a real difference in the bottom line of his business:

> Every year we lose 140 million Danish kroner in turnover through loss of contracts to our competitors. We believe that after we have educated our people in TQM and begin monitoring the customer satisfaction index and the employee satisfaction index, we will be able to reduce that.

By the end of 1992, only the Scandinavian division had started the TQM training process. The other countries outside of Scandinavia, and some within Scandinavia, had taken a first step toward TQM by starting the process of achieving ISO 9000 certification, an international quality standard which assures documentation and consistency of process.

Although the European division did not expect to begin the TQM process for several years, one of the first tangible results of the TQM thrust occurred in this division in 1992 when the UK operation brought in the head of the ISS Quality Institute to convince the Heathrow airport management of the value of the ISS TQM program. Primarily due to that competitive difference, ISS subsequently won a cleaning contract for Terminal 1 at the airport. The TQM training for the employees involved in this contract began in 1993, ahead of the rest of the European division.

ISS in 1992

Traditional cleaning and maintenance made up 83 percent of ISS 1992 revenues. The bulk of this activity was in daily office cleaning, but other specialized activities included cleaning services for the food industry, hospitals, hotels, trains, shopping malls, as well as landscaping and snow removal. Additionally, ISS was active in security services (which it began divesting in the early 90s), catering, linen service, uniform rental, the selling of cleaning products/equipment, and energy services (see Exhibits 6 and 7).

The company is organized in four divisions: Scandinavia, Europe & Brazil, North America, and Clorius. The Scandinavian management team runs the four Scandinavian countries, and the European division includes all other European countries and Brazil. The North American "division" only includes the United States, and therefore

EXHIBIT 6 ISS Activities

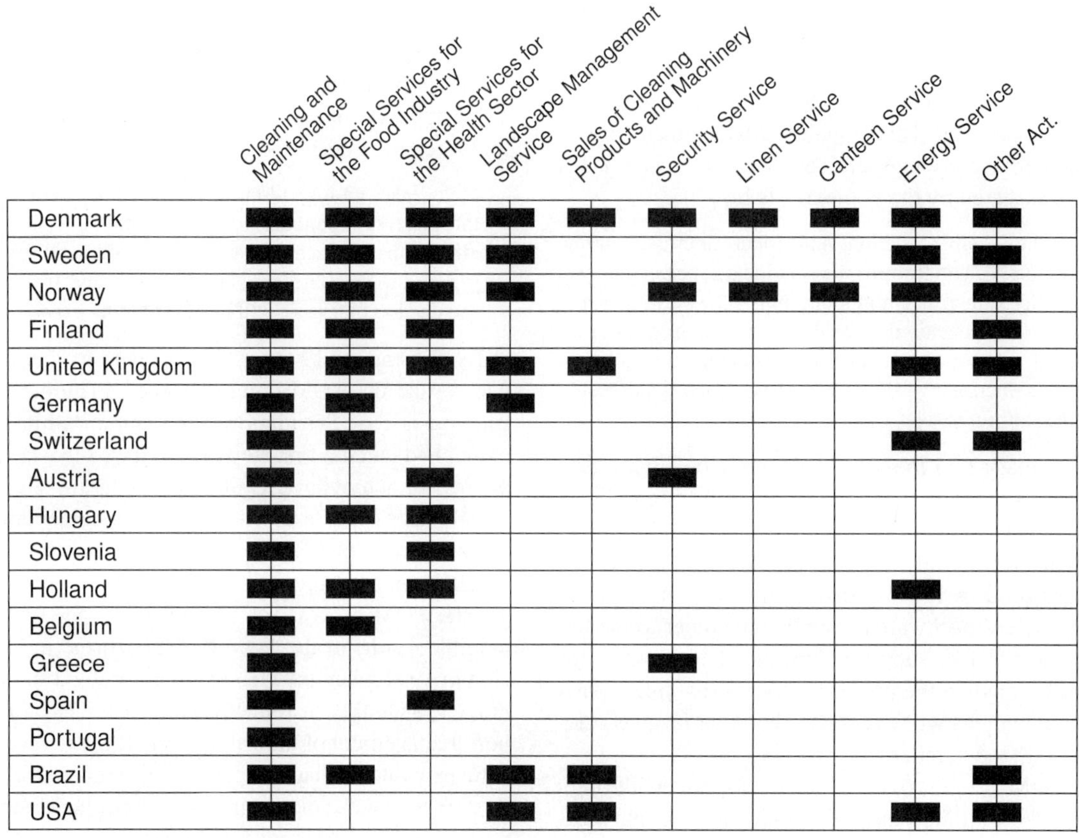

	Cleaning and Maintenance	Special Services for the Food Industry	Special Services for the Health Sector	Landscape Management Service	Sales of Cleaning Products and Machinery	Security Service	Linen Service	Canteen Service	Energy Service	Other Act.
Denmark	■	■	■	■	■	■	■	■	■	■
Sweden	■	■	■	■					■	■
Norway	■	■	■	■		■	■	■	■	■
Finland	■	■	■							■
United Kingdom	■	■	■	■	■				■	■
Germany	■	■		■						
Switzerland	■	■							■	■
Austria	■		■			■				
Hungary	■	■	■							
Slovenia	■		■							
Holland	■	■	■						■	
Belgium	■	■								
Greece	■					■				
Spain	■		■							
Portugal	■									
Brazil	■	■		■	■					■
USA	■			■	■				■	■

the division and country management are one and the same. Clorius is an energy control equipment company which has an international scope (Exhibit 8). Geographically, Scandinavia contributed 45 percent of 1992 turnover with Europe and Brazil and North America each producing 26 percent.

ISS was by far the leading company in the four Scandinavian countries in 1992 with approximately 33 percent of the contract market, i.e., the part of the cleaning market which is contracted to outside vendors. ISS was also the market leader in Austria and Greece. In the other European countries, ISS was much smaller relative to the largest local competitor. In the US, the company's share was only 1 or 2 percent of the contract market.

Beyond in-house cleaning, ISS' largest competition by far are the numerous, small cleaning companies which have the advantage of being substantially less expensive because of the minimal management and training overhead. There are only a few other multinational competitors which ISS competes with, one of which is ServiceMaster in the US. This company provides only contract management services for cleaning. The workers who perform the service are the clients' own employees. The other significant multinational competitor is BET, who is active in professional cleaning in Europe as well as many other unrelated businesses. Within each country, there are often other strong competitors of significant size.

The ISS strategy for the first half of the 90s is to concentrate on growth within the commercial cleaning market and to prioritize expansion within its current geographic base before going on to open new units in Asia

EXHIBIT 7 ISS Results by Division and Service Area 1990–1992
(amounts in DDK million)

	1992	1991	1990
Results by Division			
Turnover			
Scandinavia	5,079	4,984	3,444
Europe & Brazil	2,943	3,341	2,924
North America	3,001	3,217	2,962
Clorius	3,232	250	258
Others	10	14	22
	11,356	11,806	9,610
Operating Profit			
Scandinavia	288	305	182
Europe & Brazil	159	177	155
North America	127	133	123
Clorius	21	16	(6)
Others	(58)	(49)	(40)
	537	582	414
Results by Service Area			
Turnover			
Cleaning and Maintenance	9,432	9,449	7,303
Security Services	795	963	926
Canteen/Catering Services	310	541	594
Sales of Cleaning Products and Machinery	149	188	165
Linen Services	329	341	339
Energy Services	323	285	258
Others	18	39	25
	11,356	11,806	9,610
Operating Profit			
Cleaning and Maintenance	498	539	330
Security Services	57	56	52
Canteen/Catering Services	9	18	34
Sales of Cleaning Products and Machinery	18	16	19
Linen Services	34	32	28
Energy Services	21	18	(6)
Others	(100)	(97)	(43)
	537	582	414

Source: ISS Annual Report, 1992.

and other parts of the world. Thus, ISS will continue to emphasize the traditional office cleaning market. Additionally, there are other higher value-added—and therefore more profitable—opportunities such as the cleaning of hospitals and the cleaning of food processing facilities that will be exploited in the markets where ISS already has a strong presence. Furthermore, there is a growing demand for single point service, i.e., one vendor who can either perform or coordinate total facility management (cleaning, security, catering, snow removal, etc.) as well as serve multinational companies across borders. ISS, as one of the few multinational cleaning and facility service companies in the world, seems to be ideally positioned to take advantage of this trend.

EXHIBIT 8 ISS Organisation 1993

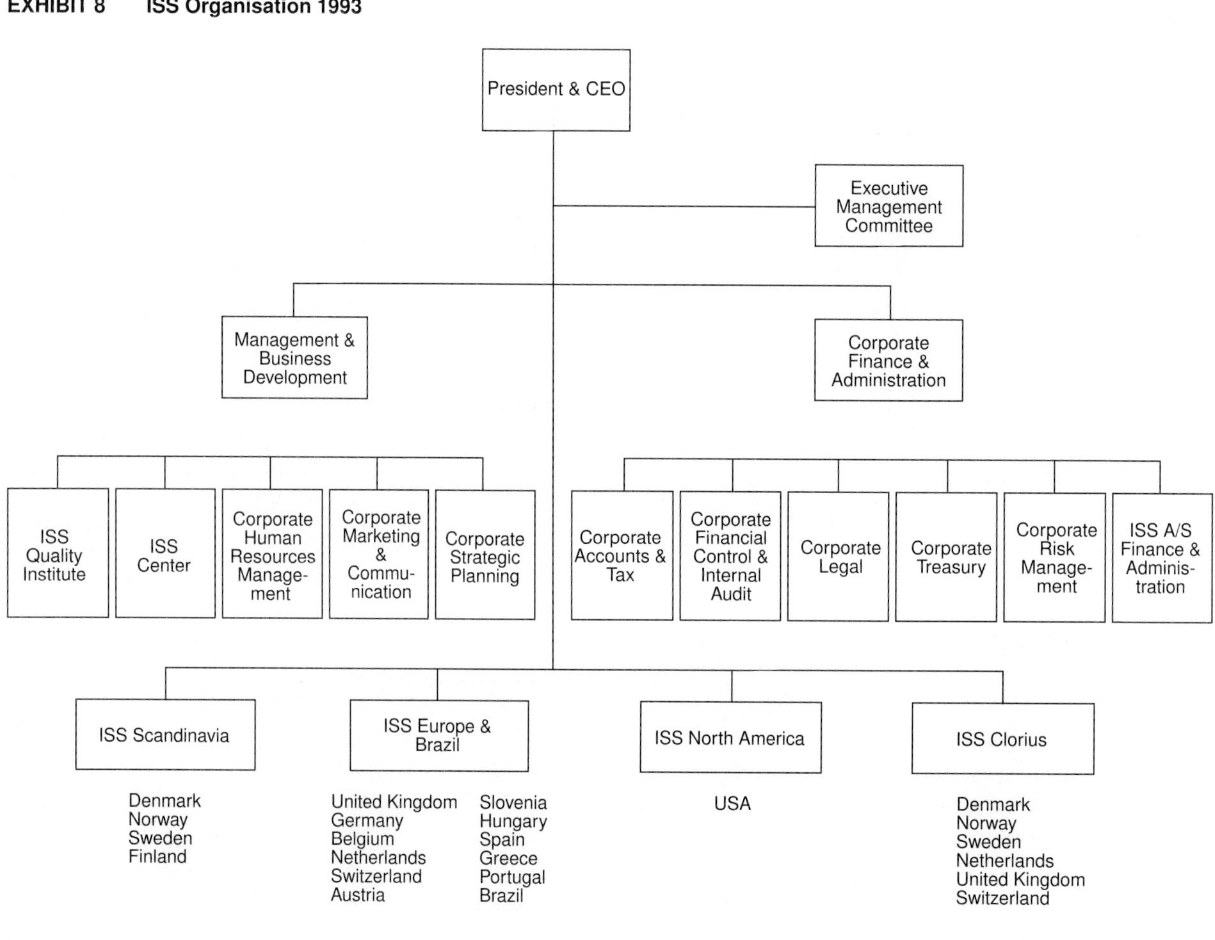

Within the Chinese Walls: The Business Unit

Andreassen has based the ISS organizational structure on the philosophy that the most efficient, profitable way to provide services is through small stand-alone companies led by a local manager who is encouraged to think of the business as his or her own. Andreassen has intentionally erected a barrier around the operating units which he calls the "Chinese Wall" to keep out top management. He explains its importance:

> Obviously the reason for its construction was that the Chinese wanted to keep the enemy out of their country . . . therefore they built this wall. Within this wall, they developed a culture entirely their own, and everyone knew it was outstanding . . . That is why I think that if you have a business . . . these people should have their Chinese Wall around them . . . They should not be managed from the top. The market should be left for them to develop. They should identify themselves with this market.

Thus, each national subsidiary of ISS is a legally separate company with the country manager carrying the title of Managing Director with his or her own board of directors. This board is normally staffed by key members of the country's management team, the head of the divisional management team, one or two outsiders who provide professional services to the country organization (i.e., the lawyer), and often another ISS country manager. The board meets three times per year to review budgets, potential acquisitions and any nonurgent policy decisions that need to be made.

The Managing Director's direct reports are typically several regional directors for the cleaning business and a

EXHIBIT 9 ISS Country Organisation The Netherlands

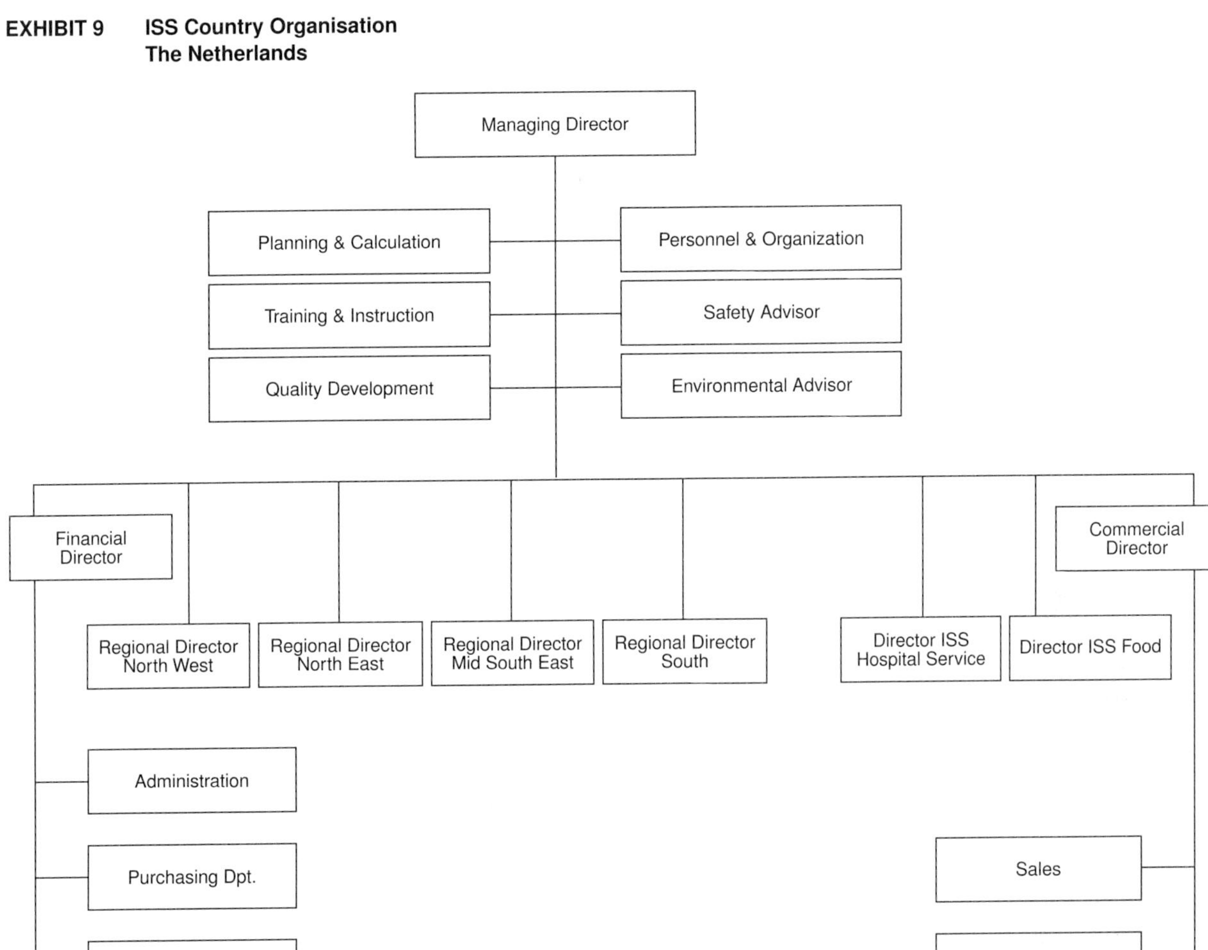

Source: ISS Netherlands.

director(s) heading up a special service such as Hospitals or Food. There are three usual levels of management under the regional director, starting with the district manager who has overall responsibility for a specified geographical area within the country, the branch manager with responsibility for the profitability and quality of coverage for an even smaller geographical area, and the supervisor who has responsibility for the daily execution of one or a few specific contracts. See Exhibit 9 for a typical country organization.

The title of "Managing Director" is considered to be a valuable tool for attracting and keeping good country managers. Not only does the title and the legal structure reinforce the philosophy that the country organization is his or her own company, it also enables the country manager to more easily call on the Managing Directors of potential customers. The title gives both professional and social prestige to the country manager in what many would consider to be an unprestigious industry. The compensation package for each Managing Director is renegotiated each year and varies by country. Like most Managing Director positions in Europe, the package includes a car such as a high-end BMW.

This arrangement has enabled ISS to hire successful managers who might otherwise not have been interested in the company. Theo Buitendijk joined ISS as the Managing Director in Holland in 1990 after working in a multinational oil company for 25 years. He remarks that

"Here it's more fun because I'm in charge of the whole thing. You can keep your independence as long as you meet your budget."

Similarly, David Openshaw used to work for ISS' largest competitor in Europe, BET, in a position with responsibility for 35 million pounds turnover (1 UK£ = US$1.76, 1991). Upon joining ISS, Openshaw became the Managing Director for a new ISS company whose mission was to build from scratch a cleaning operation in London. "The one thing that attracted me was the promise that I would have my own business . . . that I could run the business the way I wanted to run it." In two years, he was proud to note that his turnover had reached 6 million pounds.

In 1992, the country-level Managing Directors were being encouraged to create independent companies with their own Managing Directors within the country structure to focus only on Food or only on Hospitals. Taking the philosophy even further, Germany was in the process of establishing five additional independent companies under the country Managing Director to focus on daily office cleaning in the various regions of Germany. The key reason for breaking up the country units in this manner was to motivate and focus the managers of these segments.

This organizational philosophy imposed some additional costs in terms of additional management, audit, and legal fees. For this reason, some country managers were resisting the push from corporate to develop the special service businesses as separate legal entities while they were too small to support the additional overhead. On the other hand, focused activities seemed to create more profit.

The head of the cleaning business in Denmark was not pleased when the decision was made to relieve him of his responsibility for hospital cleaning in Denmark in order to combine all the hospital business in Scandinavia under one company. Yet after this happened, as related by his boss, Sven Ipsen, "His PBT is up by half a percent and his growth in turnover is better than before. He admits it's because of his new focus just on cleaning."

Waldemar Schmidt, the head of the European group, is a longtime ISS manager who originally developed the Brazilian operation. From this experience and seeing how the European countries which he now manages have benefited from the "own your company" approach, he comments, "One can easily quantify the cost of creating smaller companies . . . the value-added is something you must believe in."

The success or failure of a country manager is viewed by ISS corporate almost exclusively in terms of financial results: his or her performance against profitability and growth targets. The profitability target is a minimum of 5 percent profit before tax, and the growth target generally ranges from 10–15 percent, varying by country. The country manager's bonus is a reflection of these parameters.

The ISS requirement that its unit managers provide consistent financial returns often takes priority over any strategic objectives. Gerhard Marischka, the Managing Director of Austria, is one of ISS' "stars" because he has averaged 16 percent organic sales growth annually over the past three years and earned a profitability (before tax) above all other ISS countries, approaching 8 percent in 1991 and 1992. Strategically, however, he has had to chart a path that has not always been consistent with the overall ISS priorities. He retains his profitable security business, for example, despite the divisional decision to exit that activity. He has also not developed any significant business in either of the targeted areas of special service, Hospitals or Food, which tend to be less profitable, at least initially.

Theo Buitendijk, the Managing Director of Holland who came to ISS in 1990 from Exxon, has tried to balance the financial and strategic objectives laid out by ISS divisional and corporate managements. By doubling his sales by acquisition between 1990 and 1991 without increasing overhead, he doubled his financial returns, which allowed him to invest in building a new service area, Food. Though he is suffering a short-term drop in profitability before tax at the country level as he builds the food business, he believes it is the more profitable strategy for the long term. As a measure of his market success, in 1992, he was servicing 50 food contracts and was the market leader in that segment in Holland. In 1991, Holland reported a profit of 4.7 percent and 5.4 percent in 1992. Speaking from experience, Buitendijk comments:

> We as entrepreneurs are paid on results—that makes us risk avoiders, not risk takers. The system as it stands now doesn't stimulate focused attention to new areas . . . change is costly. Corporate says they accept the costs if you try new things . . . but I really don't know.

Within the challenging objective of meeting the financial plan, the Managing Directors have almost complete freedom to manage their business as they like. For example, Rolf Witt, the German Managing Director, used his freedom to quickly exploit the need for a service to dispose of building rubble when the former East Germany was first opened to the West. Using "petty cash", he acquired a small concern in East Germany to perform this type of work. After a period, he made a tidy profit by selling off pieces of the company such as the vehicles, which were bought by a concern in Poland. There are limits, however, to such freedom. When the former head of the Brazilian operation signed an agreement for a major acquisition committing ISS corporate resources without corporate approval, he was later asked to resign.

This local freedom also serves as a breeding ground for new ideas when the investment can be justified at the operating unit level. Andreassen explains:

> With only 43 people at headquarters, it's clear that it is not from there that development springs. Our development is based on what goes on around us. . . But we put a good deal of money into education and committee work. So you see, what we have here are companies working together, developing something new, under the leadership of corporate management, a process involving all companies, a process which does not start at the top.

One of the most important innovations springing from an operating unit was the 5 Star training program. It originated in Brazil but then was shared with Belgium and Austria, who greatly enhanced the program. This key program for supervisors and managers is now a part of the corporate human resources strategy. The five stars refer to the five levels of training (Exhibit 10) which cover the ISS philosophy, cleaning techniques, labor law, contract management, quality control, customer relations, employee relations, and other key areas.

Building Bridges: Divisional Management

The corporate management team at ISS has always been small because Andreassen "dreads bureaucracy." He feels that the primary role of the headquarters staff should be to:

> Procure the financial opportunities, check and control the company's development, and to create resources for the strategic development, training, R&D and marketing on an international basis . . . The number should be small at the headquarters office but they must be extremely qualified.

Thus, until 1989, Andreassen and his corporate staff of 50 people managed the ISS operations employing 100,000 people scattered across 16 countries. In 1989, the divisional level of management was added to reduce the span of control sufficiently so that the leadership of the company could work with the Managing Directors more closely. In 1992, the European division totaled 8 people, the Scandinavian division management numbered 22 people, and the North American division, which also served as the country management team for the United States, totaled 40 people.

The majority of the staff are oriented toward the financial function, though there are also experts to provide advice on marketing, human resource management, quality, strategy, and acquisitions. To support the management above the country level, each country pays a royalty of 1.5 percent of turnover to ISS corporate, of which 0.5 percent is forwarded to the division management organization. Waldemar Schmidt, head of the European division, points to the performance improvement in Europe to prove the value-added of divisional management: the PBT for the countries within the division more than doubled from 2 percent in 1989 to almost 5 percent in 1991.

Strategy

Both Schmidt, the head of Europe and Ipsen, the head of Scandinavia, spend much of their time developing the strategy for their areas of the world and working individually with the country managers to develop their respective business plans. They also give a lot of thought to optimizing the organizational structure, such as creating or spinning off a new operating company at the right time. Though the divisional management team is very respectful of the autonomy of the local management, their mandate is to make the division greater than the sum of its parts, the countries. The corporate and divisional management can persuade and negotiate, but for the most part, the quest for entrepreneurial freedom seems to take priority over upper management directives. The Chinese Wall works.

One example of this is the freedom which the operating companies have when they choose a supplier for their cleaning products. The ISS operating company, Darenas, provides a full line of cleaning products, but the operating units are not required to buy them, though some formerly reluctant country managers have yielded to pressure to do so. In a similar vein, corporate or divisional level strategic priorities are not normally pushed on a country manager who does not "buy in". That is why there were several countries in Europe who had little or no activity in Hospitals or Food in 1992, in spite of the corporate strategy to target these areas.

The country management can be a barrier to strategic plans from above, but there are also instances when the local manager finds the corporate strategy to be a barrier to his own initiative. The Managing Director of Mediclean, the UK hospital service company, saw an

EXHIBIT 10 Basic Constituents for a 5-Star Program

Subject	One Star	Two Star	Three Star
ISS Knowledge	Basic overview—local and international	Basic financial reports structure, ownership, etc.	Vision, mission and strategy
Function of Job	Role, responsibilities and success criteria	Role responsibilities and success criteria	Role responsibilities and success criteria
Contract Control Systems	Labor: hours/wages, social costs, numbers	Staff turnover %'s and costs, materials, machinery	Contract profitability and contribution
Cleaning Systems	Basic work methods and material standards	Machinery and equipment usage	Chemicals, technology, equipment, materials-flow
Personnel Management	Recruitment and selection	Team building and interpersonal skills	Basic pers. administration and the contract's labor relations
Risk Management, Health and Safety	Personal appearance, job safety, safety precautions, and regulations. First aid.	Hazard training and communications/signs, exits substances, storage	Loss control (both ISS and customer property) and Insurance
Customer Relations	Attitudes and professionalism	Complaint handling/ corrective action	Proactive customer relations on service quality
Quality Control	What is quality and why have it? What is a quality standard? Introduction to ISA 9000 where applicable	Quality: inspection and maintaining, identifying shortfalls and reasons, corrective action. ISO 9000 responsibilities	Taking quality to consistent, uniform delivery: 100% performance.
Training Skills	On job—one to one skills training	Refresh	Group training skill
Leadership Techniques	Motivation	Communication	Problem solving and decision making in the HR arena
ALL COUNTRIES CAN ADD COURSE MATERIAL WHICH IS APPLICABLE TO THEIR OWN LOCAL MARKET			**Extra Courses** Contract planning and rationalisation: An Introduction Basic over of time management (personal & work related)

Subject	Four Star	Five Star
ISS Knowledge	Who's who?—local and international	ISS News: Company Progress: How to keep up to date: Local and international news: The communications channels
Financial Knowledge	Basic MRS	Basic P/L, balance and budgets
Management Skills	Handling meetings	Negotiation skills
	Problem solving and decision making	Delegation, appraisal skills
		Organising
	Customer care	Customer relations
Sales	Selling add-ons	Sales techniques and service development
Contract Review	Contract planning and rationalisation	Contract analysis cycle
Human Resources	Employment law overview	Industrial relations
Training Development	Review training skills	Organising, monitoring, and assessing training

Source: ISS Netherlands.

attractive opportunity to purchase an interest in a prepared food company which sells its product to the British National Health Service. He felt it would be a strong complement to the hospital catering business he provided. The investment was not approved by divisional management because "Our strategy is not to invest in food manufacturing." The Managing Director feels that if he had been the true owner of Mediclean, he would have risked his capital on the new venture. In the end, informal ties were made with the company that allow Mediclean to enjoy most of the sought-after benefits without any risk of capital.

The divisional management has taken the lead in developing the strategy and infrastructure to meet the emerging demand by customers for single-point facilities management. The European division became a partner in 1992 in a marketing company called "Service Interface," which coordinates a number of service companies to provide an all-inclusive facility management contract. Beyond the cleaning service offered by ISS, the companies in the partnership provide catering, technical maintenance, waste management, textile services, and security services. The idea has been well received in the UK market, and Schmidt hopes to sell the idea across to other countries in Europe. He comments, "It's an interesting alternative to acquiring companies."

The overall demand for such one-stop shopping was uncertain, however. The Scandinavian division provided a similar type of "multiservice" to clients in the early 1990s by offering a complete ISS contract covering the range of available services: cleaning, security, catering, landscaping, and textiles, with one contract manager and integrated billing. The program was discontinued when it became evident that the majority of customers actually preferred dealing with multiple vendors so that they could leverage one against another to gain a better overall price. Additionally, customer decision making often occurred in different parts of the organization for the various services that ISS was providing, making smooth coordination very difficult.

Measurement

The divisional management team is responsible for setting the targets for the MRS budget for each unit manager based on the corporate guidelines for the year as articulated during the planning process. These targets, such as sales growth, contribution margin, and profit before tax, vary slightly by country and are always an improvement over the previous year's performance. This emphasis on the financials prompted one manager to exclaim, "The only vision we get from above are numbers!"

Retained earnings which are accumulated by each operating company are not its own to keep. For historical reasons, ISS Scandinavia is an exception and enjoys the right to keep the balance of the earnings of its operating companies not paid out as dividends and to reinvest the funds as it chooses. The European division was not set up with this autonomy, and therefore, in principle, its earnings are returned to corporate to be redistributed throughout ISS as headquarters sees fit.

There is some dissatisfaction with the policy which allows one division to keep its retained earnings. Its opponents believe that investment funds should be applied to the best opportunity within the entire corporation. As one manager remarked:

> When ISS Scandinavia bought the rest of the Finnish cleaning company in 1992, it was probably the best opportunity they had to grow their turnover . . . but I think there were better investment opportunities in the European division where ISS has a very small presence.

The drive for continually improving financial returns combined with an extremely conservative approach to reinvesting in the local business is a source of frustration for some business unit managers. As one remarked:

> There is no extra money to develop a business on your own. I could expand more rapidly if I got some funding from corporate. It's easier to acquire a company [than grow internally] because corporate will provide that money.

Transferring Knowledge

ISS has several formal platforms which attempt to transfer best practices among operations and geographies. Until 1991, a group of all the senior management and Managing Directors (the Top Management Conference) within ISS met annually to discuss relevant issues. As the company grew, the group exceeded 100 people, making it hard to create a participative environment for sharing. Therefore, the divisions began holding a similar meeting several times a year with the appropriate participants within their division, which limited the group to a more workable number.

In the last European Division TMC, attended by 30 managers, the group spent the first day discussing how to improve their business development capabilities by using Belgium's process as an example of one successful strategy. The second day was spent discussing methods to improve customer retention by learning from the progress that Holland had made in this area.

At the corporate level, and within the European and Scandinavian divisions, there are a number of committees which share information and make decisions on common systems. At the corporate level, the committees meet two to four times each year on the subjects of Quality, Strategy, Human Resources, Finance, and Marketing to develop general policies in these areas. The membership of these committees is drawn primarily from the divisional and corporate management. Similar committees exist in many of the same functions at the divisional level to provide a forum for sharing ideas among countries. While some within ISS see the committee structure to be one of the few available mechanisms to share expertise within the company, others are less supportive of the system. One manager commented, "The committees are not very well-liked. They're too expensive with no value."

There is no formal mechanism for sharing ideas and practices between line managers below the country management level. While contact with other ISS managers outside their own country structure is limited for managers in staff functions (i.e., finance and sales), it is practically nonexistent for line management. Thus, a district manager for office cleaning in Austria has no contact with his or her counterpart in the UK, for example. Explaining the difficulty of sharing new methods, one manager remarked, "A new idea which appears in one country has to go all the way up through the division or even corporate and back down to another country to be shared."

ISS had a matrix organization in the early 80s of corporate level product managers for each service segment, such as Food and Hospitals, whose mission was to transfer best practices across the operating units in different countries. Most of these product managers were young and inexperienced in the cleaning business; thus they spent much of their time "publishing manuals". The limitations of this approach to sharing best practices was revealed when the Hospital Service manual for Denmark was given to ISS in New York to assist them in their entry into the business. The New York management was disappointed to find that the education level of their workforce was not high enough to read the manuals and execute the complicated calculations used in the procedures. Results such as this one made it difficult to justify the value-added and, after a short time, the product manager positions were eliminated. In 1992, corporate management again proposed a matrix structure which would assign a product manager at the corporate level for two service areas. In part due to the last experience with this type of position, the division management opposed the proposal and it was dropped.

Communication within ISS seems to work best on an informal basis, with the business unit managers reaping the most benefit when sharing their experiences in new service areas. Denmark has supported a significant amount of training of managers from other countries in the Food business, both in Denmark and in their home countries. An idea for a new vacuum cleaner which could be carried on the operator's back for cleaning trains travelled from Denmark back to the UK through a chance visit by a British manager. Yet, informal sharing does have its limits. As the German country manager explains:

> I would like to be aggressive on Food but I don't have enough knowledge. I can't ask Denmark to lend me a person for 4 weeks. The royalty [paid to corporate] doesn't cover that.

Nevertheless, he does not support the idea of paying for this service because, "These things must work informally, colleague to colleague."

The most successful example of transferring learning within ISS occurred when a very experienced and multilingual planner from Denmark spent several years traveling between offices in Europe giving advice to the operations and sharing his experiences. Also, helping to share ideas on a regular basis, ISS corporate publishes a quarterly newsletter, "ISS News", which gives an in-depth review of one country's business in each issue, as well as the key events happening throughout the rest of the ISS world. Within the countries, other newsletters update the employees on the latest happenings.

Beyond the organizational difficulties, the lack of a common language inhibits the sharing between countries. With the exception of the Managing Directors and their Financial Directors, the ability to speak the most likely common language, English, is often lacking, apart from the US, the UK, and Scandinavia. This discourages common training and teamwork across countries in many cases. One manager, who has the experience to compare ISS' ability in this area with other multinational companies in other industries, feels that ISS managers have a lower level of multilingual ability than most multinational companies of its size.

Expertise

The division management provides mainly financial and marketing expertise to the countries. In the financial domain, the divisional Financial Director spends several days a year with each country performing an in-depth audit of their financial records and systems. During this visit, and as needed throughout the year, he gives advice on such matters as cash management, insurance, reduction of debtor days, and other similar concerns. The divisional level finance committee is also active in sharing financial tools between countries.

The marketing expertise at the divisional level was added in the late 80s to assist the countries in meeting the challenge of organic growth. Several years later, all Managing Directors are not yet comfortable with the new emphasis in this area. As one Managing Director expressed:

> When I'm thinking of marketing, I'm saying ooh, it costs. I'm much more operations-oriented. All the problems my people are having today, I was through years ago. I have a much more open eye and ear for operations problems than marketing issues.

In recognition of the fact that most of the country managers had grown up with ISS, building their organizations through their expertise in operations, the two most recent country manager recruits in Holland and Belgium came from marketing and sales backgrounds in nonservice industries.

The ISS sales and marketing function varies in strength and sophistication from country to country. In most country organizations, the two are combined into one function with the sales function being the stronger of the two. To target customers, an ISS salesman would typically drive through a neighborhood, noting all large buildings which were not ISS clients and any new office buildings under construction. These potential customers would then be contacted by mail or telephone to try to set up a meeting to discuss the client's needs. In some countries, ISS is the only cleaning company to have a professional sales and marketing department.

The European divisional efforts to assist in the country marketing plans have been met with mixed feelings. Though the market data which the division provides is welcomed by the countries, the feeling is that marketing is a line function, not a staff position. One country manager commented, "How can someone from the division help us write a marketing plan when they don't even know the market?"

In 1992, the European Marketing Director sponsored a study of the cleaning opportunities in the food processing segment within Europe. When the study showed a very attractive opportunity for ISS in this area, the European division proposed to its member countries that they aggressively go after the market with a pan-European salesman who could support and leverage the countries' individual efforts by selling to customers who have multiple food processing operations across Europe. This thrust met with strong resistance from the country management for a variety of reasons, but primarily because "it was too much, too fast".

Though Theo Buitendijk of Holland had the leading Food business in the European division, he opposed the plan. He argued that first everyone in Europe must get some experience in the industry so that they could properly support it. "We must not sell hot air." He remembers very well a contract he lost with a multinational in the Netherlands due to problems in the service provided by the Spanish ISS subsidiary with the same multinational client in Spain. In explanation, he says, "In professional services, we sell confidence. My customer must believe in my blue eyes. We don't sell on our name in Europe, we're too small."

Buitendijk feels that as long as ISS corporate promotes the virtues of high strategic autonomy at the country level, it will be a long time before ISS Europe can provide the consistent, high quality service in Food that he believes is needed to support a pan-European strategy. He suggests that if ISS wants to speed the implementation of these types of multiple-country strategies, "They should direct or force us . . . rather than leaving it up to each country manager." In the end, the pan-European proposal was "shelved" awaiting further market analysis and discussions. In spite of the lack of progress in Food, the European division was still working to market office cleaning services to multinationals across Europe.

The division management teams also provide other services which an individual country would not normally be able to support on its own. For example, the European division did a study for its countries to help them understand the impact of the 1992 Common Market in terms of labor law, health and safety, public sector policies, and other areas relevant to the ISS operating companies.

Beyond his strategic control and support roles, Schmidt feels the biggest help he can provide to his country managers is showing that he cares.

> It's very difficult with 25 companies to spend a lot of time with each. The most important thing is to show an interest, show that you care about them and their performance. When I receive the monthly management report, I often call people who do not even report to me and say "well done." When David Openshaw was struggling to build a business from scratch, I would send him a bottle of champagne every time his turnover increased by a million pounds. . . I also try to notice when things aren't going so well and give a call to say "what happened?"

Additionally, several Managing Directors have profited from the one-on-one assistance that divisional management has been able to provide during some rough times. When the Managing Director in Belgium was hired in 1989 from the pharmaceuticals industry, Ken Pepper, the European Chief Operations Officer worked very closely with him for a year to turn the business around. Pepper was able to add value due to his many years in line management in the UK cleaning industry. He remembers that a big part of this help was in the role of a sounding board for his colleague as he tried to apply some of his marketing ideas from the pharmaceuticals industry to ISS' cleaning business.

At the Helm: Poul Andreassen

In 1992, Poul Andreassen is preparing to retire as head of ISS within the next two years. He will leave a company which has been deeply imprinted with his management ideals. He feels satisfied with the role he has played in the first 30 years of his leadership because during that period he has laid down a network of values which have served ISS well. He explains:

> I was the right man at the right time . . . with the entrepreneurial personality and qualifications. I believe I had the right approach, maybe because of my [working class] background.

Establishing Values

ISS has been built upon a few guiding principles laid down by Andreassen from his early days: financial conservatism, respect for workers, and the professionalism of the industry. Though ISS has always functioned as an extremely decentralized organization, he has used "centralized training and information functions to, more or less, instill in the people the same attitude to handling various situations."

Andreassen characterizes ISS as a conservative company which "doesn't like to speculate or go into risky businesses." He points to the monthly MRS reports as an example of a conservative tool to keep the business on track. If the numbers did not make a good story, ISS would quickly get out of the business. ISS exited a number of businesses over the years including restaurants in Scandinavia and cleaning operations in Australia and France because of negative returns. Andreassen claims that he has the patience to suffer some losses in businesses he knows, but not otherwise.

The message to the rest of ISS concerning how failures are handled is very clear because of the transparency of the MRS reports which are widely available within many levels of the company. Andreassen comments:

> We never cut a failure before everyone expects it. I mean everyone can see the MRS, month by month, year by year. I would say it's more the other reaction . . . if I have too much patience with a company, then the other people say, hey, wait a minute. We're not going to pay a lot of money for that other business to blow it.

He feels he allows a large margin for failure, though if someone fails too often, action must be taken.

> A manager shouldn't be afraid in a given situation to make his decisions, even if he doesn't know all the prerequisites. But then again, he has to accept the fact that there is a professional hazard involved if he wants to be a leader, that if he doesn't succeed he won't have the glory. He risks losing his stars.

The financial conservatism of ISS is one reason why large amounts of funding are not made to develop businesses from scratch. Andreassen is not against new investments of this type, but he is very cautious; they must be backed by a budget and a plan. ISS' bad experience in France taught the company a strong lesson. He describes what ISS learned:

> You can't just say I want to go into this business—let me hire 10 salesmen. I saw that in Security in France. 50 salesman with all their allowances . . . He got the 50 people but certainly did not live up to the expectations for sales performance and revenue. So we had big losses and then he didn't want to stop. So it depends on how realistic the plans and profits are.

Andreassen points to the example of when David Openshaw started an ISS business from scratch in London to show that even a conservative financial policy can support the right investment:

> He came with a plan and a budget. We looked at the plan and said OK, go ahead. It's the third year now. If they come up with a plan and a budget, very few people have negative answers.

Andreassen holds his workforce in high respect and strongly believes in training as a lever for building professionalism in the firm and the industry.

> These people are trained which gives us an image, a profile in public that this is a modern company that is doing an important job. We try to build this image all the time. Not so much with lots of advertising, but by doing what we're doing. Training is also a demonstration of caring because it costs someone. People need to know that they're number 1,

> well-trained and to be told that, "You're important and this is your company."

The professional reputation Andreassen has built is recognized by the multinational clients that ISS seeks. In 1992, the company won a contract with Eastman Kodak for its whole industrial complex in Rochester, New York. The work had previously been performed by in-house employees. ISS was asked to make an offer for the job in an unusual situation where the job was not opened up for bidding. Andreassen attributes its "win" with Kodak to be due to the ISS professional image and the fact that it is subscribing to the same TQM principles that Kodak espouses to its employees.

Challenge and Stretch

Andreassen sees his personal role as that of the innovator and challenger, not an administrator. His managers have complained in the past that he moves too fast, changing direction before they have implemented the first plan. Understanding that it takes a large company more time to move, his philosophy remains that, "If you stop struggling for it, then nothing will happen." Expanding on his personal management style, he continues:

> I like new ideas, I like to stir up new things, new concepts... One of my best days is when they [the divisions or business units] ask me to come out and sit down and discuss for one or two days with them, where I challenge them... But I say to them, "This is what I am criticizing and this is what I recommend, but in the end, it is your choice."

He sees no one management style which is essential for ISS' continued development, though he believes that there needs to be a good balance between entrepreneurship and management controls.

> As an innovator, I choose to have good planning administrators among the top executives around me. But another man could come in and be a planner or an economist, for instance, and run this company on a more bookkeeping approach. Then he would need to have some aggressive people underneath him to spark the innovation, as well as someone to judge what they're doing.

Though within ISS the Managing Directors are commonly called entrepreneurs, Andreassen characterizes them differently:

> Those people are intrapreneurs, not entrepreneurs. The people that are willing to stay at ISS have more or less the same values as I . . . that they like to grow and they have talents for making this happen, but not for their own money. From the start they like to be in a company where they have some control, where they're not on their own, they like to work for other people.

Foundation for the Future

Poul Andreassen sees no change in the ISS mission as the company continues its geographic and service expansion:

> ISS' mission is to be the international market leader, within our business areas, not only regarding our product areas but also how we manage a service company, how we treat and work with our employees, how we organize, how our customer service works, how we are conceived as an investment object.

He has worked with his management team to create a shared Vision 2000 for ISS to help drive its service and personnel development into the future. It includes services for the elderly, service in the private home market, and increased partnering with the public sector.

Andreassen considers the TQM strategy to be critical to ISS' future. It will not only be a marketing tool, but more importantly, it will help integrate the ISS units through the communication which will have to take place to pursue quality.

> Training people, bringing them together, creates new ideas for new services. I think this is one of the most important benefits of TQM. The Quality Institute will be the driving wheel. The people in the special service companies will be in a group under the Quality Institute. No product management, but they themselves will have to say how can we improve our business, customer satisfaction, our value-added service.

Carrying the benefits of communication through training even further, Andreassen hopes to have an on-going training program beginning in 1994 for ISS top management at the Quality Institute to help establish a stronger network at the very top of the company.

> They will have to sit together for 14 days and get to know each other. And when they have a problem in San Francisco, they can call someone in Amsterdam, and say "Hey John, can't you send me some..."

The effort must wait until 1994, however, to avoid overwhelming the management agenda. With the restructuring of the special service companies, TQM, and the 5 Star training program all in full swing, in 1992, senior managers could not cope with another major initiative at the same time.

Andreassen feels comfortable about leaving ISS in someone else's hands. He expects his successor to be different from him and it is unclear whether he or she will come from within or outside of ISS. He is not concerned though because he has changed the image of cleaning from being a "dirty business."

> Now you can find somebody, I think you can find many, many people. Now it's a professional job. Still the top managers can choose between a beer brewery and tobacco companies or food manufacturing. I think many would prefer that to coming here. But I certainly know people I would like to see and that would be interested to follow me in this job today. They would never have dreamed of it 10 or 15 years ago.

INSEAD EURO-ASIA CENTRE *Case 5-3*

The Acer Group: Building an Asian Multinational

The Taipei-based Acer Group had just celebrated its 20th anniversary: from small beginnings, by the late 1990s Acer was producing personal computers, motherboards, peripherals, fax machines, dynamic random access memory (DRAM) microchips, application specific integrated circuits (ASICS), hybrid microelectronics, and software. It was also seeking to develop new products for the consumer electronics and communications fields. Under the dynamic and inspired leadership of its chairman and CEO Stan Shih, Acer had grown to be the number five computer company in the world, Taiwan's leading brand-name exporter, and the largest PC-compatible manufacturer in South East Asia. Acer was a leading brand name in more than 30 countries, holding top position in 13 markets including Indonesia, Malaysia, Philippines, and Thailand, as well as in Latin American countries such as Chile, Mexico, Panama, and Uruguay. Standing at eighth position in the overall US market, it was the third largest supplier to US retail channels. Acer also ranked among the top three companies globally in the monitor business and in the top five worldwide in mid- and high-end PC servers and CD-ROM drive production.

This case was written by Deborah Clyde-Smith under the supervision of Professor Peter J. Williamson. It is intended to be used as a basis for class discussion rather than to illustrate either effective or ineffective handling of an administrative situation.

Over the last three years, Acer had set industry records, with over 50 percent growth in 1993, more than 70 percent in 1994, and more than 80 percent in 1995. By 1995, PC shipments had reached 4 million units, plus an additional 1.7 million CD drives, 3.5 million monitors, and 52 million memory chips. Net income in 1995 was US$413 million on sales of US$5.83 billion (see Exhibit 1). Pre-audit results showed Acer Group revenues for 1996 would exceed last year's sales figure with PC shipments projected to hit 5.5 million. By 1996 the group was operating 80 offices in 38 countries around the world, employing more than 16,700 staff from 50 different nations. As well as establishing overseas branches, Acer's practice was to form joint ventures with local partners and promote local shareholder investment to increase its share in strategic markets, thus aiming to develop into a publicly traded local company in various different countries while maintaining a global brand.

As the year 2000 approached, Acer planned aggressive action to consolidate a position as a leading provider of world class products and components for a new information technology age. Its strategy of encouraging local investment and expanding overseas joint ventures, based on current rates of expansion, aimed at reaching its "21 in 21" goal of 21 publicly listed companies by the beginning of the 21st century, to become a consortium of borderless networked companies, a US$10 billion "company of companies".

Acer's History: 20 Years Young

Stan Shih, realising the money-making potential of the microprocessor and microcomputer industries, teamed up with four partners to found Multitech International in June 1976 (the name was not changed to Acer until 1988). The partners dropped out, but Shih in the following years built the company from a US$25,000, 11-employee beginning into a world player. The firm began by importing electronic components, publishing trade journals, and consulting on high tech issues. Up to 1980, Multitech trained engineers for Taiwan's information industry, and designed products for local manufacturers (including the Dragon Chinese language CRT terminal, winner of Taiwan's most prestigious design award) plus CRT terminals for export.

Growth Through the 1980s

In 1981, the Multitech Industrial Corporation, precursor to Acer, was established. Since the company first

EXHIBIT 1 Acer Group's Performance

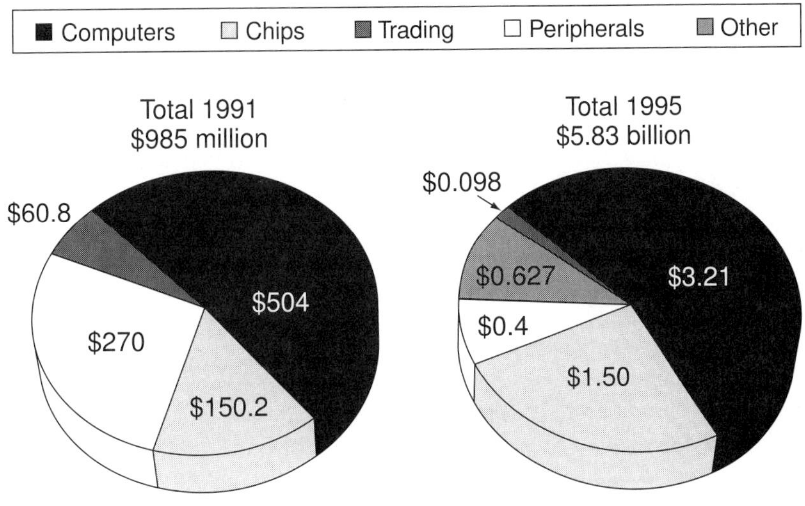

Source: Acer Group.

began building micro-based equipment in its early years, constant emphasis on R&D had led to the introduction of many innovative products, and 1981–1990 were growth years. In 1982, the firm launched an eight-bit Apple clone successful in Taiwan and exported to the UK, Germany, Hong Kong, and Singapore. In 1983, Acer was a pioneering developer of PC-compatibles with its XT/PC, and in 1984 switched to production of IBM compatible PCs which used the same microprocessors and ran the same software as the original IBM machines, and were very successful. On this basis, net profits grew by 43 percent per annum from 1984–88. In 1988, the company name was changed to Acer and it went public, coinciding with an all time high on the Taipei stock market.

The firm had achieved a reputation for innovation. Leveraging its close co-operation with the dominant American microprocessor Intel, Acer was repeatedly among the first companies worldwide to market computers on the basis of newly developed chips. In 1986 it beat IBM and was second only to Compaq to announce a 32-bit 386 PC based on Intel's 386 microprocessor, leading to considerable media attention and fanfare in the computer press. Acer was one of the first Taiwanese firms to develop its own brand for international markets, and subsequently moved more of its business away from supplying established computer companies (original equipment manufacturing or OEM) to sales of its own brands. In 1991, Acer set an industry standard by designing the world's first chip CPU upgrade technology, "ChipUp".

Storm Clouds

All was not smooth sailing, however. Shortly after becoming a public listed company in 1988, Acer had suffered a significant "brain drain," with many employees selling their stock and leaving. After 1988, profitability began to decline, and Shih became concerned about the company's heavy dependence on the PC business. In response, the decision was taken to broaden the product range by moving into more sophisticated segments of the computer industry, a move which ultimately contributed to the company's first loss-making year in 1990. In 1987, Acer had acquired Counterpoint, an American producer of multiuser systems, for US$6 million; by 1989, however, poor performance meant that most of Counterpoint's factories had to be closed and its products discontinued. In 1990 came the acquisition of Altos, another American multiuser system producer, for US$94 million: in 1992, Altos was still unprofitable.

Alliances and joint ventures had been formed with a number of western companies, the most significant being with the American firm Texas Instruments in 1989 for production of 4 megabit DRAM chips. Acer put in 58 percent of the capital, US$71.9 million, while Texas Instruments provided the technology. TI-Acer began production in

March 1992, coinciding with a price drop for DRAM chips to about a quarter of the 1989 level. This was a risky venture which was nearly disastrous: the market for DRAM chips traditionally suffers huge swings of over and under supply, and for two years Acer poured millions into the scheme. The venture did eventually prove successful, generating 80 percent of Acer's profits in 1993, and a third in 1994, while also guaranteeing Acer a steady supply of competitively priced DRAMs for its PC manufacturing operations.

In addition to problems with its American operations, Acer was trying to survive intense price cutting in the highly competitive PC market—PC prices slumped by 25–40% in 1991, and continued to fall at much the same rate in 1992. These factors combined to give Acer in 1992 its third annual loss in three years. It posted a US$2.8 million loss after tax on sales of US$1.26 billion, and the following year the Taipei stock exchange downgraded its stock, since its earnings-to-revenue ratio was not sufficient to maintain blue-chip standing. Despite the problems, however, Shih succeeded in keeping his team of experienced Acer executives, and in retaining his reputation as one of Taiwan's entrepreneurial visionaries. The challenge now was to transform Acer into one of the industry's leaders despite its slim resources.

Re-engineering the Company

To succeed Acer had to enhance efficiency, cut costs, and scale down the organisation to strengthen competitiveness. This was achieved through setting up independent business units, planning a new global business model, downsizing, diluting shareholdings, and the development of the "fast food" style logistics and assembly structure. The company shed about 8 percent of its work force (400 employees), including several layers of management at head office. Other overhead reductions included cutting inventory from a 90 to a 45 day supply—the difference between current and obsolete technology. Conventional wisdom might have dictated that Acer should close the North American operations that were proving a drain on the whole company, but senior management wanted to hold on to the dream of becoming "a leading global high tech company". Dependent upon outsiders to run his North American operation, Shih had hired Leonard Liu (formerly chairman of IBM's software development laboratories in California) as president. It was Liu who organised the acquisition of Altos, which rather than giving Acer the hoped for firm foundation in America, drained the company of US$100 million. Liu resigned in early 1992, and was replaced with Ronald Chwang, who had moved to Acer in 1986 from Intel. At this time, Shih began his re-engineering of Acer, and his willingness to try the introduction of new and innovative management strategies and to take risks succeeded in turning the company around, with rapid growth between 1992 and 1996 propelling it into the top ranks of the global computer industry and positioning the company for continued expansion in the years ahead.

Globalisation: Overcoming the Initial Hurdles

The Image Problem

In many respects, Acer had been typical of Taiwanese high-tech companies: it had benefited from Taiwan's aggressive technology programmes, such as cheap government loans, and had a factory in Hsinchu science-based Industrial Park, created by the government in the early '80s and where companies enjoyed tax advantages and government funding for innovative R&D. Yet Taiwan retained an image problem, and for this reason Shih often tried to disassociate the company from its origins in the public mind. "Taiwan's reputation is for low-end products" he commented once "even bankrupt companies in Silicon Valley have a better image than companies from Taiwan". Even within Asia, Taiwan suffered from a poor reputation, with many consumers not believing a Taiwanese company capable of sophisticated technology.

Shih admitted problems did exist: "Our (Asia's) quality is not consistent, and we have not known how to communicate our brand names effectively to the market. At Acer, we are aggressive in trying to change this image." His contention was that the best Asian companies had lower cost structures and were better prepared than the big US companies to deal with rapid change. The IT industry in Taiwan was dynamic and cost effective, with much US educated and local Chinese talent, and tremendous production capability to support new technologies. (About 60 percent of Taiwan's university population consisted of science and engineering students, compared with 44 percent in Korea and 32 percent in Japan, but Taiwanese engineers earned about half their US counterparts.) Yet the perception of low quality, low price that the "Made in Taiwan" label carried continued to affect Acer's efforts to penetrate world markets, despite the fact that its plants around the world were certified compliant with ISO 9000, the world's foremost quality assurance standard.

Acer pursued a two-pronged strategy to create a global brand image. On one level, the company contributed to government-supported campaigns to improve the perception of Taiwanese products, and to joint efforts with private enterprises: Acer co-founded the Brand International Promotional Association, and joined such government promotion efforts as Taiwan's Image Enhancement Programme (of which Shih was chairman) and brand name advertising campaigns which did enjoy some success.

The second prong of Acer's strategy was to promote its own brand image. When Acer's name was changed from Multitech in 1987, this was partly due to the company's desire to adopt a name suitable for expansion into a worldwide marketplace. Multitech was considered too long and not original enough. "Acer" comes from the Latin for "active, sharp, incisive," qualities on which the company's corporate culture was built. It also carries the connotation of winner or ace, and the name was intended to pave the way to a new corporate identity. It is short and easy to remember: it needed to be registered in over 100 different countries and have no negative implications in any of them.

Without the resources of its big rivals, Acer needed to keep the cash coming in, and Shih concentrated on the company's strengths as a small, flexible, and aggressive local manufacturer while it progressively invested to build its brand. It looked for the most cost-effective routes to brand building. The foundation for Acer's brand-building strategy was a consistent commitment to supplying high quality, innovative merchandise. Acer deployed its R&D capability toward being first on the market with technological breakthroughs which, in turn, helped the company win media attention. It used its strategic alliances with overseas companies to raise awareness of the Acer name. Contrary to the low-profile adopted by many of its Asian competitors, Acer continually used PR channels to promote its goals and achievements. As more financial resources became available, high-profile advertising (such as the displays on the luggage trolleys in international airports around the world) was stepped up. In Europe in 1991, for example, Acer's average brand name recognition rate was only 5 percent, so a massive advertising campaign was launched in 1992, with a shift from computer to more general publications. By 1995, Acer budgetted $150–$170 million on advertising worldwide, the total being split 25 percent for Central and South America, 25 percent for Asia, 33 percent for North America, and 17 percent for Europe. In late 1995, still suffering from low brand awareness in the US despite its top 10 position, Acer had determined to double its media budget, and begin broadcast advertising in addition to print campaigns.

Scarcity of International Management Experience

A further hurdle to globalisation of the company came in the shape of lack of managers with international experience: Shih conceded that Acer's top management remained too technically oriented, and needed to learn more about the market. "This is the weak point of Taiwanese companies—they are not able to exploit their technical capability to the level where it reaches their market potential . . . global expansion and decentralisation demand many qualities from managers—business sense, understanding of corporate mission, the ability to control operations and adjust to change. It is very difficult to develop such people, especially foreign managers in overseas operations," Shih noted.

Localising management abroad proved a big challenge, while cultural differences also posed communication problems. Outsiders sometimes found it difficult dealing with the intricacies of Acer's organisation, where the spreading of responsibility among several people at headquarters made decision making slow. Also, the Taiwanese practice of job rotation, in which personnel moved around frequently in order to gain experience, hindered the formation of relationships with overseas colleagues. Acer therefore began to concentrate on sending more Chinese managers overseas to train the local executives gradually in preparation for greater autonomy at a later stage: while it was not difficult to motivate Chinese managers (or those in developing countries), it was found that people from the advanced countries tended to feel they knew better than headquarters, thus hindering the development of team spirit and mutual trust.

Inadequate Access to Distribution and Market Intelligence

In the early days, by Shih's own admission, Acer lacked presence in foreign markets and had little understanding of what was needed to establish a sound presence overseas, as well as a lack of knowledge of legal systems in various countries. Following his early successes, Shih recruited managers from outside the company to oversee Acer's rapid growth in the late '80s, thus precipitating an excessively rapid expansion which he later admitted had been "beyond our capacity" and which took the company into the red between 1990–1992. These people—in particular Leonard Liu, from IBM, chairman of

Acer America—operated in a different fashion from Acer traditional culture, causing internal warfare and the loss of many good employees. Shih came to understand that Liu's appointment was a mistake, and that he had delegated too much too early. Moving back into control (after offering his own resignation, which the Board refused) Shih stopped trying to emulate IBM and instead began to shape Acer in his own distinctive fashion.

Outside the USA, Acer's infrastructure was built more gradually. In Europe, for example, Acer began selling its products to distributors in 1984, after making contact through trade fairs and advertising. It was then decided to establish a European office to improve distribution and its understanding of the rapidly expanding market. This office was set up in 1985 in Dusseldorf by Teddy Lu, previously in charge of managing relations with European customers in Taiwan, with three local employees. In the early years, the team concentrated on establishing relationships with the most efficient European distributors, and developing OEM sales. Acer Europe grew rapidly, and after three years contributed almost a third to group sales, though market share varied considerably from country to country. By 1988, it was decided that Acer should set up its own subsidiaries in markets where the potential size could justify them, thus hoping to better understand local particularities, and establish direct links to dealers and corporate accounts. By 1992, Acer had subsidiaries in Denmark, France, Italy, Germany, Holland, and the UK. Direct sales to dealers meant higher margins and brought Acer's management closer to the market.

Problems in the United States at this time were forcing most Taiwanese manufacturers to rethink distribution techniques: hence in 1991 Acer introduced the "Acros" microcomputer range to be sold through mass distribution channels including computer supermarkets. "Acros" rapidly accounted for almost half Acer America's sales, and was subsequently introduced in Germany to be sold via a big consumer electronics chain.

Reassessing Profit Potential in the Changing Computer Industry

By 1995, Stan Shih believed the personal computer was at the centre of the computer, communications, and consumer electronics products mainstream, and the industry was much different from that of the '80s, having become an open environment, an industry based on the use of standard components to create various types of systems. This Shih referred to as the "disintegrated" mode, being the opposite of the vertical integration mode used by companies such as IBM or Digital Equipment Corporation in the early days. At that time, there were no accepted industry standards for components: under the disintegrated business mode, each standard component represented an industry segment. As a result, customers benefited from a much better performance-to-cost ratio, as open systems led to greater competition in the industry. Competition had also provided opportunities for new players to find a niche in the market. Systems were relying more and more on modular open standard components, and the industry was becoming increasingly disintegrated.

In the new IT age, a change had also occurred in the infrastructure: rather than being defined by industry giants, the infrastructure was created by third parties including hardware, software, and component suppliers, the media, and end users. A further development was in the way businesses competed: technology and manufacturing leaders were now spread around the world, making technological competition increasingly global. With markets divided into segments along regional or national lines, a new environment of global co-operation and competition had emerged, with competitors forming alliances aimed at strengthening each others' business models. The large investment required to develop new products meant many companies could not survive without co-operating with rival manufacturers. As their overseas operations matured, many multinational corporations were becoming increasingly "borderless" in the way they operated their businesses.

Strategic Innovation at Acer: Rewriting the Rules of the Game

The Smiling Curve

According to Shih's philosophy, the key to success in the new age was providing value: by succeeding in value-added business segments, companies could do well in the disintegrated mode. To explain the trend, he created a chart he called his "smiling curve" (see Exhibit 2).

Value is added, Shih argues, in component production on the left side, and marketing/distribution on the right. The dotted line represents the traditional computer industry value added curve. In the early days, companies such as Acer started from the centre, sourcing the components, assembling the system, and then marketing the product. By the mid 1990s, there was no longer any value

EXHIBIT 2 The "Smiling Curve"

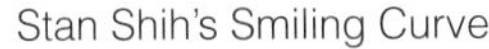

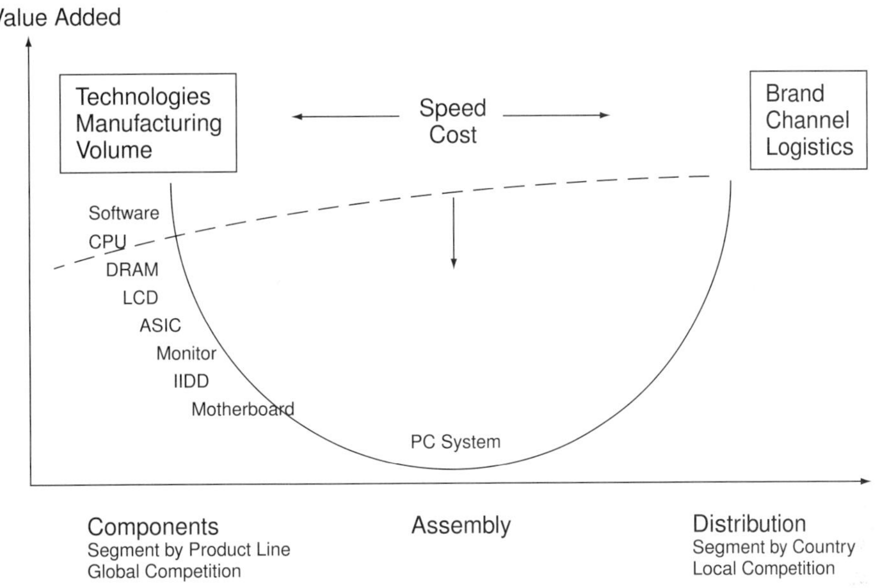

Notes to the Smiling Curve

- The dotted line indicates the growth path of traditional IT industries.
- Computer system manufacturers used to provide nearly all "value added."
- In the new IT Age, there is no "value added" in assembling a computer—anyone can make a PC today out of standard off-the-shelf components.
- "Value-added" is manufacturing key components and marketing brand name products.

Source: Acer Group.

added in assembling computers, which could be done by anyone, and to succeed in the new IT age, it was necessary to gain a top position in component segments such as software, CPUs, DRAM, ASICs, etc., as a distribution leader in a country or region.

Since universal standards meant global competition, to succeed on the left side, a company needed technology and a strong manufacturing capability, and in some areas a lot of capital. On the distribution side, success required a good image, brand name awareness, well managed channels, and effective logistics. For both sides, however, it was essential to be a leader of the segment, and Shih believed the chief factors for success in the disintegrated mode to be speed, cost, volume, and value. Speed meant fast response to changes, and fast time to market with new products; cost comprised overhead management, inventory reduction, and minimising risks. Companies with access to strong R&D, engineering, and manufacturing resources were best equipped to enter volume production quickly. Effective channels for distributing high value products were also necessary for building a strong brand name image and generating more value. On the component side, Acer was in the top five worldwide for all the segments currently pursued, and in distribution was the leader in developing countries and targeting a top five position in the US and top ten in Europe.

The Fast Food Business Model

One of the keys to Shih's re-engineering of Acer was his concept of the "fast food" model of computer supply, based on the example of the uniform quality with which McDonald's produces hamburgers worldwide: the approach being to assemble Acer products locally while

EXHIBIT 3 The Fast Food Model

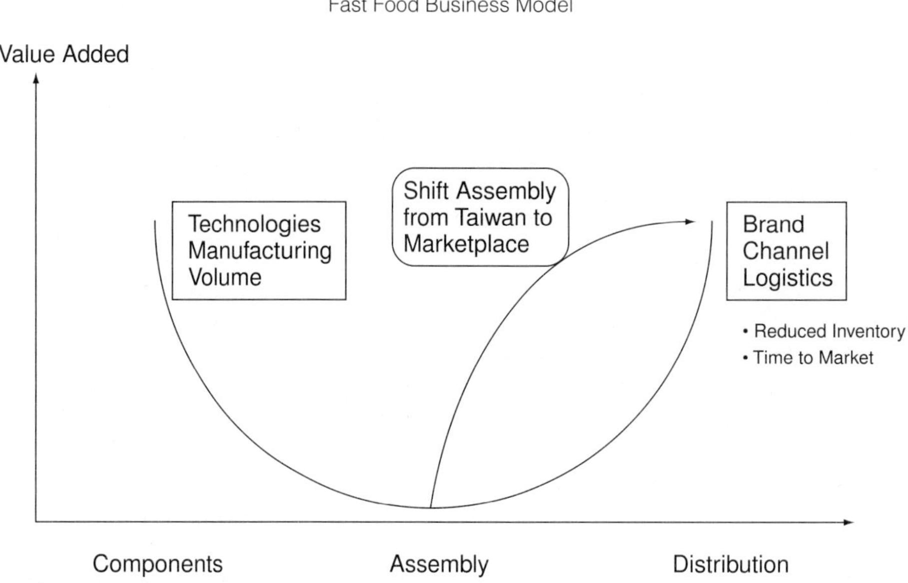

Key Words in the New IT Age

- Speed: time to market; time to volume; time to phase out; inventory turnover times; no idle time.
- Cost: low overhead; low material cost; low manufacturing cost; high productivity; no idle assets.
- Volume: economies of scale; purchasing power; marketing efficiency.
- Value: new technology; lower prices; better quality; easy to purchase/use/get support for.

Source: Acer Group

still maintaining consistency. The assembly process was consequently spread to 35 sites around the world, while tight controls were prescribed to ensure workers everywhere followed the same testing procedures. Components were prepared in large mass manufacturing facilities, then shipped to assembly sites close to local customers. Retail buyers of Acer computers were guaranteed the "freshest" ingredients—the latest technology—because Acer made them itself and sped them from Taiwan and Malaysia to its assembly sites: motherboards were flown in directly, while CPUs, hard drives, and memory were purchased locally to fill individual user requirements (Exhibit 3). This provided for economies of scale, plus the ability to tailor individual products to suit the needs of individual customers, the result being standardised quality, customisable products, and lower inventory costs. "We serve fresh PCs everywhere, not stale models." Rather than marketing computers based on six-month-old ideas and specifications, the turnaround time from idea to market dropped to only one or two months. Acer was turning over its inventory more than seven times per year, making it one of the most efficient PC manufacturers selling through retail channels. The high turnover aided Acer in achieving a 34 percent return on equity, as against an industry average of 15–20 percent. Without this decentralisation of operations, many analysts believed Acer could not have met the price cutting challenge of industry leaders such as IBM and Compaq. By 1995, Compaq had realised the advantages of local production, and had opened a few offshore sites, but Shih was dismissive, "Acer is the only company doing the fast food business right now."

Local Touch, Global Brand: A Network of Joint Ventures

The use of joint ventures to build international capability, conserve capital, and help raise awareness of the Acer brand name was a further important element of Shih's strategy: the most successful joint ventures were with

Texas Instruments on the TI Acer semiconductor plant, and with MBB, a subsidiary of the German Daimler Benz group, on a hybrid electronics firm. In 1995, Acer also had joint ventures with partners in Thailand, Indonesia, India, Mexico, Brazil, Chile, Argentina, and South Africa.

Shih regarded his "local touch, global brand" philosophy—the formation of joint ventures with local partners and encouragement of local shareholder investment—as a "key to corporate good citizenship." Since competition on the distribution side was local, alliances with strong local partners were needed to achieve eventual leadership. Acer consequently formed alliances with local partners to leverage its competitive edge in components with its partners' leading position in local markets. The philosophy also served as a means to integrate global talent and capital reserves to compete with the big names for market share.

Local touch empowered the management team in each market to decide on product configurations, pricing strategies, and promotional programmes that were right for its particular territory. These managers were mainly local to the area or country, with in most cases a single Taiwanese joining them to aid communications with headquarters in Taipei. Thus Shih's re-engineering of Acer sought to overcome its competitive weaknesses by rendering them irrelevant: "Taiwan doesn't have enough people who are really skilled in foreign languages and familiar with foreign cultures to enable us to direct a global marketing effort from Taipei . . . I turned this weak point into a great strength, a core competence." "Local touch" meant more for Shih than just local assembly—through local management and shareholder majorities, Acer aimed to become a true local identity in markets around the world, while maintaining its world-class global identity.

Pioneering Frontier Markets: Acer in Mexico and South Africa

Another way in which Acer sought to rewrite the rules of the global game was to pioneer frontier, and often distant, markets early, rather than the more traditional pattern of expansion which emphasised starting either with large, established markets or successively expanding outward from home base. Acer's approach in Mexico and South Africa provide good examples of this strategy at work.

In 1996, one in three PCs sold in Mexico was an Acer, giving it a 32 percent market share, way ahead of that of competitors such as IBM, Compaq, or Hewlett Packard, and Acer and its Mexican partner Computec Co. operated to establish a new venture to handle assembly, marketing, and distribution for all Latin America. When Computec formed in 1989 to distribute Acer computers, it discovered a gap between the high-priced PCs being sold to the corporate market by IBM and HP, and the low quality clones aimed at the private consumer, and zeroed in on the small business and home PC market. The joint venture, formed in 1992, invested heavily in marketing, and by 1993 when the price wars hit Mexico, the company had begun assembling its products in a suburb of Mexico City.

This gave Acer a crucial edge: local assembly enabled Acer to keep prices down and keep pace with rapidly developing technology—the local plant substituted components which became obsolete quickly, rather than waiting to import finished computers with up-to-date components. The Mexican management continually revised tactics (with considerable latitude from Taipei) to deal with problems such as the peso crisis of December 1994. Acer broke with the custom of quoting dollar prices and listed in pesos; while the computer market shrank by 40 percent it launched a new model, continued to buy TV time, and targeted new customers, winning contracts to supply the state-owned power company and the main public university. "We had great flexibility to make decisions and respond quickly to the market" to quote the company's general director. The next step was set to be the manufacturer of components and subassemblies such as motherboards and monitors, probably on the US border, for the North American market.

Co-operation with local markets also paid off for Acer in South Africa, where many multinationals shied away from a potentially unstable market during the transition from apartheid to majority rule. Acer's manager/investors took the risk of moving forward in their coverage of the country, which in late 1995 consisted of 5 branches, 16 distributors, and a network of 1,800 dealers, giving the brand tied second place in the market.

The Client Server Organisation

The flexible "client server" business model—which sought to harness basic human motivation for mutual support while responding to the trend toward increased dispersion and local autonomy—stressed the need to achieve independence simultaneously with co-operation among Acer group members. Following its re-engineering, strategic business units (SBUs) were formed to take primary responsibility for R&D, manufacturing, product management, and OEM sales, while regional business units (RBUs) took the lead on distribution, service and marketing. This new structure allowed for faster decision making based on changing conditions in each region,

EXHIBIT 4 Client-Server Relationships

Interaction in Acer's Client-Server Organisation

Client \ Server	RBU	SBU
RBU	Share market intelligence and marketing "best practice"	Traditional interaction: SBU provides product to RBU
SBU	Communicate market needs to SBU (sensing)	Joint purchasing, development and manufacturing of common components; shared R&D

while independent ownership and responsibility provided added motivation and incentive. Yet the objective was not to recreate a "multidomestic" structure comprising largely independent, national businesses linked to headquarters primarily through a system of financial control (the model traditionally adopted by many European multinationals). Instead, drawing the analogy from a PC network, Acer sought for each business unit to act as both a "client" and a "server" within the global network (see Exhibits 4 and 5). Thus, in addition to acting as clients for the SBU's products, the RBUs also act as "servers," providing local market intelligence and "best practice" to SBUs and other RBUs. The quasi-independent SBUs meanwhile, also act as both clients and servers to each other through joint purchasing, design, and manufacturing of common components and shared R&D.

Building the Culture of an Asian Multinational

Leadership and Vision

In any discussion of Acer's development, the force of character of Stan Shih as leader and motivator comes over as a powerful driver behind the company's success. Yet Shih, a modest man of humble origins, unlike many of the prosperous businessmen from Taiwan, did not inherit a successful business or a fortune to start one, nor did he have the political connections which facilitate such an enterprise. He always stressed his modest beginnings, but his dream was the creation of a Chinese multinational firm. In the words of Ronald Chwang, president of Acer America, "Stan is one of the few leaders in the industry with a vision. He believes in the role he wants Acer to play. He sees opportunities ahead of others."

Acer's dream in the '70s was to popularise microprocessor technology in Taiwan, in the '80s to move into the top 10 players in the world PC industry, in the '90s to be in the "top 5 in '95, 21 in '21 and 2000 in 2000". As a talented engineer, Shih always maintained his involvement with technical product development, but at the same time possessed the ability to steer his growing high-tech company through some very turbulent years in the PC market. "Technically he is very much in touch with the industry, even though he delegates a lot" (Chwang), and it was Shih's own attitudes which were largely the inspiration behind the tirelessness of his engineers, always willing to rise to the challenge of any new technology which might take the company to the front.

At the same time, Shih was deeply rooted in tradition, deriving inspiration from the ancient Chinese board game "Go", or wei chi, in which players have to follow certain strategies and consider the long-term effects of every move. "In Go, you always play from the corner, then the side, the main reason being that you need less resources to occupy the corner. As we don't have the kind of resources that Japanese or American companies have, Acer started its business in smaller markets. That gives us the advantage, because these smaller markets are becoming bigger and bigger, and the combination of many small markets is not small" said Shih. The "Go" strategy was set to become ever more as growth in smaller emerging markets took off.

EXHIBIT 5 The Client-Server Organisation
Acer Regional Business Units (RBUs)
Global Brand, Local Touch

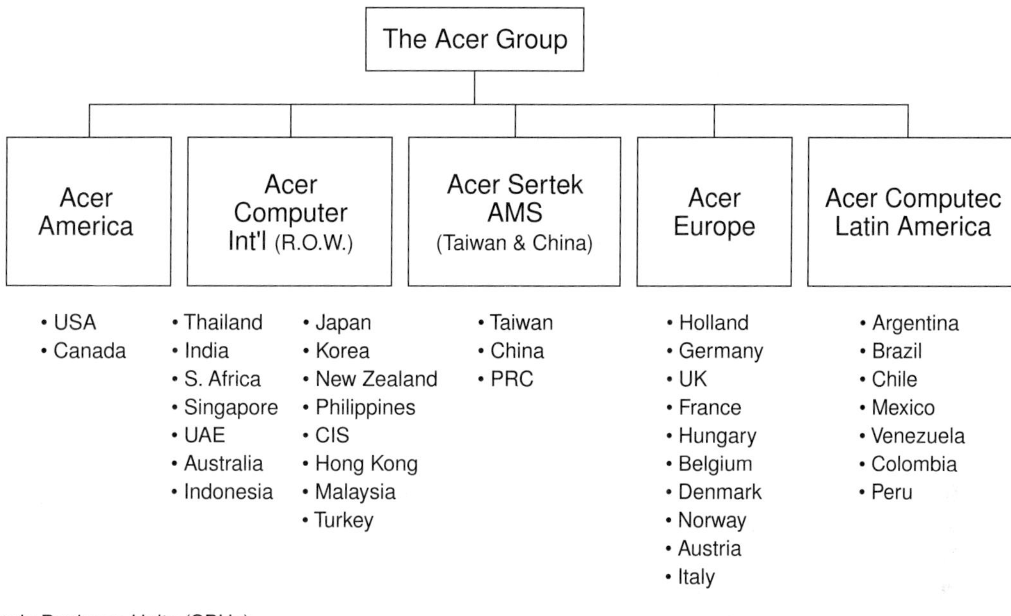

Acer Strategic Business Units (SBUs)

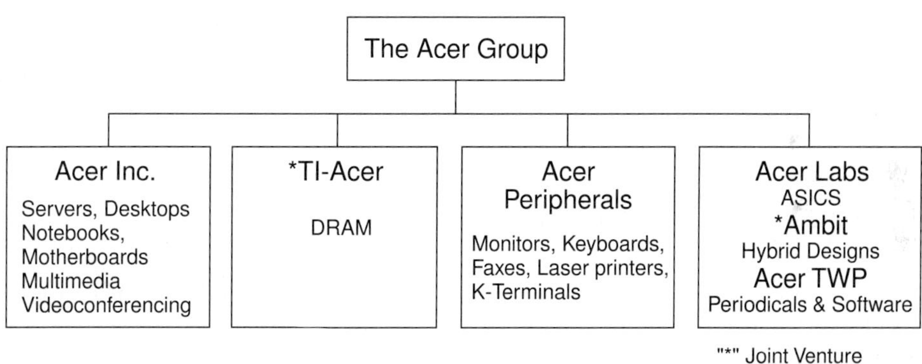

Source: Acer Group.

Shih won considerable acclaim over the years for his success with Acer, with many media and other citations and awards for his individual and corporate contributions to the computer industry and to world trade and commerce. These included being named an International CEO of the year by *Financial World* magazine in 1995, the same year in which he received the Emerging Markets CEO of the Year, presented in Washington, DC, during a joint annual meeting of the International Monetary Fund and the World Bank, for being a CEO whose "vision and company performance has best shown the pattern that can be offered as a model to other emerging markets companies around the world."

Values and Corporate Culture

Up to the mid 1980s, Acer's management motivated employees with the theme of the "Dragon Dream": Chinese children are repeatedly told of the country's former glory, and Shih's dream was to resurrect some of this greatness. (While successful and well received, it was later felt that perhaps too much patriotism was not a good thing for an aspiring multinational.) Shih introduced a flat hierarchy, with middle management involved in decision making, although this hierarchy was in fact still fairly rigid. The philosophy behind the culture was one of equality and frugality, (with Shih himself setting the example). He believed "human nature is essentially good," and the firm invested more than was usual on employee training, while exercising less control than normal over its workers. While wages were fairly modest, Acer did offer other benefits, including a potentially lucrative stock purchase plan.

Shih was not a typical all-powerful Chinese chief executive: "We don't believe in control in the normal sense. We feel there is another way to succeed. We rely on people, and build our business around them." He always listened carefully to others' views, and did not object to his top executives having a high public profile. His employees called him by his English first name, and he professed to treat every employee as his boss, as they were his shareholders and thus all equal. (Employee ownership in the company in 1995 accounted for about 30 percent.)

Corporate slogans were considered by Shih an integral part of Acer's corporate identity system for their ability to convey a company's business philosophy: Acer began with the slogan "The Microprocessor Gardeners," progressing to "Bridge the Gap for a Better Tomorrow," "Global Vision through Technology," "Technology for Everyone," and then "Fresh Technology Enjoyed by Everyone, Everywhere."

Shih felt that in general Chinese companies were infused with too much family influence, and strongly disagreed with the traditional philosophy that businesses should be handed down to sons rather than capable managers. Acer offered opportunities for committed talent from anywhere, regardless of background. Talented people, he believed, would not necessarily be happy working for a foreign company without real participation—hence the Acer vision of a progressive global partnership, with local management and local shareholder majority. "We are demonstrating a new way to run a business. It is not just new for Taiwan, it is new for the world. It is truly a 21st century approach." People in the local operations of Acer companies could be proud to contribute to their society and be a local company, and there was a common goal to become part of a world class IT company.

There is an old Chinese saying that it is better to be the head of the chicken than the tail of the ox—it is better to run your own shop than be an employee in a large enterprise (and better to be a leader in a small segment than an also ran in the mainstream.) Hence the plan was to make a lot of Acer employees heads of chickens—Taiwanese people like to be their own boss, and have a strong entrepreneurial spirit. Acer had always pursued a decentralised management model, upon which the client server structure was built, and a management philosophy stressing that fast decision making, direct communication, and a reliable organisation were the keys to success. At the heart of the client-server organisation lay a closely linked team of mature and experienced managers committed to the success of their own "piece of the Acer group" as well as to ensuring Acer's overall long-term growth. Acer's top managers were loyal and had worked together closely for a long time: through regular summits, strategies were continually outlined and new possibilities explored for contributing to overall group success.

Mutual understanding and trust, communication, and consensus were the cornerstones of Acer's management strategy: thinking and dealing in a human way, cultivating an easy working environment, providing the right motivation, setting competitive but achievable goals. "Acer's success depends on team work between managers with business sense. Corporate performance is based on people," observed Shih.

Leveraging the Multinational Network

In June 1995, Acer unveiled its new mission statement: "Provide Fresh Technology to be Enjoyed by Everyone, Everywhere." Fresh, for Shih, meant more than just "new," which could carry connotations of unproven, expensive, and risky—it meant the best high-value, low-risk, user-friendly, and affordable technology. Moreover, the "fresh" concept applied not just to technology; fresh ideas were equally important for business strategy, and the key to survival in a rapidly changing industry. Shih foresaw a shift in focus, as consumer electronics and related markets became the target for Acer brand products, his policy being to rely on the core PC technologies that Acer had always specialised in, using them in products for the home that were "digital, interactive, and smart."

In September 1995, Acer launched the Aspire line of stylish multimedia home PCs. Acer America, working closely with the California design company Frog Design, created the revolutionary Aspire look and crafted the overall design concept, while Acer Inc.'s powerful PC product expertise developed the tooling and internal PC technology. Acer Peripherals Inc. added innovative monitor and keyboard technological assistance, and much of the creative work behind the global promotion campaign was supported by Acer operations in the US, Singapore, and South Africa—a good example of the group's combination of a deep resource base plus flexible strategic design and organisational structure. The sleek grey Aspire, a radical departure from the bland look of the PC for the last 15 years, was an immediate huge hit in America, the key selling point being the innovative award-winning design, which attracted rave reviews and caused the then troubled Acer America's sales to nearly double in the fourth quarter of 1995. Having previously had an uninspiring image in the US and with nothing to lose, Acer was able to take a gamble on something radical which the market leaders were perhaps too risk-averse and complacent to attempt.

At the same time, Acer was also designing a computer aimed at markets in the developing world, the Acer Basic, a "monitorless" budget computer "for the masses" to be launched in summer 1996, on which construction costs were slashed by the use of a 100 megabyte "zip" drive instead of an expensive hard disk, and by incorporating less expensive chips and software. In 1996, Acer also planned the launch of the AcerKids and AcerEden computers aimed at families with children, "monitorless" boxes able to play a host of IBM compatible games and education programmes on audio and video disks. From these, Shih hoped to spawn a host of future information appliances to carry Acer higher up the industry's ranks. By the turn of the century, he hoped to see Acer offering everything from Internet services and software to manufacturing cellular telephones, wide-screen TVs, and digital video disc players as well as PCs and microchips, a leader in a new market of intelligent consumer products.

Some saw this as over-ambitious: shipment growth in the US cooled from 75 percent in the fourth quarter of 1995 to 25 percent in the first quarter of 1996, despite cutting the price of the Aspire in the autumn, and earnings from its chief profit maker, chips, had fallen—Shih admitted the company would fall short of its forecast of US$ 217m net profit due to the fall in memory chip prices. Acer planned to boost its name recognition with a new ad campaign—despite the Aspire's success, Acer was still outflanked in brand awareness in the West by the industry giants such as Sony, Compaq, IBM, and NEC—to expand its distribution by the end of 1997 from mass market chains to office supply and computer stores, and to renew its assault on the corporate market. At the same time, Acer was continuing its push into markets everywhere—number one in Asia, Africa, and the Middle East, number two in Latin America, number three in India. In Russia, Acer was delivering computers from a new plant in Finland, 20km from the border, in five days (instead of five weeks) with sales rising from $3.4m to $42m in 1995. Thanks to intensive advertising, Acer had higher name recognition in Russia than Compaq or Toshiba.

While US companies were turning increasingly to Taiwan's cheap, highly skilled labour, Acer was already moving to even lower cost manufacturing bases, opening plants in the Philippines and Malaysia, and with plans eventually to move into China. In March 1996, an IDC report released in Boston predicted that by the year 2000, the top three players in the PC market would be Hewlett Packard, Compaq, and Acer.

However there was also the possibility that Acer might confuse consumers with too wide a range of products, that the new products required high investment but had low margins, and might not sell. Moreover, a simple design like the AcerBasic was easily copied, and Acer might itself end up competing with low-cost imitators. But Shih believed that by steadily building a low cost manufacturing base and accumulating skill in all digital technologies, Acer always retained the option, if necessary, of returning to being a behind-the-scenes supplier of components and systems sold by the big brand names. (At this time, half the PCs Acer manufactured were still under OEM agreements for other brand names, and a good deal of its global clout had been gained through strong OEM relationships with the big American and Japanese manufacturers.) One way or another, he was determined to be a major player in the digital age.

Looking to the Future

"21 in 21"

The initial public offering in August 1995 of Acer Computer International (ACI), the regional business unit responsible for marketing and services in the Asia Pacific, Africa, the Commonwealth of Independent States, and the Middle East, and 75 percent owned by Acer Inc., met with overwhelming response and was 19 times subscribed at its close, with the 9.43 million shares available for public subscription and the 3.17 million reserved for ACI management, employees, and associates all snapped up, confounding the popular belief that US dollar offerings on the Singapore stock market tended to elicit a lukewarm response. In September, Acer announced that Acer Peripherals had applied to the Taiwan stock exchange to offer 32.3 million shares, intending to launch its IPO in March the following year, and Acer Sertek successfully followed suit in late 1996.

Shih's plan to break Acer into 21 public companies listed around the world would open investment in the company to foreigners, as Taiwan enforced strict protectionist barriers against outside capital, with no foreign institution permitted to own more than 7.5 percent of a listed company in Taiwan. Under his grand design, Acer's Latin American marketing company went public in Mexico in late 1996, and Acer America and TI Acer were to be floated within two years. These being core subsidiaries, Acer kept a 40 percent stake, but in less crucial subsidiaries, Acer's ownership might be as little as 19 percent. "Eventually Acer will have a majority of local ownership in each country, and no one will be able to say that we are a Taiwanese company." Ultimately the spinoffs would halve Shih's own stake in the group to about 5 percent.

Shih stood to gain new sources of financing and new opportunities to motivate managers with stock ownership: without majority control, however, some questioned whether he could maintain his hold over the group. "Some people talk about control with 51 percent ownership. But I control through an intangible approach, common interest." Naturally independent units would face investor pressure to protect their own interests: "To meet their requirements, we will have to provide value added." It was unheard of for the founder of a Taiwanese company to relinquish so much control, as he acknowledged: "US and Japanese companies would never do this. To them, risk is losing control. My answer is that I am willing to lose control, but make money." Once Acer was broken up, however, the group would no longer be able to use profits from units such as TI Acer and Peripherals—which together accounted for 60 percent of the group's 1995 earnings—to subsidise losses overseas, which might affect the marketability of the companies.

New Frontiers

Shih believed that Acer's strong foundation making PCs put it in an excellent position for capitalising on the anticipated convergence of the computer and consumer electronics markets in the late '90s. "We believe the industry is on the verge of a transition to new usage platforms." By the turn of the century, he wanted 15 percent of Acer's revenues to come from a line of "information appliances." Acer planned the launch of a wide-screen TV able to double as a computer monitor, with DVD players, high speed CD ROM drives, set-top boxes for cable and satellite TV, and a combined fax, scanner, and colour printer to follow the next year. Acer Peripherals was to begin work on a plant to make plasma displays for flat screen monitors and TVs, and Acer was investing heavily in telecommunications to develop wireless and integrated services digital network (ISDN) modems and video phones.

Reflecting on these developments and their future implications, Shih noted: "Revenues may be limited in the warm up stage, but the potential lies in the future. Even so, our resources will not be defocused by these efforts, as we will commit even more to the server, notebook, and many other software and peripherals technologies. We believe these are long-term investments today for securing our position in emerging markets." With the boost from these products, Acer expected to reach $10 billion in sales by 1999, and to become a "household brand name" around the globe. "Because we are from Taiwan, people do not appreciate our strengths yet. But we have patience. We have a very long-term plan: affordable fresh technology to be enjoyed by everyone, everywhere. That is our mission statement." Shih reiterated.

SECTION III Managing the Globalization Process

UNIT 6 Market Entry Strategies and Managing Political Risks

Case 6–1

THUNDERBIRD
THE AMERICAN GRADUATE SCHOOL OF INTERNATIONAL MANAGEMENT

Enron Development Corporation

On August 3, 1995, Rebecca Mark, chairman and CEO of Enron Development Corporation (EDC), hurried to the airport to catch the first leg of a flight from Houston to Bombay. Earlier that day she had received word from India that EDC's $2.8 billion Dabhol power plant project had been canceled. Given the political situation in the state of Maharashtra, the cancellation was not completely unexpected. However, if the decision could not be reversed, EDC's potential financial losses were significant. More importantly, EDC was counting on Dabhol as a beachhead that would lead to further projects in India. India's power-generating capacity was forecast to triple in the next 15 years. The cancellation of the Dabhol project could seriously undermine EDC's participation in this massive development.

This case was prepared by Andrew Inkpen with research assistance from Katherine Johnston and assistance from Professor Arvind Phatak, Temple University, for the basis of classroom discussion only and is not intended to illustrate either effective or ineffective management.

Enron Corporation

Houston-based Enron Corporation (Enron), formed in 1985 in a merger between InterNorth, Inc. and Houston Natural Gas Corp., was a leading firm in the worldwide energy industry. The firm's new slogan was "Creating Energy Solutions Worldwide" and its stated vision was to become "The World's Leading Energy Company—creating innovative and efficient energy solutions for growing economies and a better environment worldwide."

Enron was the largest natural gas company in the United States and operated the largest gas pipeline system in the world outside of Gazprom in Russia. The firm was involved in developing more natural-gas-fired independent power plants than any other company in the world. Enron owned and operated energy facilities in 15 countries and had projects under way in 15 additional countries. In 1994, the firm had revenues of $9 billion and an operating profit of $944 million. Enron's international operations had earnings before interest and taxes of $148 million in 1994, an increase of 12 percent over the previous year. International operations represented 15 percent of the company's total sales and operating income. Table 1 provides a financial summary for Enron.

Enron had five operating divisions:

- Enron Operations Corp. was responsible for U.S. interstate natural gas pipelines, operated the company's worldwide physical assets (except those

TABLE 1 Enron Financial Summary
(Dollars in Millions, Except per Share Amounts)

	Year Ended December 31				
	1994	1993	1992	1991	1990
Revenues	$ 8,894	$ 7,986	$ 6,415	$ 5,698	$5,460
Income Before Interest, Minority Interest and Income Taxes	944	798	767	715	662
Income Before Extraordinary Items	453	332	328	232	202
Total Assets	11,966	11,504	10,312	10,070	9,849
Long Term Debt	2,805	2,661	2,459	3,109	2,983
Shareholders' Equity	3,257	2,837	2,518	1,929	1,856
Earnings per Common Share	1.70	1.46	1.21	0.98	0.86
NYSE Price Range					
High	$34⅝	$37	$25	$19⅛	$15⅝
Low	27	22⅛	15¼	12⅜	12½
Close December 31	30½	29	23³⁄₁₆	17½	13⅝

Source: Enron financial statements.

owned by Enron Oil & Gas), and provided engineering, construction, and operating services expertise across all business lines.

- Enron Capital & Trade Resources Corp. conducted the majority of the firm's worldwide marketing activities for natural gas, liquids, and electric power and was responsible for U.S. power development.
- Enron Oil & Gas was involved in exploration and production activities in natural gas and crude oil.
- Enron Global Power & Pipelines (EPP) owned and operated natural gas pipelines in emerging market countries. Enron Corporation held a 52 percent ownership interest in Enron Global Power & Pipelines.
- Enron Development Corporation was involved in the development of international energy infrastructure projects such as power plants, pipelines, fuel transportation, and natural gas processing plants.

Enron Development Corporation. EDC's focus was on natural gas projects. The firm had an international reputation as a reliable provider of turnkey natural gas projects on a timely basis. All of EDC's projects were project-financed and had long-term contracts with pricing agreements reached in advance. Revenues were tied to the U.S. dollar and the host government or an outside agency held responsibility for currency conversions.

EDC's projects spanned the globe. On Hainan Island in China, EDC was constructing a $135 million 150-megawatt (MW) power plant. This independent power plant was the first developed by a U.S. company in China. After completion by late 1995, Enron would be the operator and fuel manager. In the Dominican Republic, EDC was completing the first phase of a 185MW power plant. This project had a 20-year power purchase agreement with the government. In Columbia, EDC was constructing a 357-mile natural gas pipeline for the state-owned oil company. Other projects in active development included a 478MW gas-fired power plant in Turkey, a 1,120-mile natural gas pipeline from Bolivia to Sao Paulo, Brazil, a 500MW gas-fired power plant in Java, Indonesia, and a $4 billion liquefied natural gas processing plant in Qatar.

There was a close relationship between EDC and Enron Global Power & Pipelines (EPP). The parent firm had granted EPP a preferential right to acquire all of EDC's ownership interests in completed power and gas projects outside the United States. The projects under construction in which EPP had preferential rights included the firm's interest in the Dominican Republic power project, the Hainan Island power project, the Colombia pipeline, and the first and second phases of the 2,015MW Dabhol project in India.

Market Reform in India

India's population of more than 900 million inhabited the seventh largest country in the world. Issues of language and religion played a major role in Indian culture, politics, and business. Fifteen national languages were recognized by the Indian constitution and these were spoken in over 1,600 dialects. India's official language, Hindi, was spoken by about 20 percent of the population. English was the official working language, and for many educated Indians, English was virtually their first language. Hinduism was the dominant religious faith, practiced by over 80 percent of the population. Besides Hindus, Muslims were the most prominent religious group, making up 11 percent of the population.

On a purchasing power parity basis, the Indian economy was the fifth largest in the world. Gross domestic product per capita was $1,300. After India gained its independence from Great Britain in 1947, and until the mid-1980s, the government pursued an economic policy of self-sufficiency. This policy was often referred to as *swadeshi,* a Hindi word meaning indigenous products or made in India. The term was first used by Mahatma Gandhi during the independence movement to encourage people to buy native goods and break the British economic stranglehold on India. To many Indians, *swadeshi* evoked images of patriotism and Indian sovereignty.

After decades of socialist-oriented/statist industrial policy focused on achieving self-sufficiency, India was financially strapped and bureaucratically bloated. High tariffs kept out imports and official government policy discouraged foreign investment. In the 1970s, Coca-Cola and IBM were among the multinational firms that pulled out of India. During the period 1985 to 1990, foreign investment in India averaged only about $250 million annually.

Efforts to reform the Indian economy began after the 1991 federal elections. The Indian government was on the verge of bankruptcy, and foreign exchange reserves were sufficient for only three months of imports. After considerable prodding by the IMF and Finance Minister Manmohan Singh, Prime Minister Rao introduced free-market reforms in July 1991. Singh urged that India follow the free-market models of South Korea and Taiwan in achieving rapid economic development. India's economic liberalization plan moved the economy away from its traditionally protectionist policies toward actively encouraging foreign participation in the economy. As part of the plan, the Prime Minister's office set up a special "fast track" Foreign Investment Promotion Board to provide speedy approval for foreign investment proposals. In October 1991, the government of India opened the power industry to private-sector foreign direct investment. In February 1992, the Indian government allowed the rupee to become partially convertible. In 1994, India ratified the World Trade Organization agreement on intellectual property laws.

The economic reform program had a powerful effect. By 1995, the Indian economy was growing at an annual rate of more than 8 percent, although from 1991 to 1993 growth averaged only 3.1 percent. Exports were up by 27 percent over the previous year in the April–June quarter. The country had more than $20 billion in foreign reserves, up from $13.5 billion in 1994 and only $1 billion in 1991. Food stocks were at an all-time high and inflation was under 10 percent. Tariffs, while still high and ranging from 30–65 percent, were only about one-fifth what they were before liberalization. By some estimates, the government's policies had produced up to $100 billion in new entrepreneurial projects in India since 1992. In January 1995, a delegation of U.S. executives accompanied U.S. Commerce Secretary Ron Brown on a visit to India. During the trip, Brown was asked if the CEOs from the energy sector had expressed any fears about doing business in India. Brown replied, "if they had any [fears] before they came, they certainly have been dissipated by this visit."[1]

Despite these efforts to encourage market reform and economic development, many hurdles remained. In 1995, foreign direct investment in India was only $1.3 billion, as compared to $33.7 billion in China. About 40 percent of the industrial economy remained government-owned. Perhaps the greatest impediment to both rapid growth and attracting foreign investment was the lack of infrastructure that met international standards. In particular, India suffered from a substantial electricity shortage.

Demand for Electricity

The Indian population was starved for electricity. It was estimated that many of India's industries were able to operate at only half their capacity because of a lack of electric power. Frequent power outages were taken for granted. In New Delhi, the government-owned power company imposed rotating one to two hour blackouts periodically during the summer, when demand for electricity

[1]N. Chandra Mohan, New Beginnings, *Business India,* January 30–February 12, 1995, p. 135.

TABLE 2 Power Demand Projections (at March 1995)

Current capacity	78,900 MWs
Estimated growth rate of demand to 2007	Approximately 9% per year
Total requirements by 2007	220,000 MWs
Likely rate of addition to 2007	3,000 MWs per year
Total capacity by 2007	115,000 MWs
Likely shortfall in 2007	107,000 MWs
Additional investment needed	Rs 5 trillion ($160 billion)

Source: The Economist Intelligence Unit, *India: 3rd Quarter Report, EIU,* 1995.

peaked and temperatures were often as high as 115 degrees Fahrenheit. More remote areas had no power at all. India's current annual electrical generating capacity was about 80,000MWs. Demand was expected to nearly triple by 2007, as Table 2 shows.

Virtually all of India's power was generated and managed by state-owned electricity boards (SEBs). It was widely acknowledged that these boards suffered from chronic managerial, financial, and operational problems.[2] As much as a quarter of the electricity generated was stolen. Government-run power plants typically operated at about 50 percent capacity. In comparison, the private power plants run by Tata Steel, an Indian company, operated at around 85 percent capacity.

Indian power rates were among the lowest in the world. Farmers paid less than 15 percent of the cost of electricity generated by new thermal power plants. In several states, small farmers paid nothing for electricity. Although the SEBs had been trying to raise rates, this had proved to be very difficult. In 1994, in the state of Gujarat, the opposition party encouraged farmers to blockade roads and burn government property after rural power rates were increased. The government was forced to back down and lower the amount of the increase.

Because of these problems and because all levels of government were so short of funds, the central government decided to turn to the private sector. The Electricity Act was amended in October 1991 to make this possible. However, the response from the private sector was poor. The act was amended again in March 1992 to provide further incentives, including a 16 percent rate of return to investors. In comparison, the Chinese government in 1994 announced a 12 percent rate of return cap on private power projects.

Still, potential investors remained skeptical of the central government's commitment to reform and were doubtful of the SEBs' ability to pay for privately generated power. The government took one more step. In May 1992, a delegation of Indian central government officials visited the United States and the United Kingdom to make a pitch for foreign investment in the power sector. The delegation included then power secretary S. Rajagopal, finance secretary K. Geethakrishan, and cabinet secretary Naresh Chandra. The visits were a major success. Many independent power producers (IPPs) immediately sent executives to India. By July 1995, more than 130 Memorandums of Understanding (MOUs) had been signed by the government of India with IPPs. Twenty-three of the 41 pending electricity projects bid on by non-Indian companies were led by American firms.

The Dabhol Project

In turning to the private sector for power plant development, the Indian government decided to give the first few private sector projects the status of pioneer projects; later these projects became known as "fast track" projects (of which eight such projects were eventually signed). For the fast track projects, the central government decided not to follow the standard public tendering process. Instead, it would negotiate with IPPs for individual projects. The rationale was that the government was not in a strong negotiating position, and therefore the financial risk to the IPPs had to be reduced to entice them to invest in India. At a press conference, power secretary S. Rajagopal said the first few projects "would not be allowed to fail."

EDC's Rebecca Mark met with the Indian delegation when it visited Houston. In June 1992, Mark and several other EDC managers, at the Indian government's invitation, visited India to investigate power plant development opportunities. Within days, Enron had identified a potential site for a gas-fired power plant on the western coast of India in the port town of Dabhol, 180 miles south of Bombay in the state of Maharashtra (see map in Exhibit 1). Maharashtra was India's richest state and the center of Indian industrialization. The huge port city of Bombay was the capital and the headquarters of most of India's major companies, including Air India and Tata Enterprises, the largest Indian industrial conglomerate. Firms based in Bombay generated about 35 percent of India's GNP.

EDC, acting on the government's assurances that there would not be any tendering on the first few fast track

[2] Michael Schuman, India Has a Voracious Need for Electricity: U.S. Companies Have a Clear Inside Track, *Forbes,* April 24, 1995.

EXHIBIT 1 **Map of India**

projects, submitted a proposal to build a 2,015MW gas-fired power plant. The proposed project would be the largest plant EDC had ever built, the largest of its kind in the world, and at $2.8 billion, the largest foreign investment in India. The liquefied natural gas needed to fuel the Indian power plant would be imported from a plant EDC planned to build in Qatar. The proposal was very favorably received by both the central government and officials in the Maharashtra state government. The Maharashtra State Electricity Board (MSEB) had long wanted to build a gas-fired plant to reduce its dependence on coal and oil. Other countries with limited petroleum reserves, such as Japan and Korea, had followed a similar strategy and built coastal gas-fired power plants.

EDC was the first IPP to formally submit a proposal. Later in June 1992, EDC signed an MOU with the MSEB. A new company called Dabhol Power Company (DPC) was formed. Enron held 80 percent of the equity in Dabhol and its two partners, General Electric and International Generation Co., each held 10 percent. International Generation was a joint venture between Bechtel Enterprises Inc. (Bechtel) and San Francisco-based Pacific Gas & Electric formed in early 1995 to build and operate power plants outside the United States. General Electric was contracted to supply the gas turbines and Bechtel would be the general contractor. Exhibit 2 lists the various individuals involved with the Dabhol project, and Exhibit 3 shows the timing of the various events.

Following the signing of the MOU, EDC began a complex negotiation process for proposal approval, followed by more negotiations on the actual financial details. Officially, no power project could be developed without technical and economic clearance from the Central Electricity Authority. Typically, this process could take many months, or possibly years. The Foreign Investment Promotion Board (FIPB) was the central government's vehicle for a speedy approval process. The FIPB asked the Central Electricity Authority to give initial clearance to the Dabhol project without the detailed information normally required. However, final clearance would still be necessary at a later date.

In November 1992, EDC made a detailed presentation at a meeting chaired by the central government finance

EXHIBIT 2 Individuals Involved in the Dabhol Project

Name	Title and/or Role
Lal Krishna Advani	President of the Federal BJP Party
Manohar Joshi	Chief Minister of Maharashtra, deputy leader of Shiv Sena
Kenneth Lay	CEO of Enron Corporation
Rebecca Mark	Chairman and CEO of EDC
Gopinath Munde	Deputy Chief Minister of Maharashtra with direct responsibility for the state energy ministry, BJP party member
Ajit Nimbalkar	Chairman and Managing Director of Maharashtra State Electricity Board
Sharad Pawar	Former Chief Minister of Maharashtra, voted out of office March, 1995; known as the Maratha strongman
P.V. Narasimha Rao	Prime Minister of India
N.K.P. Salve	Federal Power Minister
Manmohan Singh	Federal Finance Minister, architect of free market reforms and economic advisor to PM Rao
Robert Sutton	EDC Managing Director
Balashaheb "Bal" Thackeray	Leader of Shiv Sena

EXHIBIT 3 Timing of Events Associated with the Dabhol Project

October 1991	Government of India invites private sector participation in the power sector
May 1992	Indian delegation visits UK and U.S.; EDC invited to India by government of India
June 1992	Maharashtra State Electricity Board signs MOU with EDC
February 1993	Foreign Investment Promotion Board (FIPB) grants approval
March 1993	Power Purchase Agreement negotiations start
November 1993	Central Electricity Authority clears Dabhol project
February 1994	Government of Maharashtra signs guarantee
September 1994	Government of India signs guarantee
March 1995	Dabhol financing completed
March 1995	Maharashtra state election results announced
April 1995	Construction begins; government of Maharashtra orders a review; Munde Committee set up to investigate Dabhol Project
August 1995	Project canceled by government of Maharashtra

secretary and attended by various other senior government officials, including the chairman of the MSEB. (Note: The finance secretary was the senior civil servant in the finance department and reported directly to the finance minister.) From this meeting came a recommendation to the FIPB to approve the project. In turn, the Central Power Ministry, acting on the advice of the FIPB, asked the Central Electricity Authority to expedite the approval process. The Central Electricity Authority gave an in-principle (not final) clearance to proceed with the project since the Ministry of Finance had found the project satisfactory.

In March 1993, with the necessary government approvals largely in place, EDC was in a position to negotiate the financial structure of the deal. The most critical element was a Power Purchasing Agreement (PPA) with the MSEB. The PPA was the contract under which EDC, as the owner of the power plant, would supply power to the MSEB electric grid. Over the next year or so, Rebecca Mark visited India 36 times. Ajit Nimbalkar, chairman and managing director of MSEB, described the negotiations:

> This is the first project of this kind that we are doing. MSEB did not have any experience in dealing with international power developers. It was a complicated exercise, for the money involved is large, and so the negotiations took a long time.[3]

MSEB turned to the World Bank for advice in the negotiations. The World Bank offered to fund a team of international consultants. The MSEB chose Freshfields, a British law firm, and the British office of the German Westdeutsche Landesbank Girozentale as consultants in the PPA negotiations.

In addition to negotiating the project financial structure and gaining state and central government approvals, EDC had to obtain dozens of other government approvals, some of which were based on regulations dating back to British colonial times. For example, to get permission to use explosives on the construction site, EDC had to visit the western Indian town of Nagpur, where British Imperial forces once stored munitions.[4]

In November 1993, the Central Electricity Authority officially cleared the Dabhol project. In December 1993, the MSEB signed the Dabhol PPA. The state government of Maharashtra signed a financial guarantee in February 1994 and the central government signed a guarantee in September 1994. These guarantees provided financial protection for EDC in the event that the MSEB was unable to make its payments. The central government's guarantee, which was to become very controversial, was signed with EDC before the government's guarantee policy was announced publicly.

Structure of the Dabhol Project

Although the original plans were for a 2,015MW project, the Maharashtra government decided to break the project into two phases. Phase I would be a 695MW plant using distillate fuel instead of natural gas, and Phase II would be a 1,320MW gas-fired plant. The capital cost for Phase I would be $920 million, with an estimated turnkey construction cost of $527 million.[5] The second phase would cost about $1.9 billion.

Dabhol was broken into two phases because EDC had been unable to finalize its gas contracts and because the government had become concerned about the mounting criticism of the project. The shift from gas to distillate was done because distillate could be sourced from local refineries, helping deflect the criticism that gas imports would be a persistent drain on India's foreign exchange. Furthermore, using distillate instead of gas eliminated the need to build a port facility for Phase I.

The capital cost for Phase I included some costs for infrastructure items that would normally have been provided by the state, such as a pipeline. If these costs were deducted from the total capital cost, the cost per MW was comparable with the other fast track power plant projects. However, Dabhol was the only project that had been finalized. The other projects were still going through planning and approval stages.

The Indian government generally followed what was known as a fixed rate of return model. Investors were assured a 16 percent rate of return on net worth for a plant load factor of up to 68.5 percent. Beyond 68.5 percent, the rate of return on equity would increase by a maximum of 0.70 percent for each 1 percent rise in the plant load factor. Net worth was based on the total costs of building the power plant. The main objection against this model was that it provided no incentive to minimize the capital costs of investment.

The Dabhol project used a different model. A tariff of Rs2.40 ($1 equaled about 36 rupees) per unit (kilowatt/hour) of electricity was established. The tariff, fixed in terms of U.S. dollars, consisted of a capacity charge of

[3] Bodhisatva Ganguli & Tushar Pania, the Anatomy of a Controversial Deal, *Business India,* April 24–May 7, 1995, p. 57.

[4] Marcus W. Brauchli, A. Gandhi Legacy: Clash Over Power Plant Reflects Fight in India For Its Economic Soul, *Wall Street Journal,* April 27, 1995, A6.

[5] Ganguli & Pania, p. 59.

Rs1.20 based on the capital cost of the plant and an energy charge of Rs1.20 for the price of fuel. It was estimated that the plant would run at 80 percent capacity. By using a fixed tariff, the problems of a cost-plus system were eliminated, and consumers would not be affected by increases in the capital cost of the project. For EDC and its partners, there was an incentive to become more efficient to improve shareholder returns. Based on the capital costs per MW, Dabhol was comparable to other proposed projects in India. As to the tariff of Rs2.40, other fast track power projects had similar tariffs, as did several recently approved public sector projects. Several existing public sector plants were selling power in the Rs2.15 range (although the average tariff for state electricity boards in India was Rs1.20). Enron's projected internal rate of return on the project was 26.5 percent before tax. Dabhol was granted a five-year tax holiday and the initial purchase agreement was for 20 years. Failure to achieve electricity targets would result in substantial penalty payments by the DPC to the MSEB. In the event that MSEB and DPC could not settle disagreements, international arbitration proceedings in London would be possible as specified in the PPA.

Nevertheless, because there was no competitive bidding on the Dabhol project, critics argued that the Rs2.40 per unit was too high and that the company would be making huge profits. Kirit Parekh, director of the Indira Gandhi Institute of Development and Research, was an ardent critic:

> In the United States, power generated from gas-based plants is sold to utilities at 3–4 cents while Enron is charging 7 cents. It is a rip-off. The China Power Company, which is setting up a 2,000MW power plant in Hong Kong, and which will go on stream in 1996, is doing so at 15 percent less capital than Enron.[6]

Further criticism was directed at the company's lack of competitive bidding for its principal equipment supplier, General Electric, and its construction partner, Bechtel. Although General Electric and EDC had worked closely in the past, some critics suggested that foreign equipment suppliers were favored over Indian suppliers. EDC countered with the argument that it had awarded more than 60 contracts worth more than $100 million (Rs3.6 billion) to Indian companies.

EDC was also subject to criticism because of its plan to import gas for Phase II from its gas processing plant in Qatar. When completed, this plant would be owned by a joint venture between Enron Oil & Gas and the Qatar government. Although Enron vigorously denied it, critics suggested that Enron would make excessive profits through transfer pricing and charging arbitrary prices for the fuel. From EDC's perspective, taking responsibility for fuel supply was a means of reducing its risk, since the contract specified penalties when the plant was not able to generate electricity. Fuel supply failure would not constitute sufficient grounds for being unable to generate electricity.

The federal guarantee also came in for criticism. A World Bank report questioned the guarantee arrangement because in its opinion, it was nothing more than a loan made by the federal government on behalf of the MSEB if it could not cover its payments to Enron. EDC's Sutton countered:

> It is only after the government of India decided as a policy to give guarantees that we also decided to ask. It would have been impossible to raise money from international bankers at competitive rates without the guarantee when others are approaching the same bankers with guarantees in their pockets.[7]

The Political Situation in India

India's political process was based on a parliamentary system. At the national, or central level as it was referred to in India, the Congress (I) party formed the current government and its leader, P.V. Narasimha Rao was Prime Minister. The Congress (I) Party was the descendant of the Indian National Congress, which was formed in 1855 and became the major vehicle of Indian nationalism. From 1947 to 1989, some form of the Congress Party ruled India in an unbroken string of governments. Indira Gandhi, who had been Prime Minister since 1964, founded the Congress (I) Party after her defeat in the 1977 election. In 1980, Indira Gandhi and the Congress (I) party regained power. After she was assassinated in 1984, her son Rajiv became Prime Minister. In the 1989 election, Congress (I) lost and turned power over to a minority Janata Dal government. During the 1991 election campaign, Rajiv Gandhi was assassinated and P.V. Narasimha Rao became Congress (I) party leader. Congress (I) regained power in a minority government, and although Rao was not considered to be a strong leader by opponents or supporters, he had proven to be surprisingly resilient. The next election was scheduled for May 1996. Predictions in August 1995 were that three parties, Congress (I), Left Front, and the Bharatiya Janata Party

[6]Ganguli & Pania, p. 58.

[7]Ganguli & Pania, p. 56.

(BJP), would each get about 150 of the 543 available seats in the Lok Sabha (House of the People).

The official opposition party was the BJP. In English, this translated to the Indian People's Party. The BJP platform emphasized support for traditional Hindu goals and values, making the party less secular than the Congress (I) Party. Many of its members belonged to the urban lower middle class and distrusted the free market reforms and modern cultural values. The BJP believed it could build support among the business community that sought decentralization and deregulation but resented intervention on the part of foreign multinationals. The BJP was considered to be the front party for a Hindu fundamentalist movement led by Rajendra Singh, known as Rashtriya Swayamsevak Sangh (RSS; translation: National Volunteers Core). The RSS supported economic nationalism and promoted anti-Muslim, anti-feminist, and anti-English language views. In 1990, the RSS formed the Swadeshi Jagaran Manch, or National Awakening Forum, to promote economic nationalism. The Forum deemed the marketing of Western consumer goods frivolous and wasteful ("India needs computer chips, not potato chips"). According to the Forum's Bombay representative, "Soft drinks and instant cereals do not serve the mass of Indian people. We are not pleased with the way [Coke and Pepsi] are demolishing their rivals."[8]

The Maharashtra election. The political parties in the 25 Indian states level mirrored those at the central level, although the Congress (I) was less dominant. Only five states had a majority Congress government. In two states, West Bengal and Kerala, politics had long been dominated by the Communist Party. The BJP was particularly strong in the industrial, heavily populated, and largely Hindu northern states. Decision making was decentralized in India, and many of the states had a substantial amount of power and autonomy. For example, the World Bank had secured an agreement to lend directly to individual states.

On February 12, 1995, a state election was held in Maharashtra. Results were to be announced about four weeks later because the chief election commissioner in Maharashtra had a policy of delinking voting from the counting of votes. The incumbent Congress (I) Party and an alliance between the BJP and Shiv Sena Parties were the primary contestants. State elections were normally held every five years. In the previous election in 1990, the Congress (I) party had formed a majority government under Chief Minister Sharad Pawar. Pawar was confident of retaining power in the 1995 election.

The BJP Party was closely aligned with the national BJP Party. Shiv Sena was a Maharashtra-based party with the stated objective of protecting the economic interests and identity of Maharashtrians and safeguarding the interests of all Hindus. The official leader of Shiv Sena was Manohar Joshi, but he had limited power and openly admitted that the real authority was Bal Thackeray (sometimes referred to as Mr. Remote Control for his ability to control the party from an unofficial capacity). Thackeray was a newspaper cartoonist before he become a right-wing activist. A talented organizer and rousing orator, he set up the Shiv Sena Party in the mid-1960s to appeal to poor Hindus who resented the influence of foreigners and non-Maharashtrians, particularly those from South India. Thackeray was prone to provocative and somewhat threatening statements. He wanted to change the name of India to Hindustan and during the Maharashtra election, talked about chasing non-Maharashtrians out of the state.

The Dabhol power project was a major campaign issue leading up to the election. Election Commission norms in India prohibited a state government from taking decisions on vital matters in the run-up to an election. However, the BJP and Shiv Sena did not make this an issue in February. Had they done so, the Election Commission might have ordered the state government to defer the decision on Dabhol.

The BJP/Shiv Sena election campaign rhetoric left little doubts as to their sentiments—one of their slogans was "Throw Enron into the Arabian Sea." The BJP platform promoted economic nationalism and sovereignty and denounced the Dabhol project. The BJP attempted to isolate Chief Minister Pawar as the only defender of Enron. The Dabhol project was described as a typical case of bad government—the failure of the ruling party to stand up to pressure from multinationals, corruption, and compromising on economic sovereignty. The BJP had always been opposed to the project for various reasons: the social and environmental aspects, alleged bribes, the project's cost, and the lack of competitive bidding. The BJP/Shiv Sena campaign strategy painted the Congress (I) Party as antipoor, corrupt, and partial to foreign firms. This platform evidently appealed to Maharashtrians. On March 13 the election results were announced. The BJP/Shiv Sena coalition won 138 of 288 seats in the election and, with the help of several independent members, formed the new government. The Shiv Sena's Manohar Joshi became the new Chief Minister.

[8] *Asia Week,* India Power Down: A Major Blow to Rao's Reform Drive, August 18, 1995.

Not long after the election, Enron CEO Kenneth Lay noted, "If something happens now to slow down or damage our power project, it would send extremely negative signals to other foreign investors."[9] Other firms with power projects under way or in planning included the Swiss firm ABB, the U.S. firms AES Corp. and CMS Energy, and Hong Kong's Consolidated Electric Power Asia.

Construction Begins

On March 2, 1995, EDC completed the financing for Phase I of the Dabhol project. Phase I financing would come from the following sources:

- A 12-bank syndication led by the Bank of America and ABN-Amro (loans of $150 million).
- U.S. Export-Import Bank ($300 million; arranged by GE and Bechtel).
- The U.S.-based Overseas Private Investment Corp. ($298 million).
- Industrial Development Bank of India ($98 million).

Construction was soon under way. But, almost simultaneously, the new state government in Maharashtra, in keeping with its campaign promises, decided to put the project under review.

The Munde Committee

One week after coming to power, deputy chief minister and state BJP president Gopinath Munde ordered a review of the Dabhol project. The committee formed to carry out the review had two members from the BJP and two from the Shiv Sena. Munde, a known critic of Dabhol, was the Chairman. An open invitation to individuals to appear before the committee was followed up by letters to the MSEB and Dabhol Power Company. The committee was scheduled to submit its report by July 1.

Over the next few months, the committee held more than a dozen meetings and visited the site of the power plant. The committee was assisted by five state government departments: energy, finance, industries, planning, and law. All requests for appearances before the committee were granted. Among those making depositions were: environmental groups, energy economists, a former managing director of the Bombay Suburban Electric Supply Company, representatives of other IPPs, and representatives of the IPP Association. The Industrial Development Bank of India, a prime lender to the project, representatives from the former state government, and the Congress (I) party did not appear before the committee.

During the committee hearings, the BJP continued its public opposition to Dabhol. The issue of irregularities—a euphemism for bribes—was raised. According to a senior BJP official:

> Though it is impossible to ascertain if kickbacks were paid to [former Maharashtra Chief Minister] Pawar, even if we can obtain circumstantial evidence it is enough. The project has been padded up and if the review committee can establish that, it is sufficient to cancel the project.[10]

Allegations of bribery were vigorously denied by EDC. Joseph Sutton, EDC's managing director in India, had told delegates at India Power'95, a conference on the power sector held in New Delhi in March, "during the three years we have been here, we have never been asked for, nor have we paid any bribes."[11]

On June 11, the RSS (the Hindu fundamentalist group) issued a directive to the BJP that it would like the party to honor its commitment to the *swadeshi* movement. The economic advisor to the Central BJP Party, Jay Dubashi said:

> We think canceling this project will send the right signals. It will demonstrate that we are not chumps who can be taken for a ride. Enron probably never imagined that Sharad Pawar [former Maharashtra Chief Minister] would go out of power. They thought he would see the deal through.[12]

Pramod Mahajan, the BJP's All-India secretary, was also fervently against Dabhol, stating that "we will go to court if necessary and decide in the long-term interest of the country."[13] Mahajan also ruled out paying penalties to EDC if the project were scrapped.

Meanwhile, EDC officials were shuttling back and forth between New Delhi and Bombay, trying to convince the press and the government of the viability of the Dabhol project. At one point, the U.S. ambassador to India, Frank Wisner, met with BJP president, L. K. Advani. Advani refused to meet Enron officials. The issue was even discussed during U.S. Treasury Secretary Robert Rubin's visit to India in April. According to the Assistant Secretary of the Treasury, "we pushed for resolution of

[9] Emily MacFarquhar, A Volatile Democracy, *U.S. News and World Report*, March 27, 1995, p. 37.

[10] Ganguli & Pania, p. 56.
[11] Ganguli & Pania, p. 55.
[12] Ganguli & Pania, p. 55.
[13] Ganguli & Pania, p. 55.

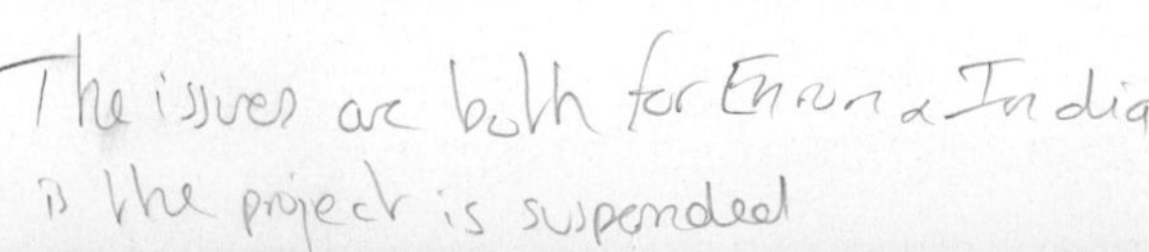

the issue."[14] In May 1995, the U.S. Department of Energy warned that failure to honor the contract would jeopardize most, if not all, other private projects proposed for international financing in India. Maharashtra had attracted more than $1 billion of U.S. investment, and more than half of all foreign direct investment projects in India were in this state. Furthermore, more than 25 percent of all FDI in India was from the United States.

In the meantime, Bechtel had not stopped construction. A spokesman for Bechtel said the company can't afford to have its 1,300 workers idled during a month-long review. "We have to meet a schedule; we have to provide power according to the power purchase agreement."[15]

Cancellation of the Dabhol Project

The Munde Committee report was submitted to the Maharashtra government on July 15, 1995. Prior to the release of the report, N.K.P. Salve, India's power minister, stressed that the "Enron contract can be canceled only if there is a legal basis for doing so, not for any arbitrary or political reason."[16] On August 2, the Indian Supreme Court dismissed a petition by a former Maharashtra legislator challenging the Dabhol project on the grounds of secrecy.

On August 3, Chief Minister Joshi (who had visited the United States in the previous month to attract investment to India) announced to the Maharashtra legislature that the cabinet unanimously agreed to suspend Phase I of the project and scrap Phase II. The following are excerpts from Chief Minister Joshi's lengthy statement in the Assembly:

> The Enron project in the form conceived and contracted for is not in the best interests of the state. . . . Being conscious of the deception and distortion in the Enron-MSEB deal which have caused grave losses, the subcommittee is clear that the project must not be allowed to proceed. The subcommittee wholeheartedly recommends that the Enron-MSEB contract should be canceled forthwith. . . . Considering the grave issues involved in the matter and the disturbing facts and circumstances that have emerged pointing to extra-commercial considerations and probable corruption and illegal motives at work in the whole affair, immediate action must be initiated under the penal and anti-corruption laws by police.
>
> The wrong choice of LNG [liquefied natural gas] as fuel and huge inflation in capital costs, along with unprecedented favours shown to Enron in different ways, including in the fuel procurement [had all resulted in an] unreasonable fuel cost to the consumers. . . . The documentary evidence obtained by the committee shows beyond any reasonable doubt that the capital cost of Enron Plant was inflated and jacked up by a huge margin. The committee believes that the extent of the inflation may be as high as $700 million. . . . Being gas-based, this project should have been cheaper than coal-based ones but in reality, it turns out to be the other way about.
>
> I am convinced that Enron, Bechtel, and GE will sell off at least 50 percent of their equity for the recovery of their expenditures on the project plus profits and the government would be a helpless spectator. The government should have sought some part of this for itself. . . . This contract is anti-Maharashtra. It is devoid of any self-respect; it is one that mortgages the brains of the state which, if accepted, would be a betrayal of the people. This contract is no contract at all and if by repudiating it, there is some financial burden, the state will accept it to preserve the well-being of Maharashtra.[17]

Other grounds were given for cancellation: there had been no competitive bidding; EDC held secret negotiations and used unfair means to win its contract; there was potential environmental damage to a region that was relatively unpolluted; the guaranteed return was well above the norm; and concerns about the $20 million earmarked by EDC for education and project development. The BJP government charged that concessions granted to EDC would cause the state of Maharashtra to lose more than $3.3 billion in the future. The committee was also outraged that loose ends in the Dabhol project were being tied up by the Maharashtra government as late as February 25, almost two weeks after the state election. In effect, the contract had been made effective by an administration that had already been rejected by voters.

When the decision was announced, Prime Minister Rao was on a trade and investment promotion trip to Malaysia. He indicated that the economic liberalization policies initiated by his government would not be affected by this decision. Sharad Pawar, the Chief Minister of Maharashtra at the time the original agreement was signed with Enron, criticized the BJP's decision to cancel the Dabhol power project:

[14] Ganguli & Pania, p. 55.

[15] *San Francisco Business Times,* May 5, 1995 Sec: 1, p. 1.

[16] Foreign Investment in India: The Enron Disease, *The Economist,* July 29, 1995, p. 48.

[17] "Indian State Axes $2.8 BN Dabhol Power Project", in *International Gas Report, The Financial Times,* August 4; Mahesh Vijapurkar, Enron Deal Scrapped, Ongoing Work Halted, *The Hindu,* August 4, p. 1.

> If the government of Maharashtra was serious about the industrialization of Maharashtra, and its power requirements for industrialization and agriculture, they definitely would have appointed an expert group who understands the requirement of power, about overall projection, about investment which is coming in the fields of industry and agriculture, legal sides, but this particular angle is totally missing here and that is why I am not so surprised for this type of decision which has been taken by the government of Maharashtra.[18]

On the day after the government's cancellation announcement, the *Saamna* newspaper, known as the voice of the nationalist Shiv Sena Party, published a headline that read, "Enron Finally Dumped into the Arabian Sea." Later that week, *The Economic Times* in Bombay reported that local villagers celebrated the fall of Enron (see Exhibit 4).

EDC's Next Steps

About 2,600 people were working on the Dabhol power project and it was nearly one-third complete. More than $300 million had been invested in the project and estimated costs per day if the project were shut down would be $200,000 to $250,000. Cancellation of Phase II was less critical because EDC had not yet secured financing commitments for this portion of the project.

A few days before the Munde Committee report was made public and anticipating a cancellation recommendation, Rebecca Mark had offered publicly to renegotiate the deal. She told the media that the company would try to meet the concerns of the MSEB. On August 3, EDC announced that while it was aware of the reported announcement in the Maharashtra Assembly on the suspension of Dabhol, the company had received no official notice to that effect. The statement, issued in Houston, said:

> [EDC] remains available for discussions with the government on any concerns it may have. . . . [EDC] has very strong legal defenses available to it under the project contracts and fully intends to pursue these if necessary. The DPC and the project sponsors would like to reiterate that they have acted in full compliance with Indian and U.S. laws.[19]

[18] All-India Doordarshan Television, 3 August 1995.

[19] Vijapurkar, p. 1.

EXHIBIT 4 Excerpts from *The Economic Times*, Bombay, August 7, 1995
Villagers Celebrate 'Fall' of Enron

The 'Fall' of Enron was celebrated with victory marches, much noise of slogans, firecrackers and dancing outside the gates of the Dabhol Power Project and in the neighboring villages of Guhagar, Veldur, Anjanvel and Katalwadi on Sunday.

The march was led by local BJP MLA, the boyish Mr. Vinay Natu, whose father, a former MLA, is said to have originally brought the Enron project to its present site. The younger Natu denies this and says it is Enron propaganda to defame his father.

Much action was expected at the project site by the accompanying police escort. If nothing else, the celebrators were expected to pull down the Dabhol Power Company signboards on the gates of the high fence. They had earlier trailered this in Guhagar when women pulled down a DPG signpost indicating the way to the site and trampled it with fury.

Instead, the processionists danced, threw gulai in the air, and burst long strings of firecrackers before moving on to the next gate. Behind the wire fences at the site stood the tense security staff of the project; in the distance on higher ground could be seen site engineers observing the proceedings through binoculars.

Lining the fence inside were hundreds of construction workers who came to see the show. These workers too come from the neighboring villages, including those where the celebrations were being held. And even among the processionists were many who on other days worked inside the fence area on pay much higher than anything they can get in their villages. The paradox of benefiting by the Enron project as well as protesting against it has been the most striking aspect of the controversy.

The local Congress leader, 'Mama' Vaidya, was most unimpressed by the show or the opposition to the project. "This backward area needs the project," he said. As to any Congress efforts in the area to muster support for the project or economic development of the area, Mr. Vaidya said there was infighting in the party and coordinated action was not possible.

At DPC itself work goes on. There's worry on the faces of engineers, but they are determined to go on until they are told by their bosses to stop. No such order has been served yet.

INSEAD EURO-ASIA CENTRE

Case 6–2

Deng's Legacy: China On-Line

When Deng Xiaoping's economic reforms began at the end of the 1970s, China possessed an extremely poor telecommunications infrastructure. Its level of telephone penetration lagged far behind countries of both the industrialised and developing world (Exhibit 1). Direct dialling, both internationally and between cities, was not possible. Telecoms equipment was decades out of date. Residential lines, available mainly to the political elite, acted more as an indication of social status than a tool for communication. Under Mao, telecommunications were seen purely as an administrative tool, and expenditure on telecoms was one of the first victims of any budget cuts. In the Maoist economic system, telecom assets were viewed as "unproductive".

With the advent of the Deng reform era, the importance of telecommunications in China's economy rose dramatically. The Chinese government embarked on an aggressive strategy of modernising and expanding the country's telecom infrastructure, dependent heavily on foreign investment and transfers of technology. By 1997, China was installing the equivalent of Canada's telephone network every year. New technologies, including cellular telephony, paging, and data communications were introduced and immediately experienced dramatic growth. Despite its rapid progress, China still lagged behind the industrialised nations in terms of the quantity and quality of services, and high growth promised to continue for several decades as China tried to catch up with the rest of the world. Lured by China's enormous untapped potential, foreign telecom firms flocked to China, keen to gain a share of this gold mine and rekindle their growth outside their maturing home markets.

This case was written by Adam Pearson, of The Boston Consulting Group, under the supervision of Jonathan Story, Professor at INSEAD. It is intended to be used as a basis for class discussion rather than to illustrate either effective or ineffective handling of an administrative situation.

EXHIBIT 1 Teledensity and GDP Per Capita in Selected Countries (1980)

	No of Telephones Per 100 People	GDP Per Capita
United States	78.8	11,867
W Germany	46.4	13,413
Japan	46.0	8,751
Hong Kong	32.6	5,086
Singapore	29.1	4,855
South Korea	7.7	1,112
Brazil	6.3	1,979
Malaysia	4.5	1,857
Kenya	2.1	425
Egypt	1.2	580
Thailand	1.1	746
Pakistan	0.4	333
China	**0.4**	**280**
India	0.4	237
Indonesia	0.3	491
Afghanistan	0.2	215
Zaire	0.1	146

Source: *United Nations Statistical Yearbook 1981, 1986;* China Statistical Yearbook 1996; World Bank.

The Chinese Telecommunications Market

The growth of the Chinese telecom market, driven by the government's modernisation programme, accelerated throughout the 1980s and the early 1990s. Growth also consistently exceeded the projections of the government's Five Year Plans. The modernisation had its effect in three respects:

- *Penetration and Usage*. Teledensity, the basic measure of the penetration of telecom services, increased tenfold between 1980 and 1995 (Exhibits 2a & 2b). The number of long distance calls grew even faster than exchange capacity, with 50 times as many long-distance calls being made in 1995 as in 1980. The growth of telecom services throughout this period was often double the rate of growth of GDP per capita. The Ninth Five Year Plan (1996–2000) planned to continue the growth of the previous 15 years, albeit at a slightly lower pace. But in absolute

EXHIBIT 2a Major Indicators for Telecommunications in China

Indicator	1980	1985	1988	1989	1990	1991	1992	1993	1994	1995	1996	2000
Teledensity												
Lines/100 People (actual)	0.4	0.6	0.9	1.0	1.1	1.3	1.6	2.2	3.2	4.7	6.2	—
Lines/100 People (target)					0.9					2.5	—	10
Exchange Capacity												
Total–Actual (million lines)	4.4	6.1	8.9	10.3	12.3	14.9	19.2	30.4	49.3	72.0	93.1	—
Total–Target (million lines)					10.0					48.0	—	174.0
Urban–Actual (million lines)	2.0	3.4	5.6	6.7	8.3	10.3	13.6	22.1	37.2	54.6	—	—
Rural–Actual (million lines)	2.4	2.8	3.3	3.7	4.1	4.6	5.6	8.3	12.0	17.5	—	—
Long Distance Lines												
Total–Actual ('000s)	22.0	37.6	68.5	87.1	112.4	151.8	234.3	420.3	615.8	735.5	—	—
Total–Target ('000s)										520.0	—	1,940.0
Long Distance Calls (million)	214	383	646	785	1,163	1,729	2,874	5,069	7,576	10,140	12,300	—
International Calls ('000s)	—	—	247	624	1,294	2,624	5,184	11,113	22,836	—	—	—
Cellular Subscribers												
Total–Actual (million)	—	—	0.003	0.007	0.02	0.048	0.18	0.64	1.57	3.65	6.86	—
Total–Target (million)												20.0
Analogue–Actual (million)			0.003	0.007	0.02	0.048	0.18	0.64	1.57	3.47	5.20	—
GSM–Actual (million)	—	—	—	—	—	—	—	—	—	0.18	1.66	—
Paging Subscribers (million)	—	—	0.1	0.2	0.4	0.87	2.2	5.6	10.3	27.7	—	—

Note: figures for targets are drawn from the appropriate Five Year Plan projections.

Source: BD Associates, Beijing; *The Chinese Telecommunications Market,* MDIS, 1996; *China Statistical Yearbook 1996;* Various other sources.

EXHIBIT 2b Growth Rates of Major Indicators for Telecommunications in China

Annual Growth Rates for the Period	1980–85	1985–90	1990–95	1995–00F
Teledensity				
Lines/100 people	6.9%	13.1%	33.2%	16.5%
Exchange capacity				
Total	6.7%	15.0%	42.4%	19.3%
Urban	10.9%	19.7%	45.9%	—
Rural	2.7%	7.9%	33.9%	—
Long Distance Lines	11.3%	24.5%	45.6%	21.4%
Long Distance Calls	12.3%	24.9%	54.2%	—
International Calls*	—	128.9%	105.0%	—
Cellular Subscribers	—	—	183.2%	40.6%
Paging Subscribers	—	—	129.3%	—

Note: Figures for 1995–2000 based on Ninth Five Year Plan projections.
*IDD call growth rates are for 1988–1990 and 1990–1994 respectively.
Source: BD Associates, Beijing; *The Chinese Telecommunications Market,* MDIS, 1996; *China Statistical Yearbook 1996;* Various other sources.

terms, purchases and installation of equipment were at an unprecedented scale. Mobile telephony, in particular, would grow extremely fast: the number of subscribers was planned to increase fivefold.

- *Range of Services.* For the first time, long-distance direct dialing, and later international direct dialing (IDD), became possible. In 1987, the first cellular networks were built using analogue technology (TACS), and in 1993, the first digital cellular networks, using the GSM standard, were constructed. Mobile networks, which are relatively easy to construct, grew much more rapidly than fixed networks, and the subscriber base more than doubled every year through the early 1990s. Paging services grew even faster than cellular networks, and by 1997 it was estimated that there were 40 million subscribers. China started launching communications satellites in 1984 and increased satellite numbers and capacity through the 1990s. During the 1990s, data networks were built and value-added services such as voice-mail, call waiting, e-mail and the internet became available.
- *Quality of telecoms services.* Before the reforms, reliability of services was very poor. Long-distance calls usually took between one to four hours to be connected. Waiting lists for residential lines were as long as two years. Progress in improving quality was slower than progress on increasing the quantity of services, because customers' expectations and usage rose faster than the rate of network expansion. In 1992, a World Bank Report on Telecoms in China found that there were still serious problems of service quality. Even then, long-distance circuits in the South of China were so congested that only 15 percent of calls got through. By the mid-1990s, the rise in service quality had not been as great as the growth in services.

The growth of telecom services was not spread evenly. It was led initially by the fastest growing regions, Guangdong province and the cities of Shanghai and Beijing, followed by the other coastal provinces. By 1991, Guangdong had four times as many lines per head as the rest of the country. Shanghai and Beijing were also far ahead of the rest of the country in terms of quantity, quality, and range of services. The development of telecom in each region mirrored the region's economic development (Exhibit 3).

Telecom Market Structure

The telecom market is divided into two parts. The first is the manufacture and supply of telecom equipment. There are a number of different categories of equipment that compose telecom networks. Fixed networks are made up of central office switching systems, which include integrated circuit technology, transmission systems, cable

EXHIBIT 3 Teledensity and Per Capita Income by Region

Province	GDP Per Capita (Rmb) (1994)	Telephones Per 100 People (1995)
Shanghai	15,204	20.8
Beijing	10,265	20.5
Tianjin	8,164	14.8
Guangdong	6,380	12.1
Zhejiang	6,149	9.1
Liaoning	6,103	7.3
Jiangsu	5,785	7.3
Fujian	5,386	7.0
Hainan	4,820	5.2
Shandong	4,473	4.0
Heilongjiang	4,427	4.4
Xingjiang	3,953	4.1
Jilin	3,703	6.4
Hebei	3,376	3.9
Hubei	3,341	4.0
Inner Mongolia	3,013	3.8
Qinghai	2,910	3.0
Shanxi	2,819	3.1
Guangxi	2,772	2.3
Hunan	2,701	3.1
Ningxia	2,685	4.4
Anhui	2,521	2.6
Sichuan	2,513	1.9
Yunnan	2,490	2.2
Henan	2,475	2.1
Jiangxi	2,376	2.4
Shaanxi	2,344	2.8
Tibet	1,984	1.5
Gansu	1,858	2.7
Guizhou	1,553	0.9

Source: *The Chinese Telecommunications Market*, MDIS, 1996; *China Statistical Yearbook 1996.*

(both fibre-optic and other materials), network access systems, microwave trunk and local loop systems, private branch exchanges (PBX) and handsets. Mobile (also known as 'cellular') and paging networks also have switching systems at their core, linked to a network of base stations, and ending with handsets or pagers. Data networks require more sophisticated cable and transmission equipment than voice telephony.

During the 1980s, most of China's equipment needs were satisfied by imports, supported by soft loans made by European governments. In an effort to build a more sustainable domestic equipment manufacturing base, China encouraged foreign equipment vendors to set up joint ventures (JVs) with Chinese companies. At the same time, it developed its own domestic manufacturing industry. With the reduction in soft loans following the Tiananmen Square incident, the proportion of equipment imported fell, replaced primarily by JV output (Exhibit 4). As its domestic industry developed, China began to export telecom equipment to a variety of countries. By 1995, it was running a trade surplus in telecom and office equipment (Exhibits 5 and 6).

The second part of the telecom market is the provision of services over the network. In China, operators typically plan and construct new networks, and then operate, service, and market the services to customers. Chinese operators derived the bulk of their income from up-front connection charges, which were very high relative to other countries. Thereafter, fees for telephone usage were very low, even in mobile telephony. During the early 1990s, the cost of a handset and connection to the mobile network was as high as $4,000, while it cost 5 cents per minute to use. This tariff structure allowed the costs of network construction to be covered very quickly, while services themselves were charged at the very low marginal cost, without extracting any consumer surplus from users. However, services provided over the network were not as advanced as those in industrialised countries, nor as advanced as the installed technology would allow. Relia-

EXHIBIT 4 Central Office Switches Installed 1990–1995
(Thousand lines)

	1990	1991	1992	1993	1994	1995
Imports	1,300	2,090	3,000	5,500	5,300	3,000
Joint Ventures	500	800	1,800	5,400	9,900	13,600
Locally Produced	0	0	250	1,000	2,400	3,500
TOTAL	**1,800**	**2,890**	**5,050**	**11,900**	**17,600**	**20,200**

Source: *The Chinese Telecommunications Market*, MDIS, 1996.

EXHIBIT 5 China's Exports and Imports of Office Machines and Telecom Equipment

	1992	1993	1994	1995
Exports ($ million)	6,344	6,528	10,023	14,506
Share of World Exports	1.8%	1.7%	2.1%	2.4%
Imports ($ million)	6,380	9,175	11,796	14,352
Share of World Imports	1.8%	2.4%	2.5%	2.4%
Sector Trade Surplus/(Deficit) ($ million)	(36)	(2,647)	(1,773)	154

Source: *World Trade Organisation Annual Report 1996* (more detailed breakdown not available).

EXHIBIT 6 Major Destinations of Chinese Telecommunications Equipment Exports
($ thousands)

	1988	1989	1990	1991	1992	1993
Hong Kong	154,512	258,703	464,017	—	1,339,312	1,641,882
Japan	8,120	18,546	28,766	—	166,070	327,520
USA	11,040	18,127	31,494	—	83,446	113,309
Singapore	1,310	4,808	8,841	—	35,379	44,329
South Korea	—	—	—	—	14,366	31,570
Malaysia	175	378	297	—	12,751	23,018
Germany	1,345	2,238	3,559	—	10,787	13,849
CIS/USSR	65	15,272	40,016	—	16,818	14,581
Greece	26	8	145	—	202	13,411
France	437	286	1,279	—	2,182	7,290
Total (World)	**233,010**	**360,034**	**646,285**	**—**	**1,768,394**	**2,332,125**

Source: *Almanac of China's Foreign Economic Relations & Trade (1990/1, 1991/2, 1994/5).*

bility and servicing of networks was also poor. In 1997, foreign companies remained strictly prohibited from operating networks, a result of the belief of the Chinese government that telecommunications is crucial to national security. However, they were involved in the construction and operation of networks through agreements with certain Chinese operators, who were keen to receive both foreign advice and, more importantly, capital.

China's Telecommunications Policy Community

There were a number of state bodies involved in the formation and execution of telecom policy in China (Exhibit 7).

- *The State Council*. At the top of the pyramid, in charge of overall policy direction, was the State Council, effectively China's cabinet. It was chaired by the Premier and comprised all the Vice-Premiers, and the heads of Ministries and State Commissions. It approved all the laws and administrative measures, as well as resolving interministerial disputes that could not be resolved lower down the hierarchy. Attached to the State Council, on an ad hoc basis, were "Leading Groups". These were subcommittees that reported to the State Council on matters of specific interest. Their formation was a sign of intense high-level interest in a particular sector or area of policy, and often led to a significant change in policy.
- *State Commissions*. Below the State Council were nine State Commissions that dealt with issues involving a number of ministries. The most important economic commission was the State Planning Commission (SPC), which was responsible for Five Year Plans, and which directed and co-ordinated economic,

EXHIBIT 7 Chinese Telecommunications Industry Policy Community (1997)

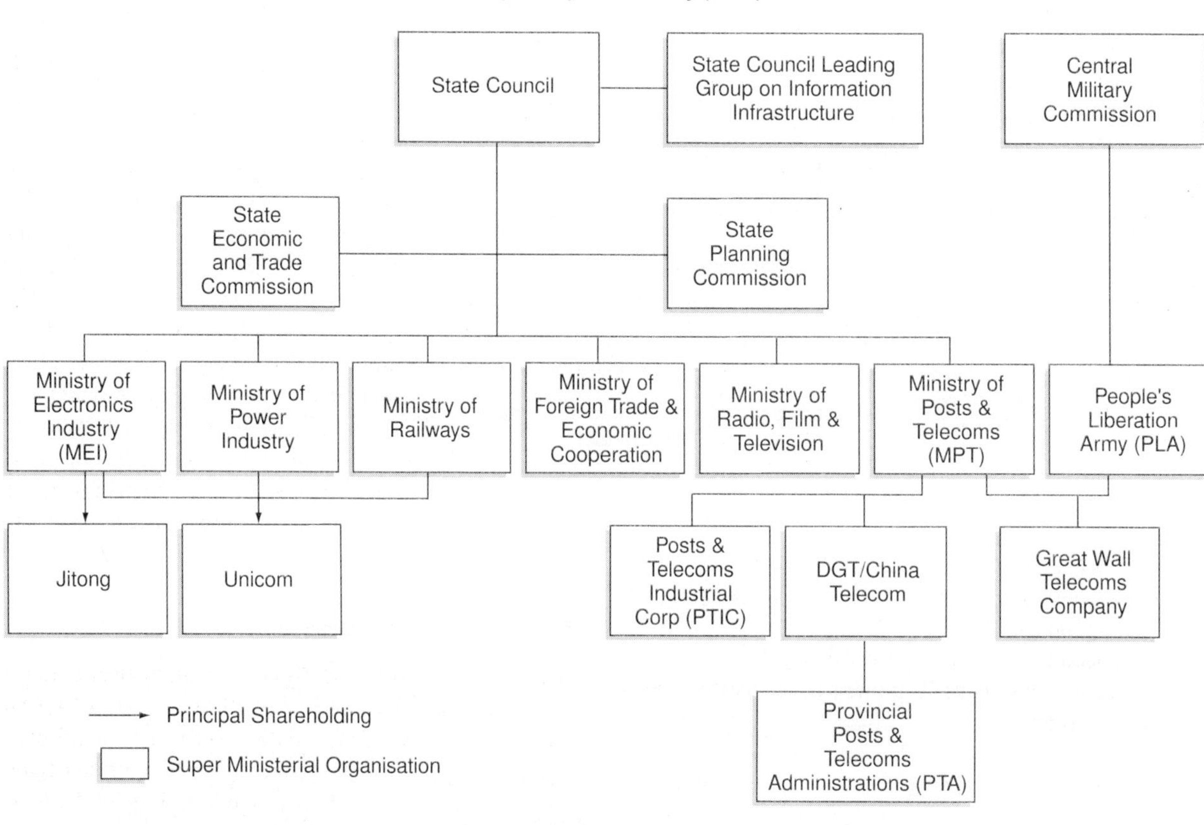

Source: Batey Burn & Co, Ltd, Beijing.

technological, and regional development. Most foreign investments larger than $30 million had to be approved by the SPC. The State Economic and Trade Commission (SETC) resolved interministerial conflicts in plan implementation through the setting of budgets and funding levels.

- *The Ministry of Posts & Telecommunications (MPT)*. The MPT historically held primary responsibility for all aspects of the management of China's public telecom network, including planning, construction, operation, and regulation. The MPT was also involved in equipment manufacture through the China Posts & Telecoms Industrial Corporation (PTIC) and other manufacturing subsidiaries. In the mid-1990s, the MPT employed 1.2 million people, about half of whom were involved in telecoms.
- *Posts & Telecom Administrations (PTAs)*. The MPT had a hierarchy of provincial and lower-level units to carry out its functions. At the provincial level these were called Posts & Telecom Administrations and at city and county level, Posts & Telecom Bureaux (PTBs). Although the MPT was highly centralised historically, its control over its branches was weakened with the modernisation and growth of the telecoms network.
- *The Ministry of the Electronics Industry (MEI)*. Until 1993, the MEI was part of the Ministry of Machine Building and Electronics Industries (MMEI). It was responsible for China's manufacture and development of electronic equipment, including telecom equipment. It was effectively the holding company of a collection of over 100 state-owned factories and JVs with foreign companies.
- *The People's Liberation Army (PLA)*. In the 1990s, the PLA was an emerging player in China's telecom market. It held control over much of the radio spec-

trum and operated its own extensive fixed and mobile private network.[1] The PLA used its substantial political power to expand its commercial telephony activities: it reported to the Central Military Commission, a Party body, which had near-equal status to the State Council.

- *The Ministry of Radio, Film, and Television (MRFT).* During the early 1990s, the MRFT began building its own cable TV network, using similar cable technologies to those employed in telephony, allowing the possibility of offering voice telephony services to its consumers. At the same time, PTAs allowed local cable TV companies to use telecom networks to transmit cable TV. The State Council subsequently encouraged the convergence of the two networks, although, as of 1997, it was not clear how this convergence would occur.
- *The Ministry of Foreign Trade and Economic Cooperation (MOFTEC).* MOFTEC worked closely with the State Council in the creation and execution of foreign trade policy. Through its power of approval over foreign investment in China, including JVs, it influenced the amount of trade being done with different countries, using its powers as an instrument of foreign policy.
- *Other Ministries.* From 1976, a number of other ministries and state organisations were allowed to set up their own private networks, which came to represent a large proportion of overall network capacity. These ministries included the Ministries of Railways, Electric Power, Coal, Water Resources, Aerospace as well as some banks and airlines.

Telecommunications Policy in the Deng Reform Era

Deng's economic reform policies in the 1980s were, for the Chinese, a very new approach to modernisation. For the first time, technology was seen as critical to achieving effective modernisation. The Chinese leadership recognised the country's backwardness in comparison to other countries, and decided to reduce the disparity by the absorption of foreign technology. This change in view arose partly from a recognition of the flaws in Maoist approaches to modernisation exhibited in the Great Leap Forward, but was reinforced by the exposure of the PLA's technological backwardness in the 1978–79 border war with Vietnam. In 1979, Deng's visit to the United States signalled the start of China's policy of greater openness to Western trade, technology and ideas.

Technology's place at the centre of China's modernisation increased telecom's importance. Indeed, Deng placed the development of the telecom infrastructure ahead of the "Four Modernisations"—industry, agriculture, national defence, and science. In addition, the "Open Door" policy, which encouraged foreign investment in China, itself promoted the development of the telecom infrastructure through the need to exchange information with the outside world. Finally, as government authority began to decentralise during the reforms, the Chinese leaders came to see an advanced telecom infrastructure as a means of increasing their control over the periphery through better gathering and dissemination of information.

Early Reforms and Modernisation: 1978–1993

The Chinese government employed a number of policies throughout the 1980s and early 1990s, as part of a first phase of telecom reform. With a shift in national economic policy in 1993, a second phase of reforms began. As is typical in Chinese policy making, some of the policies emanated from the central government bodies such as the State Planning Commission, while others were driven by pressure from different ministries pursuing their own interests.

Private network development

The earliest force to modernise China's telecom networks, in fact, came before the start of the Open Door policy, and from outside the normal policy-making domain. In 1976, a number of ministries and the PLA were allowed by the State Council to develop private telecom networks, to redress the poor quality of services they received from the MPT. In 1993, it was estimated that these networks made up 40 percent of China's total network capacity. In the late 1980s, the MPT, which only had responsibility for public networks, protested (unsuccessfully) against the building of further private networks, arguing that it was able to provide adequate services for all users. In spite of this, the State Council still allowed some ministries to continue private network development. The parallel development of private networks hastened China's telecom modernisation, but in the 1990s it

[1] A "private" network is a network controlled and operated by a body for its private use, i.e., not for the public.

also helped to break the MPT's monopoly when the ministries sought to offer their spare capacity to the public.

Financial reforms

The first reforms initiated by the State Council in the early 1980s addressed one of the biggest challenges posed by reform: the need to finance such a rapid expansion of the infrastructure. The Seventh Five Year Plan in 1985 projected a total investment to the Year 2000 of $21.7 billion, but as subsequent plans became more ambitious, independent estimates of the total investment required rose as high as $100 billion for the period 1994–2000 (total annual inflows of FDI to China in the mid-1990s were about $50 billion). The Chinese government could not be relied on to fund new investment, so a new system for funding telecom investment was introduced: one-third of investment funds came from the installment fee; one-third came from depreciation with a high rate of 16 percent; one-third came in the form of domestic and foreign loans. Only 100 million yuan per year came in the form of government grants. At the same time, responsibility for funding shifted down to the provincial PTAs. The aim was to make PTAs and local network development self-financing.

In the 1990s, the development of mobile and paging networks came to provide cashflow to finance fixed network expansion. In spite of high handset and connection costs, mobile telephony grew rapidly, creating a rich source of additional funds for the PTAs. The other source of finance was from foreign companies. This was virtually all in the form of soft loans, export credits, and vendor finance, as foreigners were strictly prohibited from holding equity or making loans to Chinese telecom operators. Until 1995, the Chinese government was able to fund the expansion of the network from these sources, although it was uncertain how long this situation could continue.

The advent of foreign involvement in equipment manufacture

Although imports provided for the bulk of China's equipment needs in the 1980s, the government encouraged the growth of its domestic manufacturing base through JVs with foreign companies. After some unsuccessful approaches to foreign companies in 1979, PTIC concluded an agreement with ITT Belgium (later part of Alcatel) to form a switch and integrated circuit (IC) factory called Shanghai Bell, China's first telecom joint venture. Two more switch/IC JVs were set up in the 1980s, with Siemens and NEC, as well as a handful of other JVs in other technologies.

The decentralisation of MPT responsibilities during the 1980s

In the early phases of telecom modernisation, the State Council maintained the MPT's de facto responsibility for planning, development, and management of the national public telecom network. But the leadership realised that with their planned expansion of the network, the financial and managerial burden on the MPT would be too great if it retained direct responsibility for both local and national networks. Therefore, they encouraged PTAs to become self-financing and to take control of local network development. PTAs retained more of their earnings that hitherto had been taken in tax or passed up to the MPT. They were also allowed to charge for installation and, later, raise the rates charged for calls. Installation fees, which ranged from $250–$750 per line, came to contribute significantly to network investment. Finally, PTAs were encouraged to seek partnerships with local government bodies and other local investors, linking network development with broader infrastructure investments. In the 1990s, PTAs grew their links with provincial and local governments, and lines of authority and allegiance started to run horizontally rather than vertically.

The reforms' overall effect was to give the PTAs in wealthier areas, such as Guangdong and Shanghai, growing financial autonomy from the MPT. Financial autonomy led to broader managerial autonomy. The richer PTAs began introducing new technologies and services, sometimes ahead of the MPT approval, and forging their own alliances with foreign companies. Foreign involvement came mostly through equipment supply and network construction, but occasionally involved "consulting" to assist in network operations, an MPT ban notwithstanding. PTAs became the pioneers of new technologies and approaches.

Despite its decentralisation during the 1980s, the MPT maintained a moderate level of control over the PTAs, as well as retaining a number of its own responsibilities. It was first charged with the development of the national public network. It developed international and intercity trunk networks (Exhibits 8 and 9), using fibre-optic cable, microwave, and satellite links. It also controlled international connections and traffic, although for some time it was denied access to receipts from international calls by the Ministry of Finance. Second, the MPT possessed a broad regulatory mandate, setting technological standards and, in tandem with other state bodies, controlling pricing in local networks and controlling PTA access to foreign exchange. Third, it redistributed funds from the richer to the poorer PTAs, and in so doing, be-

EXHIBIT 8 China's International Fibre Optic Links (1997–present & planned)

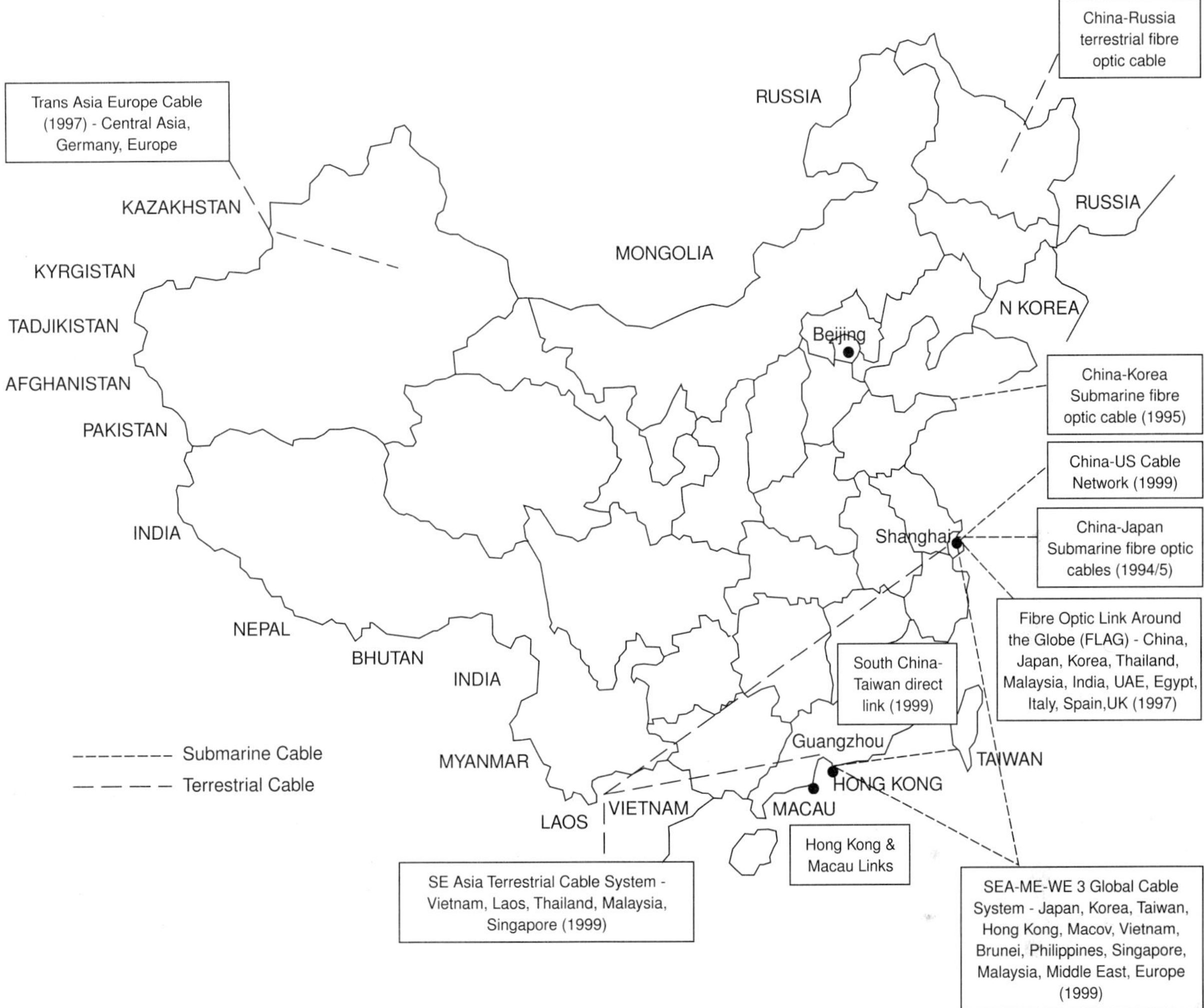

Source: The Chinese Telecommunications Market, MDIS, 1996; Press Reports.

came involved more intimately in the poorer networks' development. Finally, it retained and developed its manufacturing interests, forging alliances with foreign companies and increasing its income.

The Emerging Policy Environment: 1993–1997

The end of the MPT's monopoly: Jitong and Unicom The second phase of telecom reform and modernisation began in 1993. In December, the State Council licensed two new telecommunications operators, called Jitong and Unicom, to offer respectively data and voice telecom services. In the preceding years, the State Council had been pressurised by a coalition of ministries, led by the Ministry of the Electronics Industry (MEI), to allow them to set up new national data and voice networks, using their private network capacity. These ministries were keen to gain a share of the lucrative telecom operation market, but they also argued to the State Council that the creation of a second network would provide a number of benefits to China: the new data network would provide the leadership with a reliable information source in the

EXHIBIT 9 China's New Trunk Network for Completion During the Ninth Five-Year Plan

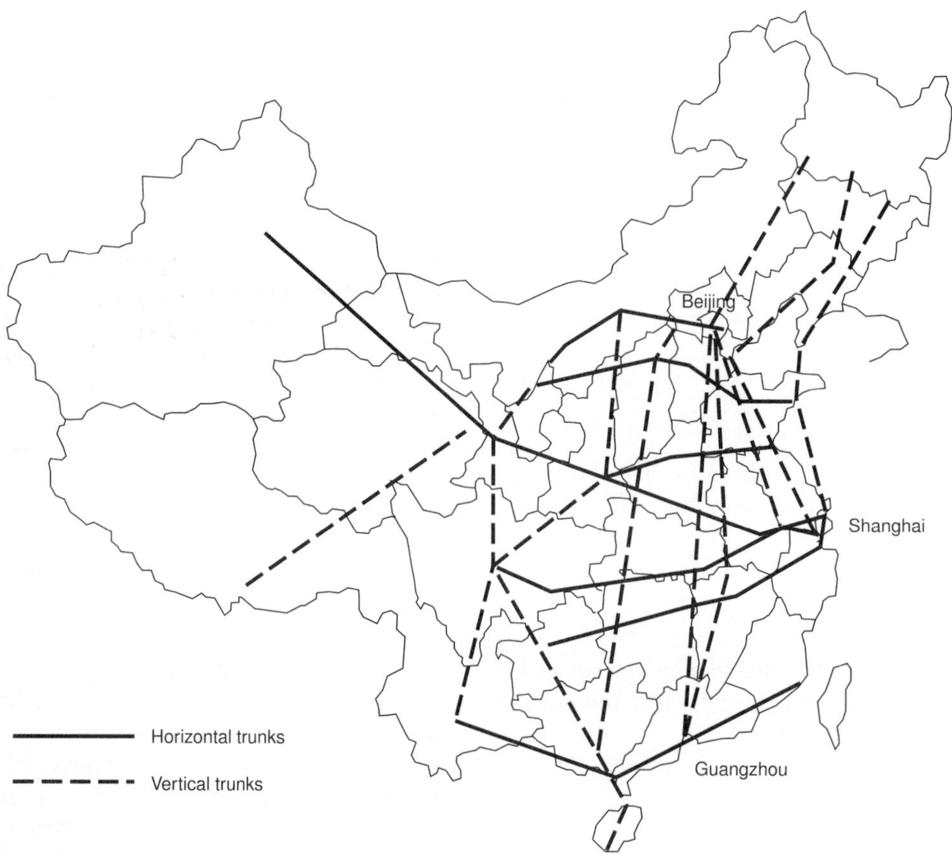

Source: *The Chinese Telecommunications Market,* MDIS, 1996.

increasingly fragmented economy; data services such as electronic payments would fuel economic growth; the voice network would add unused private capacity, and provide a competitive spur to the MPT.

In 1994, the new operators were finally launched with great fanfare and ambitious targets for the future (Exhibit 10). Unicom planned to attack the MPT's monopoly in voice telephony, while Jitong aimed to build the Chinese equivalent of the Information Superhighway, called the "Golden Projects" (Exhibit 11). Unicom was backed by the three sponsoring ministries plus four "Red Chips"[2] and a range of companies linked to ministries and provincial governments, while Jitong was held by MEI-controlled factories (Exhibit 12). Unicom's structure was particularly unusual: each shareholder was a "branch" of the company, and was allocated an area of the country in which it could develop telecom services, using Unicom as the licensed operator. While Unicom retained central control over areas such as standards, it devolved some power to its "branches," which on occasions led to branches overstepping their authority or financial limits, causing conflicts with the centre.

The two companies energetically set about finding foreign partners to help facilitate and fund their expansion. Unicom (and its shareholders) was particularly aggressive, signing 43 Memoranda of Understanding (MOUs) with foreign telecom firms in its first year. A number of these were later converted into joint ventures, most to

[2]"Red Chips" were Chinese conglomerates with investments in a wide range of industries. The Red Chips involved in Unicom were CITIC, China Merchants, China Everbright, and China Resources.

EXHIBIT 10 Unicom's Targets at Its Launch

Objectives for the Year 2000

10% of China's long distance telephone traffic

30% of China's mobile telephone traffic, including services in over 100 cities

Installation of 12 million lines (i.e., an addition of 40% on 1993 capacity)

Provision of international services

Investment of Rmb 300 billion ($34.5 billion) in 1994-2000

Further Objectives

2005:	Full national network
2010:	One of the world's largest telecom operators

From a speech by Zhao Weichen, first Chairman of Unicom, at the company's launch, July 1994.
Sources: *Business China, Far Eastern Economic Review.*

construct mobile networks. Although foreign ownership of operators was strictly prohibited, Unicom found a way around the ban by promising the partner a share in the profit stream from operation. At the same time, Unicom demanded large injections of capital from its foreign partners, sometimes demanding payment even before the deal had been closed.

Contrary to Unicom's grand ambitions, its first two years were a big disappointment. By the end of 1996 it had signed up only 60,000 mobile subscribers in 18 cities, well below its targets. It had become plagued by disagreements between its shareholders, many of whom had aims that diverged from that of Unicom itself. It had three chairmen in its first two years and staff turnover was high. The company soon acquired a reputation with foreign companies for being unprofessional and poorly managed. Unicom also faced fierce competition from the MPT and its PTAs, which employed predatory pricing and resisted Unicom's requests for connectivity to their networks. The only real success Unicom had was as a competitive spur to the MPT: as a result of its presence in certain cities, mobile prices dropped considerably, and MPT GSM networks were rapidly constructed. By 1997, the company was at last making some progress: an interagency group set up by the State Commissions was studying the company's problems and making recommendations to the State Council on how to improve both the company's external environment and internal situation. This improvement was also helped by the arrival of a new chief executive, Mme Li Huifen, who was politically well connected, and by a mediation process managed by the State Commissions to resolve disputes with PTAs. Unicom was unlikely in the near term to pose a major threat to the dominant MPT as a second carrier, but many believed that it would continue to exist and grow under the tutelage of the State Council.

Similarly, Jitong failed to live up to the perhaps oversold aspirations at its launch. The MEI focused its attention more on Unicom than Jitong, leaving the latter with little political power and a weak management structure. In addition, delays in rolling out the Golden Bridge project, intended as the platform for other ministries' and institutions' networks, led many of these organisations to set up their own networks, leaving Jitong with little to do. In 1997, the only on-going revenue source was the internet services offered over the Golden Bridge network. Some other projects remained under development. The company's potential as a profit generator remained unproven.

The emergence of the PLA

During the early 1990s, the People's Liberation Army also began to move into the telecom industry. This was part of a broader move to convert much of the military-industrial complex to civilian production, and use the income generated to supplement the defence budget. With its control of significant sections of the radio spectrum, its first move was into paging networks, which work on a wide variety of frequencies. Paging networks were not viewed by the State Council as strategically sensitive, and the PLA was allowed to start operations. The PLA quickly became one of the biggest paging operators across the country and, by late 1996, was establishing its first national paging network, based on its strength in the South-West.

The PLA started to move into cellular telephony. It formed a joint venture with the MPT, called Great Wall Communications, which signed a series of deals with foreign telecom companies to set up cellular networks, using a U.S. digital standard called CDMA. Like Unicom, its partnerships were on the edge of the law, allowing the foreign party to share in the revenues through "consultancy" fees while Great Wall remained the legal operator. In early 1997, Great Wall still awaited an operator's license, but with the MPT's support and its huge political clout, it was likely that it would soon be China's third telecom operator.

EXHIBIT 11 Jitong's Planned "Golden Projects"

Project	Objective	Bodies Involved
Golden Bridge	National public backbone network and international interface to transmit data, voice, image, and multimedia information	MEI State Information Centre Jitong Co.
Golden Customs	Foreign trade tax network, including currency settlement, domestic returns and quota management system. EDI platform, statistical database	MOFTEC Customs Department Jitong
Golden Card	Electronic financial transaction system and information service for credit cards. Aim for 200m credit cards in use within 10 years	People's Bank of China MEI, Ministry of Internal Trade Great Wall Computer Co
Golden Sea	N-ISDN data network linking top government leaders with other CCP institutions and organisations	People's Bank of China State Statistical Bureau State Information Centre
Golden Macro	State economic and policy support system. Database including statistical, economic, industrial, tax, price, investment, resource, capital information	China Export-Import Bank Ministry of Finance State Information Centre
Golden Tax	Create computerised links between work units and banks to facilitate paperless tax accounting. Introduction of Smart Cards for payment & tax	Ministry of Finance, MEI National Taxation Bureau Great Wall Computer Co
Golden Intelligence	Network linking higher education institutions to allow all teachers and researchers to exchange information and ideas	State Education Commission
Golden Enterprise	Enterprise target and quota system, national enterprise, and product database to supply macroeconomic and demand and supply data	State Economic and Trade Commission
Golden Agriculture	Agricultural supervisory, calculation and forecasting system to collect and provide trend data on agriculture	Ministry of Agriculture
Golden Health	Network linking 500 largest hospitals to distribute and facilitate information exchange within the Chinese health service	Ministry of Health
Golden Information	The development of the national statistical and targeting network into a real-time network	State Statistical Bureau
Golden Housing	Real estate information network linking banks, developer, government, and property agents	
Golden Cellular	Production and marketing of cellular equipment, and the establishment of national roaming standards and systems	MEI
Golden Switch	Development of Chinese domestic telecom switch manufacturing capabilities	MEI MPT

Source: Harvard Business School, The Hong Kong University of Science & Technology; *China's Golden Projects: Reengineering the National Economy*, 1996.

The split of the MPT and China Telecom

With the licensing of a second operator, the State Council saw the need to reform the structure of the MPT and split its commercial activities from its regulatory ones. Accordingly, it created the Directorate General of Telecommunications (DGT), also known as China Telecom, to be responsible for the construction and operation of networks, while the MPT retained its regulatory role. In reality, this split was not effective in creating a level playing field for competition. China Telecom's headquarters remained in the same building as the MPT in Beijing, and many staff had roles in both organisations. Unicom was given little protection against discrimination by PTAs. Nevertheless, the reform was

EXHIBIT 12 Ownership of Jitong and Unicom (Liantong)

Jitong's Shareholders	Unicom's Shareholders
China Electronic Appliance Corp	Ministry of Electronics Industry
China Electronic Leasing	Ministry of Power Industry
China Electronic System Engineering Group	Ministry of Railways
China International Trust & Investment Corp	China International Trust & Investment Corp
China National Electronic Device Industry Corp	China Resources Holdings
China Tong Guang Electronics Corp	China Everbright Group
China Zhenhua Electronic Industry Corp	Huaneng Group (Ministry of Power)
MEI 1st, 7th, 34th and 54th Research Institutes	China Merchants Group (Ministry of Communications)
Beijing Economic Development & Investment Corp	China National Technology Import-Export Corp (MOFTEC)
Beijing Kangxun Electronic Co	China National Chemical Import-Export Corp (MOFTEC)
Beijing Wire Communications Plant	Shanghai Scientific & Technology Investment Corp (MOFTEC)
Tianjin Communications & Broadcast Co	FOTIC (MOFTEC)
Tianjin Optical & Electronic Communications Co	Catch Communications Group (Beijing Municipal Government)
Changzhou Electronics Development Corp	Dalian Vastone Telecom and Cable
Nanjing Radio Factory	Fujian Provincial Trade Centre Group
Wuhan Zhongyang Radio Factory	Unicom Guangzhou Branch
Dongguan Tongpai Telecommunication Industry Co	
Guangzhou United Telecommunications Corp	
Shenzhen Guoye Trade Co	
Shenzhen Sangda Communications United Corp	
Zhuhai Dongda Stockholding Group	

Note: Most of Jitong's shareholders were subsidiaries of the Ministry of Electronics Industry. Names/acronyms in brackets indicate the body's controlling ministry.
Source: *Business China.*

seen as symbolic in paving the way for a more open telecom sector.

The rush into manufacturing joint ventures

Around 1993, a large number of telecom equipment manufacturing JVs were set up. This was caused partly by a reduction in soft loans funding imports, but also by a desire of the Chinese government to increase the transfer of foreign technology via JVs. In 1989, the State Council issued a directive limiting the approved list of switch suppliers to just the three that had set up switch/IC joint ventures. Foreign vendors believed that future sales success would come from creating such JVs, by winning favours with the government and *guanxi* at a provincial level. Between 1992 and 1996, more than 70 joint ventures were set up in telecommunications, some with the MPT and others with the MEI. Exhibits 13 and 14 show the investments, employees, revenues, and approximate market shares of the major foreign equipment vendors.

At the same time, in the equipment manufacture market, there appeared to be a move to consolidate China's equipment industry, and push back against further penetration of the market by foreign equipment vendors. During the preceding decade, China had transferred many technologies from foreign vendors, and had learned to manufacture some moderately advanced technologies domestically. The leading firms were Great Dragon, a grouping of MEI factories, and Huamei, a privately owned manufacturer in Guangdong, which, unusually, employed expatriates to help in its development. These firms' products did not pose an overwhelming threat to foreign vendors, but were strong in the poorer provinces, dragging the market price down. It was the stated aim of the government, however, that Chinese firms should take an increasing share of the market.

EXHIBIT 13 Key China Statistics of Major Foreign Vendors (Approximate)

	Investment in China to 1997 ($ million)	Employees in China (1997)	China Revenues ($ million)				
			1992	1993	1994	1995	1996
Motorola	480	6,000	400	1,400	2,500	3,200	—
Alcatel	—	—	—	1,200	1,300	2,000	2,000
Siemens	300	8,500	—	—	1,000	1,300	1,800
Ericsson	500	3,000	—	—	400	1,000	1,300
NEC	500	2300	—	—	—	1,000	—
AT&T/Lucent	200	1500	250	500	—	—	—
Nortel	100	—	—	300	500	500	—

No figures available on Nokia or when indicated by a dash (–). Nokia is the other large foreign equipment vendor.

Note: All available figures are approximate, unaudited or estimates; they are intended to be indicative rather than exact. Some figures include Hong Kong business (Ericsson, Motorola), or nontelecom business (Motorola, Siemens, Alcatel, NEC).

Source: Press reports (figures usually provided by vendors themselves).

The possibility of further regulatory reform

Although the MPT remained the dominant force in 1997, there were numerous signs that further change to the balance of power in the industry might be on the way. There were hints that policy was being revised at the highest level, with the creation of a Leading Group on Information Infrastructure, headed by Vice-Premier Zou Jiahua, to consider options for the future shape of the telecom industry. One change reportedly being discussed was the complete removal from the MPT of its regulatory role, and the creation of a brand new body to regulate both telephony and broadcasting. There were intermittent reports in the Chinese press that "experiments" in foreign operation of data, and even voice networks, were taking place. In May 1997, the Unicom President, Li Huifen, claimed that the State Council had approved a pilot trial of a direct foreign investment in an operation joint venture through a minority stake. While the sector was still largely closed to foreign companies, change seemed to be on the way.

The future of Hongkong Telecom

As Hong Kong's transition to Chinese sovereignty on 1 July 1997 approached, speculation about the future of Hongkong Telecom (HKT), and the role it might play in China, mounted. The highly profitable company, which dominated Hong Kong's telecom market, and controlled a large proportion of international traffic entering China, was 59 percent owned by Britain's Cable & Wireless (C&W). It was widely believed that China would not tolerate foreign control of HKT when it came under Chinese rule. However, it seemed unlikely that any Chinese investor had the funds to buy HKT. In the early 1990s, a "Red Chip" company, Citic Pacific, built up a stake of 17 percent, but it later sold down its stake to 8 percent. In May 1997, China Everbright, another Red Chip, bought Citic Pacific's share in HKT. Everbright was owned by the State Council and held a 6 percent stake in Unicom. Then in June, C&W sold a 5.5 percent stake in HKT to China Telecom, and agreed to sell further stakes until the two companies held equal shares. In return, C&W would be the major investor in a Hong Kong-quoted arm of China Telecom. This could bring "unique access to the vast opportunities" of the Chinese market to C&W, according to Dick Brown, C&W's chief executive. MPT Minister Wu Jichuan commented. "Hongkong Telecom has a lot to offer China Telecom in terms of technology and personnel expertise, and China Telecom in turn has vast opportunities in China's telecommunications market to offer Hongkong Telecom and Cable & Wireless". The deal and C&W's fortunes in China were thought to have major implications for the future of foreign operators in China.

The Environment for Foreign Equipment Vendors in China

The creation and approval of a joint venture was a long and cumbersome process, which usually took well over

EXHIBIT 14 **Approximate Market Shares in Selected Markets**

Public Switching Systems

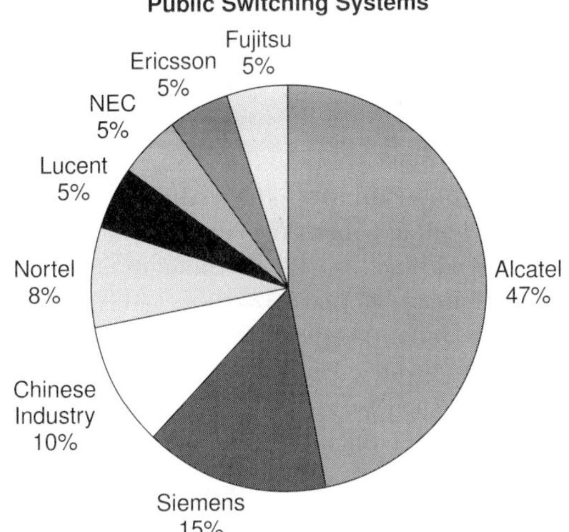

SDH Transmission Equipment

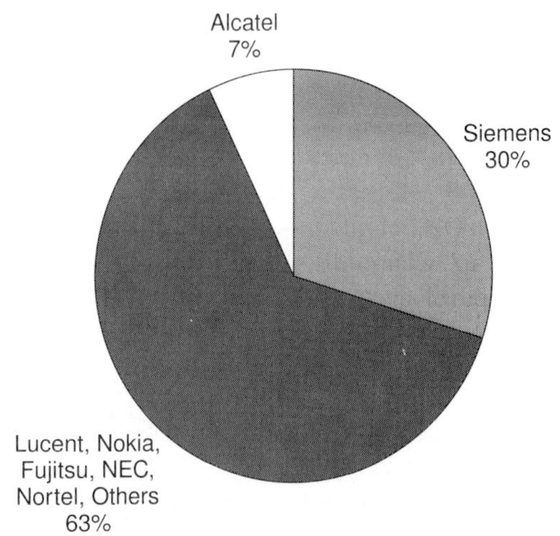

Digital Mobile Handsets

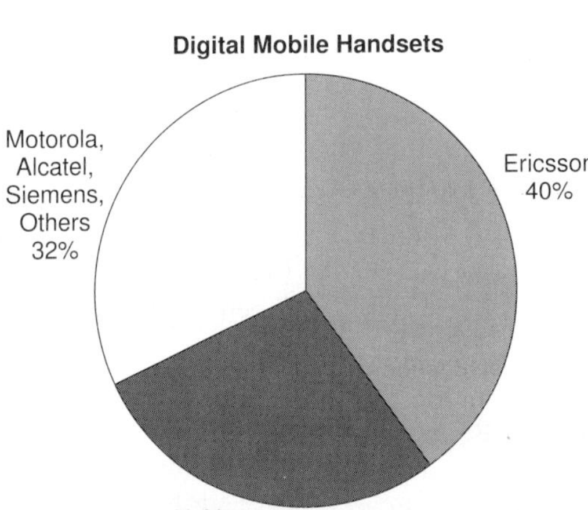

Analogue Handsets

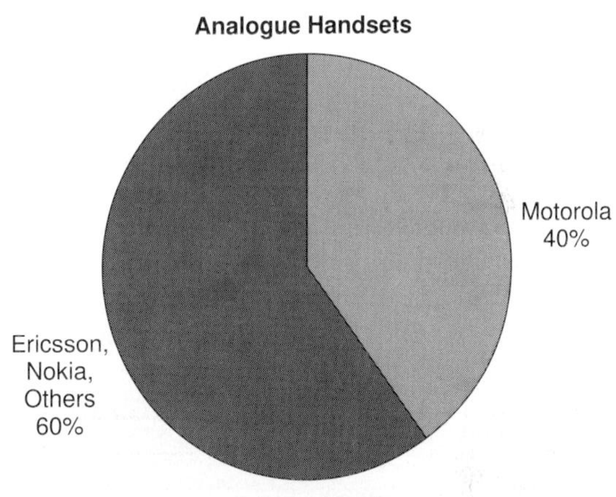

Mobile Infrastructure

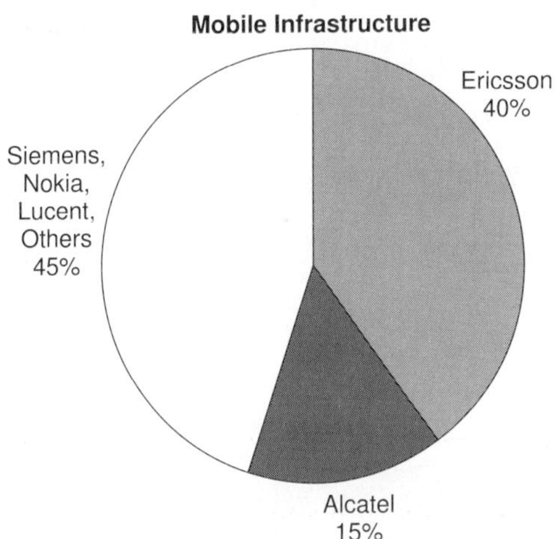

Pagers

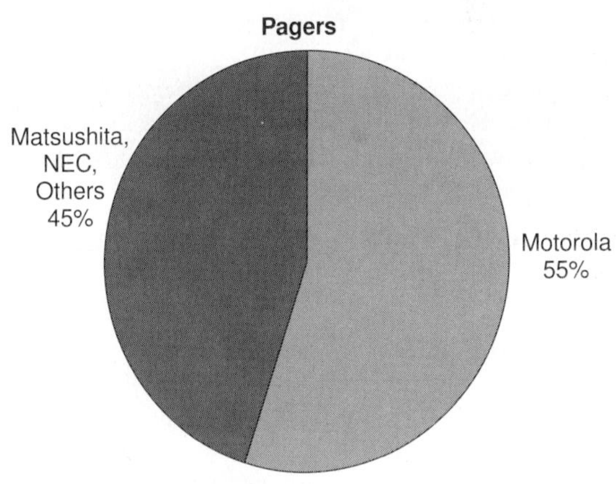

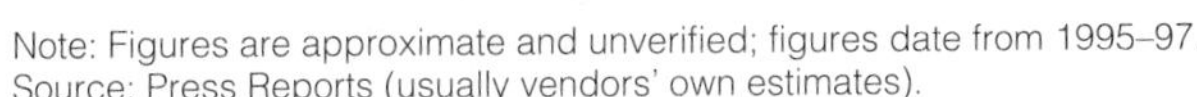
Note: Figures are approximate and unverified; figures date from 1995–97.
Source: Press Reports (usually vendors' own estimates).

a year. The first stage was the choice of a partner. Partners were chosen either for their capabilities, such as a skilled workforce or a good distribution network, or their political advantages, being either part of, or close to, the purchaser of the equipment. There was usually one Chinese partner; when there were more, they were included for their political connections. Negotiations with Chinese partners were usually tough. The Chinese tended to be formal, sticking to the agenda, but also adept at employing Machiavellian tactics to wring concessions from their prospective partner. The negotiation process was complicated by the elaborate regulatory approvals process (Exhibit 15). Although this was supposed to be purely administrative, and based on publicised regulations, in fact it was taken as an opportunity for the regulatory bodies, and often the Chinese partner, to renegotiate the terms.

Management of Joint Ventures

Joint ventures presented myriad challenges to foreign vendors. Problems varied from one case to another, but they fell into three main categories:

- *Diverging Views and Interests*. Very often partners had differing objectives that made managing the venture as one company difficult. The foreign company may have seen the JV as a means to gain market share and perhaps open the market to non-JV products, while the Chinese were often interested in the foreign company's technology and funds. The Chinese tended to have shorter payback periods than foreign companies and were unwilling to make heavy long-term investments.
- *Lack of Capabilities*. Foreign companies often had to cope with lower standards of quality, management skills, and sales and marketing skills in the Chinese partners, arising from the partners' lack of experience in a market economy. Sometimes even the Chinese partner's *guanxi,* often the reason for their choice as partner, was worse than expected and did not deliver the sales or relationships that had been hoped for.
- *Rising Costs*. In the 1990s, demand for well-educated staff, which were needed in high technology operations, rose, particularly in fast-growing regions. Competition in labour markets drove wages up dramatically, and companies found their staff being poached for inflated salaries. Sometimes, demands were made of the foreign partner to take on the Chinese firm's social costs, and perhaps surplus workers, again reflecting a divergence in the interests of the two parties.

These challenges were common to all sectors of industry, and made life very hard for foreign vendors. With a few rare exceptions, however, all foreign direct investment in China's telecom equipment market was through joint ventures, mainly as a result of Chinese government policy. Joint ventures became one of the biggest drains on profitability in the equipment vendor industry.

Taxation, Regulations, and Financial Inducements for Foreign Vendors

The Chinese government used a number of different fiscal measures to manage the market and foreign investment. As in many other emerging markets, these were focused on inducing the transfer of foreign technology and investment, and export-led growth. They fell into a number of categories:

- *Import Tariffs*. In 1997, China was not a member of the World Trade Organization (WTO), and had an average level of tariffs of 35.9 percent. During the year, this was reduced to 23 percent, the biggest single cut ever implemented by any country. It was planned they would fall further to improve the country's chances of accession to the WTO.
- *Inducements for Joint Ventures*. There were a number of fiscal inducements to set up joint ventures. JVs were tax-exempt until they earned a profit; thereafter they faced reduced corporate taxes. Imports of capital goods and raw materials for JVs were exempt of import duties. At the end of 1995, the government decided to withdraw this privilege, but the exemption was extended after a number of foreign firms claimed that their investment projects would be put in doubt by the changes.
- *Regional Tax Inducements*. In the early years of the reforms, China designated some special economic zones, free of various taxes, to encourage foreign investment, and as the reforms progressed, these zones grew. Growing regional disparities in the 1990s, however, caused the government to reverse these changes, and unify tax rates.

There were also a number of restrictions imposed by Western governments on exporting high technology to China and other communist countries during the Cold War. These were gradually eased during the late 1980s and 1990s, to the extent that most modern telecom products could be sold to, and manufactured in, China.

EXHIBIT 15 Foreign Joint Venture Approval Process

Examination & Approval Authorities

MOFTEC or COFTEC
Ministry of Posts & Telecoms
Local Planning Commission
Local Administration of Industry & Commerce

Business Registration AIC
Land Tax Bureau
Local Land Administration
Local Labour Bureau
Local Customs
Local Auditing

Project Proposal

Feasibility Study Report

Contract & Articles of Association

"20 Chops"

Letter of Intent or Memorandum of Understanding

Feasibility Study

Investigation ← *Negotiation* → *Registration*

Between 12 and 24 months

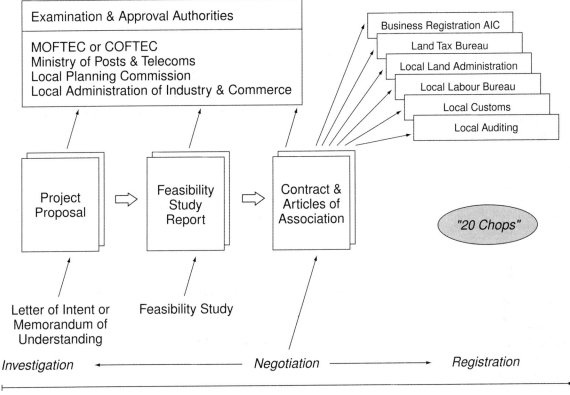

Source: Professor Phillippe Lasserre, Euro-Asia Centre, INSEAD

The Environment for Equipment Sales

The environment faced by foreign vendors was characterised by a number of features:

■ *A Huge, Decentralised Market.* China was divided into a sprawling hierarchy of provinces, cities, and counties, but even a county might have one million people. When soft loans funded most purchases, equipment and technology decisions were made at the provincial or national level, and market shares in different provinces soon became fixed. With the reduction in soft loans (in the case of mobile equipment, soft loans had never been available), lower-level units were required to generate their own funds for investment, and buying decisions were devolved accordingly. Vendors were increasingly faced with thousands of equipment purchasers.

■ *Competition.* With the influx of foreign vendors and the creation of numerous joint ventures, some market sectors were suffering from severe overcapacity. This was particularly the case in public switching, where capacity was reportedly about 30 million lines per annum with demand at only 20 million lines. Switch prices were at a third of the European level. The whole market was so competitive that new products could expect to command prices at least 20–30 percent less than normal. In nascent sectors, meanwhile, there was a scramble by all the vendors to gain market share. The high level of competition demanded that the companies' sales forces play a more active role.

■ *Regulation of Technical Standards*. China's government used technical standards partly to ensure that network development took place with compatible technologies, but also to help manage the market. In 1989, the issuing of the "switch list" punished foreign firms that had not transferred IC technology, and regulations issued by the MPT in 1995 on technical standards often favoured the products of its own subsidiaries, such as PTIC.

■ *Political Markets*. Potential customers often expected vendors to offer inducements as a way of securing a contract. There were many stories circulating about under-the-table payments, employment of relatives and other sweeteners, and all vendors claimed to have lost deals on dubious grounds. However, it was considered acceptable for foreign vendors to send clients on "factory visits" or training in the home country, among other things, as a means of building the relationship.

■ *Interministerial Rivalry*. The licensing of a new operator in 1993 to rival the MPT caused some conflicts of interests for vendors. For a time, at least, the MPT was very sensitive about its suppliers selling to the new operator, Unicom, although most vendors managed to supply both. Dealing with this issue sensitively was important to maintain relationships.

■ *Influence of Foreign Politics*. If China was offended in some way by the actions or words of a vendor's government, the vendor's business could suffer considerably. Multinational companies able to assume multiple national identities attempted to avoid this problem by changing allegiances, but such tactics tended to be of limited use.

■ *Technology*. Chinese buyers were always impressed by high technology and well-known brands. Vendors were therefore able to sell sophisticated technology that was not necessarily required. By the same token, the Chinese tended to place little value on service, and expected vendors to carry this out for free, which was not common practice elsewhere.

The Environment for Foreign Network Operators in China

Unlike equipment vendors, in 1997, foreign operators were banned from any involvement in operation of networks. In spite of the ban, Unicom and later the PLA posed a challenge to this ban by inviting the involvement of foreign operators in the operation of their networks. The ban was circumvented by the formation of joint ventures between the foreign company and a "branch" of Unicom who would build the network and then offer "consultancy" to its legal operator, Unicom. Structures such as this were allowed to exist, although they tended to be unprofitable to the foreign partner due to Unicom's aggression in deal making and the extremely low level of tariffs. In addition, foreign operators had little effective control over operations.

In August 1997, Minister of Post and Telecommunications Wu Jichian stated in an interview that "conditions are not yet ripe" to open operations to foreign companies. In particular, companies would have to wait until 2010, when the posts and telecommunications operation were separated. "It could be even quicker," he added. The high costs of posts meant that the postal service in 1996 lost seven billion yuan; telecommunications services had to be universal. In 1996, telecommunication services showed profits of 10 billion yuan, after taking into account the 7 billion in losses, and was expected to earn 12 billion yuan in 1997. The state would not give the policy of high installation fees to foreign operators. "When we have developed the service to a certain level, then the policy will disappear, which will provide an equal basis for foreign competition."

Foreign companies hoped the market would open up before the turn of the century. Accordingly, a large number of operators were present in China, building contacts, lobbying the government, and waiting for an opening. They saw a number of different pressures acting to open up the sector, to both foreign and domestic operators. Some of these pressures were functional—they were a corollary of the stated aspirations of the Chinese policy makers, a necessary condition of the fulfillment of those ambitions. Other pressures were of a broader political nature—some internal and others external. It was the balance of these pressures which foreign companies were evaluating to try to predict the timing and nature of a future opening.

Functional Pressures

■ *The Need for Investment*. In the early 1990s, independent observers believed that China's ambitious telecom expansion plans could not be achieved with its existing sources of finance. They predicted a shortfall in funds of $3 billion–$7 billion per annum, which could only be met by foreign investment in network operation, either through loans, equity investments, or Build-Transfer-Operate (BTO) projects. In 1997, however, it seemed that the pressures for raising finance had eased and that

China would be able to generate enough finance internally. Nevertheless, many operators believed that, at some point, the rapid expansion would require some foreign investment in the sector.

■ *Network Operation and Marketing Skills*. While the Chinese were very competent in the construction of telecom networks, they placed less value on and were less competent at the service and operation of those networks. Chinese operators tended to buy the best telecom equipment available, and then be unable to use it to its full potential. This led to poorer quality customer service, and low exploitation of the revenue-generating potential of telecommunications. Some senior telecom officials acknowledged this in private, recognising the strength of foreign companies in providing high quality customer service. The desire to improve services had the potential to lead to increased involvement of foreign companies in the sector.

■ *New Technologies*. The rapid development of new technologies, such as callback and the internet, and the convergence of voice, data, and video technologies posed a challenge to the established order in China's telecom industry, and could perhaps open new avenues for foreign companies. Growth of the internet was being actively encouraged by the government, although it was also fearful of the "national security" implications. The development of new technologies was proceeding so quickly, however, that it threatened to run ahead of China's regulatory authorities, most of whom came from a traditional voice telephony background.

Internal Political Pressures

■ *Economic Growth*. One of the greatest threats to the stability of the country and the ruling regime was a slowdown in economic growth. The Chinese leaders were said to be "riding the tiger's back," existing on the sufferance of a population that demanded a constantly rising standard of living. If, as the government frequently stated, telecom modernisation was a vital engine of China's growth, then it needed to maintain the momentum of telecom growth, even if that required foreign involvement for functional reasons (such as those above).

■ *Unemployment and the Problem of State Owned Enterprises (SOEs)*. The other threat to the government's stability came from unemployment, particularly the potential for job losses in China's state-owned sector. China's economic growth was both driven by, and benefited, foreign-backed enterprises at the expense of the state sector. Despite efforts to encourage foreign companies to employ large numbers of former SOE employees, further foreign investment was likely to be detrimental to employment in the state sector. This pressure was likely to make an opening up to foreign investment *less* probable.

■ *Quality of Life*. As wealth rose and the population became more educated, demands for a higher quality of life were likely to increase. There was some evidence that a consumer culture was developing in China, through media such as television discussion programmes about consumer issues. If consumer pressure on the quality of telecom services rose significantly, China would probably be forced to invite foreigners, with their acknowledged expertise, to help raise standards, in the same way that it encouraged foreign transfers of technology.

■ *Bureaucratic Politics*. The experience of the Deng reform era had shown that the development of policy was as much about the interaction of bureaucratic interests as carefully planned changes in policy. Some changes resulting from their bureaucratic battles, such as the creation of Unicom, had opened up the sector and provided opportunities for foreign companies. Even though it seemed likely that there was significant support for further opening of the sector within parts of the bureaucracy, there were also large groups who would consider such an opening as a threat to their institutional interests. Thus, opinions in the summer of 1997 were being sought on the draft Telecommunications Law as one item of the Five Year Plan 1996–2000. The Law had been drafted by the MPT and was in the hands of the State Council. The ebb and flow of discussions and conflicts within the bureaucracy and the relative power of different interests would be a major determinant of future market opening.

■ *Centre–Local Relations*. China's economic growth had been achieved largely as a result of the decentralisation of economic power to the provincial and local level. The rising wealth of some provinces had allowed them to be more bold in pushing back the frontiers of what was acceptable in China. In the telecom sector, it was provinces such as Guangdong and Shanghai that were most commonly reported to be "experimenting" with foreign operation of networks. It was therefore likely that the relative power of these provinces would be a determinant of the speed and nature of the sector's opening. Militating against this was the need of the Chinese government to balance regional economic development. In the mid-1990s, the MPT was increasingly making efforts to balance regional development in telecommunications and redistribute revenues from rich to poor provinces.

■ *National Security.* While China's leaders encouraged the growth of telecom networks, including those carrying data or internet traffic for commercial reasons, they retained concerns about the potential threats to the country's "national security" from groups using networks to spread information criticizing the government. They also cited "national security" as the reason foreign companies were barred from operating networks. National security was likely to remain a key factor in the debate over telecom liberalisation in the future.

External Political Pressures

■ *World Trade Organisation Accession*. Although China had been seeking WTO membership for 11 years, by 1997 its desire to join had reached a peak, and talk was of membership by the end of the year. Unfortunately for China, in February 1997, agreement was reached by the WTO members for a broad liberalisation of telecom services. A part of this agreement was a set of conditions concerning the openness of members' markets that went far beyond the modest and largely superficial reforms China had so far put in place. It was possible that, if China became a member, it would be given some grace period to meet any obligations before full liberalisation would be required, as has been the case for some other Asian nations. However, it was also likely that the WTO would still demand significant reform of regulation, network and market access, and the level of competition before accession was approved. The outcome of these negotiations would be an important factor in determining market openness in the future.

■ *Hong Kong.* Hong Kong's transition to China on 1 July 1997 was viewed by foreigners as a litmus test for the future of both mainland China and Taiwan. A number of foreign companies also saw it as a means of entering the Chinese telecom market. It was believed that the existing operators in Hong Kong's recently deregulated telecom market would have a unique opportunity to enter China after the transition to Chinese rule via the wealthy neighbouring province, Guangdong. Their success in operating under Chinese rule and the experience of the Chinese in allowing them to do so was thought to be indicative of the future of foreign involvement in Chinese telecom operation. In addition, C&W's ability to use its stake in Hongkong Telecom to gain a foothold in China was seen as an indicator of China's openness to foreign operations.

Case 6–3

PaintCo Brasileira Ltda.

In the first 10 years since adopting an aggressive strategy of international expansion, PaintCo had developed into a budding world player in the highly competitive paint business, with operations extending from North America to Western Europe. However, it was becoming increasingly apparent to management that the future international growth of the company would have to occur in the emerging markets of developing economies. In 1994, 70 percent of PaintCo sales were in North America and 25 percent in Western Europe, and growth in both regions had leveled off. Outside NAFTA,[1] the South American market[2] seemed to promise greater than 10 percent growth well into the 21st century.

In December 1994, CEO Hugo Deimios assigned Pat Gato the task of establishing PaintCo's presence in South America. The initial objective was to find the best long-term prospects for the company in Brazil in terms of market segments, mode of entry, level of investment, and scope of operations. Pat had to keep in mind the corporate focus on decentralized entrepreneurial operations and assess possibilities for drawing on and contributing to the knowledge, skills, and competencies of other com-

---

This version of the PaintCo Brasileira case was prepared by professors José de la Torre at the Anderson School at UCLA and John Naman at the Katz School, University of Pittsburgh. It is based on an earlier case written by professors Bruce McKern (now at Mt. Eliza Business School, Melbourne, Australia) and John Naman both then at the Carnegie Bosch Institute, Carnegie Mellon University, in 1995. It was prepared for class discussion rather than to illustrate either effective or ineffective handling of an international management situation. The names of people and organizations and other identifying information have been disguised.

[1]The United States, Canada, and Mexico signed the North American Free Trade Agreement, or NAFTA, on December 17, 1992. The agreement progressively eliminated tariffs and nontariff barriers to trade in most goods; subjected trade in services to clear rules and principles while improving market access; established rules for foreign investment; strengthened protection of intellectual property rights; and created an effective dispute settlement mechanism. After each country completed its domestic approval and implementation procedures, the NAFTA entered into force on January 1, 1994.

[2]For PaintCo, the South American region comprised Argentina, Bolivia, Brazil, Chile, Colombia, Costa Rica, the Dominican Republic, Ecuador, El Salvador, Guatemala, Honduras, Nicaragua, Panama, Paraguay, Peru, Uruguay, and Venezuela. Mexico was considered to be part of the North American region.

EXHIBIT 1 Summary Financial Statements for PaintCo, Inc.

	1990	1991	1992	1993	1994
Income Statement					
Sales	$1,727	$1,818	$1,980	$2,433	$2,577
Cost of Goods Sold	1,093	1,063	1,094	1,422	1,467
Research and Development	104	113	121	146	160
Selling and Administration Costs	204	202	211	261	284
Depreciation	158	181	202	236	254
Before Tax Income	168	259	352	368	412
Federal and Foreign Taxes	81	121	166	172	186
Operating Income	87	138	186	196	226
Other Income (net)	3	1	6	9	6
Net Income	$ 90	$ 139	$ 192	$ 205	$ 232
Common Stock					
Earnings Per Share	$2.13	$2.87	$3.80	$4.28	$4.86
Dividends Per Share	0.85	1.26	1.82	2.22	2.63
Stock Price (high-low)	20-36	24-35	30-44	39-47	39-63
Balance Sheet					
Current Assets	$ 713	$ 756	$ 823	$ 990	$1,090
Net Property, Plant & Equipment	960	1,034	1,065	1,182	1,232
Other Assets	28	54	62	85	79
Total Assets	$1,701	$1,844	$1,950	$2,257	$2,401
Current Liabilities	$ 189	$ 211	$ 219	$ 309	$ 306
Other Liabilities	11	16	15	48	46
Long-Term Debt	49	47	44	75	100
Deferred Income Tax	37	44	50	85	85
Stockholders' Equity	1,415	1,526	1,622	1,740	1,864
Total Liabilities	$1,701	$1,844	$1,950	$2,257	$2,401

Note: All Income Statement and Balance Sheet figures are in $US millions.
Source: Company Annual Reports.

pany ventures. PaintCo's board of directors, which included the venture capitalists who had helped take the company public in the 1980s, could not be expected to approve large investments with uncertain prospects, but would accept some risk for well-justified plans. Exhibit 1 provides recent financial information on the company.

As Gato was unfamiliar with the current business climate in Brazil, PaintCo's CEO engaged an outside consultant to provide her with an overview report on local business conditions. Gato would then have to determine the best means of expansion into the Brazilian market. One possibility was to establish a wholly owned subsidiary. In some European countries, however, the company had licensed a local producer to supply local demand. Another possibility would be to investigate a joint venture with a Brazilian producer as a minority or majority partner. Gato realized that the future success of PaintCo's operations in Brazil and the rest of Latin America might well depend on the results of this first strategic entry into the region. Therefore, she felt that it would be best for PaintCo to approach the situation very carefully at this stage.

The International Paint Industry

The world paints and coatings market in the early 1990s amounted to approximately 13.5 billion liters per year, valued at over $US 50 billion.[3] Paints are surface coatings

[3]Most industry data were obtained from *The World Paint Industry 1992,* Lausanne: IMD.

EXHIBIT 2 Major Players in the International Paint Industry

Rank	Manufacturer	Headquarters	Segments*
1	ICI	UK	automotive refinish; can and coil coatings; powder; specialties
2	Sherwin-Williams	US	automotive refinish
3	PPG	US	automotive OEM; coil; specialties
4	BASF	W. Germany	automotive OEM; can; coil; specialties
5	Akzo-Nobel	Netherlands	automotive refinish; coil; specialties
6	Nippon	Japan	automotive OEM; coil; specialties
7	Courtlauds	UK	can; powder; specialties; marine, anticorrosion
8	Kansai	Japan	automotive OEM; coil
9	Du Pont	US	automotive OEM and refinish
10	PaintCo	US	automotive OEM and refinish; industrial

*Note: All major manufacturers were active in the architectural/decorative segment.
Source: *The World Paint Industry 1992,* IMD, p. 36 ff. and industry sources.

used for decorative, protective, and other special functions. The major market segments were architectural paints for buildings and homes (about 50 percent of world sales) and automotive coatings (11 percent of world sales). Minor segments included industrial coatings such as for coiled steel or aluminum (9 percent), tin and aluminum can coatings (3 percent), and powder coatings for appliances and outdoor metal surfaces (2 percent). Niche markets have been developed for special functions such as extreme heat and cold resistance, marine and aviation applications, reflective and fluorescent safety uses, nonstick coatings for frying pans, and advanced plastic product packaging. In general, the higher technology products offered multiple performance features that could command higher prices and profits. Also, most market segments required multiple products—such as primer and finish coats for automotive applications—and each of these subsegments may be served by different paint manufacturers.

Worldwide, there were approximately 10,000 paint producers operating mainly in their own domestic markets. International producers, numbering closer to 100, had been growing since 1980 by acquiring small domestic manufacturers. Internationalization has been driven by desire for growth, economic pressures to spread increasing R&D costs over larger volumes, and the demanding requirements of international manufacturers who were major customers of the paint companies. For example, global auto manufacturers required consistent technologies, benefits, and performance for paints throughout the world. Exhibit 2 lists the 10 major international paint manufacturers in 1995, and Exhibit 3 shows the typical cost structure for each of the major market segments.

Globalization of the Paint Business

As its major customers expanded worldwide and paint markets developed in other countries, PaintCo was compelled to look for growth outside the United States and Europe. Foreign competitors were also entering the U.S. market and reducing the potential for profit growth at home. Yet, despite this trend toward international competition, there remained important differences between countries in terms of climate, patterns of industrialization, cultural preferences, market and distribution systems, and government regulations. For these reasons, it was important to have a strong local marketing organization, as well as local product development and manufacturing operations in some cases, in order to succeed and achieve significant market share. PaintCo had to provide to its global customers the same degree of service and product responsiveness of a local firm, plus world-class quality, advanced technology, and continuous product improvement.

These technical challenges were not new to PaintCo. The company had built its success on fundamental research into the chemistry of dyes, pigments, and various media and delivery systems for product application. PaintCo's development laboratories in the United States, Canada, and England had a well-deserved reputation in the automobile, appliance, and electronics industries for imaginative developments of surface coatings carefully tailored to customers' needs. For example, PaintCo was one of the pioneers in the use of aqueous paint solutions and dispersions for industrial applications, which were of significant benefit in reducing toxic emissions from paint shops. In many of these applications, success against other

EXHIBIT 3 Average Manufacturing Cost Structure Per Segment (percentages)

Category	Decorative	Can Coating	Auto Refinish	Auto OEM	Coil	Powder
Raw Materials	40%	50%	30%	50%	55%	55%
Direct Labor Conversion	5	5	9	7	8	10
Indirect Mfg. + Depreciation	12	13	14	13	12	10
R&D & Technical Service	3	6	8	10	8	7
Logistics & Transport	4	3	5	3	4	5
Marketing & Selling	18	8	12	6	5	5
Overheads	8	7	9	8	6	6
Profits Before Tax	10	8	13	3	2	2
Ave. World Price ($US/liter)	3.00	2.00	6.50	4.50	6.00	4.50/kg
Market Share (liters)*	50%	3%	5%	6%	1%	2%

*Note: Market share for all other industrial uses is 33%.
Source: *The World Paint Industry 1992,* IMD, p. 34.

global competitors depended on devising coatings tailored to the customer's product and also on understanding the paint application process itself.[4] This often meant working with the customer from an early stage of the customer's product development process. Innovations developed in the U.S. or European market for a major customer could often be sold to that customer's affiliates in other countries, provided PaintCo could offer local support.

PaintCo's technical strength had initially been directed solely toward the industrial sectors (including the auto refinish market), but more recently a concerted effort was made to diversify into architectural and decorative applications. Success in this segment depended less on innovative R&D and more on marketing skills, an extensive distribution system, a strong brand, and an efficient production operation. Development of these consumer-oriented skills did not come easily to PaintCo, and it encountered fierce competition from the larger, entrenched firms. In the United States, where it was among the second tier of competitors, PaintCo advertised heavily, distributed widely through hardware stores, home centers and paint specialty dealers, and operated a number of color coordination services for retail customers.

In the North American market, the auto and industrial segments accounted for about 45 percent of PaintCo's volume and some 60 percent of its profits, whereas the decorative segments were 55 percent of volume and 40 percent of profits. In Europe the mix varied by country, but there was generally a stronger emphasis on the industrial segments.

With free trade between Canada and the United States, PaintCo had rationalized its manufacturing and supply operations across the border and placed them under U.S. control. Nonetheless, the company found it necessary to maintain a Canadian development center to deal with major customers there. Sales and marketing in Canada were managed with considerable autonomy. The gradual dismantling of any remaining trade barriers to the Mexican market under NAFTA, plus the growth of U.S. foreign investment in that country, encouraged the company to expand its coverage to Mexico beyond the current sales subsidiary. Management felt that the Brazilian experience may provide a useful template for future direct entry into Mexico.

PaintCo and Brazil

PaintCo had chosen Brazil as its first country for expansion in South America for important strategic reasons. First, Brazil was the largest country in Latin America, and it offered the greatest consumer market potential. Brazil was also the most industrialized country in the region, producing a wide range of manufactured goods from steel and chemicals, to aircraft and automobiles, and was an established exporter of many industrial products. This broad range of industrial and consumer manufacturers represented a large paint and coatings market. As an important producer of chemicals and minerals, Brazil also supplied

[4]In many applications the labor and capital costs associated with applying the paint were three to four times the cost of the coating material.

many primary and intermediate raw materials for the paint industry, such as titanium dioxide and zinc oxide from Du Pont's pigment plant in Uberaba, colored chrome pigments from Glasurit do Brasil, and certain clay extenders and synthetic resins from other suppliers.

Second, before market liberalization began in 1990, restrictions on the availability of import licenses were used as a means to control and limit imports, and served as a major barrier to imports from the United States. Now import licenses were used primarily for statistical purposes. The more open market represented an opportunity for efficient international producers, both in terms of exports to Brazil and direct investment into the country.

Direct investment had become more inviting since December 1991, when Brazil removed the 60 percent withholding tax applicable to foreign remittances of profits and dividends, leaving a flat rate withholding tax of 15 percent on such transfers. In addition, Central Bank regulations were altered in January 1992 to allow foreign enterprises to register reinvested profits as foreign capital at the exchange rate in effect at the time earnings were declared. This change addressed a frequent complaint of foreign investors that the typical three-month lapse between the declaration of earnings and the registration of reinvested capital resulted in substantial depreciation of the real value of the investments, particularly with hyperinflation rates of up to 50 percent per month. Most recently, President Fernando Henrique Cardoso's anti-inflation program, the Real Plan, sharply cut inflation to about 2 percent per month by December 1994, promoting economic growth and further encouraging investment. Exhibits 4 and 5 provide data on Brazil's economy and foreign investment by sector.

Third, the emerging free trade area in the southern cone of South America, MERCOSUR, offered a market of over 200 million people and both problems and opportunities. The following excerpt from a U.S. State Department report suggested that there could be reduced opportunities for exporters, offset by strategic incentives for direct investment, either in joint ventures or wholly owned subsidiaries.

> "In August 1990, Brazil, Argentina, Paraguay, and Uruguay jointly signed a treaty creating MERCOSUR and a target date for the partial elimination of internal market barriers to some 80 percent of goods by 1995. The United States has encouraged an open and GATT-consistent MERCOSUR, and concluded a trade and investment framework agreement in 1991, whereby the United States and the four member countries agreed to consult closely on trade and investment relations.
>
> "The effects that MERCOSUR might have on U.S. exporters and investors are still unclear. For some goods, such as autos, pharmaceuticals and textiles, complete tariff reduction is planned by 2005. However, the Treaty also provides for a Common External Tariff against imports across the four countries, to be fully implemented by 2005. A number of U.S. manufacturers with local operations are rationalizing their production facilities among the four countries and seeking opportunities arising from harmonization of tariffs, consumer codes and other laws. Others, particularly exporters who do not manufacture in any of the four countries, fear that possible "upward" harmonization of non-tariff barriers could restrict their access to the larger MERCOSUR market. Lingering problems concerning the coordination of macroeconomic policies, the creation of a common external tariff and the harmonization of widely different laws in a number of socioeconomic fields threaten to delay complete implementation of the MERCOSUR Agreement by its 1995 deadline. Brazil remains determined to complete the integration process."[5]

These conditions were driving PaintCo's customers such as automobile and appliance manufacturers to expand into Brazil. Since a key rule of business for PaintCo was to serve their customers wherever they went, and preferably to get there ahead of them, this factor was critical to the decision to expand into the Brazilian market.

Over the years, PaintCo had been exporting a moderate volume of specialty industrial products to an independent Brazilian distributor, Colorado Ltda. Increasing exports to this growing market, however, was a questionable solution to Gato's problem. PaintCo's existing plant capacity was earmarked for other markets in the U.S. and Europe, and any significant growth in the South American market would soon require new capacity.

Gato learned that its Brazilian distributor would resist larger volumes unless accompanied by increased discounts to compensate for the extra costs attributable to higher volume imports. The distributor's warehouse was nearing full capacity. Financing additional space and equipment would require a long-term contract with PaintCo. Furthermore, the complicated logistics for imports required the distributor to keep a large inventory that had high carrying costs. Occasional wildcat strikes by U.S. East Coast longshoremen protesting against containerized bulk cargo threatened the already long delivery cycles for U.S. products to Brazil, in turn resulting in higher inventory costs and the potential loss of any just-in-time customers such as auto plants.[6]

Early in January 1995, Pat Gato cut short a winter vacation and returned to her office to find the consultant's report and other data on Brazil waiting for her. These included some hard data on the growing Brazilian paint

---

[5]Adapted from *Economic Policy and Trade Practices: Brazil,* U.S. Department of State, July 1994.

[6]*The Wall Street Journal,* December 5, 1994, p. A11.

EXHIBIT 4 Brazil—Key Economic Indicators

	1991	1992	1993	1994[1]
Income, Production, & Employment				
GDP at Current Prices (billions of U.S. dollars)	410	417	456	474
Real GDP Growth (annual percent)	0.9	−0.8	4.1	4.0
Per Capita GDP (current $)	2,780	2,793	2,872	2,898
Labor Force (000's)	63,200	64,400	65,600	66,900
Unemployment rate (percent)	4.15	4.5	4.4	5.5
Money and Prices (Based on local currency ratios)				
Money Supply (M2) (annual percent growth)	616	1,725	2,596	20.9
Interest Rate for Financing Working Capital (monthly nominal rate in percent)	35.0	30.7	41.2	3.9
CPI (annual percent change)[2]	475	1,149	2,489	23
WPI (annual percent change)[2]	472	1,154	2,639	24.5
Exchange Rate (official/commercial transactions)[3]	1.07	12.39	327.00	0.85
Parallel Exchange Rate (unofficial transactions)[3]	1.14	14.60	342.00	0.85
Balance of Payments and Trade (in millions of U.S. dollars)				
Total Exports (FOB)	31,620	35,793	38,783	41,400
Exports to US (FOB)	6,362	7,120	8,028	8,300
Total Imports (FOB)	21,041	20,501	25,711	28,400
Imports from US (FOB)	4,978	4,949	6,028	6,800
Total Trade Balance	10,579	14,844	13,072	13,000
Trade Balance with US	1,384	2,171	2,000	1,500
External Debt	123,910	132,260	130,000	146,000
Debt Service (paid)	8,621	7,253	8,453	9,975
Gold and Foreign Exchange Reserves	9,406	23,754	32,211	48,000

Notes:

(1) 1994 figures are annual estimates based on available monthly data up to October 1994.

(2) Refers to Consumer and Wholesale price indices, respectively.

(3) Exchange rates for 1991–93 are expressed in cruzeiros real (CR, the currency adopted on August 1, 1993, and worth 1,000 old cruzeiros) per dollar. Figures for 1994 are based on the currency adopted with the Real Plan on August 1, 1994, the Real (R). One Real = 2,750 CR. All figures are for end-of-year rates.

Source: U.S. Department of Commerce, Bureau of Economic Analysis, and IMF.

market (Exhibits 6 and 7). There was also a preliminary forecast for PaintCo sales in Brazil and other South American markets (Exhibit 8) based on what could be expected from a strong commitment to export sales or a 100-percent-owned local manufacturing subsidiary. But competition would be significant. Glasurit do Brasil Ltda. (a subsidiary of Germany's BASF) looked to be a competitor in both nonaqueous and aqueous polymers, pigments, dyes, and special-purpose amino-resins, phenolics, and polyurethanes. Strong niche players, such as Tintas Coral S.A. (an ICI affiliate), were focused exclusively on manufacturing paint and varnish from nonaqueous synthetic polymers under license from PaintCo's toughest global competitors. Another local competitor, Tintas Renner, was said to be negotiating with Hoechst to produce pigments under license. Other global players such as Akzo-Nobel, PPG, and DuPont had invested in local affiliates and were involved in both importing and manufacturing.

As Gato came to understand the situation, it became clear to her that PaintCo needed to get their expansion plans under way quickly or they might miss the current window of opportunity.

EXHIBIT 5 U.S. Direct Investment Position in Brazil
Historical Cost Basis—1992 (millions of U.S. dollars)

Category	Amount	Category	Amount
Petroleum	738	Other Manufacturing	3,514
Food & Kindred Products	1,596	Wholesale Trade	96
Chemical and Allied Products	**2,114**	Banking	1,139
Metals, Primary & Fabricated	673	Finance and Insurance	1,946
Machinery, except Electrical	1,668	Services	80
Electric & Electronic Equipment	715	Other Industries	334
Transportation Equipment	2,265	**Total all industries**	**16,908**

Note: Paints are included in Chemicals and Allied Products. The book value of all foreign direct investment in Brazil in 1992 exceeded US$40 billion.
Source: U.S. Department of Commerce, Bureau of Economic Analysis.

EXHIBIT 6 Automotive Markets for OEM Paints
Vehicle Production, Imports and Exports (thousands of units, and US$ millions)

Brazil	1989	1990	1991	1992	1993	1994
Production	1,013	914	960	1,070	1,391	1,581
Imports	0	20	24	70	190	224
Exports	187	193	342	332	378	263
Capacity Investment	$ 602	$790	$936	$1,150	$1,317	n.a.

Notes: Figures for 1994 are preliminary. Passenger cars represent about 30 percent of total production. The balance is for trucks (both light and heavy), buses and special vehicles.

United States	1990	1991	1992	1993	1994
Passenger Cars—Production	6,077	5,439	5,664	5,981	6,614
—Imports: Canada & Mexico	820	698	613	761	641
—Imports: Others	2,403	2,038	1,937	1,776	1,735
Commercial Vehicles (trucks & buses)	3,725	3,387	4,062	4,895	5,620

Spain	1990	1991	1992	1993	1994
Passenger Cars—Production	1,679	1,774	1,795	1,506	1,826
Commercial Vehicles (trucks & buses)	302	220	232	152	173

Sources: American Automobile Manufacturers Association; Brazil's National Association of Motor Vehicle Manufacturers (ANFVEA); and Booz, Allen & Hamilton, *Strategy for the Automobile Industry in Brazil.*

Exploratory Trip

On January 10, 1995, Gato sent a memo to Arthur Dobson in the controller's office and to Dr. Adrian Loyzaga, a technical operations manager, inviting them to accompany her on an exploratory trip to Brazil. Both had been previously involved in the expansion effort into Europe in the 1980s, and Adrian Loyzaga was an expert on paint production who had set up the company's operations in Spain. Loyzaga spoke fluent Spanish and had a good working knowledge of Portuguese. The memo explained

EXHIBIT 7 Brazilian Market and Industry Data

Major Brazilian Paint Market Segments

Automotive OEM	Chiefly enamel. Annual consumption estimated at 20 million liters.
Auto Refinish Market	Car registrations reached 17 million in 1993; most refinish work results from accidents. Consumption estimated at 23 million liters.
Industrial Market	Many different applications, the largest of which is for appliances such as refrigerators and washing machines. Consumption forecast at 84 million liters for 1995.
Decorative Market	Mainly latex house paints. Well-established market and highly competitive. Has two subsegments: trade (contractors and builders) and individual consumers (household, do-it-yourself). Annual consumption estimated at 240 million liters.
Other	Includes wood finishes, coil and can coatings, and specialty markets. Consumption estimated at 30 million liters.

Brazilian Paint Industry Structure and Production:

1. Total Number of Firms	50
2. Market Share of Largest Firm (est.)	21%
3. Market Share of Second Largest Firm	16%
4. Market Share of Top 10 Firms	80%
5. Estimated Consumption in 1995	400 million liters

Note: Per capital consumption in Brazil amounted to 2.7 liters, which compared with approximately 19 liters in the United States, 17 in Germany and 12 in Japan.

EXHIBIT 8 Sales Forecast for PaintCo in Brazil and South America
(Under either an intensive export effort or a 100 percent-owned manufacturing subsidiary)

Segments (in 000's of liters)	1996	1998	2000
Auto OEM (factory-applied finishes on new cars)	153	1,285	2,099
Auto Refinish (spot refinishing on cars in body shops)	2,706	2,777	3,181
Industrial (other than auto and decorative)	894	1,503	1,878
Decorative (homes & buildings)	797	1,245	1,942
Total	4,550	6,810	9,100
Proportion of Sales to Other South American Markets	10%	12%	15%

Notes: Average selling price per liter in 1994: 2.83 Reals (equivalent to US$12.60/gal)
Source: Samvest, Ltda. and corporate records.

that the expansion needed to get under way quickly and that they would need to investigate the alternatives available in Brazil. Pat summarized the objectives of the trip:

1. Review the current distributor's situation and determine the feasibility of expanding the current export arrangement.
2. Determine the feasibility of a licensing agreement with a Brazilian firm.
3. Investigate the possibility for a joint venture with a Brazilian firm.
4. Investigate the possibility of purchasing an existing Brazilian plant or firm.
5. Examine possible sites for constructing a new plant of our own in Brazil.

The memo went on to emphasize the importance of PaintCo's establishing an office in Brazil in order to keep a finger on the pulse of the market and to signal to customers, current and future, its commitment to the Brazilian and South American market. The development of relationships and understanding of the culture would be valuable for fine-tuning the overall expansion plan. However, such an expense would be hard to justify in isolation.

On January 20th, the three executives flew to São Paulo to begin their assessment, first calling on their distributor, Colorado Ltda. The tour of the distributor showed that the operation and quality of personnel were similar to PaintCo's warehouse and distribution operations in southern Europe. The compensation for managerial and sales personnel was 20–30 percent less than for the PaintCo España subsidiary, but employee benefits seemed high by U.S. standards, at around 102 percent of salaries. Colorado was, however, a relatively simple operation compared to that in Spain, with somewhat older technology and unsophisticated logistics. Loyzaga estimated that Colorado's operation could be brought up to PaintCo standards with some equipment upgrade and a training program for their personnel, as had been done in southern Europe.[7]

The team also began working with Samvest, an investment service recommended by Banco do Estado de São Paulo (BANESPA), whose Miami branch financed PaintCo's existing export trade. Samvest began screening Brazilian companies for a possible acquisition. They also recommended considering a plant location in the state of Minas Gerais rather than São Paulo. São Paulo was reaching industrial saturation, and Minas Gerais state officials were actively promoting new investments less than 300 miles away. Samvest thought that Minas Gerais offered the best location for the types of customers and markets in which PaintCo was interested. Overall, the booming regional economy promised expanding markets for all industrial and decorative segments. A U.S. International Trade Administration report noted:

> "Minas Gerais is located in southeast Brazil, about the size of France and strategically placed near the two large consumer markets of Rio de Janeiro and São Paulo. Within the state is the third largest city in Brazil, Belo Horizonte, with a population of three million and the second largest industrial center in Brazil. Those markets and its proximity to Brazil's main ports have led to its development as one of the most internationalized state economies in Brazil. While the Brazilian automotive industry is concentrated mainly in São Paulo, Minas Gerais produces 23 percent of the total vehicles and most future auto and durable goods plants are likely to be built there."[8]

The team agreed to focus on Minas Gerais and visited the region and called on several potential customers. Fiat produced 1,200 vehicles a day at its plant in Betim, outside Belo Horizonte. They were constructing a new auto line with capacity for an additional 500 vehicles a day and were planning to invest another US$40 million in a new equipment line. Autolatina, the VW/Ford joint venture with just over 50 percent of the Brazilian market, could be a major customer, although the joint venture seemed to be having difficulties in late 1994 and might break up in the near future. PaintCo could probably build on its long relationship as a supplier to Ford in the United States and Germany; and perhaps its more recent experience with SEAT, VW's subsidiary in Spain. GM's main operations were in the São Paulo area, but local officials were expecting GM to build a new plant just off the Belo Horizonte-São Paulo (Fernão Dias) highway. Several Japanese and Korean manufacturers were also considering entry or expansion of their Brazilian automotive business. The general feeling among auto executives was that pent-up demand would explode with economic stability, and that many people regarded cars as a hedge against a return of inflation. The group visited several promising plant sites and judged them to be more than adequate in terms of infrastructure and availability of labor.

The Export Option: Expanding U.S. Capacity

On their return, the team reported of their findings. First, Gato asked Loyzaga and Dobson to flesh out the numbers for extending the current export arrangement aggressively. They determined that the investment required to expand annual capacity at an existing U.S. plant by 12 million liters (one U.S. gallon equals 3.785 liters) would be $11.25 million. This was thought to be an economical increment, and that a smaller expansion would be inefficient. It was clear to the team that South American demand would be significantly below this capacity during the early years of market expansion in the region. Therefore, the team looked into the possibility of selling excess capacity in either the United States or Europe. They came to the conclusion that up to one million gallons of the plant's output might be sold in other PaintCo markets during the first few years of operations.

---

[7] In fact, the Brazilian and Spanish markets were similar in size as can be seen in Exhibit 6. The size of the total fleet in Spain was 16.7 million vehicles in 1994, which compared with 14.3 million for Brazil.

[8] *Brazil: Minas Gerais Economic Profile, 1994,* U.S. Department of Commerce, International Trade Administration.

In addition, PaintCo would have to support Colorado financially for them to make the investments in warehousing, logistics, and working capital essential to obtain a reasonable share of the Brazilian market. Thus, it was decided that a 10 percent allowance against local sales would be financed by PaintCo, up to a limit of $3 million, and guaranteed by Colorado's assets. This amount would supplement working capital provided by Colorado out of its own margins. The arrangement was thought to allow for better customer service and larger local inventories, and allay the fears of any potential buyer concerned with supply security. With sufficient investment in working capital, even the automotive OEM customers may be willing to bear the risk of long paint supply lines for their JIT production facilities in order to access PaintCo's quality products.

Finally, Loyzaga and Dobson arrived at some reasonable estimate of cost figures for the U.S. export option, shown in Exhibit 9. The transfer price to Brazil would include a contribution to U.S. overheads and R&D expenses of 10 percent, judged to be appropriate given that these sales would need occasional engineering and customer service support from headquarters.

EXHIBIT 9 Pro Forma Unit Costs and Prices on Export Sales

	$/gal
U.S. Average Sales Price	10.43
a) Cost of Goods Sold (assumed at 58 percent of sales price)	6.05
b) U.S. Overhead Charges (10 percent of U.S. sales price)	1.04
Net Transfer Price for Exports (a + b)	7.09
c) Insurance & Freight to Brazil (8 percent of shipping value)	0.57
CIF Value	7.66
d) Customs Duties (at 16 percent of CIF value)	1.22
Landed Cost	8.88
Local Freight, Distribution and S&A (22 percent of local sales)	2.77
Sales Price in Brazil	12.60
Profit Margin (7.5 percent)	0.95

Notes: Import duties are levied *ad valorem* on the CIF (cost, insurance, & freight) value of the goods. Customs surcharges include the Merchant Marine Renewal Tax, syndicate and brokerage fees, warehouse tax, and an Administration Commission, currently fixed at $50. These figures do not include the Merchandise Circulation Tax (ICM) and Industrial Products Tax (IPI) taxes levied on most domestic and imported manufactured products. These taxes and fees are equivalent to sales taxes and can amount to as much as one half of f.o.b. (free on board) prices, not including inland freight or other nontax costs. Since all sellers, foreign and domestic, pay these, they have not been included in the calculations.

Sources: *Manual de Atualizacão da Tarifa Aduaneira do Brasil,* (Brazilian tariff book). Editora Agenco, Ltda, Rio de Janeiro, R.J., Brazil and U.S. Department of Commerce International Trade Administration 10/1/94.

The Investment Option: PBL

Next, Arthur Dobson prepared a pro-forma asset statement for the alternative of establishing a wholly owned manufacturing subsidiary in Brazil that would cover the same sales volume (these figures are shown in Exhibit 10). The team had concluded that building a local plant would require immediate distribution in the São Paulo region, thus continuing to involve Colorado in order to capture its share of domestic purchases. In this case, however, the assumption was that PaintCo would have to acquire Colorado as part of the investment. Gato felt that the new subsidiary should be named PaintCo Brasileira Ltda. (PBL) to emphasize the combination of PaintCo's global brand name and local responsiveness.

The tentative PBL plan assumed (1) direct sales to the Auto OEM and key industrial customers, (2) distribution of auto refinish products through traditional "jobbers," and (3) sales of decorative paints and other industrial segments through Colorado's existing network of distributors. Samvest had mentioned the changes in franchising rules that had been passed by the Brazilian Congress, so the choice between company retail outlets and franchisees was noted, but a decision was deferred for future consideration. Either way, PBL would be positioned to expand in the profitable, but highly competitive, retail market should it choose to do so.

Based on their observations of Colorado's current operation, the team was recommending that a senior manager of Colorado be recruited to serve as the new president of PBL. Initially, PaintCo personnel would be required to staff several technical and the controller positions. Qualified people could be drawn from European or American personnel who were fluent in Portuguese or Spanish. As Brazilians were found to take up the key positions, the expatriates would be returned to their respective countries. Adrian Loyzaga listed several potential candidates to help supervise the construction and "shakedown" of the new plant.

Proposal to Acquire Colorado Ltda.

The owners of Colorado had built the business from the ground up in the 1960s. By 1995 they were mostly retired and had turned over active management to entrepreneurial younger managers in the organization. These executives were now seasoned by years of experience during recession, growth, and hyperinflation. Expanding the

EXHIBIT 10 Pro Forma Asset Statement
Establishment of 100%-Owned Manufacturing Subsidiary Initial Plant Capacity 10 Million Liters

Investment Required	Real (000s)	US $ (000s)
Land	652	767
Buildings	2,385	2,806
Plant & Equipment	4,760	5,600
Total Fixed Assets	7,797	9,173
Net Working Capital[1]	3,863	4,545
Miscellaneous[1]	1,302	1,532
Total	R 12,962	$15,249

Notes: (1) These figures are for the purchase of the current assets and other equipment of the existing distributor, Colorado, Ltda.

(2) For subsequent years, net working capital can be estimated at 25% of sales.

(3) Exchange rate in January, 1995 was 0.850 Real/$US 1.00.

Costs (in percent of sales)	1996	1998	2000
Manufacturing Cost—includes annual depreciation of Real 595,000	76%	68%	64%
Selling & Administrative Expenses	20%	16%	13%

Brazilian Taxes = 30% of before tax income, excluding withholding taxes on interest and dividends. Taxes paid to the Brazilian government would be credited against PaintCo's liability for U.S. taxes on remitted foreign earnings.

Source: Corporate records.

firm would require capital that the owners were reluctant to provide. Sale of the firm, therefore, looked to be favorable for both the owners and its management. The owners would receive payment that could be invested in U.S. dollar-denominated fixed income assets, providing them with a comfortable retirement income essentially protected against any return to hyperinflation. The entrepreneurial management would have the long-awaited opportunity to pursue a growth strategy with the technological and financial backing of an international corporation.

When the owners were approached about the possibility of a buy-out, they expressed interest subject to suitable arrangements for the existing managers and employees. Once it was understood that the plan called for the existing organization to be kept essentially intact as a decentralized unit, the negotiations proceeded as a friendly takeover. Gato then asked Samvest to advise their lawyers on creating a tentative agreement that the Colorado owners and PaintCo's board might ultimately approve. Within days, a tentative agreement was drafted for the acquisition of Colorado, including a method to arbitrate any disputes over the value of assets. Both parties agreed further that if the PaintCo or Colorado boards failed to approve the transaction, the existing export-distribution business relationship would continue as in the past.

In early March, PaintCo's CEO, Hugo Deimios, called a meeting of the executive committee to consider, among other things, the Brazilian venture. The committee consisted of senior executives representing all PaintCo product and geographic areas. Their focus was on the potential opportunities and challenges of integrating the new subsidiary into PaintCo's decentralized network of affiliates, coordinating multipoint sales to global customers such as Ford and Whirlpool (both with extensive operations in South America), and including PBL in the human resource development program. Gato presented the team's assessment of the current business climate in Brazil (see Exhibit 11 and the Appendix), and all other data collected to date, including the pro-forma asset investment estimates and a presentation on the Colorado acquisition proposal. Gato noted that other investment alternatives were still being sought out by Samvest in Brazil. A decision was deferred pending more detailed feasibility data.

Proposals from Grossman

Shortly thereafter, Samvest called Gato to report on another likely prospect. They were in contact with Sr. Victor Grossman, principal owner and manager of Grossquimica, S.A., a medium-sized manufacturer operating primarily in the industrial and decorative market segments. The management was reputedly good, although the company's technology was conventional. Samvest felt that this target seemed to fit the stated acquisition requirements and suggested that PaintCo enter into exploratory negotiations. Data on Grossquimica's recent financial and market performance is shown in Exhibit 12. The project team reassembled and returned to Brazil to meet Sr. Grossman and determine whether a good fit existed with PaintCo's strategy.

Victor Grossman opened the talks by demanding US$30 million for his company. He stated that the Brazilian market was booming and the Real Plan promised highly profitable returns for American investors. Summary data on the operation were provided to illustrate the strength of the company and its 4.8 percent market share.

EXHIBIT 11 **Wall Street's Views on Brazil**

Brazilian Plan to Open Up Investment Wins Support, Aiding Inflation Program

By Matt Moffett
Staff Reporter of THE WALL STREET JOURNAL

RIO DE JANEIRO—A government plan to open Brazil's industries such as petroleum, mining and telecommunications to foreign and other private investment got a surprisingly upbeat reception late last week from key factions within the country's often obstructionist political system.

Passage of the sweeping constitutional reforms is considered crucial to maintaining investor confidence in President Fernando Henrique Cordoso's anti-inflation program, the Real Plan. The program, which has relied heavily on a strong currency to cut monthly inflation to about 1% in December from 50% in June, has come under intense scrutiny following the collapse of the Mexican peso.

Although the reforms threaten many powerful interests, the proposals outlined by government ministers in a meeting with some key political and business groups were generally well received. "The government achieved an important point with this meeting," said Alberto Goldman, president of the Brazilian Democratic Movement Party, which will control the largest bloc of legislators in the new Congress, to be installed in February.

The package includes an opening to private investment in woefully undercapitalized state oil monopoly Petroleo Brasileitro SA. One proposal would let Petrobras and private drillers enter into risk contracts, which give drillers a stake in any Brazilian oil they find. Other proposals would permit joint ventures in refining and eliminate the state monopoly in transportation of oil and gas.

The proposals are designed to increase energy-sector productivity in a country that imports half of its daily requirement of 1.3 million barrels of oil even though it has ample oil reserves. The main reason for the lackluster production is that the company's exploration and production budget is about half the level management says it needs. Nearly a score of exploration projects have been halted for want of capital.

Also in the reform package are measures to eliminate the state monopoly on telecommunications; a proposal to offer foreign capital the same legal treatment given to Brazilian capital; a plan to open up the hydroelectric-power and mining industries to foreign capital; and measures to eliminate restrictions preventing state-owned companies from going bankrupt.

Mr. Cardoso is trying to use Mexico's peso meltdown to rally support for the legislative program, which he says is needed to support Brazil's new currency, the real. "The Mexican crisis serves as an alert on the necessity of the structural reforms that give sustenance to a strong currency," said Mr. Cardoso, who designed the Real Plan in his previous post as finance minister, before his recent election as president.

As in Mexico, Brazil made a strong currency the anchor of the anti-inflation drive; today, one real is valued at a little more than the dollar. Although in a far less dramatic fashion than in Mexico, the strong currency has deteriorated Brazil's trade balance by making exports more expensive and imports cheaper. The December trade deficit jumped to $884 million, far wider than the forecast of $47 million.

The government still posted a trade surplus of more than $10 billion for all of 1994. Nevertheless, the December deficit worried analysts. "The Mexican crisis has clearly demonstrated the problems of stabilization programs relying excessively on the exchange rate rather than on balanced fiscal accounts," said Lars Schonander, Latin American economist for Baring Securities Ltd.

He now expects the government to shift the program's emphasis, making higher interest rates and spending cuts, instead of the strong real, the pivot of its anti-inflation push. Mr. Schonander said that to give the program credibility, the government will have to use aggressive privatization and tax reform to close a budget gap estimated at $13 billion this year.

Ups and Downs
Brazil's trade balance turns negative, but inflation eases

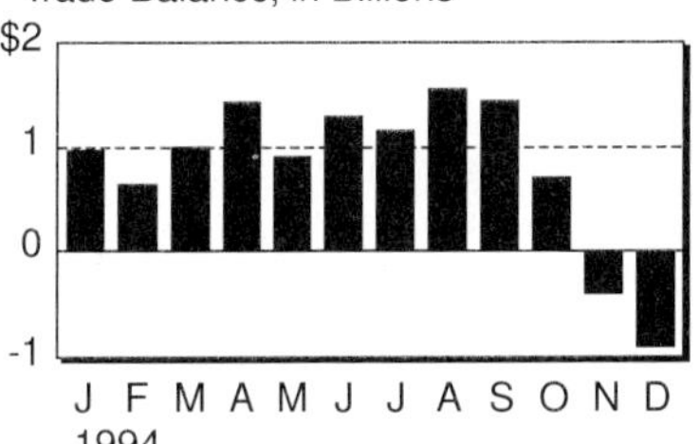

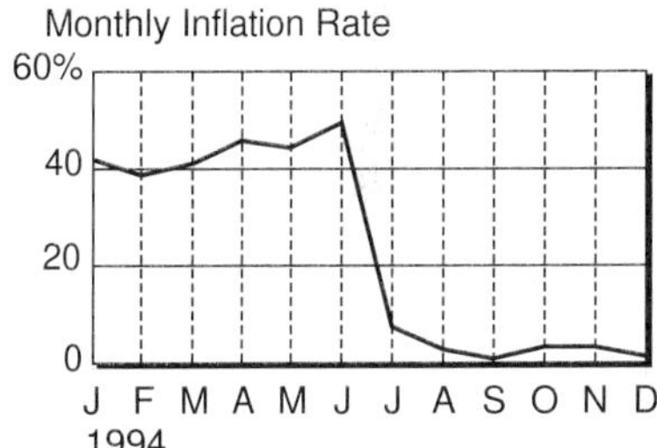

Sources: The University of Sao Paulo; government sources

Source: *The Wall Street Journal,* January 30, 1995, p. A20.

When it was pointed out that he seemed to be asking for a premium price, he responded that a such a price would be required to motivate any successful Brazilian manufacturer to sell out under the current auspicious circumstances. The benefit to PaintCo, he argued, would be a significant market share and the use of first-rate manufacturing facilities that were being operated at only 85 percent of rated capacity. Dr. Loyzaga openly remarked that a similar plant with Cowles dissolvers and filling lines could be constructed without paying a premium. Grossman countered by noting his plant would be available immediately and would not require waiting for construction and training of the work force. Besides, attempting to enter the market against entrenched competitors could be financially disadvantageous compared with beginning immediately with a large market share. Gato agreed that such a purchase would offer advantages, but "they would need to consult with headquarters before proceeding further." Pat made it clear that price was clearly going to be a hurdle that could be difficult to overcome, particularly given the question of how to combine Grossman's existing business segment strategy with PaintCo's objectives in South America.

The next day, Grossman called to say that he had discussed the matter with his directors and had developed two alternatives that might be preferable to PaintCo. First, they would entertain an offer to enter into a joint venture whereby PaintCo would acquire 51 percent of Grossquimica for US$16.8 million. The five-member Grossquimica board would be expanded by six new seats, giving PaintCo majority control. Sr. Grossman would stay on as Chairman of the Board for three years to ensure a smooth transition and the melding of the two companies and national cultures.

EXHIBIT 12 Grossquimica S.A.: Financial Statements[1]
(in millions, except as noted)

	1992	1993	1994
Sales	CR 202.1	CR 4,261.4	Real 38.3
Cost of Sales	135.3	2,729.5	25.0
Selling & Administration	36.8	752.0	6.8
Depreciation[2]	13.7	278.5	2.6
Income Before Taxes[3]	16.3	501.3	3.9
Estimated Market Share	4.8%	5%	4.8%
Employees (number)	280	290	295
Exchange Rate Per $[4]			
—Average for the Year	CR 4.51	CR 88	R 0.64
—End of Year	CR 12.39	CR 327	R 0.85

Notes:

(1) Figures for 1992–93 are in cruzeiro reals; those for 1994 are in Reals. The 1994 figures are preliminary and unaudited.

(2) Net book value of plant and equipment by end 1993; US$24 million.

(3) Grossquimica's income tax payments averaged 30 percent of income.

(4) Exchange rates for 1992–93 are expressed in cruzeiro reals per dollar, and for 1994 in Reals per dollar. See footnote in Exhibit 4 and the Appendix for more detail on exchange rate policies.

Segment Sales (percent)	1992	1993	1994
Auto Refinishes	7%	6%	6%
Appliances	4	5	3
Other Industrial Segments	12	8	6
Wood Finishes	12	13	15
Decorative	65	68	70

Source: Company records.

The other option that Grossman thought might appeal to Gato's CEO would be a licensing agreement between the two companies. PaintCo would issue an exclusive license for all of its products, and Grossquimica would produce paints to serve the Brazilian and the rest of the South American market. With access to PaintCo's technical personnel, Grossquimica would invest in a new dispersion process to produce specialty products and expand its market scope. To clarify the arrangement, Victor Grossman offered to send over a draft license agreement that the firm's executives had developed (reproduced in Exhibit 13).

Further Issues

In reviewing the new alternatives, Gato began to grasp more fully the opportunities and challenges offered by expanding in Brazil. Victor Grossman clearly thought that the prospects for Brazil and South America were good, but competition would be as tough as in other PaintCo markets. President Cardoso's anti-inflation program appeared to be working, but several years might be necessary to see how committed the government was to more open markets. If the emphasis of the Real Plan on a strong currency required higher interest rates and government spending cuts, would it be wise to make a major manufacturing investment now? The Mercosur process was due to wind up with the possible affiliation of Bolivia and Chile, but Samvest had spoken of the possibility that Chile might spurn Mercosur and join NAFTA instead. Was too much emphasis being put on exports to the rest of South America? The auto boom in the U.S. appeared to have peaked in late 1994, and the Big Three were beginning to idle some American plants in 1995. Would they scale back plans for additional capacity in Brazil?

The question of getting profits out of Brazil had not been addressed in the team's draft of the five alternatives. What form should the return on investment best take: dividends, interest on loans, high profits on exports, or royalties? Would the Brazilian government put future restrictions on hard currency transactions, or return to an artificially low exchange rate? The notes below summarize existing rules on transfers of foreign currency to foreign headquarters:

> "Since December 1991, Brazil has stuck with a flat rate surcharge of 15 percent on foreign remittance of profits and dividends (Law number 8383) and there is no longer any limit on the amount of profits remitted nor supplemental taxes on remittance of excess profits. Capital (including reinvestment), may be repatriated without payment of tax nor limitation as to period or amount. Capital gains require special permission before being repatriated and are subject to a 25 percent tax on profits. Investment capital resulting from any "debt conversion" scheme must remain in Brazil for a 12-year period before its remittance is permitted. Dividends from such investments, however, may be remitted the same as regular dividends under Law 8383. Remittances of royalties or technical service fees by a subsidiary established in Brazil to its head office abroad are permitted under Law 8383. Payments of royalties or technology fees abroad are deductible for income tax purposes by the Brazilian subsidiary.
>
> "The minimum repayment period for foreign loans is 8 years (or 10 years when qualifying for tax incentives), with a grace period of 30 months before the first repayment of principal. The loan may be repaid in equal installments throughout the remainder of the period of the loan (5½ or 7½ years, respectively). Subject to these limitations, no restrictions are imposed on the payment of loan principal and interest is freely remittable.
>
> "Brazilian income tax may be levied on a foreign exporter if there is evidence that the exporter is present in Brazil (Article 76 of Law Number 3470/58). This presence is determined basically by two interrelated factors: the closing of direct sales contracts in Brazil and the existence of either an express or tacit power of attorney granted to an agent or representative in Brazil. In such cases, the taxable income is estimated at 20 percent of the total price of the product imported into Brazil. The precise applicability of this law to any particular transaction or agent-principal relationship is best determined by a Brazilian tax lawyer."[9]

According to Arthur Dobson, the PBL subsidiary would be subject to a 30 percent Brazilian corporate tax rate. PaintCo's U.S. marginal tax rate for the equivalent capacity and revenue stream was currently 40 percent. Both rates appeared subject to small swings and changes every few years, as the respective congresses shifted priorities, changed policies, and adjusted tax formulas. It appeared unlikely that exports to Brazil would fall under Article 76 and attract an income tax of 30 percent on 20 percent of local sales, which would be prohibitive. In any event, under existing bilateral agreements, any income taxes paid in Brazil would be fully credited against U.S. tax liability. No debt conversion scheme was being contemplated either.

There were questions, however, about operating a subsidiary under inflation rates of 1 to 5 percent per month. Brazilian regulations allowed company balance sheets (particularly net fixed assets and inventories) to be adjusted

[9]Abstracted from the U.S. Department of Commerce, International Trade Administration, 1995.

EXHIBIT 13 License Agreement
(proposal submitted by Grossquimica)

This letter sets forth an agreement between Grossquimica S.A., a Brazilian corporation (hereinafter referred to as Grossquimica), and PaintCo, Inc., a U.S. corporation (hereinafter referred to as PaintCo), whereby PaintCo will provide an exclusive license to Grossquimica to manufacture and sell products under PaintCo trademarks for Latin America, subject to the following terms and conditions:

I. Products
PaintCo grants to Grossquimica exclusive rights to manufacture and sell PaintCo formulations for paints, thinners, primers, resins, and related coatings products. Grossquimica will be supplied all patents, formulas, processes, and techniques, existing and future, for all PaintCo products sold elsewhere in the world during the term of this agreement. Grossquimica will have immediate access to any new products PaintCo brings to market outside of Latin America during the term of this agreement. Grossquimica will assume full and complete responsibility for the manufacture and sale of the aforementioned products within the exclusive territory of Latin America during the term of this agreement.

II. Trademark
Grossquimica will be assigned the sole and full right to use PaintCo's trademark, or trade name, and the trademarks, or trade names, of all products sold by PaintCo elsewhere in the world in connection with any product, promotion, or publication during the term of this agreement. Grossquimica will have immediate sole and full rights to any new trademarks, or trade names, that PaintCo uses outside of Latin America during the term of this agreement. Grossquimica will assume full and complete responsibility for the use of the aforementioned trademark, or trade names, within the exclusive territory of Latin America during the term of this agreement.

III. Term of Agreement
The term of this agreement will be from _____ , 1995 through _____ , 2000.

IV. Territory
The territory encompassed by this agreement shall include all of Latin America, including the following nations and territories, and their successors: Argentina, Bahamas, Barbados, Bolivia, Brazil, Chile, Colombia, Costa Rica, Cuba, Dominican Republic, Ecuador, El Salvador, Guatemala, Haiti, Honduras, Jamaica, Mexico, Nicaragua, Panama, Paraguay, Peru, Tobago, Trinidad, Uruguay, Venezuela.

V. Confidential Information
A. Confidential information shall mean that information: (1) disclosed to Grossquimica by PaintCo in connection with or during the term of this agreement; and (2) which relates to PaintCo's past, present, and future research, development, and business activities; and, (3) which has been identified to Grossquimica at the time of disclosure as confidential information of PaintCo. It shall also mean the deliverable items specified in Paragraph I of this agreement. The term "Confidential Information" shall not mean any information that is previously known to Grossquimica without obligation of confidence, or without breach of this Agreement, is publicly disclosed either prior or subsequent to Grossquimica's receipt of such information, or is rightfully received by Grossquimica from a third party without obligation of confidence.
B. For a period of three (3) years, from termination of this Agreement, Grossquimica agrees to hold all such Confidential Information in trust and confidence for PaintCo and not use such Confidential Information other than as described in this Agreement. Grossquimica agrees not to disclose any such Confidential Information to any person other than those persons whose services Grossquimica requires who have a need to know such Confidential Information for purposes of carrying out the terms of this Agreement, and who agrees in writing to be bound by, and comply with the provisions of this Section.
C. Grossquimica agrees to secure all writings, documents, and other media that embody such Confidential Information in locked files at all times when not in use to prevent its loss or unauthorized disclosure, and to segregate such Confidential Information at all times from the materials of others.

VI. Royalty Payments
A. Grossquimica agrees to make royalty payments to PaintCo as a compensation for the license as follows:
   a. on each liter of primer a royalty of _____
   b. on each liter of enamel a royalty of _____
   c. on each liter of thinner a royalty of _____
   d. on each liter of varnish a royalty of _____
B. Grossquimica will keep separate records of all PaintCo products manufactured and sold under this agreement and those records will be open for inspection, on request, by certified public auditors employed by PaintCo.

VII. Termination

This Agreement may be terminated, without cause and without penalty, upon one hundred and eighty (180) days written notice to the other party. In the event of termination, Grossquimica will have the right to sell all products and materials in inventory under the same terms and conditions as in this Agreement or PaintCo, at its discretion, may purchase all or part of same inventory at current market prices and cause to have said inventory shipped at PaintCo's expense.

VIII. Brazilian Law

This Agreement shall be construed, and the legal relations between the parties hereto shall be determined, in accordance with the laws of the nation of Brazil and, where applicable, the laws of the state of São Paulo, Brazil. The venue of any action regarding this agreement will be São Paulo, Brazil.

If the foregoing is in accordance with PaintCo's understanding, please indicate agreement by dating, signing, and returning the enclosed duplicate of this letter of Agreement to the Contract Administrator, Grossquimica, S.A.

By: ______________________	Agreed to by: ______________________
Sr. Victor Grossman	Name: ______________________
Title: Managing Director	Title: ______________________
Grossquimica, S.A.	PaintCo Inc.
Date: ______________	Date: ______________

---

for inflation through the application of an official adjustment index (known as the "TR"). However, if social unrest occurred as a consequence of the Real Plan's austerity measures, it was possible that Brazil could return to a system of price controls. The U.S. State Department warned, "Brazilian governments in the past have not hesitated to apply price controls on a wide range of industrial products in attempts to fight inflation. Established foreign investors in Brazil, notably in the automobile and pharmaceutical industries, objected to the inflexibility of such controls, which forced them into unprofitable production and discouraged investment. There continue to be calls for selective price controls on those products having increases out of proportion to increases in production costs."[10]

As Pat Gato readied for the coming executive committee meeting, now scheduled for the first week in April, the pressing question was which alternative to recommend for expanding PaintCo's presence in Brazil. Any recommendation would also have to include what priorities should be attached to the different market segments. What, for example, should be the right price to offer for Grossquimica, if this were the entry vehicle chosen? And for what percentage? Gato was beginning to have second thoughts about the risks involved in a Brazilian venture at this time. In the last weeks of 1994, the Mexican peso had collapsed and President Clinton had, against the objections of Congress, put together a joint US–IMF $45 billion financial rescue package for the Mexican economy. These dramatic events had impacted currency markets throughout the region (the so-called "tequila effect") and initiated a broad reassessment of investment risk in the whole of Latin America. The committee members would be most aware of these facts.

As she cleared her desk to begin putting together all the data at her disposal, there were a number of technical issues Pat had to resolve as well. For example, should she use PaintCo's standard discount rate of 12.5 percent to analyze these options, or should a Brazilian country risk factor be added? Second, how should she factor future inflation and currency devaluation in her estimates? Brazil's allowance for asset revaluation might offer some protection on the value of fixed assets, but what about working capital investments? Should depreciation charges be remitted as incurred, or should they be reinvested in working capital, process improvements, and expansion? And if the market continued to grow at current rates, how should the analysis factor in additional investments in the future? Pat's assistant, Peter Garland, had prepared an initial spreadsheet with all the relevant data as an aide to the analysis. She now fired up her desktop and prepared to tackle these issues.

Pat knew that the decision to launch a new strategy of international growth in emerging markets was not going to be easy for PaintCo. Risks were abundant, yet the opportunities seemed very attractive. Just that morning she had held a telephone conversation with a senior executive from one of their major U.S. automotive customers

[10] *Economic Policy and Trade Practices: Brazil 1994*, U.S. Department of State.

who reported that, ". . . car sales have increased 25 percent since the Real Plan came into effect, mainly due to the availability of consumer credit. This is something Brazil has not had for years. We are indeed optimistic about the future for Brazil and for the rest of the Mercosur market and will be expanding our operations there accordingly."[11] Pat was convinced that her presentation to the executive committee had to explore all the options and provide a clear recommendation with a sense of both the risk and the promise implied in the Brazilian market and beyond.

APPENDIX
BACKGROUND NOTES ON BRAZIL

Profile

Geography: Area: 8,511,965 sq. km. (3,290,000 sq. mi.). Capital city (1989): Brasilia (pop. 1.8 million). Other cities: São Paulo (11 million); Rio de Janeiro (6 million); Belo Horizonte (2.3 million); Salvador (2 million); Fortaleza (1.8 million); Recife (1.4 million); Pôrto Alegre (1.4 million); Curitiba (1.4 million). Terrain: Dense forests in northern regions, including Amazon Basin; semiarid along northeast coast; mountains, hills, and rolling plains in the southwest (including Mato Grosso); and coastal strip. Climate: Mostly tropical or semitropical with temperate zone in the south.

Population (1989 est.): 150.1 million. Annual growth rate: 2.1 percent. Density: 17.6 per sq. km. (45.6 per sq. mi.). Ethnic groups: Portuguese, Italian, German, Japanese, African, Indians, principally Tupi and Guarani linguistic stock. Education: 78 percent literacy among adult population. Workforce (1989, 62.5 million): Agriculture (35 percent); industry (25 percent); services (40 percent). Trade union membership: about 6 million.

Flag: A yellow diamond on a green field; a blue globe with 23 white stars and a band with "Ordem e Progresso" centered on the diamond. The globe represents the sky and the vastness of the states and capital, and green and yellow signify forest and mineral wealth.

Natural resources: Iron ore, manganese, bauxite, nickel, uranium, gemstones, oil.

Agriculture (12 percent of GDP): Products: coffee, soybeans, sugarcane, cocoa, rice, beef, corn, oranges, cotton, wheat. Land: 17 percent arable, cultivable, or pasture.

Industry: steel, chemicals, petrochemicals, machinery, motor vehicles, consumer durables, cement, lumber, shipbuilding.

Trade (1988): Exports—$33.8 billion. Major markets—US 26 percent, Japan 7 percent, Netherlands 8 percent, Germany 4 percent, Italy 4 percent, Argentina 3 percent. Imports—$14.7 billion. Major suppliers—US 21 percent, Germany 10 percent, Japan 7 percent, Argentina 5 percent, France 4 percent.

People

With an estimated population of 150 million, Brazil is the most populous country in Latin America and ranks sixth in the world. Most of the people live in the south-central

[11]According to the figures obtained from the Brazilian automotive manufacturers association, the degree of penetration of motor vehicles in Brazil was still significantly below those in other emerging economies. The table below shows the number of inhabitants per vehicle for a few selected countries.

	1980	1990	1994
United States	1.4	1.3	1.3
Spain	4.2	2.7	2.2
Mexico	12.7	8.9	7.5
Brazil	11.8	11.1	10.4

area, which includes the industrial cities of São Paulo, Rio de Janeiro, and Belo Horizonte. Urban growth has been rapid; by 1984 the urban sector included more than two-thirds of the total population. Increased urbanization has aided economic development but, at the same time, has created serious social and political problems in the major cities. Four major groups make up Brazil's population: indigenous Indians of Tupi and Guarani language stock; the Portuguese, who began colonizing in the 16th century; Africans brought to Brazil as slaves; and various European and Asian immigrant groups that have settled in Brazil since the mid-19th century.

The Portuguese often intermarried with the Indians; marriage with slaves was also common. Although the basic ethnic stock of Brazil was once Portuguese, subsequent waves of immigration have contributed to a rich ethnic and cultural heritage.

From 1875 until 1960, about 5 million Europeans emigrated to Brazil, settling mainly in the four southern states of São Paulo, Parana, Santa Catarina, and Rio Grande do Sul. In order of numbers, after the Portuguese, the immigrants have come from Italy, Germany, Spain, Japan, Poland, and the Middle East. The largest Japanese community outside Japan is in São Paulo. Despite class distinctions, national identity is strong, and racial friction is a relatively new phenomenon.

Indigenous full-blooded Indians, located mainly in the northern and western border regions and in the upper Amazon Basin, constitute less than 1 percent of the population. Their numbers are rapidly declining as contact with the outside world and commercial expansion into the interior increase. Brazil is the only Portuguese-speaking nation in the Americas. About 90 percent of the population belongs to the Roman Catholic Church, although many Brazilians adhere to Protestantism and spiritualism.

As its geography, population, size, and ethnic diversity would imply, Brazil's cultural profile and achievements are extensive, vibrant, and constantly changing. Traditionally, Brazilian culture has developed around regional subjects, with the country's northeast normally identified with national themes, both nativist and Afro-Brazilian, while the urban centers of São Paulo and Rio de Janeiro have demonstrated a tendency toward a more international, and European-oriented expression. With the post-1964 push to a more integrated national culture, these tendencies have diminished somewhat but remain central to understanding the uniqueness of this vast nation.

History

Brazil was formally claimed in 1500 by the Portuguese navigator Pedro Cabral. It was ruled from Lisbon as a colony until 1808 when the Portuguese royal family, having fled from Napoleon's army, established their seat of government first in Salvador and later in Rio de Janeiro. Brazil became a kingdom under Dom Joao VI, who returned to Portugal in 1821, leaving his son, Dom Pedro I, as regent. Dom Pedro I successfully declared Brazil's independence on September 7, 1822, and became emperor. Dom Pedro II ruled from 1831 to 1889 when a federal republic was established.

From 1889 to 1930, the government was a constitutional democracy with a limited franchise. The presidency alternated between the dominant states of São Paulo and Minas Gerais. This period ended with a military coup by Getulio Vargas, who remained as dictator until 1945. From 1945 to 1961, Enrico Dutra, Vargas, Juscelino Kubitschek, and Janio Quadros were the elected presidents. When Quadros resigned in 1961, he was succeeded by Vice President Joao Goulart.

Goulart's years in office were marked by high inflation, economic stagnation, and the increasing influence of radical political philosophies. The armed forces, alarmed by these developments, staged a coup on March 31, 1964. The coup leaders chose as president Army Marshal Humberto Castello Branco, who was confirmed by the National Congress on April 11, 1964. Castello Branco was followed by retired Army Marshal Arthur da Costa e Silva (1967–69), Gen. Emilio Garrastazu Medici (1969–74), and retired Gen. Ernesto Geisel (1974–79). Geisel began the political liberalization process, known as *abertura* or opening, which was carried further by his successor, Gen. Joao Baptista de Oliveira Figueiredo (1979–85). Figueiredo not only permitted the return of politicians exiled or banned during the 1960s and early 1970s, but also allowed them to run for state and federal offices in 1982, including the first direct elections for governor since 1966.

However, the electoral college, consisting of all members of Congress and six delegates chosen from each state, continued to choose the president. In January 1985, the electoral college picked Tancredo Neves from the opposition Brazilian Democratic Movement Party (PMDB) as president. However, Neves became ill in March and died a month later. His vice president, the former Senator Jose Sarney, who had been acting president since inauguration day, became president upon Neves' death. Brazil completed its transition to a popularly elected government in

1989, when Fernando Collor de Mello won 53 percent of the vote in the first direct presidential elections in 29 years.

Political Conditions

Following the 1964 military coup, the 13 existing political parties were abolished, and two political organizations, the pro-government National Renewal Alliance (ARENA) and the opposition Brazilian Democratic Movement, were formed. In 1979, under a government-sponsored bill approved by the congress, this two-party system was abolished, and a multiparty system was allowed to reemerge. In 1989, more than 20 political parties participated in the campaign. The major parties were:

PMDB: *Partido do Movimento Democratico Brasileiro* (Brazilian Democratic Movement Party). The country's largest party suffered defections in the 1989 campaign. Known as the MDB from 1966 to 1979, under military-dominated governments, the PMDB includes politicians ranging from conservative to left of center. Most state governors and almost all PMDB cabinet members belong to the conservative wing of the party. PMDB popular support is strongest in urban areas.

PFL: *Partido da Frente Liberal* (Liberal Front Party). The country's second largest party; defeated in the 1989 presidential campaign, later aligned with President Fernando Collor de Mello. The PFL espouses views similar to those of the Democratic Social Party (PDS), but looks to different political leaders and maintains fewer ties to the military establishment. The PFL is strongest in medium-sized towns and the more conservative cities, especially in the northeast. It was founded in 1985 by PDS dissidents.

PSDB: *Partido da Social Democracia Brasileira* (Brazilian Social Democracy Party). Led by Senator Mario Covas, the PSDB was founded in 1988 and includes prominent politicians who quit the PMDB, PFL, and PDS over political differences with national or state leaders of those parties. The PSDB advocates adoption of a parliamentary system of government in Brazil.

PDS: *Partido Democratico Social.* Founded in 1982, the PDS is the modern version of the ARENA party, which represented Brazilian interests during 21 years of military-dominated governments (1964–85). It advocates using foreign capital for economic development. Its popular support is greatest in certain rural strongholds and among upper/middle class in urban areas.

PT: *Partido dos Trabalhadores* (Workers' Party). Formed in 1978, the PT is Brazil's "European-style" leftist party, with a clearly defined ideology and program, strict party discipline, a hierarchical structure, and internal party democracy. It is strongest among intellectuals, organized labor, and the economically disadvantaged. It draws considerable support from the liberation-theology wing of the Catholic Church and from the labor confederation, the sole Workers Central (CUT). In 1988, it won mayoralties of important industrial cities, including that of Luiza Erundina in São Paulo and Olivio Dutra in Pôrto Alegre. In 1989, PT presidential candidate Luiz Inacio Lula da Silva lost to Collor in the second-round run-off election as he did again in 1994 against Cardoso.

PRN: *Partido da Reconstrucão Nacional* (National Reconstruction Party). The PRN was created by Collor in 1989 and served as the vehicle for his 1989 presidential campaign. Collor and his advisers generally advocated free-market solutions to Brazil's economic problems. His electoral support was greatest in rural areas and in small towns across the country.

Brazil also boasts several dozen small parties, some of which (e.g., National Mobilization Party—PMN, and Christian Democratic Party—PDC) are significant in specific regions or states.

U.S.–Brazilian Relations

The United States was the first country to recognize Brazil's independence in 1822. Brazil's 19th-century leader, Emperor Dom Pedro II, admired Abraham Lincoln and visited the United States during the 1876 centennial. President Eisenhower was given a hero's welcome when he visited Brazil in 1960. Presidents Roosevelt and Truman made earlier visits; President Carter visited in 1978 and President Reagan in 1982. President Sarney visited the United States in 1986.

The United States is Brazil's most important commercial partner and largest investor. The U.S. share of Brazilian trade averages 22 percent, and two-way trade exceeded $24 billion in 1994. The growing diversification of U.S.–Brazil trade has led to trade disputes. Brazilian trade practices, including prohibition of some imports and difficult import licensing procedures, market reserve requirements on computer products, and the lack of intellectual property protection (especially patents in certain areas), led to frictions with the United States and other major trading partners. These culminated in 1988 and 1989, when the United States named Brazil in a number of formal trade actions and took retaliatory steps against some Brazilian imports under U.S. trade law. For its part, Brazil was critical of the United States for singling it out and of high U.S. tariffs on products of interest to Brazil such as steel and orange juice. Following the liberalization of Brazil's import restrictions since 1989, trade frictions have diminished.

The agreements between Brazil and the United States include a treaty of peace and friendship; an extradition treaty; a joint participation agreement on communication satellites; and scientific cooperation, civil aviation, and maritime agreements. Brazil and the United States exchange professors under Fulbright and other academic programs and carry out university cooperation projects.

Economic Conditions in Brazil

Brazil is a country rich in resources and natural advantages. To date, however, its economic performance has lagged behind its potential. Economically, it is a country of contrasts ranging from sophisticated economic centers around São Paulo to relatively undeveloped trading outposts on the Amazon. Industrial development has been concentrated in the southeastern states of Rio de Janeiro, São Paulo, Parana, and Rio Grande do Sul, but is now expanding to include the northeast and center west.

1. Past Economic Strategy

Following the 1964 coup, the Brazilian government focused on two major economic goals, high growth rates and control of inflation. In the 1970s, escalating oil prices, governmental indebtedness, and high interest rates brought the Brazilian economy to a virtual standstill, forcing reduced government expenditures and subsidies and income tax increases. Nevertheless, budget deficits have persisted. The combined public sector deficit in 1989 was at least 7 percent of GDP.

Taking office in 1985, the Sarney administration brought inflation to a halt by freezing all prices and ending indexation of wages and other facets of the economy. Real wage increases led to a consumer spending boom which created shortages and tight profit margins. This plan collapsed in November 1986, and inflation rose to record heights—1,700 percent—in 1989. In addition, high levels of imports so reduced foreign exchange reserves that interest payments on foreign loans were suspended in February 1987. Foreign indebtedness rose to $112 billion (about $18 billion held by US commercial banks), the largest of any developing country. Debt service claimed most of Brazil's balance of payments, and periodically the federal government has suspended some forms of debt service, including a *de facto* moratorium on payments to commercial banks in September 1989.

In the spring of 1990, President Collor introduced measures to stabilize and liberalize the economy. The initial phase of the program, which focused on drastically reducing liquidity and cutting inflation, appeared to be achieving its objectives. Inflation slowed nearly to zero within the first month, rising gradually to about 10 percent monthly by August. Collor put into place the administrative machinery to implement an ambitious privatization program and began to open Brazil's markets to foreign goods. However, he was impeached on charges of corruption and forced to resign in December 1992. His Vice President, Itamar Franco, assumed office but financial instability returned to Brazil with inflation soaring to more than 5,000 percent on a yearly basis by mid-1994. A new Finance Minister, Fernando Cardoso, appointed by Franco to deal with the situation, introduced the Real Plan in July 1994. Based on the plan's success, Cardoso was elected president in November 1994.

2. Agriculture, Industry, and Natural Resources

About one-half of Brazil is covered by forests. The largest rainforest in the world is located in the Amazon Basin and is so impressive in character and extent that the entire Amazon region is identified with it. Recent migrations into the Amazon region and controversial large-scale burning of forest areas placed the international spotlight on Brazil. The government has since reduced incentives for such activity and has begun to implement an ambitious environmental plan.

The agricultural sector employs 35 percent of Brazil's population and accounts for about 12 percent of its GDP and almost 40 percent of the country's exports. Except for wheat, Brazil is largely self-sufficient in food. It is the world's leading exporter of coffee and orange juice concentrate; the second largest exporter of cocoa and soybeans; and a major exporter of sugar, meat, and cotton. During the past decade, in an effort to expand its agricultural exports, Brazil began opening new regions to cultivation. The most important of these are devoted to soybean production in Mato Grosso do Sul, Rio Grande do Sul, São Paulo, Parana, and, more recently, Minas Gerais and Goias. Brazil also has expanded cultivation of sugarcane, the raw material used to produce the ethyl alcohol fuel that powers more than half of the nation's cars. Brazil's power, transportation, and communications systems generally have kept pace with development, but, in recent years, facilities in some areas have not met demand due to lack of investment and maintenance funds. The country has a large and increasingly sophisticated industrial base, producing basic industrial products such as steel, chemicals, petrochemicals, finished consumer goods and aircraft. A computer industry is also emerging. Within the past decade, industry has been the greatest contributor to economic growth. It accounts for nearly 35 percent of GDP and 60 percent of exports.

Brazil is one of the world's leading producers of hydroelectric power, with a potential of 106,500 megawatts. Existing hydroelectric plants provide 90 percent of the nation's electricity. Two large hydroelectric projects, the 12,600-megawatt Itaipu Dam on the Parana River—the world's largest dam—and the Tucurui Dam in northeast Brazil are in operation. Proven mineral resources are extensive, and additional exploration is expanding the resource base. Large iron and manganese reserves provide important sources of industrial raw materials and export earnings. Deposits of nickel, tin, chromite, bauxite, beryllium, copper, lead, tungsten, zinc, and gold, as well as lesser known minerals, are exploited. Oil exploration is less urgent now, because of Brazil's reduced dependence on oil and lower world prices. High-quality coal, especially of the coking grade required in the steel industry, is in short supply. The government is beginning to implement coal extraction and gasification projects to tap Brazil's ample deposits of low-grade coal in the south.

The Brazilian government has undertaken an ambitious program to reduce dependence on imported oil from 70 percent of the country's needs to less than 50 percent. In addition to developing hydroelectric, nuclear and coal resources, Brazil has become a world leader in the development of alcohol fuel derived from sugarcane. Brazilian gasoline is a mixture containing up to 22 percent ethyl alcohol. Its auto manufacturers began large-scale production of 100 percent alcohol-powered cars in 1979, and today more than 1.5 million are on the road. Alcohol production has not kept pace, however, leading to alcohol shortages in the early 1990s.

3. Current Policy Framework

On July 1, 1994, Brazil introduced a new national currency, the "Real" (the fifth in seven years), replacing the "cruzeiro real" at the rate of 2,750 cruzeiro reals per real. The new currency was the centerpiece of the government's economic stabilization plan, the *Plano Real,* designed to curb chronic, rampant inflation, which had reached an annual level of nearly 5,000 percent by the end of 1993. Other key elements of the stabilization plan included balancing the federal government budget, privatization of state-run industries, and strict monetary controls. Following the introduction of the new currency, nominal monthly rates of inflation fell from 50 percent in June (measured in the old currency) to 1.5 percent in September (measured in the new currency). The real rate of inflation was nonetheless higher for the first nine months of 1994 (15.87 percent per month) than for all of 1993 (13.38 percent). The Real Plan established quantitative targets on the expansion of the monetary base. Monetary policy was also constrained by the need to maintain positive real interest rates in order to roll over the domestic government debt and to prevent capital outflow. High interest rates, however, worsened the fiscal deficit.

Brazil has suffered structural deficits for many years. Provisions of the 1988 constitution which mandated substantial revenue transfers to states and municipalities, as well as mandatory federal expenditures, leave the government with discretionary control of only about 10 percent of revenues collected. Long-term stabilization will require structural reforms and revision of Brazil's constitution. The constitutional review process which began in 1993 expired in May 1994 with virtually no reforms adopted. Among the reforms considered by the Constitutional Review Congress were fiscal reforms, including a redistribution of federal, state and municipal government responsibilities, simplification of the tax system, privatization of the state-owned telecommunications and petroleum monopolies, elimination of the distinction between foreign and national capital, and permitting foreign investment in mining. Broad consensus existed on the need for constitutional reform to rectify the economic distortions of the current constitution, but there were significant differences regarding the specific reforms needed. Now that the constitutional review process was over, approval of constitutional reforms will require two votes each by the upper and lower chambers of the Brazilian Congress: a 60 percent majority is required for all four votes.

The process of economic and trade liberalization that began in 1990, slowed during 1993 and 1994, but has nevertheless produced significant changes in Brazil's trade regime, resulting in a more open and competitive economy. Imports were increasing in response to lower tariffs and reduced nontariff barriers, as well as the strength of the real relative to the dollar, and were now composed of a wide-range of industrial, agricultural and consumer goods. Access to Brazilian markets in most sectors was generally good, and most markets were characterized by competition and participation by foreign firms through imports, local production and joint ventures. Some sectors of the economy, such as the telecommunications, petroleum and electrical energy sectors, were still dominated by the government, and opportunities for trade and investment were severely limited.

Brazil and its partners, Argentina, Uruguay, and Paraguay, in the Southern Common Market (*Mercosul* in Portuguese), concluded negotiations in August 1994 for a common external tariff (CET) which went into effect on January 1, 1995. The CET levels for most products range between zero and 20 percent. The Brazilian government unilaterally lowered tariffs on some 6,000 items to the CET levels in September 1994, as part of its anti-inflationary effort. With the exception of tariffs on informatics products and some capital goods, the maximum Brazilian tariff level is now 20 percent, and the most commonly applied tariff is 14 percent. When the CET enters into force in the four Mercosul countries in January 1995, all revisions to the tariff schedule will have to be negotiated among the four partners.

The Government of Brazil ratified the Uruguay Round Agreements in 1994, and became a founding member of the World Trade Organization on January 1, 1995.

4. Exchange Rate Policy

Brazil has three exchange rates: a commercial rate, a tourist rate, and a semi-official parallel rate. The commercial rate is used for import-export and foreign investment transactions registered at the Central Bank and financial transactions linked to external debt. The tourist, or floating rate, is used for individual transactions such as unilateral transfers, travel, tourism, and transactions involving education and training abroad. The parallel rate is also used for individual transactions, but they are not recorded. All three rates fluctuate: the spread between them has diminished since the introduction of the new currency.

The measure introducing the real, established parity with the dollar. However, a surplus of dollars caused by financial activities of exporters and foreign investors, resulted in the steady appreciation of the real relative to the dollar. The Central Bank did not intervene until September, when the real reached 0.85 to one dollar. Subsequent Central Bank interventions indicate that this level is the Bank's floor.

5. Structural Policies

Although some administrative improvements have been made in recent years, the Brazilian legal and regulatory system was far from transparent. The government has historically exercised considerable control over private business through extensive and frequently changing regulations. To implement economic policies rapidly, the government has resorted to issuing decrees rather than securing congressional approval of legislation. These decrees were frequently challenged in the courts, and a number have been declared unconstitutional. Such regulatory instability makes planning difficult. In June 1994, a new antitrust law was passed to prevent "abusive pricing." The law will likely face legal challenges.

The tax system in Brazil was extremely complex, with a wide range of income and consumption taxes levied at the federal, state and municipal levels. Both payment and collection of taxes was burdensome. An effort to streamline the tax system was begun in 1991, and considerable progress has been made to improve collections. Significant further reforms will require constitutional revision.

The privatization program initiated in 1990 slowed to a near halt during 1994. The planned privatization of part of the electricity sector was abandoned entirely, while a number of planned auctions of financially troubled or noncompetitive, state-owned companies were delayed in response to lukewarm investor interest and low price offers. The pace of privatization is expected to increase significantly during 1995, under the new administration of President Cardoso.

6. Debt Management Policies

Brazil's external debt totaled approximately $146 billion at the end of 1994. Of this total, about $34 billion is medium-term commercial bank debt owed by the government. Foreign private bank debt is $63 billion, of which the U.S. share is $24 billion. In 1993, Brazil's debt service payments represented 4 percent of its gross domestic product, and 42 percent of its export earnings.

In April 1994, the government concluded a debt renegotiation agreement with foreign commercial banks, which included exchanging $35 billion in medium-term commercial bank debt for new instruments. The agreement also included rescheduling outstanding arrears. Unlike past Brady Plan debt exchanges, the Brazilian deal was closed without the support of the official international financial community since the Brazilian government was unable to reach an agreement with the IMF for a standby program. Brazil did not reach an agreement with the Paris Club during 1994 to reschedule official debt. Under Brazil's previous 1992 agreement with the Paris Club, further debt rescheduling is contingent upon the government concluding a standby agreement with the IMF.

7. Significant Barriers to U.S. Exports

Import Licenses: Although Brazil required import licenses for virtually all products, this generally did not pose a barrier to U.S. exports after 1990. Licenses are now used primarily for statistical purposes and generally are issued automatically within five days. However, obtaining an import license can occasionally still be difficult. For example, the Brazilian government has refused to grant an import license for lithium for nearly two years. In January 1992, a standard import license fee of approximately $100 was instituted, replacing a 1.8 percent ad valorem fee. The Secretariat of Foreign Trade's computerized trade documentation system (SISCOMEX), scheduled to be fully operational in January 1995, will further streamline filing and processing of import documentation.

Services Barriers: Restrictive investment laws, lack of administrative transparency, legal and administrative restrictions on remittances, and arbitrary application of regulations and laws limited U.S. service exports to Brazil. In some areas, such as construction engineering, foreign companies were prevented from providing technical services unless Brazilian firms were unable to perform them. Many service imports were restricted by limitations on foreign capital under the 1988 constitution. In particular, services in the telecommunications, oil field, and mining industries were severely restricted. Foreign financial institutions were restricted from entering Brazil or expanding pre-1988 operations. Restrictions also existed on the use of foreign-produced advertising materials.

Foreign legal, accounting, tax preparation, management consulting, architectural, engineering, and construction industries were hindered by various barriers. These include forced local partnerships, limits on foreign directorships and nontransparent registration procedures. Foreign participation in the insurance industry was impeded by limitations on foreign investment, market reserves for Brazilian firms in areas such as import insurance, and the requirement that para-statal organizations purchase insurance only from Brazilian-owned firms. Further, the lucrative reinsurance market was reserved for the state monopoly, the Reinsurance Institute of Brazil (IRB).

Other legal and administrative obstacles to foreign services suppliers were being eased. In January 1992, the government announced rules which allowed foreign remittances of trademark license fees and technology transfer payments covered by franchising agreements. The change effectively ended a 20-year ban on international franchising in Brazil.

Investment Barriers: In addition to restrictions on service-related sectors, foreign investment faced various prohibitions in petroleum production and refining, internal transportation, public utilities, media, real estate, shipping, and various other "strategic industries." In other sectors, such as the auto industry, Brazil limited foreign equity participation and imposes local-content requirements. Foreign ownership of land in rural areas and adjacent to international borders was prohibited. Foreign investors were denied "national treatment" pursuant to the constitutional distinction between national and foreign capital.

Informatics: Under the 1991 Informatics Law, prohibitions or requirements for government prior review for imports, investment, or manufacturing by foreign firms in Brazil were eliminated. However, import duties remained high (up to 35 percent) on information technology products, and Brazilian firms received preferential treatment in government procurement and had access to certain fiscal benefits, including tax reductions. For a foreign-owned firm to gain access to most of these incentives, it must commit to invest in local research and development and meet export and local training requirements. Rules governing computer software are contained in Law 7646 (the Software Law) of December 1987. It required that all software be "catalogued" by the Informatics Secretariat of the Ministry of Science and Technology prior to its commercialization in Brazil, and that in many cases software must be distributed through a Brazilian firm. The law contains provisions to deny cataloguing of foreign software if the Secretariat determines there was a similar program of Brazilian origin. However, this provision was no longer applied. A draft law has been introduced into Brazil's Congress to eliminate these three requirements.

Government Procurement: Given the significant influence and size of the state-controlled sector, discriminatory government procurement policies were an important barrier to U.S. exports. For example, procurement practices in the computer, computer software, and digital electronics sector may have significant adverse market access implications for U.S. firms, particularly firms not established in Brazil.

Article 171 of the 1988 constitution provides for government discrimination in favor of "Brazilian companies with national capital." On June 21, 1993, Brazil adopted procurement legislation, Law Number 8666, requiring open bids based upon the lowest price. However, later that year the government introduced new regulations which allow consideration of nonprice factors and give preferences to telecommunications, computer, and digital electronics goods produced in Brazil, and stipulate local content requirements for eligibility for fiscal benefits. In March 1994, the government issued Decree 1070 regulating the procurement of informatics and telecommunications goods and services. The regulations require federal agencies and para-statal entities to give preference to locally produced computer products based on a complicated and nontransparent price/technology matrix. It is not possible to estimate the economic impact of these restrictions upon U.S. exports. However, free competition could provide significant market opportunities for U.S. firms. Brazil was not a signatory to the GATT Government Procurement Code.

8. Export Subsidies Policies

In general, the Brazilian Government did not provide direct subsidies to exporters, but offered a variety of tax and tariff incentives to encourage export production and to encourage the use of Brazilian inputs in exported products. Several of these programs have been found to be eligible for U.S. countervailing duty provisions in the context of specific subsidy/countervailing duty cases. Incentives included tax and tariff exemptions for equipment and materials imported for the production of goods for export, excise and sales tax exemptions on exported products, and excise tax rebates on materials used in the manufacture of export products. Exporters also enjoyed exemption from withholding tax for remittances overseas for loan payments and marketing, and from the financial operations tax for deposit receipts on export products. In October 1994, the Brazilian government issued Decree Law 674, granting exporters a rebate on social contribution taxes paid on locally acquired production inputs.

An export credit program, known as PROEX, was established in 1991. PROEX was intended to eliminate the distortions in foreign currency-linked lending caused by Brazil's high rates of inflation and currency depreciation. Under the program, the government provided interest rate guarantees to commercial banks which finance export sales, thus ensuring Brazilian exporters access to financing at rates equivalent to those available internationally. Capital goods, automobiles and auto parts, and consumer goods were eligible for financing under the PROEX program.

9. Protection of U.S. Intellectual Property

Brazil's regime for the protection of intellectual property rights was inadequate. Serious gaps existed in current statutes with regard to patent protection for pharmaceuticals, chemicals, and biotechnological inventions; trademarks and trade secrets; and copyrights. Legislation has been pending before the Brazilian Congress for several years to address many of these areas. The Brazilian government has made a commitment to bring its intellectual property regime up to the international standards specified in the Uruguay Round Trade Related Aspects of Intellectual Property (TRIPs) Agreement. As a result of this commitment, the U.S. government terminated the "Special 301" investigation initiated in May of 1993, and revoked Brazil's designation as a "priority country" for trade retaliation. Brazil remains under Section 306 monitoring.

Brazil is a signatory to the GATT Uruguay Round Accords, including the TRIPs Agreement. Brazil is a member of the World Intellectual Property Organization and a signatory to the Berne Convention on Artistic Property, the Universal Copyright Convention, the Washington Patent Cooperation Treaty, and the Paris Convention on Protection of Intellectual Property.

Patents: Brazil did not provide either product or process patent protection for pharmaceutical substances, processed foods, metallurgical alloys, chemicals, or biotechnological inventions. The Industrial Property Bill passed in 1993 by the Chamber of Deputies and currently pending before the Senate would recognize the first four of these categories and extend the term for product patents from 15 to 20 years. The Brazilian government announced in early 1994 that it would support amendments to the bill which would bring its provisions into conformity with TRIPs provisions, including those on compulsory licensing, domestic requirements, and parallel imports.

Trade Secrets: Brazil lacked explicit legal protection for trade secrets, although a criminal statute against unfair trade practices can, in theory, be applied to prosecute the disclosure of privileged trade information. The Industrial Property Bill pending in Congress included civil penalties and injunctive relief for trade secret infringement.

Trademarks: All trademarks, as well as licensing and technical assistance agreements (including franchising), must be registered with the National Institute of Industrial Property (INPI). Without such registration, a trademark was subject to cancellation for nonuse. The pending Industrial Property Bill included significant trademark revisions which will improve trademark protection.

Copyrights: While Brazil's copyright law generally conformed to international standards, the 25-year term of protection for computer software fell considerably short of the Berne Convention standard of the life of the author plus 50 years. Enforcement of copyright laws has been lax. Current fines did not constitute an adequate deterrent to infringement. The U.S. private sector estimated that piracy of video cassettes, sound recordings and musical compositions, books, and computer software continued at substantial levels. Since 1993, enforcement of laws against video and software piracy has improved, and foreign firms have had some success in using the Brazilian legal system to protect their copyrights. The government had also initiated action to reduce the importation of pirated sound recordings and videocassettes.

Semiconductor Chip Lay-out Design: A bill introduced in 1992, and still pending before the Congress, will protect the lay-out designs of integrated circuits. Amendments to the draft law were expected to bring its provisions into conformity with the TRIPs text.

Impact on U.S. Trade: In early 1994, the U.S. pharmaceuticals industry estimated losses of $500 million due to inadequate intellectual property protection. The U.S. software industry claimed losses of $268 million, and estimated that less than 50 percent of the software in use in Brazil was legally obtained. The Motion Picture Export Association of America estimated its annual losses due to motion picture piracy in Brazil at $39 million.

10. Worker Rights

Brazil's Labor Code provided for union representation of all workers (excepting military, police, and firemen), but imposed a hierarchical, unitary system funded by a mandatory "union tax" on workers and employers. Under a restriction known as "*unicidade*" (one per city), the code prohibited multiple unions of the same professional category in a given geographical area. It also stipulated that no union's geographic base could be smaller than a municipality. The 1988 constitution retained many provisions of the 1943 Labor Code. The *unicidade* and union tax provisions continued to draw criticism from elements of Brazil's labor movement and from the International Confederation of Free Trade Unions (ICFTU).

In practice, however, *unicidade* had proven less restrictive in recent years, as more liberal interpretations of its restrictions have permitted new unions to form and, in many cases, compete with unions and federations that had already enjoyed official recognition. The sole bureaucratic requirement for new unions was to register with the Ministry of Labor which, by judicial decision, was bound to receive and record their registration. The primary source of continuing restriction was the system of labor courts, which retained the right to review the registration of new unions, and adjudicate conflicts over their formation. Otherwise, unions were independent of the government and of political parties. Approximately 20 to 30 percent of the Brazilian workforce was organized, with just over half of this number affiliated with an independent labor central. (Mandatory labor organization under the Labor Code encompassed a larger percentage of the workforce. However, many workers were believed to have minimal if any contact with these unions.) Intimidation of rural labor organizers by landowners and their agents continued to be a problem.

The constitution provided for the right to strike (excepting, again, military, police and firemen, but including other civil servants). Enabling legislation passed in 1989 stipulated that essential services remain in operation during a strike and that workers notify employers at least 48 hours before beginning a walkout. The constitution prohibited government interference in labor unions but provided that "abuse" of the right to strike (such as not maintaining essential services, or failure to end a strike after a labor court decision) was punishable by law.

Source: United States Department of State, Washington, DC, 1995.

UNIT 7 Alliances, Partnerships, and Acquisitions

Case 7–1.

Northrop Grumman and the Advanced Technology Transit Bus Program

On July 16, 1998, Lockheed Martin Corporation announced the termination of its attempt to acquire Northrop Grumman corporation and create the leading player in the world's defense industry. The dissolution of the merger agreement, first announced on July 3, 1997, was made in response to the "fundamental objections" raised by both the Justice Department, primarily on antitrust grounds, and the firms' principal customer, the U.S. Department of Defense.

The merger with Lockheed Martin had been Northrop Grumman management's response to a strategic dilemma it faced in the midst of the dramatic industry consolidation under way since the end of the Cold War. Raytheon Corporation had first acquired the military electronics operations of Texas Instrument for $3 billion in 1996, and had followed with an agreement early in 1997 to buy Hughes Electronics' defense operations from General Motors for $9.5 billion. These had been two highly contested transactions in which Northrop, following its own merger with Grumman in 1994, had failed in its decade-old ambition to reach the top ranks of the industry. Boeing's acquisition of Rockwell's defense and space business and McDonnell Douglas, and the earlier consolidation of Lockheed and Martin Marietta meant that the U.S. industry was closing ranks around a handful of major players. A similar trend was under way in Europe, although the European industry was still more fragmented than its North American counterpart.

With the collapse of the Lockheed deal, Northrop Grumman stood as a distant fourth in the aerospace/defense sector behind Boeing, Lockheed Martin, and Raytheon. Its total size in 1998 was approximately 20 percent that of Boeing's and one-half that of Raytheon's. In a climate of reduced defense expenditures and higher technology costs, the future seemed to call for larger firms that could maximize synergy and efficiency.

The ATTB Program

Simultaneously with these developments, Al McDonald, Vice President for Business Development at Northrop Grumman, had to reach a decision on what strategy he would recommend to top management regarding the upcoming request for manufacturing bids on an advanced technology transit bus. The first prototype for an ATTB, designed and built by Northrop Grumman, had been introduced in October 1996 at a major public unveiling in Los Angeles and had attracted considerable attention. Since then, five other vehicles had been built and delivered by the company, and were being subjected to a series of road tests nationwide. Although this product did not fit Northrop Grumman's core defense business, McDonald was convinced that there was a large market for these technically superior buses worldwide.

Northrop Grumman did not possess many of the key skills and abilities necessary to take such a product to market. And even if it did, the question of strategic fit would argue against major investments in this field. Furthermore, the Grumman Corporation had already suffered an earlier disastrous experience in the public transport industry, and many senior executives were reluctant to try again. So it seemed that some sort of alliance would be best. Yet, in spite of many efforts to this effect, no potential partner had emerged. The questions that Al needed to answer before Northrop Grumman's Corporate Strategy Group included how to proceed, with or without a suitable partner, and how to structure such a deal to everyone's satisfaction.

This case was prepared by Professors José de la Torre and Wesley B. Truitt, and by Ms. Barbara Lewis, at the Anderson School at UCLA as a basis for class discussion. The authors are grateful for the generous contributions made by a number of senior Northrop Grumman executives, particularly Mr. Robert L. Graham, but they retain all responsibility for the case content and any errors or misrepresentations of facts that may remain. Revised, April 1999.

Background

In mid-1991, Ronald Wilson, then Chief Engineer of the Los Angeles County Metropolitan Transportation Authority (LACMTA), approached a number of local aerospace companies with the unusual idea of developing a light-weight transit bus. His concept was to use an "aerospace" approach—that is, total system design, employing lightweight materials and using advanced control technologies—to accomplish a revolution in urban transport. Wilson called on Joe Sparkman, Manager of Advanced Systems in Northrop Grumman's Business Development Department, at the company's Aircraft Division in Hawthorne, California. After an initial discussion of potential characteristics and functional parameters, Joe carried out some preliminary analysis on the validity of such a concept. Satisfied that it was possible, he approached his boss, Al McDonald, with the recommendation that broader discussions continue with Wilson and his staff. McDonald agreed and gave the go-ahead for further talks.

The next meeting was held in October 1991 at Northrop Grumman's Hawthorne facilities. Wilson and his engineering and operations staff at LACMTA presented the case for a new generation of transit buses to be designed and built in the United States for the American market. The buses currently in operation on the streets of most American cities were based on designs from the 1950s or 60s, with some modifications made over the years to accommodate the availability of new components. They were generally very heavy, and exhibited high maintenance costs and low levels of fuel efficiency. Compared to European buses, which were much newer in design, they were less attractive, less comfortable and less efficient.

LACMTA's goal was to initiate an effort for a brand new design, "starting with a clean sheet of paper." They wanted aerospace industry involvement because they knew that aerospace engineers understood lightweight materials and were expert at total system design and integration (Wilson was a retired U.S. Air Force colonel). In their mind, the new bus would have to result in significantly lower operating costs as well as be driven by three major design considerations:

- *Light weight:* reduce the average weight by approximately one-third from the 30,000 pounds level that was characteristic of current buses;
- *Low emissions:* meet the Clean Air Act emission standards coming into force across the nation, but also go beyond in order to meet heightened air quality standards being mandated for Southern California;
- *Low floor:* meet the accessibility standards established by the Americans with Disabilities Act, and reduce "dwell" time (the time required to load and unload passengers at each stop).

LACMTA believed that an aerospace company could achieve these design goals better than the current bus industry. Their preliminary discussions with the four major U.S. bus manufacturers had confirmed that the latter had little interest in making the required changes, nor were they financially or technologically capable of doing so. Ronald Wilson understood that LACMTA did not know enough about the technical issues to write a Request for Proposal (RFP) for such an unorthodox product, so outside experts were engaged for this purpose.

Corporate Strategy and Core Competencies

When Kent Kresa took over as Chairman and CEO of Northrop in 1989, it was established that the company would remain principally a defense contractor and adhere to its core competencies related to this field. These included systems integration, computerized control systems, advanced electronics, and the use of lightweight materials. It was also determined that Northrop Grumman would explore applications of those core competencies in fields other than defense. McDonald had been part of the Strategic Planning Group which had developed these ideas for Mr. Kresa's review and approval, and he had a relatively good insight into the new CEO's thinking. As a result, Al concluded that the bus project fit Kresa's guidelines rather well. He understood the corporate culture and politics, and felt that "the bus could be made to fly."

More fundamentally, the Cold War had ended, the Soviet Union had ceased to exist, and the future of U.S. defense requirements was in flux. With this in mind, Northrop Grumman was searching for new opportunities for the application of its capabilities beyond its traditional Defense Department customer base. Many in the Aircraft Division, particularly in the marketing area, viewed the advanced technology bus as an excellent opportunity to test the company's capabilities to break out of pure defense programs and to apply Kresa's vision of alternative technology applications to a real test case. (See Exhibit 1 for a summary of Northrop Grumman sales by product category in recent years.)

Program Funding and Political Climate

Funding for the program initially came from LACMTA under a U.S. Department of Transportation (DOT) grant. It was clearly understood at LACMTA and among the members of the Los Angeles County Board of Supervisors that this was likely to become the largest R&D program ever funded in the United States for a transit vehicle. The effort could be justified because Los Angeles County had the second largest bus ridership and the longest route structure of any major American city. The Los Angeles bus system was also one of the nation's highest cost-per-mile operators; thus the motivation for a substantial reduction in operating costs.

The RFP was drafted during the spring of 1992 in a cooperative effort between LACMTA's engineering department and Northrop Grumman's Aircraft Division. The major design parameters were as follows:

1. A 40-foot long transit bus (about 13 meters); the industry standard.
2. Maximum unit price of $300,000 in 1992 dollars.
3. Passenger capacity of 43 seated and 29 standing, plus 2 wheelchairs.
4. Fully compliant with ADA requirements for disabled-person boarding.
5. Light-weight composite structure, noncorroding.
6. Curb weight at least 10,000 lb less than equivalent current bus.
7. Low emissions (2.5 gm/bhp-hr NOx and 0.05 gm/bhp-hr PM)[1] as per California's Air Resources Board (CARB) Low Emission Vehicle requirements.
8. Extended product life (25 years instead of the 12 currently in practice).
9. Vehicle management system for driver-command, high quality performance.
10. Low operating and life-cycle costs.
11. Self-diagnostics and rapid fault isolation.
12. Ergonomically designed operator's station.
13. Maintenance-friendly modular design.

[1]Emissions are measured in grams per brake-horsepower per hour of particulate matter.

EXHIBIT 1 Northrop Grumman Annual Sales by Product Category, 1992–1998
($ millions)

	1998	1997	1996	1995	1994	1993	1992
Net Sales							
B-2		$1,615	$1,725	$1,914	$2,392	$2,881	$3,212
Surveillance Aircraft		1,073	1,104	1,179	754	—	—
Boeing Jetliners		858	569	569	483	531	549
Airborne Radar		668	560	—	—	—	—
Marine		590	496	—	—	—	—
F/A—18		551	715	822	817	641	610
Electronic Countermeasures		384	398	351	357	372	378
Space		328	315	—	—	—	—
Airspace Management		297	223	—	—	—	—
C-17		276	249	244	121	—	—
Information Technology & Services		1,002	905	822	120	—	—
All other		1,511	1,348	1,371	1,667	638	801
Total	$8,902	$9,153	$8,607	$7,272	$6,711	$5,063	$5,550
Net Income	$ 194	$ 407	$ 264	$ 277	$ 35	$ 96	$121
Total Assets	$9,536	$9,677	$9,645	$5,642	$6,047	$2,939	$3,162
Long-Term Debt	$2,562	$2,500	$2,950	$1,163	$1,633	$ 160	$160

Note: Figures for 1995–97 have been restated to account for recent acquisitions in the information technology area; 1998 figures are year-end estimates.
Source: Annual Reports.

Four companies indicated interest in bidding after the RFP was released: Northrop Grumman, Hughes Aircraft, Lockheed, and TRW. Hughes eventually joined the Northrop Grumman team as a subcontractor. The three remaining teams submitted proposals in November and the LACMTA staff reviewed and scored them, narrowing the competition to Northrop Grumman and TRW. Northrop Grumman was judged to be several points higher than TRW, mostly on technical merit. Consequently, the engineering staff recommended that they be declared the winner.

The LACMTA Board reviewed the staff evaluation and scheduled a vote for a meeting to be held on December 17, 1992. TRW was invited to make a presentation to the Board in order for them to counter the staff's recommendation. In the end, the Board's vote was 7 to 1 in favor of the staff's recommendation. A contract was negotiated and signed in early 1993 for a Phase I effort (concept definition/preliminary design) at a contract value of $3.8 million. The funds were provided by the Federal Transit Administration (FTA) and LACMTA on an 80/20 split, that is, 80 percent by the federal agency and 20 percent local funding.

Thus, in January 1993, Northrop Grumman became the prime contractor of the LACMTA's Advanced Technology Transit Bus program. This presented Northrop Grumman's corporate management with a dilemma. While they had approved undertaking the program and liked the idea of having won the contract, especially one involving their local government, they were concerned that the bus program might "confuse" their principal customer, the U.S. Department of Defense (DOD). With the Cold War ended, a new CEO at the helm, and funding for the company's largest program (the B-2 bomber) in constant political trouble, the company saw some serious risks to its future customer base. What if DOD, as a result of the bus program, thought that Northrop Grumman was less committed to the defense business?

As a result, Corporate decided to downplay the bus publicly, while the Aircraft Division helped to bring the project to reality and sustain it. Northrop Grumman's Washington office was to make sure the federal government requested, authorized, and appropriated their 80 percent share of the necessary funding during each subsequent year for the program. LACMTA understood this very well and directed its own Washington lobbyists to work the bus program aggressively among congressional corridors, in close cooperation with Northrop Grumman's office. A number of key Aircraft Division marketing and program management people provided behind the scenes support. Due to these joint efforts, approximately $41 million in federal funds were appropriated for the program over the next five years. This, together with LACTMA's local share, brought the total ATTB R&D program to just over $51 million. Northrop Grumman was not required to make any investment of its own funds.

Two key political factors enabled this to happen: California's legislative clout in Washington and a cooperative Administration of the same political party. California's two Democratic senators, Barbara Boxer and Diane Feinstein, were briefed on the program and supported it. In fact, Senator Boxer became the program's main champion. Facing re-election earlier than Feinstein, she had coined the slogan "Build a Bomber, Build a Bus" during her election campaign. When first briefed on the ATTB, she was pleased to learn that her slogan now had a real basis. With large reductions in DOD spending, both senators sought new programs to reinvigorate the state's depressed economy. Senator Feinstein was a member of the Senate's Appropriations Committee. She worked hard to secure the first increment of federal funding specifically earmarked for the ATTB by adding $6.25 million of unrequested and unauthorized funds to the DOT's 1993 fiscal year appropriation. By November 1993, the DOT agreed to support the program, giving it official national status.

During the following year, the DOT's leadership included the ATTB R&D program as part of their "request" in the President's budget submittal to Congress for fiscal year 1994. The LACMTA/Northrop Grumman team in Washington once again worked assiduously to enact these funds. The Clinton Administration's Secretary of Transportation, Federico Peña, took a personal interest in the bus program, hailing it in speech after speech as an excellent case for federal and local partnership and a fine example of "defense conversion." That same year, in April, Northrop acquired the Grumman Corporation.

Initial Progress and Project Development

At the start of Phase I, Al McDonald held a two-day off-site meeting with all participating firms to develop team spirit and agree on communication protocols. The designation of an "Integrated Product Team" would follow standard Northrop Grumman practice in such cases, emphasizing collaboration and total quality concepts. One company (TMC of Roswell, New Mexico) was a bus manufacturer, giving the team credibility in the customer's eyes and also at the corporate office. Other partners included Hughes Aircraft (electronic systems, controls display and intelligent highway systems), FMC Corporation (hybrid drive systems), Detroit Diesel (alternate fuel engines) and Allison Transmission Division (drive components).

Phase I preliminary design activity was completed in October 1993, and LACMTA and Northrop Grumman had a design (and more importantly a model) of the bus to show government officials. The bus was viewed as "politically correct" in several dimensions: it had low emissions, it complied with the Americans with Disabilities Act, and it was a shining example of successful defense conversion. Senator Boxer became an enthusiastic spokesperson, stating that "This bus will be built right here in Southern California."

While appreciative of the support, LACMTA and Northrop Grumman worked aggressively to prevent the bus from becoming a political program associated with any one party. They were also concerned not to build exaggerated expectations in terms of jobs and other economic development outcomes. And, of course, there was the persisting question of how DOD would view this effort.

By December, LACMTA awarded Northrop Grumman the Phase II engineering and manufacturing design contract without competition. The program was proceeding well, on cost and on schedule. The successful political effort was viewed as critical to the program's future viability. Northrop Grumman had assembled a team of 18 companies working contractually as suppliers, three of which were minority- or women-owned. With the on-time and on-cost completion of Phase II, the Phase III contract for prototype construction was again awarded without competition the following year. Federal funding continued, although each year it was an increasing struggle.

Potential Markets

The U.S. domestic bus market has fluctuated between annual sales of 2,000 and 3,000 units of the standard, large city transit buses (38′–45′ in length) and an additional 400–500 units of medium buses (33′–38′) since the mid 1980s (see Exhibit 2). At a unit price around \$300,000,[2] new bus annual sales exceeded \$1 billion a year. The top 40 transit bus customers in the country (each roughly corresponding to a city authority) represented more than 80 percent of the total national bus fleet and annual procurement. The remaining customers, representing hundreds of smaller communities and transit systems, standardized their requirements around the larger customers in order to save on procurement and logistics costs. Other buyers, such as intercity bus lines, airport authorities, rental car agencies, school districts, etc., represented the balance of sales.

Federal regulations mandating alternate-fueled vehicles caused a significant decline in bus deliveries in 1992. Due to intense price competition and the lack of proactive cost cutting strategies, several manufactures, including BIA and TMC[3] were acquired, while others, such as Flxible, had gone bankrupt without completing their outstanding orders. The remaining players were mainly assemblers who operated with outdated technology, delivering products that were sold only under specification waivers. The industry was generally considered a graveyard for major vehicle manufacturers.

In June 1995, Sparkman and McDonald visited the world transit expo in Paris to view the competition and assess the market outside the United States. The European market was estimated to be approximately 10,000 buses per year, or nearly four times the size of the U.S. market. European built buses were considered to be excellent in quality, although they were mostly made of steel and aluminum and were powered by conventional diesel or gasoline engines.[4] Weight did not seem to be a major issue in Europe, but low operating costs were critical. In addition, emission problems were beginning to emerge as a political issue in the wake of some significant political gains made by various "green" parties, particularly in France and Germany.

None of the major European companies expressed any interest in working with Northrop Grumman on the ATTB program, fearing among other things high start-up costs. These companies included Mercedes-Benz, Volvo, Mann, Iveco, and Renault. Only Volvo and Mercedes-Benz appeared to have any interest in penetrating the U.S. market. But due to "Buy American" provisions governing public procurement in the United States, plus tariffs and other restrictions, the

[2]According to the American Public Transit Association, average costs for a sample of buses ordered in 1997–98 ranged from \$358,000 for "long" buses (over 45′ in length), \$354,000 for intercity buses, \$277,000 for standard (38′–42′) buses, and \$252,000 for medium buses (33′–38′).

[3]TMC was first acquired by Canada's Novabus, which in turn was acquired by Volvo in 1998.

[4]Over 80 percent of all new buses delivered in the United States in 1997 were diesel powered. Compressed natural gas accounted for an additional 19 percent. All other energy sources represented less than 1 percent of deliveries.

EXHIBIT 2 U.S. Bus Deliveries
(1987–1997)

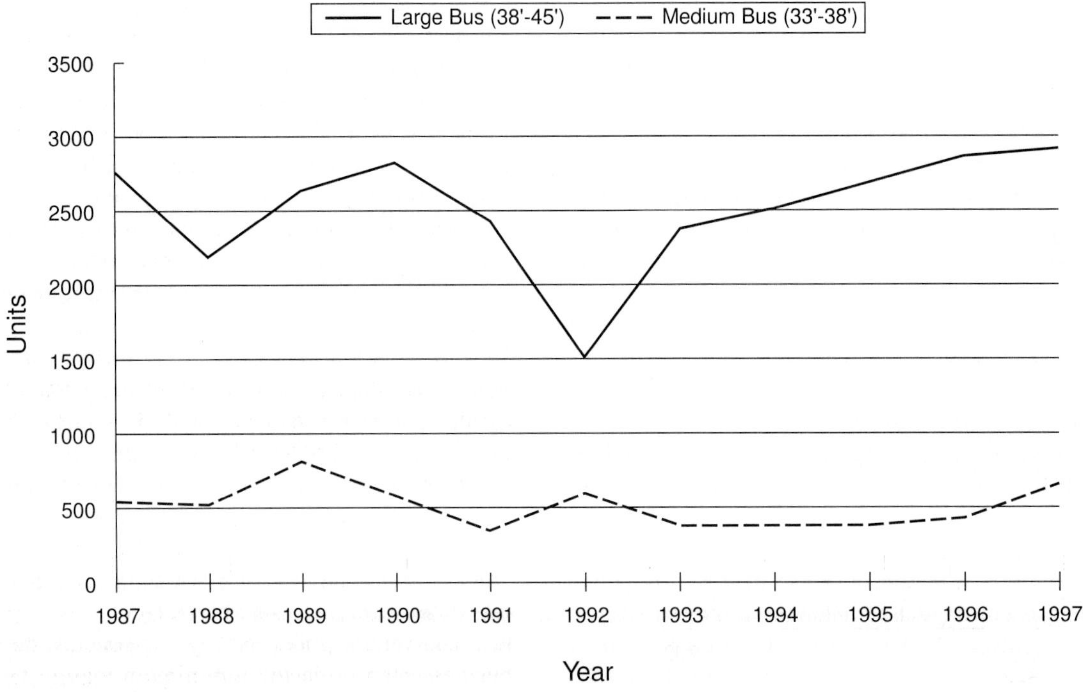

Source: American Public Transit Association, 1998.

U.S. market was essentially closed to non-U.S. based producers, unless they would set up local manufacturing subsidiaries or entered into a joint venture with an American company. Volvo had successful partnerships with two Hungarian firms, Ikarus and NAB Industries Ltd., and had recently acquired Canada's Novabus.

In Asia, most markets were supplied by Japanese or Korean companies. These markets, however, generally required smaller buses and were organized differently than the typical European or North American transit authority. Japan was a closed market and Northrop Grumman's trading company partner there had indicated that no Japanese firm was interested in the new bus product. The Koreans, particularly Samsung, were aware of the ATTB program and expressed some interest in eventually becoming a licensed producer or coproducer. All markets for new procurement outside Europe and North America were estimated to amount to over 10,000 buses annually. Exhibit 3 shows a sampling of the fleet sizes in 25 major world cities.

The Northrop Grumman team estimated that the ATTB could be expected to capture 30 percent of the domestic urban transit bus market in the United States within five years of domestic production and delivery. Its penetration of international markets would depend on the availability of domestic partners in each area, and on the characteristics of local transit systems.

With an eye to the future, Northrop Grumman had formed the Rapid Transit Review Board in 1992. This board consisted of 20 transit agencies from across the country that participated as a design review team for the life of the R&D program. These agencies included most of the largest transit bus users in the United States and represented a geographically diverse set of user conditions, both topographical and climatic, and population densities. The board was intended to develop a customer base for the product, ease any fear associated with the introduction of new technology, and establish a linkage that would permit a smooth transition to production and operation. The RTRB was viewed by the ATTB team as critical to the future success of the program, since Northrop Grumman had no plans to spend any marketing dollars to attract attention to the new product or to develop its market.

EXHIBIT 3 Existing Bus Fleets for Selected Cities (1995)

Asia	
Seoul	8,500
Shanghai	5,300
Delhi	3,500
Beijing	3,000
Bombay	3,200
Tokyo	1,800
Taipei	1,400
Calcutta	1,300
Australia/South Africa	
Sydney	1,400
Capetown	700
Middle East	
Cairo	3,100
Istanbul	2,300
Europe	
London	5,200
Paris	4,000
Stockholm	1,900
Athens	1,800
Madrid	1,800
Warsaw	1,700
Munich	1,600
Budapest	1,600
Bucharest	1,200
Barcelona	800
South/Central/North America	
Mexico City	4,000
Montreal	1,800
Rio de Janeiro	700

Source: Jane's Urban Transport System, 1996–7.

Product Characteristics, Costs, and Benefits

On October 8, 1996, after nearly four years of development, the first prototype ATTB was rolled out at Northrop Grumman's E1 Segundo, California, facility. Present were Secretary Peña, Senator Boxer, and a number of senior LACMTA officials, including a beaming Ronald Wilson. The bus was a standard 40 feet in length, had the stated seating capacity, and weighed 21,000 lb. Its power was derived from an engine operating on compressed natural gas which, in turn, powered an electric generator. The latter provided electric power to all four wheel motors, accessories (such as air conditioning), and control equipment. The bus was capable of operating on alternative fuels. There were four wheels instead of the standard six. It had a low floor, with all mechanical equipment placed on the roof, was largely made of glass composite material and had fewer heavy mechanical components. The driver had an array of electronic equipment in the "cockpit" controlling most bus functions and accessories.

A total of six prototypes were delivered by the end of 1997. Road testing in Los Angeles County and other geographic locations was scheduled for most of 1998, and this would complete the R&D program.

The ATTB was estimated to have a selling price of about $337,000 per unit, slightly higher than the average price of a conventional bus. Although there were considerable uncertainties regarding projected costs depending on factors such as production rates, final design parameters, and vendor prices for key components, the ATTB business plan projected a minimum margin target of 20 percent on sales. The domestic industry's average profit margin was less than 10 percent. Northrop Grumman believed that the ATTB's operating cost efficiencies allowed for a premium price. This fact, combined with significant lower production costs due to its unique technologies and processes, would justify the higher margin expectations.

LACMTA projected, for example, that the ATTB would result in operating cost reductions in the order of 25–30 percent relative to conventional buses. The cost benefits of introducing such a product into their fleet would include:

1. Lower fuel consumption, reduced component wear, and increased reliability.
2. Ergonomically designed operator's area permitting longer hours for drivers.
3. A flat floor enabling easy entry and exit and reducing "dwell" time by up to 80 percent.
4. Fast removal and replacement of components, reducing out-of-service vehicles by 50 percent.
5. Longer life (twice that of a standard bus) due to corrosion-free components, thereby reducing capital costs per operating passenger-mile.

LACMTA estimated that if it replaced its entire fleet of 2,100 buses with the ATTB, it would save $8 million a year on fuel and $1.8 million a year on brake repairs alone. In addition, the bus's lower weight would reduce damage to streets, highways, bridges, and terminal infrastructure, savings that would accrue to the municipality operating the transit authority.

Future Production

Northrop Grumman had stated from the beginning that it could make no commitment to put the bus into production. In addition to the question of strategic fit, management realized that the company lacked many of the skills necessary to succeed in this business. Chief among these were high-rate manufacturing skills to operate a line making thousands of these products per year, as opposed to the much smaller numbers involved in a typical aircraft program. Also, the tight cost requirements associated with commercial production might not come handily to Northrop Grumman's manufacturing facilities. Finally, the company had no experience in marketing this type of product, nor in dealing with a multitude of customers that would be spread widely across the nation and, perhaps, globally. The need to warrant products and provide service and performance guarantees were markedly different in commercial markets than in defense procurement programs. Investment, however, was not a problem. Initial estimates were that a factory and capital equipment necessary to manufacture up to 1,000 buses per year would cost less than $50 million.

There were a number of options available to Al McDonald and his team. One was to complete the test program and then stop, hand over the final results to LACMTA, and move on to other activities. A second set of options revolved around the concept of licensing the technology. Any number of U.S. or overseas manufacturers might be interested, although none had demonstrated an overwhelming desire to do so. Part of the problem was that the ATTB's technology would be entirely foreign to any standard vehicle manufacturer. Skills in metal bending and conventional mechanics would not be very applicable to composite materials, modular fabrication, and systems integration. Although technically all drawings and product specifications belonged to LACMTA and the DOT, who had funded the program, Northrop Grumman retained the know-how essential to put such a product into production. The U.S. government and LACMTA wanted this product built, and senior Northrop Grumman executives did not feel that the ownership issue would be critical as long as their ultimate objective was met.

A third option was to enter into a joint venture with either a U.S. or a foreign manufacturer who possessed the necessary skills. Preliminary discussions with a host of U.S.-based companies had shown little prospects or interest. Northrop Grumman was concerned about the political implications of an alliance with a foreign company on a DOT-funded project. But neither had any of the major European companies signaled an interest to pursue this possibility.

In defining the criteria by which any such partner might be selected, a number of characteristics had been mentioned as being critical to the choice. These included bus manufacturing experience, high-rate vehicle production expertise, financial resources, the availability of U.S. operations (or the willingness to build such a facility), and the company's reputation and acceptability to the municipalities that would be the likely customers. In addition, access to foreign markets might be an attractive feature of a partner, but only at a second stage in the business development.

Finally, there was the possibility of taking the plunge and entering the bus business directly. This was by far the least popular alternative internally. It was suggested that Northrop Grumman could not produce the bus inside one of its operating divisions given overhead rates and DOD cost sharing issues. Instead, a separate subsidiary would have to be established and the requisite skills purchased in the market. But corporate opposition to any major investment in this product would likely doom any such initiative. Exhibits 4–6 list the companies that had been identified as potential partners for either licensing, joint venture, or acquisition in the ATTB program. Exhibit 7 is a picture of the bus prototype.

Test Program Results

By the Fall of 1998, the six prototype vehicles had virtually completed a rigorous test program. Some had been in operation on the streets of Los Angeles, carrying passengers on normal routes, while others had performed similar tests in Phoenix, Minneapolis, Boston, New York City, and Washington, D.C. One vehicle spent several months undergoing simulated road testing at the National Vehicle Test Center in Pennsylvania. These tests put the vehicles through every topographical, climate, route size and length, and other environmental and operating conditions to which the bus might be exposed if it were to enter normal service in North America.

Results of the test program were positive. No systemic failures were encountered, although there were failures

EXHIBIT 4 Existing Bus Manufacturers

U.S. Companies	Location	Advantages	Disadvantages
Flxible	Ohio	Bus manufacturing experience	Once owned by Grumman; Out of business
Gillig	California	Bus manufacturer; 21% U.S. market share in 1997	Weak; No interest; Small; Low tech
Neoplan	Colorado	LACMTA bought some of their buses and had problem with natural gas; Strong technology	Small (6% of U.S. market in 1997); German-owned; parent may not approve
Mercedes Benz	Alabama	Financially capable; Largest bus manufacturer in world	Only autos and SUVs made in U.S.; Possible cannibalization of existing products
TMC	New Mexico	Bus manufacturing experience; Worked with Northrop on ATTB	Owned by Novabus; U.S. factory closed in 1997
No. American Bus Co.	Alabama	Bus manufacturing; 9% market share	Small, Low-tech and financially weak
Motor Coach Industries (MCI)	Chicago	Bus manufacturing experience; 3% U.S. market share in 1997	Low tech; subsidiary of Dina (Mexico); low financial capacity
Canadian Companies			
Bombardier	Montreal	Financially capable; Diversified, hi-tech company	No bus experience; Rate production
Orion	Ontario and U.S. (NY)	Bus manufacturing experience; 18% of U.S. bus market in 1997	Conventional technology; subsidiary of Western Star Trucks (B.C.)
New Flyer	Manitoba and U.S. (MN)	Bus manufacturing experience; 17% of U.S. bus market in 1997	Conventional technology; small and low tech
Novabus	Ontario	Bought TMC to establish U.S. presence; 14% U.S. market share in 1997	Financially weak; Small; Low tech Acquired by Volvo in 1998
European Companies			
Ikarus	Hungary	High-rate production	Financially weak; Small; Low tech
Iveco	Italy	Financially capable; High-tech; Largest Italian manufacturer	No interest in expansion beyond Europe
Mann	Germany	Financially capable; Leading edge technology in Europe	No interest in expansion beyond Europe
Mercedes Benz	Germany	Financially capable; Largest bus manufacturer in the world	Concerned about cannibalization of existing products
Renault	France	Bus manufacturing experience; Largest in France	State owned; No interest; Old technology; Financially troubled
Volvo	Sweden	Financially and technically capable; Wants U.S. market entry; 2nd largest bus manufacturer in Europe	Conventional technology; concerned about cannibalization

EXHIBIT 5 Other Vehicle Manufacturers

Companies	Country	Advantages	Disadvantages
BMW	Germany	Expanding into all types of passenger vehicles; High-rate production; Aerospace history; Has plant in South Carolina	No bus experience
Caterpillar	U.S. (IL)	Financially capable; High-rate production; Might seek diversification	No passenger vehicle manufacturing experience
DaimlerChrysler	U.S. (MI)	Surplus cash; Kresa was a member of Chrysler's board and Vice-Chair Lutz served on NG's board	No prior bus experience; merger into DaimlerChrysler may change focus
Fiat	Italy	Cash rich; Provide European base	No bus experience; Focus on European vehicle production
Ford	U.S. (MI)	Surplus cash; International opportunities; Might desire coach division	No transit bus experience (built only school buses)
GM	U.S. (MI)	Surplus cash; North American vehicle focus; International opportunities	Sold off coach division in 1980s; May be reluctant to re-enter
Honda	Japan and U.S. (OH)	Cash rich; U.S. opportunities; May want coach division	No bus experience
John Deere	U.S. (IL)	Financially capable; High-rate production; Might seek diversification	No passenger vehicle manufacturing experience
Kawasaki	Japan	Financially and technically capable	No large vehicle manufacturing experience
Mazda	Japan and U.S. (MI)	Financially and technically capable; Access to Japan	May have no interest
Mitsubishi	Japan	Financially and technically capable; automotive experience	May have no interest
Nissan	Japan and U.S. (TN)	Cash rich; U.S. opportunities; May want coach division	No bus experience
Samsung	Korea	U.S. opportunities; Northrop subcontractor; Considered Korean auto production; Wants diversification	No vehicle experience; Affected by Korean crisis
Toyota	Japan and U.S. (KY)	Cash rich; U.S. opportunities; May want coach division	No bus experience

EXHIBIT 6 Aerospace Manufacturers

Company	Country	Advantages	Disadvantages
Aerospatiale	France	Advanced technology	No bus experience; Financially weak; State owned; Member of Airbus consortium
Alenia	Italy	Advanced technology	No bus experience
Allied Signal	U.S. (NJ)	Cash rich; Northrop Grumman relationship; High-rate production; Major vehicle component manufacturing	No bus experience
Boeing	U.S. (WA)	Northrop Grumman is subcontractor on 747	No bus experience
British Aerospace	U.K.	Northrop Grumman relationship; High-rate production	No bus experience
CASA	Spain	Northrop Grumman relationship; Advanced technology	No bus experience; Small; State owned; Financially weak
Dassault	France	Privately owned; Advanced technology	Northrop Grumman rival; Financially weak; No bus experience; No vehicle experience
DaimlerChrysler Aerospace (DASA)	Germany	Financially and technically capable	Parent company may not view favorably
Lockheed Martin	U.S. (MD)	High-rate experience; Advanced technology	No bus experience
Raytheon	U.S. (MA)	High-rate experience; Advanced technology	No bus experience
Textron	U.S. (RI)	Financially and technically capable; High-rate experience	No bus experience
TRW	U.S. (OH)	Parent company in vehicle component manufacturing; Wanted ATTB program; Advanced technology; California facilities	No bus experience

EXHIBIT 7 ATTB Prototype

detected in various subsystems and components. For example, the electrical systems overheated in downtown Los Angeles during the summer months because the temperature inverters had been placed in the engine cavity. A design change will place them on the roof, where ambient temperatures are much cooler. On two occasions a suspension mount pulled loose due to manufacturing defects, but repairs were successfully undertaken. None of the failures encountered, normal for any test program, was considered to be critical.

On the contrary, in some respects the vehicles performed better than expected. The computer control system and the integration of the heating/cooling system, for example, were far superior to expectations. It was also discovered that the composite material of the bus shell was a better insulator than anticipated, leading to easier floor heating in the Minneapolis winter testing and to greater air conditioning efficiency in Phoenix, exceeding performance ratings by 25 percent. In the end, all 13 design parameters outlined at the outset of the R&D project had been validated.

LACMTA's Request for Manufacturing Proposals

The political environment in Los Angeles had shifted significantly since 1994. This was partly the result of major failures in cost control by LACMTA in connection with the multibillion dollar subway construction project under way since the late 1980s. Significantly behind schedule and grossly over budget, the prospects for completion of the ambitious underground transit project were dim. In the meantime, the neglect of the bus system had resulted in an aging bus fleet (over 40 percent of the fleet was over the 12 year-old design limit), a number of disastrous experiments (hundreds of methanol/ethanol-fueled buses suffered repeated engine failure), and an irate public that relied on buses for 91 percent of all public transportation in the county. LACMTA struggled each day to find the 1,805 buses it needed to operate its full route schedule.[5]

After Mayor Richard Riordan appointed Julian Burke as the new CEO for LACMTA in the summer of 1997, the strategy shifted away from expensive rail systems and toward greater use of surface vehicles. Recently, nearly 500 new compressed natural gas buses were added to the fleet. An additional 223 of these were to be delivered by the summer of 1999. And the agency has committed itself publicly in September 1998 to add another 2,095 modern buses to its fleet over the next six years.

By November 1998, LACTMA was preparing to release an RFP for volume production of ATTBs. The RFP was to provide for the purchase of at least 500 ATTB buses over a period of five years for LACTMA's own use. Also included in the RFP would be an ancillary procurement of up to 150 ATTBs for New York City, Washington, D.C., Baltimore, and Santa Monica, California. Thus, the RFP would package a procurement of more than 130 buses per year for the five cities. Other city transit authorities wanted to participate in this initial procurement, but both LACMTA and Northrop Grumman felt that a five-customer launch order may stretch management to the limit. Additional city orders could be entertained after the program was under way. The RFP assumed a factory site in the Los Angeles area.

From Northrop Grumman's standpoint, the ATTB contract would be completed on December 15, 1998, with the delivery of the remaining three prototypes to LACMTA. The ATTB office at Northrop Grumman would then be virtually shut down. All specialized tools would be placed in storage, and the remaining 17 people who had worked on the program would be reassigned or laid off. Corporate management believed that the company should not take the lead in bus production, but a two-year search for a strategic partner had yielded no results to date.

Northrop Grumman had stressed its willingness to provide technical support, experience, and manufacturing "know-how" to whichever firm stepped forward as prime contractor, whether it involved the company or

[5]During the 1984 Summer Olympics, the county had an active fleet of 2,600 buses.

not. They would be willing to turn over existing plans, drawings, and other relevant documentation, as well as make available its key personnel to a winning bidder. Fees for these services would have to be negotiated with the new bus company owners, but Northrop Grumman had declared to the FTA and to LACMTA that they would "not drop the ATTB." Time was running short on a decision, however, and the risk that the team responsible for the project would soon disband was a serious threat to the continuity of the bus program.

Case 7–2

Fiat and Peugeot's SEVELNORD Venture (A): Laying the Foundations for a Second Success

On one of Turin's first warm spring days in March 1991, Roberto Rossi of Fiat Auto and Roland Picard[1] of Peugeot Automobiles SA were spending the day at Fiat's renowned Mirafiori plant preparing for the next meeting of the Directors' Committee of the companies' two joint ventures, SEVEL and SEVELNORD.

The two companies had been working closely together since 1978, the starting date of the first SEVEL joint venture, which produced a very successful line of commercial vans. At the top of the current agenda was the second venture, SEVELNORD, due to begin minivan production in 1994 (refer to Exhibit 1). Since the agreement had been signed in 1988, much had already been decided about the framework of the second venture: location, operating structure, design, and production methods. But, on the following day, the Directors' Committee would have to finalize its industrial investment plan, which would have considerable financial implications. The plan would clearly set the venture into an irreversible mode.

Before committing to such a high level, Roberto Rossi and Roland Picard, who jointly presided over the Directors' Committee, felt it would be useful to review their relationship and their achievements, in the hope of drawing some lessons for future decisions. They formed a small team to prepare the review, with Giovanni Bianchi representing Fiat and Jean Pierre from Peugeot.

As the final version of this presentation started taking shape, all four individuals felt good about the probable outcome of the Directors' Committee meeting. They were confident that the two partners would find the needed inspiration to answer the remaining questions.

SEVEL Italie: A Working Success

Fiat Auto and Peugeot had been successfully working together for over a decade. Their first joint venture, known as SEVEL (*Société Européenne de Véhicules Légers and Società Europea Veicoli Leggeri*), had begun in 1978 as a cooperative effort to develop and manufacture a new line of commercial vans. The first vehicles were produced and marketed in late 1981 under five brands: the Fiat Ducato, Peugeot J5, and the Citroën C25, as well as models for subsidiaries Alfa Romeo and Talbot.[2] Both Fiat and Peugeot (which also owned Citroën) bought the vans from SEVEL Italie (SI) and distributed them independently through their own network. The model met with immediate success. Between 1981 and 1988, production increased from 250 vehicles per day in 1982 to 700 per day in 1988, exactly double the originally planned maximum volume of 350 vehicles a day.

In order to manage the project, which was known internally as the X2/12, the two companies adopted a uniquely balanced management structure. A new factory was built in Val di Sangro near Pescara, Italy,[3] specifically for the venture. Both companies had contributed equally in terms of research and development, engineering

[1]The names of all managers and as well as some of the data presented in this case have been modified to assure confidentiality. The rest of the information discussed is factual.

This case was prepared by Research Associate Mary Schweinsberg under the supervision of Professor Francis Bidault as a basis for class discussion rather than to illustrate either effective or ineffective handling of a business situation.

[2]Alfa Romeo and Talbot are owned respectively by Fiat and Peugeot SA.

[3]Val di Sangro was a highly automated, state-of-the-art assembly facility, conducting three phases of production: body-in-white, painting, and final assembly.

Body-in-white defined: the foundation of the car which serves as the structural frame. It encompasses the outer "skin" of the car and has important aesthetic requirements. Body-in-white consists of many manufacturing processes such as lines of stamping and dies, component subassemblies like underbody, engine compartment, roof, etc. After body-in-white is assembled, it moves through painting and into final assembly for power train, exterior trim and internal finishing.

EXHIBIT 1a SEVEL Italie: Variations of the X2/30

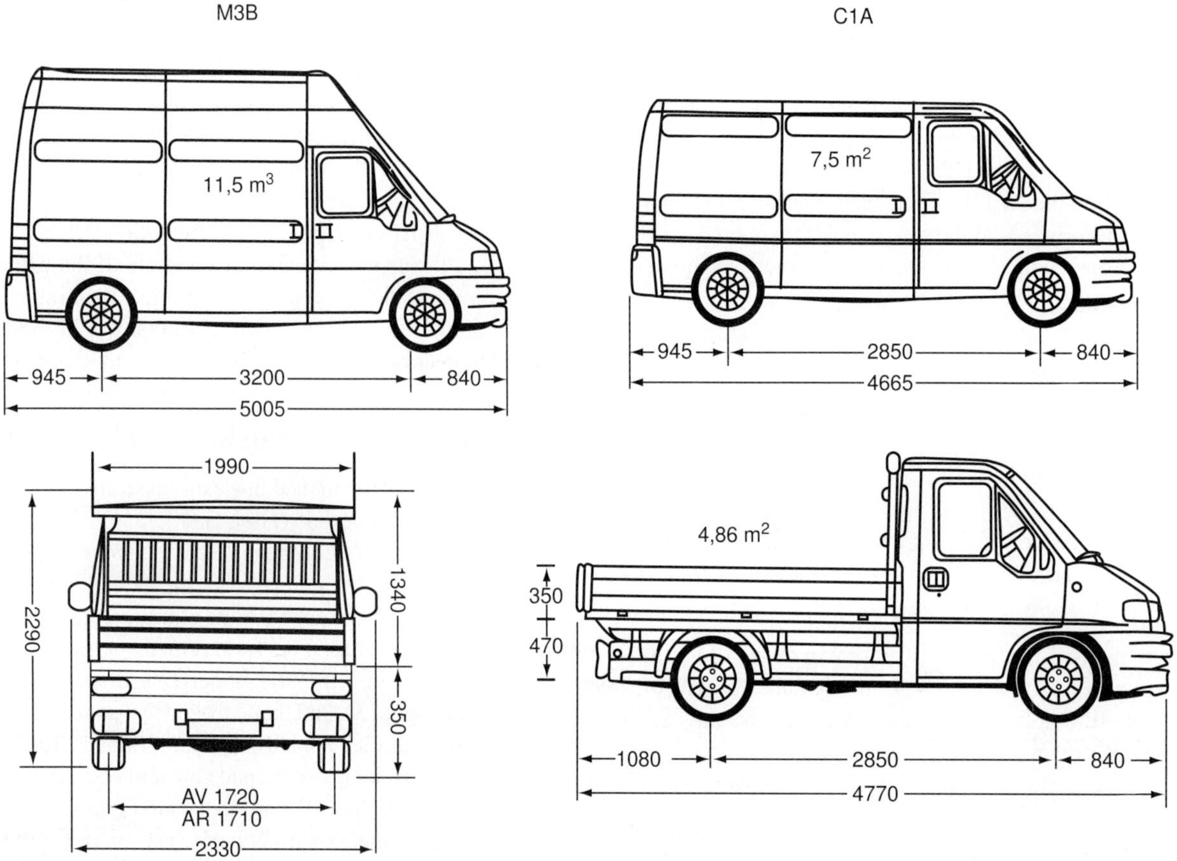

M3B
C1A
11,5 m³
945
3200
840
5005
7,5 m²
945
2850
840
4665
1990
2290
1340
350
AV 1720
AR 1710
2330
4,86 m²
350
470
1080
2850
840
4770

EXHIBIT 1b SEVELNORD: The UG Project. Vehicle Marketed as the 806, Ulysse, Evasion and Zeta

ULYSSE
5 places
6 places
7 places (5+2 sur demande)
8 places (5+3 sur demande)

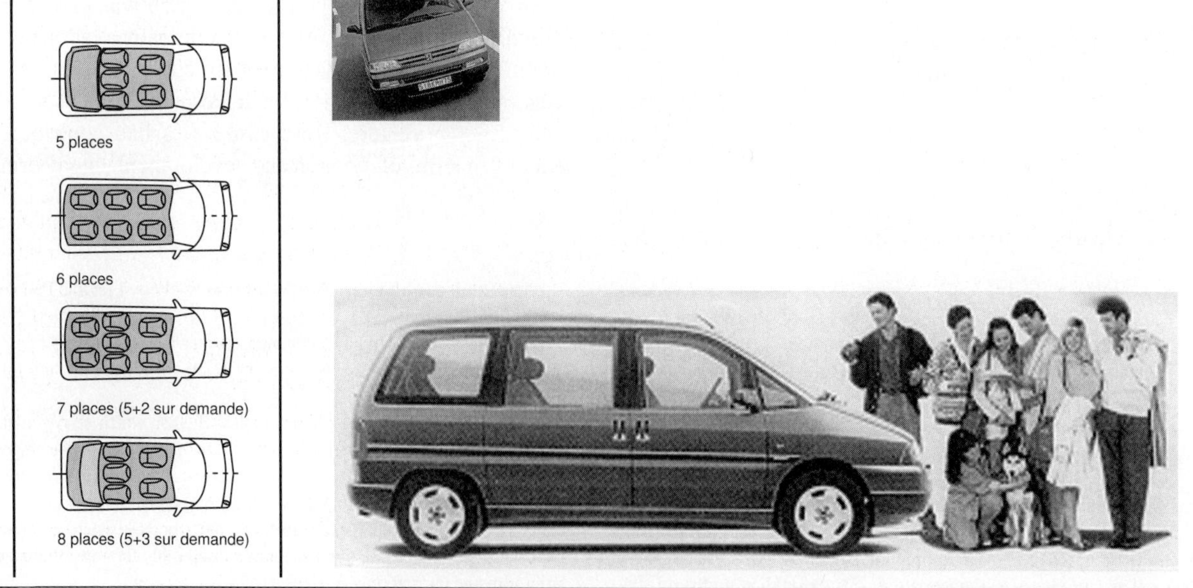

EXHIBIT 2 Split of Responsibilities for the SEVEL Italie and SEVELNORD Projects

Peugeot (independantly)	**Peugeot** Support to SEVEL:	SEVEL Joint Ventures	**Fiat** Support to SEVEL:	**Fiat** (independantly)
Feasibility Studies	Financing	Through Joint Committees:	Financing	Feasibility Studies
Marketing	Product Engineering	Product Planning	Product Engineering	Marketing
Distribution		Technical Engineering		Distribution
Service		Logistics Policy		Service
	to SEVELNORD:	Quality Policy	*to SEVEL Italie:*	
	Production Engineering	by Plant Management:	*Production Engineering*	
	Purchasing Services	Production Management	*Purchasing Services*	
	Quality Mgmt Tools	Purchasing	*Quality Mgmt Tools*	
	Corporate HR	Quality	*Corporate HR*	
		Personnel & Organization		
		Logistics		
		Accounting, Finance & Control		
		Maintenance		

and investment. It was decided that Fiat would manage the new plant within its own production system, i.e., relying on Fiat's procedures for purchasing and accounting. The plant took on a hybrid nature: legally it was an independent company,[4] but at the same time, many of its corporate functions did not exist as they were carried out by the parent companies (refer to Exhibit 2).

To assure that operational management would be suitable for both parties, it was decided that Fiat would appoint the director of the plant, while PSA would appoint the deputy directors for quality control, product coordination (logistics), and administration and control. These three managers guaranteed that Peugeot could closely monitor key points in the production process. For instance, Peugeot's quality manager could stop production if he felt that the product did not meet Peugeot's standards.

A series of steering committees was devised to allow joint planning and decision making in order for both companies to be involved with decisions[5] beyond normal plant management (refer to Exhibit 3). There were four levels of coordination, with both companies having equal representation at all levels. The system established in 1978 was still in place in 1991.

1. A *"Board of Directors" (BD)* existed—as formally dictated by law—however, most major decisions took place at the level of the Directors' and Steering Committees, with the BD mainly ratifying results. Because the BD was the theoretical representation of shareholders—in this case the parent companies themselves—its members were selected from the senior executives of Fiat Auto and Automobiles Peugeot. In the unlikely event of unresolvable differences, the issues would be taken to the executive committees of the parent companies before going to the Board of Directors. In fact, while all decisions needed to be issued through the BD, issues having important strategic or financial consequence would be decided at the highest level of the parent companies.

[4]Unlike a regular factory within the Fiat industrial complex, the SEVEL plant was set up as an independant company, with a separate balance sheet and profit statement.

[5]French was adopted (unofficially) as the working language of the joint venture; however all contracts and minutes from committee meetings were issued in both a French and Italian version.

EXHIBIT 3A The Fiat–Peugeot SEVEL Italie Joint Venture: Utility Vehicles

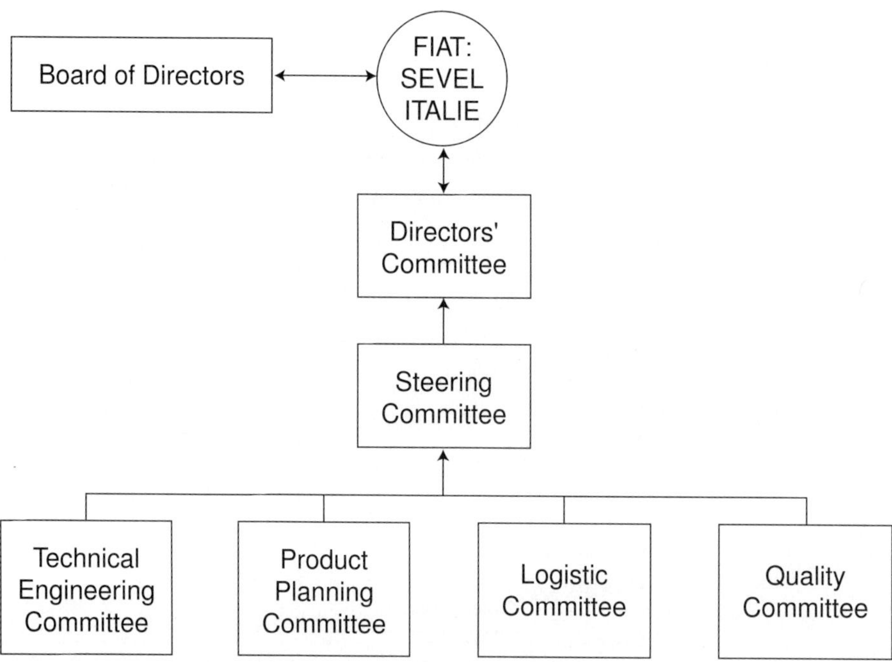

2. The *"Directors' Committee" (DC)* was the principal executive board, consisting of eight members (four from each parent). Its function was to examine broader operational and strategic issues, including new product development, finance, production volumes, employment levels, investment, profitability, and budgeting. In the early life of the model, much of the operational and design control was delegated to the Steering Committee. In case of disagreement at the SC level, the DC served as an arbitrator.

3. During the initial start-up and product launch, the *"Steering Committee" (SC)* would manage most nonfinancial tasks for the DC. It was co-chaired by the two directors of the joint venture (one nominated by each parent company), with 10 members from each parent company. This committee reviewed operational and guidance issues such as new products and styling. They were also in charge of bringing the product to market: product launches, by country, as well as the required volumes, etc. The SC tried to resolve a maximum number of operational issues and, when needed, to prepare recommendations for the Directors' Committee. Once a new product had come to market and was running smoothly, the SC would be disassembled.

4. The last level was composed of subcommittees known as the *"Joint Committees" (JC)*. These groups were responsible for the design and overall implementation of the project. There was a JC for each main task, with specialists from both companies represented: technical engineering, product planning, logistics (including marketing), quality. These subcommittees were empowered to make decisions, and issues would be escalated to the Steering Committee only in the event of disagreement at this level.

Roland Picard reflected:

> On the manufacturing side of the venture, we put everything together; we make all the big decisions together and then we delegate the execution of the decision to one of the two partners. It's a different story on the marketing side, but for manufacturing, it's the key to success. . . because big companies like Fiat or Peugeot simply are not used to having someone else tell them what to do.

EXHIBIT 3B The Fiat–Peugeot Joint Ventures: Utility Vehicles and Minivans

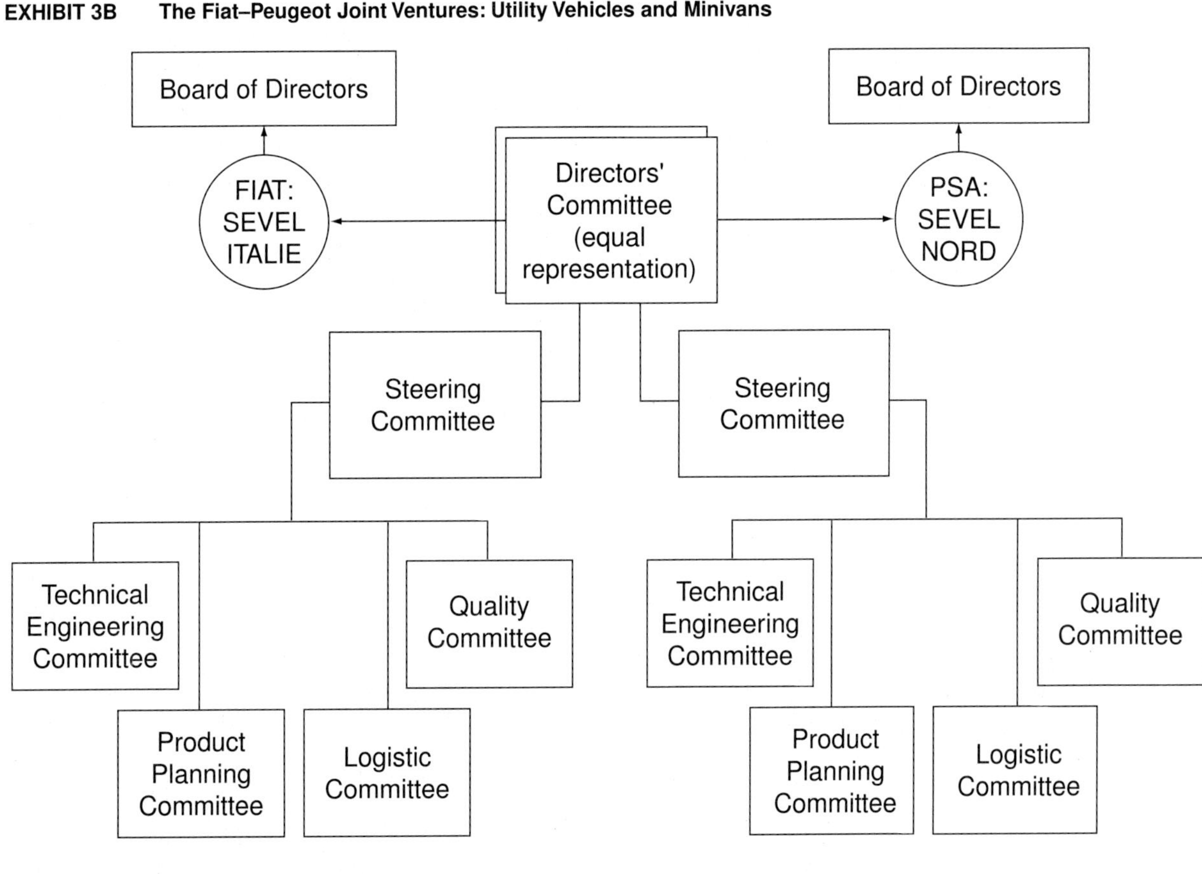

SEVEL Italie: Financing and Investment

At the onset of the venture, the parent companies decided that each would be responsible for 50 percent of its financing. The original venture agreement was signed in 1978 and would last through 1993, with the possibility to renew five years prior to the end of the contract. The theoretical duration of ownership of the plant (known internally as Val di Sangro, VDS) was open-ended.

The purchase price paid by each parent to take a vehicle off the assembly line at VDS was based on costs and invoiced in Italian lire. A cost-plus system was agreed upon in the 1978 accord, whereby costs were assigned to the vehicle in three tiers:

1. *Variable costs* were those derived directly from each unit produced, i.e., materials, labor.
2. *"Budgeted Fixed Costs" (BFC)* were those arising from the yearly operating budget of the VDS plant. These costs would be split in proportion to the number of vehicles each company was scheduled to build in that year. Examples of budgeted costs included management staff expense (such as production engineering, logistics, quality, and general administration) and utilities not directly linked to the assembly process. These costs would nevertheless vary from year to year and were identified through the annual budget process.
3. The last tier of unit cost was known as *"Capacity Fixed Costs" (CFC),* which was primarily the factory and equipment amortisation. Given the financing terms of the venture, total amortisation was to be split evenly between the two parents. In practical terms, every year, each partner would pay half of the total amortisation scheduled for that period, regardless of the number of vehicles taken off the line. Thus the CFC per unit charged to a partner actually depended on the number of units ordered by that partner from the factory in any given year.

Because each partner had financed half of the investment, each was thus entitled to half of the maximum production capacity, known as the "reserved capacity." However, if one partner could not order up to its "reserved capacity," it could try to sell any portion of the remaining capacity to the other partner, assuming this partner had higher than expected sales.

Changes in CFC costs per unit were identified through the annual budget process; any amortisation adjustment resulting from overcapacity of a partner was reimbursed at the end of the year.

Product development was not a permanent function on the SEVEL Italie (SI) project, but was provided by each parent company's engineering department. The two companies then balanced their R&D expenditures through a system of reciprocal billing (conducted on a trimester basis) to ensure that each partner paid half of the development cost. But, if one parent required a product design or attribute that the other parent did not want, it was designed then and financed entirely by the parent wanting the option.

As with product development, process engineering and product planning were conducted by the parent companies outside the normal framework of SI, and the expenditures were equalized on a regular basis. Process engineering determined the production methods and identified optimal production capacities and limitations. Given the increases in production at SI over time, process engineering played a crucial role in the venture's expansion and profitability through efficient production methods. As the plant itself was managed through Fiat's industrial system, Fiat headed the process engineering initiative. However, small modifications and design changes done after the new model introduction were often carried out by the joint committee in charge of product engineering.

According to Fiat Auto's Giovanni Bianchi:

> The structure at SEVEL allows for a high degree of flexibility. . . the parent companies don't need to be involved in all operational issues. The systems in place allow them to become involved only as the need arises. . . plus the fact that we outsource design tasks back to the parent companies means we produce this vehicle for much less than it would normally cost.

Because SEVEL Italie was organized as an independent company, even vehicle components supplied by the parent companies were "purchased" and invoiced in the currency of origin.

Between 1978 and 1988, the utility vehicle market in Europe doubled from 400,000 to 800,000 vehicles. During this period, the VDS plant was continually increasing its production capacity beyond what had been originally planned. The circumstances dictated that both companies needed to work closely together to solve problems related to meeting increasing demand. During that time, the two companies were able to expand the scale of their production in proportion to market needs.

The 1988 Agreements

In 1988, an addendum to the original agreement was signed by Fiat and Peugeot extending the life of the SEVEL Italie venture. SEVEL would introduce the X2/30 to replace the X2/12. It would be marketed under the name Peugeot Boxer, Citroën Jumper, and the Fiat Ducato through their respective distribution networks.

Shortly after the X2/30 accord, the two companies announced the creation of another venture: an agreement to develop and produce a minivan for passenger transportation. The project was code-named U6 and would lead to the launch of the personal minivan (the U60) in the spring of 1994. The agreement also mentioned the joint development and production of a commercial minivan (the U64) derived from the U60, to be launched at a later date. The passenger minivans would be marketed under four brand names: the Peugeot 806, the Citroën Evasion, the Fiat Ulysse, and the Lancia "Z" (or Zeta); each version was to be sold through the respective partner's distribution network.

The Advent of the Minivan in Europe

The personal minivan in Europe had a shaky beginning. In the spring of 1984, Renault—through a cooperation with Matra Automobile—introduced the Espace. The minivan concept was virtually unknown in Europe at the time (and just coming into its own in the United States), and the launch of the Espace was seen as somewhat of a gamble. In fact, Renault sold only 9 of these vehicles during the first month after its launch; although eventually 5,923 units were sold during the first year, well under the volume target (50 vehicles a day or 11,000 units) that the two companies had set. By 1986, the personal minivan concept was catching on, with approximately 17,000 vehicles sold in Europe, and, by the late 1980s, production of the Espace had reached 40,000 vehicles per year. Renault was claiming a 70 percent repurchase rate for the model. By end 1991, Renault Espace sales for the year were expected to reach 45,500 vehicles (refer to Exhibit 4). The Matra factory (which manufactured the car for Renault) had added a third shift to its production, and there was a waiting period of several months after ordering a new Espace.

EXHIBIT 4 The Minivan Market in Europe

Company and Make		1984	1985	1986	1987	1988	1989	1990	1991 forecast
Renault Espace	PV*	2,703	14,039	16,932	21,819	28,814	37,816	44,310	45,538
	CV*	0	249	1,246	1,626	1,403	1779	2,004	1,066
Chrysler Voyager	PV	0	0	0	6	1,409	6,365	15,141	17,367
+Dodge Caravan	CV	0	0	0	0	20	184	396	477
+Plymouth Voyager									
Mitsubishi Space Wagon	PV	4,129	5,131	6,572	8,594	8,400	7,080	9,538	8,371
	CV	0	21	1,348	1,195	1,045	980	748	346
Nissan Prairie	PV	8,763	7,386	9,245	7,523	5,424	6,705	6,025	5,492
	CV	29	135	846	787	355	205	533	359
Toyota Previa	PV	0	0	0	0	0	0	3,133	13,150
	CV	0	0	0	0	0	0	50	970
Chevrolet Astro	PV	0	0	0	27	81	206	286	422
	CV	0	0	0	174	402	357	1,136	719
Pontiac Trans Sport	PV	0	0	0	0	0	1	1,272	3,357
+Oldsmobile Silhouette	CV	0	0	0	0	0	36	131	127
+Chevrolet Lumina									
Ford Aerostar	PV	0	0	0	2	47	181	486	461
	CV	0	0	0	0	2	48	165	79
G M C	PV	0	0	0	0	1	2	10	8
	CV	0	0	0	1	7	1	11	12
Mazda MVP	PV	0	0	0	0	1	0	4	1
Serena	PV	0	0	0	0	0	0	0	0
TOTAL		15,624	26,961	36,189	41,754	47,411	61,946	85,379	98,322

*PV = Personal Vehicle
CV = Commercial Vehicle

Renault was clearly the market leader, but the competition was starting to heat up.

With the success of the Espace and a new niche market identified, major car producers were scrambling to introduce minivans in Europe. The Nissan Prairie and the Mitsubishi Space Wagons (also considered minivans) already had a substantial market share by 1986. By 1990, Chrysler's Voyager (launched in 1988) was a strong competitor, and Toyota obtained instant market share with the Previa introduced in 1990.

By the late '80s, other car producers were announcing their intention to enter the market. Key players included Nissan, whose Serena was scheduled to come to market in 1992, a Ford–Volkswagen joint venture also in 1994 and Honda in 1995.

Two questions, however, were still looming on the horizon: How big was the minivan market in Europe? And could the market support so many competitors?

Projection of the Minivan Market Development

Despite the relative success of the minivan in Europe, the minivan market was still considered to be primarily a niche market, competing against large family vehicles and luxury 4-wheel drive vehicles, such as the Volvo stationwagon and the Range Rover Land Cruiser. Between 1988 and 1993, minivans were expected to grow from 0.34 percent to 1.2 percent of all newly licensed cars in Europe. But, industry observers disagreed over its future importance, with estimated sales by the year 2000 ranging from 400,000 to 800,000 units.

Estimates on growth in the minivan segment were highly debatable. Critics argued that minivans were limited to a narrow market segment—primarily large or affluent families. Moreover, given the increasingly congested traffic conditions in Europe, some considered these vehicles impractical for parking and general maneuverability, i.e., this market could easily reach a plateau. However, initial market growth had largely exceeded expectations and some of the observers believed that the trend would continue.

The Personal Minivan Market as Seen by Fiat and Peugeot

Like other car manufacturers concerned about the future, Fiat and Peugeot studied this growing market segment in order to get an understanding of its potential. Initially, the conclusions of their market research—conducted independently of one another—were comparable regarding the market size, with sales estimates reaching between 350,000 and 450,000 units by the year 2000, but differed in terms of sales by country and the timing of market development. The two companies then worked together to arrive at a market forecast acceptable to both groups (refer to Exhibit 5).

One major concern for Fiat was the fact that the minivan concept had not yet "caught on" in Italy, the country which accounted for approximately 60 percent of its total annual sales. Fiat officials felt confident that at some point Italians would become enamoured of the minivan idea, just as the French had discovered the Espace in the mid-1980s. But, it was unclear when this would happen.

In 1988, the two companies identified the Espace and the Voyager as the main market leaders. Ford and Volkswagen, who announced their new joint venture to co-produce a personal minivan, were also potentially strong competitors, but details about their project were sketchy.

Development of the Minivan: the U6 Project

In 1987, Peugeot had been working on a personal minivan project. The level of investment (estimated FF 10 billion) and resources needed to make the endeavor profitable required that the company find another partner to help bring the product to market. Given its track record with the SEVEL initiative, Fiat seemed the logical partner. In 1988, the two companies came to an agreement to jointly enter the minivan market.

The design of a minivan presented many difficulties from a technical point of view. Neither automaker had design experience with this type of vehicle. While technically a passenger car, many of its specifications resembled those of utility vehicles. Bringing such a vehicle to market would not be easy.

The Structure of the Venture

The two companies structured the management of the new venture exactly like the original SEVEL. The two partners agreed that a new factory would be built, and they opted for the northern French town of Valenciennes. Hence, the new venture became known as SEVEL-NORD (SN). In fact, SN became the mirror image of SEVEL Italie in many respects. The new plant functioned within the industrial system of Peugeot, with the plant's deputy directors for logistics, quality, and administration/control to be named by Fiat.

The steering committees were also structured identically to the first SEVEL, with a Board of Directors, a Directors' Committee, a Steering Committee and a series of Joint Committees. The DC and SC were shared for the two ventures, as many of the issues they addressed were similar, such as billing and payment conditions. The other committees often shared the same members, with the exception of the BD, which had a distinct set of members. For the sake of convenience, SC and DC meetings for both ventures were often held on the same date and place (refer to Exhibit 3B).

Like the plant at Val di Sangro, the Valenciennes factory was financed equally by both partners with an open-ended duration of ownership. The method of amortisation was virtually identical to that of SEVEL Italie. Each company would amortise 50 percent of the factory investment. The amortisation expenses were to be passed on to the four brands in the unit price paid to the plant.

Marketing, Distribution, and Sales

Perhaps the greatest differences between the first and second SEVEL projects arose because of the marketing and sales aspects of the two ventures. The X2/12 and X2/30 were supplied with engines manufactured by the respective parent, giving the vehicles a distinct attribute of that brand. Moreover, while the companies had felt some competitive pressure from each other, the market demand in Europe had always exceeded supply.

For the U60, a different marketing approach was used. The U60, marketed across the four brands, was virtually identical for all four models—only the front grill and tail-lights being unique to each make. The new minivans would be marketed widely across Europe and, while each company had relatively strong sales and distribution positions in certain countries (Peugeot in the UK and Fiat in Germany), the four brands would be competing in the same markets. Moreover, European law prohibited price and market-sharing coordination between the two car makers.

EXHIBIT 5 Total Projected Personal Minivan Sales (Europe)

Country		1994	1995	1996	1997	1998	1999	2000	2001	2002	2003
Italy	Vol*	16.0	24.5	31.8	38.6	42.4	44.2	45.8	47.0	50.0	55.2
	%	1.0	1.4	1.7	1.9	2.0	2.0	2.0	2.0	2.1	2.3
Germany	Vol	43.6	48.0	67.0	83.5	91.3	93.8	98.8	99.3	103.7	104.0
	%	1.4	1.5	2.0	2.4	2.5	2.5	2.6	2.6	2.7	2.7
France	Vol	57.1	64.0	77.7	85.8	90.0	95.1	99.1	102.8	106.0	109.4
	%	2.9	3.2	3.7	3.9	4.0	4.1	4.2	4.3	4.4	4.5
Great Britain	Vol	15.5	24.6	34.4	41.8	49.3	50.2	53.1	56.2	58.8	58.8
	%	2.9	3.2	3.7	3.9	4.0	4.1	4.2	4.3	4.4	4.5
Spain	Vol	8.1	10.8	13.5	16.2	16.5	20.2	21.8	22.5	25.3	25.8
	%	0.9	1.2	1.5	1.7	1.7	2.0	2.1	2.1	2.3	2.3
Holland	Vol	8.2	9.9	11.5	13.0	14.3	15.4	15.7	15.8	15.8	16.0
	%	1.9	2.2	2.4	2.6	2.7	2.8	2.9	3.0	3.1	3.2
Belgium &	Vol	12.9	15.1	16.3	17.4	19.1	20.7	21.6	23.0	24.4	25.1
Luxembourg	%	3.1	3.4	3.5	3.6	3.8	4.0	4.1	4.3	4.5	4.6
Switzerland	Vol	12.2	12.7	13.6	14.4	15.1	15.6	15.5	15.7	15.6	15.8
	%	4.6	4.6	4.7	4.8	4.8	4.9	4.9	5.0	5.0	5.1
Ireland	Vol	0.3	0.3	0.6	0.8	1.0	1.2	1.3	1.5	1.6	1.6
	%	0.4	0.4	0.7	0.9	1.1	1.2	1.4	1.6	1.7	1.8
Austria	Vol	10.5	11.2	12.1	13.1	14.0	14.8	15.0	14.9	15.1	15.3
	%	3.8	4.0	4.1	4.3	4.5	4.7	4.8	4.8	4.9	5.0
Denmark	Vol	0.1	0.2	0.4	0.7	0.8	1.0	1.1	1.3	1.4	1.5
	%	0.1	0.2	0.4	0.6	0.7	0.8	0.9	1.1	1.2	1.3
Finland	Vol	1.0	1.1	1.4	1.8	2.0	2.6	3.0	3.4	3.6	3.8
	%	1.4	1.5	1.7	1.9	2.0	2.3	2.5	2.6	2.8	3.0
Norway	Vol	0.8	1.1	1.4	1.7	1.9	2.4	2.5	2.6	2.7	2.8
	%	0.9	1.2	1.6	1.7	1.8	2.0	2.1	2.3	2.3	2.3
Sweden	Vol	2.8	4.3	5.2	5.7	6.6	6.8	7.5	8.4	8.8	8.4
	%	1.8	2.5	2.9	3.1	3.3	3.2	3.4	3.5	3.6	3.4
Greece	Vol	0.0	0.1	0.2	0.3	0.3	0.3	0.5	0.9	0.9	1.0
	%	0.0	0.0	0.1	0.2	0.2	0.2	0.3	0.5	0.5	0.6
Portugal	Vol	0.2	0.7	1.0	1.3	1.6	2.2	2.6	2.6	2.7	3.0
	%	0.1	0.3	0.4	0.5	0.6	0.8	0.9	0.9	0.9	1.0
Europe	Vol	189.3	228.6	288.1	336.1	366.2	386.5	404.9	417.9	436.4	447.5
	%	1.6	1.9	2.2	2.5	2.6	2.7	2.8	2.8	2.9	3.0

*Volume in thousands.

% is the proportion of minivan sales to total vehicle sales in that country.

Existing Fiat/Peugeot Market Share

Historically, the two home markets had generated the largest percentage of vehicle sales for each company. In 1991, approximately 60 percent of Fiat's sales originated in Italy, and France accounted for 38 percent of PSA's sales. In terms of market share, PSA was traditionally well represented in the UK, Spain, Germany, and the Benelux countries. Fiat too maintained a strong presence in all European markets, particularly Germany, Portugal and Greece, though its total European sales were some 150,000 vehicles fewer than those of PSA (refer to Exhibit 6). Both car manufacturers believed that minivan sales would be roughly proportional to their traditional market shares.

In 1991, the Espace was the market leader. For example, in France it held nearly 76 percent of the market. The Voyager had 14 percent of the French market, the Toyota Previa and Nissan Prairie claimed 5 percent and 2 percent, respectively. Furthermore, Ford and Volkswagen hoped to obtain an overall 25 percent share of market in Europe, and Nissan was aiming to capture 7 percent with its upcoming Serena.

Project Status in 1991

By the beginning of 1991, the project was falling into place. The design of the minivan was nearing completion, and some of the factory buildings were under construction. As with the X2/12 project, research and design were "outsourced" to the parent companies, with expenditures balanced on a trimester basis. Peugeot took the lead on the U60 development just as Fiat had taken the lead for the X2/12.

SEVELNORD was a state-of-the-art plant which conducted three phases of production: body-in-white, painting, and final assembly. All parts required for the minivans were brought in either from other Fiat and Peugeot facilities, or from independent suppliers. Approximately 75 percent of parts and components were provided by suppliers other than Peugeot or Fiat; careful attention was given to choosing suppliers so that each parent company's traditional purchasing

EXHIBIT 6 Vehicle Sales by Country
1991 Forecast
('000)

	Peugeot		Citroën		Fiat*		Lancia	
	Units	% of Market	Units	% of Market	Units	% of Market	Units	% of Market
Italy	81.7	4.3	43.0	2.3	633.9	34.4	119.2	7.1
France	314.6	18.3	195.9	11.4	117.0	5.4	11.7	0.6
England	142.7	8.0	80.8	4.5	60.5	3.1	0.2	0.0
Germany	100.2	3.1	63.8	2.0	104.6	3.1	10.6	0.3
Belgium&Lux	32.5	8.0	22.4	5.5	15.4	2.7	2.9	0.7
Netherlands	30.5	7.8	20.8	5.3	26.5	4.7	1.4	0.3
Spain	75.0	10.5	72.3	10.2	56.8	5.7	7.5	0.8
Portugal	16.3	6.7	17.7	7.3	37.5	15.5	3.7	1.6
Switzerland	13.4	5.1	7.0	2.7	14.5	4.4	2.2	0.8
Austria	12.0	4.2	9.2	3.2	11.4	3.8	1.0	0.4
Denmark	6.4	7.8	5.8	7.0	8.9	6.2	0.0	0.0
Sweden	3.0	2.4	2.3	1.9	0.5	0.2	0.0	0.0
Norway	3.4	5.5	1.5	2.4	0.8	0.9	0.0	0.0
Finland	2.8	5.0	1.1	1.9	1.7	2.5	0.0	0.0
Greece	8.8	5.9	8.0	5.4	1.7	9.4	0.3	2.2
Ireland	3.4	5.0	1.2	1.9	3.0	3.6	0.0	0.0
Total Europe	846.7		552.8		1,094.8		160.8	

*Includes Alfa Romeo.

sources were evenly balanced. From an accounting standpoint, all parts were purchased from outside suppliers; even the parent companies were seen as "third party" suppliers.[6]

Project Financing

Major preproduction expenses—such as new product engineering and industrial processes—were paid by the parent companies and were not included in the unit "cost" of the vehicle. Because PSA had started the project on its own before Fiat became a partner, Fiat reimbursed approximately one-half of the R&D and planning studies performed by Peugeot until the date of the agreement. From that point on, the usual expenditure policy went into effect. Similarly, the capital expenditures (factory and equipment) were to be shared 50/50 between the two partners.

Rossi often told managers new to the venture:

> There is no way we can or we try to identify every hour of work that is spent on this project. It is basically understood that the partner which takes the lead on a project is going to spend more time and money on it. . . and that these two [SEVEL] initiatives will balance out over time.

The terms of vehicle price were defined in the 1988 accord. Once again, the approach used at SEVEL Italy was put into place: the three-tiered unit cost system, 50–50 amortisation of plant expenses, and pro-rata budgeted fixed costs.

Currency Arrangements

The unit price for all vehicles produced at the SEVEL-NORD factory was to be stated in French francs. For Fiat, this brought on an element of currency exposure. However, the establishment of a common monetary policy in Europe, with the prospects of the ECU, implied that European currencies would remain relatively stable against one another.

In 1988, the French franc was equal to 216 Italian lire. All profitability studies were carried out at a rate of 220. As of March 1991, the French franc was equal to 218 lire.

The Climate of Cooperation

Another aspect of the venture was the importance of ensuring a flow and exchange of ideas between the partners. The managers involved in the SEVEL ventures felt confident that the structure of the cooperation was an effective one. Jean Pierre explained:

> You know, even if we did not have the same reserved production capacity—and here, common sense prevails—if one of the parents were the majority shareholder, it would not impose a definition of the product on the other. . . because these people sit down at the same table every month and exchange their ideas, and their product evolves because of the two partners.

His counterpart at Fiat, Giovanni Bianchi, added:

> It's true, we work well together—maybe it's because our companies are from "Latin-based" societies in terms of culture and language; it's difficult to say, but our two companies are very compatible.

According to Pierre, the effectiveness of the cooperation went even beyond the current project:

> . . . one of the strong points about this cooperation is experience. It has been the synthesis of experience for the people in product development as well as for those in product planning—at each stage of development. I attend all the joint committee meetings, and on the product design level there is an extraordinary exchange of experience. . . we find solutions together. Whether it is Fiat or Peugeot that has the idea—both groups come out ahead. This kind of cooperation, you can't measure it, it has repercussions on the overall experience for everyone in product planning—across all products—at PSA and at Fiat. There is an exchange of experience that is extremely rich.

Preparing for the Future

It was early evening as the four managers finished preparing the presentation they would give the next day. The copresidents of the Directors Committee had decided to spend approximately half of the next day's meeting going over the comprehensive report that documented the joint venture's history, analyzing their contractual policies and their *modus operandi*. Roberto Rossi would open the meeting, and he felt sure that the DC members would be impressed with the venture's accomplishments. He and Mr. Picard were optimistic that, given the track record of the two SEVELs, whatever roadblocks there might be for the venture could be removed.

---

[6]This situation explained the high percentage of variable cost in the total cost per vehicle produced. All transaction prices for U60 and U64 components contained a profit margin for the supplier.

INSEAD

Case 7–3

General Electric & SNECMA (A)

In the 1960s General Electric (GE) and SNECMA (*Société Nationale d'Etude et de Construction de Moteurs d'Aviation*) were independently making efforts to enter the commercial aircraft engine market. The impact of political constraints, market demands, product development, and technological advances, led both companies to discuss a possible strategic alliance. Discussions had started around 1969 and by October 1971 were getting close to a decision point.

Civilian Markets and Competition for Jet Engines

Pioneering efforts to develop a jet engine for aircraft gained momentum in the early 1940s, simultaneously in Europe and in America. The engine development focused on military applications. Several companies involved in the manufacture of turbines and aeroengines were pursuing R&D efforts in jet engine technology.

This led to the manufacture and development of turbojets in Britain, Germany, and subsequently in the United States. The first jet engine built in the U.S. was by GE, in 1942. After World War II, development of jet engines continued rapidly in the U.S. and Britain, for military applications. The German industry was disbanded and did not restart until 1956. In France, SNECMA, the national aeroengine company, benefited from technology transfers from Germany and developed a family of engines for the Mystère and Mirage fighter planes. The Soviet Union also drew on German experience and started its own jet engine development programmes for both military and civilian applications. The principle of jet engine operations is outlined in Exhibit 1.

By the 1960s General Electric, Westinghouse, the Allison division of GM, and Pratt & Whitney were pursuing product development efforts in America, Rolls Royce in the U.K., Motoren and Turbine Union in West Germany, and SNECMA in France. Applications were primarily military.

This case was written by L.N. Krishna, Research Associate, under the supervision of Yves Doz, Professor at INSEAD. It is intended to be used as a basis for class discussion rather than to illustrate either effective or ineffective handling of an administrative situation.
 Financial support from the INSEAD Alumni Fund European Case Programme is gratefully acknowledged.

The development of jet engines for commercial application was initially a spin off from military engines. In the United States, most of the R&D funds came from the Department of Defence. However, initial efforts to develop jet-powered airliners took place in Britain. But the first such aircraft, the De Havilland Comet, was plagued by accidents stemming from its pressurization systems. Further, sweptwing aerodynamics were not fully mastered. This led aircraft manufacturers to continue to develop slower, propeller-driver planes, and, over time to equip these with "turboprops," i.e., kerosene-fuelled turbines driving conventional propellers, replacing the conventional radial piston engines.

The commercial jet engine market really developed in the early 60s with a second generation of jet-powered airplanes partly derived from military transport and tanker planes in the U.S. (e.g., the Boeing 707). In Europe, the U.K. was uncertain of its development plans, following the Comet failure in the 50s, but developed several aircraft types using Rolls Royce engines. In France, Sud Aviation developed the Caravelle using Rolls Royce's Avon turbojets. In the U.S., Boeing was steadily developing new airframes, with Pratt & Whitney as the supplier of engines. In particular, Pratt & Whitney developed the JT3D and JT8D engine family to equip the Boeing 707 and 727. Exhibit 2 presents a summary of which engines equipped which airframes (see Exhibit 2).

The normal development cycle of an aircraft engine spans over ten years, while that of an airframe lasts around five years. The approach adopted by aeroengine manufacturers has been to forecast the trend of aircraft needs and technological development over the next decade and begin development of an engine to meet the future requirement. The aircraft engine manufacturer normally forms an agreement with an airframe manufacturer, for engine prototype testing on an existing airframe. Hence a manufacturer of commercial engines faces a period of "uncertain" market demand, between the time it has to launch its own development and that at which airframe manufacturers start their own projects making use of its engine. Newcomers to the civilian engine markets may even have to demonstrate the performance and reliability of their engines through extensive flight tests before an aircraft manufacturer commits to using the new engine on one of its new programmes. To limit the risks, the approach of commercial aircraft manufacturers had been to develop an airframe around a model of engine that had already been proven reliable and durable in military service, which also meant that the jet engine makers did not normally develop new engines specifically for civilian markets.

EXHIBIT 1 Jet Engine Designs

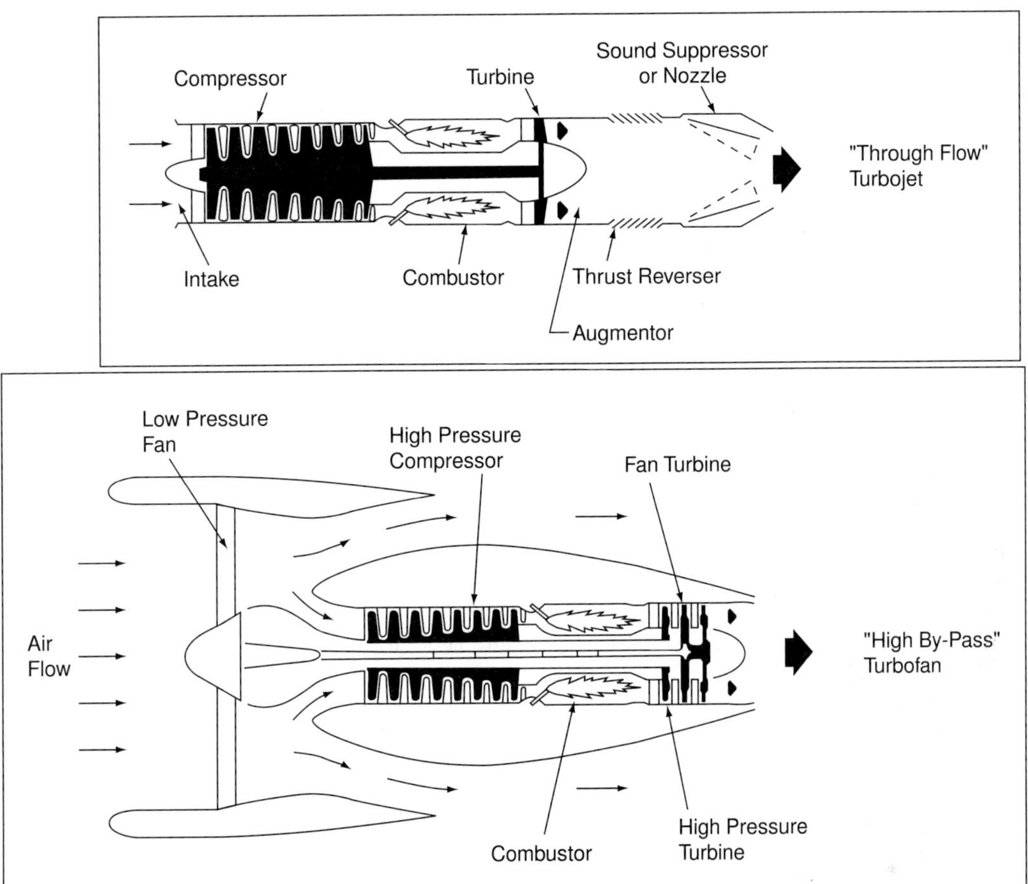

In a through flow turbojet (top), 100 percent of the air intake passes through the combustion chamber. Subsequent to the first phase of the operating cycle, namely compression, the compressed air is sprayed with fuel in the second phase of the operating cycle. The air-fuel mixture expands on ignition. The expanding air propels a turbine that serves to suck in air at the intake stage and drive the compressor. The expanding air is then ejected at high velocity. Consistent with Newtonian principle of "action-reaction" on bodies, the aircraft is propelled forward.

In a by-pass turbofan jet engine (bottom), a low pressure fan compresses the air. A portion of the compressed air is directly ejected around the turbojet at a relatively high velocity. The remaining portion of the compressed air enters the combustion chamber of the "core" and is mixed with fuel and ignited as in a conventional turbojet. Since the turbine has to drive the large fan in addition to the compressor, it comprises several stages.

General Electric's Entry into Civilian Engines

The corporate culture of GE valued superiority in technology and in engineering standards. The corporate policy was to expand into areas of high technology, high growth potential, and high cost of entry. According to industry observers "GE tracks technology and awaits opportunity." Between the 1940s and the 1960s, GE worked in close coordination with the Department of Defence for developing new engines and upgrading existing engines for military applications. GE was not historically a supplier of aeroengines, but had a strong background in manufacturing turbines of various types, which allowed

EXHIBIT 2 U.S. Commercial Jet-Powered Transports

	Model Designation	Popular Name or Sub-Type Designation	Number of Passengers	Capacity Cargo, lb	Powerplant: Number Make & Model	Maximum Speed, mph
Boeing	707–120		100–181	19.200	4 P&WA JT3C–6	600
	707–120B		100–181	25.000	4 P&WA JT3D–3	600 +
	707–220		100–181	19.200	4 P&WA JT4A–3	600 +
	707–320	Intercontinental	108–189	28.200	4 P&WA JT3D–11	600 +
	707–320B	Intercontinental	189	28.200	4 P&WA JT3D–3B	600 +
	707–320C	Intercontinental	189	96.800	4 P&WA JT3D–3B	600 +
	707–420	Intercontinental	108–189	28.200	4R-R.R Co 12	600 +
	720		88–167	16.680	4 P&WA JT3C–7–12	600
	720B		167	20.500	4 P&WA JT3D–3	600 +
	727–100		70–131	12.830	3 P&WA JT8D–1,7 ou 9	600 +
	727–200		120–178	21.00	3 P&WA JT8D–1,7 ou 9	600 +
	727–100		113		2 P&WA JT8D–7 ou 9	586
	727–200		125		2 P&WA JT8D–9 ou 15	586
	2707–300	Prototype SST	298		4 GE4	1.800
	747		374–490	62.000	4 P&WA JT9D–3	640
	747B		374–490	62.000	4 P&WA JT9D–7W	640
McDonnell Douglas	DC–8	Series 10	116–176	20.850	4 P&WA JT3C–6	580
	DC–8	Series 20	116–176	20.850	4 P&WA JT4–A–9,–11	600
	DC–8	Series 30	116–176	20.850	4 P&WA JT4–A–9,–11	600
	DC–8	Series 40	116–176	20.850	4R-R.R Co 12	600
	DC–8	Series 50	116–176	20.850	4 P&WA JT3D–3,3B	600
	DC–8	Series 61	259	20.850	4 P&WA JT3D–3B	600
	DC–8	Series 62	189	66.665	4 P&WA JT3D–3B	600
	DC–8	Series 63	259	42.580	4 P&WA JT3D–3B	600
	DC–9	Series 10	90	66.665	2 P&WA JT8D–1 ou 5	
	DC–9	Series 20	56–90	23.845	2 P&WA JT8D–9	
	DC–9	Series 30	115	26.534	2 P&WA JT8D–7	
	DC–9	Series 40	125	30.836	2 P&WA JT8D–9	
	DC–10	Series 10	270–343	30.400 (2)	3 GE CF–66	597
	DC–10	Series 20	270–343	30.400 (2)	3 P&WA JT9D–15	597
	DC–10	Series 30	250–345	4.600 (1)	3 GE CF–50A	600 +
Lockheed	L–1011–1	TriStar	256–345	32.280(2)	3R-R RB. 211–22–02	620
	L–1011–8	TriStar	256–345	33.090(2)	3R-R RB. 211–56	615

Abbréviations: GE = General Electric
P&WA = Pratt & Whitney Aircraft
R-R = Rolls-Royce
(1) = Cubic feet of cargo space
(2) = Belly compartments only
Source: *Aviation Week & Space Technology*, March 9, 1970.

it to enter the jet engine business early. In the late 1940s, GE developed the "variable stator" technology, a significant breakthrough which allowed stator blades to change incidence in flight, thus improving the thrust of the engine, and reducing fuel consumption.

In 1953, GE began decentralising its divisions. The company was divided into 50 departments, each under a general manager. Though this necessitated the duplication of several production facilities, it greatly enhanced management effectiveness.

Under the sponsorship of the Vice President of Aerospace and Defense group, GE's jet engine business underwent major growth and achieved significant innovations. GE achieved a breakthrough in the development of an improved static rotor technology that could find potential applications for commercial aircraft. GE also developed the turbofan by-pass engine and a project for a high by-pass engine.[1] The new high by-pass technology took shape as a high thrust engine for the military transport aircraft Lockheed Galaxy C5A. As the largest transport plane built to date, the C5A Galaxy was a prestigious project for both airframe builders and aeroengine manufacturers. In the mid-1960s GE developed a commercial version of the C5A's engine, and labelled it CF6. The CF6 engine consumed about 30–35 percent less fuel than earlier engines, and the engine noise was substantially lower.

The Vice President for the Flight Propulsion laboratory department, Gerhard Neumann,[2] believed the CF6 could be an ideal power plant for the projected new "wide body" aircraft, the Douglas DC10 long-distance trijet, the Airbus A-300 medium-range twinjet, and in due course for the Boeing 747. He was the champion of new applications. In 1968, the Flight Propulsion department of the Aerospace and Defence Group became a separate Aircraft Engine Group under the leadership of Gerhard Neumann. Contacts with Douglas led to the CF6 selection for the DC10. Both American and United Airlines decided to equip their DC10s with CF6s, in 1968. Since 1965, GE was also working on another U.S. defence funded project for the development of an engine for the B-1 strategic bomber. GE was also doing pioneering work toward developing an engine for a supersonic transport plane, again funded by the U.S. government.

In the meantime, Pratt & Whitney developed the JT9D turbofan engine for the Boeing 747 project, offered as an alternative to Lockheed's Galaxy. GE and Pratt & Whitney were competing for the engine choice. When the Galaxy contract was awarded to Lockheed and GE, Boeing and Pratt & Whitney decided to adapt their designs for an equivalent class of commercial transport aircraft, the Boeing 747, which Pan Am was encouraging Boeing to build. Pratt & Whitney, however, had done only preliminary design work on the JT9D when Boeing launched the 747s, forcing Pratt & Whitney to "rush" development to meet Boeing's schedule for the 747's flight test programme and airline delivery dates. This created some uncertainty on the Boeing 747 programme. Rolls Royce undertook to develop a large complex three-spool engine, the RB211, making use of composite materials, for the Lockheed L–1011, a large trijet designed to compete against the DC10. Rolls Royce's programme was technologically ambitious and expensive, and quickly ran into development difficulties.

In the late 1960s GE had only about 2 percent of the commercial jet engine market, while Pratt & Whitney controlled nearly 90 percent of the market, the remainder being served by Rolls Royce (excluding the Soviet Union, which developed its own engine types often derived from British and German designs). Pratt & Whitney's superior experience, marketing relationships with airlines, which dated back to the 1930s, and large base of engines in service made it a formidable leader.

Yet following the technical difficulties of Rolls Royce with the RB 211 for the L–1011, and those of Pratt & Whitney in rushing the development of the JT9D for the Boeing 747, the policy of airframe manufacturers became to develop at least two sources of power plants for each of their aircraft models. Each engine was certified to be used on the airframe, usually at the engine supplier's expenses, and the choice of engines was offered to the airlines. Boeing thus tested and certified the CF6 on its 747 and started offering it to airlines as an alternative to the JT9D, providing an opening to GE in addition to the DC10. Lockheed remained committed to the Rolls Royce engine.

GE obtained orders from Lufthansa, Swissair, KLM, Air France, and Alitalia in Europe, and Toa Domestic and Thai Airways in the Far East. This led GE to start putting in place a worldwide service and maintenance network for its CF6 engine.

The US Market for Civilian Jet Engines

In the United States, the market in airline passenger, cargo, and mail traffic was projected to reach over $20 billion revenue ton miles, and the net sales of aircraft was expected to reach around $3 billion in the mid 1970s (Exhibit 3). Despite these growth expectations, the U.S. market caused aircraft engine manufacturers several concerns:

- The domestic U.S. air transport markets were becoming saturated. Although deregulation and lower fares might relaunch traffic growth, more growth was expected in Europe and the Far East, which, compared to the United States, were still quite underdeveloped markets.

[1]A high by-pass turbofan has a high proportion of the total airflow going through the turbofan assembly (by-passing the combustion chambers). For subsonic flight this reduces noise and pollution levels, as well as improves fuel economy. Conversely, the pressures and temperatures in the combustion chambers of a high by-pass engine have to be higher than a lower by-pass engine to offset the smaller airflow going through the engine core.

[2]An anti-nazi German engineer who had joined General Chennault's "Flying Tigers" and fought against the Japanese in China during World War II before becoming a U.S. resident.

EXHIBIT 3 U.S. Scheduled Airline Traffic & U.S. Transport Sales, Growth Trends

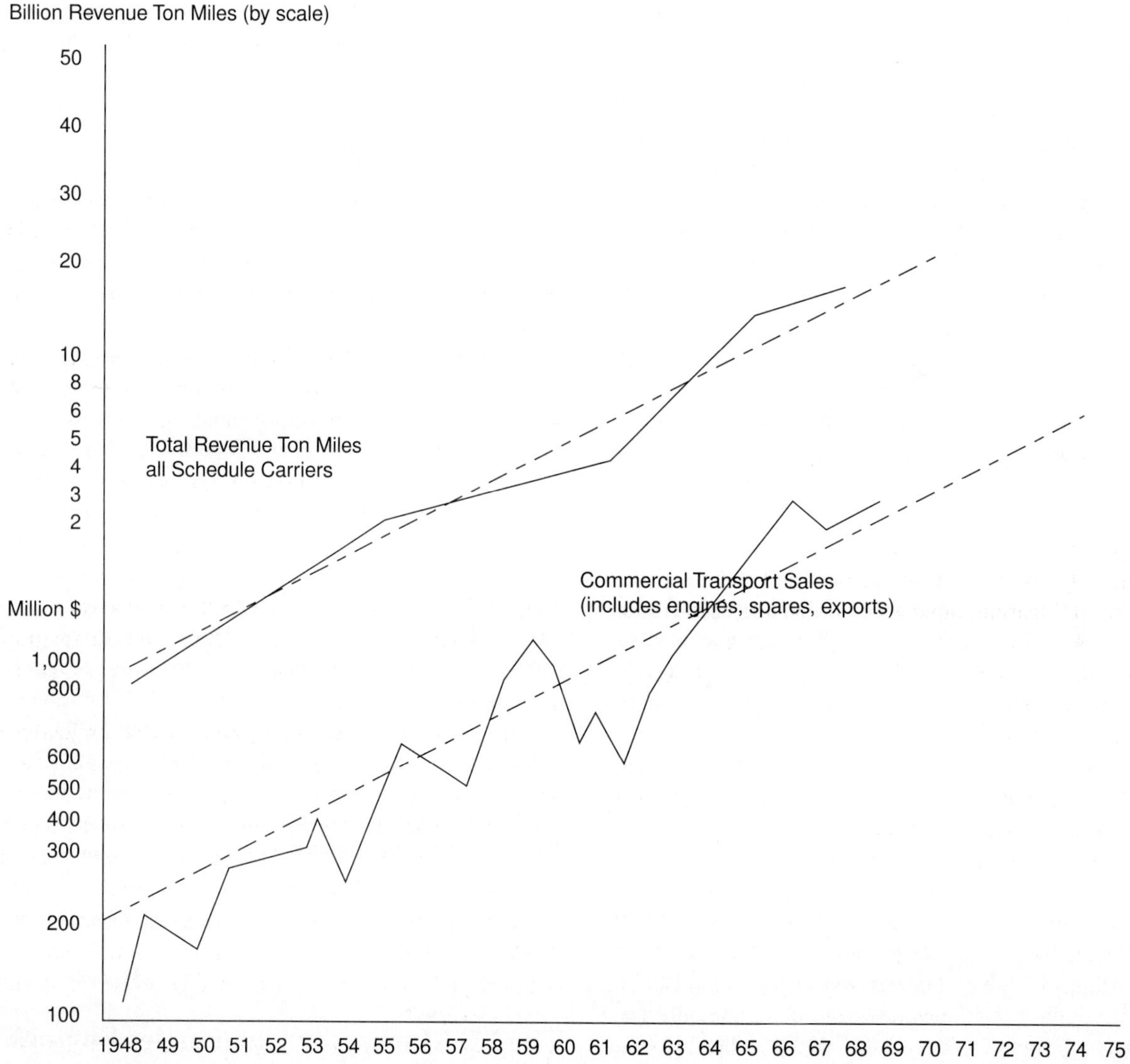

Billion Revenue Ton Miles (by scale)

50
40
30
20
10
8
6
5
4
3
2

Total Revenue Ton Miles
all Schedule Carriers

Million $
1,000
800
600
500
400
300
200
100

Commercial Transport Sales
(includes engines, spares, exports)

1948 49 50 51 52 53 54 55 56 57 58 59 60 61 62 63 64 65 66 67 68 69 70 71 72 73 74 75

Total U.S. Airline traffic—passenger, cargo, and small—is showing a slackening in growth rate. The return to trend is reflected in the drops in U.S. commercial transport sales, which soared above the trend as airlines added capacity to meet the surge in traffic.

Source: *Aviation Week*, March 9, 1970.

- The likely deregulation of the U.S. airline industry in the 70s would increase the uncertainty of the market for aircraft, engines, and spares, cut the profits of airlines, and push them to demand lower equipment prices.
- The growing aircraft market segmentation led aircraft engine manufacturers to identify more limited categories of airframes which they thought had potential. They focused engine development efforts around the particular categories of aircraft, which they anticipated the market would need 15–20 years hence. This resulted in a smaller potential market share for each type of engine, with a life cycle spread over a longer period.
- The increasing sophistication of commercial aircraft designs might further reduce the interchangeability of engine types and make it more difficult to plan for all-purpose engines suitable for multiple aircraft types.[3] A specific engine family might therefore have to include more subtypes.
- Specific flying speed (e.g., the fact that most new military planes were supersonic) and characteristics like stall margin, rapid acceleration and deceleration of aircraft, increasingly reduced the possibility of engine design spillovers from military to commercial aircraft, except in the case of military transport planes as had been the case in the 1960s. However, no major new U.S. military transport programme was expected in the 1970s. Development of new engines for commercial applications thus called for substantial investment of funds, which the U.S. Department of Defence was unwilling to spend.
- The fact that aircraft manufacturers were now likely to offer several types of engines as a choice for airlines (e.g., both the CF6 and the JT9D on the B747) meant price competition for new engine sales would be fierce. Engines would be bought by airlines separately from airframes. The normal life span of an airliner was around 15 years, and the cost of the engines was around 25 percent of the total cost of the plane at the time of purchase. During the life span of the airliner, the cost of spares and the cost of replacement of engine parts amounted to nearly 75 percent of the cost of the plane. Further, profit margins were usually higher on spare parts and maintenance services than on new engines. Hence the aircraft engine manufacturers played a significant role both in the development of airframes and in the marketing efforts of airframe manufacturers.

[3]For example, an aeroengine manufacturer had to predetermine the engine orientation and mounting, at engine design concept stage—whether fuselage mounting, tail mounting, wing mounting (twin engine or four engine versions).

Europe as a Potential Market

Beyond the export of American airframes to Europe, which involved a large number of aircraft, the potential market centered around the emergence of Airbus Industrie as an attempt to revive the European civilian aircraft industry.

In the mid-1960s, the French aircraft manufacturer Sud Aviation (now Aérospatiale) was working on the design of an enlarged Caravelle, called the "Galion," with about 300 seats. Although no decision had been made, the British industry had been approached as a possible partner. In the wake of the prestigious Anglo-French Concorde project, which was vigorously supported by De Gaulle, the Galion project did not receive much government funding. In the late 1960s the enthusiasm of the French and the British for the Concorde waned; the project was short of funds. Both partner companies sought financial help from Germany.

Germany was skeptical about the Concorde project, but was optimistic on the revival of the "Galion" project. German companies were working on an aircraft similar to the "Galion" and were willing to join France and Britain on a common project. The three governments decided upon launching the Galion project (renamed Airbus) with substantial funding from Germany. The champions of the Airbus project were Messrs Ziegler (the head of Sud Aviation), and Béteille, who was already working on the Galion project.

The Airbus A300 project, a large twin engine aircraft, called for an engine of the thrust level of the GE's CF6, Pratt and Whitney's JT9D or Rolls Royce's RB 211 2H version.

Rolls Royce, short of funds and skeptical of the market for Airbus in Europe, withdrew its support for engine development. It preferred to ally with Lockheed, which it thought would take over the European market. This contributed to a British withdrawal from the project. Both Pratt & Whitney and GE were trying to supply to Airbus Industrie. France and Germany preferred an American engine. However, the French in particular realized that the potential of Airbus enabled them to bargain for local content in Europe and technology transfer to French firms, on the part of either Pratt & Whitney or General Electric.

Despite the fact that Pratt & Whitney retained an 11 percent equity holding in SNECMA, the French company preferred GE since GE was willing to part with some technology, unlike Pratt & Whitney, which only sought to share financial risk. Further, Pratt & Whitney was in financial difficulties over the Boeing 747 project. GE was willing to license the manufacture of a portion of the CF6 engine to SNECMA, with SNECMA acting as a subcontractor. The French government in particular was keen to increase the French content of Airbus, including its engines, and exerted pressure on Air France, as a launch customer, to push for local content.[4]

Airbus Industrie was in favour of a GE–SNECMA collaboration. The move appealed to the French who were looking for technology transfers. It was also supported by the Germans. Both nations' airlines, Air France and Lufthansa, favoured Airbus planes with GE engines. SNECMA started the production of certain parts of the CF6 engine, under license from GE, with technical assistance and quality control from GE. Altogether SNECMA supplied about 27 percent of the manufacturing value of the CF6–50 version used on Airbus, mainly the compressor and other "cold" parts of the engine.[5] The collaboration was later extended to the whole CF6 programme, as a way of encouraging Air France to select CF6 on the Boeing 747s it was ordering. GE was also willing to enlist Rohr, the supplier of engine nacelles for the DC10, to supply similar nacelles for the Airbus A300, thus minimizing the engine installation difficulties.

SNECMA's Background

SNECMA resulted from the 1945 nationalization of the Gnome et Rhône company, itself the result of the 1915 merger of Gnome and the Rhône radial aircraft engine makers. During World War II the Gnome & Rhône company had been producing its "14" range of radial engines, mainly used on French planes and after 1940 various axis power aircraft.

Starting in 1945, SNECMA benefited from the work of a group of ex-BMW engineers working first in Constanz and then in France, before being fully integrated into SNECMA.[6] They developed the "ATAR" family of military jet engines, which equipped the Mystère and Mirage fighter planes developed by the Dassault company, starting in 1954. Several thousand units of the ATAR family had been manufactured by 1971, serving the needs of the French airforce and of a variety of export customers (e.g., India, Israel, Brazil, Belgium, South Africa, Australia, Argentina, Switzerland, etc.).

These military activities dwarfed the civilian activities of SNECMA, which accounted for less than 10 percent of its total sales, and even less in the manufacture of new engines. Pratt & Whitney had granted SNECMA the licence to its JT10D engine, which was used by SNECMA to power military prototypes, but the growth of the ATAR product range made reliance on the Pratt & Whitney engine unnecessary.

Despite the ATAR's success, SNECMA's management, however, was concerned with the overdependence of the company on one product family and on the military business (another major product, the "Larzac" smaller turbofan, was also used mainly for military planes). To diversify internationally, and toward the civilian markets, was one of SNECMA's key strategic objectives.

The 10-ton Engine

The aircraft engine manufacturers were of the opinion that beyond the large Airbus A300, the European market needed a twin jet of 150-seats for short-haul flights, with a high by-pass turbofan engine. The required engine thrust for such new 150-seat aircraft was about 10 tons, much less than that of the CF6.

Both the leading aeroengine manufacturers, Pratt & Whitney and Rolls Royce, were approaching the European market. In 1972, Pratt & Whitney signed a collaborative agreement with MTU of West Germany and with Fiat of Italy, for developing an engine with 11,000 kg of thrust. Rolls Royce was independently following a programme on the development of a similar thrust engine, called the RB231. Their effort was centered around a derived derated version of their three-spool high thrust engine, the RB211–524 used to power the Lockheed L1011. However, the technical and financial difficulties

[4]Air France was also a not insignificant buyer of Boeing 747s, which could be equipped with CF6 engines. So was Lufthansa.

[5]SNECMA's role for the engines mounted on Boeing 747s was more limited, leading to an average SNECMA involvement in the CF6 program as a whole of about 8 percent of the total programme value.

[6]During World War II, BMW had been one of the pioneers in the development of jet engines, used on the first German jet fighters and bombers in 1944–45.

EXHIBIT 4 General Electric's Market Forecast for Jet Engines

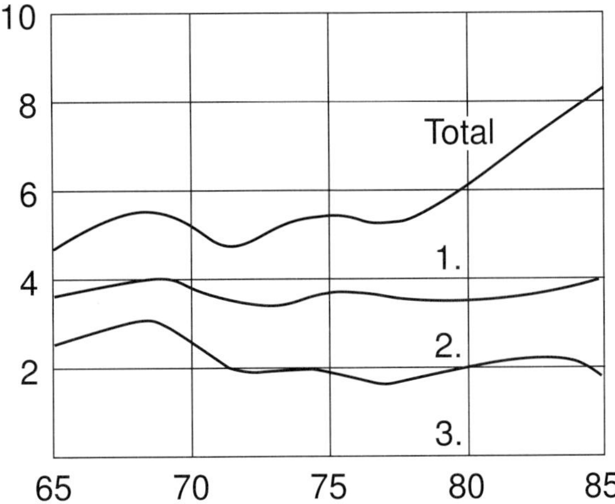

1. Civilian Sector
2. Military Exports
3. U.S. Defense

Billion U.S. dollars of 1975 base value; excludes the Soviet Bloc.

Source: *Interavia* 8/78 survey of jet engine market.

faced in the RB211 programme left few resources to develop a new engine.

GE estimated the cumulative total new installation market for the "10 Ton" engine at around 5,000 engines; it felt that between 1978 and 1993 at least 2,500 aircraft of 150-seat capacity would be manufactured. In addition to the new aircraft market, a potential market existed for the remotorisation of the Boeing 707s and DC8s and for the Dassault Mercure 200 (an existing Dassault project in the 150-seat category). In Europe and in America, the governments were increasingly likely to enforce noise and pollution control legislation vigorously. The maximum permissible engine noise was to be around 100 dB. This aspect, in addition to the criteria of fuel economy, reliability, and durability, led to expect a growing market demand for the new class of engine. GE expected that noise regulation would lead to the early replacement of some JT8D engines and of some earlier Rolls Royce designs, such as the Rolls Royce Spey. Exhibits 4 and 5 show GE's forecast for market development, and the likely competitive products for the 1980s.

GE's Approach

GE decided to develop a whole new engine rather than scale down its CF6, since the high by-pass engines were a new generation. GE's engineers felt that Rolls Royce's adaptation of an existing engine was unlikely to offer major performance advantage, while the joint Pratt & Whitney/MTU project remained uncertain.

GE had now developed an efficient engine for the B–1 strategic bomber. The engine prototype, coded F–101, was on trial. Although the B–1 was a supersonic bomber, its design had been optimized for very long-range subsonic cruise, hence the F–101 core could provide the basis for a fuel efficient subsonic commercial engine. GE decided to use the high pressure turbine and combustion chambers of the B–1 engine for the new 10-Ton engine. The F–101 provided for fewer stages of compressors than the CF6 core and did not have to be scaled down. The U.S. government had spent well over $100 million on the B–1 engine development project. GE was aware that obtaining approval from the U.S. government to use

EXHIBIT 5 Plans for the Second Generation of Turbo Fan Engines of High By-Pass Ratio

	CFM56*	Rolls Royce RB211 535	Pratt & Whitney JT10D 132	General Electric CF6 32
Core of Turbine, Derived From	F–101	RB 211 22 B	(new type)	CF6 6
Thrust at Take Off (kg)	10.885	16000	14.515	16.330
Diameter of Fans	173	188	192	193
Length (cm)	243	269	338	371
Bypass Ratio	5.9	4.4	6.2	4.7
Weight (kg)	2090	3215	2925	3110
Expected Due Date	Oct. 1979	Oct. 1981	Dec. 1981	mid-1981

*Proposed GE-SNECMA engine.

the F–101 core technology for commercial applications was going to be difficult. The B–1 bomber was yet to be introduced into operation; hence the issue would be viewed by the U.S. government as a sensitive defence secret. However, the company felt it could obtain the government's approval of the request.

To turn the F–101 into a high by-pass airline engine, GE had to develop the low pressure fan and turbine sections. They were keen on cutting the product development cycle, since protracted product development projects not only involved excess expenditures, and longer potential paybacks, but also increased the uncertainty of acceptance by an airframe manufacturer. The timing of development of a new aircraft in the 150-seat segment was uncertain during the 70s, since the Boeing 727–200 and the extended fuselage versions of the DC9, as well as the BAC Trident in the U.K., served this market segment for the time being. However GE believed both Airbus Industrie and Boeing were potential customers for the engine, as each would develop a new 150-seat airliner.

The Potential Collaboration

GE, however, was faced with a funding problem. With only a small share of the large engine market, the CF6 had to be discounted in order to win sales over Pratt & Whitney on the B747, and it still required large investment for further development and manufacturing scale-up. Although GE's top management was clearly and strongly committed to GE's entry into the commercial jet engine business, corporate resources were also scarce. GE had been investing in a series of new businesses, among which were plastics, computers, nuclear engineering, and jet engines, all of which were in need of large investments and R&D expenditures.

The CF6 subcontracting relationships had led GE's operational managers to become more familiar with SNECMA. SNECMA was evaluating GE, Pratt & Whitney, and Rolls Royce as potential collaborators. As part of the CF6 product support plan, SNECMA had a team of engineers at the Boeing plant and at the Airbus plant. It did not have any marketing expertise and lacked direct interface with airlines, unlike other manufacturers. Further it lacked the technical strength for product development of the entire engine for commercial applications. Finally the manufacture of commercial jet engines requires an extensive after sales service network, product support facilities and spare parts management programme; all fields in which SNECMA lacked expertise and had no international infrastructure whatsoever.

Toward mid-1971 Rolls Royce declared bankruptcy and went into receivership. SNECMA was increasingly interested in seeking collaboration with American-based manufacturers to enter the "10-ton" market segment.

Informal contacts had started around 1968 about the potential need for a "10-ton" engine between Mr. Claude Lomas, GE's jet engine representative in France, and Mr. Malroux at SNECMA. Through these contracts GE became aware that SNECMA had been independently considering the need for a "10-ton" engine mainly in the context of Dassault's "Mercure 200" project, a French twin jet airliner project.

Starting work on the CF6 in France had also convinced GE's engineers that SNECMA was a reliable subcontractor whose technical competencies could be trusted. GE was pleasantly surprised with the dedication to quality and reliability shown by SNECMA, and by their understanding of complex technologies.

These considerations led Messrs. Claude Lomas and Malroux to suggest a top management meeting between their two companies. Gerhard Neumann met with SNECMA's President, René Ravaud, in 1971. Both men developed a mutual respect for each other's priorities and found they could interact easily at a personal level. They respected each other's integrity. It transpired that SNECMA possessed technology for the low pressure fan and turbine that could be integrated with the F–101 core, with minimum new product development efforts. The French government appeared willing to provide SNECMA with an "advance" of about $500 million to SNECMA for development efforts.[7]

Around the same time Japan was also investigating the possibility of developing a 10-ton engine. MITI (Ministry of International Trade and Industry) and NAL (National Aerospace Laboratory) were working on the technology of the CF6 and the JT9D engines.

By October 1971, a series of discussions between senior executives at GE and SNECMA had increasingly focused on a few difficult issues.

Issues in a Potential Collaboration

Beyond the general issues of concern with the development of a new engine for an uncertain market, a cooperation with SNECMA would raise some difficult issues for GE.

Technology Choice

SNECMA was partly owned by Pratt & Whitney, who had a say in SNECMA's policies. Further, GE was concerned with the risk of strategic information technology leakage to Pratt & Whitney.

Furthermore, the collaboration with SNECMA was going to make the use of classified F–101 technology even more difficult. The F–101 core was barely in its prototype testing phase in 1970. Hence, it was unlikely the U.S. government would consent to release of F–101 technology for commercial use. In the eyes of the U.S. Department of Defence, the Western European industry was not effectively protected against industrial and military espionage from the Soviet bloc. How the U.S. Department of Defence could agree to a collaboration with SNECMA was quite unclear.

Secondly, the F–101 core was planned to be integrated with "the low pressure" system developed by SNECMA. Though the French had a proven design record for low pressure compressors and low pressure fans, the compatibility with the F–101 core was uncertain, particularly if specific F–101 technological parameters could not be communicated to the French.

The idea of combining the technologies to create a new 10-ton engine had been generated during the discussions between Gerhard Neumann and René Ravaud. Despite the support from their engineers, the idea was still only a broad "concept." The strategic alliance difficulties centered around translating this "concept" into reality, given the limits the U.S. government would impose on technology transfer to the French.

Duration and Mutual Interest

GE was of the opinion that with the passage of time it would lose its technology lead, since competitors were also pursuing R&D plans vigorously. It was necessary, then, to get commercial benefit from early technology superiority. Since the 10-ton engine was a new market segment, the company had to develop a reliable prototype engine as early as possible in order for the aircraft manufacturers to begin focusing their airframe design on a 150-seat aircraft. However, the actual timing of the launch of a new 150-seat aircraft by the aircraft manufacturers was quite uncertain. Hence GE could not forecast precisely the period when the market would actually emerge for the new engine.

Once an alliance was started, though, the life cycle of a jet engine might keep it operating for several decades, until the last engines of the new types were retired by a Third World air cargo company or by a smaller air force!

Both companies were competitors in the manufacture of military engines, so they needed to identify a strategic fit that could be a compromise between their commonality of interests in the commercial aircraft engine segment, and the need to ensure their independence in the military aeroengine segment. Further, GE was a publicly traded company upholding its shareholders' interests, while SNECMA was a government-owned company.

[7]The practice, on the part of the French government, was to lend funds for product development to be paid back by the manufacturer over time in proportion to the number of engines sold. The government thus bore a large share of the financial risk of development projects in the aerospace industry, since if the new product did not sell well, the government would not recoup its investment.

Relative Performance

Although GE's management had been impressed with the technical competence of SNECMA, its government-owned status was of concern to GE: Would a joint venture with SNECMA be as competitive as GE alone? Would GE be dragged into supporting "full" employment policies that led to inefficiencies? Would SNECMA strive for productivity improvements?

Marketing and Sales Issues

The success of the CF6 was leading GE to build a sales and service network worldwide. Such a network is expensive to set up and maintain. A jointly made 10-ton engine could be sold and supported via that network, but it was not clear that SNECMA would be satisfied without an involvement in sales and marketing, nor that GE was willing to share its network fully with SNECMA.

Funding Risks

Although the F–101 core required comparatively little further development, and SNECMA was going to benefit from government loans to develop its part of the engine, the appropriated funding was likely to be insufficient to cover further detailed development and testing, and the production start up and scale up. As one of the very first engines dedicated to the civilian market, the new "10-ton" project was unlikely to benefit from more government funding, at least in the United States. The only significant civilian programme ever, the RB211, had bankrupted Rolls Royce!

Competitive Risks

Both GE and SNECMA feared that Pratt & Whitney would do its best to extend the life of the JT8D by developing new, more fuel efficient, and higher thrust versions. While noise reduction was a more difficult issue technologically, it was unclear whether the U.S. government would really force engines into early retirement because of noise levels. Further, the rest of the world was not likely to follow U.S. regulation immediately. Noisier aircraft could thus still be used, and resold to countries less concerned with noise regulation for use between them or on their domestic routes. Both the Boeing 727 and Douglas DC8 were very successful plane designs, in widespread use. How easily they would be superseded by a new design, even with quieter and more efficient engines, was not clear.

INSEAD

Case 7–4

Electrolux: The Acquisition and Integration of Zanussi

In recounting the story of Electrolux's acquisition of Zanussi, Leif Johansson, head of Electrolux's major appliance division, had reasons to feel pleased. Through financial restructuring and operating improvements Zanussi had, in only three years since the acquisition, gone from a massive loss of Lit. 120 billion in 1983 to a tidy profit of Lit. 60 billion in 1987 ($1 = Lit. 1,170 = SEK 5.85 in 12/87)—a turnaround that astounded outside analysts and was perhaps more impressive than the expectations of even the optimists within Electrolux. More important was the progress made in integrating Zanussi strategically, operationally, and organizationally within the Electrolux group, while protecting its distinct identity and reviving the fighting spirit that had been the hallmark of the proud Italian company. Having been the first to suggest to President Anders Scharp that Electrolux should buy financially troubled Zanussi, Johansson had a major personal stake in the operation's continued success.

By early 1988, however, the task was far from complete. Not everything was going well at Zanussi: the company had recently lost some market share within Italy to Merloni, its archrival, which had taken over domestic market leadership following its acquisition of Indesit, another large Italian producer of household appliances. There had been some delays in Zanussi's ambitious programme for plant automation. Moreover, a recent attitude survey had shown that, while the top 60 managers of Zanussi fully supported the actions taken since the acquisition, the next rung of 150 managers felt less motivated and less secure. It was not clear whether these

---

This case was prepared by Sumantra Ghoshal and Philippe Haspeslagh, Associate Professors at INSEAD, and Dag Andersson, Nicola De Sanctis, Beniamino Finzi, and Jacopo Franzan. It is intended to be used as a basis for class discussion rather than to illustrate either effective or ineffective handling of an administrative situation. The cooperation of the Electrolux company and its executives is gratefully acknowledged.

Financial support from the INSEAD Alumni Fund European Case Programme is gratefully acknowledged.

problems were short-term in nature and would soon be resolved, or whether they were the warning signals for more basic and fundamental maladies.

Though Leif Johansson felt it useful to review the integration process, his concerns focused on the next stage of the battle for global leadership. The industry was changing rapidly with competitors like Whirlpool and Matsushita moving outside their home regions. At the same time some local European competitors like GEC-Hotpoint in the UK or Merloni (Ariston) in Italy were making aggressive moves to expand their shares in a relatively low-growth market. The Zanussi takeover and the subsequent acquisition of White Consolidated in the United States, catapulted Electrolux to the top of the list of the world's largest producers of household appliances.

The challenge for Johansson now was to mould all the acquired entities into an integrated strategy and organization that would protect this leadership role and leverage it into a profitable worldwide operation.

Electrolux

In 1962, Electrolux was on a downward curve. Profits were falling and the company had not developed any significant in-house research and development capability. Compared with other appliance manufacturers such as Philips, Siemens, GEC, and Matsushita, it had a limited range of products: the core business was made up of vacuum cleaners and absorption-type refrigerators. These refrigerators were increasingly unable to compete with the new compressor-type refrigerators developed by the competitors, and sales of the once highly successful lines of vacuum cleaners were rapidly declining.

That same year ASEA, a company in the Wallenberg network (an informal grouping of major Swedish companies in which the Wallenbergs—the most influential business family in Sweden—had some equity shares) sold Electro-Helios to Electrolux for shares and thereby became a major shareholder. Electro-Helios was a technological leader in compressor-type refrigerators and a significant producer of freezers and cooking-ranges. This led to a major expansion of Electrolux's role in the Swedish household appliance market, but the company found itself in financial difficulty again due to rapid expansion of production capacity during a period of severe economic downturn.

In 1967 Hans Werthén was appointed CEO of Electrolux. In the next two decades he and the other two members of what was known as the "Electrolux Troika", Anders Scharp and Gösta Bystedt, would manage to develop the company from a relatively small and marginal player in the business into the world's largest manufacturer of household appliances.

Growth through Acquisitions

At the core of the dramatic transformation of Electrolux was an aggressive strategy of expansion through acquisition. At the beginning, Electrolux concentrated on acquiring firms in the Nordic countries, its traditional market, where the company already had a dominant market share. Subsequent acquisitions served not only to strengthen the company's position in its household appliance activities, but also to broaden its European presence and open the way to entirely new product areas. Exhibits 1A and 1B illustrate Electrolux's diversification and major acquisitions between 1964 and 1988.

With more than 200 acquisitions in 40 countries, and 280 manufacturing facilities in 25 countries, the Electrolux Group had few equals in managing the acquisition

EXHIBIT 1 A 1987 Turnover by Product Line (in millions of Swedish crowns)

White goods	28,476
Aluminum products	5,853
Vacuum cleaners	5,571
Forestry products	2,394
Food-service equipment and vending machines	2,356
Building materials	1,810
Cleaning services	1,761
Garden products	1,756
Air-conditioners	1,739
Components	1,717
Car safety equipment	1,711
Leisure appliances	1,619
Kitchen and bathroom cabinets	1,286
Laundry services and goods protection	1,132
Industrial laundry equipment	1,128
Industrial products - White	1,074
Materials handling equipment	1,068
Commercial refrigeration equipment	1,040
Sewing machines	790
Commercial cleaning equipment	633
Sterilization and disinfection equipment	462
International mining	360
Agricultural implements	236
others	1,458

Exhibit 1 B Major Acquisitions and Divestments (1962–1988)
(Sales billion Swedish crowns)

Date	Company	A/D*	Activities/products
1962	ElektroHelios	A	white goods
1964	Gelinge	A	sterilization equipment
1967	Atlas	A	white goods
1967	Elektra	A	ranges
1968	Flymo	A	garden products
1968	ASAB	A	cleaning services
1968	Electrolux Corp.	D	vacuum cleaners
1969	Kent	A	commercial cleaning equipment
1969	Quatlass	A	food-service equipment
1970	Euroclean	A	commercial cleaning equipment
1972	Krett Siegas	A	absorption refrigerators
1973	Facit	A	office machines
1973	Waxcator	A	industrial laundry equipment
1973	Ballingstov	A	kitchen & bathroom cabinets
1973	Vaxjo Rostfritt	A	disinfection equipment
1974	Eureka	A	vacuum cleaners
1974	Emerson Quiet Kool	A	air-conditioners
1975	Tvattman	A	laundry services
1976	Martin	A	kitchen ranges
1976	Tornado	A	vacuum cleaners
1978	Therma	A	white goods, commercial appliances
1978	Husqvarna	A	sewing machines, white goods, chainsaws
1978	Partner	A	chainsaws
1979	Jonsered/Pioneer	A	chainsaws
1979	Tappan	A	household appliances
1980	Oceanic	A	radio/TV
1980	Voss	A	kitchen ranges
1980	Columbus Dixon	A	commercial cleaning equipment
1980	Granges	A	metals
1981	Hugin	A	cash registers
1981	Norlett	A	garden products
1981	Progress	A	vacuum cleaners
1981	Paris-Rhone	A	vacuum cleaners
1981	Lequeux	A	sterilization products
1981	Granges Kraft	D	hydro electric power
1982	Volund	A	industrial laundry equipment
1983	Camping Freeze	A	caravan refrigerators
1983	ZK Hospital	A	disinfection products
1983	Facit	D	office machines
1983	Hogin	D	cash registers
1983	Platzer	D	(Granges division), contractors
1983	Emerson Quiet Kool	D	air-conditioners
1984	Klippan	A	safety belts
1984	Sumak	A	commercial refrigeration equipment
1984	Zanussi	A	household & commercial appliances, industrial products
1985	Zanker	A	washing machines
1985	Beljer Bygg	A	building materials
1985	Duo-Therm	A	air-conditioners
1985	Staub/Bernard/Moteur	A	garden products
1985	Metalverken/Wirsbo	D	(formerly Granges divisions), metal tubes
1986	White	A	household appliances, industrial products
1986	Gotthard	A	scrap recycling
1986	Poulan/Weed Eater	A	forestry & garden products
1987	Tricity/Stott Benham	A	white goods, food service equipment
1987	Design and Manufacturing	A	dishwashers
1987	Oceanic	D	radio/TV
1988	Corberb/Domar	A	white goods
1988	Alpeninox	A	food-service equipment
1988	Britax/Kolb/Cooldrive	A	safety belts
1988	Alcatel	A	vacuum cleaners
1988	A & E Systems	A	caravan enhancements
1988	Bruynzeel	A	materials handling equipment
1988	United Hermetica	A	compressors

*A = acquisition D = divestments

and integration processes. The company generally bought competitors in its core businesses, disposing of operations which either failed to show long-term profit potential or appeared to have a better chance of prospering under the management of another company. In addition, Electrolux always tried to ensure that there were sufficient realisable assets available to help finance the necessary restructuring of the acquired company. Thus, from the beginning of the 1970s up to 1988, the group made capital gains from selling off idle assets of more than SEK 2.5 billion.

At the same time, flexibility had been maintained in order to pick up new product areas for further development. A typical example of this was the chain-saw product line that came with the acquisition of the Swedish appliance manufacturer Husqvarna in 1978. By developing this product line through acquisitions and in-house development, Electrolux emerged as one of the world's leading chain-saw manufacturers with about 30 percent of the global market. Another example was provided by the new business area of outdoor products (consisting mainly of forestry and garden products), which had been grown from the small base of the Flygmo lawnmower business through the acquisition of firms like Poulan/Weed Eater in the US and Staub/Bernard Moteur in France.

The two most notable departures from the strategy of buying familiar businesses had been the 1973 acquisition of Facit, a Swedish office equipment and electronics maker, and the 1980 purchase of Gränges, a metal and mining company. Both companies were in financial trouble. Electrolux had difficulty in fully mastering Facit. After having brought the profit up to a reasonable level, it was sold off to Ericsson in 1983. The borrowing necessary to buy Gränges, combined with the worldwide economic downturn and rising interest rates, pushed Electrolux into a sobering two-year decline (1981–1983) of its profit margin. However, through the Gränges takeover Electrolux also acquired new businesses for future growth. An example was the manufacturing of seat belts, now concentrated in the subsidiary Electrolux Autoliv. Nevertheless, the acquisition of Gränges would be the last diversifying acquisition.

Even though Electrolux had dealt with a large number of acquisitions, specific companies were seldom targeted. In the words of Anders Scharp, "You never choose an acquisition, opportunities just come." The company made it a practice to simulate what the merger combination with other companies would result in should they come up for sale. The financial aspects of an acquisition were considered to be very important. The company usually ensured that it paid less for a company than the total asset value of the company, and not for what Electrolux would bring to the party.

Based on their experience, managers at Electrolux believed that there was no standard method for treating acquisitions: each case was unique and had to be dealt with differently. Typically, however, Electrolux moved quickly at the beginning of the integration process. It identified the key action areas and created task forces consisting of managers from both Electrolux and the acquired company in order to address each of the issues on a time-bound basis. Such joint task forces were believed to help foster management confidence and commitment and create avenues for reciprocal information flows. Objectives were clearly specified, milestones were identified, and the first phase of integration was generally completed within 3–6 months so as to create and maintain momentum. The top management of an acquired company was often replaced, but the middle management was kept intact. As explained by Anders Scharp, "The risk of losing general management competence is small when it is a poorly performing company. Electrolux is prepared to take this risk. It is, however, important that we do not change the marketing and sales staff."

Electrolux Prior to the Acquisition of Zanussi

The activities of the Electrolux group in 1984, prior to the acquisition of Zanussi, covered 26 product lines within five business areas, namely: household appliances, forestry and garden products, industrial products, commercial services and metal and mining (Gränges). Total sales revenue had increased from SEK 1.1 billion in 1967 to SEK 34.5 billion in 1984. The household appliance area (including white goods, special refrigerators, floor-care products and sewing machines) accounted for approximately 52 percent of total Group sales in 1984. Gränges was the second largest area with nearly 21.5 percent of total sales. The third area, industrial products, provided heavy equipment for food services, semi-industrial laundries, and commercial cleaning.

By the 1980s Electrolux had become one of the world's largest manufacturers of white goods with production facilities in Europe and North America and a small presence in Latin America and the Far East. The Group's reliance upon the Scandinavian markets was still considerable. More than 30 percent of sales came from Sweden, Norway, and Denmark. European sales, focusing mainly on Scandinavia and Western Europe, constituted 65 percent of total Group sales. The United States had emerged as the single most important market with 28.9 percent (1987) of total sales.

Electrolux's household appliances were manufactured in plants with specialized assembly lines. Regional manufacturing operations were focused on local brands and designs and established distribution networks. Sales forces for the various brands had been kept separate, though support functions such as physical distribution, stocking, ordertaking, and invoicing might be integrated. With increasing plant automation and product differentiation, the number of models and the volume produced in any given plant had risen sharply. As described by Anders Scharp, "We recognized that expansion means higher volumes, which create scope for rationalization. Rationalization means better margins, which are essential to boost our competitive strength."

One important characteristic of Electrolux was the astonishingly small corporate headquarters at Lilla Essingen, 6 km outside the centre of Stockholm, and the relatively few people who worked in central staff departments. The size of headquarters was a direct outcome of the company's commitment to decentralization. "I believe that we have at least two hierarchical levels fewer than other companies of the same size," said Scharp, "and all operational matters are decentralized to the subsidiaries." However, most strategic issues such as investment programmes, and product range decisions were dealt with at headquarters. The subsidiaries were considered to be profit centres and were evaluated primarily on their returns on net assets as compared with the targets set by the corporate office. Presidents of the diversified subsidiaries reported directly to Scharp, while others reported to the heads of the different product lines.

The Acquisition of Zanussi

In June 1983, Leif Johansson, the 32 year old head of Electrolux's major appliance division, received a proposal from Mr. Candotti, head of Zanussi's major appliance division in France, from whom he had been "sourcing" refrigerators for the French market. The proposal called for the investment of a small amount of money in Zanussi so as to secure future supplies from the financially troubled Italian producer. The next day Johansson called Anders Scharp to ask "Why don't we buy all of it?", thereby triggering a process that led to the largest acquisition in the history of the household appliance industry and in the Swedish business world.

Zanussi

Having begun in 1916 as a small workshop in Pordenone, a little town in northeast Italy, where Antonio Zanussi produced a few wood-burning cookers, Zanussi had grown by the early 1980s to be the second largest privately owned company in Italy with more than 30,000 employees, 50 factories, and 13 foreign sales companies. Most of the growth came in the 1950s and 1960s under the leadership of Lino Zanussi, who understood the necessity of having not only a complete range of products but also a well-functioning distribution and sales network. Lino Zanussi established several new factories within Italy and added cookers, refrigerators, and washing-machines to the product range. In 1958 he launched a major drive to improve exports out of Italy and established the first foreign branch office in Paris in 1962. Similar branches were soon opened in other European countries, and the first foreign manufacturing subsidiary, IBELSA, was set up in Madrid in 1965. Through a series of acquisitions of Italian producers of appliances and components, Zanussi became one of the most vertically integrated manufacturers in Europe, achieving full control over all activities ranging from component manufacturing to final sales and service. It is rumoured that, during this period of heady success, Zanussi had very seriously considered launching a takeover bid for Electrolux, then a struggling Swedish company less than half Zanussi's size.

The company's misfortunes started in 1968 when Lino Zanussi and several other company executives died in an aircrash. Over the next 15 years the new management carved out a costly programme of unrelated diversification into fields such as colour televisions, prefabricated housing, real estate, and community centres. The core business of domestic appliances languished for want of capital, while the new businesses incurred heavy losses. By 1982, the company had amassed debts of over Lit. 1,300 billion and was losing over Lit. 100 billion a year on operations (see Exhibit 2 for the consolidated financial statements during this period).

Between 1982 and 1984, Zanussi tried to rectify the situation by selling off many of the loss-making subsidiaries, reducing the rest of the workforce by over 4,400 people, and focusing on its core activities. However, given the large debt burden and the need for heavy investment in order to rebuild the domestic appliance business, a fresh injection of capital was essential, and the company began its search for a partner.

EXHIBIT 2 Consolidated Financial Statements for Zanussi Group
(in million SEK)

	1980	1981	1982	1983
Consolidated Income Statement				
Sales	3,826	4,327	4,415	5,240
Operating Cost	−3,301	−3,775	−3,957	−4,654
Operating Income Before Depreciation	525	552	458	586
Depreciation	−161	−98	−104	−130
Operating Income After Depreciation	364	454	354	456
Financial Income	192	330	284	279
Financial Expenses	−407	−489	−647	−627
Income After Financial Items	149	295	−9	108
Extraordinary Items	−53	−228	−223	81
Income Before Appropriations	96	67	−232	189
Appropriations	−53	−42	−409	−382
Income Before Taxes	43	25	−641	−193
Taxes	−7	−7	−10	−10
Net Income	36	18	−651	−203

	1980	1981	1982	1983
Consolidated Balance Sheet				
Current Assets (excl. inventory)	1,559	1,987	1,811	2,108
Inventory	965	1,054	999	956
Fixed Assets	1,622	1,539	2,366	2,902
Total Assets	4,146	4,580	5,176	5,966
Current Liabilities	1,590	1,832	1,875	2,072
Long-Term Liabilities	1,273	1,441	1,864	2,349
Reserves	259	301	472	627
Shareholders' Equity	1,024	1,006	965	918
Total Liabilities and Shareholders' Equity	4,146	4,580	5,176	5,966

The Acquisition Process

The process of Electrolux's acquisition of Zanussi formally commenced when Enrico Cuccia, the informal head of Mediobanca and the most powerful financier in Italy, approached Hans Werthén on November 30, 1983, about the possibility of Electrolux rescuing Zanussi from impending financial collapse. It was not by chance that the grand old man of Mediobanca arrived in Sweden. Mr. Cuccia had close links to the Agnelli family—the owners of Fiat, the largest industrial group in Italy—and the proposal to approach Electrolux came from Mr. Agnelli, who wanted to save the second largest private manufacturing company in his country. As a board member of SKF, the Swedish bearing manufacturer, Agnelli had developed a healthy respect for Swedish management and believed that Electrolux alone had the resources and management skills necessary to turn Zanussi around.

In the meanwhile, Electrolux had been looking around for a good acquisition to expand its appliance business. Its efforts to take over AEG's appliance business in Germany had failed because the conditions stipulated for the takeover were found to be too tough. Later, Electrolux had to back away from acquiring the TI group in the U.K. because of too high a price-tag. Zanussi now represented the best chance for significant expansion in Europe. "It was a very good fit", recalled Anders Scharp. "There were not many overlaps: we were strong where Zanussi was weak, and vice-versa." There were significant complementarities in products, markets, and opportunities for vertical integration. For example, while Electrolux was well established in microwave-ovens, cookers, and fridge-freezers, Zanussi was Europe's largest producer of "wet products" such as washing-machines, traditionally a weak area for Electrolux. Similarly, while Electrolux had large market shares in Scandinavia and Switzerland where Zanussi was almost completely absent, Zanussi was the market leader in Italy and Spain, two markets that Electrolux had failed to crack. Zanussi was also strong in France, the only market where Electrolux was losing money, and had a significant presence in Germany where Electrolux had limited strength except in vacuum cleaners. Finally, while Electrolux had historically avoided vertical integration and sourced most of its components externally, Zanussi was a vertically integrated company with substantial spare capacity for component production that Electrolux could profitably use.

From November 30, 1983, until December 14, 1984, the date when the formal deal was finally signed, there ensued a 12-month period of intense negotiation in which, alongside the top management of the two companies, Gianmario Rossignolo, the Chairman of SKF's Italian subsidiary, took an increasingly active role. The most difficult parts of the negotiations focused on the following three issues:

Union and work force reduction. At the outset, the powerful unions at Zanussi were against selling the company to the "Vikings from the North." They would have preferred to keep Zanussi independent, with a government subsidy, or to merge with Thomson from France. They also believed that under Electrolux management all important functions would be transferred to Sweden, thereby denuding the skills of the Italian company and also reducing local employment opportunities.

In response to these concerns, Electrolux guaranteed that all Zanussi's important functions would be retained within Italy. Twenty union leaders were sent from Sweden to Italy to reassure the Italians. The same number of Italian union leaders were invited to Sweden to observe Electrolux's production system and labour relations. Initially, Mr. Rossignolo signed a letter of assurance to the unions on behalf of Electrolux confirming that the level of employment prevailing at that time would be maintained. Soon thereafter, however, it became obvious that Zanussi could not be made profitable without workforce reductions. This resulted in difficult re-negotiations. It was finally agreed that within three months of the acquisition Electrolux would present the unions a three-year plan for investments and reduction in personnel. Actual retrenchments would have to follow the plan, subject to its approval by the unions.

Prior commitments of Zanussi. A number of problems were posed by certain commitments on the part of Zanussi. One major issue was SELECO, an Italian producer of television sets. A majority of shares in SELECO were held by REL, a government holding company, and the rest were owned by Zanussi and Indesit. Zanussi had made a commitment to buy REL's majority holdings of SELECO within a period of five years ending in 1989. Electrolux had no interest in entering the television business but finally accepted this commitment despite considerable apprehension.

Another major concern was the unprofitable Spanish appliance company IBELSA owned by Zanussi. Zanussi had received large subsidies from the Spanish government against a commitment to help restructure the industry in Spain, and heavy fines would have to be paid if the company decided to pull out. Once again, Electrolux had to accept these terms despite concern about IBELSA's long-term competitiveness.

Nevertheless, there was one potential liability that Electrolux refused to accept. In the later stages of the negotiations, an audit team from Electrolux discovered that a previous managing director of Zanussi had sold a large amount of equipment and machinery to a German company and had then leased them back. This could potentially lead to severe penalties and large fines, as the actions violated Italian foreign exchange and tax laws. Electrolux refused to proceed with the negotiations until the Italian government had promised not to take any punitive actions in this case.

Financial structure and ownership. Electrolux was not willing to take over majority ownership of Zanussi immediately since it would then be required to consolidate Zanussi into group accounts, and the large debts would have major adverse effects on the Electrolux balance sheet and share prices. Electrolux wanted to take minority holdings without relinquishing its claim to majority holdings in the future. To resolve this issue, a consortium was organized that included prominent Italian financial institutions and industrial companies such as Mediobanca, IMI, Crediop, and a subsidiary of Fiat. The consortium took on a large part of the shares (40.6 percent), with another 10.4 percent bought by the Friuli region. This allowed Electrolux to remain at 49 percent. While the exact financial transactions were kept confidential since some of the parties opposed any payment to the Zanussi family, it is believed that Electrolux injected slightly under $100 million into Zanussi. One third of that investment secured the 49 percent shareholding, and the remainder went toward debentures that could be converted into shares at any time to give Electrolux a comfortable 75 percent ownership. An agreement with over 100 banks which had some form of exposure to Zanussi assured a respite from creditors, freezing payments on the Italian debt until January 1987. At the same time the creditors made considerable concessions on interest payments.

One of the most important meetings in the long negotiation process took place in Rome on November 15, 1984, when, after stormy discussions between the top management of Electrolux and the leaders of the Zanussi union, a document confirming Electrolux's intention to acquire Zanussi was jointly signed by both parties. During the most crucial hour of the meeting, Hans Werthén stood up in front of the 50 union leaders and declared: "We are not buying companies in order to close them down, but to turn them into profitable ventures . . . and, we are not the Vikings, who were Norwegians, anyway."

The Turnaround of Zanussi

It was standard Electrolux practice to have a broad but clear plan for immediate post-acquisition action well before the negotiation process for an acquisition was complete. Thus, by August 1984, well before the deal was signed in December, a specific plan for the turnaround and the eventual integration of Zanussi was drawn up in Stockholm. As stated by Leif Johansson, "When we make an acquisition, we adopt a centralized approach from the outset. We have a definite plan worked out when we go in, and there is virtually no need for extended discussions." In the Zanussi case, the general approach had to be amended slightly since a feasible reduction in the employment levels was not automatic. However, clear decisions were taken to move the loss-making production of front-loaded washing-machines from France to Zanussi's factory in Pordenone. On the other hand, the production of all top-loading washing-machines was to be moved from Italy to France. In total, the internal plan anticipated shifting production of between 600 and 800 thousand product-units from Electrolux and subcontractors' plants to Zanussi, thereby increasing Zanussi's capacity utilization. Detailed financial calculations led to an expected cost savings of SEK 400–500 million through rationalization. Specific plans were also drawn up to achieve a 2–3 percent reduction in Zanussi's marketing and administrative costs by integrating the organization of the two companies in different countries.

Immediate Post-Acquisition Actions

On December 14, a matter of hours after the signing of the final agreement, Electrolux announced a complete change in the top management of Zanussi. The old board, packed with nominees of the Zanussi family, was swept clean and Mr. Gianmario Rossignolo was appointed as Chairman of the company. An Italian, long-experienced in working with Swedish colleagues because of his position as chairman of SKF's Italian subsidiary, Rossignolo was seen as an ideal bridge between the two companies with their vastly different cultures and management styles. Carlo Verri, who was Managing Director of SKF's Italian subsidiary, was brought in as the new Managing Director of Zanussi. Rossignolo and Verri had turned around SKF's Italian operations and had a long history of working together as a team. Similarly, Hans Werthén, Anders Scharp, Gösta Bystedt and Lennart Ribohn joined the reconstituted Zanussi board. The industrial relations manager of Zanussi was the only senior manager below the board level to be replaced. The purpose was to give a clear signal to the entire organization of the need to change work practices.

Consistent with the Electrolux style, a number of task forces were formed immediately to address the scope of integration and rationalization of activities in different functional areas. Each team was given a specific time period to come up with recommendations. Similarly, immediate actions were initiated in order to introduce Electrolux's financial reporting system within Zanussi, the clear target being to have the system fully in place and operative within six months from the date of the acquisition.

Direct steps were taken at the business level to enhance capacity utilization, reduce costs of raw materials and components purchased, and revitalize local sales.

Capacity utilization: It was promised that Electrolux would source 500,000 units from Zanussi including 280,000 units of household appliances, 200,000 units of components, and 7,500 units of commercial appliances. This sourcing decision was given wide publicity both inside and outside the company, and a drive was launched to achieve the chosen levels as soon as possible. By 1985, 70 percent of the target had been reached.

Cost cutting in purchases: Given that 70 percent of production costs were represented by raw materials and purchased components, an immediate programme was launched to reduce vendor prices. The assumption was that vendors had adjusted their prices to compensate for the high risk of supplying to financially distressed Zanussi and should lower their prices now that that risk was eliminated. A net saving of 2 percent on purchases was achieved immediately. Over time about 17 percent gains in real terms would be achieved, not only for Zanussi, but also for Electrolux.

Revitalizing sales: Local competitors in Italy reacted vigorously to the announcement of Electrolux's acquisition of Zanussi. Anticipating a period of inaction while the new management took charge, they launched an aggressive marketing programme and Zanussi's sales slumped almost immediately. After consulting with Electrolux, the new management of Zanussi responded with a dramatic move of initially extending trade credit from 60 to 360 days under specified conditions. Sales surged immediately and the market was assured once and for all that "Zanussi was back."

Agreement with the Unions

In the next phase, starting from February 1985, the new management turned its attention to medium and long-term needs. The most pressing of these was to fulfill a promise made to the unions before the acquisition: the presentation of a complete restructuring programme. This programme was finalized and discussed with the union leaders on March 28, 1985, at the Ministry of Industry in Rome. It consisted of a broad analysis of the industry and market trends, evaluation of Zanussi's competitive position and future prospects, and a detailed plan for investments and workforce reduction. The meeting was characterized by a high level of openness on the part of management. Such openness, unusual in Italian industrial relations, took the unions by surprise. In the end, after difficult negotiations, the plan was signed by all the parties on May 25.

The final plan provided for a total reduction of the workforce by 4,848 employees (the emergency phone number in Italy!) to be implemented over a three-year period (2,850 in 1985, 850 in 1986, and 1,100 in 1987) through early retirement and other incentives for voluntary exit. In 1985, as planned, the workforce was reduced by 2,800.

Paradoxically, from the beginning of 1986 a new problem arose. With business doing well and export demands for some of the products strong, a number of factories had to resort to over-time work and even hired new skilled workers, while at the same time the original reduction plans continued to be implemented. Management claimed that there was no inconsistency in these actions since the people being laid off lacked the skills that would be needed in the future. With the prospect of factory automation clearly on the horizon, a more educated and skilled workforce was necessary, and the new hires conformed to these future needs. Some of the workers resisted, and a series of strikes followed at the Porcia plant.

Management decided to force the issue and brought out advertisements in the local press to highlight the situation publicly. In the new industrial climate in Italy, the strategy proved effective and the strikes ended. In 1987, the company made further progress in its relationship with the unions. In a new agreement, wage increases were linked to productivity, and no limits were placed on workforce reductions. Further, it was agreed that the company could hire almost 1,000 workers on a temporary basis, so as to take advantage of the subsidy provided by the government to stimulate worker training through temporary employment. It was clear that Zanussi management benefitted significantly from the loss of union power that was a prominent feature of the recently changed industrial scene in Italy. However, its open and transparent approach also contributed to the success by gaining the respect of trade union leaders, at both the company and national levels.

Strategic Transformation: Building Competitiveness

The new management recognized that, in order to build durable competitive advantage, more basic changes were necessary. The poor financial performance of the company before the acquisition was only partly due to low productivity, and sustainable profits could not be assured through workforce reduction alone. After careful analysis, three areas were chosen as the focal points for a strategic transformation of Zanussi: improving production technology, spurring innovations and new product development, and enhancing product quality.

Improving production technology. Recalling his first visit to Zanussi, Halvar Johansson, then head of Electrolux's technical R&D, commented: "What we found on entering Zanussi's factories was, in many respects, 1960s technology! The level of automation was far too low, especially in assembly operation. We did not find a single industrial robot or even a computer either in the product development unit or in the plant. However, we also discovered that Zanussi's engineers and production personnel were of notably high standards." As part of a broad programme to improve production technology, Electrolux initiated an investment programme of Lit. 340 billion to restructure Zanussi's two major plants at Susegana and Porcia.

The Susegana restructing proposal foresaw an investment of Lit. 100 billion to build up the facility into a highly automated, high-capacity unit able to produce 1.2 million refrigerators and freezers a year. The project was expected to come on stream by the end of 1988. The Porcia project anticipated a total investment of about Lit. 200 billion to build a highly automated, yet flexible plant capable of producing 1.5 million washing-machines per year. This project, scheduled for completion in 1990, was the largest individual investment project in the history of the Electrolux group. When on stream it would be the largest washing-machine factory in the world. Both projects involved large investments to build flexibility through the use of CAD-CAM systems and just-in-time production methodology. As explained by Carlo Verri, "The automation was primarily to achieve flexibility and to improve quality, and not to save on labour costs."

Implementation of both the projects was somewhat delayed. While the initial schedules may have been over-optimistic, some of the delays were caused by friction among Zanussi and Electrolux engineers. The Electrolux approach of building joint teams for implementation of projects was seen by some Zanussi managers as excessive involvement of the acquiring company in tasks for which the acquired company had ample and perhaps superior capabilities. Consequently, information flows were often blocked, resulting in, for example, a more than one-year delay in deciding the final layout of the Susegana factory. The delays were a matter of considerable concern to the top management of Electrolux. On the one hand, they felt extensive involvement of Electrolux's internal consultants to be necessary for effective implementation of the projects, since Zanussi lacked the requisite expertise. On the other hand, they acknowledged Zanussi's well-established engineering skills and the need to provide the local engineers with the opportunity to learn and to prove themselves. They also worried about whether the skill-levels of the local workforce could be upgraded in time for operating the new units and looked for ways to expedite the training process.

Innovation and new product development. Zanussi had built its strong market presence on the reputation of being an innovator. This ability had, unfortunately, languished during the lean period. Both Rossignolo and Verri placed the greatest emphasis on reviving the innovative spirit of the company, and projects that had idled for years due to lack of funds were revitalized and assigned high priority.

The results were quite dramatic and a virtual torrent of new product ideas emerged very quickly. The most striking example was a new washing-machine design—the "Jet System"—that cut detergent and water consumption by a third. The product was developed within only nine months, and the new machine was presented at the Cologne fair in February 1986. Through a direct television link with Cologne, Carlo Verri himself presented the assembly line at Pordenone where the "Jet-System" was to be mass produced. By July 1986, demand for the new machine had reached the level of 250,000 per year, and the company was facing delivery problems.

While the "Jet System" was the most visible outcome of the new emphasis on innovation, other equally important developments were in the pipeline. For example, the company developed a new rotary compressor to replace the reciprocating compressors that were being used in refrigerators. A major drive was also underway to improve product design and features through the introduction of IC chips. Interestingly, most of these proposals came not from the sophisticated and independent research centre of the company, but from development groups located within the line organizations which produced the products. How to maintain the momentum of innovation was a major concern for Verri, particularly as the company moved into the larger and more complex projects necessary for significant technological breakthroughs.

Enhancing product quality. Quality enhancement was viewed as the third leg of the strategy for long-term revitalization of Zanussi. At Electrolux, high quality was viewed as an essential means of achieving the primary objectives of the company: satisfied customers, committed employees, and sound profitability. Zanussi had a good reputation for quality, but the standards had slackened during the turmoil faced by the company for almost a decade prior to the acquisition. Committed to the policy that quality levels must be the same within the group no matter where a product was produced, Electrolux initiated a major drive to enhance product quality at Zanussi and set extremely ambitious targets to reduce failure rates and post-sales service requirements. The targets were such that incremental improvements did not suffice for their attainment, and a new approach toward quality was necessary. The technical staff of Electrolux provided requisite guidance and assistance and helped set up the parameters for a series of quality improvement programmes launched by Zanussi.

Carlo Verri was involved in these programmes on an almost day-to-day basis. First, he headed the working group that set up the basic policy on quality for the entire Zanussi organization. In accordance with this policy, a Total Quality (TQ) project was started in May 1986, and a series of education and training programmes were introduced in order to diffuse the new philosophy and policy to all company employees. Supplier involvement was an integral part of the TQ project. As described by Verri, "Supplier involvement was crucial. Zanussi's suppliers had to demonstrate their commitment to effective quality control. This meant that all the procedures for quality assurance, for tracking down failures, etc., had to be approved by us. In other words, suppliers had to have the capability to provide self-certification for the quality of their products. They had to provide service within days rather than weeks, given that our plants were becoming automated. Our gains in flexibility and quality through new production techniques could be lost if the suppliers did not become equally efficient."

Organizational Revitalization; Changing Attitudes

One of the biggest challenges faced in the turnaround process lay in the area of revitalizing the Zanussi organization. During the troubled years the management process at Zanussi had suffered from many aberrations. Conflicts had become a way of life, and information flow within the organization had become severely constrained. Most issues were escalated to the top for arbitration, and the middle management had practically no role in decision making. Front-line managers had become alienated because of direct dealings between the workers and senior managers via the union leaders. Overall, people had lost faith in the integrity of the system, in which seniority and loyalty to individuals were seen as more important than competence or commitment to the company.

In addition, the acquisition had also created a strong barrier of defensiveness within the Zanussi organization. In its own acquisitions Zanussi typically eliminated most of the middle management in the acquired companies. As the acquired company it expected similar actions from Electrolux. Moreover, some Zanussi managers were not convinced of any need for change. They believed that Zanussi's financial problems were caused not by any strategic, operational, or organizational shortcomings, but by the practices of the previous owners, including diversion of overseas profits through a foreign holding company in Luxembourg.

Finally, most of the managers were also concerned that both Rossignolo and Verri, with their backgrounds in the Italian subsidiary of a Swedish company, "were closer to Stockholm than to Pordenone."

In an attempt to overcome these barriers, Verri and the entire executive management group at Zanussi participated in a number of team-building sessions that were facilitated by an external consultant. These meetings gave rise to a number of developments that constituted the core of the organizational revitalization of Zanussi.

Statement of mission, values, and guiding principles. One of the direct outcomes of the team-building meetings was a statement of mission, values, and guiding principles developed to serve as the charter for change (see Exhibit 3). The statement identified the four main values of the company: to be close to the clients and satisfy them through innovation and service; to accept challenges and develop a leader mentality; to pursue total quality not only in production but in all areas of activity; and to become a global competitor by developing an international outlook. Apart from these specific points, the statement also confirmed the new management's commitment to creating a context that would foster transparent and coherent behaviour at both the individual and company levels under all circumstances. As described by Rossignolo, "We adopted the Swedish work ethic—everybody keeps his word and all information is correct. We committed ourselves to being honest with the local authorities, the trade unions, and our customers. It took some time for the message to get across, but I think everybody has got it now."

Management development workshops. In order to improve the flow of information among senior managers and to co-opt them into the new management approach, a set of management development workshops was organized. The 60 most senior managers of Zanussi, including Verri, participated in each of three two-day workshops that were held between November 1985 and July 1986. The next tier of 150 middle managers of the company were subsequently exposed to the same programme.

Middle management problems. An organizational climate survey in 1987 revealed an interesting problem. The top 60 managers of the company confirmed strong support for the mission statement and the new management style. Conversely, the 150 middle managers, who seemed to feel threatened by the changes, appeared considerably less enthused. Their subordinates—about a thousand front-line managers and professional employees—like the top management, fully approved the change and

EXHIBIT 3 Mission Values and Guiding Principles of Zanussi

Mission

To become the market leader in Europe, with a significant position in other world areas, in supplying homes, institutions, and industry with systems, appliances, components, and after-sales services.

To be successful in this mission, the company and management legitimization must be based on the capability to be near the customer and satisfy his needs; to demonstrate strength, entrepreneurship, and creativity in accepting and winning external challenges; to offer total quality on all dimensions, more than the competition; and to be oriented to an internal vision and engagement.

Values

Our basic values, ranked, are:

1. To be near the customer;
2. To accept challenges;
3. To deliver total quality;
4. With an international perspective.

Our central value, underlying all of the above, is transparence, which means that Zanussi will reward behaviour which is based on constantly transparent information and attitudes, safeguarding the interests of the company.

Guiding Principles

1. A management group is legitimized by knowing what we want, pursuing it coherently, and communicating our intent in order to be believable.
2. Shared communication means shared responsibility, not power and status index.
3. The manager's task is managing through information and motivation, not by building "power islands."
4. Time is short: the world will not wait for "perfect solutions."
5. Strategic management implies:

- Professional skills;
- Risk-taking attitudes and the skill to spot opportunity;
- Integration with the environment and the organisation, flexibility, and attention to change;
- Identification with the mission of the firm, and helping in the evolution of a culture that supports it;
- Team work ability;
- Skill in identifying strengths and weaknesses.

Policies to be Developed

Specific policies were being developed in the following area to support the implementation of the above mission, values and guiding principles: personnel, image and public relations, administration, purchasing, asset control, legal representation, R&D and innovation, and information systems. Members of senior management were assigned responsibility for developing policies in each of these areas, with completion expected by the end of 1986.

demanded greater involvement. In response to this problem, it was decided that the 60 top managers should establish direct communication with the 1,000 front-line managers, by-passing the middle management when necessary. The decision was made known within the organization, and a clear signal was sent to the middle managers that they should get on board or else they would risk missing the boat. At the same time, a special training programme was launched for the front-line managers and professional employees in order to broaden their management skills and outlook.

Structural reorganization. Before the acquisition, Zanussi was organized in five "sectors," with the heads of each sector reporting to the managing director. The sectors, in turn, controlled the operating companies in their business areas. In practice, the sector managers were closely involved with the day-to-day operations of the companies under their charge. Both the managing director at the corporate level, and the different sector managers had strong staff organizations to support their activities.

Verri abandoned the sector concept, even though the operating companies continued to report to the former sector managers who were now called managing directors. However, staff at the sector level were virtually eliminated, and the operating companies were given full responsibility and authority for taking all operating-level decisions. Similarly, staff at the corporate level were also reduced very substantially, and the heads of planning, finance and control, organization and human resources, general administration, and legal and public affairs all reported directly to Verri. The four managing directors, the five heads of major corporate staff departments, and Verri constituted the executive management group of Zanussi. As Chairman, Rossignolo concentrated primarily on external relations.

Integration of the Two Companies

As described by Leif Johansson, "With the acquisition of Zanussi, the Electrolux group entered a new era. In several respects we were able to adopt a completely new way of thinking." Much of the new thinking emerged from the discussions and recommendations of the task forces that had been appointed, involving managers from both companies, to look at specific opportunities for integrating the activities of the two organizations. In total, eight such task forces were formed: two each for components, product development, and commercial appliances, and one each for the marketing function and management development. Each of these task forces had met three to four times, typically for half a day each time. Their recommendations formed the basis for the actions that were taken to integrate the production and sales operations of the two companies, rationalize component production, and develop specialization in product and brand development within the entire Electrolux group. At the level of individuals, a bridge had been built between the top management of Electrolux and the senior management team of Zanussi, and further actions were underway for creating similar understanding and mutual respect among managers lower down in the two organizations.

Electrolux Components Group (ECG)

Following Electrolux's acquisition of White Consolidated in the United States in March 1986, an international task force consisting of managers from Electrolux, White, and Zanussi was created to explore the overall synergies that could be exploited within the activities of the three companies. The task force concluded that integration opportunities were relatively limited at the level of finished products because of factors such as differences in customer preferences and technical standards and the high transportation costs. However, at the component level there were many similarities in the needs of the three companies, implying greater scope for standardization and production rationalization. As a result of this analysis, the Electrolux Component Group was formed at the beginning of 1987 as part of the newly created industrial products division at Electrolux. (See Exhibit 4 for an overall view of the group in 1987.) The group was made responsible for the coordination and development of all strategic components used by Electrolux worldwide. Since over 50 percent of the group's component production came from Zanussi, Verri was appointed head of this group in addition to his responsibilities as managing director of Zanussi, and the group headquarters were located in Turin, Italy. In order to preserve and enhance the competitiveness of the component sector, it was decided that 50 percent of the component group's sales must be made to outside parties, and at least 20 percent of the internal requirement for components must be sourced from outside the newly formed group.

Integration of Production

At Electrolux, production, sales, and marketing had traditionally been integrated market by market. After the acquisition of Zanussi, all these activities will be

EXHIBIT 4 Electrolux Group Key Data

1. Group Sales and Employees World Wide

	Sales SEKm	No of Employees
Nordic Countries		
Sweden	11,128	29,456
Denmark	1,735	3,078
Norway	1,505	1,299
Finland	1,445	1,563
	15,813	35,396
Rest of Europe		
Great Britain	6,377	10,589
France	5,098	8,753
West Germany	4,045	3,317
Italy	3,684	15,282
Switzerland	1,818	1,814
Spain	1,445	2,851
Netherlands	1,238	1,016
Belgium and Luxembourg	913	1,040
Austria	392	958
Portugal	96	193
Others	604	41
	25,710	45,854
Asia		
Japan	707	1,175
Saudi Arabia	215	738
Hong Kong	152	1,340
Phillipines	150	525
Kuwait	147	2,220
Taiwan	119	2,178
Malaysia	72	1,833
Thailand	56	15
Singapore	50	556
Jordan	28	137
Lebanon	22	35
Others	720	1,729
	2438	12,481

	Sales SEKm	No of Employees
North America		
USA	19,488	29,750
Canada	1,580	2,150
	21,068	31,900
Latin America		
Brazil	302	6,215
Venezuela	208	1,032
Peru	181	750
Colombia	104	1,865
Mexico	66	1,735
Ecuador	34	232
Guatemala	24	31
Others	443	198
	1,362	12,058
Africa		
	414	
Oceania		
Australia	497	2,216
New Zealand	114	557
Others	14	—
	625	2,773
Total	**67,016**	**140,462**

2. Sales by Business Area

	1987 SEKm	1986 SEKm	1985 SEKm	% of Total 1987 Sales
Household Appliances	39,487	31,378	19,200	58.6
Commercial Appliances	5,619	4,250	3,348	8.3
Commercial Services	2,893	2,504	2,266	4.3
Outdoor Products	4,475	2,909	2,990	6.6
Industrial Products	11,784	9,087	9,232	17.5
Building Components	3,172	2,962	2,652	4.7
Total	**67,430**	**53,090**	**39,688**	**100.0**

EXHIBIT 4 (continued)

3. Operating Income after Depreciation by Business Area

	1987 SEKm	1986 SEKm	1985 SEKm	% of Total 1987 Sales
Household Appliances	2,077	1,947	1,589	49.2
Commercial Appliances	484	349	260	11.4
Commercial Services	169	172	132	4.0
Outdoor Products	421	241	373	10.0
Industrial Products	910	474	657	21.5
Building Components	164	138	126	3.9
Total	**4,225**	**3,321**	**3,137**	**100.0**

reorganised into international product divisions and national marketing/sales companies.

The larger volumes from the combined operations made it feasible to switch to a system in which large-scale specialised plants, equipped with flexible manufacturing technology, would each produce a single product for the entire European market. This new "one product-one factory" strategy was exemplified by the new plants in Susegana and Porcia. Each of the product divisions carried full responsibility not only for manufacturing, but also for development and internal marketing of their products. In order to coordinate long-term development among these 43 divisions, three coordinators were appointed for "wet," "hot," and "cold" products respectively. Based in Stockholm without staff, each of these coordinators would be on the road most of the time.

Integration of Sales/Marketing

Similarly, it was decided to create single umbrella companies over the separate sales/marketing organisations in all countries. Given the longstanding history of competition between the Electrolux and Zanussi organisations, this would turn out to be a difficult and complex process. It was planned that in each country the stronger organisation would absorb the weaker one. This did not mean, however, that the head of the larger organisation in each country would automatically receive the top slot in the combined organisation. A number of complaints arose on both sides over this issue, which became a source of much irritation. For example, it was because of this that Candotti, who had been the first to approach Electrolux for investment in Zanussi, resigned. In what remained a source of considerable frustration, Zanussi continued to operate through directly controlled sales companies in Germany, France, Denmark, and Norway.

Coordination among the marketing companies was achieved through an equally lean coordinating structure reporting to Leif Johansson, with an Italian manager coordinating all European countries and a Swedish manager looking after the rest of the world.

To facilitate operational coordination between sales and production, a number of new systems were developed. One, the Electrolux Forecasting and Supply System (EFS), involved the automatic coordination of sales forecasts and delivery orders. By 1988 computer links with EFS would be established in all European Sales subsidiaries and factories. The Zanussi evaluation system was changed to that of Electrolux, in which both sales and factories were assessed on the basis of return on net assets (RONA) rather than on a profit and cost basis. An overall RONA target of 20 percent was set for the Group as a whole.

Brand Positioning and Product Development

One of the consequences of Electrolux's history of international expansion through acquisitions was a proliferation of brands, not only in Europe but also in the US, where the acquisition of White had brought a number of brands. The task of coordinating these brands, some of which were local, others regional, and a few international, would fall to the two marketing coordinators, working closely with Leif Johansson and a task force involving product styling and marketing managers. The challenge was complicated by the fact that even the international brands did not always have the same position from market to market. Zanussi, for example, was not a brand name in Italy itself, where its products sold as "Rex." And its image in Sweden was not nearly as upscale and innovative as in other countries like the United Kingdom.

The approach chosen in Europe was to group the brands in four brand-name families, each targeted at a particular customer profile and destined to become a separate design family (see Exhibit 5). Two of these families would be international brands, based respectively on Electrolux and Zanussi, and the other two would regroup a number of local brands (see Exhibit 6). The goal was to develop an integrated pan-European strategy for each brand-name family. For the international brands, the strategy would involve high-scale production of standardized products in focused factories and coordinated positioning and marketing across different countries. For the families representing a collection of national brands, the products would again be standardized as far as possible so as to allow manufacturing on a regional scale; but each brand would be "localized" in its country through positioning, distribution, promotion, and service.

Exhibit 5

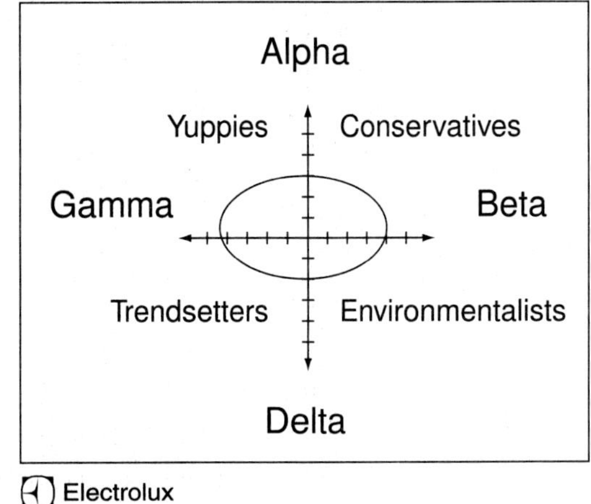

Mutual Respect and Understanding Among People

Since the acquisition Anders Scharp, Lennart Ribohn, and Leif Johansson had ensured that they jointly visited Pordenone at least once every two months for a two-day review of Zanussi's activities and progress. Hans Werthén and Gösta Bystedt also visited Zanussi, though much less frequently. The visitors would typically spend some time touring one or another of Zanussi's facilities and then move on to preplanned meetings with Zanussi's top management. Over time these meetings had built a strong bridge of mutual respect between the two groups and helped diffuse some of the early apprehensions. As described by a senior manager of Zanussi, "The top management of Electrolux really understand numbers. They look at a few key numbers and immediately grasp the essentials. That was very good training for us—we had the habit of analyzing and analyzing, without coming to any conclusions . . . Besides, the top two or three people in Electrolux have the ability of immersing themselves in a particular problem and coming up with a solution and an implementation plan. They are also so obviously excited by what they do, their enthusiasm is very contagious." For most senior managers at Zanussi these meetings provided stronger evidence than could any words that the top management of Electrolux did not consider the acquisition as a conquest but rather as a partnership. "We have had a lot of exchanges, and have learnt a lot from them, but we have not had a single Swedish manager imposed on top of us here."

At the next level of management the joint task forces had helped build some relationships among individuals, but the links were still weak and apprehensions remained. "We don't know them, but our concern is that the next level of Electrolux managers may be more bureaucratic and less open. To them we might be a conquest", said a senior manager of Zanussi. "In the next phase of integration, we must develop bridges at the middle, and I frankly do not know how easy or difficult that might be."

Future Requirements

Whereas the acquisition of Zanussi and White Consolidated had catapulted Electrolux into a clear lead in the industry, the race was far from over. After initially failing to reach agreement with Philips in 1987, Whirlpool had come back in early 1988 agreeing to buy out 53 percent

EXHIBIT 6 The Brand-Name Families

α
Alpha

β
Beta

Husqvarna

ZAKKER

therma

Zoppas (Belgium, Italy)

γ
Gamma

Elektro Helios

ATLAS

Elektra

FAURE (Quelle)

CASTOR

privileg

VOSS

Zoppas (Norway, France)

STRÖMBERG

MARYKEK

δ
Delta

ZANUSSI

of Philips's appliance operations as a first step to taking full control. Upon full completion Whirlpool would have paid or assumed debt totalling $1.2 billion for activities which in 1987 were generating $70 million pretax preinterest income on sales of $2 billion. The Japanese had started moving outside South East Asia. In the meantime, local European competitors such as GEC and Merloni were ensuring good returns and, more importantly, were gaining back market share.

All of this was taking place in a mature industry highly dependent on replacement demand. Industry analysts expected that, even in a moderately growing economy, appliance shipments would be on a downward trend for the next couple of years. Given the concentration of buyers and the shift toward specilised retailers, raw materials price increases were more and more difficult to pass on.

UNIT 8 Network Organizations on E-business

INSEAD

Case 8–1

Nexia International

In October 1995, Nexia International, a network of independent accounting affiliates, lost its Norwegian member firm to a medium-sized competitor who had lured it with promises of more international referral work. Yet, referral work between Nexia affiliates had grown dramatically in recent years, almost tripling between 1991 and 1994 to over $5.6 million. Moreover, the network's fee income had grown from $405 million to $562 million by 1994, pushing it up from 14th to 12th position[1] in the world rankings of accounting and professional service firms. The stunning growth was partly attributable to the 23 new members that joined the network between 1991 and 1994 and to increased fee income contributed by member firms already in the network.

Nigel Hodges, executive director of Nexia International, was concerned about member firms with a small percentage of international business. How could Nexia involve and stimulate those less active members?

> "We don't believe we're in the race for size, but to strengthen ties in order to give better service. . . We'd like to get stronger in South America, we're trying to do more in Asia/Pacific. . . We want better ties more than volume. We're not after market share, but better service for the medium-sized client."

That strategy had been followed since Nexia's creation, and Hodges wanted to ensure that Nexia's structure was appropriate to sustain its targeted objectives for 1996. It aimed to become a leader in the medium-sized businesses' market, rank in the top 3 or 4 international accounting networks of medium size, and help its member firms reach top 10 ranking in their respective domestic markets. Projections to reach fee income of $650 million in 1996, reduce cost-sharing contributions to a smaller percentage of fee income, and increase referral business to over $6 million, were to be achieved through more extensive geographical coverage in each of its five regions.

Affiliated under the name Nexia International for their international business, the network's independent member firms practiced locally under their own partnership's name. As a nonequity alliance, the network's members pooled some financial resources to gain access to a wider spectrum of competencies and answer the demand in the industry for expanded services. The worldwide coverage offered to network members opened greater international service opportunities.

In 1994, Nexia International had members in 68 countries and correspondents in 5 countries[2] operating 292 offices, 881 partners and 7,769 staff in total. Most business was concentrated in Europe, which contributed 49 percent of fee income, followed by 30 percent in the United States and 18 percent in the Asia Pacific region. The core business for all of Nexia's member firms was financial audit, representing 63 percent of fee income. Tax business was next at 19 percent, while 10 percent of their business came from management consulting. Other specialties, such as environmental services represented 8 percent of fee income.

Nexia International: The Creation of a Professional Services Network

Nexia International was formed in 1990 through the merger of two international accounting and auditing networks: Spicer & Oppenheim International (SOI) and Neville Russell International (NRI). A 1990 defection of the UK partners of SOI to a Big Six firm, and the subsequent closing of

---

This case was written by Marie-Claude Reney under the supervision of Mitchell P. Koza, Associate Professor of Business Policy at INSEAD, Fontainebleau, France. It is intended to be used as the basis for class discussion rather than to illustrate either effective or ineffective handling of an administrative situation.

[1] *International Accounting Bulletin,* Dublin, Ireland: Lafferty Publications Ltd., December 19, 1994, p. 6.

[2] A correspondent status was available to countries that wished to join the network but did not generate enough fee income to cover the minimum charges for full membership.

SOI's U.S. member firm due to financial difficulties, produced an opportunity in these two important countries. Competing accounting firms could fill the void by servicing these clients.

Of medium size with a solid reputation, SOI ranked 12th worldwide with 50 offices around the world and fee income of $419 million in 1990. Over 70 percent of its worldwide business was concentrated in Europe. Serving middle market clients and the United Kingdom's growing owner-managed businesses, the Spicer & Oppenheim International network was the result of a 1987 merger of the major UK accounting firm of Spicer & Pegler with the American accounting firm of Oppenheim, Apper, Dixon & Co.

NRI was a comparatively small international accounting network, ranked 23rd in 1989, with fee income of $147 million. Neville Russell International's origins went back to the early 1900s in the United Kingdom where it started in audits for insurance companies such as Lloyd's. Its business had grown to include many large charities and other small and medium clients in various industries. The Neville Russell partnerships began expanding internationally in the early 1980s. Among its affiliates were three U.S. firms: Clifton, Gunderson & Co, Wolf & Co and Lowrimore, Warwick & Co. NRI offered solid representation in the United Kingdom and some coverage in the United States and in a few countries where SOI was not yet present.

The executives of both networks recognized the need for a global solution to serve foreign clients and multinational corporations as well as small and medium-sized clients with some international presence. After the merger, Nexia's international coverage spanned 57 countries for a combined fee income of $415 million, placing it in 14th position worldwide. In May 1991, at Nexia's first annual International Council meeting in Hamburg, Germany, the merged firms of SOI and NRI adopted a new name. The name Nexia was chosen for its ease of pronunciation and its lack of connotation with any object or person making it easier for global branding and increasing "global" credibility. The logo featured a circle representing the world of Nexia and a prominent red dot representing the client as the focus of the firm.

By 1994, the network had achieved its objective of increasing referrals across borders by $2 million going from $3.7 million in 1991 to more than $5.6 million for 1994. It also reduced the percentage of fee income that members needed to contribute toward international expenses in keeping with the necessity for cost reduction. To facilitate learning between network members, Nexia International developed training programs and seminars, and expanded an international secondment program.[3]

The Worldwide Accounting and Professional Services Industry

As of 1994, the top 32 accounting firms generated over $43 billion in fees around the world and employed approximately 500,000 people (see Exhibit 1). Fee income for the group increased by 11 percent following the recession, between 1990 and 1993, whereas growth for most Big Six firms was less than 2.5 percent a year. The largest geographical markets were Europe and the United States with a little over 40 percent of fee income generated in each area. In the late 1980s, a consolidation wave in the accounting industry reduced the number of the largest accounting firms from eight to six. After these megamergers, the industry was dominated by what became known as the Big Six, which generated $33.5 billion in fee income for 1994. Over 70 percent of the Big Six firms' business remained in audit and tax, except for Arthur Andersen, which had slightly less than 50 percent of its business in consulting as of 1995.

Accounting companies often group buyers of auditing services into two segments. First, are the publicly traded companies. These clients seek an audit signed by an accounting firm with an international reputation that the capital markets will recognize and accept. The second market segment includes companies of different sizes that are not publicly traded.

In the 1990s, the accounting industry's traditional core business, auditing, was approaching stagnation. Audit and accounting services represented in excess of 60 percent for most accounting firms. The Big Six firms, already auditing most of the top 1,000 firms in the world, courted clients from each other in order to gain market share. Audit quality was perceived as similar from one Big Six firm to the next so clients were in a position to apply strong pressure to force accounting firms to reduce audit fees. Audit work was in danger of being viewed by the client as a commodity. These pressures lowered margins to the point where accounting firms sought to reduce greatly their high dependence on the audit business.

To increase profitability, firms branched out into other business areas such as consulting and corporate finance. Audit, in this view, was the door opener that let accounting

[3]Secondment was a program aimed at sending qualified personnel to member offices that needed those skills or aimed at training personnel in areas different from the one where the individual was posted.

EXHIBIT 1 Comparative Data for Global Accounting Networks, 1994

Firm's Name	Fee Income ($million)	Year Over Year Growth Rate (%)	Fee Income per Partner in $ Millions (ranking)	Number of Partners (ranking)	Total Staff	No. of Countries with Member Firms	No. of Countries with Correspondents	Number of Offices Worldwide
Arthur Andersen	6,738	12.0	2.677 (1)	2,517 (6)	72,722	74	38	358
KPMG	6,100	1.7	1.016 (6)	6,003 (1)	72,704	123	13	829
Ernst & Young	6,015	3.0	1.151 (3)	5,228 (2)	66,525	121	5	682
Coopers & Lybrand	5,500	5.4	1.068 (5)	5,150 (3)	68,000	130	4	758
Deloitte Touche Tohmatsu Int'l	5,200	4.1	1.130 (4)	4,600 (4)	56,600	126	0	684
Price Waterhouse	3,975	2.3	1.237 (2)	3,213 (5)	50,122	114	4	450
BDO Binder	1,155	0.4	0.653 (7)	1,770 (7)	16,445	67	7	458
Nexia	562	11.7	0.638	881	7,769	68	5	292

Source: Compiled from a variety of tables in *International Accounting Bulletin,* December 19, 1994, and Nexia internal documents.

firms into a company to introduce new services. The Big Six firms were, at times, prepared to take lower margins on the audit business in order to gain access to the client. For example, Coopers & Lybrand (C&L), one of the Big Six firms, was branded by some industry observers a low seller of audit services because their sales revenue per client were amongst the lowest in the industry. This led some competitors to believe that C&L was selling at below-cost prices. C&L vehemently denied the allegation that they were affecting the profitability structure of the industry, stating that some audit proposals from competitors were as low or lower than theirs. "We all thought that the competition would be less when we went from eight to six, but it has just gotten worse," stated Michael Henning, CEO of Ernst & Young International.

Competition was described as cutthroat as the large international firms sought revenue, squeezing out some smaller accounting firms. The "Big 20" medium-sized accounting firms, called the Mid Tiers, responded with cut-rate introductory fees to attract new clients mostly in the medium-sized market. This caused a "polarization of accounting markets, forcing smaller accounting firms to go for smaller clients."[4]

While auditing was a mature sector, competition in consulting was fierce. It could come from other business advisory experts such as bankers, merchant bankers, management consultants, and lawyers, and industrial sectors such as computer manufacturing where companies like IBM and Unisys offered consulting services. However, accounting and consulting advice were not homogeneous services and could not be sold in the same standardized manner as audits. Furthermore, there was resistance among large clients to give nonaudit work to their auditors. This created enormous pressure on the knowledge and skill requirements of the professionals in accounting and consulting firms. Expanding consultancy services seemed to be an answer to slow growth in certain countries within the traditional markets of accounting and auditing. But achieving success in both businesses was no easy matter.

Decentralized Webs of Independent Local Firms or Centralized Hubs?

Internationalization in the accounting industry had historically been driven by internationalization of the customer, saturation in the home audit market, the audit review becoming a commodity and the audit being the entry through the client's doors to sell other products. In some firms, international expansion was achieved through the acquisition of already established networks. For others, such as Arthur Andersen and Price Waterhouse, fast global penetration by acquisition was not the objective. Unlike their competitors, Arthur Andersen and Price Waterhouse grew through developing their own foreign offices, while others hooked up with networks of varying sizes. In both cases—the rollout method of Arthur Andersen or the acquisition mode of other networks—the ambiguity of relationships with foreign partners as well as national culture differences posed thorny operational problems.

Clients need consistent quality advice for their operations around the world, and they need to keep up-to-date on world business. Firms need global quality standards. This push toward harmonization and uniformity of techniques and procedures led some firms to increase control through centralization of key activities. Yet centralizing firms often faced subsidiaries that would fight to retain independence and autonomy. It appeared to some players that a collection of national partnerships was not suitable for integrated international business. In the future, accounting firms would perhaps resemble partnerships from the outside while being controlled as corporations.

The international accounting firms adopted several organizational models in answer to the internationalization challenge. Centralized structures with dominating headquarters were less common. Looser federations with varying degrees of decentralized decision making prevailed. Arthur Andersen distinguished itself from Price Waterhouse and the other Big Six firms with the only worldwide, integrated structure where worldwide partners in a Swiss *Société Coopérative* shared world profits of Arthur Andersen & Co. At $8.1 billion in revenue for the year ended August 31, 1995, Arthur Andersen & Co, SC, posted a 21 percent gain on its fee income over the prior year. Such a substantial increase secured its leadership position in the industry. Its sophisticated worldwide accounting system for partner compensation logged all work between offices, including work for prospective clients, which was also taken into account in the bonus calculation.

The remaining Big Six firms were structured as federations of affiliated independent accounting partnerships with more or less centralized international services. Most networks required exclusivity of membership within a country or market in most countries except for KPMG where several partnerships could compete in the same market. Most firms shared costs according to different formulae, either in the form of a percentage of fee income or by

---

[4] *European Accountant*, John Doherty, September 1990, p. 2.

splitting the total bill of running international operations. Price Waterhouse set up a hybrid structure where member firms around the world were financially autonomous except in Europe and Asia where it created profit sharing pools for those members. Several firms organized themselves along service lines such as audit, tax, and consulting. More sophisticated firms also included divisions along industry groups. Specialists in industries such as health care, telecommunications and hotel management, would form multidisciplinary teams with an audit, tax, and management consulting specialist from the sector.

Mid Tier International firms offered an alternative to clients who did not wish to do business with the Big Six accounting firms. Mid Tier referred to the medium-sized accounting firms that followed the Big Six in fee income and in size. This group of about 18 firms generated a little over $9.1 billion in fee income for 1994, which represented 27 percent of the Big Six's business. The 7th ranking international accounting network in the industry was BDO Binder generating fee income of $1.2 billion, directly behind Price Waterhouse at $4 billion in fee income for 1994. Among the Mid Tiers, Nexia took 6th place behind BDO, Grant Thornton International, Moores Rowland International, RSM, and Summit International. Following Nexia, Horwarth International earned $509 million and the next 11 firms generated less than $500 million each in fee income. Most were organized as loosely integrated federations of accounting partnerships that shared referrals across their domestic borders. Following the Mid Tiers were smaller domestic associations of independent firms and single practice firms.

What differentiated Mid Tier firms among themselves was the network approach they adopted: a simple directory or a network of more or less integrated services. The directory approach only provided a listing of members around the world. Among the five firms that preceded Nexia, BDO offered a number of centralized services to its members while RSM offered a hybrid service-directory approach. The others offered a directory listing. BDO, the top firm in the Mid Tier group was strongest in Germany, its country of origin. Its worldwide referral business was substantial at over $20 million and originated mostly (85 percent) from Germany. The loss of BDO's UK firm, Binder Hamlyn, to Arthur Andersen, showed that partnerships remained vulnerable to poaching. The second ranking network in the Mid Tier group, Grant Thornton International, was strongest in the United Kingdom and Canada. Its referral business, at about $1.3 million, was quite low compared to Nexia's $6 million and the more than $4 million generated by Horwarth International and PKF, two smaller networks. Most of the other firms in the Mid Tier group generated less than $2 million in international referral work within their network.

One of the biggest threats to the accounting profession in the 1990s remained its exposure to damages claims, escalating in the United States and threatening Continental Europe. Partners in accounting and professional service firms were particularly vulnerable to litigation as they were "jointly and severally liable" with all the partners in the partnership. Unlike medical doctors, typically responsible for their own acts, accounting partners were responsible for the work of a team and liable for the work of their partners' teams. This led to greater difficulty in recruiting applicants to the profession with the litigation threat looming. "Outstanding legal claims against the [Big Six] firms total about $30 billion in America; in London, a claim for $11 billion over the audit of Bank of Credit and Commerce International grinds against Price Waterhouse and Ernst & Young." [5]

In order to protect themselves, the Big Six firms in the United States incorporated themselves in 1994 under a limited liability partnerships (LLP) structure. KPMG in the United Kingdom incorporated its audit business in 1995. It was the only UK accounting firm to do so. KPMG surveyed its clients before incorporation and found that most agreed with the idea, except for a few clients who did not want to see that pot of gold vanish. Incorporation of firms in the face of rampant litigation risked changing the organizational structure of accounting networks that would no longer be able to function as partnerships. The danger could be seen as the potential loss of personal responsibility that prevailed in a partnership. "[. . .] the idea of personal liability means that people outside can have confidence in you. It's to do with credibility and trust," stated David McDonnell, national managing partner of Grant Thornton UK.[6] Managing a partnership as a corporation would create the difficulty of trying to reconcile local professional judgment with centralized control and procedures.

Nexia International: The Design and Coordination of a Professional Services Network

Nexia International Limited, the umbrella organization for the international network, was a corporation registered in

[5]Idem, p. 63.

[6]*Accountancy,* UK publication, Aug 94, p. 44.

Amsterdam. Its incorporation protected the name Nexia from misuse should any of its member firms leave the Nexia network or become insolvent. The management of the international network of Nexia was centralized in the hands of the International Secretariat and the International Board of Directors. An International Council ensured a democratic platform for member firms. A representative from each member firm held a single vote irrespective of the size of the firm. At the Board level, the most active countries were represented, while certain regions such as Africa and South America shared the same director. At the local level, member firms retained financial independence and decision-making autonomy within their partnership. Independence was often considered critical to member firms. It weighed in Nexia International's selection of a member firm.

There were three types of members in the Nexia International network: full members, representatives and correspondents. In 1995, full members paid membership fees according to the following formula: the greater of a minimum of £2,500 ($ 3,950) per year[7] or a percent of the member's annual fee income. Membership fees provided access to two professional advisory bodies in audit and tax, an information technology committee, some publications developed by the professional committees (to be purchased by member firms) and an international marketing and communications program. Membership fees also financed the development of training programs, the organization of an annual conference and specialized seminars, international secondment assignments, and worldwide information technology configurations.

Member firms held approval authority of Nexia's appointments in the International organization, the annual budget and the audited accounts voted on in the International Council. Full members entered into a membership agreement that required them to comply with the international network's quality standards for referred work. An exclusivity agreement ensured that all referral work was directed to Nexia International members. Potential international referral work was one primary reason firms sought membership in the network. Their "policy of having exclusive membership or representation in each country ensures that Nexia International offers stability and continuity in the service rendered to its clients."[8] In most countries, Nexia guaranteed exclusive representation in a member firm's domestic market. This meant that clients of a given member firm would have their work handled by member firms in those markets with an introduction and follow-up from their lead accounting firm.

Exceptions to exclusivity were made for very large countries such as Canada and the United States, because it was difficult for any one firm to cover all of the United States or all of Canada with the resources of a Mid Tier independent accounting firm. New markets were also excluded because several member firms were usually needed to provide the resources necessary to develop these new markets. This was especially the case in Central and Eastern Europe, where qualified personnel were not always available or required further training. This development work offered opportunities for cooperative work between members. In 1995, for example, Calan Ramolino & Associés, the Nexia French member firm, participated in the development of an office in Vietnam. Several other firms from the Asia Pacific region had taken an equity position in this venture.

The status of representative was offered to accounting firms in new markets (for example, Central European and Eastern European firms), smaller markets, or in less developed countries. Valid for a two to three year period, representatives were still bound by the exclusivity agreement and the same work standards as full members. Their membership fees were £1,500 ($2,370) annually. Although they could not vote on Council, they could attend the Council meeting and contribute. As of 1995, there were 15 representatives throughout the network.

In countries where there were neither full members nor representative firms, there might be correspondent firms. This status did not require exclusivity or adherence to the network's international standards. It was a relatively flexible agreement for representation that was adapted to local situations.

One benefit sought from being a member of an accounting network was referral of international work between member firms. Audit work for the foreign subsidiary of a client or tax advice for a multinational company were the most frequent kinds of referrals. Referral work at Nexia was compensated with a commission fee, whereas most other accounting networks did not remunerate referrals. Opportunities for international work increased as member firms grew and were able to service more clients with international business. In 1994, France sent 48 percent of the worldwide referral business to other member firms, while 19 percent was from the United Kingdom and 8 percent from the Netherlands. Work received from other member firms went disproportionately to the Netherlands (20 percent), and France and the United Kingdom both received 14 percent.

[7]At a rate of $1.58 for £1.

[8]Nexia International promotional material.

The challenge for medium-sized accounting firms in getting business from large corporations, usually the biggest generators of international work, also affected Nexia International. While the Big Six firms were nimble enough to enter the medium-sized and owner-managed markets, the reverse could seldom be said of medium-sized accounting firms going after large corporations. A partner from a Big Six firm questioned the value of belonging to a medium-sized international network that expected referrals of international business. He felt that most of those medium-sized accounting networks had affiliates with not enough international clients to justify paying such high membership fees. Some Nexia members voiced the opinion that the amount of international work generated in the network was not sufficient.

Referral work was not the only reason why firms joined an international network. Some accounting firms, especially smaller ones, felt that belonging to an international network brought prestige and credibility in their domestic market. It served to attract clients that prefer an accounting firm that provides access to international resources, services, and expertise. Conferences and seminars provided regular opportunities to meet with members from other countries and served as training opportunities in a variety of topics such as audit, tax, export, mergers and acquisitions, and many others. A "club" feeling was reported at these conferences and seminars where time for social activities contributed to the bonding between participants. An international secondment program centralizing exchanges of qualified personnel between member offices allowed specialists to share their expertise and for trainees to practice in a country other than their usual posting and also further contributed to the development of ties between member firms.

Up to 1994, technical training was only available to managers and partners in Europe. Difficulties arose when Europe tried setting up a program for all junior accountants. There was great diversity, not only in language and culture, but also in technical knowledge and training due to the differences in recruitment policies of the different European countries. It was decided to maintain the training only at the manager level and above since managers and partners would be the ones interfacing with clients. In 1995, an international course on business development was inaugurated for all senior managers and partners in the network. Member firms choose whom they send to this course and other training programs. Each firm assumed the cost of its own participants. The course helped participants develop skills in managing problems that arose in international business. It aimed "to teach managers how to sell Nexia International to their national clients," explained Nexia's European Regional Chairman, Frédéric Mazière.

Membership Selection

Regional chairmen scouted potential member firms according to their regional development plan. Regional chairmen visited potential member firms with the Executive Director, some board members and/or partners of other member firms that understood or had an interest in that new market. For example, when the time came to select an American accounting firm with a strong presence in New York, several of the Canadian partners visited potential members with Gene Temkin, the North American Regional Chairman, and Nigel Hodges. Several potential member firms were typically preselected on the basis of their high professional quality and financial stability before the trip.

Accounting firms ranked in the top 10 of their market were preferred if they were serving medium-sized businesses as well as some international clients. Ideally, they were independent firms and agreed to work exclusively with Nexia International (for details, see Exhibit 2). A short list was prepared for the Board to make its final selection. Once a member firm was selected, the Executive Director asked the partners of the potential firm to organize a board meeting with all their partners. Hodges stressed the importance of consensus among the partners early-on:

> "This helps to fend off potential takeover attempts by other firms, such as the Big Six, since recruiters will often contact members of the executive and not talk to other partners. If all those other partners have been sold to Nexia International early on, they are less likely to agree to a switch.[9] They need to be enthusiastic about being in a network. It pays at the end of the day".

A high level of commitment from member firms at the time of selection reduced future tensions and the necessity of involvement by international management. In managing relationships with affiliates and between affiliates, the Executive Director had limited authority when confronted with undesirable behavior. Because of the autonomy and independence bestowed on all member firms, the decision-making bodies for international network

[9] All partners of a member firm typically needed to be involved in the "joining a network" decision.

EXHIBIT 2 Selection Criteria for Member Firms

1. Exclusivity in the accounting firm's country.
2. High quality professional firm.
3. Independent firm serving medium-size businesses including international clients.
4. Preferably in the top 10 in their market.
5. Financial stability of the firm.
6. Good location and office.
7. Commitment.

Source: internal Nexia documents, 1994 and 1995.

strategy were not member firms on issues beyond professional quality standards.

The case of a member firm doing work for its client in another member firm's territory had arisen often. Instead of introducing the client to the relevant network affiliate, the member firm did the work by itself, sometimes establishing a new subsidiary, and thus also retaining all fees. The Board was advised of the situation by the Executive Director, who had responsibility to identify and resolve the situation.

The International Council

Overall authority rested with the International Council. Each country could send one representative to the council, except in the case of countries with more than one member firm. All the member firms in those countries elected a chairman representing that country. Representatives of members in good standing and paying full membership fees held one vote per country. They approved all appointments, annual budgets and audited accounts. Annual Council meetings, chaired by the Chairman of the Board, were held after the fall Board meeting and were followed by the international affiliates' annual conference.

With only 40 percent majority required to pass a motion in Council, countries not represented on the Board could organize and outvote the Board's decisions in the Council. However, as Nigel Hodges stated, "I am too closely connected [to the partners of the member firms] to let that happen. I am constantly visiting and in touch with all the regions. Then, who are the others to say no to a project . . . That's where the referrals come from, the countries represented on the Board." For those partners who do not attend the Council meeting, Nigel Hodges sent "a synopsis of important issues discussed at the Council Meeting, leaving out the political discussions, to all the offices in the network."

The International Board of Directors

Partners from the largest firms around the world were elected to the Board of Directors of Nexia International Limited. Composed of nine directors and a chairman in 1995, it represented the Netherlands, Germany, Saudi Arabia, Canada, Italy, France, Singapore, the United Kingdom, and the United States,[10] those countries contributing 85 percent of total business in the network as well as most of the technical contributions and participation. The Board of Directors met three times a year for regularly scheduled meetings that lasted about two days. The Board contained a minimum of seven members and a maximum of fourteen. The Chairman was elected for a minimum of three years and a maximum of four, with one reelection period allowed. Board members were elected by the Council for approximately three years with one-third of the board being replaced every year.

The Board was responsible for the overall direction of the network, maintaining quality standards, and allocating funding for international initiatives. It was accountable to the International Council. The Board was also a forum where members' views may be expressed and problems discussed. It selected new member firms from proposals by the regional chairmen. It reviewed reports on members' financial status and quality of work prepared by the International Audit Committee. Member firms may be expelled if they did not meet quality standards and/or were not in a healthy financial position. Proposals from the regions and the various international committees were reviewed by the Board. Budgets for projects were evaluated by the Board and then ratified by the International Council.

The International Secretariat

Nexia's 1995 International Secretariat was composed of Eppo Horlings, Chairman of the Board, Patrice de Maistre, Honorary President, and Nigel Hodges, Executive Director. To facilitate coordination, the International Secretariat was traditionally located in the country where the Chairman practiced. In the fall of 1994, it was moved to Amsterdam from Paris when Eppo Horlings replaced Patrice

[10]There were two directors from the United States.

de Maistre as Chairman. The International Executive Director, appointed by the Board, was responsible for the day-to-day management of the network's international activities and the implementation of the international strategy set by the Board. This included overseeing projects and handling administrative issues with the assistance of only two staff, a General Secretary and an Assistant. He visited member firms to maintain and increase the network's visibility among affiliates. As of 1995, not all qualified professionals in member firms were aware of the network.

Communications between member firms were mostly limited to a needs basis. When a client needed work done in another country, typically the partner-in-charge called the affiliated firm in the country in question. If the partner did not know anyone in that country, the directory could help in locating a partner with the required specialty. For that purpose, the Secretariat maintained a Who's Who directory of the partners in every member firm. It provided information on their specialty and the sectors in which they had experience.

A quarterly newsletter, NexiaLink, available to all member firms' staff, provided information on recent events throughout the network. Contributions from all offices were welcomed and covered such topics as developments and trends in the accounting profession, selected news of the business community around the world, and marketing ideas.

Regional Chairmen

Member firms in the network were grouped into 5 regions: Europe, Asia Pacific, North America, South America, and the Middle East, headed by a Regional Chairman. Regional chairmen were required to give regular feedback to the Board on activities in their region. After formulating project proposals on behalf of members in their region, regional chairmen discussed these projects with the Executive Director to ensure harmonization with the network's objectives. Approval was obtained from the Board for projects and annual budgets. These were put to a vote at the annual Council meeting to determine the level of investment in the proposed activity. Regional chairmen were responsible for the development of their region's client base and developed projects that would foster cooperation among member firms. In Europe, the European Training Group (ETG), the European Audit Group (NEAG), and the European Environmental Services Group (NESG) were examples of cooperative efforts "that are the cement of a network," told Frédéric Mazière. These regional working groups furthered awareness and involvement in the network by the partners of member firms.

To increase Nexia's participation in activities with regional economic institutions, conferences were held within the region to discuss trends, economic perspectives, and other developments, often with the participation of the region's board member and Regional Chairman. Owen Pierce, the Regional Chairman for the Asia Pacific region, commented:

> "The location is chosen with the aim of supporting an existing member or promoting Nexia International in an area in which it is not yet represented. As an example we met in Shanghai, China in 1994 and in Ho Chi Minh City, Vietnam in 1995. In both of these cases, the seminars were arranged to give our members the opportunity to further their knowledge and their contacts in the country concerned."

With the help of the International Secretariat, promotional seminars were conducted in each region aimed at familiarizing staff and clients on "how Nexia International can help them expand." Thematic seminars in specialty areas such as tax, exporting or international business also attracted potential clients and stimulated existing ones.

Professional Committees

Three permanent, specialized committees—audit, tax, and information technology—acted as advisory bodies in their respective areas of specialization. All member firms had free access to their services and may send representatives to those committees from all regions. Every year, the committees prepared and published new materials in their specialty for use by member firms. Regional chairmen and professional committee chairmen were reimbursed by the International Secretariat for their expenses incurred in the course of their duties. Time for their activities in the international network was donated to Nexia International by their respective member firms. Regional chairmen and committee members conducted their work for the member firms in which they were partners while serving a regional office or international committee.

The International Audit Committee set minimum reporting standards and conducted quality control reviews of all Nexia International member firms. Six volunteers constituted the committee, with John Mellows of Neville Russell in London as Chairman, in 1995. Nexia International employed two full-time auditors, formerly with the UK Institute of Chartered Accountants, to oversee the annual quality control reviews of each member firm and the reviews of potential members. The Committee helped member firms with coordination of international tenders.

The International Tax Committee included tax specialists from several member firms (France, Germany, the United States, Turkey, New Zealand, and the UK) and the committee's Chairman. It provided a team of tax specialists to coordinate and support member firms in tax activities throughout the network. They met three times a year to discuss tax support to members, and upcoming tax publications, such as a book on value added taxes entitled VAT. Member firms could sell or give away these publications to clients and prospects. Regional and international tax conferences organized by the International Tax Committee helped tax specialists throughout the network to stay abreast of tax developments in corporate and personal tax, financial and estate planning, double taxation, etc. To supplement these, a bimonthly newsletter circulated articles submitted by members on international tax issues.

The tax committee's meetings were held at different member firms in order to allow interested member firms to benefit from the expertise of tax specialists visiting on the premises. While visiting, the committee members could act as speakers in seminars for partners, employees, clients, and contacts. They also offered complimentary overall international tax review to a client of the member firm they were visiting, conducted by a group of the committee's members.

Other than providing auditing procedures software and other electronic technical tools, the Information Technology Committee maintained an electronic mail link between Paris, London, and Amsterdam, and planned to include worldwide membership by December 1995. The committee supported projects that required a larger investment of time and resources than were available from individual member firms. As of 1995, not all member firms were equipped to do computerized financial statements and audits, posing a potential problem when referring a client. Other computerized applications had to be developed to remain technologically competitive with industry trends.

Nexia International: Concrete Actions in Integrating the Network

The directors of Nexia International and its regional and professional chairmen sought to strengthen ties between member firms. Although the International Secretariat brought all members together, additional links were needed, in their view, to achieve the maximum potential of the alliance. In some regions, substantial cooperative work was already done; in others, it was more limited. "The sharing of expertise and skills is a major advantage of belonging to the network," echoed Owen Pierce. Nexia International wanted and encouraged members to become involved in joint projects as much as they could. "Members [. . .] are expected to play their part in pursuing the activities of the region," stated Owen Pierce.

Environmental Services

During 1993, the U.S. member firms of Nexia International conducted a survey in the United States, one of the countries with the most stringent environmental legislation, on environmental issues. It showed that "over half of businesses viewed green measures as a compliance issue."[11] Patrice de Maistre saw this concern for protecting the environment as a way to diversify into a growing new service area and encouraged the Board to allocate resources to the development of an environmental program. Nexia jumped ahead of its competitors in this area as only one Big Six firm seemed to be offering environmental services and one Mid Tier firm created a referral network for environmental services.

In 1994, Nexia International Europe launched the Environmental Services Group. Its vision was to provide one-stop shopping for all the environmental services executives required. Following the June 1992 United Nations Earth Summit attended by 178 countries, the EU had set standards such as the eco-management and audit scheme (EMAS) forcing executives in the public and private sectors to review their national and international policies in order to comply with new legal requirements. Nexia believed that clients would be increasingly interested in integrating environmental policy in their business strategy. Nexia International Europe environmental specialists forged links with other environmental experts and participated in various environmental committees to keep up with rapid changes in the environmental legislation. They established relations with European universities to carry out research on environmental matters in order to develop services to their clients. Led by Nexia International's Spanish member firm, Audihispana, environmental specialists in Denmark, Germany, the United Kingdom, and the Netherlands trained consultants and auditors from other Nexia European member firms in environmental regulation compliance. They offered train-

[11] *European Accounting Focus*, London, March 1994, p. 6.

ing courses and seminars to help companies with their environmental programs.

A manual of environmental impact assessment and the environmental audit had been developed. To promote these services, Nexia International Europe Environmental Services produced a brochure presenting the products and services offered, such as environmental impact assessment surveys, environmental accounting and reporting, eco-audits, and several others.

Audits of Central and Eastern European Aid Programs

The PHARE audits, another example of a team approach, involved both Western and Eastern European member firms from the Nexia network. These audits of aid programs for economic reform in Eastern European countries were assigned to Nexia International and supervised by the European Commission in 1994 and 1995 with a renewal option for another year. In 1994, Nexia teams from France, the Czech Republic, Greece, Poland, and the Netherlands participated. Seven PHARE audit assignments (five in Hungary and two in Romania) were planned for the second half of 1995. Although much enthusiasm and cooperation were present in such projects, the question of responsibility came up repeatedly. Which of the participating partnerships would sign for the PHARE audits and take responsibility for it? In the fall of 1995, after many years of debate and opposition, network members agreed that the name Nexia International could be signed for international work.

Computerized Audit Process Analysis

In the Information Technology area, CORISAN, an audit risk analysis program was created with the participation of four different accounting firms, including the Dutch member of Nexia International, Horlings, Brouwer & Horlings. Through cooperative work, a computer program was designed to control the audit process and provide a review of the planning, conducting, and evaluating stages of an audit. Another computer project was developed jointly with the Information Technology Committee. Intended for quick access of worldwide auditing standards, "we have developed an auditing and financial reporting standards data retrieval system that allows members to key in a word [on a computer] and get the policy and standard on that item. For example, the word 'stock' can be typed up, giving the user the worldwide standard associated with the query," explained John Mellows, Chairman of the International Audit Committee.

Developing the Corporate Finance Business

To take advantage of the growth potential in the area of corporate finance, Gene Temkin, a director of Nexia International and a mergers and acquisitions specialist in Chicago, decided to put together an M&A seminar for partners in Nexia member firms. "There were people from eight different countries attending: two partners from Scandinavia, one from France, one from Toronto, one from New York, one from Chicago and two from Israel. We discussed franchising, financing and sales opportunities." Temkin saw great potential for cross-referrals of clients between service lines and the possibility to involve a large number of Nexia member firms. As Temkin explained,

> "Corporate finance is an easy specialty to market since the process is the same worldwide, unlike tax and audit that have their own local specialties. As corporate finance involves a transaction, this facilitates renumeration of referral work even though the ultimate goal was the client's satisfaction in achieving that transaction. What we want to offer is transaction support to the client. It extends the counseling we provide to our clients, we are not only offering auditing services."

Along with Philip Chamberlain, a tax expert from the London office of Neville Russell, Gene Temkin invited members of the network to help them set up a corporate finance committee. He stated,

> "The M&A seminar was so popular that we decided to formalize things a bit and propose the creation of an ad hoc committee. I envision it as working together on a needs basis. Many partners from affiliates [that did not attend the first meeting] wanted to be on the committee. Since we cannot accommodate everyone, there will be 6 to 8 members on a rotating basis that will commit to being available to fly around to the affiliates that need help. We will bring the expertise to their area."

The corporate finance committee proposal was accepted at the Board level and voted on favorably at the 1995 annual Council meeting. It aimed to provide every member firm with assistance in corporate finance work, succession planning, asset sales etc.

Following the enthusiasm for this initiative in corporate finance, Nigel Hodges wondered whether Nexia International could levy greater membership fees to help its members scale down their high proportion of audit business in favor of other business activities such as management consulting, corporate finance, information technology consulting, legal services, etc. Other issues concerned him and the Board: Was Nexia International providing its members with the tools they required for effective and efficient global networking? Could Nexia International sustain future growth with its expansion policy of recruiting single practice affiliates rather than acquiring larger networks? What were the best ways to insure member firms' quality and commitment to Nexia International's goals? How should it deal with firms wanting and needing to expand outside their domestic markets into other member firms's markets?

INSEAD

Case 8–2

PixTech, Inc (A)

It was May, in the South of France. Jean-Luc Grand-Clément descended to his wine cellar to choose a bottle. Perhaps the puzzle of matching region, grower, and vintage to the evening menu would divert his thoughts for a time from business plans that had preoccupied him all day. The next day he planned to board a Tokyo flight to begin his third visit to Asia of the year.

Grand-Clément was the Chairman, CEO and co-founder of the five-year-old development firm, PixTech, and the architect of a global technology alliance of firms sharing an interest in independently entering flat panel display (FPD) production. As 1997 had unfolded, the demands on Grand-Clément's diplomatic skills seemed to accelerate with the seasons. After years of evolution in relatively low tech applications such as digital watches and gas pumps, FPDs had erupted onto the high technology scene in the late 1980s as a critical enabling technology for laptop computers. FPD technology was evolving at a blistering pace that exceeded even the early, unprecedented speed of semiconductor development in the 1970s. By the end of 1997, worldwide FPD sales neared $13 billion. Many observers believed that the thin film transistor (TFT) approach (more commonly known as AMLCD: active matrix liquid crystal display) had locked in the technological trajectory for high tech FPD development for an unforeseeable period well into the 21st century.

PixTech and a few other companies, however, dared to promote an alternative "no compromise" technological solution known as Field Emission Display (FED). PixTech and its alliance partners had built their network as part of a plan to telescope the precommercialization phase of FED development. PixTech's managers hoped at the same time to establish dominance of an industry patent base covering the solutions to key technical challenges in FED development and manufacturing. In the U.S., Motorola and Raytheon had joined the coalition; in Japan, Futaba. Grand-Clément intended his coming swing through Asia to advance discussions with new potential partners, customers, and alliance members.

Yet the technical feasibility of FED technology, its potential as a leapfrog beyond TFTs, and the long-term viability of PixTech's alliance approach to FED development remained controversial. TFT technology continued to advance, anticipating and meeting market demands in new applications such as desktop monitors, and meeting theoretical demands in blue sky applications such as large screen television. Venture capitalists (VCs) in the U.S. had funded several startups that pursued independent FED research programs, vying with the PixTech Alliance to commercialize FEDs first. Many TFT producers—the consumer electronics giants of the U.S., Japan, and Korea—had started their own development programs as a hedge against the FED's success. The future picture appeared . . . well . . . fuzzy. A little like some competitors' prototypes . . . Grand-Clément smiled inwardly.

The FPD Industry, LCD Technology, and Alternative Technologies

Flat panel displays are thin electronic screens that replace traditional cathode ray tubes (CRTs) in a number of high technology display applications. Since the late 1980s OEM manufacturers of products such as laptop computers, small televisions, personal digital assistants

---

This case was jointly prepared by Professors Yves Doz of INSEAD, Peter Smith Ring of the College of Business, Loyola Marymount University, and Stefanie Lenway and Thomas Murtha of the Carlson School of Management, University of Minnesota. It is based on a major research project on the global flat panel display industry being conducted by Professors Lenway, Murtha and their colleagues with the support of an Alfred P. Sloan Foundation Grant; and on interviews with PixTech executives conducted by all four authors. The case study was prepared as a basis for class discussion rather than to illustrate either effective or ineffective handling of an administrative situation.

Financial support from the INSEAD Alumni Fund European Case Programme is gratefully acknowledged.

(PDAs), medical devices, and industrial instrumentation have regarded FPDs as critical components. The U.S. government targeted FPDs as strategic materials and subsidized their manufacture on U.S. soil, citing military uses that include aeronautical instrumentation and navigation systems as well as portable information devices and head mounted displays for infantry. In 1997, technology observers expected FPD applications to phenomenally increase in future years, as electronics products that relied on visual interface with users multiplied in the market. Flat desktop computer monitors had just appeared. Well-heeled or well-connected technophiles could order a flat, wall hanging television. Information-intensive industries such as investment services were beginning to refit their workplaces. Flat TVs seemed poised to launch into the early, enthusiast phase of mass market expansion. In the years to come, futurists imagined that exotic new products would emerge such as household robots with FPDs as faces.

LCD Technology

In the 30 years before LCDs moved into high volume production for laptops, many in the R&D community worked to develop the technology as a substitute for the CRT. The relatively sudden emergence of the laptop computer application added resources and urgency to the drive to improve LCD technology, although observers disagreed about whether the direction of progress would ultimately lead to television-style video capabilities.

FPD manufacturing involves sandwiching a thin layer of chemicals, such as liquid crystal, between two glass substrates. In addition to the glass sandwich, each finished display incorporates drive electronics, control electronics, a mechanical package, and a power supply. Most finished FPDs have a depth of four inches or less. The displays produce images by electrically charging the chemicals to activate microscopic picture elements, called pixels. In 1997, pixel counts for single screens ranged from 120,000 to over one million pixels for the largest displays. LCD displays work by using electric charges to reorient slender, elongated rod-like liquid crystal molecules to block or allow rays from a backlight to pass through. Liquid crystal molecules have both the free-flowing properties of a liquid and the spacial regularity of a solid.

Technology progressed rapidly to improve the early "passive matrix" LCDs (PMLCDs) for laptops, but the higher-performing AMLCDs soon began to supplant them in advanced products. PMLCDs use row and column driver chips to apply electrical current to row electrode stripes while applying appropriate voltage to individual pixels on column electrode stripes. This twists the liquid crystal, orienting it at pixels to either block or allow light to pass from a display's backlight. The approach requires scanning an entire display to change the voltage of any given row or column. The resulting response rate limitations can lead to shadows and muddy images.

The AMLCD manufacturing process involves coating glass with a thin film of microscopic transistors for FPDs' back plates (Thus the term, TFT). This process associates a transistor or diode with each pixel. The transistors act as switches that driver chips attached to the edges of a display can turn individually on and off at lightning speed to twist the liquid crystal. The fast response rate contributes to the crisp display image that users at first associated with top-of-the-line laptops. By 1997, the AMLCD approach was pervasive down to middle price points.

As LCD technology advanced, manufacturing techniques and capital requirements increasingly resembled those of the semiconductor industry. TFT displays' extreme susceptibility to failures caused by microscopic contaminants required manufacturers to house their lines in ultrafiltered clean-room atmospheres. As the sizes of substrates increased, rigorously disciplined, "bunny-suited" human operators filled fewer positions in the work force, and the role of automation grew. The average size of on-site engineering staffs increased as well.

Not surprisingly, the supporting industry infrastructure included many suppliers with experience in semiconductor manufacturing processes, equipment, and materials. The supply chain consisted of component manufacturers (e.g., color filters and driver chips), materials (glass substrates, chemicals), and equipment makers (e.g., chemical vapor deposition and microlithography machines; test equipment). New facilities cost upward of one-half billion U.S. dollars for plant and equipment. Between 1991 and 1996, facilities came on line using five successive generations of production equipment, (referred to as gen 0, 1, 2, 2.5, and 3), each based on a larger glass substrate. Depending on a company's past experience, the newness of the technology included, and the local industry context, plants required up to six months or more to achieve commercial yields. New plants typically consumed up to US $100 million worth of materials each month during the ramp-up period.

The large-scale efficiencies of new plants contributed to broad cyclicality of prices for FPDs, as capacity grew by substantial increments whenever a firm added a new line's production to the market. Costs continued to decline due to productivity improvements. In part, these productivity improvements resulted from optimizing each new generation substrate size to yield greater numbers of individual panels. The sizes of finished FPDs continued to increase at the same time, as the leading-edge laptop makers used screen size and quality to differentiate their products. The typical laptop screen grew in size from under 9" diagonally to 12.1" FPDs, which were manufactured 6-up on gen 3 lines. The evolution of market preferences for screen sizes, along with manufacturers' plans for new applications such as desktop monitors and flat screen TVs, added complexity to the cost and pricing picture. Newer, larger FPDs not only cost relatively less to make but also entered the OEM market at lower prices, considered on a per-square-inch basis. As the most popular laptop screen sizes increased and new generation production equipment came on line, many manufacturers were forced to cut the new sizes from smaller substrates processed on older lines. This lowered yields by a factor of 2 or greater. For example, in 1996 many manufacturers converted lines optimized for 4-up 10.4" display to make 2-up 12.1" displays, despite the waste of materials.

At first most of the companies involved in commercial scale FPD manufacturing located their plants in Japan. These included IBM and Toshiba, who created the alliance Display Technologies, Inc. (DTI), Sharp, Hitachi, NEC, and Matsushita. All of these companies consumed some proportion of output as components in their own products. Alone among the firms in Japan, Hosiden pursued a pure merchant strategy. In late 1995, a number of Korean firms surprised the market by bringing commercial-scale plants on line (resulting in precipitous price declines in global markets). These companies included Samsung, LG, and Hyundai. Another Korean conglomerate, Daewoo, entered the business by purchasing Toshiba's original PMLCD lines. Chungwha Picture Tubes also started PMLCD production in a Taipei suburb to serve the needs of Taiwan's giant laptop assembly industry.

The phenomenal expansion of LCD capacity in Asia both attracted and deterred potential entrants considering facilities in the EU and U.S. Potential entrants needed to evaluate the impact of the cost, pricing and profitability roller coaster, size of capital investment, manufacturing complexity, the pace of technological change, uncertainty about future functionalities, disagreements among leading consultants about demand forecasts, the deep pockets of current producers, and the concentration of production facilities in Japan. AMLCD prices had dropped dramatically and looked as if they would continue to drop through the end of 1999. 10.4" displays dropped from $1,500 to $500 from 1994 to 1995, and occasionally sold for as little as $350 in early 1996. 12.1" inch displays sold for about $740 in Spring 1996 and would sink to $380 during 1997. Korean prices dropped to $280 as producers passed through the won depreciation.

In 1997, Sharp enjoyed the highest worldwide sales of all LCDs— around $2.3 billion. DTI was second with $1,125 billion, but leading the market in profitability and share of high-end displays for leading-edge laptops. NEC was third with $1,083 billion. Samsung had risen rapidly from zero sales in 1994 to $700 million in 1997, but still lagged behind the top three plus Hitachi. LG had also risen rapidly from zero sales in 1994 to around $400 million in 1997. Observers expected LG to rise to number two behind DTI by 1999 with a market share of 12.8 percent.

The consulting group DisplaySearch projected, in light of price declines, that AMLCDs would account for 70 percent of total FPD sales of about $30 billion by 2002. PMLCDs would decline to 20 percent of the market. Revenues from sales of small LCDs for products such as camera viewfinders, small TVs, PDAs, and pachinko reached $1 billion by September 1997. DisplaySearch expected these revenues to increase by almost $500 million in 1998. The U.S. and Japanese firms with production facilities prospered in their downstream product markets. DTI partners Toshiba and IBM, for example, respectively held the first and second market share positions in laptops. New FPD markets lay ahead in desktop monitors, health care instrumentation, automotive navigation, wall-hanging television, and many other areas. But how rapidly would these markets expand? What price points would ignite growth in the new product areas? Could AMLCD technology improve rapidly enough to meet the differing requirements of these future markets? Or would the technology butt against natural limitations that would bound its growth and leave it vulnerable to leapfrog technologies?

Alternative Technologies

Jean-Luc Grand-Clément was not alone in believing in the possibility of a leapfrog. Many, in fact, did not question the possibilities, but rather the question of which frog or frogs and how many frogs would leap farthest, fastest, and most persistently. Every engineer and entrepreneur interested in new technologies had a pet LCD performance anomaly to bandy about in discussions at technical meetings or with visiting analysts or researchers. Liquid crystal would, of course, slow down in low temperatures, and eventually seize up entirely. Now that automobiles rarely required a warming up before driving in freezing weather, imagine having to bring a hot water bottle down to the car in the morning to loosen up your high tech instrument displays. And when a jet fighter turned at mach speed, surely liquid crystal would smear and distort like an old lava lamp from the American '60s. Certainly the crisp, almost super real images and colors of AMLCDs would make television presentations appear wooden, more like a computer game than life. And unlike CRTs, which gradually lose clarity over their lifetimes (engineers call this "graceful degradation"), when an LCD FPD's backlight burns out, the display blinks out immediately. And those viewing angle problems!

Three alternative technologies: the FED, the electroluminescent display (EL), and the plasma display panel (PDP) appeared to offer promise in the race to address such issues. LCD makers also continued to leverage their investments and knowledge with well-financed research programs that continued to improve the AMLCD. They also hedged their bets by assigning top young researchers to alternative R&D programs. The next few paragraphs describe each of the technologies. Exhibit 1 provides PixTech's evaluation of the comparative qualities of each, as well as AMLCD.

Plasma display panels (PDPs) ionize a low-pressure inert gas, usually neon or argon, to produce richly colored images with smooth motion. The technique is similar to that of neon signs. When sufficient voltage is applied between a pixel's row and column electrodes, the gas achieves a plasma state and discharges light. Fujitsu, Sony, NHK, and Matsushita, among others, made major investments in this technology, including outright purchases of U.S. development companies. Several had shown 42" prototypes that critics assessed as very inviting to the eye. Engineers were working feverishly to reduce their weight, power consumption, and manufacturing cost.

Electroluminescent displays (ELs) produce images by bombarding a layer of phosphors with electrons, operating much as CRTs do. The manufacturing process sandwiches a thin film of luminescent phosphor between two sheets of glass attached to rows and columns of electrodes. EL displays have a long history in industrial instruments, and are impervious to temperature extremes and vibration. They produce a sharp image and have replaced CRTs where space is at a premium, such as in hospitals. EL displays could produce images in a limited spectrum of multiple colors. State-of-the-art EL manufacturing required fewer process steps and a much smaller capital investment than rivals. Manufacturers were considering whether to challenge AMLCDs by developing full-color. Planar Systems of Portland, Oregon, and Sharp were principal EL producers.

Field Emission Displays (FEDs) had drawn several well-financed startups—including PixTech—into an R&D race to realize the dream of creating and commercializing an FPD that would offer the CRT's familiar "warm" image and motion characteristics. Like a CRT, an FED incorporates a cathode and an anode enclosed within a vacuum. In a conventional color CRT the cathode consists of three electron emitters spaced at an appropriate focus distance behind the anode. (As CRTs increase in diagonal screen size, the focus distance also increases, necessitating ever deeper TV sets). The phosphors coating the anode emit light when electrons from the cathode strike it. Image and motion reproduction takes place as the three cathode rays repeatedly, instantaneously scan a CRT's anode, row-by-row to successively light the pixels. FEDs reduce the focus distance between the anode and cathode, using millions of microscopic electron emitters instead of just three. Powered by row and column driver chips, the electron emitters target individual pixel groupings.

In addition to promising "television-style" video, prototype FEDs operated over the relatively wide temperature range from -35C to 85C and offered nearly 180 degree viewing angles. The technology also offered the potential for extremely high luminance, which would help to counteract display washout from ambient light. Manufacturing required fewer process steps than AMLCDs, and developers hoped to achieve cost economies of at least one third.

In addition to PixTech, other development firms are working on FEDs including Candescent Technologies, FED Corp., Micron Technologies, and SI Diamond Technology. In the United States, government initiatives had spurred FED development through the U.S. Display Consortium (USDC), a nonprofit public-private consortium primarily oriented toward manufacturing equipment and materials, and the U.S. Defense Department's Advance Research Project Agency (DARPA). (Alliance members Motorola and Raytheon were not part of this initiative). Outside the U.S. and EU, Canon, Sony, Toshiba, and Samsung were investing in FED R&D. Futaba was a member of PixTech's alliance.

Manufacturing approaches used either high or low-voltage phosphors. Conventional CRTs have always used high voltage. But high voltage FEDs required the use of spacers to maintain a uniform gap of about one millimeter between the two glass plates comprising the display in order to prevent arcing or flashing. Spacer technology

EXHIBIT 1 FPD Technologies

Characteristics	CRT	PMLCD	AMLCD	FED
Viewing Angle	Very wide horizontal and vertical	Limited horizontal and vertical	Wide horizontal, limited vertical	Very wide horizontal and vertical
Video Speed	High speed over full temperature range	Unable to display video images with good quality	Adequate speed over full temperature range	High speed over full temperature range
Brightness Range	From low to very high, easy to dim	From low to medium, limited dimming capabilities	From low to medium, limited dimming capabilities	From low to very high, easy to dim
Dynamic Range*	High	Very limited	Limited	High
Operating Temperature	Wide range	Very limited range due to liquid crystal	Limited range due to liquid crystal behavior	Wide range
Power Consumption	High	Current industry standard	Current industry standard	Comparable to current industry standard
Manufacturability	Mature process offering lowest cost	Fewer process steps AMLCD	Complex process	Fewer process steps than AMLCD

*Dynamic range results from a combination of contrast and peak brightness.

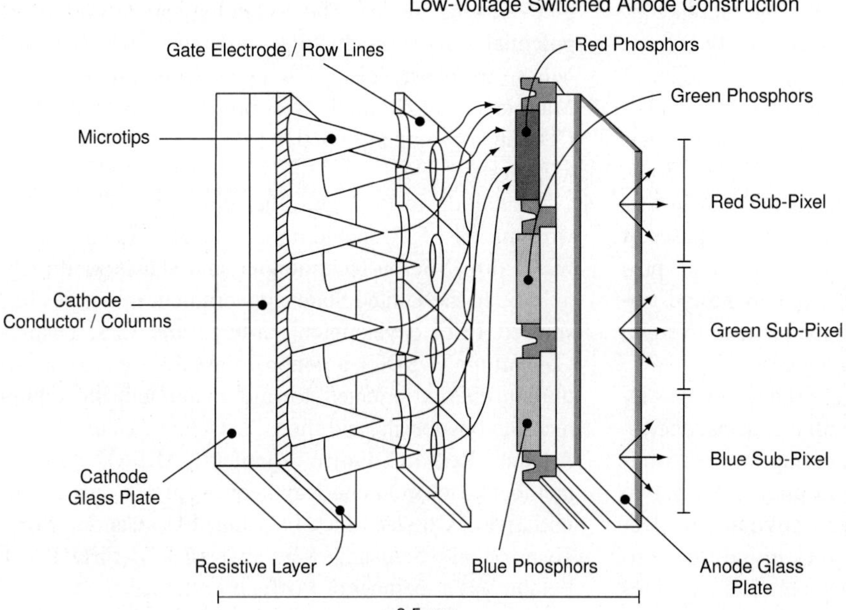

Note: Arrows show path for electrons when displaying red image.

has presented an extraordinary R&D challenge because of the need for both strength against vacuum implosion and microscopic scale for invisibility. Low voltage phosphors did not require such challenging spacer technology. The low-voltage phosphors required significant additional development in order to achieve the bright images and rich colors that were an important basis of the FED's expected appeal PixTech planned to use low-voltage phosphors for displays smaller than 8".

Pixtech's Genesis

Jean Luc Grand-Clément and Michel Garcia founded PixTech on June 28th, 1992. Grand-Clément was serving as an advisor to the Advent Venture Capital Fund when he encountered FED technology in a government laboratory development program in late 1991. PixTech became Grand-Clément's second start-up. He had served as CEO, then Chairman, of European Silicon Structures (ES2) from 1985–91. ES2 supplied application-specific integrated circuits for cell-based and full custom CMOS products. The European electronics firms that co-owned ES2 included British Aerospace, Nokia, Matra, Philips, and Siemens. Grand-Clément held managerial positions within Motorola between 1967–1978 and 1982–1985. During the interim, he served as Managing Director of Eurotechnique, an electronic components JV between the diversified French group Saint Gobain and National Semiconductor. Grand-Clément holds the diploma of the Ecole Nationale Supérieure des Telécommunications, Paris. (Exhibit 2 provides background information on other key employees).

In late 1991 Grand-Clément visited the Laboratoire d'Electronique de Technologie et d'Instrumentation (LETI); a research facility of the Commissariat à l'Energie Atomique (CEA), the French atomic energy agency. There he met Robert Meyer who was championing work on FED technology. The meeting was fortuitous. Thomson, the diversified electronics French group, had provided major funding for FED research at LETI since 1988, but had just announced plans to withdraw support. The approximately 25-member staff was being reduced to six. Grand-Clément's visit with Meyer convinced him that FED technology represented a real commercial opportunity. He persuaded Advent to provide LETI with critical interim funding. "We can do better than this," Grand-Clément reflected, considering the state of progress in FED technology at the time.

Between Christmas 1991 and June 1992, Grand-Clément created a business plan and obtained seed funding (in significant part from Advent) to start PixTech, S.A. In September 1992, PixTech obtained an exclusive, 25-year license from CEA for the LETI technologies. The LETI Agreement provided PixTech with all FED technology developed to

EXHIBIT 2 Key Employees at PixTech

Francis Courreges was appointed EVP in July of 1995. He was VP Marketing and Sales from 1993 to 1995, having joined the company in 1993. Mr. Courreges was a cofounder of ES2, and served as Manager of direct write technologies for MOS and gate array products from 1985 to 1991 and VP of Marketing from 1991 to 1992. Prior to joining ES2, Courreges was a product engineering manager at Sierra Semiconductor from 1984 to 1985. He was also employed at Electronic Arrays, National Semiconductor, and Eurotechnique. Courreges is a graduate of Ecole Nationale Supérieure des Arts et Metiers, and holds M.S. and Ph.D. degrees in Material Sciences from Stanford University.

Michel Garcia is a cofounder of PixTech. He was appointed VP, Industrial Partners in August, 1995. Prior to this appointment, he served as VP of Equipment Engineering since the founding of the company. In 1986, Mr. Garcia founded Microsolve, a semiconductor processing equipment start-up. He managed the firm for five years. From 1981 through 1985, he was operations manager at Eurotechnique. Between 1977 and 1979 he was a process engineer at Motorola. Mr. Garcia is a graduate of the Ecole Nationale Supérieure d'Electronique et de Radioélectricité de Grenoble. He also received a degree of Doctor of Microelectronics from Grenoble University.

Dieter Mezger was appointed President on March 25, 1998. From 1990, until his appointment at PixTech, Mezger was president of Compass Design Automation, a wholly owned subsidiary of VLSI Technology, Inc. in 1984, Mezger had established that firm's European beachhead in Munich. Before joining VLSI, Mezger had spent 15 years with Texas Instruments, finishing his tenure there as Manager, Sales and Marketing Europe. Mezger has a BS in engineering from the University of Stuttgart.

Thomas M. Holzel was appointed VP of Marketing and Sales for PixTech in July, 1995. From 1988 to 1995 he served as Marketing Manager of Display Devices at Motorola. In 1981, he founded Arcturus, Inc., a firm that developed the first computer compatible large screen displays, and served as its President from 1981 to 1988. Before founding Arcturus, Mr. Holzel served as Director of Industrial Marketing at Advent Corporation. Mr. Hozel is a graduate of Dartmouth College, with a degree in economics.

date by CEA and LETI. LETI and PixTech committed themselves to share the results of all future FED work through joint patent ownership. PixTech gained the right to sublicense the technologies. The organizations thereafter cooperated closely on FED development.

PixTech also agreed to pay CEA royalties, with minimum payment obligations that began in 1996. Failure to meet the minimum would trigger conversion of the agreement to nonexclusive status. The agreement obligated PixTech to compensate CEA based on a proportion of sub-licensing revenues and proceeds from sales of products developed from the technology.

In January, and again in March of 1993, Grand-Clément leveraged PixTech's seed funding by raising over $2 million from European and U.S. contacts. But PixTech needed significantly more venture capital to realize its objectives. Grand-Clément knew the difficulty of generating funding from European sources on the necessary scale, especially given the technological and commercial risk involved in the PixTech start-up. Most European VCs lacked the expertise to evaluate PixTech with full confidence. But as Executive Vice President Francis Courreges observed, "If the U.S. venture capitalists put money into us, the Europeans will do the same." The founders incorporated PixTech, Inc. as a U.S. corporation in Delaware on October 27, 1993, facilitating U.S. capital market access. One month later, on November 30, PixTech, Inc. acquired 100 percent beneficial ownership in PixTech, S.A. In December 1993, April 1994, and June 1994, PixTech raised a total of over $10 million in U.S. venture capital markets. In July 1995 PixTech raised more than $20 million of additional capital through a public stock offering on the NASDAQ exchange. Exhibit 3 presents a chronology of PixTech's development highlights to date.

EXHIBIT 3 Highlights of PixTech's Corporate History

1992	Company founded in June.
	Exclusive licenses for the FED technology obtained from LETI.
1993	U.S. incorporation. The original French company became a wholly owned subsidiary of the U.S. corporation.
	Raytheon demonstrates the first high voltage FED at 3500 foot-lamberts using PixTech FED cathodes in June.
	World's first 6-inch color FED publicly demonstrated in July.
	Futaba of Japan becomes an FED Alliance partner in November.
	PixTech signs a technology partnership agreement with Texas Instruments.
1994	PixTech raises $13 million, which was used to purchase manufacturing equipment and to lease space in Montpellier from IBM in February.
	Start-up of the 270 x 350 mm FED glass substrate line at Montpellier in November.
	FED Alliance agreement with Raytheon was signed.
1995	In February, PixTech produced their first defect free 5-inch color FED.
	Motorola joined the FED alliance in June.
	PixTech carried out a successful IPO on NASDAQ as PIXT in June which raised $13 million.
	In December, PixTech shipped the first commercial FED product.
1996	TI terminated its relationship with PixTech in March.
	At the May Society for Information Display trade show, PixTech publicly demonstrated its 10.5″ full color FED.
	PixTech began a large display R&D project with a CRT manufacturer in September.
	PixTech signed a subcontracting agreement with Unipac to manufacture FEDs.
1997	In February PixTech announced the closing of an additional round of financing. $17 million was raised through a public offering in Europe; $5 million from United Microelectronics Corp. (Unipac's parent) and $2 million from a private placement with Motorola.
	On July 23rd, PixTech announced receipt of an order for 50,000 5.2 inch FEDs over a five-year period from a U.S. manufacturer of portable medical equipment.
	On October 7th, Raytheon announced a two-year extension of its cooperative agreement with PixTech.
	On November 13th, PixTech and Sumitomo Corporation signed an agreement whereby Sumitomo will distribute PixTech's products on an exclusive basis in Japan and on a non-exclusive basis elsewhere in Asia. Sumitomo also provided PixTech with a $10 million loan to finance manufacturing equipment at Unipac.

Strategy at Pixtech

Four critical needs drove resource allocation at PixTech: needs for funding, endorsements, production capacity, and a strong intellectual property base. The last issue lay at the core of PixTech's strategy. In Grand-Clément's vision, PixTech would "create a strong patent regime," and behind it build a patent base "strong enough to entice others to take part in our alliances." Grand-Clément set a course that depended on rapidly expanding and protecting technology that would position PixTech patents at the center of any developments leading to FED commercialization. The FED alliance would accelerate, leverage, and diversify the development process and create a powerful coalition of organizations that would share an interest in appropriating the revenues from commercialization.

PixTech would develop its initial revenue stream by sublicensing its technology. Simultaneously the company would build capabilities to profit directly over the long term by entering the market. Grand-Clément planned to target high margin market segments. The company would develop a manufacturing process, plant, and partnerships for components and materials.

PixTech based its selection of alliance partners on the need for resources to complement its technology base. PixTech sought big partners. In Grand-Clément's view, "Big companies put more money into a start-up than venture capitalists do. They also provide endorsement for the technology." Moreover, they sought partners who would manufacture displays, not PC assemblers like Compaq or Hewlett Packard, companies that provided funding for Candescent.

The FED Alliance

In March 1997 the Alliance included PixTech, Futaba Corporation, Raytheon Company, and Motorola, Inc. Futaba and Raytheon had joined in 1994, and Motorola in 1995. Texas Instruments, the first partner, had departed in 1996 after nearly three years. Robert Galvin, former Motorola CEO, had suggested to Grand-Clément that PixTech ally with a major company to create a critical mass of production to legitimate the technology. Courreges viewed the Alliance objectives as follows: to meet the challenge inherent in funding start-up businesses in capital-intensive, high-tech industries; to accelerate development by creating a critical mass of resources; to gain market acceptance for FED technology from equipment suppliers, materials suppliers and end users; and to create manufacturing capacity.

The management team shared a vision of how an alliance strategy could contribute toward these objectives, agreed on the ideal selection criteria for partners and had outlined a set of governing principles. But they lacked experience in the alliance-building process. The search for partners proved opportunistic rather than calculated.

Initial Steps: A Deal with Texas Instruments

Texas Instruments (TI) joined the Alliance in June 1993, signing a three-year contract. The companies came in contact through a PixTech board member and his acquaintance who worked at TI as a project manager in the IC Division. The manager was just wrapping up a successful assignment when he learned from his acquaintance about FEDs' potential as $500 alternatives to the $1,500 AMLCDs that TI used in its notebook computers. He became an advocate. Building on his successful record, he pushed to bring TI into PixTech's new FED Technology Alliance to secure a stake in the research and further developments.

The decision to go ahead was tactical, speculative, and isolated from the corporate strategy process. The new project was not housed in the division responsible for marketing notebooks but was funded on an annual appropriation basis in the IC division. At the time, the division enjoyed an extremely positive cash position and had the discretion to divert funds to entrepreneurial projects. Work on alternative FPD technologies was already underway there. The division built an FED lab and PixTech transferred its technology. As long as annual IC profits remained strong, funding continued. The commitment to manufacture—a key element in PixTech's alliance agreements—appeared unlikely to reach the implementation phase within the three-year term of the agreement.

The rapid emergence from the lab of a working 10" prototype changed the picture. TI began to investigate the industry in greater detail, along with the financial and market implications of entering production. One study found that AMLCDs were selling under $1,500 in global markets and that prices would continue to decline. Other studies suggested that capacity growth would outstrip demand for the foreseeable future. At the same time, IC profits began to flatten.

By early 1996 PixTech managers were hearing rumors that TI planned to leave the laptop market, but would delay the announcement until it found a buyer for the business. The possibility remained that TI would stay in distribution with OEM machines by Sharp or Taiwanese companies such as Acer. PixTech anticipated that TI would honor the Alliance contract terms. Any announcement that TI would leave the Alliance would likely have an adverse impact on PixTech's stock. Unless TI publicly linked the decisions to leave the Alliance and the PC market, the announcement could also damage the technology's growing credibility. Nonetheless, TI announced its departure from the alliance, three months early, in March 1996.

PixTech management still believed that the benefits from the alliance with TI outweighed the costs. Management regarded TI's early termination of its participation as a breach of the Alliance agreement, and in the settlement, PixTech retained title to the technology advances achieved during the relationship. In addition to the technical and financial advantages that PixTech derived, management also developed a broader framework for alliance management. The agreement's end also freed PixTech to reach manufacturing agreements with Taiwanese firms, a move that TI had proscribed.

The Alliance Governance Framework

The TI alliance allowed PixTech to test the effectiveness of its strategy. Grand-Clément reflected, "ES2 taught me that mixing customers and owners is not a good thing, in particular because representatives from big partner companies do not bring the right attitudes to the Board of a small, new venture. Gaining the credibility of big, visible, producers of displays was key. The key purpose of the alliance was to build barriers toward potential competitors by fast accumulation of know-how on how to make the technology work. We wanted partners who would put their hands in their pockets very deeply, not so much by investing into PixTech as by doing their own efforts."

The TI agreement set the precedent for all future Alliance agreements. But PixTech searched thereafter for partners with deep, long-term strategic commitments to the FED business. The essential features of the Alliance governance structure provided each member with a license to all PixTech and LETI technology. Members also received license rights to all technology developed by other Alliance members. Members were entitled to know-how transfers from PixTech and the other members and gained access to PixTech's Montpellier manufacturing facilities. Know-how transfers provided members, in PixTech's terminology, not only with PixTech's own technology, but also with "background technology" developed earlier by each member that enabled them to accelerate learning, and with new technology developed by the alliance members. The Alliance patent base exceeded 300 patents and applications in 1997, and could reliably be expected to exceed 350 by the end of 1998. Members received technology updates throughout their three-year terms of membership, along with an option to renew for two years. Raytheon planned to sign a two-year extension soon.

In addition to licenses for technology and background technology improvements, PixTech received a license fee, technology transfer fees based on performance milestones, a technology update fee over the three year period and royalties based on product sales. PixTech received 5 percent of sales on the first $120 million of each partner's FED sales, and further royalties on a sliding scale declining in 0.5 percent increments for each additional $100 million until the rate reached its minimum at 1.5 percent. Partners' intrafirm sales were valued at market prices. PixTech forecast cumulative proceeds of about $40 million from each partner. PixTech, along with all Alliance members, received technology from other members free of royalties.

Unlike the TI case, Grand-Clément decided that PixTech should originate the drafts for all future alliance agreements. "In the TI case, their lawyers insisted on drafting the agreement, and this led to endless pain. The first agreement was difficult, but then we began to leverage what we had gotten. PixTech's lawyer now drafts all agreements, because each big company deals with patents, technologies, etc., in its own way, which may not suit us. We also want to be careful to have good penalty clauses. Big firms believe they can breach contracts with small ones easily, pick their brains, and not need them anymore. But our success depends on their success almost entirely."

Details of the agreement structure differ in each partner's case, mainly as a function of the background technology that each contributed. After June 1998, PixTech would gain the right to sublicense the pooled technology contributed by all Alliance members except TI. PixTech agreed to obligations to Alliance members regarding sublicensing income. Other members, however, did not generally have third party sublicensing rights. The partners have signed multiple bilateral agreements among themselves. No overarching agreement exists. PixTech, however, facilitates meetings among all the partners.

Every six weeks, six–eight engineers from each member attend a two-day technology meeting. During the first day each partner presents a progress report on its R&D projects. During the second day the group brainstorms, critiques technical issues that need work, and assigns responsibility for specific projects. Grand-Clément set up ground rules from the beginning to create an atmosphere of openness among the partners. "Every question can be asked," he said. "If a presenter makes an incomplete technical presentation, someone will call him or her on it." Each partner demonstrates a credible commitment to sharing by opening its R&D labs to the other partners. Courreges commented, "You can't know everything. But if you can see everything, there is a better chance of understanding. People take time to trust one another. If there is no access to the labs, then you know that you don't know everything that is going on." Firms have applied to join the alliance but failed because of reputations for taking more than they contribute. PixTech has agreed not to bring new partners into the alliance without the agreement of all others. But no one partner has formal veto power over new members.

Partners take turns hosting meetings at their locations, providing an opportunity for all to visit each facility. PixTech also often hosts teams of engineers from its partners, and sends its own engineers to work at partners' facilities (as do all of the partners). This helps PixTech sustain its alliance leadership and allows a first-hand understanding of each partner's efforts. Grand-Clément attends carefully to the unfolding alliance dynamics, reminding one partner, for example, to "patent more," to make its advances more accessible to the others.

Grand-Clément decided in his early vision for the alliance not to establish a joint R&D lab where engineers from each of the partners would work together. He feared that such a place would limit the engineers in their sources of ideas. Grand-Clément believes his decision was fortuitous: multiple groups working separately and exchanging information openly have generated "tremendous creativity" . . . more than would have been generated by a single group working in one place. "Each group sees a problem from a different perspective. Success stems from the direct and open communication among the engineers aimed at solving technical problems fast," according to Grand-Clément. "Managers tend to get in the way."

Futaba

Futaba, based in Mobara, Japan, joined the Alliance in 1994. The company began FED R&D in 1989. Like PixTech, the company based its approach on Charles "Capp" Spindt's cathode microtip, an advance that emerged from the Stanford Research Institute in the 1960s. By 1993, Futaba had constructed a 5" prototype line and started construction on a $50 million R&D facility. Futaba's interest in FEDs stemmed from technical limitations it encountered in Vacuum Florescent Display (VFD) research. Primarily alphanumeric formatted displays, VFDs were the workhorse for automotive dashboards and had deeply penetrated the instrumentation, audio-video equipment and personal communications markets. Futaba owned over 50 percent of the world VFD market. FEDs seemed promising as a replacement technology, particularly since VFDs could not meet the demand for full color, high luminance, high resolution, and low power consumption that auto industry technology roadmaps specified for the year 2000.

Futaba emerged from humble beginnings and continued to describe itself as "a little company in the countryside." The company's founder established the firm following World War II by reverse-engineering scarce radio vacuum tubes and making them at home. He carried the finished tubes to Akihabara, Tokyo's electronics district, and bought the parts for more tubes with the proceeds from the sales. Futaba entered VFDs in 1962. Futaba did not belong to a keiretsu and relied primarily on its own financial resources. Some Futaba managers viewed the FED decision as a "bet the company" move. Others saw few options, due to the impending VFD obsolescence. Management estimated that entry costs of $300–$500 million. In 1995, Futaba's sales were about $900 million.

Futaba brought the Alliance core competencies in low-voltage phosphor, vacuum, and display production technologies. The company made its own VFD manufacturing equipment. Futaba joined the Alliance to gain access to PixTech's cathode patents. Management viewed the relationship as strictly a technical agreement. But PixTech's strong intellectual property regime necessitated accession to the Alliance. Shortly after joining, Futaba sent a technical and manufacturing team to Montpellier for six months to evaluate the operation. PixTech had sent three-person teams to Futaba, usually for two months and specific projects.

Language barriers and time-zone differences created coordination challenges. But no Alliance member ever complained that Futaba failed to carry its weight. The company had a reputation in Japan for shyness and was reticent to publicize progress. The company exhibited monochrome FEDs at the 1997 Society for Information Display (SID) meeting. Subsequently it sampled Japanese auto manufacturers with monochrome displays for traffic information, guidance, and instrumentation. This market was thought to promise high volume but low margins.

Raytheon

In 1988, Robert Meyer, the LETI inventor who had made important advances on Spindt microtips, presented his technology at Raytheon Electronics Systems in Quincy, Massachusetts. He requested a contract, $25 million, and complete autonomy. Raytheon managers were reluctant to take the risk, but appreciated the technology's potential. Since 1951, Raytheon had produced very bright monochrome CRTs for high performance aircraft systems such as the F111, F–15, F–16 and S3A. In the early 1990s the U.S. Defense Department began to fund programs to qualify AMLCDs for cockpit displays. Raytheon management recognized a threat to its CRT business.

Raytheon investigated the various FPD technologies and judged AMLCD reliability as poor and subject to physical limitations. Management concluded that catching up in AMLCDs could involve a multibillion dollar investment in a technology with a dubious future. FEDs, on the other hand, would allow Raytheon to redeploy capabilities associated with its high performance CRTs. Raytheon engineers had made advances in sealing vacuum tubes and creating materials that reduced contaminants that otherwise build up inside CRTs as a byproduct of usage. Raytheon's capabilities in these materials, called "getters," would help address lifetime problems that plagued FEDs.

Raytheon engineers started FED research in 1990. As work progressed they encountered scintillation, or flickering problems. PixTech's approach eliminated this problem, thereby removing a key obstacle to progress. Recognizing that PixTech had made significant improvements to the LETI technology, Raytheon joined the Alliance in June 1994. Raytheon's engineering team regarded the informal technology sharing in the Alliance as a great advantage, particularly since each member brought different core competencies to the relationship. They perceived clear distinctions among the markets each alliance member proposed to serve. Raytheon also became a PixTech customer for custom cathodes. Raytheon concentrated its internal efforts on anodes, focus grids and tube sealing, which allowed the company to leverage its CRT expertise.

Motorola

The Motorola FPD initiative in Phoenix, Arizona, grew out of a long-standing personal interest of Robert Galvin, former CEO and son of founder Paul Galvin. Galvin envisioned displays as key components in products yet to be imagined. This vision created a companywide understanding of displays as the human interface with multiple technologies in multiple businesses. Because displays could play a central role in product differentiation, the corporate strategy demanded a manufacturing capability. According to one industry analyst, "Motorola saw the future as a combination of software, which they had for telecom networks, semiconductor hardware, which they mastered, and human interface technologies, including displays, which they did not really master. Display leadership was in Japan, which Motorola saw as a major problem. Together with satellite-based communications, displays became one of Motorola's key priorities."

Motorola's initial foray into display manufacturing failed. In 1992, Motorola and InFocus Systems each invested $15 million to launch Motif, a strategic alliance created to manufacture active addressing PMLCDs. Motif planned to use Motorola's Active Addressing Integrated Circuits (AAICs) to improve PMLCD response time. The partners believed that this approach would equal AMLCD quality while undercutting costs by 30–50 percent. Both partners decided to close the alliance in October 1994, just weeks before the plant was to shift into volume manufacturing.

The Motif experience left its mark on Motorola. Management critiqued the Motif investment as inadequate and ill-timed. The AMLCD technology improvement rate surprised management. They had underestimated the effort required to enter the FPD business. The Motif debacle left one particularly painful, important lesson. Motorola could not get into this business by combining existing technology with existing firm capabilities, no matter how unique. FPD manufacturing would require the company to create new distinctive competencies.

Late in 1994 Motorola created a task force to rethink the display business. The task force recommended that Motorola stay the course. In early 1995, Motorola created the FPD division, staffed with vice president and general manager Pete Shinyeda and a secretary. Motorola also committed to a $100 million pilot production facility to produce small and medium-sized displays. CEO Chris Galvin took an active interest in the project, and placed Shinyeda among his most proximate reporting relationships. The FPD Division joined other Motorola start-ups in the Automotive, Energy and Components Sector. Other divisions in the sector included the Automotive and Industrial Electronics Group, Component Products Group, Energy Products Division, and Motorola Lighting, Inc.

Shenyeda's early experiences with the Alliance helped him to brush aside his initial skepticism about the value of the collaboration. He regarded his own engineering team as well-qualified to work out any problems with Spindt tip cathode technology. On the other hand, he was concerned that the difficulty of some of the technical issues would slow the technology's time-to-market. Shinyeda concluded that "500 people sharing information" accelerated the learning curve. He was also worried about obtaining intellectual property rights to certain enabling technologies. The PixTech Alliance offered an immediate solution.

The FPD Division first built a 6" pilot line in Chandler, Arizona, to address cycle time and process development issues. The first tools were installed in a new 275,000 square feet facility in January 1996. Motorola expected to ramp up in 1998 and enter full production at an annual capacity of about 15,000 displays by 1999. The company would build a high-volume facility as soon as their manufacturing architecture is proven and the new displays find market acceptance.

Other Partners

Ideally, Grand-Clément thought, the FED Alliance should include six large corporate partners. After approaching over 20 EU companies, success continued to elude Grand-Clément in Europe. "European companies were too risk-averse and too planning-oriented," he reflected. We had trouble accessing the top, and middle-level executives are the most risk averse. We have to convince the engineers and sell strategically to the top, overcome NIH syndrome . . ." Grand-Clément expected the coming Asian travels to open new horizons.

In Japan, he would press his search for a partner in addition to Futaba. In fall 1996, PixTech had signed a large screen-FED (LS-FED) codevelopment agreement with a major CRT maker. PixTech had acquired Pano Corp, a leading Santa Clara-based research group with expertise in high-voltage FEDs, which would make larger screens possible. The time was right to add a first-class Japanese CRT maker to the Alliance. Grand-Clément had established promising preliminary contacts with Sony and Matsushita. He hoped this trip would take these forward.

Several other factors added a sense of urgency to the Japan leg of the trip. Canon, Fujitsu, and Toshiba appeared to be rapidly progressing on variants of FED technologies. Grand-Clément understood that these competitors had achieved product simplifications that could reduce costs and improve yields. In 1996, Canon had registered over 100 patents on derivatives of FED technologies, many quite interesting. The Canon approach to FED technology, called a surface conduction electron emitter (SCE), used easy-to-manufacture, superfine particles rather than microtips. The approach showed promise as an alternative to PDPs for sizes 42" and larger.

Korea raised even more difficult issues. In the past, two major Korean companies had applied to join the Alliance. In both cases, Motorola's reservations stalled negotiations. Several chaebols, or diversified industrial groups, operated FED research programs. But the direction of the research remained unclear. Samsung's program raised the most serious concerns, involving an estimated 60 or more researchers. Motorola was concerned that Korean partners would not contribute as much to the Alliance knowledge pool as they might gain. Grand-Clément also worried that some partners might join the Alliance to monitor and perhaps stifle the technology.

PixTech's Manufacturing Partners

In November 1994, PixTech opened its first pilot line in a 28,000 square feet (2,600 square meters) Montpellier facility leased from IBM. Nearly one-third of the building contained clean rooms ranging from class 10 to 1,000. In February 1995, PixTech produced its first defect-free display. In 1997, manufacturing was primarily focused on improving yields to achieve efficiencies needed for high-volume, highly automated manufacturing. When management considered building a new manufacturing facility in 1996, they considered three scenarios:

- Expand operations in Montpellier. Difficulties included barriers to raising capital and French government ministerial indifference to technology startups.
- Build a plant in the U.S. Even more capital would be needed, in an environment where VCs might not be interested in waiting a long time for low returns.
- Manufacture in Taiwan with a subcontractor who would bear the costs of facilities.

In late 1996 the firm signed a manufacturing subcontracting agreement with Unipac of Taiwan. PixTech would send a team of manufacturing people to Taiwan to work with Unipac for at least six months. Unipac, an affiliate of United Microcomputer (UMC), already manufactured 5.6" AMLCDs for portable TVs, video phones, and the transportation market. Unipac's management was eager to diversify its manufacturing capabilities and regarded the contract as an opportunity to leverage its AMLCD experience. Thin film deposition, photolithography, driver circuitry, and driver attachment required similar capabilities for AMLCDs and FEDs. These similarities created a 70–80 percent overlap of manufacturing processes between FED cathodes and AMLCDs. Unipac's managers were not interested in directly entering the FED business, characterizing the company purely as a foundry. From PixTech's point of view, the opportunity appeared ideal for building a high volume, low cost manufacturing competency without incurring high start-up

Exhibit 4 PixTech's Financial Performance
(in thousands)

	Year Ended December 31			Period from June 18, 1992 (date of inception) through Dec.31, 1997
	1995	1996	1997	1997
Revenues				
Cooperation and License Revenues	$9,865	$5,440	$1,932	$25,210
Product Sales	808	791	745	2,381
Other Revenues	840	1,413	1,142	3,938
Total Revenues	11,513	7,644	3,819	31,529
Cost of Revenues				
License Fees and Royalties	1,314	45	181	1,540
Gross Margin	10,199	7,599	3,638	29,989
Operating Expenses				
Acquisition of Intellectual Property Rights	3,111	—	—	4,765
Rsearch and Development	12,527	15,848	15,497	53,239
Marketing and Sales	1,688	1,089	1,496	5,174
Administrative & General Expenses	2,151	2,703	2,419	10,301
	19,477	19,640	19,412	73,479
Income (Loss) from Operations	(9,278)	(12,041)	(15,774)	(43,490)
Interest Income	466	428	750	2,020
Interest Expense	(493)	(362)	(280)	(1,211)
Foreign Exchange Gains (Losses)	280	256	54	654
Loss Before Income Tax Benefit	(9,025)	(11,719)	(15,250)	(42,027)
Income Tax Benefit	2,720		586	5,734
Net Loss	$(6,305)	$(11,719)	$(14,664)	$(36,293)
Net Loss Per Share	$(0,82)	$(1,44)	$(1,12)	
No of Shares (thousands)	7,697	8,137	13,140	

costs. Uncertainty remained at the panel-assembly level. FEDs required a vacuum between the cathode and anode plates, an area in which Unipac did not have experience. PixTech agreed to provide unique FED sealing tools to Unipac. In addition to this agreement, Unipac's parent acquired a $5 million equity position in PixTech.

PixTech's management knew that the company would need to manufacture FED products to survive in the long run. They believed that a delicate linkage existed between FED manufacturing and R&D. "You can only learn about the limits of a technology by manufacturing," explained Courreges. PixTech's people would help Unipac people adapt and would themselves learn Unipac's manufacturing techniques. Grand-Clément planned to settle these points on his Taiwan visit.

PixTech was also developing a series of partnerships with firms that supplied it with key components: lithography, getters, and phosphors. PixTech was working with Rhone-Poulenc and Nichia, the world's top two phosphor suppliers. PixTech had also established a partnership with SAES-Getters, the world leader in getter technology. PixTech developed these partnerships as a member of ESPRIT, the public/private R&D consortium funded in part by the European Union. Exhibit 4 shows PixTech's financial performance to date.

Conclusion

How widely would FED technology be adopted? For what products? These things remained unclear. AMLCD technology continued to improve, fueled by years of experience and billions of dollars in manufacturing and R&D investments. Could PixTech actually succeed as an FED manufacturer? PixTech and its partners had yet to build the capacity needed to meet orders of 50,000 displays per month. All high-volume AMLCD manufacturers had done so already. Relentless process improvements in AMLCD manufacturing continued to drive costs down. Grand-Clément also worried about Canon's new SCE approach. This product simplification could bring LS-FPD production costs in line with those of CRTs.

As he ascended from his wine cellar, a bottle of 1986 Mas de Daumas Gassac in hand, Grand-Clément's thoughts returned to the upcoming meetings. He was pleased with PixTech's progress to date. Grand-Clément believed that the company had learned from its early mistakes. Things had not gone as smoothly, or as fast, as he would have liked. As with all startups, progress was partly "*une question de patience.*" Grand-Clément had planted his new vineyard, breaking new ground. The coming vintage, like the weather, remained uncertain.

Case 8–3

Aspect Development, Inc. (A)

Visitors to Aspect were likely to be surprised by the intensity of the excitement and level of activity in its premises, particularly given its setting in a quiet residential district of Mountain View, California. Early one evening in September 1995, Chairman and CEO Romesh Wadhwani met with his Internet Strategy Group to discuss the company's plans to offer access to its electronic components information service over the Internet. As he listened to Craig Palmer, John Ashbaugh, and Mark Nixon aggressively thrash out ideas, Wadhwani could not help thinking how far the company had come since its beginning in 1991.

The company prided itself as being the leading worldwide provider of component databases and parts information management software for OEMs (original equipment manufacturers) in the electronics industry. In a market where many others had failed, Aspect had managed to anticipate and redefine customer needs well ahead of the competition. The company's 1994 revenues of $10 million represented a 120 percent jump over 1993 figures. With an ambitious growth target to reach $100 million in revenues by 1998, Wadhwani and his team had to generate and implement avenues for expansion very quickly. The main issue before them was the role that Internet access and distribution could play in this expansion.

Background

Romesh Wadhwani founded Aspect in 1991 with about $100,000 in capital. A Ph.D. in electrical engineering from Carnegie Mellon University, he had managed two previous high technology startups before striking out on his own. As CEO of Cimflex Teknowledge, a factory automation company that provided shop floor control and integrated robotics systems, Wadhwani had considerable exposure to the electronics industry. This background had led him to believe that there was an urgent but unaddressed business need for supplying and managing information on electronic components. He noted,

> "Looking at the electronics industry, it became clear that parts content in products was climbing, while the labor content was rapidly declining. It looked like managing parts information might become a significant problem for electronic companies. I thought it might be a very good business opportunity, and I did my own market survey for three months by visiting 25 major electronic companies. There was a reasonably strong validation of the need for an integrated, enterprisewide approach to managing components information. On this basis, I went ahead and started Aspect. . . . Our vision has evolved over the past years, but our mission has always been to be the leading worldwide provider of components information systems."

This case was written by Dr. T.C.A. Bashyam and Professor Uday Karmarkar at The Anderson School at UCLA in order to provide the basis for classroom discussion, not to illustrate positive or negative administrative practices. The authors wish to thank Romesh Wadhwani and his senior management team at Aspect Development, Inc. for their support and hospitality during the preparation of this case. Some information has been disguised to protect confidentiality. EXPLORE and VIP are trademarks of Aspect Development, Inc.

EXHIBIT 1 The Market for Business Information

The market for business information is large and growing...

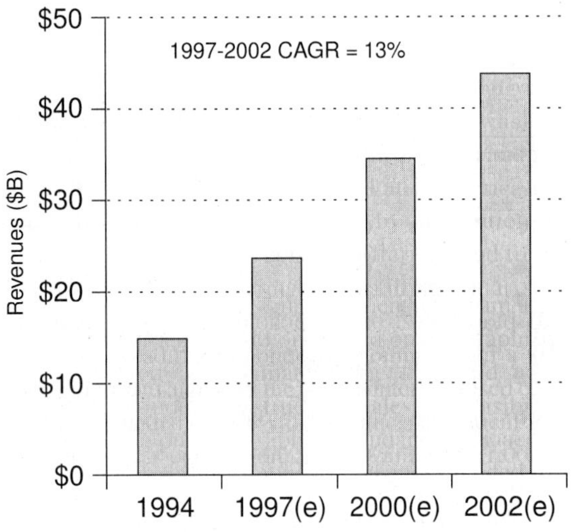

Growth Drivers:

- ♦ Product proliferation
- ♦ Digitization of information
- ♦ Computerization

...with prominent companies serving different vertical segments

Financial Information Services	• Reuters Holdings • Bloomberg Financial Markets
Business/Legal Information Services	• Value Line • Dow Jones • Dun & Bradstreet • Thomson Corporation • Reed Elsevier • Ziff-Davis
Consumer Research	• Nielsen Media Research
Aeronautical Information Services	• Jeppesen (Times Mirror)
Component Information Services	• Aspect Development

Source: Cowles/Simba Information.

Products and Markets

Aspect produced and marketed a Components Information System, which was essentially a catalog database of electronic components (such as microprocessors and memory chips) that electronic design engineers could use to search and select components for new products, similar in spirit to *Consumers Digest*. The database contained information on technical characteristics (e.g., operating temperature, speed, package type, etc.) for over 1 million electronic components.

By 1995, the market for business information was expected to exceed $16 billion (see Exhibit 1). The component information segment of this market was very small (less than 0.4 percent, or about $30–50 million in total). Of this total, the North American market accounted for about 50–55 percent, Europe for 30–35 percent, with the balance mainly in Asia. Aspect's customers included 40 of the 200 largest electronic companies in the world, such as IBM, Kodak, L.M. Ericsson, Siemens, and 3Com. Users of Aspect's product within these companies consisted primarily of design and procurement engineers.

Aspect created and maintained its database by gathering parts data in various formats (paper datasheets, CD-ROMs, and online) from electronic component manufacturers such as Intel and Motorola. Exhibit 2 displays a component datasheet from National Semiconductor available from that company's Internet site (in this case, for a microprocessor used in fax machines). Aspect entered data taken from sources such as these in a standard

EXHIBIT 2 Sample Data Sheet for Electronic Components

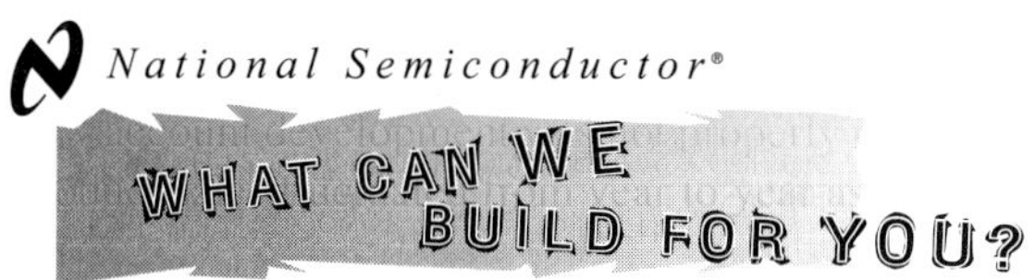
National Semiconductor®
WHAT CAN WE BUILD FOR YOU?

NS32FX200 Series 32000/EP Microprocessor

Generic Part Number 32FX200

General Description

The NS32FX200, NS32FV100 and NS32FX100 are highly integrated system chips designed for a FAX system based on National Semiconductor's embedded processors-NS32FX161, NS32FV16 or NS32FX164. The NS32FX100 is the common core for all three system chips. The NS32FV100 and NS32FX200 offer additional functions. Throughout this document, references to the NS32FX100 also apply to both the NS32FV100 and the NS32FX200. Specific NS32FV100 or NS32FX200 features are explicitly indicated. The NS32FX200, NS32FV100 and NS32FX100 feature an interface to devices like stepper motors, printers and scanners, a Sigma-Delta CODEC, an elapsed-time counter, a DMA controller, an interrupt controller, and a UART. The NS32FX200 is optimized for high-end FAX applications, such as plain-paper FAX and multifunctional peripherals. The NS32FX100, is optimized for low-cost FAX applications. The NS32FV100 is optimized for thermal paper FAX machines with Digital Answering Machine support.

Features

- Direct interface to the NS32FX161, NS32FV16 and NS32FX164 embedded processors
- Supports a variety of Contact Image Sensor (CIS) and Charge Coupled Device (CCD) scanners
- Direct interface to a variety of Thermal Print Head (TPH) printers. Bitmap shifter and DMA channels facilitate the connection of other types of printers
- Supports two stepper motors

Features (Continued)

- Direct interface to ROM and SRAM. The NS32FX200 and NS32FV100, in addition, interface to DRAM devices
- Programmable wait state generator
- Demultiplexed address and data buses
- Multiplexed DRAM address bus (NS32FX200 and NS32FV100)
- Supports 3V freeze mode by maintaining only elapsed time counter
- Control of power consumption by disabling inactive modules and reducing the clock frequency
- Operating frequency:
  - Normal mode: 19.6608 MHz-24.576 MHz in steps of 1.2288 MHz (NS32FX200)
  - Normal mode: 19.6608 MHz-24.576 MHz in steps of 1.2288 MHz (NS32FV100)
  - Normal mode: 14.7456 MHz-19.6608 MHz in steps of 1.2288 MHz. (NS32FX100)
  - Power Save mode: Normal mode frequency divided by sixteen
- On-Chip full duplex Sigma-Delta CODEC with:
  - Total harmonic distortion better than -70 dB
  - Programmable hybrid balance filter
  - Programmable reception and transmission filters
  - Programmable gain control
- On-Chip Interrupt Control Unit with:
  - 16 interrupt sources
  - Programmable triggering mode
- On-Chip counters, WATCHDOG™, UART, MICROWIRE™, System Clock Generator, and I/O ports
- On-Chip DMA controller (NS32FX200-four channels, NS32FX100, NS32FV100-three channels)
- Up to 37 on-chip general purpose I/O pins, expandable externally
- Flexible allocation of I/O and modules' pins
- 132-pin JEDEC PQFP package

Source: National Semiconductor.

format into a database at its data factory in India. By 1995, Aspect had catalogued information on components from over 500 electronic component manufacturers.

The company's Components Information System consisted of two parts. The first was a database called VIP (for Very Important Parts) that contained indexed technical data and digitized datasheets for electronic components. The database was packaged and distributed using CD-ROMs and tapes. Tapes stored searchable technical information on parts, while CD-ROMs contained original datasheets from component vendors in digitized format. The second part of Aspect's system was a software called EXPLORE, which enabled customers to search for components and compare across vendors included in the VIP database.

An Aspect user such as an electronic design engineer could query the VIP database using a search window provided by the EXPLORE software looking, for example, for vendors of memory chips with access time in the 25–35 nanosecond range. EXPLORE would then return a list of alternative vendors that met these specifications. In addition to providing indexed technical information on components, VIP also contained scanned datasheets, application notes,[1] and magazine articles providing in-depth information pertaining to any component chosen by the user.

Prior to the advent of third-party catalogues such as that provided by Aspect, component manufacturers developed their own libraries of datasheets (and databooks) and distributed them to potential customers. Some of these sheets were digitized (on CD-ROMs or online documents), but most were paper publications. There was little consistency across datasheets, even when provided by the same manufacturer. Searching for components involved physically locating datasheets from each manufacturer for potentially usable parts, and then comparing the data manually for feasibility, performance, and cost.

In addition to these search features, customers could also use the EXPLORE software to integrate their own internal proprietary and historical information on various components and suppliers with the external technical information obtainable from VIP. Thus, EXPLORE would allow a design engineer and other users within the customer's organization to conduct searches in both VIP and internal databases with multiple technical parameters to find the ideal component for their design. A purchasing engineer might use EXPLORE, for example, to find all memory chips coming from California-based manufacturers that had a quality rating of 10 on the customer's internal supplier qualification system. Aspect had designed EXPLORE to give customers the flexibility to add, organize, update, and maintain proprietary technical and business information on components and their suppliers that could be searched in parallel with the VIP database. Given this ability to merge technical with business information (such as supplier quality, delivery history, etc.), Aspect positioned EXPLORE as a Component Supplier Management (CSM) system.[2]

When the company first started in 1991, Aspect did not possess its own database of electronic components. Instead, it licensed and resold a database called CAPS, published by a competitor, IHS Communications Products. Aspect resold CAPS with a proprietary software search engine called Component Information System (CIS) designed for a networked environment. The system that IHS sold directly, in contrast, would work only in stand-alone personal computers. Craig Palmer, Aspect's Marketing Vice President explained,

> "Our first business model was to take the IHS data and make it accessible to a large enterprise in a modern client-server system. We soon decided, however, that in the long term it made sense to have our own data. Besides, IHS also reacted to our move by developing a client-server system, which would have made them a direct competitor for our product. For protection, as well as for offensive purposes, we thought that it made sense to start our own data factory.
>
> It took a whole year for us to create the VIP database and get enough parts to make it useful for end users. We have an iron-clad agreement with IHS to supply us the CAPS data until 1997, at which time I do not expect them to renew. By that time we should be more current than them."

Aspect sold the CIS software along with CAPS between 1992 and the first half of 1995. The first commercial version of their own EXPLORE-VIP combination was introduced in the second quarter of 1995. Although sales of EXPLORE-VIP were growing, the company also sold CAPS to OEMs who wanted access to both the VIP and CAPS data.

Obsolescence of electronic components combined with frequent product introduction required Aspect to update its database periodically. Every two months, Aspect sent 30 to 60 CDs and a set of tapes to its customers whenever a new release of the VIP database was announced. Customers usually had a bank of 10 CD changers, each of which could hold 6 CDs. New parts would be added across a whole range of CDs and tapes, necessitating a complete changeover for each new release of the VIP database. Customers followed a three step process for updating their data. First, they loaded the EXPLORE software from tapes into a hard disk. Second, searchable technical information on tapes would be transferred into the database created by the software. Finally, CDs containing datasheet images were loaded into the CD changer.

Benefits of EXPLORE and VIP

A recent study by British Aerospace showed that 70–80 percent of an end product's cost in the electronics industry was determined during the component selection phase of the new product development cycle. Judicious component selection could translate into a direct cost advantage when a product was launched in the marketplace. A design engineer using EXPLORE software could select components keeping procurement criteria in view. For exam-

---

[1] Application notes were suggestions from a manufacturer on how to use its components.

[2] Potentially, Aspect could sell EXPLORE as a separate product, without the VIP database, given its generic ability to organize information. On the other hand, the VIP database was useless without the EXPLORE software.

ple, designers could select parts from a preferred supplier with the best combination of price and quality. They could also select parts that were already approved by procurement or parts used by a different design group within the same company. In those cases, a customer could consolidate procurement volumes, shrink its supplier base and derive scale economies in procurement. Aspect estimated that IBM, which spent about $12 billion annually on purchasing electronic components, could save 5–10 percent on procurement costs by having designers select parts based on such criteria.

In addition to controlling end product costs, EXPLORE could reduce time-to-market for new products by enabling higher levels of design reuse. This was because the software could be used to create a central "knowledge repository" of reusable design elements, similar to the functionality provided by Lotus Notes for document archival and management. Reusable design elements could include hardware designs from past projects, system and architectural models, algorithms, software models and supplier information. Thus, EXPLORE enabled customers to reuse their intellectual capital from one design project to the next. Aspect estimated that 50–70 percent of any new design project had already been done elsewhere within the organization.

A study conducted by Aspect showed that an OEM with 500 EXPLORE users consisting of design engineers, component engineers, EDA librarians,[3] and manufacturing engineers could save about $5 million annually. These savings were attributed to six sources:

1. Reduction in the cost of components by enterprisewide volume consolidation of functionally equivalent parts.
2. Savings from increased reuse of preferred parts and suppliers. Each new part that a designer decided to use would cost an OEM between $10,000–$50,000 to set up in its procurement function due to costs associated with vendor qualification, inventory, and obsolescence.
3. Increased design engineer productivity arising from faster part searches. Aspect estimated that a designer could save an hour on average for each part search in VIP compared to searching manually through paper datasheets.
4. Increased component engineering productivity arising from faster development of procurement documents.
5. Higher EDA librarian productivity due to increased design reuse, fewer new parts requiring libraries to be set up, and faster generation of EDA libraries consequent from avoiding manual data entry.
6. Enhanced manufacturing engineering productivity due to easy access to supplier contracts and manufacturing information.

Competition in the Components Information Systems Market

Over the past few years, four firms had attempted to provide a components information system for the electronics industry. The first was Cahners, a publishing company which first entered the market with a Computer-Aided Part Selection (CAPS) database in 1990. Soon thereafter, IHS Communications Products, a Colorado-based company, introduced a competing product called IC-Masters. IHS later acquired Cahners' CAPS database in 1993 to gain the lead in the market. The third player was a company called ExpertViews, later renamed ViewPoint when acquired by R.R. Donnelley, and which went out of business in early 1994. Finally, Motorola introduced an online components information system called EnGenius in 1993, which allowed users to access a components database over the Internet. This company failed and closed down a year later.

IHS published a wide variety of databases and had about $100 million in annual sales, of which the electronic components database accounted for $15 million. It appeared that IHS customers were not entirely happy with its database since it did not simplify their components search process relative to traditional processes of searching through datasheets and databooks. Craig Palmer elaborated:

> "IHS thought they had a lock on the market even though their product had a number of gaps from an end-user's perspective. They took whatever semiconductor vendors could give them in the form of paper datasheets, and all they did was to convert paper documents into an electronic format. There were at least two problems with that approach. First, there was no prioritization of component information in their database based on the type of designs customers were currently undertaking. Second, it was difficult to compare components from different vendors. Vendors seldom describe the technical characteristics of their parts in exactly the same way. For example, different vendors may use

[3]EDA tools are software that designers use to visualize and simulate their product designs. These tools required a designer to input component information in a special electronic format. EDA librarians are specialists that convert functional specifications of components into libraries of electronic files that can be automatically imported into EDA tools.

EXHIBIT 3 Sample Classification Structure in the VIP Database

IC
(Integrated Circuit)

Microprocessors	Memory	Programmable Devices	Logic	Interface Devices	Analog Devices
• Microprocessor • Microcontroller • DSP • DSP Peripheral • Serial IO/Comm controller • Timer/RTC Clock • DMA Controller • Memory Controller • Bit-slice Controller • Memory Management Unit • Graphics/Video Controller • Clock Generator • Storage Controller • Multifunc Peripheral • Math Coprocessor • Display Controller • Interrupt Controller • Bus Controller	• DRAM • PROM • SRAM • FIFO	• PLD • FPGA	• Gate • Flip-flop • Bus Driver • Shift Register • Mux/Demux • Counter • Arithmetic Circuit • Delay Line • Decoder/Driver • Prescaler/Mono. Mult • Clock Driver	• Line driver/receiver • Display Driver • Peripheral Driver • MOSFET Driver • Drive Electronics • Level Translator	• Operational Amplifier • Buffer Amplifier • Comparator • Sample & Hold Circuit • Instrumentation Amplifier • ADC • DAC • Positive Voltage Regulator • Negative Voltage Regulator • Analog Switch • Voltage Reference • Motion Control Electronics • Position Converter • Isolation Amp. • Dual Voltage Reg. • Power Mgmt. Ckt. • DC-DC/PWM/Reg. • PLL/Freq. Synthesis • Special Function

Note: This chart illustrates the classification structure in a "high-level" class called Integrated Circuits. "Lower subclasses" (e.g., DSP) are refinements of "mid-level" classes (e.g., Microprocessors).

Source: Aspect Development.

different terminology to describe the same characteristic (e.g., clock speed vs. clock frequency) of a component like a microprocessor. Since IHS did not develop a standard framework for describing electronic components, search results in their product were, therefore, not an accurate comparison between vendors."

This understanding of IHS' weaknesses enabled Aspect to design its own products. Aspect's approach was to develop a logical framework for classifying parts and describing technical characteristics that would enable consistent comparison of components from different vendors. This was achieved by creating a *parts classification scheme* and a *data dictionary,* which together provided a hierarchical view of the information in the VIP database (see Exhibit 3 for an example of Aspect's parts classification scheme). Thus, microprocessors from vendors such as Intel, Motorola, or National Semiconductor would be described by a common terminology, and their technical characteristics could be compared by a user on an "apples to apples" basis across manufacturers.

Aspect further differentiated its product from IHS by ensuring that information from their database was immediately compatible with electronic design automation (EDA) tools that engineers would use after selecting components. EDA software tools would convert functional specifications of components in a product design into engineering layouts and mathematical models that would enable the designer to visualize his/her design and simulate functional performance for the product. Since IHS data were not EDA-sensible, a designer would have to re-enter manually all the data in IHS to

EXHIBIT 4 Aspect Development's Organization and Key Executives

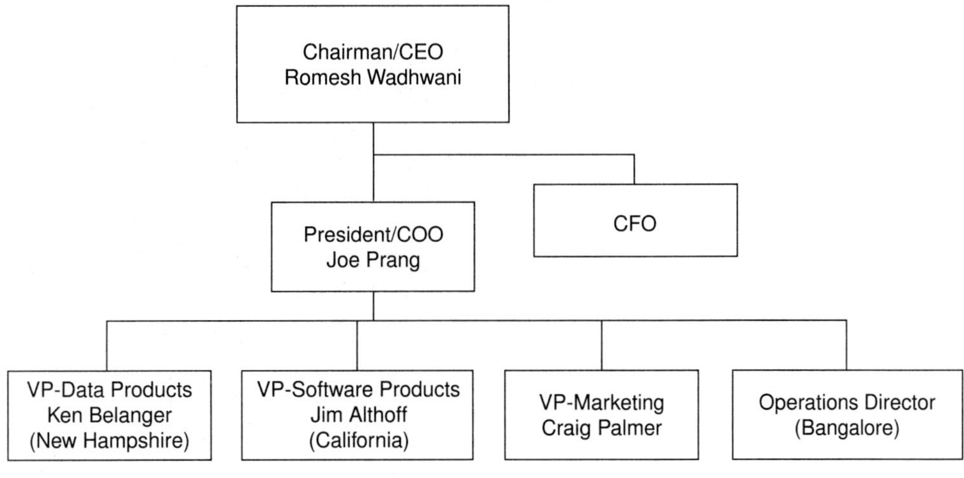

Source: Aspect Development.

create computer-aided design (CAD) files for the chosen components prior to using EDA tools.

Organization

The data and software sides of Aspect's business were organized as separate divisions, each under a Vice President (see Exhibit 4). The *Data Products Division* under Ken Belanger was responsible for creating and maintaining the VIP database. Belanger had worked previously at Wang Laboratories in supply chain management and component engineering. In 1989, he joined ExpertViews as its fourth employee, where he was in charge of both software and data development. He moved to Aspect when ExpertViews closed down in 1991, becoming Aspect's seventh employee and bringing with him other members of his team. The division was headquartered in New Hampshire (ExpertViews' former location), where it employed 30 people doing essentially data capture and database design. Most data entry was done in Bangalore, India, where the company had a 70-person staff.

From an operational point of view, the East Coast of the United States had a good overlap with business hours in India. Although salaries and hourly compensation were much lower in India than in the United States, productivity differences reduced some of the cost savings, particularly when inefficiencies caused by distance and communication problems were factored in. Aspect estimated that overall labor unit costs were about 30 percent lower in Bangalore than in New Hampshire. Mr. Wadhwani discussed the roles of both facilities:

> "Our data capture is highly engineer-centric, unlike data entry for airlines or financial services. Just because guidelines for data capture are established in New Hampshire, it does not mean that you could use data technicians for data entry. There are many interpretation issues during data entry, in addition to process issues relating to how you capture data, how you assure quality, and how you integrate streams of data into the database. Of the 70 people in our Indian operation, nearly 50 hold engineering degrees, with the others being technicians. Each technician entering data is guided by an engineer who provides specialized knowledge as needed. Our Indian operations are saving us $3–4 million a year, money that we use for software development."

The *Software Products Division* was responsible for specifying, developing, releasing, and supporting EXPLORE. Before joining Aspect in 1992, Jim Althoff had held several senior management positions at VLSI Technology. He and Belanger had jointly conceived the idea of EXPLORE as an object relational system during the course of consulting projects for Hewlett-Packard and L.M. Ericsson. The division employed 35 engineers in Mountain View, California.

EXPLORE had evolved from a previous software product called CIS, which was a standard client-server relational system with hard-coded tables. EXPLORE, being an

EXHIBIT 5 Enterprise-wide Information Infrastructure Needs

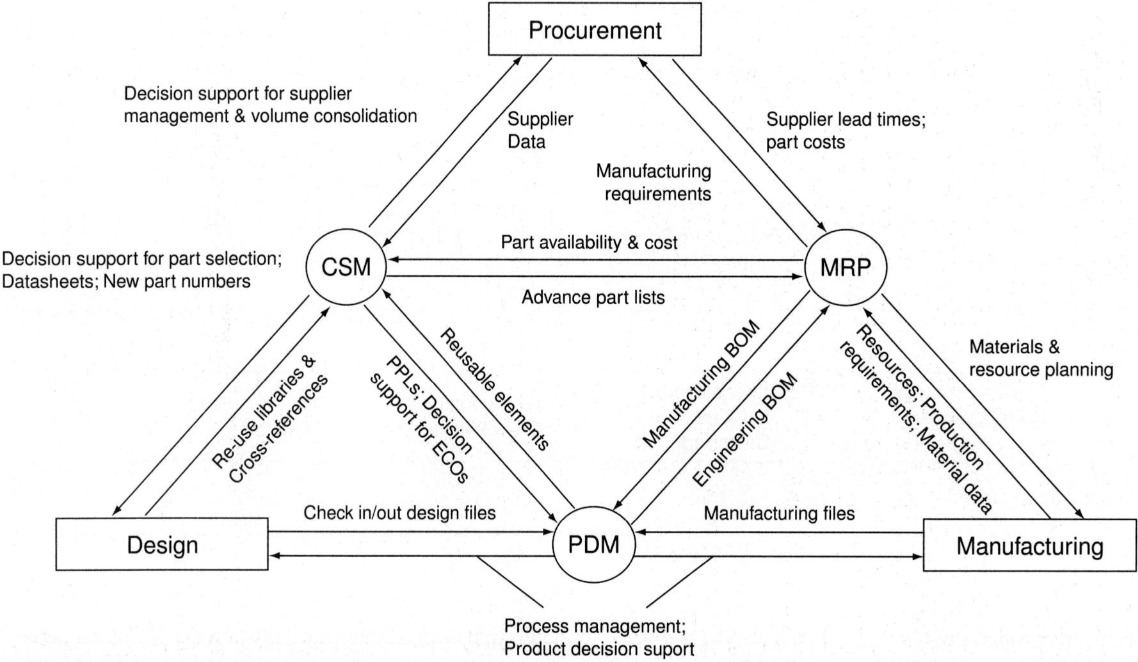

Note: Component supplier management (CSM) systems such as Aspect's EXPLORE software link design and procurement functions, while complementing existing manufacturing resource planning (MRP) and product data management (PDM) systems. PPLs are procured parts lists; ECOs are engineering change orders; and BOM are bill of materials.

Source: Aspect Development.

object-relational system, was much more flexible and powerful than CIS. It allowed Aspect to create new application modules for customers using the same core technology. For example, many companies wanted a supplier information system that would generate purchase orders, track incoming components, commit budgets for particular vendors, and track supplier quality metrics like on-time deliveries. (Exhibit 5 shows how the company's current CSM software fit into an enterprise-wide information infrastructure.) One option for Aspect was to add a new group of EXPLORE users by building a product line that would consist of the EXPLORE engine with the default component information system application, the VIP database, and optional applications such as a supplier information system.

At present, Aspect upgraded the EXPLORE software every three or four months to include added functionality. For example, in one version Aspect had added a comparison window that allowed users to pull search results into a spreadsheet and highlight differences between components on different technical attributes. The prospect of an online product would require designing an Internet front-end to the EXPLORE software. These two major development projects would be incompatible given the company's current resources.

Data Production Processes

The database production process consisted of two distinct phases (see Exhibit 6 for a schematic of the process). The VIP database was actually a family of discrete databases, one for each top level class (such as Integrated Circuits or Mechanical Parts) in Aspect's parts classification scheme. Aspect had to create, update and maintain all the databases included within VIP. A number of steps had to be performed before any data was captured in a database. These **preproduction** activities were market analysis, sourcing, production planning, procure-

EXHIBIT 6 Production Processes and Locations

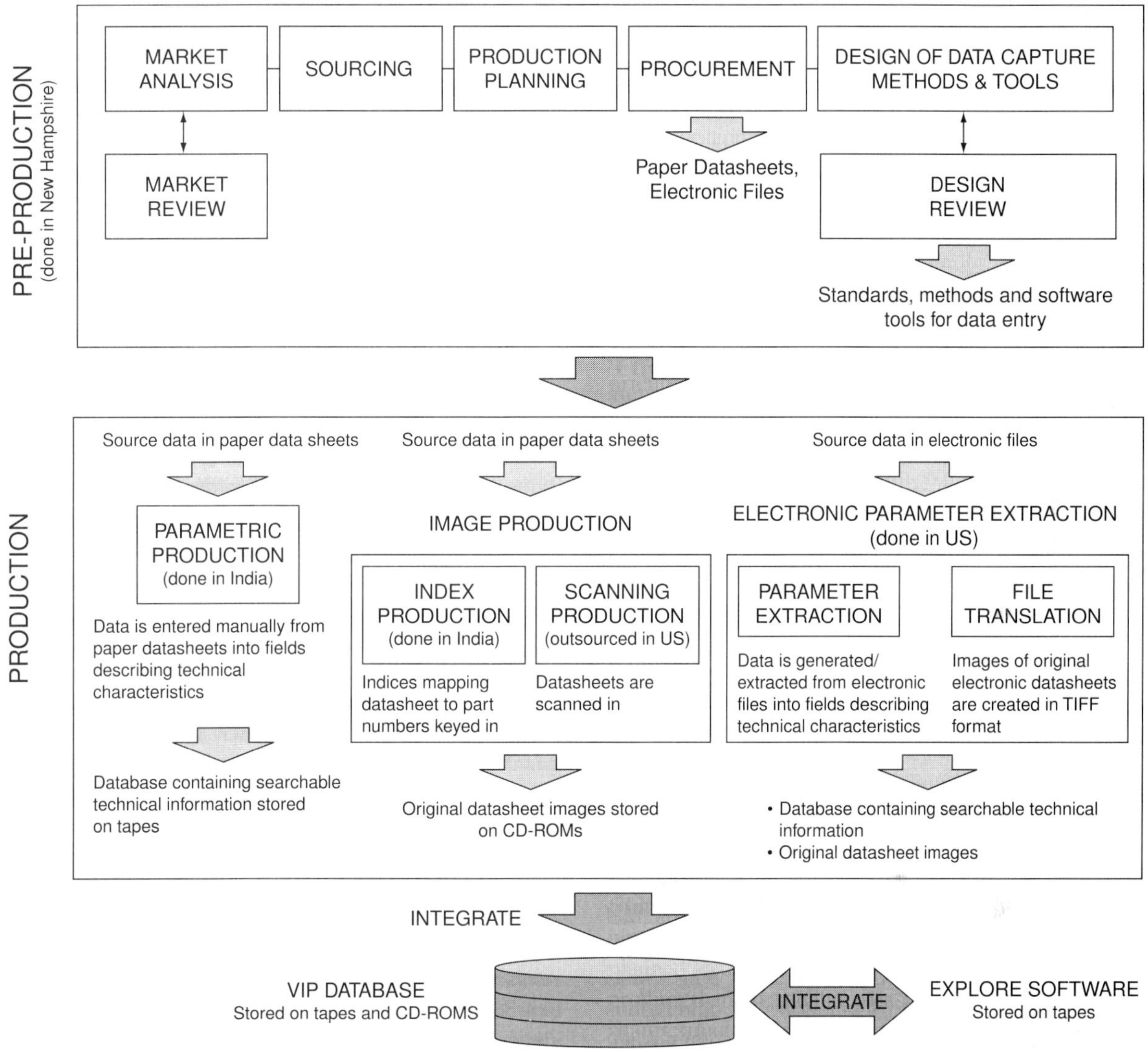

Source: Aspect Development.

ment, and design of data capture tools and methods. All preproduction was done in New Hampshire.

Market analysis determined which component vendor's data would be contained in the database. This decision was based on three sources: trade publications, preferred parts lists provided by Aspect's customers, and an in-house analysis of component usage trends in the electronics industry.

Sourcing related to establishing partnerships with the list of vendors determined by market analysis. Vendors provided Aspect with information in paper or electronic form (CD-ROMS or online files), but the format was rarely consistent even from the same source. For example, documents that Aspect obtained from Motorola were composed in 14 different versions of MSWord. Aspect's goal was to obtain electronic files from vendors on a prerelease basis, so that they had the latest component information in electronic form before anybody else.

In *production planning* Aspect assigned priorities to vendors and their parts data every month. The objective was to determine a production plan that quickly reached a critical mass of components that would make the database meaningful to a customer. The decision to include or exclude a vendor or component was not always clear cut.

Procurement referred to acquiring electronic files and hard copy documents from the target list of vendors as determined by the production plan. Aspect maintained a contact database, where they recorded orders placed with vendors for each document and electronic file. They also barcoded incoming databooks or electronically stamped files and inspected all documents against orders.

Design of data capture tools and methods involved determining what information would be captured, rules by which the information would be obtained, methods to normalize information across vendors, and standards to be employed. In addition, it designed rules for quality assurance. This step resulted in a 30–40 page specification document for each major part type.

Although preproduction activities appeared straightforward, they had often determined success or failure in the data industry. According to Craig Palmer, poor population strategy was attributed to the failure of ViewPoint, and to some extent, that of EnGenius:

> "ExpertViews' approach was to do an incredibly deep data capture for each part type so that a designer could automatically generate EDA-compatible files such as symbols directly from their data. They were capturing 10,000 fields per part and after a $5 million investment they had only about 1,000 parts in their database. They failed rapidly!
>
> "We believe that having a critical mass of components, with an appropriate breadth and depth of information, is a key success factor for our business. Both EnGenius and ExpertViews had a rather grandiose view for content. EnGenius attempted to allow users to not only search and select for components, but also enable Internet access and include graphical information like EDA-compatible symbols and footprints. It is not easy to accumulate all that. They spent so much time per part that, in the end, they had too narrow a coverage. We got broad fast and then knocked off the depth issue level by level as revenues came in. That proved to be a viable way to break into the business. I do not think EnGenius or ExpertViews figured that out in their business model."

Once the preproduction steps were completed, the database was ready for data entry during the **production** phase. This phase consisted of three simultaneous but separate processes called parametric production, image production, and electronic parametric extraction. In addition to populating its database with searchable technical characteristics of components, Aspect also provided original datasheets from vendors in electronic format. That way, after choosing a component, users could get more detailed information from a vendor's datasheet. In 1995, the VIP database contained 40–50 gigabytes of searchable technical data along with 50–60 gigabytes of datasheet images stored on CDs.

Parametric production referred to the manual capture of searchable technical information on parts from hard copy documents. For new databases, this consisted of a pilot production step followed by volume production. During pilot production of a new database, a team from Bangalore visited New Hampshire for a two- to three-month training program. Pilot production enabled transfer of data capture methods and tools developed in New Hampshire during preproduction to the Indian team. In addition, pilot production also facilitated a test run for data capture tools and specifications, and for determining production rates (parts captured per month). It also helped to anticipate problems that may arise during full-fledged data entry in India. For example, pilot production would sometimes reveal that having two people enter data would be better than fifteen, because interpreting data from datasheets in exactly the same way would be difficult across a large group.

Once the pilot was completed successfully, the first production run would be launched in India. During this step, data was not entered part by part; rather it was entered based on relationships between the data, whereby a lot less data was actually keyed in. Data generation tools were used to expand and create data based on those relationships. During the first production run, there was 100 percent inspection of data in the form of electronic checks and visual proofing, before the database was released to Quality Assurance. That department of nine people repeated the full visual and electronic checks. Once satisfied at this level, the database was shipped to New Hampshire physically using tapes or over the Internet. The database would then be integrated with the EXPLORE software and again subjected to quality tests. Only then would approval be given for volume production.

During volume production, data would be entered and inspected in India continuously, and shipped to New Hampshire where it would go through additional checks and integrated with the rest of Aspect's data. When there were enough new parts for a new release of VIP, Aspect would announce one. The new database would be stored on tapes and CDs and shipped to customers. A new release could refer to a new database for a new category of parts (say, medical electronics components) or updates of existing databases.

Image production referred to the digitization of original datasheet images from vendors. These images were linked to components in the VIP database. Once a designer chose a component, they could also view a detailed datasheet electronically. In the first step of image production, carried out in India, indices that pointed to a given datasheet were added to the appropriate part. The second step, where paper documents were scanned in, was outsourced within the United States, although there were ongoing efforts to integrate the scanning operation within Aspect.

Datasheet images were stored and shipped to customers on CDs. There were about 800,000 such pages on CDs in 1995. Many parts would be referenced by three–four pages within one datasheet. Sometimes, one datasheet would represent 30 to 40 parts differentiated by minor variations. For datasheets and databooks that were available in electronic form from vendors, Aspect had a separate *electronic parameter extraction* process to obtain searchable technical characteristics and integrate them into the database. For example, Aspect's military database was produced with information obtained directly from the government on CDs and tapes or downloaded from electronic bulletin boards. Aspect had developed page recognition software and parsers, which organized pages of information according to pre-established rules. The extent to which this was feasible was determined by the extent to which source files were in a standard format. Some electronic file formats required manual data entry, nonetheless.

Quality and Performance Issues

Production targets for adding parts to the VIP database were based on market analysis and empirically determined production rates. There was a tradeoff between the effort required to keep certain categories of parts current versus that necessary to expand the breadth of VIP by adding new databases on new part categories. Production rates during the startup phase for new databases and vendors were significantly lower compared to existing databases for which tools and processes had already been developed. Cycle time for hard copy documents, as measured by the time it took from receiving paper documents to having parts appear in the database, was about two months. Aspect's goal was to reduce cycle time to two weeks by the end of 1995. Correspondingly, Aspect shipped a new release of VIP every two months, but envisioned doing so every two weeks if it were to update customers over the Internet.

Aspect used two dimensions to evaluate its product: data quality and database quality. Data quality was essentially a measure of accuracy and was defined by errors per record and errors per field. Database quality was a system performance metric. It measured (1) *currency,* defined by the time interval between publication of a document and its availability at a customer site, and (2) *completeness,* the match between Aspect's database and customers' preferred parts lists. According to Belanger,

> "We have a well-defined, documented process, and we are trying for ISO 9000 certification. We use very sophisticated tools throughout our design, development, quality assurance, and integration processes. For ensuring data quality, we have electronic tools that are data driven. When fed rules about what you want to check for in a particular record and its relationships to other records, those tools can automatically detect duplicate records, duplicate keys, and null values, and check data types, spellings, and syntax. Many such tools are tightly integrated into our process from data capture design to data delivery to an end user."

Although Aspect still resold the CAPS database to some customers, it did not assure its quality since they believed that IHS faired quite badly on the 4 C's of the data business: currency, correctness, consistency, and completeness. CAPS included obsolete data and it took them 6 to 9 months to get new data into their database. Information in CAPS did not include many vendors and was sparsely populated. Palmer commented that,

> "CAPS was developed with a publisher's perspective, as opposed to an engineer's perspective. We consistently define what attributes describe each part type, and search results in our database are true comparisons across vendors. We also use international standards to develop our database to ensure correctness and every part points to its datasheet. In CAPS, misspellings are common, and a part points to a family of datasheets and databooks, which you must then flip through in order to get to the right datasheet."
>
> "We are currently running 200,000–300,000 new parts per quarter, about twice the run rate for IHS. We will have about 1 million parts by year end, all of which are no older than 1994. CAPS has 1.6 million parts of which 60 percent will soon be obsolete."

Pricing and Financial Issues

Aspect's revenue streams were derived from data (VIP) and software (EXPLORE) sales and consulting fees. Aspect's software sales were associated with its core engine,

EXPLORE and a number of customized decision support systems built around it. In addition, customers could also purchase interfaces for EDA tools[4] and training, consulting, and documentation services.

Pricing for the EXPLORE product was based on the number of simultaneous users, as well as on the total number of users in a customer site. EXPLORE's pricing structure was similar to other client-server software, and comprised of three license fees corresponding to the Oracle server, EXPLORE server and EXPLORE clients, respectively. The total for the three licenses could range from $80,000 for a system with 10 total users and 5 simultaneous users, to $1.6 million for a system with 1,000 total users and 100 simultaneous users. Aspect also charged a flat 16 percent annual maintenance charge for EXPLORE.

VIP data was priced at an annual subscription based on the number of simultaneous users. However, a customer could buy either all the VIP data or just some class of parts. Prices for a complete family of VIP databases ranged from $50,000 for 2 simultaneous users to $370,000 for 50 simultaneous users. Extra charges applied for EDA interfaces.

Since customers often paid their entire subscription and maintenance charges for a contracted period up front, Aspect had some flexibility in recognizing revenue. Deferred revenue was sometimes plowed back into the data side of the business. Aspect's software and data development expenses were together 45 percent of revenues, whereas marketing and sales accounted for 35 percent and administrative expenses for an additional 10 percent. Aspect's cost structure was very similar to that of software companies in their early stage of development.

Initial capital for Aspect was provided by Mr. Wadhwani, who owned 40 percent of the company. Dun and Bradstreet and Sequoia Capital together contributed an additional 40 percent. The remaining 20 percent of the equity was held by Aspect employees. Exhibit 7 provides an abridged balance sheet and income statement for the company's last year.

[4]EDA interfaces were software modules that converted components data from VIP into files that were compatible with EDA tools. Since there were several vendors of EDA tools (Mentor Graphics, Cadence, Synopsis, and Epic to name a few), Aspect users had to specify the vendor for their EDA tool in order to buy the right interface.

The Internet Decision

At a senior management meeting in September 1995, Mr. Wadhwani laid out Aspect's achievements to date and presented his outlook for the future:

> "About a year ago, we began the work of expanding our mission. One of the first things we did was to get a better understanding of the enterprise information architecture that our customers are going to be implementing in the next few years using client server technology. We decided to use EXPLORE's positioning as the link between design and procurement (see Exhibit 5) as the cornerstone of expanding Aspect's mission. Also, design reuse is a recent thrust for many large electronics companies, and it turns out to be something that EXPLORE enables extremely well. Thus, we expanded the mission from 'component information systems' to 'component supplier management (CSM) and design reuse.' In doing that, we achieved two things: we expanded our potential market and we matched the needs of customers more closely to the capabilities of EXPLORE.
>
> "Over the next three to five years, we hope to expand our market in several ways. First, we will develop information management systems for other vertical markets, like mechanical components (e.g., gears, pulleys, bearings, etc.) and software products. Second, we will further penetrate electronic OEMs because we are a long way from 100 percent penetration in the top 100 companies, particularly outside North America. Third, EXPLORE's flexibility creates opportunities for us to build application modules on top of our core EXPLORE software. Our strategy is similar to MRP system vendors who started off with a simple infrastructure and then built shop floor control modules, order entry modules and so on. Now, a full function MRP system may have 100 to 200 application modules within it. We want to progressively build a family of standard application modules which leverage the underlying capabilities of EXPLORE. We will develop 10 to 12 high value modules in the time period and keep increasing the value proposition of our EXPLORE software.
>
> "Examples of such EXPLORE-enabled applications include: (1) supplier performance management, which enables an OEM to determine which supplier is performing to what level for each component and rank them, (2) EDA library management to help company librarians manage design libraries required by their EDA tools, and (3) volume consolidation that will allow OEMs to remove functionally similar components and, by so doing, increase the volumes they bid and thereby reduce unit costs. The value proposition for such applications could be gigantic for our customers. In the next 12 to 18 months, we will build the first half-dozen of those applications. Leveraging EXPLORE to develop new enterprise applications is a major growth avenue for our company that focuses on process-driven applications rather than on the underlying infrastructure."

Exhibit 7 Aspect Development Financial Statements (in $ thousands)

Balance Sheet as of December 31, 1994

ASSETS	
Current Assets	
Cash and securities	$3,050
Account receivables	$1,980
Subtotal	$5,030
Other assets	$4,880
Total Assets	$9,910
LIABILITIES AND STOCKHOLDERS' EQUITY	
Current Liabilities	
Accounts payables	$480
Leases payables	$1,130
Deferred revenue	$2,750
Subtotal	$4,360
Stockholders' Equity	
Stock at par and pain-in capital	$8,500
Accumulated deficit	($2,950)
Subtotal	$5,550
Total Liabilities and Equity	**$9,910**

Profit and Loss Statement for the Year 1994

REVENUES	
Product Licenses	$3,675
Subscription and Maintenance	$3,350
Consulting	$1,420
Hardware, Services and Other	$1,685
Total Revenue	$10,130
EXPENSES	
Cost of Revenues	$1,265
Research and Development	$5,020
Selling, General and Administrative	$4,850
Total Expenses	$11,135
NET INCOME	($1,005)

Source: Aspect Development.

In this perspective, providing Internet access to components information was merely one of several growth avenues for Aspect. Craig Palmer, who had been asked to lead the Internet strategy taskforce for the company, summarized his views on his expectations from an online components information service as follows:

> "Our current focus is not on selling small systems to small and medium size companies, which is what our competition does. We may attack that segment head on both through an online service and a scaled down "EXPLORE light" product distributed through alternative channels. Right now, we have about 10,000 EXPLORE users within our client sites. However, they do not have a full deployment of EXPLORE. By developing new applications on top of EXPLORE, we could add about 100,000 users from design, manufacturing, and procurement just within our existing customer base"
>
> "Two years ago, the Internet was not a viable information distribution medium. Things are different today, which is why we are interested in online distribution for our database. Looking back, EnGenius actually had a decent vision for delivery. They failed on the data side since their database was too narrow, while the infrastructure for online data delivery was not there yet. Back then, Internet access for designers was not very common. In many cases, the only option was modem access, which was too slow for the graphics-intensive information that EnGenius provided. Besides, there were not enough parts in EnGenius anyway. That service did not add up to something that people would pay for. However,their business model is feasible for us today since we have the required content while the Internet is much more widespread in our target market."

A number of issues surfaced during the discussion. Some raised questions about the feasibility of an online system given the frequency of up-dating of the information and the large size of the databases (see Exhibit 8). It was generally agreed that Aspect's core clients, the 40–50 largest electronic companies around the world, might not be affected either way. On the other hand, the goal of greater penetration of smaller companies and, particularly, non-U.S.-based companies might be positively associated with an Internet-based product. But some participants in the discussion argued that channel costs would not likely change. Aspect had always relied on a direct sales force for the most part, and this would probably not change given the difficulties of explaining the value proposition of the product online. The main impact would be, without question, on their pricing models.

Exhibit 8 Competitive Segmentation Between Online and Package Technologies

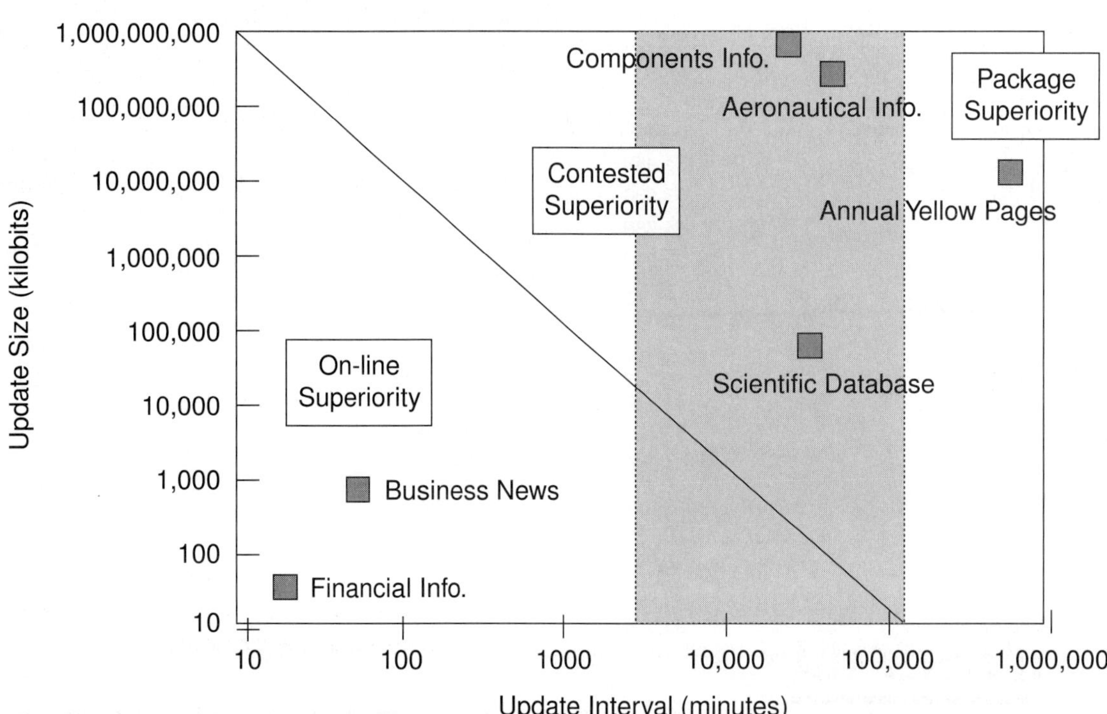

Source: T. C. A. Bashyam, "Service Design and Price Competition in Business Information Services," *Operations Research,* 1999.

Software license sales, for example, could be affected negatively, since online products would not require the EXPLORE software.

By the end of 1994, Aspect had a backlog of $15 million in orders and was generating a modest profit. As he considered the results of the meeting, Palmer remarked that, "A year later we are working on our fourth profitable quarter in a row. By the end of this year, we will have about 200 employees and $25–30 million dollars in sales. It is going to be difficult for us to move in all these directions at once, but we may have no choice in the matter. The future may look very promising, but there are hectic times ahead." In a brief respite from a challenging session, Palmer cheered as a fellow employee slam-dunked a basket during a vigorous game on the courts outside.

SECTION IV

Managing Global Operations

UNIT 9 Managing the Global Marketing Function

INSEAD

Case 9–1

Procter and Gamble Europe: Ariel Ultra's Eurobrand Strategy

One Sunday night in July of 1989, Claude Meyer and his delivery team for Ariel Ultra were on a train speeding from Brussels to Paris. They had spent 18 months developing P&G's first compact laundry detergent for the European market, and now, as they were finalizing the details of a meticulously planned pan-European launch, they learned that Unilever was about to launch a similar product in France—two months ahead of P&G.

Meyer, European Regional Vice President for laundry products, and his team were brainstorming responses to their longtime rival's pricing tactics, package sizes, and a premium-niche marketing strategy, all of which differed significantly from P&G's European plan. As the train sped toward Paris, they debated whether to change their approach to the French market to meet Unilever's challenge, or continue with their original intention to implement a consistent Europewide strategy.

P&G Europe: Background and History

Twenty years earlier, the problem of responding to Lever's launch would have been less complicated. At that time, each fully integrated major European subsidiary was structured as a microcosm of P&G in the United States, often headed by expatriate American managers, and typically reflecting the unique culture, values, marketing practices, and financial discipline that P&G had developed to become the leading consumer packaged goods company in the United States. Within that strong corporate framework, however, subsidiary General Managers (GMs) became "the kings in their countries." Each GM had a clear mission to adapt P&G's proven products for their local market, and to use the company's time-tested brand management approach to gain leadership in their country. Selecting from a portfolio of products, typically originating in P&G's domestic operations, they built local positions that fit with their specific country needs and market opportunities.[1]

This case was written by Professor Christopher A. Bartlett at Harvard Business School, Ph.D. candidate Alice de Koning at INSEAD, and Professor Paul Verdin Affiliate Professor at INSEAD and at Catholic University of Leuven, as the basis for class discussion rather than to illustrate either effective or ineffective handling of an administrative situation.

[1]In several instances, European product formulations and brand names became more successful than the U.S. transplants. For example, while Tide detergent did not do well, a European laundry formulation with a localized brand name, Ariel, was introduced in several markets in the 1960s. The formula, packaging, and position differed from one country to the next, but the brand became P&G's flagship detergent in Europe.

A small regional office in Brussels was created to control some central research capabilities housed in the European Technical Center (ETC), and later extended its role to provide minimal coordination of subsidiary activities. (Despite its development into a broad-based regional headquarters, it was still referred to as ETC.) Under this model, P&G's European subsidiaries developed into independent, largely self-sufficient, and highly entrepreneurial operations with a sense of internal competition among the GMs that helped drive rapid growth through the 1960s and 1970s. ETC's role in this period was primarily to provide administrative oversight and support as called for by the GMs.

Although the majority of senior management in P&G Europe in this era were U.S. expatriates, by the late 1970s a "cadre" of promising young local managers were offered the opportunity to spend a few years in P&G's Cincinnati headquarters before moving back to Europe. The ultimate career goal of many was to become a subsidiary GM—each the "king" in their home country's operation. It was about this time that P&G's traditional organization model began to change.

European Integration: Round One

During the last half of the 1970s, the political and economic entity of the European Community finally began to develop into reality. It was triggered in part by the 1974 oil shock, and the resulting economic downturn, and subsequent competitive pressures forced many companies to consider the value of better cross-market coordination within Europe. Because petrochemicals were the base of many of its raw materials, P&G was particularly impacted by these changes, and by the late 1970s, under the leadership of Ed Artzt, Group Vice President for Europe, the company was making its first serious attempts at pan-European coordination of the autonomous subsidiaries. ETC began gaining clout.

The first organizational group to take a clear step toward European integration was the product development division (PDD) headed by Wahib Zaki, a dynamic leader who was concerned about the inefficiencies and duplications caused by the fact that most PDD staff were located in the subsidiaries. Zaki recognized that by gaining consensus in product formulas, he could not only reduce product development time and costs, but could also leverage the strong development capabilities residing in several subsidiaries. As a first step, Zaki created Euro Technical Teams of PDD staff from the country organizations, assigning them to joint European projects.

In 1980, with the support of Ed Artzt, he further formalized this European link by having subsidiary-based product development staff report to two bosses: a PDD director at ETC and their local subsidiary GM. The change did not come easily however, as a German PDD manager recalled: "As a junior person, I was in a very difficult position. ETC expected me to get my GM into line on European developments, and the GM expected me to hold off ETC on standard formulations . . . Only strong people could handle the situation."

Nonetheless, by the early 1980s, a number of other functions also began exerting more Europewide coordination. Purchasing was a classic example. Raw materials represented a major portion of P&G's product costs, yet there were major discrepancies in the prices charged for chemicals sold to the country organizations, often by the same suppliers. Recognizing the potential economies, ETC purchasing staff negotiated a European price for large-volume supplies and developed a list of preferred suppliers. Predictably, local resistance was strong, and purchasing agents in the subsidiaries often ignored the European contracts and recommendations. Again, with senior management's support, ETC formalized the initial loose links in 1982 by centralizing the purchasing responsibility for key bulk ingredients and relocating many core purchasing activities to Brussels.

During the same period, the size and role of the regional finance manager's staff also increased. With a mandate from Artzt to gain tighter control of overhead expenses that were running more than 50 percent higher than equivalent expense levels in the United States, the European finance staff began taking a much more active role in tracking and controlling subsidiary costs. And soon after, manufacturing and engineering followed suit, with ETC staff taking a stronger role in subsidiary plant policy, resulting in a more matrixed relationship with subsidiary managers responsible for these operations. (See Exhibit 1 for a representation of the organization in 1982.)

The most difficult challenges in providing more effective coordination were undoubtedly felt by the marketing activities that had been so strongly rooted in the national subsidiary organizations. The first serious attempt at coordinating European marketing strategy was the so-called "Pampers experiment" of the late 1970s, in which a manager from the German subsidiary was moved to ETC and given responsibility for overseeing the marketing activities for disposable diapers across all subsidiaries. The experiment ended in failure when subsidiary GMs, no longer feeling responsible, withdrew local support for the brand. Eventually, management

EXHIBIT 1 P&G Europe Organization Chart, 1982 (Abbreviated Form)

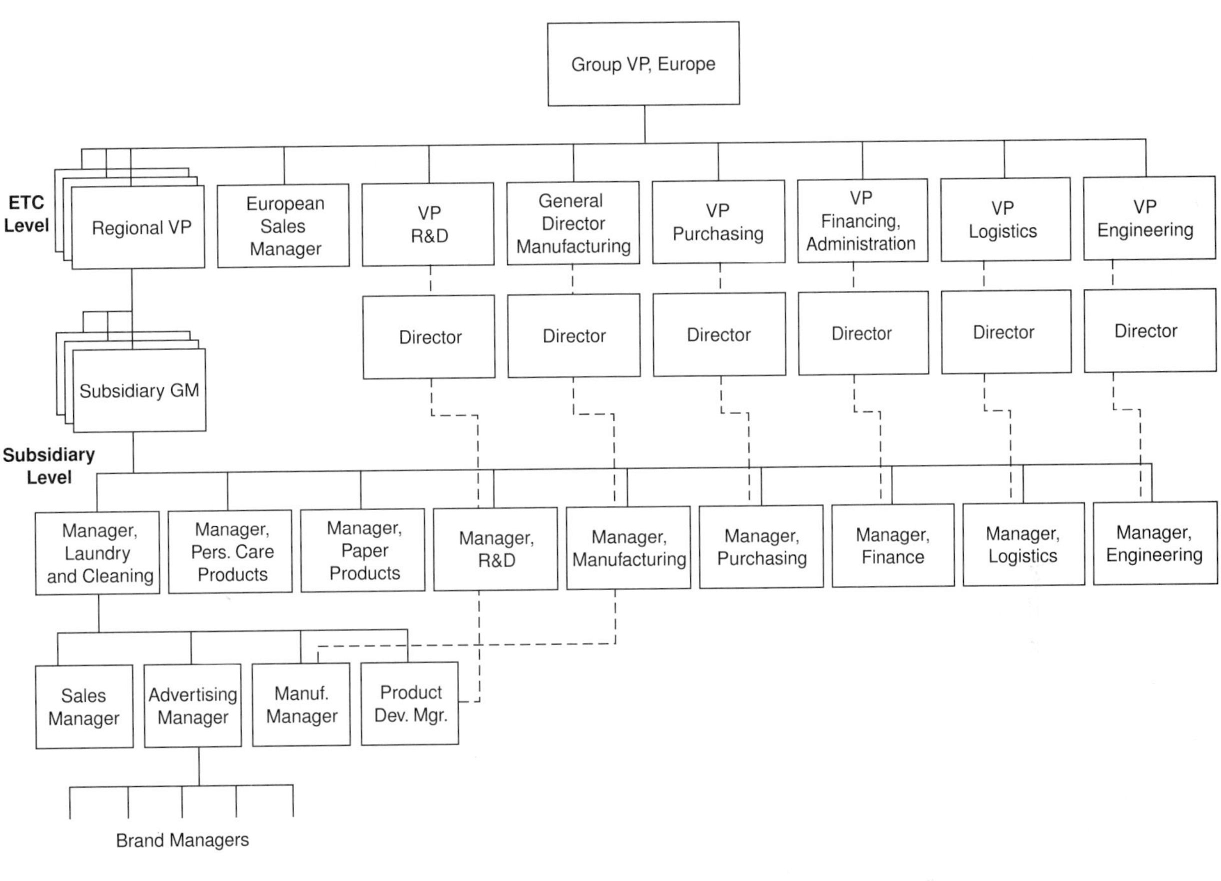

decided to abandon the experiment, and in the early 1980s, responsibility for marketing remained firmly in the hands of subsidiaries.

The Birth of Euro-Branding: The Vizir Launch

Despite the failure of the Pampers experiment, ETC management remained convinced that some form of coordinated European marketing strategies were vital if the company was to eliminate the diseconomies of its product and brand fragmentation. (Ariel, for example, was produced in nine different plants, had nine different formulas, and was positioned for low- and high-temperature washes, depending on the market.) Even more worrying was the increasing frequency of competitive leapfrogging, as companies like Unilever, Henkel, and Colgate took advantage of P&G's uncoordinated roll-out of products and won first-mover advantages in new markets—often by imitating a successful P&G strategy in another country. (A classic example was Colgate's entry into the French disposable diaper market by replicating P&G's German Pampers strategy, and beating P&G into that market by two years.)

Learning from failure of the centralized Pampers experiment, management at ETC decided to build on the success of the Euro Technical Teams to create a coordinated marketing approach. The opportunity to create a pan-European launch strategy using the first Euro-Brand Team (EBT) came with the development of Vizir, a heavy-duty liquid laundry detergent developed for the European market. Led by the brand manager from Germany, the designated lead country for the new product category, the Vizir EBT was composed of the marketing managers from all participating subsidiaries and key

European functional managers from ETC (product development, manufacturing, purchasing, etc.). But the EBT role was still largely informal, and because subsidiary GMs were still responsible for country profitability, they could disagree with proposals made by the EBT or even completely ignore its negotiated agreements. In the end, the GMs in three key countries—United Kingdom, Italy, and Spain—decided to opt out of the coordinated European launch of Vizir.

Although it successfully defined the Euro-brand concept, in terms of market share and profitability, Vizir did not come up to expectations. This was due partly to the unanticipated simultaneous launch of a competitive product from Henkel, and partly to the underestimation of the difficulty of converting consumer usage habits to the unfamiliar liquid form. Still, the organization, learning from Vizir, turned its attention to a variety of other brands with potential for cross-market coordination, and the concept of Euro-branding was established.

European Integration: The Second Thrust (1985–1989)

By the mid-1980s, most managers in P&G Europe realized how difficult cross-market coordination was. While the informal matrix approach and integrative teams had helped, the inbuilt conflicts continued to create confusion and tension, often without significant compensatory gains. As they searched for effective ways of capturing the potential benefits of integration, managers at ETC gradually began to assume more direct control, and many of the dual-reporting relationships were abandoned. For example, in 1987, the European-level manufacturing, engineering, and purchasing functions were combined to create an ETC-based Product Supply Operations (PSO) function. Although local plant managers worked as European units, they were bound by local union and national government pressures (which, in part, GMs were expected to deal with) to continue to report to GMs on day-to-day issues.

Two years later, the product development organization also eliminated its dual reporting structure, requiring instead, subsidiary laboratory staff to report only to PDD managers in Brussels. Unsurprisingly, subsidiary GMs expressed concern that they no longer had responsibility for the consumer research and market testing that was housed in their local development groups and which, they felt, was vital to their ability to tailor product features, advertising copy, and marketing strategies.

The power shift in marketing was not as clear, although there were many at ETC pushing for stronger regional management. The most aggressive move in this direction had been taken some years earlier by the European Vice President responsible for the paper category.[2] Concerned about P&G's slow penetration of the disposable diaper markets in southern European countries, in 1985, he essentially revived the earlier Pampers experiment by appointing a manager with Europewide responsibility for brand strategy and profitability. The new manager quickly recognized that the problem was that the southern markets faced much tougher competitors than that which existed in Germany, long regarded as Europe's benchmark operation for diapers. As a result, he concluded that P&G would have to substantially upgrade the product attributes and marketing approaches that had previously been based on the successful German Pampers strategy. By 1986, a new upgraded product (e.g., using higher absorption materials) and an aggressive new marketing strategy (e.g., creating differentiated boy/girl products) resulted in a major success for new Pampers Europewide. It was a success noted with interest by other European VPs. (See Exhibit 2 for the organization in 1989.)

In the eyes of ETC managers, the European coordination efforts were paying off, as P&G Europe's profits finally began to rise in the late 1980s.

> "In 1988, Europe achieved $100 million in profits after only $25 million in 1985 . . ." said Claude Mancel. "This is impressive growth especially since profit was growing faster than revenues. We felt we were entering the golden years of growth."

An Emerging European Laundry Products Strategy

It was in this context that Claude Meyer began to develop his new European laundry products strategy. Meyer was the European VP for the Central Europe region (France, Belgium, Switzerland, and Austria) who also had Europewide responsibility for laundry products. Reporting to him were the four country GMs, and, on a matrixed basis, the laundry category managers from all the European subsidiaries.

---

[2] Since the early 1980s, each of the three European VPs responsible for key regions was also given oversight for one of the major product categories—paper products, detergents and cleansers, and personal care products.

EXHIBIT 2 P&G Europe Organization Chart, 1989 (Abbreviated Form)

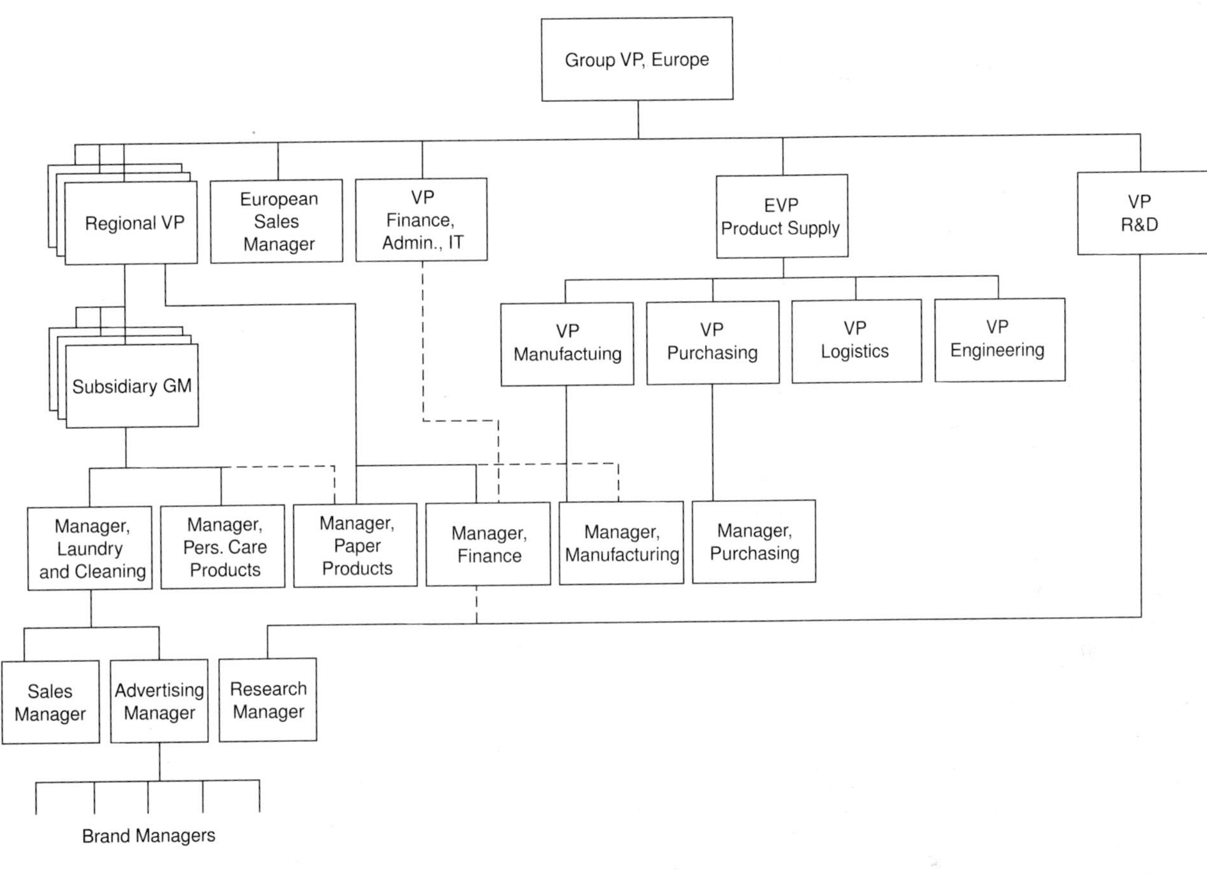

Particularly from the viewpoint of the GMs, the economic logic and strategic imperative for a strong European approach to laundry products was less clear and compelling than for the more standardized, capital-intensive disposable diaper business. Differences in washing habits, phosphate legislation, competitor mix, packaging standards, and even perfume preferences had made the standardization of detergent products difficult in the past. Even Liquid Ariel, the second-generation liquid laundry detergent that followed Vizir, was a single Euro-formula for only a short time before ETC management gave in to local pressures to adapt perfumes, package sizes, and promotion strategies. Yet Meyer was convinced that P&G could help lead the convergence of laundry practices and preferences if he could find the right product around which to rally the European organization.

Meanwhile, laundry product development had become increasingly coordinated on a European basis throughout the 1980s. In the search for European efficiencies, Claude Mancel, Vice President of R&D for Europe, continued to redirect his R&D resources away from their traditional role of supporting country-specific adaptations of existing products and toward major new product development with Europewide potential. Since early 1985, the laundry group under the leadership of Rinert Schoene had been focused on developing a concentrated detergent powder in single-dose sachets, its first major new product development effort since the work on heavy-duty liquids in the late 1970s and early 1980s.

The sachet was a product born of a concept originally developed for the Vizir marketing program. In response to Vizir's perceived usage problems—liquids did not work in detergent dispenser drawers and sometimes ran down into the washing machine's sump—PDD had developed a plastic dosing ball that could be filled with detergent and placed right in amongst the laundry in the machines. The advertising copy positioned this adaptive innovation as taking the detergent to "the heart of the wash." In both consumer perception and actual performance terms, the idea turned out to be a powerful and effective one, and PDD wanted to capitalize on it. Subsequent development efforts resulted in the concentrated powder in sachets also designed to be placed "in the heart of the wash."

The Compact Challenge: Responding to Attack

In June 1987, Kao, P&G's major competitor in Japan, launched a revolutionary new detergent that, within six months, had captured almost 30 percent of the Japanese market. Appropriately, the new product was called Attack, and its uniqueness came from a new technology that condensed hollow detergent particles to deliver the same washing power with less than one-third the dosage volume of regular powder. Sold in small, squat boxes, the new compact formula, Attack, had great appeal in a country where storage space was limited. The success of the product was so immediate that many in P&G—including Ed Artzt, now head of P&G's International Division—immediately began to wonder if there was potential in other countries.

At about the same time as the Attack launch, *Advertising Age* published a story that greatly bothered Artzt. It highlighted the simple truth that "international competitors all knew what P&G's new products would be, simply by monitoring the company's activities in the United States." In order to show that innovation and leadership in P&G should no longer reside exclusively in the United States, Artzt encouraged Europe to be the first to replicate the Attack success. He also recognized that P&G needed a response to the growing and apparently unstoppable European environmental movement that was increasingly focused on detergent producers, and felt that this product had potential to meet such pressures.

When Artzt laid down his challenge to the European management team, they were in the middle of their test market for the sachets they had been developing for over two and a half years. While intrigued by Attack's success, they questioned whether the concept had the same potential in Europe not only because European detergents were already highly concentrated, but also due to the fact that European consumers were less space-conscious than their Japanese counterparts. Besides, they told their boss, the new Ultra Packs that they had worked so hard on actually contained a new concentrated Ariel formula. But Artzt was not impressed and reiterated his challenge at each meeting. He pointed out that the sachets were expensive to manufacture, that their bulk negated the advantage of compactness, and that historically, consumers had not embraced the concept of a predosed detergent. He pushed them to develop a product that had "true Attack potential."

Mancel took the challenge back to PDD where Schoene and his team began to rethink Ariel Ultra as a free-flowing compact detergent. By adjusting the formula and removing 10 percent of the fillers, the PDD team made the product even more compact. Eventually, despite their years of work and investment, Schoene's laundry team decided to kill the sachet project and redirect the resources to Ariel Ultra compact. They recognized that the powerful "heart of the wash" concept they had been developing would allow them to deliver more concentrated cleaning power using less powder per wash. Schoene and his team then designed a reusable cloth dosing dispenser that would serve the same function as the Vizir dosing ball. By delivering the product directly into the wash rather than through the European drum machines' normal dispensing cups, they found that they could achieve better washing performance than conventional detergents with one-third less powder.

When they presented the new Ariel Ultra concept to Artzt, they immediately won his full approval. (See Exhibit 3 for product concept and packaging evolution.) The only moment of hesitation came a few months later when Unilever (which had learned about the sachet project, but not about its demise) launched Surf sachets in Italy. At that time, a few senior executives wanted to reconsider sachets, but Meyer and Mancel were not swayed. "Ultra concentrated powder was the first, big, continuous European initiative," said Meyer. "This was our chance to prove that the new organization could work."

The Ariel Ultra Delivery Team

With the Ultra concept defined, Meyer and Mancel were committed to speedy development and launch, and by May 1988 had appointed a full-time delivery team. The core members were Charles Murray, a PDD manager who had been involved in the product's development, Peter Williams, formerly a plant manager in the United Kingdom and now a member of PSO, and Rob Ratcliffe,

EXHIBIT 3 Evolution of Ariel Ultra Concept and Package: 1987–1990

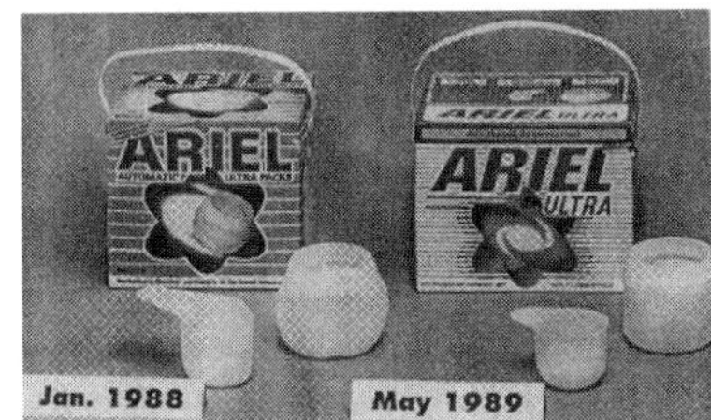

the financial analyst on Meyer's small two-person ETC staff. They were to report to Meyer, who set them the objective of market testing by January 1989, and launching by September of the same year.

Murray and Williams immediately shared the responsibilities and began driving initiatives back into their respective organizations. Murray focused on chemical specification, process development, and packaging, while Williams led initiatives in materials purchasing, manufacturing, and engineering. They soon co-opted others from PDD and PSO into three subteams to focus on major developmental issues: one group worked on an agglomerator that was key to the production process, another conducted consumer research to fine tune the product design, and the third focused on unresolved packaging issues.

One result of the cross-unit collaboration was a faster, more efficient development process. For example, by working with materials purchasing specialists in PSO, the chemical development experts in PDD were able to adapt the formula to take into account material availability and cost effectiveness. And from the PSO perspective, early involvement gave the purchasing team the time to ensure guaranteed supply of scarce specialty chemicals at guaranteed prices.

With regard to marketing, rather than giving Europewide responsibility for laundry products, as paper products had done, Meyer decided to create a task force that was a modified form of the Euro-Brand Team structure developed for the Vizir launch. In this way, he hoped to engage the marketing managers located in each country. Learning from past experience, Meyer imposed two conditions on membership: first, the task force would discuss only European-level issues—country-specific issues were off the agenda; and second, the marketing managers could participate only on condition that they had the power to commit their local organization to any decisions made. These two conditions ensured that the monthly meetings would not get bogged down in details, or have to reopen earlier decisions that had subsequently been vetoed by a general manager, as happened too often in the old EBTs days. Furthermore, the marketing task force was led by Meyer himself, not a subsidiary GM as had been the practice in the old EBTs days. Finally, Meyer was careful to keep subsidiaries well informed. As one GM recalled, "The agendas were published before meetings, and I discussed everything with the marketing manager. If I had to, I would call ETC to get more information. Before he left for the meeting, the marketing manager and I would agree on what positions he would take and what range of commitments would be acceptable."

The Euro-Brand Controversy

Given the pressure to launch in 18 months' time, Williams and Murray soon realized that only one formula could be developed for a test launch of Ariel Ultra. This would be quite a shift from the practice with the regular Ariel detergents, which typically came in a variety of country-specific formulas—phosphate and nonphosphate, various densities, several perfumes, and a whole range of package sizes and designs—reflecting the various washing machine designs, consumer habits, and historical GM dictates. Mancel and PDD supported a single formula, built to the highest common factor specifications for all European markets, citing the long-held P&G creed that its products were demonstrably better than the competition and offered consumers "superior total value." But the improved performance and the fast launch potential of a single European formula came at a cost: the phosphate substitute alone was estimated to increase raw material costs by $1 per case. Unfortunately for Meyer, Mancel and the Ultra delivery team, the benefits they were promising—offering a superior formula, removing production complexity, increasing organizational speed—were largely unquantified, and some were unquantifiable. With the worry that if they slowed down to study scale and efficiency benefits, a competitor might beat them to market with a compact detergent, the ETC group urged management to accept the potential savings "as an act of faith." In a company with a long and deeply held tradition of making decisions based on hard facts, this was a lot to ask of the organization.

Meyer saw a single formula as just the first step; he wanted to develop an integrated Ariel Ultra strategy for Europe. In response to this objective, Williams and Murray were working to achieve a single package size, consistent pricing policy, and common brand image and positioning. In this initiative, the biggest question was whether P&G should try to convert the whole market to compact detergent, or take a more conservative flanker strategy. If a conversion strategy was preferred, pricing and packaging would be targeted at attracting existing, satisfied regular detergent users; if a flanker strategy was used, P&G would have to create a premium-priced, high-margin niche, up-market from regular detergent. Because it was difficult to forecast either the conversion costs or potential economies of the former strategy, the debate about the desirability of conversion again proceeded on little hard data.

Mancel and Schoene's PDD laundry group became strong advocates of the full conversion option. They argued that the company could make huge market share gains with the better performing product and the more convenient package size they had developed. They were also aware that their counterparts at Unilever were also probably developing a compact detergent, and that the first mover would have a huge advantage in defining the market characteristics.

Dissension Among the GMs

While the GMs were excited about the general prospect of a major new product innovation, not all of them were optimistic about Ariel Ultra. One GM described his concerns:

> "Centralized groups like PDD had very different goals and interests from subsidiary level managers. It's fine for Meyer and Mancel to say they can't quantify the potential savings, but there is no European detergent category profit center. Because of P&G's structure and incentives, GMs have to be as interested in delivered cost as in product performance."

To the GMs, the concept of a single formula posed serious questions about a Euro-brand strategy that minimized local differences in market conditions. If Ultra was to meet the tough environmental standards in Germany, Scandinavia, and the Netherlands, for example, it would need a phosphate-free formula, and that would add about 10 percent to the product cost. But subsidiary GMs in the United Kingdom, Spain, France, and other countries where phosphate was not restricted, were very disturbed about the single-formula principle, arguing that they felt they could not justify the higher price to their consumers. As a result, this added cost would come right off their bottom line at an estimated loss of $25 million for Europe.

The GMs also argued that ETC underestimated enduring differences in country-to-country consumer behavior. Preference for powder or liquid and dominance of high- or low-temperature washes varied widely; national differences in perfume preference were regularly confirmed in test panels; the buying behaviors of French consumers loading up their cars at *hypermarchés* contrasted with that of the Dutch housewife bicycling to the corner store to make her purchases; and the wide differences in local pricing structure would seem to block any attempt at Europewide pricing. ETC's influence on pricing was also sensitive, since this was one key tool the GM controlled to manage subsidiary profitability on which he was judged. (See Exhibit 4 for a summary of market differences.)

Furthermore, the GMs pointed out, P&G's competitive position differed from country to country. In the Dutch, United Kingdom, and French markets, Unilever was a major competitive force; Germany was the home market for Henkel; and Colgate was a strong and sometimes disruptive factor in France. (See Exhibit 5 for a summary of competitive differences.) The GMs argued that these differences would affect the specific impact of marketing policies, even if a similar strategy was adopted throughout Europe.

Indeed, despite Attack's success in Japan, several GMs remained unconvinced that the compact detergent concept was even viable in their markets. The Italian GM, for example, pointed to the limited acceptance of the previous generation of liquid laundry detergents as evidence that conservative Italian consumers would not see value in detergents being compact. In France, according to local management, consumers were accustomed to bulk purchases of heavy packages—mineral water, for example—and did not value compact

EXHIBIT 4 Cross Market Comparisons of Selected Washing Practices—1988

						Type of Wash (as % of Total Loads)			Main Package Sizes			
	Market Size $ Millions	% Share for Powder	% Share for Liquid	% Households with Washing Machines	Total Loads Per Week	% High Temperature Wash (+60F)	% Low Temperature Wash (−60F)	% Handwash	Powder (kg)	Liquid (liters)	Average Dose Per Wash (grams of powder)	Anti-Phosphate Laws?
France	1,233	80	20	85	4.8	36	57	7	5.0	3.0	220	No
West Germany	1,271	90	10	84	3.8	40	55	5	3.5	2.0	190	Yes
Italy	750	88	12	93	7.9	36	33	31	4.8	3.0	240	Yes
United Kingdom	1,141	65	35	87	6.6	26	60	14	3.0	2.0	150	No
Belgium	208	85	15	90	4.8	40	55	5	3.5	2.0	215	No
Holland	280	80	20	93	5.4	42	52	6	3.0	2.0	170	Yes

EXHIBIT 5 Market Size and Competitive Positioning—1988

	Market Size $ Millions	P & G Brands	P & G Market Share	Lever Brands	Lever Market Share	Henkel Brands	Henkel Market Share	Colgate Palmolive Brands	Colgate Palmolive Market Share
France	1,233	Ariel Bonux Vizir	31.0	Omo Persil Coral Skip Wisk	28.4	Super X Xtra Mir Le Chat	19.1	Paic Genie Axion Gama	14.1
West Germany	1,271	Ariel Raz Dash Vizir	27.5	Sunil Coral Omo	16.1	Persil Weisser Riese Perwoll	39.6		
Italy	750	Dash Ariel	31.2	Bio Presto Surf	13.2	Dixan Perlana	15.2	Axion 2	1.9
United Kingdom	1,141	Ariel Bold Fairy Raz Dreft	48.4	Persil Radion Surf Wisk	37.2				
Belgium	208	Ariel Dreft Dash Vizir	45.2	Omo Radion Coral	11.2	Dixan Persil	13.0		
Holland	280		25.2	Omo Sunil All Robijn	22.0	Dixan Persil White Reus Fleuril	21.5		

EXHIBIT 6 Competition in the French Detergent Market: Market Share by Brand, 1988

Company (Brands)		Share (%)
Procter & Gamble (Bonux-machine, Bonux-handwash, Lava, Dash, Ariel, Vizir, Ariel-liquid, Bonux-liquid)		31.0
of which Ariel-powder	11.5	
Ariel-liquid	3.5	
Lever (Omo, Persil, Skip, Coral, Lux, Wisk, Skip-liquid, Omo-liquid, Coral-liquid)		28.4
of which Skip-powder	9.5	
Skip-liquid	2.5	
Henkel (Super-Croix, X-Tra, Mir-woolens, Mir-coloreds, Mohair, Mir-express, Le Chat-machine, Super-Croix-liquid, Mir-coloreds-liquid)		19.1
Colgate-Palmolive (Paic, Genie, Axion, Gama)		14.1
Store Brands		7.4
Total (representing 8,000 million FF)		100.0
of which liquid	30.0	

Source: *Points de Vente,* Oct. 1, 1989 and *L'Expansion*, 23 Nov/6 Dec 1989.

packaging. And in Germany, large surface area hypermarkets did not create the premium for shelf space that was evident in countries like Holland that had many more smaller stores.

Finally, several GMs reacted strongly against ETC's favored conversion strategy. Arguing that they had excellent market position and profitability with existing products, they saw no reason to jeopardize their existing profitable situation. A conversion strategy was highly risky and, they suggested, could send consumers to a competitor's traditional product. Some GMs were more cautiously optimistic about the alternative flanker strategy, however. Such was the case in France, for example. The French subsidiary's detergent line had historically suffered poor profitability, primarily due to the pressures of a highly competitive market in which four major manufacturers each battled to promote more than 20 brands (see Exhibit 6). While the French GM was intrigued by the possibility of a potential profit boost from a high-margin premium-niche market, he also wanted to keep the shelf space allocated to the existing product range to block new entrants and squeeze out weaker competitors.

This debate about Ultra's proposed strategy was important to the GMs, due to the fact that laundry detergent was a bread-and-butter product for them. While European profits had risen dramatically in the late 1980s (see Exhibit 7 for a graphic—but uncalibrated—representation used by ETC management to show the link between new product initiatives and profitability), the GMs were conscious of continued pressure to achieve profit improvement. And, as they frequently reminded the staff groups, if ETC-driven strategies and initiatives failed, the results and responsibility would show up on the subsidiaries' bottom line.

Resolving the Differences

While the delivery team wanted to engage the subsidiary managers in discussions about the new product, they also wanted resolution with unanimity. Having been involved in the Vizir launch when four key countries simply opted out of the European roll-out, Meyer and Mancel both wanted to avoid such a situation at all costs. But they could not afford to make too many concessions to individual countries to win their cooperation. Above all, they were committed to making Ultra a true Euro-brand.

The ETC leaders decided they would have to coerce key subsidiary personnel into thinking on a European scale. In one tactic, Meyer ensured that various Europewide marketing projects were assigned to subsidiary representatives on the marketing task force. The United Kingdom marketing manager, for example, took a lead role in package design, working with PDD to develop a strong unified image for all Europe. Another strategy was commitment to a concentrated European outreach program to engage subsidiary management in the launch planning. Meyer, Murray, and Williams visited each country organization, setting up meetings focused on

EXHIBIT 7 Growth of European Profit Against Product Initiatives
Unscaled Representation 1980/81—1988/89

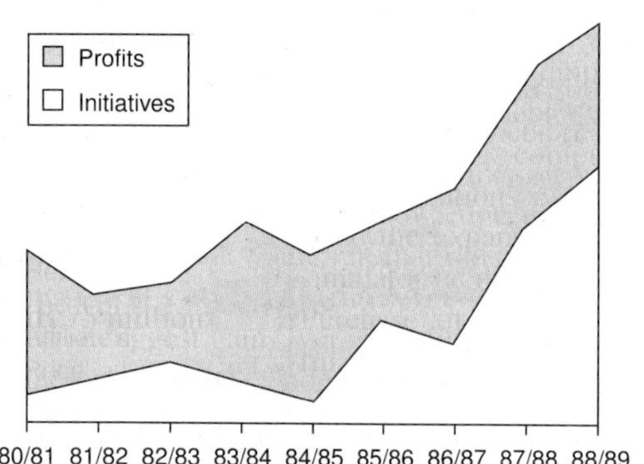

country specific issues of the launch. Murray recalled the difficulty of some of these meetings:

> "We deliberately included managers from all functions because we wanted to dilute the subs' marketing side. They were usually the strongest opponents to the European policies, and we wanted to soften the confrontations."

As Meyer recalled,

> "This slow process was actually a cultural adjustment. People need time to change. Going too fast would kill the organization." But the objective of the various discussions was always to get agreement on and commitment to a European strategy for Ultra. As one manager said: "That's how we work here. We disagree, we argue, but once a decision is made, we get on with it."

On the sensitive positioning issues, the marketing task-force compromised on the two competing proposals by deciding to launch with a flanker strategy, but with a long-term goal of achieving conversion. Some at ETC questioned the logic of this decision. For example, PDD laundry team leader, Rinert Schoene, felt that such a decision would prevent the company from promoting the new product as strongly as it could for fear of implying that compact was the "new improved" Ariel and the traditional product was the "old inferior" Ariel. Nonetheless, he and his ETC colleagues went along with the two-stage compromise.

Other key policies were also resolved through negotiation, with ETC yielding to local subsidiary demands where they needed to. On packaging, for example, it was agreed that marketing needed to educate consumers about the compact concept by creating "equivalent-to-regular" package sizes. Since sizes varied from country to country—Dutch and English consumers made frequent purchases of small quantities (1- or 3-kilo packages), while French and Italian consumers bought large packages (typically 5- and 8-kilo packages)—two or three standard Euro-packs were deemed infeasible. However, Williams managed to insist on a single package design and single "footprint" (i.e., consistent box base dimensions to simplify setups on the packaging lines). In addition, the task force agreed to adopt a broad range of standard pack sizes from which countries could select.

On pricing policy, the marketing task force rejected ETC's proposal for equivalent cost-per-wash pricing due to the subsidiaries' need to improve margins. Instead, they decided to price slightly above the cost per wash for regular, but below for liquids like Vizir, which had been premium priced. Because of national differences in everything from competitive rivalry to recommended dosage, any thought of a single pricing standard was dismissed. However, the task force agreed to a consistent policy of pricing at a cost of about 15 percent higher per wash than the established local price of regular Ariel, and clearly below the 30 percent premium typically charged for liquids.

The most controversial issues to resolve between ETC and the subsidiaries turned out to be the "highest common factor" product formulation. Its most vocal and persistent opponent was John O'Keefe, GM of the U.K. subsidiary, who felt that Ultra's phosphate-free compact formula was just too expensive for his market. Months of passionate discussions followed between O'Keefe, Meyer, and Mancel, with little visible progress. Initially, Harold Einsmann, P&G's European VP, did not interfere in the debate, although it was widely known that he was strongly in favor of a single formula. Eventually, a number of forces intervened to push the issue toward resolution. First, Henkel launched Bright White, positioned as an environmentally friendly "green" product. Soon after, Sainsbury, the U.K. supermarket chain, launched an own-brand nonphosphate detergent. Then, Williams and Murray responded to the GMs' pressure by promising formula improvements that would reduce the nonphosphate cost premium from one dollar to 50 cents a case. When O'Keefe finally conceded that a nonphosphate flanker strategy could be made to work in the United Kingdom, Einsmann confirmed the decision: P&G would make a single compact formula, a decision for Europe that he acknowledged may not have been optimal for each country.

The Roll-Out

One point on which the task force was in unanimous agreement was the need for an early launch of Ariel Ultra. Meyer developed a launch schedule based on some specific principles—the need to establish lead markets, a commitment to matching Lever's initiatives, and a principle of launching Ultra in every country before adding a second compact brand. The speed of the roll-out would depend on the rate at which plant capacity could be converted, but the objective was to reduce sequencing delays to a minimum. And, beyond agreeing that conversion to compact was a long-term goal, no specific timing was set for the two-phase strategy. Indeed, with the exception of P&G Holland, most countries adopted a "wait-and-see" perspective on their commitment to full conversion.

The German Launch

Operating on the principle that roll-out speed was more important than country-tailored launch precision, the task force proposed launching on market information obtained from a few quick test markets. As Williams described it:

> "Our test marketing was a 'no negatives' check and a quick 'how to sell' test, not the traditional P&G six to eight month test market in each country designed to define the business potential of the product concept."

In February 1989, only six weeks behind schedule, a minimal set of market and consumer tests was launched in Saar for Germany, Monte Carlo for France, and Carlyle for the United Kingdom. Even before all the test results were in, Ariel Ultra was launched nationally in Germany in May. The German marketing group launched a 2-kilo size compact, fully equivalent to a regular 3-kilo size, and developed an advertising message designed to attract attention by initially emphasizing Ultra's benefits to the environment, then subsequently promoting product performance. This emphasis on less packaging and fewer chemicals was particularly relevant in Germany since P&G's German rival, Henkel, had positioned itself as a "green" company in its environmentally sensitive home market.

The French Launch

In the European roll-out plans, Meyer had scheduled France for a September launch, timed for *la rentrée* when families returned from vacation and children went back to school. While the French marketing manager, Alain Lorenzo, and his team were open to the compact concept and were keen for a new product that might regain the momentum they had experienced with the liquid detergent introductions of the early 1980s, they still had lingering doubts about Ultra's potential. Lorenzo pointed out that the recent introduction of a concentrated fabric softener had not been a big success in France, illustrating, in his view, that compactness was not a big advantage to the French consumer. He explained:

> "France is a 'bulk-size' country. The success of the *hypermarché* has meant that consumers are not so concerned with small boxes. They bring their cars and load up. In fact, our most successful recent promotion has been a double pack of two 8-kilo boxes of Ariel!"

Still, the Monte Carlo test market went ahead, offering the 3-kilo box of Ariel Ultra, promoted as roughly equivalent to the popular 5-kilo box of regular detergent, and the 5-kilo box as doing the same number of washes as 8 kilos of regular. In keeping with the overall strategy, both were priced slightly higher per wash than the regular, but lower than the liquid. While not specifically referring to Ultra's nonphosphate formula, the launch positioning featured an environmental theme.

Early test results suggested positive market response (see Exhibits 8 and 9), and by June, the French launch proposal was sent to Cincinnati for approval. The plan reflected the fact that distribution in France was dominated by the *hypermarchés* with 85 percent of P&G France's sales being made through only 1,000 stores. While suburban *hypermarchés* did not face the same shelf space constraints as small stores in city centers, it was always hard to slot in a new brand. Yet Lorenzo and his team felt they could argue that, because Ariel was such a major brand and because P&G was committed to educating consumers on the new concept, compact could eventually lead to increased turnover per meter of shelf space.

In terms of message, ETC's delivery team convinced the French team to follow the innovative advertising campaign that had induced a high level of trial in Germany. Although the French market was less "green" than the one in Germany, they felt the environmentally sensitive campaign would be a viable counter to Henkel, which had recently bought the French brand "Le Chat,"

EXHIBIT 8 Ariel Ultra France: Test Market Results

1. Shipments

Cumulated results after four months exceed objectives by + 16 percent. The slow test market start in months one and two reflect the late break of advertising (week seven) and the need for consumer education. These are fully addressed in our national plan. (MSU = Market share for Ultra.)

	Monthly Objective	Actual	Index vs. Objective	
	Msu	Msu	Msu	Cumulative
March 1989	3.5	1.8	51	51
April	2.4	2.4	100	76
May	2.7	4.2	156	98
June (estimate)	3.0	5.0	167	116

2. Sales Offtake (Sales Panel)

This panel of five big stores represents 40 percent of the test area total turnover.

Offtake buildup was slow in the first weeks and increased substantially after the start of advertising, sampling, and in-store demonstrations.

Cases/week	Ariel Ultra	Ariel Powder	Ariel Liquid	A. Ultra as a % of Ariel Powder	Total Ariel Index vs. Base	
					Month	Cumulative
Base (prev. 6 months)	–	645	327	–	100	100
March	63	594	271	11%	96	96
April	145	561	309	26%	104	100
May	232	658	275	35%	120	107
June	368	621	284	59%	131	113

and was building on that brand's established "pure" image to promote it as the dominant environmentally sensitive product line.

Lever's Launch

In late June 1989, soon after its launch plans had been completed, the French team was stunned to hear through the industry grapevine that Lever was planning to launch Skip Micro in July of that year. They assumed that their old rival had monitored Ultra's launch in Germany and its test market in France, and decided to capture first-mover advantage in the French market.

In the weeks before the official launch, Murray obtained a package of Skip Micro and ordered an analysis of its contents. The analysis suggested that Lever had achieved the compact form by simply removing the "fillers" from the formula for regular phosphate-based Skip. Murray also concluded that Unilever's new product offered poorer performance than either regular Skip or Ariel.

When Skip Micro was launched in July, the Ultra team faced an even more troubling issue. The new product came in 2.2 kilo packages, which Lever advertising claimed were equivalent to 5 kilos of regular. To educate consumers about the compact concept, Skip's ad theme was "2.2 = 5." Equally troubling was their decision to price Micro below the 5-kilo pack of regular. This would appear to be a better value product for consumers than Ultra if the French team implemented the planned 15 percent price premium strategy. After a thorough analysis, however, P&G researchers concluded that a much larger dose of Skip Micro was required to achieve equivalent cleaning power, resulting in a cost per job even higher than that of Ultra.

From P&G's perspective, it was not clear what Lever was hoping to achieve. Lorenzo suggested that, as num-

EXHIBIT 9 Ariel Ultra France: Market Research Results

1. Early Brand Evaluation Study

French results are satisfactory and in line with those obtained in Germany and are generally higher than those obtained by Ariel Liquid 12 weeks after the start of advertising.

% of Surveyed Group	Monte Carlo (4 weeks after advert)	Ariel Ultra Saar, Germany (4 weeks after advert)	For Reference: Ariel Liquid Monte Carlo (12 weeks after advert)
Ever Used[a]	14	9	14
Ever Purchased[a]	8	6	7
Purchase Intent (regularly/occasionally)	45	52	32
Brand Awareness	64	65	57

[a]Note: Percentage of users exceeds percentage of purchasers due to sample distribution.

2. Early User Reaction Study

Run among users four weeks after their first purchase, these results evidence an excellent acceptance.

	Tele Monte-Carlo	For Perspective: Saar, Germany
Repurchase intention (% of sample)		
Would Definitely Repurchase	59	69
Would Probably Repurchase	36	24
Total	95	93
Overall Rating		
Excellent %	59	20
Very Good %	36	49
Comparison with Usual Brand (cleaning)		
Better Than Usual Brand	47	60
As Good as Usual Brand	51	32
Average Number of Scoops Per Load	1.5	1.3
Average Consumption	140 g	120 g
% Consumers Having Bought Second Pack	41	32

ber two competitor, they were simply trying to protect their detergent position in the French market. (The number three competitor in the laundry market usually did not make money.) At ETC, more complex theories emerged. Both Mancel and Meyer thought their competitor probably knew its product was inferior and speculated that Unilever's French GM simply may have wanted to induce consumers to try compact and then reject it, thereby damaging the valuable segment P&G hoped to develop. Yet another scenario suggested that Lever was buying time, using a quickly developed, lower quality product to gain first-mover advantage, but planning to upgrade the formula as quickly as possible.

How to React?

As the train pulled into Gare du Nord, Meyer and his delivery team were still trying to figure out how the rules surrounding the planned September launch had changed and what implications these changes had for Ariel Ultra's success in France and Europewide. At some point, Unilever's product would define the French consumers' perception of compact detergent, perhaps negatively. Should P&G make public their internal studies that disputed Lever's claims about Skip Micro's performance? Would that further discredit compact? Worse still, might there be a backlash against P&G?

More specifically, Meyer wondered if the team should modify its carefully planned launch strategy. Lorenzo and his local brand manager felt strongly that the plans had to be significantly changed in order to respond to the Skip Micro challenge. For example, they argued that Unilever's pre-emptive strike had effectively obsoleted Ultra's proposed positioning of its 3-kilo box as the equivalent to 5 kilos of regular. They suggested that plans for the 3-kilo box be scrapped and that a new 2-kilo box be substituted. Despite the fact that this size was not among the standard European package options, they argued that at 10 percent smaller than Skip Micro's 2.2-kilo package, the 2-kilo size would support Ultra's compact image.

Responding to a consensus that P&G should not match Unilever's "2.2 = 5" claims which they judged misleading to consumers, the French managers proposed simply dropping the equivalency claims that had been proposed for the European positioning of Ultra, substituting a more general message, *"Beaucoup de lavage—peu de lessive"* ("Lots of cleaning—little powder)". They also felt they would have to price the new 2-kilo pack significantly below that of a 5-kilo pack of regular, although, at the recommended dosage, Ultra's cost per wash would still be 10–15 percent higher. Finally, they argued that the planned environmental theme should be moved into the background, and that a more performance-based message replace it in the launch advertisements.

These were significant changes to Ultra's packaging, positioning, pricing, and promotion strategy, that Meyer and the ETC delivery team had so carefully constructed, and they were not at all convinced that such last-minute deviations from the European roll-out plans were either wise or necessary. Would this be the beginning of yet another unraveling of what looked like P&G's best chance at developing a true Eurobrand?

As his ETC lieutenants hailed a taxi for the French office, Meyer's mind turned from the complexities of the actual decisions to the subtleties of how they should be made. If there were differences in perspectives, as there seemed to be, how should they be resolved? What impact did all the recent changes in the ETC subsidiary relationships have on the roles and responsibilities of the key players?

Case 9–2

Hewlett-Packard: Global Account Management (A)

In a November 1989 interview, John Young, President and Chief Executive Officer of Hewlett-Packard, summarized the situation in the computer and electronics industry that was the mainstay of his $11. 9 billion multinational corporation by stating that, "Customers no longer want a box, they want solutions." In Young's view, the industry was moving from an era in which the product defined the solution to one in which the customer defined the solution. A pure technological focus was no longer appropriate as customers were demanding more standardization and support. In addition, industry growth was slowing in the United States, which represented just less than half of the global market for computers and electronics.

Customer relations and sound management principles had been central to Hewlett-Packard's (HP) success since 1939, but a strong emphasis on technology had moved HP toward a more product-focused approach to the business. For example, HP management decided in the mid-1970s that the company was growing too fast and falling behind despite record earnings. As a result, the company refocused on product leadership. This focus was maintained until the mid-1980s when HP's computer revenue projections were beginning to peak, and there was a growing concern over the structure and focus of the organization's profit centers. In 1984, the company began to shift to a new sales strategy focused on markets rather than product lines.

While product focus had played an important role in HP's strategy and was considered one of their strengths in delivering technology to customers, market conditions were rapidly changing, and technical excellence in itself was no longer sufficient to sustain competitive advantage. In 1989, Mr. Young initiated a campaign to get HP back to its roots and encouraged a return to a customer-

---

This case was prepared by Tammy Madsen, Ph.D. candidate, under the direction of Adjunct Professor George S. Yip at the Anderson School of Management at UCLA, as the basis for class discussion rather than to illustrate either effective or ineffective handling of an administrative situation.

focused strategy. As a result, HP began to rethink its strategic approach and to establish a balance between customer, geographic, and product-focused strategies. Challenges were particularly evident in HP's largest division, the Computer Systems Organization.

Computer Systems Organization

The Computer Systems Organization (CSO) consisted of six main groups: Systems Technology, Workstation Systems, Systems and Servers, Integrated Systems, Computer Order Fulfilment/Manufacturing, and Sales and Marketing. Products supported by the CSO included the HP9000 and HP3000 systems and servers that were designed to coexist with or serve as an alternative to mainframe computing. CSO was also responsible for the development of HP's Reduced Instruction-Set Computing (RISC) platform used with network operating systems and workstations. Other CSO responsibilities included HP's "Open View," a network and system management software that had been named one of the top 20 information products of the last 20 years by Data Communications Magazine. CSO's sales and marketing staff were responsible to the managers of each product segment, but were also responsible for the geographic sales operations.

One of the main internal challenges HP faced was shifting the sales force from a product focus to a customer focus. HP's sales activities were structured on geographic lines, with sales performance measures being based on product quotas. The organization structure and sales practices created barriers between sales regions and geographies, and limited development of new business and alternative sales channels. Sales and account managers' performance evaluation was based on product quotas within a specific geographic region, so that they had no incentive to develop business outside their geographic boundaries even if it would benefit HP or the customer. Regional boundaries also created barriers to coordination as managers in different regions had no incentive to cooperate or coordinate activities. Performance was driven by product quotas and not by accounts. This also limited development of new business opportunities and alternative channels of distribution. As third-party channels were beginning to play a large role in the industry, HP wanted to establish the appropriate strategy to maximize the opportunities presented by alternative channels and to capture this channel business.

One CSO executive, Greg Mihran, Manager, Industry Marketing, and a 14-year HP veteran, summarized HP's position as follows:

> "HP has a long history of success with a product-oriented, country-based sales and support organization. While considerable progress has been made during the past two years toward an account focus, ongoing efforts to adjust the balance between account and geographic strategies continued. It seemed evident, however, that the right answer was somewhere in between these two extremes. Both strategies must coexist to ensure success and respond to the complex mix of country and global account priorities."

Franz Nawratil, Vice President and Manager, CSO Worldwide Marketing and Sales, also identified the need for a more global approach to the business. In 1990, Mr. Nawratil, with the support of several sales and account managers, developed a proposal to restructure HP's sales activities to support the needs of the changing global market. The proposal focused on the establishment of a global account management program, and emphasized balancing geographic and global forces. In mid-1990, Mr. Nawratil was working to gain the support of upper management in order to initiate the program.

Hewlett-Packard: Company Background

HP was incorporated in 1947 as successor to a partnership formed in 1939 to design, manufacture, and service electronic products and systems for measurements and computation. The company was committed to a set of core values: leadership in technology, quality, and customer service, financial stability, and uncompromising integrity in all business dealings. HP sold nearly all of its products to businesses, research institutes, and educational and healthcare institutions, and was one of the United States' largest exporters. HP's basic business purpose was to provide the capabilities and support needed to help customers worldwide improve their personal and business effectiveness. The company employed over 92,000 people in 1990 and operated product divisions in 53 cities and 19 countries, had over 600 sales and support offices in 110 countries, and generated revenues of $13.2 billion. Net revenue grew by 11 percent in 1990, following a 21 percent increase in 1989. That year, HP experienced a slower net revenue growth in most of its product areas and declines in operating profit and net earnings when compared to those reported in 1989 (see Exhibit 1).

HP was organized into five strategic industry segments (see Exhibit 2): Computer Systems, Computer Products, Test and Measurement, Measurement Systems, and Component Products. A sixth segment focused on Geographic Operations, which encompassed three main worldwide sectors: Europe, Asia Pacific, and the Americas.

EXHIBIT 1 **Consolidated Balance Sheet**
(In millions, except share amounts)

	For the years ended October 31		
	1990	1989	1988
Net Revenue:			
Equipment	$10,214	$ 9,404	$7,709
Services	3,019	2,495	2,122
	13,233	11,899	9,831
Costs and Expenses:			
Cost of Equipment Sold	5,072	4,513	3,494
Cost of Services	1,921	1,578	1,338
Research and Development	1,367	1,269	1,056
Selling, General, and Administrative	3,711	3,327	2,859
	12,071	10,687	8,747
Earnings from Operations	1,162	1,212	1,084
Interest Income and Other Income (expense)	66	65	135
Interest Expense	172	126	77
Earnings before Taxes	1,056	1,151	1,142
Provision for Taxes	317	322	326
Net Earnings	**$ 739**	**$ 829**	**$ 816**
Net Earnings Per Share	$ 3.06	$ 3.52	$ 3.36

Several groups or divisions existed within each segment, as was the case with the Computer Systems Organization. The CSO was HP's largest division, and the Global Account Management Program was proposed for implementation in this segment (see the Appendix for a description of these industry segments).

Product focus and technical excellence had played a dominant role in HP's strategy throughout the 1970s and early 1980s. By 1985, HP's contacts with customers consisted primarily of engineers talking to engineers. But during the latter half of the 1980s, chief executives, financial officers, and marketing directors became increasingly involved in purchasing decisions, resulting in the need for more "business-to-business" marketing. As a result, HP launched a new integrated advertising campaign that positioned HP as the company always looking to solve problems. This approach was very successful and opened new computer business channels, some of which management had not been aware.

Industry Trends

By 1990, HP was still battling with attaining a balance between a product focus and a customer focus. Furthermore, HP had to wrestle with ambiguity in its dealing with competitors—the company needed to be competitive at the customer level but cooperative at the standards level. In addition to the market demand for standardization, four product trends that shaped the 1980s came to dominate the industry: (1) RISC technology, which enabled parallel processing and allowed the user to perform software functions with fewer instructions than with non-RISC based technologies; (2) open systems management platforms, which were software systems that allowed multiple applications to be integrated on a single distributed system and to share various facilities; (3) network computing, which allowed the user to hook multiple computers to a single network in conjunction with a network server, allowing individual work stations to use common software and data; and (4) Unix operating systems, more powerful and flexible than DOS, for personal, mini, and main frame computers. Strategically, HP had positioned itself to benefit from these major industry trends.

In addition, in 1990 the industry was moving away from a geographic focus to more of a customer focus with an emphasis on global strategy. As customers demanded more standardization, hardware producers were being driven into complex and occasionally secret alliances. For example, AT&T, creator and owner of the Unix operating system, teamed up with Sun Microsystems to promote its

EXHIBIT 2 Hewlett-Packard Organization Structure, 1990

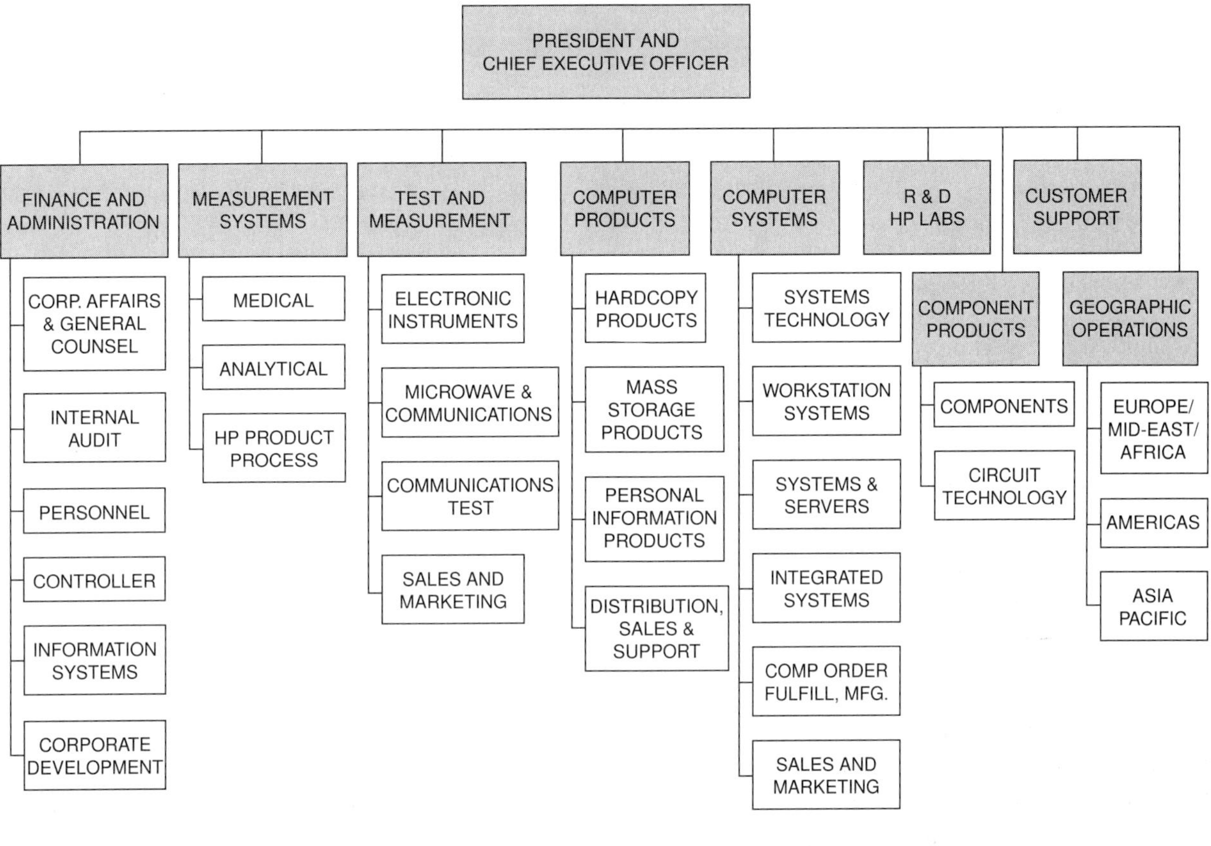

standard. On the other side of the fence, IBM, Digital Equipment, and a few others were trying to promote another version of Unix, possibly the one used by Steve Jobs, Apple Computer's founder, in his new workstation. These two groups then began to discuss working together on a common version of the operating system.

Customers also wanted to work with vendors that provided consistent service and support across geographic regions and industries. Multinational customers demanded that vendors be strategic partners who could demonstrate an understanding of specific international needs and deploy solutions to these needs on a global basis. HP executives increasingly saw the need for "one platform common across vendors and across many industries." While competitors appeared to be interested in taking a more global approach to the business, one of HP's senior executives indicated that ". . . the industry looked at 'global' as a buzzword." Many at HP, nonetheless, saw the need to integrate the current geographic approach with a global strategy.

Alternative sales channels such as dealers, two-tier suppliers, systems integrators, or resellers had become prevalent throughout the industry. Thus, companies needed to identify strategies that would maximize these alternative channels and the opportunities presented by them. In HP's case, the organization needed to couple industry/customer focus with an all-channel strategy as well as develop ways to measure and develop alternative channels.

Furthermore, organizations throughout the industry were involved in different forms of cost reduction independent of the shift in customer needs and demands. HP, for example, had been reducing headcount through attrition and early retirement packages since late 1988.

HP maintained manufacturing plants, research and development facilities, warehouses, and administrative offices in the United States, Canada, West Germany, France, Spain, Italy, Switzerland, The Netherlands, Australia, Singapore, China, Japan, Hong Kong, Malaysia, Mexico, and Brazil. HP had a strong market presence in Europe with net revenue from European operations equal to approximately five billion dollars. HP's market participation was weaker in Latin America but strong in Asia. The geographic distribution of HP's orders was 46 percent in North America, 35 percent in Europe, and 19 percent Asia Pacific, which included Latin America.

Account Management Program

HP's account and sales management program in 1990 was product focused and organized on geographic lines, and supported approximately one thousand accounts worldwide. Under this structure, sales responsibility did not extend beyond geographic boundaries and, according to one executive, the amount of business tended to shift up and down from year to year.

The organization structure consisted of four levels. First, there were field operations managers for each of the three worldwide sectors: Europe, Asia Pacific, and the Americas. Second, each sector was divided by countries and/or regions, and managers were identified for each country or region. The number of country/region managers was a function of country size and business. For example, the United States was divided into four regions: west, south, mid-west, and east. Each country or region manager reported to a field operations manager. Third, the regions or countries, depending on size, were further divided into areas, with area sales managers reporting to the country or region manager. Fourth, district sales and account managers reported to the area sales managers. Just as area sales manager responsibility did not extend beyond the area geographic lines, district manager responsibility did not extend beyond district lines. District managers were designated as the major account managers for the largest accounts in their districts, but were also responsible for the entire geographic area. In addition, there were approximately eight sales representatives per district manager. Minimal interaction occurred between regions and districts, and there were no mechanisms in the system to encourage interaction across areas, districts, or regions.

In addition to the field operations sales and account structure, headquarters account managers were located at corporate headquarters. Headquarters account managers reported to the product divisions while the rest of the sales staff reported to the geographic operations. Account managers utilized these contacts to gather information and determine if HP had sufficient resources to support their customers. One of the executives interviewed indicated that since the headquarters account managers reported directly to the different product divisions, they did not always act in the interests of the district or region managers. As a result, many of the geographic sales managers were not sure if they could trust or would benefit from the use of a headquarters account manager.

Performance Measures and New Accounts

Under the geographic structure, performance measures were based on product quotas. Managers focused on meeting product line targets within their designated region, area, or district. For many years HP had set sales quotas and tracked performance by product lines solely within geographic boundaries. This was an important metric to quantify product performance, but lacked clear differentiation of account quotas and expenses. Expenses and account quotas were reported and managed together within all other product quotas and costs in each country and region. As a result, within the product focus structure, it was difficult to differentiate individual account performance at any level, and there was a lack of a complete measure of global account performance. In 1990, when HP began to shift to more customer focus, one senior executive indicated that it was very difficult to get the sales team to shift to an account orientation while they still were required to satisfy product line targets.

These metrics did not facilitate the development of new accounts outside regional boundaries. Area and district managers had no incentive to provide information to other district or area sales managers regarding new account development, as their primary focus was meeting product quotas within their own designated region or district. In many ways, different regions, areas, and districts competed with each other. Ken Fairbanks, a District Sales Manager, indicated that if managers wanted to help develop business for a customer in another region, the manager was forced to use a "tin cup approach." For example, if an account manager for the U.S. Northwest region needed to coordinate activities for his customer in another region in the United States, he or she had to provide an incentive to the account manager in the other region if they wanted any assistance. Mr. Fairbanks indicated that he would have to "beg" for support if he had to approach managers in other regions. Managers often spent considerable amounts of time trying to convince managers in other regions of the benefits that would result from their support. Given the lack of incentives for managers in different regions to coordinate activities, new account development was not properly pursued, and product sales fluctuated from year to year as a result.

Concerns and Opportunities

Account managers identified this lack of synergy between regions as a major limitation to developing new business and to achieving a shift to greater customer focus. They argued that a system was needed that would integrate the current geographic approach with a more global customer focus. In addition, HP needed to maximize opportunities presented by alternative channels. This would also entail defining ways to measure these alternative channels.

Second, a quota system that integrated an account focus measure was necessary. As long as sales managers and representatives were measured on product line targets only, without a link to specific accounts or complete global measures, they would lack the incentive to shift to a customer orientation.

Third, district or local account managers tended not to utilize headquarters account managers for the reasons given earlier. Region, area, and district account managers needed headquarters staff who had incentives to assist the account manager in all sales activities—and not just in the product lines they represented, provide accurate information from headquarters, and represent the account manager's interests at headquarters.

Finally, a formalization of the account executives' roles was needed. Liaisons with key executives had been established on an informal basis and institutional formalization of these linkages would facilitate service and support efforts for the major accounts.

The Global Account Program Proposal

In 1990, Franz Nawratil put together a steering committee composed of several account managers to initiate the development of a global account-focused strategy proposal. The mission of the committee was to develop a global account-management approach that provided direct customer support for key global accounts. The proposal focused around five fundamental strategies as summarized by Mr. Mihran, one of the committee's members:

1. Establish and communicate clear, high-level business objectives for the program.
2. Refine the structure of the worldwide sales organization to match the requirements of multinational customers.
3. Select the right set of global accounts within strategic industries.
4. Empower and reward the best possible global account managers.
5. Capture and track all performance variables within the program.

Another goal of the proposal was to address the issue of the balance needed between customer and geographic strategies. In addition, Mr. Nawratil wanted to integrate an all-channels development and measurement strategy within the global account proposal. Global accounts would be treated as a separate market or channel of distribution. This channel would be considered in conjunction with several other channels when setting overall profitability targets for HP's computer business. One executive interviewed indicated that the global account program vision was to, "establish a long-term, strategic partnership with a select group of industry-leading customers through the successful deployment of cooperative computing systems on a worldwide basis."

The proposed objectives of the program were intended to ensure that all its elements were "win-win for all concerned, to be one company to the customer throughout the world, to establish clear ownership and accountability within HP, and to develop and manage the Global Account as a unique business." In addition to the five strategies summarized by Mr. Mihran, the proposal targeted three critical factors:

1. Capture global market share in strategic industries by increasing HP revenues faster than all other competitors.
2. Achieve the highest possible ranking of customer satisfaction within HP's target marketplace.
3. Operate effectively within the current culture of HP to attract and retain the best possible personnel on a worldwide basis.

Organization Structure

The proposal entailed modifications to the existing organization structure and would create a new position, the Global Account Manager (GAM), located at the same level as the area sales manager. GAMs would be responsible for directly managing HP's relationship with the global account, including:

1. Responsibility for worldwide customer sales and support.
2. Assure that HP was perceived as one company at all customer sites.
3. Accountability for worldwide customer satisfaction.
4. Act as the HP business manager for the global account.
5. Work with the appropriate senior management to ensure HP was properly organized and resourced to service the opportunities identified in the global account.
6. Establish a close working rapport with the assigned executives, both primary and supporting, and communicate account status when appropriate.

According to the proposal, GAMs would report to the country/region and industry managers, but also to a field operations global accounts sales manager (GASM), who would be responsible for all global accounts business within that field operation. The global accounts sales manager for the field operation would report to the field operations manager and to the head of the global accounts program. This dual reporting structure was seen as critical to the overall success of the program. Although GAMs should be measured on the worldwide performance of a single account, the country managers would continue to be measured on the total performance of a single geography. Thus, while GAMs would be empowered to make decisions independent of geography, they would also be responsible for making appropriate business decisions given the environmental and competitive conditions in each country or region. In addition, GAMs would be required to reside in the country where the global account was headquartered.

The committee also proposed that the global account headquarters staff should report directly to the GAM, while district sales managers and sales representatives should have dual reporting to the GAM and their local area sales manager. The proposal suggested that such a dual reporting relationship would provide the GAM with the solid-line authority required to manage account decisions effectively, but also would reinforce geographic responsibilities for the sales force. See Exhibit 3 for the proposed organization structure.

In order to empower managers and assure the appropriate vision, global account managers would be responsible for the growth and health of the entire program including all sales and expense metrics. Global account managers would set revenue and cost targets, and these targets would be reviewed at an annual quota-setting meeting. Once the targets were agreed upon, individual account targets would be set for each geography such that the collective sum of these targets would support the total program objectives. This would allow the GAMs to pursue some accounts at more aggressive cost levels in order to fund investment in others. This flexibility was essential to the program since it allowed success in one global account to directly support another.

Executive Roles and Responsibilities

Headquarters account managers (HAMs). The committee also redefined the headquarters account management program. The proposal stated that the mission of the headquarters account management program should be to "champion the critical needs and significant opportunities of the global account within HP headquarters and to establish HP as a strategic vendor of Cooperative Computing Systems through long-term sales growth and customer satisfaction." HAMs would be field-funded by GAMs and would dual report to the GAM and the CSO product division headquarters. In this way, HAMs could assume global responsibility and ownership. The proposal indicated that each HAM would also be responsible for global account development, issue resolution and customer satisfaction, strategic deal ownership and management, and sales and marketing goal congruence. The proposal also emphasized that HAMs should provide a focused channel for product divisions, a strategic partner for account assigned executives (see below), be advocates for the customer at HP headquarters, and the main representatives for the global account manager. The proposed structure would empower the HAMS with the authority and tools needed to accomplish these objectives.

Account assigned executives (AAEs). The GAM proposal also included provision for account assigned executives (AAEs). District sales managers and area sales managers had often established alliances with headquarters executives to assist in account development efforts and to ensure HP had the resources to support opportunities identified in a particular account or product line. The GAM proposal attempted to formalize this tradition into the structure by defining two types of AAEs: those "permanently assigned" to an account, and those "focused assigned" for a limited period of time and specific purpose. According to the proposal, the purpose of the AAE was to "define and encourage the active involve-

EXHIBIT 3 Proposed Sales Organization Structure—GAM Program

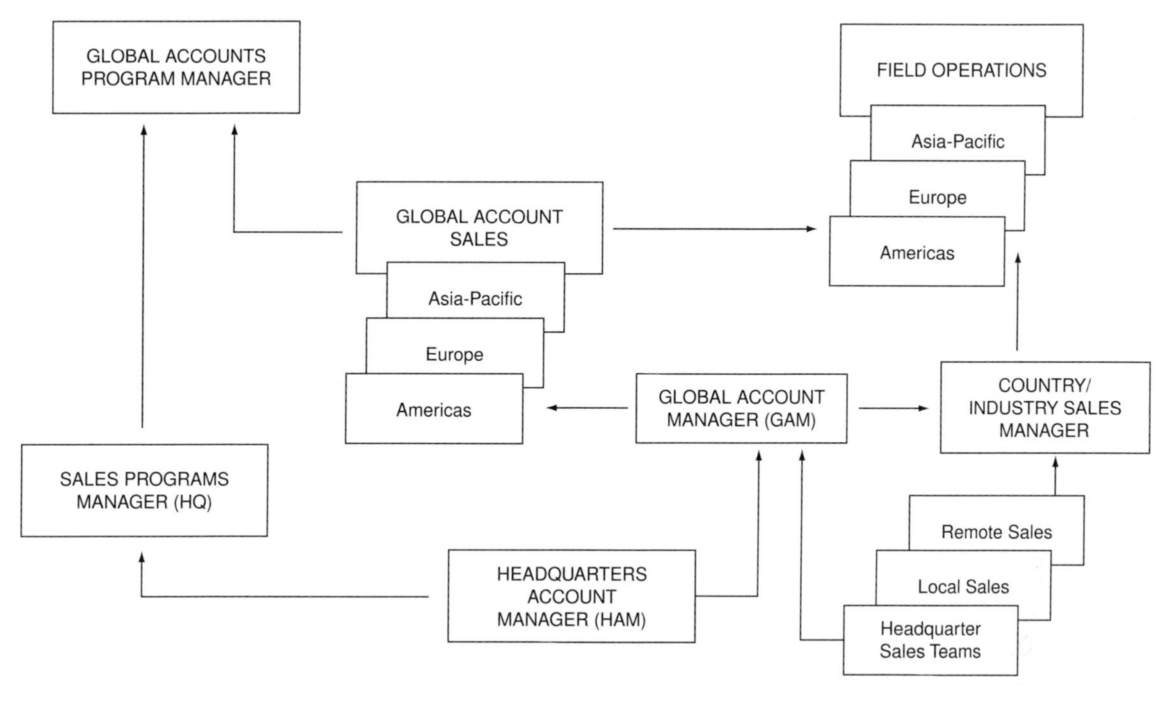

ment of key HP executives in current or target major accounts that are considered crucial to HP's long-term success within selected strategic industries." The goals of the AAEs would be to establish HP as a strategic supplier to the target, and to ensure sales growth and customer satisfaction. The proposal defined the responsibilities of the AAEs as follows:

1. Foster personal rapport with key customer executives.
2. Develop and champion HP sales opportunities.
3. Top-down issue resolution for the sales process.
4. Participation in account planning and review meetings.
5. Mentor and coach the HP account manager and sales team.

The selection of AAEs would be based on strategic responsibility or expertise, organizational position and influence, and individual personality and style. The intent of the proposal was to match the needs of key customer executives and customer business culture, with the appropriate HP account managers and sales teams. Exhibit 4 describes the AAE process. The proposal identified two types of *permanently assigned executives:* primary and supporting. Primary executives would be the highest level HP executives involved with an account and would take the lead in most HP executive activities. The supporting executive's main role would be to help the primary executive when the needs of an account required additional focused management expertise or interface.

The *focused account executive* was defined as an HP executive assigned to an account for a limited period of time. There were three types of focused account executives identified: deal executive, technology executive, and functional executive. The deal executive would be associated with an account during the life of a big deal. Deal executives would be involved with all aspects of a deal and would be selected based upon a technology or functional linkage. The technology executive would be primarily associated with an account that required a strong understanding of specific HP strategy, products, or technology. Last, the functional executive's main role would involve association with an account that required strong functional understanding of how HP does business in terms of finance, manufacturing, human resources, or communications. An issue for the entire AAE concept was what levels of executives should be

EXHIBIT 4 Proposed AAE Process

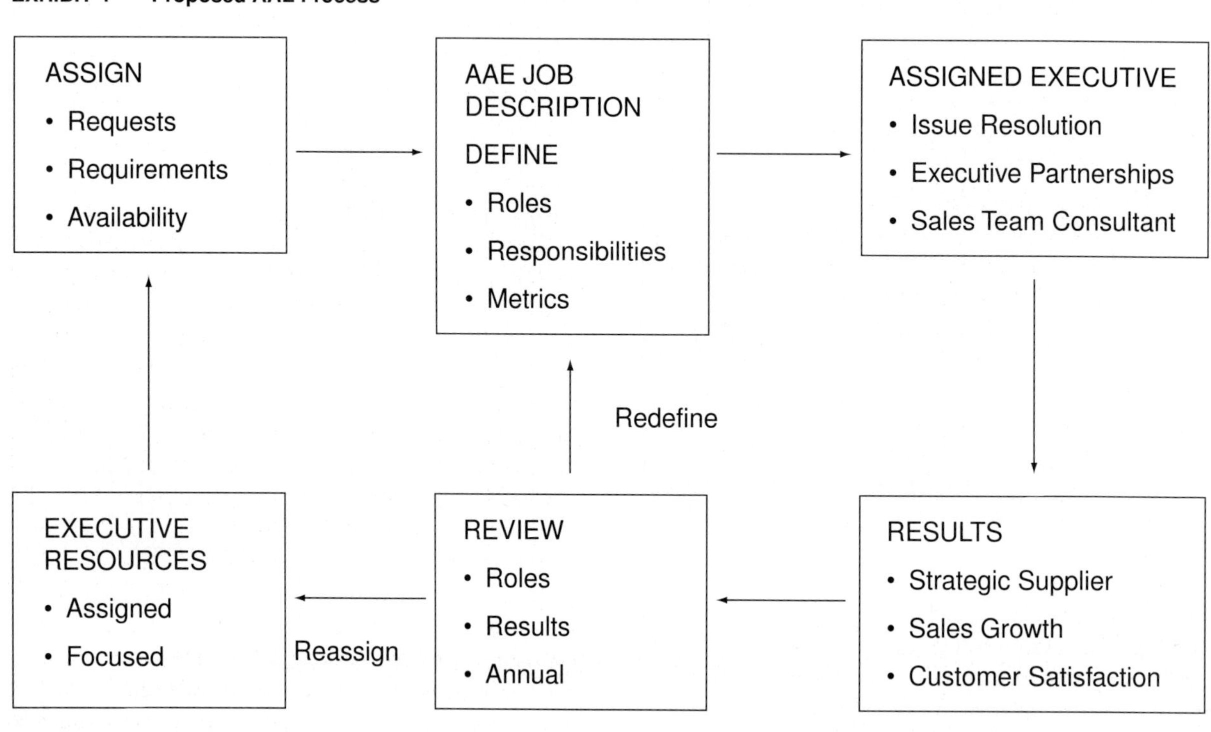

selected for the different roles. For instance, should HP's CEO, John Young, take on an AAE role and, if so, under what circumstances?

Identifying Global Accounts

The proposal also addressed the issue of how to identify the global accounts. The proposal specified that global accounts should be selected based on specific industries where HP could be the most successful over the long-term. Critical dimensions of account selection involved the analysis of several parameters including long range projections of industry segment performance, evolving business conditions and needs within those segments, and HP's ability to deliver solutions for those business problems. Additional selection criteria could include:

1. The Global Account (GA) customer understood what was required for competitive advantage.
2. The GA customer had a serious open systems client/server commitment to HP.
3. The GA customer demands were consistent with worldwide sales and support programs.
4. The GA customer was seeking working relationships with HP executives.
5. Annual HP computers sales plus service revenue > \$10 million for the global account.
6. The GA customer had significant computer sales across two or three HP fields.
7. HP had the opportunity to develop a defensible position as a strategic supplier.
8. A committed assigned executive was in place or being recruited.
9. The account was in a global strategic industry segment.

The GAM proposal emphasized that the program should also provide specific customer benefits for the designated account, such as: (1) HP premier status; (2) a consistent worldwide approach from HP; (3) access to key HP executive and resources; (4) the ability to influence HP strategy and direction; and (5) mutual account planning and implementation.

Performance Measures/Quota System

One of the key issues of the global account management proposal involved how to measure performance in global accounts. The committee believed it essential to have a worldwide measurement system with metrics that could be obtained easily and measured by the GAM. In addition, many account managers emphasized the need to restructure the quota system to reflect the shift to a global customer focus. Thus, a management quota integrating an account focus with geographic dimensions would be essential. Such a management quota system would also have to provide incentives to the Global Account Managers to sustain as well as expand customer liaisons.

The proposed quota system included an all-channels measurement model for global accounts. The GAMS performance ratings would be based on an all-channels strategy that included all goods sold in (direct and indirect) and all goods sold out. Direct goods involved goods for which customers paid HP directly. Indirect goods involved goods sold through third parties such as distributors, dealers, systems integrators, or two-tier suppliers.

The proposal identified two additional metrics that also seemed critical to the success of the program: (1) the selling cost envelope (SCE) and (2) the account-specific field selling cost mode (FSC). The FSC concept involved identifying costs associated with worldwide implementation of the global account sales team and supporting programs. Field selling costs included the following:

1. Sales representative cost module by country: worldwide average sales representative cost was estimated at $400,000.
2. Customer support staff: support staff costs would average about $200,000.
3. Global Account Manager and Headquarters Account Manager: the average cost for a HAM was approximately $200,000. For example, a sales representative in Los Angeles may cost approximately $450,000, while the cost of a sales representative in India was approximately $80,000.
4. Additional consulting, program, telesales, and administrative personnel.
5. Special porting or customer project expenses.
6. Additional expenses such as sales meetings and travel.

Costs for items four through six above would depend on scope and needs of each account as well as location. The proposal indicated that GAMs would be responsible for identifying these costs and the level of support required for a global account. GAMS would also define the SCE.

The SCE measured all the selling costs associated with obtaining a list order. Based on previous account and product performance, HP estimated that the SCE would be equal to 45 percent of the total list price. This measure would fit for a collective of global accounts as well as for individual accounts. One executive indicated that some accounts might run higher while others might run lower. The 45 percent was based on previous business performance, and HP felt strongly that accounts should be able to meet or beat this proxy measure. Together the FSC and SCE would enable HP to identify costs at the account level as opposed to just the industry level. The proposal indicated that the goal of these metrics was to understand the full costs associated with implementing the Global Account Program for any major account.

The committee indicated that identification of the FSC and SCE would enable HP to determine if an account merited the use of a full-time GAM or half-time GAM. In addition, GAMs would be responsible for identifying the level of support needed for an account, such as the appropriate sales staff level. This included determining whether the account could afford a full-time HAM or half-time HAM. The intent of the proposal was to develop a program that allowed global account sales quotas and expense targets to be compiled by country and held separately within that country so that quotas or expenses were less likely to move in or out of the global accounts channel to other channels.

The Quota System

GAMs would be responsible for setting an overall sales objective for the upcoming year through detailed analyses of account quotas by country and, in turn, country quotas by product line. GAMS would also be responsible for developing, in conjunction with the country manager, global account management quotas, SCE, resource and channels plans on a yearly basis. The proposal indicated that once these quotas were established, the GAMs would be required to identify the level of sales and support personnel needed to achieve them. In order to ensure that the process provided a profitable investment for HP, GAMs would be required to meet a specific objective that tracked worldwide FSCs and discount expenses. Mr. Mihran gave an example of how this might work:

> "For example, let's say that a global account's worldwide sales quota is projected to be $100 million list price, and

> that the GAM is targeted to spend only $40 million to achieve that goal. If average worldwide discount for the account is calculated to be 20 percent, then $20 million is left to invest in resources and program expenses. This process allows the GAM to make important investment decisions around the world independent of local implications. Each sales representative may, therefore, be managed to a quota loading best suited for the specific sales situation in that country."

In addition, global account quotas and quotas for non-global accounts would be combined to form the country and industry quotas. Country and industry managers could keep the global quotas and funding separate from their other accounts. Resource allocations within each country or industry would be reviewed every quarter. If allocations were not at the appropriate levels, or if additional allocations were necessary, then the GAMs were to adjust the allocations.

The Situation in the Fall of 1990

With the proposal in hand, Mr. Nawratil was seeking support from upper management to initiate a global account management pilot program. In October 1990, Mr. Nawratil met with Mr. Lew Platt, Vice President and General Manager, CSO, to discuss the proposal and request his support. Mr. Nawratil and Mr. Platt wondered what the major internal and external challenges would be. HP definitely needed something to improve its global presence, enhance its account development, improve alternative channels development, and encourage cooperation and value-added activity across geographic areas.

APPENDIX: DESCRIPTION OF INDUSTRY SEGMENTS

Computer Products

The Computer Products Organization (CPO) was composed of four main groups: Hardcopy Products, Mass Storage Products, Personal Information Products, and Distribution, Sales and Marketing. Products supported by CPO included the HP Deskjet 500 Printer for PCs and Macintosh Computers. This particular printer was one of HP's top selling products. More than 90 percent of CPO's sales were through alternative channels (resellers), and HP was focused on maximizing opportunities in key resale segments such as high-volume retail outlets as well as more specialized, high-value-added resellers. The distribution, sales, and marketing staff were responsible to the product segment, but they were also tied to geographic operations.

Test and Measurement Group

HP's Test and Measurement Group was composed of four main subgroups: Electronic Instruments, Microwave and Communications, Communications and Test, and Sales and Marketing. The primary focus of this group was on the development of test and measurement equipment used in the design of high speed electronic products such as modular oscilloscopes. The group also developed equipment for the fast growing optical communications market as well as products that telecommunications manufacturers used to vary their transmission equipment.

Measurement Systems

The Measurement Systems Organization consisted of three groups: Medical, Analytical, and HP Product Processes. HP's Medical Group designed and developed several measurement systems for medical applications such as small, low cost fetal monitors, defibrillators, and central station monitors that provide patient information from bedsides to a central location. The Analytical Products Group designed analytical instruments and systems for use in research and development, quality control, and analytical service laboratories.

Component Products

The Component Products Groups was organized around two main groups: Components and Circuit Technology. The Components Products Group developed products such as a silicon chip set that enables users to move information among workstations, mainframes, and supercomputers at greater speed than previous products.

UNIT 10 Managing the Global Finance Functions and Risks

Case 10-1

China Southern Airlines

Concomitant with the rapid growth of the Asian economies has been the dramatic expansion of the area's aviation industry. Just as Asia's new industrialisation has increased the demand for cargo capacity and business class travel, the parallel development of a large middle class has led to the emergence of a segment of the population who can afford to travel solely for leisure. The continuation of these pressures, coupled with the easing of travel constraints in previously restricted countries, will serve to drive demand growth beyond the turn of the century. According to IATA[1] forecasts, India, China, Indonesia, and Vietnam are likely to see the greatest increase in the demand for airline services. For the region as a whole, the 10.1 percent growth seen in the last decade is expected to slow to a still quite extraordinary 7.4 percent between now and 2010.[2]

This explosive demand has created both opportunities and problems for the region's carriers. The Asian aviation industry is somewhat unique in that major airline hubs are in close proximity, and a large number of various-sized airlines share the market. Competition has served to keep prices in check while putting pressure on carriers to maintain high levels of service and quality. The fact that most Asian airlines are either wholly or partially publicly owned has, in some cases, constrained their ability to get the necessary funding for the upgrading of facilities and purchasing of new planes. On the other hand, the apparently boundless potential of the market, the increasingly liberal attitude of Asian governments to privatisation, and the willingness for Asian and Western fund managers to put funds into investment opportunities in Asia, present many opportunities for companies seeking investment funds.

The China Southern Airline's IPO

China Southern Airlines (CSA) is one of the six government owned airlines currently operating in China. One of the largest of the Chinese airlines (in terms of passengers, routes, flights, etc.), it is the dominant domestic carrier in southern China. The economic reforms begun by the late Chinese leader Deng Xiaoping led to substantial changes within the company, as it attempted to quickly modernise its planes and management structure and procedures. The removal of government funding made the partial privatisation of the company inevitable.

The first foreign investment into China's aviation industry occurred when American Aviation Investment Company purchased 25 percent of China Hainan Airlines paving the way for additional foreign investment. The successful IPO[3] of China Eastern Airlines in February 1997, along with a host of other Chinese infrastructure firms during the past two years, gave CSA's senior management a great deal of hope that their public listing, planned for July 1997, would be a resounding success.

As in the case of China Eastern, CSA planned to offer shares simultaneously on the Hong Kong and New York stock exchanges. For the company's management and workers, the listing represented far more than an infusion of much needed cash. It served as international recognition of the success of the modernisation work done by the company to date, as well as a vote of confidence in the Chinese economy, in general, and the future of CSA, in particular.

In late April 1997, with less than three months to go before the listing of CSA shares, Mr. Li Yong Zhen, the Company Secretary and Director of Investor Relations,

This case was written by Professor Timothy Devinney and Kris Vogelsong, MBA, as a basis for class discussion and not for the purpose of illustrating either the good or bad handling of a specific management situation. Some facts from the actual situation have been altered.

[1]International Air Transport Association.

[2]IATA, *Asia Pacific Air Transport Forecast 1980–2010*, January 1997.

[3]Initial Public Offering.

and Mr. Yu Yan En, the Chairman of CSA, prepared for the final series of presentations and meetings with potential investors. Although interest in Chinese IPOs has been strong, and the news of reactions to CSA's floatation quite positive, everyone knew that this final foray would be make or break for CSA's prospects of securing major investments from the unit trust and mutual fund managers of Europe and America's major investment houses.

The Evolution of the Chinese Aviation Industry

Following the Revolution in 1949, the commercial aviation industry in China became the sole possession of the Civil Aviation Administration of China (CAAC), an arm of the central government in Beijing. The CAAC owned or leased all commercial aircraft operating in China. It operated all civil, cargo, and mail service flights and was responsible for the administration of all the airports and the air traffic control system throughout the country.

Before the initiation of economic reforms in 1978, the demand for CAAC services was very low with few prospects for growth. In 1978 the total CAAC fleet consisted of only 98 aircraft operating on 162 routes and serving 2.3 million passengers. As a basis of comparison, 275 million passengers flew in the United States during 1978.[4]

The 1980s saw the beginning of a long overdue reorganisation of the Chinese aviation industry. Through a series of reforms in the early 1980s, the industry was split into six administrative bodies based roughly along geographic lines. However, the Chinese aviation system still remained under the complete control of the CAAC.

The performance of each of these administrative bodies was evaluated individually in an attempt to encourage operating efficiency and profitability. By 1985 the number of airline passengers flying on Chinese airlines reached 7.5 million (see Exhibit 1). Despite these efforts, service on Chinese airlines remained pitiful throughout the decade. In a 1988 survey rating airline service quality CAAC services were ranked 46th of the 46 airlines analysed.[5] In belated recognition of the general poor service being meted out by China's airlines, the CAAC launched an initiative in 1993 aimed at improving the service of Chinese airlines. Among the many service aspects to be addressed were luggage handling, on-time arrivals and departures, ticketing services, and fare refunds.

EXHIBIT 1 Airline Volumes in China (1980–1996)

Year	Passengers Carried (millions)	Cargo and Mail Carried (000 tonnes)	Total Traffic (billions of tonne kilometres)
1980	3.4	89	0.4
1985	7.5	195	1.3
1990	16.6	370	2.5
1991	21.8	452	3.2
1992	28.9	575	4.3
1993	33.8	694	5.1
1994	40.4	829	5.8
1995	51.2	1,011	7.1
1996	55.6	1,150	8.1

Source: CAAC.

During the early 1990s, the CAAC gradually turned over the management of the majority of the industry to the six regional administrative bureaux, effectively creating six major Chinese airlines. Each of the former administrative bodies was given management independence with the CAAC acting as a national regulatory body.

Air China was formed from the Beijing bureau and was designated the Chinese "flagship carrier." As such, it received the most lucrative and the largest number of international routes. Routes were also allocated to China Southern, China Southwest, China Northern, China Northwest, and China Eastern, based approximately on geographic lines. Each airline was subsequently granted certain international destinations, and all were authorised to fly from their Chinese hub cities to Hong Kong. The distribution of passengers by airline is presented in Exhibit 2.

In the last decade, the aviation industry grew even more rapidly than the Chinese economy in general (see Exhibit 3 for some general statistics on China). By 1996, 142 commercial airports were servicing 55.6 million passengers (an almost 100 percent increase from the 28.9 million passengers flown in 1992). On average, one Chinese person in twenty-four flew in an aeroplane during 1995. This growth is even more startling when one considers the fact that, as is the case in developed countries, air travel in China is generally more expensive than other forms of transport.

[4] *Statistical Abstract of the United States*, Washington DC: GPO, 1979, p. 654.

[5] http://www.chinanews.org/ChinaToday/

What makes the Chinese transport market unique is the very poor level of infrastructure supporting the other transportation options. Passenger trains provide the only real alternative to air transport and, although they are inexpensive, they are generally crowded and slow. For example, a train ride from Guangzhou to Beijing typically takes 34 hours as compared to 3 hours by plane. The cost of a one-way economy class airline ticket is approximately RMB 1,500 while a rail ticket in a sleeper cabin costs between RMB 512 and RMB 973.

According to CAAC plans, China will begin an era of intense air travel infrastructure construction. In total, the CAAC blueprint calls for another 41 airports to be built in provincial capitals and major coastal towns by the year 2000. Between 2000 and 2005 new airports are on the books for Guangzhou, Zhuhai, and Shenzhen. Current expansion of the airport at Beijing will increase capacity to 35 million passengers annually while Shanghai's new international airport will be able to handle 20 million passengers per year.

EXHIBIT 2 Aircraft and Passengers of Major Chinese Airlines (1996)

	Aircraft	Passengers Carried (millions)
Air China	47	6.68
China Southern	73	15.21
China Eastern	38	6.50
China Southwest	26	5.65
China Northern	28	4.88
China Northwest	19	3.08

Sources: CAAC, http://www.intercpt.demon.co.uk/fleets.html.

The growth of the commercial aviation industry in China is almost solely attributable to the growth of the Chinese economy and increasing personal income. This growth has resulted in an increased demand for business travel as well as a boom in leisure travel both within China and to and from China. Four factors are recognised as driving the increased demand for aviation services in China:

- A relaxation of restrictions on overseas travel by Chinese nationals.
- Increased travel to China by overseas Chinese (especially from Taiwan, Singapore, the USA, Canada, and Australia).
- Increased business and tourism demand from overseas nationals.
- A gradual shift within China from other forms of travel to air travel.

The role of tourism in the expansion of Chinese aviation will increase in the coming decades. Estimates for tourism into China indicate that by the year 2020 annual tourism could exceed 140 million visitors.

EXHIBIT 3 Economic Indicators for China (1981–1996)

	Average 1981–91	1990	1991	1992	1993	1994	1995	1996
Population (billions)	1.09	1.14	1.16	1.17	1.19	1.20	1.21	1.22
Population Growth (percent)	1.5	1.4	1.3	1.2	1.2	1.1	1.1	1.0
GDP Per Capita (RMB)	1,152	1,622	1,867	2,273	2,912	3,755	4,810	5,569
GDP Growth (percent)	NA	3.8	9.2	14.2	13.5	11.8	10.2	9.7
Industrial Output Growth (percent)	12.8	5.2	12.8	24.7	27.3	24.2	20.3	14.5
Retail Sales Growth (percent)	7.5	2.5	13.2	16.5	27.4	31.1	28.3	19.4
Consumer Price Growth (percent)	NA	3.1	3.4	6.4	14.7	24.1	17.1	8.3
Export Growth (nominal, percent)	13.4	18.2	15.8	18.2	8.0	31.9	22.9	1.5
Import Growth (nominal, percent)	11.1	−9.8	19.6	28.3	19.0	11.3	14.2	5.1
Exchange Rate (RMB/$US)	4.8	4.8	5.3	5.5	5.8	8.6	8.4	8.3

Source: International Monetary Fund, *International Financial Statistics*, various years. Department of Foreign Affairs & Trade, Commonwealth of Australia, *Country Economic Brief*, China—August 1997, China—August 1993. All growth rates are real unless otherwise indicated.

Despite the modernisation of the Chinese aviation industry, concerns still abound about the general calibre of aircraft maintenance, the skill and training of pilots and flight crews, and the quality of the air traffic control system. For example, between 1953 and 1978, 62 accidents resulting in airliner hull loss were recorded, while the years 1979 to 1996 saw an additional 45 crashes.[6] Although the safety situation has improved in recent years, concerns still abound. For example, as a consequence of an Australian Civil Aviation Safety Authority report issued in January 1997 citing lax safety standards, Air China and China Eastern Airlines are now required to undergo extra safety inspections in order to continue to fly in Australia.

Even though CSA was not cited in this report, it has not been without its problems. In November 1992, a CSA 737–300 crashed into a mountain at 7,000 feet just before making an approach at Guangzhou's Baiyun airport. There were no survivors as all 133 passengers and 8 crewmembers were killed. In 1996, the company lost two helicopters and their crews.

The CAAC

Today, the CAAC is the sole regulatory body for commercial aviation within China and maintains a substantial oversight of virtually all airline operations including: route allocation and pricing, aircraft acquisition, fuel prices, airport operations, and the certification of aircraft maintenance and safety.

Although, having substantially divested itself of airline operations, the CAAC maintains a shareholding in all major Chinese airlines. In addition, the China National Aviation Corporation (CNAC), an affiliate of the CAAC, owns portions of two overseas airlines—35.9 percent ownership in Dragon Air (majority owned by the Swire Group, the parent of Cathay Pacific) and 51 percent ownership in Air Macau. Exhibit 4 presents the organisational structure of the CAAC.

The CAAC is the final arbiter with respect to route rights and pricing. It determines which airlines will be allocated which routes with the locations of the airlines' main or regional hubs playing an important role in the determination of route rights. Foreign carriers are not permitted to operate on China's domestic routes. Airfares are determined wholly by the CAAC for domestic routes and in consultation with foreign governments in the case of international routes. Fares are published and apply to non-Chinese, with Chinese citizens receiving a discounted rate. The CAAC levies a 10 percent tax on domestic flights and a 6 percent tax on international flights.

Among the various regulatory and aviation related activities performed by the CAAC, the organisation operates two supply companies, the China Aviation Oil Supply Company (CAOSC) and the China Aviation Supplies Import and Export Corporation (CASC).

The CAOSC is the only jet fuel supply company in China, and all airlines are required to purchase their fuel from one of its seven regional branches. The CAOSC sets a uniform price throughout China, although the actual cost to deliver fuel to different locations varies. Prior to 1994, Chinese jet fuel prices were generally below international jet fuel prices. Since then, the Chinese jet fuel prices have been substantially above international prices with current CAOSC charges set at 25 percent above international market prices. Jet fuel shortages are known to occur in China, resulting in flight delays and cancellations. Such shortages have not affected CSA since 1993.

The CASC supplies aviation equipment including aircraft, engines, spare parts, and other flight equipment. Because it possesses the only licence to import or export aircraft, all aircraft purchased in China must go through the CASC. Airlines must first lodge formal applications with the CAAC asking for approval to purchase aircraft. Once the airline receives the approval of both the CAAC and the State Planning Commission, it negotiates the terms and conditions with the manufacturer in conjunction with the CASC. The CASC receives a commission on each aircraft purchased. CSA, Air China, and China Eastern are permitted to import jet engines directly from the manufacturer provided they are for their own use.

China Southern Airlines

CSA operates an extensive route network within China, serving 68 destinations with over 270 routes within China. The company's main hub is Guangzhou[7] in Guangdong province in southeastern China. From Baiyun International Airport in Guangzhou, CSA services 56 domestic routes and 14 international destinations, as well as Hong Kong. CSA also operates from nine other hubs—Wuhan, Haikou, Changsha, Zhenghou, Xiamen, Zhuhai, Shantou, Shenzen, and Guilin. CSA services all

[6]http://www.pongnet.nl/avnsafety/.

[7]Guangzhou was called Canton in the older Wade-Giles method of Chinese/English translation.

EXHIBIT 4 Structure of the Civil Aviation Administration of China

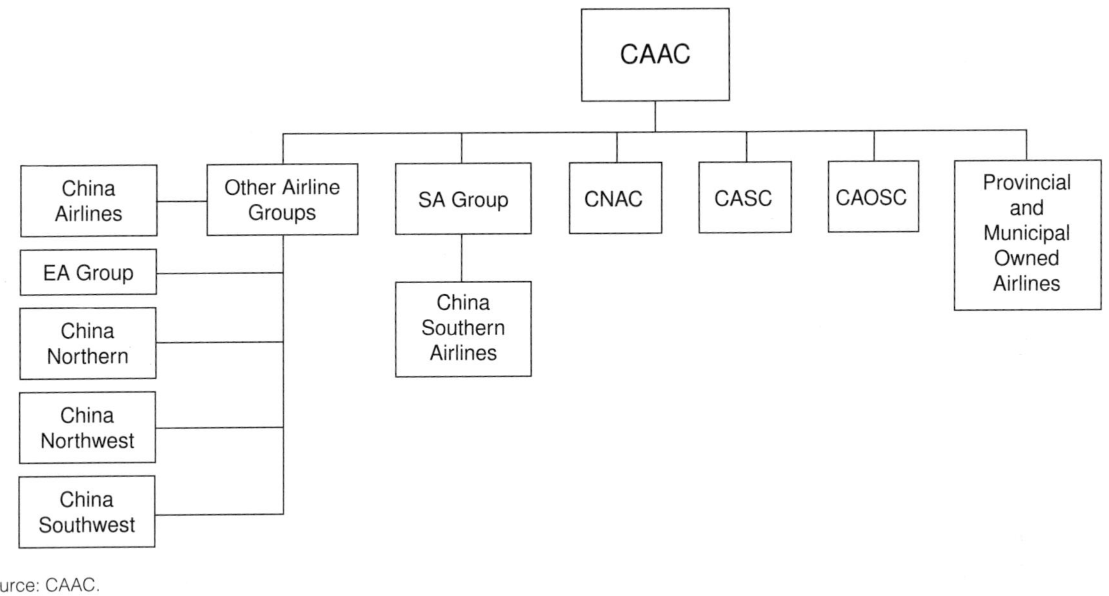

Source: CAAC.

of China's provinces and regions except Inner Mongolia, Tibet, and Ningxia. (CSA's route structure is presented in Exhibit 5).

One thousand of the company's approximately 2,445 flights per week originate or arrive at Baiyun International Airport in Guangzhou. In addition, the company services international destinations such as Manila, Singapore, Osaka, Amsterdam, and Los Angeles. CSA has a fleet of 84 aircraft with an average age of 4.5 years (see Exhibit 6) and employs slightly more than 10,000 people (see Exhibit 7). Its aircraft fleet is one of the youngest in the world. In comparison, the U.S. carrier Delta Airlines has an average fleet age of 11.2 years, while the German carrier Lufthansa maintains its average fleet age at 5.5 years. Almost all the aircraft operated by CSA are leased with terms customary for aircraft lease arrangements.

In addition to its flagship, China Southern, CSA maintains 60 percent ownership in four regional carriers: Xiamen Airlines, Shantou Airlines, Guangxi Airlines, and Zhuhai Airlines. It also owns or is a joint venture partner in a flight school for pilots, a flight catering company, a helicopter operator, a flight services company, and an information systems company specializing in reservations and airline information systems, and a finance company. The company's organization structure and ownership stakes are illustrated in Exhibit 8.

CSA's aircraft maintenance functions are performed by GAMECO, a joint venture between CSA, Lockheed, and Hutchinson. GAMECO performs all types of aircraft maintenance from inspections to major overhauls. GAMECO was the first aircraft maintenance facility in China to receive repair certification by both the CAAC and the U.S. Federal Aviation Administration (FAA). Payments for GAMECO services to CSA aircraft are payable in 50 percent U.S. dollars and 50 percent Renminbi. In 1996 GAMECO recorded revenue of RMB 352 million of which 90 percent was derived from CSA. In addition to servicing the CSA fleet, GAMECO also provides maintenance services to 17 other Chinese airlines and 7 international airlines. Five other companies within China also provide commercial aircraft maintenance services.

CSA believe they have a competitive advantage based on the training of their pilots and flight crew. Prior to 1993, CSA recruited most of their pilots from the CAAC Aviation College and the Chinese Air Force. Due to concerns about a shortage of qualified pilots, CSA established a joint venture pilot training program known as the China Southern West Australian Flying College. Would-be pilots must pass a CAAC examination to obtain a pilot's license. One hundred pilots were expected to complete the training program by February 1998.

EXHIBIT 5 China Southern Airlines' Route Structure, 1997

Source: China Southern Airlines.

Note: Map not to scale. The location of cities is approximate and distance between them not representative of the actual distances. Small cities serviced by regional carriers are not shown.

Ticket sales and reservations are managed through independent sales agents and CSA's network of sales offices. The company has sales offices in all of its route base cities. Additionally, CSA has sales offices in such cities as Beijing and Shanghai. International sales offices are located in Bangkok, Manila, Hanoi, Ho Chi Minh City (Saigon), Singapore, Kuala Lumpur, Penang (Malaysia), Jakarta, Surabaya (Indonesia), Vientiane (Laos), Osaka, Amsterdam, and Sharjah (UAE). Approximately one-quarter of all ticket sales are made through this network. Within China, CSA pays agents a commission of 3 percent of the ticket price. Agents outside China receive a 9 to 12 percent commission. Ticket sales and reservations in Hong Kong are handled by the China

EXHIBIT 6 **Distribution of Aircraft Held by China Southern Airlines**

Aircraft Model	Number	Average Age (years)	Passenger Capacity
Boeing 777-200	4	0.53	380
Boeing 767-300	3	3.73	270
Boeing 757-200	25	5.61	200
Boeing 737-500	18	4.10	132
Boeing 737-300	23	3.43	145
Boeing 737-200	5	8.58	128
Saab 340B	4	NA	36
An-12	2	NA	NA

Source: China Southern Airlines.

EXHIBIT 7 **Distribution of Personnel of China Southern Airlines**

Personnel Type	Number
Pilots	1,151
Flight Attendants	1,793
Maintenance Personnel	1,552
Sales and Marketing	3,752
Administration	2,408

Source: China Southern Airlines.

EXHIBIT 8 **Organisation Structure of China Southern Airlines**

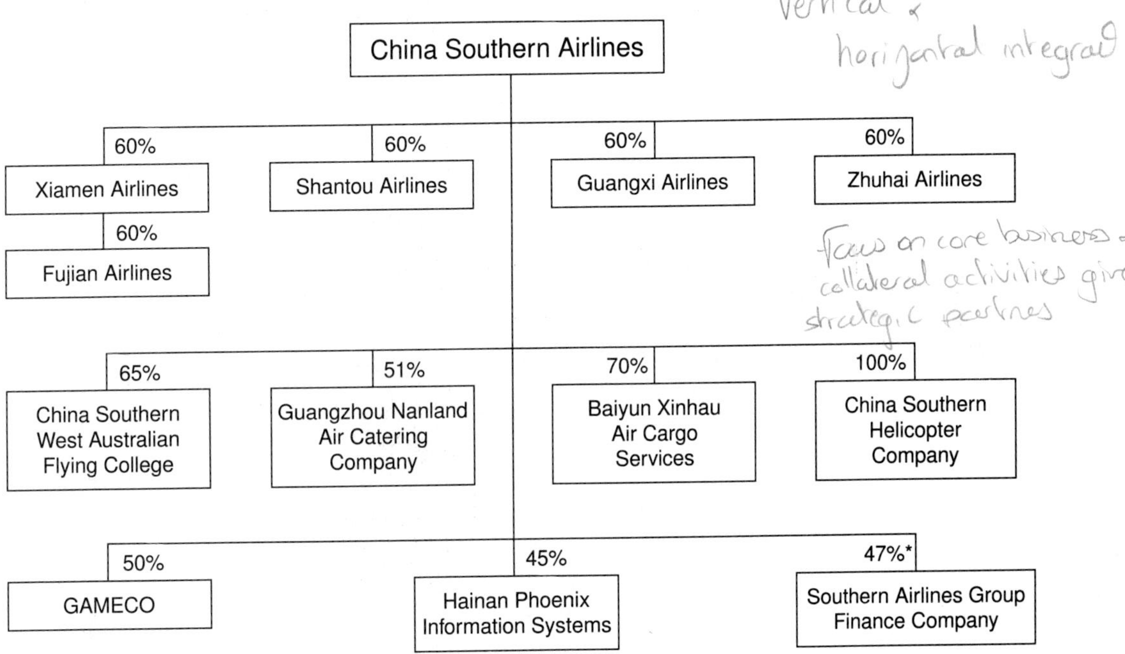

*Includes 17% held through CSA's subsidiaries.

Source: China Southern Airlines.

EXHIBIT 9 Operating Characteristics—China Southern Airlines (1992–1996)

	1992	1993	1994	1995	1996
Available Seat Kilometres (ASK)	10,625	13,610	18,095	21,100	23,712
Revenue Passenger Kilometres (RPK)	9,166	10,302	12,843	15,387	16,743
Aircraft in Service	59	79	84	82	84
Operating Cost Per ASK (RMB)	0.27	0.31	0.37	0.38	0.39
Market Share (percent)	31.6	29.4	29.8	28.0	27.4
Income Per Share (RMB)	0.06	0.10	0.05	0.10	0.33

Source: China Southern Airlines.

National Aviation Company (CNAC) for which they receive a 12 percent commission. The company also has sales agreements with airlines throughout Asia, USA, Europe, and Africa.

The financial and operational performance of the company has been excellent from a market share, revenue growth, and profit perspective, while asset utilisation rates remain roughly in line with industry averages. Exhibit 9 illustrates CSA's recent operational performance while Exhibit 10 presents CSA's share of passengers and cargo of major clinical airports. Exhibit 11 contains the firm's financial statements.

EXHIBIT 10 China Southern Airlines' Market Share at Chinese Airports, 1996 (percent)

	Passengers	Cargo
Beijing	13.2	10.5
Guangzhou	52.6	49.9
Shanghai	12.7	4.0
Shenzhen	35.9	31.1
Chengdu	7.1	9.4
Kunming	11.2	11.6
Xiamen	64.6	56.8
Haikou	38.0	35.1
Xian	6.2	4.0
Chongqing	9.1	10.5

Sources: CAAC, China Southern Airlines.

CSA's Strategy and Plans for the Future

CSA has long been viewed as the most "developed and . . . aggressive" of the Chinese airlines having been allowed by the CAAC to "stretch the rules and be a pioneer for the development of the whole industry."[8]

According to company documents the business strategy followed by CSA is:

> Continued expansion and rationalization of its operations with a view of increasing the profitability of its route network and the utilization rates for its aircraft. Continued focus on meeting international standards of service with fully integrated flight training, aircraft maintenance, and air catering operations. Continued investments in the Company's aviation infrastructure, including information systems.

Although the company's core focus is the development and solidification of its domestic business, international routes are seen as important "feeders" to local routes. CSA's recent signing of a code sharing agreement with the U.S. carrier Delta Airlines was a reflection of this strategy.

On the domestic front, CSA's strategy includes adding additional routes and substantially expanding its cargo and mail transport businesses. In 1996 the company dedicated one of its Boeing 737 aircraft solely to cargo and mail transport.

The company had approval to acquire 13 Airbus A320–200 aircraft by 1999. In addition CSA is seeking approval for an additional three Airbus A320–200 and three Boeing 777–200 aircraft. Its four subsidiary airlines also plan for expansion through the year 2000. The total acquisition plans among the subsidiaries are for sixteen Boeing 737 aircraft of varying configurations (10 737–700s and 2 each of the 737–500, 737–200, and 737–300 class of aircraft).

[8]Anthony O'Connor, The Tearaway, *Airfinance Journal,* July/August, 1996, pp. 16–19.

EXHIBIT 11a **Consolidated Income Statement—China Southern Airlines (RMB million)**

	1992	1993	1994	1995	1996
Operating Revenue	3,858	5,107	7,592	9,032	11,387
Less Operating Expenses	*2,833*	*4,282*	*6,626*	*7,940*	*9,322*
Operating Income	**1,025**	**825**	**997**	**1,092**	**2,064**
Equity Income from Affiliated Companies	16	21	37	13	55
Gain (loss) on Sale of Fixed Assets	168	13	17	(54)	45
Interest Expense	(306)	(416)	(921)	(920)	(1,062)
Exchange Gain (loss), Net	(891)	(637)	95	238	312
Other, Net	26	53	31	131	20
Exceptional Item	—	—	—	—	(173)
Income (loss) before Taxation and Minority Interests	**38**	**(141)**	**226**	**500**	**1,260**
Taxation	166	406	(41)	(125)	(376)
Minority Interests	(66)	(41)	(82)	(148)	(158)
Net Income	**138**	**225**	**104**	**227**	**727**

EXHIBIT 11b **Consolidated Balance Sheet—China Southern Airlines (RMB million)**

	1992	1993	1994	1995	1996
Cash	632	2,339	1,902	1,710	2,714
Other Current Assets	1,504	1,455	1,490	1,594	1,892
Fixed Assets, Net	4,342	8,652	11,320	12,754	16,039
Total Assets	**8,212**	**14,906**	**19,228**	**21,200**	**25,971**
Current Bank and Other Notes Payable	611	902	1,366	2,255	2,366
Current Installments of Obligations under Finance Leases	192	259	440	570	778
Long Term Debt	638	3,256	5,257	4,652	5,982
Obligations under Finance Leases (excluding current obligations)	4,581	6,374	6,761	7,066	9,545
Other Unspecified Liabilities and Minority Interests†	1,519	3,382	4,568	5,594	5,224
Owners' Equity	**671**	**733**	**836**	**1,063**	**2,076**

†These unspecified liabilities and minority interests include minority equity interests, accounts payable, sales in advance of carriage, taxes payable, amounts due to related companies, accrued expenses, provisions for major overhauls, deferred expenses and other liabilities. The individual accounts cannot be specified for all the years.

Source: China Southern Airlines. The above financial information is estimated based on CSA's best judgement. Independent auditors have not examined these financial statements.

Competition

CSA faces a large number of competitors both within China and internationally. Domestically, the primary competitors of CSA are Air China and China Eastern. Although CSA has no single direct international competitor, because of CSA's designation as China's "South East Asian" carrier it competes against China Airlines, Malaysian Airlines, Thai Airlines, Singapore Airlines, Vietnam Airlines, Qantas, and Hong Kong carriers, Cathay Pacific and Dragonair. Comparative summary information on these airlines is given in Exhibit 12 with financial and operational statistics to be found in Exhibits 13 and 14.

EXHIBIT 12 Summary Statistics for Selected Asian Airlines

Airline (Country)	Aircraft	Government Ownership (percent)	Passengers Flown (1996) (millions)	Employees	Stock Price (April 1997)
Air China (China)	47	100	6.68	15,000	NL
China Eastern (China)	38	65	6.80	NA	HK$ 2.43
China Southern (China)	73	100	15.21	10,656	NL
China Airlines (Taiwan)	47	71.5	6.40	8,251	NT$ 38.73
Malaysian Airlines (Malaysia)	83	0	NA	22,546	RM 5.55
Thai Airways (Thailand)	71	93	14.30	22,000	THB 38.00
Singapore Airlines (Singapore)	87	53.8	12.00	27,516	S$ 7.20
Vietnam Airlines (Vietnam)	30	100	2.57	NA	NL
Qantas (Australia)	98	0	18.60	30,080	A$ 2.67
Cathay Pacific (Hong Kong)	59	0	10.90	15,500	HK$ 12.05
Dragonair (Hong Kong)	11	35.9	NA	1,181	NL

Sources: Company reports, Bloomberg, http://www.intercpt.demon.co.uk/fleets.html, CAAC. NL = Not listed.

EXHIBIT 13 Performance of Chinese Airlines

Airline	1994	1995	1996	1997E	1998E	1999E
China Eastern						
Revenue (RMB million)	5,836	6,616	7,286	8,812	10,108	11,594
Expenses (RMB million)	4,433	5,116	5,847	6,998	8,107	8,210
Tax Rate (percent)	34.1	36.3	28.4	33.0	33.0	33.0
Load Factor (percent)	55.0	57.8	55.5	52.7	51.9	51.8
Shares (billions)	3.00	3.00	3.00	4.87	4.87	4.87
China Southern						
Revenue (RMB million)	7,592	9,032	11,387	13,943	16,894	20,151
Expenses (RMB million)	6,626	7,940	9,322	10,964	13,245	15,744
Tax Rate (percent)	18.0	25.0	29.8	33.0	33.0	33.0
Load Factor (percent)	57.5	58.7	59.4	58.5	58.1	58.4
Shares (billions)	2.20	2.20	2.20	3.37	3.37	3.37

Source: Goldman Sachs.

EXHIBIT 14 Performance of Selected Asian Airlines (1994–1999E)

Airline	1994	1995	1996	1997E	1998E	1999E
China Airlines						
Revenue (NT$ million)	43,227	47,193	50,747	57,479	63,980	71,064
Expenses (NT$ million)	42,227	46,649	49,234	53,787	58,674	64,210
Tax Rate (percent)	70.0	4.3	15.0	15.0	15.0	15.0
Load Factor (percent)	77.9	78.0	80.2	83.3	84.6	85.5
Shares (millions)	1,128	1,298	1,457	1,657	1,657	1,657
Malaysian Airlines						
Revenue (RM million)	4,081	4,780	5,713	6,485	7,293	8,178
Expenses (RM million)	3,938	4,435	5,032	5,763	6,320	6,919
Tax Rate (percent)	52.4	15.0	7.2	4.4	11.1	9.0
Load Factor (percent)	63.9	63.9	62.3	60.3	66.0	65.9
Shares (millions)	700	700	700	770	770	770
Thai Airways						
Revenue (THB million)	58,579	63,755	72,798	78,022	82,920	93,221
Expenses (THB million)	53,946	55,260	63,434	68,600	73,875	82,501
Tax Rate (percent)	26.3	27.9	29.6	30.7	30.0	30.0
Load Factor (percent)	65.8	69.2	68.7	68.1	69.1	69.9
Shares (millions)	1,400	1,400	1,400	1,400	1,400	1,400
Cathay Pacific						
Revenue (HK$ million)	27,215	30,454	32,381	34,109	37,431	42,523
Expenses (HK$ million)	23,099	26,198	28,125	29,778	32,590	36,670
Tax Rate (percent)	18.8	14.5	12.8	15.0	15.0	16.0
Load Factor (percent)	69.0	69.5	70.6	74.1	74.0	73.7
Shares (millions)	2,864.5	2,864.5	3,437.5	3,437.5	3,437.5	3,437.5
Singapore Airlines						
Revenue (SG$ million)	6,236	6,556	6,890	7,222	7,766	8,484
Expenses (SG$ million)	5,417	5,625	5,845	6,326	6,620	7,129
Tax Rate (percent)	8.0	4.1	5.1	4.0	5.0	5.0
Load Factor (percent)	69.5	69.8	69.4	70.5	71.4	71.1
Shares (millions)	1,283	1,283	1,283	1,283	1,283	1,283
Qantas						
Revenue (AU$ million)	6,531	7,163	7,600	7,834	8,038	8,422
Expenses (AU$ million)	6,051	6,692	7,096	6,609	6,798	7,140
Tax rate (percent)	34.1	43.7	38.5	37.4	40.0	40.0
Load factor (percent)	63.3	65.9	64.3	64.6	65.3	65.8
Shares (millions)	1,000	1,000	1,035.5	1,111.7	1,111.7	1,111.7

Source: Goldman Sachs, Deutsche Morgan Grenfell.

Intra-China Rivals

The six largest Chinese airlines controlled 70 percent of the passenger traffic in 1996 with another 20 airlines controlling the remaining 30 percent.[9] CSA's most direct competitors are Air China, operating from Beijing and China Eastern Airlines, operating from Shanghai. As of March 1997, CSA operated 35 domestic routes that were also operated by China Eastern and 20 domestic routes that were also operated by Air China. Since prices are fixed by the CAAC, the companies compete on seat availability, ticketing and reservations, in-flight service, flight scheduling, safety, and on-time performance.

Wang Zhi, a senior member of the planning department at the CAAC, expressed the CAAC's general view of the industry when he said, "on average, the scope of airlines is too small. . . . From the point of view of efficiency, this is bad. . . . We must have more co-operation and mergers."[10] Given that many Chinese airlines are regional carriers established by provinces or municipalities, mergers are difficult due to the complexity of negotiations required between large airlines and municipalities. Additionally, provinces and municipalities tend to adopt a parochial view toward their airlines and do not wish to risk reduction or elimination of unprofitable routes. Still other localities are operating profitable regional airlines and do not wish to give up these profit streams.

Air China

Air China is the Chinese "flag carrier" and the largest passenger and cargo airline in China. The company maintains an impressive flight schedule to 26 countries in Europe, Africa, America, South East Asia, and the Far East. In addition, the company services more than 60 domestic locations. Beijing is the hub for its domestic and international services and the airline also operates subsidiary airlines with hubs in Tianjin and Inner Mongolia.

Air China stresses the company's air safety record and quality in-flight service in attracting new customers. Each of its approximately 1,000 pilots must pass an annual examination. Its emphasis on safety has recently been tarnished by the Australian government's imposition of a safety watch on the airline and the January 1997 collapse of the front landing gear of a Boeing 747 landing in New York from Beijing.

The carrier has adopted many of the marketing practices used by Western airlines such as a frequent flyer program and special lounges for club members. One promotion even offered free mobile phone hire for patrons flying to the United Kingdom.

Financial data is not available on Air China at the present time, although a public float is rumoured. Estimates place the worth of the firm's assets at RMB 19.3 billion, and 1996 profits at around RMB 470 million on revenue of RMB 11.5 billion.[11]

China Eastern Airlines

China Eastern Airlines (CEA) operates from its primary hub at Shanghai's Hongqiao International Airport. In 1995, China Eastern's flights accounted for one-third of the airport's traffic. Its route network includes 44 domestic and international destinations accounting for 1,100 flights per week. It flies to Hong Kong from 12 locations in China. CEA has a larger international route structure than CSA—its 15 international destinations include the United States, Belgium, Spain, Germany, Japan, South Korea, Thailand, Singapore, and Australia. Flights to Japan and Hong Kong make up almost half of CEA's revenue. CEA's international destination exposure opens it to more direct competition than CSA with both regional and international rivals.

Listed on the Hong Kong Stock Exchange and the New York Stock Exchange in February 1997, the company was planning to list on the Shanghai Stock Exchange in November 1997. The Hong Kong and New York share listings raised RMB 2.1 billion, while the total funds to be raised through all three offerings is estimated to exceed RMB 2.8 billion.[12] These funds will be used primarily to purchase additional aircraft and payoff existing loans.

Prior to its partial privatisation, CEA initiated a reorganisation similar to that subsequently used by CSA. All nonairline-related activities of the company were assigned to a holding company called the EA Group. All airline-related assets and liabilities were assigned to China Eastern Airlines with the EA Group serving as the parent holding company. As part of this reorganisation, the airline adopted a new motto to emphasise the new corporate spirit of the firm: *Reform driven, market-oriented, safety preconditioned, and profitability-aimed.*

The EA Group participates in over 30 joint ventures and foreign funded enterprises engaging in air passenger

[9] *China Securities Bulletin,* 19 November 1997.
[10] *Ibid.*

[11] *Flight International,* 22 October 1997, p. 22.
[12] http://www.irasia.com/listco/hk/chinaeast/.

and cargo transportation, air transportation agents, tourism, hotel services, air catering, real estate, import and export services, advertising, and foreign exchange.

China Eastern plans to grow by building on their dominant presence in Shanghai. The company believes its commitment to safety will help it achieve its financial goals that include controlling operating costs. China Eastern has only had one safety incident in recent years, where two passengers were killed when a China Eastern jet overran the runway at Fuzhou airport.

The airline is currently experiencing a shortage of qualified pilots, which may limit its future growth. The CAAC has granted China Eastern the right to acquire China General Aviation Corp. a small airline based in Taiyuan; it is speculated that this acquisition was an attempt to secure additional pilots.

International Rivals

Due to the substantial growth in international air traffic to and from China, new foreign competitors continue to enter the market. Although these competitors can not operate on China's domestic routes, the rapid opening of China's economy has spurred 64 foreign airlines from 38 nations to enter the market, including 8 of the world's top 10 air cargo companies.

China Airlines

Supported by an NT$400,000 investment, China Airlines (CA) began flying two military surplus aircraft from Taipei to Kaohsiung in 1959. The conflict in Vietnam drove much of the company's early growth as contracts were given to parachute supplies into Laos beginning in 1961. Throughout the 1960s, additional contracts were awarded to China Airlines to fly South Vietnamese government officials and U.S. military personnel. In 1966, a regularly scheduled service from Taipei to Saigon was established. After the conflict in Vietnam ended, the carrier began to focus on regional routes to and from Taipei. The airline grew with the economic expansion in Asia and the significant growth in the Taiwanese economy. As Taiwan became a major exporter of goods, an impressive cargo business was built up to complement the carrier's passenger trade.

In 1988, 26 high-ranking military officials established the China Aviation Development Foundation to assume supervisory management of the company. In 1993, the company was partially privatised in order to fund additional expansion. Although the government still holds majority ownership, the company's stock is traded on the Taiwan stock exchange.

The carrier currently operates with high load factors (the highest in Asia) on heavily contested routes and currently does not have any alliances with other airlines, although it is seeking a strategic partner by offering a 16 percent ownership stake to a would-be suitor.

CA flies to 35 cities in 20 countries and aims to expand this to 50 cities in 25 countries in the next 10 years. Their route structure includes 15 destinations in Asia, four in Europe, six in North America, two in Australia/New Zealand, plus a handful of cargo only destinations. It has recently developed a highly profitable route network in the rapidly expanding Indonesian market and further growth in both services offered and profits are expected. In order to meet the company's increasing demand, the carrier plans to add 7 new planes in 1997 and 11 more in 1998 with a goal of operating 67 aircraft by 2003.

The biggest issue facing CA is its safety record. The company's accident rate has been shocking by any set of standards. During the last 30 years, the airline has seen 11 of its planes crash. In the last 10 years, there have been 4 crashes killing 323 people. Some of these crashes include:

- 1989: A China Airlines jet flying in Taiwan took a wrong turn after take off and crashed into a mountain, killing all 54 people on board.
- 1993: A China Airlines aircraft overran the runway in Hong Kong. The Boeing 747 spent two weeks floating in the harbour; no passengers were killed.
- 1994: A China Airlines Airbus A300 stalled at 1,800 feet when a member of the flight crew accidentally turned on the auto pilot just before landing at Nagoya in Japan. The plain hit the ground tail first 100 meters from the runway and burst into flames. All 264 passengers and crew died.

After the crash in Japan, the airline tripled its pilot training time, bought new flight simulators, and hired Lufthansa as a safety consultant.

Despite the safety problems surrounding the airline, it still controls over 30 percent of the Taiwanese market, but its greatest potential for growth lies with the Chinese mainland. Direct flights are not currently permitted between the People's Republic of China (PRC) and Taiwan. However, this may change in the future and CA will be in a good position to serve major routes within China.

Malaysian Airlines

Malaysian Airlines (MAS) is the national airline of Malaysia and has operated as a public corporation since being privatised in 1985. The airline was formed from one plane in 1947 and grew rapidly after the formation of Malaysia in 1963. In 1966, the governments of Malaysia and Singapore jointly took control of the fledgling airline purchasing the 30 percent stake held by Qantas and the British Overseas Airways Corporation (the predecessor of British Airways). In 1966, the airline consisted of 21 aircraft and 2,400 staff operating on a domestic route network. International flights to the Philippines, Australia, and Taiwan soon followed. In 1971, the Malaysian-Singapore partnership was dissolved, and the firm emerged in its present form in 1972. Since then, the company has expanded rapidly, servicing 34 domestic and 27 international destinations with 37 aircraft by 1988. In 1991, Beijing was added as the MAS's 81st destination.

With its main hub in Kuala Lumpur, MAS now services 110 domestic and international routes. Codes sharing alliances with Virgin Atlantic, British Midlands, and Canadian Airlines along with increased international flights have spurred recent growth within the firm. Record profits have been recorded in the last two financial years with double-digit growth rates in revenue, earnings, and dividends in 1996.

The company's expansion plans are far from over as the firm has ordered 20 additional aircraft scheduled for delivery during the next five years. A new airport in Kuala Lumpur is expected to increase both efficiency and service for the airline. The Ministry of Finance has given MAS a five-year tax holiday, although they refused to justify the reasoning behind this favouritism.

Thai Airways

Thai Airways (THAI) began in 1951 when the Thai government purchased shares in three airlines and amalgamated their fleets. For the remainder of the decade, the airline focused on the domestic market. In 1960, THAI formed an alliance with Scandinavian Airlines Systems (SAS) and began to serve 10 regional destinations with propeller-driven aircraft. Beginning in 1966, the firm instituted a program of international route expansion using jet-propelled aircraft. By 1970, THAI was carrying 500,000 passengers and had become Asia's third largest airline. Intercontinental routes were established in 1971 with service to Sydney and Copenhagen. Other cities quickly followed, and by 1979 demand was high enough for the carrier to begin purchasing Boeing 747s. In the following year it began flying to North American destinations. THAI's current route network includes destinations in more than 60 countries including, Athens, Beijing, Berlin, Guangzhou, Helsinki, Hanoi, Jakarta, Katmandu, Manila, Johannesburg, Los Angeles, Melbourne, Osaka, Shanghai, Taipei, and Vientiane.

THAI is another national carrier that has issued an IPO, although the airline is not completely privatised. After recording a net profit of THB 791 million in the first quarter of 1992, the company issued 100 million shares at an initial price of THB 60 per share. The sale was highly successful, as the offer was oversubscribed, and the influx of funds was used to significantly reduce borrowing. The company had plans to issue another 250 million shares before the end of 1997 reducing the government's ownership to 76 percent. These proceeds will be used to help finance a THB 20 billion, five-year expansion plan. Pending the success of the 1997 float, another 500 million shares will be sold before the end of the century.

THAI is attempting to rationalise and modernise its operations. The airline is currently in the process of selling between 14 and 17 of its older aircraft, generating an estimated profit of between US$250 to US$300 million. It is also negotiating with United Airlines, Air Canada, SAS, and Lufthansa about a possible global airline alliance. The expectation is that the synergies from such an alliance could increase profits and market share through code sharing agreements, marketing programmes, and savings resulting from cost sharing.

Singapore Airlines

After the break-up of Malaysia-Singapore Airlines in 1972, Singapore Airlines (SA) took over the entire international network of 22 cities and the aircraft that serviced them. In 1978, a major expansion was launched with the addition of 19 new aircraft. In 1989, a global alliance between Swissair, Delta Airlines, and Singapore Airlines saw Delta (2.74 percent) and Swissair (0.62 percent) take ownership stakes in the carrier. SA took small, reciprocal, ownership stakes in each of its partners (5 percent in Delta and 3 percent in Swissair). SA has continued to grow throughout the 1990s and now serves over 70 destinations including 13 in Europe, 5 in North America, 9 in Australia/New Zealand, and 44 in North and Southeast Asia.

As one of the first foreign airlines to recognise the vast potential of the Chinese aviation market, SA has, today, more destinations in greater China than any other foreign carrier, including Beijing, Shanghai, Xiamen, Macau, Kaoshsiung, Guangzhou, Hong Kong, Taipei, and Hangzhou. In addition to flight services, SA has established a joint venture with the Beijing Capital International Airport wherein it provides flight-catering services to 16 domestic and 6 international airlines as well as operating all ground handling services.

Service excellence has been an important component of the company's success. Numerous awards are presented to the airline each year, giving credibility to the company's claim as the world's best airline. Safety has never been a problem for the carrier due, at least partially, to the very young fleet it maintains. The average aircraft in SA's fleet is currently less than five years old. Even more amazing is the fact that the carrier has managed to earn a profit every year since its inception. The carrier continued to grow in 1996, recording a revenue increase of 4.8 percent on a 9.3 percent increase in revenue passenger kilometres.

Vietnam Airlines

Watch Us Take Off was the slogan used in Vietnam airline's (VNA) recent advertising campaign. It also could be used to describe the carrier's recent growth. In 1996, VNA flew 2.6 million passengers. It is literally the fastest growing airline in the region with passenger traffic increasing 18 percent between 1995 and 1996 and a whopping 53 percent increase between 1994 and 1996. Although a veil of secrecy surrounds state run enterprises in Vietnam, turnover for 1996 was estimated at US$450 million compared to US$400 million for 1995.[13] Profit figures are unavailable.

Until 1989, VNS was under the control of the Ministry of Defense. After 1989, the company was placed under the control of the Civil Aviation Administration of Vietnam (CAAV), where it remained until 1993 when control was transferred to the Prime Minister. While under the control of the ministry of defence and the CAAV, the carrier maintained a fleet of Soviet-era aircraft manufactured by Tupolev, Yakovlev, and Ilyushins. These aircraft constrained the airlines' ability to fly long-haul routes and created a costly maintenance structure. Commercial air transport was not a priority in Vietnam, and by 1991 VNA was only carrying 462,000 passengers.

A fleet modernisation program was begun as the economy and air transport began to expand in the early 1990s. The current VNA fleet consists of five Tupolevs,[14] five Boeing 767–300s, 10 Airbus A320s, 2 Fokker 70s[15] and a variety of turboprop aircraft including 6 ATR72s.[16] The Tupolevs are used for routes within Vietnam, Cambodia, Laos, and the loss making Hanoi-Guangzhou route. The other Soviet-era aircraft are used for charter flights, while the Western aircraft are used for certain domestic and all other international destinations. VNA's route structure is limited. Intercontinental destinations include Amsterdam, Sydney, Berlin, Moscow, Melbourne, Paris, and Vienna. Its regional destinations include Hong Kong, Bangkok, Singapore, Guangzhou, Osaka, Dubai, Seoul, Manila, Taipei, and Kuala Lumpur. The airline also services 15 domestic locations. VNA operates hubs in Ho Chi Minh City, Danang, and Hanoi.

The CAAV is planning a massive expansion of the airline infrastructure and has put enormous effort behind the modernisation of VNA. CAAV plans call for the redevelopment of many airports not used since the Vietnam War along with increasing the passenger capacity at Ho Chi Minh City to six million passengers per annum. VNA intended to replace its Russian-built planes with either Boeing or Airbus aircraft in early 1998. Further fleet expansion plans call for 40 aircraft by 2000 and 70 to 80 planes by 2005.

VNA's sole joint venture is with Cathay Pacific. Flights between Hong Kong and Hanoi (11 per week) and Hong Kong and Ho Chi Minh City (14 per week) are serviced jointly by Cathay Pacific and VNA. The joint venture also covers such ancillary activities as flight catering. VNA has also begun instituting modern flight safety, service, and marketing practices, including a planned frequent flyer programme.

In the first quarter of 1997 Vietnam Airlines flew 711,600 passengers (290,800 were foreigners) of an expected three million passengers for the year.[17] Expectations are for continued rapid growth of international traffic to Vietnam. As the population and economy continue to expande, the number of passengers could reach 17 million by 2010.[18] Within this booming market, VNA currently competes with 25 other carriers but holds a 40 percent market share. Destinations to Northern Asia constitute 70 percent of the carrier's revenues.[19]

---

[13]Jeremy Grant, *Vietnam Airlines in Careful Ascent,* Financial Times, 30 January 1997, p. 29.

[14]These Russian-built aircraft carry between 160 and 180 passengers and are flown primarily by former Soviet-bloc national airlines. Approximately 1,000 were built, starting in 1966, most of which are still in service.

[15]An 80-seat jet aircraft first produced in 1994 by the former Dutch aircraft manufacturer, now a component supplier to Airbus.

[16]A common French-built commuter aircraft introduced in 1988. This twin-propeller-driven aircraft has a maximum capacity of 72 passengers.

[17]Saigon Times Daily, *Vietnam Airlines Passenger Growth in First Quarter,* 11 April 1997.

[18]Reuters News Service, *Vietnam Airlines Continues Meteoric Rise in 1996,* 8 January 1997.

[19]Le Hung Vong, *Vietnam Airlines Spreads its Wings Despite Competition,* Saigon Times Daily, 11 December 1997.

Apart from an embarrassing ordeal in 1992, when a former airforce pilot hijacked an aeroplane and dropped antigovernment leaflets from the cockpit, VNA has enjoyed a clean safety record.

Qantas

Qantas is the dominant air carrier in Australia with substantial international and domestic operations. Begun in 1920 by offering joyrides in rural Australia, Qantas has grown to become one of the world's most recognisable airlines. The airline now services 5 continents with 104 destinations in 29 countries. In 1996, the company added new routes in Asia, including destinations in Indonesia (Denpasar), China (Beijing via Shanghai), and India (Mumbai). Additional flights were added on routes to Thailand, Vietnam, Hong Kong, Singapore, and the Philippines. 1996–97 also saw additional code share agreements with Japan Airlines, Asiana, and Aircalin (formerly Air Caledonie). In 1993, the Australian government sold 25 percent of Qantas to British Airways, an arrangement that has developed over the decade and now includes code sharing and other arrangements with British Airways and its US partner American Airlines. The government sold its remaining stake in the airline in 1995.

An increased emphasis on profitability, market share, and operating efficiencies has followed the carrier's successful privatization. Cost-cutting measures and increasing revenue are expected to continue, but profitability is constrained by the high labour costs in Australia. As a result of these expanded services, international capacity was up 7.3 percent versus traffic growth of 9.3 percent compared to an increased capacity in the domestic market of 4.9 percent versus traffic growth of 3.8 percent. All these factors combined to increase revenue by 3.1 percent and push the average aircraft utilisation rate to a very respectable 12.2 hours per day.[20]

Qantas has an excellent reputation as a safe airline, having never had a crash. This is a rather remarkable achievement considering it is now the oldest operating airline in the world. Qantas continues to invest heavily in safety in order to protect its enviable safety reputation.

[20]Deutsche Morgan Grenfell Securities Australia, *Qantas Airways Ltd*, 21 August 1997.

Cathay Pacific

Cathay Pacific (CP) was founded in 1946 as a venture between an American and an Australian businessman utilising two military surplus DC–3s. In 1948, additional investors, including the shipping giant Butterfield & Swire, joined the organisation, providing much-needed funds for aircraft purchases. By 1976, the airline was operating 15 jet aircraft serving routes in Asia, Australia, and the Middle East. 1986 saw tremendous changes for the carrier as it expanded its route network to Rome, Paris, Beijing, San Francisco, Auckland, Denpasar, and Amsterdam. That same year CP was listed on the Hong Kong Stock Exchange. Its listing broke all Hong Kong subscription records as it attracted more than HK$51 billion in applications.

Today, CP operates 47 destinations on five continents including, Bahrain, Bangkok, Jakarta, Kuala Lumpur, London, Manila, Manchester, New York, Osaka, Perth, Seoul, Singapore, Sydney, Taipei, Tokyo, Toronto, and Zurich. Its steady increase in passengers—9.8 million in 1994, to 10.4 million in 1995 and 10.9 million in 1996—has pushed its aircraft utilisation rate to over 11 hours per day.

CP operates nearly all flights from its hub in Hong Kong where growth has been constrained due to the capacity limitations of the aging Kai Tak airport. A new airport was expected to begin operations in April 1998. Although this will add much needed gate capacity, the cost of the facility will increase CP's ground operations costs. CP has begun a programme of fleet expansion recently placing a firm order for another 13 Boeing and Airbus aircraft, for delivery before May 1999.

In addition to Cathay Pacific operations the company also owns 75 percent of Air Hong Kong, an all-cargo carrier, as well as other holdings including an interest in the very profitable Dragon-air. Cathay is majority owned by Swire Holdings (43.9 percent) and CITIC (25 percent).

Dragonair

Dragonair (DA) was formed in 1985 to link Hong Kong with eight cities in the People's Republic of China. The airline was an immediate success and has generated substantial profits for its owners. Known for its punctuality and the quality of its equipment and maintenance, DA is able to charge a price premium relative to Chinese airlines operating on the same routes. The company utilizes only Airbus aircraft, none of which is more than four years old.

Today, the airline serves 27 destinations on Chinese and short haul regional routes. Nearly one-third of the passengers carried between Hong Kong and the PRC in 1996 flew with the company. DA's busiest destinations are Beijing (14 flights weekly) and Shanghai (16 flights weekly). Other mainland destinations include Tianjin, Chengdu, Kunming, Wuhan, Xiamen, Haikou, Guilin, Xian, Qingdao, and Chongqing. International destinations include Hiroshima, Dhaka, Kaohsiung (Taiwan), and Phuket.

DA shareholdings have always been closely held. As of April, 1997, Swire holds 25.5 percent of the company, CITIC Pacific 28.5 percent, the CNAC 35.86 percent, and the Chao family (the original founders) 5.02 percent. Despite its minority ownership of DA, Cathay Pacific still wields considerable influence over the company and shares its management and technical expertise and reservation and ticketing operations (Cathay's CUPID system). DA is considered the star of CNAC's holdings, making up more than 40 percent of the organisation's revenues.

In addition to its flight operations, DA owns 32 percent of the equity stake in the flight kitchen operated by LSG Lufthansa and 100 percent of Hong Kong International Airport Services Ltd.

APPENDIX: THE CHINA SOUTHERN AIRLINES OFFER

The company will float an allotment of shares on the New York and Hong Kong stock exchanges. The float will involve two types of shares. The Hong Kong listing will be in H shares while ADSs will be listed in New York. Goldman Sachs is acting as the global coordinator with the support of other Wall Street powerhouses such as Credit Suisse, Paine Webber, and Smith Barney.

The float will allow the purchase of 31.9 percent of the company's equity, as follows:

New York. 20,600,000 American Depository Shares (ADS)[21] are to be issued. Each ADS represents 50 H shares. The share price is US$30.66 per share based on an exchange rate of HK$7.7465 to US$1.00 on 23 July 1997.

Corporate Investors. A consortium made up of several large Hong Kong companies (Cheung Kong Holdings, Hutchison, New World, Sun Hung Kai Properties, and Tai Fook Group) agreed to purchase 290,447,000 H shares. Investment funds affiliated with Goldman Sachs agreed to purchase another 32,200,000 H shares.

The SA Group

As part of the float the company has undergone a restructuring whereby the former company (SA Group) maintained majority shareholder interest in the new company (CSA). The SA Group is a wholly owned state enterprise under the control of the CAAC. Substantially all of CSA's directors, supervisors, and executive officers are closely affiliated with the SA Group either through employment or directorship.

Under the restructuring agreement CSA assumed all airline and airline related businesses, assets, and liabilities, while the SA Group retained all nonairline related businesses, assets, and liabilities. Further to the agreement, CSA will continue to sell or rent housing to its employees at below-market rates. The SA Group will compensate CSA for such services through a fee of RMB 85 million per year for the next 10 years.

Over-allotment Option

CSA has granted a 30-day option to purchase a maximum of 3,090,000 additional ADSs at the initial price, minus discounts and commissions to cover over-allotments. If the over-allotment option is granted, the total equity share of the float will be 35 percent (the maximum allowable foreign ownership stake).

Shareholder Rights

Shareholders in Chinese companies do not have the same rights as those in Western countries. Specifically, shareholders may not sue a corporation, its directors, its supervisors, its officers, or its other shareholders under any circumstances. Instead shareholders must rely on appropriate agencies of the Chinese government to resolve any dispute that may arise. Chinese securities regulations are incomplete and evolving, therefore, uncertainties in shareholder rights in China Southern may arise and enforcement of arbitration is uncertain.

[21] American Depository Shares (ADS) are shares of overseas companies traded on exchanges in the United States. Actual foreign shares are held as collateral against the ADS. ADS allow U.S. investors to invest in overseas shares without establishing a foreign exchange account or special custody arrangements. ADS are traded on major U.S. exchanges and all transactions are in U.S. dollars.

Use of Proceeds

The float was expected to raise US$580 million after commissions and expenses. The proceeds from the float would be allocated in the following manner:[22]

RMB 2,360 million	Payments for acquired aircraft and related equipment
RMB 1,366 million	Repayment of debt
RMB 130 million	Purchase of computerised flight operations systems
RMB 100 million	Fund the expansion of flight simulator facilities
RMB 75 million	Purchase of a computerised financial management system

The balance would be used to construct airport facilities at the new airports in Haikou and Xhengzhou, construction of an air catering facility in Hubei province, and working capital requirements.

Proceeds from the sale would be deposited in U.S. denominated short-term securities at a Chinese bank until required.

[22]The exchange rate for the summer 1997 was approximately RMB 8.3 per US$1.0.

Source: Goldman Sachs and China Southern Airlines.

Case 10–2

SouthGold

The release of Nelson Mandela from Pollsmoor prison in 1990 and the victory of the African National Congress (ANC) in the 1994 elections presaged vast political and social changes in the country. Ending decades of oppression for the majority black population, the rise of the administratively inexperienced ANC was looked on at the time with a mixture of hope and misgiving. The ANC, and President Mandela personally, promised a new beginning for the nation's blacks—better roads, schools, health care, and housing. Mandela's powerful personality and his willingness to accommodate South Africa's business community did much to instill confidence in the government's management of the economic and social change that was both necessary and inevitable.

This case was written by Professor Timothy Devinney as a basis for class discussion and not for the purpose of illustrating either the good or bad handling of a specific management situation. The assistance of Elizabeth Fulcher, MBA, is gratefully acknowledged.

However, there was no doubt that sections of Mandela's government and party still held to their Marxist ideology and were less than happy with the velvet glove that the ANC's top echelon were applying to economic reforms, particularly those relating to the mining industry. At the Institute of International Research's African Mining Summit in June 1998, Dr. Zola Skweyiya read a speech in abstensia for the Minister of Minerals and Energy, Peneull Maduna, outlining the government's policy proposals with respect to mineral rights.

> Minerals are a form of natural resource which is property belonging to all South Africans, therefore, they should be held in trust by the state. . . . [T]his country had laws that prohibited black people access to minerals, prospecting and mineral rights. I am convinced that state ownership of mineral rights is the most appropriate vehicle to promote black participation in the industry.

Robert Viljoen, SouthGold's Chief Financial Officer, was at that meeting and remembers the reaction.

> I could hardly forget the speech. We had just listed the company on the Johannesburg Stock Exchange (JSE) and the team was pretty high. There had been a lot of change in the industry and the interaction between the government and the industry was quite positive. Dr. Skweyiya's speech was a bit of a bombshell. Many of my industry colleagues were quite hostile to the government's position and you could imagine the tenure of the private conversation that followed the speech.
>
> Personally, I think there is much more to Mr. Maduna's position than a redress of past racial injustice. What he is saying is that the status quo is not in South Africa's best interest as a nation. The concentration of mining ownership, not just in the hands of the whites but in the hands of a small set of powerful interests, is not good for the country as a whole. It thwarts legitimate investment and development and stifles innovation. The fact that our mining industry fell behind, particularly in the area of gold mining technology, during the waning years of apartheid was due, to no small extent, to an unwillingness to confront the status quo, both socially and in business.

South African mining companies were notorious for their conservative bent. They relied on sheer market power to control the price for key commodities—such as diamonds, manganese, platinum, and chromium—while utilizing the power of the state to protect their market and control costs—through preferential access to resources, protectionism, and breaking the unionism of black laborers. This conservatism could be seen in every aspect of the business but was most obvious in the structure of the mining companies and their approach to risk.

Of all the world competitors, South African mining companies were the least likely to utilize modern risk-reduction techniques in the management of their operations. According to a recent World Gold Council report, South African gold companies account for around 22 percent of gold hedging activity while their North American and Australian competitors dominate with around 35–40 percent each.[1] This fact is made abundantly clear in their profit figures. In 1997, the average price received for South African gold was $362 per ounce, around $10 above the spot price. Australian companies, the world leaders in mineral commodity hedging strategies,[2] were receiving $460 per ounce, while the North American firms were receiving $385 per ounce. In this year, only 5 of 30 operational gold mines in South Africa showed a profit.[3]

According to Janet Smyth, a hedge specialist from Warburg Dillon Read hired onto Viljoen's team,

> "The lack of an organized hedging strategy was hardly an issue when gold was $500 an ounce. However, with today's price and the current cost of operating a mine in South Africa, the difference between life and death for a company in the short term is likely to be its treasury operation. I see treasury as having two roles. First, we need to control the cash flow to give the company the breathing space it needs to restructure the mining operations to meet the reality of today's prices. Second, we need to protect the assets of the company so that fluctuations in the price of gold do not have adverse impact on our cost of capital."

Sam Mbuli, a graduate of London Business School and another of Viljoen's team members, echoed this sentiment.

> "We want this company to be a global player and scale is clearly important. Currently, we are a respectably sized company but if we cannot control our cash flow and hence our cost of funds, we will not be able to expand operations at a cost that is profitable."

[1] Ian Cox and Ian Emsley, *Utilisation of Borrowed Gold by the Mining Industry: Development and Future Prospects,* Research Study No. 18, World Gold Council, 1998.

[2] It is estimated that more than 60 percent of Australia's gold reserves are hedged.

[3] Kenneth Gooding, South Africa: Finding a Way Forward for Gold, *Financial Times,* 15 August 1997.

The three person team of Viljoen, Smyth, and Mbuli had a daunting task—to build from the ground up a hedging strategy that allowed SouthGold to develop into something more than a middling player in the international gold mining industry.

SouthGold

SouthGold was formed in June 1998 as the merger of the mining assets of Southreef, Southern Africa Resources (SAR) and Zamines. Southern Africa Resources was a small, diversified mining company wholly owning and operating two gold mines outside Johannesburg in Guateng province—Carlton and Venterspost. It also held minority interest in a number of other ventures including zinc, nickel, and aluminum mines. Southreef was solely focused on the operation of a single mine, also known as Southreef. It received about 30 percent of its revenue from the provision of exploration services to other mining companies. Zamines was a diversified Zambian mining company with interests in gold, coal, and copper. It owned two open-pit mines west of the Zambian capital of Lusaka. The Dunblaine mine was still in operation while the Mumbwa mine had been closed more than 30 years ago but was showing promising prospects based on recent exploration of adjoining territory.

According to Richard Riks, the Managing Director of SouthGold and the visionary behind the formation of the company, the creation of SouthGold was

> ". . . a way of gaining focus and scale so as to be able to compete in the globalizing South African mining industry. The power of the American, Canadian, and Australian gold mining companies, and the sophistication they bring to both the operational and financial performance aspects of their business indicated to us that the days of small speculative mines were over. We had to change and do so quickly and in a radical way."

This sentiment was echoed by Robert Viljoen.

> "1994 was not only a time of political change but also the beginning of a corporate reawakening. Until then, South African mining companies fell into two categories, the giants—like Anglo American, Gencor, and Billiton—who mined everything in sight and dominated the Johannesburg Stock Exchange (JSE), and the single mine operations that were little more than speculative ventures. The little old ladies kept their pensions in Anglo American, while the speculators loved Southreef and SAR. After 1994, it became obvious that neither Anglo American or Southreef could continue to operate as before. Hence when Richard approached me in late 1996 about merging the operations of his company

(Southern Africa Resources) and mine (Southreef), it was really a no-brainer."

The addition of Zamines' open-pit mining operation with SAR's and Southreef's deep mine operations was a combination of a statement of vision and lucky timing. Both Riks and Viljoen thought a three-mine operation was probably too small to be a force in the local market but had difficulty in attracting other mining companies into the new venture. Much of this was due to a labyrinth of cross-holdings in the South African mining sector. However, in mid-1997 Zamines was in need of cash and looking for an opportunity to sell its Dunblaine operation. It had first approached Gold Fields of South Africa and Anglo American, both of whom were busy with their own reorganizations and were less than enthusiastic about taking over an aging open pit mine in Zambia. Riks and Viljoen approached Zamines with a proposal to purchase not only the Dunblaine mine but also the dormant Mumbwa mine. Southreef had conducted a series of tests on the Mumbwa tract in 1995 and estimated that with the investment of new technologies developed in Australia, the mine was potentially viable. Both Riks and Viljoen were also interested in experimenting with open-pit mining techniques to diversify the knowledge base of their new company and prepare for potential overseas opportunities.

By June 1997, plans were in place to integrate the operations of Southreef and SAR while taking on the new operations in Zambia. New offices were let in the Sandal section of Johannesburg clear of the crime-ridden CBD. Both Southreef and SAR headquarters were situated in the same building and tactical teams formed to integrate systems and functions. In preparing the new company for operation, SAR sold its minority holdings in nongold operations to Billiton for 48 million Rand in late 1997.

On June 1, 1998, shares of the newly formed SouthGold began trading on the JSE. The ownership shares were distributed such that shareholders of Southreef received 40 percent, and shareholders of SAR 50 percent of the new company. As part of the agreement with Zamines, it received 10 percent of SouthGold along with a payment of 50 million Rand (all executed on the 1st of June). In total, 65 percent of the company was held by outside investors, i.e., nondirectors and excluding Zamines' holding.

Both Riks and Viljoen view the prospects of the company as quite positive. The Carleton and Venterspost mines have had slow degradation of their gold value but are expected to maintain the current level of output for at least 5–6 years. Southreef is clearly the gem of the company. Providing the highest yield it is also the youngest of the mines in operation and has not seen a serious decline in the grade of ore. Because it is at a rather shallow depth it is approximately 15 percent cheaper per ton of milled ore to operate than Carleton and Venterspost. The Dunblaine operation, being an open-pit mine utilizing cheaper Zambian labor, is about 30 percent cheaper to operate but suffers from an additional transport cost of about 10 percent due to distance from Zambia to the South African ports of Capetown and Port Elizabeth.

EXHIBIT 1 Summary of SouthGold Operations

	1998	1997
Area Mined (000 sq. meters)	120	119
Tons Milled (000)	462	566
Yield (grams per ton)	8.74	7.10
Production (kilograms)	4,043	4,003
Production Costs (Rand per kilogram)	40,535	37,510
Revenue (Rand per kilogram)	50,696	53,613
Revenue (Rand million)	214.3	215.2
Cost of Sales (Rand million)	161.7	150.6
Administration (Rand million)	6.6	12.3
Tax (Rand million)	5.7	18.0
Capital Expenditure, Actual (Rand million)	15.1	18.2
Shares Outstanding	23,376,411	19,395,237
Year End Share Price (Rand)	6.06	8.10

Note: All numbers are done on an appropriation basis.
Source: SouthGold Annual Report, 1998.

Exhibits 1 through 5 provide a snapshot of the financial and operational performance of SouthGold. These for 1998 are actual figures with those from 1997 being best estimates for the merged entity had it existed earlier.

Mining and the New South Africa

Until the 1990s, South African mining houses were like the metal they took from the ground—a prized and protected asset. Finely attuned to their unique environment, these companies and their white oligarchy were lords of all they could see. With government sanctioned access to cheap land and labor resources, a protected home market,

EXHIBIT 2 **SouthGold's Reserves and Resources**

		Tons (metric millions)	Grade (grams/ton)	Gold (metric tons)
Ore Reserves				
Proved	1998	1.4	10.98	15.37
	1997	1.5	10.27	15.41
Probable	1998	6.7	12.01	80.47
	1997	3.7	17.25	63.83
Total	1998	8.1	11.83	95.82
	1997	5.2	15.25	79.30
Mineral Resources				
Measured	1998	1.9	9.53	18.11
	1997	1.7	9.64	16.39
Indicated	1998	11.4	9.50	108.30
	1997	8.4	9.35	78.54
Total	1998	13.3	9.50	126.35
	1997	10.1	9.40	94.94

Note: *Mineral resources* are a mineral deposit that may eventually be legally and economically mined. It includes *ore reserves,* which represent that part of the mineral resource that technically can be mined under the condition operating presently. These estimates are confidence-based estimates following standards accepted by the Geological Society of South Africa and the Johannesburg Stock exchange. The numbers exclude any estimates for the Mumbwa mine.

Source: SouthGold Annual Report, 1998.

EXHIBIT 3 **SouthGold Mining Operations (1998)**

	Carleton	Dunblaine	Mumbwa	Southreef	Venterspost
Location	Guateng	Zambia	Zambia	Guateng	Guateng
Tons Milled (000)	102	129	NA	96	135
Gold Value (grams/ton)	9.60	4.91	NA	16.75	6.08
Mining	Deep Shaft	Open pit	Open Pit	Deep Shaft	Deep Shaft
Currently Operating	Yes	Yes	No	Yes	Yes
Exploration Ongoing	Yes	No	Yes	Yes	No

Source: SouthGold.

EXHIBIT 4 SouthGold Income Statement (millions of Rand)

	1998	1997
Revenue	214.3	215.2
Cost of Sales	(161.7)	(150.6)
Operating Profit	*52.6*	*64.6*
Administration	(6.6)	(12.3)
Interest Expense	(15.0)	(13.5)
Other Income-Net (including sales of assets)	4.0	15.9
Profit before Tax	*35.0*	*54.7*
Tax	(5.7)	(18.0)
Profit after Tax	*29.3*	*36.7*
Capital Expenditure Appropriation	(19.9)	(17.2)
Profit Available	*9.4*	*19.5*
Dividends	(9.1)	(9.1)

Source: SouthGold Annual Report, 1998.

EXHIBIT 5 SouthGold Balance Sheet (millions of Rand)

	1998	1997
Assets	*343.9*	*314.3*
Fixed Assets	289.9	201.6
Investments	0.6	0.3
Long-term Loans (unsecured)	0.6	0.4
Inventories	18.9	17.4
Accounts Receivable	4.9	2.8
Cash	29.0	91.8
Liabilities	*91.7*	*62.4*
Accounts Payable	21.5	17.2
Notes and Loans Payable	15.7	17.2
Long Term Debt	39.0	15.3
Deferred Revenues and Other Liabilities	15.5	12.7
Shareholders' Equity	*252.2*	*251.9*
Capital Stock	251.9	241.5
Retained Earnings	0.3	10.4

Source: SouthGold Annual Report, 1998.

and a limited set of world competitors, the joint forces of externally imposed trade sanctions and internally imposed protectionist measures created an environment where two sorts of firms thrived. The giants, such as Anglo American Corporation and Gencor, controlled vast empires that spanned mining of all sorts as well as financial services.[4] The limited investment opportunities open to South African companies as well as the limited liquidity available because of trade sanctions imposed on the white regime led to economic autarky. Isolated and under the umbrella of the giant corporations, there existed a mass of small and highly risky speculative ventures. These small mining houses normally consisted of a whole or partial share of a single mine and were financed with some combination of bullion loans,[5] high-risk equity, or investments from the major mining firms.

In a world of limited investment opportunities, the South African mining companies bought and sold operations on what seemed to be a daily basis, valuing and revaluing assets for tax purposes. According to conventional practice, the "corporation" only invested in the mine and never really operated it. The mine would be listed as a separate entity and would pay fees and dividends to the "corporate" investor. Such activities led to a Peyton Place of cross-shareholdings and a pyramid of ownership aimed at deterring hostile takeovers while making the industry unfathomable to any but an absolute insider.[6]

The last decade of the 20th century brought political and economic change at home as well as integration into a global economy that had been evolving dramatically while South Africa stagnated. The expanding mining operations of the states of the former Soviet Union as well as developing countries and traditional competitors such as Australia, the USA, and Canada were eroding South Africa's dominant position in gold. Although still pos-

[4]It is worth noting that even today, the South African mining industry is dominated by a few large players—Anglo American/DeBeers, Gencor/GFSA, Anglovaal and JCI—and two family groups—the Oppenheimers (Anglo American/DeBeers) and the Hersov and Menell's (Anglovaal).

[5]A bullion loan is one denominated in ounces of gold. A company would receive an amount of gold to be sold on the market (or an agreed dollar loan) for which it agreed to repay in ounces of gold plus interest subject to a specified schedule. Bullion loans are normally made at the gold lease rate. Traditionally, the gold lease rate has been far below the rate for lending cash as a reflection of the fact that the forward price of gold has normally been in excess of the spot price.

[6]Here is just one simple example of such cross holdings. The Rembrandt Group owns 40 percent of GFSA Holdings Ltd., which owns 43 percent of Gold Fields, which owns 37 percent of Driefontien Ltd., which, together with Gold Fields, owns 40 percent of Asteroid Ltd., which owns 40 percent of GFSA Holdings Ltd.

EXHIBIT 6 South African Gold Production (metric tons)

Year	Western World Production	South African Production	Year	Western World Production	South African Production
1960	1,066.8	664.6	1991	2,627.1	601.6
1965	1,281.5	949.6	1992	2,928.9	615.1
1970	1,226.0	968.5	1993	2,794.4	620.4
1975	956.2	713.3	1994	2,817.3	583.2
1980	961.8	675.2	1995	3,026.8	523.6
1985	1,235.5	672.1	1996	3,079.5	495.8
1990	2,516.2	606.4	1997	3,592.5	492.2

Source: Chamber of Mines of South Africa.

sessing almost 40 percent of the world's reserves, South Africa's proportion of gold production has been declining steadily (see Exhibit 6). At the same time, the importance of gold to the South African economy was declining. In 1980, gold production accounted for more than 15 percent of South Africa's gross domestic product (GDP). By 1997, this figure was under 3 percent of GDP and is still falling.

Although the industry has been restructuring and downsizing for more than a decade one could hardly call its approach radical. Faced with the problem of having to spend more money to get ore from older and deeper mines while the price of the final commodity fell continually on the open market, marginal mines were closed and the mineworkers sent packing. Between 1987 and 1997, 180,000 gold miners were laid off with an additional 50,000 estimated to have lost their jobs in 1997.[7] However, in spite of these layoffs the need to pull more ore from the ground to produce the same amount of gold increased costs by more than 10 percent in 1997.[8]

According to *The Economist,* "if nothing else this miserable performance has concentrated minds wonderfully,"[9] and 1998 appeared to be the year when all that concentration reached a head. In addition to the formation of SouthGold, two giant corporations were formed plus a host of smaller entities. The integration of the gold holdings of Anglo American Corporation led to the creation of the world's second largest gold company—Anglogold—controlling 9 percent of world output. Gold Fields (first known as Goldco) represented the merger of the gold operations of GFSA and Gencor. Finally, Consolidated African Mining acquired the assets of JCI Gold to move from the second tier to the first tier of players. Add to this group, Avgold—the integration of Anglovaal, West Areas, and Target Exploration Company formed in 1996—and one has well over 80 per cent of South Africa's gold mining assets in four companies (see Exhibit 7).

What is interesting about these changes is that they are not being carried out by a group of rampaging financial raiders but by the participants themselves—yet another sign of the insularity of the industry. The notable exception to this is Randgold—which has been likened

EXHIBIT 7 South Africa's Top Gold Mining Companies (excluding SouthGold)

Company	Assets (Rand millions)
Anglogold	22,056.4
Gold Fields	14,759.0
Avgold	1,898.4
Consolidated African Mining	1,619.0
Randgold	1,343.9
West Rand Consolidated	190.8
Kalahari Goldridge	122.6
Amalia Mining	71.9

Note: All figures for FY ending December 1997. Gold Fields' figures are for FY ending June 1998. Consolidated African Mining figures are for March 1998 and reflect the merged operations of JCI Gold. Kalahari Goldridge is partially owned by West Rand Consolidated, however, West Rand Consolidated numbers exclude this ownership.

Source: Reuters.

[7]Golden Handshake, *The Economist,* 26 July 1997; Kathy Chenault, A Tremor in the Mines, *Business Week,* 23 March 1998.

[8]South African Chamber of Mines, *Industry Overview 1997.*

[9]A New Vein, *The Economist,* 27 September 1997.

by industry insiders to the wildebeest that is isolated by the pride of lions. In 1994, Julian Baring of Mercury Asset Management, forced the removal of the directors and instilled a new team. Under the new executive director, Mr. Peter Flack, Randgold began a restructuring program aimed at: eliminating the management contracts between the mining companies and the mining finance houses; eliminating management layers; restructuring via merger; and exchanging mineral rights so as to colocate mining operations.[10] Unlike its rivals, which have sought integration and scale, Randgold has been restructured into a number of small companies more akin to the second tier Australian and Canadian gold producers. Mr. Baring's views were quite clear. "The fees previously paid to shareholders of the mining houses will accrue to the shareholders of the individual mines. . . . and the mining houses will have to maximize the share price of their underlying mines, rather than their management fees."[11] According to some, the Randgold restructuring is a model driven by managerial efficiency—its head office staff was cut from 128 people to just 14—as opposed to efficiency by sheer scale and the removal of miners. [12]

Gold and the Management of Risk

As noted earlier, South African mining houses were quite lax in their management of risk. Historically, they would control cash flow fluctuations in two ways. First, they would share resources with other mining companies reducing their dependence on the output of a single commodity or mine. Hence the complicated ownership arrangements found in the traditional diversified South African mining company. Second, they would push the risk down onto the mining operation with the headquarters serving a purely administrative and financial function. The headquarters would then charge fees associated with management contracts. These fees were fairly inflexible and provided the mining house with a steady stream of income.

In the case of deep mine gold production a third option was available. Unlike their open-pit competitors, the South African gold producers could vary production through the veins they mined and the speed of production. Open-pit mines were cheaper to operate overall but were inflexible in terms of production. In other words, large amounts of ore needed to be milled to achieve a specific amount of gold and the amount of ore necessary was not easily predictable *ex ante*. In the case of deep-pit mining, it was easier to target what was being mined, and output was subject to finer tuning.[13]

Three new realities were making financial hedging more important for the South African companies. First, as the grade of ore declined and the cost of operating their mines increased, the ability to fine tune production was becoming less important. Second, pressure from international investors, made starkly clear from the Randgold case, was forcing a change in thinking about the nature of the industry in total and putting the traditional management contract at risk. Finally, the supply and demand structure of the gold market was going through fundamental change that required a different outlook on the role of the mining company.

Although the demand for gold has traditionally been far in excess of the amount mined (see Exhibit 8), the growth in competition, along with the dramatic sales of gold bullion by the major central banks—it was estimated that between 1990 and 1997 central banks sold 1,410 tons of gold [14]—have created enormous downward price pressure. According to Rhona O'Connell, founding partner of T. Hoare and Company, "the gold gap (between supply and demand) will increase by an average of 100 tons a year over the next 10 years. There is scope in the mining industry for annual hedging of 220 tons and then, should the desire be there, there is scope for central banks to feed 300 tons into the market to keep the balance."[15] It is equally likely that the full-scale integration of the European Union's central banks under the European Central Bank, along with the desire to trade a nonearning asset gold for earning assets will lead to continued net sales of gold by the world's monetary authorities.

The number of risk management instruments used by gold mining firms and financial managers has grown dramatically over the last several years. According to O'Connell around 9 percent of world production is cur-

---

[10]Kenneth Gooding, South Africa: Gold—the Ground Shifts for a World Leader, *Financial Times,* 15 September 1997.

[11]Ibid.

[12]The South African Mining Industry, *Engineering and Mining Journal,* April 1998.

[13]Kenneth Gooding, South Africa: Anglogold puts Brave Face on Drop in Prices, *Financial Times,* 27 November 1997.

[14]Patrick Laurence, South Africa: Precious Little Cheer as Gold Loses its Luster, *Financial Times,* 16 July 1997.

[15]Melanie Cheary, South Africa: Growing Gold Gap Seen Filled by Hedges, *Reuters News Service,* 28 July 1997.

EXHIBIT 8 World Gold Supply and Demand (1990–2001, in tons)

	Demand	New Mine Supply	Shortfall in Supply	Official Holdings
1990	2,146	2,133	13	35,750
1991	2,293	2,159	134	35,712
1992	2,528	2,232	296	35,351
1993	2,472	2,289	183	35,103
1994	2,459	2,278	181	34,938
1995	2,732	2,269	463	34,819
1996	2,630	2,346	284	34,675
1997	2,851	2,402	449	34,053
1998[e]	2,949	2,510	439	33,703
1999[f]	2,960	2,530	430	33,453
2000[f]	3,144	2,540	604	32,903
2001[f]	3,254	2,580	674	32,253

Note: The World Gold Council surveys account for less than 100 percent of world gold demand. Actual demand may be as large as 20 percent above the stated figures. 1998 figures are estimates. Figures from 1999–2001 are author's estimates based on information from ABN Amro.

Source: Anglo American Corporation; World Gold Council; International Monetary Fund, *International Financial Statistics,* 1998; ABN Amro, *Gold—1999 Outlook,* 1998.

rently hedged in some way, shape or form.[16] Cox and Emsley [17] estimated that 65 percent of this is driven by mine hedging with the remainder being split between speculative and inventory activity. However, in spite of this there is quite a diverse range of approaches. Many companies, both large and small, engaged in no risk management whatsoever and publicly declared that they were doing so in order for their shareholders to capture the full benefit of the increase in the price of gold and to chose to reduce their risk through their own diversification policy. As Pierre Lassonde, president of Euro-Nevada explains,[18]

> "We will not do it. If our shareholders want to play the gold market—because that's what you're doing—they can go out themselves and do it. We don't think it's management's role to basically guess or bet what the gold price will be next year. If you're wrong, it's going to cost you a ton of money."

Other companies, most notably the Canadian giant American Barrick, hedged almost all their production. Still others, such as Barrick's main North American competitor, Newmont Mining, come out somewhere in between. Newmont hedges about 20 percent of its production.[19]

Of the South African companies, both Anglogold and Gold Fields have active hedging strategies. Anglogold's strategy has been geared around controlling the price received from active mines whereas Gold Fields' approach has been directed at the development and expansion of operations (e.g., it hedged 90 tons of gold related to its Beatrix mine). The most interesting hedge was JCI's (now part of Consolidated African Mining) South Deep expansion where the entire planned output of the mine was presold in forward contracts. However, in spite of this activity, the active management of risk is far less likely in the smaller mining houses of South Africa.

Risk Management Instruments

The risk management instruments available to SouthGold include *gold financings* (such as bullion loans), *forward sales* and *spot deferred contracts,* and *futures* and *options* on both gold and currency (and options on the futures contracts). According to Cox and Emsley approximately

[16]Ibid.

[17]Ian Cox and Ian Emsley, *Utilisation of Borrowed Gold by the Mining Industry: Development and Future Prospects,* Research Study No. 18, World Gold Council, 1998.

[18]Keith Damsell, Canada: Barrick May Be Doing It, but That Doesn't Mean Gold Hedging Is The Way To Go, *National Post,* 20 January 1999.

[19]Paul Simao, USA: Top Gold Producers Force Investors to Hedge Bets, *Reuters News Service,* 10 September 1998.

75 percent of risk management activity was in forward sales and spot deferred contracts, 20 percent in options, and the remainder in loans.[20]

Gold financing is mostly associated with the financing of new mining ventures or long-term capital improvements. For example, Southreef had financed a portion of its initial investment in the development of the Southreef mine with a five-year 20 million Rand bullion loan, virtually all of which has been paid off. The relatively low cost of borrowing in gold versus currency make such loans attractive in high interest rate periods but less attractive in situations like that prevailing today.[21] Other instruments that have been used by international gold companies include gold indexed offerings and trusts.

A gold indexed offering is literally what it says, of which the most common example is the gold-indexed bond. One traditional bond is denominated in a specific amount of gold and pays the holder interest based on an interest rate and the face value of the instrument (e.g., it might pay 2.5 percent on a face value of $1,000). The holder has the right to redeem the offering after a specific date for a specified amount of gold (or its cash equivalent). In most situations, the longer the offering is not redeemed the greater the redemption value in gold. Another example relates the interest rate to the price of gold. When First Toronto Mining took over the Australian gold mining firm Forsayth NL in 1989, it offered three common shares and one C$5 gold-indexed bond for every 10 shares of Forsayth. The bonds came due five years after the issue. Paying an initial rate of 6 percent, they would rise by one percentage point a calendar quarter for each C$25 increase in the price of gold above the C$400 an ounce base price. The maximum interest rate was 25 percent.[22]

Gold trusts are normally reserved for larger operations due to the complexity of their initial setup. A typical trust instrument entitles the holder to a percentage of the mine's output, with the exact percentage being based on the price of gold. Barrick Resources was a clear innovator in this area, financing two mines—Renabie in 1983 and Camflo in 1984—with the first such trusts in Canada.[23] However, with the general decline in the value of gold, the rise of bullion lending, and the growth of equity gold funds, such trusts have declined in importance.

"Accelerated selling" such as through forward sales and spot deferred contracts are the instruments of choice for gold firms attempting to hedge their price risk. Forward contracts commit the seller to deliver a specified amount of gold on a specific date at a price preset by the agreement. Settlement of the contract occurs on the delivery date. Forward sales are private contracts, normally of a relatively short duration, that can be tailored to the individual needs of the parties. The parties can settle these contracts earlier than the delivery date subject to negotiation. Normally, gold forward prices are in excess of the spot price at the time of the contract—a situation known as contango.[24] The premium reflects the difference between lending cash for interest (such as the LIBOR) and lending gold, the gold lease rate. Exhibit 9 provides information on the historic spot and forward prices for gold along with LIBOR and the gold lease rate.

Spot deferred contracts are virtually identical to forward sales with the exception that the seller has control over the delivery date. For example, such a contract might specify that the first delivery date for 20,000 ounces of gold at a price of $310 an ounce to be 2 January 2000 and the last delivery date as 2 January 2009. When 2 January 2000 arrives, the company has the choice of delivering the gold at $310 an ounce or deferring to the next delivery date, e.g., one-year hence. The price set for the new delivery date would be based on the spot price on 2 January 2000 plus the forward premium existing at the time. Spot deferred contracts are effectively identical to closing out one forward position and opening another. However, they are effective tax management instruments (since no gains and losses need to be recorded when they are "rolled over") for companies with strong balance sheets or large uncollateralized assets.

Both spot deferred contracts and forward sales are handled privately through specialized banks and financial houses.

Futures contracts are similar to forward contracts but are rarely used by mining companies due to the fact that they are marked-to-market on a daily basis. This requires daily settlement and is antithetical to the cash flow management needs of the gold producers. Options are a more obvious choice since they allow the producer to protect itself from price fluctuations, hence implicitly purchasing balance

[20]Ian Cox and Ian Emsley, *Utilisation of Borrowed Gold by the Mining Industry: Development and Future Prospects*, Research Study No. 18, World Gold Council, 1998.

[21]See, Jessica Cross, *New Frontiers in Gold: The Derivatives Revolution*, London: Rosendale Press, 1994.

[22]Allan Robinson, Australia: Change of Plans by First Toronto Brings $157.7 Million Forsayth Bid, *Globe and Mail*, 26 August 1989.

[23]Peter Tufano and Jon Serbin, *American Barrick Resources Corporation*, Harvard Business School Case 9–293–128, 1993.

[24]The reverse situation, when the spot price is greater than the forward price is known as backwardation.

EXHIBIT 9 Gold Spot, Forward and Future Price, Gold Lease Rate, and LIBOR (1990–1999)

	Gold Price (Spot, $US/oz.)	Gold Price (Forward, $US/oz.)	Gold Price (Future, $US/oz.)	Gold Lease Rate (percent)	LIBOR (percent)
January 1990	411.45	422.59	N/A	0.75	8.43
July 1990	356.80	369.89	370.00	1.95	8.38
January 1991	366.10	375.63	365.80	1.18	7.63
July 1991	368.00	373.73	370.00	0.65	6.44
January 1992	356.75	364.83	356.70	0.79	4.25
July 1992	343.00	349.18	344.40	1.27	4.00
January 1993	329.70	334.96	330.00	1.02	3.63
July 1993	377.00	380.75	379.10	0.68	3.50
January 1994	382.00	392.92	381.60	0.54	3.50
July 1994	385.50	394.58	387.30	0.79	5.25
January 1995	374.85	385.59	375.50	1.21	7.00
July 1995	384.15	387.70	385.50	2.16	5.99
January 1996	406.20	414.45	405.60	1.62	5.51
July 1996	380.20	384.77	381.60	1.81	5.79
January 1997	344.10	349.11	344.50	1.45	5.60
July 1997	333.70	342.07	335.30	2.40	5.91
January 1998	302.20	311.13	295.00	1.82	5.77
July 1998	296.70	303.40	298.10	1.76	5.78
January 1999	285.30	291.73	288.30	0.81	4.97

Note: All interest rates and futures and forward prices are for six months ahead.
Source: Bloomburg, Reuters, Peter Tufano.

sheet and income statement insurance.[25] Mining firms traditionally buy put options—which gives them the right to sell gold at a specified price up to a specified date (in the case of American-style options[26])—or use a "collar." A collar is achieved through the financing of the purchase of put options with the selling of call options. Call options give them the right to buy gold at a specified price up to a specified date. The call option's exercise price would be above the puts option's exercise price, insuring the trader that they would be selling the commodity within the range between the two exercise prices. Because of the offsetting premia of the two positions, the firm is able to either insure itself costlessly or at a very low price. By varying the exercise prices and the number of puts and calls purchased, the firm can determine how much upside and downside risk it wishes to take. Exhibit 10 presents the future and forward prices for gold up to December 1999 and Exhibit 11 provides information of a selection of options on futures traded on the Chicago Mercantile Exchange.

SouthGold's Risk Management Strategy

Like most small South African companies SouthGold and its predecessors, Southreef and SAR, were not

[25]Option contracts can be either privately arranged or purchased and sold through organized exchanges. For example, the Chicago Mercantile Exchange and the South African Futures Exchange trade both gold and rand futures and options on these futures contracts.

[26]American-style options allow the holder to exercise them at anytime up to the maturity date. European-style options can be exercised only on the maturity date. In our discussion we will refer to American options. It should be kept in mind that many types of options do exist. The most used "exotic" options include the Asian option (the exercise price is compared to the average spot price over the life of the option), the exploding option (the option exists until some preagreed barrier price is reached, at which point the options ceases to exist), and the binary option (the payout is all-or-nothing depending on whether or not the underlying assets price meets a predetermined condition).

EXHIBIT 10 Gold Futures Prices, Gold Lease Rates and Rand/$US Forward Rates (as of January 30, 1999)

End of Contract Date	Gold Price (future, $US/oz.)	Gold Lease (Rate (percent)	Rand/US$ Forward Rate
February 1999	288.4	0.60	6.14
March 1999	285.6	0.66	6.19
April 1999	289.2	0.71	6.24
May 1999	—	—	—
June 1999	291.1	—	—
July 1999	—	0.81	6.37
August 1999	295.1	—	—
September 1999	—	—	—
October 1999	294.8	—	6.51
November 1999	—	—	—
December 1999	296.6	—	—
January 2000	—	1.42	6.65

Source: New York Mercantile Exchange, Kitco, Reuters.

sophisticated derivatives operators. Both South Reef and SAR had begun aggressively forward selling gold only two years ago and Southreef's mine development was partially funded with a bullion loan. For example, in 1999 SouthGold was guaranteed sales of over 67,000 ounces gold at $399 an ounce on its U.S. dollar contracts and $307.78 on its Rand denominated contracts (assuming a 6 Rand to the U.S. dollar exchange rate) (see Exhibit 12). However, as Janet Smyth notes, the imbalance between the price of SouthGold's dollar and its Rand forward sales is quite telling.

> "It was fairly obvious that when Robert and Richard entered into these contracts they were concerned about guaranteeing continuity of sales at a price rather than getting a complete insurance contract. The failure to protect the Rand denominated contracts against a decline in the currency was clearly an oversight. One of the first things I did on coming here in November was to buy six month call options with an exercise price of 6.15 Rand to the dollar to protect us from a further decline in the 1999 Rand denominated contracts. Clearly this cost us some money, but we could not afford to have to sell 10 percent of our production at fairly close to our operating costs. We weren't losing money but we certainly weren't making as much as was possible. There was too much reliance on the fact that our cost of production would fall in line with our revenues."

For SouthGold the question of the development of a hedging strategy to match with the development of the company was critical.

For Riks and Viljoen the prospect of bringing on line the Mumbwa mine was alluring but it was obvious that the cost of production was going to be at least 10 to 20 percent higher than the Dunblaine operation. Jonathan Wright, SouthGold's Director of Technical Operations, felt that it was not unreasonable to expect a yield of 2.5–3.5 grams of gold per ton of ore from Mumbwa with a total mineral resources reserve on the order of 2–3 million metric tons. With this level of reserves the mine could be operational for 5 to 7 years. However, with such a yield it was unclear whether the mine was viable at today's gold prices, especially given the estimated 25 million Rand start up cost.

Similarly, the developments in the South African and Zambian economies were worrying (see Exhibits 13 and 14). Viljoen in particular was worried about the declining value of the Rand, with its potential to affect the company's Rand denominated forward sales, both those fixed as of today and possible positions the company would take in the future. He was also intrigued by a recent Intermoney report on the South African Rand that highlighted that the growing forex trade in the Rand makes its short run movements with gold tenuous.[27] "We always assumed that as the gold price fell so, too, would the Rand, thereby protecting our production cost base. I don't think we can so readily rely on this tendency as we once had."

Sam Mbuli, however, was concerned about the value of the Zambian Kwacha (see Exhibit 15), which had been falling dramatically since early 1998. SouthGold clearly gained from the lower cost of production this entailed but Mbuli was concerned about the possibility of a general economic collapse that could affect as much as 20 percent of SouthGold's production and investment. Noted Mbuli, "I can imagine what would happen if we attempted to finance the production of the mine with a bullion loan or a large tranch of forward sales and the government passed a law restricting gold sales by foreign entities."

[27] Intermoney, *South African Rand 1999—Blowing in the Wind*, London: Independent Economic Analysis, 1998.

EXHIBIT 11 Examples of Options on Futures Contracts

Expiry Date (1999)	Contract (1999)	Exercise Price	Call (price)	Put (price)
March 12	April	250	N/O	N/O
July 9	August	250	43.0	1.4
November 12	December	250	N/O	N/O
March 12	April	260	29.2	0.4
July 9	August	260	34.0	2.0
November 12	December	260	40.0	2.3
March 12	April	290	3.5	4.3
July 9	August	290	10.4	7.8
November 12	December	290	16.6	8.6
March 12	April	310	0.4	21.2
July 9	August	310	3.8	20.4
November 12	December	310	7.8	18.9
March 12	April	330	0.1	40.8
July 9	August	330	1.7	37.1
November 12	December	330	2.8	32.9
March 12	April	350	N/O	N/O
July 9	August	350	0.8	57.0
November 12	December	350	1.8	51.4

Note: Prices on 30 January 1999. When transacted prices not available the price is the average of the bid and asks. N/O implies a contract is not offered.

Source: New York Mercantile Exchange.

EXHIBIT 12 SouthGold's Forward Sales of Gold

For the 12 Months Ending December 31	Ounces Sold (000)	Kilograms Sold	Price in $US per Ounce	Price in Rand per Kg
1999	49	521	399	65,140
2000	41	273	386	67,571
2001	39	224	399	74,943
2002	34	145	401	81,114
2003	19	586	401	86,507
2004	7	229	419	96,876

Source: SouthGold Annual Report, 1998.

EXHIBIT 13 Selected Economic Indicators for the South African Economy (1990–1997)

	1990	1991	1992	1993	1994	1995	1996	1997
Gross Domestic Product (millions of Rand)	276,060	310,074	341,765	382,199	431,088	484,614	542,741	594,858
Exports of Goods & Services (millions of Rand)	70,714	74,220	79,105	91,233	103,098	121,857	149,361	165,185
Imports of Goods & Services (millions of Rand)	54,046	58,726	65,285	76,155	95,275	120,947	142,283	158,353
Net Income and Overseas Transfers (millions of Rand)	−10,332	−8,568	−8,635	−8,320	−8,209	−8,826	−12,365	−13,368
Government Deficit (millions of Rand)	10,457	13,987	26,423	28,342	38,690	23,465	28,563	28,129
Consumer Price Index	100.00	96.4	93.5	93.3	95.8	103.00	100.5	103.6
Mining Production Index	100.00	99.1	99.5	102.5	100.9	99.3	98.8	100.9
Mining Employment Index	100.00	97.4	102.4	100.6	100.8	101.7	97.9	94.3
Population (millions)	37.07	38.01	38.82	39.63	40.44	41.24	42.39	N/A

Source: IMF, International Financial Statistics Yearbook, Washington, DC 1998.

EXHIBIT 14 Selected Economic Indicators for the Zambian Economy (1990–1997)

	1990	1991	1992	1993	1994	1995	1996	1997
Gross Domestic Product (millions of Kwacha)	113,300	218,300	569,600	1,482,100	2,240,700	2,998,300	3,969,500	5,155,800
Exports (millions of Kwacha)	42,300	75,000	147,100	420,900	806,500	1,082,300	1,237,400	1,552,000
Imports (millions of Kwacha)	41,700	67,300	178,400	450,600	905,200	1,228,200	1,710,400	2,196,000
Government Deficit (millions of Kwacha)	9,800	98,400	N/A	N/A	83,900	203,200	29,300	N/A
Consumer Price Index	100.00	193.2	519.8	1,497.4	2,300.2	3,086.8	4,515.2	5,635.4
Mining Production Index	100.00	90.1	100.8	92.0	76.8	N/A	N/A	N/A
Population (millions)	8.07	7.39	7.55	7.72	7.90	9.37	8.28	N/A

Source: IMF, International Financial Statistics Yearbook, Washington, DC 1998.

The SouthGold team of Viljoen, Smyth, and Mbuli clearly had its work cut out for it. Both Riks and Viljoen agreed that a long term risk management strategy needed to be in place by March 1999. Until this strategy was clearly defined any question of the opening of the Mumbwa mine had to be delayed at considerable cost to the company. As Riks summed it up, "all up, the Zambian operations cost us around 65 million Rand. Unless we could get this operation going our investment will decline further in value as the Kwacha collapses. The future of this company depends less on getting gold from the ground than getting a handle on the management of risks we face with respect to our revenue base."

EXHIBIT 15 South African Rand and Zambian Kwacha—US Dollar Exchange Rates (1990–1999) and Six Month Forward Rand Rates

	Rand Per $US	Kwacha Per $US	Forward Rates Rand/$US
January 1990	2.55	13.8	N/A
June 1990	2.66	30.3	N/A
January 1991	2.54	42.8	2.65
June 1991	2.89	64.6	3.02
January 1992	2.79	89.0	2.96
June 1992	2.82	172.2	2.90
January 1993	3.07	325.0	3.19
June 1993	3.17	522.1	3.45
January 1994	3.40	635.8	3.52
June 1994	3.63	690.0	3.73
January 1995	3.54	690.0	3.63
June 1995	3.68	920.1	3.79
January 1996	3.65	978.0	3.80
June 1996	4.35	1,265.0	4.52
January 1997	4.68	1,290.0	4.79
June 1997	4.47	1,310.0	4.78
January 1998	4.86	1,480.0	5.14
June 1998	5.15	1,945.0	6.32
January 1999	6.05	2,580.0	6.43

Source: Bloomberg, Reuters. Kwacha data before January 1993 estimated from IMF, *International Financial Statistics,* various issues.

UNIT 11 Managing Global Manufacturing and Logistics

Case 11–1

BOK Fibers International

BOK Fibers International (BFI) was a "strategic business unit" within the Fibers Division of BOK NV, a diversified multinational company active in a variety of chemical fields and based in Holland. In 1995, the Fibers Division had total sales of $2.9 billion, and an operating income of $250 million. These figures represented 17 and 12 percent, respectively, of the parent company's total sales and operating profits. The Division's six business units were structured around specific technologies or product/markets and served primarily European customers. BFI was the division's unit responsible for all textile and industrial fiber operations outside the European economic space. BFI was one of the division's best performing business units, accounting for over 20 percent of overall division sales and for a third of its total profitability.

After many years of successful operations, BFI's financial performance had taken a turn for the worse in the early 1990s (see Exhibit 1 for details). Part of the problem was due to the increase in competitive pressures from new producers in Asia and a rise in capacity investments by other competitors in BFI's main markets outside Europe. But another important factor was the rapid drop in tariff and other quantitative import barriers among many developing countries around the world as they adopted market-based economic policies. BFI's network of affiliated companies were the beneficiaries as well as the victims of this new liberal "world order."

A case in point was the rate of economic change buffeting Latin America since the mid-1980s. BFI's Latin American operations represented the largest share of the unit's global revenues, followed by its operations in Japan, India, and East Asia. The rapid spread of market-oriented policies throughout the region and the growing tendency towards economic integration had surfaced serious management coordination problems given the structure of BFI's Latin American operations. As a result, BFI's managing director, Hans Schmidt, was interested in finding ways through which it could increase coordination among their various affiliates and, as a result, yield higher profits for the group as well as for the individual participating companies.

Company History

The BOK Group was established as a result of a series of mergers that characterized the European chemical industry in the postwar period. The first of these was the merger of two Belgian companies—Oostende Chemische Groep and Belgische Pharmaceutieke—in 1952, which created a diversified chemical firm known as Belpharm-Oostende. In the late 1950s, the Board of Belpharm-Oostende decided to enter various downstream product markets such as plastic derivatives and coatings in order to realize opportunities for forward integration of the company's technologies, as well as to take advantage of the expected concentration in the chemical industry that would result from increased levels of technological development.

In 1960, Belpharm-Oostende was acquired by Koninklijke Chemische Fabrieken (KCF), a diversified group based in Holland with activities in chemical fibers, plastics, processed foods, and consumer products. KCF was itself the result of a series of previous mergers involving both Dutch and German companies in the field of petrochemical derivatives and downstream products. KCF brought needed managerial and marketing skills to the new company, plus a more international orientation that

---

This case was prepared by Professors José de la Torre and Sriram Dasu together with Mr. Nasser Sagheb (MBA 1988), at the Anderson School at UCLA as a basis for class discussion. The authors are grateful for the generous contributions of a number of senior executives in the company here called BOK NV and their affiliates in Latin America. All case data, names, and figures have been disguised to preserve corporate confidentiality, but they retain the essence of the original facts and relationships. The authors maintain all responsibility for the case content and any errors or misrepresentation of facts.

EXHIBIT 1 BOK Fibers International—Financial Performance, 1989–95
(in millions of U.S. dollars)

	1989	1990	1991	1992	1993	1994	1995
Total Sales	$466	$432	$487	$632	$710	$659	$653
Operating Profit	$123	$75	$107	$144	$122	$90	$75
Return on Sales (%)	26.4%	17.4%	22.0%	22.8%	17.2%	13.7%	11.5%

Source: Company records.

included affiliates throughout the world. These skills and businesses had to be integrated into the more technical and research culture that prevailed at Belpharm-Oostende, an inherently conservative company. The resulting organization was renamed BOK and regrouped into eight major divisions, one of which was BOK Fibers.

Capitalizing on a number of industry innovations, KCF had established or acquired subsidiary companies in Germany, France, and Spain throughout the early and mid-1950s. A North American subsidiary was set up in 1957 in Georgia, followed by two Latin American affiliates in Mexico and Argentina. After the merger with Belpharm-Oostende, BOK's newly established Fiber Division continued its international expansion throughout the 1960s with investments in Sweden, India, and Thailand, the establishment of three additional Latin American affiliates in Colombia, Brazil, and Ecuador, and a number of licensing agreements with similar firms in Japan and other East Asian countries.

Beginning in the early 1970s, the fiber industry underwent a series of capacity crises that led to severe losses and major shifts in competitive position among many of its key players. Simultaneously, Asian producers, particularly in India, Pakistan, Taiwan, Hong Kong, and Korea, began major investment programs in synthetic fiber production that threatened the established producers. Exhibits 2 and 3 show the evolution of production of man-made fibers since 1970. Of these totals, "cellulosic" fibers accounted for nearly the same tonnage in 1995 (3.2 million) as they did in 1970 (3.6 million). Production of "synthetic" fibers, however, had grown rapidly from 4.8 to 18.3 million tons in 1970–1995, accounting for 85 percent of all man-made fiber production. This dramatic shift in synthetic fiber production to emerging markets followed an earlier and similar shift in the textile and clothing industries.

Throughout this period, BOK's fiber business changed accordingly (see Exhibit 4). The eventual sale of its North American subsidiary (it had always been too small to compete adequately in that market) and the successive streamlining and rationalization of European operations led to a very different mix of businesses in 1995 when compared to 1970.

Major expansion through acquisitions in other areas of business such as paints and coatings, pharmaceuticals and specialty chemicals, characterized BOK's strategy throughout the decade of 1985–95. Driven in part by the growing integration of European markets, as well as by the global consolidation taking place in many of these sectors, the company had expanded to a level of nearly $20 billion in sales by 1996. As a result, the Fibers Division had lost some of the preeminence it had enjoyed within the old KCF structure.

The Latin American Affiliates

BFI had five affiliated companies in Latin America, each of which had different competitors and corporate structure.[1]

Mexico. Fibras Textiles S.A. (Fitex) was the oldest and largest of these companies. A joint venture with the powerful Omega Group, one of Mexico's strong diversified industrial conglomerates, Fitex was founded in 1957 in order to supply synthetic fibers to the growing textile market in that country as well as to the Central American region. Production later expanded to cover industrial fiber products in order to serve the growing automotive, tire, and other related industries setting up facilities in Mexico. With a total capacity of 150,000 tons (of which 80 percent were in synthetic textile fibers) and over 5,000

[1]The names, locations, and circumstances of the subsidiaries in question have been disguised to maintain confidentiality. Care has been given, however, to retain all relevant proportions and relational characteristics.

EXHIBIT 2 Distribution of World Production of Synthetic Fibers, 1970–1995
(in percentages)

	1970	1975	1980	1985	1990	1995
By Physical Type						
Yarn	50	51	45	46	47	54
Staple	50	49	55	54	53	46
	100	100	100	100	100	100
By Chemical Type						
Polyamide	40	33	30	26	24	18
Polyester	34	45	47	50	54	57
Polyacrilic	21	19	19	18	15	12
Other	5	3	4	6	7	13
	100	100	100	100	100	100
Polyester Fiber by Geographical Source						
W. Europe	28	19	14	14	11	8
United States	40	41	36	23	17	15
Japan	19	13	12	10	8	6
Other	13	27	38	53	64	71
	100	100	100	100	100	100

Source: Company records.

employees, Fitex was BOK's largest operating company outside of Western Europe. It commanded approximately 30 percent of the local market in competition with other international and domestic companies. Fitex was the second largest textile fiber manufacturer in Mexico.

BOK owned 40 percent of Fitex and had a technical agreement by which polyester fiber and other relevant product and process technologies were provided to the joint venture through various means, including the presence of a technical director seconded from BOK Fibers to Fitex. The Omega Group held the majority shares and was responsible for the management of the company.[2] Omega was a highly diversified group with activities ranging from steel production to consumer products, and they owned majority shares in two other fiber producers—in cellulose and nylon fibers, respectively—in collaboration with two U.S.-based chemical companies with which BOK competed in other markets. All three independent companies were managed under a common legal umbrella by Omega (Grupo Textil Omega, S.A. de C.V., a fully-owned subsidiary of the Omega Group) and shared the same top management and administrative services (e.g., a common managing director and financial director, as well as accounting, legal, personnel, and related services). The three operating subsidiaries, however, had separate facilities, technical and marketing staffs.

Fitex occupied its own manufacturing site in Monterrey, Mexico, and operated its own independent technical and commercial organization. The latter consisted of two sales forces for textile and industrial products, respectively, that reported to Fitex's Marketing Director. The current Technical Director at Fitex had been on the job for nearly five years and had previously served as plant manager for one of BOK's largest plants in Germany. Fitex had always been profitable, and the relationship between BOK Fibers'

[2]Foreign investment regulations in effect at the time of the establishment of Fitex required foreign companies wishing to invest in Mexico not to exceed 49 percent ownership, except in special cases. For petrochemicals and derivatives, the foreign investor's ownership was limited to 40 percent. These regulations had been rescinded as a result of the general liberalization of economic activity in Mexico that began in the late 1980s, a process later confirmed by Mexico's agreements under its adoption of OECD and NAFTA rules.

EXHIBIT 3 World Production of Man-Made Fibers, 1970–95

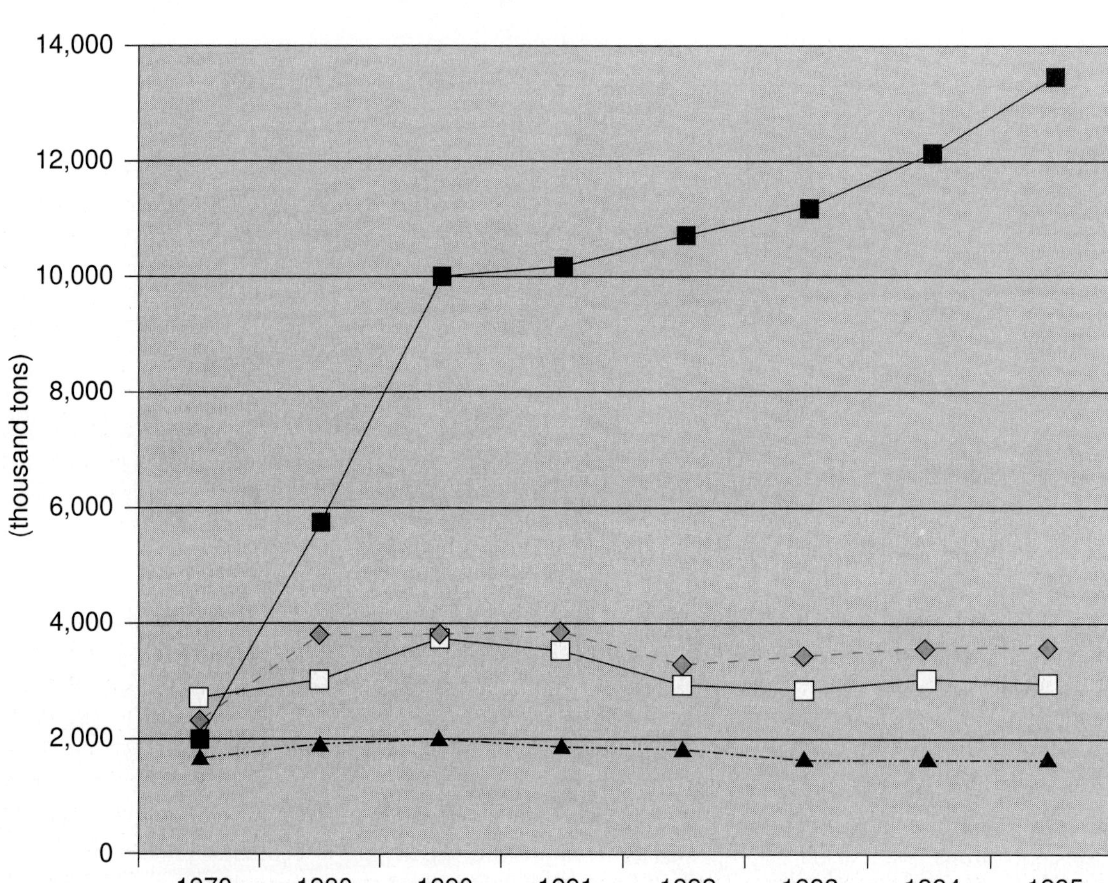

EXHIBIT 4 Distribution of BOK's Fiber Business, 1970 and 1995

	1970	1995
European Textile Fibers	66%	27%
European Industrial Fibers	20	24
Non-European Fibers	9	22
Engineering Plastics	0	12
Specialty Fibers	0	8
Non-fiber Products	5	7
Total	100%	100%

Source: Company records.

and Omega's management had been extremely cordial over the years. The current Managing Director of BFI had previously occupied the post of Technical Director at Fitex and knew the partner's top management well.

In recent years, Fitex had developed a booming export market to the United States and Canada. This was expected to grow in the aftermath of the signing of the North American Free Trade Area (NAFTA). The December 1994 economic crisis had seriously affected the company, particularly in terms of the collapse of domestic demand. The subsequent devaluation of the peso, however, was likely to give a boost to exports, both in terms of direct fiber exports as well as increased demand from Fitex's domestic textile and clothing client firms selling into foreign markets.

Colombia. This was one of BOK's earliest markets in South America, one with a long textile tradition. Colombia had an extremely efficient and competitive textile industry since the 1920s, although it was smaller than those in Mexico or Brazil. In the early 1950s, a gradual shift from natural to man-made fibers began to gather speed, and the two largest textile firms in the country (Textiles Antioqueños and Coltex) decided to integrate backwards into man-made fibers. They sought foreign partners and approached KCF, BOK's predecessor. As a result, a joint venture was established in which BOK owned 60 percent of the equity, and each of the two Colombian partners and customers owned 20 percent.

BOK-Andina, as the company was known, was managed by BFI and had grown over the years to dominate the domestic market with a market share in excess of 60 percent. Its plant with a capacity of 60,000 tons was located in Medellín, the center of Colombia's textile industry. The company's two local partners jointly accounted for approximately one-third of total sales, and had never become involved in day-to-day management decisions. The bulk of the remaining sales went to other smaller textile firms in Colombia as well as some exports to Venezuela, Ecuador, and the Caribbean. The signing of the Andean Pact had given the company the opportunity to extend its sales to other countries in the region, primarily Peru, but lingering protectionism in textile markets had prevented BOK-Andina from taking advantage of this situation.

BOK-Andina, while still profitable, has lost considerable ground financially in recent years. The government's recent commitment to open borders and international competition had a severe impact on market share and prices. Competition from neighboring textile and clothing firms had increased significantly, affecting BOK-Andina's domestic customers. In fact, one of its local partners, Textiles Antioqueños, had gotten into financial difficulties and had been exploring the possibility of selling its 20 percent share in the company in order to raise cash for its operations. There were also rumors of foreign chemical companies looking into the Colombian market for investment possibilities. The second local partner, Coltex, was part of a large financial holding headquartered in Bogota that had indicated an interest in taking action to improve the company's performance. Local management was, therefore, under pressure to find ways in which BOK-Andina's plant could be made more competitive in the new economic environment.

Brazil. KCF had also been approached in the late 1950s by an investment group from Brazil with the view of establishing a major textile fiber operation in that country. Company management was, however, concerned with what they considered high political risks associated with foreign investments in Brazil and chose not to enter with a direct equity investment. Instead, a licensing agreement was concluded between BOK Fibers International and Mr. Arturo Gomes, titular head of the Gomes family enterprises. This agreement provided for technology transfer and other technical assistance for the construction of a synthetic fiber plant named Polyester de Brasil, or Polybra, in the state of Minas Gerais. In exchange, Polybra would pay BFI a fixed minimum payment and royalties on sales.

Polybra operated autonomously from BFI since its inception. Although the terms of the agreement called for the presence of several BFI personnel in Brazil and for regular exchanges of technicians, no BFI staff had been posted to Brazil on a full-time basis after the initial shake-down of the plant in 1959. A balance-of-payments crisis in the early 1970s, however, made it impossible for Polybra to honor its financial commitments to BFI. As a result, BOK agreed to convert its royalty receivables into a minority interest of 25 percent in Polybra in 1975. Since then, additional expansion requirements and the multiple commitments of the Gomes family had caused BFI to increase its share of the equity in the business to 55 percent by 1991. Together with this shift in control, BFI had been obligated to staff some of Polybra's key management positions, including both the general manager and technical director. By 1995 the plant had a capacity of 95,000 tons and a market share in excess of 30 percent in Brazil.

BOK Fibers had subsequently opened another Brazilian subsidiary focused on industrial fibers. This company operated under the name of BOK Fibras do Brasil and was 100-percent owned by the parent company. It was located in the state of Sao Paulo and had a capacity of nearly 50,000 tons, serving a variety of industrial and automotive customers.

The Brazilian market had traditionally been fairly closed, with high tariff barriers and other quantitative restrictions. Recently, however, unilateral decreases in tariff protection as the result of the liberalization policies of the Franco and Cardoso governments, together with commitments to freer markets undertaken under the auspices of the WTO and Mercosur agreements, had impacted Polybra's performance. Sales of other BFI affiliates in South America into the Brazilian market, for example, had caused severe problems for the company. Among the largest of four local textile fiber manufacturers, Polybra had suffered heavily as Brazil had embraced a more liberal market-based economic system.

Others. BOK Fibers had two other affiliates in Latin America making textile fibers. A small company in Ecuador (15,000 tons in capacity) was started in the late 1970s to serve primarily local textile firms. BOK held a 49 percent interest in this company in partnership with local passive investors. BOK had originally held a 50 percent share in an Argentine company that produced both textile and industrial fibers (total capacity of about 50,000 tons), but had sold out its interest to their local partner some years ago, retaining only a technical licensing agreement. Both these firms were included in regional meetings dealing with marketing or technical issues. BFI management was of the opinion that if the problems afflicting their major Latin American textile fiber operations could be resolved, this would provide a blueprint for tackling similar problems elsewhere.[3]

[3]Given their relatively small size these two companies are not considered in the rest of this analysis. Similarly, other textile fiber affiliates in South and East Asia are not discussed further in this case, although some of them were experiencing similar problems in the early 1990s.

EXHIBIT 5 Market and Competitive Conditions in Mexico, 1995

A. Markets

The total size of the Mexican market in 1995 was approximately 400,000 tons of polyester fiber and 200,000 tons of other fibers, including industrial uses. Key figures regarding Fitex's competitive position in Mexico are shown below.

	Flat Yarn	Texturized Yarn	Other Fibers
Total Market (tons)	90,000	310,000	200,000
Main Competitors	4	6	12
Fitex:			
- capacity (tons)	30,000	90,000	30,000
- 1995 production	28,500	80,000	27,000
- capacity utilization	95%	89%	90%
- market share	32%	26%	37%[1]

B. Environment

Historically, Mexico had conducted its monetary affairs conservatively, except during periods immediately preceding presidential elections. Following the international debt crisis in 1982, rapid increases in inflation resulted. These were brought under control with an austerity economic program imposed at the end of 1987. Simultaneously, the Salinas administration launched a series of market initiatives designed to reduce the role of the state in the economy and modernize its productive sectors. Central to this program was a process of import liberalization, a fairly strong currency and broad privatizations. High inflows of foreign capital kept the peso overvalued and resulted in a large trade deficit. Eventually, the situation came to a crisis at the end of 1994, when the Zedillo government was forced into a major currency devaluation followed by a significant contraction of the domestic economy. Figures for domestic economic growth and inflation (wholesale price index with 1990=100), average foreign exchange rates, and a calculated "competitiveness factor" for the last six years are shown in the table on the following page.

[1]Applies only to the relevant segments in which Fitex competes.

EXHIBIT 5B (continued)

	1990	1991	1992	1993	1994	1995
Economic Growth	4.4%	4.2%	3.6%	2.0%	4.5%	(6.2%)
Price Index	100.0	120.5	136.7	148.8	158.9	221.1
- annual change	*23.3%*	*20.5%*	*13.4%*	*8.9%*	*6.8%*	*39.1%*
Exchange Rate[2]	2.813	3.018	3.095	3.116	3.375	6.419
- annual devaluation	*12.5%*	*6.8%*	*2.5%*	*0.7%*	*7.7%*	*47.4%*
Relative Competitiveness[3]	107.9	121.2	134.1	145.0	142.9	104.5

C. Future Expectations

Mexico is considered a stable country committed to democratic political reforms and a market economy within the context of NAFTA. They are actively seeking free trade pacts with other Central and South American countries. The country has a successful and diversified textile industry that will benefit greatly from implementation of the NAFTA accords. Reasonably conservative fiscal and monetary policies are expected under the Zedillo administration to lower inflation rates in the context of a free floating currency. Forecasts for economic growth, annual inflation, and average exchange rates relative to the US$ for 1996 thru 2000 are given below.

	Actual	Projections				
	1995	1996	1997	1998	1999	2000
Economic Growth	(6.2%)	5.0%	4.0%	3.5%	2.5%	4.0%
Price Index	221.1	276.4	331.6	364.8	419.5	461.5
- annual change	*39.1%*	*25.0%*	*20.0%*	*10.0%*	*15.0%*	*10.0%*
Exchange Rate[2]	6.419	8.025	8.447	8.891	11.855	13.172
- annual devaluation	*47.4%*	*20.0%*	*5.0%*	*5.0%*	*25.0%*	*10.0%*
Relative Competitiveness[3]	104.5	104.5	119.2	124.5	107.4	106.3

[2]Rates are in terms of New Pesos per U.S. dollar, averages for the year.
[3]This is a ratio of the domestic price increases at wholesale or producers level to the external devaluation of the currency (in terms of its value in dollars), both relative to their values in 1989. If greater than 100, the country's exports are losing competitiveness relative to the base year, and vice versa.

Exhibits 5 thru 8 provide additional information on the market and competitive conditions in each of these three countries, as well as in other key markets in South America with BFI affiliates or to which the BFI affiliates exported at one time or another. Exhibit 9 shows recent financial data on the textile fiber operations of each of the three principal affiliates.

Products and Manufacturing Process

All three affiliates manufactured the same range of basic synthetic textile fibers. Sales volume was dominated by two commodity-type fibers: (1) "F" was a polyester flat yarn with a weight of 76/24; and (2) "T" a polyester texturized yarn weighing 167/36.[4] These products were sold on the basis of technology and price, with financial terms, delivery and local service being next in importance. Competition was intense and margins were thin. Therefore, capacity utilization and production efficiency were critical to profitability.

In addition, there existed a number of specialty products, derived from the two main fibers by further processing,

[4]These designations mean that the first product consisted of 24 filaments twisted together in a smooth yarn with a total weight of 76 grams per meter of length, whereas the second was a heat-treated, texturized yarn (a process that added volume and texture to the final textile product) with 36 filaments weighing 167 grams per meter.

EXHIBIT 6 Market and Competitive Conditions in Colombia, 1995

A. Markets

The total size of the Colombian market in 1995 was approximately 110,000 tons of polyester fiber and 50,000 tons of other fibers, including industrial uses. Key figures regarding BOK-Andina's competitive position are shown below.

	Flat Yarn	Texturized Yarn	Other Fibers
Total Market (tons)	30,000	80,000	50,000
Main Competitors	2	1	4
Fitex:			
- capacity (tons)	20,000	40,000	10,000
- 1995 production	19,500	40,000	7,000
- capacity utilization	97.5%	100%	70%
- market share	65%	50%	67%[1]

[1]Applies only to the relevant segments in which BOK-Andina competes.

B. Environment

Colombia's government had pursued a prudent macroeconomic policy for several years. The country did not become highly indebted in the 1970s and, therefore, was not unduly affected by the 1982 crisis. Debt servicing has been kept at reasonable levels, and a successful export diversification strategy begun in the 1970s has isolated the country from extreme swings in the prices of its basic commodity exports, oil and coffee. In parallel to this, a realistic exchange policy has kept the value of the Colombian peso in constant real terms and economic growth on a high level. On the political front, however, the country has been gripped by a major Marxist insurgency for several years, one that had resisted multiple attempts at peace negotiations. This fact, together with the continued influence of the drug cartels lent an aura of instability to the country. Major indicators for the 1990–95 period are shown below.

	1990	1991	1992	1993	1994	1995
Economic Growth	4.3%	2.0%	4.0%	5.4%	5.8%	5.7%
Price Index	100.0	127.6	153.3	175.1	205.1	242.3
- annual change	*26.6%*	*27.6%*	*20.1%*	*14.2%*	*17.1%*	*18.1%*
Exchange Rate[2]	502.3	633.0	759.3	863.1	844.8	912.8
- annual devaluation	*23.8%*	*20.1%*	*16.6%*	*12.0%*	*(2.2%)*	*7.4%*
Relative Competitiveness[3]	96.4	97.6	97.8	98.2	117.6	128.5

[2]Rates are averages for the year in pesos per U.S. dollar.
[3]This is a ratio of the domestic price increases at wholesale or producers level to the external devaluation of the currency (in terms of its value in dollars), both relative to their values in 1989. If greater than 100, the country's exports are losing competitiveness relative to the base year, and vice versa.

EXHIBIT 6 (continued)

C. Future Expectations

Colombia is considered a stable democracy with two strong parties who often alternate in government. Two large Marxist insurgency groups persist in the mountainous regions and continue to disrupt political life throughout the country. Drug trafficking is also a very serious problem affecting both the rule of law as well as the trade balance. The textile industry is strong, highly concentrated, and internationally competitive. Financial policy is expected to continue its conservative orientation with annual inflation matched by devaluations in the peso. A free-floating regime, however, may result in swings from parity if other capital flows such as illicit trade or foreign investment become dominant. Forecasts for the economy for 1996–2000 are shown below.

	Actual	Projections				
	1995	1996	1997	1998	1999	2000
Economic Growth	5.7%	5.0%	4.0%	5.0%	4.5%	5.0%
Price Index	242.3	285.9	343.1	404.9	465.5	535.4
- annual change	*18.1%*	*18.0%*	*20.0%*	*18.0%*	*15.0%*	*15.0%*
Exchange Rate[2]	912.8	1,074	1,342	1,790	2,237	2,632
- annual devaluation	*7.4%*	*15.0%*	*20.0%*	*25.0%*	*20.0%*	*15.0%*
Relative[3] Competitiveness	128.5	128.9	123.8	109.5	100.8	98.5

[2]Rates are averages for the year in pesos per U.S. dollar.
[3]This is a ratio of the domestic price increases at wholesale or producers level to the external devaluation of the currency (in terms of its value in dollars), both relative to their values in 1989. If greater than 100, the country's exports are losing competitiveness relative to the base year, and vice versa.

EXHIBIT 7 Market and Competitive Conditions in Brazil

A. Market

The total size of the Brazilian market in 1995 included approximately 300,000 tons of polyester fiber and an equal amount of other fibers, primarily for the industrial sector. Key figures regarding Polybra and BOK Fibras do Brasil respective positions are as follows:

	Flat Yarn (Polybra)	**Texturized Yarn** (Polybra)	**Other Fibers** (BOK Fibras)
Total Market (tons)	75,000	225,000	300,000
Main Competitors	4	3	8
Polybra/BOK FdB:			
- capacity (tons)	25,000	70,000	50,000
- 1995 production	22,500	68,000	37,000
- capacity utilization	90%	97%	74%
- market share	30%	30%	41%[1]

[1]Applies only to the relevant segments in which BOK Fibras do Brasil competes.

EXHIBIT 7 (continued)

B. Environment

Brazil had experienced more than half a dozen stabilization plans in the last decade. After a period of sustained and rapid economic growth (albeit with high inflation) throughout the 1960s and 1970s, the large foreign indebtedness of the country was a major liability in the post-1982 environment. Inflation oscillated between a rate of about 100 percent annually in the mid-80s, to highs exceeding 2000 percent a year in the early 1990s. Dramatic currency devaluations did not always keep up with inflation, and new currencies were introduced periodically. The latest stabilization plan was introduced in August 1994 by then Finance Minister Fernando Cardoso, who was later elected president on the strength of his success in combating inflation. Figures for GDP growth, domestic inflation (wholesale price index with 1990=1), average exchange rates for each year, and a calculated "competitiveness factor" for the last six years are given in the table below.

	1990	1991	1992	1993	1994	1995
Economic Growth	−6.4%	1.2%	−0.9%	4.3%	6.1%	4.1%
Price Index	1.0	5.0	55.0	1,173	28,280	44,548
- annual change	*2,704%*	*400%*	*1,000%*	*2,033%*	*2,311%*	*57.5%*
Exchange Rate[2]	24.8/m	148/m	0.0016	0.032	0.639	0.918
- annual devaluation	*95.8%*	*83.2%*	*91.0%*	*94.9%*	*95.0%*	*30.4%*
Relative Competitiveness[3]	116.3	97.6	96.9	105.9	127.8	140.1

C. Future Expectations

Brazil is a large unstable democracy that emerged recently from two decades of military rule. There is great political fragmentation with deep opposition to the government's market liberalization program, but the success of Cardoso's Real Plan has strengthened his hand. The economy is the largest and most diversified in Latin America. The large textile industry is characterized as both diversified and competitive, with a strong design content.

Financial management is likely to be erratic in the future. The strong currency will put pressure on the trade balance, but foreign investment is likely to pick up considerably, especially as a result of planned privatizations of state-owned companies. Elections at the end of 1998 could undermine the government's resolve and, if accompanied by continued government fiscal deficits, may entail a collapse of the stabilization program with a return to high inflation. Forecasts for key economic indicators for 1992–1996 are given below.

	Actual	Projections				
	1995	1996	1997	1998	1999	2000
Economic Growth	4.1%	5.0%	4.0%	3.0%	2.0%	4.0%
Price Index	44,548	49,003	51,453	52,482	60,354	75,443
- annual change	*57.5%*	*10.0%*	*5.0%*	*2.0%*	*15.0%*	*25.0%*
Exchange Rate[2]	0.918	1.020	1.074	1.193	1.591	1.871
- annual devaluation	*30.4%*	*10.0%*	*5.0%*	*5.0%*	*25.0%*	*15.0%*
Relative Competitiveness[3]	140.1	138.7	138.4	134.1	115.7	122.9

[2]Rates are averages for the year in Reais per million US$ (1990–91) and Reais per US$ (1992–2000).

[3]This is a ratio of the domestic price increases at the wholesale level adjusted by the external devaluation of the currency (in terms of its value in dollars), both relative to their values in 1989. If greater than 100, the country's exports are losing competitiveness relative to the base year, and vice versa.

EXHIBIT 8 Market and Competitive Conditions in Other Countries

The total size of the polyester fiber market in other principal countries of the region can be summarized in the table below. Some of these countries were highly developed and had a strong domestic fiber industry, e.g., Argentina, where a BFI licensee had a significant market position. Others had little in the form of fiber production, yet they possessed a competitive textile sector such as Ecuador and Peru. Finally, a few smaller countries had little in the form of a domestic fiber or textile industry and imported these from other countries in order to supply their own garment manufacturers, as was the case with most Central American and Caribbean producers.

	Flat Yarn	Texturized Yarn	Other Fibers
Central America	15	40	10
Caribbean Nations	10	30	-
Argentina	35	80	75
Chile	20	50	30
Ecuador	10	35	25
Peru	25	70	35
Venezuela	15	30	50
Total	130	335	225

In terms of access, Mexico had preferential tariffs in serving the U.S. and Canadian markets, although full tariff remission would not take effect until 1999. Mexico and Colombia would have some logistical advantages in serving the Central American and Caribbean markets, and Mexico had signed free trade agreements with several countries in the area, notably Costa Rica and El Salvador. Both Mexico and Colombia had a free trade agreement with Venezuela. Bolivia, Colombia, Ecuador and Peru were all part of the Andean Common Market with certain tariff advantages for firms trading inside that area. Finally, Brazil and Argentina were members of the Mercosur agreement which would allow for free trade among its four members (these two plus Uruguay and Paraguay) by the year 2000, and included Chile and Bolivia as associate members.

Below are the relative competitiveness indices for five countries (1989=100).

	1990	1991	1992	1993	1994	1995
Argentina	103.7	111.4	113.8	114.9	116.9	124.4
Chile	106.8	113.8	122.2	118.5	123.3	140.4
Ecuador	99.8	108.4	114.3	127.1	131.3	138.2
Peru	107.6	106.2	103.7	95.8	102.3	110.2
Venezuela	94.1	95.0	97.5	99.1	107.9	143.0

which were proprietary to BFI and where smaller volumes could be compensated by higher margins. For simplicity, we consider here two distinct products ("F1" and "F2"), both based on further processing of "F" yarn by subjecting it to a series of additional treatments involving twisting and/or dyeing of the raw yarn. Similar processing could be applied to texturized ("T") yarn resulting in two other specialties designated "T1" and "T2" respectively.[5]

[5]In reality, the product portfolio of all three companies was more complex than depicted here, but this simplification captures the essence of the coordination and logistics problems faced by BFI at the time.

The manufacturing processes for these fibers is diagramed in Exhibit 10. A number of raw materials (petrochemical derivatives such as DMT, PTA, and glycol) were first processed in an autoclave at high temperature and pressure to produce different concentrations of the basic chemicals in the form of "chips." These were later crystallized and dried before being put through a high temperature extrusion process, and then spun and wound into bobbins. The head of the extruder contained as many pinholes as filaments were required (24 or 36, respectively, in the two products above). The weight of the yarn was determined by the number of filaments, the size of the pinholes in the extrusion head, and the tension in the spinning/winding step.

EXHIBIT 9 **Financial Results for BOK's Latin American Affiliates, 1995**
(In thousands of US$ and percentages)

	Fitex, Mexico		BOK-Andina, Colombia		Polybra, Brazil*	
	(US$ '000)	(%)	(US$ '000)	(%)	(US$ '000)	(%)
Sales Revenue						
Flat Yarn	55,940	21.0	49,320	32.6	51,530	26.7
- F1	*1,860*	*0.7*	*3,240*	*2.1*	*2,280*	*1.2*
- F2	*2,590*	*1.0*	*4,630*	*3.1*	*2,970*	*1.5*
Texturized Yarn	144,290	54.0	82,050	54.2	141,520	73.3
- T1	*6,350*	*2.4*	*7,160*	*4.7*	*10,820*	*5.6*
- T2	*13,260*	*5.9*	*9,350*	*6.2*	*16,150*	*8.4*
Other Fibers	66,760	25.0	20,130	13.3	0	0.0
Total Revenue	266,990	100.0	151,500	100.0	193,050	100.0
Variable Costs						
Direct Labor	11,550	4.3	5,170	3.4	10,040	5.2
Raw Materials	115,500	43.3	79,010	52.2	85,330	44.2
Utilities	16,170	6.1	7,110	4.7	5,860	3.0
Packaging & Supplies	11,550	4.3	4,520	3.0	6,690	3.5
Specialties Fixed Costs	2,400	0.9	2,000	1.3	1,600	0.8
Tariffs	60	0.0	1,380	0.9	240	0.1
Sub-Total	157,230	58.9	99,190	65.5	109,760	56.9
Fixed Costs						
Indirect Labor & Admin.	32,425	12.1	21,500	14.2	30,200	15.6
Maintenance	11,620	4.4	3,460	2.3	4,650	2.4
Sales and Logistics	5,775	2.2	2,080	1.4	2,510	1.3
Depreciation	16,170	6.1	7,620	5.0	5,860	3.0
Royalties and R&D	10,240	3.8	6,220	4.1	10,380	5.4
Sub-total	76,230	28.6	40,890	27.0	53,600	27.8
Total Expenses	233,460	87.4	140,080	92.5	163,360	84.6
Before-tax Income	33,530	12.6	11,420	7.5	29,690	15.4
Less Income Taxes	10,394	3.9	3,997	2.6	9,798	5.1
After-tax Income	23,136	8.7	7,423	4.9	19,892	10.3
Assets & Liabilities						
Current Assets	90,780	40.1	56,810	37.7	55,018	37.4
Net Plant & Equipment	135,500	59.9	93,926	62.3	92,082	62.6
Total Assets	226,280	100.0	150,736	100.0	147,100	100.0
Payables & Short-term Debt	21,360	9.4	18,634	12.4	14,092	9.6
Long-term Debt	75,450	33.3	25,451	16.9	59,844	40.7
Capital Account	129,470	57.2	106,651	70.8	73,164	49.7
Total Liabilities	226,280	100.0	150,736	100.0	147,100	100.0

*Figures do not include the activities of BOK do Brasil.

Source: Company records.

EXHIBIT 10 **Basic Manufacturing Processes for Polyester Filament Yarn**

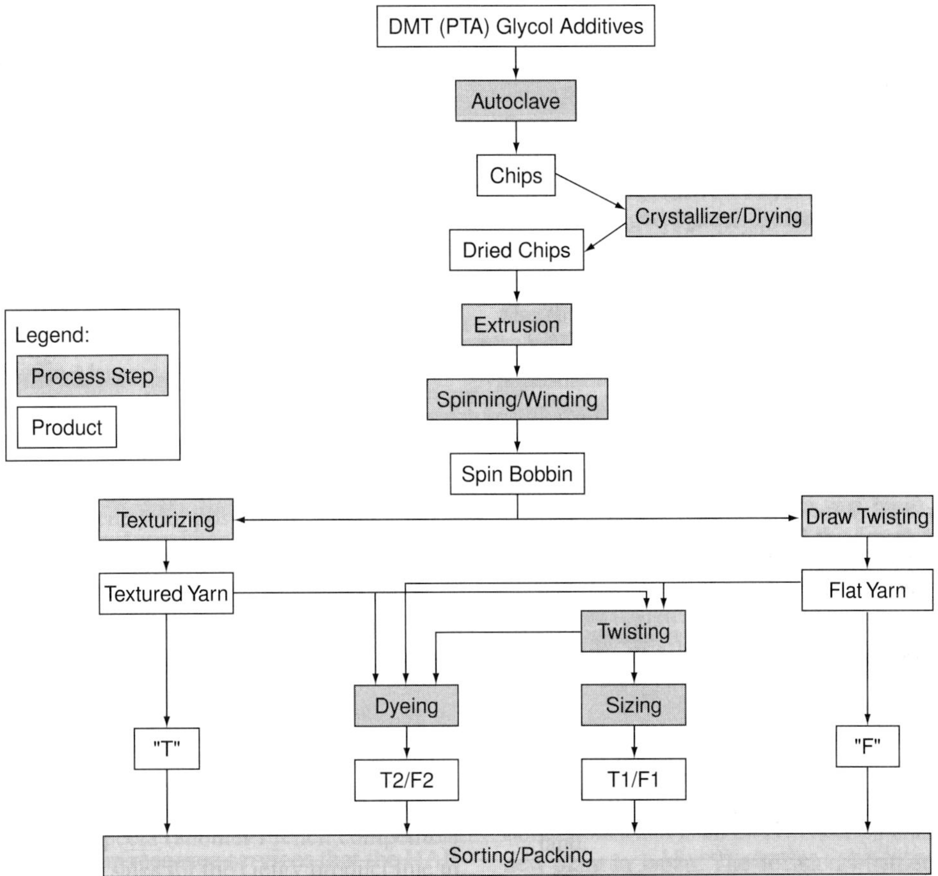

The production process for both products was identical. However, since the unit weight of polyester "flat yarn 76/24" was roughly one-half that of "texturized yarn 167/36", and line speeds were similar for both products, approximately one-half as much tonnage of flat yarn, relative to texturized yarn, could be produced in a given time interval. As a result, the capital investment for producing one ton of flat yarn per year was nearly double the investment necessary to produce one ton of texturized yarn. Relative prices reflected this difference as well as the material content in both types of yarn.

These extrusion/spinning/winding steps were critical to the quality and economics associated with the final product. The correct balancing of the production line was more an art than a science, where the experience and knowledge of the operators, particularly the plant engineers, was extremely valuable. For this reason, BOK Fibers and its affiliates tended to have dedicated lines to each major product. While it was technically possible to convert a line producing flat yarn to texturized yarn, for example, the numerous calibrations necessary, the time and expense involved, and the loss of substandard product produced before the correct new balance was obtained, argued against such product shifts except for the long term.

At this point, the spun and wound fiber could be sold directly as commodities, or processed further. Although demand was overwhelmingly for commodity fibers, a small percentage of customers wanted a yarn that had special characteristics that could translate into a unique final product. This could be done by submitting the yarn to a series of processes whereby it would be twisted, sized, and/or dyed to specific customer requirements. The additional variable cost of these processes were insignificant when compared to the higher prices obtainable, particularly when the product was designed by BOK's engineers for a single customer application. There were, however, sizable set-up costs associated with such specialty products. Typically, large customers bought commodity products and carried out their own further processing when necessary. On the other hand, smaller, niche firms preferred such specialties as it aided them in differentiating their own end products from competitors.

The last steps in production consisted of sorting and packaging the various products for distribution to either the domestic or export markets.

Cost Structure

Production costs for **commodity products** were divided into fixed and variable costs. As illustrated in the financial statements shown in Exhibit 9, variable costs consisted of five major categories:

Direct labor costs were relatively small, representing between 3 and 7 percent of total costs. Direct labor costs for any given quarter depended on the productivity of that plant (number of man-hours per ton of output) for that period, the wage rate at the start of the analysis, and the cumulative level of wage inflation in the country since then. This, of course, was translated into dollars at the prevailing exchange rate. While direct labor was a variable cost in the long run, it was impractical (or illegal) to hire and fire production workers at will in order to smooth fluctuations in production levels. Therefore, the plant manager was required to fix the work force for a given period at least one quarter in advance. If demand did not materialize, then adjustments in the level of the work force could be made for the following quarter.

Raw materials had a critical impact on costs. Their incidence ranged from 45 percent to 65 percent of total costs depending on the year and the country. Not all countries produced their own chips, and then some who did also relied on foreign suppliers for some of their other raw materials. The breakdown for the three operating subsidiaries was as follows:

	Percent of Domestic Raw Material Purchases	Manufactured Own Chips
Mexico	100%	Yes
Colombia	0	No
Brazil	80	Partially

Local raw material costs were determined by the rate of utilization of raw materials at each plant for each period (an efficiency measure of raw material yield), the proportion of imported versus domestic raw materials, and the dollar cost of domestic materials when local prices were translated at current exchange rates. International raw material prices were the same for all companies. Furthermore, tariffs on imported raw materials were usually quite small.

Utilities varied directly with volume of production, and there were no apparent economies of scale. Utility costs varied between 4 and 10 percent of total, partly the result of differences in efficiency and in utility rates among countries. Brazil, for example, with nearly unlimited access to hydroelectric power, had much lower rates than either Colombia or Mexico.

Packaging and supplies also varied directly with production volume and ranged between 4 and 7 percent of total costs for different years and countries.

Sales and transportation costs referred to domestic sales, distribution, transportation and logistics, which were nearly constant for all countries at about $30 per ton. These charges applied to all sales, including export sales in order to compensate for higher packaging costs. International transport costs were considered separately.

Fixed and semi-fixed costs consisted of four additional categories:

Indirect labor and administration costs were a function of both the level of direct labor and the size of the plant. For the smallest plant, i.e., BOK-Colombia, these costs represented nearly five times their direct labor costs. The largest, more efficient plant, Fitex in Mexico, typically had indirect labor and administrative costs that averaged about three times its direct labor bill.

Maintenance costs were a function of size and economies of scale. A minimum amount of maintenance was necessary irrespective of size and capacity utilization. Variations ranged between 2 and 6 percent of total costs.

Depreciation was estimated on a straight line basis. Investments per kilogram of capacity depended on the product type: about $1/kg for texturized yarn, and $2/kg for flat yarn. Total investment in fixed assets was translated into local currency and depreciation was calculated on a replacement cost basis (i.e., net of inflation), and retranslated into dollars for comparison. Given the flexibility for designing a plant on the basis of multiple production lines for different products, no economies of scale in plant cost were assumed to exist. Plant life was estimated at 20 years.

R&D and technology costs involved primarily the payment of royalties and management fees to BOK. The parent company charged a technology fee of 3 percent of sales for updating of both product and process technologies, as well as the annual technology seminar held by BOK's technical staff for exchanging technical and best practice information. Any charges for BOK personnel assigned to a local affiliate would be included under administrative expenses. Finally, each of the affiliates undertook some development work on their own to accommodate the needs of their major customers and adapt products to local requirements.

The production of **specialty products** entailed additional set-up costs not applicable to the commodity products on which they were based. Every time a local plant wished to manufacture a certain quantity of specialties, an incremental fixed cost was incurred that represented the engineering time and other waste associated with starting, balancing, and monitoring such a production run. These fixed costs were similar for all plants, and were amortized over the relevant production volume. No additional variable costs were associated with the production of specialty products over and above the variable cost of the base commodity.

Based on 1995 total expenses for the three operating companies, variable production costs for the basic commodity fibers were approximately as shown below (in $/ton). Specialty products variable costs were similar to these, except for the separate set up costs associated with them and reported separately in the income statements.

	Flat Yarn	Texturized Yarn	Other Fibers
Mexico	$1,750	$1,540	$2,150
Colombia	2,400	1,850	2,500
Brazil	2,000	1,720	2,150 (BFI do Brasil)

Exhibit 11 presents data on **transportation and tariff costs** for any combination of shipment arrangements. Transportation costs reflected the relative shipping volume and other cartel accords that may apply to specific routes. These rates may vary over time. Tariffs were those in effect at the time between Latin American trading partners. The Mercosur free trade area will give, for example, Brazilian producers duty-free access to the Argentine market. Colombia and Peru had preferential tariffs in the context of the Andean pact, and Mexico and Colombia had negotiated (together with Venezuela) a duty-free agreement that will be implemented through 2005. Further changes along these lines were possible, as other agreements come into play or existing agreements are abandoned.

Demand Characteristics and Competition

The markets for the various kinds of products in each country are shown in Exhibits 5–8. The market for flat yarn products was nearly identical in all four countries and was made up principally of commodities. However, there existed the possibility of developing a number of proprietary specialties that could represent as much as 15 percent of the total demand for BOK-branded flat products. The same could be said for the market for texturized yarn products, except that in this case specialties could capture as much as 20 percent of total BOK sales. The price premium obtainable in specialty products could go as high as 15 percent above the referenced commodity price for F1 and T1 products, and 25 percent for F2 and T2 products.

In the "old days" domestic prices were driven mainly by domestic costs and local competition, since imports were either forbidden or significantly discouraged through high tariffs and import licensing requirements. Margins, therefore, were more than adequate to cover all costs and yield attractive profits. Since 1990, prices and quantities were increasingly determined by the low cost

EXHIBIT 11 Transport and Tariff Costs for Major Countries

Shipment Costs—Including Freight, Insurance, and Port Fees, 1995 (in US$ per metric ton)

Shipping From:	Mexico	Colombia	Brazil	Europe	Asia
To:					
Mexico	**X**	$240	$70	$250	$320
Colombia	$300	**X**	$240	$260	$370
Brazil	$350	$260	**X**	$220	$420
Argentina	$280	$320	$80	$220	$420
Chile	$240	$280	$100	$240	$340
Peru	$300	$150	$200	$280	$340
Venezuela	$180	$120	$180	$200	$380
United States	$50	$180	$220	$140	$180

Prevailing Tariff Rates, 1995 (percentage of landed costs)

Shipping From:	Mexico	Colombia	Brazil	Europe	Asia
To:					
Mexico	**X**	15%*	15%	15%	15%
Colombia	13%*	**X**	7%	13%	13%
Brazil	20%	10%	**X**	20%	20%
Argentina	10%	10%	5%*	10%	10%
Chile	11%*	11%	11%*	11%	11%
Peru	13%	0%	13%	13%	13%
Venezuela	10%*	0%	10%	10%	10%
United States	3%*	6%	6%	6%	6%

* = All these rates are subject to change as the respective treaties among these countries take effect. See text and Exhibits 5–8 for details.

producer, provided it had sufficient capacity to supply the market.

Competition to the local BOK affiliate in each market came from three sources: local independent suppliers (sometimes affiliated with other international companies), other BOK affiliates exporting into that market, and production from any number of foreign suppliers, mainly in Asia. Some degree of customer loyalty existed, primarily due to the difficulties associated with switching supply sources. For a textile firm to incorporate a new fiber source with different specifications into its manufacturing process could entail significant switch-over costs and waste until production stabilized. There were also some advantages in dealing with a local supplier, particularly in terms of delivery, service, currency risk, and financing. Therefore, a local customer of a domestic BOK affiliate would not switch suppliers indiscriminately, and only in response to significant price/cost savings.

Given that fiber technology was such a critical demand factor, a new supplier approaching a local BFI customer would face less resistance if it were a BOK-affiliated company than would be the case for an independent supplier, whether local or foreign. The reason was that the BOK sister company would be able to provide the same technology and product quality as the local BFI affiliate, thus incurring low technical switch-over costs for the textile manufacturer. It could not, however, provide the same level of service as the domestic-based BFI affiliate could offer. Therefore, corporate management estimated that a foreign-based BFI-affiliate wishing to take market share away from one of its sister companies, must price at least 3 percent below the domestic company in order to overcome the natural loyalty and service advantage enjoyed by the latter. For every percentage point below that, the exporter could expect to gain an additional 5 percent of the domestic company's market.

Non-BOK domestic suppliers, on the other hand, could deliver on the service aspect, but were unable to guarantee the same product quality or characteristics. Since product characteristics and consistency had a higher value to the costumer than other service attributes, the switching-cost threshold in the case of a non-BOK domestic suppliers was estimated to be slightly higher at 5 percent. Furthermore, for each percentage point below that level, the non-BOK supplier would gain 4 percent of the domestic BFI company's market.

Finally, a foreign, non-BOK supplier would face both disadvantages—technology and service—when competing against a local BFI affiliate. As a result, it would be required to offer significantly larger price concessions in order to obtain a comparable share of the market. These were estimated at 7 percent for the minimum threshold, and a slope of 2.5 percent market share loss for every percentage price discount above that level. Exhibit 12 shows the estimated demand substitution schedules for all three types of competitors.

The demand for specialty products, however, behaved differently. Only BOK affiliates could supply these specialties as they were proprietary to the company, subject to the same switching costs that applied to commodities. Specialties were substitutes only for commodity products of the same type sold by BOK companies in their domestic markets, within the maximum volume and price limits specified above. If specialty prices rose above the stipulated ratios relative to commodity prices, the market for specialties tended to shrink rapidly.

Costs and Benefits of Coordination

As senior management pondered these issues, they considered how to resolve the conflict of low coordination among its subsidiaries. In March 1996, Hans Schmidt held a regional meeting in Cancun, Mexico, with the general managers and marketing directors from all five companies attending, plus a few key staff from BFI in Europe. He opened the meeting with a global review of the state of the industry and the deteriorating results for BFI. It was obvious to all those present that cross-border exports at discounted prices was a contributing factor. But other trends such as a rise in regional buying by industrial customers (particularly in the automotive sector) required better coordination across countries. Finally, the threat of new competitive entrants into the region was common to all the affiliates.

In order to facilitate the discussion, Schmidt had contracted with a consulting group to prepare an analysis of what might be the benefits that could be expected from a regional restructuring of the company's operations. Exhibit 13 summarizes these results. The consultants started by defining three possible organizational models. The first was denominated "*Old World*." Under this model each of the three main subsidiaries[6] satisfied its domestic demand first, and then would export to non-competing markets, such as the United States or Chile, to the extent it had any excess capacity and could meet local prices. Parallel imports from one affiliate to another's home market were difficult due to strong protectionist tariffs in all countries. In this case, the model simply estimated total group profits made from domestic sales by each of the companies. To the extent that there were any exports, net income from export sales (that is, export revenues net of transportation and tariff costs, less variable production costs) were added to that firm's results.

This model was included for comparative purposes under conditions that assumed a continuation of current macroeconomic trends. Current economic thinking in the region would make it highly unlikely that any of the major countries would revert to autarkic protectionist policies. Therefore, the "old world" results were a look at the past and merely provided a benchmark against which other organizational models and economic conditions could be tested.

The second model consisted of a world in which tariffs were significantly reduced and all firms were free to compete in all markets, subject only to competitive forces and their desire for profit maximization. This "*Wild West*" model allocated markets to producers on the basis of their cost competitiveness, subject to the substitution schedule described earlier. A number of iterations were run each quarter, and the model gradually converged on an efficient

[6]The analysis included only the three main subsidiaries—Mexico, Colombia, and Brazil—although its findings should be generalizable to the group as a whole, provided similar conditions existed in other markets. In all instances, the models estimated profits for each of the three companies over a 20-quarter period, solving for the equilibrium solution for each quarter and then moving on to the next. The figures reported here are the sum of all quarterly profits for all three companies over the full five years of each run.

EXHIBIT 12 Demand Substitution Schedule as a Function of Competitor's Prices

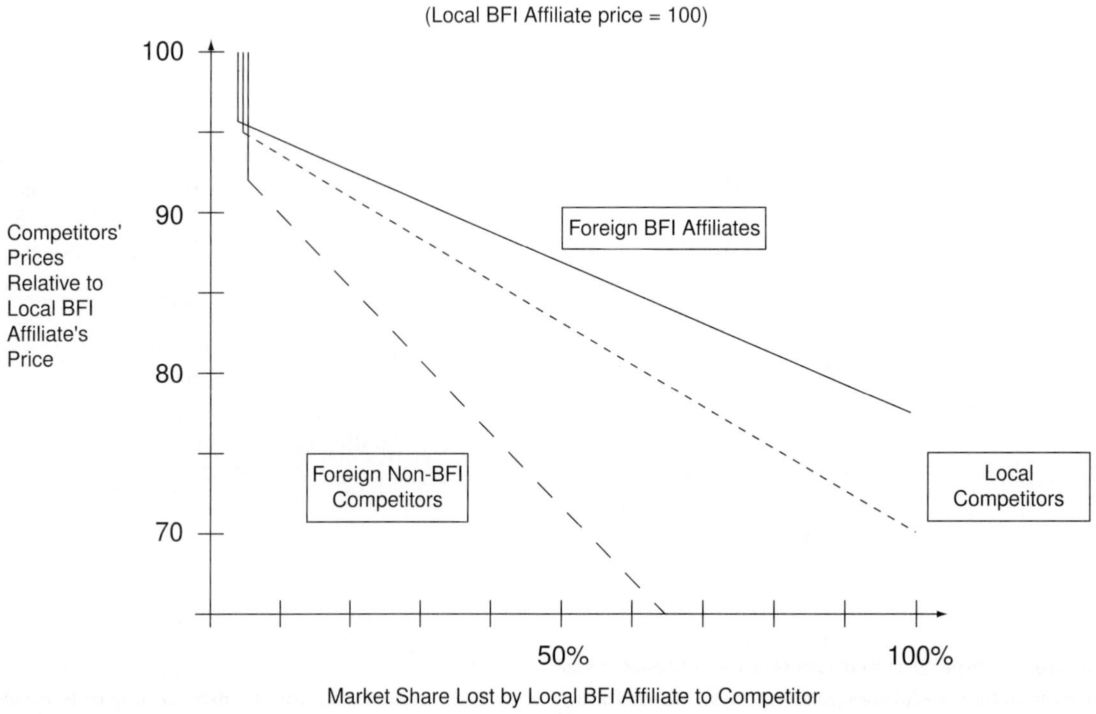

(Local BFI Affiliate price = 100)

solution with each player adjusting prices and quantities in different markets in response to economic conditions and competitors' moves. Each company maximized its own financial results constrained only by competition and its short-term productive capacity. Individual companies had no loyalty to the group and strived to maximize only their own interests.

The third model was labeled "*Central Control*" and assumed the existence of an all-knowing central power that was able to allocate markets to producers in a way that maximized total profits for the group. Individual companies had no capacity for independent decision in this model. They supplied the markets which were assigned to them by the central authority and served all customers in their respective territories, irrespective of the source of supply. Under this arrangement there were no penalties associated with imported BOK products since the provenance of the goods was opaque to the final customer; the buyer was serviced as if the local subsidiary were actually manufacturing the product. The model allocated markets to producers in an iterative sense every quarter, as before, but this time it allowed for production specialization, collaboration, and trading off of market positions among the group companies with the objective of maximizing group results. In fact, the network functioned as if it were a single unit with multiple plants.

The base case in Exhibit 13 compares all three organizational models under a set of common economic variables that can best be described as a continuation of existing conditions, that is, a five-year projection of "business as usual." Under these assumptions, the "old world" model yielded a five-year total contribution of $538 million for the group. The adoption of a liberal market regime in the region, together with a "wild west" competitive structure, would reduce this figure to $418 million. Most of the loss would come from increased price competition (and reduced margins) among different producers, not all of which would be compensated by ef-

EXHIBIT 13 Summary of Simulation Results—Wild West versus Central Coordination
(in millions of US$ per five-year simulation period and percent)

	Simulation Model		Profit Improvement from Central Coordination	
	Wild West	Central Control	($)	(percent)
Economic Scenarios				
1. Base Case*	$418	$481	$63	15.1%
2. Aggressive Asian Competitor	$361	$459	$98	27.1%
3. Stable Economic Conditions (all countries observing PPP rates)	$375	$485	$110	29.3%
4. Only Mexico Observes PPP Rates	$225	$427	$202	89.8%
5. Hemispheric Free Trade	$400	$481	$81	20.3%
6. Export Limits Set at 10% of Domestic Production	$418	$458	$40	9.6%
7. Capacity Expansion**				
- in Mexico	$444	$517	$73	16.4%
- in Colombia	$433	$514	$81	18.7%
- in Brazil	$504	$571	$67	13.3%

*For the base case under "Old World" rules (see text), total profits equalled $538 million.

**Assumes an addition of 2,500 tons of capacity for flat yarn and 5,000 tons for texturized yarn in each country, respectively, all under the base case scenario.

Source: Company records.

ficiency gains. If the three BOK firms were forced into a centrally controlled regime, however, their joint return would rise to $481 million as both cost efficiencies would be obtained from production specialization, and price competition between BOK affiliates would be avoided.

For each of the last two organizational models the consultants then ran a number of environmental and economic scenarios in which they would vary any combination of the following parameters for each country: inflation rates, foreign exchange regimes, economic growth, tariff rates for finished goods and/or raw materials, transportation costs, and the degree of domestic and foreign (i.e., extra regional) competition. Over 100 such simulations were conducted with the "central control" model always outperforming the "wild west" model (the exhibit shows only a sample of these cases). However, individual firms were not always better off in the collaborative model. For example, if a country pursued an aggressive foreign exchange policy designed to keep its currency undervalued, it might pay for the BOK affiliate located in that country to follow a "wild west" policy and ignore the rest of the group. In other words, what was always best for the group was not necessarily best for all its members.

Finally, it was obvious to Schmidt and his team that the "central control" model was highly unrealistic, since such level of organizational efficiency would be extremely difficult to achieve. Plus there would be costs associated with coordinated actions that were not estimated by the model such as, for example, the acquisition and deployment of a sophisticated management information system capable of allowing for such network optimization. However, the consultants argued that the "central control" model provided a rough measure of the potential benefits that may obtain from a collaborative strategy in terms of economies of scale, better utilization of plant capacity, and sales and price coordination.

In addition, there were other potential benefits from collaboration—such as the availability of a broader product range, the ability to serve multinational customers on a regional basis, central buying of materials and equipment, potential reductions in inventories, better cash management and improved control of foreign exchange risk and exposure, sharing of know-how and best practices among the units, etc.—that were not estimated in the consultants' analysis. Schmidt felt that these figures would provide an incentive to the assembled executives to begin discussions on a strategy of coordination and how to implement it.

Management's Choices

One possibility was to institute a system of loose linkages among the five affiliates in the region. These linkages might involve assigning specific geographic markets to each of them, in which the designated firm would have sales priority. It might also include a set of bilateral agreements to coordinate production of specialties and certain formulations on a voluntary basis designed to improve productivity and cost efficiency. Finally, information exchanges on capacity planning and export activities, particularly when involving each other's markets, would round out this option.

A second option called for a more intense and formal connection among the companies. This might involve the creation of a "trading company" that would be jointly owned by all firms and to which they would delegate all "international" sales, that is, sales outside the local territories of each of the five companies. This would require an agreement on the definition of local territories similar to that envisioned in the first option, but with more teeth.[7] To cement such a relationship, the firms would undertake an exchange of shares among them, whereby up to 20 percent of each company's stock would be held by its regional partners, and they would adopt common planning mechanisms. The latter would include capacity, marketing, and financial planning, and some degree of harmonization of accounting standards and human resource systems and policies.

Finally, a third option was put on the table involving a full merger of all companies into a single structure. Such a merger would include the creation of a regional holding company structure, the transfer of the ownership in all local companies to the holding, and the restructuring of the ownership in the holding to reflect the valuation of the five companies and the respective shares of the different owners in these. While complex in principle, there were no technical or tax obstacles to such a transfer. Eventually, the holding company might enter into an initial public offering (probably in the United States) in order to raise additional capital for expansion and to provide liquidity to its shareholders. Together with such a capital restructuring, the group would have to undertake a reassessment of its management structure and processes. This would be left to a later stage, but it clearly involved centralizing certain functions at the regional level, while other tasks would remain essentially local.

There were a number of considerations affecting the feasibility of such restructuring. One would be the attitude of the various owners. They would be required to exchange their relatively large (sometimes controlling) shares in a domestic company for a smaller, minority position in a regional organization. This loss of control would be compensated by a larger and more dynamic organization, and one presumably with greater value and liquidity. But it was not obvious that they would do so happily.

Another obstacle might be the current management, since the new organizational structure emerging from the merger would shift power in directions that were not necessarily in their immediate interests. There were five country managers and a full set of financial, marketing, technical, and sales directors at present whose jobs might be in jeopardy. How to compensate them and convince them of the value of the new structure would be an issue.

Finally, there was the issue of how local governmental authorities might react to any of these moves. On the one hand, the recent climate of economic liberalization would probably lead to a supportive attitude towards a more competitive solution. But anything short of a full merger might entail antitrust risks, particularly as the liberalization process itself had given new impetus to nascent competition agencies in the region, particularly in countries such as Mexico and Brazil.

---

[7]The use of "territories" in this context was not necessarily equivalent to national boundaries. For example, it was generally accepted that the Mexican company's territory encompassed the rest of North America where it had clear logistical and tariff advantages due to NAFTA. Similarly, Brazil might have a priority claim on the rest of Mercosur, except for the position of the Argentine licensee. In any event, these definitions would have to be agreed upon under either of the proposed schemes.

Case 11–2

BMW: Globalizing Manufacturing Operations

BMW's new plant at Spartanburg, South Carolina, was a source of pride. In a record-breaking 24 months, BMW had put together a state-of-the-art facility. By September 1995, only a year after the first vehicle (a 318i model) had rolled off its assembly line, BMW management was considering expanding the plant's capacity ahead of schedule. This was to accommodate a faster ramp-up of production of the Z3 roadster—a brand new 2-seater which was produced only at Spartanburg (see Exhibit 13). Eberhard Von Kuenheim, chairman of the BMW Supervisory Board and former CEO, took pride in this accomplishment.

> "The United States is the largest, most competitive, and dynamic consumer market in the world. If BMW cannot thrive in the U.S. market, it will ultimately suffer the same fate in Europe.
>
> "I do not think the Japanese have anything to teach BMW. We plan to produce a brand new model at our American plant. The Japanese would consider that too risky in a new factory with a new workforce. Their transplants began by making models already produced in Japan to make it easier to develop factory skills and establish high quality practices before they dared to introduce a new model."

For Spartanburg, the challenge of producing a brand new model had become even more arduous by an unexpected surge in the demand for the Z3. An astute advertising campaign for the Z3 as James Bond's car in the movie "Golden Eye," favorable reviews in trade journals, and the car's relatively low price had created high demand for the Z3. In September 1995, as the first Z3s were being produced, Al Kinzer, President of BMW Manufacturing Corp. (BMW MC), was under pressure to formulate a strategy for dealing with this unexpected demand. He was proud of what had already been accomplished at Spartanburg and wanted to be sure that this short-term pressure would not cause a long-term setback for BMW MC.

The History of BMW

Traces of BMW's origin may be found in its logo: a rotating propeller in blue and white, the colors of Bavaria. In 1913, Karl Rapp opened an aircraft engine design shop near Munich and called it RAPP-Motorenwerke. It became Bayerische Motoren Werke in 1917. After WWI, the Treaty of Versailles prohibited German firms from producing aircraft and aircraft engines. BMW sought other engine-making opportunities, and in 1922 began producing a small engine for the Victoria motorcycle. One year later BMW began production of the R 32 motorcycle.

In late 1928, BMW acquired the struggling Eisenach Vehicle Factory, just north of Munich. Eisenach had been making cars since 1899. When BMW took over, the factory was producing a single model, a licensed version of England's Austin Seven. This car would become the first BMW automobile, known as the 3/15 or "Dixi." In the years that followed, BMW moved quickly, introducing several new models and enlarging its engines from 1.2 liters to 3.5 liters. During the 1930s, BMW established its reputation as a maker of high-quality, sporting motor vehicles. By winning famous races—such as Italy's Mille Miglia in 1939—BMW's fame spread. When WWII broke out, BMW was forced to build engines for the German Luftwaffe, and ceased all auto and motorcycle production. Its factories were dismantled after the war, but BMW survived by making kitchen and garden equipment. The Eisenach plant, where all BMW cars had been produced, was in the eastern zone, which later became East Germany.

Shortly thereafter, BMW rebuilt its bombed-out Munich plant and began producing motorcycles again. In 1948, the company introduced a one-cylinder motorcycle, which sold well as cheap transportation in postwar Germany. But that did not pull BMW out of trouble. BMW cars produced in the 1950s were too large and expensive for the postwar economy, and sales were disappointing. As motorcycle sales also began to decline, BMW was again on the verge of bankruptcy. In 1959, Herbert Quandt bought control of BMW for $1 million. Quandt was a visionary who set a new direction for

This case was prepared by Sibel Berzeg, Michael Maier, and Juan Carlos Páez, Georgetown MBA '96, under the guidance of Professor Kasra Ferdows, Georgetown University School of Business, as a basis for class discussion rather than to illustrate either effective or ineffective handling of an administrative situation. The information presented in this case does not necessarily represent the opinion of BMW AG.

BMW, concentrating on sport sedans. He was determined to build a car for the driver, as opposed to the rider. The first of the "new range" of BMWs was launched in 1961. This niche strategy proved successful, and in 1966 BMW expanded by purchasing the ailing auto-manufacturing company Hans Glas.

Over the next two decades, BMW grew considerably. It climbed from 69th to 11th place among Germany's top industrial corporations, and its market value reached almost $9 billion. Still, BMW was small compared to the big U.S. auto makers: it was one-third the size of Ford, and one-fourth the size of GM. The Quandt family still owned 60 percent of BMW, and many believed that this allowed the company to accept moderate short-term returns in exchange for long-run profit potential. BMW was one of only two auto manufacturers that had continuously shown a profit for 30 years. From 1984 through 1994, sales grew almost 8 percent annually, while profits grew approximately 1.5 percent annually. Although the overall trend was upward, in 1990 and 1993 BMW's profits declined. In 1994, sales and profits increased substantially. This was partly due to the acquisition of the Rover Group (UK), but even after adjusting for that, sales and profits grew at a healthy rate throughout 1994 (see Exhibit 1).

BMW 1995

BMW had 34 wholly owned subsidiaries—14 in Germany and 20 dispersed around the world. It also had more than 130 foreign sales operations. Before the Spartanburg plant, BMW's manufacturing activities were essentially concentrated in seven plants in Germany. These included a motorcycle plant in Berlin, a tooling plant in Eisenach (now a part of reunified Germany), and a plant in Steyr, Austria (three hours south of Munich by car). The plant in Austria was BMW's largest facility for production of its 4 and 6-cylinder engines. BMW also operated various so-called "kit factories" outside Europe. Kit factories assembled either complete knockdown kits (CKDs) or semi-knockdown kits (SKDs). BMW's oldest and most sophisticated SKD plant was located in Rosslyn, South Africa (near Pretoria). In Thailand, Indonesia, and Malaysia, local partners assembled BMW cars under joint manufacturing agreements (see Exhibit 2). In 1994, two new assembly plants were established, one in the Philippines and another in Vietnam, to avoid high tariffs, taxes, and trade restrictions. The kits supplied from Germany were exempt from these restrictions because they were augmented with locally purchased components and complied with local content and value-added regulations.

EXHIBIT 1 BMW Group in Figures

		1990	1991	1992	1993	1994
Sales	DM million	27,178	29,839	31,241	29,016	42,125
Rover Group Contribution to Sales	DM million	-	-	-	-	10,173
Percent Change in Sales	%	2.5	9.8	4.7	-7.1	45.2
BMW Automobile Sales	units	525,866	552,660	594,895	535,492	568,733
Rover Group Automobile Sales	units	-	-	-	-	391,700
BMW Motorcycle Sales	units	29,701	32,187	35,675	35,031	44,203
Workforce		70,984	74,385	73,562	71,034	109,362
Investment	DM million	2,066	2,123	1,975	2,214	3,543
Investment as a Percent of Sales	%	7.6	7.1	6.3	7.6	8.4
Cash Flow	DM million	2,780	2,831	2,880	2,567	3,569
Fixed Assets	DM million	6,707	6,748	6,834	7,151	11,748
Total Assets	DM million	22,501	25,405	27,504	30,295	38,693
Shareholders' Equity	DM million	5,860	6,392	6,718	7,025	7,922
Material Cost	DM million	15,749	17,472	18,542	17,368	24,694
Personnel Cost	DM million	5,314	5,823	5,387	6,245	8,425
Net Income	DM million	696	783	726	516	697

Source: BMW Annual Report 1994.

EXHIBIT 2 BMW Plants

	Workforce	Production Capability	Capacity (per day)	Plant Area (in sq.m.)
Munich, Germany	11,700	3-series, 6, 8 and 12 cylinder engines	850 cars, 950 engines	450,000
Dingolfing, Germany	17,528	5-series, 7- and 8-series, axles and central part supply	900 cars	1,500,000
Regensburg, Germany	7,420	3-series sedan, coupe, and convertible, components	700 cars	1,420,000
Landshut, Germany	3,056	components and parts	n/a	320,000
Eisenach, Germany	212	tooling	n/a	85,000
Berlin, Germany	511	R and K series motorcycles, motorcycle engines	150 engines	195,000
Steyr, Austria	2,116	4 and 6 cylinder engines	1,600 engines	206,000
Rosslyn, South Africa	2,920	parts and electronics, kit assembly	n/a	n/a
Spartanburg, U.S.	591	3-series, Z3 roadster	120 cars	135,000

December 1994

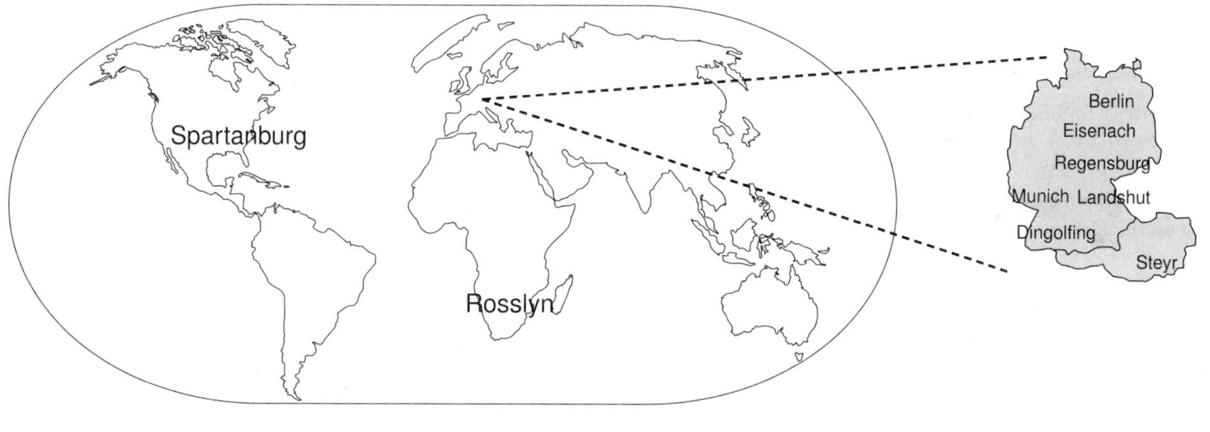

BMW's market share in Germany had increased in recent years to 6.7 percent; but the figure for the United States was a disappointing 0.9 percent (see Exhibit 3). The German market was served by 800 exclusive dealerships, while the much larger U.S. market was served by only 354 dealers, only 30 percent of them exclusive.

BMW in the United States

BMW of North America, Inc. (BMW NA) was established in 1975. The "yuppie" generation's preference for imported cars in the early 1980s made the United States the fastest growing market for BMW. By 1994, the

EXHIBIT 3 **1994 BMW Unit Sales by Country**

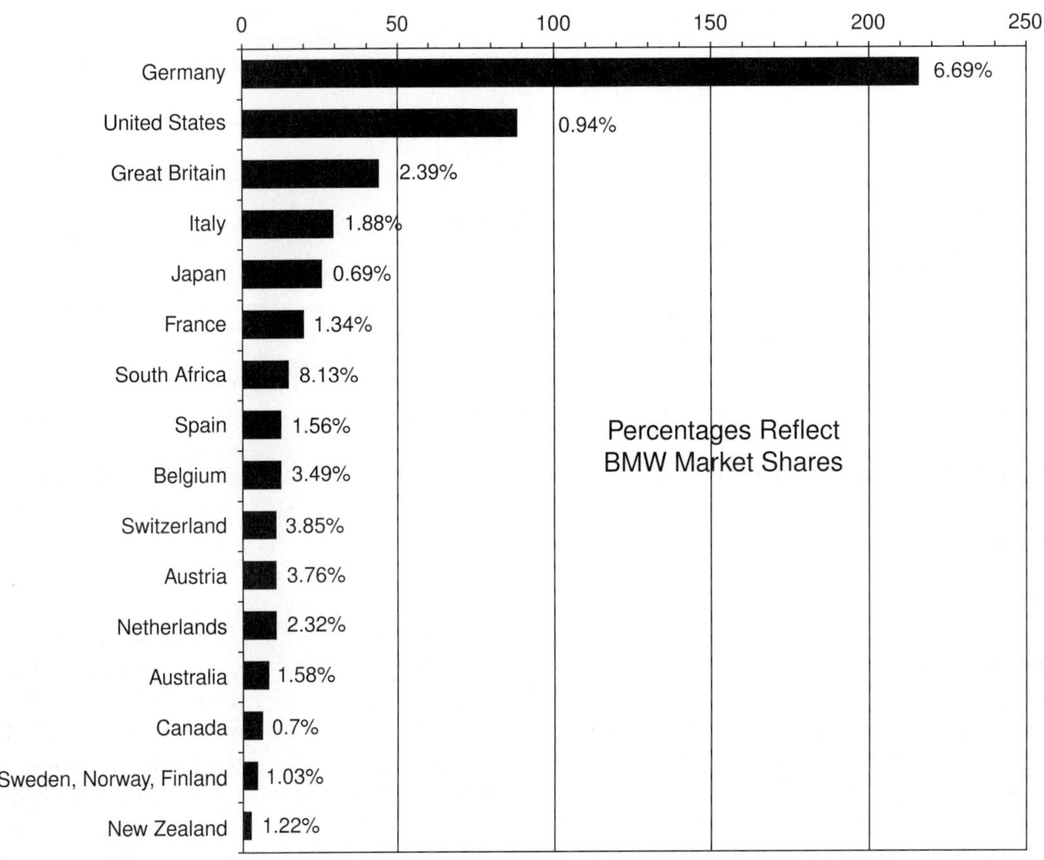

United States was BMW's largest export market. BMW exported 84,500 units, 14.7 percent of its total automobile production, to the United States that year. Accordingly, the trends in the U.S. market in the late 1980s and early 1990s had a huge impact on BMW. Between 1986 and 1991 the United States automobile industry experienced a 24 percent decline in sales (20 percent between 1986 and 1989). The stock market crash of 1987 and the Tax Reform Act of the same year (which directly affected deductions and depreciation on luxury vehicles), made owning a luxury car less affordable. Also, a "luxury tax" of 10 percent was levied on cars selling for more than $30,000, and the "gas guzzler" tax was doubled. By 1989, total BMW sales in the United States had fallen to 65 percent of the 1986 level. By 1991, BMW realized that there were serious limitations to its export strategy in the U.S. market (see Exhibit 4).

Meanwhile, Japanese automobile manufacturers had started to introduce a new group of lower-end luxury cars. In 1986, Honda introduced the Acura, and in 1989, Nissan introduced the Infiniti and Toyota introduced the Lexus. These strong models were favorably reviewed, and quickly established a reputation for quality, service and reliability among U.S. consumers. The Japanese undertook an aggressive strategy to gain market share and drastically undercut BMW's prices with similar product offerings. While BMW's least expensive 3-series in 1990 was $25,000 to $35,000, Acura's most affordable model was $22,000 to $29,000. Both Lexus and Infiniti offered a range of models priced from the low $20,000s to the upper $30,000s. The Japanese manufacturers were also outspending BMW in advertising (Lexus' 1991 advertising budget was double that of BMW). Although these luxury models

EXHIBIT 4 Sales Trends by Region

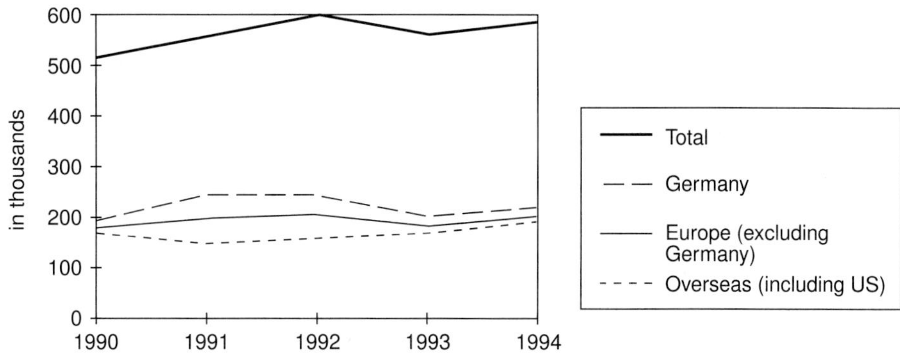

were imported from Japan, Japanese manufacturers had set up impressive factories in the United States and were rapidly expanding production in these factories (see Exhibit 5 and 6).

At the same time, a soaring German mark and high labor costs in Germany were putting more pressure on BMW. The mark had appreciated against the dollar over the previous 10 years (see Exhibit 7). With most of its costs denominated in marks and virtually all of its manufacturing activities concentrated in Germany, BMW had no operational hedge, and currency fluctuations were eating into its profit margins. With an average of $22.32 per hour, wage rates in Germany were 45 percent higher than those in the U.S. ($15.38). Also, Germans worked an average of 1,647 hours per year, 16 percent fewer hours than workers in the United States. Higher fringe benefits, longer vacations, and higher absenteeism further contributed to elevated labor costs in Germany—making them among the highest in the world. Direct labor constituted about 15 percent of BMW's total production cost. It was estimated that BMW's production cost in Germany exceeded U.S. production cost by 30 percent due to Germany's more expensive labor, materials, and overhead functions.

All this pointed to the need for more aggressive measures to maintain and increase market share in the United States. In 1991, BMW's German plants were operating at capacity—550,000 units per year. Any significant increase in output would require further investment in production facilities. As Eberhard Von Kuenheim, BMW's soft-spoken, aristocratic chairman at that time, put it, "an American factory is a logical next step for BMW because, among other things, it would reduce our exposure to exchange-rate fluctuations." Thus, plans for establishment of a U.S. factory went into high gear. In the interim, BMW repositioned its 5- and 7-series luxury models by cutting prices. Although this reduced profitability for these models, it allowed the company to maintain its market share in the early 1990s (see Exhibits 8 and 9). In 1994, BMW began to import its 3-series coupe (or "compact") to the United States. With a sticker price of $20,000, this car was the least expensive BMW on the market. It was BMW's first attempt to appeal to a more price-sensitive consumer, which meant that BMW had to sacrifice its usual high profit margins.

Manufacturing in the United States

Von Kuenheim's objectives for the U.S. plant went beyond reduction of short-term costs and exposure to currency fluctuations. He stated that expanding production to the U.S. would help BMW "maintain, secure, and build up its position in the U.S. luxury-car market, the world's biggest." To achieve this position, Von Kuenheim believed that BMW should develop a flexible and technologically advanced plant and take full advantage of being close to the demanding American consumer.

On June 22, 1992, BMW announced that it would set up a manufacturing plant in Spartanburg, South Carolina. This announcement was the result of a long process during which BMW narrowed its choice from 215 possible locations to four. Spartanburg triumphed over competing sites partly due to an attractive incentive package from the South Carolina state government, which included reduced building and infrastructure costs. Furthermore, the BMW plant was granted free-trade status as a part of the

EXHIBIT 5 Transplant Car Factories in the U.S.*

	Production Launch	Location	Products	- Employ ment	1994 Capacity (cars only)	Ownership
Auto Alliance Intern. Inc.	1987	Flat Rock, MI	Mazda MX-6, 626 Ford Probe	3,800	240,000	Ford 50%, Mazda 50%
Diamond Star Motors Corp.	1988	Normal, IL	Mitsubishi Eclipse and Galant Chrysler Sebring, Dodge Avenger, Eagle Talon	3,900	240,000	Mitsubishi 100%
Honda of America Mfg. Inc.	1979	Marysville, OH	Accord sedan, coupe, motorcycles, TRX	10,100	380,000	Honda 100%
	1982 (cars)	East Liberty, OH	utility vehicle, Civic sedan and coupe		220,000	
		Anna, OH	car and motorcycle engines		575,000 engines	
New United Motor Mfg. Inc. (NUMMI)	1984	Fermont, CA	Toyota Corolla, Tacoma pick-up, Geo Prizm	4,600	370,000	GM 50%, Toyota 50%
Nissan Motor Manufacturing Corp. USA	1983	Smyrna, TN	Altima, Sentra, 200SX coupe, compact pickups engines and components	6,000	450,000	Nissan 100%
Subaru-Isuzu Automotive Inc.	1989	Lafayette, IN	Isuzu pickup, Rodeo, Honda Passport, Subaru Legacy	2,220	170,000	Fuji 51%, Isuzu 49%
Toyota Motor Mfg. USA Inc.	1988	Georgetown, KY	Camry, Avalon, engines and axles	6,000	400,000 cars, 500,000 engines	Toyota 100%
Mercedes Benz US Intern. Inc.	1997 (planned)	Vance, AL	sport utility vehicle	n/a	60,000 to 80,000	Daimler-Benz 100%
BMW Manufacturing Corporation	1994	Spartanburg, SC	3-series, Z3 Roadster	2,000 (by 1997)	90,000 (by 1997)	BMW 100%

Source: Ward's Automotive Yearbook 1994/1995.

Greenville-Spartanburg airport's free-trade zone. This meant that BMW would not pay U.S. duties on parts imported from Germany or elsewhere unless the final product was sold in the United States. The free-trade zone status would provide considerable savings on duties which would only be paid at the vehicle's final destination—be it the United States or another country. Financing charges would also be reduced as duties would be paid only after the completed car had left the factory.

The South Carolina site also provided other advantages: it offered easy access to highways and rail, it was close to the big port of Charleston, and was only 10 minutes from an international airport. Also, the cost of living in the region was considerably lower than many other areas in the United States.

In 1994, BMW AG (Germany) established the BMW Manufacturing Corporation as a wholly owned subsidiary with headquarters in Spartanburg, SC. BMW MC was in charge of manufacturing operations and various corporate functions such as human resources, finance, and purchasing for North America. This did not affect BMW North America (headquartered in New Jersey), which was still responsible for marketing and sales in the U.S.

EXHIBIT 6 Production Data of Japanese Transplants in the United States

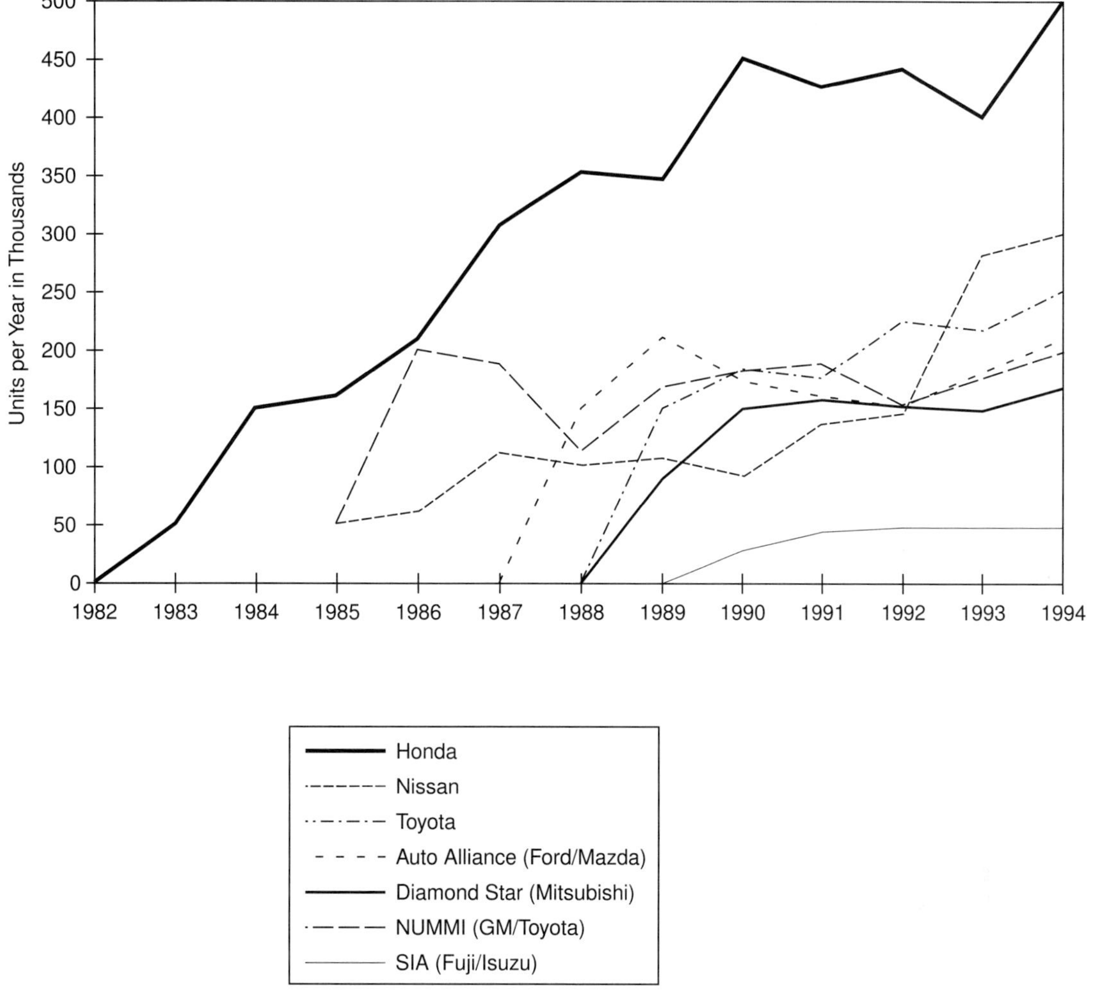

Building a Plant in the United States

Press releases, a vision statement, and interviews by several BMW officials all indicated an ambitious goal for the newly created BMW MC:

> To quickly develop a flexible, technologically advanced plant which satisfies BMW's stringent quality standards. Using a single assembly line, this plant would be capable of producing different models—including a brand new one.

Quick

With only 24 months between the laying of the groundwork for the plant and the start of production, the Spartanburg plant was built in record time (see Exhibit 10). BMW initially invested $400 million in Spartanburg, which included construction of a 1.2 million-square-foot plant. This was followed by an additional $200 million investment in tooling, bringing the total investment to $600 million. The Spartanburg plant was designed to

EXHIBIT 7 Exchange Rate Index

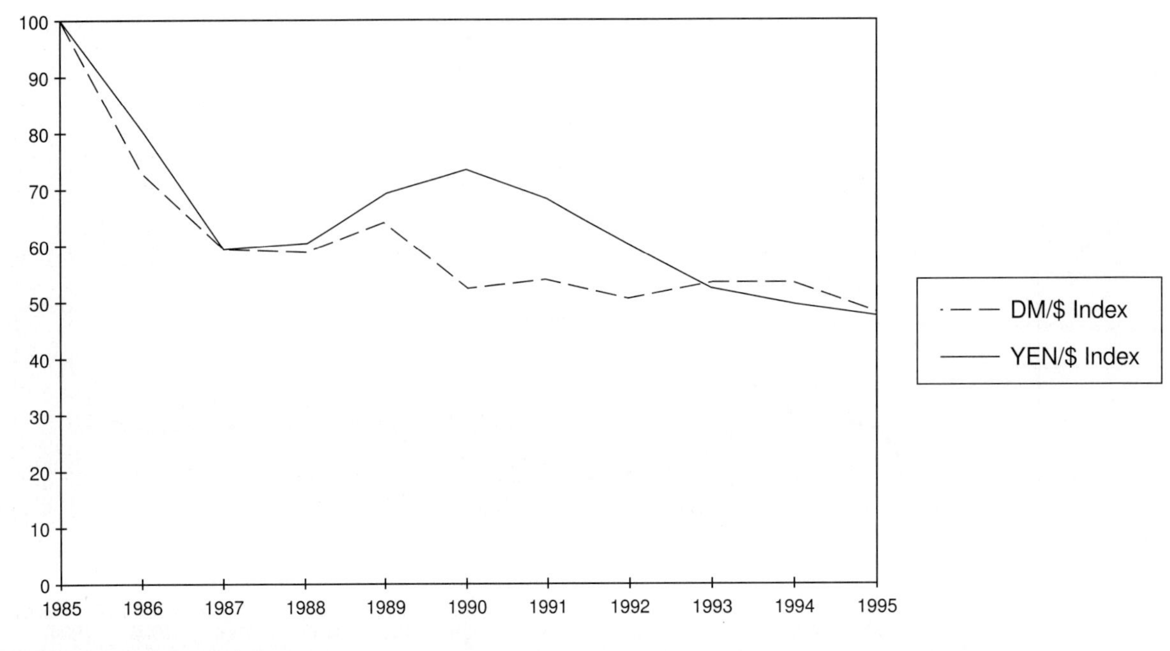

EXHIBIT 8 Sales Trends by Models

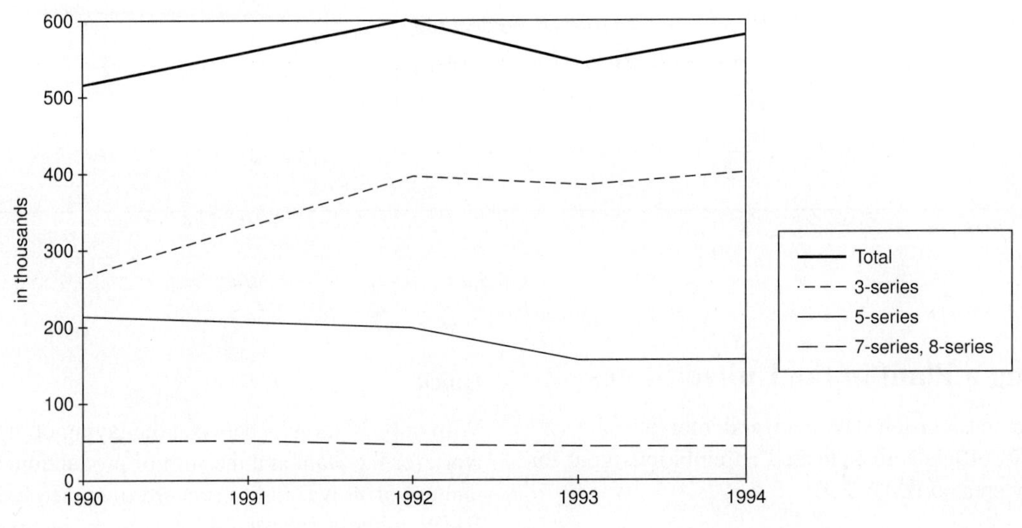

EXHIBIT 9 Competition in 1994

Make	Model	Manufacturing Location	Price Range
BMW	3-series	Spartanburg, US, Munich and Regensburg, Germany	$25,125–39,250
	5-series	Dingolfing, Germany	$38,875–47,950
	7-series	Dingolfing, Germany	$56,400–84,400
	8-series	Dingolfing, Germany	$68,550–98,500
	Z3 Roadster (1995)	Spartanburg, US	$28,000
Cadillac	DeVille	Hamtramek, MI	$33,615–38,615
	Seville	Hamtramek, MI	$42,055–45,955
Honda	Acura Legend	Sayama, Japan	$34,185–41,885
Jaguar	XJ6, Vanden Plas	Coventry, UK	$52,330–59,980
	XJ12	Coventry, UK	$72,330–73,780
Mercedes	C-Class	Sindelfingen and Bremen, Germany	$30,375–35,375
	E-Class	Sindelfingen and Bremen, Germany	$40,475–81,275
	S-Class	Sindelfingen, Germany	$71,075–133,775
	SL-Class	Bremen, Germany	$85,675–120,575
Nissan	Infiniti G20	Oppama, Japan	$19,950–20,850
	Infiniti J30	Tochogo, Japan	$37,400
	Infiniti Q45	Oppama, Japan	$50,900–57,500
Toyota	Lexus ES 300	Tsutsumi, Japan	$31,670
	Lexus SC 300	Motochi, Japan	$38,470–39,370
	Lexus SC 400	Motochi, Japan	$45,570
	Lexus LS 400	Tahara, Japan	$51,670

Source: Wards Automotive Yearbook 1994/1995.

EXHIBIT 10 Chronology of Events

June 1992	BMW AG of Germany announced the intention to build an assembly plant in Spartanburg, SC.
September 1992	Groundwork for the plant began.
April 1993	Construction work on buildings began, followed by production facilities and interior.
January 1994	First production associate hired.
June 1994	First imported BMW arrived at port in Charleston and was prepared at the plant for delivery to U.S. dealers.
September 1994	The first 3-series BMW (318; Sedan) built in the U.S. rolled off the assembly line.
November 1994	Official plant opening ceremony took place.
March 1995	First cars are shipped to U.S. dealers.
September 1995	First Z3 roadster comes off the assembly line.

produce 300 cars a day, with future expansion to 400 cars per day. Plans called for the production of the 3-series models 318 and 328. Assembly of the 4-cylinder 318i sedan was scheduled for September 1994, and production of the second model—the 6-cylinder 328 sedan—was scheduled for the fall of 1995. BMW planned gradual expansion of the plant from 100 vehicles per day at the end of 1995, to 300 vehicles by the first quarter of 1997 and 400 vehicles per day in 1998. This was still considerably smaller than a production rate in a typical auto assembly plant, which was over 1,000 vehicles per day (see Exhibit 5).

Flexible

While most automobile plants, including BMW's German plants, were built with a high degree of hard automation, Spartanburg focused on manufacturing flexibility. The layout was designed to support a flexible team working environment rather than transfer-line automation. In a radical departure from tradition, the body shop, the paint shop, and the assembly line were all located under one roof. The plant layout was L-shaped to allow for a higher degree of integration between the production line, quality control and supporting functions. Also, to facilitate communication, the assembly line was in the form of a lower-case "e" (instead of the typical "s" or "u" shapes), meaning that the final part of the assembly line curved back to the middle of the shop. Testing operations were located in the middle leg of this "e" (see Exhibit 11). In addition to bringing the assembly-line workers closer to each other, the "e"-shaped layout reduced required space by 40 percent and sharply reduced construction costs.

The Spartanburg plant had only 25 robots installed in the plant: one in the assembly line (used for windshield adhesive application), a few in those welding operations that needed a high degree of speed and accuracy (much of the welding was still done manually), and the rest in the paint shop.

Technologically Advanced

The new facility in Spartanburg was state-of-the-art. It integrated all the concepts BMW had learned from auto makers around the world. The U.S. plant's fully automated paint shop had a water-borne system, which was used in BMW's Regensburg plant in Germany, and an experimental line to test new innovations. BMW was the first car manufacturer that used water-based paint on four of the five paint layers. Only the clear top coat was solvent-based.

Forty percent of the total initial investment in Spartanburg was for the paint shop. The water-borne system was environmentally safer but trickier to launch and operate. First, the car body had to be thoroughly cleaned to remove all residues. Next, a special coat was applied by lowering the entire body into a water-diluted paint in a giant cathode dip bath. This layer was baked onto the automobile, and after cooling, the underbody protection was applied, followed by a base coat. High-speed atomizers were used to create an ultra-fine mist that was drawn to the body of the car by high-tension electrostatic charge. The final top coat was then applied and hardened in a drying oven. All paint layers were applied by robots to maintain consistent thickness. In all, BMW used 18 colors of primer and 32 base coat colors, all of which were water-based. This was a color spectrum unheard of in auto assembly plants.

BMW had also studied Harley-Davidson's success with powder coating and GM's ground-breaking acrylic powder system. The paint shop in Spartanburg was designed with provisions to allow powder coat equipment to be added later.

Scheduling the daily production at the paint shop also posed a challenge. Painting was done in batches based on colors. Operations before painting (in the body shop) and after painting (final assembly) were done in series based on orders. Synchronizing painting with these operations was not easy. The master production schedule at Spartanburg was based on sales orders, and suppliers delivered parts in the exact sequence in which they were used both in the body shop and the assembly line. There was a stacker or "post office," which was located between the paint shop and the assembly line. The post office had four levels that each held six rows of four cars for a total of 96 vehicles. The post office could reshuffle the cars into the desired sequence necessary for either painting or assembly-line production. All this required sophisticated material handling and scheduling systems.

Besides the paint shop, the rest of the Spartanburg plant was also designed to be friendly to the environment. It recycled corrugated cardboard, office paper, aluminum cans, scrap metal, glass bottles, plastic bottles, solvents, rags, and used oil. The total amount of recycled materials was 180 tons in 1994. It also used a cogeneration system to produce some of its own energy. The gas turbines were equipped with nitrogen oxide reduction technology which reduced emissions to less than 10 percent of the federal standard for stationary gas turbines. The plant operated an on-site wastewater pretreatment plant that cleaned the waste water before releasing it into the community waste water treatment.

BMW Quality

> Production ramp-up will be deliberately slow to absolutely ensure first-time quality.
>
> —Al Kinzer, President of BMW MC.

EXHIBIT 11 Spartanburg Plant Layout

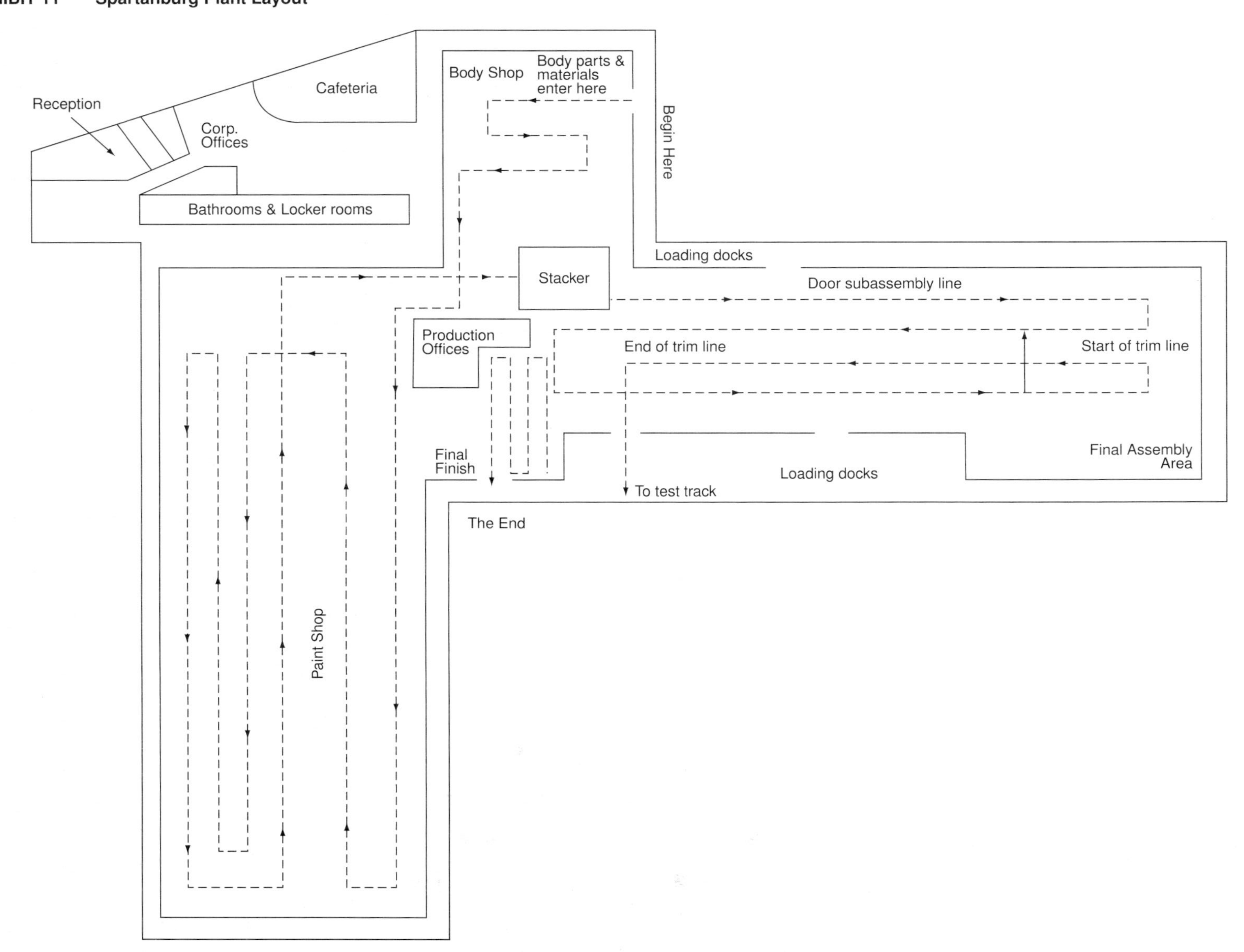

Everyone at BMW was conscious that an important asset of BMW was its quality image. Part of this image, historically, was built on the German reputation for high quality work. The Spartanburg plant had paid careful attention to this concern and had developed several systems for quality control. For example, suppliers were screened carefully and were held responsible for meeting strict quality standards (Spartanburg did not perform incoming inspection).

Within the plant, team members checked each other's work throughout the production process and final quality checks were performed at the end of the assembly line by workers from each shop. Production errors were referred back to the person (or the "associate," as everyone was called in BMW MC) who installed the system or part; he or she was solely responsible for the rework. This system distinguished between person-based and system-based errors, and identified major systemwide quality problems.

Spartanburg had a separate "Import Car Processing" (ICP) line that served as a final check for all imported BMW's from Germany destined for dealers in the Southern United States (BMW also had two other ICPs in the U.S.). In addition to extensive checks, installation of custom items such as radios, compact disc players, and computer equipment was performed in the ICP. When this operation started in Spartanburg in July of 1994, the line prepped approximately 20 vehicles per week. This rate increased rapidly to 60 vehicles per day, and reached 100 vehicles per day by February 1995.

Single Line—Different Models

In July 1994, BMW R&D chief, Dr. Reitzle, announced the introduction of a new sports car for the model year 1996. Named Z3, the two-seat roadster was unveiled at the Detroit Auto Show in January 1995. Code-named E36/7, the two-seater was based on a 3-series platform. The original model was made of steel and had a canvas top, with a hardtop option to follow. Though the car's striking body matched no other BMW, key pieces of Z3—engine, transmission, suspension, seats, steering—were taken from parts used in other BMW models. The Z3 used the same underbody and wheel base as the 3-series coupe. The car was powered by a 1.8 or 1.9 liter, 4-cylinder engine with 115 HPs—the same as in the 318 sedan. Even the planned 6 cylinder version of the Z3 was to use an existing engine—the one used in the 328 sedan.

Through the development of the Z3, BMW officials tried to remove costs from the design and manufacturing processes. "This car will be a big step forward for us in design for manufacturability and assembly," stressed Reitzle. Aware of the need to catch up with the world's leaders in overall efficiency—Toyota, Honda, and Ford—Reitzle said the Z3 program would spearhead BMW's drive to lower design cost, shorten the development cycle, and increase production efficiency. "We can't afford to wait until the cost pressure from the market gets worse," he stated. "Germany's auto industry cannot expect to keep up with Japan's in productivity unless we act now."

One example of this improved design for manufacturability was the reduction in the "hits" that body panels required at Spartanburg. "Hits" refers to the number of times a die (or press) must stamp a panel before it assumes its final shape. At BMW, major body panels generally required seven hits; for the Z3, the average was only four hits—which meant that the final shape was achieved using four dies instead of seven. Dies were expensive, and reducing their numbers generated large savings—especially in a small-scale operation such as Spartanburg.

BMW estimated the world market for all roadsters to be 150,000 to 160,000 units per year, of which the Z3 was expected to capture 20 percent. This small market implied that the location chosen for production of the new model would have to supply the world market of 100 countries. Because of its flexible assembly process and lower expected costs, Spartanburg was the prime candidate. But, if selected for the Z3, Spartanburg would have to produce the 318 sedan, the 328 sedan, and the Z3 roadster simultaneously. In addition, the Z3 had to be produced in 74 country-specific variations to accommodate the differences in exhaust systems, safety features, lights, steering, and other requirements. All this would demand enormous flexibility from the single assembly line at Spartanburg.

There were also the usual concerns about the risks of producing a brand new model in a brand new plant—especially a plant outside the "home base." Would there be enough time for Spartanburg to develop the necessary engineering competence to support the introduction of a new model—particularly one that encompassed many innovations for BMW? It was argued that since Regensburg produced all the 3-series models—including the Coupe—it was a logical place to introduce the new Z3. Regensburg could solve the inevitable problems of introducing a new model while Spartanburg focused on the standard 318 and 328 models. The Z3 could then be relocated to Spartanburg to take advantage of cost differences. But eventually this argument was not accepted, and BMW decided to introduce the Z3 at Spartanburg.

Globalizing BMW's Manufacturing Network

There were many within BMW who felt that the repercussions of creating a U.S. plant went beyond Spartanburg and the U.S. market; this move had far-reaching consequences for BMW's entire manufacturing network. BMW had to reconfigure its global supplier network, create a unique and effective work culture, and design mechanisms for necessary knowledge transfer.

Building a Global Supplier Network

NAFTA granted tariff exemption within North America for all goods manufactured with a local content of at least 65 percent. That provided BMW with a strong incentive to develop local suppliers in the United States. Many high quality parts and components could be found in the United States at lower prices than in many other countries: stampings, frames, seats, fasteners, glass, and interior and exterior trim could all be purchased in the U.S. for less than in Europe. Eventually, BMW planned to import only engines and transmissions from Germany. "We are looking to develop an adequate U.S. supplier base. It is inefficient to use suppliers halfway around the world because it drives costs up," said one BMW MC executive.

Developing a local supplier base was no easy task. Although Spartanburg wanted to choose suppliers that were also supplying BMW's other plants, it could not simply favor German-based suppliers with U.S. operations or global suppliers with a German base. It wanted to identify the best supplier and when appropriate, encourage U.S. suppliers to form joint-ventures with German firms. Spartanburg also wanted to work closely with its suppliers. In late 1994, it held an unprecedented 2 1/2-day seminar for over 100 suppliers' quality control managers, and another seminar for suppliers' account managers (to handle operational details such as details of BMW's payment system). Supplier representatives were often invited to the new plant to show assembly-line workers the best way to handle their parts and systems, and plant employees often visited the suppliers' plants.

The procurement office in Spartanburg had the responsibility for all North American procurement activities. Although this office interacted directly with its German counterpart, it had no reporting relationship with Germany and was managed separately. Nevertheless, in 1995 a group of German engineers was still in Spartanburg to assist in the development of the supplier network and to ensure global coordination.

Spartanburg's attempt to enlist local suppliers ran counter to a very strong industry trend to rationalize the network of suppliers. Like other car manufacturers, BMW faced the issue of choosing suppliers who could deliver parts and components to the company on a global basis—thus providing more consistent quality as well as an improved bargaining position for the company. The so-called "tier one" suppliers provided more complete subassemblies and helped in product development. Chrysler's LH program used 230 parts and materials vendors and the Ford Mustang was targeting 180. BMW was aiming for 100 tier one suppliers. More than 60 tier one suppliers were already committed to Spartanburg and nearly half planned to set up facilities close to Spartanburg. Of the 60, only a few (eight) were based in Germany. Some, like Robert Bosch Corp., were large multinationals that had operated in the United States for a long time.

High on the priority list for BMW was a drastically enhanced role for the suppliers in the design and manufacture of its models. This included buying more completed subassemblies from top-tier suppliers. To enhance the supplier's role in design, cross-functional procurement teams had been formed with designers, engineers, manufacturers, and purchasers. An important objective was to build in more quality control and to work on friendlier terms with the 100 systems suppliers. The teams involved the suppliers at the concept stage of new models, and enlisted them to look for ways to reduce costs and improve manufacturability. They also helped to change the traditional cost orientation of the purchasing function. In fact, somewhat unlike other auto makers, BMW did not mandate extreme and continuous cost-cutting by the suppliers. There were only clauses in the contracts for "negotiating cost adjustments."

Tier one suppliers were expected to assume responsibility for more complete subassemblies. Eventually, 20 of them were expected to provide 80 percent of all BMW's purchased parts. A sun roof, for example, which used to be assembled by BMW from 60 different purchased parts, now came semi-assembled from one supplier, with only three subassembled pieces. This integrated approach was estimated to yield a cost reduction of at least 20 percent and perhaps as much as 40 percent in some cases. "Non-systems suppliers ultimately run the risk of becoming subsuppliers" said Dr. Reitzle, BMW's head of R&D.

Creating a New Culture

One of the most important objectives for Spartanburg was to develop a new atmosphere in which employees could be creative and productive. This work atmosphere would be different from the traditional one found in Germany. In a sense, Spartanburg presented BMW with a unique opportunity to experiment with a new format combining the best of German and American traditions. The results were extraordinary.

The entrance to the Spartanburg plant—spacious, impeccable, and very organized—reminded a visitor of a German setting. To the left, two assistants diligently and efficiently took in visitor information and provided name tags. To the right, a series of pictures showed the history of the development of Spartanburg, from groundbreaking to the present. Straight ahead was a huge inviting corridor which led to the production area. At the end of the corridor, a BMW Z3 roadster prototype hung from a movable wall.

To the left, another wide corridor led to the open area which housed all BMW MC corporate offices. There were three small conference rooms on this corridor, which were the only closed rooms throughout the Spartanburg plant. The corporate office layout resembled that of a Japanese corporation—80 desks were tightly packed across a large open room creating small clusters of barely discernible work units. Somewhere within each cluster, a small signpost indicated the appropriate corporate function—finance, public relations, human resources, etc. There were no cubicles, walls, or separations of any kind.

At the corner closest to the window, at a desk slightly slanted with a view of the whole room, sat Al Kinzer, President of BMW MC. Mr. Kinzer dressed exactly the same as everyone else in the office and the plant. At Spartanburg, BMW tried to erase the difference between office and manufacturing employees by having all employees—including managers—wear a white uniform with a BMW emblem. Only those employees whose specific duties required special gear departed from this common uniform.

There was no division between this large area and the rest of the plant. Sitting at their desks, managers and office workers could see part of the paint shop, some of the assembly shop, and the impressive Z3 prototype hanging from the movable platform. The hanging car stood in front of another set of offices which housed plant operations, including plant procurement and manufacturing support functions. Interestingly, these offices were located in the geographic center of the plant, surrounded by the body shop, the paint shop, and the assembly line. Initially, they were supposed to be completely open, but due to noise problems glass walls had been erected to surround the office area. The very layout of the building conveyed the message that there should be no difference between office and production workers.

This philosophy of equality and a shared environment extended to all facets of life at Spartanburg. All employees lunched at the same cafeteria—an enormous hall seating close to 1,200 people. Three lunch shifts were necessary due to capacity constraints, but, in general, office workers lunched with production workers and corporate staff. Also, workers from all areas shared the same rest rooms and locker rooms.

All employees were organized into teams. A typical team had 20 members and was composed of smaller teams of four to five people. Teams had rotating leaders who were democratically selected by the team members. Each team worked on a section of the car and put an identifying signature on its work. Teams were also responsible for their own quality control. Teammates always checked each other's work systematically, and corrected their own mistakes. If the error had originated outside of the team, they called on the team that had signed the part to correct the mistake. As Bobby Hitt, Spartanburg's manager of Community Relations, said "we all have bad days. Teams allow us to tell the difference between someone having a bad day and a recurring mistake which might be happening due to larger, systemwide problems."

At Spartanburg, BMW recruited workers who were new to auto production and trained them from scratch—not only in manufacturing cars, but also in team-building and conflict resolution. It also instituted a carefully designed compensation program. Benefits were the same for production, staff, and managerial positions. For example, a perfect attendance bonus of $100 was given for every 20 consecutive work days. All other bonuses depended on overall plant performance regardless of the employee's rank.

Transferring Knowledge Between German and American Operations

To provide sufficient engineering support in the ramp-up phase of the plant, BMW formed an engineering group of 40 German engineers. They were linked to Germany and to suppliers by a CATIA system—an on-line CAD system. The engineers served in the United States on a rotating basis. They were responsible for design, quality and reliability tests, and export homologation, Reitzle explained.

Each management position in production was filled with two persons: a U.S. manager and a German manager. German managers provided expertise as well as assistance during the startup process. Meanwhile, they also learned the innovations which were introduced in Spartanburg and eventually, upon return to Germany, would transfer this knowledge to other BMW plants. All these

German managers were expected to return after two years, leaving the U.S. manager in charge.

Reitzle planned to expand BMW MC's design engineering group from 40 to 150 in a few years. All would be networked via CATIA with engineering headquarters in Munich. This, Reitzle explained, would allow virtual real-time engineering between the United States and Germany. BMW also had a small design studio in California, which would be on-line with this system.

In general, transfer of knowledge and systems between the United States and Germany posed a cultural challenge. BMW in Germany was highly hierarchical, whereas the new culture at Spartanburg emphasized a flat organization (see Exhibit 12). According to Bobby Hitt, to ensure better communication, BMW tried to standardize managerial positions across BMW's plants and administrative offices. In this way, everyone could easily identify his or her counterparts in the other BMW operations. But since Spartanburg's organization and culture were markedly different, it was difficult to match the positions between Germany and the United States. This presented a trade-off: imposing a hierarchy in Spartanburg would improve communication with Germany, but it would also inhibit its unique culture.

The Dilemma

By September 1995, as the first Z3s were leaving the assembly line, the huge success of the new car had already created a new challenge. The original manufacturing plan for Spartanburg called for a gradual ramp-up of production of the Z3, continuation of production of the 318 model, and later production of the 328. But the strong demand for the Z3 was forcing major changes to this plan. Already, instead of the 328, Spartanburg was to focus on producing more Z3s. However, due to larger differences between the Z3 and the 318 (than between the 328 and the 318), this ramp-up would have to be slower than for the 328 model. Spartanburg's production for 1995 would therefore not reach the planned 20,000 units. Instead it would be under 16,000 units, of which only 6,000 were Z3s. Plans called for expansion of Z3 production to 35,000 units in 1996, but even that would not satisfy all the demand. The entire production planned for 1996 had already been sold by BMW's dealers.

There were also other reasons to expand production at Spartanburg. In September 1995, Bernd Pischestrieder, the newly appointed CEO of BMW AG, had made an announcement that due to pressures on margins, volume levels would have to increase to maintain profitability. Especially troublesome was the Z3 situation: "It's a question of capacity more than anything else, and the capacity [at Spartanburg] is limited." Not meeting the demand was troubling, especially since 1996 was the only year in which the Z3 would have only one competitor, the Mazda Miata. Mercedes, Porsche, and Audi were all planning to introduce roadsters in 1997.

But how should Spartanburg respond to the pressure to expand the Z3's production? Al Kinzer knew that he had to formulate a response quickly. This was the main topic

EXHIBIT 12 BMW Manufacturing Corporation Organization Chart

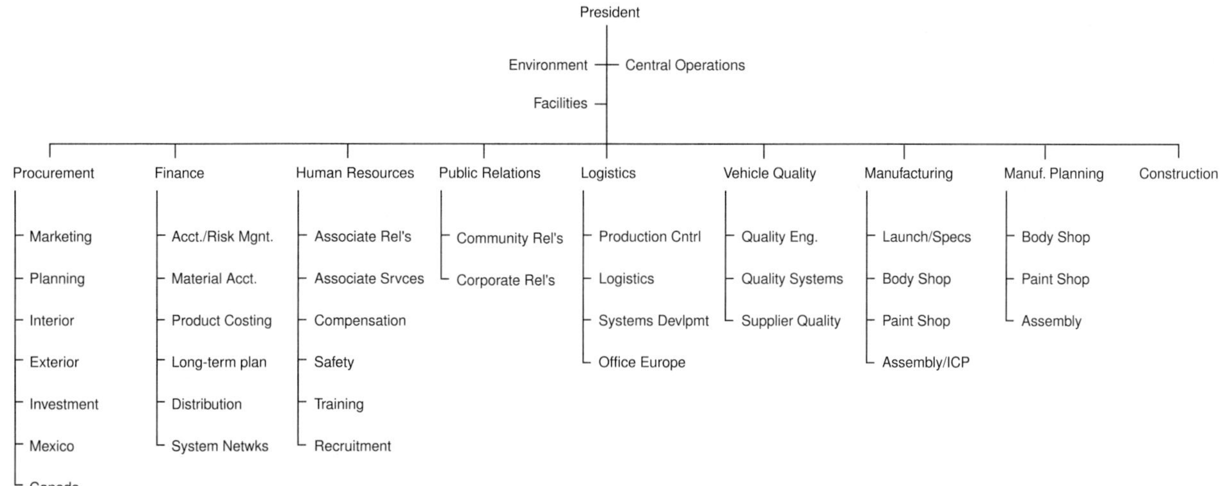

of discussion during the board meeting that was to be held the following week in Munich.

Kinzer narrowed his options to three: one was to gear up for higher production of both the Z3 and the 3-series models. This required an additional investment of $200 million, bringing the total at Spartanburg to $800 million. This rate of growth was phenomenal and demanded careful management attention. New construction would add about 300,000 square feet of manufacturing space to the 1.2 million square foot plant. The expansion would increase the daily capacity of the body and assembly areas from 300 units to 400. The plant's paint shop was already rated at 400 units per day. This investment would allow BMW to expand the body and assembly departments while maintaining the plant's single line production concept. Furthermore, Spartanburg would have to move to two shifts by November 1995, instead of February 1996, as originally planned.

Another option was to send the 318 back to Germany's Regensburg plant. Regensburg had recently cut back work hours and had excess capacity. By concentrating all its energy on the Z3, Spartanburg would become a specialized plant for the roadster. Meanwhile, Regensburg could easily supplement production of the 318, albeit at a somewhat higher cost.

The third option was to resist market pressure. Kinzer understood that quality was the most important element of BMW's strategy. For 85 years BMW had been able to rely on a carefully constructed base of German engineers, and had gained a leading reputation for technical excellence and quality. The risk of capitulating to market pressure and increasing production levels was the possibility that quality problems would develop. Even the smallest failure in Spartanburg's quality would have far-reaching consequences—corporate headquarters might lose confidence in the plant's capacity to supply BMW-quality vehicles. Worse, the public might decide that U.S.-made BMW's did not deserve the premium price tag or might demand only German-made BMWs.

EXHIBIT 13 The Z3

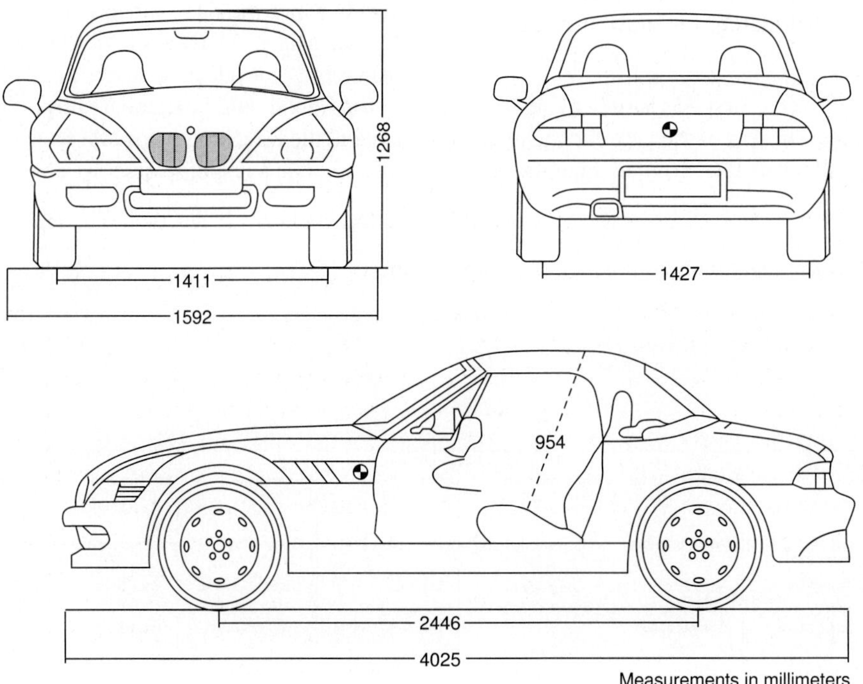

UNIT 12 Managing Research, Knowledge, and New Product Development

THESEUS
INTERNATIONAL MANAGEMENT INSTITUTE

Case 12–1

Salomon: Strategic Entry into the World Snowboard Market

In the fall of 1995, Jean-Luc Diard, head of Salomon's snowboard development project, was looking at the feedback from the first field tests of Salomon's prototype snowboard and binding. Over the past year, the company had carried out an intensive research program in order to understand the needs of the snowboarding community and define a family of products to satisfy those needs.

The idea of developing a snowboard and related accessories was not new at Salomon. The possibilities had already been investigated in the late 1980s and then again in the early 1990s. However, it was not until the fall of 1994, when the global market for snowboarding equipment started being commercially significant, that a more concentrated effort was initiated. At this stage, Jean-Luc Diard was encouraged to look into the snowboarding market in more depth.

After conducting some preliminary market research in the United States, Salomon acquired a small but legitimate company producing snowboarding clothing under the brand name "Bonfire" at the end of 1995. The company's owner, Brad Steward—a U.S. snowboarding guru, also joined Salomon, thereby strengthening its marketing force. In the early summer of 1995, Salomon had already set up a snowboard development team, including board and binding development (boot development was initiated in the spring of 1996). By late fall the same year, the team had come up with the first prototype board and binding.

Looking at the results from the first field tests, it was obvious that Salomon was clearly on target to develop a very exciting product for an attractive market. However, several issues still existed which Jean-Luc would have to resolve prior to a full-blown market introduction. First, which brand to use for the product launch needed to be decided. The choice was between Bonfire, with its avant-garde and hard-core image, and Salomon, known for being an innovator in the high-end alpine ski market. Second, decisions related to organizing sales and marketing, product development, manufacturing, and logistics had to be determined. The alternatives were whether to (1) locate the business within Salomon's existing network of product development and manufacturing centers; (2) establish an independent business unit with its own new product development and manufacturing center (similar to Taylor Made for golf equipment); or (3) outsource the business to external companies.

Salomon Worldwide

In 1947, François Salomon, his wife Jeanne, and son Georges set up a small shop producing metal edges for skis in Annecy's old town. As skiing in the French Alps increased in popularity, the company's activities also experienced rapid growth. By the year 1952, the Salomon business was producing around 700 km of ski edges per year.

This early growth was further enhanced by a series of innovations. In 1965, Salomon commercialized a cable-free ski binding. By the year 1972, the company had become a world leader in ski bindings. Having established a dominant position in ski bindings, Salomon decided to enter the alpine ski boot business in 1974 by launching a major product development project. After five years in development, the new boot was introduced in 1979. At the time of its introduction, Salomon's rear-entry boot concept, "*Salomon Equipe,*" was considered revolutionary. The boot was a significant improvement over the conventional "buckle" ski boots, as they were much easier to use. Thus, over the next few years, the company grew into one of the largest producers of alpine ski boots.

In 1980, Salomon entered the cross-country market by introducing an integrated boot and binding combination, the "*SNS*" (Salomon Nordic System). Salomon's position

---

This case was written by Dr. Jukka Nihtila under the supervision of Prof. Francis Bidault. It is intended to be used as a basis for class discussion rather than to illustrate effective or ineffective handling of an administrative situation.

in the ski business was further strengthened through the 1993 acquisition of San Giorgio, an Italian ski boot manufacturer. Salomon not only acquired a second production site, but it also gained access to the whole "ski boot cluster" of Montebelluna. Almost 80 percent of the world's ski boots were being produced in this small Italian town.

In the mid-1980s, Salomon decided to complete its product range in the alpine ski business by developing its own line of skis. Called "*Equipe8000,*" this new family of skis for the high-end market was introduced in 1990. The Salomon skis, based on a new technology called "*monocoque,*" became an immediate success, as they were a vast improvement on the "sandwich" structure used in conventional skis. In the monocoque structure, the skis were constructed in a modular manner from prefabricated elements, thus significantly enhancing the ease of manufacture. In terms of product performance, the new structure gave the skis a more evenly distributed flexibility, which enabled them to have a better grip on hard-packed snow. By the 1992/93 season, Salomon skis had captured 20 percent of the high-end ski market.

The winter sporting goods business depended heavily on weather conditions. To reduce the risk of losses incurred by snowless winters, Salomon decided to balance its activities between winter and summer sports. In 1984, the company diversified into the golf equipment business through the acquisition of Taylor Made, an American golf equipment manufacturer established in 1979 by the golf "pro," Gary Adams. The company rapidly became a market leader in golf clubs, which were distinguished by their "metalwood" technology. By the early 1990s, the golf equipment activity represented some 28 percent of Salomon's net sales. However, difficulties in the market, especially in Japan, slowed the growth of the golf equipment business.

In order to extend its presence in summer sports, Salomon entered the market for hiking (trekking) boots in 1991. In their first full season (1992/93), the boots captured a 4.4 percent market share with net sales of 56 million French francs; by 1994/95 the figures were 6 percent and 90 MFFr, respectively. Again, Salomon's key to success was its new innovative technology. By developing a new type of nonskid outer sole—called "Contragrip," not only could the boots grip more firmly on wet, slippery downhill surfaces, but their wear rate also improved.

In 1994, Salomon again decided to diversify further by entering the bicycle component market through the acquisition of the French company, Mavic. This company, already established since 1890, was a leading manufacturer of high-end bicycle rims. The bicycle market was especially interesting for Salomon because of its size and future growth potential. Annually, over 90 million bicycles were sold around the world, with 40 percent of them devoted to recreational use. Altogether, the global bicycle market was approximately 40 billion French francs, of which bicycle components represented some 40–50 percent. In comparison, the global winter sports market was 11 billion and the golf equipment market 22 billion French francs (see Exhibit 1).

Company Structure

With an annual turnover of 4 billion French francs (1995/96), Salomon had become one of the major players in the design, manufacture, and distribution of sports equipment (Exhibit 2). Although the company's growth in recent years had been quite stable, Salomon did experience a serious decrease in sales and profits in 1990 and 1991 (Exhibits 2 and 3). This was mainly due to a series

EXHIBIT 1 Salomon's Market Position by Product Line During the 1994/95 Season

Brand	Product Line	Rank	Market Share
Salomon	Alpine Bindings	1	44%
	Alpine Boots	2	24%
	Alpine Skis	5 (2*)	8%
	Cross-country Bindings	1	61%
	Cross-country Boots	1	42%
	Hiking Boots	5	6%
Taylor Made	Gold Clubs (Metalwoods)	2	11%
Mavic	Bicycle Rims	1	N/A

(*) Rank in terms of value. Salomon skis were positioned on the high-end market.

EXHIBIT 2 **Salomon Worldwide Net Consolidated Sales, 1988/89–1994/95** (in millions of French francs).

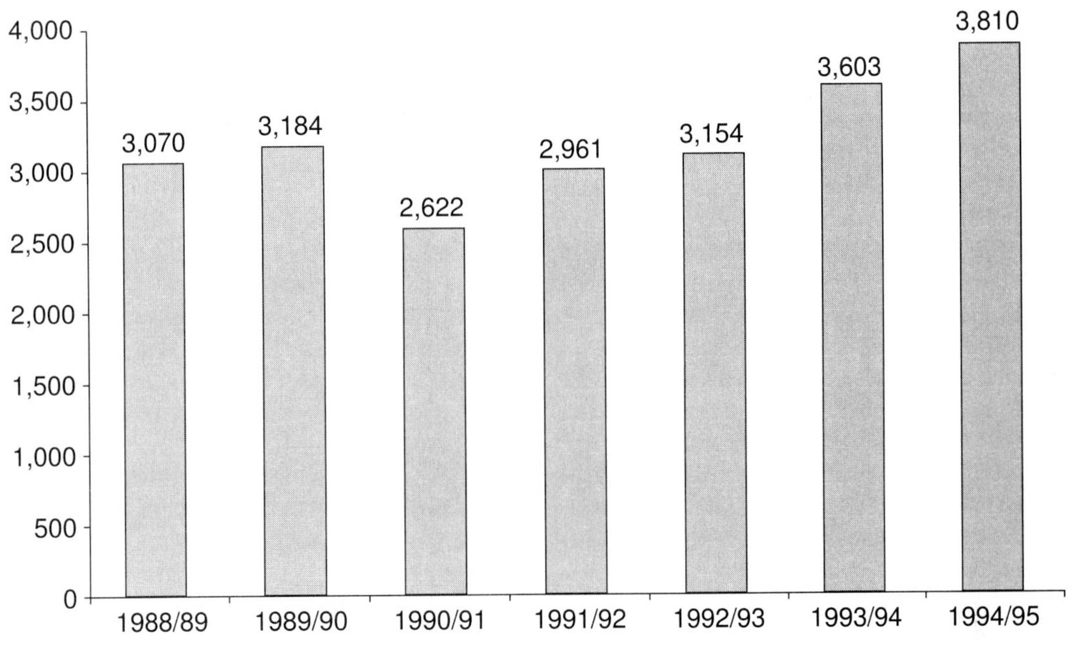

EXHIBIT 3 **Salomon Worldwide Net Results, 1988/89–1994/95** (in millions of French francs).

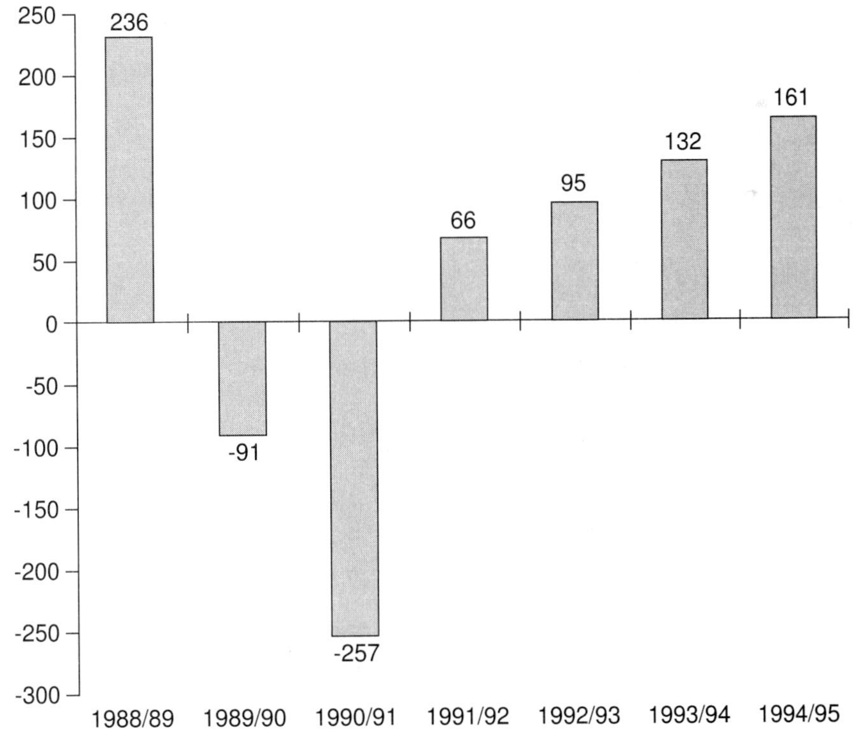

EXHIBIT 4 Salomon Worldwide Sales by Activity, 1992/93–1994/95

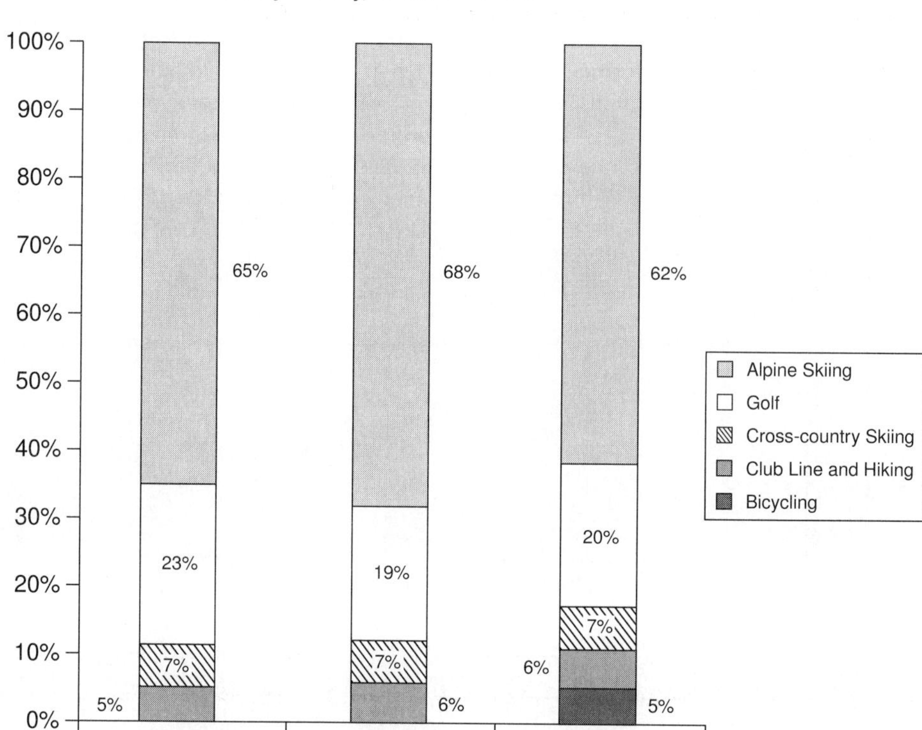

of poor winters as well as the economic downturn. As can be seen from the distribution of activities in Exhibit 4, the company's original focus area—alpine skiing—still accounted for the highest proportion of its business, i.e., a total of 62 percent of net sales. Golf was the second largest sector with 20 percent of net sales. The three other business units—cross-country skiing (7 percent), accessories and hiking equipment (6 percent), and bicycle components (5 percent)—each represented a relatively minor portion of net sales. However, these areas were expected to grow significantly in the following years.

Geographic distribution of sales was split quite evenly between Europe and Japan (Exhibit 5). The former represented 37 percent of total sales volume and the latter 36 percent. In 1994/95, the North American market provided 27 percent of Salomon's worldwide sales.

Salomon's structure is shown in Exhibits 6, 7, and 8. Salomon S.A., the parent company, was headquartered in Annecy Metz-Tessy, France, and the corporate functions of finance, marketing, and planning were located there. Several production sites for winter sports equipment were also located in the Annecy region: Rumilly, Serrières, and Prairie. The Rumilly site was developed in the early 1990s as the prime manufacturing facility for the newly developed monocoque ski. Later, product development for alpine skis and bindings as well as binding production was moved to this site. Salomon's boot development and production was split between Chavanod, Serrières, and Montebelluna in Italy. Serrières had been the prime site for ski boot development and production until the acquisition of the Italian ski boot manufacturer, San Giorgio, in Montebelluna. From then on, Montebelluna had provided another important center of expertise in ski boot production. Serrières has been gradually converted to the manufacture of Mavic bicycle components. In addition to its own facilities, Salomon operated a net-

EXHIBIT 5 Salomon Worldwide Sales by Geographic Region, 1992/93–1994/95

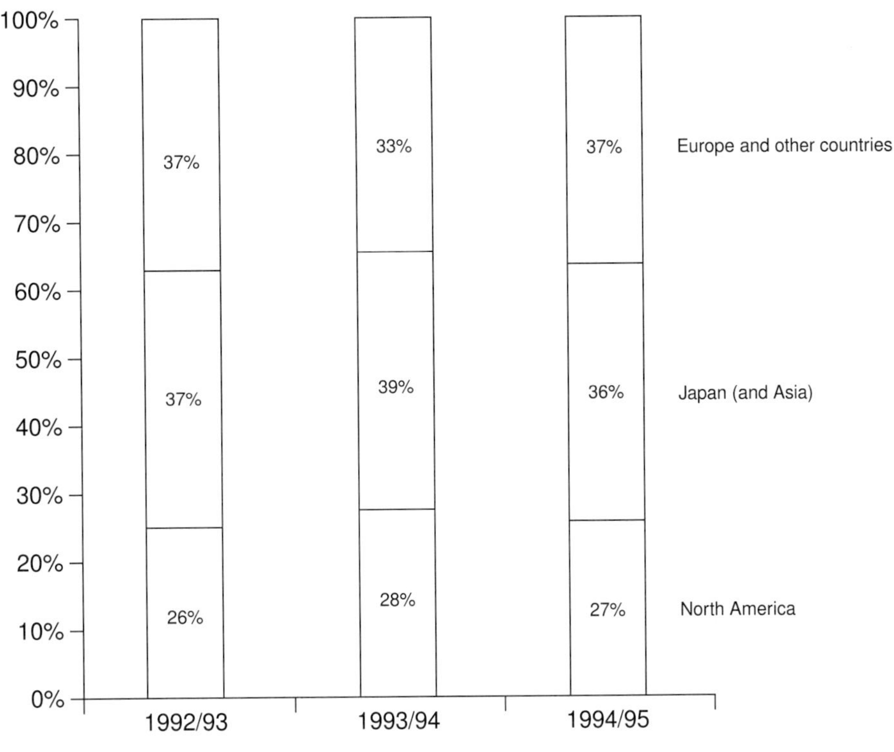

work of subcontractors in Europe, North Africa, and Southeast Asia.

The golf equipment manufacturer, Taylor Made, operated as an independent subsidiary. The company's product development and production (assembly) were performed at two different sites, both of which were close to its main markets. One center was located in Carlsbad, California, USA, and the other one was in Tokyo, Japan. Likewise, the bicycle component manufacturer, Mavic, functioned as an independent subsidiary of the Salomon group. This unit's operations were situated in France, the product development center in Saint Trivier and two production sites in St Trivier and Serrières.

Salomon controlled its entire distribution channel (Exhibit 6). With the exception of Spain and Korea (with branch offices), and Salomon & Taylor Made Japan (with 87 percent ownership), all the distribution companies were fully owned subsidiaries of Salomon S.A. Every Salomon subsidiary distributed winter sports equipment. Golf equipment was distributed by Taylor Made (in the United States and Great Britain) as well as by Salomon Canada Sports Ltd., Salomon & Taylor Made Co. Ltd. (in Japan), and Salomon Sports AB (in Sweden). Bicycling equipment was distributed by the Mavic subsidiary's logistics network.

Salomon History and Culture

Salomon's strong entrepreneurial background was still very much in evidence. Until 1978, Georges Salomon had run the company essentially single-handedly. The company's culture up to that point reflected his low profile and hands-on management style. When Salomon began diversifying outside the ski business, additional professional managers were brought into the company. Simultaneously, the company's recruitment policy began to include graduates from the best engineering and business schools in France. For example, Jean-Luc Diard,

EXHIBIT 6 Salomon Organization Structure

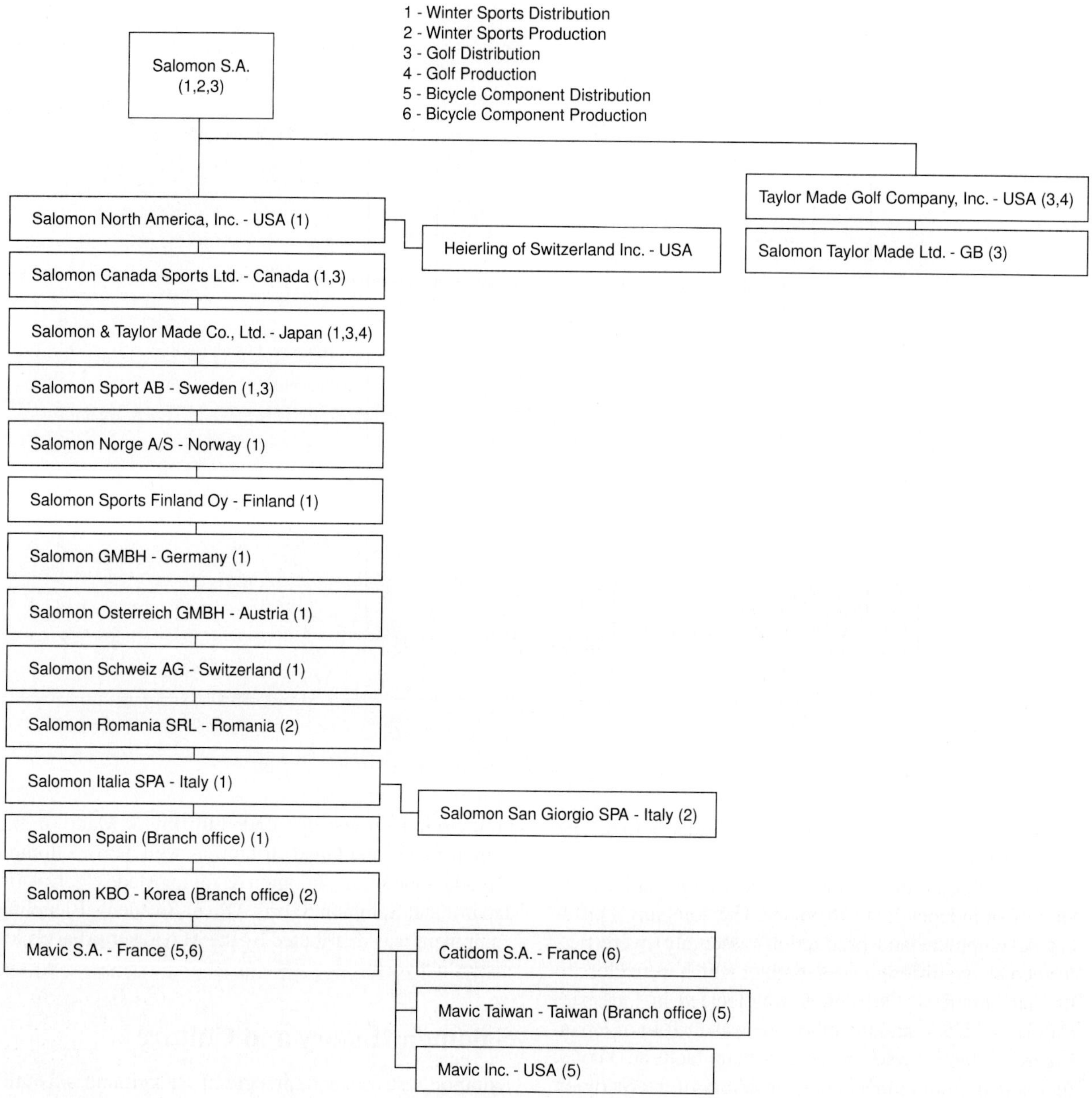

1 - Winter Sports Distribution
2 - Winter Sports Production
3 - Golf Distribution
4 - Golf Production
5 - Bicycle Component Distribution
6 - Bicycle Component Production

Source: Salomon Annual Report 1994/95.

Exhibit 7 Location of Salomon Operations in 1995

Saint Trivier (France)
R&D Center: Bicycle components (Mavic)

Serrières (France)
Production: Alpine boots

Carlsbad (US)
R&D Center: Golf clubs
Production: Golf club assembly

Tokyo (Japan)
R&D Center: Golf clubs
Production: Golf club assembly

Rumilly (France)
R&D Center: Alpine skis and bindings
Production: Alpine skis and bindings

Chavanod (France)
R&D Center: Alpine, cross-country and hiking boots

Annecy Metz-Tessy (France)
Salomon S.A. headquarters

Annecy Prairie (France)
Production: Aluminum components for alpine bindings

Cesardes (France)
Surface Treatement: Alpine skis and bicycle rims

Montebelluna (Italy)
R&D Center: Alpine boots
Production: Alpine, cross-country and hiking boots

Subcontractors:
Italy: Alpine and hiking boots
France: Alpine and cross-country bindings
Romania: Alpine, cross-country and hiking boots
Czech Republic: Cross-country and hiking boots
Morocco: Cross-country boots
South East Asia: Hiking boot components

hired in 1984, was a graduate of ESC Paris, one of the country's top business schools. Jean-Francois Gautier joined Salomon in 1990, initially as a managing director, from the French consumer appliance company, Thomson Brandt. He then gradually started taking over the CEO's responsibilities from Georges Salomon.

Jean-Francois Gautier became CEO of Salomon when Georges Salomon left the company in 1991. The management structure at that time included an executive board (CEO Gautier and executive vice-president Bernard Salomon, son of Georges) and a supervisory board comprised of the company's main investors and members of the Salomon family.

The Salomon company's ability to implement sophisticated innovative ideas served to distinguish it from its competitors. In addition, Salomon became expert at identifying, integrating, and commercializing new technologies originating from external sources (other entrepreneurs and companies). The diversification process that took place during the late 1980s and early 1990s also enabled the company to evolve (from a limited focus on ski bindings and boots) into a sports equipment manufacturer that featured a range of "freedom action sports." Given its French origins and size, Salomon became a global company very early on, because management quickly realized the potential of the overseas market and having a global presence.

Finally, Salomon benefited from the fact that most of its employees, including management, were enthusiastic users of Salomon, Taylor Made, and Mavic equipment. Alpine skiing was especially popular since most of the company's sites were near Annecy, which was located in the heart of the French Alps. Their own high rate of

EXHIBIT 8 Salomon Organization

- CEO
  Jean-Francois Gautier
  - Operations
    - Boots
      Jean-Pierre Dimier
    - Bicycle Components
      Bernard Salomon
    - Skis and Bindings
      Philippe Regnier
  - Development
    - Snowboards/In-line Skates
      Jean-Luc Diard
    - Golf
      Jean Hue
    - Skis
      Maurice Legrand
    - Alpine Boots and Bindings
      Roland Petrini
    - Bicycle Components
      Bernard Salomon
    - Hiking/Cross-Country/Club-line
      Henri De Rocca-Serra
  - Markets
    - Asia
      Jean-Rene Belliard
    - North America
      Gilles Descamps
    - Europe
      Alain Compiegne
  - Functions
    - General Secretary
      Anne-Marie Berrette
    - Finance and Administration
      Jean-Paul Bertrand
    - Human Resources
      Jacques Descamps
    - Salomon Brand
      Thierry Paris
    - Logistics and Information
      Didier Pichon
    - Legal/IPR
      Clotilde Turleque

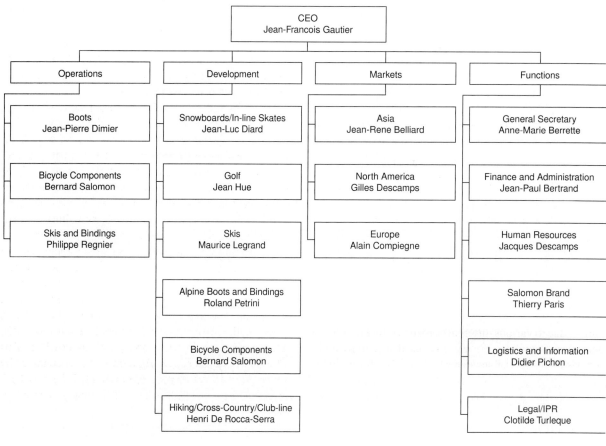

Source: Salomon Annual Report 1995/96.

participation gave Salomon personnel an excellent understanding of the market, how their products were perceived by customers, as well as how they were being used.

To summarize, Salomon's values centered on entrepreneurship, innovation, having a global presence, as well as enthusiasm for sports and outdoor activities.

The Snowboard Industry

During the time period between the mid-1980s and the 1990s, snowboarding became one of the most popular winter sports. Most estimates projected that, by the turn of the century, around 20 percent of winter sports participants would be snowboarders.

According to some industry observers, snowboarding already existed as far back as the late 1920s. Although a man named M.J. Burtchet claimed to have built the first snowboard—using plywood—in 1929, there is no official record of such a board. Generally, credit for the first snowboard design (in 1963) has gone to Tom Sims, a skateboard champion from New Jersey, USA. The board, constructed for a high school woodworking class project, was a skateboard redesigned to slide on snow.

In the mid-1960s, Sherman Poppen invented a board shaped like a small water ski, which was called "the snurfer." It had a rope attached to the tip to facilitate steering and a rough surface for traction. The Brunswick Company commercialized this product, and over one million snurfers were sold in the late 1960s. One of those snurfers was given to a surfing enthusiast named Jake Burton Carpenter for Christmas in 1969. He then decided to develop the concept further and succeeded in designing his own snowboard version that later evolved into a commercial product, Burton Snowboards.

The early snowboards were made of solid wood. Consequently, they were quite heavy and not very flexible. Other drawbacks included the primitive bindings, which were merely an adaptation of sailboard foot straps, and the fact that these boards did not have steel edges. In 1971, Dimitrije Milovitch, a surfing enthusiast from Long Island, New York, developed a snowboard based on a surfboard design. The board, later named the "Winterstick," consisted of pressure-molded foam wrapped in fiberglass. The board had metal edges, which made it possible to use on groomed slopes and hard-packed snow. During the 1970s and '80s, improvements in snowboard design evolved rapidly, soon approaching the style and shape of modern snowboards. This achievement was largely due to the work of early innovators such as Jake Burton, Tom Sims, and Chuck Barfoot.

However, getting ski resorts to accept this sport came about much more slowly. As late as the mid-1980s, snowboarding activity usually had to take place in the back country, as the sport was banned at most ski resorts. At this stage, there was often a hostile relationship between alpine skiers and snowboarders—in the United States as well as the more conservative European ski resorts—due to various differences in the culture of the two activities. Snowboarders were accused of significantly increasing the risk of accidents both on and off the slopes because of their reckless behavior. Another factor was that snowboarders did indeed want to be distinctive from the alpine skiing community. They sought to be highly visible by typically wearing nontechnical clothing, for example, baggy worn-out pants and sweaters. Also, the media industry reacted quickly, producing several snowboard specific magazines such as *Snowboarder, Skating,* and *SnowSurf* by the late 1980s. Simultaneously, various snowboard videos—including *Apocalypse Snow I* and *II, Cowabunga,* and *Off the Lip*—further strengthened the identity of the snowboarding community.

Gradually, throughout the latter part of the 1980s and the early 1990s, ski resort owners realized that snowboarding was a growing sport and that it was in their economic interests to welcome boarders. Also, the snowboarding community increasingly gained acceptance amongst alpine skiers. This change in attitude occurred more easily because skiers began trying and then eventually even switching over to snowboarding. However, the cultural gap between the two activities was still not totally eliminated.

For some time, there were two basic approaches to snowboarding: the alpine and the freestyle method (Exhibit 9). Alpine riders focused on making carved turns mostly on groomed trails. They also competed in slalom and giant slalom races, similar to alpine ski races. In freestyle, the rider descended a slope or a half-pipe while attempting as many tricks and jumps as possible. This method was developed by Tom Sims who, encouraged by the success of skateboarding, constructed the first half-pipe in 1982. At first, this idea was strongly opposed by

EXHIBIT 9 Types of Snowboarding

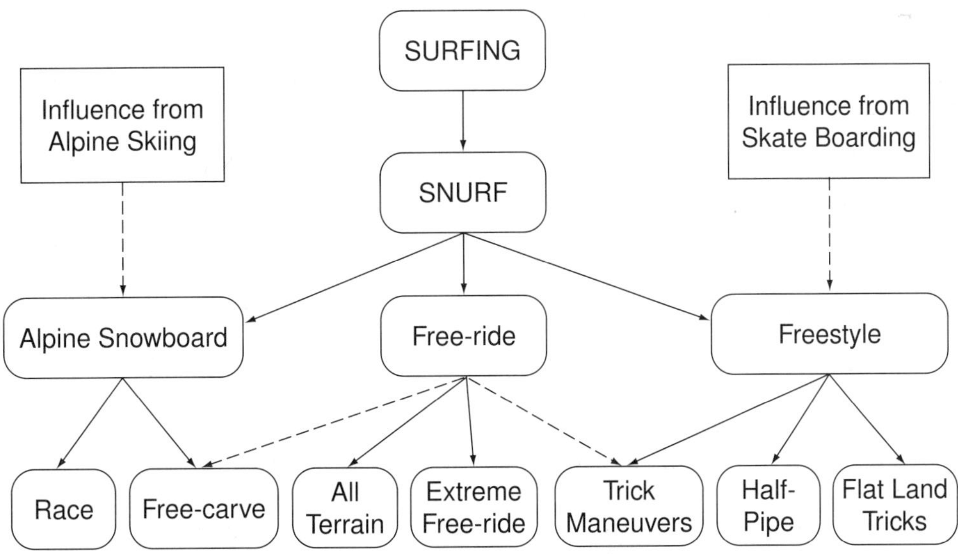

many snowboarding enthusiasts—an ironic fact in retrospect, as the half-pipe concept with its exciting acrobatic maneuvers, speed, and leaps proved fundamental to the sport's success and popularity. In more recent years, a new development in snowboarding called free-riding emerged. The idea—as the name suggests—was to use the entire mountain as a snowboarding playground. Some ski resorts also constructed in-bound obstacle areas specifically designed for the free-ride method. Freestyle and free-ride became the two most popular and practiced methods.

As in alpine skiing, snowboarding was driven by individual pro riders. However, in this sport the order or standing of the riders was not defined by an official ranking based on a series of competitions. Instead, a rider's popularity was based on his or her reputation as a free-ride performer, which was mainly communicated by word-of-mouth and through the media (ads, press releases, videos).

In terms of culture and values, snowboarding differed significantly from traditional alpine skiing. There was less emphasis on performance and technique. Instead, this sport focussed on the challenge. Snowboarding also stressed having fun, and recreation over competition. To sum it up, snowboarding brought a new approach to winter sports in the mountains.

The Markets for Snowboards

Snowboarding was one of the fastest growing segments in the sporting goods industry. During the 1994/95 season, a combined total of 7 million pairs of skis and snowboards were sold worldwide (Exhibit 10), down only slightly from the previous year's figure of 7.12 million. Of this amount, snowboards accounted for approximately 420,000 in 1993/94, whereas around 800,000 snowboards were sold the following season, an increase of almost 100 percent. In 1994/95, the number of boards sold in the three key geographic markets was evenly divided, with one-third in North America, Japan, and Europe, respectively.

North America

North America, the birthplace of snowboarding, continued to be the largest single market in terms of snowboarding shops, participants, and suppliers. In 1993, the total snowboarding population was some 1.8 million. Snowboarding was practiced in 524 ski resorts throughout the United States, the major hubs being Vermont, Colorado, Utah, Southern California, Tahoe (Nevada), and Seattle (Washington). In Canada, the major areas for snowboarding were Quebec, Alberta, and British Columbia. The dominant

EXHIBIT 10 Development of the World Ski and Snowboard Market (1987/88–1997/98)

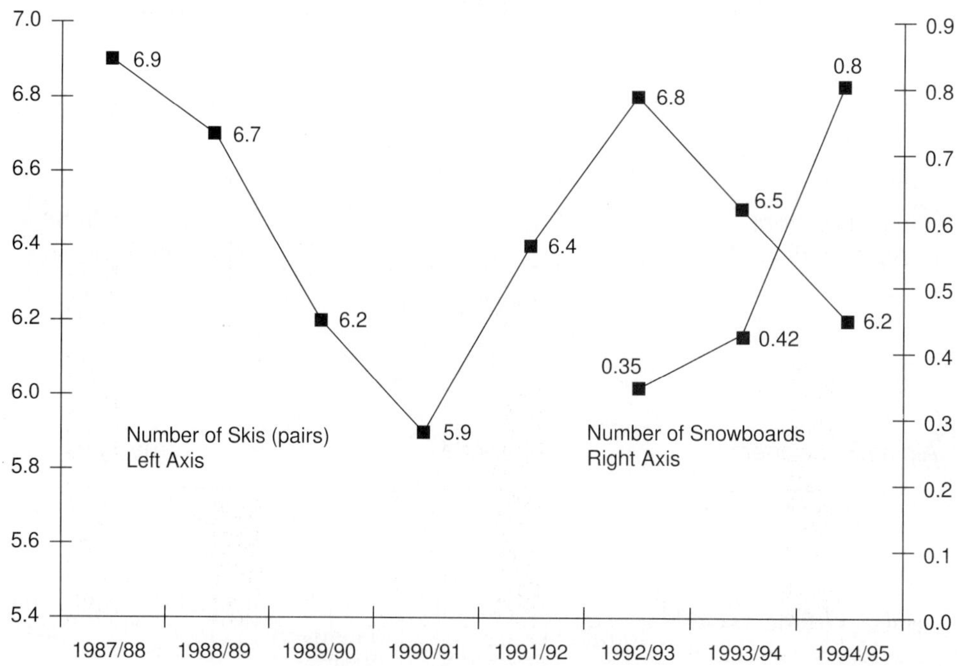

boarding styles were freestyle and free-ride (Exhibits 11 and 12). Only 10 percent of snowboarders favored alpine riding, but it was slowly gaining popularity, especially in the eastern areas. The North American market was dominated by six brands: Burton, K2, Morrow, Mervin Manufacturing (Lib Tech and Gnu), Ride, and Sims. Much of the snowboarding equipment was produced in the United States.

Japan

Approximately 80 percent of the terrain on Japan's four main islands was mountainous, which included over 700

EXHIBIT 11 Share of the Snowboard Market Soft/Hard Boots

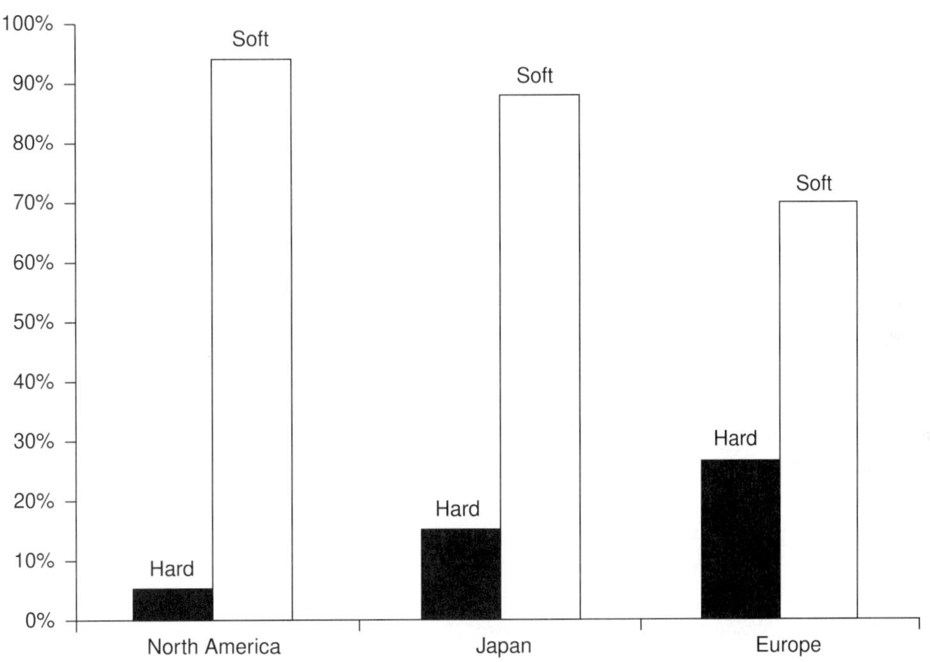

EXHIBIT 12 Snowboarding Style Preferences by Main Markets

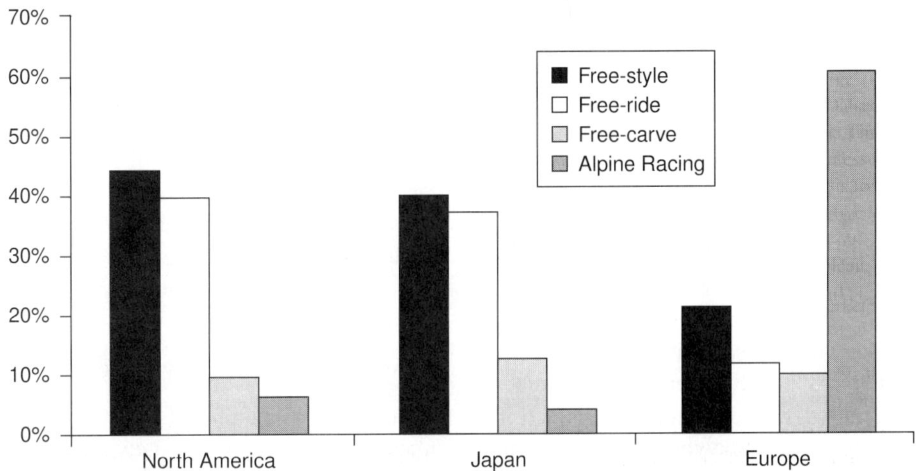

ski resorts. In 1994/95, the total Japanese snowboarding population was some 700,000 people. The sport grew during the early 1990s at a very fast rate. Simultaneously, the ski market declined. As for equipment, there was a strong preference for foreign boards over the few domestic brands. Free-ride was the most popular method in Japan, although it differed from North America and Europe since it was forbidden to ride anywhere except on official trails in Japanese ski resorts. As seen in Exhibits 11 and 12, only 15 percent of the snowboarders used alpine-style hard boots.

Europe

Skiing had been a traditional part of the European culture for a long time. Then snowboarding began challenging this tradition and rapidly succeeded in being appreciated and accepted. Most snowboarding took place in the many resort areas in the Alps, although the sport was growing more popular in the North European ski resorts as well. In 1993/94, the total number of snowboarders in Europe was around 550,000. The countries with the largest number of snowboarders were Germany (18 percent), Austria (11 percent), and Switzerland (16 percent). Due to a longstanding history of skiing in Europe, alpine riding was more popular there than in the other snowboarding markets. Almost 30 percent of snowboarders used hard boots (Exhibits 11 and 12). There were several European snowboard manufacturers: e.g., A Snowboards, F2, Nidecker, and Rossignol. However, the major North American brands were also very strong in the European market.

Snowboarding Demographics

In terms of demographics, the snowboarding community was evolving. The largest group consisted of teenagers between the ages 13 and 17 (Exhibit 13), especially in North America and Europe. In Japan, snowboarders tended to be slightly older, typically young adults between 20 and 25 years of age. However, the fastest growing segment was an even older group, i.e., adults between 24 and 36 years old (*SportStyle,* 1998). Another strong growth area was in equipment for young children from 5 to 10 years old. The breakdown between male and female snowboarders was similar in the United States and Europe: approximately 80 percent men and 20 percent women. In Japan, however, female riders accounted for around 40 percent of the total snowboarding population (Exhibit 14).

Snowboarders frequently had a skiing background. In North America (Exhibit 15), 75 percent of snowboarders took up the sport after having been skiers. Yet, only 37 percent continued to practice the two sports simultaneously. A survey also revealed that only a scant minority (6 percent) wanted to try skiing after snowboarding if they had had no skiing background previously.

Snowboarding Products

The snowboarding industry consisted of four types of related products: snowboards, bindings, boots, and apparel (clothing). Each style of snowboarding (alpine, freestyle, and free-ride) required different equipment. Riders practicing freestyle or free-ride used soft boots, strap (high-back), or step-in bindings, and a short (typically between 150 and 160 cm) flexible snowboard with a rounded tip and tail. An alpine rider used harder plastic boots and a plate binding. The alpine board was longer than the board used in freestyle. It was also less flexible and had a flat tail.

The snowboarding business, like all the other winter sports, needed to come up with genuine innovations. However, it was often difficult for the consumer to distinguish between a real technical innovation and a mere "unique selling proposition" (USP). One innovation that did dramatically affect the industry, however, was the application of monocoque technology to snowboard manufacture. This technology, which was originally developed by Salomon for alpine skis, provided several technical advantages over the traditional sandwich method. The main merits of monocoque technology were having flexibility that was evenly distributed, improved manufacturability, and an elegant look. However, this technology did require an expensive upfront investment in molds.

The most recent developments in snowboard bindings focused on a step-in soft boot and binding system. The main benefit of this system was that making the attachment was easier. However, it was estimated that some 95 percent of snowboarders still used the conventional attachment method (*San Francisco Business Times,* 1996). Developments in snowboarding boots centered around achieving a more customized fit, better shock absorption, and using new lighter materials.

Competitors in the Snowboard Market

There was a vast number of snowboarding equipment manufacturers. According to a study made in 1995 by the U.S. market research company, Morgan-Horan Inc., Burton was

EXHIBIT 13 Age Distribution of the Snowboarding Population by Main Markets

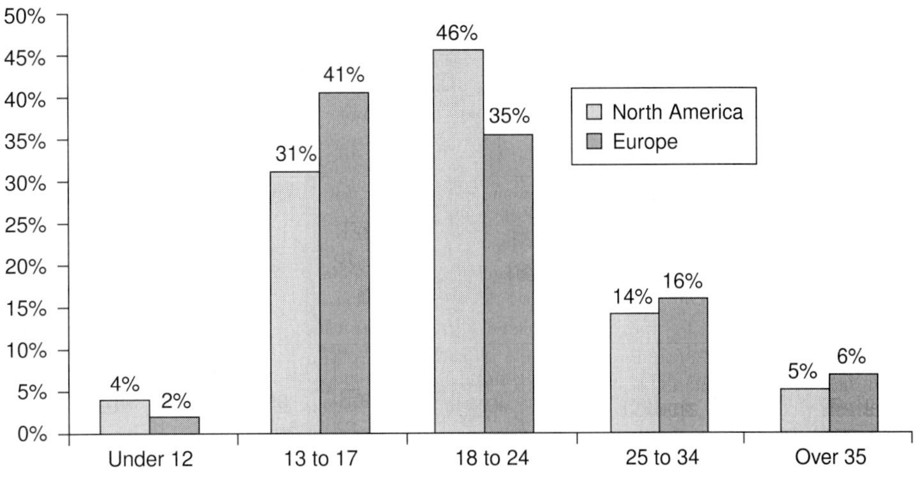

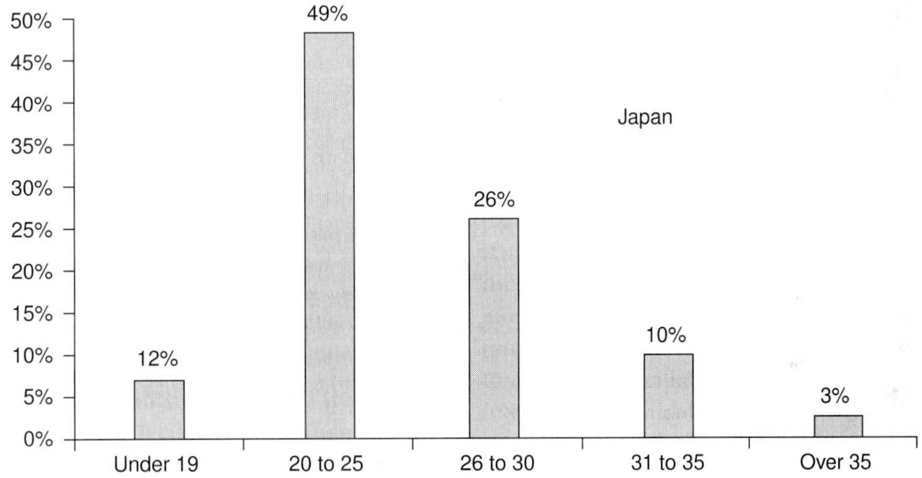

the clear market leader in snowboards. The company ranked at the top both in terms of the number of retailers carrying the brand and in market share (Exhibits 16 and 17). The U.S. alpine ski manufacturer, K2, held second place. The combined market share of Burton and K2 was almost 50 percent. In snowboarding boots, Burton was again the market leader, with Airwalk in a close second position (Exhibits 18 and 19). Together, these two companies accounted for over 65 percent of the boot market.

The industry players came from a variety of backgrounds. Some of them, such as Burton, Ride, Sims, Nidecker, and other pioneers of the industry started off as snowboarding companies. Recently, many ski equipment manufacturers had also entered the business—e.g., K2 and Rossignol. Yet another group of companies had their roots in other kinds of sporting goods—such as F2 in windsurfing, Santa Cruz in skateboarding, and Vans Inc. in sneakers.

EXHIBIT 14 **Gender Demographics of the Snowboarding Population by Main Markets**

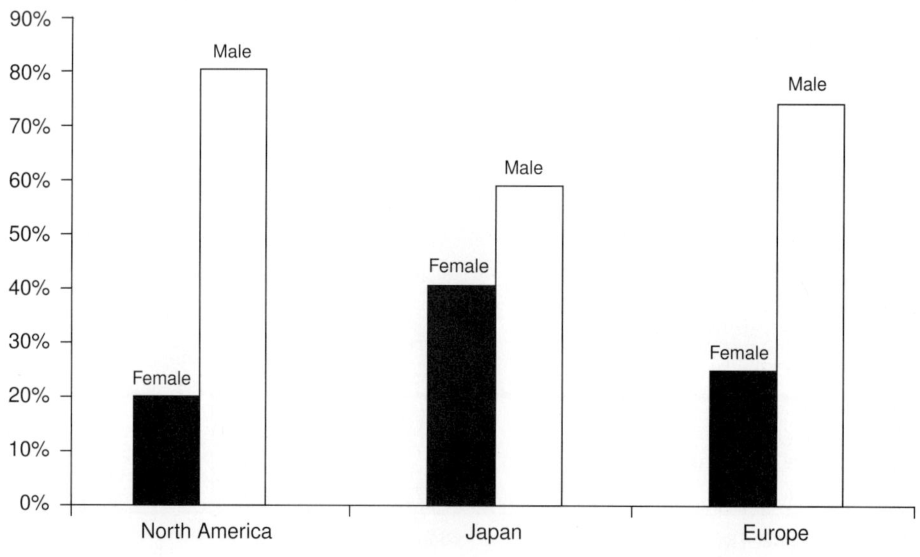

EXHIBIT 15 **Skiing Background of North American Snowboarders**

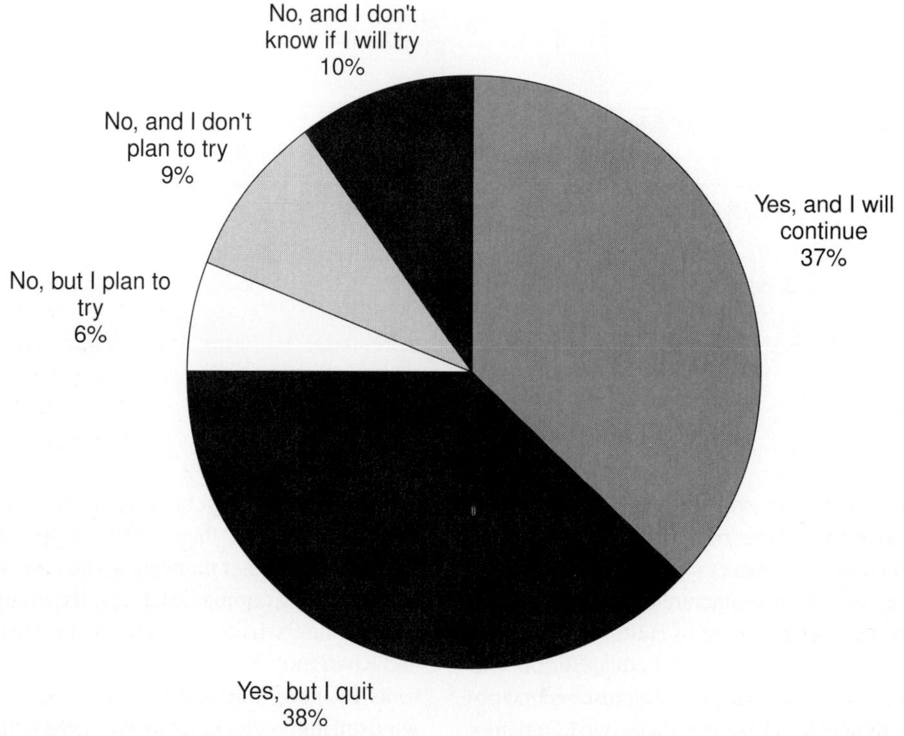

EXHIBIT 16 Snowboard Brands Carried by Retailers, 1995

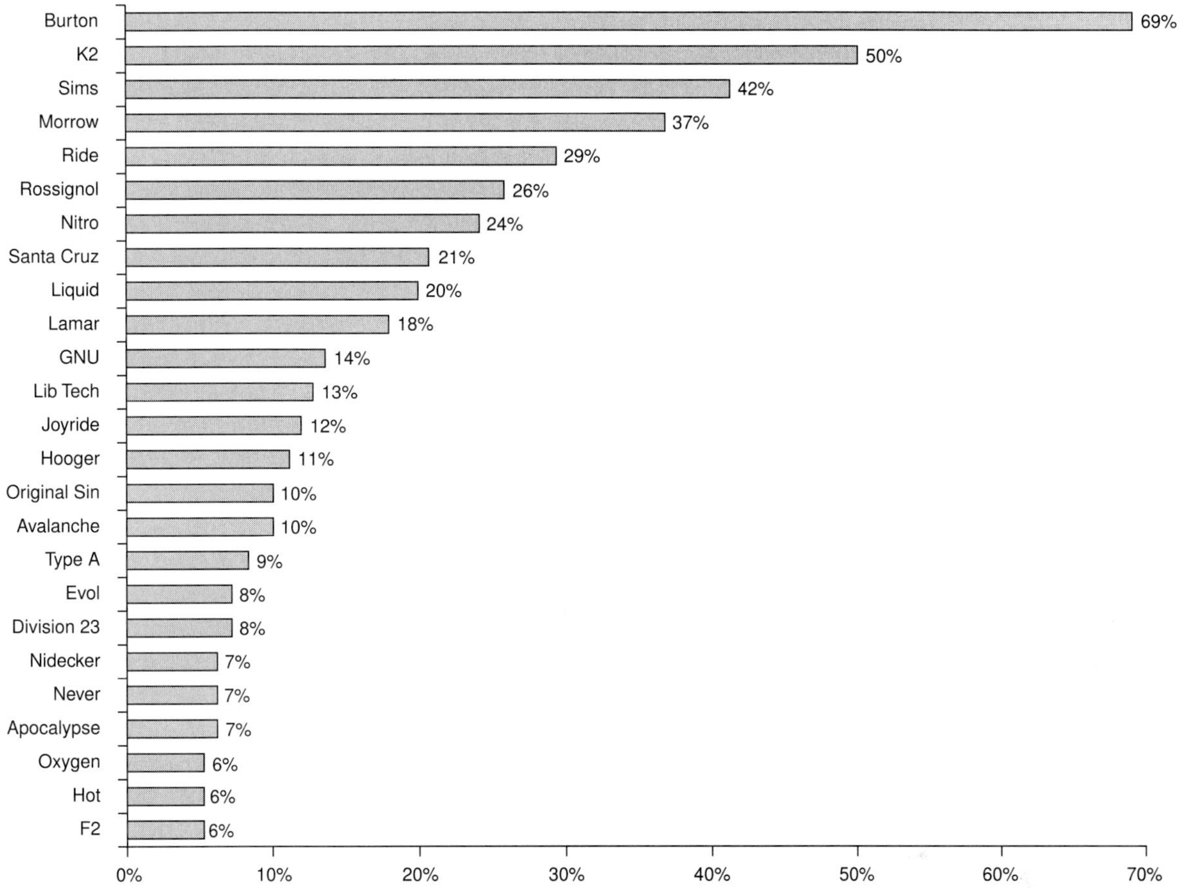

Burton	69%
K2	50%
Sims	42%
Morrow	37%
Ride	29%
Rossignol	26%
Nitro	24%
Santa Cruz	21%
Liquid	20%
Lamar	18%
GNU	14%
Lib Tech	13%
Joyride	12%
Hooger	11%
Original Sin	10%
Avalanche	10%
Type A	9%
Evol	8%
Division 23	8%
Nidecker	7%
Never	7%
Apocalypse	7%
Oxygen	6%
Hot	6%
F2	6%

0% 10% 20% 30% 40% 50% 60% 70%

Source: Morgan-Horan, Inc.

Many of the snowboarding companies were offering a complete product portfolio that included snowboards and bindings (snowboards were mainly sold with bindings), boots, and apparel. This trend was enhanced by the increasing importance of rental equipment. A similar pattern was occurring in the ski industry, where it was estimated that up to 50 percent of the market was in rental equipment. Many snowboarding companies also had their own product line of related apparel, which was perceived as a high-growth segment.

Winter sports equipment retailers played an important role in the snowboarding industry. The retailers consisted of two main groups: specialized snowboarding shops and chain stores. Especially during the initial growth period, most snowboarding equipment—unlike alpine ski equipment—was purchased from specialty stores. This trend, which was still true to a certain extent, could be explained by several factors. First, even at the lowest price point, a snowboard was a \$150 to \$200 retail item that had to be selected, configured and set up for the individual rider. Therefore, the level of knowledge required by the sales personnel needed to be higher. Inevitably, knowledge and experience were typically higher in a specialized shop than in a chain store. Second, some of the less known and lower volume hard-core or cult products were available only in specialized shops. Third, the major snowboarding brands were directly related to snowboarding enthusiasts, which meant that they were more likely to be found in specialty shops than in chain stores. Frequently, these specialty shops also sold skates,

EXHIBIT 17 Snowboard Brands by Market Share, 1995

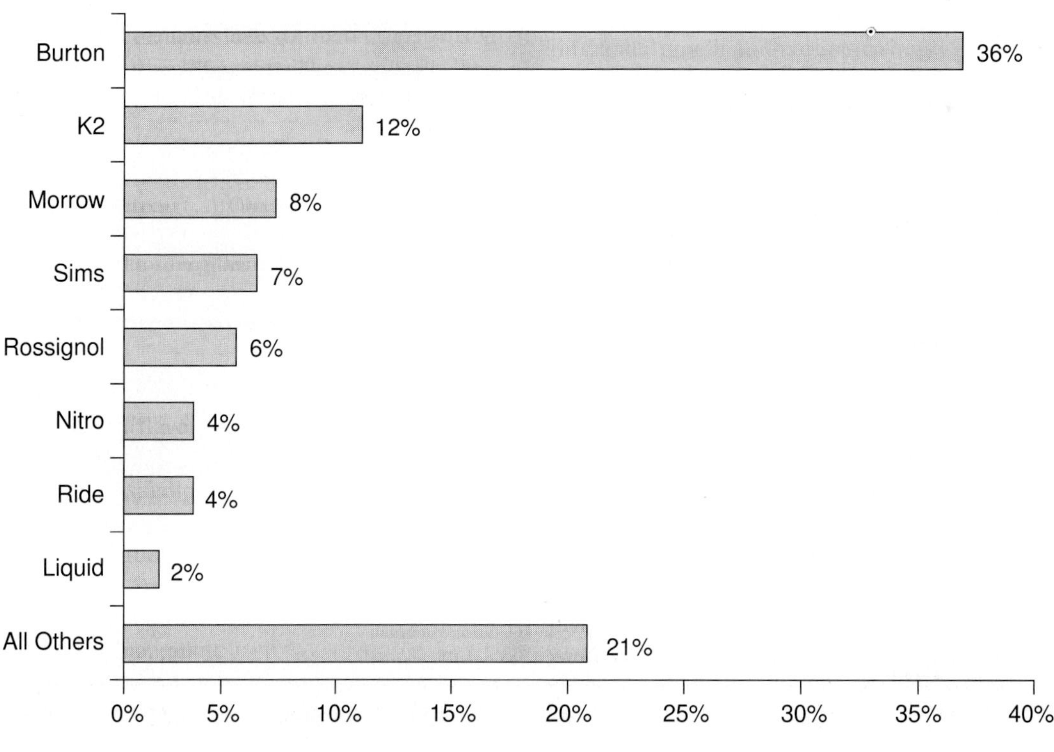

Source: Morgan-Horan Inc.

skateboards, and related apparel in the same line. Specialty shops also contributed considerably to snowboarding's success because of their cultural impact. Shop owners and personnel were often experienced snowboard gurus and charismatic individuals. Thus, the shops became popular sites for "hanging around" and discussing the latest news related to snowboarding.

More recently, general purpose sporting goods chains (e.g., Intersport) recognized that snowboarding was a significant business and started selling snowboarding equipment. These stores typically focused on established brands with a proven track record and money to back up their brands with efficient marketing and public relations. They offered fewer brands and only ones that were well established.

As an industry, snowboarding was changing from being in an initial phase of exponential growth to a period of heavy consolidation. According to some observers, the industry was experiencing the same cycle that the ski industry had seen a few years earlier: tremendous growth; overzealous manufacturing, marketing, and distribution; and leveling out. It was estimated that there would be only around 40 viable companies producing snowboarding goods (*SportsStyle,* 1998) by the year 2000. However, these survivors were likely to maintain a lucrative business, as snowboarding would continue to experience a steady growth rate.

Snowboard Development at Salomon

A small group of people at Salomon had been pursuing the idea of developing a snowboard since the late 1980s. In fact, by that time the company had already produced a snowboard prototype. A full project had not yet been launched because the consensus was that it would be difficult to dominate the field with just a board. It seemed more suitable to enter the market through accessories such as bindings, boots, and apparel. This reasoning was analo-

EXHIBIT 18 Snowboard Boot Brands Carried by Retailers, 1995

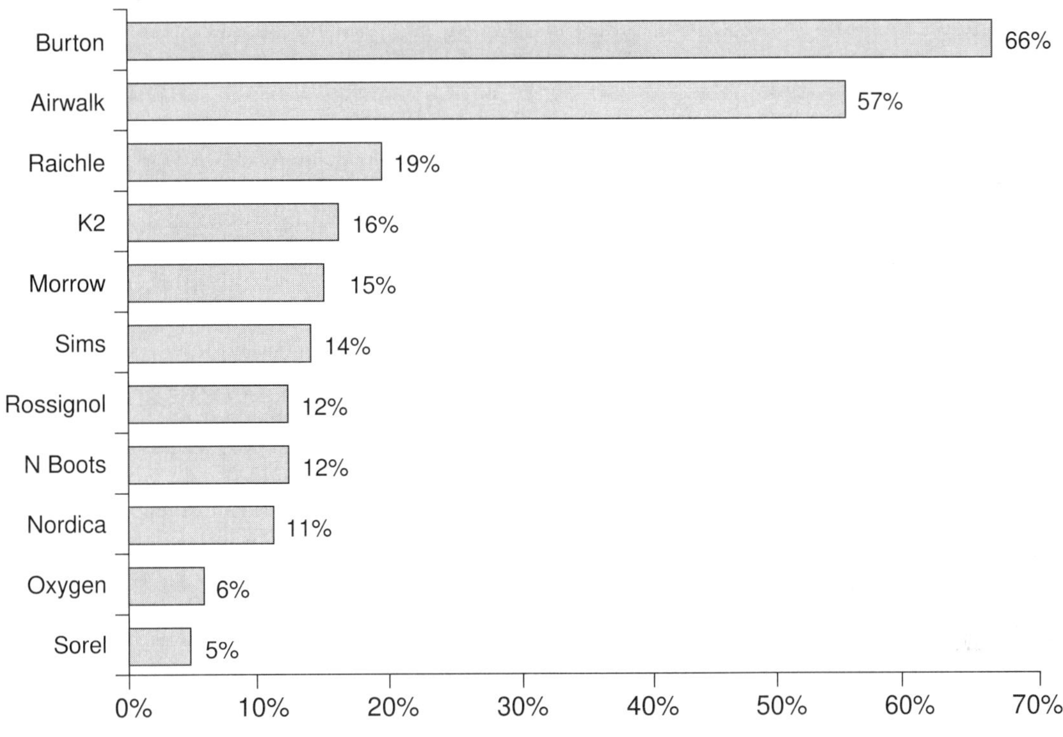

Source: Morgan-Horan Inc.

gous to the bicycle market, which was largely dominated by the big equipment manufacturers, such as Shimano and Campagnolo, rather than by systems integrators.

In 1989, Salomon also started a project to develop a snowboard binding, specifically a step-in release binding for snowboarding. Unfortunately, the logistics related to bindings for a snowboard were different from the requirements for alpine skis. A snowboard was considerably shorter than an alpine ski, and both legs were attached to a single board. Therefore, the likelihood of twisting the knees in a fall or receiving a leg injury was minimal. Because the demand for creating a release binding for snowboarding was considerably lower than expected, Salomon halted its development project when the company underwent an overall restructuring process in 1990.

In 1992, Bernard Salomon and Marc Vial initiated a study on diversification possibilities. This study looked into the snowboarding business as well. However, based on the product-focused approach that was used, the study concluded that the snowboarding market was not yet sufficiently interesting for Salomon. Additionally, at this time the skiing business started to emerge from its 1990/91 downturn and, in particular, the Japanese market was booming. Consequently, the company's diversification project was discontinued.

A few years later, by the fall of 1994, the global market for snowboarding equipment had become significant (with an annual sales volume of 600,000 to 700,000 snowboards). So, Jean-Luc Diard proceeded to look into the snowboarding market once again. During that fall season, he and Joel Bordeau assessed what the company actually knew about the business. They concluded that instead of focusing exclusively on the snowboard, a more global approach to the sport would be appropriate. It would not be limited to the different products—the board, binding, and boot—but would also include the development of a brand suitable for the market. At this

EXHIBIT 19 Snowboard Boot Brands by Market Share, 1995

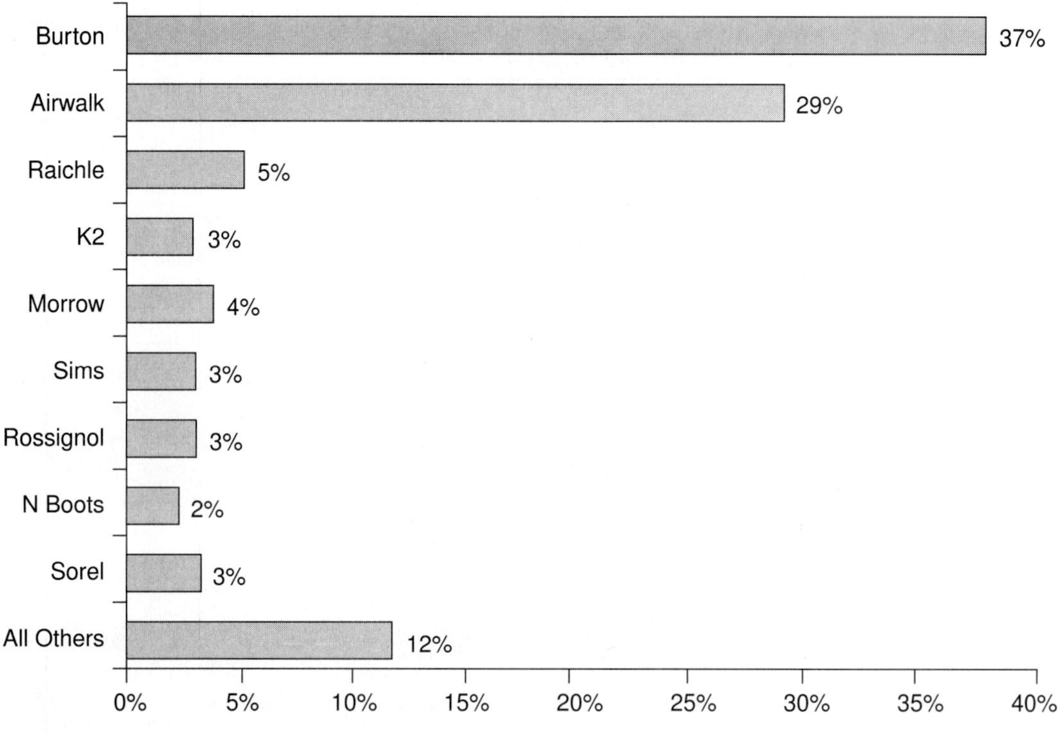

Source: Morgan-Horan Inc.

same time, Salomon was holding discussions with Burton, a leading snowboard manufacturer, about the possibilities of collaborating at some future date. However, these discussions were terminated in 1994.

Since the United States was the main market for snowboarding, Jean-Luc decided to focus market research efforts in North America. His team worked together with a young American "snowboarding guru," Brad Stewart, who was considered a major figure in the sport. Brad also had established a small, but legitimate, brand of snowboard-related clothing called Bonfire. In 1995 Salomon acquired Bonfire, and at that time Brad Stewart joined Salomon. Throughout the spring of 1995, the team then conducted a series of interviews in North America in order to understand the snowboarding culture and market. The acquisition of Bonfire was finalized in December 1995.

In the market study, the development team interviewed young snowboarders in the United States and made every effort to use their input in a definition of the product. The team also contacted a number of specialized shops, namely the snowboarding chain Boards and Blades to assess the feasibility of their idea. Initially, snowboard riders and retailers were skeptical about Salomon's ability to create a competitive product. However, the snowboarding community, including the specialty shops, gradually realized that the company did not want to impose its existing designs on the market. Indeed, they discovered that Salomon was committed to listening seriously to snowboard users, so that they could have a real influence on the development of new products. This realization then encouraged snowboarders to be much more receptive to the idea of a Salomon board and to provide valuable feedback.

Thus, early in the summer of 1995, Salomon officially established a snowboard project and a team to pursue it. Jean-Luc Diard reasoned that because the world of snowboarding was significantly different from that of alpine

EXHIBIT 20 Salomon's Value Chain

	R&D	Manufacturing	Marketing	Sales and Logistics	Brand
Golf	Carlsbad; Tokyo	Carlsbad; Tokyo	Carlsbad	Salomon and Taylor Made Network	Taylor Made
Bicycle Components	Saint Trivier	Saint Trivier	Saint Trivier	Mavic Network	Mavic
Alpine Skis	Rumilly	Rumilly	Metz-Tessy	Salomon Network	Salomon
Alpine Boots	Montebelluna	Montebelluna; Serrières; Subcontractors	Metz-Tessy	Salomon Network	Salomon
Alpine Bindings	Rumilly	Rumilly	Metz-Tessy	Salomon Network	Salomon
Nordic Boots and Bindings	Chavanod	Montebelluna; Subcontractors	Metz-Tessy	Salomon Network	Salomon
Hiking Boots	Charvanod	Montebelluna; Subcontractors	Metz-Tessy	Salomon Network	Salomon
Snowboard (development and prototype manufacture) → 1996	Boulder; Rumilly; Montebelluna	Rumilly; Montebelluna	Boulder; Portland; and Boston	N/A	N/A
Snowboard (operations) 1996 →	?	?	?	?	?

skiing, the engineers needed an in-depth understanding of the snowboarding culture. He found a French globe-trotter, Eric Metro, to head up the snowboard development. In addition to his engineering background at Dynastar and Aerospatiale, Eric was also an enthusiastic surfer. The snowboard team comprised a number of Salomon engineers in Annecy and a small group of Bonfire personnel in the United States. Bruno Borsoi, another experienced board rider and engineer with considerable background at Nordica and Ferrari, was put in charge of boot development. The binding team consisted of engineers from Salomon's binding development. Additionally, Jean-Luc employed one marketing person from Boards and Blades to participate in the project. By late in the fall of 1995, the team had already come up with a first prototype board and binding.

As Jean-Luc scanned the feedback from the first field tests, he became even more confident that the project was right on target, both from a product and a technology perspective. He was still concerned, however, about certain issues related to the brand and its place in the organization. In order to expedite the decision-making process, Jean-Luc began setting up a table that would examine the current state of affairs in Salomon's organization (Exhibit 20).

Case 12–2

INSEAD

Nestlé, S.A.

With worldwide sales of SFr 35.2 billion in 1987, Nestlé was the second largest food company in the world, and the largest Swiss company. While it had diversified into cosmetics, pharmaceuticals, and pet foods during the previous decade, Nestlé's core business still remained the processing of agricultural raw materials into food products. A summary of the company's financial results for recent years is provided in Exhibit 1.

This case was written by Professor Arnoud De Meyer at INSEAD. It is intended to be used as a basis for class discussion rather than to illustrate either effective or ineffective handling of an administrative situation.

Financial support from the INSEAD Alumni Fund European Case Programme is gratefully acknowledged.

EXHIBIT 1 Nestlé, S.A.—Summary of Financial Performance and Activities, 1983–1987
(in millions of Swiss Francs, except per share data, and %)

	1987	1986	1985	1984	1983
Operating results					
Consolidated Sales	35,241	38,050	42,225	31,141	27,943
Cost of Sales & Distribution	21,625	24,447	na	na	na
Marketing, Administration and R&D	9,965	9,932	na	na	na
Trading Profit	3,651	3,671	4,315	3,206	2,883
Net Profit after Taxes	1,827	1,789	1,750	1,487	1,261
Cash Flow (PAT + depreciation)	3,011	2,946	3,081	2,491	2,171
Balance Sheet Items					
Current Assets	16,241	15,820	15,236	16,407	13,868
Fixed Assets	8,902	9,275	9,952	8,067	6,621
Short-term Liabilities	7,547	8,119	8,858	7,651	6,092
Other Liabilities	4,939	4,775	5,092	3,834	3,277
Shareholder's Equity	12,657	12,201	11,238	12,989	11,120
Per Share Values					
Net Profit	537	526	515	480	430
Dividend	150	145	145	136	125
Price Range (in thousands)					
—bearer shares	11.4-7.2	9.9-7.3	9.2-5.6	5.6-4.5	4.9-3.7
—registered shares	5.5-3.9	5.1-3.9	5.0-3.3	3.3-2.8	3.0-2.3
Other figures					
Trading Profit/Sales	10.4%	9.6%	10.2%	10.3%	10.3%
Net Profit AT/Sales	5.2%	4.7%	4.1%	4.8%	4.5%
Net Profit/Equity	14.7%	15.3%	14.4%	12.3%	11.9%
No. of Shares (millions)	3.2	3.2	3.2	3.1	2.9
Total Employment (thousands)					
—administration and sales	65	66	63	57	59
—factory personnel	98	96	92	81	81
Ave. Exchange Rate (SFr/$)	1.49	1.79	2.45	2.36	2.10

Source: Company reports.

Beginning in the early 1970s, Nestlé had embarked on an ambitious acquisition program which included, among others:

1973: Stouffer (USA): Frozen foods, ice cream, food service, hotels
1977: Alcon (USA): Ophthalmic products
1978: Chambourcy (France): Refrigerated products, desserts
1979: Beech-Nut (USA): Baby foods
1984: Warner Cosmetics (USA): Perfumes and cosmetic products
Ward Johnson (USA): Chocolate and confectionery products
1985: Carnation (USA): Food products
Hills Bros. (USA): Coffee
1986: Herta (Germany): Cold cuts

Exhibit 1 *(continued)*

Geographical Distribution of Sales and Personnel, 1987

	Sales	Personnel
Europe	43.1%	43.3% (9.5% in Switzerland)
North America	28.5	23.2
Asia	13.0	8.0
Latin America & Caribbean	10.0	17.8
Africa	3.0	4.4
Oceania	2.4	3.3
	100.0%	100.0%

Subdivision of Sales by Product Group, 1987

Drinks	30.1%
Dairy Products	17.9
Culinary Products	11.7
Frozen Foods & Ice Cream	10.5
Chocolate & Confectionery	7.9
Refrigerated Products	7.9
Infant Foods & Diet Products	5.7
Pet Foods	4.3
Pharmaceutical & Cosmetics	2.2
Subsidiary Products/Activities	1.0
Hotels & Restaurants	0.8
Total	100.0%

Sales in main markets, 1987 (in millions of Swiss francs)

United States	9,298
France	4,160
West Germany	3,827
Japan	2,266
United Kingdom	1,852
Brazil	1,628
Spain	1,522
Italy	939
Switzerland	872
Canada	760
Total	27,124 (= 77% of total sales)

Source: Annual Reports

In addition, many smaller companies were acquired in recent years, and Nestlé held important interests in a few other companies, most notably a substantial minority participation in L'Oréal, the French-based multinational cosmetic products company. In 1988, Nestlé was back on the acquisition trail with its bids for Buitoni, the Italian pasta and food products company, and Rowntree, one of Britain's premier confectionery manufacturers.

The pattern of acquisitions over the past 15 years displayed certain important characteristics. First, while Nestlé had entered new industries via this route, i.e., pharmaceuticals with Alcon, the thrust of its acquisition program had been the consolidation and expansion of its presence in the food industry. Second, while Nestlé had acquired companies worldwide, it has spent a disproportionate amount on purchases in the United States, consistent with Nestlé's desire to expand its presence in the American market. The purchase of Carnation in 1985, for example, was Nestlé's largest single acquisition, following which North America's share of Nestlé's sales climbed from 24.1 percent in 1984, to 37 percent in 1985. The Carnation acquisition contributed largely to Nestlé's 1985 total revenue growth of 35.7 percent over 1984.

With 383 production facilities in over 50 countries (see Exhibit 2) and no more than one-third of its sales from any one continent, Nestlé could be categorized as a truly global company.

EXHIBIT 2 Nestlé's Worldwide Positions in 1987

● Local Production[1]

◑ Local Production and Imports

○ Imports[2]

Region	Country	Number of Factories (total 383)	Condensed Milk	Milk Powder	Other Milk Products	Infant Formulae	Cereal Food for Infants	Baby Foods	Coffee Extracts	Roast and Ground Coffee	Other Preparations for Drinks	Liquid Drinks	Chocolate Confectionery and Biscuits	Dehydrated and Canned Culinary Products	Frozen Foods	Ice Cream	Refrigerated Products	Products for the Foodservice Trade	Pet Food	Pharmaceutical Products
Europe	Austria	3	●			◑	●	○	○	●	○		○	◑				◑	○	○
Europe	Belgium	5	○	○	○	○	●	○	○		○	○	◑	○	◑	○	◑	○	○	◑
Europe	Denmark	4		●	●	●	◑	○	○		◑	○	○	○	●		○	◑	○	○
Europe	Spain	23	●	●	●	●	●	●	●	●	●	●	◑	◑	◑	●	◑	●	◑	◑
Europe	France	31		●	●	●	●	◑	●		●	◑	◑	◑	◑	●	●	●	●	◑
Europe	Greece	4	◑		◑	○	○	○	○	●	○		●	◑				◑	○	○
Europe	Italy	13	◑		◑	◑	●		◑	●	◑	○	◑	◑				◑	◑	○
Europe	Norway	5	●	●		●	●	◑	○		●	○		○	◑			◑	◑	○
Europe	Netherlands	7	●	●	●	●			◑		◑		○	◑	○			◑	○	○
Europe	Portugal	6	●	●	●	◑	●		●	●	●	○	●	◑	●	○		●		○
Europe	Germany	31	●	●	◑	◑	●	●	●	●	●	●	◑	◑			●	◑	○	○
Europe	Republic of Ireland	1	○		○				○	○		○	◑	◑	○		○	◑	○	○
Europe	United Kingdom	19	●	●	●	●	○		◑	○	●	●	◑	◑	◑		◑	◑	◑	○
Europe	Sweden	6				●	●	●	○	●	○	●		◑	●		●	◑	○	○
Europe	Switzerland	13	●	●	●	●	●		●		●	○	◑	◑	◑	●		●	◑	○
Europe	Turkey	1	○	○		○			○		○		●							
North America	Canada	15	●	●	◑				◑	●	◑	●	◑	◑	◑			◑	◑	◑
North America	United States	66	●	●	◑		●	●	◑	●	◑	●	◑	◑	●	●	●	◑	●	●
Asia	Saudi Arabia	1	○	○	○	○	●	○	○		○		○	●	○			○	○	○
Asia	South Korea	1					●				●			●						○
Asia	India	2	●	●		●	●		●					●				●		
Asia	Indonesia	2	●	●	●	●	●		●		●			◑				◑		
Asia	Japan	4	●	●	●			○	◑	◑	◑	◑	○	◑	○			◑	◑	○
Asia	Malaysia	5	●	◑	◑	◑	●		◑		●	●	●	◑				●	○	○
Asia	Philippines	3	◑	◑	◑	◑	●		●		●			●				●		○
Asia	Singapore	1	◑	○	○	○	○		○		●	○	○	◑	○			◑	○	○
Asia	Sri Lanka	2	●	◑	○	◑	●		○		●			○				◑		
Asia	Taiwan	1	○	○	○	○	●		◑		●			○				○		○
Asia	Thailand	4	●	○	◑	○	●		◑		●		●	◑				●		○
	Argentina	6	●	●	●	●	●		●	●	●		●	●		●		●		◑
	Belize	1	○	○	○	○	○	○	○		○	●		○						
	Brazil	17	●	●	●	●	●	●	●	●	●	●	●	●	●	●	●	●		◑
	Chile	7	●	●	●	●	●	●	●		●		◑	●	●	●	●	●		○

EXHIBIT 2 ***(continued)***

● Local Production[1]

◑ Local Production and Imports

○ Imports[2]

Region	Country	Number of Factories (total 383)	Condensed Milk	Milk Powder	Other Milk Products	Infant Formulae	Cereal Food for Infants	Baby Foods	Coffee Extracts	Roast and Ground Coffee	Other Preparations for Drinks	Liquid Drinks	Chocolate Confectionery and Biscuits	Dehydrated and Canned Culinary Products	Frozen Foods	Ice Cream	Refrigerated Products	Products for the Foodservice Trade	Pet Food	Pharmaceutical Products
Latin America	Colombia	3	●		●	●	●		●		●		●	●			●	●		○
	Ecuador	3		●	●	◑	●				●	●	●	●			●	●		○
	Guatemala	1	○	○	○	○	●				●			●						
	Jamaica	2	●		●	○		○	○		●	○		●						○
	Mexico	12	●	●	●	●	●		●		●			●	●	●	●	●		◑
	Nicaragua	1		●																
	Panama	2	●			◑	○	○	○		○	●	○	◑				◑		○
	Peru	2	●	●		◑	●		●		●			●				●		○
	Puerto Rico	1	○	○	○		○	○	○		○	●	○	◑	○			◑	○	◑
	Dominican Republic	2	●	●		○	○	○			●			●				●		○
	Surinam	1												◑						
	Trinidad and Tobago	1	◑	○	◑	○	○	○	◑		◑	◑		○				●		○
	Uruguay	1		○		○	○		●	●	●		○	○						◑
	Venezuela	2			●	●	●		●		●			●				●		○
Africa	South Africa	12	●	●	●	◑	●	●	◑	●	●	●	●	●			●	◑	○	○
	Ivory Coast	2	○	○		○	◑		●		◑			◑						
	Ghana	1	●				●				●							●		
	Kenya	1				●	●		○		●			●						
	Nigeria	1	○	○		○	●				●			◑						
	Senegal	1	●	○		○	○		○		○			○						
	Tunisia	1	○			○	●				●					●				○
	Zimbabwe	1	●	●		●	●		○		●									
Oceania	Australia	14	●	●	●	●			◑	●	●	●	●	◑	●	●		◑	●	○
	Fiji	1	○			○	○		○		○		○	◑				○	○	
	New Zealand	3	●		●				◑		●		●	●	○			●	○	○
	Papua New Guinea	1	○	○	○	○	○		○		○		○	◑				○	○	

[1] May represent production in several factories.

[2] May, in a few particular cases, represent purchases from third parties in the market concerned.

Countries within the continents shown according to the French alphabetical order.

The Early Development of R&D at Nestlé

Since the end of the Second World War, research and development (R&D) activities at Nestlé evolved from being highly centralized to form a dispersed international research and technology development network. The origins of this transformation could be traced to the merger with Maggi of Switzerland in 1947.

Prior to that time, Nestlé's R&D efforts were limited to basic scientific research and some process development work centralized at their laboratory in Vevey, Switzerland. The merger with Maggi raised the issue of integrating the R&D work being carried out at Maggi with similar efforts at Nestlé. An initial attempt to transfer all R&D efforts to the central facilities in Vevey was not successful in the sense that Maggi's research potential was lost in the larger facility. As a result, R&D activities at Maggi were returned to its original center in Kempttal, where they were allowed to proceed, subject to control of headquarters in Switzerland.

Following this experience, as new companies with their own R&D facilities were acquired, the practice of allowing their R&D efforts to remain in the "home" environment was continued. Thus, a number of new Nestlé-controlled R&D centers emerged throughout Europe. Although financed from Switzerland, these centers did not always enjoy the same visibility or prestige as Vevey, and were left much to their own devices.

The turning point for R&D at Nestlé came in 1969, with the creation of the Department of Technological Development. The importance of other corporate R&D units as sources of product technology was recognized and supported. Thus, Nestlé undertook an active role in developing and enhancing the expertise of these centers and in coordinating their activities.

The Department of Technological Development, as well as all research centers, were soon thereafter incorporated into Nestec Ltd. (Nestlé Products Technical Assistance), a wholly owned subsidiary, headquartered in Vevey, with a 1988 staff of several hundred people active in providing assistance in all aspects of corporate activities (product development, marketing, production, engineering, personnel training, etc.) to all Nestlé companies worldwide.

With a corporate staff of fewer than 20 people, Nestec's R&D Department had a mandate to provide technological assistance to all food production centers throughout Nestlé, and to develop technological know-how for the group as a whole. As General Manager, R&D, Dr. Brian Suter explained, "The role of Nestec is to manage a portfolio of projects for the corporation as a whole, participate in the establishment of corporate strategy, and ensure that R&D will respond to the requirements of that strategy."

As a result of the success of the policy of enhancing R&D facilities attached to new acquisitions, coupled with Nestlé's international expansion, Nestec took an active role in establishing new Technological Development Centers around the world that would develop products based on raw materials available locally. The number of these centers, mostly known by the suffix "Reco" (for Research Company), doubled since 1975, to reach a total of 16 centers, operating 21 facilities in ten countries (see Exhibit 3). Of these, seven were established directly by Nestlé (not including the soon to be opened AfriReco in Abidjan, Ivory Coast), while most others had been obtained as a result of acquisitions.

In addition to this emphasis on technology development, basic scientific research remained an important element of Nestlé's R&D strategy, as was evident from the inauguration of the new Nestlé Research Center (NRC) above Lausanne, Switzerland, in 1987. The NRC combined all scientific research under one roof, with the exception of a small operation in Tours, France, which was part of FranceReco and carried out research in plant genetic engineering. The company's rationale for this move to centralize basic research (as opposed to product development) was that it was consistent with the nature of research in the nutritional sciences. According to this view, there was a close interdependence among the various relevant disciplines, and proximity of activities would greatly enhance the effectiveness of overall nutritional research efforts.

Whatever diversity might exist in the system, Nestlé placed great emphasis on avoiding R&D duplication. Each center was specialized in a particular Nestlé product line or technology, and any R&D related to a product was carried out by the center best qualified for that activity. Given the geographical dispersion of the Technological Development Centers, one of Nestec's most important roles was coordinating these many activities.

Organization of R&D at Nestlé

Exhibit 4 depicts the structure of R&D management at Nestlé. One of the functional responsibilities of the Managing Director of Nestlé was R&D, for which he was directly accountable to the Board of Directors of the corporation. Furthermore, the General Manager of R&D at

EXHIBIT 3 Nestlé's Global Research and Development Network

Scientific Research

The two centers at La-Tour-de-Peilz, near Lac Leman, and Orbe were moved to the new Nestlé Research Center, above Lausanne. The main fields of scientific research at Nestlé were:

* Basic research in nutritional sciences, biochemistry, immunology, and toxicology;
* Biological studies in the areas of microbiology, molecular biology, biochemistry, and fermentation to develop an understanding of future human nutritional needs and assist technological process developments;
* Nutritional evaluations to understand the physiological effects of products on the human body, metabolic unit; and
* Fundamental scientific research on the composition, physical and sensory properties of nutrients.

The Tours center in France, managed under the FranceReco umbrella, carries out research in plant genetic engineering.

Technological Development

The role of the Technological Development Centers (or Recos) was to develop new products from locally available raw materials for worldwide use. In order to avoid duplication of efforts, each center had been assigned unique missions in terms of products and technologies.

1. **Linor, Orbe, Switzerland**
   Established in 1958, expanded in 1965 and 1978.
   Areas: Instant coffee, decaffeination technology, cocoa-based instant drinks, cereal-based dehydrated products, fermentation technology, packaging.
2. **Alpura-KoReco, Konolfingen, Switzerland**
   Dates from 1974.
   Areas: Long conservation dairy products, powder milk, soya-based products, aseptic filling technology.
3. **VitoReco, Kempttal, Switzerland**
   Originates from the Maggi merger. Developed in 1958; renamed VitoReco in 1975, and moved to new facilities in 1980.
   Areas: Dehydrated culinary products, pasta, culinary aids, meat aroma, bouillon.
4. **Food Technology Group, La-Tour-de-Peilz, Switzerland**
   Areas: Food service products (for hotels and restaurants), bakery products, microwave processing technology.
5. **Chocolate Technology Group, Broc, Switzerland**
   Areas: Chocolate and confectionery.
6. **DeReco, Germany**
   There were two centers within this organization.
   Ludwigsburg: Cold sauces, instant desserts, drinks, coffee mixtures.
   Weiding: Baby foods in jars, fresh dairy products, desserts.
7. **FranceReco, France**
   Besides the Tours research facility mentioned above, there were three other centers. The Beauvais center was developed from the Maggi merger and the Gervais acquisition. The center at La Meauffe originates from the Claudel acquisition.
   Beauvais: Frozen foods and ice cream, dehydrated culinary products, sterilized products.
   La Meauffe: Fresh cheese, soft and semi hard cheese, refrigerated milk-based products.
   Béziers: Specialty vegetable oils.

Nestec was a member of the General Management body of the Nestlé group (equivalent to an executive committee). This high-level representation in the executive and top decision-making offices of Nestlé was a sign of the importance attributed to R&D by the corporation. In fact, Nestlé considered itself (and was considered by competitors) as being strong in technology. The company did not provide publicly data on R&D expenditures or employment, so it was difficult to obtain any quantitative measure of Nestlé's dedication to R&D.

Nestec. Headquartered in Vevey, Switzerland, Nestec's R&D Department played the key role of coordinating Nestlé's worldwide R&D efforts. The heads of all the Recos and the NRC were considered part of the R&D management team. All technology assistance

EXHIBIT 3 *(continued)*

8. **DomeReco, Corbie, France**
This center belonged to Gloria pet foods and was obtained as a result of the Carnation acquisition.
Area: Pet foods.

9. **LondReco, Hayes, England**
This center developed from Crosse & Blackwell's research facility, purchased in 1960.
Areas: Sterilization technology, pickles, refrigerated culinary products, liquid sauces, aseptic filling technology.

10. **NordReco, Bjuv, Sweden**
Developed from the center obtained through the Findus acquisition in 1962.
Areas: Frozen food, refrigerated culinary products, agronomy research, dietetic and baby foods, culinary products, fish and meat sourcing and handling.

11. **NovaReco, Robbio, Italy**
Areas: Long conservation cheese, processed cheese, semi-hard and hard cheese, packaging.

12. **HispaReco, Badajoz, Spain**
Established by Nestec.
Areas: Agronomy research (fruit and vegetables), vegetable-based frozen and sterilized products.

13. **CalReco, California, USA**
CalReco was Carnation's R&D center, which was integrated into Nestec in 1985.
Areas: Chocolate based drinks, nutritional drinks, culinary products, food industry products, ice cream, pet foods.

14. **WestReco, USA**
Three centers established by Nestec in the USA.
Marysville, Ohio: Coffee (instant, roast and ground), tea, soya-based products.
New Milford, Conn.: Dairy products, refrigerated and dehydrated culinary products, fruit juices and drinks, meat aromas, dietetic products for adults. Established in 1981.
Fulton, N.Y.: Chocolate and confectionery, chocolate-based drinks, cocoa. Established in 1984.

15. **LatinReco, Quito, Ecuador**
Established by Nestec in 1983.
Areas: Dehydrated culinary products, infant cereals, malnutrition studies, agronomy research.

16. **EastReco, Singapore**
Established by Nestec in 1983.
Areas: Dehydrated culinary products, soya-based products, fermentation products, agronomy research.

17. **AfriReco, Abidjan, Ivory Coast**
In the process of being established by Nestec.
Areas: mainly dehydrated culinary products.

Source: Company reports.

requests from Nestlé's operating companies throughout the world were channeled through Nestec to the appropriate Reco. It was Nestec's responsibility to ensure that duplication of R&D efforts did not take place, and that new projects were assigned to the most qualified centers. It was possible, however, for Nestec to assign certain projects to more than one center if they were to complement each other's activities. As Mr. S. Brengou, the Director of FranceReco, explained, "even if two centers work on the same product, they often approach the problem in two different ways, using different technologies."

Nestlé Research Center. NRC was Nestlé's central research laboratory in Lausanne, engaged in basic research in all major areas of biological and nutritional sciences. The activities of this center could be categorized into three broad areas:

EXHIBIT 4 Nestlé, S.A. Partial Organizational Chart

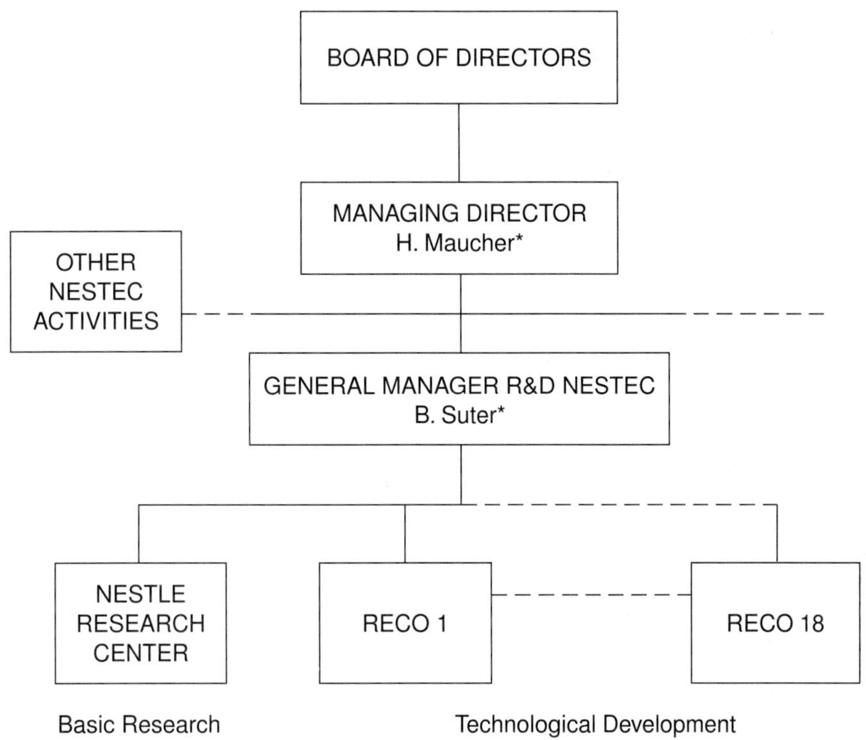

Source: Company reports.

- enlarge its knowledge of nutritional science through in-house research and collaboration with nutritional and medical research institutes around the world;
- find better uses for raw materials of vegetable and animal origin, and reduce the use of additives through basic knowledge of composition, functional and sensory properties; and
- use of plant and molecular biology for obtaining new and improved raw materials and nutrients.

Recos. The Recos were Nestlé's centers for the development of technology into products and processes. Each center's area of specialization was generally predetermined in order to prevent duplication of efforts. For the seven centers directly established by Nestec, their specialization had been determined partly as a function of the local climate and raw materials availability. However, the specialization of each "acquired" center had evolved historically.

For example, FranceReco's two centers at Beauvais and La Meauffe had developed from the Maggi merger and the Claudel acquisition, respectively. Thus, it was natural that the Beauvais center specialized in culinary products and La Meauffe in cheese, their respective areas of specialization under Maggi and Claudel. Similarly, the work on ice cream at Beauvais was a development of the activities of Gervais after its acquisition.

Although all the Recos were managed under the Nestec umbrella, there was no hard and fast "Nestlé Model" of an R&D center. All Recos followed certain

Nestlé norms in terms of lay-out, communication, planning, and reporting, but the internal operations of each center were very much determined by historical and cultural influences particular to it. Sometimes local requirements would lead the Recos to fulfill more than an R&D function. In EastReco in Singapore, for example, the task of the technological center included also Quality Assurance activities for the whole of the Far East region, ensuring that all products in all factories were produced to Nestlé's standards. Somewhat unexpectedly, this side activity provided a lot of very useful information about product performance and market needs to the Reco. The knowledge thus acquired, for example, on the level of pesticides in Thai raw materials, would help the Reco to devise products and processes for such a situation.

Two characteristics of the corporate R&D organizational structure at Nestlé were of special interest. First, although most Technological Development Centers were located at or near production facilities run by the national operating company, they were managed separately through Nestec. This separation of management was seen as overcoming the danger of a short-term R&D mentality that could result from local control. The Reco manager and the local country manager were thus hierarchical equals, and a high level of informal contact was encouraged between them.

Secondly, all the Recos were managed as profit centers. Their revenues came from a "fees plus percent margin" that these centers charged for activities undertaken at the request of Nestec, whether in terms of their R&D missions or their rendering technical assistance services. Nestec's income was derived from receiving a percentage of revenues from the operating units for the services that it provided to them; and it allocated any profits to supporting long-term projects or investments such as the new NRC. The percentage charge was not uniform, however, and varied from product to product and unit to unit. Nestec, thus played the role of a broker by putting customers (operating units) in contact with the appropriate suppliers (R&D Centers or other technical assistance services), and charging the customers a fee for services rendered.

The objectives of Nestlé's R&D activities were twofold: (1) to develop basic scientific know-how in all aspects of the nutrition field, the main task of NRC; and (2) to develop technological know-how in food processing and production for continuous improvement of existing products as well as for the development of new products, the task of the Recos. It was up to Nestec R&D to orchestrate the multiple sites and resources to deliver on both counts.

Site Selection and Specialization

For those R&D centers that were inherited as part of an acquisition, their previous expertise in a given field and proximity to a production facility usually determined the mission assigned to them in the corporate R&D portfolio. An example of this type could be seen in NordReco, which was developed from the initial facilities of Findus in Sweden, a specialist in frozen foods acquired in 1962. Similarly, DomReco in France, which was obtained as a result of the Carnation acquisition, was assigned work mainly in the development of pet food products, its area of specialization under Carnation management.

The issue of site selection and specialization became more critical in those centers directly established by Nestec. According to Dr. Suter, one of the most important factors in site selection was proximity to a production facility. Since a principal function of these centers was the development of new products, constant communication between the development center and production was considered essential for efficiency.

Another factor of more recent importance to Nestlé was the establishment of development centers in regions of strategic interest to the company. This explained the creation of LatinReco in Ecuador and the new center under development in the Ivory Coast. Given the differing tastes and eating habits of the people in these regions, it was important to develop products based on local preferences and raw materials as these markets developed.

Geographical and environmental factors played a role in site selection as well. For example, the fact that three different climatic regions existed in Ecuador (coastal tropical, high elevation temperate, and central plains) was an important factor in the location of LatinReco. Within a relatively small area, different types of vegetables and cereals could be grown and developed for production, and later introduced in practically any Latin American country. Another example was the presence of an extensive irrigation system near the site in Spain selected for HispaReco, which became known as the "California" of Europe.

Also important to site selection were local restrictions on work permits for foreign nationals. Nestlé relied heavily on expatriates in the initial staffing of management positions in new centers. Less restrictive work permit regulations were cited as a factor in selecting Singapore over competing locations as the site for EastReco.

Site specialization was also related to these factors. The different climates in Ecuador, once again, made it a prime candidate for developing special expertise in the area of vegetable-based culinary products. Local raw materials also played an important role in site specialization. Given the importance of soya in Southeast Asia, Singapore had been given the mandate to develop soya-based culinary products. A farm in neighboring Malaysia had solved the problem of limited agricultural land in Singapore.

Although in certain areas, such as dehydrated culinary products, more than one center was engaged in R&D activities, this did not necessarily imply duplication of efforts. Each center in these cases typically had developed an expertise in specific types of raw materials or technology, which it developed for worldwide utilization. Also, on projects where Nestec assigned tasks to more than one center, a project leader was usually selected and given overall responsibility.

Sales volume did not seem to play a significant role in either the site selection or specialization decision. Ecuador and Singapore, for example, were not sources of sales revenue for Nestlé. Japan and Brazil, on the other hand, were countries which were major revenue earners for the company (fourth and sixth in 1987, respectively) but had no Recos.

A critical issue in the decision whether to establish a new center or expand an existing one concerned the relationship between the size of an R&D facility and its effective management. According to Dr. Suter, efficiency was at maximum with a size of 60 to 150 people. Mr. Zettl, Director of EastReco, was also of the opinion that a Reco of 150 people was about the maximum which could be handled efficiently. At Nestlé the size of Recos ranged from 20 in the smallest, to 250 in the largest.

Four of the Recos (FranceReco, WestReco, CalReco, and Linor) had more than 200 employees. Of these, however, FranceReco and WestReco comprised a number of independent centers, while CalReco was obtained as a result of the Carnation acquisition and was not under the control of Nestec until late 1985. The 450 people at NRC in Vevey constituted a much larger center than thought optimal, but the company argued that it was composed of various groups arrayed by disciplines and, as such, it could be considered as if it were several centers operating under one roof.

Cooperation with external organizations was a complementary part of the global R&D mission at Nestlé. Aside from the links between the Nestlé Research Center and various institutes around the world, some Recos had developed working relationships with local research organizations, as was the case with universities in Ecuador and Singapore. Any such cooperation, however, was based on specific needs or the requirements of a given project. Nestlé rarely supplied funds to external research centers for general scientific research.

Budgeting, Planning, and Control of R&D

The global R&D budget was developed at Nestec with input from all parties. The most important element of the budget was manpower. It was, therefore, not surprising that the Director of Technological Development at Nestec had final authority to fix the number of total man-hours for each center in a given year. This decision was reached after consultation with all center directors and a review of R&D plans and projects for each center. Within this budget, there was an allowance of 3 percent (in man-hours) for "free creative activities", to be used for nondirective work at the center directors' prerogative.

The decision to use man-hours as a unit of measure was noteworthy. Given international variations in the cost of scientific personnel and the rate of currency fluctuations, man-hours were a readily comparable unit of measure for R&D activities against which output and efficiency could be evaluated at all centers, regardless of their location. Furthermore, since 60–65 percent of the cost of R&D was labor, control over the number of man-hours provided an effective means of control over the budget. However, although the total number of man-hours was fixed by Nestec, the mix of employees at each center (i.e., the relative number of scientists, engineers and technicians) was left to the center directors. Faced with a trade-off between obtaining a uniform unit of measure for all centers and full budget control, Nestlé opted for the former.

Since most of the R&D at the Recos was of an applied nature, planning of R&D projects was very important to the success of product development at Nestlé. In its capacity as the supervising body, Nestec played an important role in defining and assigning R&D projects to various centers. In addition to handling requests from operating companies for technical development, Nestec had the responsibility of setting priorities based on corporate objectives in the face of limited resources. Consequently, an extensive planning process was put in place to define each center's activities for the year.

Through a series of meetings with the operating and geographic units, marketing and production staffs, and the Reco directors, Nestec developed a full R&D program which was finalized along with the budget in August of each year. The plan took into account requests from the operating units, and established priorities based on corporate objectives for the coming year. Furthermore, Nestec would attempt to balance short and long-term projects at each center. The final proposal for each Reco was drawn up by the director of the center in close cooperation with Nestec coordinators, whose responsibility was to ensure the fit between Reco R&D plans and corporate objectives.

A preliminary draft of the plan was circulated to various departments for review and comment. Most often it was approved without much change, an indication that the Nestec coordinators had ensured beforehand that the R&D plans met corporate objectives for the coming year as identified by all interested parties.

One participant in the R&D planning process called it an example of "participative centralization." The central body, Nestec, interpreted corporate objectives and market requirements, evaluated projects, set up priorities, and developed R&D plans with inputs from all parties. The unique aspect of this arrangement was that, unlike the classical centralized system, Nestec R&D was a small organization which carried out no research. Market data was obtained through discussions with the operating units, thus effective communication became a crucial element in the functioning of the planning system.

To keep track of the status of all projects, each center maintained a standard project file through which information was communicated to Nestec. The file contained data such as project status, expenditures, milestones, completion time, and other vital data. In addition, each center supplied a full report on its activities and progress every four months. Nestec gathered these reports and provided a summary to the General Management body.

Centers were also requested to submit a "Special Report" once on each project, generally at its conclusion. This report contained all major research findings, the reasons for the project's failure if unsuccessful, or manufacturing specifications if successful. These reports were also used to evaluate the quality of the work carried out at different centers and, in certain situations, they could provide some protection against patents claimed by others. On average, between 100 and 200 Special Reports were submitted to Nestec each year.

Another element of control at Nestlé, was the frequent visits by Nestec staff to R&D centers. Each center was visited at least twice a year by either the director or his deputy, in addition to numerous visits by the project coordinators. Although the main purpose of these visits was to keep communication lines open and reinforce personal contacts within the R&D organization, they also served to provide first-hand information about center operations.

The staff at Nestec also controlled what information from the various reports it received would be of interest to different centers and transmitted the findings accordingly. Glossaries (annotated lists) of important notes and communications that each center submitted during the years were also made available to all centers which could then use them to request additional data from the appropriate center. Proper diffusion of these reports was an important element of communicating technical information around the world.

Communication Policies

The view at Nestlé was that a system of centralized R&D management and independent research centers could not succeed unless it was supported by extensive communication between all interested parties (Nestec, the Recos, the operating companies' production and marketing staffs, etc.). A number of policies had been introduced in order to achieve this despite the geographic dispersion.

The main element of this policy was the collection and distribution of activity reports from the centers by Nestec as described above. The efficient distribution of information contained in these reports was a major concern to most center directors. A second element was the twice-yearly Nestec staff visits to each center. For example, the centers were encouraged to arrange from time to time special functions to familiarize the Nestec staff with the culture of each country and environment.

A yearly meeting of all Reco directors was held in Switzerland to discuss general issues and ideas. This not only enhanced Reco-Nestec communications, but it also provided opportunities for inter-Reco contact and familiarization. In fact, telephone conversations, discussions, and visits between managers in different Recos were always encouraged, and seemed to be a common practice. For example, Mr. Zettl, director of EastReco, stated that he normally took advantage of being in Europe for the yearly directors' meeting to visit one or more European Recos and factories, and he stressed the fact that most of his colleagues had already visited EastReco, although it had been in operation for only four years.

More technically oriented meetings (analytical, microbiological, etc.) were also held frequently, which brought together technical specialists from around the world on a regular basis. Discussions of new ideas and products between marketing, production, and R&D staffs were also strongly encouraged by Dr. Suter, a practice enshrined with a special name: "Trialogue."

Job rotation was another element of Nestlé's policy to promote communication within the company. Employee transfers between the Recos and production facilities supported the efficiency of R&D activities. Furthermore, periodic visits by key production personnel to different R&D centers developed their awareness of R&D and vice versa.

Communication at Nestlé, however, went beyond these formal meetings and visits. Directors of Recos which shared common areas of research were in constant contact with one another. For example, the staff at NordReco, HispaReco, FranceReco, and VitoReco (all centers working on frozen and/or culinary products) met regularly outside formal channels. At times, samples of new products were sent to interested centers by the center that had developed it. Nestlé's policies encouraged this type of contact. For travel within Europe, for example, no higher approval than the Reco director was required. This multitude of contacts, reinforced through telephone communication and the fact that most of the directors had known each other for some time, greatly contributed to the efficiency of information diffusion within Nestlé R&D.

The open communication style had filtered down to the internal operations of the Recos as well. In FranceReco, extensive formal and informal arrangements existed by which people at the various local centers met to discuss R&D issues, or even to taste and rate products. For example, various project leaders at Beauvais gathered two or three times a year to carry out what had been termed as "Cross Work." They listed issues that had to be solved against the technologies that might be used. This often provided a guideline about technologies which FranceReco needed to master and those which it could obtain from other centers. Sometimes a certain technique or approach from one domain was applied to another, as was the case when a design technique employed for making ice cream was successfully applied to some frozen food products.

Mr. Brengou emphasized that FranceReco worked mostly on the basis of informal communication. "There is a conflict between structure and the flexibility required in this domain [food research]," he stated. A similar statement was made by Mr. Zettl: "R&D requires teamwork, and a team can only work if everybody works more or less at the same level. A natural hierarchy will establish itself on the basis of competence."

Human Resource Management Issues

The international nature of R&D at Nestlé posed special problems in terms of human resource management which required careful attention. Issues ranging from salary compensation in different countries, to training of local researchers, the hiring of expatriates, and motivation of researchers in remote sites had led Nestlé to follow deliberate human resource management practices designed to eliminate or minimize any problems associated with international R&D.

Recos. As Nestlé considered itself an international company, it had no specific rules about the nationality of R&D center directors. There was no deliberate attempt to assign local nationals to project leader or director positions; nor was there a practice of hiring Swiss nationals for these positions. Aside from competence, human and technical skills, two major criteria were considered in staffing these positions: language skills and work experience in at least two or three different countries. It was thought that these requirements would provide managers with an appreciation of different cultures and made them more effective in dealing with local researchers.

A common practice encouraged by Nestec was to fill technical position vacancies at Recos with new graduates in order to develop personnel. Exceptions were made for those areas where a Reco did not have expertise in a field and experienced professionals were sought from outside. In general, the proportion of expatriate personnel at most R&D centers ranged from 5–10 percent for most European centers, to about 25 percent for centers in Singapore and Ecuador.

These guidelines had to be seen in a dynamic context. EastReco, for example, was started mainly by expatriates. Their number peaked at 22, and was subsequently reduced to 13 (out of about 120 employees) by 1987. Eventually, it was expected to drop to about 6 to 8. The replacement of expatriates by local personnel had gone somewhat slower than expected in this case. For many Singaporeans, a job at Nestlé was viewed as a reference for future employment and not as a long term career. The degree of company loyalty that existed in other Nestlé sites had not yet flourished in Singapore and, due to EastReco's recent founding, there were few role models of successful Singaporeans who had a long period of service with the company. The opposite was the case in France, where Mr. Brengou expressed his regret at not being able to attract more qualified foreign nationals to FranceReco.

Nestec R&D Staff. Certain qualities were deemed essential for anyone aspiring to a position at Nestec R&D, given the key role this organization played in the system. Interpersonal skills, considerable experience within Nestlé, age (maturity), willingness to travel, and competence in a domain in which Nestlé was active were among the most important qualifications. Age and experience were related to both know-how and credibility; while competence in a specific domain ensured that all areas of critical knowledge were represented in Nestec. Yet, as the staff at Nestec R&D was small and the fields of R&D at Nestlé were many, extreme specialization was less important than a broad technical competence.

Nestec staff were expected to be in constant communication with R&D centers. This involved at least two yearly visits to each center and annual or semiannual seminars with directors and project leaders. Furthermore, since they performed coordinating as well as supervisory roles, the Nestec staff were on call to handle any problems that may arise on a given project. In general, it was felt that only people with intimate knowledge of the company through many years of experience in various production or R&D capacities were capable of performing this role.

Remuneration. Salary proposals for R&D staff at the centers were typically made by the local directors and sent to Nestec for approval. Since it was recognized that headquarters could not often judge the appropriateness of these salary recommendations, the country managers were consulted. In fact, R&D center directors were required to discuss and coordinate employee salary levels with the respective country managers. The compensation of the directors was determined by the Nestec General Manager after consultation with the country managers.

Training and continuing education. The training and development of local researchers and staff was left to the center director, whereas project leaders were required to attend initial courses at the training center in Switzerland. Thus, the center directors were free to influence their employees' professional development according to their own priorities. For example, new technical recruits at FranceReco were sent to work in a production facility during the first three months of their employment. Mr. Brengou believed that a satisfactory performance in a production center was a prerequisite to a satisfactory performance in R&D. Mr. Zettl, on the other hand, was concerned about the impact on his staff of technical training in Switzerland. A training stint in Switzerland could be used as a reference to apply for a job in other Singapore companies.

Corporate Culture

It appeared that a major reason for Nestlé's R&D success was the existence of a "Nestlé family culture." Despite the great distances that separated the sites, the open communication policy implemented in the company had contributed to the development of a closely knit network of R&D centers. This identification with Nestlé was best summed up by Mr. Brengou when he said that "here one becomes Nestlé."

In spite of this corporate identification, there was no "standard" Nestlé R&D center. National characteristics and the historical background of each center were often evident in its internal operations. FranceReco, for example, employed its chefs in positions of project leadership and as heads of product development teams, whereas in other centers chefs were employed only to produce prototypes. At the Beauvais center, there were a few "tasting rooms" where employees gathered to taste and rate new recipes, and the chefs often presented their daily experiments with recipes to the employees at 11:30 A.M. (there were typically about 15 recipe experiments at Beauvais every day).

Perhaps the best description of the Nestlé R&D environment was that it consisted of a multicultural society with common goals and values. The motivation to develop products for worldwide use, and Nestlé's policy of reinforcing personal contacts reduced nationalistic barriers. At the same time, however, individual Reco cultures were reinforced through activities such as the get-togethers organized by Recos during the Nestec staff visits.

Some Concerns About the Future of R&D at Nestlé

The main concern of Nestec executives and Reco directors was improving the efficiency of R&D at Nestlé. While there were no convincing methods of measuring R&D efficiency, there were constant discussions about how to improve it. This included a consistent effort to see that R&D projects were linked to clear business objectives, while striving not to lose the "creative touch".

Extensive use of electronic and data processing equipment was one approach. Mr. Brengou mentioned that he felt FranceReco was slow in adopting information systems. His center, however, was moving ahead with this process and he expected to see computer terminals all over the place within five years. Although computers were used for technical support (e.g., statistical analyses), some chefs had even begun to employ computers to obtain data such as calorie values and product costs for the recipes they developed. Dr. Suter felt that although use of information systems has spread gradually at Nestec R&D, experimentation with electronic conferencing was under consideration. Yet, he felt this could not replace personal contacts.

Two areas of concern brought up by Mr. Brengou were the more efficient use of the Nestlé Research Center and better management and distribution of the extensive technical reports generated worldwide. There were concerns also on the future ability of Nestlé to maintain its R&D culture and style. Nestec was constantly involved in preserving a delicate balance between centralized control and motivating the R&D centers to develop their own "personality". According to Mr. Zettl, there was a basic attitude of trust between the central organization in Vevey and the Recos. "They don't jump on us all the time," he said. "We get the necessary freedom, but on the other hand we have to perform according to Nestec's standards. Nestec's management is very gentle but it can become very tough if something goes wrong."

The issue was particularly important when dealing with R&D centers obtained as a result of acquisitions. How could a center that had previously operated autonomously, within a different culture, be integrated into Nestec? A case in point was the ongoing integration of CalReco, obtained as part of the Carnation acquisition, into Nestec's policies and procedures. Under Carnation's management, the R&D center was engaged in activities spanning a greater part of the food world. This was inconsistent with Nestlé's policy of center specialization. Some R&D activities at CalReco would, therefore, have to be adapted to a new mission. Such redirection of activities would be a difficult task to impose on the new affiliate without affecting national sensitivities and motivation.

Similar problems had already occurred at the time of the integration of the German centers. Mr. Suter acknowledged the seriousness of these issues and cautioned that the integration or establishment of a new R&D center into the "Nestlé family" would take about five years before it became effective. Mr. Brengou added that "[R&D coordination] at Nestlé works because people know each other, because most of them have made their entire career at Nestlé," a situation not shared with new companies or other countries. Mr. Zettl agreed and warned that it might require more than a decade to create this culture in EastReco. As Nestlé's acquisitiveness continued, the complexity of the company's R&D management system would rise accordingly.

INSEAD

Case 12–3

Managing Knowledge at Booz-Allen & Hamilton: Knowledge On-Line and Off

As 1998 came to a close, Chuck Lucier could look back at the past five years with a sense of satisfaction. A senior partner of Booz-Allen & Hamilton, Lucier had been named the firm's first Chief Knowledge Officer (CKO) in March 1994. Since then, the firm had:

- Augmented its collection of provincial libraries—stocked with paper and CD-ROM resources—with an integrated, state-of-the-art knowledge management intranet called Knowledge On-Line, or KOL (see Exhibit 1);
- Institutionalized the practice of knowledge sharing and reuse on KOL, allowing associates and senior associates to better leverage the experience of the firm and allowing principals to spend less time reinventing the wheel and more time serving the client;
- Launched an award-winning general management journal, *Strategy and Business*, disseminating and demonstrating the quality of leading-edge thought being generated in the firm.
- Experimented with a variety of models for innovation teams; learning a great deal along the way about how to bring together experts from inside and outside the firm to test and improve consulting products and leading-edge ideas.

This case was written by Charles Galunic, Associate Professor, and John Weeks, Assistant Professor at INSEAD. It is intended to be used as a basis for class discussion rather than to illustrate either effective or ineffective handling of an administrative situation. We are grateful for the support of the CIMSO Centre at INSEAD and Mr Claus Nehmzow.

EXHIBIT 1 Practices and Global Offices

The knowledge management program had met all of its aims and had done so more quickly than anyone had predicted. Indeed, the major pieces had been put in place in fewer than three years and had generated measurable success. Publications and media mentions were up five-fold in that time and, more importantly, profits and revenues had doubled and growth had outpaced that of the industry as a whole. Since 1997, they had been maintaining, tweaking, and honing KOL.

Reflecting on what they had achieved, Lucier wondered now if the firm had become a victim of its own success. They had made tremendous progress, but there was still work to be done to unleash the creativity of their key assets—each other—and to bring more consistently their breakthrough ideas quickly to market. It was time to go beyond KOL as it existed today. But in what direction?

Vision 2000 and the History of KOL

As originally envisioned five years earlier, knowledge management was one plank of Booz-Allen's plan for self-renewal known as Vision 2000, or V2K. Announced in 1994, V2K represented over a year's worth of analysis and self-assessment in the firm. Booz-Allen was one of the oldest and proudest management and technology-consulting firms.[1] It was founded in 1914 by Edwin Booz. With degrees in psychology and economics, Booz went to work for himself straight out of college, performing studies and statistical analyses for businesses. He was joined by James Allen (the firm's third employee, an economist with business college training) in 1929, and in 1935 by Carl Hamilton, who had extensive management experience in lumber and forest products. By 1947 the firm employed over 100 people and had bookings of US$2 million. Following the firm's publication in the *Harvard Business Review* in 1957 of an article introducing the concept of the "Product Life Cycle," *Time* magazine in 1959 called the firm "the world's largest, most prestigious management consulting firm." With headquarters in McLean, Virginia, the firm is now a private corporation (after a brief stint of public ownership in the 1970s), and, in the fiscal year ending March 1999, its 8,800 employees, spread across 100 offices worldwide, generated sales of roughly US$1.5 billion. The firm is growing at a rate of 15 percent a year. This is in the context of an estimated US$80 billion in sales of the management consulting industry as a whole. The industry is growing at a rate (which varies by country) of 10–30 percent.[2]

Booz-Allen was divided into two business groups: the Worldwide Commercial Business (WCB), which served major international corporations, and the Worldwide Technology business, which primarily served various U.S. government agencies but also some overseas governments. The focus of Vision 2000—and this case—was the WCB (see Exhibit 2). Lucier led the formulation of V2K on behalf of Brian Dickie, the president of the commercial business at the time. It contained four planks. The first concerned client relationships and a move toward deeper relationships with fewer clients and a move away from selling individual projects. The second plank was a shift in focus to work which would integrate Booz-Allen's three functional competencies: strategy, operations management, and information technology. Other firms may be able to equal Booz-Allen in one or two of those areas, but the firm saw as its competitive advantage the ability to deliver a truly integrated service offering, that its competitors could not match. The third plank was a revamped system for developing internal talent. And the fourth was something only vaguely understood at the time: "knowledge management."

Knowledge management supported the other three planks: facilitating the knowledge sharing necessary to

[1]The founding dates of the first management consulting firms: Foster Higgins, 1845; Sedgwick, 1858; Arthur D. Little, 1886; Booz-Allen Hamilton, 1914.

[2]Biswas, S. and D. Twitchell. *Management Consulting: A Complete Guide to the Industry.* New York: Wiley, 1999.

EXHIBIT 2 Practices and Global Offices

Communications Media & Technology

Operations Management

Financial & Health Services

Consumer & Engineered Products

Information Technology

Strategic Leadership

Energy, Chemicals and Pharmaceuticals

Global Offices (over 100)

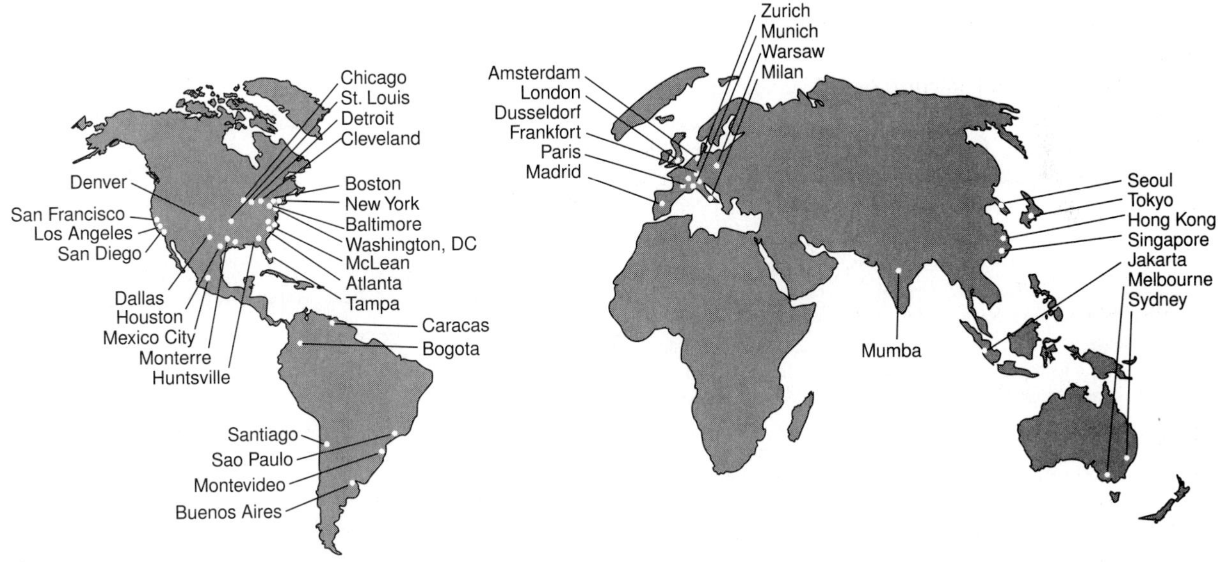

integrate work across the firm's geographical sectors,[3] its three functional practices,[4] and its four industry practices;[5] marketing the leading edge ideas that would make clear to clients why a deep relationship with Booz-Allen was valuable; and giving consultants the tools they needed to more quickly grow their skills. But it wasn't an easy sell. As talk about knowledge management had become more widespread—building on the interest generated by groupware technologies and academic notions of learning organizations—so had cynicism. Predictions of performance improvements had been inflated in the management literature, as had the utopian promises of a new approach to epistemology. Lucier, however, saw substance behind the rhetoric and sought to strip away from the philosophical musing and the technological enthusing a simple point. The firm could not deliver on its strategy unless it changed the way it managed its knowledge. "The big part of motivating an organization like this to change," he said, "is to build a compelling case on the need for change, and that requires you to be pointed." His efforts secured approval for the knowledge management program and the role of CKO for Lucier. Dickie was equally pointed: "Fine," he told Lucier, "you recommended this thing, now you come figure out how to do it."

Knowledge Management the Old-Fashioned Way

The knowledge management program aimed to change three areas of the organization. The first was the collection of libraries the firm maintained. Most offices had one, sometimes overseen by one of the 30 Booz-Allen librarians, other times by a local secretary. As assistants to research, the librarians were valuable resources. As libraries, the collections of paper and CD-ROM documents were poorly indexed and unevenly stocked. People who had been with the firm for many years noted that the typical library experience was one of two scenarios.

> "You enter the library and this wonderful woman who had been at the firm for 100 years would go through our physical files and pull out for you every document that was relevant—but few of which were competitive—and you'd sift through this pile of documents 100 feet high, and you'd get so frustrated that you'd decide, 'Oh to hell with this, I'm just going to create my own way to do it because I don't have time to look at all this stuff.'" (Principal)

Or, you would find out that the library had nothing on your subject and that you needed instead access to the private libraries kept by people who had worked on particular assignments in that area. Related to this, was the second area of change: the capture and sharing of the firm's intellectual capital (IC). The bulk of this IC was made up of learning done during the course of client engagements. Each partner kept documents relating to the assignments he or she had worked on in personal filing systems. As one senior European staff member recalls, "the nearest thing we had to knowledge management in 1990 was a cupboard which had photocopies of some of the documents that had been done. That was maintained by the clerk who ran the Xerox machine—that was our knowledge storage system." The problems with such an admittedly inexpensive system were indexing and incompleteness. It was hard to find documents relating to a particular industry or approach, and anyway the most relevant documents were not publicly available. This was for two reasons. The first was client confidentiality. Like all large consultancies, Booz-Allen maintains so-called "Chinese walls" to protect client data in cases where it worked for two competing firms. The firm also maintained strict guidelines protecting sensitive client information—regardless of competitor involvement. The important documents relating to client work, possibly containing sensitive client information, were closely kept by the team who had worked on the assignment. And because the threat of violating the "Chinese wall" policy was real, partners always had a legitimate excuse not to share documents. As a senior partner put it:

> "The partner controlled knowledge because he was sitting on the confidential client reports. Nothing was in the public domain. If you wanted to learn from his experience, you had

---

[3]The geographical sectors were: the Atlantic (including Europe and North America), Latin America, and Asia Pacific/Japan.

[4]The functional practices were: Strategic Leadership Practice (SLP, focusing on CEOs and top executive teams on topics such as business unit and corporate strategy, people strategies, and leadership); Information Technology Group (ITG, focusing on client's information technology needs); and Operations Management Group (OMG, focusing on competitive analysis, operations strategy, business process redesign, strategic sourcing, supply chain management, and technology choice and deployment).

[5]The industry practices were: Consumer and Engineered Products Practice (CEP, focusing on global companies whose primary products are tangible goods, such as aerospace, airlines, and automotive manufacturers); Communications Media and Technology Practice (CMT, focusing on telecommunications, media, entertainment, information, computers, and electronics businesses); Energy, Chemicals, and Pharmaceuticals Practice (focusing on the fields of energy, natural resources, chemicals, and pharmaceuticals); and Financial and Health Services Practice (FHSPC, focusing on financial services institutions and health care organizations and insurers, with separate managing partners for each subpractice).

to interview the partner and he would look at his reports and maybe pass on some comments. Maybe. But he was Mr. Control".

The second problem was that even when a consultant found the right person and convinced him or her to share documents, the documents could not be understood by someone who hadn't been part of the assignment. Copies of presentations given to clients, reports written for clients—these were too context-specific to be of general use. "They didn't impart any knowledge at all," one principal complained.

As a result knowledge was being created, but it was trapped in what some called "small pyramids:" local structures with a partner at the top accumulating industry wisdom and cultivating client relationships but remaining insular. These were a vestige of the firm's highly decentralized past where Booz-Allen was little more than a shared brand name for individual partners who owned client relationships. The old way of doing business—uncompetitive in an age when clients demand an integrated offering from Booz-Allen spanning geography and functional offerings—had started to change in 1987 with a new partner compensation system that aligned the interests of partners with those of the firm as a whole. The need for change was as acute when trying to establish new client relationships, as when building on prior ones. Helmut Meier, managing partner of the CMT practice, summed up the trend:

> "In the past it was sufficient to deliver smart bright young guys, who basically said 'we don't understand your business but that doesn't matter because we are smart, and we will deliver great analytics.' That's no longer viable. Today you just don't survive without providing, from the start, strong know-how, understanding of the clients, understanding the industry issues, and providing routinized methodology and creating solutions."

At a time when growth and a 15–20 percent staff turnover rate meant that at any given time roughly one-third of its consultants were new to the firm, this shift in client expectations presented a considerable challenge that the knowledge management program aimed to address.

The third targeted area of change was the marketing of Booz-Allen. As Lucier saw it, "What consulting firms market, at least in part, is their leading edge ideas, their knowledge." Two issues arose. The first was the fragmented nature of ideas in the firm. There were no structures in place to provide a synthesis of what Booz-Allen knew and believed about a given subject. As one consultant put it, "We weren't generating a view about what we, Booz-Allen, thought about a particular topic." Furthermore, the "small pyramids" mentality meant that opportunities for triangulation on a particular idea from people who had experience with various aspects of it, were being missed. Instead, the firm generated, and regenerated, multiple strategies and methodologies in the same area with no attention given to the costs of duplicated effort. Some put this down to culture: using the ideas of others was seen as uncreative and dangerously close to the practice of reselling off-the-shelf solutions to clients that Booz-Allen's second-tier competitors indulged in. The second issue was one of idea dissemination. Booz-Allen didn't want to return to the "publish or perish" days of its distant past, but there was a concern among many partners that too little publication of ideas was going on and that brand-recognition was suffering as a result. Fairly or not, there was a widespread perception that McKinsey had an unfair advantage in getting its consultants' work published in the *Harvard Business Review* and that HBR had little real competition in the marketplace. "Booz-Allen people had kind of given up," was a sentiment echoed by many. Chuck Lucier and the Core Knowledge Team that he put together over the course of 1994 aimed to attack each of these three fronts.

The Change Process

The simple fact of the appointment of someone as senior as Lucier to the position of CKO was the first important step in the change process. As Claus Nehmzow, a Vice President, put it:

> "Creating the CKO position and filling it with a senior partner who would be respected by the partnership, who carried some weight, was, I think, the cornerstone to making the thing successful. I mean there was no way that we could have done anything just coming from a purely technological perspective, or just coming from some group. It was important to have a senior partner to convince the rest of the partnership that this was somewhere we want to put our money."

The Core Knowledge Team was made up of individuals hand picked from each of the practices, by the practices themselves and vetted by Lucier. The criteria for the job was that the candidate have some background in, and passion for, "building the institution" and, importantly, a willingness to spend two years of their careers developing this service within Booz-Allen. Since none of the team members were partners themselves and it was understood that no one would make partner on this basis—client service and growth remaining the *sine qua non* of consulting—a strong intrinsic motivation was necessary, and the decision was not a simple one. Nevertheless, Lucier managed to attract a dedicated and energized group of people (some of whom simply welcomed the chance to have a stable lifestyle, a respite from the constant travel of consulting work).

Early on, the team realized that its toughest challenge would not be implementing a new technology: it would be changing the organization. Convincing still skeptical minds about the value of knowledge management would be key. This placed a premium on delivering demonstrable results quickly, and it meant that, early on, effective marketing of the program was essential. Their initial focus, then, was twofold: to initiate the lengthy process developing new intellectual capital and to rapidly put in place an IT system to facilitate knowledge sharing and automate some elements of basic training.

Innovation Teams

Lucier solicited the views of everyone in the firm about what constituted its leading edge IC. "I told people that we were going to pick five subject areas where we were going to marshal the firm's resources to really accelerate our progress in those five areas." By the summer of 1994, some 25 different areas were suggested and it proved impossible to reduce them to five. Instead, they selected four as so-called High Impact Products (or HIPS) of primary interest for the firm, and ten more as Special Interest Groups (SIGS) that were slightly less critical areas and that were given smaller budgets by a factor of four. The HIPS were: (1) business process reengineering (BPR), (2) customer care, (3) management measurement systems, and (4) new organizational models or forms. The SIGS included such topics as: sourcing and value engineering, marketing, war gaming, electronic commerce, postmerger integration, and growth.

The idea was for each topic to have one member from each organizational unit plus four or five people who were especially enthusiastic about the topic. This meant teams of 12–15 members each: a number that, in retrospect, was felt to be probably too large. Levels of commitment varied widely as did attendance at the meetings scheduled every six weeks or so. The teams demanded consultants' most precious resource: time. They brought less tangible reputation benefits to participants and a chance to shape the direction of the firm. The large team size reflected the belief that it was important that the teams incorporate a wide diversity of members. One of their goals was to consolidate the knowledge and practices within the firm. Lucier explains:

> "In large part, the reason I wanted all of the different organizational units to be involved was that each focused on a different set of clients and did, for example, business process reengineering, each in their own way. So we had one approach to BPR that we used in our Financial Services Group that was a little bit different than we used in Energy and Chemicals, and so on. So what this did was that it forced those guys to get together. And what we discovered was that we were learning the same lessons five or six times. So we got a lot of power from getting all of the experts together and actually agreeing on how we wanted to do this".

In the end, about 100 of Booz-Allen's 150 partners participated. The deliverables varied by team and included marketing materials (to attract clients), selling documents (to convince clients), and formal approaches and best practices (methodologies for specific topic areas, to be used by other partners and staff members). The overall cost at this stage was US$2 million. Some of these innovation teams (as the HIPS and SIGS were known collectively) migrated into the individuals' practices over time. Others, having achieved their aims, were disbanded, while new ones had emerged.

Knowledge On-Line 1.0

At the same time that topic areas for the innovation teams were being selected, work was underway on a pilot of a delivery system. Several trial systems for knowledge sharing had already been developed at a local level to meet various needs. One such program, for example, had been developed by Jan Torsilieri and a team of IT professionals, within the Information Technology Group.

> "I was a senior associate and I didn't want people to have to deal with what I experienced in my past—reinventing the wheel. It was a very emotional thing. I wanted people to have access to each other's thinking. It was stupid that we didn't do this."

Another had been developed by Mary Beth Sasso within the Financial and Health Services Practice. There the emphasis was on both sanitization and putting the confidential deliverables in a computer database.

> "The partners felt that there were so many clients with whom Booz-Allen had long-term relationships that we had to be able to centralize and store the actual reports we had given to the clients. Since the clients referred back to those reports, we had to be able to refer back to them as well."

Both Torsilieri and Sasso would be recruited into the knowledge management effort, their early efforts providing an important impetus to the development of KOL.

The goal with the first version of KOL was to avoid a long and drawn out IT project. Lucier put Aron Dutta in charge of formulating the mechanics of the system.

> "My directive to Aron was I wanted something that was up and operating within six months. And I didn't want it to be fancy, I just wanted something that was going to work 100 percent of the time."

It was decided to leverage an electronic bulletin board system that most of the firm already had access to. Initially, resumes, company policies, and other documents already in the public domain were put on the system along with the materials being generated by the innovation teams. Only the abstracts of documents were indexed, and they were the only thing translated into English—the actual documents remained in whatever language they had been written in and were available for download but could not be viewed on-line. As Lois Remeikis, a member of the core knowledge team, says, "to launch the thing, we were much more interested in content and change than we were in the technology. We figured we'd get the technology right later on when we had the time to think about it."

The pilot version of KOL was ready in December 1994. The full roll out across the firm was completed in March 1995. Over 500 documents were available on the system at that point. By all accounts, people were impressed. When it was first shown off in a partners meeting, one team member recalls, "people cheered because the content was great." A strong emphasis went into marketing KOL both on the day of its release and before. One member explains:

> "As we moved from the 'pilot' to going live with the first version of KOL, we asked each practice for their resumes. We wanted the resumes of every single individual and we said if you got them to us by whatever date, they would be live on the system. We also went to each of the offices, told them when we were rolling KOL out, and invited people who are at the lower levels in the organization but who are up and comers—people who other people respect—to a special event prior to the launch. These were people selected by their offices as being leaders at different levels within our organization whose job was to go back on the day we launched this and promote it to all their colleagues."

On the day of the launch, kiosks were set up with multimedia presentations; glossy brochures were distributed. The event was staged, as one team member explains, "in a way that we just had never done things around here."

> "We really treated it as a marketing event and put people in all of the different WCB offices and made a special event day out of it. So that we would be present in these offices and raise awareness that this was here, this had happened, this wasn't just a dream. I think it was really effective. It flagged in peoples' minds that this thing was here, and it was real, and it was ready to use."

KOL 1 was, by all accounts, a success. Greater functionality would arrive in the next version, but the acceptance garnered at this stage was essential in convincing skeptics of the value it offered.

The Second Year

The Fall of 1995 marked the first issue of *Strategy and Business*. Lucier hired Joel Kurtzman, a former senior editor from *Harvard Business Review,* to edit this competitor to *HBR*. The journal won the Folio Editorial Excellence award given by the business publishing industry and, by 1997, had a circulation of 60,000. Its status as a bona fide journal boosted Booz-Allen's publishing profile not only with clients but also with consultants inside the firm. It signaled a change in approach that manifested itself in such ways as an increase in the number of Booz-Allen presentations at conferences and books published. In the Spring of 1996, KOL 2.0 was released. Whereas the first version of KOL had been based on a relatively unsophisticated technology, version 2.0 was state-of-the-art at that time. Its implementation was Netscape's first mission critical intranet account. The design still emphasized reliability and speed (of particular importance was the ability for consultants dialing in over phone lines from hotels and client sites to face a reasonable response time) over bells and whistles. The system contained the following features (see Exhibits 3–6):

Offices A "yellow pages" listing the location of Booz-Allen offices and the personnel who resided there.

Business Operations Information about the mission, goals, and policies of the firm including recruiting information and calendars, and various human resource data (pension fund information, internal newsletters, events, etc.).

Practices/Teams A description of the organizational structure of the firm in terms of its practices (which were often spread across geographical locations). Links to information on team members and to basic

EXHIBIT 3 Home Page

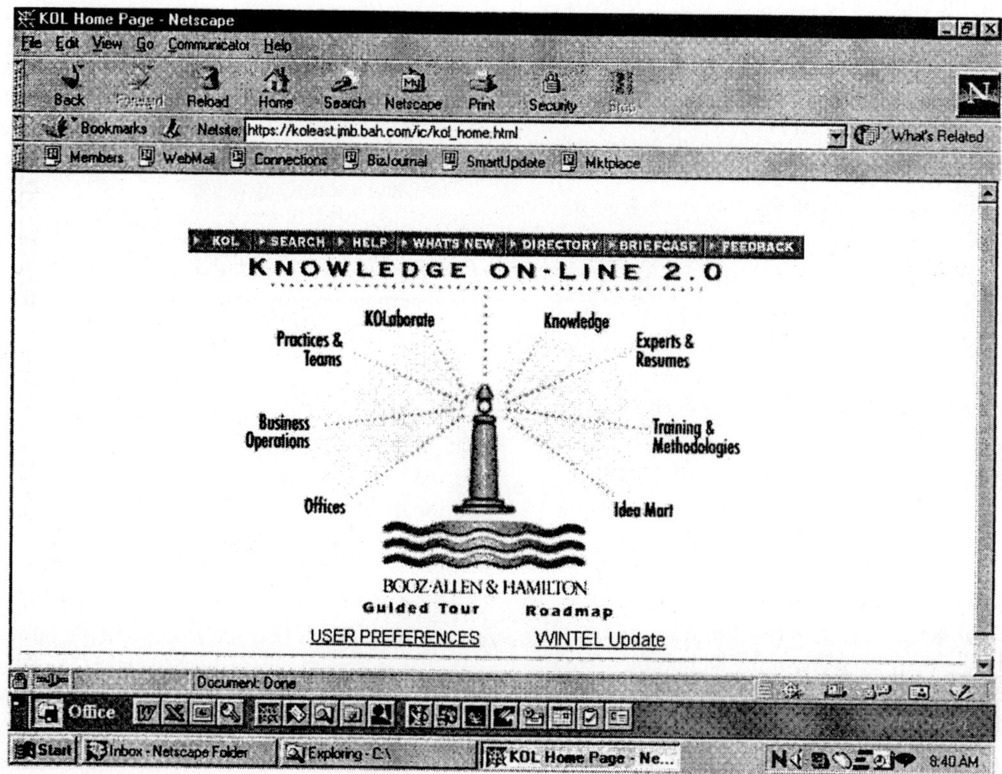

descriptions of their activities. Qualifications (or "Quals") describing ongoing and completed projects, listing participating members. Quals were a useful way of identifying who had experience in a particular area and also formed an important part of a client proposal demonstrating Booz-Allen's experience.

KOLaborate A discussion group system for special interest groups and ad hoc teams where members could post ideas and reactions in real-time and maintain a "virtual" discussion. The groups were controlled: individuals must apply to the group's moderator to join the discussion. Groups could form easily with a partner's approval if some topic of common interest existed that required real-time discussion. Some 100 KOLaborate forums were created, after perhaps a slower than expected uptake of the technology.

Knowledge The intellectual capital of the firm, with abstracts arranged according to practice and cross-practice categories (which reflected the work of the innovation teams). Typically users employed the search feature to find a list of abstracts concerning a particular person or subject area and then, based on those abstracts, decided which documents to download for viewing.

Experts and Resumés A more detailed database on people in the firm, containing backgrounds and experiences.

Skills and Methodologies Developmental materials such as computer-based tutorials on such topics as multiple linear regression, interviewing skills, and basic finance. Also listings of training opportunities.

In addition, KOL provided online help, an opportunity to provide immediate feedback on the systems operations, and links to internet-based content such as directory and information services.

Accompanying the new technology were new practices to ensure that the knowledge generated in client projects

EXHIBIT 4 WCB Knowledge

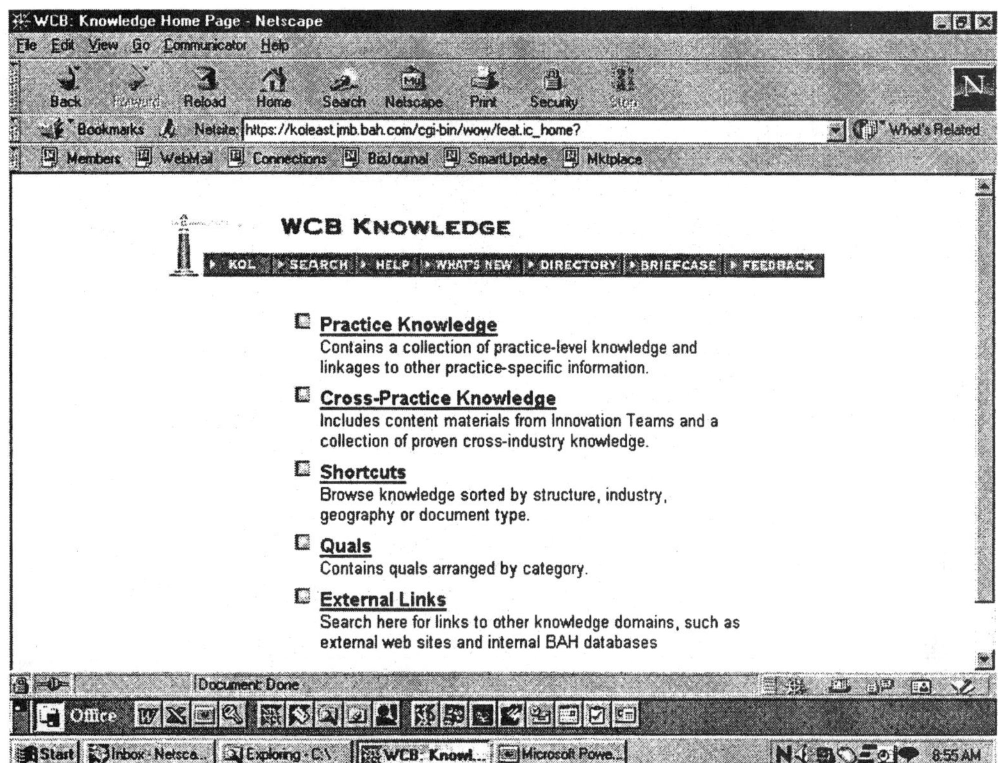

was captured and shared. Twelve knowledge managers, dedicated to particular practices, worked with project teams to ensure that, where appropriate, sanitized and generic lessons learned were entered into the system. There was a strong emphasis on quality control. As one partner said:

> "You don't want just anything to get posted there. We definitely have a different view at Booz-Allen than some others who suggest you let everyone post anything and you create a free market. Absolutely not! That wastes everyone's time: all knowledge is not created equal. We definitely have strict quality standards."

After they received officer (partner) approval, documents were eventually posted by the knowledge managers and their teams—collectively known as the Information Professionals Community, or IPC—who worked with IT people to make sure KOL remained well-organized and properly maintained.

The process from client project to intellectual capital could take quite a while. Even before the period of anywhere from one week to two months required to groom documents for KOL, there were often delays in getting the documents from consulting teams in the first place. No time was allocated to consultants for this work. They were expected to capture the knowledge in the so-called "beach time" between client projects. A consultant explained, "say if we were on the project together and I was on the beach for a week and you were staffed on something else, then I would be expected to co-ordinate it and to get input from you." During prosperous periods there was little beach time, and so this often left only evenings and weekends for KOL work. The IPC found themselves having to chase material. One knowledge manager noted:

> "I've always viewed myself as the conscience of the practice. I mean people don't naturally do this. People won't naturally write up a description of their project just because

EXHIBIT 5 Experts and Resumes

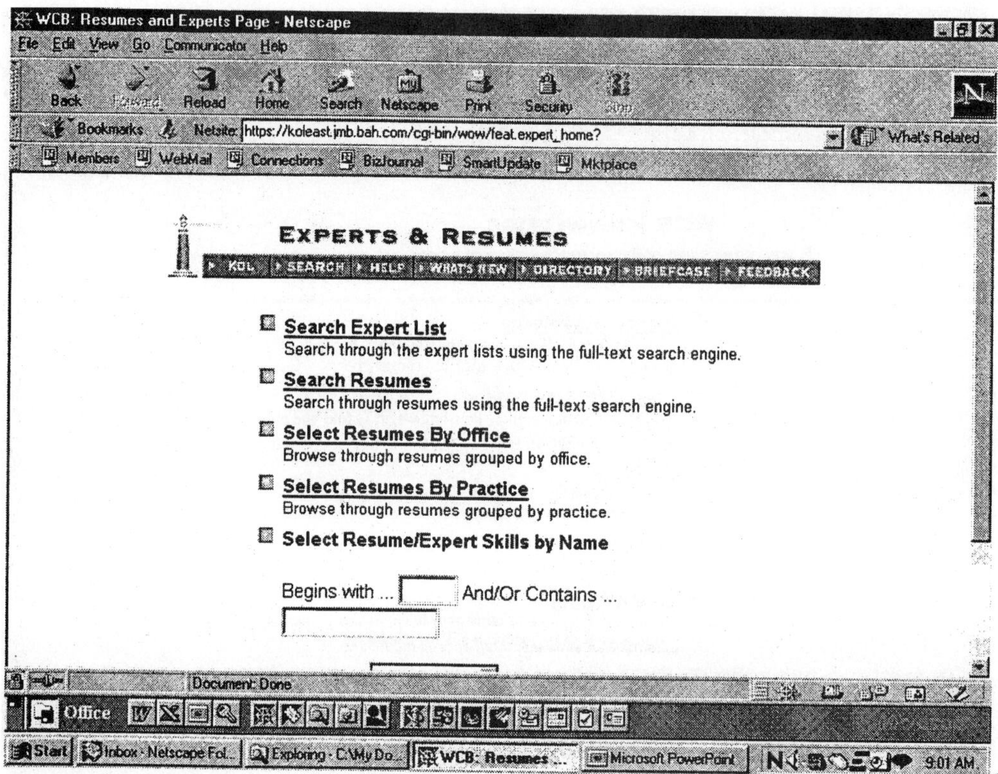

they know it's the right thing to do. I mean, most, a lot of this work happens on weekends and evenings, and the team finishes one project, they immediately roll onto another project. The last thing they want to do is all the clean up. And so, as I said, I feel that one of my main roles is to convince people that this is something that they really need to do. But that's tough going."

The job of persuasion was made easier by the firm's reward structure. Some practices offered awards for excellent contributions. These ranged from tombstones for the consultant's desk to the CMT practice's award of $50,000 to a winning team for them to spend on learning-related activities of their choice (the only restriction being that they must report their learning back to the practice as whole). But, more significantly, developing intellectual capital had become one of the four criteria used when determining promotion and bonuses. For junior consultants, this meant how well do they used KOL to leverage the experience of the firm, adopt best practice, and avoid duplicating previous efforts. For principals and partners, this meant they were contributing to the system, building the firm's IC. Practices varied in the emphasis they put on IC, but in several well-known cases, failure to contribute to KOL had cost people a promotion.

"I've been with the firm for almost 15 years, it used to be that if you got a Viewpoint written you were an expert, and you couldn't get promoted as a partner unless you wrote a Viewpoint. Viewpoints are these internally published 10 to 20–pagers on a particular topic. That's not enough any more. You need to start getting some press in the outside business world. Hell, now that we've got people writing books left and right, I can imagine that someday you will need to be known as writing a book."

Knowledge management, then, was supported by both carrot and stick. The importance of these motivating factors was revealed by the deluge of IC submitted just before the appraisal cycle started.

EXHIBIT 6 Skills and Methodologies

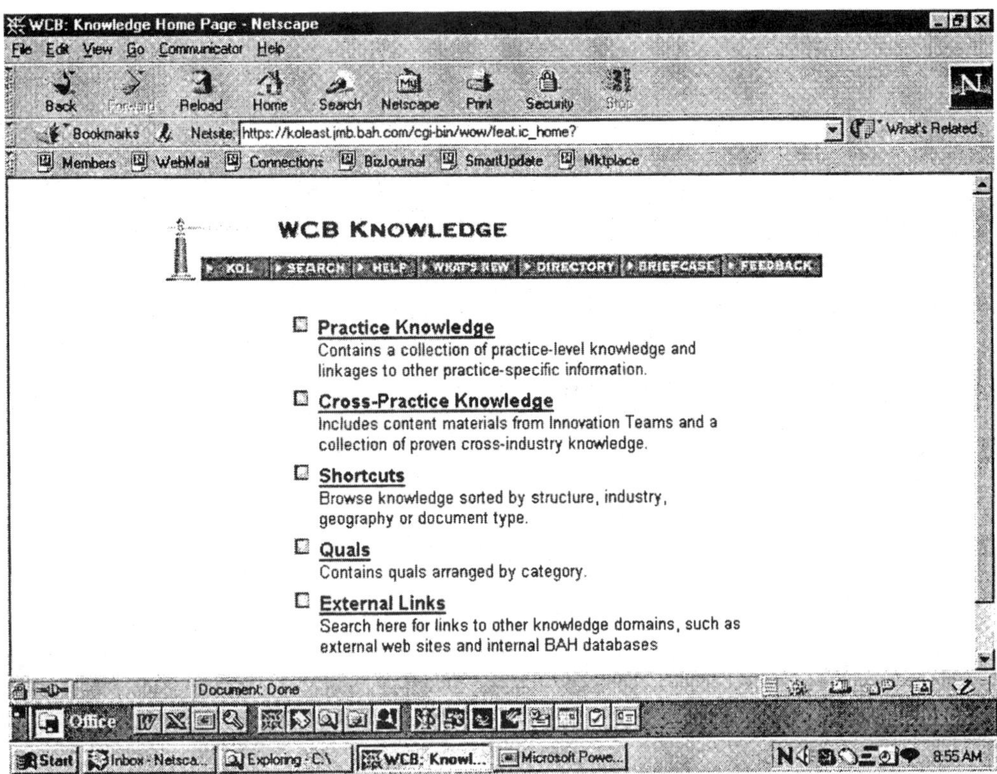

Some claimed that the culture of Booz-Allen reinforces these extrinsic rewards. A senior partner described that "the culture always reinforced the idea that if you are seen as a thought leader that was important. And in fact one of the most derisive things you can say about somebody in the firm is that they are content free." Knowledge reuse was also culturally consistent. "The culture encourages people to borrow good ideas," another said. Indeed, people were so comfortable using the IC on KOL that, when pressed for time, there could be a temptation to rely on KOL instead of going to the experts themselves. KOL was viewed by some in the IPC as almost too successful. "Junior staff are heavy users of this thing, and to some extent I think they look for more than we would ever want to have on KOL. KOL is designed to be only one element of the knowledge management program, not the be all and end all."

The foci of the knowledge management program were knowledge capture and knowledge sharing. A senior partner noted, "KOL is best viewed as a kind of passive collector of stuff that we're doing in pursuit of our mission, not a mission in itself. And I react negatively to the idea of preparing specific IC for KOL." The idea, Lucier explains, was not to create a new R&D effort but to mobilize the knowledge already being generated in the firm. A consultant added, "The starting point is always client work. So you start with presentations that are made to a client and things that were described to the client. You're not expected to just dream up a whole set of new ideas." Instead, the goal of having, for example, client reports systematically sanitized and contextualized, frameworks and approaches captured and disseminated, and public domain documents such as HR policies getting much greater visibility, was to ensure—to use the cliché of knowledge management—that Booz-Allen now knew what Booz-Allen knew.

Knowledge Management in Practice

The impact of the knowledge management program and the use of KOL varied considerably by level in the firm. Junior consultants were most likely to use the computer-based training facilities and the information about the firm as they tried to quickly socialize themselves in Booz-Allen. Senior Associates and Principals were more likely to use the system when preparing proposals for clients or starting a project. They used it to get ideas, to see previously used methodologies, to gather quals to list on the proposal, and so on. The intent here was to ensure that they were able to direct their time and attention in the most productive manner. A principal in the London office gave the following example of what the new approach to knowledge management helped him avoid:

> "One of the projects I did—this was before KOL—had a sales force management module to it. It took about four weeks for me to create the model which was still rough and, shortly after the assignment had finished, I discovered that somebody who was seated three desks away from me, had built a similar model six months previously. So pretty much what took me four–six weeks I could have done in a couple of days and I could have spent two weeks perfecting. That didn't happen because (a) it was difficult to get hold of, but also (b) the information was within the mind of people that had it and therefore it was individual property. I don't mean legally, I just mean in the connotation. So therefore the company didn't actually own it."

KOL could help reduce the amount of time consultants had to spend on the tedious parts of their work so that they could focus on the areas that brought the firm revenue. Lucier explained it this way:

> "What we're trying to do with this program is actually to channel peoples' creativity. In other words, what I'm telling you is I don't want you to build a new and better approach to do, say, business process reengineering, I really don't. I want you to use the existing approach—I don't want you to go create a new one. What I want you to do is I want you to be able to figure how to make change happen at your clients. That's where I want you to spend your time and worry about your creativity."

Another partner pointed out that KOL freed up time in another way, "when your documents were available for download over the system, you had to field far fewer telephone calls answering the same questions over and over about what you did and how."

Overall, it was clear that KOL had changed the way people in the junior ranks worked.

> "When I was an associate and a senior associate said, 'We've got to have a deck [presentation] for this client by Monday afternoon,' and then Monday afternoon came round and he said, 'Show me what you've got,' if I was to say I only have these three slides but I spent the first four hours checking KOL, my tail would've been chewed raw, and I would have been there till midnight writing. Whereas the reverse is now the case. If someone goes to an associate Monday afternoon and says, 'What have you got?' and he says 'Here's this framework I came up with' and he says, 'Well did you check KOL?' If the answer was 'No,' they would then be spending the evening being sure of what was on KOL."

The organizational change surrounding knowledge management has been successful at this level.

> "Partners use the system quite differently. For one thing, they use it less. The user statistics tracked by the knowledge team show that while two-thirds of the firm's professional staff log on to the system at least once in a given month, only about one third of partners do. Partners are net contributors to the system: they are more likely to post than to browse.
>
> They're not going to log on, they're just not going to. In general they're not going to spend their time looking through different documents on a topic to find the one they want. They're going to call their secretary or they're going to call the principal or senior associate on the team and say, 'You know, I remember that the post merger integration team put together a CEO-level discussion document on post merger integration. I'm about to go a client, can you go get that thing for me?'"

This was an issue of time, but it also reflected the fact that, generally speaking, the higher up you were in the organization, and the more senior, the better were your personal networks for getting information. Also at the partner level, KOL was intended more to provide know-who than know-how. KOL served as an enhanced yellow pages. It demonstrated who the firm's experts were in a given area and how to reach them.

What KOL was not designed to do was to replace those experts. As Torsilieri explained:

> "It's an entry point basically into something, into a content. And then if you really need to explore it you've got to get a hold of the expert and develop that relationship."

The danger of someone, especially a junior staff member, pulling a deck off KOL, changing a few words, and presenting it to a client was a worry shared by many. One principal noted:

> "Although you should be wary of just pulling up a document off KOL, giving it a light tailoring, and speaking of it at a client presentation, we all know of people who have done that. Best practice is that you use KOL as stimulation and to

get ideas at the start of a project about how you're going to run the project, what are the issues that other people have encountered, and the pitfalls that you can avoid. But I guess that there is the temptation when you're pressured by deadlines, to pull something off and if it suits—or if it's close to suiting—just run it."

Such fears had led some partners to restrict the level of detail they put on KOL to ensure they did not mislead anyone into thinking that all of the knowledge could be made explicit and downloaded. In this way they ensured that information did not get misused. Another principal told the following story of a close call.

"I was sitting in my office late at night, this was about a year and a half after KOL had been launched, and I had a couple of associates that were brand new, walk into my office. They said, We've heard you know a lot about how to organize *xyz*. And so we've pulled this stuff of yours off KOL, and we've got a proposal written that's due tomorrow, can you look at it? I flipped through this document which was on the face of it beautiful. Beautiful graphics, beautiful headlines, but it made no sense because they had cobbled together a bunch of stuff that they didn't understand. It was terrible. And the lesson from that is that the content that's out there is only as good as the peoples' ability to use it well."

In the end, the system worked: KOL generated a starting point and initiated a human contact. But what if the person hadn't been there at that hour?

The culture was considered to both help and hinder at this level. A principal put it this way:

"So, our junior people are very willing to share. And they're very willing to use each others' stuff because they're trying to develop themselves. By the time they become senior they're still willing to share because that's the kind of firm we are. But they're very resistant to using the expertise of others by the time they get to be senior partners, because what that really means is that you've got to use the physical being."

The resistance to reaching out was not fear of being rejected by someone who selfishly won't make time.

"In my experience, unless people are on vacation or in some very difficult situation, they would typically get back to you. Or at the very least point you in the direction of somebody else in their team."

Instead, it seemed to be a combination of not wanting to impose on others, take advantage of the norms of teamwork, and the healthy confidence in one's own ability that came with making partner in a firm like Booz-Allen.

"Partners still believe that they're smarter than the other guy and that they can figure it out. And if they were just given the deck they are thinking, 'yeah, there's some stuff that they've done, I'm sure that's helpful—just get me a couple of charts and then I'll be able to take it from there.' "

Stories like the following one were still relatively more common for junior members of the firm.

"Let me give you an example, a very recent history. I have a client who was recently promoted. He was a middle manager type a few years ago and he has now become Head of Marketing for a financial services company and I'm going to meet him for lunch. And he said 'I've got an issue about the cost of processing X and I'm thinking of using IT solutions.' So I e-mailed another colleague of mine who worked on the same assignment and who is a technology specialist and I said what do you know about this subject. He gave me a few things but he couldn't come to the meeting I'd set up. So he suggested another person. That other person knew another person who I didn't know existed. And within three e-mails that person is now coming to my meeting with a kit bag and potential solutions. The guy didn't know me from Adam."

Nonetheless, the norm at the junior levels was still to use KOL to deliver "know-what" rather than "know who."

One downside of this was that besides often being misleadingly incomplete, documents could become outdated on KOL. In response, BAH was making a concerted effort to periodically prune the system. Documents that were outdated, had been superseded, or had not received substantial use (which the IPC monitors) were pulled from the system, leaving behind as concise and accurate a statement on best practices within the firm as possible. The IPC organization, and particularly local knowledge managers, headed this effort. This was often a very demanding process—contributors to KOL may lose face if their documents were not pulled with tact. There was, of course, a natural tendency to resist. One IPC member recalled:

"We had actually gone through all of the intellectual capital that resided within our section of KOL. It was an incredibly painful process. We looked at usage statistics—if they hadn't been downloaded and they were either out of date because there was something more current or they were out of date just because the issue was no longer relevant to our clients, we went to them and said 'Listen, here's the things we think we can chop.' Either the authors or those content experts said 'Fine, get rid of it,' or they said 'No,' or 'Keep it on, but put a note in the abstract saying here's why it's still in the system.' This was sometimes legitimate but sometimes for political reasons or ego."

Thus far with KOL 2 there have been several cleanings carried out by individual practices (FHSPC recently removed about 15 percent of their documents, for example).

Looking Ahead

As Lucier reflected on the upcoming Beyond 2000 strategy process, it was clear that KOL had been a success story. But it was also clear to him that there were many views about the direction the knowledge management program should head. Some felt that radical steps, such as selling client's access to KOL were called for. Many felt that the biggest gains were behind them and that, as one principal put it, "we should just do more of the same and more aggressively, particularly in Europe." In part, this would mean enhancing the content on KOL. It was widely felt, for example, that what KOL was missing were the lessons learned not from individual projects—the system was excellent at capturing those—but across multiple projects.

> "The primary limitation of the system at the moment is the fact that it is based on project output. You've got lots of reasonably disparate pieces of information about different projects, but if you were interested in a topic, say, data warehousing, no one has synthesized all of the pieces of work we've done in that area and put it down in one place. You don't find that."

Another element of content that was missing was information about how the various projects and methodologies worked in practice for the client. You still had to contact the team who had done the work to get that context. Also, there was no facility for people to interactively comment on the pieces of IC to build up a database of opinions, experiences, modifications, and qualifications to what was on the system.

As the internet had taken hold and portal services such as Yahoo! and Excite had become more feature-laden, some in Booz-Allen would like to see KOL keep up with more advanced searching capability, personalization, online viewing of documents, and multimedia. Some were frustrated by the amount of time that it took for IC to appear on the system. KOL contrasted sharply to the Internet where things were posted quickly and meant to have a short shelf life. The IC on KOL was meant to hold its value over time and underwent careful quality checks. As a result, many consultants found themselves using the Internet more than the intranet when searching for up-to-date information.

Other voices in the firm argued, though, that the necessary changes required more than tweaking the existing technology: they required a change of behavior. Some said that KOL, which focused on knowledge capture and sharing, needed to be complemented with ways of increasing the amount and quality of creative thought in the firm. One principal used football (soccer) as a metaphor:

> "There are two ways of scoring in football: via open play or via a set piece. KOL is set piece activity. You arrange your forces, you look on KOL, you get the information, and you do something with it. Open play is when you're interacting with the client, you're talking with them, you're using the knowledge you've gained from KOL but at the same time you need to have an understanding and a grasp and KOL doesn't help you there. It gives you facts, but it doesn't necessarily explain them well. And when you're sitting with a client or sitting with your colleagues you get to detect that you've got some facts but you may not understand them."

The solution may be more interactive technologies—like KOLaborate, if it were to get a critical mass of users. It may mean lowering the quality controls in some areas of KOL to allow more voices and shorter lead times.

But some felt that the answer was not technology at all: it was getting people to bring the firm's experts into their projects. "That is the hurdle that we're facing," one core knowledge team member said, "How do we formalize something to encourage or force people to use the experts? It's the thing that we're starting to deal with now. I mean it's a problem that we know exists within the firm. We're trying to fix it."

Lucier and Torsilieri studied a broad range of knowledge management efforts in America and Europe and found that few delivered tangible bottom- line results. The reason, they postulated, was that too many were more concerned with feel-good, bottoms-up systems that enabled everyone to share their views. Too few focused on the much more profitable side of centrally developing best practice and using the knowledge management system to disseminate that best practice. In an age of information-overload, the real problem was often too much content, not too little.

It was a luxury to have these problems, Lucier knew, a testament to how far the firm had come already. And only one thing was certain: the discussions ahead would be intense and interesting.

UNIT 13 Managing People in the Global Company

Case 13–1

The Anderson School at UCLA

Federal Express, Inc. (A)

In December 1988, Fred Smith, Chief Executive Officer (CEO) of Federal Express, Inc. (Fedex), faced a decision which might dramatically increase the size and scope of his company. Tiger International, the parent company of the world's largest international freight company, Flying Tigers, had approached Smith with an offer to sell the whole company to Fedex. The proposition was tempting for Smith, who had modestly expanded Fedex internationally since 1984 via the purchase of several small international courier companies. The potential acquisition of Flying Tigers provided a tremendous opportunity for Fedex. Through this acquisition, Fedex would become the largest international cargo company in the world and would gain access to the highly coveted Asian market, where scarce landing rights were almost impossible to obtain.

However, the contemplated purchase of Flying Tigers was not without associated problems. Fedex would have to absorb 6,500 Tiger employees, most of whom were unionized, into its own nonunion organization; the number of foreign countries served would triple; and the number of foreign employees would double, straining Fedex's administrative staff and challenging the company's strong centralized organization. Moreover, none of Fedex's foreign acquisitions had yet become profitable, and major expansion of the company's international network could endanger its domestic operations by draining cash to subsidize foreign operations.

This case was prepared by Professor David Lewin with the collaboration of Ms. Debra Dalle, MBA student at the Anderson School at UCLA, and Mr. Charles W. Thomson, Vice President, International Personnel, Federal Express Corporation. Financial support was provided by the UCLA Institute of Industrial Relations, David Lewin, Director, and the UCLA Center for International Business Education and Research, José de la Torre, Director.

Smith needed to make his decision quickly, because other companies, including the industry's largest, United Parcel Service (UPS), also found Flying Tigers attractive and could well try to outbid Fedex. Acquisition of Flying Tigers by UPS almost certainly would mean that Fedex would never be able to get the routes necessary to becoming a viable force in the international market. However, Smith had not built Fedex by avoiding difficult decisions, and he would not be easily dissuaded from his goal of making Fedex an important player overseas.

Company History

On April 1, 1973, Fedex picked up its first packages for overnight delivery; there were six packages in all, four of them test packages. Three years passed before Fedex achieved profitability, during which time the company struggled to stay afloat. That initial struggle was instrumental in creating the strong corporate culture that continued to exist at Fedex. Smith and his company emphasized people and service (see Exhibit 1), and that commitment led to the company's startling growth in the decade following its creation (see Exhibit 2). By 1989, Fedex remained the largest enterprise in the United States built on venture capital, and one of the most successful. It employed 80,000 people and earned gross revenues in excess of $5 billion. Throughout its history, Fedex has been especially aggressive in the

EXHIBIT 1 Statement of Corporate Mission

Federal Express is committed to our People-Service-Profit philosophy. We will produce outstanding financial returns by providing totally reliable, competitively superior, global air-ground transportation of high priority goods and documents that require rapid, time-certain delivery. Equally important, positive control of each package will be maintained using real time electronic tracking and tracing systems. A complete record of each shipment and delivery will be presented with our request for payment. We will be helpful, courteous, and professional to each other and the public. We will strive to have a completely satisfied customer at the end of each transaction.

EXHIBIT 2 Federal Express Corporation: Selected Consolidated Financial Data
(Years ended May 31st; in millions, except as indicated)

	1988	1987	1986	1985	1984
Operating Results					
Revenues	3,882.8	3,178.3	2,573.2	2,015.9	1,436.3
Operating Expenses	3,503.4	2,813.6	2.229.2	1,757.3	1,247.6
Operating Income	379.5	364.7	344.0	258.6	188.8
Operating Income (expense)	(77.1)	(52.9)	(38.9)	(46.3)	(11.9)
Income before Taxes	302.3	311.9	305.1	212.3	176.8
Income Taxes	114.6	144.9	112.4	73.5	51.4
Income from Operations	187.7	167.0	192.7	138.7	125.4
Losses, Discontinued Operations	0.0	(232.5)	(60.8)	(62.7)	(10.0)
Net Income (loss)	187.7	(65.6)	131.8	76.1	115.4
Per Share					
Net Earnings Per Share	3.56	(1.27)	2.64	2.94	2.74
Average Shares Outstanding (thousands)	52,670	51,905	49,840	46,970	45,448
Financial Position					
Current Assets	630.0	507.5	613.3	423.1	328.1
Property and Equipment	2,231.9	1,861.4	1,551.8	1,346.0	1,112.6
Other Assets	146.6	130.6	111.3	130.3	85.0
Total Assets	3,008.5	2,499.5	2,276.4	1,899.5	1,525.8
Current Liabilities	572.1	503.7	431.9	316.9	255.9
Long-term Debt	838.7	744.9	561.7	607.5	435.2
Stockholders' Equity	1,330.7	1,078.9	1,091.7	812.3	717.7
Operating Data					
Average Daily Express Package Volume	877,543	794,392	550,306	406,049	263,385
Average Pounds Per Package	5.3	5.1	5.3	5.6	5.5
Average Revenue Per Pound ($)	3.10	3.33	3.40	3.45	3.80
Average Revenue Per Package ($)	16.32	16.97	17.92	19.19	21.03
Average Number of Employees	48,556	41,047	31,582	26,495	18,368
Aircraft Fleet at Year End					
McDonnell Douglas DC-10s	21	19	15	11	10
Boeing 727s	68	60	53	53	47
Cessna 208s	109	66	34	9	0
Fokker F- 27s	5	0	0	0	0
Vehicle Fleet at Year End	21,000	18,700	14,500	12,300	9,000

adoption and development of "progressive" human resource policies.

Fedex was the creation of Frederick W. Smith, son of a Southern entrepreneur. Smith learned to fly when he was 15, and his passion for aviation continued through his years at Yale in the early 1960s. Upon graduation, he went to Vietnam with the Marines, and gained his first managerial experience there, first as a platoon leader and later as a captain. Joining the military in the 1960s was a significant decision for Smith. Well educated young men with trust funds were not particularly well represented in the U.S. armed for.ces at that time, and Smith went against popular sentiment by volunteering for military service. In so doing, he fought side by side with working class men of varied races and backgrounds. Smith credited his military experience with the close attention he later gave to rank and file employees in his companies.

His first business venture was Arkansas Aviation Sales, a company based in Little Rock, which repaired and maintained private aircraft. His father took the company over in 1967, and Smith in turn took control of it when he returned from military service. Under Smith's direction, the company emphasized the sale of used corporate aircraft and de-emphasized aircraft maintenance, which resulted in major financial success. Nevertheless, Smith grew increasingly dissatisfied with the business and, in the early 1970s, began to look for another business which could benefit from his knowledge of the used aircraft market.

While at Yale, Smith wrote a term paper which outlined his belief that there was an under-served market for a timely and efficient high priority package delivery system. Though he received a "C" grade on that paper, Smith felt that his core idea was valid, and he began seriously to think about the possibility of starting a new air courier service company. At that time, the small package delivery business was shared by the industry leader, UPS, which primarily transported items that were not time-sensitive; Emery Air Freight, which specialized in overnight deliveries; the Parcel Post service offered by the U.S. Post Office; and several airlines, each of which accepted small packages for next-plane-out delivery. Overnight delivery services were expensive and virtually unknown to small businesses and individual consumers.

Smith was convinced that there was a large, untapped market for a reasonably priced, reliable package air delivery system. He rethought the concept of overnight delivery and took advantage of the latest technology to provide a completely new service to customers who had not previously considered overnight delivery. He conceived of Fedex primarily as a service company, and only secondarily as a transportation company; that is, customers would primarily be buying a service. The central components of the new system were as follows:

Ownership of airplanes. In 1973, when Fedex was established, there were no companies with aircraft dedicated to small package deliveries. Other courier services contracted with freight companies and commercial airlines on an as-needed basis to carry their packages from point to point. Ownership of airplanes allowed Smith to develop a hub and spoke system, making it far easier to control the operation from beginning to end. However, this also meant that volume was critical, since flying an airplane with only a few packages aboard was prohibitively expensive.

Computerized tracking of packages. No other delivery service was able to tell its customers exactly where a package was located at any point in the delivery process. The use of new technology provided Fedex with far more information about its operations than competitors had about theirs, and Fedex continuously used this information to streamline its operating processes. This monitoring also gave Fedex customers a feeling of security, which no other courier service could match.

100 percent quality. For Fedex this meant that every package had to be delivered on time and that every customer inquiry had to be handled in such a way that the customer was fully satisfied. Smith realized early in the development of the company that 98 percent, or even 99 percent, accuracy would leave thousands of customers dissatisfied, and would undermine the company's commitment to absolute reliability. This commitment to quality was still apparent in numerous aspects of Fedex's culture. For employees, the commitment to 100 percent quality meant that every individual action was important, since there was no margin for error. Employees were individually responsible for their parts of the 100 percent quality goal.

Commitment to employees. Smith believed that Fedex's primary sales force was its couriers, since they had the most contact with customers. Fedex recruited and trained its employees based on the premise that their individual efforts were critical to the success of the company, and with the promise that those efforts would be rewarded by attractive compensation packages, substantial opportunities for promotion, and lifetime employment. Unlike other courier service companies, Fedex rarely used contract employees and consequently was better able than its competitors to control the image and performance of its workforce. This high commitment to employees also provided Smith with a strong defense against the unionization of Fedex's work force, which he felt would limit the company's flexibility in making operational changes and reduce its control of the package delivery system.

Fedex struggled to survive during its first few years, and was close to bankruptcy more than once. Smith worked continuously to keep the business a going concern. He invested his inheritance in the company and borrowed money whenever and wherever he found it. Stories from the early days of Fedex have become part of the company's culture and illustrate the commitment of Smith and his employees to keeping the company in business. When Fedex ran short of cash and credit, pilots charged jet fuel on their personal credit cards to keep the airplanes flying. Not all of the stories told about the early years of Fedex reflect favorably on Smith, however. For example, Smith's sisters sued him for "raiding" the family trust fund to pay Fedex's bills.

Smith also lobbied the U.S. Congress hard to change FAA regulations which prohibited Fedex from flying the large airplanes that were required to provide the efficiencies necessary to the company's survival. The commercial air carriers fought just as hard to prevent these changes in FAA regulations. Smith won a major battle in 1977, with the Congress's passage of a domestic all-cargo deregulation statute. Without that legislation, Fedex could not have achieved rapid growth rates or attained its present size. While Smith was fighting to keep the company alive, Fedex undertook numerous advertising campaigns designed to create customer awareness of the new service it was offering. The company's motto, "Absolutely, positively, overnight!", began to catch on with the public, and in 1976, the company posted its first profit.

Fedex's profits grew rapidly during the early to mid-1980s (see Exhibit 2), but profitability declined following the company's introduction of "Zapmail" in 1983. A point-to-point fax service, Zapmail was subsequently rendered obsolete by the introduction and diffusion of inexpensive fax machines during the late 1980s. Zapmail required a large capital investment in specialized equipment; when Fedex wrote off that equipment in 1987, it suffered a substantial loss. By 1988, however, Fedex had achieved a 50 percent share of the overnight mail and package delivery market and experienced its most profitable year. Also by 1988, Fedex employed 50,000 people, roughly 10 percent of whom worked outside the United States.

Operations

Fedex offered express delivery of packages up to 70 pounds in weight to most of the world. In the United States, such packages would be delivered by 10:30 A.M. the next day, and the company was presently attempting to institute overnight delivery to most of the world. This delivery system was based on a hub and spoke configuration. The process started when a local courier either picked up a package from a customer or the customer delivered the package to a Fedex drop-off location or office. Usually customer pick-ups must be made by 5:00 P.M. and drop-offs by 6:00 P.M. for next day delivery. The packages were then delivered to the local airports where Fedex airplanes transported them to appropriate hubs. During the flights, employees began electronic package sorting, and this continued after the aircraft were unloaded at the hubs. Typically a Fedex airplane was on the ground for about three hours during which time it was reloaded with packages bound for its original take-off point; the aircraft then made the return trip. Fedex trucks waited at the airports to load packages for final sorting into individual courier routes. This process was a 24-hour-a-day operation requiring both full-time and part-time employees.

Throughout the operation, packages were tracked by the bar-codes imprinted on their labels. Individual couriers carried bar-code readers with which they checked packages in and out as they were transferred. These bar-codes were connected to computers accessed by customer service representatives, who could then inform customers about where their respective packages were in the system at virtually any point in time. In addition to delivering packages, couriers carried Fedex shipping materials and labels preprinted with customer names, addresses, and account numbers to expedite the consignment of packages and ensure efficient package handling.

Fedex continually evaluated its operations with a view toward making the system more efficient. Employees were encouraged to offer suggestions for improving their jobs and, more broadly, operating processes. Individual customer service representatives and couriers were given autonomy to make on-the-spot decisions to deal with operating problems and customer concerns. However, Fedex's corporate office in Memphis, Tennessee, made all policy decisions and provided for standardized employee training programs, performance evaluation procedures and operating processes. The company slogan, "Make It Purple!" (a reference to Fedex's unusual purple and orange color scheme), exemplified Fedex's emphasis on companywide adherence to standardized operating policies and practices.

The success of Fedex was built on its commitment to the motto, "People–Service–Profits." Fred Smith understood that without the dedication of its employees, Fedex could not deliver on its promise of high quality service to customers. Smith underscored this point in a Fedex policy statement:

> "Our customers' perception of quality is critical. A positive interaction adds value—a negative experience can be devastating. And the kicker is, we can't recall a bad experience with a customer like a manufacturer can recall a

faulty part, fix it, and put it back into service so it works right the second time. So in trying to understand the service side of quality, one must necessarily grasp the significance of the human side of quality."

Competition

Fred Smith had started Fedex in the belief that there was a market for overnight delivery service which was not being adequately provided by existing companies. However, by the 1980s and following Fedex's success, a number of existing and new carriers began to compete directly with Fedex for dominance of the overnight package delivery business.

United Parcel Service. UPS was the oldest and largest private delivery company in the United States and remained the nation's largest ground package delivery service. In 1986, its average daily volume of delivered packages was 8.3 million. UPS was a privately held company, and its employees had been unionized since 1927. The company delivered packages to virtually every location in the United States and had local operations in many countries. Until 1991, packages had to be dropped off at a UPS facility for shipment unless the sender had established a UPS account and paid a weekly fee for regular site pickups. UPS had been slow to integrate computerized tracking system and company-owned aircraft into its operation and had often contracted for these services. Although it had offered its two-day "Blue-Label" service since 1953, UPS did not aggressively market this service until the late 1970s. Furthermore, the company did not offer an overnight delivery service until 1982.

United States Postal Service. The U.S. Postal Service (USPS) instituted its overnight "Express Mail" service in 1978; by 1986, it was handling 40 million pieces per day. The USPS offered attractive prices, and outgoing express mail could be picked up by the regular mail carrier for next day delivery, dropped off at a local post office, or deposited in special post office boxes located in many commercial areas. Employees were civil servants who were subject to government regulations and compensation programs. Individual packages handled by the USPS could not be tracked until and unless they failed to arrive at their destination.

Emery Air Freight. Emery was the leading air-freight forwarder at the time that Fedex entered the package delivery market in 1973. Most of Emery's shipments were handled through contracts with airlines, freight companies and local delivery services, and it had limited international exposure. Any business could call Emery for local pick-up of packages without having established a prior account. The service was relatively expensive and there was minimal tracking of packages. In an effort to counter Fedex, Emery instituted regular overnight service with competitive pricing in 1978. By 1986, Emery's daily volume was 42,000 pieces. One year later, Emery merged with Purolator, a company which specialized in ground package delivery. Following the merger, the new company accounted for 12 percent of the total overnight delivery market in the United States.

Airborne Freight, Inc. Airborne began in business as a traditional freight forwarder, much like Emery. However, it was quicker than Emery to respond to the threat posed by Fedex and quicker to adopt Fedex's practices of using computerized package tracking, owning its own aircraft, and offering on-call package pick-up. Airborne was involved in both domestic and international delivery services. By 1986, its express service handled 105,000 pieces per day.

Commercial Airlines. Most U.S. commercial airlines had offered some form of next-plane-out, small package delivery service whereby packages were shipped from airport to airport on regularly scheduled flights. These carriers had always sold cargo space on commercial flights, but their cargo operations were not set up to handle priority packages. Further, it often took several hours, sometimes days, to retrieve cargo that had been shipped on particular flights. Various small package delivery services contracted with local delivery companies to provide door-to-door service if customers did not want to pick up or drop off packages at airports. However, the cost of these services had traditionally been high, and package tracking capabilities had been limited. Most airlines stopped marketing these services during the mid-1980s. Although still available, these services were usually assigned very low priority by commercial air carriers.

Human Resource Policies

The strong emphasis placed on human resources at Fedex was one of the company's most notable features, and the personnel function, headed by Senior Vice President James Perkins, was one of only four staff functions that reported directly to the CEO (see Exhibit 3 for a diagram of

EXHIBIT 3 Federal Express Corporation: Corporate Organization Chart

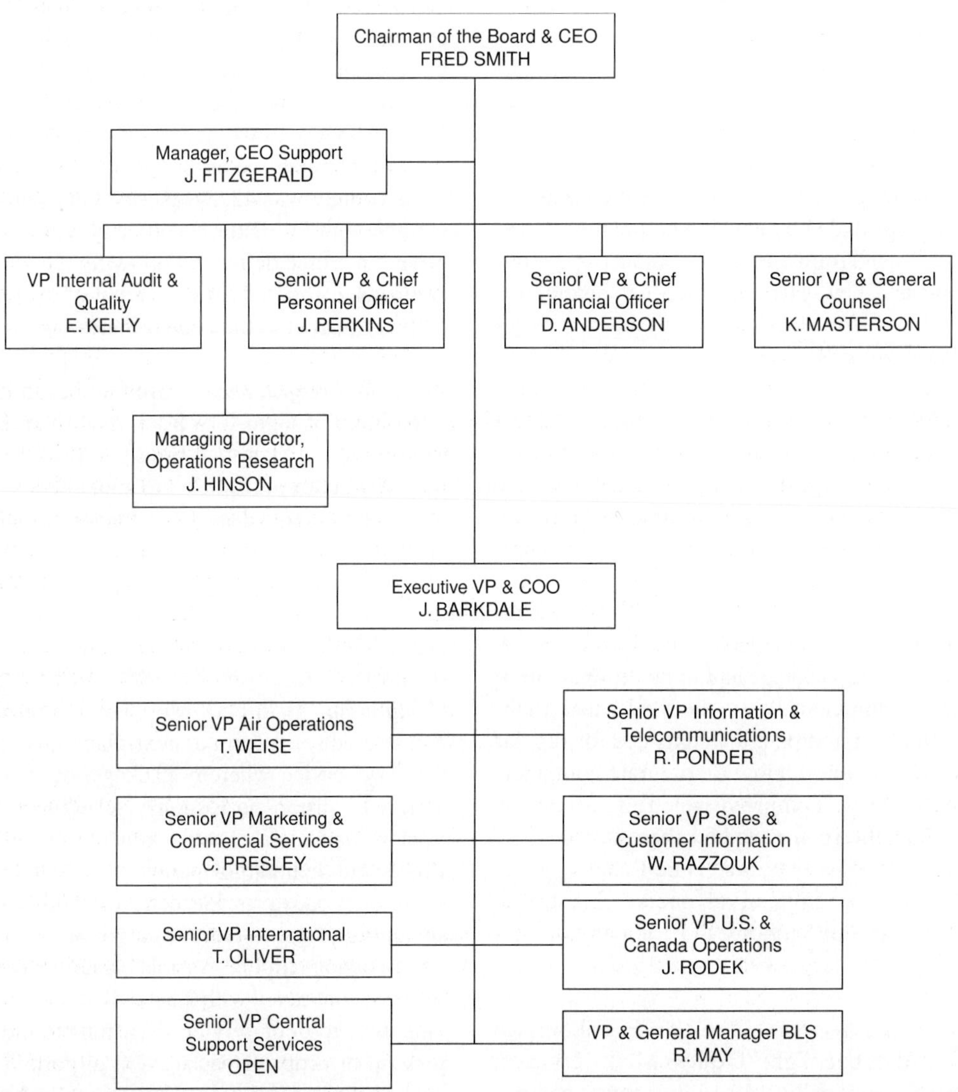

Fedex's organization chart). Fedex continually evaluated and revised its human resource policies, yet these policies continued to reflect the strong culture which Fred Smith imparted to the company on its founding in 1973. Many companies claim that "people are our most important resource," but relatively few companies actually formulated policies on the basis of this belief. Fred Smith commented:

> "The problem of consistently keeping people first is hard work. Putting people first in every action, every planning process, every business decision, requires an extraordinary commitment from every manager and every employee. Every company says it's a people company. Fedex's challenge is to infuse that philosophy with action. Putting this somewhat ideal philosophy into practice means we must look for a multitude of ways to replace talk with action."

Virtually every Fedex statement of company policy, list of instructions, or explanation of operations began with a reference to people. Rather than selecting one or two "progressive" human resource policies—such as management by objectives or employee involvement and participation—as touchstones of the company's human resource strategy, Fedex employed a portfolio of human resource policies which it believed fit closely with its overall business strategy and objectives. Among these human resource policies were the following.

Employee recruitment and training. Fedex searched the labor market for energetic recruits who possessed entrepreneurial spirit. This was true for all types of new hires, ranging from couriers to pilots. Most new employees were given three months of orientation training, which included job-specific skills as well as immersion in company policies and procedures. Training was continuous, though dependent in part on an employee's career goals. Most employees received several weeks of formal training each year, both to learn about new procedures and technology and to acquire and hone the skills necessary for advancement within Fedex. Leadership training for supervisors, managers, and executives was provided on a regular basis and was regarded as one of the key components of the company's portfolio of training programs.

No lay-off policy. Lifetime employment was an unusual (and declining) practice among U.S. companies, but Fedex followed a no-layoff policy in order to retain its experienced workforce, increase employee loyalty, and reduce the incentives for employees to become unionized. This policy was severely tested during the economic recession of the early 1980s, but no layoffs took place despite another company policy authorizing layoffs in the case of extreme financial constraints. This fact had become one of the often-cited internal stories about Fedex's culture and it gave credence to the concept of lifetime employment. However, there was some flexibility in this policy in that Fedex employed temporary as well as casual "on-call" employees who did not have lifetime employment. Stated differently, lifetime employment applied to the core work force, but not the peripheral work force at Fedex.

Promotion from within. At Fedex, most supervisory and managerial positions were filled from the existing workforce—that is, from within. This feature of the company's internal labor market was used by Fedex to attract and recruit job applicants, and the company believed that it was especially helpful in attracting high quality recruits. Promotion from within was also intended to insure that those who were promoted to supervisory and managerial position would understand the problems of their subordinates and would be thoroughly familiar with the company's culture.

Grievance procedures and voice. The "Guaranteed Fair Treatment" (GFT) procedure and the "Survey-Feedback-Action" (SFA) plan were two formal mechanisms through which employees could express their concerns and dissatisfaction to the management of Fedex (see Exhibits 4 and 5). The GFT was a progressive three-step process through which employees could file written appeals and was open to any employee who felt that he or she had been treated unfairly; this included supervisory and management personnel. Most written complaints were resolved at the first level, but approximately 650 complaints annually would go to the next two higher levels for settlement. The SFA was an annual survey of employee opinions about workplace and organizational practices which required managerial responses in the form of action plans to address employee concerns. In addition, Fedex has an "open door" philosophy which encouraged employee communication with management. All of these policies were designed in part to obviate the need for unions and unionized grievance procedures.

Compensation and financial participation. Fedex's compensation levels were competitive with those of other firms in its industry, though it attempted to stay a bit ahead of median pay rates in the labor markets and communities in which it operated. Annual compensation incorporated both fixed and variable components. Pay increases were based in part on changes in labor market rates and in part on individual merit, as determined through annual performance appraisals. Further, all full-time employees were eligible to participate in the company's profit-sharing plan. Thus, Fedex's compensation philosophy could be said to reflect a combination of pay for inputs and pay for outputs.

Performance appraisal. At Fedex, each employee's job performance was evaluated twice annually by his or her supervisor. An employee who received a negative performance evaluation or who had violated company policies must follow a "performance improvement program," which was jointly agreed to by both the employee and his or her manager. The purpose of the program was to enhance employee job performance and/or correct substandard behavior. The last stage of this process

EXHIBIT 4 Federal Express Corporation: Sample "Survey-Feedback-Action" Form

How To Answer: Read each statement carefully. Then to the right of each statement mark which best expresses your agreement or disagreement with the item. Mark only one answer to each item, and remember to respond to all items. Remember that "workgroup" means all the persons who report to the same manager as you do regardless of job title.

1	I feel free to tell my manager what I think.	SA*	A*	AD*	D*	SD*	U*
2	My manager lets me know what's expected of me.	SA	A	AD	D	SD	U
3	Favoritism is not a problem in my work group.	SA	A	AD	D	SD	U
4	My manager helps us find ways to do our jobs better.	SA	A	AD	D	SD	U
5	My manager is willing to listen to my concerns.	SA	A	AD	D	SD	U
6	My manager asks for my ideas about things affecting our work.	SA	A	AD	D	SD	U
7	My manager lets me know when I've done a good job.	SA	A	AD	D	SD	U
8	My manager treats me with respect and dignity.	SA	A	AD	D	SD	U
9	My manager keeps me informed about things I need to know.	SA	A	AD	D	SD	U
10	My manager lets me do my job without interfering.	SA	A	AD	D	SD	U
11	My manager's boss gives us the support we need.	SA	A	AD	D	SD	U
12	Upper management (directors and above) let us know what the company is trying to accomplish.	SA	A	AD	D	SD	U
13	Upper management (directors and above) pay attention to ideas and suggestions from people at my level.	SA	A	AD	D	SD	U
14	I have confidence in the fairness of management.	SA	A	AD	D	SD	U
15	I can be sure of a job as long as I do a good job.	SA	A	AD	D	SD	U
16	I am proud to work for Federal Express	SA	A	AD	D	SD	U
17	Working for Federal Express will probably lead to the kind of future I want.	SA	A	AD	D	SD	U
18	I think Federal Express does a good job for our customers.	SA	A	AD	D	SD	U
19	All things considered, working for Federal Express is a good deal for me.	SA	A	AD	D	SD	U
20	I am paid fairly for the kind of work I do.	SA	A	AD	D	SD	U
21	Our benefit programs seem to meet most of my needs.	SA	A	AD	D	SD	U
22	Most people in my workgroup cooperate with each other to get the job done.	SA	A	AD	D	SD	U
23	There is cooperation between my workgroup and other groups in Federal Express.	SA	A	AD	D	SD	U
24	In my work environment we generally use safe work practices.	SA	A	AD	D	SD	U
25	Rules and procedures do not interfere with how well I am able to do my job.	SA	A	AD	D	SD	U
26	I am able to get the supplies or other resources I need to do my job.	SA	A	AD	D	SD	U
27	I have enough freedom to do my job well.	SA	A	AD	D	SD	U
28	My workgroup is involved in activities to improve service to our group's customers.	SA	A	AD	D	SD	U
29	The concerns identified by my workgroup during the last year's SFA feedback session have been satisfactorily addressed.	SA	A	AD	D	SD	U

*Scale: SA=Strongly agree; A=Agree; AD=Sometimes agree/disagree; D=Disagree; SD=Strongly Disagree; U=Undecided/Don't know.

EXHIBIT 5 Federal Express Corporation: Guaranteed Fair Treatment Procedure

We have found that in an open environment, people are more apt to take part, offer suggestions for improvement, question decisions and surface concerns. The Guaranteed Fair Treatment Procedure (GFTP), our in-house avenue for airing grievances, is one way we listen to our people. Every week the CEO, COO, Chief Personnel Officer and two Senior Vice Presidents, on a rotating basis, review grievances under Step 3 of GFTP.

The Guaranteed Fair Treatment Procedure affirms your right to appeal any eligible issue through a process of systematic review by progressively higher levels of management. Though the outcome is not assured to be in your favor, your right to participate within the guidelines of the process is guaranteed.

The Guaranteed Fair Treatment Procedure is a three-step process, which require specific actions to be performed by specific individuals within a designated time frame. The steps are identified as follows:

1. MANAGEMENT REVIEW
   - **Complainant** submits written complaint to a member of management (manager, senior manager, or managing director) within 7 calendar days of the occurrence of the eligible issue.
   - **Manager, Senior Manager, and Managing Director** review all relevant information; hold a telephone conference and/or meeting with the complainant; make decision to either uphold, modify, or overturn management's action; and communicate their decision in writing to complainant and personnel matrix.
2. OFFICER REVIEW
   - **Complainant** submits written complaint to an officer (Vice President or Senior Vice President) of the Division within 7 calendar days of Step 1 decision.
   - **Vice President and Senior Vice President** review all relevant information; conduct additional investigation, when necessary; make decision to either uphold, overturn, modify management's action, or initiate a Board of Review; and communicate their decision in writing to complainant with copy to personnel matrix and the complainant's management.
3. EXECUTIVE REVIEW
   - **Complainant** submits written complaint within 7 calendar days of the Step 2 decision to the Employee Relations Department who investigates and prepares the GFTP case file for Appeals Board review.
   - **Appeals Board** reviews all relevant information; makes decision to either uphold, overturn or modify senior management's decision, or take other appropriate action; responds in writing to complainant within 3 calendar days of the decision with copy to personnel matrix and the complainant's chain of command.

consisted of a one day paid leave during which time the employee stayed home and considered whether or not to remain with the company. If the employee decided to stay with Fedex, he or she must present a plan to the appropriate supervisor outlining the steps to be taken to improve job performance. Fedex also maintained a Leadership Evaluation Awareness Process (LEAP) for the purpose of identifying candidates for management positions with the company. The assessments derived from this program were used to fill middle and senior management vacancies, including positions from which Fedex executives eventually retired.

Recognition. In addition to maintaining certain incentive compensation programs, Fedex recognized outstanding employees through such programs as the "Bravo Zulu" award. Based on a U.S. Navy flag which means "well-done," this award was given to employees in recognition of their special efforts, particularly in the areas of teamwork and cooperation. The award included "Bravo Zulu" certificates, small cash payments, and vouchers that could be used for restaurants and tickets to theatrical or sporting events. Supervisors may confer such awards whenever they felt that certain employees had rendered exceptional performance.

Communications. Fedex employees were distributed throughout numerous locations in the United States. The company's communications programs were designed to promote a feeling among employees that they were part of a unified team even while being geographically separated. Fedex maintained its own television network and transmited daily broadcasts to each of its distribution centers in the United States. These broadcasts were also videotaped and played back in employee cafeterias during work breaks. Broadcast messages included the previous night's service record, the company's stock performance, workplace safety updates, and other items. Fred Smith often appeared on the company's television network, particularly when Fedex had been in the news. In this way, employees were made to feel that they got most of their information about the company from internal rather than external media sources.

Expansion Opportunities and Issues

Although Fedex grew rapidly in the domestic market during the 1970s and 80s, to the point where it became a major business success story, a critical question facing the company in late 1988 was whether or not it could expand internationally while preserving its impressive service record. Arnetta Green, Manager of International Personnel at Fedex, expressed her concern about this matter:

> "We are still learning how to work with the different countries in which we have offices; I can't imagine how we will cope with double the non-U.S. employees we already have. And, we have had very little exposure to Asian countries. I don't know how we can translate our training materials into Asian languages without at least a year's lead time, and it doesn't look like we will get more than a few months."

Charles Thomson, at the time Vice President for Human Resources of Flying Tigers, expressed concern about how unionized pilots in his company, who were accustomed to exercising considerable autonomy, might react to the more highly structured and centralized Fedex organization.

> "By and large, the pilots of Flying Tigers were angry at the prospect of the merger. The company had just enjoyed its most profitable year, and many pilots felt that, instead of rewarding the employees, management was selling them off."

Despite these concerns, Fred Smith was convinced that Fedex should seriously pursue additional acquisitions in order to launch the next phase of the company's development. Smith believed that if Fedex chose not to become a major global business player, the company's share of the international market would erode and its core domestic business would increasingly be threatened by stronger, global competitors. However, Smith wondered if acquiring Flying Tigers was the best way to achieve international expansion and future business success.

Case 13–2

Federal Express, Inc. (B)

On August 7, 1989, Federal Express Corporation (Fedex) completed a long-awaited merger with Flying Tigers. Fedex had made the decision to acquire Flying Tigers only three weeks after learning that the company was for sale, in December 1988. The acquisition added 6,500 employees to the Fedex payroll, expanded the company's fleet of cargo-carrying jet aircraft by 39 and, most importantly, included international landing rights which would provide Fedex with access to previously unavailable world markets.

Fedex executives expected the merger to go smoothly. After all, their company was one of the great success stories in American business, the "darling of Wall Street," whose very name had become synonymous with overnight delivery. In contrast, Flying Tigers steadily lost money during the early and mid 1980s, and the business faced significant financial challenges if a buyer could not be found. Moreover, Fedex executives thought that Flying Tiger employees would be grateful to be rescued by such a strong, high-profile company as Fedex. However, only two years after the acquisition, Fedex's stock price fell for the first time in its history and the company's declining earnings were primarily attributed to the acquisition of Flying Tigers and to subsequent international expansion. It appeared that Fedex had failed to assess the complexity of its new organizational arrangements to the point that the company's motto, "People–Service–Profit," was called into question.

International Expansion

Fedex began its expansion into the overseas delivery market in 1984 with the purchase of Gelco Express, a courier firm based in Minneapolis, which served 84 countries. Other acquisitions followed, primarily in Eu-

---

This case was prepared by Professor David Lewin with the collaboration of Ms. Debra Dalle, MBA Student at the Anderson School at UCLA, and Mr. Charles W. Thomson, Vice President, International Personnel, Federal Express Corporation. Financial support was provided by the UCLA Institute of Industrial Relations, David Lewin, Director, and the UCLA Center for International Business Education and Research, José de la Torre, Director.

rope and Asia, although the worldwide shortage of landing slots restricted Fedex's access to the international market. Fedex did not become profitable in the United States until it reached a daily volume of 25,000 packages, and Fedex executives believed that the company needed to achieve similar volumes in each country that it served in order to be profitable in those locations. However, it could not do so without having reliable, efficient services to market to its customers. Fedex's commitment to international expansion thus meant that it would have to subsidize foreign operations until it obtained the desired business volumes.

The acquisition of Flying Tigers increased Fedex's cargo fleet by 25 percent and vastly enhanced the company's access to foreign markets, especially in Asia, which had provided Flying Tigers with two-thirds of its revenue. Prior to the acquisition, Fedex operated in 27 countries where it employed 14,000 people; following the acquisition of Flying Tigers and subsequent purchases of several local delivery companies, the number of countries served by Fedex increased to 108, and the number of employees working abroad increased to 20,000. Although Fedex's revenues from international operations doubled in the two years following the merger, operating losses from foreign operations increased to more than $200 million annually by 1991. Fedex's net earnings declined from $184.5 million in fiscal 1989, to $115.8 million in fiscal 1990, and to $5.8 million in fiscal 1991 (see Exhibit 1). Further, Fedex's profit projections for the early 1990s had been revised downward, and senior Fedex executives were uncertain about when, if at all, international profitability would be achieved.

Foreign Operations

With the acquisition of Flying Tigers' landing rights, Fedex was able to create an international hub and spoke network based on the system that had proven successful in the United States. Fedex has hubs in Brussels, Frankfurt, Anchorage, and, perhaps most important, Tokyo. The basic operating system was the same: couriers picked up packages from customers or customers dropped them off at Fedex offices, the packages were transferred to central sorting facilities located near airports, the sorting of packages began and continued on flights to the appropriate hubs, and packages were routed to their destinations and delivered by couriers to customers. Exhibit 2 shows an organization chart for Fedex's international operations.

Nevertheless, it was more difficult to implement a hub and spoke system globally than domestically because geographical distances were too great to allow every package to go through a single hub. The number of possible routes through which a package could transit increased dramatically with additional service areas. Fedex had limited operations and facilities in many areas of the world, so that a single courier had to cover a wider area than was typically necessary in the United States. In addition, holidays abroad occurred on different dates than in the United States, other countries often celebrated more official holidays than the United States, and business hours varied widely abroad and were often different from those customary in the United States.

To illustrate, Fedex tried to cut off package deliveries at 5:00 P.M. in foreign countries, yet in Spain and in certain other countries the business day normally extended to 8:00 P.M. Most Europeans were not as time-sensitive as U.S. customers, and paying extra for a 10:30 A.M. delivery was not as important to European as to U.S. businesses. Further, modes of customary transportation varied widely abroad. Fedex vans, which were a familiar sight in U.S. cities had to be supplemented by (Fedex) motorcycles in Singapore. More importantly, reliance on air transport, which characterized Fedex's entrance into the U.S. market, might not be appropriate in all regions. In Asia and Africa, for example, a U.S.-type delivery system may work well because those regions were geographically similar to the U.S. In Europe, however, distances were shorter and trucking was the preferred method of transport. In fact, Europe probably had the best road and train systems in the world. Fedex was not established as a trucking company, and had not devoted much attention to operational efficiencies in trucking. These examples illustrate the challenges Fedex faced to adapt its operations (and work practices) to foreign locations.

Fedex's culture, human resource policies, and operations were closely integrated in the United States. The company had a commitment to 100 percent on-time delivery and could only achieve this goal if it had full cooperation from its employees. With international expansion, full employee cooperation or high commitment had been more difficult to achieve and, as a result, efficiency and quality of service had suffered. Fedex's domestic strategy had centered on complete control of the delivery system. In the United States, Fedex employees and equipment handled every component of the delivery process—a process that was continually monitored and modified to increase efficiency.

EXHIBIT 1 **Federal Express Corporation: Selected Consolidated Financial Data**
(Years ended May 31st; in millions, except as indicated)

	1991	1990	1989	1988
Operating Results				
Revenues	7,688.3	7,015.1	5,167.0	3,882.8
Operating Expenses	7,408.5	6,601.5	4,742.5	3,503.4
Operating Income	279.8	413.6	424.4	379.5
Other Income (expense)	(238.9)	(195.2)	(126.1)	(77.1)
Income before Taxes	40.9	218.4	298.3	302.3
Income Taxes	35.0	102.7	131.9	114.6
Income from Operations	5.9	115.8	166.5	187.7
Other Income (loss)	0.0	0.0	18.1	0.0
Net Income (loss)	5.9	115.8	184.6	187.7
Per Share				
Net Earnings Per Share ($)	0.11	2.18	3.18	3.56
Average Shares Outstanding (thousands)	53,350	53,161	52,272	52,670
Financial Position				
Current Assets	1,282.8	1,315.4	1,100.1	630.0
Property and Equipment	3,624.0	3,566.3	3,431.8	2,231.9
Other Assets	765.6	793.3	761.5	146.6
Total Assets	5,672.5	5,675.1	5,293.4	3,008.5
Current Liabilities	1,493.8	1,240.2	1,089.1	572.1
Long-term Debt	1,826.8	2,148.1	2,138.9	838.7
Stockholders' Equity	1,668.6	1,649.2	1,493.5	1,330.7
Business Segment Information				
U.S. Domestic Revenue	5,057.8	4,784.9	4,144.8	n.a.
International Revenue	2,630.5	2,230.2	1,022.1	n.a.
U.S. Domestic Operating Income	671.2	608.1	467.1	n.a.
International Operating Losses*	(391.4)	(194.5)	(42.7)	n.a.
U.S. Domestic Identifiable Assets	4,032.1	3,798.4	3,007.3	n.a.
International Identifiable Assets	1,640.1	1,876.7	2,286.1	n.a.
Total Worldwide	5,672.2	5,675.1	5,293.4	
Operating Data				
Average Daily Express Package Volume	1,309,973	1,233,628	1,059,882	877,543
Average Pounds Per Package	5.5	5.3	5.4	5.3
Average Revenue Per Pound ($)	3.11	3.14	3.04	3.10
Average Revenue Per Package ($)	17.08	16.53	16.28	16.32
Airfreight Average Daily Pounds	2,880,106	3,310,494	4,019,353	n.a.
Average Revenue Per Pound ($)	1.17	1.12	1.06	n.a.
Average Number of Employees	81,711	75,102	58,136	48,556
Aircraft Fleet at Year End				
Boeing 747s	18	19	21	0
McDonnell Douglas MD-11s	1	0	0	0
McDonnell Douglas DC-10s	27	26	24	21
McDonnell Douglas DC-8s	0	6	6	0
Boeing 737-200s	0	0	0	0
Boeing 727s	149	130	106	68
Cessna 208s	194	184	147	109
Fokker F-27s	26	19	7	5
Vehicle Fleet at Year End	32,800	31,000	28,900	21,000

*Includes a $121 million charge in 1991 related to restructuring of U.K. operations.

EXHIBIT 2 Federal Express Corporation: International Operations

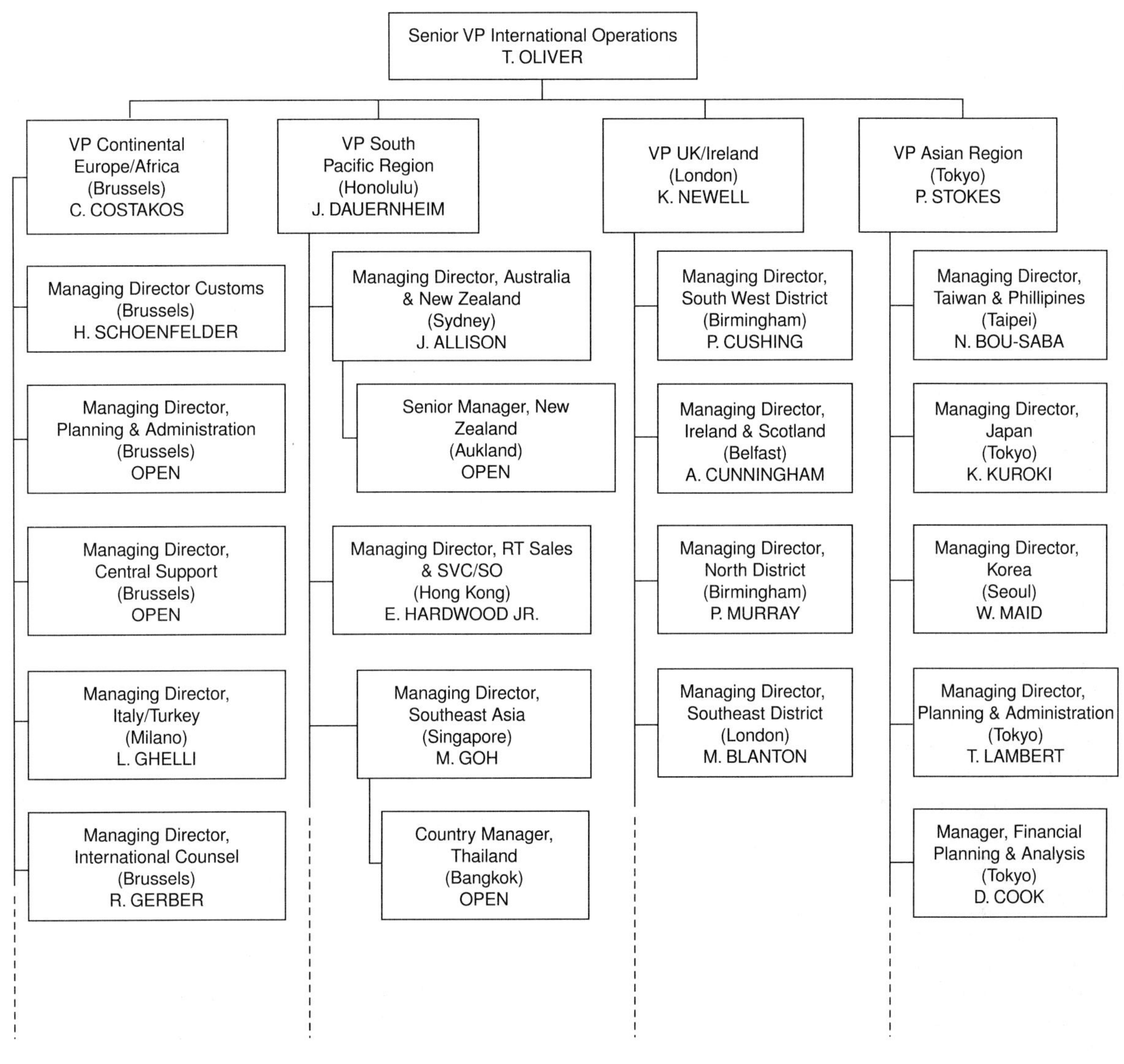

In contrast, Fedex's international strategy was based on the acquisition of existing companies and the export of domestic policies to foreign locations. The tendency had been to buy local delivery companies, primarily for their road authority or delivery system, with little concern for the kind of products being delivered by those companies. Fedex now found itself with vehicles and drivers accustomed to carrying pianos or produce, rather than packages, in limited geographical areas. Fedex wanted to establish itself abroad as quickly as possible by buying existing local companies, but may have underestimated the difficulty of integrating so many disparate companies into one integrated system. Thus, Fedex found the export of its domestic business strategy and operating policies to be much more difficult than originally anticipated by senior management.

Despite the acquisition of Flying Tigers, Fedex had neither sufficient aircraft nor landing rights in foreign

EXHIBIT 2 continued

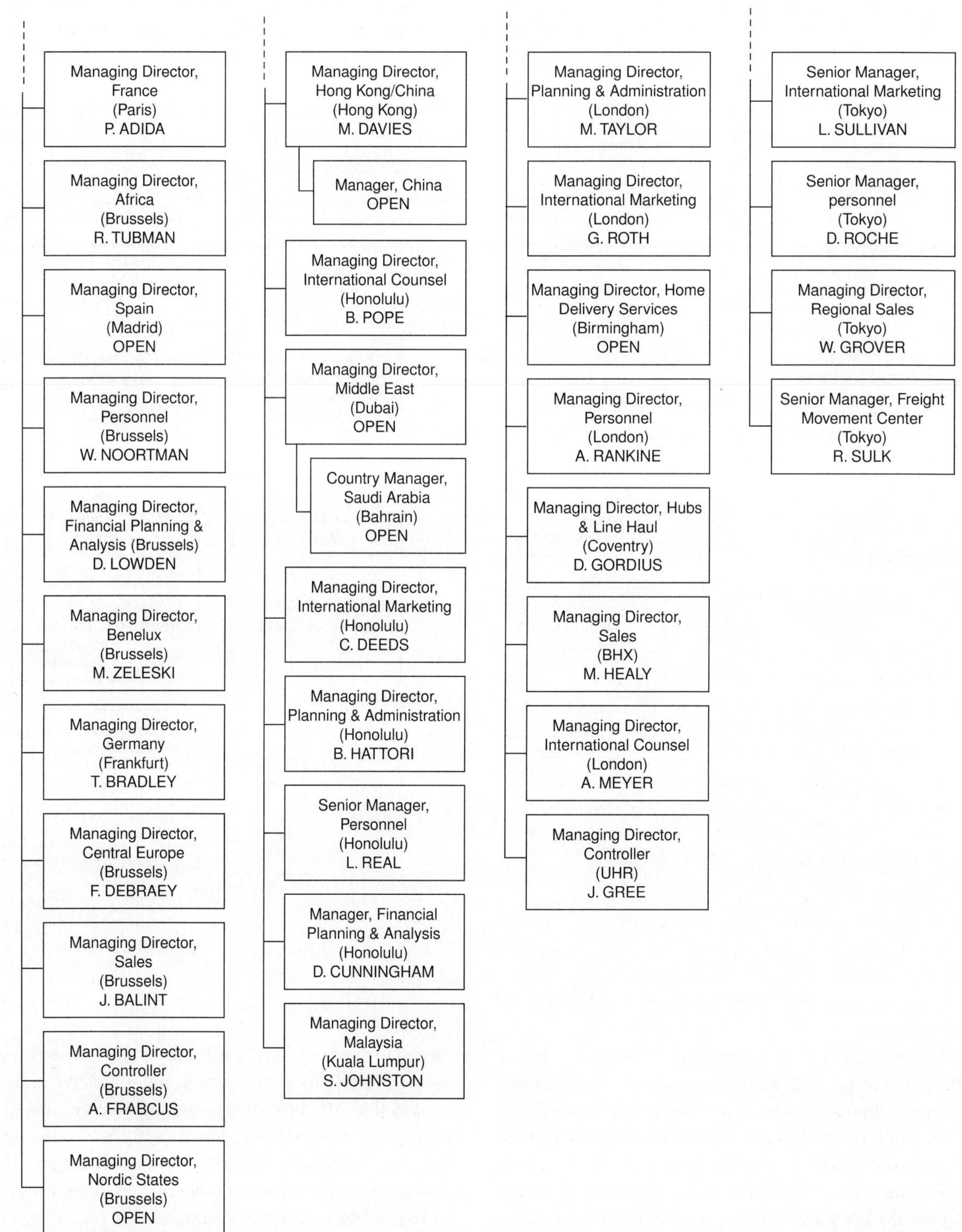
Managing Director, France (Paris) P. ADIDA
Managing Director, Africa (Brussels) R. TUBMAN
Managing Director, Spain (Madrid) OPEN
Managing Director, Personnel (Brussels) W. NOORTMAN
Managing Director, Financial Planning & Analysis (Brussels) D. LOWDEN
Managing Director, Benelux (Brussels) M. ZELESKI
Managing Director, Germany (Frankfurt) T. BRADLEY
Managing Director, Central Europe (Brussels) F. DEBRAEY
Managing Director, Sales (Brussels) J. BALINT
Managing Director, Controller (Brussels) A. FRABCUS
Managing Director, Nordic States (Brussels) OPEN
Managing Director, Hong Kong/China (Hong Kong) M. DAVIES
Manager, China OPEN
Managing Director, International Counsel (Honolulu) B. POPE
Managing Director, Middle East (Dubai) OPEN
Country Manager, Saudi Arabia (Bahrain) OPEN
Managing Director, International Marketing (Honolulu) C. DEEDS
Managing Director, Planning & Administration (Honolulu) B. HATTORI
Senior Manager, Personnel (Honolulu) L. REAL
Manager, Financial Planning & Analysis (Honolulu) D. CUNNINGHAM
Managing Director, Malaysia (Kuala Lumpur) S. JOHNSTON
Managing Director, Planning & Administration (London) M. TAYLOR
Managing Director, International Marketing (London) G. ROTH
Managing Director, Home Delivery Services (Birmingham) OPEN
Managing Director, Personnel (London) A. RANKINE
Managing Director, Hubs & Line Haul (Coventry) D. GORDIUS
Managing Director, Sales (BHX) M. HEALY
Managing Director, International Counsel (London) A. MEYER
Managing Director, Controller (UHR) J. GREE
Senior Manager, International Marketing (Tokyo) L. SULLIVAN
Senior Manager, personnel (Tokyo) D. ROCHE
Managing Director, Regional Sales (Tokyo) W. GROVER
Senior Manager, Freight Movement Center (Tokyo) R. SULK

locations to enable it to transport packages using only its own carriers. In countries where the market was small, Fedex used local couriers and leased space on existing air carriers, which made the standardization of operating procedures and methods more difficult to manage. Fedex specified service standards in its contracts with local companies, and employed on-site managers to monitor compliance. Although Fedex made serious efforts to train employees of local couriers in the company's operating procedures and methods, there was no guarantee that only those employees who had undergone such training would be those picking up or delivering packages for the company. In addition, links to centralized customer service centers were often difficult and sometimes impossible to maintain in foreign locations.

Because of all this, Fedex had difficulties in consistently guaranteeing delivery times to its foreign customers. Therefore, it was hard for Fedex to impress those customers with the quality of service on which the company built its reputation and market share in the United States.

Competition

While some of the difficulties which Fedex experienced abroad stemmed from the varied environmental and cultural characteristics and work practices in the countries in which it operated, other difficulties may be attributed to sharp competition for the services which Fedex provided. Contrary to its experience in the United States in the 1970s, major competitors existed in international markets, which were strongly entrenched and competitive. Among the most important were the following.

DHL. DHL was established in San Francisco in 1969 and was presently the largest of all international delivery service companies. Like Fedex, DHL offered door-to-door service and computerized tracking of packages. For the most part, the company contracted with local delivery services and freight forwarders, although it owned and operated some aircraft and delivery vehicles. Unlike Fedex, DHL sought early on to gain a strong presence abroad, especially in Europe and Asia, and it did so during roughly the same period in which Fedex was building its strong presence in its domestic market. By 1989, DHL controlled approximately 45 percent of the entire international express delivery market, and its name became as well known in Europe and parts of Asia as Fedex's name had become in the United States.

United Parcel Service. UPS had also expanded aggressively abroad in the 1980s, and was operating in 150 countries by 1990. The company followed essentially the same policies and procedures abroad as it did in the United States (described in the A case).

TNT. TNT was a large Australian conglomerate which expanded aggressively in the international delivery business during the 1980s, with $300 million in sales for 1990. TNT's "SkyPak" service offered overnight delivery to most of the world, and the company relied heavily on subcontracted freight and courier services. TNT had been marketing an international "business mail" service, which standardized mail service for businesses throughout the world. TNT was the second largest delivery company in Europe (after DHL) at the time, and had been mentioned as a possible candidate for purchase by Fedex.

Psychology of a Merger

When Fedex acquired a company, it attempted to insure that human resource practices in general, and compensation and benefit programs in particular, were at least as attractive as those offered by its competitors. At the same time, Fedex also attempted to achieve a certain standardization and consistency of human resource polices and practices across acquired companies—perhaps analogous to Fedex's attempts to achieve standardization of operating procedures and methods across countries. There was understandable tension between the two sets of employees involved in any acquisition. Fedex had found that its own employees tended to view themselves as "better" than the employees of acquired companies, while the latter often resented the fact of their having been taken over by Fedex. Further, employees of acquired companies often worried about their job security and their "fit" with the new organization. For its part, Fedex's management was concerned about the possibility that employee resentment and conflict associated with international expansion and acquisition would translate into specific problems of discipline and insubordination, and, more broadly, threaten Fedex's strong organization culture.

Although, Fedex faced these problems all around the world, with numerous local variations, they were particularly evident in the acquisition of Flying Tigers. Flying Tigers' management and employees were proud of their company and unhappy that the business was sold. Flying Tigers got its name from the group of pilots who founded the company after World War II, during which many of them had flown in and around China and the Pacific theater. The company had built its reputation on the willingness of its pilots to fly anything (including live tigers) anywhere in the world, as evidenced by their motto: "If you can get it to the airport, we'll fly it!" The company's culture was based on a strong sense of individualism. Flying Tiger employees had not only lost their company identity after they were acquired by Fedex, but also their union representation. Even though Fedex's human resource policies included grievance procedures and employee opinion surveys, the formerly unionized Flying Tigers' employees were suspicious of policies set down by management rather than agreed to through collective bargaining.

At the same time, Fedex's management and employees were equally proud of their company and, understandably perhaps, tried to overlay Fedex values, systems, and processes on Flying Tigers personnel. In the opinion of Charles Thomson, Vice President of International Personnel for Fedex, who had come from the Flying Tiger organization, this was a mistake.

> "In the early days of the merger, Fedex badly misjudged the heavy freight market and customer base that was Flying Tiger's main business, and that initially cost the company a great deal of business. Fedex lost many key Flying Tigers employees who chose not to join Fedex because they felt that no one would listen to them or take advantage of their expertise. Fedex also initially imposed [on them] many personnel policies and procedures in the international area that were unworkable because of local customs. After a rough first year, Fedex recognized its mistakes and took actions to correct them."

Human Resource Policies

Because business operations had to be modified to reflect customary practices, rules and laws prevailing in those regions of the world into which Fedex had expanded, many of the company's human resource policies also had to be modified. Given the considerable heterogeneity among countries in which Fedex operated, each country presented certain distinct problems in so far as the adaptation of Fedex's human resource policies and practices to them was concerned (see Exhibit 3 for a Fedex personnel organization chart, and Exhibit 4 for a summary of selected human resource policies and practices in nine countries).

Employee recruitment and training. Fedex was generally considered to be an attractive employer by job applicants in the United States, and the company had usually been able to attract high quality applicants for domestic jobs. However, employee recruitment abroad had proven to be far more difficult for Fedex. In Hong Kong and certain Western European nations, for example, unemployment levels were so low that most companies, especially service companies, had major difficulties in filling entry level positions. In Japan, where there was considerable enthusiasm about the type of services which Fedex provided, there was little cultural respect for the kinds of jobs which Fedex offered. As an example, the job of courier was not viewed in the same positive light in Japan as in the United States. Further, the employment of women in Japan continued to be restricted to certain labor markets and job groupings, such as office clerical jobs, and this cultural feature served to restrict the labor supply available to Fedex in filling operating and delivery jobs in its Japanese subsidiary.

Employee training, which was vital to Fedex's efforts to provide a uniform image and standardized services and procedures to customers, was not a traditional human resource practice in several of the foreign countries in which Fedex has acquired delivery companies. In these countries, moreover, local managers were often not well educated or formally trained, and the expatriate managers brought to these countries from the United States by Fedex were typically not provided language or cultural training. Even if appropriate training programs for foreign nationals and expatriate managers had been established by Fedex, the speed with which the company expanded its business to these foreign locations made it extremely difficult for the training programs to be translated into local languages and carried out in parallel with the rate of business expansion.

Furthermore, in some foreign locations new employees were frequently obtained through employment contractors on an as-needed basis. In those locations, different people often showed up for work each day, thereby making systematic training impossible. This situation prevailed in Italy, for example—until a Fedex customer sent Fred Smith a photograph of a Fedex "employee" sitting in his truck on a lunch break. The employee's shirt was unbuttoned, his feet were on top of the dashboard of the truck, and a cigar dangled from his mouth. At that point, Fedex decided that the use of contract employees, though convenient and available at relatively low cost, came at too high a price in terms of maintaining the company's desired service and quality image.

No lay-off policies. Employment-at-will was a far more prevalent practice in the United States than in most

EXHIBIT 3 Federal Express Corporation: Personnel Organization

- Senior VP & Chief Personnel Officer
J. PERKINS
  - VP Human Resource Development
L. MCMAHAN
    - Managing Director, Human Resource Development
L. DEBERRY
    - Managing Director, Leadership Institute
S. NIELSEN
    - Managing Directors, Management Preceptor
J. SLANGERUP
V. FIFER
  - VP Personnel Services
F. KENNY
    - Managing Director, HRA, Employee Relations, EEO
W. KIMBROUGH
    - Managing Director, Safety & Health Programs
F. RINE
      - Senior Manager, Safety, Health & Fire Protection
F. BROWN
      - Senior Manager Safety & Health Central & Western
C. LOVINSKI
      - Senior Manager Safety & Health Eastern & Southern
K. TULLOS
  - VP Personnel Administration
S. PRIDOY
    - Managing Director, Personnel Information Services
J. CHANDLER
    - Manager, Personnel Division Administration
A. SCURLARK
  - VP International Personnel
C. THOMSON
    - Managing Director, Personnel Europe
A. RANKNE
    - Senior Manager, Personnel Asia Pacific
D. ROCHE
L. REAL
    - Senior Manager, Americas Region Personnel
W. BENNET
    - Senior Manager, International Benefits
H. COLLINS
    - Manager, International Training
A. GREEN
    - Managing Director, Personnel
W. NOORTMAN

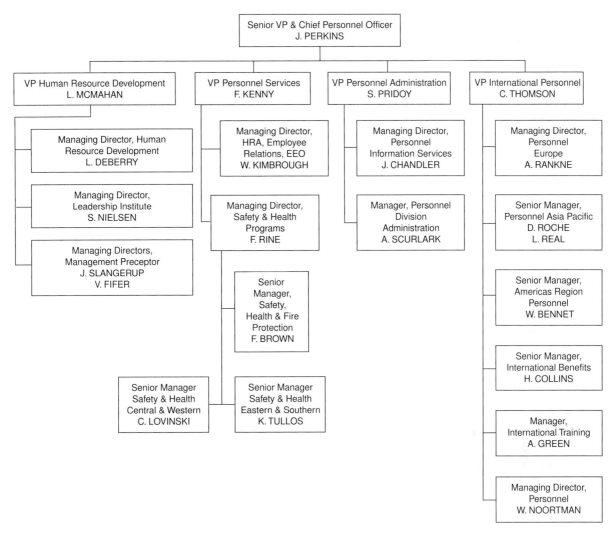

other countries, so that Fedex's no-layoff policy was relatively attractive to job applicants in U.S. labor markets. However, lifetime or continuous employment was common in Japan and many European nations, and in these countries employers also traditionally had greater (customary or legal) obligation to their employees than was the case in the United States. In Italy, for example, a company was legally mandated to provide nine months of severance pay to an employee when he or she left a company. This requirement held even if the employee's exit from the firm was entirely voluntary. For management employees, mandated severance pay could be even more burdensome. To illustrate, one of Fedex's Italian managers chose to leave the company after three years of employment. Although Fedex wanted him to stay with the company, Fedex was nevertheless compelled to pay him $130,000 in severance pay. Not only was Fedex's no layoff policy a weaker labor market incentive abroad than it was domestically, but the policy had sometimes created a financial burden for Fedex. This occurred whenever Fedex acquired a company and found that it did not need all of the acquired company's employees.

Fedex's acquisition of Flying Tigers, for example, resulted in a surplus of pilots which the company never-

EXHIBIT 4 Summary of Selected Human Resource Policies and Practices in Nine Countries

	Employment Contracts	Minimum Pay	Maximum Hours	Minimum Annual Holiday	Employee Participation
Belgium	Certain terms must be in writing	Yes	8 per day; 40 per week	4 weeks	Works councils
France	Written contracts	Yes	10 per day; 39 per week	2.5 days per month	Codetermination; works councils; employee unions
Germany	Fixed-term agreements	Collective agreement	8 per day; 48 per week	18 days	Codetermination; works councils; employee unions
Japan	Written contracts	Yes	46 per week	20 days maximum	Employee unions
Ireland	Employees may require written statement of terms from employees	No	No	3 weeks	Codetermination
Italy	Written contracts	Collective agreement	8 per day; 48 per week	Collective agreement	Works councils; national collective bargaining agreements
Mexico	No	Yes	8 per day; 48 per week	6 days first year; additional 2 days per subsequent year	Collective bargaining in some industries; mandatory profit-sharing
Spain	No	Yes	9 per day; 40 per week	2.5 days per month	Codetermination; employee delegates and committees
U.K.	Written statement of terms of employment	No	No	No formal requirements	No formal requirements

Sources: David Lewin and Daniel J. B. Mitchell, "Systems of Employee Voice: Theoretical and Empirical Perspectives," *California Management Review, 34* (Spring 1992), pp. 95–111; Trevor Bain, "Employee Voice: A Comparative International Perspective," presented to the Forty-Fourth Annual Meeting of the Industrial Relations Research Association, New Orleans, LA, January 1992; James B. Dworkin and Barbara A. Lee, "The Implications of Europe 1992 for Labor-Management Relations," in Harry C. Katz (ed.), *The Future of Industrial Relations* (Ithaca, NY: New York State School of Industrial and Labor Relations, Cornell University, 1991), pp. 1–24.

theless was obligated to absorb because of its no lay-off policy. It also created a serious challenge to Fedex's preference for remaining a nonunion company, given that Flying Tigers' pilots were fully unionized. Although Fedex was not required to recognize or bargain with the Flying Tigers pilots' union, it was necessary to merge its own pilot seniority list with that of Flying Tigers. This process was accomplished through third-party arbitration. As a result of this decision, some Fedex pilots fell hundreds of places in the combined seniority list, with consequent loss of status, assignments to new equipment, and reductions of pay rates and certain fringe benefits which were linked to pilot seniority. It was hardly surprising, therefore, that dissatisfaction rose among Fedex pilots. Indeed, some pilots sued Fedex over what they considered to be a breach of their original contracts with the company, and Fedex pilots sought to have the Air Line Pilots Association (ALPA) certified by the National Labor Relations Board as their bargaining representative—efforts which proved to be unsuccessful.

Promotion from within. The policy of promotion from within had been applied consistently by Fedex in the United States, except to certain functional specialties, such as finance and legal affairs, which demanded specialized expertise obtained externally. Further, most managerial positions at Fedex were filled from within the company, usually by people who began their careers in entry-level positions. While Fedex attempted to follow this policy abroad, it had often found it necessary to staff key managerial positions with U.S. personnel. In 1991, Fedex employed approximately 200 expatriate managers overseas. Over time, Fedex intended to reduce the use of expatriate managers and increase the hiring and promotion of foreign national managers, but this would depend heavily on the company's rate of foreign expansion and its ability to adapt local customs and practices to Fedex's organization culture and management development programs.

The criteria for selecting employees for promotion varied considerably among countries. In the United States, most promotion decisions were based on individual ability and merit, and Fedex had formalized these criteria through its Leadership Evaluation Assessment Process (LEAP). By contrast, in many Asian countries, age and length of service (seniority) were the main criteria used to make promotion decisions. Moreover, in Asia, lateral (as distinct from vertical) "promotions" and transfers were more common and important than in the United States. Fedex faced the seniority-in-promotion issue immediately upon its acquisition of local delivery companies in Asia, whose employees had been hired long before Fedex came on the scene. Expatriate managers employed by Fedex in Asia were often younger than many of the employees they managed, and this created tension in employee relations. Recognizing such tension, Fedex planned to reduce its use of expatriate managers and increase its use of local personnel in Asian countries. However, Fedex's ability to respond to local customs in this regard would depend in part on the rate of business expansion and on the successful implementation of employee training and management development programs.

Grievance procedures and voice. The "Guaranteed Fair Treatment" (GFT) procedure and the "Survey-Feedback-Action" (SFA) plan were conflict resolution mechanisms which were developed and refined by Fedex in response to the needs of U.S. employees and managers. Inherent in these policies was an American value system which prized equality and individual rights. However, Fedex had difficulty in exporting these procedures because the value systems prevailing abroad were often very different from those found in the United States.

For example, the three-step GFT procedure allowed an employee with a grievance to file the written complaint initially with his or her supervisor or manager. If the employee was unhappy with the disposition of the grievance at this stage, it was then presented to the next level of the procedure, namely a management committee. If the employee continued to remain unsatisfied with the disposition of the grievance at this level, an International Appeals Board will hear and rule on the grievance; decisions rendered at this level of the GFT were final and binding. Most grievances filed by U.S. employees of Fedex were resolved at the first step of the GFT. However, the GFT had proven to be unworkable in Asian countries or in Italy, where supervisors and managers believed that they would lose the respect of their employees if they made decisions which were overturned by their superiors—that is, they would lose "face." Recognizing this, Fedex instituted a two-step grievance resolution process in these countries in which the employee's supervisor or manager and the manager's superior served jointly as the first step, and the International Appeals Board served as the second and final step. Supervisors in these countries apparently believed that their authority would not be threatened by this new process, largely because their decisions could not be overturned by their immediate supervisor or manager. That is, if a local manager's decision was overturned at the second step of the GFT, it could be attributed to senior company management or company policy, rather than being taken as a "direct" reprimand of the local supervisor or manager.

The SFA plan also needed to be modified for use in certain foreign countries. In Germany, for example, where work rules and other business matters were subject to consultation with legally mandated works councils, the SFA was viewed with great suspicion. Even though the surveys initiated under this plan were anonymous, the works council at Fedex Germany was concerned that the company might have a method of identifying employee-respondents and that "complaining" employees would receive unfavorable treatment. In Asian countries, every survey question was typically answered with a check in the middle column, which was labeled "sometimes agree, sometimes disagree." Asian employees were especially uncomfortable about criticizing their supervisors and managers, and they also doubted that the confidentiality of their responses would be preserved. Fedex responded to these concerns with extensive training in the purposes and uses of the SFA, and it worked with local employees to revise and reword survey questions so as to promote respondent understanding and useful survey responses. Significant improvement in foreign employees' acceptance of the SFA plan had occurred as a result of these efforts.

The open door policy maintained in the United States by Fedex, although available to all employees worldwide, was still not widely used abroad. In the United States, the company had established a casual atmosphere; employees were on a first-name basis, and executives regularly mingled with employees and solicited their opinions and suggestions. Managers and workers in European and Asian countries were often uncomfortable with this type and level of informality. To illustrate, when Charles Thomson visited a newly acquired company in Brussels, he behaved as he would in the United States. He arrived early, took off his coat, walked around the facility and chatted with employees. Later, Thomson discovered that his behavior had damaged his image among managers in Brussels. He had spoken to employees who were not his direct reports and without their managers being present, and his casual manner and attire offended these managers. When Thomson subsequently apologized for these offenses and remarked that he had merely been attempting to earn the employees' respect, a local Brussels manager responded by saying "of course they respect you, you're a vice-president from America." To the extent that respect was associated with a title and not the person who held the title, the efficacy of an open-door policy in these cultures would be in doubt.

Compensation and financial participation. Fedex had a stated policy of paying competitive compensation rates, and its financial participation policies reflected the company's strategy of motivating employees to work hard for the success of the company. As Fedex expanded abroad, it found it necessary to modify existing compensation packages so that they would be in accord with the company's compensation policy. In many countries, this resulted in the raising of pay rates and levels beyond those that prevailed previously (in the acquired companies). To illustrate, Fedex's salaries were about 30 percent higher than those paid by Flying Tigers for comparable positions, 35 percent higher than those of equivalent positions in Japan, and 40 percent higher than those of equivalent positions in Mexico. Although newly acquired employees were generally pleased to receive pay raises, some employees resented the implication that the companies for which they had previously worked had not treated them "fairly" in so far as compensation was concerned. This practice also significantly increased the fixed costs of these acquired companies and sometimes turned a profitable operation into an unprofitable one.

In certain foreign countries, moreover, legislation sometimes forced Fedex to pay more for employees in certain job specialties than it did for similar employees in the United States. For example, Canadian legislation required companies to follow a policy of comparable worth, that is, equal pay for work of equal value. In practice, this meant that jobs which were judged to have the same or similar value based on assessments along several internal job dimensions (factors) must be classified at the same level and paid the same wage or salary. The effect of this policy was to raise labor costs and reduce pay flexibility. To illustrate, if secretaries and couriers were judged to occupy jobs of the same internal value, Canadian law required Fedex to compensate occupants of these jobs at the same rates. This resulted in higher pay for secretaries employed by Fedex in Canada than for secretaries employed by Fedex in the United States—and also in lower pay for couriers employed in Canada by Fedex than for those employed in the United States. If shortages of one or another occupational specialty occurred in Canada, Fedex and other companies could not selectively raise the pay for the occupational specialty in question without raising the pay for other jobs judged to be of comparable value—jobs for which shortages may not exist and which were therefore relatively easier to fill.

Financial participation and incentive compensation programs practiced by Fedex in the United States had also proven to be less successful abroad. For example, in Singapore an incentive program which offered a holiday abroad to the salesperson with the highest dollar volume of sales failed to attract any interest. Upon investigation, it was discovered that the sales personnel viewed the program as having one winner and many losers, and that employees were so averse to losing that the single prize offered by Fedex did not serve as an incentive to achieve high sales. In fact, employees in many of the countries in which Fedex operated preferred group rewards over individual rewards, and Fedex has recently established group incentive plans in some of those countries. Unexpectedly, these plans had been so successful that Fedex intended to introduce them in the United States.

In recent years, Fedex has relied more heavily on variable pay as part of total employee compensation in order to tie compensation more closely to the performance of the business. Its overall goal was approximately 25 percent variable and 75 percent fixed compensation for employees. While there were some countries and cultures in which a relatively large proportion of compensation in the form variable pay was acceptable, in other countries it was not only distasteful but unworkable. In Italy and Brazil, for example, the Doctrine of Acquired Rights (which also governed severance pay) stated that an employer could not lower an employee's pay. Implicit in the policy of variable compensation was the notion that an individual employee's pay may vary year to year, based on both individual and company performance. Since Italian and Brazilian laws allowed pay to go up, but not down, Fedex's variable pay plan was unworkable in those countries.

In the United States, Fedex often used overtime hours to insure that packages were handled expeditiously and delivered on time. Fedex's U.S. employees looked favorably on such overtime work, which was compensated at a 50 percent pay premium (that is, one and one-half times the base rate). By contrast, Fedex discovered that German employees tended to value personal time over increased income. As a result, Fedex's German employees consistently refused to stay on past their "normal" work hours, shifts, and days, declining overtime pay in favor of leisure. This reduced Fedex's operational flexibility and increases its costs of doing business in Germany. A sufficient number of employees had to be hired to meet peak, rather than average, capacity in order to guarantee package delivery times in Germany.

Evaluation. In countries which had stronger group values and weaker individual values than those prevailing in the United States, resistance to individually oriented pay, incentive compensation, performance appraisal, attitude surveys, and conflict resolution programs was often observed. This had been Fedex's experience in many of the countries into which it had recently expanded, including several in both Asia and Western Europe. Indeed, and to take an extreme example, individual initiative, which was so highly prized in the United States, was regarded as insubordination in India, where an important characteristic of that nation's culture was to please one's superior. A human resource strategy, policy, or practice mounted by Fedex or any other U.S.-based company which did recognize this and other cultural and value differences was likely to result in negative consequences for the business—as Fedex had vividly discovered.

Fedex's Future Abroad

By 1991 Fedex was operating in 127 countries where it employed 17,000 people, and the company expected to be operating in 170 countries by the end of 1992. Fedex's share of the international delivery market stood at about 10 percent in 1991, but operating losses from the company's foreign operations mounted during the early 1990s. Several factors contributed to these losses, including a restructuring of Fedex's business in the United Kingdom, which resulted in a $121 million charge against 1991 income; higher-than-anticipated repair costs to aircraft obtained through the acquisition of Flying Tigers; expenses associated with continued purchases of new local companies; and the adjustment of operating and human resource policies and practices in those companies to comport with Fedex's requirements. On balance, Fedex's foreign expansion had proven to be far more costly and taken longer than was originally anticipated. This rapid expansion posed special difficulties for Fedex's international personnel executives and professionals, who continuously scrambled to staff the new organizations abroad and to coordinate human resource policies and practices in widely varying locations.

Indeed, issues of organizational structure and decision making had become paramount as Fedex continued its foreign expansion. Although there were several Fedex regional offices in foreign locations, most major decisions continued to be made by senior U.S. executives at the company's headquarters in Memphis, Tennessee. The present and planned rapid growth of Fedex's international business may require greater regional (if not country-by-country) authority, autonomy, and responsibility. Should this occur, however, it could well bring about a major cultural change in the company, which even with a worldwide work force of 90,000 employees had sought to maintain a single, strong cultural identity. Whereas Fedex recognized the pressures on it to adopt and adapt to local customs as it expanded abroad, its goal had been to make all of its offices "purple," that is, to bring all employees into the Fedex "family." However, some softening of this position may be in the offing. For example, Thomas Oliver, Senior Vice President for International Operations, said in April 1991 that "it's not necessary for Federal Express to own and operate every aspect of this thing. It's totally impractical." Chuck Thomson had indicated that Fedex was exploring several joint ventures abroad which, should they materialize, were likely to alter Fedex's organizational structure, decision-making systems, and culture.

In 1990, Fedex received the Malcolm Baldridge National Quality Award for Excellence, becoming the first service company to be so honored. That award was given largely in recognition of Fedex's domestic business operations. Fred Smith characterized the award as "a beginning rather than an end." He went on to say that,

> "Since we were awarded the Malcolm Baldridge National Quality Award, I have been asked many times if this means that we have now achieved the ultimate level of quality. My answer is that the receipt of this award is simply our 'license to practice.' I believe that another profound series of improvements lie ahead."

Smith continued to believe in the Fedex motto, "People–Service–Profit." He added, "When people are placed first, they will provide the highest possible service, and the profits will follow." Smith continued to head and champion his company, and he remained committed to a strong international presence for Fedex despite the losses which the company had experienced abroad during the last several years.

The central decision making, organization culture, and human resource policies which had served Fedex well at home, may be inappropriate to the international marketplace. Customizing these characteristics of Fedex's domestic business to fit local conditions, customs, and laws abroad may be insufficient to create the reputation for consistent high quality service which Fedex required to succeed in the international marketplace. Chuck Thomson and his personnel staff, in particular, faced the twin challenges of integrating foreign employees into Fedex's culture while adapting that culture to fit foreign environments. Though he believed that there was no simple way of meeting or managing these challenges, Thomson also believed that developing effective responses to them was critical if Fedex was to be a successful global business in the 1990s.

Case 13–3

Nizhlak: The Top Management Team

In 1991, following an attempted coup by hard-line communists against the government of Mikhail Gorbachev, the Union of Soviet Socialist Republics (USSR) collapsed into a loose confederation of independent states. The dissolution of the USSR and the abdication of absolute power by the Communist Party of the Soviet Union led to a period of economic and social chaos as the rigid system of state economic planning and social control quickly fragmented. Although by 1998 the Russian Federation had adopted a new constitution and elected Boris Yeltsin president for a second time, it was clear that the path to economic and social reform in Russia was not going to be as smooth as some had hoped.

However, in spite of the upheaval and Russia's inexperience with the institutions of capitalism and representative democracy, many foreign firms looked on the former USSR as a land of opportunity. Possessing vast natural resources, a highly skilled and literate workforce, and key technologies that had grown out of its cold-war conflict with the United States, Russia, to many, deserved serious consideration as an investment opportunity.

Nizhny Novgorod

The city of Nizhny Novgorod was the third largest city in Russia. It is located 260 miles southeast of Moscow at the confluence of two rivers, the Oka and the Volga (see Exhibit 1). Formally known as Gorky, Nizhny Novgorod was, before the collapse of the USSR, one of many "closed" military-industrial cities. For most Westerners, Gorky was known for being the location of Nobel prize winner Andre Sakharov's internal exile. However, the city boasted a heavy concentration of defense-related industrial facilities, including aerospace, pharmaceuticals, radio and electronics, machine tools, and chemical and petrochemicals. Exhibit 2 presents a snapshot of Nizhny Novgorod.

With the city closed to foreigners and nonessential residents until 1990, the population of Nizhny Novgorod was unique to say the least. Because of the preponderance, even in 1998, of military armaments factories and technological facilities and institutes, the city still maintained an aura of "security consciousness." However, for exactly the same reason, there was a high concentration of skilled and educated workers and a network of related business operations rarely found in other cities in Russia.

Like many places in Russia, the population was split in its attitude to foreign investment. Some Russians, remembering the days of the imperial USSR, remained suspicious of foreign business people. A common complaint was that following the collapse of the USSR and opening of country to foreign investment, foreign companies moved in and bought up valuable companies and assets at bargain basement prices. Individuals expousing this viewpoint were likely supporters of Communist and Ultra Nationalist political parties and politicians such as Alexander Lebed and Vladimir Zhirinovsky. Other Russians, particularly the young, well educated, and entrepreneurs operating small ventures, welcomed the opening of Russian society to foreign money and influence. These individuals were less likely to be politically active

---

This case was written by Professor Timothy Devinney as a basis for class discussion and not for the purpose of illustrating either the good or bad handling of a specific management situation. The assistance of Dr. A. Schmidt and Ms. I. Petrova, MBA, is gratefully acknowledged.

EXHIBIT 1 Map of Western Russia

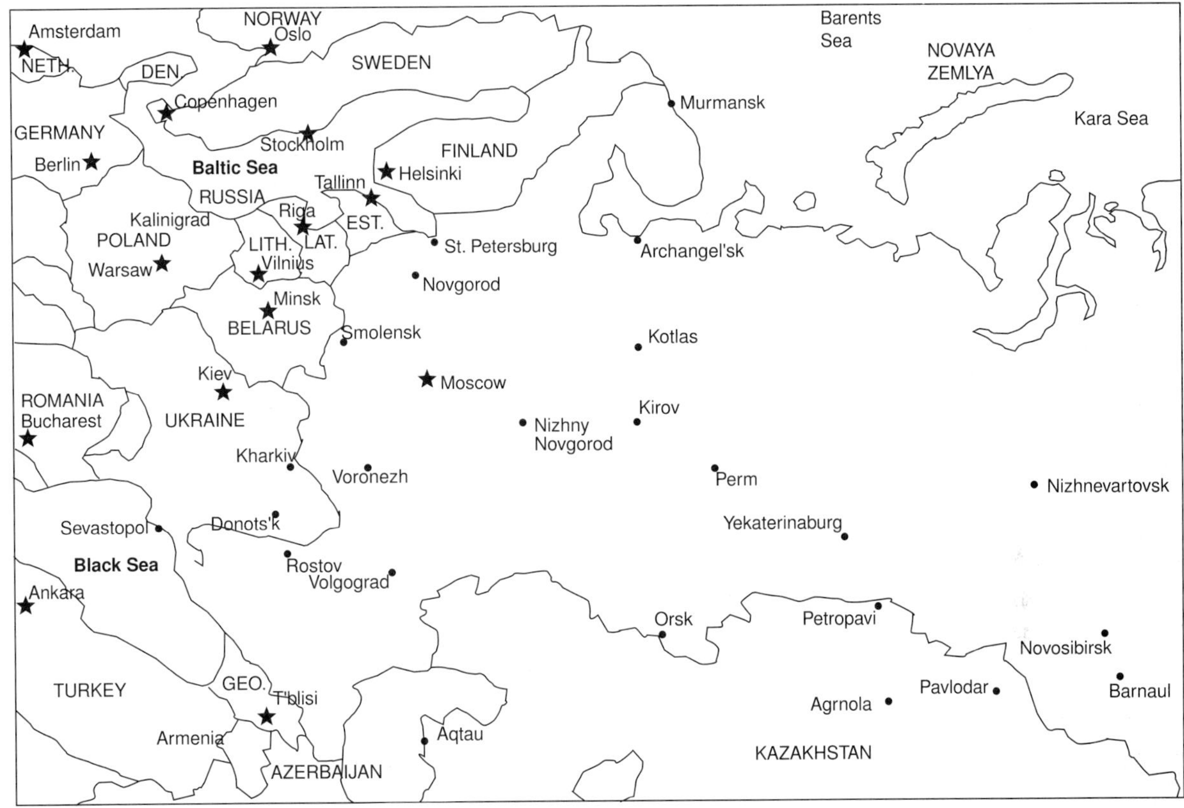

Source: Adapted from http://www.lib.utexas.edu/Libs/PCL/Map_collection/commonwealth/Russia.94.jpg.

but were generally sanguine about the erratic liberalizations occurring under the Yeltsin administration.

There was a strong German presence in Nizhny Novgorod, and the rapport between local political and business leaders and their German counterparts was quite positive. Although American business people appear better able to work with the city's growing army of entrepreneurs, German corporations have had greater success with the larger state-run and former state-owned enterprises. Some of this appeared to be due to a difference between American and German management styles, however, the greater willingness of German firms to provide direct financing for their ventures seemed to have created a lot of good will. In a reflection of the growing German presence in the city, Lufthansa began twice weekly flights between Frankfurt and Nizhny Novgorod—the first scheduled commercial international flights into the city.

The Nizhlak Joint Venture

Nizhlak was a joint venture company between Bayern Farben AG (BF) and AO Roschimprom (Aktsionernoye Obschestvo Rossiyskaya Chimicheskaya Promyshlennost). Founded with capital of 350 million roubles (approximately DM 100 million), it was a private joint stock company with equal shares being held by BF and AO Roschimprom. BF's contribution consisted of is DM 45 million in cash and the equivalent of DM 5 million in equipment and deferred royalty payments. AO Roschimprom was contributing RUR 10 million in land, RUR 10 million in cash, and RUR 5 million in deferred material costs. The remainder of their contribution (approximately RUR 150 million) was being financed by loans to AO Roschimprom from the Investment Fund for Central and Eastern Europe, the International Finance

EXHIBIT 2 An Overview of Nizhny Novgorod

Territory:	74,800 square kilometres. The main city is Nizhny Novgorod. It is surrounded by eight small cities in the district: Dzerzhinsk, Balakhna, Zavolzh'e, Bor, Kstovo, Bogorodsk, Gorodets, and Pavlovo.
Population:	Nizhny Novgorod district: 3.7 million Nizhny Novgorod city: 1.4 million
Education Levels:	62 percent of the population has a high school degree or some university education. 20 percent have a university degree and 13 percent have some post graduate experience.
Transportation:	The district has 8,000 kilometres of roads (almost 4 times the Russian average). The rail density is 3.3 times the Russian average. The Volga and Oka rivers are navigable and the district is connected to the Baltic Sea, the White Sea, the Black Sea, the Sea of Azov, the Caspian Sea, Moscow, St. Petersburg, and the Ural district via waterways. An international airport serves 30 former republics and 10 regional airlines.
Economic Development:	Private enterprise represents 90 percent of industrial production and more than 40 percent of commodity, retail, and service operations.
Foreign Investment:	US$60 Million (1995). The largest investors were: USA, Germany, Finland, Cyprus, Turkey, UK, and Switzerland.

Source: Nizhny Novgorod Regional Committee of State Statistics.

Corporation, and the European Bank for Reconstruction and Development.

Nizhlak would be responsible for the manufacturing and marketing of specialty paints using BF pigments and technology. Specialty paints were used for automobiles, ships, planes, electrical equipment, and consumer goods. Nizhny Novgorod, with the Gorky Automobile plant, the Factory of Specialized Automobiles, several shipbuilding concerns, defense facilities, and a myriad of consumer product companies, represented a potentially lucrative market for BF's high quality paints.

Bayern Farben, although small in total size compared to companies like Du Pont, PPG, Kansi, Hoechst, and BASF, was one of the largest specialty paint companies in Europe. A dedication to a specialized market in what was otherwise a heavily fragmented industry had led to superior profit performance over the last 10 years. Founded in 1923, BF specialized early on in providing paint to the German military. Following the Second World War, with its traditional market destroyed and its founder jailed by the Allies for complicity with the Nazis in the use of forced labor, BF, under new management, branched out into the developing fields of automobile and aircraft paints. With the fall of communism in Eastern Europe, BF moved quickly to establish operations in the Czech Republic, Poland, Romania, and the former East Germany. It also had operations in Thailand, Indonesia, and China.

AO Roschimprom was founded in 1935 and was one of the largest chemical companies in Russia. The company owned six plants involved in various types of chemical production throughout the former USSR. AO Roschimprom marketed more than 100 products ranging from liquid chlorine and ethylene to laundry detergents and linoleum. Its products were exported to more than 40 countries and 30 percent of its revenues were export earnings.

A former state-owned enterprise; it was privatized in 1995. To date, the sophistication of AO Roschimprom's production operations and the quality of its products had saved the company from many of the difficulties normally associated with privatization. Since 1995, the firm had reduced its workforce by 20 percent and managed to eke out its first profit in 1997. Nizhlak represented AO Roschimprom's first foreign joint venture (excluding deals done with old East European and CIS companies) and its initial foray into the paints business.

The management structure of Nizhlak is presented in Exhibit 3. A two-member oversight board who reported to both BF and AO Roschimprom nominally was to oversee the JV. These individuals were jointly responsible for ensuring that the wishes of the parent companies were communicated to the JV and that unbiased reports of the JV's performance were presented to the parent companies' management and Board of Directors. The Managing Director was a position assigned to a Russian, subject to the approval of the parent companies' Board of Directors upon the joint recommendation of the Co-Chairmen. Although the JV agreement did not specify the nationality of the six operational Directors, it was initially agreed that three of the team would be German—the Directors of Finance, Marketing and Accounting and Control—while Russians would hold the remaining positions—the Directorships of Operations, Research and Development, and Human Resources. This was based upon the differential expertise that the JV partners felt they had in these areas. The Directors were chosen by the parent companies subject to the approval of the Co-Chairmen and the Managing Director.

EXHIBIT 3 The Nizhlak Joint Venture Management Team Structure

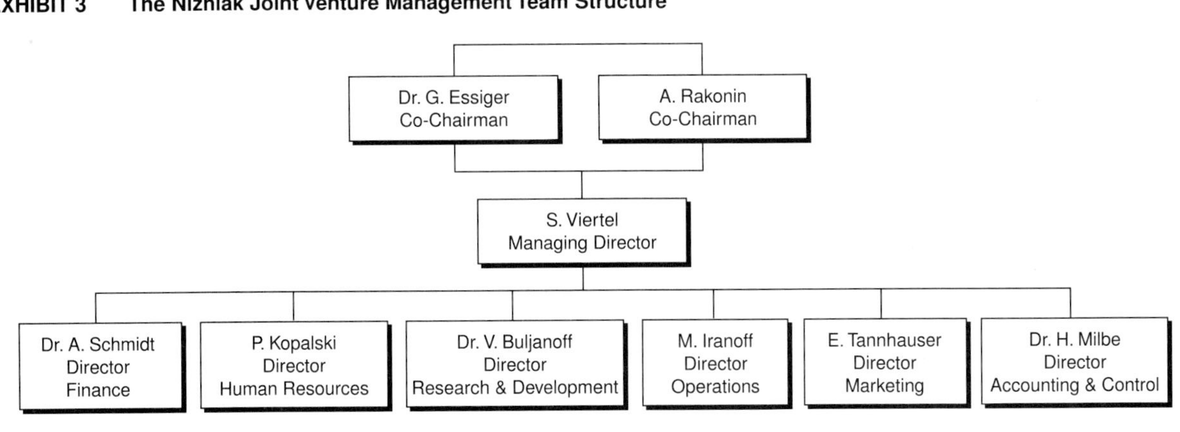

The Nizhlak Management Team

The Bayern Farben Team

Dr. Harmut Milbe was a native of Dresden. He earned a doctorate in chemistry from Universität Dresden. He spent 18 years with Deutsche Chemie (DC) until it was purchased by BF in 1993 as part of the general restructuring of the East Germany economy by the Treuhandanstalt. Although trained in engineering and science, he spent the last 10 years while at DC working as an accountant and controller (all at the Meissen plant outside Dresden). After the purchase by BF, Dr. Milbe was responsible for assisting in the achievement of the ISO9001 certification for the Meissen facility. The company recently sent him to a four-week executive program at Harvard Business School. He was fluent in German, Russian, and Polish and had passable English. He was divorced with three children, and he was 54 years old.

Dr. Augustus Schmidt was a native of Munich. He was a graduate of the Universität Augsburg in physics and earned a doctorate in economics from Universität München. After receiving his doctorate, he spent 10 years at Bayerische Vereinsbank in Munich working on syndicated loans for developing countries. During this period, he worked extensively in Eastern Europe. He joined BF five years earlier as a General Manager in Finance, handling the corporate finance aspects of BF's acquisitions and expansion in Eastern Europe. He was fluent in German and English, married with two children, he was 49 years old.

Ms. Eva Tannhauser was a native of Ratzeburg outside Hamburg. A graduate of Hochschule für Kunst (College of Art), Bremen, in fine arts, she had an MBA from St. Gallen in Switzerland. Following her studies in Bremen she worked for three years with Burston Marsteller as an advertising copy editor. After her studies at St. Gallen, she worked for Beiersdorf in Hamburg as a product manager for three years. After this she worked for two years in Leverkusen as a marketing manager for the Agfa Gevaert Group, a division of Bayer specializing in film and photographic products. For the last two years she had been a General Manager in Marketing for BF operating from their Munich headquarters. She was fluent in German, French, and English. She was 39 and single with one child.

Dr. Guido Essiger was born in Qingtao, China, where his parents served as medical doctors attached to a German Protestant charity. Just before the Japanese capture of Qingtao the family moved to Plauen in Saxony. After the defeat of Germany and the establishment of the German Democratic Republic, he and his mother (his father had been killed in the defense of Breslau, now Wroclaw in Poland) escaped into West Germany, where she established a small medical practice in Regensburg. A graduate of Universität Regensburg in chemistry, he had a doctorate in chemistry from Universität München. Dr. Essiger had worked for eight years with BASF in Ludwigshafen and Vienna. For the last 18 years he held various positions with BF including serving as the General Manager of Quality Assurance. He spent most of the last five years overseeing the successful establishment of a joint venture operation in Tianjin, China. He was fluent in German, Chinese, and English. He was 59 years old and married with five children.

The AO Roschimprom Team

Dr. Vassili Buljanoff was a native of Moscow. He earned a doctorate in chemistry from Moscow State University. He spent 10 years with Nizhegorodpolymer as a chemist. In 1991 he moved to the recently formed private company, Acrylat, where he was responsible for overseeing chemical quality control. AO Roschimprom hired him specifically for the position of Director of Research and Development for the Nizhlak venture. He was fluent in Russian and English. He was married with one child, and was 51 years old.

Mikhail Iranoff was a native of Moscow. He graduated from Moscow State University with a degree in mathematics. He spent the last 15 years with AO Roschimprom, first as a plant operations foreman and then a plant manager in Irkutsk and most recently as the plant manager of the ethylene plant in Bor. Before joining AO Roschimprom, he worked at the USSR Academy of Sciences as a mathematician specializing in linear programming algorithms. He was fluent in Russian and had passable English. He was divorced with one child. He was 49.

Pyotr Kopalski was a native of Minsk, was a graduate of the Minsk Polytechnic Academy with a degree in economics. He joined AO Roschimprom following his graduation in 1960 and held numerous positions in the company. He spent his first 12 years with the company in Moscow—five years handling export sales to the Middle East and seven years in military and government procurement. He moved to Nizhny Novgorod in 1982 and spent the last five years dealing with personnel matters associated with the privatization of the company. He was fluent in Russian, Polish, and had passable English. He was 54 years old and married with one child.

Sergei Viertel was a native of St. Petersburg. His family was one of the founding families of Brunnental (Kriwojar) colony on the Volga River in 1855. They were subsequently removed to Smolensk during the civil war that followed the revolution. They moved to St. Petersburg in 1960 when his father secured a job as a medical doctor. Sergei Veirtel graduated from M. I. Kalinin Polytechnic Institute of Leningrad (now St. Petersburg State Technical University) with a diploma in engineering in chemistry. After receiving his degree, he worked for a short time at the Russian Academy of Sciences in Moscow. He joined AO Roschimprom in 1988 as a chemist and quickly moved into the ranks of management. He was responsible for implementing the company's first modern quality control system and subsequently had been given responsibility for the technical upgrading of a number of the firm's factories. He was 41 years old and married with one child. He was fluent in Russian and German and had passable English.

Anatoly Rakonin was a native of St. Petersburg. He was a graduate of the Frunze Military Academy and one of the youngest tank commanders in the Soviet army. He had a stellar military career serving as the Soviet military attaché in France, Cuba, Spain, and Egypt. After retiring from the military in 1990, he joined AO Roschimprom as its liaison with Russian army procurement. He was fluent in Russian, French, and English. He was 61 years old and married with two children.

INSEAD

Case 13–4

Ciba-Geigy—Management Development

On the short hop from Orly, Arnold Delage, soon to become Managing Director of Ciba-Geigy's French subsidiary, was looking forward to his dinner meeting later that evening in Basel, Switzerland (headquarters to Ciba-Geigy). He and the top management of the parent company's Pharma Division were scheduled to review candidates for the position of Sales and Marketing Manager for the French subsidiary's pharmaceutical business, an important position since this division accounted for over a quarter of total French sales and had shown rapid growth in recent years.

Until recently, Delage had been general manager of Ciba-Geigy's French Pharma Division and President of Laboratories Ciba-Geigy, the pharmaceutical subsidiary of Ciba-Geigy in France, with sales of more than FF 2 billion. René Lamont, the current Managing Director of Ciba-Geigy in France, was scheduled to retire at the end of the year, and Delage had been chosen by Ciba-Geigy's top management to succeed him, a selection announced in early December.

This case was initially prepared by Martine van den Poel, Research Associate under the supervision of Yves Doz, Professor of Strategy and Management. It is intended to be used as a basis for class discussion rather than to illustrate either effective or ineffective handling of an administrative situation.

> Delage had had a successful career with Ciba-Geigy. A Frenchman, he joined Esso-Africa upon graduation from INSEAD 15 years ago, and worked in Switzerland (Geneva) and in Madagascar, in sales and marketing positions for four years. He was subsequently recruited by Ciba-Geigy and, after a year at Pharma Division's headquarters in Basel, was sent to Hong Kong in a sales and marketing management position. After four years in the Far East he was appointed Marketing Manager in Belgium, where he successfully launched a number of new pharmaceutical products. He was then promoted to Pharma Division Manager in Belgium, a position he held for three years. Mr. Delage was then posted to the much larger French Pharma Division as Marketing Manager, where he continued to supervise a number of new product launches and was subsequently promoted to Pharma Division Manager. During the past two years he considerably strengthened the management of the French Pharma division.

Delage's appointment to Managing Director of Ciba-Geigy France had opened the position of Pharma Division Manager within the French subsidiary. Jules Breton, an experienced manager recently hired by Delage from Sanofi (a major French pharmaceutical company where he had held the position of president and general manager of one of its subsidiaries) to head the French division's marketing efforts, was promoted to replace him. The position of Pharma Marketing Manager therefore became vacant. Delage and Breton presented the candidacy of Pierre Dumont, a Frenchman who had recently been recruited from Specia (another French competitor) to head marketing and sales for the Geigy product line in France. Pharma Division headquarters in Basel had suggested several other candidates. Among them, their preference was for Michel Malterre, a Swiss national from Montreux, currently heading Pharma marketing in West Africa and based in Abidjan, Ivory Coast.

Such decisions as the appointment of key executives in subsidiary companies were usually the result of joint agreement by divisional management in Basel and the local managing directors, and were often debated at the highest levels within the company. A long-standing corporate commitment to human resource and management development ensured that such choices received considerable attention and that all relevant aspects were carefully weighed before a decision was reached.

The Company and its Organization

Ciba-Geigy resulted from the 1970 merger between two long-standing Basel chemical companies: Ciba (created in 1884) and Geigy (created in 1758). Both companies were active competitors in certain business areas, e.g., dyestuffs, pharmaceuticals, industrial chemicals, and agro-chemicals. In other areas, their activities were complementary. Both were strong internationally, although Geigy had a stronger worldwide presence in agro-chemicals and Ciba a wider experience in pharmaceuticals.

The management styles and structures of the two companies, however, differed widely. Ciba was centrally managed by one person, Dr. Kappeli, its chairman. He relied on strong and entrepreneurial division managers to control Ciba's widely diversified activities. In contrast, Geigy had been organized in a three dimensional organizational structure where businesses, national subsidiaries, and corporate functions were managed by an Executive Committee regrouping Geigy's top management. Following the merger, the Geigy structure was retained, it comprised the following units (see Exhibit 1):

1. A divisional structure covering the seven main product areas;
2. A geographic structure with 80 group companies organized in a loose administrative way into six main regions: North America, Western Europe, Latin America, Africa/Middle East, Eastern Europe, and Asia/Australia; and
3. Ten central corporate functions (legal, finance, technology, etc.) at group headquarters in Basel, Switzerland.

Group companies, generally 100 percent-owned, were responsible for all Ciba-Geigy activities in a given country, the local development of Ciba-Geigy's businesses, and for overall financial results within their territories. Administrative functions were thus centralized locally to serve all local units. In addition, government relations and membership in industry and trade associations could be made more effective. The product divisions and the Executive Committee (*Konzernleitung*) coordinated and integrated the group companies' activities.

Product divisions were responsible to the Executive Committee for the worldwide management of their businesses and their overall results. Research and development, production and marketing of products were specific responsibilities of the divisions. Divisional plans and budgets for the group companies were discussed with headquarters' divisions in Basel, and coordinated with the group companies' managing directors. Major investment projects in the group companies were reviewed

EXHIBIT 1 Corporate Organization

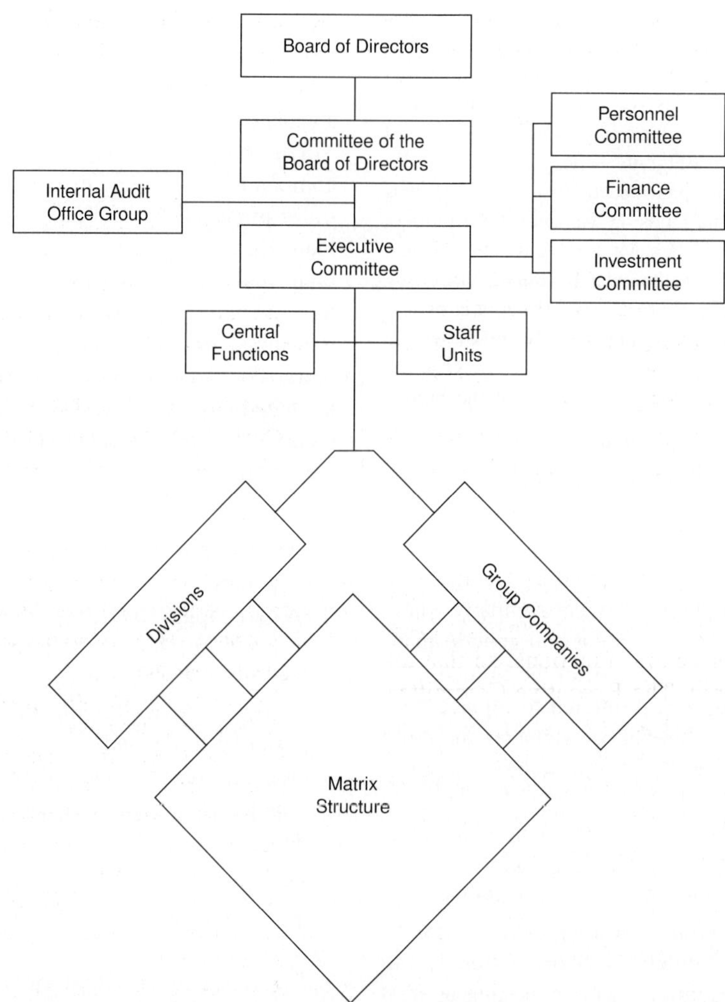

Central Functions

- Research
- Technology, Switzerland
- Technology, group
- Finance
- Control and management services
- Personnel, Switzerland
- Information and promotion
- Legal services
- Commercial services
- Superannuation fund and property
- Protection of health and environment

Product Division

- Pharma
- Self medication
- Ciba Vision
- Crop protection
- Animal Health
- Seeds
- Textile dyes
- Chemicals
- Additives
- Pigments
- Polymers
- Composites
- Mettler Toledo

Staff Units

- Central secretariat
- Regional services
- Management development
- Corporate planning

by the product divisions, which were also responsible for business development on a worldwide basis.

Divisional management also participated in establishing the organizational structure of, and in nominating candidates for top positions in their corresponding divisions within group companies. Product divisions were managed through divisional management committees reflecting the main functions of a division.

The group company managing director had to operate within the framework of policies and guidelines set from the center, and to harmonize plans between the various central units (divisions and central functions) and local requirements. The divisional heads within each group company were administratively responsible to the managing director, but were also functionally responsible to the corresponding division in Basel.

The *Executive Committee,* in Basel, was constituted by 10 members and was responsible for group policy, structure, resource allocation (plans, budgets, investments), management systems and guidelines, and the evaluation of the performance of individual units.

Each member of the Executive Committee was overseeing, as a "patron," a number of countries and one or two divisions or central functions, so that all major units were covered. The Executive Committee met as a group frequently. The preparation and negotiation of decisions involving several divisions, group companies, and/or central functions could be delegated by the Executive Committee to regional staffs. These provided an intermediate level between the group companies and the Executive Committee, since all 80 or so group companies could not effectively be supervised directly by the individual Executive Committee members.

Central Services fell into two categories: Executive Committee staffs and corporate functions. They formulated, for the approval of the Executive Committee, opinions, guidelines, and procedures specific to their field, commented on functional plans and budgets to the heads of group companies, and participated in the nomination of group companies' functional executives. Central functions and staffs also placed their specific expertise at the service of group companies.

Two key Executive Committee staff functions were Corporate Planning and Management Development (the latter is described below in detail). Recently, planning had acquired more prominence with the redefinition of Ciba-Geigy's businesses into about 30 "corporate segments," and the establishment of a corporate strategic plan drawn from a bottom-up planning process at segment level rather than only at divisional level. The corporate planning staff at Ciba-Geigy employed only four people, and was directly responsible to the Chairman of the Executive Committee. Franz Hartmann, its director, explained the changes in corporate strategy and the way resources were allocated that had transpired over the past few years:

> "During the 1970s and early '80s the resource allocation process in Ciba-Geigy was not very sophisticated. It was rather informal since there were few financial constraints. The real beginning of strategic planning occurred in 1984, in the sense of it being more than simple operational planning with a longer-term horizon. The economic crisis in the early 1980s forced us to put more emphasis on actual strategic thinking and less on number pushing. We introduced portfolio approaches, which reflected the growing differentiation among our businesses and the need to account for different success factors in how, and by whom they were managed. As a result, the divisions moved from worldwide segment strategies to local portfolios of segments. During the 1990s there was growing delegation in operational matters by the Executive Committee to divisions and group companies. We were now introducing new tools such as value-based assessment, to better drive the segment strategies.
>
> "This segment approach questions the divisional structure. We will need to implement substructural changes to fit the segments and reallocate functional responsibilities within divisions. We were also going to need better managers and more general managers. We were now recruiting more and more MBAs and putting a lot of emphasis on young people and training, sending them abroad early in their careers to take up responsibility. In fact, we have been forced to look outside to find general managers for some of our new activities.
>
> "One implication of all this is that there is going to be a lot more internal competition within the firm. Changes are being made in the role of the group company managers. Originally, they were mainly administrators, political agents, and caretakers. They now play a key role in difficult trade-offs among divisions within their companies on issues of employment, investment, plant location, and so on. They are increasingly being asked to contribute to the planning dialogue between local and headquarters division management." [See Exhibits 2 and 3 for corporate information.]

Management Development at Ciba-Geigy

Dr. Leopold Luthi, was a lawyer who joined Geigy in 1967, worked in various line management positions in

EXHIBIT 2 Group Sales and Financial Highlights (SFr Millions)

	1994	1995
Sales by Operating Sector and Division		
Health Care	8,745	7,998
-Pharmaceuticals	6,105	5,828
-Self medication	938	1,049
-Ciba Vision	1,094	1,121
Agriculture	4,765	4,805
-Crop protection	4,037	3,880
-Animal health	491	709
-Seeds	237	216
Industry	8,538	7,896
-Textile dyes	1,316	1,083
-Chemicals	1,216	1,081
-Additives	2,222	2,067
-Pigments	1,091	1,026
-Polymers	1,238	1,238
-Composites	399	391
-Mettler Toledo	1,056	1,010
Group total	22,048	20,699
Financial Highlights		
Group after Tax Profit	1,913	2,156
Operating Profit	2,729	3,046
-Health Care	1,689	1,895
-Agriculture	727	969
-Industry	928	834
-Unallocated	−615	−652
Group Operating Cash Flow	2,754	2,335
Wages, Salaries, Bonuses, and Welfare Benefits	4,095	3,719
Research and Development Expenditures	2,151	1,985
Capital Expenditures	1,375	1,276
Current Assets	18,472	17,305
Long-term Assets	13,372	13,165
Short-term Liabilities	9,989	7,173
Long-term Liabilities	6,129	6,063
Capital	15,726	17,234
Earnings Per Share (SFr)	68.10	75.40
Dividends Per Share (SFr)	17.00	20.00
Average Price-Earnings Ratio	11.5	13.5
Number of Employees at Year-End	83,980	84,077
Geographic Distribution of Sales		
Europe	55.8%	58.2%
The Americas	42.8	40.9
Other	18.6	18.8
Less Intersegment Sales	(17.2)	(17.9)
Total	100%	100%

Source: Annual reports.

EXHIBIT 3 Location of Major Affiliates

Region	Major Affiliates and Agencies
Europe	Austria, Belgium, Czech Republic, Denmark, Finland, France, Germany, Greece, Hungary, Ireland, Italy, Netherlands, Norway, Poland, Portugal, Romania, Russia, Slovenia, Spain, Sweden, Switzerland, Turkey, United Kingdom
North America	Bermuda, Canada, United States
Latin America	Argentina, Brazil, Cayman Is., Chile, Colombia, Dominican Republic, Ecuador, Guadaloupe, Guatemala, Mexico, Peru, Uruguay, Venezuela
Africa	Egypt, Ivory Coast, Kenya, Morocco, Nigeria, South Africa, Zimbabwe
Asia	Bangladesh, China, Hong Kong, India, Indonesia, Iran, Japan, Malaysia, Pakistan, Philipines, Saudi Arabia, Singapore, South Korea, Taiwan, Thailand, Vietman
Oceania	Australia, New Zealand

Note: Headquarters are located in Basel, Switzerland.

the Agchem division for over 15 years, and later became Head of Management Development for Ciba-Geigy. He explained the early development of the management development (MD) function in the company as follows:

> "A separate staff unit was created called 'Executive Development' whose role was to assure a supply of qualified managers for line management positions. The unit was to report directly to the Executive Committee. The idea was to make management development planning an automatic component of the yearly divisional and regional plans. At the beginning we overestimated the possibility of developing precise instruments of measurement and evaluation from which to derive the development potential. In fact, a formal system would not work. Line managers might comment quite differently on their people according to whether they evaluated current performance or future development potential.
>
> The units in Basel and abroad started to work on MD plans, we discussed these plans with them, and we started to present them to the chairman of the Executive Committee and to the unit's 'Patron'. One of the early issues was to get comparability of people and profiles on a lateral basis among the units. We had about 1,000 executives included in our MD program. At the beginning, the system we developed worked mainly with the executive group within each

EXHIBIT 4 Typical Annual Job Rotations, Total and International, 1990s

	Total	Of Which		International Rotations			
				From:	HQ	Group Co.	Group Co.
	Rotations	Local	International	To:	Group Co.	HQ	Group Co.
Executives	96	76	20		3	8	9
Potential Executives	185	154	31		14	5	12
Total	281	230	51		17	13	21

company where the immediate preoccupation with succession was the highest. We later expanded the process to reach those young men and women of high potential in the organization, and to increase the supply of them over time."

Currently, the management development staff unit at corporate headquarters employed 14 people, roughly half of them working in management education, running and organizing in-house and external training courses, and the other half dealing with succession planning, recruitment, job rotations, MD plans, etc.

The Central Management Development program focused on some 2,100 employees (2 percent of total employment) of the company, the so-called executives and potential executives. In addition to slightly over 100 senior executives in top management positions, the executives occupied the 1,000 or so most senior management positions in Ciba-Geigy worldwide (400 in Basel and 600 abroad) including Directors, Deputy Directors, and Vice Directors of the parent company, and the top management positions within the group companies. The potential executives, numbering about 1,000, were employees at lower and middle management levels who, in the opinion of their supervisors, were likely to advance some day to an executive position. The final responsibility for appointments and selection to the list was with line management: the Executive Committee for executive appointments, and the various group company, divisional, and central function heads for the potential executives.

This corporate wide management development program had several objectives:

1. Planning executive successions for the whole group on the basis of corporate, divisional, and group company MD planning reports;
2. Identifying potential executives and plan their next development steps;
3. Monitoring the quality and age structure of each unit's executive and potential executive population;
4. Setting up career moves and job rotation for both executives and potential executives totaling about 300 per year (see Exhibit 4);
5. Coordination of the moves of obsolete executives into new positions to give them new incentives and added motivation; and
6. Educational development of all executives and potential executives through internal (in-house) and external (business schools) management courses.

As such the role of the MD unit was *conceptual* (policy and system development); *pedagogical* (assignment and coordination of management training activities); and *advisory* (to the Executive Committee). It follows that the three mainstays of Ciba-Geigy's MD program were the MD plans, its training programs, and its role in executive appointments.

Management Development Plans

Drawn up every two years by the heads of every group company and every division and function of the parent company, each MD plan showed the current executive positions in the organization, indicated future moves and candidates for job rotations, proposed internal successors and offered positions for outside candidates, showed potential executives, and defined action programs (see Exhibit 5 for examples). Upon receipt of an MD plan, the MD staff at headquarters would first discuss it with the appropriate unit head, and then present it to the Chairman of the Executive Committee and to the unit's patrons. In the case of an MD plan for a group company, it would also be discussed with each corporate division or function as far as its corresponding local subunit was concerned. Dr. Luthi added:

"The way in which the various group companies are handling this question varies a great deal. In the U.S. and Italy, for example, the local group company's Executive

EXHIBIT 5 MD Succession Charts
Key for MD Planning Signs

Title / Name	Key management position: key manager
Title / Name	Key management position which is also an executive position : executive
Title / Name	Key manager with potential for advancement*
Title / Name	Key manager who could assume greater responsibility at the same organizational level*
Title / Name	Key management position which could be abrogated when present holder leaves*
Title / Name	Key management position which is expected to become vacant within the next 5 years*
Title / Name	Potential key manager
○	Key manager or potential key manager in position outside the organization unit represented by the chart
- - - - - - - - - →	Possible move (e.g., for successor candidate)
——————→	Definite move (i.e., decision already made)

*These descriptions can also be used for key managers in executive positions.

Committee discusses the plan and then holds additional discussions with the various divisional management committees. The whole system permeates the group company. In Mexico they are now going to do a two-day human resource planning meeting in Cuernavaca. One day is going to deal with the strategic plan, and another day with implications in terms of the MD plan. That is good because they can couple the two systems very closely.

"Other countries do it with a lot more secrecy. They do not discuss this as a group, only face-to-face with the relevant managers. It is very important for us in Basel to have the confidence of line management. Therefore, we have to assure them that each unit's MD plan will be treated with appropriate confidentiality . . ."

"A critical element in the successful implementation of our objectives is the full commitment and backing of the Chairman of the Executive Committee and its members. The general managers of large group companies come personally to Basel to discuss the management development plan with the Chairman of the Executive Committee, the patrons and our staff."

EXHIBIT 5 (continued) MD Chart for Medium Group Company

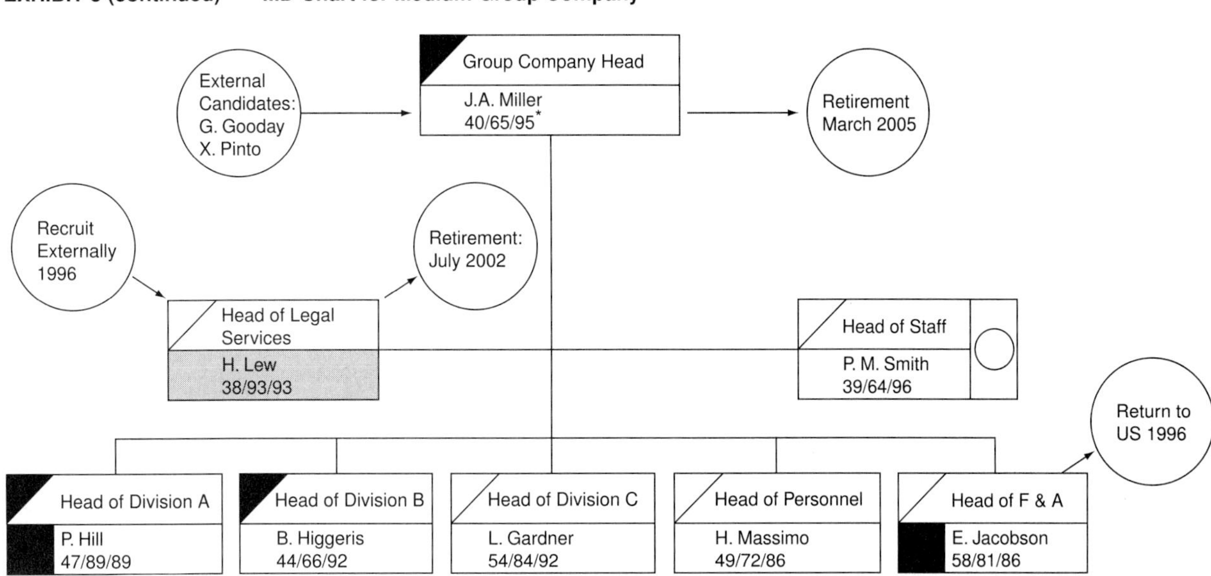

*X/Y/Z figures below names mean: X, year of birth; Y, year when joined Ciba-Geigy, and Z, year when appointed to current position. Therefore Mr. J. A. Miller was born in 1940, joined Ciba-Geigy in 1965, and has been head of the group company since 1995 (in the example given above)

Note: It is suggested that this chart show the top management organization and the succession situation for the company head and for any other key management positions not shown on the divisional/functional charts. The successor situation for the heads of divisions and functions is usually best shown on their respective charts.

"Putting full responsibility for MD plans with line managers makes the plan adaptive. Rather than try to forecast centrally what managerial profiles would be required, when and in what numbers, the process is designed to develop, cultivate, and track a large inventory of diverse people, from which could be extracted those with the skills required for a particular position at any point in time."

Management Training Programs

Ciba-Geigy put more emphasis and devoted more resources to management training than most companies. The main Ciba-Geigy management course was a two-week program offered to all newly promoted executives of Ciba-Geigy worldwide. Prior to this course many new executives had taken a group orientation course and a basic management course, each one week long. Ciba-Geigy's top management was active in teaching these courses. Senior management seminars were organized every few years in various countries (with a total of 450 participants) to discuss the strategies and profitability of Ciba-Geigy. These in-house central training programs (see Exhibit 6) were the backbone of the company's educational efforts, covering a large number of participants, emphasizing Ciba-Geigy specific topics and concentrating on general management issues.

Each division, function, or group company had its own more specific and more function-oriented training program with basic management courses. Management seminars at various business schools around the world were viewed as important supporting elements, where the emphasis was on the individual needs of the participant, exposure to other firms and industries, and addressing more general business topics.

Executive Appointments

Appointments to all 1,100 executive positions were decided by the Personnel Committee, which consisted of three members of the Board of Directors and three members of

EXHIBIT 5 (continued) **MD Chart for Large Group Company**

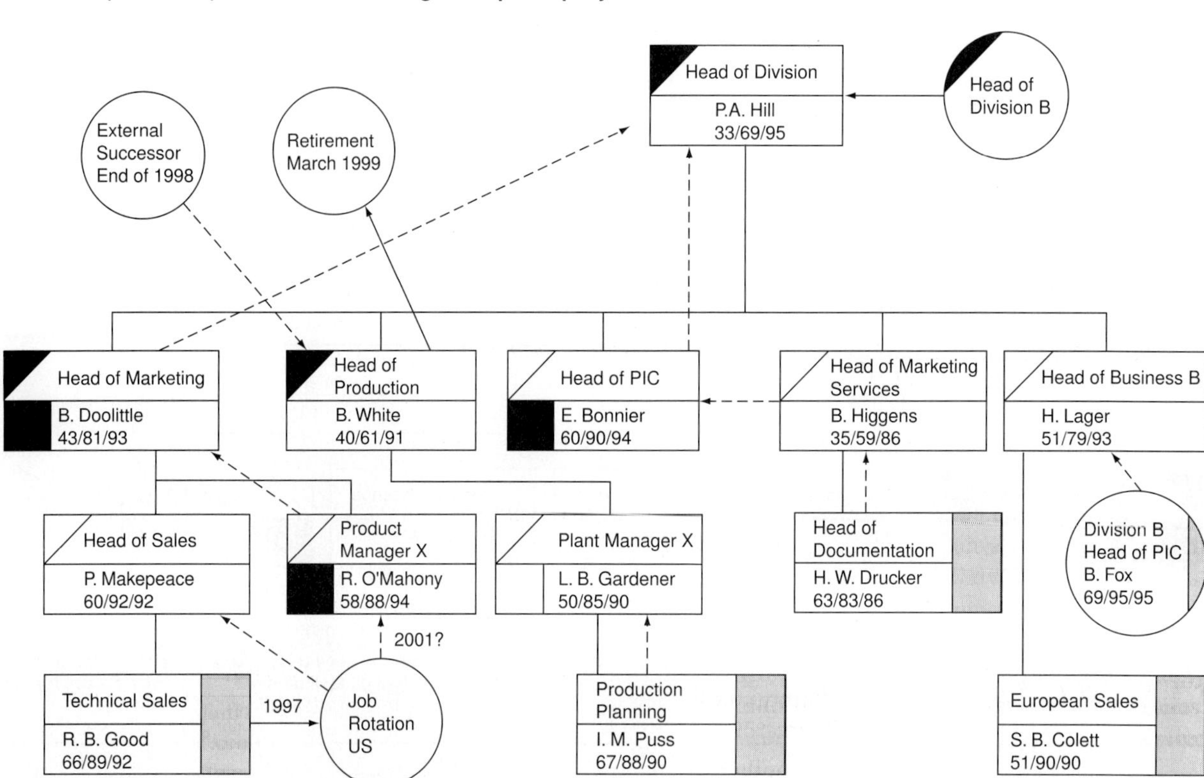

the Executive Committee. The Personnel Committee met every Thursday to recommend top appointments; its decisions went next to the full Executive Committee for their approval. The head of the MD unit met every Monday morning with the Chairman of the Executive Committee to review all pending MD matters. From time to time, this Monday meeting also reviewed individual cases for both executive and potential executive appointments and dealt with possible crises. The meetings could include other executives as appropriate.

Based on the MD plans and numerous discussions with division, function, and group company heads, the MD unit prepared a list of candidates for promotion. For some divisions, such as Pharma, and for positions below that of Group Company Division Head, the preparation of such lists was often delegated to the divisional MD Manager. Dr. Luthi commented:

> "Decisions are taken in person-to-person discussions, and not exclusively based on the personnel files of the candidates. Our approach is not only an appraisal of the current job performance, but also considers suggestions regarding the job someone could take over in the future. Personal judgments of the line managers on candidates are critical; they know the task and the job and they are the person's direct boss. Yet for any particular promotion someone has to write a broad list of candidates, not only coming from the specific line organization, but also from other divisions, other group companies, other functions and eventually from outside Ciba-Geigy. The list is based mainly on the MD plan, but we can put additional candidates of a given background on the list. The process builds on the inventory of suitable candidates."

The product divisions were a centralizing element in MD planning. As they had worldwide profit responsibility and were responsible for worldwide strategies, they had a strong interest in the quality and choice of the people in the different group companies. Therefore, when a divisional executive in a group company came up for a promotion appointment, the Executive Committee expected the head of the group company and of the parent division to provide a joint proposal.

EXHIBIT 6 Internal Management Training and Orientation Programs

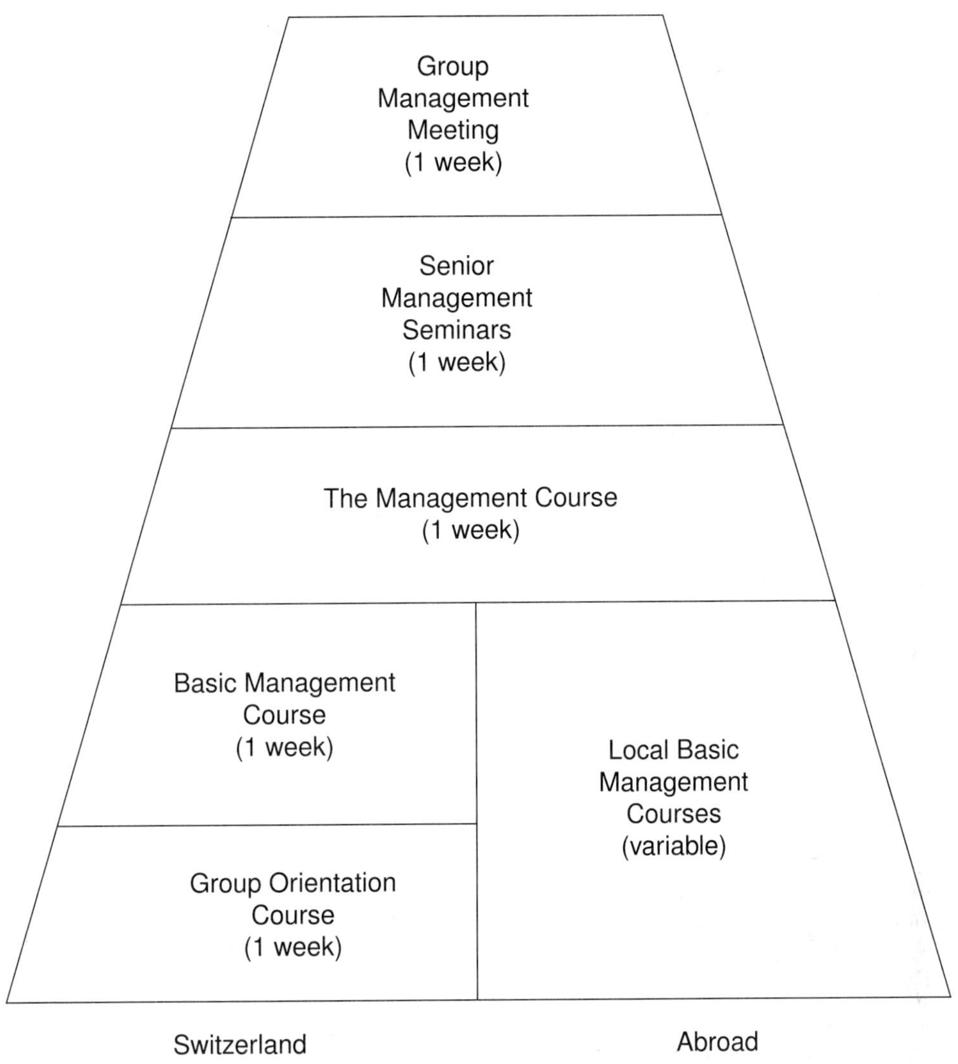

Management Development in the Pharma Division

While some Ciba-Geigy divisions were facing a slowdown in profitability and low growth prospects, others, such as the Pharma division, were growing rapidly. Divisional management was concerned that there would be a shortage of executives and potential executives to fill future positions. Alfred Steiner had been head of management development for the Pharma division for the past three years, and prior to that a member of the corporate MD staff for seven years. He explained the situation:

> "Five years ago a new Pharma division head developed a strategy to branch out more broadly into the health care market, rather than stay exclusively in ethical pharmaceuticals. This diversification led divisional management to become overburdened, and to the realization that what the division had as available potential executives was in no way sufficient to staff our needs for the next five to ten years given the new growth targets. In fact, the division realized that it

had too few potential executives even for current replacement alone.

"The new division head approached Dr. Luthi with a suggestion for an MD function within the Pharma division. When I first came to the Pharma division I soon realized that the secretary of the division's management committee had sat down over a weekend to get the MD plan done. The forms were filled in, but not taken very seriously. The official MD planning system was conceived as a corporate instrument with too restrictive definitions for actual development purposes in critical stages. Potential executives were 35 to 40 years old, but by that age a career is almost over in development potential! We had to change that process."

"Another problem we found is that the MD plan reflects today's organizational structure and does not project requirements into the future. The organization is changing constantly, you can't do tomorrow's succession planning based on an interpretation of today's structure. Therefore, it is not a real plan; it remains a mere inventory, not an action program. But at least it shows us who are the potential executives and what they may become."

Steiner set out with an action plan for management development in the Pharma division. Several goals were formulated such as achieving an even ratio between executives and potential executives, since currently the former far out numbered the latter. He also initiated a program to recruit 40 young people each year, mainly MBAs, and put them on a fast track development. This was a major change from Ciba-Geigy's traditional recruitment policy. Finally, systematic MD planning was instituted that would account for different profiles of executives needed for the traditional drug business versus new business sectors and acquisitions.

In total the MD unit in Pharma dealt with nearly 600 people, 330 executives and 250 potential executives on a worldwide basis, covering operations in over 60 countries. The MD action plan was specifically tailored to the needs of the Pharma division as Mr. Steiner remarked:

"Obviously, what we developed here would not apply to Ciba-Geigy as a whole since other divisions face different management development and competitive problems . . . The Pharma division is growing fast but competing head-on with other companies like Hoechst, Glaxo, or MSD. If we want to compete successfully for executives, we have to offer salary levels comparable to those offered by our main competitors. Clearly we have a conflict between the salaries our division has to pay and those other divisions want to pay. Also, as a rule, the most profitable divisions believe that they should have a higher standard of living."

The Pharma Division in France

Pharma division operations in France had always been rather autonomous. In the old days, the French Pharma Division had been headed by Dr Henri d'Encausses, a pharmacist and the Mayor of Gaillardon, a village in Southern France. He gladly entertained visiting executives from headquarters, but carefully protected his autonomy. In this he had the implicit support of the company's Managing Director, Antoine Roux, who ran the French subsidiary quite successfully and kept headquarters at bay. Middle managers were caused to think that Basel was trying to influence the group company unduly. Since his thinking was often ahead of that in Basel, Mr. Roux maintained his advantage and kept the management of the French company close to his chest.

Tensions grew eventually between Roux and divisional and corporate management in Basel, and he was replaced by René Lamont, a French speaking Swiss national of English origin, who had been head of the French Pharma division for three years. Lamont was succeeded in this role by Maitre Guillaume, a French lawyer, who was appointed at age 65, and occupied the position only for two years until Delage's arrival. Lamont was a skillful negotiator who did much to improve communications between headquarters and the French company.

Neither Lamont nor Guillaume had a strong feeling for management development. They did not have the necessary potential executives to fill new positions and let an enduring weakness develop in their supply of managers. When Delage came back to France, for instance, he was the only manager with a marketing background and a good knowledge of English. Lamont and Guillaume had satisfied corporate MD formal requirement by drawing up MD plans when requested, but concrete implementation actions rarely followed these plans and little was done to recruit and develop potential managers. Delage strengthened the French Pharma Division considerably. First, he spent much time in the field improving the quality of the medical representatives' force, by training, selection, and replacement. He then created two positions of product line managers—one for Ciba products, the other for Geigy's—to provide additional sales and marketing management competence and support, and replaced several of the weaker product managers. As a result, the Pharma organization in France was much improved (see Exhibit 7).

EXHIBIT 7 French Pharma Division Sales and Marketing Structure

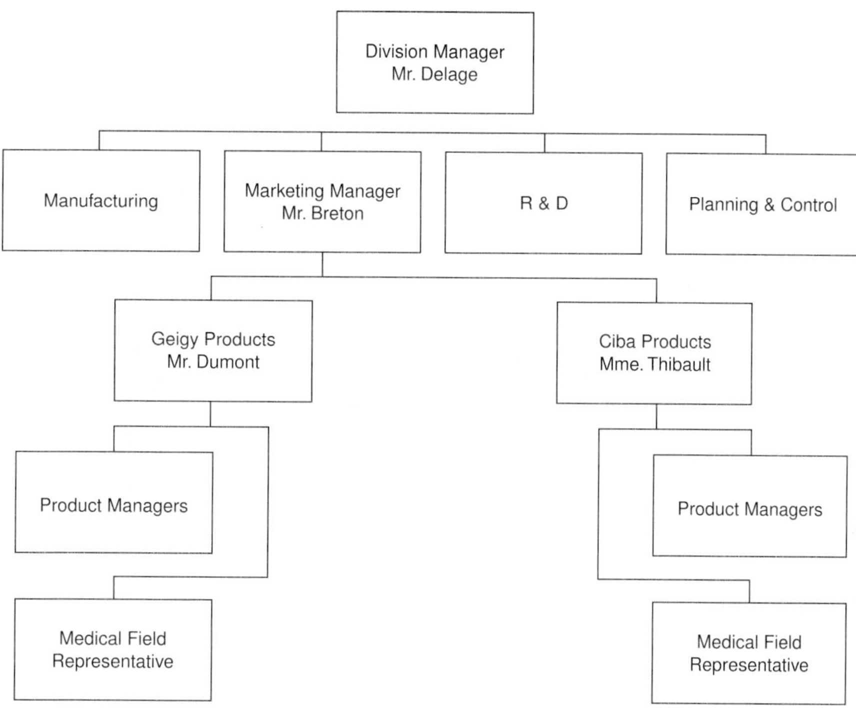

The Choice of a New Marketing Manager

When Lamont retired, Delage was chosen to replace him in competition with a Swiss expatriate. Among many factors in the decision it was felt that national feelings in France would favor a Frenchman to head the local group company. According to H. Grunwald, Pharma's European regional manager:

> "Delage is a prototype of a successful career within Ciba-Geigy Pharma. He has been successful wherever he was. Delage is the type of person we really like. Among possible candidates he was closest to the ideal profile: a Frenchman to head the French group company, but with good experience of headquarters, several successful assignments abroad, and a clear perspective on relationships with Basel. We want that type of person in key positions abroad. He already was an ideal division manager who understood the Ciba-Geigy philosophy well. There is nothing worse than having key people in group companies who know nobody in Basel, are not known to headquarters, and lack an understanding of the company's culture."

The only issue with Delage's appointment, was that he had been division head in France for less than two years and, in reviewing the French MD plan, the Executive Committee had put a hold on him. Yet, since no other candidate came close to his profile, he was selected.

Finding a new Pharma division head to replace Delage was more difficult. Two years ago, while head of the division, Delage had proposed hiring Charles Mortier as marketing manager for Pharma France. Nobody from the French Pharma division was well qualified for the job, and the only candidate suggested by the corporate MD unit was a Swiss manager then in Canada, Paul Aubert, who worked in another division and was not well known to the Basel Pharma division management. Mortier had a good track record with a U.S. pharmaceutical company in

France, where his career progression had been stifled, and he was a seasoned marketing and sales manager. After much discussion, his appointment was agreed by all parties. But after barely a year with Ciba-Geigy, Mortier went back to his former employer, lured by a promotion as marketing manager and a financially attractive offer. Soon thereafter, the U.S. company introduced a product in direct competition to Ciba-Geigy's very successful Voltarene.

Delage then hired Jules Breton from Sanofi to become the new marketing manager. In the interim, following Mortier's departure, Delage had to step back into this role, spending about 60 percent of his time on marketing and sales issues in addition to his division management responsibilities until Breton's arrival. Breton was more a general manager than a marketing specialist so that a year later, with Delage's appointment as managing director, the opportunity came to promote him as division head. According to Steiner, "there was no better candidate. We are reluctant to go out on the market for division heads, and Breton knew the French market and his people well. He did not, however, know headquarters nor the Ciba-Geigy culture, and he was not well known to headquarters' management. But we decided we could live with this."

Breton and Delage then suggested Dumont as a replacement for Breton as marketing manager. Dumont had been recruited from Specia (a French competitor) to take responsibility for the marketing of the Geigy line of pharmaceutical products. He was a pharmacist with an additional degree in political science (from "Science-Po", a prestigious *grande école* in Paris). Following military service, he had joined Boehringer-Ingelheim in Reims as product manager for OTC (over-the-counter) drugs. A year later, he joined a Specia subsidiary, overseeing two products which between them accounted for over 50 percent of the subsidiary's sales. He became responsible for all product managers at Specia and was very successful. He was then offered to head a newly acquired market research subsidiary that would create a marketing "methodology" to advise and assist line managers. Seeing himself more as a line manager, he was not very pleased with this new position when he was approached by an executive placement firm on behalf of Ciba-Geigy. Following interviews and discussions with Mortier and Delage, he decided to join the company.

By the time Dumont came on board, Mortier had left the company and for the next six months (until Breton actually arrived on the job) the French Pharma Division had no marketing manager. Delage, in addition to his divisional management duties, concentrated most of his attention on the Ciba products, where rapid product line management turnover had created problems. Dumont was immediately given full responsibility for the Geigy product line with little supervision. This included a marketing and sales force of about 120 people, supported by a service staff of more than 20 people. He handled them successfully, continuing the 20 percent per annum real rate of growth started under Delage. According to Dumont, the quality of the products, the commitment of management, and the financial means of Ciba-Geigy explained that continued success.

In less than one year, Dumont had created a good impression at headquarters. According to Grunwald, the Pharma European regional manager, "he attended meetings in Basel and left good impressions everywhere; he elicited positive feelings and was known within headquarters." Nonetheless, headquarters routinely initiated a wider search for candidates. According to Steiner: "We were asked 'why not go with Dumont?' by Delage and Breton. Our initial reaction was that we do not really know Dumont very well since he has been in the company only a few months. At first sight he seems very young—he was born in 1962—but maybe we are getting old. We wanted to look at who else we had. Delage knew all of them anyway."

Dumont had been very successful in France and knew both the techniques of marketing and the specific character of the French pharmaceutical markets extremely well. The French pharmaceutical market was considered one of the most difficult for foreign competitors, among European markets. France had some strong national competitors, such as Specia, with extensive positions on their domestic market, but little international presence. Furthermore, prices were tightly controlled and complex administrative and political procedures governed the registration of new drugs. In a price inelastic market, margins were slim. The new Socialist government in France was about to initiate discussions with foreign pharmaceutical companies with the objective of granting price increases only to those which agreed to increase local investment and employment levels.

The French market was one of the largest national markets for Ciba-Geigy's pharmaceutical products. Among the group companies, France had had the most success with Voltarene, and this product now accounted for a substantial proportion of Ciba-Geigy's sales in France. Steiner and Grunwald drew up a profile of an ideal candidate. According to them, international exposure and headquarters experience were desirable characteristics that Dumont lacked. Together, they designed a more formalized profile to assess candidates (see Exhibit 8). This blank profile would be sent to each senior manager within Ciba-Geigy who knew the candidates.

EXHIBIT 8 Candidate Profile Form

Group Company Division Marketing Management Evaluation Grid	Education				Experience						Personality							
	Professional Education	MBA or Management Seminars	Knowledge of English	Knowledge of Local Languages	Several Years of Successful Line Management Experience	Pharma Marketing Management	Market Research	Planning and Control	International Management Experience	Local Market Experience	Analytic Skills	Creativity	Overall Management Skills	Leadership Capability	Overall Balance	Development Potential	Career Development Aspect	Availability
Inidividuals																		

Steiner reviewed the files of possible candidates from outside the French company and came up with a total of about 40 names drawn from among 600 Pharma managers, worldwide. He then analyzed these, employing three main criteria to pare the list down: suitability for the position; availability; and career development considerations. The requirement for full "perfect" fluency in French quickly eliminated all but six candidates. Only three of these were considered as "genuine" candidates by Steiner and Grunwald, and they were submitted to Delage.

Delage quickly brushed aside one candidate who looked perfect on paper, but whom he knew personally from a previous position in the Pharma division and whom he did not consider suitable for the position. Another candidate turned out not to be available, having been in his current position only nine months and not being easily replaceable there. This left one possible candidate: Michel Malterre. Malterre, however, had been slotted to move to Greece as Pharma marketing manager there in one year and was not, therefore, technically available.

Malterre was a 36 year-old, French-speaking Swiss, a lawyer by training, and currently marketing manager for the Pharma division in West Africa. He had started with Ciba-Geigy in 1986, and for the next two years was legal assistant to the Pharma division's manager for planning, information, and control in Basel. During the civil war in Nicaragua, the International Committee of the Red Cross (Geneva) had asked Ciba-Geigy for Malterre's detachment on leave to Central America, where he had worked with the Red Cross prior to his joining the company. After four months spent organizing medical relief programs there, often flying in helicopters through combat zones, he returned to his job in Basel. The company's Executive Committee was interested in the value of lending executives to nonprofit organizations for humanitarian purposes and asked Malterre to make a detailed presentation of his experience upon his return.

Malterre was then named product manager for anesthetics in Switzerland, after which he was appointed to the secretariat of the Chair of the Executive Committee for five years. He then applied for a line job and was sent to the Ivory Coast to market pharmaceutical products. Over the past three years he was quite successful in developing sales in West Africa and had developed good relationships with local health officials and ministers. His MD plan called for his transfer to Greece in the next year.

Headquarters executives were sensitive to various aspects of Malterre's career. According to Grunwald, "Malterre has worked in Pharma, at corporate level and abroad. His big disadvantage is not to be French, but his mother tongue is French. He is well experienced in the Ciba-Geigy organization, and knows the French group company, since most products sold in West Africa were manufactured in France."

SECTION

Synthesis and Integration

UNIT 14 Organizational and Strategic Redirection

Case 14–1

AB Thorsten (1)

By late July 1996, Mr. Anders Ekstrom awaited with a certain amount of impatience for a decision from corporate headquarters in Montreal, Canada, on his proposal to begin manufacturing XL–4 in Sweden within the next year. After several months of preparation, Mr. Ekstrom was anxious to finalize this matter and return his attention to his many other responsibilities as President of AB Thorsten, a wholly owned subsidiary of Roget Industries Ltd., a large diversified Canadian company.

Roget's History and Operating Philosophy

Roget Industries Ltd. was one of the largest industrial companies in Quebec, Canada. Founded in the 1920s, the company originally produced a simple line of chemical products for sale in Canada. By 1996, it had expanded to produce more than 200 complex, specialty chemicals in 21 factories located throughout Canada, the United States, and a few European countries.

Mr. André Juvet, Chairman of the Board and President of Roget, believed that the company's organization (see Exhibit 1) was the result of careful planning:

> "Until the mid-1960s, we were organized with one large manufacturing division here in Canada, and one large sales division with a small department devoted to export markets. However, exports grew fast and domestic markets became so complex that we were forced to create three main product divisions, each with its own manufacturing plants and sales organizations.
>
> "At first, the United States had been our largest foreign market, but beginning in 1975, anticipating the establishment of the Canada–United States Free Trade Area, we integrated all North American operations into one organization, and gave each division direct responsibility for its international operations. As sales to other markets expanded, each division gradually set up foreign subsidiaries to take over the business in certain areas. For example, in Industrial Chemicals we have two European subsidiaries—one in the United Kingdom serving the British and Continental markets, and one in Sweden, which serves all Scandinavia and Eastern Europe. The U.K. and Swedish companies account for 9 percent and 5 percent of divisional sales, about a third of which originate in Canada. The domestic department of the Industrial Chemicals Division handles all exports, whether they go to our subsidiaries or to independent agents in countries where we have no direct presence.
>
> "Our organization is designed to provide individual profit responsibility at all levels. Mr. Gillot, for example, is responsible for profits for all industrial chemicals; Mr. Lambert is responsible for profits from North American

This case is based on an earlier series entitled AB Thorsten (A–C) prepared by Professors Gordon Shillinglaw and Charles Summer at the International Management Development Institute (IMD), Lausanne, Switzerland.

EXHIBIT 1 Roget Industries Ltd.—Organization Chart

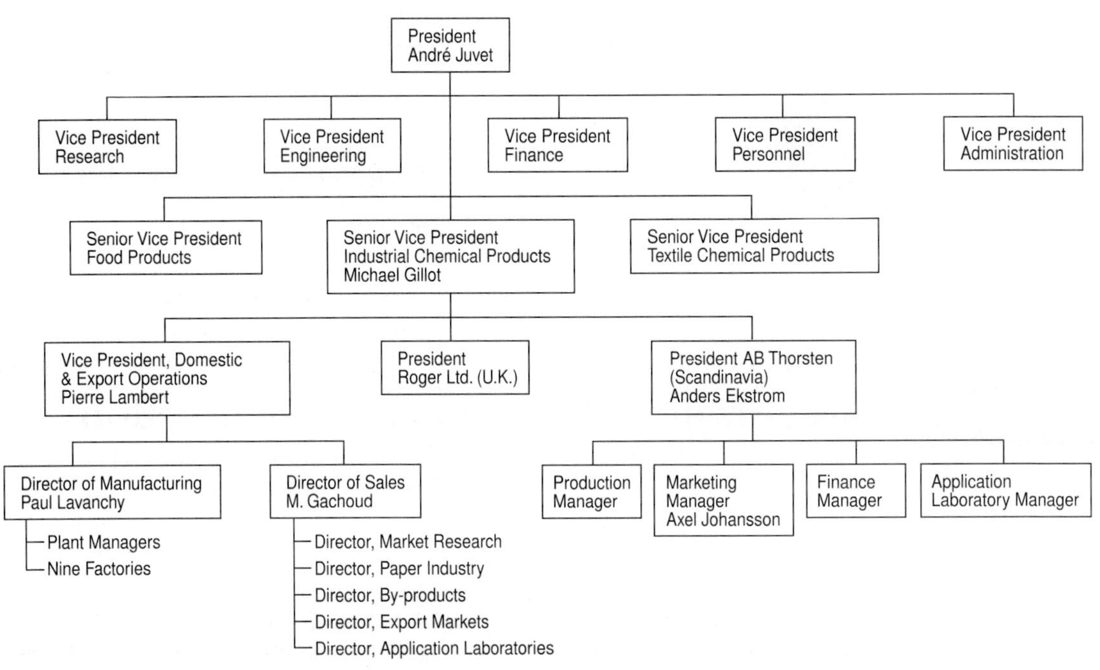

operations (manufacturing and sales) and from export sales; and Mr. Ekstrom is responsible for profits in his geographic area from both imported and locally made products. We also utilize a liberal bonus system to reward executives at each level, based on the profits of their divisions. This structure, together with a policy of promotion from within, helps stimulate managers in Roget to a degree not enjoyed by some of our competitors. It also helps to keep executives in an industry where experience is of great importance. Most of our managers have been in the starch chemicals business all of their lives. It is a complex business, and we feel that it takes many years to learn it.

"We have developed certain policies—rules of the game—that govern relationships with our subsidiary company presidents. These are intended to maintain efficiency within the whole Roget complex, while at the same time they provide subsidiary managers with sufficient autonomy to run their own businesses. For example, a subsidiary manager can determine what existing Roget products he wants to sell in his part of the world market. Export sales will quote him the same price as they quote agents in all countries. He is free to bargain, and if he doesn't like the price he need not sell the product. Second, we encourage subsidiaries to propose to division management in Montreal the development of new products. If these are judged feasible we will proceed to manufacture them in Canada for supply to world markets. Third, the subsidiary president can build his own manufacturing plants if he can justify the investment."

Company Background: AB Thorsten

AB Thorsten was acquired by Roget in 1978. During the first 10 years of Roget's ownership, Thorsten's sales first grew from Skr. 50 million to about SKr. 170 million, but dropped again at the end of that period. With cumulative losses threatening the viability of the company, the board of AB Thorsten decided that the only alternative to closing down or selling the company was to hire a totally different management team to overhaul and streamline operations. On advice of the Swedish directors, and with the help of a local executive search firm, Mr. Anders Ekstrom, a 38-year-old graduate of the Royal Institute of Technology, was hired as President. He had a total of 16 years of experience in production engineering for a large machinery company, as marketing manager of a British subsidiary in Sweden and, more recently, as division manager in a large paper company. As Ekstrom described his experience:

"Working for the paper company, the European subsidiary of a large U.S. firm, was particularly valuable to me. I knew little of modern financial methods and strategic planning prior to my working with them, as most of my training and experience had been on the technical side. As I came into contact with executives trained in many top U.S. business schools, I came to realize that these were the kind of tools I needed to be successful, those needed to operate our industry with maximum productivity. Fortunately, my previous employer was committed to executive training and sent me to a number of courses in which I was exposed to these analytical tools. Sure enough, they have been invaluable to me and to Thorsten. A few executives in Roget are familiar with them, but even there such methods are relatively unknown among many managers. I am proud to have learned such management techniques and they give me confidence in managing Thorsten—for the benefit of the company and for the benefit of Sweden's productive capacity."

Ekstrom had been president of AB Thorsten since early in 1989. Since that time the same team had constituted Thorsten's Board of Directors: Mr. Michael Gillot, Senior Vice President in charge of Roget's Industrial Chemical Products Division; Mr. Ingve Norgren, a prominent Swedish banker; Mr. Ove Svensen, a Stockholm industrialist with considerable international experience; and Ekstrom. Swedish corporation law required any company incorporated in Sweden to have Swedish directors, and Roget management felt fortunate in having found two such distinguished individuals to serve on the Thorsten board.

Ekstrom recognized that there were risks associated with his joining Thorsten:

"I like the challenge of building a company. If I do a good job here, I will have the confidence of Norgren and Svensen as well as of Roget's management in Montreal. Deep down inside, succeeding in this situation will teach me things that will make me more competent as a top executive. So I chose this job even though I had at the time (and still occasionally get) offers from other companies."

In the following years, Thorsten sales increased to over Skr. 500 million, and profits had reached levels that Roget's management found highly satisfactory. Both Ekstrom and Norgren attributed this performance to: (a) an increase in industrial activity in Scandinavia since the 1990–91 recession; (b) changes in production methods, marketing strategy, and organization structure made by Ekstrom; (c) the hiring of a competent executive team by Ekstrom; and (d) Ekstrom's own ambition and hard work. Ekstrom's knowledge of modern planning techniques—sophisticated market research methods, financial planning by use of discounted cash flows and incremental analysis, and, as Ekstrom put it, "all those things I learned from my former American employer"—had also contributed to the successful turnaround in Thorsten.

Initial Proposal for Manufacture of XL–4

In September 1995, Ekstrom informed the Thorsten board of directors that he proposed to study the feasibility of constructing a facility in Sweden to manufacture XL–4, a proprietary Roget product used in paper converting processes. He explained that he and his customer engineers had discovered a new way of helping large paper mills adapt their machines at moderate cost so that they could use XL–4 instead of traditional substitute products. Through this innovation, Ekstrom and his team estimated that large paper mill customers would be able to realize dramatic savings in material handling and storage costs, primarily due to substantially shorter drying times, as well as in fuel economy. In their judgment, Ekstrom reported, Thorsten could develop a market in Sweden almost as big as Roget's present worldwide market for XL–4. Roget's Industrial Chemicals Division was then producing XL–4 at the rate of 600 tons a year, and less than 3 percent of this was sold in Scandinavia. According to Ekstrom, Mr. Gillot and the other directors seemed enthusiastic. Gillot reportedly said, "Of course, go ahead with your study and when you have a proposed plan, with the final return on investment, send it in and we will consider it thoroughly." Ekstrom continued:

"During the next six months, we did the analysis. My market research department estimated the total potential market in Sweden at 800 tons of XL–4 per year. We interviewed important customers and conducted trials in the factories of three big companies. These proved that with the introduction of our machine designs the large cost saving would indeed materialize, and would overwhelm the small investment costs associated with making the necessary changes. We determined that if we could sell the product for Skr. 185 per kg., we could capture one-half of the market within a three-year period.

"At the same time, I called the head of Corporate Engineering in Montreal and asked for his help in designing a plant to produce 400 tons of XL–4 per year, and in estimating the cost of the investment. This is a routine thing. The central staff divisions are advisory and always comply with requests for help. He assigned a project manager and

EXHIBIT 2 AB Thorsten Proposal to Manufacture XL–4 in Sweden—Financial Summary (in thousands of Swedish crowns)

Year	Description	After-tax Cash flows*	Present Value at 8%
0	Equipment	(70,000)	
	Working Capital	(5,600)	
	Total	(75,600)	(75,600)
1	Cash Operating Profit	10,500	
	Working Capital	(200)	
	Total	10,300	9,537
2	Cash Operating Profit	16,000	
	Working Capital	(700)	
	Total	15,300	13,117
3	Cash Operating Profit	21,500	17,067
4	Cash Operating Profit	21,500	15,803
5	Cash Operating Profit	21,500	14,633
6	Cash Operating Profit	14,500	9,137
7	Cash Operating Profit	14,500	
	Recovery Value of Equipment and Working Capital	21,500	
	Total	36,000	21,006
	Project Grand Total	**65,000**	**24,701**

Financial Conclusions

Net Present Value to the Corporation	Skr. 24,700
Payback Period (years)	4.3
Internal Rate of Return	15.70%

*From Exhibits 3, 4 and 5.

four other engineers to work on the design of factory and machinery, and to estimate the cost. At the same time I assigned three people from my staff to the project. In three months this joint task group reported that the necessary plant could be built for about Skr. 70 million.

"Our calculations, together with a complete written explanation, were mailed in early April 1996 to Mr. Gillot. I felt rather excited, as did most of my staff. We all know that introduction of new products is one of the keys to continued growth and profitability. The yield on this investment (15 percent) was well above the minimum 8 percent established as a guideline for new investments by the Roget Vice President of Finance. We also knew that it was a good analysis, done by modern tools of management. In the covering letter, I asked that it be put on the agenda for the next Board meeting."

The Board meeting was held in Stockholm on April 28, 1996. The minutes show on the agenda "A Proposal for Investment in Sweden" to be presented by Mr. Ekstrom and members of his staff. They also quote from his remarks as he explained the proposal to the other directors:

"You will see from the summary table (Exhibit 2) that this project is profitable. On an initial outlay of Skr. 70 million for plant and equipment and Skr. 5.6 million for working capital, we get a rate of return over 15 percent and a net present value of Skr. 24.7 million.

"Let me explain some of the figures underlying this summary table. My second chart (Exhibit 3) summarizes the operating cash flows that we expect to get from the XL–4 project. The sales forecast for the first seven years is shown in the first row. The forecast was not extended beyond seven years because our engineers estimated that the technology of starch manufacture will improve gradually, so that major plant renovations will become necessary at about the end of the seventh year. Actually, we see no reason why demand for XL–4 will decline after seven years, as we shall see in a minute.

"The estimated variable cost of Skr. 100 per kg represents the full operating cost of manufacturing XL–4 in Sweden,

EXHIBIT 3 Estimated Operating Cash Flows from Manufacture and Sale of XL–4 in Sweden

	Year							
	1	2	3	4	5	6	7	Total
1. Sales (tons)	200	300	400	400	400	400	400	2,500
				Skr Per kg				
2. Sales Price	200	185	185	185	185	185	185	
3. Variable Costs	100	100	100	100	100	100	100	
4. Profit Margin	100	85	85	85	85	85	85	
				Thousand Skr				
5. Contribution	20,000	25,500	34,000	34,000	34,000	34,000	34,000	215,500
6. Promotion Costs	13,000	7500	5000	5000	5000	5000	5000	45,500
7. Before-tax Profit	7,000	18,000	29,000	29,000	29,000	29,000	29,000	170,000
8. Depreciation	14,000	14,000	14,000	14,000	14,000	0	0	70,000
9. Taxes Payable	(3,500)	2,000	7,500	7,500	7,500	14,500	14,500	50,000
10. Net Cash Flow	10,500	16,000	21,500	21,500	21,500	14,500	14,500	120,000

including out-of-pocket fixed costs such as plant management salaries but excluding depreciation. These fixed costs must of course be included because they are incremental to the decision. We feel certain that we can enter the market initially with a selling price of Skr. 200/kg, but full market penetration will require a price reduction to Skr. 185/kg at the beginning of the second year. The total contribution resulting from these figures is shown on the fifth line. The next two rows list the market development and promotion expenditures that are needed to launch the product and achieve the forecasted sales levels, and the resulting net operating cash flows before tax.

"The cost of the plant can be written off for tax purposes over a five-year period, at the rate of 20 percent of original cost each year. Subtracting this amount from the before-tax cash flow and multiplying by the tax rate (50 percent) yields the tax payable on row 9. When this is subtracted from the before-tax cash flow, it yields the after-tax cash flow on the last line.

"A proposal of this kind also requires some investment in working capital. Our estimates on this element (Exhibit 4) is that we will need about Skr. 8 million to start with, but some of this can be deducted immediately from our income taxes. Swedish law permits us to deduct 60 percent of the cost of inventories from taxable income. For this reason, and given a tax rate of 50 percent, we can get an immediate reduction of Skr. 2.4 million in the taxes we have to pay on our other income in Sweden. We'll need small additional amounts of working capital in the next two years, so that altogether our requirements will add up to Skr. 6.5 million (net of taxes) by the end of our second full year of operations.

"Now, let's come back to the issue of what happens after 2004. Seven years is a very conservative estimate for the life of the product. If we limit the analysis to seven years, we'll be overlooking the value of our assets at the end of that time. At the very worst, the plant itself should be worth Skr. 30 million after seven years (Exhibit 5). We'd have to pay tax on that, of course, because the plant would be fully depreciated, but this would still leave us with a net value of Skr. 15 million for the plant. The working capital should also be fully recoverable. After paying the deferred tax on inventories, we'd get Skr. 6.5 million back on that. The total value at the end of seven years would thus be Skr. 21.5 million.

"As I said earlier, however, we have chosen to be conservative in these calculations. It is quite probable that with a small additional investment the plant could be refurbished and XL–4 production could continue for many years. In conclusion, it seems clear from these figures that we can justify this investment on the basis of sales to the Swedish market alone. There is, however, the possibility of expanding sales to the rest of Scandinavia and Eastern Europe, but we have not incorporated these in our analysis. Our Group Vice President for Finance has laid down the policy that any new investment should yield at least 8 percent. This particular proposal shows a return of 15 percent. My management and I strongly recommend this project."

Ekstrom told the case writer that while he was making this proposal he was sure that it would be accepted, and that Gillot had said "that it seemed to him to be a clear case." The minutes of the Board meeting show that Gillot asked a few questions, mainly about the long-term

Exhibit 4 Estimated Working Capital Required for XL–4 Sales in Sweden
(In thousands of Swedish crowns)

	(1) Inventory at Cost	(2) Other Current Assets Less Current Liabilities	(3) Working Capital [1+2]	(4) Change from Previous Year	(5) Tax Credit [30% of Change in (1)]	(6) Net Funds Required [4–5]
Year 0	8,000	0	8,000	8,000	2,400	5,600
Year 1	9,000	(500)	8,500	500	300	200
Year 2	10,000	(500)	9,500	1,000	300	700
Year 3+	10,000	(500)	9,500	0	0	0
Total	10,000	(500)	9,500	9,500	3,000	6,500

Exhibit 5 Estimated End-of-Life Value of Swedish Assets
(in thousands of Swedish crowns)

Estimated value of plant	30,000	
Less tax on capital gain	15,000	
Net value of plant		15,000
Terminal value of working capital	9,500	
Less payment of deferred taxes on special inventory reserves	3,000	
Net value of working capital		6,500
Net value of Swedish assets after 7 years		21,500

likelihood for sales of more than 400 tons a year, about the expansion to other Scandinavian and East European markets, and about sources of funds. Ekstrom added:

> "I explained that we in Sweden were very firm in our judgment that we would reach 400 tons a year on the first year, but felt constrained to show a conservative estimate of a three-year transition period. If sales to other countries took off in the future, an expansion of the plant's capacity could be undertaken at a fraction of the total costs now envisaged. We also showed him how we could finance any expansion by borrowing in Sweden. That is, if Roget would furnish the initial capital requirements from Canada, and if demand surpassed the 400 ton level, any funds needed for further expansion would easily be lent by local banks. The two Swedish directors confirmed this. The Board then voted unanimously to approve the project."

Disagreement between Parent and Subsidiary

About a week later, Gillot telephoned Ekstrom: "Since my return to Montreal I have been through some additional discussions with the production and marketing people here. They think the engineering design and plant cost are accurate but that you are too optimistic on your sales forecast. It looks like you will have to justify this more." Ekstrom related his reaction:

> "I pushed him to set up a meeting the following week. This meeting was attended by me and my marketing and production directors from Sweden, and four people from Canada: Gillot, Lavanchy [Director of Manufacturing], Gachoud [Director of Sales], and Lambert [Vice-President for Domestic and Export]. It was one of the worst meetings of my life. It lasted all day. Gachoud argued that they had sales experience from other countries and that in his judgment our market potential and share estimates were too optimistic, that the whole world market for Roget was only 600 tons a year (see Exhibit 6), and that it was inconceivable that Sweden alone could take 400 tons. I told him over and over how we arrived at these figures, but he just kept repeating the overoptimism argument.
>
> "Lavanchy then said that the production of this product was very complicated and that he had difficulties producing it in Canada, even with trained workers who had years of experience. I told him I only needed five trained production workers and that he could send me two men for two months to train Swedes to do the job. I impressed on him that 'if you can manufacture it in Canada, you can manufacture it for us in Sweden until we learn, that is, if you don't have confidence in Swedish technology.' He repeated that the difficulties in manufacturing were great. I stressed that we were prepared to learn and take the risk. Somehow I just couldn't get through to him.
>
> "By 6 P.M. everyone was tired. Lambert had backed up his two production and sales officials all day, repeating their arguments. Gillot seemed to me to just sit there and listen, occasionally asking questions. I cannot understand why he didn't back me up. He seemed so easy to get along with at the earlier board meeting in Stockholm—where he seemed

Exhibit 6 Estimate of World Market for XL–4 and Current Sales, 1995

	Potential Market (percent of world paper production)	Current Sales of XL–4 (percent)
Sweden	12	1.7
Finland	7	0.5
Norway	3	0.2
Russia	10	0
Rest of Europe	20	8.6
Canada	15	54.8
United States	13	28.5
Rest of the World	20	5.7
Total	100	100

decisive. Not so at this meeting. He seemed distant and indecisive; an ineffective executive.

"Finally, Gillot stopped the meeting without reaching a solution and said that he hoped all concerned would do more investigation of this subject. He vaguely referred to the fact that he would think about it himself and let us know when another meeting would be held."

Objections from a Swedish Director

Ekstrom returned to Stockholm and reported the meeting to his own staff, and to the two Swedish members of his Board. "They, like I, were really disappointed. Here we were operating with initiative and with excellent financial techniques. Roget management had often emphasized the necessity for decentralized profit responsibilities, authority, and initiative on the part of foreign subsidiary presidents. One of my men told me that they seem to talk decentralization and act like tin gods at the same time." Mr. Norgren, the Swedish banker on Thorsten's board, expressed surprise at the outcome and commented further:

"I considered this carefully. It is sound business for Thorsten, and XL–4 will help to build one more growth company in the Swedish economy. Somehow, the management in Montreal has failed to study this, or they don't wish the Swedish subsidiary to produce it. I have today dictated a letter to Mr. Gillot telling him that I don't know why the project is rejected, that Roget has a right to its own reasons, but that I am prepared to resign as a director. It is not that I am angry, or that I wish to dictate decisions for the worldwide Roget group. It is simply that, if I spend my time studying policy decisions, and those decisions do not serve the right function for the business, then it is a waste of time to continue. Furthermore, I fail to understand the role of Thorsten's board. Why bother to discuss and vote on proposals, if they are going to be rejected elsewhere?"

Ekstrom added, "while I certainly wouldn't bring these matters out in a meeting, I think those Canadian production and sales people simply want to build their empire, and make money in Roget Canada. They don't care about Thorsten and Sweden. That's a smooth way to operate. We have the ideas and the initiative, and they take them and get the payoff."

After Mr. Gillot received Norgren's letter, he contacted Messrs. Lavanchy, Gachoud, and Bols, the company's CFO. He told them that the Swedish XL–4 project had become a matter of key importance for the group because of its implications for company profits and the morale and autonomy of the subsidiary management. He asked them to study the matter and report their recommendations in one month. He also wrote Ekstrom, "Our corporate staff is studying the proposal. You will hear from me within about six weeks regarding my final decision."

Report of Roget's Director of Manufacturing

A month later, Lavanchy gave Gillot a memorandum explaining his reasons for opposing the Swedish plant proposal:

"At your request, I have reexamined thoroughly all of the cost figures that bear on the XL–4 proposal. I find that manufacture of this product in Sweden would be highly uneconomical for two reasons: (1) overhead costs would be higher; and (2) variable costs would be greater.

"As to the first, suppose that Thorsten does sell 400 tons a year so that our total worldwide sales rise to 1,000 tons. We can produce the whole amount in Canada with essentially the same capital investment we have now. If we produce 1,000 tons, our fixed costs will decrease by Skr. 12/kg.[1] That means Skr. 7.2 million in savings on production for domestic and export to countries other than Sweden (600 tons a year), and Skr. 12 million for worldwide production including Sweden.

"Second, if we were to produce the extra 400 tons in Canada, we could schedule longer production runs, have

[1]For simplicity, all figures have been translated into Swedish crowns at the prevailing rate of approximately Skr. 5 per Canadian dollar. Total fixed costs in Canada were C$ 3.6 million in 1996, the equivalent of Skr. 18 million a year at current exchange rates. Divided by 600 tons, this equals Skr. 30,000 a ton (or Skr. 30/kg). If spread over 1,000 tons, average fixed cost would drop to Skr. 18/kg.

lower set-up costs and larger raw material purchases, thus allowing savings in material handling and purchase prices. My staff has studied this and concludes that our average variable costs will decrease from Skr. 95 to Skr. 93 per kg. This difference means a saving of nearly Skr. 1.2 million on Canadian domestic production, or Skr. 2 million for total worldwide production, assuming that Sweden takes 400 tons a year. Taxes on these added profits are comparable in Canada and Sweden, about 50 percent of taxable income.

"In conclusion, the new plant should not be built. Ekstrom is a bright young man, but he does not know the adhesives business. He would be head over heels in costly production mistakes from the beginning. I recommend that you inform the Thorsten management that it is in the company's interest, and therefore it is Roget's policy, that he must buy from Canada."

Exhibit 7 Comparison of Economic Gains between Two Alternative Proposals for the Manufacture of XL–4 (in thousand of Swedish crowns at 8 percent discount rate)

	Made in Sweden	Made in Canada
Present Value of Investment	−76,385	−7,183
Present Value of Operating Profits	88,540	29,295
Present Value of Residual Assets	12,545	4,318
Net Present Value	24,700	26,430
Payback Period	4.3 years	2.5 years
Internal Rate of Return	15.7%	60.0%

Report of Vice President of Finance

A few days later, Gillot received the following memorandum from Eric Bols, Roget's CFO:

"I am sending you herewith a complete economic study of the two alternatives which have been raised for producing XL–4 within the Roget group. The Swedish management has proposed constructing a plant in Sweden, while Messrs. Lavanchy and Lambert on our Canadian staff have proposed producing here in Canada.

"First of all, I should state that I agree that this kind of matter must be resolved by the highest authority. Industrial chemicals is not the only group within the company which has such location problems, and Mr. Juvet [Roget's CEO] is concerned that any precedent set here would also apply to other divisions.

"After thorough analysis, it is clear that the Roget Group will benefit substantially by producing total world requirements for XL–4 in Canada, including the 400 tons per year which Swedish management estimates it will need over the next seven years. Not only will the Roget group of companies gain the Skr. 1.7 million difference between the net present values of both proposals, but the really important factor is that we would have to furnish only Skr. 7.2 million in initial capital funds, while in Sweden it would cost Skr. 76.4 million to build a new plant and stock it (see Exhibit 7).

"The importance of this factor can be demonstrated. The internal rate of return on investment is 60 percent for the Canadian project because of the low initial investment, while it is 15 percent for the costly Swedish investment. Stated in another way, Sweden is asking us to invest Skr. 69.2 million more than necessary. If invested in Eurodollar bank certificates averaging 8–9 percent return, these funds would grow to more than Skr. 120 million after seven years. This shows the opportunity cost of committing needless money in Sweden. Such money is, in effect, wasted, because the internal rate of return is so much lower in Sweden.

Exhibit 8 Estimated Variable Costs of Manufacturing XL–4 in Canada for Shipment to Sweden (In Swedish crowns)

Variable Costs Per Kilogram	
Manufacturing	93
Shipping from Canada to Sweden	25
Swedish Import Duty	20
Total	138

"Another way to see the importance of initial capital is to look at the payback period. It would take the group over four years to get its money back in Sweden but only two and one-half years in Canada. Exhibit 8 provides an estimate of variable costs of manufacturing and shipping incurred to supply Sweden from Canada, taken from Paul Lavanchy's report. Exhibits 10 through 12 are constructed exactly as Mr. Ekstrom performed his analysis, and provide the figures that are summarized in Exhibit 9. They show operating profits, working capital requirements, and the salvage value of assets at the end of seven years, expressed in Swedish crowns at current exchange rates to facilitate comparison. There is, of course an exchange risk associated with these flows, but one that would apply equally to any future dividends from Sweden.[2]

"Finally, I must call attention to my position as compared with that of Mr. Lavanchy. He and I agree on the most important issue—that it would be much more profitable to manufacture in Canada. But we differ on one point. It is not correct that there would be savings in fixed costs. Since our plant is already built, there would be no actual money costs one way or the other under either of three alternatives: produce in Canada, produce in Sweden, or simply not produce

[2]See Exhibit 13 for historical data on the Swedish crown/Canadian dollar exchange rates and relative inflation rates in both countries.

Exhibit 9 **Roget's Proposal for Manufacture of XL–4 in Canada for Export to Sweden and Other World Markets** (In thousands of Swedish crowns)

Year	Description	After-tax Cash Flows*	Present Value at 8%
0	Working Capital	(5,400)	(5,400)
1	Cash Operating Profit	300	
	Working Capital	(1,000)	
	Total	(700)	(648)
2	Cash Operating Profit	3,900	
	Working Capital	(1,000)	
	Total	2,900	2,486
3	Cash Operating Profit	7,500	5,954
4	Cash Operating Profit	7,500	5,513
5	Cash Operating Profit	7,500	5,104
6	Cash Operating Profit	7,500	4,726
7	Cash Operating Profit	7,500	
	Recovery Value of Equipment and Working Capital	7,400	
	Total	14,900	8,694
	Project Grand Total	41,700	26,429

Financial Conclusions

Net Present Value to the Corporation	Skr. 26,429
Payback Period (years)	2.5
Internal Rate of Return	60.0%

*From Exhibits 10, 11 and 12.

Exhibit 10 **Estimated Operating Cash Flows from Manufacture of XL–4 in Canada for Shipment to Sweden**

	Year 1	2	3	4	5	6	7	Total
1. Sales (tons)	200	300	400	400	400	400	400	2,500
Skr Per kg								
2. Sales Price	200	185	185	185	185	185	185	
3. Variable Costs	138	138	138	138	138	138	138	
4. Profit Margin	62	47	47	47	47	47	47	
Thousand Skr								
5. Contribution	12,400	14,100	18,800	18,800	18,800	18,800	18,800	120,500
6. Promotion Costs	13,000	7500	5000	5000	5000	5000	5000	45,500
7. Savings*	1,200	1,200	1,200	1,200	1,200	1,200	1,200	8,400
8. Before-tax Profit	600	7,800	15,000	15,000	15,000	15,000	15,000	83,400
9. Taxes Payable	300	3,900	7,500	7,500	7,500	7,500	7,500	41,700
10. Net Cash Flow	300	3,900	7,500	7,500	7,500	7,500	7,500	41,700

*These are savings incurred in sales to other markets due to more efficient purchasing and production scheduling (600 tons × Skr2,000 per ton)

Exhibit 11 Estimated Working Capital Required for Manufacture of XL–4 in Canada for Sale in Sweden
(In thousands of Swedish crowns)

	(1) Inventory at Cost	(2) Other Current Assets Less Current Liabilities	(3) Working Capital [1+2]	(4) Change from Previous Year	(5) Tax Credit [30% of Change in (1)]	(6) Net Funds Required [4–5]
Year 0	5,000	1,000	6,000	6,000	600*	5,400
Year 1	5,500	1,500	7,000	1,000	0	1,000
Year 2	6,000	2,000	8,000	1,000	0	1,000
Year 3+	6,000	2,000	8,000	0	0	0
Total	6,000	2,000	8,000	8,000	600	7,400

*Based on finished goods inventory of Skr. 2 million in Sweden.

Exhibit 12 Estimated End-of-Life Value of Canadian and Swedish Assets (in thousands of Swedish crowns)

Terminal Value of Working Capital	8,000	
Less Payment of Deferred Taxes on Special Inventory Reserves	600	
Net Value of Working Capital after 7 years		7,400

Exhibit 13 Exchange Rates and Relative Inflation in Canada and Sweden, 1990–1995

	Exchange Rates			Inflation Rate Indices (1990=100)			
				Canada		Sweden	
	Skr/US$	C$/US$	Skr/C$	CPI*	PPI*	CPI*	PPI*
1990	5.698	1.160	4.911	100.0	100.0	100	100.0
1991	5.530	1.156	4.785	105.6	99.0	109	101.7
1992	7.043	1.271	5.541	107.2	99.5	112	101.0
1993	8.304	1.324	6.272	109.2	102.7	117	108.1
1994	7.462	1.403	5.319	109.4	108.6	120	112.3
1195	6.658	1.365	4.877	111.8	117.3	123	121.0

*CPI = consumer price index; PPI = producers price index.

additional XL–4 at all. You will notice, therefore, that I do not include any depreciation cost in my calculations.

"I hope that this analysis is of help to you in formulating a divisional policy on construction of manufacturing plants around the world. It seems to me that it should be the policy of Roget to construct plants whenever and wherever the group as a whole will gain most benefits, taking into consideration worldwide supply and demand, rather than conditions in any one country or one part of the group. That is, we should produce at the point where the cost of production is lowest.

"We in Finance have the highest respect for the Swedish management. Mr. Ekstrom, particularly, is an outstanding manager with great financial expertise himself. In this case, he has simply not had complete information from our group. I trust that he will understand that this is not a personal rejection, but one that is for the good of the group as a whole."

INSEAD EURO-ASIA CENTRE *Case 14–2*

Henkel Asia-Pacific

It was January 9, 1994. Ulrich Lehner leaned back in his business class seat on a Lufthansa flight from Hong Kong back to Germany. He had lost count of the number of flights he had made over the last two years as chairman of Henkel Asia-Pacific Ltd. "Too many," his wife would say. "Not enough," he thought to himself, given the tasks the board in Düsseldorf had assigned him. In November 1991 he had gone to Asia to set up a regional headquarters in Asia that would strengthen Henkel's position there and to develop new ideas and strategies for the company in the fastest growing region of the world.

The office had been established with a small team of highly dedicated Germans who hoped to make Henkel grow as fast as possible in the coming years. A comprehensive strategy for the company's future in Asia had been developed and adopted in 1992. The first steps toward rationalising Henkel's diverse activities in the region were taken and a large number of new ventures initiated, mainly in China. Within the company, Asia had moved from relative obscurity into the limelight.

The president and most other board members had travelled to Asia and supported Lehner's work. A recent visit of supervisory board chairman to China had convinced him that Henkel should spare no money to increase its exposure in Asia. Back in Düsseldorf most of the diversified chemical firm's divisions and strategic business units (SBUs) had suddenly begun to develop new ideas for Asia. On the corporate level the company, after a recent spate of acquisitions, had declared Asia to be the only priority investment area apart from East Germany and Eastern Europe. Following the launch of new projects, expectations about the rewards to be had from the Asia Pacific region had risen significantly. The 1992 strategy paper had targeted an 80 percent increase of sales within five years. In the meantime this figure had been substantially increased.

For Lehner, leaving Hong Kong this time was not merely a routine trip back to Germany; it was his final departure from Asia as the chairman of the regional office. He was returning to headquarters to take over an important function in the corporate finance department, where he had spent most of his life before coming out to Asia. The company had already announced that he would replace the current finance director on the board of managing directors following the latter's retirement within the next year or two. In fact, this decision was public knowledge within the company at the time of Lehner's appointment to the Asia Pacific post.

Lehner's successor as chairman of Henkel's Asian operations, Mr. Veit Müller-Hillebrand, had already been posted to Hong Kong. Both Lehner and his successor had spent sufficient time together to ensure a smooth transition. Together they had visited all subsidiaries and met with most of the company's important contacts and joint venture partners.

While Asia had gained visibility in Henkel and a good structure had been put in place, Lehner was not sure whether his successor's job would be any easier than his had been. Had the SBUs and the local subsidiaries really accepted the need for a regional strategy? Was the regional office already sufficiently staffed? And how far had the company gone with the implementation of new organisational initiatives and the realisation of the new joint ventures in China? Had adequate attention been paid to the growing local competition and to competitors from the US, Europe and Japan? With China absorbing most of the regional office's resources, had Japan been neglected? What would happen to the regional push if China turned inward again and all the new investments had to be written off?

The Henkel Group

Henkel was founded in 1876 as a bleaching powder company that over time grew from Düsseldorf, Germany, into a conglomerate of more than 200 companies operating in 56 countries and with business relationships with more than 100 other countries. In 1993 the company recorded a turnover of DM 13.9 billion and a profit of DM 375 million.

Of the parent company Henkel KGaA the Henkel family owns 100 percent of the ordinary shares (with voting rights) and 1/3 of the preferred shares (without voting rights, but entitled to a higher dividend). The other shares are widely scattered and quoted on various stock exchanges. The family is represented on the supervisory board, as are the workers, management personnel, and bankers. Konrad Henkel is the honorary chairman of both the supervisory board and the shareholders' committee. No one in the Henkel family, however, is a member of the management board that runs the group. The management board consists of the president and CEO,

---

This case was prepared by Hellmut Schütte, Affiliate Professor of International Management at INSEAD. It is intended to be used as a basis for case discussion rather than to illustrate either effective or ineffective handling of an administrative situation.

five members (each in charge of a business division), a finance director, a director in charge of research and development (R&D), and a personnel director.

Henkel considers itself a specialist in applied chemistry, selling 11,000 products worldwide to industrial customers and end consumers. It is the world's largest producer of oleo chemicals made from natural fats and oils, of metal treatment products, and of adhesives. Research and development are important for the company, which spends DM 400 million annually on this sector. All nine managing directors held PhDs, though not necessarily in the natural sciences, and all had risen within the company's ranks. In recent years, Henkel researchers have laid major emphasis on environmental protection issues. This emphasis has made Henkel a leading firm in the industry's switch to the bio-degradable surfactants that serve as raw materials for liquid and powder detergents.

In Europe Henkel ranks among the top companies for detergents, cleaning agents, personal care and cosmetic products, and competes head on with Unilever, Procter & Gamble, L'Oreal, Colgate, and others. Persil, a universal detergent launched in 1907 as one of the first branded products in the world has remained Henkel's largest single product and the market leader in Germany. (The brand, however, is owned by Unilever in the UK and France.)

Henkel's product range is split into five divisions and one separate unit, a joint venture with Ecolab in the area of institutional hygiene. In the early 1990s the divisions were further subdivided into SBUs.

Business	Percentage of Sales	No of SBUs
Chemical Products	28	14
Metal Chemicals	5	1
Industrial Adhesives and Technical Consumer Products	16	8
Cosmetics/Toiletries	10	4
Detergents/Household Cleaners	31	4
Institutional Hygiene	10	J.V.
Total	**100**	**31**

Henkel has substantial shareholdings in Degussa in Germany, and in Clorox, Ecolab, and Loctite in the US, but no direct influence on the operational management of any of these firms.

During the last 10 years Henkel's growth came to a large extent from a very high number of acquisitions, especially in Europe and the US. Henkel had also been quick to move into Eastern Europe after the collapse of communism. Eleven joint ventures in Russia, Poland, Hungary, the CSFR and Slovenia in 1992 already produced sales of DM 500 million in 1992. In this year, the last major acquisition—of Barnängen from Nobel of Sweden—boosted Henkel's position in the cosmetics' field, but put some strain on the company's finances. Henkel's conservative equity ratio had deteriorated to less than the 40 percent that had been the company's long-standing golden rule. While Henkel management announced the reestablishment of the ratio over the medium term, it did not categorically rule out further acquisitions.

Henkel's diversified product mix had by and large shielded its profit performance from cyclical swings. Profitability was seen as acceptable, but was below that of Unilever or Procter & Gamble in terms of return-on-investment. This was one of the reasons why Henkel had recently launched a "cost chase" across all parts of the company. On the personnel side a "cultural evolution" had been launched to change the conservative and paternalistic attitudes then particularly pervasive in Germany. This was considered necessary in order to make the employees more customer- and performance-oriented, to reduce hierarchy, and to streamline the organisation. In line with Henkel's long-standing mission of being an attractive and supportive employer, the company avoided large-scale reductions in the number of personnel—which became common in Germany in 1993—and opted instead for more socially acceptable measures. At the end of 1993, Henkel employed 40,500 people worldwide, of which 16,700 were employed in Germany.

Germany remains Henkel's most important market, although other European countries such as France, Italy, and Spain have gained importance. Henkel's American operations, which included Nopco, Emery, and Parker & Amchem, represent its second largest single market. The table below shows a regional sales breakdown according to the location of customers and the Henkel company that delivers the products:

Henkel Group Sales 1993 (total DM 13.9 billion): Shares by Region (in percent)

Region	Sales by Location of Customer	Production by Location of Company
Germany	29	35
Rest of Europe	48	47
North America	12	12
Latin America	4	3
Africa, Asia, Australia	7	5
World	**100**	**100**

Given the stagnation in Europe and the prospects of slow growth in the Americas, Henkel became increasingly aware that it had to significantly boost its exposure in Asia if it was to continue to grow and prosper.

Henkel in Asia

Henkel's earliest activities in Asia date back to the 19th century when the company's founder, Fritz Henkel, started to trade with China. Yet it was only after the Second World War that the company began to invest in the region, though its expansion remained limited in comparison with the growth of activities in Europe and the United States.

In the 1980s Henkel found itself involved in a large number of mostly small operations in Asia Pacific. Some of these were only sales offices, while others also had manufacturing activities. Some subsidiaries (in Henkel jargon called "VU"= verbundene Unternehmen) were 100 percent-owned, while others had been set up as joint ventures. In addition, Henkel had concluded a number of licensing contracts with a variety of partners in Asia, and certain businesses were represented by agents and distributors, often operating in parallel with the local Henkel organisation. This situation was the result of the SBUs, or their organisational predecessors in Düsseldorf pursuing independent strategies in the countries concerned.

The situation became somewhat confusing when Henkel acquired companies that had a number of subsidiaries in Asia and sold its institutional hygiene business in the region. These moves forced Henkel's local operations to integrate certain new businesses while letting go of other parts. This process was not always easy, due to the existence of local joint venture partners.

The overwhelming majority of Henkel's business in Asia was conducted by the chemicals division, and all of the 10 country managers in Asia reported directly to Mr. Dieter Ambros, the board member in charge of the chemical division. As Henkel had introduced a matrix organisation, Ambros also had responsibility for the regions of Asia and North America.

In 1985 Ambros sent Mr. Leonhardt to Singapore to open a regional office that would ensure that the company stayed in closer touch with the region. The office consisted only of Leonhardt and his secretary. Though Leonhardt was Ambros' "man on the spot," he did not report to him directly, but to one of the directors in Düsseldorf working with Ambros. Leonhardt's task was to represent headquarters in the ASEAN subsidiaries and the operations in Australia and New Zealand. Japan was not considered part of the region and the operations in Taiwan, Korea and Hong Kong/China were not deemed in need of any special attention. Leonhardt took care of the subsidiaries' board meetings, looked after the joint venture partners, and tried to co-ordinate activities of general concern to the VUs. His involvement in day-to-day operations was limited, not least by long serving expatriate country managers, who jealously guarded control over their area of responsibility. In 1989 Leonhardt returned to Düsseldorf and the regional office was closed.

During Leonhardt's tenure in Singapore the idea was born and implemented to strengthen product development, adaptation, and technical services in the region. A number of specialists were brought in from Germany for extended periods to support the sales activities in selected countries. Costs for these experts were carried by the chemical division, but their services were not always appreciated. The exception was the Thai subsidiary, to which most of the technicians were assigned and which therefore benefited considerably from their efforts. The last specialist was recalled to Düsseldorf in 1993.

From 1989 on the Asian region was again entirely coordinated from Germany, by the chemicals division, where Ambros was in charge. But the growth in the region, increasing competitive pressures from both local and international rivals, and the need to integrate certain activities regionally rather than linking individual Asian operations with headquarters, made the task of co-ordination more demanding. It had also become clear that the Asia Pacific region offered excellent opportunities for other businesses as well; the adhesives and the metal treatment divisions, for example, had made major inroads into certain markets. As a result the chemical division was less dominant in the region.

In the fall of 1989, awareness was growing within Henkel that individual SBUs or countries were doing well in Asia, but that few synergies and hardly any trade existed between the various businesses and subsidiaries. In 1989, Henkel achieved a turnover of DM 354 million in the region with a profit ratio that was above the company's average. The Henkel board decided to develop an overall Asia strategy and hired McKinsey consultants to lay the groundwork by conducting a study of opportunities in the region. In defining the region, Japan was excluded, since it required the development of a separate strategy. Henkel nevertheless recognised the influence of Japan and Japanese competitors on the region.

The study was carried out and its results presented in 1990, a year during which the attention of German industry had been drawn toward East Germany and Eastern Europe following the fall of the Berlin Wall and the reunification of Germany. McKinsey was very positive, almost bullish, on the potential of the region for Henkel, noting that the company was presently underrepresented in the Asia Pacific region compared to its competitors. The McKinsey consultants, who felt that with better coordination and minimal additional investment substantial profits could be achieved, recommended that Henkel take a closer look at downstream (=branded consumer) products. Up until that point, this type of product had only been sold in very limited quantities in the region.

The McKinsey study identified Taiwan and Korea as the countries with the best short-term potential for Henkel, and Thailand and Indonesia as those with the best long-term potential. China was considered to be of "less interest to Henkel," though the study reported that the country ". . could be of great interest in the long run."

The study recommended improved technical support (in the form of extensive product adaptation by qualified chemists in several new centres of competence) as well as increased local production (on account of imports from Germany). McKinsey also felt that a number of partnerships needed to be re-evaluated and renegotiated. Finally, the establishment of a regional organisation was proposed as a means of overcoming "the lack of decision-making competence in, and isolation of, the individual VUs. . ."

During the months that followed discussions in Düsseldorf focused on the structure of this regional organisation, particularly on the question of whether or not to include Japan in Henkel's definition of the Asia Pacific region. In terms of turnover Japan represented by far the largest individual country with about DM 150 million. Japan had the best technology, the most critical customers, and faced a very specific problem: the existence of a brand new, expensive and dedicated plant producing sophisticated chemicals for which demand had disappeared.

In Malaysia, the second largest Henkel country in Asia, a new investment in a major fatty alcohol facility in joint venture with Japanese, Korean, and local partners was in the pipeline. Some of the output would find its way to other Henkel operations in Asia, including Japan. And opportunities in China appeared too appealing to pass up. After numerous visits by Henkel managers from a variety of SBUs the first projects became more concrete.

In the fall of 1991, the Henkel board appointed Lehner as head of the Asia-Pacific region and sent him to Hong Kong to set up a regional headquarters. He was also asked to develop concrete proposals for a regional strategy.

Establishing Henkel Asia-Pacific Ltd (HAP)

On November, 1 1991, Henkel announced the establishment of a new legal entity as a management holding with headquarters in Hong Kong. In a press release the holding group's objectives were defined as: the centralisation of management; the intensification of advisory services; and the re-enforcement of the management of subsidiaries and joint ventures. Lehner became chairman of this holding and all the heads of the subsidiaries reported directly to him, including Japan. The region consisted of 11 countries—Australia, China, Hong Kong, Indonesia, Japan, Malaysia, New Zealand, Philippines, Singapore, South Korea, Taiwan, and Thailand. One thousand six hundred people were employed in 15 subsidiaries that generated sales of about DM 450 million (see Exhibit 1).

A small team of German managers surveyed Henkel's activities in the region and generated ideas for the future. Then, in July 1992, Henkel Asia Pacific (HAP) invited board members and other key managers from Düsseldorf and the heads of the subsidiaries in the region for a presentation of Henkel's Asia Pacific strategy.

The presentation was based on the assumption of continued high growth and a tendency towards further integration in the region. Given the importance of Japan in the region, due consideration would be given to that country. On the other hand, China was seen as the country with the

EXHIBIT 1 Employees in Asia-Pacific, 1991

Henkel Australia	150
Shanghai Henkel	33
Guangzhou Henkel	5
Henkel Peking (Rep. Office)	6
Henkel Chem. Hong Kong	44
Henkel Indonesia	245
Henkel Hakusui (Japan)	321
Henkel Korea	19
Henkel Daesung (Korea)	18
Henkel Oleochem (Group Malaysia)	289
Henkel New Zealand	19
Henkel Philippines	38
Henkel Singapore	26
Henkel Taiwan	57
Henkel Thailand	309
Total	1,589

EXHIBIT 2 Opportunity Matrix for Henkel in Asia Pacific

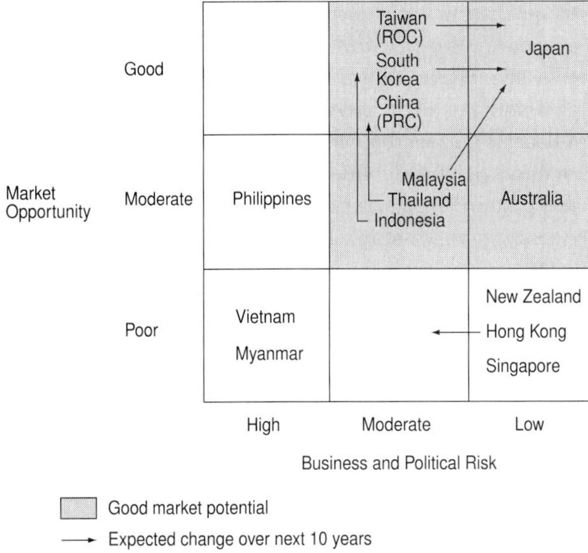

greatest potential for expansion. A HAP assessment of the various markets in Asia is shown in Exhibit 2.

As far as new ideas for the various product groups and SBUs were concerned, the HAP team stressed that no separate Asian product strategies would be developed, and that instead they would be considered in the framework of global strategies generated by the SBUs. In fact, all the product-related ideas presented during the meeting had been discussed in advance with both the product groups as well as with the country managers concerned. Not surprisingly, the meeting went very well and most of the proposals were accepted in one form or another.

By classifying their proposals into "Must do," "Option 1," and "Option 2," the team established a priority list. "Must do" issues mainly concerned the various ill-defined areas of responsibilities that needed to be sorted out before any proper strategy could be implemented. "Must do" issues also dealt with some pending operational issues. "Option 1" was concerned with the generation of internal growth, and "Option 2" with the opportunities for external growth through acquisitions and partnerships.

Most attention was paid to organisational changes and functional strategies. The main points are summarised below.

Organisation

1. Business teams will be formed per SBU with members from Europe, the US, and the Asia Pacific region. These teams will be in charge of co-ordinating and leading the regional business activities in the specific product category. "Asian Desks" will be established in some SBUs staffed by managers concentrating their efforts entirely on the region. Twelve of those managers would be immediately assigned to these tasks and become members of the business teams. As a rule, these managers would not be newly hired Asia experts, but rather consist of existing staff within the SBUs who had dealt with Asia in the past, though not exclusively. The business teams would have to look after marketing strategies, resolve conflicts between competing subsidiaries (VUs), allocate technical support and production facilities, etc.
2. Responsibility for product strategy and profit would be shared by the SBUs and HAP. They were also in charge of strategy implementation and control. By arguing that profits result from sales to the customer, as opposed to sales from Henkel headquarters, or Henkel VUs to another VU, transfer pricing disputes were to be minimised. The respective VUs would have to implement the SBU strategy, optimise production capacity, maximise contribution through active marketing and sales, and minimise their costs.
3. The various partnerships had to be streamlined and, whenever possible, consolidated under one roof. In some countries wholly-owned subsidiaries and joint ventures (both called VUs) existed side-by-side with independent agents selling Henkel products and manufacturers under license to produce other Henkel product lines. The ideal would be to build "Henkel clones" over a period of time.

Manufacturing

A regional production system had to be established. While some of the existing facilities were underutilised, production capacity in Asia was inadequate in certain product categories. Economies of scale required the rationalisation of some facilities. A first regional production meeting would have to be scheduled and a regional production audit commissioned.

Accounting/Finance

In order to compare costs across the region, Henkel had to introduce a unified and standardised accounting and reporting system that would also facilitate transfer pricing discussions. In the past, the independence of the VUs had led to a variety of different software and hardware systems. Under the leadership of HAP these would gradually be standardised. In addition, there was a call for the optimisation of the financial structure of some of the VUs. Better management information systems would improve opportunities for global and regional purchasing.

Technical Service

There was widespread recognition that the provision of professional technical services was essential to boost sales in the region. Nevertheless, the establishment of a large regional technical centre was not recommended, since this was likely to lead to a duplication of efforts. All VUs would have to set up technical service facilities sufficient for their own local needs. Moreover, regional centres of technical competence would be established. Japan, for example, would take the lead in chemicals for the leather industry, while Indonesia in those for the textile industry. Singapore would be in charge of metal cleaning chemicals.

Headquarters in Germany would be required to accelerate the development of new products or applications for the region. More staff would be assigned to service the specific needs of the Asia Pacific region. The number of visits by technical experts from Düsseldorf to advise and train local staff, and hold regional seminars, would also be increased.

Human Resources

The former emphasis on the development of individual VUs in the various countries had led to a low profile for Henkel as a recruiting organisation and to limited career opportunities for local staff. These weaknesses had to be overcome through the establishment of a regional human resource strategy and the development of a regional corporate culture. As a first step, a more systematic assessment of management potential and needs had to be undertaken, and compensation packages brought in line. Local and regional training programmes were also to be launched.

There was also an initiative to institutionalise an internal regional job market for Asian managers that would foster cross-border job rotation. The situation in which most VUs were directed by expatriates would be overcome by a mechanism—referred to as the "Tandem Principle"—that would oblige the established expatriates to train an Asian manager to take over his position at the end of an assignment. Long-term expatriates would have to accept local compensation packages after eight years. Bonuses for the VUs' managing directors would depend on both the results of the respective VU and its contribution to the region.

Expansion of Existing Operations

From 1991 sales of DM 450 million, Henkel aimed to increase the existing business in the region to DM 850 million by 1996. (These figures are exclusive of exports from Asia Pacific, Malaysia in particular, to markets outside the region.)

In 1991, 75 percent of the HAP business came from the chemical side (oleo chemicals, organic specialities, and care chemicals), 14 percent from adhesives (industrial and consumer adhesives) and 11 percent from metal chemicals (chemicals for treating metals, in most cases during the production process). Adhesives were expected to grow fastest, representing 20 percent of Henkel's total sales in Asia Pacific in 1996. The share of chemicals was projected to fall to 69 per cent.

Sales by country in 1991 were as follows: Japan's sales were the largest with 34 percent, followed by Australia, Indonesia, and Thailand each contributing around 10 percent. In 1996 Japan was still expected to have the highest sales, although its percentage of total sales would drop to 29 percent. Indonesia, Thailand, and Korea would each contribute 10–11 percent respectively.

Henkel's existing operations in China were expected to grow from DM 29 to DM 109 million in 1996, then representing 13 percent of HAP's sales. In 1991 they were small scale and scattered, and consisted of:

1. *Business development:*
   Henkel Beijing Representative Office (mainly adhesives)
2. *Trading (indent business and ex-stock):*
   Henkel Chemicals Hong Kong with service offices in China (mainly chemicals)
3. *Local manufacturing and marketing:*
   Shanghai Henkel Chemicals (mainly metal chemicals)
4. *Local manufacturing and marketing:*
   Guangzhou Henkel Chemical Products (mainly metal chemicals)

Exhibit 3 provides an overview of Henkel's existing activities in the Asia Pacific region.

The operations that sold products of DM 450 million in 1991 had by 1993 grown to DM 615 million. This pace of development was the fastest recorded by Henkel worldwide during this period.

EXHIBIT 3 Henkel Asia-Pacific by Product-Groups

	Henkel Australia	Henkel Shanghai	Henkel Guangzhou	Henkel China	Henkel Indonesia	Henkel Japan	Henkel Korea	Henkel Daesung	Henkel Malaysia	Henkel New Zealand	Henkel Philippines	Henkel Singapore	Henkel Taiwan	Henkel Thailand
Oleo-chemicals	X			X	X	X	X		X		X		X	X
Textile Auxilliaries	X			X	X	X	X		X		X		X	X
Leather Auxilliaries				X	X	X					X		X	X
Plastic & Coating Additives	X			X	X	X	X		X	X	X		X	X
Pulp & Paper Additives	X									X			X	X
Mining/ Oilfield Chemicals	X				X									
Cosmetic & Pharm. Raw Materials	X			X	X	X	X		X	X	X		X	X
Fine Chemicals	X					X								
Food-Additives	X													X
[Toll-manufacturing for Ecolab]		X			[X]	X		X			[X]		[X]	
Metal Surface Treatment	X	X	X	X	X	X	X			X		X	X	X
Consumer Adhesives	X			X	X	X	X			X				X
Industrial Adhesives				X	X	X	X			X	X		X	X

Henkel China = Henkel Peking Office + Henkel Chemicals Hong Kong

New Projects for China

The activities of the HAP office, the visits of board members and major shareholders to China at the beginning of the 1990s began to have an impact on the various SBUs at the Düsseldorf headquarters. There was a dramatic increase in interest in selling into or investing in the country. Of all the "newcomers," the detergent division was the first to become involved in China with an investment in an existing plant in Tianjin. After a period of search and negotiation that lasted for several years, a joint venture agreement was concluded with HAP's assistance. Henkel took a 20 percent share, which was complemented by a 10 percent participation from DEG, the German government-owned investment bank. The operations of the joint venture started in 1993 with 1000 people. Persil was also among the brands launched and relaunched. Sales in 1993 were DM 65 million and a small profit was made. At the beginning of 1994 Henkel increased its share in the venture to 45 percent.

As Henkel's largest division the detergent group carried a lot of weight. Its decision to invest in China was a major one for Henkel, not least because of the large capital outlay required.

Many years earlier Henkel had decided to concentrate the detergent business on Europe where it held a very high market share. The logic behind this concentration was that Henkel, as an integrated producer, was involved in both upstream and downstream activities. Consequently, companies like Procter & Gamble and Unilever were at once Henkel's competitors in end products and its customers for raw materials. The strength of Henkel's position in Europe allowed the company to pursue this policy. Outside Europe, however, Henkel felt it would be better to act solely as a supplier. This decision had led, years earlier, to Henkel's withdrawal from the detergents' markets, most notably in Brazil.

In the early 1990s Henkel began to reconsider its policy and to see detergent as a global business. This new attitude was in part influenced by the aggressive strategies of Henkel's competitors in the Asia Pacific region, which was thought to account for 25 percent of the world demand. In view of this, Henkel felt it could not afford to miss out on the growth in Asia. In fact, after the start of the first venture the division was keen to find further projects in China. A project proposal for Vietnam was also discussed.

The cosmetics division had become equally restive. In contrast to their colleagues from the detergents division they had already established a small presence in eight countries in Asia Pacific through a number of distribution and license agreements with companies such as Inchcape in Thailand and Lucky in Korea. Henkel's main brand was Fa. The cosmetics division had also assigned their own representative to HAP office in Hong Kong. Investments so far had, however, been limited. Due to recent acquisitions in Europe the division felt it would be difficult to find large funds for a rapid expansion in Asia, even for China, which was seen as a priority country.

Henkel therefore agreed to form a new joint venture with a small Hong Kong agency to which it had previously granted all distribution and licensing rights for China. This company was owned by a former Henkel employee from Hong Kong with good contacts in China. The venture, in which Henkel took a 90 percent share, was called Henkel Cosmetics China. It would both manufacture and market a variety of products utilising existing Chinese plants.

The chemical division was in the process of constructing a new major plant in Shanghai. In partnership with four Chinese organisations Shanghai Henkel Oleochemicals would produce surfactants and other raw materials for detergents, shampoos, soaps, etc., as of the end of 1994. Henkel had taken a 70 percent share in the venture. In light of China's fast growing automobile sector Henkel Shanghai Teroson was founded to market protective coatings, sealants and adhesives for motor vehicles. The adhesives and metal chemicals divisions had further projects under consideration and negotiation.

In early 1994 almost all of Henkel's 31 SBUs appeared to be searching for business opportunities in China.

HAP's Organisation and Functions

With so many ventures and partnerships under discussion, the co-ordination of Henkel's activities in China became a matter of concern. Traditionally, Henkel Chemicals Hong Kong had covered China. If anyone could claim some expertise on China it was this VU that employed 44 people. Therefore the idea was born to convert this office into an umbrella organisation for China called Henkel China. Although this was quickly realised, the move was opposed by those divisions that, while not yet active in China, were then aggressively pursuing various projects in the country. These divisions argued that Henkel Chemicals Hong Kong only had experience in chemicals and adhesives, but not in their fields. They would therefore rather remain independent from the Henkel China office.

The discussion of the organisation of the China activities had a direct impact on HAP's role as a regional office. So far most of the new projects had either been initiated or supported by the office. However, due to China's unforeseen growth, and Düsseldorf's strong interest in the country, Lehner and his team had, in fact, spent most of their time and energy on that country. Expectations were emerging that in the years to come Henkel's business in China alone could equal that of all the other countries combined.

Should the VUs in China be first of all co-ordinated within the country and only later integrated into a regional co-ordination body called HAP? How would Taiwan or a "Greater China" concept fit into such an organisation? What would be the implications in terms of layers and bureaucracy? Alternatively, with all the activities in China and the location of HAP in Hong Kong, was the regional office in fact evolving into a *de facto* China office?

The reluctance of the detergents' division to operate under a China umbrella raised the more fundamental issue of their relationship to HAP, as well as the rationale for the existence of HAP. Because of the size of its projects and their importance, the division was reluctant to share any responsibility with other parts of the organisation. Nevertheless, they welcomed the administrative and human resource services that the HAP office could provide. There was also the issue of reporting lines. Under Lehner, HAP still reported to Mr. Conrad, the board member who was in charge of both chemicals and Asia. The detergent project in China had been personally championed by the board member heading the detergent division, who did not see a need to have his representative in Tianjin come under the HAP umbrella.

While most VUs were pleased with the establishment of HAP in Hong Kong, the Japanese resisted and stressed that their market had little in common with the region, with the possible exception of Korea and Taiwan. They saw their operation as more in line with medium-sized European VUs, which were not asked to report to a regional office. It was therefore important to assess and redefine the role of HAP at regular intervals as Müller-Hillebrand, the successor to Lehner, had at the beginning of 1994. For Müller-Hillebrand, HAP carried out the following functions,

Integrative function:

- Translation of SBU strategies into an integrated Asia Pacific strategy.
- Promotion of synergies across businesses and countries.
- Provision of services (technical, legal, financial, human resources).

Strategic operative function:

- Direction of Henkel's regional strategies and support implementation.
- Co-ordination between VUs, SBUs, and corporate functions.
- Support for the exploitation of new business opportunities.

Since the opening of the HAP office much had been done to fulfil these tasks for Henkel in the region. An overall regional strategy had been developed, proposed and accepted. A regional production network was beginning to emerge and a regional accounting system had been agreed upon. A regional office for corporate purchasing had been established at HAP.

Key countries in the region were taking over technological leadership as "Centres of Business Competence." Not all Asian desks had been staffed as planned, but certain managers concerned had moved from headquarters to Kuala Lumpur, Bangkok, or Singapore. Many operational issues had been tackled such as those related to the new plant in Japan. The decision whether or not to open a representative office in Vietnam had to be made soon.

Due to the enormous workload, the initially small team of a chairman and four managers plus support staff had grown, though only slightly (see Exhibit 4.) The HAP's operational costs had therefore remained reasonable. The HAP office was, however, still exclusively staffed with expatriate managers and most of the VUs in the region were still headed by expatriates.

Müller-Hillebrand now reported to Lehner, who would soon be on the board as finance director without representing any specific product division. With Lehner's background in Asia the region would have sufficient backing in Düsseldorf.

Henkel's Asia Pacific Strategy

But there were more than organisational issues on Müller-Hillebrand's mind as he looked from his office desk over the bustling Hong Kong harbour.

EXHIBIT 4 HAP 1992—Organisation Chart

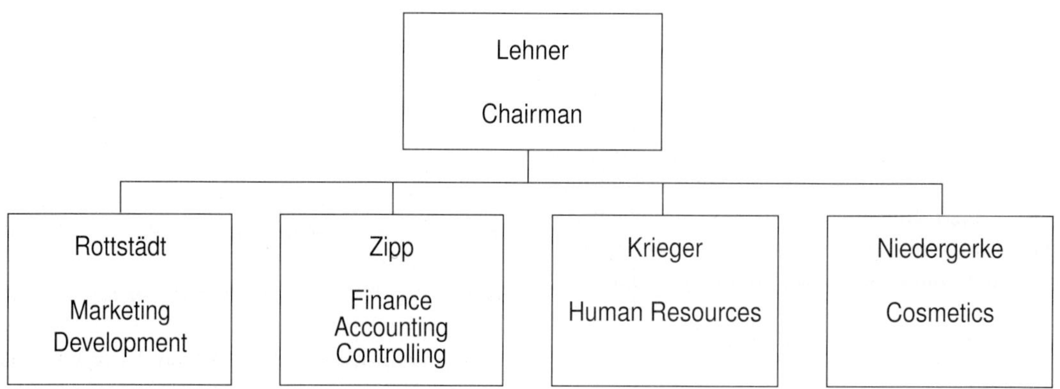

HAP 1994—Organisation Chart

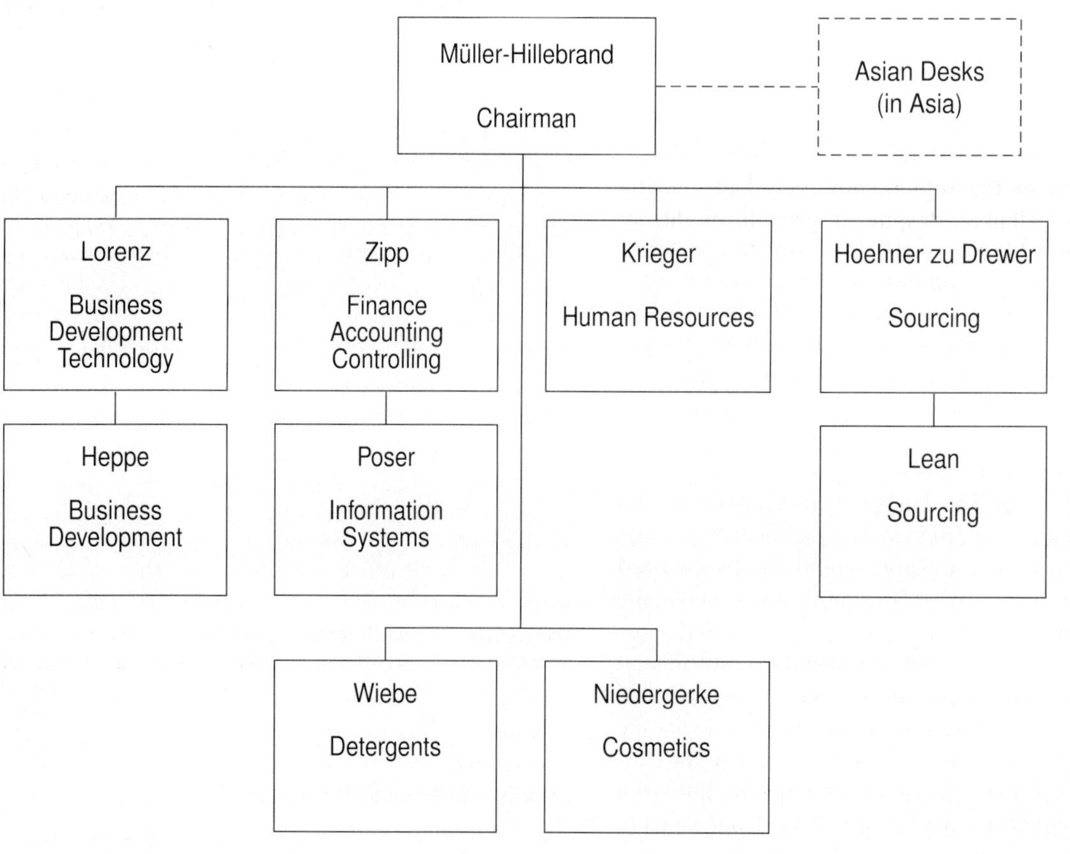

Strategically the region had gained in importance for Henkel, but its total share in its worldwide sales and profits was still tiny. Much of Henkel's growth in the region now depended on progress in China and its future development. What would happen with Henkel's Asia Pacific strategy if a prolonged crisis was to hit the country? Had Japan, Indonesia, or Thailand been neglected as a result of the emphasis on China? Was success in Asia possible—as some would argue—without being successful in Japan?

When in 1992 Henkel's strategy for Asia Pacific was formulated, two objectives were set:

1. To strengthen Henkel's position in the region.
2. To adequately participate in the region's growth.

Both these statements were open to interpretation. Henkel's position certainly had improved compared with past performances, but compared to its competitors there was no evidence that its position had really been strengthened. Competing in so many product areas across so many countries with limited market data made any serious benchmarking exercise extremely difficult. Reports and newspaper articles on competitors' activities in the region, however, had created some fear that Henkel, despite its growth, might, in fact be falling behind.

It was also unclear what was really meant by "adequate participation" in the region's growth. What was the yardstick by which Henkel's growth was to be measured: GNP growth, industrial growth, growth of the chemical industry, growth in sectors in which Henkel already competed or could compete?

On an aggregate level several surveys had shown that 20–25 percent of all chemicals in the world were sold in Asia. There was consensus that this percentage would increase considerably over the coming decades on account of declining shares held by Europe and the United States. Henkel still had only 4.4 percent of its business in Asia.

Incremental moves spread over 31 SBUs would not be enough to rectify this situation. To become a truly global player Henkel would have to come up with alternative strategies. As the new chairman of Henkel Asia Pacific what could Müller-Hillebrand do to launch a second campaign in favour of the region?

INSEAD

Case 14–3

Alfa Laval Agra (A)

Late in 1996, having studied the results of the year so far, Staffan Bohman, the CEO of Alfa Laval Agri (Agri), a branch of Alfa-Laval, and the world's leading supplier of milking equipment and farm supplies to dairy farmers, was again worried. While his policies seemed to have brought growth, margins were not what he wished, and he feared being caught in profitless growth. He was even more concerned as he felt substantial progress had been accomplished, but his parent company was raising the performance hurdle further. For the past years, he had been trying to push growth through better customer responsiveness, higher efficiency, and innovation, and wondered what he could learn from his experience so far to guide next steps (Exhibit 1).

He had been appointed CEO in 1991, before Tetra-Pak, a SWF 7 billion family business in liquid food processing and packaging, had bought Agri. A longstanding manager at Alfa-Laval, Bohman knew this subsidiary did well in comparison with the group, despite turbulence in its environment. After decades of rapid growth, driven by the development of dairy farming and the industrialization of milk processing, Agri had successfully weathered the imposition of milk quotas by the EEC. Fortunately, in the early 1980s, Bohman's predecessors had anticipated the milk overproduction, and entered the after market of consumables, accessories, and maintenance, which was already profitable,[1] offered higher margins and less volatility than new equipment sales in capital goods—i.e., milking systems (Exhibit 2). Hans Ekdahl, then

This case was written by Marie-Aude Dalsace, Research Associate, under the supervision of Yves L. Doz, The Timken Chaired Professor of Global Technology and Innovation, Professor of Business Policy at INSEAD. It is intended to be used as a basis for class discussion rather than to illustrate either effective or ineffective handling of an administrative situation.

[1]By the end of the decade the after market accounted for some 40 percent of Agri's sales.

EXHIBIT 1 Chronology of Events Alfa-Laval Agri, 1880s–1996

1880s	First cream separator; First dealer network
1920s	First milking machine in the US. Entry in Poland, Finland
1930s	WWII: shortage of Agri's equipment in US
1960s	AB Separator becomes Alfa-Laval The group questions to discontinue Agri
1970s	Construction of the European Community and of the Agricultural policy Reorganisation at HQ level first: creation of the Scandinavian region Branching out to the after market Acquisition of a detergent company, license with Archimedes in Poland
1980s	Milk quotas in Europe; Crisis in the US; drop of sales (-50%) and layoffs at Agri Entry in the after market, followed by rapid growth Reorganisation at MC (market company) level: Agri gets its own MCs Awareness that the accounting system does not locate costs or show profits Partnership with a stall manufacturer Fall of the Berlin Wall, Entry in South America Quality and growth challenge
1990	GATT negotiations, Change in the Agricultural Common Policy in France
1991	Drop in turnover in European MCs (−20%) SB takes charge of Agri. 20MCs, Turnover = SEK 60M TP acquires Alfa-Laval First growth challenge: invest out of NA and WE, launch new generation of products JV with Archimedes in Poland, Entry in Asia Four managers replaced in the management team
1992	TQM in plants for quality, service and controls/measurement Second Brands regionalised Activity regained in India and Poland (acquisition of Archimedes) WE= drop of 20% in turnover, Cooling = 8% of the sales
1993	Launch of direct distribution After market compensates for the drop in capital goods European market created Tetra-Laval created with 4 Industrial Groups
1994	Region organisation and new divisions created (product centers) Agri Council becomes EGM, Product teams become virtual companies New R&D head: project management; steering groups; pilot countries, new budget SAP R/3 starts at HQ Intensive expansion in emerging markets with Tetra-Laval's support
1995	Change in the regions' organisation, Reflection on TQM Growth in emerging markets proves costly; New demand from Tetra-Laval
1996	Audit of Agri, Matrix organisation put in place ABC analysis launched

EXHIBIT 2 Sales Split per Product Type (%)

Agri group 1988	Milking Systems 36%	Feeding Syst. 8%	Cooling 8%	M* 8%	Others 9%	Parts 34%
Scandinavia 1988	Milking Systems 21%	Feeding Systems 14%	M* 16%	Others 14%	Parts 35%	
Group strategic mix 1995	Milking Systems 26%	Feeding Systems 11%	Cooling 8%	M* 8%	Others 10%	Parts 37%

*M=Manure handling

Deputy Managing Director and in charge of the after market,[2] recalls:

> "In 1984, the implementation of the milk quotas in Europe had us cut staff[3] by 30 percent (1,000 jobs throughout Europe and at the headquarters in Tumba). It cut new equipment sales in the EEC by half, we sold a plant, and lowered costs level by opening Agri's first distribution center in Europe."

The industry had drastically concentrated (Exhibit 3), leaving Agri the acknowledged leader with four secondary international competitors: a German (Westfalia), a British (Fullwood), and two American companies (Boumatic and Surge). The aftermath of the European crisis had stressed some of Alfa Laval' s strengths: the power of its global size, international scope, and components manufacturing centralized in Tumba, as well as its outstanding engineering.

In the late 80s, Agri took advantage of two growth opportunities: first, the fall of the Berlin wall, in November 1989, opened the economy of Central and Eastern European countries where it had a historical presence. Second, dairy farming was to gain momentum with urbanization and rising living standards in Asia, Latin America, and the Middle East. Farmers' invested in milking equipment to achieve better productivity, hygiene, and increase milk quality. Given Agri's market position and distinctive strength these markets could offer a huge potential away from the "traditional" ones (North America and Europe) where Agri made 95 percent of its turnover.[4] Indeed, the company brought considerable strength to the milking equipment business.

Technological Leadership and Innovation

Since its creation in 1878, in Sweden, Alfa Laval (then called AB Separator) had a reputation of leader and innovator. One of its founders, Gustaf de Laval, an engineer, had imagined a continuously functioning centrifugal

[2]Hans Ekdahl was appointed CEO of Agri in January 1999.

[3]Many of the staff cuts in Tumba, the Swedish headquarters were older workers and technical personnel with a background in farming and agriculture.

[4]Eastern Europe including Russia and India had a potential of 70 million dairy cows not counting 35M buffaloes in India, twice as much as North America and Western Europe altogether.

EXHIBIT 3 Evolution of the Number of Dairies in 6 countries (source FAO)

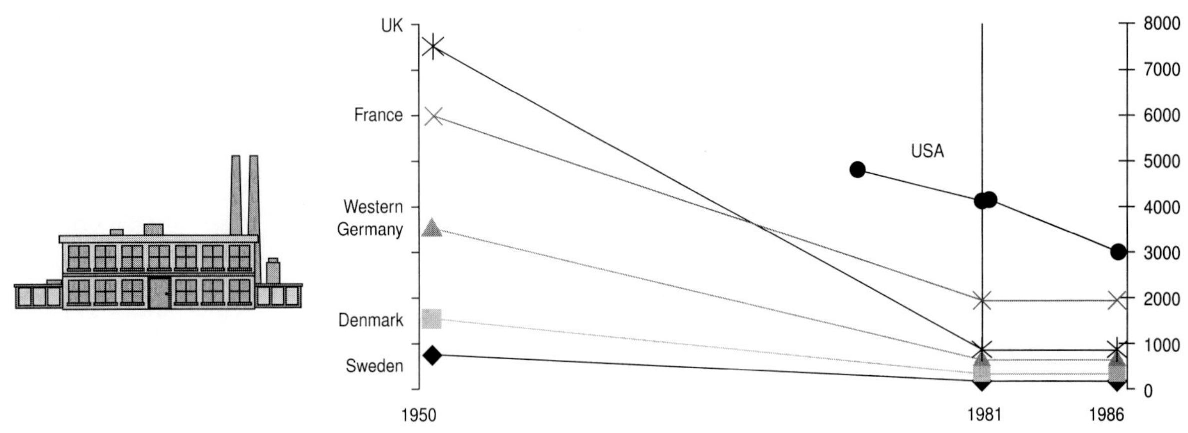

separator, to separate the cream from the milk. He had bought the Hamra farm in Tumba, on the outskirts of Stockholm in 1894, to have a pilot site to test equipment and breed a top-quality herd. In 1889, he had acquired the worldwide patent for a piece of equipment that made better use of the centrifugal force. The "Alfa" patent was soon to turn this hand-driven separator into an all time best seller with 12 million units sold worldwide. This success built the company's position, which immediately sought other applications to separate yeast or oil. Then in the 1920s, the US subsidiary developed and sold the first automatic milking machine thus revolutionizing the farmers' working conditions and the whole dairy industry.

After World War II, the company's diversification in activities such as flows and plate heat exchangers brought it progressively to a leadership position in the process industry from chemicals to food with highly engineered products. In the 1960s, AB Separator changed its name to Alfa-Laval, thus stressing its wider range of activity, and keeping a trace of the roots of its success, the Alfa patent.

Distribution Channels and Subsidiaries

As early as the 1880s, Sweden's domestic market had proved too limited for the separator, and the company had its first overseas manufacturing sales-distribution subsidiary in the United States in 1883. It managed the dealers whose strong customers and market knowledge had helped gain power over the "center"—the headquarters. In addition, the two world wars had made the supply of Alfa Laval's goods more difficult in the United States. In milking equipment, the dealers had started to buy from Agri's competitors and to build and sell their own customized milking systems. Moreover, they considered the group did not offer a product range that allowed them to be competitive in the whole of their market (Agri's products were positioned in the middle range of the U.S. market). They used this as a reason not to be fully loyal to Alfa Laval.

Following the United States, AB Separator had established its presence in other countries through "market companies"—subsidiaries in charge of the sales and distribution channels for capital goods installations. They managed the interface between the distribution channels (mostly dealers) and the head office, and had an acute market and customer knowledge. In countries where the market potential had been limited, AB Separator had either worked through dealers, farmers' co-operatives or local agents, and frequently combined all three, according to the local context.

In 1963, Agri's product portfolio in traditional markets consisted basically of high-end milking machines and plants where a farmer could mechanically milk some 10 to 20 cows. Shortly thereafter, Alfa-Laval's management decided to introduce other brands to Agri's business, either to protect its high market share in new equipment (50 percent on average) or to better control its distribution channels by fighting lower-end suppliers. Alfa Laval acquired a Euro-

EXHIBIT 4 Evolution of Agri's Markets and Technologies in Capital Goods

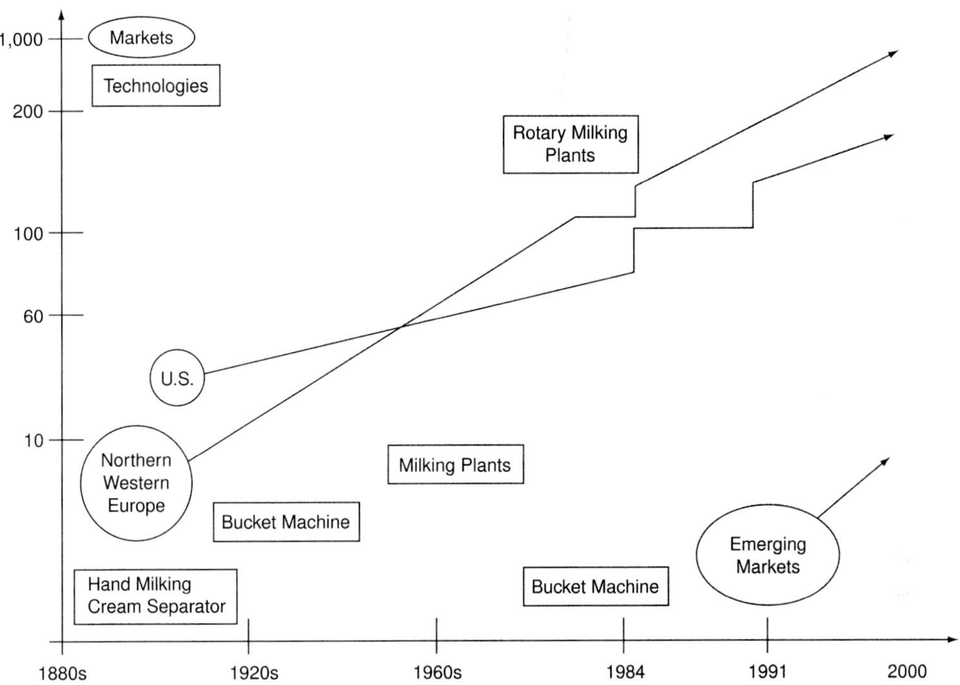

pean supplier of capital goods, Manus, that gave Agri access to the lower end of the market and strengthened its distribution network in Sweden, France and Holland. However, not all market companies saw this in a positive light: "We should not fight among ourselves but with our competitors," said one of the managing directors.

As Agri expanded geographically and accessed new markets and segments, it faced growing difficulties coping with the increasing variety of demand (see Exhibit 4). Not all customers were equally knowledgeable in milking techniques and equipment (education was critical in emerging markets) and Agri's technological competence was challenged by a new herd with huge potential, buffaloes. Agri did not cope well with all these challenges. More diverse milking system designs were needed, but the center largely ignored it. As a result, one manager commented that,

> "The design of a milking system requires an artistic flair. The center was doing it well, but it was not profitable. The market companies had to adapt each design to their local demands. Each installation was then too much of a unique design, each time excessively customized."

However, at the end of the 1980s, Agri had adjusted its offering to access large herds in East Germany, and had served developing markets such as South America with unusually "low-tech" equipment: it was producing and selling cooling tanks to refrigerate the milk (a stainless steel container with a compressor to keep milk at a low temperature for conservation); or "bucket machines" (a bucket with a mechanical milking device) to milk one cow at a time. But these technologies were easily accessible to local companies that rapidly launched their own competing lines. Agri discovered a new battlefield with harsh price competition and low margins. However, within a few years, Agri had captured up to 45 percent of market share thanks to its brand name, historical link with the markets, or quality of its service or presence, as compared to those of local competitors.

In the midst of the crisis due to the new European agricultural policy, a central distribution center had been established in Sweden. It had been a revolution for the market companies. They used to require high levels of stock to serve and service their local customers in order to make up for the center's lack of market responsiveness. Erik Jenssen,[5] then Managing Director for the Danish market company, said:

"I was the first to be reluctant to this change. But then, we had to cut costs. As a result, in Denmark, we reduced our assets by up to 60 percent (. . .). One thing was to lower the inventories, the other was to become more professional. Agri realized it needed to strengthen its logistics and this was a major step for the company."

Engineering Excellence

By the 1980s, Alfa Laval had grown into a huge conglomerate with products ranging from food production, chemical separators and plate heat exchangers, to milking machines. Its' image was blurred by the variety of its activities, but the group was widely acknowledged as a technology leader. Agri's image and reputation within Alfa Laval was less attractive.

As Staffan Bohman put it:

"Agri was the odd bird in Alfa Laval, a branch selling milking equipment and consumables to less qualified and less knowledgeable customers. Its image within the Alfa Laval group was bad, although it was bringing above average profits and thus supporting other activities."

Agri did not fit in Alfa Laval's tradition of highly engineered products and complex systems. The acquisition of a detergent company in the United States in the 1970s–(to provide consumables and help guarantee quality and cleanliness in milking–(had hardly improved this "low tech-low end" image within the group. Engineering excellence became a mixed blessing for Agri. When it benefited from the technical expertise of the group, its products were too complex and too engineered for the often basic needs of farmers. When it did not benefit, Agri suffered. Moreover, Alfa Laval had early on centralized all activities and product development at the group's headquarters, also located in Tumba. Some market company managers overseas saw the proximity to the Swedish market company, located about 20 kilometers from Tumba, with concern:

"New products were too 'Scandinavian'. It was difficult to develop products for other markets as the United States with herds of up to 5,000, or much smaller ones elsewhere, from a headquarters dominated by Europe where most farms had 30 to 100 cows. Only a few products used in some less developed European markets could be sold in the emerging countries."

Agri was torn between a high-end product positioning in capital goods and an increasingly growing low-end segment. A gap had progressively opened between the center and the customers, and internal links had been strained as Agri expanded geographically. The perceived inadequacy of the center's products to the increasingly differentiated farmers' needs had led the market companies and the bigger dealers to create local solutions, with little attention to norms and quality. Thus, 80 percent of costs were incurred in the market companies, which did their own engineering and fixed problems with their own local resources. Over the years, they had relegated Agri's headquarters to a role of components supplier, ordering parts of milking systems they would assemble according to the local farmers' needs. The U.S. dealers had learned to "cherry-pick" among several suppliers, and the market companies had built direct relationships with Alfa Laval's own suppliers, thus getting better prices on components. Management had tried many times to address a rising claims rate that was reaching 6-7 percent, but the lack of a clear strategy had never allowed implementation of these policies. Customers were also complaining about Agri's service and distribution. As one manager put it,

"At that time [in the 1980s], a big installation would be completed only after six to nine deliveries, and the farmers saw the cost this implied for Agri. They concluded that this was the cause of Agri's high prices. Moreover, it was difficult for the center to sell a whole system because the market companies were customizing so much."

Professional Management

In the 1970s, Alfa Laval was part of the Investor Group—the Wallenberg family holding company that was a major shareholder in many leading Swedish companies. Over the decades this had brought high quality management practices and control systems to Alfa Laval. Once Agri started to develop sales of consumables, parts and service to farmers, it was re-organized around three divisions: "capital goods" (selling systems and equipment), "after market" (dealing primarily with consumables), and "second brand" handling Manus' product line (later renamed United Brands). All R&D, production, logistics and other functions were centralized in Tumba—a move that had helped increase functional efficiency.

However, this was sometimes in conflict with the geographic organization of market companies. They showed little concern for profitability apart from that at the local level. The accounting system did not allow allocation of product and system costs precisely between market companies and central functions. Therefore, costs and revenues per product line were hard to isolate, and no control system or procedures permitted to develop a clear picture of the financial reality. Moreover, historically, all functions had been independent: production and marketing were separate from sales, each optimizing product and process innovations as a function of their own preferences.

In the early 1980s, Alfa Laval implemented a better way to measure the profitability of various units and product lines, and the group reorganized its distribution structure which gave Agri its own market companies. In 1991, a computerized sales support system had been created for Sweden, Germany, Holland, and Denmark in an attempt to rationalize sales activities and control costs. This system was meant to increase efficiency in administrative matters, but the center was too weak to face the reluctance of the market companies to set it up. Implementation lagged, and the tool was partly discarded. It was considered too much of a "center's idea".

New Owners

Tetra-Pak, a Swedish private group specialized in liquid processing and packaging had acquired Alfa-Laval at the end of 1991. Its main interest was in the food processing engineering skills of Alfa-Laval, which were complementary to its activity. But Tetra-Pak had also seen the potential to develop the Agri business[5] into a more global company, and the synergies between their two activities: the quality control of the milk production chain, "from teat to pack." In 1993, four consolidated industrial groups were created around one new entity, Tetra-Laval: Tetra-Pak (liquid packaging), Alfa-Laval (industrial activities), Agri and Food (non-liquid food processing). This acquisition and structure strengthened Agri. The company now had a parent with a drive for growth that would allow long-term investments and support a more aggressive strategy. Tetra-Pak would build on its own growth strategy, especially in emerging markets. The group immediately gave Agri a mandate to expand into emerging countries. Tetra-Pak would help Agri become a full supplier of complete systems and to become more customer oriented. With a customer base of 1,500, Tetra-Pak had a good knowledge of operations and customer management. It helped Agri renew its concern for its diversified customer base of 600,000 farmers worldwide.

This obviously put pretty tough demands on Staffan Bohman. Tetra-Laval would invest in Agri, but would demand high returns and expect strategic synergies with its milk processing equipment business. He knew that unless he complied to the new owners' demand of profitable growth with a return on capital of a minimum 20 percent, Agri could be divested. But he was also sure of Tetra-Pak's strong commitment to Agri's success, especially in those markets where they were already present: Asia and South America.

Initial Difficulties

When Staffan Bohman took charge of Agri, sales had again been cut drastically in Europe: farmers had withheld their investments in capital goods until the GATT agreements and the changes in the EC's Common Agricultural Policy had settled. Once again, the European market companies suffered an average drop in turnover of 20 percent per year in 1991 and 1992, and even 50 percent per year in the UK. Concurrently, demand in the United States had flattened, as the government had lowered its support and guarantees on the price of the milk. This situation deepened the crisis between Agri and its distributors that demanded products to improve their profitability.

If his familiarity with Agri's financial figures had initially made him confident in Agri's future (Exhibit 5), Staffan Bohman was in for a rude awakening. He had been confronted with a market crisis and some internal difficulties he had no means to anticipate. He visited Agri's major customers who told him harrowing stories of missed delivery dates, incomplete shipments and poorly fitted installations that required endless maintenance. There were also stories of inaccurate bills, poor maintenance, and product designs that were perhaps fine for Scandinavia but did not meet the local farmers' needs. One distributor summed it up for him:

> "You may believe Agri is doing fine, but the reality is that it is an arrogant, old-fashioned company selling yesterday's products at excessive prices in ways that do not meet customer needs."

To a certain extent, Agri was paying the price of its rapid growth pre-1984, when demand in capital goods was strong. Farmers had invested heavily in milking

[5] Agri's sales then accounted for as little as 10 percent of Tetra-Pak's.

EXHIBIT 5 Agri Group 1982–1992

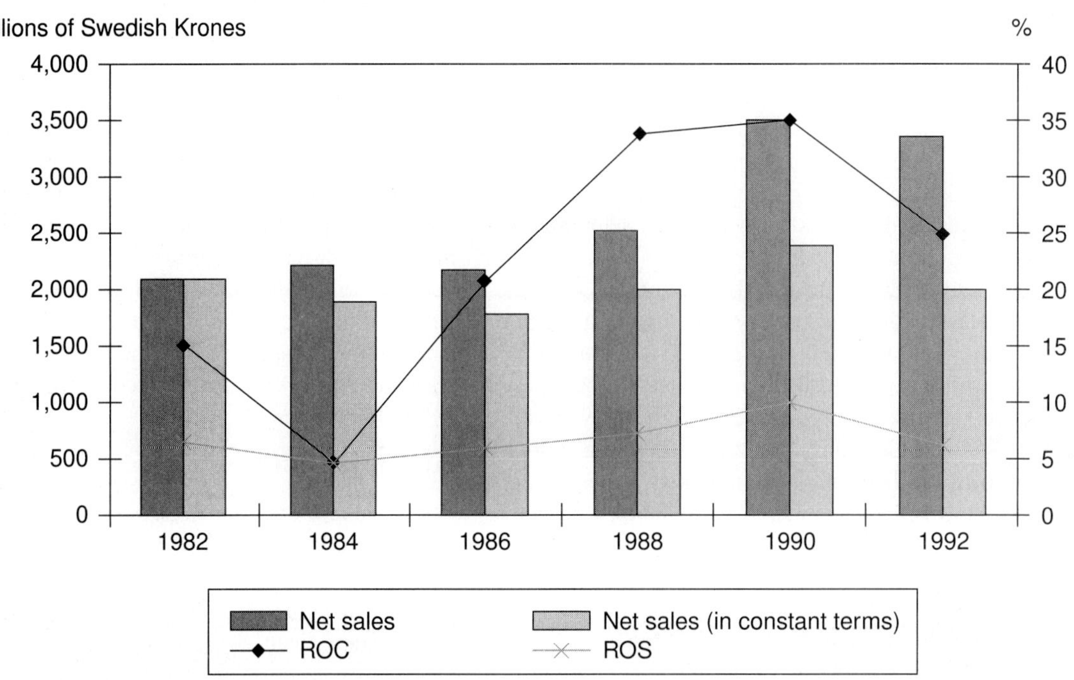

Note: In 1996, the average rate of exchange was 6.71 Swedish kroner (SEK) per US$. For the decade 1982–92 this rate fluctuated between SEK 8.60 per $ in 1985, and SEK 5.82 per $ in 1992.

equipment to reach more profitability and meet the EEC's requirements to produce quality milk. Agri had positioned itself with high prices and high quality products. Moreover, it had not paid sufficient attention to the consequences of the rapid diversification of its markets. One key executive commented:

> "While it was convenient to blame the culture of over-engineering, of highly customized solutions that permeated the whole of the Alfa Laval group, problems also ran deep in Agri itself. This culture was probably derived from other industrial groups within Alfa Laval, who often did 'one-off' engineering projects, the technologies of which were more complex than Agri's."

The "First Growth Challenge"

Building Credibility of the Center and Increasing Market Responsiveness

In December 1991, Staffan Bohman launched a strategic plan, the "first growth challenge," where he announced a set of measures aimed to tackle the most visible problems. Staffan Bohman faced two difficulties in this endeavor: first, he was reporting to his predecessor (who would be assigned to another position in early 1993); and second, many changes had been announced by former top management teams but never implemented, thus undermining the center's credibility. Staffan Bohman decided to commit himself strongly, affirm the value of his vision of Agri, and push change through the organization from top to bottom, and from the center to the market companies.

He took over the Agri management team, a team composed of the 12 top managers, announced the departure of three and the retirement of a fourth. They were respectively heads of agri export, capital goods, research and technical management, and second brands. Instead, for the first time in Agri, he appointed four senior market company people respectively from the United States, Germany, Spain, and Finland. In order to build the credibility of this rejuvenated management team, Staffan Bohman chose those who were either managing directors locally or their direct reports, people who had field expertise and a research or technical background. New hires in production and logistics were to improve Agri's competence in this weak function.

Staffan Bohman said:

> "Some of these executives had really acted as eye openers to me during the first years. The reality of Agri's situation was absolutely not visible from where I stood before, as Agri's—and later Group—controller. I was in a difficult situation where I had to defend my predecessor and also acknowledge a reality that I had to report to him. As the crisis in the U.S. market was at its peak and urgently needed to be solved, I had to look for things I would not have looked for otherwise."

This first integration ever of market company people into Tumba sent a positive and strong signal of change to the market companies. They were represented at the headquarters, their concerns were now to be heard. Moreover, the new Agri management team would foster communication among all top management and clarify the strategic direction for the group.

The R&D strategy had also to be revamped. The milking systems' main problem was their complexity with regard to farmers' needs. Most of the warranty claims were still caused by poorly designed products, or premature product releases that generated quality problems, stressing Agri's lack of market understanding. Staffan Bohman appointed Hans Ekdahl as head of R&D, marketing, and production for the non-after-market areas. A year later, in 1994, Hans Ekdahl hired a new head for the R&D department, Jan Ove Nilsson, a former Siemens Medical R&D manager, to whom Staffan Bohman said: "we have a lot of money but we lack ideas." Surprisingly enough, Nilsson found out that there were ideas, but that there was no global approach to R&D that allowed for their exploitation. A structure with rigorous guidelines for product releases and R&D management had already been put in place, and was to be developed further. Jan Ove Nilsson participated in the change of the whole R&D process. He created systematic procedures for the development of new products, and an approach to product development that Tetra-Laval had implemented, that involved the field. For all launches, pilot countries (and their market companies) were chosen according to their potential interest in a product and availability of resources. In one of them the project was "home-based," another would test the concept and validate, or not, the pre-study and evaluation of the market potential. It was new to Agri to refuse to launch a product, and it proved a good source of savings. The marketing launch and the training packages for the sales forces and dealers were prepared concurrently. As a result of these rationalizations, the R&D allocation was increased from 2 percent of the turnover to 3 percent.

In emerging markets, Agri was technologically challenged by the unique characteristics of each market. In Morocco, for example, climatic conditions (high temperatures) provoked distension of valves and pressure variations problematic for milking machines' pumps. In India, a country where the market company promised to be the largest during the next millenium, Agri had had to learn how to milk buffaloes. Agri was able to leverage Alfa-Laval's 70 years of knowledge of the Indian market and local resources, hiring the local top management of Alfa-Laval's former trading company, Vulcan Laval. Said a local manager:

> "Agri hired and trained milkers and technicians, and learnt from them to develop the adequate milking system for buffaloes. We did it in three years and it is now a large business that exports to Italy and Brazil. "This is Agri's strength: its dedication and presence."

At a strategic level, Staffan Bohman decided to increase sales by 50 percent in four years, and to accelerate its international expansion in emerging markets. Within three years, the number of market companies increased from 20 to 30. New market companies were established in countries where a turnover of at least SWF 2 million could be rapidly achieved, with an average SWF 10 million turnover potential in the long run. Prior to that, an agent would be appointed, as in Pakistan for example, and the local Agri structure would benefit from Tetra-Pak's presence and logistics.

Regaining Technological Edge and Efficiency

The second priority was to regain Agri's historical technological edge on competitors. The issue was a difficult one since Agri was still "the" all time leader in terms of market share, market presence, size, etc. But Agri's relative market share in capital goods had decreased by 5 percent, to the profit of Westfalia (that had reached 30 percent). It was also facing harsh competition in the after market where Agri's technological advantage was less of an asset, as compared to often aggressive commercial strategies. Staffan Bohman first pushed change from the center to the distribution channels, to rebuild Tumba's credibility, and second aimed to reconstruct Agri's image with its customer base. In 1992, he launched TQM at plant and then at group level. He wanted to enforce routines, procedures, evaluation and

EXHIBIT 6 **Agri's Profit and Loss Accounts, 1983–1996**
(In millions of Swiss francs)

	1983	1984	1985	1986	1987	1988	1989	1990	1991	1992	1993	1994	1995	1996
Net Sales	**560**	**510**	**502**	**491**	**516**	**583**	**681**	**790**	**747**	**770**	**864**	**940**	**990**	**1,018**
Gross Margin	249	219	210	207	227	250	298	339	327	331	371	420	431	438
Gross Margin (%)	*44.5*	*42.9*	*41.8*	*42.2*	*44.0*	*42.9*	*43.8*	*42.9*	*43.8*	*43.0*	*42.9*	*44.7*	*43.5*	*43.0*
Factory Results	-1	-8	-8	-2	-1	1	3	5	1	3	3	0	0	2
Sales, R&D and Administrative Costs	-187	-194	-179	-166	-179	-196	-226	-255	-258	-253	-280	-310	-328	-335
Net Operating Income	**61**	**17**	**23**	**39**	**47**	**55**	**75**	**89**	**70**	**81**	**94**	**110**	**103**	**105**
Operating capital (OC)	270	325	255	216	170	166	197	219	210	195	240	250	264	270
OC Turnover	2.1	1.6	2.0	2.3	3.0	3.5	3.5	3.6	3.6	3.9	3.6	3.8	3.8	3.8
ROS (%)	*10.9*	*3.3*	*4.6*	*7.9*	*9.1*	*9.4*	*11.0*	*11.3*	*9.4*	*10.5*	*10.9*	*11.7*	*10.4*	*10.3*
ROC (%)	*22.6*	*5.2*	*9.0*	*18.1*	*27.6*	*33.1*	*38.1*	*40.6*	*33.3*	*41.5*	*39.2*	*44.0*	*39.0*	*38.9*

Note: In 1996, the average exchange rate was SwF 1.236 = 1US$. For the preceding decade, these rates fluctuated between a high of SwF 2.457 per $ in 1985, and a low of SwF 1.183 per $ in 1995.

EXHIBIT 7 **Market Potential Worldwide of Dairy Cows & Buffaloes (1997 Forecast)**
Total = 292 million among which 70 million are buffaloes.

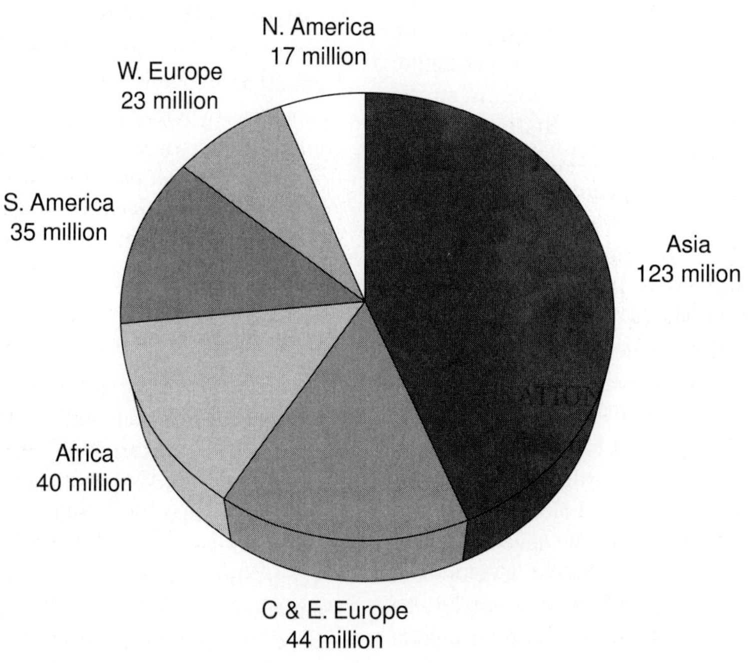

controls to solve the milking systems' quality problems, and thus decrease the claims rate and the need for the market companies to compensate for the center's lack of quality products and market responsiveness. Claims rate, service level, inventory turnover rate, and throughput started to be measured at the plant level.

The third area where Staffan Bohman had found room for improvement of its global efficiency was by a better use of Agri's human resources and trimming costs. Staffan Bohman had set up project teams in 1992, in an attempt to increase exchanges and develop motivation through joint work. These were to gather product and factory managers with product development people, who were to identify, discuss and develop propositions to solve their common issues. After a few months, their main frustration was that they had no decision power to implement change: Tumba's critical eye on their results and reports finally rejected all their proposals. But the increased use of job rotations from—and to—the field had created better relationships across the organization and fostered mutual learning. Slowly, concern for global issues had started to develop within Agri.

At field level, Agri reorganized its distribution structure in order to take out all sources of extra cost and inefficiency. Erik Jenssen, former managing director of the Danish market company, commented:

> "In Europe, we took out 60 to 80 technical people in the field, who were serving the dealers when those should have taken care of the farmers' problems themselves. They were a big cost for Agri without much added value."

Then at group level two other distribution centers were created to centralize what proved to be a costly function. They now could save on capital, and the group would have a better control on distribution costs relative to when each market company used to manage its own stock and warehouse. One distribution center was located in Kansas City, where Agri had set up its R&D Center for Hygiene and one in Germany, to serve Central and Western Europe.

In parallel, for the first time, the Second Brands' division was restructured to achieve economies of scale, and regionalised: Manus was to remain European, and two recently acquired brands, Universal and Nu-Pulse, would be sold in the United States and in Asia-Pacific, respectively.

By the end of 1993, financial results had improved (Exhibit 6), external growth opportunities had been seized, and the after market was profitable, accounting for nearly 50 percent of Agri's total turnover. Despite obvious progress, the group remained too centralized with all 30 market companies inefficiently reporting to the three divisions at the center. But some key issues were still to be handled. Agri was still delivering 90 percent of its turnover in its traditional markets despite the potential in emerging markets (Exhibit 7). An order for a complete milking plant could consist of more than 300 items, and 95 percent of the orders were sent out incomplete giving rise to customer and distributor complaints. Installation costs remained high, as the missing components had to be made up at the last minute, causing delays and cost overruns. The market companies were still incurring 80 percent of Agri's total costs without control from the center, and the group's accounting structure was still opaque.

Building a New Organization

1994: Shifting the Internal Balance

Staffan Bohman discussed with Tetra-Pak colleagues on their recent regional organization and reflected on the lack of vertical communication within Agri. He found the idea of the regions valuable for his company in terms of efficiency through decentralization, and decided to work on its implementation. He said:

> "The company had grown fast and more market companies were still to be created. It was impossible to continue to work in the same way. The Scandinavian region, created in the 1970s within Agri, had worked successfully . . . I asked for the advice of a retired manager from that region and we both worked to create a matrix at group level."

Bohman reorganized the company around six regions, one of which, AgriExport, was dedicated to serving and supporting commercial activities in emerging markets where there were no market companies such as in some parts of Asia, Africa, South and Central America. The other ones were North America; Northern, Central, and Western Europe; and Oceania/Southern Africa. Each was responsible for "growth, profitability, market penetration, total quality, and day to day management of operations in the field." The three distribution centers split their geographic scope of activity: Sweden took charge of Norway, Finland, the Baltic States (where Agri was just entering through three old established Alfa-Laval companies), Poland, and Russia. Germany took Central and Eastern Europe, and the US became responsible for the Americas and Japan.

The regions worked in a matrix with the three product divisions in Tumba that kept strategy, product development, market support, and product positioning. The heads of the leading market companies became region managers and monitored the other local market companies. These were gathering in "regional meetings" with their manager, where, as one market company manager put it:

> "We brainstormed, shared ideas and worries; it had been a filter toward Tumba. The decision-making process had changed, and I was worried about this when it was launched. But it all went smoothly, as we all trust our regional directors will report to the center. And they are responsible for the market companies' results anyway."

This matrix increased the exchanges between the regional managers, who started to agree on company-wide projects thus building a global spirit. They benchmarked each other and created processes to enhance the management of their respective market companies. Some found the endeavor difficult, and underlined many conflicts of interest because of the diversity of their markets or resources. But it was the first time that joint decisions were made. These regional meetings proved efficient and invaluable for Agri, bringing the company together and building a common awareness of the company's reality: marketing competencies were not being developed as they should, most knowledge was in the market companies, and the group was not reaching economies of scale.

Economies of scale was one of Staffan Bohman's main concerns. In an attempt to rationalize the products' reference system worldwide, and harmonize procedures and systems, a new CFO was hired with responsibility for IT. He started to implement the SAP R/3 enterprise integration platform at headquarters in Tumba, but as one manager commented:

> "It was not a success. People are not literate enough, or maybe the strategy was all too ambitious? However, it made field administration more effective for people, or stock management less costly. It built sales tracking systems that later helped build a customer database . . . yes, it was a basis for future steps."

Meanwhile, Staffan Bohman decided to keep on changing procedures and reporting to reach a more distributed supervision. He rejuvenated the idea of the Agri Council of 1991. He changed the team and renamed it "Executive Group Management" (EGM). It consisted of a "virtual management team" of 11, which gathered corporate people, division and region managers. They developed a strategic perspective on major issues and made all the decisions regarding the product mix. Staffan Bohman's clear strategy and concrete propositions helped them motivate and push their people to implement all decisions. They reviewed each functional area to find out whether the new organization called for adjustments in staffing and/or allocation of resources. The direct benefits of this group were two-fold: it gave more voice to country managers in the corporate policy, an opportunity they had never been given before, and quality of the dialogue throughout Agri was enhanced, allowing more decisions to be carried out. The EGM was filling the void of the project teams that were now increasingly cross-functional. The results, the better definition of roles and responsibilities, and the clearer distribution of power were building the confidence of all parties on the change process. A major shift in mentality started to occur according to Hans Ekdahl:

> "People in Tumba learned a lot on the field, we learned more about products than before. The regional managers got some power and were allowed to focus on the field, to create a more meaningful dialogue with the market companies. People in the center used to see market companies too much as customers versus them being a part of the company. This EGM and the organization of the regions made it possible to get decisions carried through into the market companies."

In an internal survey, market company employees expressed satisfaction with the changes that had occurred within Agri since 1991. The center had gained overall credibility as products' quality improved, the number of claims and the lead-time in delivery dropped, service level increased and the inventory turnover rate improved.

Strengthening Position in Emerging Markets

Growth was essentially achieved through expansion into emerging markets and better penetration of traditional ones. First, in emerging markets, Agri had developed a strategic two-step approach that had established its presence and built its market in capital goods. A manager of the Indian market company illustrated this:

> "Agri would first sell a cooling tank to a village and, in the meantime, inform and educate the farmers on hygiene and milking techniques. Then it would train sales people, and later sell a milking machine to a group of farmers for US$1,000 that would pay off in two to three years. The concern here is to educate small farmers, and to target large farms with herds of over a thousand heads in the short term,

EXHIBIT 8 Channels of Distribution by Product Group and Herd Size

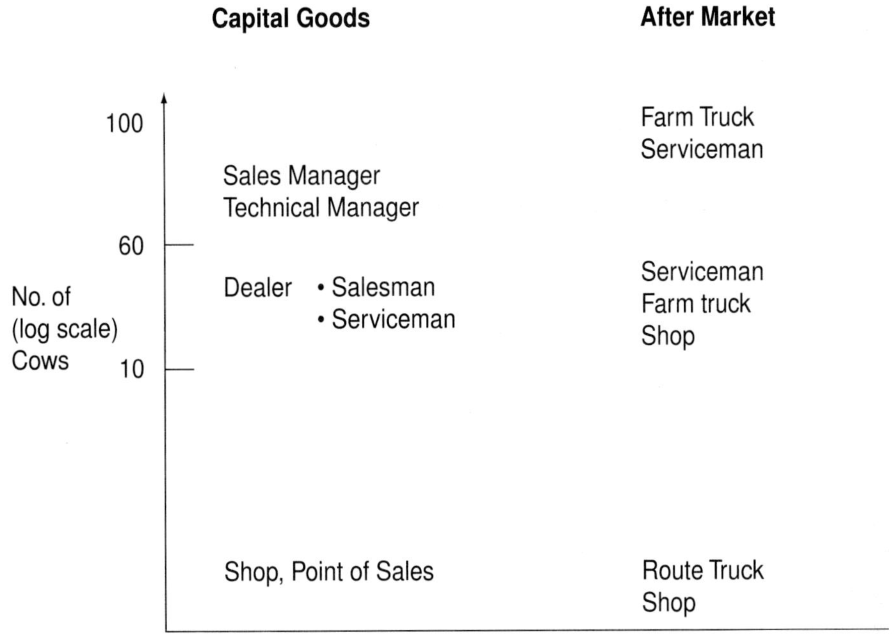

as was done for tractors 15 years ago. When market acceptance is reached, it will be a booming business for Agri. Our turnover has already doubled every year since the cooling tanks' factory opened in 1995."

Staffan Bohman was concerned that this strategy was costly in terms of management capacity from Tumba and the break-even point was slowly reached. The Indian market company was only to be profitable after four years of investment and efforts. The Ukrainian one would become profitable after five years and an investment of SWF 1 million, but its market share would reach 70 percent in three years. But Bohman knew Agri's long-term growth opportunity in these markets exceeded those in the traditional markets.

Second, in more mature markets, where Agri carried both product lines, the structure of distribution had been frequently adjusted to allow Agri to find a local optimal solution. In Poland for example, the managing director had benchmarked other market companies to set up the structure illustrated in Exhibit 8.

In the country's 16 districts, the dealers in capital goods had been supplemented with sales and technical managers who supervised the districts to reach the upper segment of the bigger farms. They serviced it with farm trucks. In the after market, they had route trucks to supply smaller farms and local "hardware" stores where farmers bought their small equipment (gloves, sponges, detergents, brushes, etc.).

Finally, in those emergent markets, Agri could enter a give-and-take relationship with Tetra-Laval. Tetra-Pak's local established leadership was indeed a competitive advantage for Agri, and Agri enabled Tetra-Pak to control and guarantee the milk's quality from the cow to the processing into cheese. For example, in India, Agri would control "on farm processing" units in farms producing up to 10,000 liters per year. Tetra-Pak would deal with those from 10,000 liters upward.

In 1995, Staffan Bohman could look back with some satisfaction over the past four years: he was granted an ISO 9000 certification in Tumba, and could reap some fruits of the TQM endeavor he had implemented on his arrival. The European domination on products had decreased, the center had enhanced market awareness and tolerance for diversity so Agri had entered more aggressively the segment of bigger herds in the United States or former state farms in Eastern Europe (in Russia especially). But in the United States, Agri was still struggling despite progress made in deliveries, product quality, and the introduction of second brands the dealers had called for. The company had not yet reached economies of scale, had to improve on operational efficiency, and make a better use of its resources. In a first attempt, Staffan Bohman adjusted the one-year old regional structure to Agri's international expansion. Three of the six regions were modified: one region was created for the Americas, one for Asia/Pacific, one for "India, Middle East, Africa" (IMEA). The three European regions basically remained unchanged. He realized that even if outstanding on many aspects, the regional organization did not address the issue of the opaque cost structure. There was still the risk of product proliferation and of having each region work independently. Staffan Bohman thought it was now time to put equal emphasis on all dimensions of the existing matrix and create a better balance in the organization: the market companies had to be more committed to the group.

1996: The Matrix Organization

Staffan Bohman had recently read "The Discipline of Market Leaders" by Treacy and Wiersema, a book that had a deep impact on him as he could identify many of his actions with the book's framework. He relied on some of the key ideas to present Agri's new objectives: investing more on technology, reducing the costly complexity of all processes, and further improving the quality of the dialogue between the center and the market companies. He announced in 1996 that,

> "We have gradually adjusted the organization structure of the company to changes in how we work in the market place, to the increased size of our company, the larger number of market companies, and to the global shift of milk production away from traditional markets. This has mainly affected our market organization and resulted in the present regional structure, which has turned out to be an outstanding success: our sales in emerging markets have increased five-fold in three years. This requires a centralized management of the product lines. We must improve their profitability and build on responsibility at all levels. If we succeed, then we will be able to optimize our resources and become a true global force in the milking industry".

Within nine months, Staffan Bohman structured the matrix around three divisions and nine business units (BUs) located in Tumba (Exhibit 9). He renamed the two main divisions "Milk Production Systems," and "Farm Supply and Service." Each was respectively built around five and four business units, headed at 60 percent by managers coming from central staff. Two support units (one for Purchasing and Logistics, the other for Market Communications) would support the BUs and market companies. The functional organization was blended in this matrix, as each new division or BU gained responsibility for P&L, business development, global marketing support, assortment policy, purchasing, product development, sourcing, production, and quality assurance. The third division was still responsible for Agri's second brands.

A Clear Definition of the Tasks and Goals for Improved Efficiency

The market companies responsibility was clearly separated from that of the BUs: they were to be the link between the customer and the BU in order to increase responsiveness and build market knowledge at the center. They would have to provide the BUs with market information if they wanted their local needs to be answered. The BUs were to work on product development or modifications, and develop the marketing strategy and all technical tools to support the market companies' sales effort. The center was in charge of sales and product promotion, and pricing policy according to the BU's recommendations.

The challenge that Agri faced was to build some cooperative and trustful relationships between all, to build on the emerging "Agri spirit," and to have the market companies accept to comply to new constraints. Staffan Bohman told them:

> "Dealing with product proliferation requires centralization of product management even if I am aware we would need to serve older installations with specific parts.[6] We want to improve the product-line profit, increase our market pene-

[6]An installation had a life time of 15 to 20 years.

EXHIBIT 9 Organisation Chart, 1996

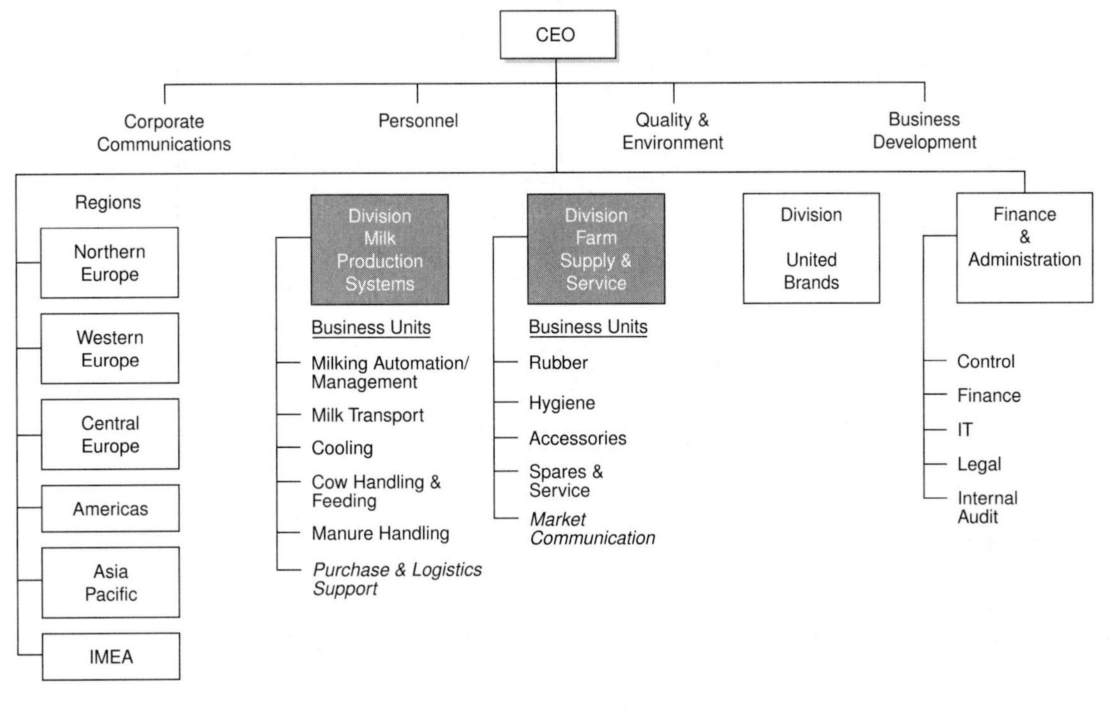

tration, and put more efforts in the after market. Both the market companies and the business units will have full accountability of the product lines, and we all have to optimize our global use of resources, and reach economies of scale."

On the launch of the matrix, the BU's first task was to clean up all product lines, to progressively put systems in place, and to streamline the distribution centers' activity. These actions would clarify the true cost structure and helped Agri to manage its resources better. The benefits of a tighter control on product lines and costs showed rapidly. In capital goods, the number of combinations in milking systems was scheduled to drop from 100,000 in 1996, to 3,500 within two years. Some market companies such as that in Poland were to rationalize and save as much as 70 percent on some of their production costs. Thereafter, the suppliers policy was concurrently revamped. Agri had managed up to 8,000 suppliers worldwide in the past, and reduced these to some 3,500 thanks to this rationalization. In the meantime, Staffan Bohman started an Activity Based Costing (ABC) analysis, first at the center, then in the market companies. However, its results would not be available before 1998.

Making Matrix Management Come Alive

Within the matrix, regional meetings gathered people from different market companies to work jointly on a product, a range of products, or to build common sales actions at the regional level. In capital goods for example, regional marketing meetings were organized twice a year, either at the center or in the region. They aimed at developing new products, and eventually assigned a pilot country for its launch. Each market company in the region was highly involved in the pre-project (a market potential analysis) and development phase, working with the project manager in Tumba to test its feasibility. But national specificities and the independent nature of the market companies were to create difficulties. Some of the projects demanded co-operation of all market companies that was not always reached. The smallest market companies sometimes did not have the required resources to carry it out. Some BU managers would also participate in these yearly or bi-yearly meetings with the market companies to get a feel for the markets' problems or to present their strategy and get feed back. But some market companies said:

> "The BUs are based in Sweden, thus too Scandinavian and not receptive to the other regions' needs or expectations. They reinforce the center. Moreover, they do not co-ordinate their actions, and it is difficult for a market company to work with them."

The BUs met to plan and budget their actions, coordinate projects, and allocate resources according to their degree of commitment to it. New projects were developed by the former product teams that had become "virtual companies;" they reported their new ideas to the BUs that, if feasable, would then hire market company employees to gain knowledge on a specific issue. For example, the BU Milk Automation hired market company people from Australia, New Zealand, Denmark, Holland, and Sweden to develop a project. Short-term rotation assignments were also organized—usually from the center to the market companies.

Agri faced difficulties managing the new split of responsibilities between the BUs and the market companies. On the one hand, the BUs were accused of reinforcing the center, of thinking too "Scandinavian" thus not listening to other demands. On the other hand, the market companies were reluctant to stop customizing, and to report to "non-knowledgeable" people at the center who were constantly asking for market information.

Some managers continuously reinforced this message:

> "It is the BUs' responsibility to have equipment suitable for the markets. Each BU must be able to see—and work on—the applications of its products on the farm. They must take full responsibility over the products, and release the right ones for each market. Each enhancement or change must be done by the BU. The market companies must see that BUs remain aware of the field, they have more frequent visits of BU people, and the market companies come to Tumba to share market information. Communication between them is difficult as the BUs have to comply to many demands. The market companies are aware of the support of the BUs, but they must fully use group products, be aware that they offer optimal solutions for good milking conditions as opposed to customization."

The implementation of the matrix organization was difficult because of Agri's long-time internal dysfunctions between the center and the market companies. It would take more to get the company together and build a true common "Agri-culture" or "Agri-spirit" with a global concern for cost control. Among the key recurrent questions around this new organization, Staffan Bohman and the EGM were cautious of not falling back into being again too component oriented. Increased coordination among the BUs was essential in order for the to fit the milking, feeding, or stalling systems together, and for the creation of compact milking systems.

In the summer of 1996, Staffan Bohman could acknowledge some progress toward better relationships between and among regions and BUs. There were new knowledge flows and increased cost transparency. The market companies had clearer targets about market share or service concepts, and they had identified specific executives in the organization that held the competencies they lacked, and on whom they could rely. The matrix interfaces were becoming Agri's backbone.

Responding to Increased Competition

Staffan Bohman knew Agri had to secure its long-term market position through technological innovation. The threat of technology challengers in milking equipment or consumables was looming in Europe, and competition was harsh both in the United States and in emerging markets. The new organization had created an opportunity to decentralize the R&D department that now belonged the different BUs. It had given more focus to and accelerated product development cycles, and developed routines and procedures to aid in this process. A research team on cooling was set up at their distribution center in Groeningen; research on chemicals was based in Kansas City, the center for Hygiene; and for United Brands, a team of eight people had been created after the acquisition of the American Germania. The market companies were especially happy with the many new products in Hygiene, but complained new products in capital goods were still at development or test stage. Among them, was a milking robot that would revolutionize the milking industry in Agri's traditional markets to a similar extent that the first milking machine had in the 1920s. Some competitors were already marketing it, but Agri was confident in its distinctive strengths. Staffan Bohman had turned the company into a full service supplier, from milking equipment to manure handling, ventilation, feeding or farm supplies. He was proud of his achievement, but was aware he had to bring the company further if he wanted to ensure its future.

INSEAD

Case 14–4

Rank Xerox (A)

With his team's last major working session approaching, in Copenhagen in early May 1993, managing director of Rank Xerox's Dutch subsidiary, Mike Van Bachum, was worried. The team needed to decide which organisational solution it should recommend to Bernard Fournier,[1] managing director of Rank Xerox, to improve European customer operations.[2] That recommendation had to be acceptable not only to Fournier, but also to his bosses, in Rank Xerox's parent company, the Xerox Corporation.

In the wake of Rank Xerox's poor financial results for 1991, Fournier had appointed Van Bachum to head a special task force, dubbed Team A, composed of a dozen senior managers from various parts of Rank Xerox, to rethink the organisational design. With Rank Xerox missing its return targets several years in succession, Fournier knew he had to secure rapid financial improvement through cost cutting, resource sharing, and so on. But he was also aware that for the company to achieve sustained revenue growth, it would have to become more customer responsive and flexible. Furthermore, the parent company, Xerox, had just redefined its strategic intent as "The Document Company" and reorganised itself along divisionalised product lines, leaving Rank Xerox with the task of finding an adequate response to "align" its organisation to the new product structure.

The joint challenges—one a cost problem, one a reorganisation problem—certainly overlapped. Yet the stakeholders differed, as did the balance of personal and organisational risks at stake. What might be the trade-offs? Could a solution be found that would satisfy all the stakeholders and that would be consistent with the new strategic intent of the company? These were some of the issues that preyed on Van Bachum's mind as the May 1993 deadline approached.

Xerox: Company Background

In 1949, The Haloid Company, later renamed the Xerox Corporation, introduced its first commercial xerographic copier. Without the capital resources to expand abroad, the company entered into two joint ventures: in 1956, with the English motion picture firm, the Rank Organisation; and, in 1962, with Fuji Photo Film in Japan.

In 1959, Xerox launched its first automatic, plain-paper copier, the 914. This technological breakthrough, combined with the inspired strategy of charging customers per copy (rather than renting or outright selling), ignited the spectacular growth not just of Xerox, but of a whole industry. The 914 has been dubbed the most successful commercial product in history.

A barrage of patents assured the product's position in the market. As the current CEO (and former head of Rank Xerox), Paul Allaire, once put it, "Xerox grew from a high-tech start-up to one of the country's biggest corporations in large part because we were the only game in town."[3] This led to easy growth throughout the 1960s, with sales becoming the dominant function.

With no competitors against which to gauge performance, Xerox focused on internal standards: machines were compared against one another for quality, and sales results were measured against those of the previous period. The company failed to respond to growing customer dissatisfaction with product reliability, service quality, and pricing policies.

This case was written by Jean-Louis Barsoux, Senior Research Fellow, and Yves Doz, Timken Professor of Global Technology and Innovation, both at INSEAD. It is intended to be used as a basis for class discussion rather than to illustrate either effective or ineffective handling of an administrative situation.

Research for the case was funded by the Corporate Renewal (CORE) Initiative at INSEAD.

[1]Bernard Fournier's career started in 1966 when he joined Rank Xerox France as a systems analyst. Six years later he became marketing manager, and four years after that, deputy general manager, operations. From 1980–81 he was based in Rank Xerox headquarters as regional manager for Africa and Eastern Europe. He then returned to France, as general manager, and became chairman and general manager in 1983. In 1987, he was assigned to the United States as president of Xerox Americas Operations, and in June 1989, was appointed head of Rank Xerox.

[2]Rank Xerox also controlled a Technology and Research Centre, located in Welwyn (UK), which was mainly responsible for the development of mid range copiers for various U.S. divisions, and several industrial sites in Europe (Mitcheldean in the UK, Venray in the Netherlands, and Lille in France). These industrial and technical operations were not directly affected by the organisational choices considered here.

[3]"The CEO as Organizational Architect: An Interview with Xerox's Paul Allaire." *Harvard Business Review,* September–October 1992 p. 108.

So, when the patent protection was effectively lifted in the mid-1970s,[4] Xerox came in for a rude awakening. The lucrative copier market attracted IBM and Eastman Kodak in the United States, and a host of Japanese manufacturers led by Canon. From 1976 to 1982, Xerox suffered a staggering decline in its domestic market, with its share of copier installations dropping from an estimated 80 percent to 13 percent, and return on assets falling down to 8 percent.[5]

In the mid-1980s, Xerox began a sustained effort to recapture its leading position in the world copier market, and to create a platform for future growth. As a result of its Leadership Through Quality programme, Xerox addressed underlying problems regarding product development, cost control in manufacturing, and customer service, and actually won back market share from Japanese rivals. Xerox pulled back to 19 percent of overall share of installed machines by 1990, and increased its return on assets to 14 percent.[6]

Industry Outlook

Xerox's main competitor, Canon, did not share the same strategy. Canon was the originator of the personal copier market, and it held about 70 percent of the global market share for personal copiers in 1992. Xerox, focused rather on the high end of the market, such as major accounts and printing establishments. Their main rivalry was in the mid volume market. Furthermore, Canon sold its products primarily through a dealer network. Xerox, on the other hand, had its own sales force. Canon's main source of revenue was from equipment sales, while Xerox had traditionally made its money from the recurring sales of service, parts, paper, and rentals. This accounted for almost two-thirds of Xerox's revenues.

As Finance Director Bill Goode, put it: "The core reprographic market is flattening out. It is a mature business. The real battle ground is in the mid-range. At the low end it is commodity pricing and indirect channels. At the high end, the technology and the services provided are real differentiators."

In 1992, the photocopier industry was already in the midst of a radical shift in technology. The central force was the transition from conventional light lens technology to digital technology. Once digitised, documents need no physical storage space. Text and images can be manipulated at will, then printed or transmitted around the world. Increasingly, then, digital, colour, and networked products would be performing the copying, printing, scanning, and faxing functions.

The problem, from Xerox's point of view, was that digital products were unlikely to yield the high service margins the company had enjoyed from its optical products. While it was true that new software and upgrades would provide revenue for digital products, cornering that business was likely to prove difficult in the face of a software standard open to all comers.

Another problem with pursuing a digital strategy, was that Xerox would become more like a computer company and would start to move into the same territory as Hewlett-Packard, IBM, and Siemens, where competition was tougher and margins smaller. Xerox's long-standing problem with high selling, administration, and general expenses (SAG) would not make this an easy transition.

Xerox 2000

In 1990, the new CEO, Paul Allaire, set up the Xerox 2000 project to assess the major product forces likely to shape the company's business (summarised in Exhibit 1), and to consider the strategic alternatives open to Xerox in the latter half of the 1990s. The culmination of this reflection was the repositioning of Xerox as *The Document Company.*

This concept reflected Xerox's position at the intersection of electronic and paper-based information, and its document concept encompassed both. Pursuing a digital strategy would enable Xerox to switch from being a copier, printer and facsimile producer to being a "solution seller." Xerox would increasingly be working with customers to improve the production, management and use of documents as a productive tool in their business. The company's strategic intent became: "To be the leader in the document market by providing document services that enhance business productivity."[7]

It was clear that reaching this vision would require a fundamental change in what Allaire termed the "organisational

---

[4]The Federal Trade Commission filed a monopoly complaint against Xerox in 1973. The outcome, two years later, was that Xerox agreed to license its copier patents to other manufacturers.

[5]Kearns, D, and Nadler, D. (1992) *Prophets in the Dark: How Xerox Reinvented Itself and Beat Back the Japanese,* New York: Harper Collins, p. 134–135.

[6]Kearns, D, and Nadler, D. (1992) op. cit., p. 246.

[7]From Paul Allaire's comments to the Senior Management Meeting, February 4, 1992, in "Xerox 2000: Putting It Together," p. 2.

EXHIBIT 1 The Expected Evolution of Xerox Products

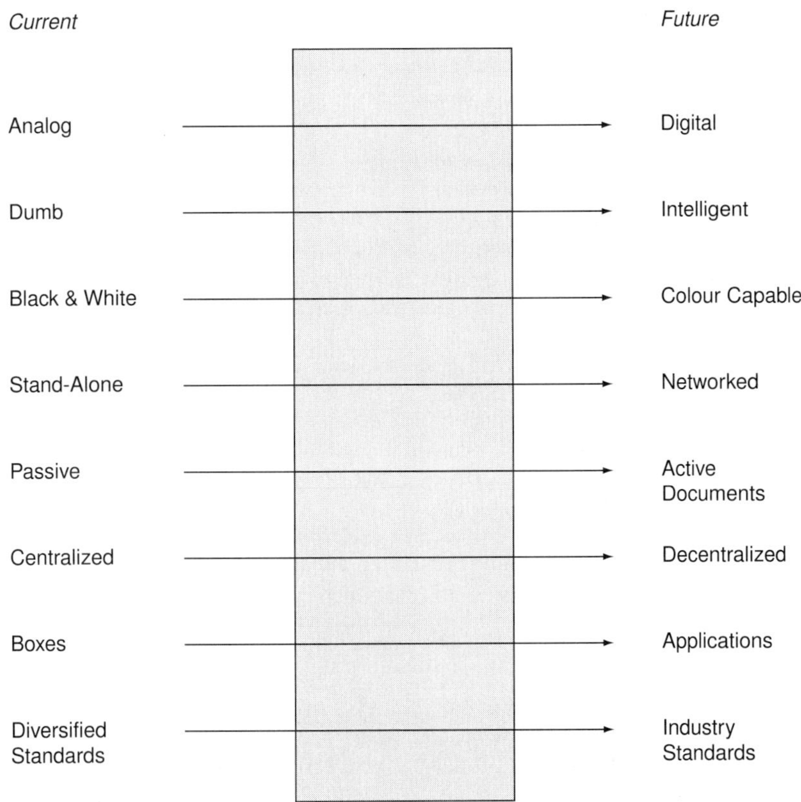

Source: Xerox Toward the Year 2000—Internal Company Document.

architecture of Xerox"—which included process improvements and behaviours, as well as structure. The business divisions model emerged as the organisational form considered to provide the best platform for the document company.

The idea behind this model was to move away from the narrowly functional and highly centralised organisation of the past. Decision making would be moved out from the corporate centre to the business divisions, and thus closer to the customer.

The business divisions model was initially based on the notion of a single client interface, but multiple product divisions. Three customer operations divisions—United States, Americas Operations, and Rank Xerox Customer Operations—were each responsible for managing the customer relationship in a specified geographical area. They were responsible for delivering Xerox products and services and improving customer satisfaction. But behind these customer operations, there were nine independent business divisions, each offering a distinct set of products and services (see Exhibit 2). The new structure was sometimes referred to as the "9+3" solution: nine business divisions and three customer operations divisions all reporting directly to top operations executives at the Xerox corporate office (Exhibit 3).

It is worth adding, that although the business divisions would normally market their products through the three customer operations divisions (of which Rank Xerox was one), the Xerox 2000 initiative left open the possibility that certain divisions could establish their own customer interface (Exhibit 4).

This new approach was driven by the recognition that the company needed to do a better job linking markets and technologies. Central to that approach was the notion of "end-to-end" responsibility, whereby single units or teams have complete responsibility for a set of Xerox

EXHIBIT 2 Breakdown of the Business Divisions

The nine newly created business divisions, defined by product and business segment, were positioned as follows:

1. **Personal Document Products:** targets small businesses and individual consumers, via retail, direct mail, and catalogue channels. Core products are copiers, fax machines for the home office and small businesses.
2. **Office Document Systems:** focuses on office document printers, especially the high-value end of the market (exploiting full colour applications). Core products are desk, work group, and departmental printers chiefly linked to personal computers.
3. **Office Document Products:** pursues both the light lens reprographics market and the digital copying market which is destined to replace it. It is also present in the plain paper fax market. Its core products are convenience, work group, departmental copiers (including colour copiers). This is the heart of the copier business.
4. **X-Soft:**produces publishing and graphics software needed for collaborative document applications and management services.
5. **Advanced Office Document Services:** offers advanced document services for the office market. This is a high-tech business division which produces scanning, image enhancement and recognition products. Currently, these are minority products but they are set to become commercial sector products in the future.
6. **Document Production Systems:** offers business productivity solutions in the dedicated operator printing market, and drives the transfer of offset printing to reprographics. This business division focuses on electronic publishing systems, and very high volume copiers and duplicators. The key product is called Docutech.
7. **Printing Systems:** concerned with large data centre printing, and non-impact printing solutions to small and medium data centres. The core products are mid range and high range electronic printers, especially those which hook onto mainframes and minicomputers. This is a big business for Xerox.
8. **Xerox Engineering Systems:** this is a discrete division which is dedicated to the engineering document market, with its unique requirements and size of plans. It develops and designs specially adapted copiers, printers and plotters.
9. **Xerox Business Services:** responds to demand for full document management and operational services at customer sites. This involves taking over complete responsibility for running the print room facility, with Xerox implanted in the customer's business. This is an important growth area.

products and services, targeted at a particular set of market needs.

The idea was for each business division to resemble a stand-alone business. Each division was responsible for the entire value chain, from the definition and development of products to the control of distribution channels for sales, and had full profit and loss responsibility. The mission for each business division was to achieve a dominant position in its designated market.

Each business division consisted of a set of "business teams" each headed by a general manager. These business teams were responsible for an offering, or a set of offerings. Again the guiding principle was "end-to-end" accountability, with clear line of sight to customers. The theory was that each team should have the training, the tools and the information it needed to assume total responsibility for its work environment and the satisfaction of its customers. The expectation was that these smaller, more autonomous units, will encourage entrepreneurial behaviour and increase customer responsiveness.

An additional merit of the divisional structure was deemed to be its flexibility over time. As new markets or new technologies emerged, a new business team, and eventually a new division, could simply be created. It was also possible to split or eliminate a business division without affecting the basic architecture of the company. This adaptability was important in view of the evolution of products, notably the transition from conventional optical technology to digital technology—with Xerox anticipating that growth in revenues from digital equipment would go from around 40 percent in 1993 to 80 percent by the year 2000.

Rank Xerox: European Operations

Formed in 1956 to bring the benefits of the newly invented plain paper copying technology to European users, Rank Xerox quickly expanded to operate throughout the continent. By 1992, it stood as one of Europe's top 150 companies, with 26,000 employees and an annual turnover of \$5.0 billion (as against \$7.2 for Xerox U.S.).

The existing Rank Xerox organisation was structured as a group of 15 independent national operating companies (OpCos for short). Country managers of the largest OpCos (France, UK, Germany) reported directly to the managing director. The smaller OpCos were clustered by region and reported to one of four regional general managers (Exhibit 5).

EXHIBIT 3 The Business Divisions Model

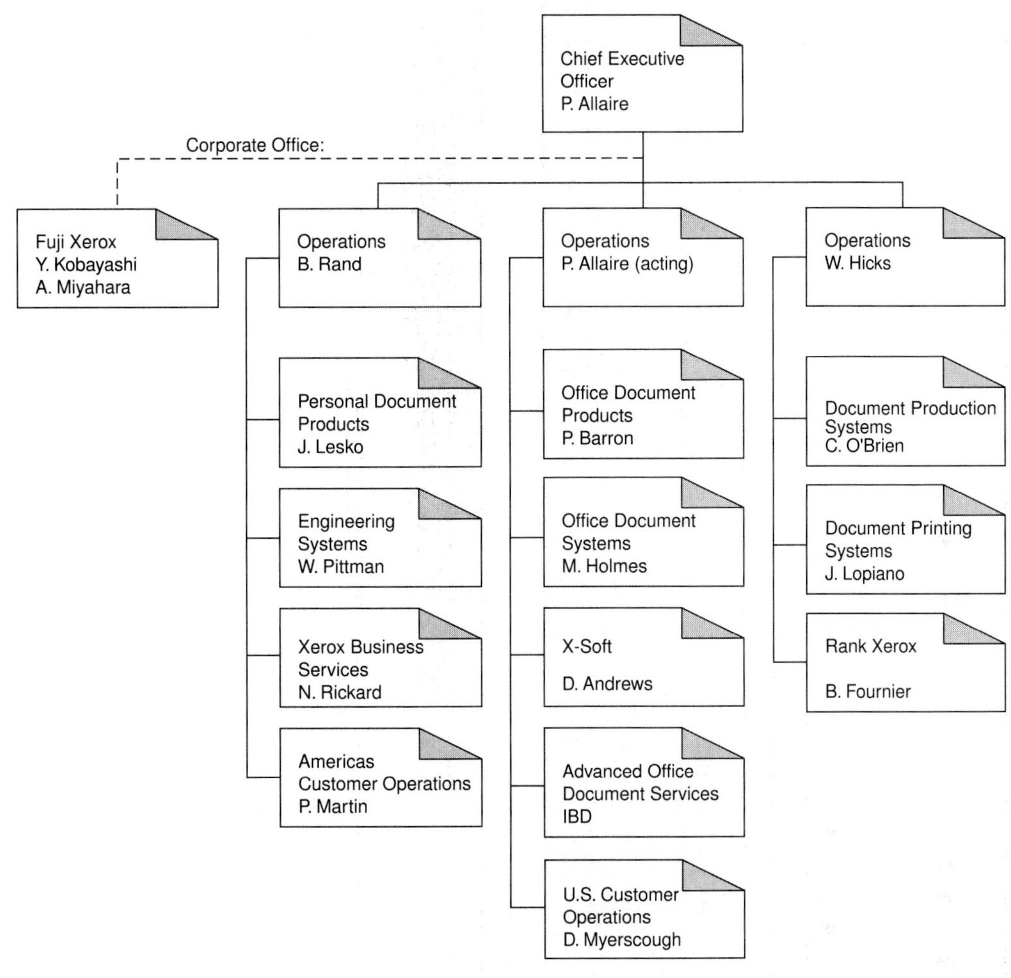

Source: Xerox 2000: Putting it Together (the "9+3" solution)—Internal Company Document.

The OpCos of Rank Xerox were traditionally organised by separate functions (sales, service, administration). This presented something of a problem both upstream and downstream. Downstream, the functional organisation meant that sales people, account management people, and service people were all working for the same customer, but did not know their Rank Xerox colleagues who were also dealing with that customer.

Upstream, the functional organisation now allowed insufficient interface with the business divisions. This was the responsibility of the European Headquarters (EHQ) in Marlow. The prevailing structure of Rank Xerox provoked doubts about the capacity of Rank Xerox HQ and operating companies to effectively serve the global business divisions.

Quite independently of relations with the global business divisions, there were also doubts about the effectiveness of the current organisation *per se*. To start with, the EHQ with its staff of 1,500, was thought to be too large. In conversation with Bill Goode, Rank Xerox's Director of Finance, Bernard Fournier revealed his concerns: "There are far too many people based in Marlow. We waste so much time and energy just administrating those people. It makes us very inward looking. If we started again with a clean sheet, I can't see much reason why the EHQ should be any bigger than about 60 people."

EXHIBIT 4 The Relationship between Business Divisions and Customer Operations

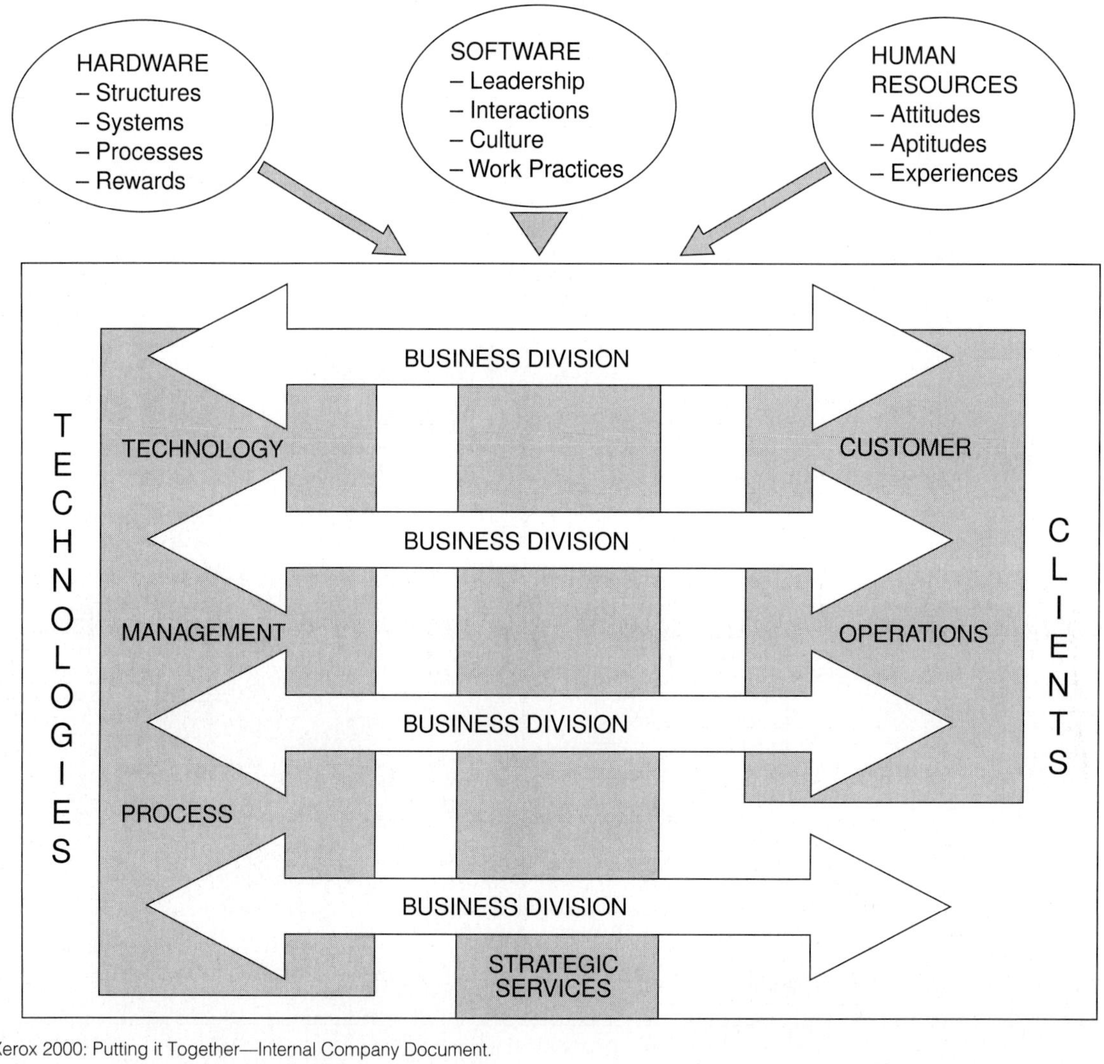

Source: Xerox 2000: Putting it Together—Internal Company Document.

Within the operating companies too, it was considered that there were too many people dealing with process rather than the customer, and too many layers separating managers from customers. This partly stemmed from a strong control culture. As Fournier saw it: "Reporting requirements are still heavy. The gains we made by halving them last year are going to be wiped out by the increase we can expect from the new Xerox organisation." And he continued, "But I still think that the problem is more psychological than anything else. There is a lack of trust. Our culture encourages everyone to be informed about everything. Tremendous managerial energy is spent on ensuring everybody is operating within the expense budgets. That emphasis on the numbers means we sometimes lose sight of what really matters."

Although efforts were being made to delegate authority, simplify work processes, and develop initiative within the OpCos, old habits were dying hard. Privately, Fournier revealed his concern: "Developing initiative is fine in theory, but the context inhibits it. There's a lack of energy. There's a curious lack of dissatisfaction with the way things are—no real desire to do things differently. People are empowered in principle, but it doesn't seem to change much in reality."

EXHIBIT 5 The Rank Xerox Organisation Structure

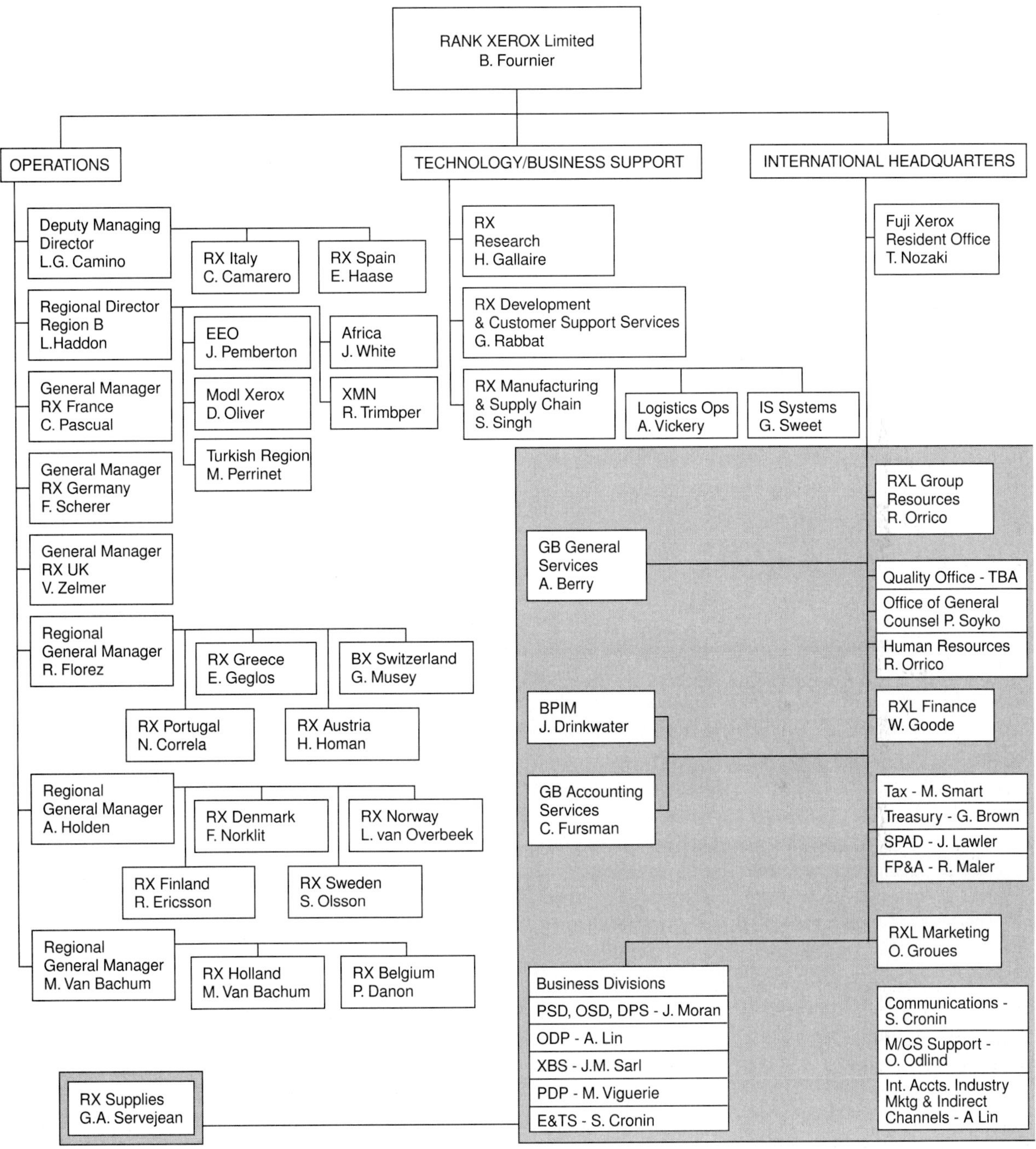

Source: Organisation Announcement (13/1/93)—Internal Company Document.

Rank Xerox's Recent Performance

Over the past few years, Rank Xerox's unsatisfactory performance had manifested itself in a variety of ways. Internal studies, carried out by the Xerox Quality Implementation Team, comparing the various parts of Xerox, showed that Rank Xerox was less profitable than its Xerox marketing counterpart in the United States. Whereas Xerox (U.S.) had achieved a ROA of close to 20 percent in recent years, the comparable rate for Rank Xerox was well below this level and looked unlikely to improve in the context of enduring European recession.

Extrapolating from existing improvements in ROA, Rank Xerox could expect to improve its ROA by 5–6 percent by 1996. But in order to remain an attractive distribution channel for the newly formed product divisions, Rank Xerox needed to do significantly better than that. Even assuming reasonable growth, Rank Xerox would still have to make up a cost gap of some $200m by 1996.

Rank Xerox also had problems with market share, with Japanese competitors pricing at borderline levels to capture market share. In all three of its largest markets (France, Germany, and UK), it was behind the market leader, Canon. Exhibit 6 shows the company's position in terms of market share for these countries and for the other European Operations.

Despite making notable advances in service quality, and winning the European Quality Award in 1992, there was still evidence of customer dissatisfaction. One consultant, charged with assessing Rank Xerox's customer orientation, found that:

> "RX underperforms in areas related to: supporting rather than controlling the front line; giving those dealing with customers the freedom to act; trust; and ensuring that each customer requirement has a front line owner. On the other hand, the organisation performs well against characteristics deemed *not* to be customer responsive: focusing on financial performance; limiting front line authority to ensure control; clarifying functional demarcation lines; and leaders providing the answers."[8]

The same consultant's report also identified that employee satisfaction was suffering: "There seemed to be overwhelming agreement that Rank Xerox is suffering due to unmotivated employees, and that correcting this problem is an immediate priority."

While Rank Xerox's overall performance left something to be desired, the picture was not all bleak. Among the OpCos there were islands of high performance. Rank Xerox fared better in some countries than others, notably Holland, Belgium, Austria, Switzerland, Denmark, and Portugal. These OpCos had ROAs of 20 percent and above, while Rank Xerox as a whole was well below those levels. They were also the best performers on other dimensions: in terms of revenue per employee, service productivity and sales productivity, as well as customer satisfaction and employee satisfaction.

Change Processes and Alternatives

In September 1992, Fournier launched the Rank Xerox 2000 initiative. After extensive consultation with his staff on the major problems to be addressed, he formed two task teams to undertake a close review of the way Rank Xerox worked. Their mission would be to make recommendations on how the company could be reorganised to meet the current and future challenge of the Rank Xerox 2000 strategy.

The objectives, as presented by Fournier in slide form, were threefold:

1. To make the new organisation:
   - *Cost effective*—$200m cost gap.
   - *Flexible*—simplification of processes and more productivity.
   - *Synergetic*—shared resources and skills at all levels.
   - *Proactive*—closer to the customer and empowered.
2. To position Rank Xerox for 2000
   - That is, to move closer toward the idea of "The Document Company".
3. To restructure in line with Xerox Business Divisions organisation

Team A's mission was to propose a new structure for the Operating Companies of Rank Xerox. Meanwhile, Team B would investigate ways of streamlining the shared activities at the company's European Headquarters (EHQ) in Marlow, England.

Conscious of the disparate interests at stake, Fournier felt it necessary to open up the strategic thinking process. Each team therefore consisted of 10 or so representatives drawn from across the European OpCos. This would help to legitimise the proposed solution and would enhance the likelihood of buy-in and ownership.

Team B's mandate was to look at the role and structure of the European Headquarters. The team's objective was to identify and eliminate activities and layers that did not

---

[8]From consultant's communication to Xerox's top management on Rank Xerox Customer Reponsiveness, 14/8/91.

Exhibit 6 Market Position within Each OpCo

Source: Latest MDMs—Internal Company Document.

EXHIBIT 7 Sample of Team B Output
Customer: Office Document Products

Outputs	Valued Added	What if Bypassed?
QUALITY:		
Provision of support programmes and training.	Expertise	
HUMAN RESOURCES:		
Allocation for provision of administrative and international services.	International expertise and support.	
FINANCE:		
Allocation: Systems produced and supported.	Transactions facilitated.	More work in XC or ELC but might give rise to small synergy savings.
Price files produced and business results analysed.	Decisions enabled.	
MARKETING DIRECTORATE:		
Allocation		
MARKETING-ODP & OPS SUPPORT:		
Business Management Product Planning and Marketing. Product Lifecycle/Classification.	Develop an implementation plan for ODP strategy for Op Units.	Lost opportunity.
Activity and Pricing. Supply/Demand.	Provide market analysis to all BDs.	Lost opportunity.
Coverage & Channels Planning & Support. Field Support. Best Practices Sharing. Determine RX Customer requirements. MARCOM	Develop services strategies.	Lost opportunity.
MARKETING-COMMS TRAINING:		
Fully nationalised and validated 16 European configurations.	Enable RX revenue of $2.2B for reprographics and $124M for . facsimile.	Current activities would have to be done in U.S. at higher cost.

add direct value. Also, where possible, functions should be transferred to the field organisations.

The task facing team B, led by Ralph Orrico, Rank Xerox's Head of Human Resources, was essentially tactical rather than strategic. To be effective it would require a thorough reassessment of what internal services were provided, which internal customers they were aimed at, and whether those customers felt they were getting good value. This would provide a better picture of the value of the functions and major processes performed across Rank Xerox. On this basis, it would then be possible to determine which of these activities needed to be centralised. Exhibit 7 gives a flavour of the output.

Within four months, in early 1993, Team B had come up with recommendations for how to reduce the size and scope of headquarters. As expected this re-engineering exercise resulted in some job losses among head office staff. But it also produced short-term savings of $50 million which went a long way toward closing the $200 million shortfall identified previously, as well as building confidence in improving the performance of Rank Xerox.

Team A's mission, which was based on the premise that EHQ would no longer act as intermediary between OpCos and business divisions, was working in parallel with Team B. When Team B finished, a number of its longer term recommendations were integrated into Team A's activities. Team A was given eight months to come up with recommendations. The rest of this case will deal with the challenge facing team A.

Team A

One of the dangers of relying on insiders for recommendations was that they might be unduly influenced by the existing configuration of Rank Xerox. So Fournier signalled his willingness to consider and implement even radical recommendations by giving team members assurances of job security. He also emphasised the need to look outside Xerox for successful models to emulate, benchmarks to attain, and advice from academic experts. Most importantly, he appointed a relative newcomer to Rank Xerox, Mike Van Bachum, to head the team.

Van Bachum had headed ICL in the Netherlands until 1987. Within Rank Xerox, he was seen as something of a maverick. But, as General Manager of Rank Xerox Holland, he had cut costs by over $100 million while improving customer service. This had been achieved through a variety of "hard" and "soft" measures.

First, he had significantly altered the proportion of direct to indirect people: while the number of administrative staff was squeezed, the number of sales people went up from 100 to 150. He had then created semi-autonomous workgroups (6 to 7 people) responsible for their own territory and work allocation. He had also replaced the process-oriented technical director with a more people oriented manager; and had encouraged the middle managers to be more supportive and to play less of a policing role.

These measures had enabled Rank Xerox Holland to increase its revenues by 8–10 percent more than other OpCos per annum—without incurring a corresponding increase in SAG costs. While it was generally assumed that SAG grows at the same rate as revenues, Rank Xerox Holland had managed to restrict SAG growth to half of revenue growth. What was more, this productivity jump had not come at the expense of customer satisfaction. Brand awareness had increased and perception of service quality for Rank Xerox (NL) was joint top with Miele in the Netherlands.

When he appointed Van Bachum to lead Team A, Fournier had several things on his mind. In conversation with Van Bachum, he revealed the extent of his concerns: "We have a performance crisis—in terms of volumes, revenues, costs, and returns. And the external environment is not going to get much easier. But I'm not just concerned with cost savings—we also have to unleash entrepreneurial energy to improve customer responsiveness and retention at the local level. We need to revitalise not just rationalise, without forgetting that we need to establish better coordination between product line and geographic management."

In its first few meetings, Team A made an effort to chart Rank Xerox's existing problem, using the quality management methods that had become Xerox's usual problem analysis tool. Exhibit 8 summarises the team's assessment of where the company stood and what weaknesses needed addressing.

Individuals were also assigned the task of collecting benchmark information. On the one hand, they were to look within Rank Xerox to identify best practices and to assess the productivity improvements achievable in Europe within a relatively short time horizon. On the other hand, they were to scan the external environment to compare how other global players, such as DEC, Hewlett-Packard, ABB, Andersen, and Canon, structured and coordinated their European operations.

The Alternatives

Some months later, team members reported their findings regarding alternative organisation structures, based on external visits and benchmarking. Three relevant models had been identified. Operations could be reorganised by product, by industry or else, by geography, as was currently the case.

1. The Divisionalised Model

A divisionalised structure would align in an obvious way with the recently established business divisions of Xerox in the United States. Most business divisions—certain smaller divisions might be grouped to obtain critical mass—would have their own marketing and sales, and possibly service and management organisation, in Europe and select the local delivery and service channels best suited to their product characteristics.

In such an organisation, product lines manage the flow of resources, skills, and information in an integrated pan-European or even worldwide fashion. Operational strategic direction would flow directly from the divisions to their sales and service teams in the various locations. This would provide the most direct connection between the product divisions and their respective customers.

Country general managers would become mostly coordinators/facilitators across divisions, focusing on customer satisfaction and quality of coverage, while seeking the proper balance between products and functions within their territory. They might also keep administering local activities that provided services to various product divisions, such as service and solution development. They would assume responsibility for legal matters and

EXHIBIT 8 Snapshot of Rank Xerox's Weaknesses

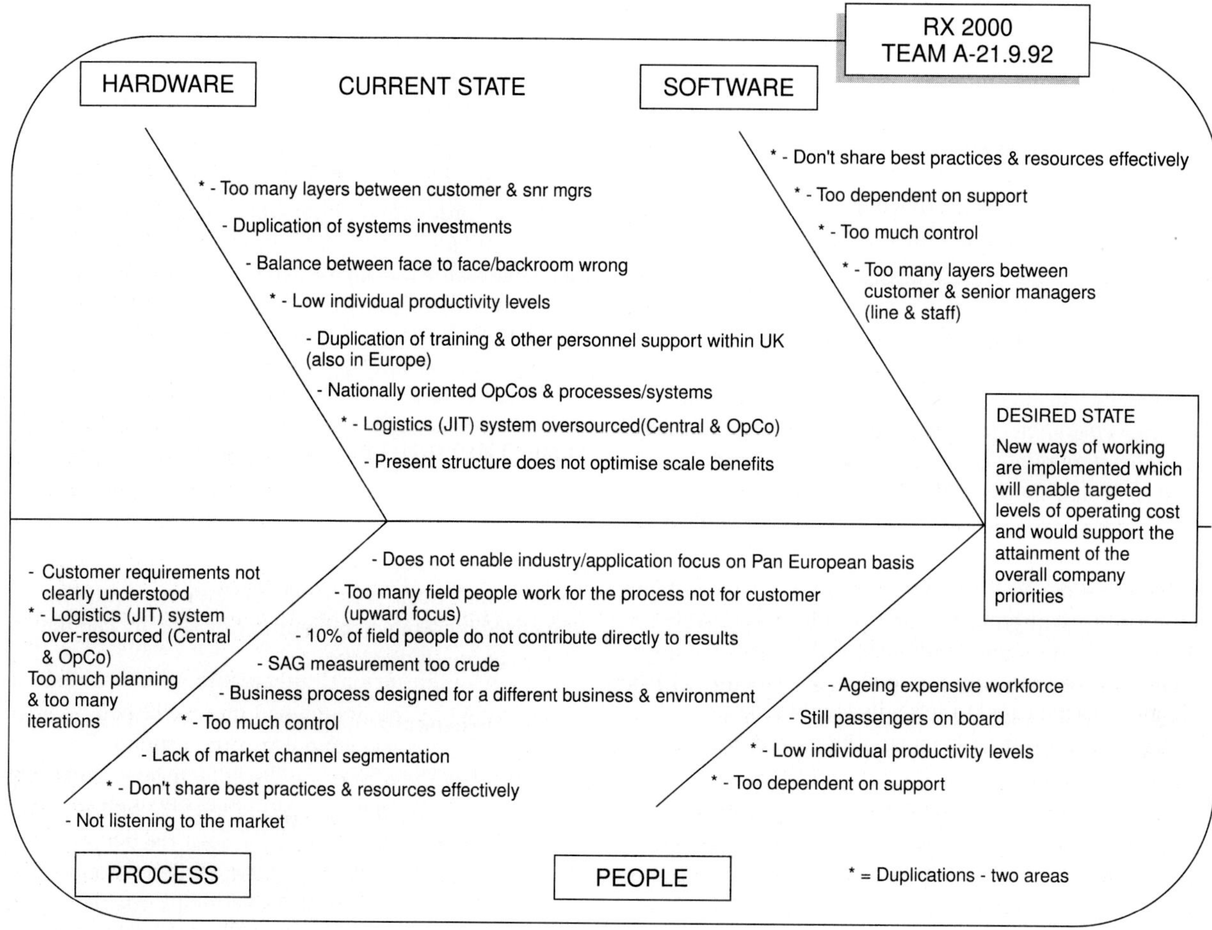

Source: Rank Xerox 2000: Team A—Internal Company Document.

physical facilities. But budgets, strategy, and profit and loss responsibility would fall to the local division heads, under the guidance of their pan-European bosses.

2. The Vertical Industry/Market Model

With digital technology, customised "solutions", and software products assuming increasing importance for Xerox, adopting the marketing strategy of certain computer and computer service companies was also an option.

Instead of focusing on product lines, this model would be aligned according to key vertical markets, that is, customer industries requiring similar hardware and software products (obvious examples being the printing industry, engineering services, small enterprises and so on).

Industry general managers could be dispersed throughout Europe depending on local industry strengths. For example, small enterprises might be located in Italy, oil and gas in Norway, automotive in France, chemicals in Germany, and financial services in the UK. Market and investment strategy, and annual planning would all be carried out at the industry level. The industry general manager would provide the basic "line of sight" for customers, procure products from the U.S. product divisions, and provide the divisions with market information.

Country general managers (heading up a country or cluster of countries) would assume responsibility for customer base care, employee development, operational support, and PR in their respective areas. They would essentially take on a facilitator role, while profit and loss responsibility would reside with industry heads on a local and pan-European basis.

Depending on the more or less local or pan-European nature of the industry they served, each industry division could be more or less decentralised. Some, say "education" might be organised nationally; others, say "small enterprises" broken into a series of smaller regional units within each country; others still, in particular industries dominated by a handful of multinational companies, could be organised by account in a pan-European fashion.

3. The Revised Geographic Model

This option was the closest to the existing organisation and reaffirmed the predominance of the geographic dimension as an organising principle. According to that model, sales, service, and customer administration could be grouped into relatively small independent local business units (LBUs) on a regional basis within each OpCo.[9] Each LBU would comprise no more than about 400 people and was expected to serve its local market.

The activities of LBUs would be co-ordinated by national OpCos, certainly for the largest countries (France, Germany, and UK) and perhaps by newly created cross-national OpCos regrouping LBUs from the smaller European countries. This form would allow both the number of LBUs and OpCos to be adjusted with market evolution, and avoid duplicating key processes in all the LBUs. LBUs would draw on OpCo support for accounting and finance, logistics, and personnel, and minimise the number of their own direct employees.

The role of the OpCo would be to integrate the strategic objectives of the business divisions with the local customer requirements served by the LBUs. But responsibility for business objectives (profit and loss, ROA, customer satisfaction, market share) would shift from the general manager of the OpCo to the LBU general managers, on a geographic basis, and to the local business division manager on a line of business basis.

[9]Although the OpCos obviously had regional branches, the three way functional specialisation (sales, service, customer administration) ran deep into them to the "front-line" dealing directly with the customer.

Choosing Between Alternatives

The team then spent time reviewing these options in some detail and developing a set of design criteria that the new structure should satisfy. Taking their cue from the earlier work done by the Xerox quality implementation team, they built on the four basic dimensions previously identified: more energy, more responsiveness, better customer focus, and improved competitiveness. These were broken down into a set of 24 criteria (see Exhibit 9).

The team also noted that some remarkably successful companies followed each of the three models. Hewlett-Packard, for instance, had moved closer to the divisionalised model, although finally retaining a matrix organisation in Europe. Apple and several other computer companies operated with a vertical industry model, and several companies, most notably Andersen Consulting and Gemini, were moving in that direction. Most U.S. multinational companies active in Europe, however, retained the geographic model of organisation.

Within Rank Xerox, at least two interesting local initiatives were started in parallel with Team A's work. The French OpCo had put in place a product division structure, with representatives of the business divisions interacting with the regional directors in a kind of matrixed process. While the French had presented their approach to Team A, they had not drawn strong support.

Mike Van Bachum, in particular, was quite concerned with the need to go beyond a mere organisational realignment to placate U.S.-based divisions, and to use the opportunity to achieve a real quantum leap in customer and market responsiveness. The French management organisation might not have a real impact on front line responsiveness. The second experiment was taking place in Scandinavia. A new regional director, faced with a performance crisis in most countries (except Denmark), decided to merge support functions across countries. Accounting and control, for example, would be managed on a regional basis, as a single functional organisation for the whole Nordic region. While accountants and controllers would remain physically in the various countries, they would now be part of a multicountry function, and report to the regional unit, not to the local OpCo. While both of these experiments were interesting, it was still early to draw conclusions from them.

As Team A deliberated the general merits, drawbacks, and "unknowns" of the various options, in the spring of 1993, additional elements of information emerged. These concerned the preliminary results of the cross-country

EXHIBIT 9 Design Criteria for the New Structure

1. Release "this is my business" entrepreneurial spirit.
2. Promote business accountability at lowest levels possible (shift from costs centre to profit centre).
3. Enable every employee to know how their actions impact profit of the organisation (be a meaningful part of something they care about).
4. Retain/develop the capability to attract the best quality people.
5. Minimise organisational barriers along value-added chain (minimise hand offs).
6. Rapid response to customers requirements. Rapid introduction of new products (launch), solutions and services.
7. Provide natural boundaries for accountability and responsibility (define the playing field/align planning and implementation).
8. Minimise the number of levels between the top and bottom of the company.
9. Ensure that central utilities support revenue generating organisation (vs. control).
10. Meet the specified requirements of business divisions IHQ/fiduciary and legal.
11. Enable Rank Xerox to anticipate and respond to customer's unique requirements (current and latent).
12. Ensure the appropriate decisions are made at customer contact point.
13. Enable Rank Xerox to co-ordinate resources to respond to customer's buying patterns (integration).
14. Enable Rank Xerox to co-ordinate resources to respond to customers' service requirements.
15. Nurture core competencies.
16. Enable Rank Xerox to capture productivity potential by focussing on key business processes.
17. Enable Rank Xerox to anticipate and respond to local markets (as well as be viewed as a local company on a worldwide basis).
18. Ensure the flexibility to be big or small, when advantaged.
19. Ensure that operational overhead (labour & other) is minimised and is reduced by at least $200M.
20. More effective linkages to BD's.
21. Optimise resource sharing by establishment of competency centres.
22. Enable better resource identification to minimise BD allocated cost and enable better resource utilisation/support.
23. Enable future flexibility.
24. Enable Rank Xerox to be easy to do business with.

Source: Rank Xerox 2000: Team A Status—Internal Company Document.

comparisons of OpCo efficiency within Rank Xerox. Two sets of statistics had been compiled. The first set compared the staffing levels and output in all 15 European OpCos. This showed work productivity rates by process area, based on the Corporate Process Architecture: market to order, order to collection, product maintenance, supply chain, finance/leasing, and information management. The difference between the highest and lowest performers revealed the potential productivity improvements for each process area. In addition to this, a strong correlation was found between productivity and quality of performance. This suggested that greater work output per employee within Rank Xerox did not come at the expense of excellence (see Exhibit 10).

The second set of statistics, was a more detailed revenue analysis of productivity in just four countries: the UK, France, Holland, and Austria. From the outset, the Operating Company in Holland was known to be among the most productive—indeed, that had been one of the reasons for selecting its country manager to head Team A. The analysis considered performance from various angles and showed that Holland outperformed the other countries on just about every critical success factor (see Exhibit 11).

The business strategy of the four OpCos was also examined. For example, Rank Xerox Holland was seen to have grown its business faster than domestic GDP growth by maintaining a superior level of orders from its key account customer base and by pursuing large bulk contracts with high minimum billing quantities and rich product mix. This helped RX Holland to achieve exceptionally high salesforce productivity scores.

A significant finding of the benchmarking studies, in terms of reforming the Rank Xerox organisation, was that the larger OpCos (France, UK, Germany) did not appear to benefit from any perceptible economies of scale. Operating Companies scoring highest on productivity and profitability tended to be among the smaller ones. This posed a real dilemma for Team A. On paper, it seemed feasible to consolidate certain processes across borders into larger pools in the pursuit of savings. Yet, in practice, high productivity came from organising activities into smaller, less complex units.

EXHIBIT 10 **Comparing the OpCos on Productivity Versus Service Response and Customer Satisfaction**

a) Service response and productivity are not traded off

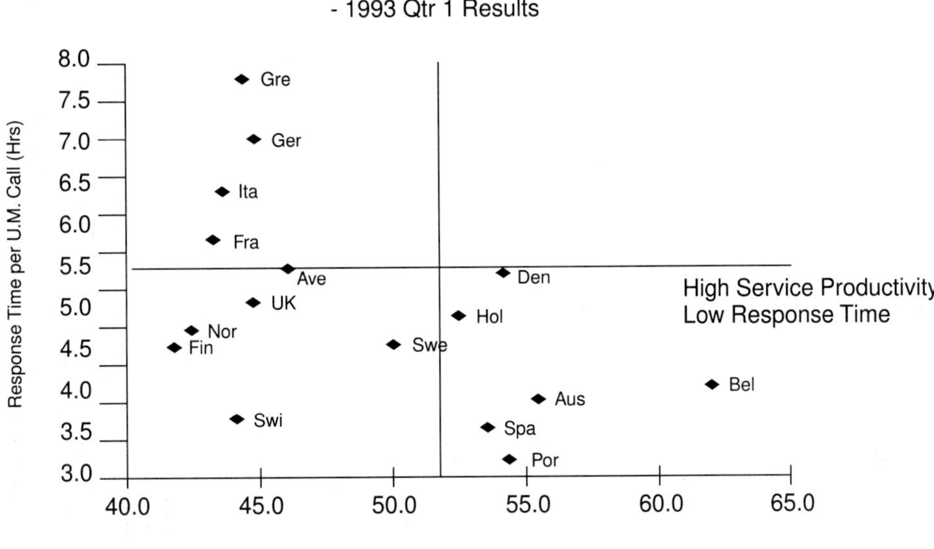

b) Customer satisfaction and productivity are not traded off

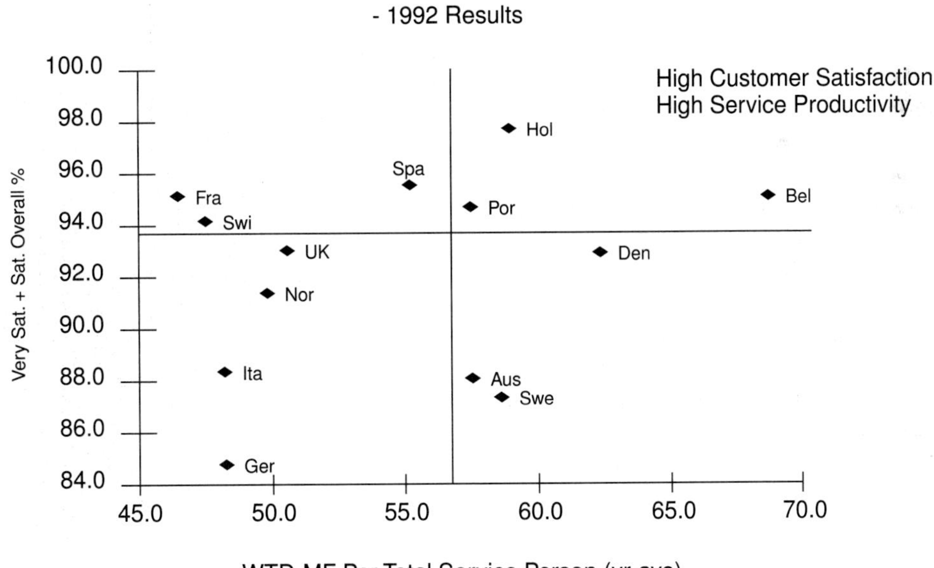

Source: Responses based on the 1992 Competitive CSMS for Reprographics. Rank Xerox Recommendations (26/3/93)—Internal Company Document.

EXHIBIT 11 Comparing the OpCos on Critical Success Factors (1992)

	UK	France	Holland	Austria
Salesforce Productivity (Equip Ref/QBS)*	385	412	483	396
Sales Heads % Total	22	24	25	29
SAG % Rev	31	28	23	29
OP Inc % Revenue	16	15	27	19
Revenue/Head ($K)	170	180	260	216

*Equipment revenue per quota bearing salesperson.

Source: RX 2000: Operating Company Comparison—Internal Company Document.

The X Factor

With few meetings left before presenting the team's recommendations to the board, Mike Van Bachum found himself in a difficult position. The team needed to make a convincing case for one model. But a number of uncertainties remained.

For example, it was not clear to what extent each of the models addressed the challenge of promoting accountability and initiative at lower levels. Personal experience made Van Bachum acutely aware of the need to push down decisions to the level where they belonged. On the other hand, he also realised that it would be difficult to accomplish because of what he saw as "the lack of trust and the tendency to delegate problems upward."

Nor was it clear how each of the models would align with the business divisions. The industry and the revised geographic models, in particular, raised a number of questions. The newly appointed business division managers were already growing impatient with what they saw as Rank Xerox's high costs and lack of transparency, and several were considering setting up their own channels in Europe, altogether bypassing Rank Xerox. The division managers seemed to have the ear of top management and there was a growing concern, on Team A's part, that they would only be given one chance to address all of Rank Xerox's difficulties.

Each of the models would also require Rank Xerox managers to take on new roles. And Van Bachum was unsure whether the company had the managers it needed to meet the various requirements. It was not clear, either, that the OpCo general managers, who constituted the backbone of the Rank Xerox organisation and management team, would support the changes Team A contemplated.

Finally, the models differed considerably in terms of clarity and complexity. Did the company require a model which would be implemented identically throughout Europe, or could it afford diversity?

Past experience made Van Bachum conscious of the need for radical change, not simply window dressing. The model had to be flexible enough to allow interpretation according to local needs and capabilities; yet the breadth of choice should not allow units to escape the change.

As the May 1993 deadline approached, Van Bachum was getting increasingly nervous as to which of the approaches that his team had been discussing for the past six months should be implemented. Which structure should the team recommend?

Index